The Cambridge Handbook of Compliance

Edited by

BENJAMIN VAN ROOIJ
University of Amsterdam & University of California, Irvine

D. DANIEL SOKOL
University of Florida

CAMBRIDGE
UNIVERSITY PRESS

CAMBRIDGE
UNIVERSITY PRESS

University Printing House, Cambridge CB2 8BS, United Kingdom

One Liberty Plaza, 20th Floor, New York, NY 10006, USA

477 Williamstown Road, Port Melbourne, VIC 3207, Australia

314-321, 3rd Floor, Plot 3, Splendor Forum, Jasola District Centre, New Delhi - 110025, India

103 Penang Road, #05-06/07, Visioncrest Commercial, Singapore 238467

Cambridge University Press is part of the University of Cambridge.

It furthers the University's mission by disseminating knowledge in the pursuit of education, learning and research at the highest international levels of excellence.

www.cambridge.org
Information on this title: www.cambridge.org/9781009280129
DOI: 10.1017/9781108759458

First published 2021
First paperback edition 2022

A catalogue record for this publication is available from the British Library

Library of Congress Cataloging in Publication data
NAMES: Rooij, Benjamin van, 1973– editor. | Sokol, D. Daniel, editor.
TITLE: The Cambridge handbook of compliance / edited by D. Daniel Sokol, University of Florida; Benjamin van Rooij, University of California, Irvine School of Law.
Description: Cambridge, United Kingdom ; New York, NY : Cambridge University Press, 2021. | Series: Cambridge law handbooks | Includes bibliographical references.
IDENTIFIERS: LCCN 2020046954 (print) | LCCN 2020046955 (ebook) | ISBN 9781108477123 (hardback) | ISBN 9781108759458 (ebook)
SUBJECTS: LCSH: Corporation law – Criminal provisions. | Commercial crimes – Prevention. | Financial institutions – Corrupt practices. | Tort liability of corporations. | Business ethics. | Industrial hygiene – Law and legislation. | Industrial safety – Law and legislation. | Consumer behavior. | Compliance auditing.
CLASSIFICATION: LCC K5216 .C36 2021 (print) | LCC K5216 (ebook) | DDC 346/.065–dc23
LC record available at https://lccn.loc.gov/2020046954
LC ebook record available at https://lccn.loc.gov/2020046955

ISBN 978-1-108-47712-3 Hardback
ISBN 978-1-009-28012-9 Paperback

Contents

PART IX ANALYSIS OF PARTICULAR FIELDS

Figures

Tables

Contributors

Saed Alizamir (Yale University)

James Alm (Tulane University)

Robert J. Apel (Rutgers University)

John Armour (University of Oxford)

Miriam H. Baer (Brooklyn Law School)

Stephen M. Bainbridge (University of California, Los Angeles (UCLA))

Florentin Blanc (Organisation for Economic Co-operation and Development (OECD))

Arjan Blokland (Leiden University)

Megan Brownlee (University of Amsterdam)

Jesse Bull (Florida International University)

Stephanie M. Cardwell (University of Texas at San Antonio, University of Queensland)

Chirantan Chatterjee (Indian Institute of Management Ahmedabad (IIMA))

Li Chen (Cornell University)

Jeffrey Cisyk (Charles River Associates)

Cary Coglianese (University of Pennsylvania)

Heith Copes (University of Alabama at Birmingham)

Pascal Courty (University of Victoria)

Douglas Cumming (Florida Atlantic University)

Robert Dannhauser (The Investment Integration Project)

Kevin E. Davis (New York University (NYU))

Anne Leonore de Bruijn (University of Amsterdam)

Henk Elffers (Netherlands Institute for the Study of Crime and Law Enforcement)

Naomi Ellemers (Utrecht University)

Yuval Feldman (Bar Ilan University)

Adam D. Fine (Arizona State University)

Garry Gray (University of Victoria)

Sean J. Griffith (Fordham University)

Richard S. Gruner (John Marshall)

Fiona Haines (University of Melbourne)

Todd Haugh (Indiana University)

David Hess (University of Michigan)

Wim Huisman (Free University of Amsterdam)

Arynn A. Infante (Portland State University)

Sofia Johan (Florida Atlantic University)

Justin Johnson (Cornell University)

Elena Kantorowicz-Reznichenko (Erasmus University Rotterdam)

Vrishali Kanvinde (Meadows Mental Health Policy Institute)

Yotam Kaplan (Bar Ilan University)

Muel Kaptein (Erasmus University)

Matthias Kasper (University of Vienna)

Kees Keizer (University of Groningen)

Jay P. Kesan (University of Illinois)

Vikramaditya S. Khanna (University of Michigan)

Sang-Hyun Kim (Yale University)

Erich Kirchler (University of Vienna and IHS-Institute for Advances Studies Vienna)

Marieke Kluin (Leiden University)

Emmeke B. Kooistra (University of Amsterdam)

Donald C. Langevoort (Georgetown University)

Hau L. Lee (Stanford University)

Siegwart Lindenberg (University of Groningen and Tilburg University)

Kristin Lloyd (Florida State University)

Donald Macrae (XDG Consulting Ltd)

Veronica Root Martinez (University of Notre Dame)

Colin Mayer (University of Oxford)

John Mendeloff (University of Pittsburgh)

Stephan Muehlbacher (Karl Landsteiner University of Health Sciences)

Suresh Muthulingam (Pennsylvania State University)

Daniel S. Nagin (Carnegie Melon University)

Jennifer Nash (Harvard University)

J. S. Nelson (Villanova University)

Jessica M. Nolan (University of Scranton)

Theo Nyreröd (EconAnalysis AB)

Giuseppa Ottimofiore (OECD)

John Pachter (Smith Pachter McWhorter PLC)

Johannes Paha (Justus-Liebig-University Giessen)

Jordan Paradise (Loyola University Chicago School of Law)

Christine Parker (University of Melbourne)

Alex R. Piquero (University of Miami and Monash University)

Nicole Leeper Piquero (University of Miami)

Greg Pogarsky (University at Albany SUNY)

Elizabeth Pollman (University of Pennsylvania)

Andrea Polo (Luiss University, Pompeu Fabra University, EIEF, Barcelona GSE)

Travis C. Pratt (University of Cincinnati)

Alex Raskolnikov (Columbia University)

Christopher P. Reinders Folmer (University of Amsterdam)

Melissa Rorie (University of Nevada Las Vegas)

Whitney Sanders (University of Texas at Dallas)

Galit A. Sarfaty (University of British Columbia)

Natalie Schell-Busey (Rowan University)

Saba Siddiki (Syracuse University)

Frédérique Six (VU University Amsterdam)

D. Daniel Sokol (University of Florida)

Eugene Soltes (Harvard University)

Jonathan E. Soeharno (University of Amsterdam)

Giancarlo Spagnolo (Stockholm School of Economics, University of Rome)

Shauhin A. Talesh (University of California, Irvine)

Cody W. Telep (Arizona State University)

Florence Thépot (University of Glasgow)

Dane Thorley (Brigham Young University)

Jessica Tillipman (George Washington University)

Stacey Tovino (University of Oklahoma College of Law)

Judith van Erp (Utrecht University)

Benjamin van Rooij (University of Amsterdam & University of California, Irvine)

Elianne F. van Steenbergen (Utrecht University)

Kenneth E. Wallen (University of Idaho)

Liam Wells (Erasmus University Rotterdam)

Christopher Yukins (George Washington University)

1

Introduction: Compliance as the Interaction between Rules and Behavior

Benjamin van Rooij and D. Daniel Sokol

Abstract: Compliance has become important in our contemporary markets, societies, and modes of governance across very different public and private domains, stimulating a rich body of empirical work and practical expertise. Yet, so far, we do not have a comprehensive understanding of what compliance is and what mechanisms and interventions play a role in shaping it, or how compliance shapes various fields. Thus far, the academic knowledge of compliance has remained siloed in different disciplinary domains, and along different regulatory and legal spheres and different mechanisms and interventions. This chapter, which is the introduction to *The Cambridge Handbook of Compliance*, offers a comprehensive view of what compliance is. It takes a broad approach in seeing compliance as the interaction between rules and behavior. It discusses what different mechanisms and interventions are at play in shaping such compliance. And it reflects on the different methods for studying compliance and their inherent limitations.

The 2020 Coronavirus pandemic presented one of contemporary humanity's largest behavioral challenges. In order to contain the spread of the virus, human behavior had to change fundamentally. And it had to do so rapidly and most likely for a prolonged period of time. At the core of this behavioral change operation were sets of rules about hygiene, consumer behavior, and social distancing and isolation. Some of these behavioral changes were adopted in private organizations, directed at employees, at members, or at customers. And some were governmental, directed at businesses, at public organizations, and at the general public. To contain the spread of the virus, these rules (and, in some cases, formal government mandates) could be effective only if individuals and organizations followed them. In other words, to fight the Coronavirus required a worldwide effort to boost compliance. This crisis thus presents a good example of how important compliance has become in our contemporary markets, societies, and modes of governance.

Prior to this crisis, compliance had already become a highly important issue across very different public and private domains, stimulating a rich body of empirical work and practical expertise. Often this work across fields was done in isolation from other fields. For example, there has been much attention paid to compliance in the corporate world. As countries have adopted legal incentives or duties for corporations to develop compliance and ethics management programs, like the US Federal Sentencing Guidelines of 1991, corporations have

This research was made possible through a generous grant from the European Research Council (ERC-2018-CoG - HomoJuridicus - 817680).

instituted a range of compliance measures, including codes of conduct, dedicated compliance officers, training programs, and whistleblower protection rules both for core financial crime-type functions such as audit that fundamentally impact board governance (Chhaochharia and Grinstein 2007; Iliev 2010; Alexander et al. 2013) and across other more specialized areas (Coglianese and Lazer 2003; Parker and Gilad 2011; Parker and Nielsen 2009b; Van Rooij and Fine 2019).

Compliance has become an industry complete with its own professional organizations and is creating an ever-growing stream of jobs. While some of these jobs are purely legal and about setting up systems of rules and codes of conduct, corporations have also turned to auditors, management consultants, behavioral economists, psychologists, and organizational scientists to understand how they can effectuate these rules in practice.

There has also been much attention paid to compliance in the public sector. Governmental regulators, including environmental, tax, antitrust, data protection, and occupational health and safety, have increasingly moved from a pure law enforcement to a compliance perspective, where they try to understand how they can best stimulate regulated actors to change their conduct as required (Gray and Silbey 2012, 2014; Kagan and Scholz 1984). Regulators have developed specialized compliance units that focus on behavioral change, and some even have behavioral specialists with backgrounds in psychology, behavioral economics, or other social sciences. In the criminal justice sphere, compliance has always been vital, although the term is less used.

Criminal justice has always conceptualized how best to reduce criminal behavior and thus is always about how the law can shape human and organizational conduct. Here, police and prison and parole authorities, and to some extent also prosecutors, have teamed up with criminologists, psychologists, sociologists, and other social scientists to understand what enforcement strategy and what other interventions may work best to reduce crime.

Another good example is compliance in the medical world, where much attention has gone out to whether patients comply with doctors' orders (Memon et al. 2017; Jin et al. 2008; Reardon et al. 2011; Costa et al. 2015) and whether medical workers comply with hygiene norms (Erasmus et al. 2010; Labrague et al. 2018; Gammon et al. 2008). Compliance in health has also focused on how government and the private sector can nudge individuals to be healthier through various compliance schemes (Bachireddy et al. 2019).

All of this shows that compliance is everywhere. Yet, so far, we do not have a comprehensive understanding of what compliance is and what mechanisms and interventions play a role in shaping it, or how compliance shapes various fields. So far, the academic knowledge of compliance has remained siloed in different disciplinary domains, and along different regulatory and legal spheres and different mechanisms and interventions. The aim of this *Handbook* is to bridge these silos and show a comprehensive view of what compliance is, how we can best study it and what different mechanisms and interventions are at play in shaping it.

This *Handbook* takes a very broad view of compliance. It sees compliance as *the interaction between rules and behavior*. We can portray it in a simple formula, with R for rules and B for behavior:

$$R \longleftrightarrow B$$

By taking this broad approach, the *Handbook* spans the different disciplinary perspectives. First, it takes a broad approach to rules (the R in the formula). These can include legal rules in formal legislation. Here we can think of the criminal law rules that are binding formal law, violations of which constitute misdemeanors or felonies punishable with governmentally backed sanctions. In another category of formal rules are the administrative law regulatory rules that guide individual and organizational behavior through administrative sanctions. And there are private law rules, too, most notably those flowing out of tort liability and contracts; these also guide human conduct but their enforcement goes through private law enforcement mechanisms. Our broad approach to rules may also include rules that are directly related not to the formal legal system but to private ordering. Here we can think of internal organizational rules that bind organizational members. Or we can think of informal rules as they exist, for instance, between doctors and patients (where patients are asked to follow doctors' orders), in sports (the rules of the game), and within communities.

Second, the *Handbook*'s broad approach also spans different forms of behavior (the B in the formula). It includes both individual and organizational conduct, and sees that most behavior is a combination of both. As such, it does not see organizational behavior as solely that of the organization but also as the sum of the interactions among the individuals in the organization. And individual conduct is always embedded in the broader social, organizational, and cultural settings in which individuals exist, where there is always an influence of social norms (Cialdini 2007; Cialdini and Goldstein 2004; Elster 1989; Goldstein et al. 2008; Schultz et al. 2007) and social learning processes (Akers 2017; Akers et al. 1979). The *Handbook* covers both clearly deviant and unacceptable behavior, often framed in society as done by "criminals" or "bad people," and behavior that, while in violation of the rules, may be quite common and done by "good people." Here, by combining the criminological approaches that focus on deviancy and the other social science approaches, including, for instance, social psychology (Ariely 2012), behavioral economics (Jolls et al. 1998; Thaler 2015), and behavioral ethics (Feldman 2018; Bazerman and Tenbrunsel 2012), the *Handbook* shows that there are remarkable communalities among these studies and that the distinction between good and bad people breaking rules may not be as stark as some hold (Feldman et al. 2019). Finally, the *Handbook* covers a range of behaviors, including street crime, fraud, bribery, cybercrime, intellectual property rights infringement, traffic violations, medical errors, doping in sports, human rights violations, unsafe food production, and occupational health and safety violations.

A core aspect in the *Handbook*'s approach to compliance is the interaction processes between rules and behavior. The two arrows (←→) in the formula show that we take a bidirectional approach to such interaction processes. On the one hand, we look at how rules come to shape behavior. For many this is how compliance is traditionally understood: how people respond to rules and come to adapt their behavior to the rules. But the *Handbook* also follows a growing body of research in sociology and anthropology that looks in the opposite direction, namely, at how people's responses to rules shape the meaning and functioning of such rules (Edelman et al. 1991; Edelman and Talesh 2011; Talesh 2009; Talesh and Pélisse 2019; Lange 1999; Falk Moore 1973). The *Handbook* thus combines the instrumental view of law, where law is seen in terms of its function in achieving a certain behavioral goal, with a constructive view of law, where society constructs what law means and the functioning of law (Griffiths 2003). Here, our approach is similar to the way in which Anthony Giddens' sociological theory combines structure and agency in a reflexive manner through the idea of structurization (Giddens 1984, 1990).

The largest part of the book looks at how rules come to shape behavior. Here the focus of the field of compliance is markedly different from the traditional view in the field of law. In existing legal scholarship and education, the relationship between legal rules and human behavior is often backward-looking, with discussions about what the appropriate law is for behavior that has happened in the past. This presents an *ex post* view of law and behavior, where law comes after behavior. In such a view, the behavior is given, and the core question is legal and normative (van Rooij in press). The view on compliance in this *Handbook* is mostly *ex ante*, where law seeks to shape future conduct (Darley et al. 2001). Such a view is focused on what mechanisms play a role in how law comes to shape behavior (behavioral mechanisms) and what interventions (behavioral interventions) can successfully activate such mechanisms. The *ex ante* view of law and behavior requires an empirical analysis as well as causal inference in order to gain knowledge about the functioning of such mechanisms and processes, before developing a normative view about which legal and other interventions are to be promoted. The nature of empiricism varies across fields, mostly notably between quantitative and qualitative approaches. However, even within quantitative approaches, the nature of how to structure research and the types of question that different fields ask vary.

The *Handbook* shares much of the available empirical knowledge we have about how rules shape behavior. As such, it forms the basis for an *ex ante* approach to law and a behavioral jurisprudence that corrects legal assumptions about behavior, just like the field of behavioral economics did for traditional neoclassical economic thought (van Rooij in press). The *Handbook* looks at different mechanisms and interventions at play in how rules shape behavior. As a general structure, the Handbook first looks at punishment, incentives (such as tort and positive incentives), legitimacy (including procedural justice and the general duty to obey the law), social norms, shame (neutralization of shame), capacity for compliance (including legal knowledge and self-control), opportunity for rule violation, cognitive processes, and finally organizational processes.

For each of these different parts of the *Handbook*, there are complex interactions between different behavioral mechanisms and different behavioral interventions. Consider, for instance, punishment. Punishment as a behavioral intervention, in different forms, can shape behavior in different ways through different behavioral mechanisms. And some of these are positive, in that punishment, if it works well, can reduce rule-breaking, and some are negative, in that punishment can result in more crime. See Table 1.1 for an overview.

On the positive side, punishment can deter people from breaking rules because they can come to fear punishment (Nagin 2013; Nagin et al. 2009; Nagin and Pepper 2012; Schell-Busey et al. 2016; Simpson et al. 2014). It can incapacitate: people cannot break rules when

TABLE 1.1 *The potential behavioral effects of punishment*

Positive		Negative
		Erode positive social norms
		Strengthen negative social norms
End impunity (set a norm)		Disperse illegal behavior
Be a specific deterrence		Cause criminogenic effects
Be a general deterrence		Cause brutalizing effects
Reassure compliers	→ Behavior←	Make people evade detection
Incapacitate		Enhance blame shifting
Rehabilitate		Undermine procedural justice
Shame		Stigmatize offenders
		Enhance neutralization

they are locked away from society (Cohen 1983; Kessler and Levitt 1999; Miles and Ludwig 2007; Travis et al. 2014) or when professionals are debarred or when organizations lose licenses or are closed down. It can rehabilitate offenders by forcing them to go through treatment for underlying causes that made them commit offenses (Lipsey and Cullen 2007). Punishment can also shame people and activate social and personal pressures on people to motivate them to correct their conduct (Kahan and Posner 1999; Makkai and Braithwaite 1994; Van Erp 2011). And, of course, punishment can set a norm and end impunity as well as reassure those that are complying that they are not doing so without reason (Gunningham et al. 2005; Thornton et al. 2005).

On the negative side, depending on the type of punishment, the execution of such punishment, the type of behavior, the type of offender, and the existing social norms and social and economic conditions, there are ways that punishment can make behavior worse. Punishment can erode existing positive social norms (Gneezy and Rustichini 2000) and strengthen negative social norms (Cialdini 2007; Cialdini et al. 2006; Schultz et al. 2007). Imprisonment can have criminogenic (Cullen et al. 2011) and stigmatizing (Alexander 2012) effects, making ex-cons more likely to reoffend, in part because prison socializes them in how to commit crime and in part because the stigma of being an ex-con keeps them from the employment, housing, and educational opportunities they need to lead a law-abiding life. Punishment can also result in a cat-and-mouse game, where the higher the punishment, the more people are incentivized to try to evade getting caught (Plambeck and Taylor 2015). Strong and violent punishment, like capital punishment or lifelong imprisonment, may also have brutalization effects in pushing offenders toward more violent crime (Cochran and Chamlin 2000; Cochran et al. 1994; Shepherd 2005; Marvell and Moody 2001). And law enforcement can result in offenders seeking elaborate ways to avoid detection (Gray and Silbey 2014). Punishing one offender may also create opportunities for other offenders and thus displace and disperse offending; at worst, there can be a Hydra effect where eliminating one offender creates many others (e.g. Ryan 1998). In order not to face strong punishment, offenders can seek to shift blame to others and to neutralize their own shame and guilt (e.g. van Rooij and Fine 2018). And finally, punishment can backfire if it is done in a procedurally unfair manner that undermines people's sense of legitimacy and their willingness to obey rules out of a sense of obligation (Nagin and Telep 2017; Jackson et al. 2012; Tyler 2017; Walters and Bolger 2019).

All of this shows how just one particular intervention we use in law to shape behavior can trigger many different behavioral mechanisms and have both positive and negative effects, depending on the circumstances of the punishment, the offense, the offender, and the wider context. The contributions in the *Handbook* cover distinct interventions and mechanisms, or aspects of each, as that is mostly how the existing literature has developed. A full reading of the *Handbook* will show the necessary comprehensive picture of how these different aspects of how rules shape behavior interact.

To study compliance and the interaction between rules and behavior requires both legal and empirical analysis. The legal analysis studies what interpretations of rules exist and may also establish how such interpretations may leave room for discretion and interpretation in practice. The empirical analysis looks both at what the behavior is in response to the rules and at how, in practice, the rules come to be interpreted and applied, what different influences there are on such behavior, and how these influences come to interact and shape the behavior. The combination of the two styles gets us past the debate of "Does law matter?" to "How does law matter?".

The empirical methods used to study compliance present fundamental challenges for research. A first problem is practical and ethical. While, for some, compliance research involves behavior that is not clearly illegal or legal, much other compliance research is about finding out whether there was legal or illegal behavior. Studying illegal behavior through surveys is highly challenging as most people who break the law do not want to share this with researchers (Parker and Nielsen 2009a). At the same time, for most types of illegal behavior (with the exception, for instance, of homicides, which are normally reported to the authorities), reliance on enforcement data to establish patterns in rule-breaking is problematic as this makes it impossible to know whether enforcement detection has improved or whether illegal behavior has gone up. Part of this is due to shifts in enforcement where behavior that was once prosecuted may no longer be a priority. Doing experiments has the advantage that real rule-breaking can be directly observed, but the disadvantages are that laboratory experiments may have low external, or real-world, validity and that field experiments are possible only in certain areas of conduct but not in many others. Ethnography, finally, allows for direct observation of illegal behavior and complex processes in real life, but it has the disadvantage that it is hard to generalize to a larger set of cases or populations.

Another issue is what the research focuses on. Much scholarship assesses compliance with a limited set of rules, and at one or two or maybe three points of time (here, of course, exceptions are research data using automated monitoring or satellite monitoring, such as when measuring pollution emissions or contact movement for public health, governmental inspection data, or studies using publicly traded company data). Such research, whether through surveys, experiments, or governmental data, gets us a clear picture of behavior with regard to the selected rules at the given times. Yet, the reality of compliance is that individuals and especially organizations face a multitude of rules and do so often on a continual basis. What this means is that compliance research, where no continuous data or data across different sets of legal rules are available, may come to show a static picture of something that is inherently dynamic (Wu and van Rooij 2019). Put differently, the more complex the situation to be studied, the more difficult it is to create a set of testable hypotheses that capture its richness.

Yet another challenge in the study of compliance is how to establish a causal relationship among the rules, the behavior, and the different mechanisms and interventions that can shape individual and organizational responses to rules, and here methods that allow for more causal inference (experimental and natural experimental designs) may have trouble capturing the complexity of how a multitude of mechanisms are at play in reality, while those that capture such reality (ethnography and, to a lesser extent, enforcement data and nonexperimental surveys) allow for less causal inference.

In all of this, scholars also face ethical challenges if, through their study of people, they come to know of illegal behavior that, in most instances, they cannot protect as privileged information. This is especially so for studies that use direct observation of real behavior, such as field experiments and ethnography (Parker and Nielsen 2009a).

To study compliance means to embrace the inherent limits of empirical methods. The *Handbook* provides a state-of-the-art overview of the different approaches to capturing compliance and making causal inferences about the influences at play. The *Handbook* does not favor one method over another but, rather, sees that all methods have inherent advantages and disadvantages and that researchers must make choices about the generalizability, simplicity, and preciseness of data (Fine and Elsbach 2000).

The Cambridge Handbook on Compliance seeks to bring together knowledge about rules and behavior from across the legal and social science disciplines. In doing so, it also seeks to stimulate legal thinking and theory, to focus more on the question of how law comes to shape behavior, and thus more on the *ex ante* approach to law's influence on future conduct (Darley et al. 2001). Here, it is hoped that the massive body of knowledge contained in its chapters will help to clarify assumptions that exist in law about human and organizational conduct. These include, for instance, assumptions about whether people know the law, how people respond to punishment, how people respond to the law's other incentives such as tort, whether people make individual and amoral and rational decisions in response to legal rules, and whether organizations (both private and public) respond to the law just like individuals do. It is hoped that this body of knowledge will show which assumptions in law require correction and that compliance scholars stand at the forefront in capturing and changing flawed legal assumptions about behavior and in building a behavioral jurisprudence (van Rooij 2020).

The *Handbook* also hopes to reduce some disciplinary siloes by introducing work from certain approaches and fields to others. All too often, researchers across fields are unaware of related work (albeit with some different assumptions and research questions), which can prevent potential policy steps from being fully informed. Indeed, one hope for the *Handbook* is that its use is not merely academic but will influence policy across a number of legal and regulatory fields. Chapter authors do not merely discuss the extant literature. Rather, they take care to synthesize the literature and provide some overall thoughts on existing gaps of research as well as potential policy prescriptions where appropriate. As the use of data analytics and machine learning play a larger role in empirical research across fields over time, this may lead to new use of existing data sets or of new data sets being developed.

Ultimately, while each *Handbook* chapter can be read independently, the overall collection of work is itself a distinct product that can help challenge certain previously held beliefs of both researchers and policymakers. One basic divide is that those researchers who focus on government-related compliance often do not understand how some of the assumptions and research focuses of private organizational compliance and governance differ in certain respects. Nor do they always understand some of the similarities. If we have identified new research questions for researchers and policymakers and challenged some prior beliefs, we have done our jobs as editors.

REFERENCES

Akers, R. L., M. D. Krohn, L. Lanza-Kaduce, and M. Radosevich. 1979. "Social Learning and Deviant Behavior: A Specific Test of a General Theory." *American Sociological Review* 44:635.

Akers, Ronald. 2017. *Social Learning and Social Structure: A General Theory of Crime and Deviance*. Abingdon, UK and New York: Routledge.

Alexander, Cindy R., Scott W. Bauguess, Gennaro Bernile, Yoon-Ho Alex Lee, and Jennifer Marietta-Westberg. 2013. "Economic Effects of SOX Section 404 Compliance: A Corporate Insider Perspective." *Journal of Accounting and Economics* 56(2):267–90.

Alexander, Michelle. 2012. *The New Jim Crow: Mass Incarceration in the Age of Colorblindness*. New York: New Press.

Ariely, Dan. 2012. *The (Honest) Truth about Dishonesty: How We Lie to Everyone–Especially Ourselves*. New York: HarperCollins UK.

Bazerman, Max H., and Ann E. Tenbrunsel. 2012. *Blind Spots: Why We Fail to Do What's Right and What to Do about It*. Princeton, NJ: Princeton University Press.

Bachireddy, Chethan, Andrew Joung, Leslie K. John, Francesca Gino, Bradford Tuckfield, Luca Foschini, and Katherine L. Milkman. 2019. “Effect of Different Financial Incentive Structures on Promoting Physical Activity Among Adults: A Randomized Clinical Trial.” *JAMA Network Open* 2 (8):1–13.

Chhaochharia, Vidhi, and Grinstein Yaniv. 2007. “Corporate Governance and Firm Value: The Impact of the 2002 Governance Rules.” *Journal of Finance*, 62 (4):1789–825.

Cialdini, Robert B. 2007. “Descriptive Social Norms as Underappreciated Sources of Social Control.” *Psychometrika* 72 (2):263–8. doi: 10.1007/s11336-006-1560-6.

Cialdini, Robert B., and Noah J. Goldstein. 2004. “Social Influence: Compliance and Conformity.” *Annual Review of Psychology* 55:591–621. doi: 10.1146/annurev.psych.55.090902.142015.

Cialdini, Robert B., Linda J. Demaine, Brad J. Sagarin, Daniel W. Barrett, Kelton Rhoads, and Patricia L. Winter. 2006. “Managing Social Norms for Persuasive Impact.” *Social Influence* 1 (1):3–15.

Cochran, John K., and Mitchell B. Chamlin. 2000. “Deterrence and Brutalization: The Dual Effects of Executions.” *Justice Quarterly* 17 (4):685–706.

Cochran, John K., Mitchell B. Chamlin, and Mark Seth. 1994. “Deterrence or Brutalization: An Impact Assessment of Oklahoma’s Return to Capital Punishment.” *Criminology* 32:107.

Coglianese, Cary, and David Lazer. 2003. “Management-Based Regulation: Prescribing Private Management to Achieve Public Goals.” *Law & Society Review* 37 (4):691–730.

Cohen, Jacqueline. 1983. “Incapacitation as a Strategy for Crime Control: Possibilities and Pitfalls.” *Crime and Justice*:1–84.

Costa, Elisio, Anna Giardini, Magda Savin, Enrica Menditto, Elaine Lehane, Olga Laosa, Sergio Pecorelli, Alessandro Monaco, and Alessandra Marengoni. 2015. “Interventional Tools to Improve Medication Adherence: Review of Literature.” *Patient Preference and Adherence* 9:1303.

Cullen, Francis T., Cheryl Lero Jonson, and Daniel S. Nagin. 2011. “Prisons Do Not Reduce Recidivism: The High Cost of Ignoring Science.” *Prison Journal* 91 (3 suppl.):48S–65S.

Darley, John M., Kevin M. Carlsmith, and Paul H. Robinson. 2001. “The ex ante Function of the Criminal Law.” *Law and Society Review* 35 (1):165–90.

Edelman, Lauren B., and Shauhin A. Talesh. 2011. “To Comply or Not to Comply – That Isn’t the Question: How Organizations Construct the Meaning of Compliance.” In *Explaining Compliance: Business Responses to Regulation*, edited by Christine Parker and Vibeke Lehmann Nielsen, 103–22. Cheltenham, UK: Edward Elgar.

Edelman, L. B., S. Petterson, E. Chambliss, and H. S. Erlanger. 1991. “Legal Ambiguity and the Politics of Compliance: Affirmative Action Officers’ Dilemma.” *Law & Policy* 13 (1):73–97.

Elster, Jon. 1989. “Social Norms and Economic Theory.” *Journal of Economic Perspectives* 3 (4):99–117.

Erasmus, Vicki, Thea J. Daha, Hans Brug, Jan Hendrik Richardus, Myra D. Behrendt, Margreet C. Vos, and Ed F. van Beeck. 2010. “Systematic Review of Studies on Compliance with Hand Hygiene Guidelines in Hospital Care.” *Infection Control & Hospital Epidemiology* 31 (3):283–94.

Falk Moore, S. 1973. “Law and Social Change: The Semi-autonomous Social Field as an Appropriate Subject of Study.” *Law & Society Review* 7 (4):719–46.

Feldman, Yuval. 2018. *The Law of Good People: Challenging States’ Ability to Regulate Human Behavior*. New York: Cambridge University Press.

Feldman, Yuval, Melissa Rorie, and Benjamin van Rooij. 2019. “Rule-Breaking without Crime: Insights from Behavioral Ethics for the Study of Everyday Deviancy.” *The Criminologist* 44 (2):8–11.

Fine, Gary Alan, and Kimberly D. Elsbach. 2000. “Ethnography and Experiment in Social Psychological Theory Building: Tactics for Integrating Qualitative Field Data with Quantitative Lab Data.” *Journal of Experimental Social Psychology* 36 (1):51–76.

Gammon, John, Heulwen Morgan-Samuel, and Dinah Gould. 2008. “A Review of the Evidence for Suboptimal Compliance of Healthcare Practitioners to Standard/Universal Infection Control Precautions.” *Journal of Clinical Nursing* 17 (2):157–67.

Giddens, Anthony. 1984. *The Constitution of Society: Outline of the Theory of Structuration*. Berkeley: University of California Press.

Giddens, Anthony. 1990. *The Consequences of Modernity*. Stanford, CA: Stanford University Press.

Gneezy, Uri, and Aldo Rustichini. 2000. “A Fine Is a Price.” *Journal of Legal Studies* 29 (1):1–17.

Goldstein, Noah J., Robert B. Cialdini, and Vladas Griskevicius. 2008. "A Room with a Viewpoint: Using Social Norms to Motivate Environmental Conservation in Hotels." *Journal of Consumer Research* 35:472–82.

Gray, Garry C., and Susan S. Silbey. 2012. "The Other Side of the Compliance Relationship." In *Explaining Compliance: Business Responses to Regulation*, edited by Christine Parker and Vibeke Lehmann Nielsen, 123–38. Cheltenham, UK: Edward Elgar.

Gray, Garry C., and Susan S. Silbey. 2014. "Governing Inside the Organization: Interpreting Regulation and Compliance." *American Journal of Sociology* 120 (1):96–145.

Griffiths, John. 2003. "The Social Working of Legal Rules." *Journal of Legal Pluralism* (48):1–72.

Gunningham, Neil, Dorothy Thornton, and Robert A. Kagan. 2005. "Motivating Management: Corporate Compliance in Environmental Protection." *Law & Policy* 27 (2):289–316.

Iliev, Peter. 2010. "The Effect of SOX Section 404: Costs, Earnings Quality and Stock Prices (August 26, 2009)." *Journal of Finance* 65 (3):1163–96. https://ssrn.com/abstract=983772 or http://dx.doi.org/10.2139/ssrn.983772.

Jackson, Jonathan, Ben Bradford, Mike Hough, Andy Myhill, Paul Quinton, and Tom R. Tyler. 2012. "Why Do People Comply with the Law? Legitimacy and the Influence of Legal Institutions." *British Journal of Criminology* 52 (6):1051–71.

Jin, Jing, Grant Edward Sklar, Vernon Min Sen Oh, and Shu Chuen Li. 2008. "Factors Affecting Therapeutic Compliance: A Review from the Patient's Perspective." *Therapeutics and Clinical Risk Management* 4 (1):269.

Jolls, Christine, Cass R. Sunstein, and Richard Thaler. 1998. "A Behavioral Approach to Law and Economics." *Stanford Law Review*:1471–550.

Kagan, Robert A., and John T. Scholz. 1984. "The 'Criminology of the Corporation' and Regulatory Enforcement Strategies." In *Regulatory Enforcement*, edited by Keith Hawkins and John M. Thomas, 67–95. Boston: Kluwer-Nijhoff Publishing.

Kahan, Dan M., and Eric A. Posner. 1999. "Shaming White-Collar Criminals: A Proposal for Reform of the Federal Sentencing Guidelines." *Journal of Law and Economics* 42 (S1):365–92.

Kessler, Daniel, and Steven D. Levitt. 1999. "Using Sentence Enhancements to Distinguish between Deterrence and Incapacitation." *Journal of Law and Economics* 42 (S1):343–64.

Labrague, L. J., D. M. McEnroe-Petitte, T. Van de Mortel, and A. M. A. Nasirudeen. 2018. "A Systematic Review on Hand Hygiene Knowledge and Compliance in Student Nurses." *International Nursing Review* 65 (3):336–48.

Lange, B. 1999. "Compliance Construction in the Context of Environmental Regulation." *Social & Legal Studies* 8 (4):549–67.

Lipsey, Mark W., and Francis T. Cullen. 2007. "The Effectiveness of Correctional Rehabilitation: A Review of Systematic Reviews." *Annual Review of Law and Social Science* 3:297–320.

Makkai, Toni, and John Braithwaite. 1994. "Reintegrative Shaming and Compliance with Regulatory Standards." *Criminology* 32 (3):361–85.

Marvell, Thomas B., and Carlisle E. Moody. 2001. "The Lethal Effects of Three-Strikes Laws." *Journal of Legal Studies* 30 (1):89–106.

Memon, Khalida Naz, Nudrat Zeba Shaikh, Rafique Ahmed Soomro, Shazia Rehman Shaikh, and Anza Mansoor Khwaja. 2017. "Non-compliance to Doctors' Advices among Patients Suffering from Various Diseases: Patients Perspectives: A Neglected Issue." *Journal of Medicine* 18 (1):10–14.

Miles, Thomas J., and Jens Ludwig. 2007. "The Silence of the Lambdas: Deterring Incapacitation Research." *Journal of Quantitative Criminology* 23 (4):287–301.

Nagin, Daniel S. 2013. "Deterrence in the Twenty-First Century." *Crime and Justice* 42 (1):199–263.

Nagin, Daniel S., and John V. Pepper, eds. 2012. *Deterrence and the Death Penalty*. Washington, DC: National Academies Press.

Nagin, Daniel S., and Cody W. Telep. 2017. "Procedural Justice and Legal Compliance." *Annual Review of Law and Social Science* 13:5–28.

Nagin, Daniel S., Francis T. Cullen, and Cheryl Lero Jonson. 2009. "Imprisonment and Reoffending." *Crime and Justice* 38 (1):115–200.

Parker, Christine, and Sharon Gilad. 2011. "Internal Corporate Compliance Management Systems: Structure, Culture and Agency." In *Explaining Compliance: Business Responses to Regulation*,

edited by Christine Parker and Vibeke Lehmann Nielsen, 170–95. Cheltenham, UK: Edward Elgar.
Parker, C., and V. Nielsen. 2009a. "The Challenge of Empirical Research on Business Compliance in Regulatory Capitalism." *Annual Review of Law and Social Science* 5:45–70.
Parker, Christine, and Vibeke Lehmann Nielsen. 2009b. "Corporate Compliance Systems: Could They Make Any Difference?" *Administration & Society* 41 (1):3–37.
Plambeck, Erica L., and Terry A. Taylor. 2015 [online]. "Supplier Evasion of a Buyer's Audit: Implications for Motivating Supplier Social and Environmental Responsibility." https://doi.org/10.1287/msom.2015.0550; 2016. *Manufacturing & Service Operations Management* 18 (2):184–97.
Reardon, Gregory, Sameer Kotak, and Gail F. Schwartz. 2011. "Objective Assessment of Compliance and Persistence among Patients Treated for Glaucoma and Ocular Hypertension: A Systematic Review." *Patient Preference and Adherence* 5:441.
Ryan, Kevin F. 1998. "Clinging to Failure: The Rise and Continued Life of the U.S. Drugs Policy." *Law and Society Review* 32:221.
Schell-Busey, Natalie, Sally S. Simpson, Melissa Rorie, and Mariel Alper. 2016. "What Works? A Systematic Review of Corporate Crime Deterrence." *Criminology & Public Policy* 15 (2):387–416.
Schultz, P. Wesley, Jessica M. Nolan, Robert B. Cialdini, Noah J. Goldstein, and Vladas Griskevicius. 2007. "The Constructive, Destructive, and Reconstructive Power of Social Norms." *Psychological Science* 18 (5):429–34.
Shepherd, Joanna M. 2005. "Deterrence versus Brutalization: Capital Punishment's Differing Impacts among States." *Michigan Law Review*:203–56.
Simpson, Sally, Melissa Rorie, Mariel Elise Alper, Natalie Schell-Busey, William Laufer, and N. Craig Smith. 2014. "Corporate Crime Deterrence: A Systematic Review." *Campbell Systematic Reviews* 10 (4):5–88.
Talesh, Shauhin A. 2009. "The Privatization of Public Legal Rights: How Manufacturers Construct the Meaning of Consumer Law." *Law & Society Review* 43 (3):527–62.
Talesh, Shauhin, and Jérôme Pélisse. 2019. "How Legal Intermediaries Facilitate or Inhibit Social Change." *Studies in Law, Politics, and Society* 79:111–45.
Thaler, Richard H. 2015. *Misbehaving: The Making of Behavioral Economics*. New York: W.W. Norton & Company.
Thornton, Dorothy, Neil Gunningham, and Robert A. Kagan. 2005. "General Deterrence and Corporate Environmental Behavior." *Law & Policy* 27 (2):262–88.
Travis, Jeremy, Bruce Western, and Steve Redburn. 2014. *The Growth of Incarceration in the United States: Exploring Causes and Consequences*. Washington, DC: National Academies Press.
Tyler, Tom. 2017. "Procedural Justice and Policing: A Rush to Judgment?" *Annual Review of Law and Social Science* 13:29–53.
Van Erp, Judith. 2011. "Naming without Shaming: The Publication of Sanctions in the Dutch Financial Market." *Regulation & Governance* 5 (3):287–308.
Van Rooij, Benjamin. 2020. "Behavioral Jurisprudence: The Quest for Knowledge about the ex-ante Function of Law and Behavior." *Jerusalem Review of Legal Studies* 22(1):57–77.
Van Rooij, Benjamin, and Adam Fine. 2018. "Toxic Corporate Culture: Assessing Organizational Processes of Deviancy." *Administrative Sciences* 8 (3):23–61.
Van Rooij, Benjamin, and Adam Fine. 2019. "Preventing Corporate Crime from Within." In *The Handbook of White Collar Crime*, edited by Melissa Rorie, 229–45. New York: John Wiley and Sons.
Walters, Glenn D., and P. Colin Bolger. 2019. "Procedural Justice Perceptions, Legitimacy Beliefs, and Compliance with the Law: A Meta-analysis." *Journal of Experimental Criminology* 15 (3):341–72.
Wu, Yunmei, and Benjamin van Rooij. 2019. "Compliance Dynamism: Capturing the Polynormative and Situational Nature of Business Responses to Law." *Journal of Business Ethics*:1–13.

PART I

Compliance Concepts and Approaches

2

Compliance as Costs and Benefits

Vikramaditya S. Khanna

Abstract: This chapter explores the conceptual, measurement, and incidence issues surrounding the costs and benefits of compliance. At the conceptual level, foundational questions are not fully resolved. For example, when speaking of compliance, do we mean compliance with the law or something else (e.g., an ethical code or industry standard)? What a firm is complying with will influence the costs and benefits being considered. Further, are the costs and benefits to be assessed from the perspective of the firm or from the perspective of society? Which one is chosen will impact what are viewed as costs and benefits. At the measurement level, assessing the effects of various compliance initiatives is a fraught exercise as attested to by a voluminous literature. It will typically require the use of multidisciplinary approaches with challenging questions about the unit(s) of measurement, the presence of counterfactuals, difficult to measure items, and difficult to operationalize trade-offs along with many potentially questionable assumptions. Further, embedded within measurement issues will be legal policy choices and structures that influence how, and by whom, the measurement is conducted. Finally, questions of incidence are important but are not often addressed in the literature. For example, if the costs of compliance fall disproportionately on smaller businesses, then what impact does that have on the political sustainability of the compliance initiative, the equity of it, and the competitive structure of the sector subject to these initiatives? Bringing together these considerations allows for a richer and more nuanced understanding of the costs and benefits of compliance and also encourages us to develop more careful theoretical models with which to analyze, and more reliable evidence-based research with which to assess, compliance initiatives.

2.1 INTRODUCTION

The literature on compliance has grown dramatically over the last two decades as instances of corporate misbehavior have garnered greater global attention.[1] Whether one looks at the

[1] *See, e.g.*, GEOFFREY P. MILLER, THE LAW OF GOVERNANCE, RISK MANAGEMENT AND COMPLIANCE (WOLTERS KLUWER, 3RD EDITION, 2020); Luigi Alberto Franzoni, *Tax Evasion and Tax Compliance*, *in* 4 ENCYCLOPEDIA OF LAW AND ECONOMICS 51 (BOUDEWIJN BOUCKAERT AND GERRIT DE GEEST, EDS., EDWARD ELGAR, UK AND UNIVERSITY OF GHENT, BELGIUM, 1999); John Robert Graham, Jillian Grennan, Campbell R. Harvey, and Shivaram Rajgopal, *Corporate Culture: Evidence from the Field* (June 26, 2019), available at SSRN: https://ssrn.com/abstract=2805602; Sean J. Griffith, *Corporate Governance in an Era of Compliance*, 57 WILLIAM & MARY LAW REVIEW 2075 (2016); Wouter P.J. Wils, *Antitrust Compliance Programmes & Optimal Antitrust Enforcement*, 1 JOURNAL OF ANTITRUST ENFORCEMENT 52 (2013); Veronica Root Martinez, *Complex Compliance Investigations*, 120 COLUMBIA LAW REVIEW 249 (2020); Rosa M. Abrantes-Metz and D. Daniel Sokol, *Antitrust Corporate Governance and Compliance*, *in*

United States or across the world, this greater attention has focused regulatory and business efforts on developing and implementing compliance programs to reduce the incidence and severity of wrongdoing.[2] In addition, because compliance represents the confluence of a number of related, yet distinct, areas – corporate liability and governance, business ethics, information systems, technology, accounting, and yet others – it has become one of the most actively debated and discussed areas of research inquiry.[3] In spite of this, there are few scholarly works that provide a broad overview of the costs and benefits of compliance. This chapter aims to provide one such overview and, in the process, provide additional insights and some potential areas for future research.

One matter that should be addressed early on is what does compliance mean? Although one could provide many definitions, I rely on an approximate one for this chapter – compliance involves gathering relevant information about the thing(s) with which you wish to comply and your responses to that information.[4] But this just starts our inquiry into compliance as costs and benefits, which involves conceptual, measurement, and incidence questions. This makes it a complex inquiry with a tantalizingly broad array of questions.

For example, at a conceptual level, a foundational question is "compliance with what?" – the law or something else? Similarly, when we say costs and benefits, do we mean costs and benefits to individual actors (or corporations) or to society? Further, when exploring measurement or assessment questions, we are forced to examine what tools we use to do this – is a multidisciplinary approach most useful (and, if so, which disciplines) and how are the trade-offs and choices operationalized (and can this be done in a theoretically parsimonious manner)? Relatedly, what role should the law (e.g., legislatures, the judiciary, regulators) have in structuring the measurement or assessment of compliance efforts? What about the role of private parties providing compliance and related services? In addition, should we closely examine who bears the costs of compliance (i.e., its incidence)? For example, if there are consistent and persistent differences (e.g., smaller versus large businesses, new entrants versus incumbents) then what does that do to the political sustainability of compliance efforts and to other matters of interest (e.g., competition, entrepreneurial activity)? Of course, all of these questions cannot be fully answered in this short chapter, but identifying the contours of these questions and probing at them may help to facilitate the development of ways to address these critical issues.

Oxford Handbook of International Antitrust Economics (Roger D. Blair and D. Daniel Sokol, eds., Oxford University Press, 2013); Chapter 1 in this volume; Josephine Nelson, *Paper Dragon Thieves*, 105 Georgetown Law Journal 871 (2017); John Armour, Brandon L. Garrett, Jeffrey N. Gordon, and Geeyoung Min, *Board Compliance*, 104 Minnesota Law Review 1191 (2020).

2 *See* Miller, *supra* note 1; D. Daniel Sokol, *Monopolists Without Borders: The Institutional Challenge of International Antitrust in a Global Gilded Age*, 4 Berkeley Business Law Journal 37 (2007); Greg Distelhorst and Richard Locke, *Does Compliance Pay? Social Standards and Firm-level Trade*, 62 American Journal of Political Science 695 (2018). Goldman Sachs also discusses its global compliance efforts on its website (see www.goldmansachs.com/careers/divisions/global-compliance/) and there is a Baker & McKenzie website dedicated to the topic (see *Global Compliance News*, https://globalcompliancenews.com/).

3 There are new courses in the curricula of law and business schools focused on compliance as well. In addition, there are symposia focused on these topics. *See, e.g.*, Veronica Root Martinez, *Investigating Intersections of Corporate Governance and Compliance* (October 23, 2019), University of Chicago Law Review, *in press*, available at SSRN: https://ssrn.com/abstract=3474334. There is also the annual Compliance Net conference; see www.compliancenet.org/.

4 *Cf.* Miller, *supra* note 1. Although I envisage the information gathering to take place in a formal compliance process, it is undoubtedly the case that informal gathering of information (even outside of a formal process) is important and significant.

Section 2.2 begins the inquiry by examining some of the most pertinent conceptual questions in order to provide us with a sense of the topography of the compliance terrain. Section 2.3 pushes forward on the most difficult of issues – measuring and assessing compliance efforts – and notes some insights that existing research provides. Section 2.4 examines the thorny issue of incidence and what impact that may have on the design of compliance efforts and their implementation. Section 2.5 concludes.

2.2 CONCEPTUAL QUESTIONS

Although the topic of compliance generates substantial discussion across multiple areas of scholarly inquiry, there have been few papers that examine some challenging conceptual questions. Section 2.2.1 explores how the question of "compliance with what?" influences our thinking on the costs and benefits of compliance. Section 2.2.2 delves into the question of whose costs and benefits concern us most and what we are willing to count in the cost–benefit calculus.

2.2.1 *Compliance with What?*

The concept of compliance implies that there is some standard against which one is comparing activity to determine whether it "complies." Within the compliance literature, this standard seems capable of meaning different things.[5]

For most scholars, compliance would mean, at a minimum, compliance with the law. Typically, this means state, federal, and perhaps foreign or international laws and regulations.[6] With this focus, the costs and benefits we may consider are likely to be those associated with setting up systems to monitor for behaviors that might violate these rules and the harms (and bad publicity) avoided when fewer violations occur. This, however, is not the only thing with which firms might comply.

Many firms may also comply with a range of nonlegal standards, for example statements of corporate policy that are designed to enhance the efficiency of the firm and perhaps reduce waste or theft by employees.[7] Yet other firms may want to meet the procurement standards of an important customer or contracting party (e.g., Walmart's procurement standards) or meet manufacturing or preparation standards (e.g., ISO standards, "organic" food).[8] Beyond this, some firms may want to comply with ethical or other standards such as environmental, social, and corporate governance (ESG) standards.[9] Firms may be interested in complying with

5 *See, e.g.*, Miller, *supra* note 1.

6 *See, e.g.*, Franzoni, *supra* note 1; Griffiths, *supra* note 1; Abrantes-Metz and Sokol, *supra* note 1.

7 *See, e.g.*, Miller, *supra* note 1.

8 *See, e.g.*, *HSBC and Walmart Join Forces on Sustainable Supply Chain Finance Programme*, AP News, April 17, 2019, available at: https://apnews.com/Business%20Wire/8be2ad54cf0242ddaf69dcee60924347; Michael P. Vandenbergh, *The New Wal-Mart Effect: The Role of Private Contracting in Global Governance*, 54 UCLA Law Review 913 (2007); Sarah L. Stafford, *Private Policing of Environmental Performance: Does It Further Public Goals?*, 39 Boston College Environmental Affairs Law Review 73 (2012); Margaret M. Blair, Cynthia A. Williams, and Li-Wen Lin, *The New Role for Assurance Services in Global Commerce*, 33 Journal of Corporation Law 325 (2007–8); Jeanne C. Fromer, *The Unregulated Certification Mark(et)*, 69 Stanford Law Review 121 (2017). Of course, we might be interested in whether these private governance efforts have desirable effects. For some discussion see Richard Locke, Fei Qin, and Alberto Brause, *Does Monitoring Improve Labor Standards?: Lessons from Nike*, 61 Industrial and Labor Relations Review 1 (2007).

9 *See, e.g.*, Cristiano Busco, Costanza Consolandi, Robert G. Eccles, and Elena Sofra, A *Preliminary Analysis of SASB Reporting: Disclosure Topics, Financial Relevance, and the Financial Intensity of ESG Materiality* (March 4, 2020), available at SSRN: https://ssrn.com/abstract=3548849; Linda M. Lowson, Esq., *SEC ESG Noncompliance: Where the Rubber Meets the Road*, 24 Journal of Applied Corporate Finance 57 (2012).

these nonlegal standards to enhance profitability, to project an image or reputation to customers, employees, or other stakeholders, and for intrinsic reasons as well (e.g., firm owners may believe in the standards perhaps as a moral or religious matter).[10] Indeed, in the last two years the world's largest asset managers (e.g., BlackRock) have stated that they want their investee firms to make long-term sustainable value a core part of their strategy.[11] This, along with other matters, has led to considerable interest and growth in ESG ratings, firms pursuing integrated-ESG businesses, and funds investing mainly in "good" ESG firms.[12]

Thus, firms often have incentives to meet nonlegal standards and may set up internal systems to gather information on matters that aid in complying with these standards. Here, costs and benefits are likely to be broader than when the concern was simply complying with the law. But that still leaves opens the question of whose costs and benefits are to be considered.

2.2.2 *Whose Costs and Benefits?*

The simplest starting point is whether we focus on the *social* as opposed to *private* costs and benefits of compliance.[13] This often depends on what question is being asked. If one is thinking about whether compliance systems for particular industries or sets of issues are desirable then social costs and benefits seem most important. However, if one is thinking about whether firms are likely to implement compliance systems then private costs and benefits may be of greater importance.

Let us begin by asking what the private costs and benefits of compliance activities are to the firm. These would typically be the costs of adopting compliance systems, beyond those the firm would otherwise have, to address the issue with which the firm wishes to comply. These costs would most likely include those associated with setting up the incremental compliance system (e.g., hiring and training personnel, technology costs, time of executives spent on compliance matters) and the costs associated with avoiding (taking) decisions because of compliance concerns that otherwise would have been taken (avoided).[14]

[10] See cites in *infra* note 12. Firms and their owners sometimes espouse particular views. *See, e.g., Burwell* v. *Hobby Lobby*, 573 U.S. 682 (2014).

[11] *See Letter to CEOs*, Larry Fink, Founder, Chairman and CEO of BlackRock, Inc., January 17, 2018, available at: www.blackrock.com/corporate/investor-relations/larry-fink-ceo-letter.

[12] For empirical papers *see, e.g.*, Florian Berg, Julian Kölbel, and Roberto Rigobon, *Aggregate Confusion: The Divergence of ESG Ratings* (August 17, 2019). MIT Sloan Research Paper No. 5822-19, available at SSRN: https://ssrn.com/abstract=3438533; Tim Verheyden, Robert G. Eccles, and Andreas Feiner, *ESG for All? The Impact of ESG Screening on Return, Risk and Diversification*, 28 Journal of Applied Corporate Finance 47 (2016); Soh Young In, Ki Young Park, and Ashby H. B. Monk, *Is "Being Green" Rewarded in the Market?: An Empirical Investigation of Decarbonization and Stock Returns* (April 16, 2019), Stanford Global Project Center Working Paper, available at SSRN: https://ssrn.com/abstract=3020304; Jyothika Grewal, Clarissa Hauptmann, and George Serafeim, *Material Sustainability Information and Stock Price Informativeness*, 162 Journal of Business Ethics 1 (2020). For the rise of ESG funds, *see* Jeff Benjamin, *As Pandemic Rages On, ESG Funds Shine Brightly*, Investment News, April 19, 2020, available at: www.investmentnews.com/as-pandemic-rages-on-esg-funds-shine-brightly-191673.

[13] The distinction between social and private costs and benefits is ubiquitous in much scholarship. *See, e.g.*, Steven Shavell, *The Fundamental Divergence between the Private and the Social Motive to Use the Legal System*, 24 Journal of Legal Studies 575 (1997); A. Mitchell Polinsky and Steven Shavell, *The Economic Theory of Public Enforcement of Law*, 38 Journal of Economic Literature 45 (2000). For a discussion of social costs and benefits in the context of Sarbanes-Oxley, *see* John C. Coates and Suraj Srinivasan, *SOX after Ten Years: A Multidisciplinary Review*, 28 Accounting Horizons 627 (2014).

[14] For some general approaches to compliance costs, *see* Coates and Srinivasan, *supra* note 13; Peter Iliev, *The Effect of SOX Section 404: Costs, Earnings Quality and Stock Prices*, 65 Journal of Finance 1163 (2010); William Wilson Bratton, *Enron and the Dark Side of Shareholder Value*, 76 Tulane Law Review 1275 (2002).

On the private benefits side, the expected penalties, bad publicity, and lost sales avoided due to incremental compliance efforts should be counted.[15] Further, if compliance leads to other changes at the firm that generate benefits then those should be counted too. An example is compliance efforts identifying employees who were not complying with the matter at issue but also were creating other costs to the firm that were unlikely to be identified without the additional scrutiny afforded by increased compliance efforts.[16]

Although focusing on private costs and benefits has the advantage of relative simplicity, one suspects that most policy reform is interested in assessing the social costs and benefits of incremental compliance efforts. If that is our focus then the types of things we count as costs and benefits not only change but also increase.

Let us start with social costs. These include the private costs for setting up compliance systems, but some of these costs may generate employment in the compliance sector, which may be viewed as a partially offsetting social benefit. We can also include potential errors associated with compliance decisions. For example, if a compliance system prohibited some behavior that in fact was compliant with the relevant standard then the social benefits lost from this error should be counted as social costs.[17] The size of this error cost would vary with what was prevented – blocking a useful vaccine might have large costs, but blocking an additional sale of a refrigerator less so. Similarly, if a compliance system led to behavior which was in fact noncompliant, and would not otherwise have occurred, then that should count as a social cost. Some scholarship suggests that compliance systems may erroneously "license" noncompliant behavior that would not otherwise have been undertaken had its compliance status remained uncertain.[18]

Compliance systems may also have spillover effects that impact other firms. For example, poor compliance with anti-corruption norms by some firms could push toward more corruption in that sector (a negative externality).[19] Similarly, superior compliance might lead to other firms adopting similar practices and hence to less wrongdoing. Although challenging to measure, these too should be counted in the social analysis.

Moving toward examining social benefits also raises a host of issues to consider. For example, we should include – as social benefits – the social costs of wrongdoing avoided by incremental compliance efforts. But this is not the same as the private benefits of reduced expected penalties because the expected penalties may not reflect the full social costs of wrongdoing and not all instances of wrongdoing are eventually detected and punished.[20] For example, the full social costs of costly sanctions (e.g., prison) and enforcement actions are not

15 *See, e.g.*, Jonathan M. Karpoff, D. Scott Lee, and Gerald S. Martin, *The Cost to Firms of Cooking the Books*, 43 Journal of Financial and Quantitative Analysis 581 (2008).

16 *See, e.g.*, Christopher R. Yukins, *Feature Comment: Enhancing Integrity – Aligning Proposed Contractor Compliance Requirements with Broader Advances in Corporate Compliance*, 49 Government Contractor 166 (2007). It is also argued that such integration improves the efficiency of the compliance system as its own system. *See id.*

17 *Cf.* Shavell, *supra* note 13; Polinsky and Shavell, *supra* note 13; Michelle Burtis, Jonah B. Gelbach, and Bruce H. Kobayashi, *Error Costs, Legal Standards of Proof and Statistical Significance* 25 Supreme Court Economic Review 1 (2017).

18 *See, e.g.*, Nelson, *supra* note 1; Todd Haugh, *"Cadillac Compliance" Breakdown*, 69 Stanford Law Review Online 198 (2017); Chapter 9 in this volume.

19 This notion is often seen in the corruption literature where the perception that more people are corrupt makes it more likely that another person will decide to engage in corrupt activities. *See* Pranab Bardhan, *Corruption and Development: A Review of Issues*, 35 Journal of Economic Literature 1320 (1997).

20 *See* Polinksy and Shavell, *supra* note 13.

typically reflected in the private benefits of reduced expected penalties.[21] Thus, the firm's private benefits are related to social benefits, but not in a very simple manner.

In addition, superior compliance systems may not only reduce the instances and severity of wrongdoing but also generate an environment that boosts employee morale. Employees may be more motivated at firms that avoid wrongdoing and indeed at firms that engage in socially responsible or "moral" activities.[22] This might be socially beneficial both because employees are happier and because, amongst other things, it enhances productivity.[23] Similarly, engaging in certain socially responsible activities or greater compliance may also change the likelihood of enforcement scrutiny (or its intensity) and that may be valuable (the so-called "halo" effect).[24] This latter benefit is only a social benefit if the lesser attention is correlated with a firm that engages in less harmful behavior, but if it is used to muddy the waters and cover up for a firm that is engaged in harmful behavior then the "halo" effect is a social cost and a private benefit.[25]

Yet another benefit of superior compliance is that it may enable greater risk-taking, which may well be socially beneficial. This might seem counterintuitive because people usually associate more compliant behavior with less risky behavior. Although true at some level, it may be useful to think of good compliance as also being similar to having a good product safety testing department. If a firm is thinking of developing a new product that has some risks (for which the firm will bear some liability or lost sales), then which type of safety testing department is more likely to result in the firm taking the chance to develop the risky product? Presumably, the better a firm's safety testing department, the more likely the firm's developers are to try risky products because they anticipate that the safety testing department will block the products with the worst risks (or reduce the risks with the product) before it gets to the market (something a weak safety testing department is less likely to do). In some sense, a better compliance department is like having better brakes on your car: you feel more comfortable driving faster in a car with good brakes than in one with weak brakes.

In addition to this, sometimes compliance activity may result in unexpected advantages to the firm. This is thought to be more likely when a firm's compliance system is integrated into

21 *See id.*; Gary S. Becker, *Crime and Punishment: An Economic Approach*, 76 Journal of Political Economy 169 (1968). Moreover, sometimes expected penalties on firms do not address some social losses. For example, if the injured party is a doctor then the social costs are the salary he foregoes when injured, the physical pain and suffering, and the activity he cannot do (e.g., treating patients). The inability to treat patients is rarely within expected penalties, but the former costs are.

22 *See* Alex Edmans, *Does the Stock Market Fully Value Intangibles? Employee Satisfaction and Equity Prices*, 101 Journal of Financial Economics 621 (2011); Leonard Berry, Ann M. Mirabito, and William Baun, *What's the Hard Return on Employee Wellness Programs?*, Harvard Business Review (December 2010), available at SSRN: https://ssrn.com/abstract=2064874.

23 *See* Edmans, *Stock Market*, *supra* note 22; Claudine Madras Gartenberg, Andrea Prat, and George Serafeim, *Corporate Purpose and Financial Performance*, 30 Organization Science 1 (2018). Greater employee satisfaction or well-being is likely related to employee retention too; see Chitrabhanu Bhattacharya, Sankar Sen, and Daniel Korschun, *Using Corporate Social Responsibility to Win the War for Talent*, 49 MIT Sloan Management Review 37 (2008).

24 *See* Harrison G. Hong, Jeffrey D. Kubik, Inessa Liskovich, and José Scheinkman, *Crime, Punishment and the Value of Corporate Social Responsibility* (October 14, 2019), available at SSRN: https://ssrn.com/abstract=2492202; Mary Hunter McDonnell and Brayden King, *Order in the Court: The Influence of Firm Status and Reputation on the Outcomes of Employment Discrimination Suits*, 83 American Sociological Review 61 (2018); N. Craig Smith, Daniel Read, and Sofia Lopez, *CSR Halo: The Gift that Keeps on Giving?* (March 6, 2018), INSEAD Working Paper No. 2018/07/ATL/Social Innovation Centre, available at SSRN: https://ssrn.com/abstract=3135132; Sue A. Cooper, K. K. Raman, and Jennifer Yin, *Halo Effect or Fallen Angel Effect? Firm Value Consequences of Greenhouse Gas Emissions and Reputation for Corporate Social Responsibility*, 37 Journal of Accounting and Public Policy 226 (2018).

25 *See* Smith et al., *supra* note 24; Cooper et al., *supra* note 24.

the firm's operations and may help identify more efficient ways to do things or perhaps new business lines.[26] This would be a private and social benefit.[27]

Finally, the length of the items considered as social costs and benefits might give one the impression that social, not private, costs and benefits should be our focus. Although social net benefits are important, ignoring private ones is myopic. Focusing on private costs and benefits may be critical in thinking of how to incentivize firms to engage in compliance when it is socially desirable, but perhaps not privately desirable.

2.3 MEASURING AND ASSESSING COMPLIANCE EFFORTS

Even though conceptual issues raise a number of fascinating questions, an even greater challenge awaits those interested in measuring and assessing a firm's compliance efforts. Indeed, regardless of whether we are measuring social or private costs and benefits, there are a number of issues to address.

Section 2.3.1 briefly discusses some methodology and measurement questions. Section 2.3.2 examines how one might engage in cost–benefit analysis and underscores the many discretionary choices made in such analyses. Section 2.3.3 explores what the role of the law should be in guiding the use of this discretion. For example, how should the law (or enforcement authorities) treat self-reporting efforts and steps that might aid law enforcement (e.g., providing information on potentially culpable individuals)? Should the law rely on (or delegate) some issues to professional bodies whose members work in the compliance space? Section 2.3.4 delves into the issue of tying executive compensation to compliance efforts. If executives' compensation is not in some sense dependent on compliance results then their incentives to push for compliance are weaker than they might otherwise be.[28] Finally, Section 2.3.5 makes concrete some of these issues by exploring two live issues – how to use bounties and how to internally structure reporting lines from compliance to other departments (e.g., should the chief compliance officer (CCO) report to the General Counsel (GC) or to the board or chief executive officer (CEO)).

2.3.1 *Methodologies and Measurement*

First, what sorts of methodologies might we use for measurement and assessment? In light of the fact that we are exploring how legal and business structures influence organizational activity, it seems that our focus would be on looking at things from multiple perspectives or from a multidisciplinary point of view. This might mean relying on economics or behaviorally informed economics for many things, but also lessons from internal agency, psychology,

[26] *See, e.g.*, Kent D. Miller, *A Framework for Integrated Risk Management in International Business*, 23 JOURNAL OF INTERNATIONAL BUSINESS STUDIES 311 (1992); Yukins, *supra* note 16.

[27] Compliance efforts may be particularly valuable in building a reputation and enhancing firm credibility. *See* Henry Hansmann and Reinier Kraakman, *Hands-Tying Contracts: Book Publishing, Venture Capital Financing and Secured Debt*, 8 JOURNAL OF LAW, ECONOMICS AND ORGANIZATION 628 (1992).

[28] *See* Karl Hofstetter, Eugene F. Soltes, and Reinier H. Kraakman, *Compliance, Compensation and Corporate Wrongdoing* (May 1, 2018), Conclusions from a Roundtable at Harvard Law School of May 18, 2018, available at SSRN: https://ssrn.com/abstract=3373718. Connecting compensation to ESG goals has generated discussion. *See* Faizul Haque and Collins G. Ntim, *Executive Compensation, Sustainable Compensation Policy, Carbon Performance and Market Value* (January 1, 2020) BRITISH JOURNAL OF MANAGEMENT, in press, available at SSRN: https://ssrn.com/abstract=3512600; Faizul Haque, *The Effects of Board Characteristics and Sustainable Compensation Policy on Carbon Performance of UK Firms*, 49 THE BRITISH ACCOUNTING REVIEW 347 (2017). To the extent that the "Balanced Scorecard" influences compensation, it too is noteworthy, see *infra* note 35.

and sociology on how individuals and groups behave.[29] Moreover, given that most compliance involves measurement and gathering of information, we may bring in insights from accounting, information systems, and technology.[30] These are vast fields of scholarly inquiry that have devoted considerable attention to issues relevant to assessing compliance efforts. A summary of these literatures is not attempted here, but rather a nod to the multidisciplinarity of the inquiry seems warranted to underscore that measurement and assessment require considerable thought.[31]

Bringing these various perspectives together is challenging not only because they sometimes do not directly speak with each other but also because the units of measurement are often different and sometimes difficult to compare.[32] For example, how does one measure benefits from estimated harms avoided? Measuring counterfactuals is notoriously difficult and becomes more so in compliance because there may be more than one type of counterfactual to measure.[33] In addition, it is often challenging to get easy commensurability – for example economic costs versus improvements in the environment (or climate risk changes).[34] However, although these challenges are very real, they are not necessarily insurmountable. Multiple papers have explored how one might make progress on these issues.[35] Indeed, perhaps one of the most fascinating issues is how regulatory agencies conduct cost–benefit analysis under these conditions.

[29] *See, e.g.*, Abrantes-Metz Sokol, *supra* note 1; Jonathan Jackson, Be Bradford, Mike Hough, Andy Myhill, Paul King Quinton, and Tom Tyler, *Why Do People Comply with the Law? Legitimacy and the Influence of Legal Institutions*, 52 British Journal of Criminology 1051 (2012).

[30] *See, e.g.*, Priscilla Ann Burnaby, Martha A. Howe, and Brigitte Muehlmann, *Detecting Fraud in the Organization: An Internal Audit Perspective*, 3 Journal of Forensic & Investigative Accounting 195 (2011); Clive Lennox, Petro Lisowsky, and Jeffrey A. Pittman, *Tax Aggressiveness and Accounting Fraud*, 51 Journal of Accounting Research 739 (2013); Urs Gasser and Daniel Markus Häusermann, *E-Compliance: Towards a Roadmap for Effective Risk Management* (March 15, 2007), available at SSRN: https://ssrn.com/abstract=971848; Kenneth A. Bamberger, *Technologies of Compliance: Risk and Regulation in a Digital Age*, 88 Texas Law Review 669 (2010).

[31] *See, e.g.*, D. Daniel Sokol, *Understanding Corporate Compliance and Wrongdoing in Interdisciplinary Context*, 34 Managerial and Decision Economics 437 (2013).

[32] *See, e.g.*, Haque and Ntim, *supra* note 28; Haque, *supra* note 28; cites in *infra* note 35.

[33] Concerns with counterfactuals have occupied a great deal of scholarly space. *See, e.g.*, Allan F. Gibbard and William L. Harper, *Counterfactuals and Two Kinds of Expected Utility*, in Foundations and Applications of Decision Theory 125 (Clifford Hooker, James J. Leach, and Edward McClennen, eds., Dordrecht: D. Reidel, 1978); Damien Geradin and Ianis Girgenson, *The Counterfactual Method in EU Competition Law: The Cornerstone of the Effects-Based Approach*, in Ten years of effects-based approach in EU competition law: State of play and perspectives 211 (Jacques Bourgeois and Denis Waelbroeck, Eds., Bruylant, 2012).

[34] The incommensurability debate has a long historical pedigree. For some recent contributions *see, e.g.*, Alon Harel and Ariel Porat, *Commensurability and Agency: Two Yet-to-Be-Met Challenges for Law and Economics*, 96 Cornell Law Review 749 (2011); Christine A. Desan, *The Key to Value: The Debate over Commensurability in Neoclassical and Credit Approaches to Money* (March 1, 2020), Law and Contemporary Problems (2020), *in press*, available at SSRN: https://ssrn.com/abstract=3556127.

[35] In principle, "Balanced Scorecards" attempt to do this. *See* Robert S. Kaplan and D. P. Norton, The Balanced Scorecard: Translating Strategy into Action (Boston, MA: Harvard Business School Press, 1996). There is a great deal of commentary (often critical) on these scorecards. *See* Arthur M. Schneiderman, *Why Balanced Scorecards Fail*, 3 Journal of Strategic Performance Measurement 6 (1999); Michael C. Jensen, *Value Maximisation, Stakeholder Theory, and the Corporate Objective Function*, 7 European Financial Management 297 (2001); Dennis Campbell, Srikant Datar, Susan Kulp, and V. G. Narayanan, *Using the Balanced Scorecard as a Control System for Monitoring and Revising Corporate Strategy* (September 5, 2002), Harvard NOM Working Paper No. 02-35, available at SSRN: https://ssrn.com/abstract=328880. Integrated risk management bears some similarity to this but is different in the sense that it attempts to integrate risk management into business decision-making. *See* Miller, *supra* note 26.

2.3.2 *Prior Research on Cost–Benefit Analysis*

Cost–benefit analysis (CBA) is often required (or encouraged) in regulatory rule-making and review as well as in how scholars and commentators assess such regulation. However, there are still significant concerns with conducting CBA even for areas where there is some agreement on units of measurement and methodologies such as financial regulation or securities regulation.[36]

Coates explores issues raised in financial regulation and what that tells us about assessments under CBA.[37] He focuses on several case studies (including disclosures under Sarbanes-Oxley and heightened capital requirements for banks) where it appears that financial agencies proposing a new rule need to engage in quantified and judicially reviewed CBA.[38] Coates argues that quantified CBA involves "no more than 'guesstimation,' entailing: (a) causal inferences that are unreliable under standard regulatory conditions; (b) the use of problematic data; and/or (c) the same kinds of contestable, assumption-sensitive macroeconomic or political modelling used to make monetary policy."[39] He then argues that CBA should itself be subject to cost–benefit analysis (i.e., engaging in CBA should only be pursued where its costs exceed its benefits).[40] In the context of financial regulation, Coates finds that CBA is likely to have few benefits because finance is, in the USA, social, political, and economic and is going through long-term structural changes.[41] These features mean that it will be difficult to usefully estimate effects of financial regulations and that forecasting in such situations will not serve to discipline regulatory behavior.[42] Moreover, the likely costs of such analysis (e.g., resources, camouflage of interests, partisanship) are likely to exceed its benefits.[43] This all suggests that mandating judicially reviewable CBA of financial regulation is not worth the candle. However, Coates is quick to add that voluntary CBA conducted by regulatory agencies, that does not stress quantifiable analysis, may well be useful, in part, to develop tools to conduct more meaningful CBA in the financial regulation context.[44]

To the extent that similar issues may plague the CBA of compliance initiatives, they may well be subject to similar critiques. If so, that makes engaging in CBA of compliance more problematic, especially given the range of costs and benefits noted in Section 2.2. However, that does not mean that it is not worth it (as Coates himself notes),[45] but rather that how one may wish to engage in this assessment may require some way to guide discretion.

2.3.3 *Guiding Discretion: Law, Enforcement, Private Parties*

If relying on the legislature or the judiciary is difficult, then perhaps one could move toward looking at regulators or regulatory initiatives to guide us in thinking about issues

36 For examples in the context of Sarbanes-Oxley, *see* Coates and Srinivasan, *supra* note 13; Dhammika Dharmapala, *Estimating Firms' Responses to Securities Regulation Using a Bunching Approach* (October 31, 2016), University of Chicago Coase-Sandor Institute for Law & Economics Research Paper, available at SSRN: https://ssrn.com/abstract=2817151.

37 *See* John C. Coates, IV, *Cost-Benefit Analysis of Financial Regulation: Case Studies and Implications*, 124 Yale Law Journal 882 (2015).

38 *See id.*

39 *See id.* at 887.

40 *See id.*

41 *See id.* at 888.

42 *See id.*

43 *See id.* at 888–9.

44 *See id.* at 889.

45 *See id.*

(e.g., self-reporting or cooperating with law enforcement as part of compliance efforts). For example, the US Department of Justice's (DOJ) FCPA Unit produced a manual providing some guidance on what it considers useful features in a compliance program.[46] We have seen similar initiatives at other regulators in the USA and elsewhere – most recently in 2019 with the release of the DOJ's manual for evaluating compliance programs.[47] Although earlier guidance was quite broad and often did not provide much information on how to assess the costs and benefits of compliance or to determine whether compliance programs would receive any enforcement credit, the 2019 manual provides considerably more detail.[48]

Another source of guidance might be private parties who provide compliance advice to their clients (e.g., law firms, accounting firms, other consultants). These entities may well possess some useful information for assessing and measuring the costs and benefits of compliance and may be a group that regulators and firms could go to for some information.[49] However, prior scholarship has expressed quite a bit of skepticism about whether these parties are likely to be very helpful in assessing compliance programs.[50] Although they may have fairly good information, their incentives may not align. The matrix of relationships among consultants, law firms, regulators, and the regulated firms can create incentives to turn compliance into something of a form of insurance with large payoffs for the professionals.[51]

In the end, it seems that to make progress on assessing the effectiveness of compliance efforts one would want evidence-based research that helps in understanding what aspects of compliance programs seem to "work" and why and what can be replicated elsewhere. There is some research that goes down this path, but more would be highly valuable.[52]

2.3.4 *Executive Compensation and Compliance*

Although the steps noted so far may aid in the process of measuring and assessing the costs and benefits of compliance, it seems incomplete not to consider things that firms can do to

[46] *See* FCPA Guide, Criminal Division of U.S. Department of Justice and Enforcement Division of U.S. Securities and Exchange Commission (2012), available at: www.justice.gov/criminal-fraud/fcpa-guidance.

[47] *See* Criminal Division, U.S. Department of Justice, Evaluation of Corporate Compliance Programs (2019), available at: www.justice.gov/opa/pr/criminal-division-announces-publication-guidance-evaluating-corporate-compliance-programs.

[48] On discussion of earlier guidance, *see, e.g.*, Peter Reilly, *Incentivizing Corporate America to Eradicate Transnational Bribery Worldwide: Federal Transparency and Voluntary Disclosure Under the Foreign Corrupt Practices Act*, 67 Florida Law Review 1683 (2015).

[49] *See* Scott Killingsworth, *The Privatization of Compliance* (May 29, 2014). RAND Center for Corporate Ethics and Governance Symposium White Paper Series, Symposium on "Transforming Compliance: Emerging Paradigms for Boards, Management, Compliance Officers, and Government" (2014), available at SSRN: https://ssrn.com/abstract=2443887.

[50] *See, e.g.*, Todd Haugh, *The Criminalization of Compliance*, 92 Notre Dame Law Review 1215 (2017); Kimberly D. Krawiec, *Cosmetic Compliance and the Failure of Negotiated Governance*, 81 Washington University Law Review 487 (2003); William S. Laufer, *The Compliance Game*, in Regulação do abuso no âmbito corporativo: o papel do direito penal na crise financeira (Saad-Diniz, D. Brodowski, and A. Luiza, eds., São Paulo: LiberArs, 2015) [*hereinafter Game*].

[51] *See* Haugh, *supra* note 50; Krawiec, *supra* note 50; Laufer, *Game*, *supra* note 50. Further, one might doubt that courts would be willing to delegate fully to private parties on compliance standards.

[52] *See* Sally S. Simpson, Melissa Rorie, M. Alper, Natalie Schell-Busey, William S. Laufer, and N. Craig Smith, *Corporate Crime Deterrence: A Systematic Review* (Campbell Collaboration), 10 Campbell Systematic Reviews 1-106 (2014); Brandon L. Garrett and Gregory Mitchell, *Testing Compliance* (February 10, 2020), Law and Contemporary Problems, *in press*; Duke Law School Public Law & Legal Theory Series No. 2020-14, available at SSRN: https://ssrn.com/abstract=3535913; D. Christopher Kayes, David Stirling, and Tjai M. Nielsen, *Building Organizational Integrity*, 50 Business Horizons 61 (2007).

incentivize their employees to be more interested in compliance. After all, setting up a great information-gathering system might flounder if employees display little interest in it. Of course, encouraging and inculcating norms to be law-abiding and socially responsible is likely to be useful, but so might making some portion of executive compensation depend on compliance performance. This has not been discussed in much depth in legal scholarship,[53] but in the field of ESG compliance we have witnessed a great deal of interest in the notion of tying compensation to ESG metrics in some manner.[54] Of course, generating metrics for assessing whether a firm meets certain thresholds for ESG involves many of the same issues as general compliance (albeit in a more directed manner). Steps taken to design and maximize these sorts of metrics could provide useful templates for assessing compliance.

2.3.5 *A Few Examples: Of Bounties and Reporting Lines*

Finally, as a way to add concreteness to the commentary, I discuss two recent examples of compliance-related matters to highlight how some of the considerations noted in this chapter map out in the context of specific decisions – whether and when to give bounties for information provided by whistleblowers and when the compliance officer should have a direct report to the board as opposed to the GC. Both questions turn on matters related to how information is likely to flow within a firm, which in turn depend upon structures within the firm and incentives therein.

In the context of bounties for whistleblowers, these can be useful features of a firm's compliance program but they need to be designed carefully. This is in large part due to the uncertainty surrounding the underlying wrong (uncertainty in the definitional sense – statutes and regulations are often quite vaguely worded and can be interpreted in many ways and there are many of them).[55] This uncertainty may lead individuals in the firm to hoard information and become reluctant to share it. This is because uncertainty about the value of information may make some individuals reluctant to share it with others because they do not know if the information might harm them and they do not know if the other person will provide that information to authorities in order to obtain a bounty.[56] Reluctance to share information can have negative effects within the firm such as: (i) making it more difficult to detect, deter, and prevent wrongdoing, which in part depends on gathering and sharing information, and (ii) increasing the likelihood of fraud by hurting firm performance because reluctance in sharing information with each other makes it harder to work cohesively together within a firm, which should lead to weaker firm performance (a key predictor for fraud).[57] This suggests that either bounties should be targeted to more clearly defined wrongs (thereby reducing some uncertainty) or perhaps they should have other features of bounty design (e.g., differentiating between internal and external whistleblowers or varying bounty by firm size)

53 *See* Hofstetter, Soltes, and Kraakman, *supra* note 28.

54 *See* Haque and Ntim, *supra* note 28; Haque, *supra* note 28; David M. Silk Andrea K. Wahlquist, David E. Kahan, and Erica E. Bonnett, *ESG and Incentive Compensation Programs*, May 1, 2020, Memo, Wachtell, Lipton, Rosen & Katz, on file with author. To the extent that the "Balanced Scorecard" influences compensation, it too is noteworthy, see *supra* note 35.

55 This builds on some of my related research; *see* Vikramaditya Khanna, *Designing Bounties in Light of Uncertainty*, Draft (2021).

56 *See id.* There may be some individuals who might be more inclined to provide information to authorities too. *See id.*

57 *See id.*

that might address such concerns.[58] This is not to suggest that bounties cannot be useful, but rather that designing something as well-known as bounties can raise multiple problems.[59]

In the context of whether the CCO should report to the board or the GC, it seems that dividing the tasks traditionally associated with the GC's office between a CCO (who reports to the board) and the GC may often impose costs on the firm.[60] These costs include weaker information gathering and duplication of effort, as well as the potential for even greater wrongdoing.[61] This is because some employees may be more reluctant to share their information with an independent CCO than with the GC for a variety of reasons including, but not limited to, because conversations with the GC are more likely to fall within the firm's attorney-client privilege than conversations with the CCO and because of the uncertainty in the definition of wrongdoing.[62] To the extent that this leads to a reduction in sharing of information, it is likely to make it harder to detect, deter, and prevent wrongdoing as well as undermining firm performance leading to increased incentives to commit fraud. These costs would need to be balanced against the potential gains from having compliance run by someone who reports directly to the board and is thus more independent of top management than the GC.[63] Which way this balance comes out may vary across firms and sectors. This discussion, much like that for bounties, underscores that designing and assessing compliance systems is not easy and may require some degree of context-driven choices rather than a one-size-fits-all approach. Moreover, attention needs to be paid to structures for gathering information, incentives to gather and provide information, and how the presence of more independent individuals may affect these considerations.[64]

2.4 INCIDENCE OF COMPLIANCE

Thus far, the analysis has not focused on how the incidence of the costs and benefits of compliance may affect its operation and its political sustainability. However, incidence questions are important because they influence how constituencies experience the compliance process and the likelihood that they may organize and influence the process (e.g., via lobbying).[65]

Let us assume that certain compliance measures tend to be a greater burden on some firms compared to others. This may be because some costs are larger, in an absolute sense, for some

58 *See id.*

59 *See* David Freeman Engstrom, *Bounty Regimes*, in RESEARCH HANDBOOK ON CORPORATE CRIME AND FINANCIAL MISDEALING (JENNIFER H. ARLEN, ED., EDWARD ELGAR, 2018; A. Mitchell Polinsky, *Private Versus Public Enforcement of Fines*, 9 JOURNAL OF LEGAL STUDIES 105 (1980); Geoffrey Christopher Rapp, *Mutiny by the Bounties? The Attempt to Reform Wall Street by the New Whistleblower Provisions of the Dodd-Frank Act*, 2012 BRIGHAM YOUNG UNIVERSITY LAW REVIEW 73 (2012).

60 *See* Vikramaditya S. Khanna, *An Analysis of Internal Governance and the Role of the General Counsel in Reducing Corporate Crime*, in RESEARCH HANDBOOK ON CORPORATE CRIME AND FINANCIAL MISDEALING (JENNIFER H. ARLEN, ED., EDWARD ELGAR, 2018). For a discussion of the Chief Compliance Officer, see Miriam H. Baer, *Compliance Elites* (April 20, 2020), FORDHAM LAW REVIEW, *in press*; Brooklyn Law School, Legal Studies Paper No. 633, available at SSRN: https://ssrn.com/abstract=3581025.

61 *See id.*

62 *See id.*

63 *See id.*; Anette Mikes, *Risk Management at Crunch Time: Are Chief Risk Officers Compliance Champions or Business Partners?* (May 30, 2008), available at SSRN: https://ssrn.com/abstract=1138615.

64 *See* Khanna, *supra* note 55; Khanna, *supra* note 60.

65 *See, e.g.*, Vikramaditya S. Khanna, *Corporate Crime Legislation: A Political Economy Analysis*, 82 WASHINGTON UNIVERSITY LAW QUARTERLY 95 (2004); Yael V. Hochberg, Paola Sapienza, and Annette Vissing-Jørgensen, *A Lobbying Approach to Evaluating the Sarbanes-Oxley Act of 2002*, 47 JOURNAL OF ACCOUNTING RESEARCH 519 (2009).

firms than for others or because the absolute costs may be similar but the effect of that on firms may be quite different.

For example, small and large firms may bear similar costs of complying with Sarbanes-Oxley Section 404, but to a smaller firm these costs might be very large relative to their profits or sales and put them in a more precarious financial position compared to a large firm.[66]

On the other hand, even if some firms bear absolutely greater compliance costs than others (leading one to think that they would oppose such costs), they may still find it in their economic interest to prefer to bear these costs because they operate as entry barriers for their competitors.[67] The anti-competitive effects of certain compliance costs may be significant in some industries and present us with an odd trade-off of sorts:[68] greater compliance costs for some areas (e.g., financial sector firms) might trigger concerns for different areas (e.g., concentration in the financial sector leading to competition concerns amongst others).

In addition, the extent to which the costs of compliance have a bigger effect on smaller firms might lead to some depressive effects on entrepreneurial activity because many startups are fairly small and higher compliance costs could be a greater concern for them (just like any additional costs would be).[69] Of course, compliance expenditures might create new business opportunities for some firms, but one suspects that this may happen less frequently than compliance costs endangering some startups.[70]

Although the differential incidence of compliance costs creates potentially interesting effects, it is also likely to impact how groups respond to compliance efforts via their own lobbying efforts. For example, it may be that some firms that consider themselves more negatively affected than others may lobby for exemptions (as in the case of SOX Section 404) or they may "cut corners" or lobby against the compliance initiatives at the legislative, regulatory, or enforcement levels. This may sometimes lead to socially desirable outcomes, but at times may result in rent-seeking, perverse incentives, and a patchwork of often difficult to understand, and navigate, exemptions.[71] Such complex structures tend to favor those who are larger and may lead to further concerns about erecting entry barriers for newer and smaller firms.[72] Although this is not always something that results from increased compliance obligations, it is something to be vigilant about.

66 *See* Coates and Srinivasan, *supra* note 13; Iliev, *supra* note 14; Jagan Krishnan, Dasaratha Rama, and Yinghong Zhang, *Costs to Comply with SOX Section 404*, 27 AUDITING: A JOURNAL OF PRACTICE & THEORY 169 (2008); Dharmapala, *supra* note 36. *But see* John L. Orcutt, *The Case Against Exempting Smaller Reporting Companies from Sarbanes-Oxley Section 404: Why Market-Based Solutions Are Likely to Harm Ordinary Investors*, 14 FORDHAM JOURNAL OF CORPORATE AND FINANCIAL LAW 325 (2009).

67 *See generally* Simeon Djankov, Rafael La Porta, Florencio Lopez-de-Silanes, and Andrei Shleifer, *The Regulation of Entry*, 117 QUARTERLY JOURNAL OF ECONOMICS 1 (2002); Leora Klapper, Luc Laeven, and Raghuram Rajan, *Entry Regulation as a Barrier to Entrepreneurship*, 82 JOURNAL OF FINANCIAL ECONOMICS 591 (2006).

68 *See* Djankov et al., *supra* note 67; Klapper et al., *supra* note 67.

69 *See, e.g.*, Viral V. Acharya and Krishnamurthy V. Subramanian, *Bankruptcy Codes and Innovation*, 22 REVIEW OF FINANCIAL STUDIES 4949 (2009); H. Sapra, Ajay Subramanian, and Krishnamurthy V. Subramanian, *Corporate Governance and Innovation: Theory and Evidence*, 49 JOURNAL OF FINANCIAL AND QUANTITATIVE ANALYSIS 957 (2014).

70 For examples of startups working in the compliance space, *see RegTech Startups Transforming Compliance*, DISRUPTION HUB, 23 January 2017, available at: https://disruptionhub.com/regtech-10-innovative-startups-making-compliance-easier/.

71 On the potentially perverse effects of exemptions, *see* Louis Kaplow, *Optimal Regulation with Exemptions*, 55 INTERNATIONAL JOURNAL OF INDUSTRIAL ORGANIZATION 1–29 (2019). For discussion on exemptions for smaller issuers under Sarbanes-Oxley, *see* Orcutt, *supra* note 66.

72 *See* Klapper et al., *supra* note 67.

Before concluding, I want to underscore that progress has been made on many of the issues noted in this chapter. Thus, although the inquiry into the costs and benefits of compliance is quite challenging, this does not mean that it cannot be done tolerably well or that it should not be done. Rather, with careful theorizing and evidence-based research, one can surely make progress on the core issues discussed in this chapter. Moreover, as we gain better knowledge about what works in compliance and how this maps on to compliance costs and benefits, our compliance systems should get better. This suggests that more research should facilitate the development of better compliance systems even across a wide and fast-developing terrain.

2.5 CONCLUSION

This chapter's aim was to explore some of the issues implicated when examining the costs and benefits of compliance. This involves challenging and, as yet, not fully resolved conceptual, measurement, and incidence questions. On a conceptual level, we must first answer questions such as "comply with what?" to understand the range of our inquiry. Options include not only complying with the law but also complying with nonlegal standards (e.g., corporate policy, ESG standards, and so forth). After this, we need to make a distinction between social and private costs and benefits. Although these concepts overlap, there are many differences that in turn change the nature of what we are asking about when examining the costs and benefits of compliance. These conceptual questions, however, only begin the inquiry.

This is because, perhaps, the most difficult questions arise in measuring costs and benefits and assessing whether compliance is effective in some sense. Here there are myriad issues requiring careful thought, ranging from what methodologies and units of measurement are to be used to how one should operationalize cost–benefit analyses in ways that might be meaningful (as opposed to cosmetic) and useful to those looking to design effective compliance systems. In addition to these questions, the analysis suggests that greater attention should be paid to how compliance affects compensation and to the structure of information flows, and the incentives for gathering information, within the firm. Overall, greater reliance on evidence-based research seems critical to getting a better understanding of the costs and benefits of compliance.

Finally, this chapter briefly explores questions on the incidence of costs and benefits of compliance. Incidence will impact how parties respond to compliance efforts and how sustainable they are. If the costs of compliance fall in ways that create distinct groups with demarcated interests then there is the risk of extended lobbying efforts at legislative and enforcement levels as well as concerns about firms attempting to "cut corners," which naturally impacts enforcement activity. More broadly, incidence questions also raise issues about whether compliance efforts are serving as entry barriers to certain sectors or making entrepreneurial activity more difficult – thereby exacerbating market competition and innovation concerns. Indeed, one of the more paradoxical aspects of compliance is that enhanced compliance with respect to some issues might worsen other concerns one might have (e.g., competition) that themselves are the subject of compliance discussions.

The analysis thus suggests that the question of compliance as costs and benefits is fraught with difficult questions that raise thorny issues for anyone interested in compliance and with social welfare more generally. The analysis suggests that substantial progress can be made with more evidence-based research, but an important starting point for analysis will be to address many of the conceptual, measurement, and incidence questions raised in this chapter.

3

The Professionalization of Compliance

Eugene Soltes

Abstract: In the last three decades, compliance has grown from an ad hoc job function into a sophisticated profession. In this chapter, I describe the development of the field and current challenges in the design of effective compliance programs. I discuss several opportunities, particularly around the use of data and analytics, that have the potential to enhance compliance efficiency and efficacy.

3.1 INTRODUCTION

Every day, hundreds of thousands of compliance officers around the globe seek to prevent and detect conduct that can legally and reputationally jeopardize organizations. Even organizations outside the most heavily regulated industries of financial services, health care, and defense often have a designated chief compliance officer (CCO) supported by sizable teams that help manage the compliance function. These employees often have prior regulatory or enforcement experience (e.g. former Assistant United States Attorney (AUSA), Federal Bureau of Investigation (FBI) Special Agent, outside counsel) and hold designations attesting to their expertise in helping mitigate or investigate various kinds of misconduct (e.g. certifications in fraud examination, anti-money laundering, and integrity programs). Over just a few decades, compliance has grown from an ad hoc position into a respected profession in itself.

In this chapter, I describe how the compliance profession came into being, the challenges facing the industry, and the opportunities for compliance leaders going forward.

3.2 CREATING THE COMPLIANCE PROFESSION

Following a series of corruption scandals in the 1970s and 1980s, numerous defense contractors banded together to create a series of internal policies that could better prevent and respond to misconduct within their organizations. These self-regulatory efforts staved off additional external regulation and offered an appealing alternative for both companies, which saw added legislation as disruptive, and policymakers, who viewed self-regulation as an efficient and cost-effective means of enhancing firm accountability.[1]

As companies grew their internal compliance programs, regulatory and enforcement bodies also began acknowledging and crediting firms' efforts. In 1991, officials at the United States Sentencing Commission (USSC) began rewarding self-regulatory compliance efforts by stating that a company with a compliance program that was "generally effective in preventing and detecting criminal conduct" could qualify for significantly reduced sanctions.

[1] This history is provided in considerably more detail in Soltes 2018b.

By the late 1990s, leaders at the Department of Justice (DOJ) followed with a series of memos urging prosecutors to consider a firm's compliance program when determining whether to charge the firm for misconduct.[2]

Along with "carrots" offered to organizations that invested in compliance, firm leaders also saw the growing "sticks" facing companies that engaged in malfeasance. Corporations have long been subject to criminal sanctions for misconduct (*New York Central & Hudson River Railroad* v. *United States*, 1909). However, beginning in the early twenty-first century, sanctions became an increasingly common, and increasingly punitive, response to business misconduct. In 2000, US authorities assessed criminal fines against corporate entities totaling a quarter of a billion dollars. Less than two decades later, in 2017, corporate criminal fines had grown forty-fold, reaching over $10 billion by US authorities alone.

Notably, the growth in enforcement was not limited to firms headquartered in the United States or solely US agencies. The extraterritorial reach of US enforcement meant that firms based outside the United States and engaging in business largely outside the United States could still face punitive sanctions by US authorities (e.g. for using dollars wired from a US bank). As evidence, by 2019, eight of the ten largest fines for violation of the US Foreign Corrupt Practices Act (FCPA) were issued against firms headquartered outside the United States. Professional compliance increasingly became a global phenomenon as enforcement agencies outside the United States also pursued cases and sanctioned firms (e.g. European Union (EU) and anti-trust; Sokol 2017).

This growth in criminal sanctions often followed corporate scandals and public concern, which further drove new regulation, which in turn expanded compliance programs (Haugh 2017a: 1231–3). Increased sanctions also raised the value of the "carrots" associated with implementing compliance programs. Firms with an effective compliance program potentially qualified for a declination or reductions in US criminal sanctions of up to 95 percent. While some heavily regulated industries like financial services and pharmaceuticals had long had extensive compliance functions due to the nature of their regulatory environment, public and even private firms began hiring personnel and often establishing entire departments, akin to marketing or finance, focused on organizational compliance.

The basic objectives of compliance programs are threefold. First, organizations encounter different regulatory, reputational, and ethical issues, and compliance assesses which of these risks are pertinent for the organization to mitigate. Second, based on the different risk areas, compliance programs seek to prevent misconduct, with the benefit of averting regulatory incursion or reputational damage. Third, compliance seeks to detect misconduct through monitoring and surveillance, to manage and mitigate the potential consequences.

These objectives are frequently interdependent. For instance, by appropriately assessing the risks facing the firm, the organization can direct resources toward preventing the most consequential types of misconduct within the company. Likewise, a firm that can prevent most misconduct can be better positioned to investigate and respond to allegations of misconduct in a timely manner.

The types of misconduct that compliance officers seek to mitigate vary considerably across industries, geographies, and firms. A compliance department may consider not only the legal

[2] See Memorandum from Larry D. Thompson, Deputy Attorney General to Heads of Department Components, to United States Attorneys (January 20, 2003); Memorandum from Eric H. Holder, Deputy Attorney General, Federal Prosecution of Corporations to all Federal Prosecutors (June 16, 1999); and Memorandum from Mark Filip, Deputy Attorney General, Principles of Federal Prosecution of Corporations to Heads of Department Components, United States Attorneys (August 28, 2008).

Areas for Compliance Management

Anti-Bribery	Exchange Listing Requirements
Anti-Money Laundering	Financial Reporting
Antil Trafficking	Human Rights
Competition and Anti-Trust	Insider Trading
Data Privacy	License and Permitting
Economic Sanctions	Product Safety
Employment Law	Workplace Safety
Environmental Policy	

FIGURE 3.1 Compliance risk areas

and regulatory risks specific to its company's industry but also those outside the regulatory environment that may still adversely impact the company's public reputation (e.g. purchasing goods produced by laborers who are incarcerated). Furthermore, while there may not be criminal firm sanctions associated with a leader harassing an employee, the reputational damage associated with such conduct may lead compliance to prioritize the prevention and detection of such conduct. Figure 3.1 gives an overview of the most common risk areas managed by compliance. Notably, firms may shift focus over time as both regulation and public expectations change. Given the considerable number of risk areas that are of potential concern, compliance in practice within many companies becomes "backward" looking, with the main priority being the most recent issue that drew regulatory scrutiny or public criticism within their firm or industry. Although such a practice may not be appropriate or conceptually desirable, it reflects compliance leaders' limited ability to concretely address many risk areas simultaneously.

Most compliance program initiatives can be divided between prevention and detection activities. Prevention initiatives include codes of conduct, policies, and procedures that describe regulations and cover key risk areas, as well as training to ensure that employees are educated on them. Detection measures include monitoring, investigative procedures, whistleblowing hotlines, and data analytics.[3] Some of these compliance processes are required or recommended by legislation. For example, the Sarbanes-Oxley Act (SOX) of 2002 requires firms to provide employees with a process to anonymously report alleged accounting misconduct (i.e. a hotline), and the Equal Employment Opportunity Commission (EEOC) requires firms to investigate claims of a hostile work environment.

Compliance departments are organized in ways that vary according to managerial approaches and regulatory requirements. Compliance leadership is often subsumed within the general counsel (GC) role, or can be an independent position that reports to legal counsel, the board of directors, or the chief executive. Many compliance functions are also fulfilled by departments outside of compliance, including legal counsel and human resources (HR). For example, HR may be responsible for investigations related to harassment, and legal may be involved in investigations where there is a desire to assert attorney–client privilege over aspects of the process. The rapid growth in regulation and the desire for cost-efficiency has led firms to supplement or even replace internal programs with outside support. A large third-party compliance industry offers compliance services including training programs, hotline services to receive whistleblowing reports, investigative services, and software for compliance analytics.

3 For more on the development of a compliance program, see Soltes 2018a.

3.3 CHALLENGES FACING COMPLIANCE

While it is difficult to ascertain the average cost of compliance programs across companies, one estimate suggests that the average multinational spends in excess of $3.5 million a year supporting its compliance program. This is likely a significant underestimate, given that compliance entails many indirect costs, such as time spent on compliance training. In spite of these considerable annual expenditures, most firm leaders fail to have a clear sense of the impact and returns associated with their compliance efforts.

Much of the growth in the focus on compliance programs arises from the notion of "effective compliance" alluded to by regulatory and enforcement agencies.[4] For example, the DOJ notes that the "adequacy and effectiveness" of a compliance program and "remedial efforts" to "implement an adequate and effective corporate compliance program or to improve an existing one" (US DOJ 2019) are taken into account when determining whether to bring charges and in negotiating agreements with firms. Yet there is no explicit guidance or consensus on what is actually meant by *effective* compliance. The DOJ Fraud Section provides an extensive set of questions to aid prosecutors in examining a compliance program, while the Department of Health and Human Services lists over 550 metrics to consider when "measuring compliance program effectiveness," but neither of these documents explicitly defines the standard of effectiveness. Similarly, there is no authoritative list that comprehensively defines the initiatives that comprise an effective compliance program. This is in part due to the fact that appropriate compliance efforts are a dynamic reflection of variable risks based on business type, location of operations, incentives faced by employees, and the surrounding regulatory environment.

The lack of clarity around what constitutes "effectiveness" is not only a regulatory but also a managerial challenge. In an effort to respond expediently to the perceived need to have a compliance program, many firms target their efforts toward fulfilling requirements "on paper," without adequately understanding the actual impact on employees in practice. For instance, the most common metric used to assess compliance and ethics training programs is the rate of completion (Deloitte/Compliance Week 2017), a measure that overlooks how much employees actually learn from the training, or how such training impacts behavior. Other metrics may be even more ambiguous, such as the number of calls that are collected by a firm's whistleblowing hotline. A lower number of calls could indicate that there are few instances of alleged misconduct. On the other hand, fewer calls could also reflect a culture where employees feel uncomfortable reporting potential misconduct, or even one where such behavior has become an accepted norm.

In many instances, compliance officers make efforts to find measures and interpret data, but, as these examples show, defining and assessing effectiveness is complex and requires more than descriptive data that poorly correlates with outcomes. However, finding causal measures of effectiveness is critical to understanding whether a compliance program has an impact on organizational culture and behavior, and whether the organization's resources are being put to good use. Put more simply, firm leaders cannot effectively manage what they cannot effectively measure. Effectiveness does not imply that a program must be "perfect." As the USSC notes, "the failure to prevent or detect the instant offense does not necessarily mean that the program is not generally effective . . ." (USSC 2014: §8B2.1(a)). Instead, compliance programs ought to be "reasonably designed, implemented, and enforced so that the program is generally effective in preventing and detecting criminal conduct" (USSC 2014: §8B2.1(a)).

[4] For discussion on the growing reference to "effective compliance," see Soltes 2018b and Chen and Soltes 2018.

Risk scoring and measures focused on outcomes can better assess whether a program is ultimately achieving its goals or merely seeking to superficially satisfy regulatory requirements "on paper."[5]

One of the primary challenges associated with innovating within compliance programs is that many organizations approach compliance as an extension of the legal function with a defensive, litigation-focused mindset. Many, if not most, compliance leaders are attorneys by training, and compliance teams often sit within a firm's legal group. The resulting legal orientation exhibits itself through a focus on contractual obligations around appropriate employee behavior. However, these legal "check the box" approaches often fail to properly motivate or incentivize the desired conduct.

One example of an inappropriately legalistic "check the box" exercise is the attestations that employees are required to make in which they agree to follow their firm's code of conduct. This typically includes a provision that employees report any behavior they observe that violates the organization's code of conduct. In spite of signing such attestations, most employees indicate in follow-up surveys that they do not report observed violations, in direct contradiction to the provisions they have signed (Soltes 2019b). Employees often describe a range of concerns that lead to nonreporting, including fear of retaliation, concern that the report will not be taken seriously, aversion to becoming involved, and concern about getting a colleague fired. Thus, simply signing contractual codes of conduct is insufficient to assure appropriate and compliant employee behavior. At best, such signatures are a "check the box" exercise that serves to insulate the firm from potential liability.

Further, a gap between how individuals intend to behave and how they actually behave in practice has long been demonstrated in the psychological literature, which shows how strongly individuals are influenced by their surrounding environment and social norms.[6] Compliance practices that predominantly focus on addressing conduct through legal contracts and enforcement risk not only overlook psychological influences on behavior but even create counterproductive cultural norms where individuals learn to circumvent the goals of compliance programs. One notable instance is Intel's antitrust compliance program, which was once profiled as a best-practice example in the *Harvard Business Review* (Yoffie and Kwak 2001). The program employed an approach that was not dissimilar to the one employed by regulatory and enforcement agencies during their examinations process. Intel's leadership conducted random audits where Intel investigators would go to a division unannounced, seize emails and papers, and use these records to conduct interviews with managers. Ultimately, this compliance effort created an environment in which employees saw company policies as a bureaucratic and arbitrary process to be managed (e.g. finding loopholes to circumvent such obstacles). Just a few years after the "best practices" profile, Intel came under investigation for antitrust violations, ultimately incurring a $1.44 billion fine – the largest ever imposed on a firm. As the New York State Office of the Attorney General noted: "[W]hatever the intention, the actual effect of the program was to school Intel executives in cover-up, rather than compliance" (Haugh 2017a: 1217). The Intel example illustrates the importance of considering the objectives of compliance in preventing and mitigating misconduct and understanding that the challenge cannot be met solely through aggressive monitoring and enforcement. Instead, compliance requires cultivating an organizational culture that fosters

5 For further discussion, see Chen and Soltes 2018.

6 One of the most celebrated studies to explore this phenomenon is Darley and Batson 1973.

genuine understanding of and commitment to the longer-terms goals associated with the spirit of compliance.

From a broader perspective, compliance seeks to preserve and sustain an organization's integrity. To that end, compliance leaders are often viewed as protectors of a firm's reputation. However, compliance teams do not have full control over the many factors and decisions that can contribute to – or undermine – firm integrity, such as hiring decisions, incentive design, and business strategy. For example, a compliance department can disseminate a policy prohibiting retaliation against whistleblowers, but authority to actually follow the policy both explicitly and implicitly lies with individual managers scattered throughout the organization, and each manager may have other personal or business priorities. Or compliance leaders may design training describing how employees are expected to treat one another with respect and care, but a CEO or other senior leader may undermine this message through their own language and conduct.[7] In such situations, compliance leaders find that their "span of accountability" – the firm's integrity – is greater than their "span of control,"[8] leaving a gap between the tools available to compliance leaders and the decision rights needed to actually support the goals of the program in practice.

Companies use varied approaches and efforts to reduce this gap. CCOs in different organizations may report to the GC, the CEO, or the board of directors, with differing implications for firm communication, leadership, and attorney–client privilege.[9] Placing compliance under the GC may enhance information sharing, reduce duplicated efforts, and offer information gained from internal "whistleblowers" the protection of legal privilege. On the other hand, placing compliance under the board or CEO may offer compliance greater independence and reduce the potential conflict between protecting the firm (which often seeks less documentation of potential allegations of misconduct) and fostering more compliant conduct (which requires transparency around potential deviant conduct). Regulatory and enforcement authorities have historically preferred to separate compliance and legal, and even required such division of responsibilities in settlements with companies.[10]

Conflicts over the span of control for compliance extend beyond senior management and the legal department. Most compliance programs focus only on a subset of legal and regulatory risks like bribery (e.g. FCPA and domestic corruption), insider trading, and embezzlement. However, compliance conceptually covers a much broader set of legal, regulatory, and reputational risks, some of which are managed by other parts of the firm. HR typically leads training and investigation processes around harassment and discrimination, security officers address issues of cyber- and physical security, and the marketing department may handle product quality concerns that originate in consumer complaints.

When compliance concerns and processes are spread across departments, the firm may miss emerging problems or trends, or incorrectly believe that an issue falls under the responsibility of another unit. Wells Fargo, for example, received complaints from both

7 One report found that while most organizations "require" compliance training, under half of them had a system in place to sanction employees through compensation or advancement (DLA Piper, "2017 Compliance & Risk Report").

8 See Soltes, "Spans of Control and Accountability," Harvard Business School Background Note, 9-11-066. When spans of accountability are greater than spans of control, managers may be more inclined to engage in collaboration and creativity to help overcome this gap. For a thoughtful discussion on how such gaps can empower individuals, see Simons 2010.

9 In the DLA Piper Survey, 39 percent of compliance officers report to the CEO, 34 percent to the GC, 12 percent to the board (usually audit), and 16 percent to others within the organization.

10 The merits of different organizational structures are discussed in detail in Khanna 2018 and Ostlund 2017.

customers and staff about the creation of fraudulent accounts without customer permission. However, the organization did not bring together the information it had from disparate sources and thus was not able to appreciate the magnitude of the developing problem. Bringing a range of issues together under a single compliance or risk leader can mitigate challenges around centralizing information and responsibility but is practically difficult to accomplish given entrenched divisional leaders who often seek to guard their own power and resources.

A further challenge to compliance is the dynamic nature of compliance risks and how they differentially impact various subunits of an organization. Even if a program is appropriately designed, it may not continue to adequately confront new risks and regulations. For example, rising concerns about data privacy led to the EU's General Data Protection Regulation (GDPR), which dramatically tightened privacy restrictions on personal data beginning in 2018.[11] Norms of appropriate conduct also vary geographically, posing an additional challenge to firms that operate across diverse locations. While companies may desire to present a single unified set of guidelines, such as a single code of conduct, to all employees, the same policies may resonate differently or be interpreted differently between offices.[12] Bribes, for instance, are more likely to be considered an acceptable business practice in some emerging markets,[13] but US anti-bribery regulation (FCPA) applies globally to any firms with transactions conducted in or through US jurisdiction, including banking transactions through US banks and emails routed through US servers. In other cases, laws in different jurisdictions may even conflict with one another, leaving compliance departments to choose between different risks. The United States, for example, has established sanctions that prevent US citizens, businesses, and foreign entities that conduct business in US markets from doing business in Iran. Breaking these sanctions can result in serious monetary and criminal penalties as well as denial of foreign companies' ability to operate in US markets. At the same time, the EU passed a regulation (EU Blocking Regulation) that prohibits individuals and companies within the EU from ceasing to conduct business in Iran simply to comply with US sanctions. Thus, EU-based countries are potentially placed in the position of violating either US or EU law.[14]

Although the complexity of regulation has grown considerably and the costs of not managing these risks have exploded, compliance initiatives and strategies have not similarly adjusted. The majority of organizations continue to rely on the same core tools – hotlines, codes of conduct, and training – despite evidence of the limited effectiveness of those tools. With the exception of financial services, where there has been a considerable growth of "regtech" to manage certain risks (e.g. anti-money laundering), the third-party compliance space has not seen much innovation, either. One possible reason for this is the lack of competition for third-party services.[15]

11 For an excellent description of GDPR compliance costs, see Stapp 2019.

12 As an example, most organizations seek to have one code of business ethics translated into different languages to account for a global workforce.

13 As an example of how norms can vary across markets, EY found in its Global Fraud Survey that 19 percent of managers can justify cash payments to win business when helping a business survive a downturn in emerging markets, but only 6 percent could justify such payments in developed markets (EY, "15th Global Fraud Survey," 2018).

14 The EU is also developing a special purpose entity (INSTEX) to further trading with Iran around US sanctions. See www.fcpablog.com/blog/2019/6/24/practice-alert-new-ofac-compliance-guidelines-collide-with-e.html.

15 As just one example, more than 80 percent of hotline providers for large publicly traded firms are provided by two companies. See also Soltes 2019a.

Overall, despite the rapid growth of the compliance industry, there are numerous challenges facing the compliance profession that offer many more opportunities for new and more innovative approaches.

3.4 INNOVATING WITHIN COMPLIANCE

In an effort to design more effective programs, an increasing number of firms are considering new initiatives to better prevent and detect noncompliance. Three of these innovations that have garnered the most interest are data analytics, behavioral nudges, and different organizational leadership styles.

Data analytics offers an opportunity to address several of the main barriers to effective and efficient compliance. In principle, compliance leaders have access to vast amounts of internal information that – with the right analysis – can more readily uncover misconduct and provide better metrics for assessing compliance programs. Moreover, data analytics can model the factors surrounding misconduct, generating insight into the situations where misconduct is likely to occur, and targeting and tailoring compliance programs toward areas and employees with the highest risk. Data can assist, for example, in better targeting audits of high-risk transactions that may be suspected bribes. Compliance departments can examine the parties, timing, mode, and other factors involved in payments, and develop a risk profile of transactions that may be problematic and warrant the resources for careful scrutiny (EY and Anheuser-Busch InBev 2018).

Data analytics also has the potential to enhance compliance training. For a company with tens of thousands of employees, annual training on topics like anti-bribery requires considerable effort, particularly in terms of the opportunity cost of employee time. Training is often delivered on a routine schedule, rather than when employees might most benefit, and across the organization rather than targeted toward specific employees. Analysis can examine employee travel schedules and types of deal to pinpoint which employees are most likely to encounter bribery risks, and when those risks are most likely to appear. This information can allow compliance to target training to the most high-risk employees. For instance, analytics can identify an employee traveling abroad to pitch a foreign minister on a potential contract, and compliance can then target anti-bribery training to that employee shortly before the trip.

Most firms do not currently leverage their data to drive their compliance programs, in part because these methods come with their own challenges. First, the data produced by growing firms and compliance programs has outpaced analytic expertise – notably empirical knowledge that has not traditionally been part of compliance and its legally focused evolution. Second, compliance leaders may have difficulty gathering data that is spread around the firm, such as the information on employee roles and travel schedules. This synthesis challenge is compounded by privacy issues related to HR data, particularly in the EU under GDPR.

Nonetheless, firms stand to benefit greatly if they are able to build their analytics capabilities and successfully connect compliance with other departments to produce relevant datasets, metrics, models, and monitoring. With a data-driven system in place, analytics can assess and improve the effectiveness and efficiency not only of individual initiatives but of the compliance program as a whole. Eventually, organizations with enough data may even begin to compare and examine the effects of differing compliance structures between firms.

Another field that can contribute to innovative compliance is behavioral and organizational psychology. As the Intel antitrust experience illustrates, a legally directed compliance program cannot adequately assess – and therefore cannot adequately influence – human behavior among employees. However, organizations can draw from behavioral psychology to introduce "nudges," small changes to organizational structures and process designs that can produce major effects (Haugh 2017b). Nudges may be especially influential in areas with organizational and psychological barriers, such as the barriers to whistleblowing.

The breadth of challenges associated with improving and sustaining firm integrity necessitates engagement from leadership across the organization. As compliance moves from a strictly legal function to a behavioral influence unit, it will be important to educate board members and senior leadership about new approaches. Within firms where senior leadership and board members hold ultimate accountability for compliance, these constituencies will need to grow their understanding in parallel with compliance to adequately assess new initiatives. Moreover, these leaders hold authority to reorganize and delegate resources to adapt and sustain more innovative compliance programs. To begin this journey, company decision-makers need to first understand what new compliance initiatives aim to accomplish, what impediments they face, and what metrics can track impact and progress over time.

3.5 CONCLUSION: COMPLIANCE OF THE FUTURE VERSUS COMPLIANCE OF THE PAST

Driven by expanding regulation and increasing risk for firms, compliance has developed rapidly from an informal role into its own industry and profession. Yet, the recent rate of growth – in personnel, costs, and complex organizational structures and processes – is unsustainable. As William Laufer noted in illustrating the dramatic growth of compliance, JP Morgan "supports more compliance, risk, and fortress control professionals than all uniformed NYPD officers, and more than three times as many FBI special agents across all U.S. field offices" (Laufer 2018: 393–4).

Not only has the field experienced outsized expansion but there is little evidence that ever-larger compliance departments adequately – let alone efficiently – address the full spectrum of integrity risks facing organizations. In order to move forward, compliance must begin working smarter rather than harder, shifting focus from growth and investment toward evidence-based initiatives and metrics that reflect real impact.

To develop more efficient and effective compliance, traditional legal expertise needs to be complemented by greater expertise in technology, data analytics, and behavioral psychology. As the risks and scope of compliance expand, technology will be pivotal to sifting through large amounts of information and directing limited resources to key areas – as well as tracking which efforts prove most effective. Meanwhile, psychological approaches recognize the human factors underlying integrity, and seek to remove barriers to compliance by aligning organizational processes with behavioral tendencies.

Whether these cross-disciplinary solutions are developed in-house or by third-party providers, the emphasis will need to be on smart, efficient designs that can create tailored and timely interventions, and ease the pressure on overgrown yet overburdened compliance departments. Companies that can adapt in the near future to incorporate these elements are likely to benefit greatly from improved compliance efficacy, while those that cannot will increasingly be overwhelmed by ever-growing regulatory and reputational risks. Compliance professionals find themselves in an increasingly critical and dynamic field, with the opportunity to lead their firms' continual efforts to cultivate high-integrity organizations.

REFERENCES

Chen, Hui, and Eugene Soltes. 2018. "Why Compliance Programs Fail: And How to Fix Them." *Harvard Business Review* 96 (2) (March–April): 116–25.

Darley, John, and Daniel Batson. 1973. "'From Jerusalem to Jericho': A Study of Situational and Dispositional Variables in Helping Behavior." *Journal of Personality and Social Psychology* 27 (1): 100–8.

Deloitte/Compliance Week. 2017. "In Focus: 2016 Compliance Trends Survey."

EY Fraud Investigation & Dispute Services and Anheuser-Busch InBev. 2018. "You Can't Monitor What You Can't Measure," *Fraud Magazine* (March/April).

Haugh, Todd. 2017a. "The Criminalization of Compliance." *Notre Dame Law Review* 92 (3): 1215–70.

2017b. "Nudging Corporate Compliance." *American Business Law Journal* 54: 683–741.

Khanna, Vikramaditya S. 2018. "An Analysis of Internal Governance and the Role of the General Counsel in Reducing Corporate Crime." In *Research Handbook on Corporate Crime and Financial Misdealing*, ed. Jennifer Arlen. Cheltenham, UK: Edward Elgar.

Laufer, William. 2018. "A Very Special Regulatory Milestone." *University of Pennsylvania Journal of Business Law* 20: 392–428.

Ostlund, Grant A. 2017. "Should We Separate the General Counsel & The Chief Compliance Officer?" *Law School Student Scholarship*: 889.

Simons, Robert. 2010. *Seven Strategy Questions: A Simple Approach for Better Execution*. Cambridge, MA: Harvard Business Review Press.

Sokol, D. Daniel. 2017. "Troubled Waters between U.S. and European Antitrust." *Michigan Law Review* 115 (6): 955–77.

Soltes, Eugene. 2018a. "Designing a Compliance Program at AbInBev." Harvard Business School Case 118–071, March.

Soltes, Eugene. 2018b. "Evaluating the Effectiveness of Corporate Compliance Programs: Establishing a Model for Prosecutors, Courts, and Firms," *NYU Journal of Law & Business* 14 (3): 965–1011.

Soltes, Eugene. 2019a. "Accenture's Code of Business Ethics," Harvard Business School Teaching Note 119–049, January.

Soltes, Eugene. 2019b. "Where Is Your Company Most Prone to Lapses in Integrity?" *Harvard Business Review* (July/August).

Stapp, Alec. 2019. "GDPR After One Year: Costs and Unintended Consequences," May 24, post on blog "Truth on the Market," https://truthonthemarket.com/2019/05/24/gdpr-after-one-year-costs-and-unintended-consequences/.

United States Department of Justice Criminal Division (US DOJ). 2019. "Evaluation of Corporate Compliance Programs." Guidance Document, updated April 2019.

United States Sentencing Commission (USSC). 2014. "2014 Federal Sentencing Guidelines Manual."

Yoffie, David B., and Mary Kwak. 2001. "Playing by the Rules: How Intel Avoids Antitrust Litigation." *Harvard Business Review* (June).

4

From Responsive Regulation to Ecological Compliance: Meta-regulation and the Existential Challenge of Corporate Compliance

*Christine Parker**

Abstract: This chapter revisits the significance of responsive regulation for theories of compliance. It shows how responsive regulation's theory of compliance recognises both multiple motivations for compliance and plural actors who help negotiate and construct compliance. It argues that responsive regulation theory implies responsive compliance and that this can help build possibilities for deliberative democratic responsibility and accountability of both businesses and regulators. This is the idea that I previously labelled the meta-regulation of the 'open corporation'. This chapter concludes that since business activity and indeed human development now face the existential challenge of socio-ecological disruption and collapse in which profit-oriented commercial activity is a significant driver, theories of compliance need to expand to concern themselves with how whole markets and industries can be made responsive to both social and ecological embeddedness. Regulatory compliance scholars need to pay attention to how networks of interacting business, government and civil society and social movement actors can influence business activity profoundly enough to shift the very nature of 'business as usual'. The chapter therefore proposes the need for 'ecological compliance' as a development of Ayres and Braithwaite's analysis of compliance.

4.1 INTRODUCTION

The study of business compliance with social, environmental and economic regulation is inherently paradoxical. Business organisations in capitalist societies[1] are legally constituted as for-profit entities. Yet regulation is aimed at making commercial entities responsible and accountable to non-commercial public interest goals. On the one hand, the very idea of 'regulation' implies that external authorities must force business firms to comply via the threat of harsh sanctions. On the other hand, the word 'compliance' implies that business firms can and must be trusted to operate responsibly within parameters of social justice, ecological

* I am grateful to Professor Fiona Haines for many fruitful discussions about our idea of 'ecological regulation'.

[1] For the purposes of this short chapter, I include a variety of capitalisms in this generalisation including the state-capitalism of China, the oligarchic capitalism of many countries in the former Soviet bloc, liberal market economies and so on, thus meaning that most of the world is now capitalist of one variety or another. But note that these different capitalisms feature different styles of regulation of business entities. See Hall and Soskice 2001; and for application to regulatory capitalism, Levi-Faur 2006.

sustainability and economic fairness. 'Compliance' occurs only where businesses organise and govern themselves internally in such a way as to ensure that workers are treated well, that the environment is not harmed, that the limits of fair competition are not breached and that they meet a host of other social, environmental and economic responsibilities that might harm their profits, at least in the short term (Parker 2002).

This paradox of regulation and compliance is reflected in regulatory compliance scholarship and practice. As Ayres and Braithwaite (1992: 20) put it, 'there is a long history of barren disputation within regulatory agencies, and more recently among scholars of regulation, between those who think that corporations will comply with the law only when confronted with tough sanctions and those who believe that gentle persuasion works in securing business compliance with the law'. Ian Ayres and John Braithwaite's (1992) *Responsive Regulation* proposed a principled way to transcend this stand-off. Since the publication of *Responsive Regulation*, business regulation has proliferated (even despite apparent neo-liberal commitment to deregulation; see Braithwaite 2008: viii). Yet despite the many public interest benefits achieved, the challenge of ensuring that commercial activity operates within social, ecological and economic boundaries remains overwhelming. Haines and Parker (2018; Parker and Haines 2018) have called this the challenge of 'ecological regulation'. This chapter proposes the need for 'ecological compliance' as a development of Ayres and Braithwaite's analysis of compliance.

Section 4.2 summarises responsive regulation's theory of compliance, focusing on the famous responsive regulation pyramid of enforcement and compliance. Section 4.3 argues that responsive regulation necessarily requires an expanded concept of 'responsive compliance', in which both business firms and regulators are responsive to deliberative democratic accountability through the involvement of plural business, state and civil society actors in responsive regulation to activate and enforce compliance with public interest goals. I previously referred to this as the meta-regulation of the 'open corporation' (Parker 2002). Section 4.4 shows that business activity and indeed human development now face the existential challenge of socio-ecological disruption and collapse in which profit-oriented commercial activity is a significant driver. In this context, 'ecological regulation' and thus 'ecological compliance' are necessary developments in responsive regulation. Theories of compliance must expand to concern themselves with how whole markets and industries can be regulated and made responsible to public interest goals by networks of interacting business, government and, crucially, civil society and social movement actors. Regulatory compliance scholars need to pay attention to how these networks can influence business activity profoundly enough to shift the very nature of 'business as usual'.

4.2 RESPONSIVE REGULATION'S THEORY OF COMPLIANCE

4.2.1 *Responsive Regulation*

Ayres and Braithwaite's (1992) *Responsive Regulation* both describes and prescribes how regulatory enforcement action best promotes compliance in practice. It proposes that in order to be effective, efficient and legitimate, regulatory policy should take neither a solely deterrent nor a solely cooperative approach: 'The basic idea of responsive regulation is that government should be responsive to the conduct of those they seek to regulate in deciding whether a more or less interventionist response is needed. In particular, law enforcers should be responsive to how effectively citizens or corporations are regulating themselves before deciding whether to escalate intervention' (Braithwaite 2002: 29). Broadly speaking, theories that seek to explain regulatory compliance can be divided into three categories (Nielsen and Parker 2012; Winter and May 2001): those that see people as motivated by economic *calculative motivations*, the fear of detection of violations and application of sanctions (Simpson 2002: 22–44); those that see people as motivated by *social motivations*, the desire to earn the respect and approval of significant others (Gunningham et al. 2003; Rees 1997); and those that see people as motivated by *normative motivations*, their sense of moral duty to comply and their agreement with the legitimacy of particular regulation (which can include evaluations of both the substantive and the procedural justice of regulation) (Tyler 2006).

Ayres and Braithwaite (1992: 30–5) show that different people have different motivations for complying (or not complying) with the law at different times, and that the same person (or firm) can have multiple, potentially conflicting, motivations for compliance at the same time. Responsive regulation therefore proposes a normative theory about the way these plural motivations for compliance interact with one another and respond to plural deterrent and cooperative regulatory enforcement strategies. It does this by proposing that enforcement strategies should be arranged in a hierarchy or 'regulatory pyramid' with more co-operative strategies deployed at the base of the pyramid and progressively more punitive approaches utilised only if, and when, co-operative strategies fail (see Figure 4.1). To make sure that they start as many 'positive spirals' of reactions and counter-reactions as possible, regulators should generally start enforcement from a presumption of being co-operative. Regulatees showing the will and ability to repair any harms they have caused and to reform themselves to come into compliance should be rewarded with less harsh enforcement (Ayres and Braithwaite 1992: 19). If regulatees fail to respond in kind to offers of co-operation, the regulator should go on to 'somewhat punitive' action 'only reluctantly and only when dialogue fails, and then escalate to even more punitive approaches only when the more modest forms of punishment fail' (Braithwaite 2002: 30). When regulatees become willing to co-operate, the regulator should, according to Ayres and Braithwaite, be able to forgive a history of wrongdoing (Ayres and Braithwaite 1992: 33) and de-escalate down the pyramid to less harsh enforcement.[2]

4.2.2 *The Responsive Regulation Pyramid*

Responsive regulation theory claims that this pyramid of enforcement activates different (potentially contradictory) motivations so that they interact to support compliance, and discourage resistance, game-playing and abuse in two main ways: First, the application of the pyramid of enforcement strategies makes it beneficial for rationally calculating regulatees to be virtuous (Braithwaite 2002: 33). It is more rational for those who are motivated by calculations as to what is to their own benefit to 'voluntarily' comply than it is to resist and not comply where the regulator will otherwise escalate up the enforcement pyramid. The claim here is that the fact that people and firms have 'multiple selves' (Ayres and Braithwaite 1992: 30–5) means that once they agree to negotiate with a regulator (albeit for self-interested reasons), their better self can be brought to the fore through social and normative appeals. Second, beginning with enforcement strategies lower down the pyramid means that the regulator is normatively

2 For a more detailed analysis and empirical test of this theory, see Nielsen and Parker 2009. This part of this chapter is based on this analysis.

justified if and when they must use deterrence (to appeal to rational actor motivations) further up the pyramid. The staged deployment of enforcement strategies from lower to higher is designed to avoid breaking down regulatees' moral commitment to comply with the law: '[B]y resorting to more dominating, less respectful forms of social control only when more dialogic forms have been tried first, coercive control comes to be seen as more legitimate' (Braithwaite 2002: 33).

The pyramid of enforcement strategies is the most well-known aspect of *Responsive Regulation*. It is intuitively attractive because it translates the challenge of regulating for the public interest onto a human, interpersonal relationship scale in which co-operation, or at least accommodation, between business and regulators is possible much of the time. In this sense, the motivating rationale of *Responsive Regulation* is not just more responsive regulators but also more responsive regulatees. As Valerie Braithwaite (2009) has argued, regulation is a relationship in which the regulatee can display more or less committed or dismissive and defiant 'motivational postures' towards regulators. The challenge for responsive regulators is to deal with wrongdoing while nurturing consent and commitment. To put it another way, responsive regulation implies 'responsive compliance'.

Yet the pyramid is only one chapter of the *Responsive Regulation* book. The significance of the responsive regulation theory of compliance goes beyond what it says about how dyadic encounters between enforcement officials and regulatees can best promote compliance. As Section 4.3 shows, responsive regulation also presumes a context of plural participation in regulation where other market, state and civil society stakeholders (beyond the regulator and regulatee) are recruited to the process of responsive regulation and responsive compliance.

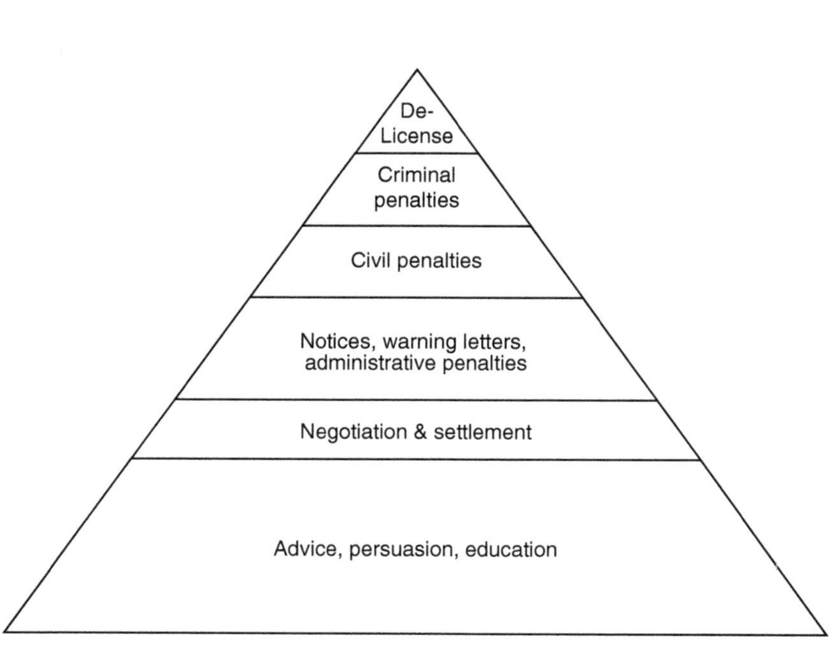

FIGURE 4.1 Responsive regulation pyramid
Source: Based on Ayres and Braithwaite 1992.

4.3 META-REGULATION: 'RESPONSIVE COMPLIANCE' IN DELIBERATIVE DEMOCRACY

4.3.1 *Plural Participation in Constructing Compliance*

Responsive Regulation sits in a tradition of qualitative social science research in regulatory studies which points out that compliance and non-compliance are not objective stable phenomena based on rules set out by official agencies and then implemented or breached by businesses and individuals. Rather, compliance is the interaction of plural actors and influences that constructs how regulation is implemented, what it means in practice and, ultimately, whether business activity can itself be made responsive and accountable in deliberative democracy (Braithwaite 2008). The very meaning of compliance (and non-compliance) in each particular circumstance is interpreted, negotiated and co-constructed by plural actors, including official government regulators (through monitoring and enforcement action: Hutter 1997), multiple individuals and units within each business firm (Gray and Silbey 2011; Heimer 2013) and a host of third-party business and civil society actors. These can include supply chain partners for each business (who might require certain accreditations in order to contract), rating agencies, banks, insurers, auditors and accreditation agencies (who may assess businesses on various social and environmental responsibility and compliance indicators), public interest groups, social movements (who might campaign on specific issues) (Rodriguez-Garavito 2017) and individual citizens (Parker and Nielsen 2011: 6–8). It has been suggested that these business and civil society third parties can construct second and third 'faces' to the regulatory pyramid (see Gunningham and Grabosky 1998: 398; Grabosky 2013). But for Ayres and Braithwaite (1992: 54–100) it was the participation of civil society groups in responsive regulation negotiations between government enforcement agencies and businesses in individual cases as well as a broader context of vibrant deliberative democracy that were crucial to holding both regulators and businesses democratically accountable thus ensuring the achievement of public interest goals.

For many commentators, the negotiation of compliance between government, industry, third-party and civil society actors is, however, an opportunity for corruption and capture. Tombs and Whyte (2013) argue that the negotiation of enforcement and compliance via responsive regulation pyramids will tend to depoliticise substantive conflict between the conduct of business and the demands of public interest regulation. The focus of much interpretive compliance research is on revealing and uncovering the politics of compliance, that is, the power relations that result in one set of actors' understandings of compliance being socially constructed as more legitimate than others (see, e.g., Edelman 2016; Shamir and Weiss 2012). *Responsive Regulation*, by contrast, seeks to transcend these politics by seeing the process of negotiation and construction of compliance as both instrumentally valuable and normatively desirable in achieving what I label here 'responsive compliance'.

4.3.2 *Instrumental Value of Plural Participation in Responsive Compliance*

Let's consider first the instrumental value of plural, negotiated processes of constructing compliance. Responsive regulation theory points out that official regulators do not necessarily have the capacity to effectively activate regulatees' plural motivations for compliance on their own. There is likely to be a higher rate of business compliance with the law when a plurality of actors (public and private) utilise their plural resources and relationships with regulatees to activate the plurality of motivations for compliance than when regulatory agencies rely on official powers alone. Different stakeholders will have different types of relationship with regulatees, different sources of influence over regulatees and therefore the ability to activate a range of different motivations that regulatees might have for complying with legal regulation. For example, an official fair work regulator may not have sufficient power and influence to persuade a celebrity chef who runs a chain of restaurants to prioritise putting in place accounting systems to ensure that all staff are paid fairly, and they may not have the staff and authority to audit all the books in detail. But third parties such as employees and labour unions may be able to blow the whistle on wage theft and appeal to banks, institutional investors, media outlets and customers to withdraw support until the chef ensures that proper systems are put in place in all restaurants in the chain. This can have a moralising and socialising impact on a whole industry far beyond what the regulator could achieve in inspections. Similarly, regulators might not be able to levy a heavy enough fine to deter a large and profitable firm from price-fixing behaviour, but they can ensure media publicity that names and shames the company and then expect industry peers, rating agencies, consumer groups and other stakeholders to levy informal financial and reputational sanctions that motivate compliance (Van Erp 2011).

This plural responsive regulation has been extended by Gunningham into the concept of 'smart regulation' in which markets, civil society and other institutions and resources can be harnessed or 'enrolled' (Black 2003) by government agencies to act as surrogate regulators using a range of regulatory instruments to achieve public interest goals more effectively, legitimately and efficiently. Smart regulation conceptualised this as another 'face' to the pyramid (Gunningham and Grabosky 1998: 398; see also Gunningham, Kagan and Thornton (2003) extending to the idea of social, economic and legal licences to operate). Even where regular inspection by a government agency may not be a possibility, 'social stakeholders', such as neighbours, activist organisations and the general public, may fill the void, bringing complaints or acting to shame recalcitrant business into compliance. 'Economic stakeholders', including shareholders and institutional investors, banks, insurance agencies and customers, may also demand compliance with public interest goals (see also Nielsen and Parker 2008). If enough influential social and economic stakeholders all expect compliance, regulatees will come to see compliance as appropriate and desirable for its own sake, without calculating reasons for compliance (Nielsen and Parker 2008).

4.3.3 *Democratic Desirability of Plural Participation in Responsive Compliance*

Responsive Regulation sees plurally negotiated compliance as not merely a pragmatic necessity but also a normatively desirable opportunity for the democratic accountability and legitimacy of regulatory activity and the sustainable achievement of public interest goals through compliance. *Responsive Regulation* is clear that deliberative, participatory democracy should permeate both the making and the implementation of law and regulation. Ayres and Braithwaite (1992: 18) explicitly state that the theory is intended to be a normative one based on civic republican theory. That is, it is built on an ideal of societies with strong states, strong markets and strong civil society, in which there are many opportunities for all those affected to participate in deliberative mechanisms and all (public and private) exercises of power are contestable by plural actors (see Pettit 1997; see also J. Braithwaite 2008; V. Braithwaite 2009). A whole chapter of *Responsive Regulation* (Ayres and Braithwaite 1992: 54–100) demonstrates both formally in economic theory and substantively as a matter of political theory that 'tripartism' of market, state and civil society is necessary for democratic accountability in regulation. That is, public interest group participation in the dialogue of responsive regulation is necessary to hold both regulators and businesses accountable for their negotiation of the exercise of regulatory and compliance discretion in each particular case.

4.3.4 *Meta-regulation and the Failure of Responsive Compliance*

The Open Corporation (Parker 2002) looks at responsive regulation from the other side of the equation, the experience and capacities of large business firms which should be subject to accountability and responsibility via regulation. That is, what does responsive compliance require? In *The Open Corporation* I demonstrate (on the basis of original field work and meta-review of compliance literature) that it is necessary to make businesses permeable to both state and civil society influence in a democratic society through requiring internal compliance systems, leveraging the agency of corporate insiders (e.g., environmental managers, in-house lawyers and compliance professionals) who institutionalise social and environmental values inside the company, making it more responsive to stakeholders who contest corporate decisions and actions. I argue that this is possible only where there is meta-regulation by the state of the company's internal responsibility systems to ensure accountability, responsibility and reflexive action in the 'open corporation'.

The 'open corporation' (Parker 2002) is a marriage between management and democracy and law – formal government regulation, democratic and stakeholder action, and internal corporate self-regulation all interact through an iterated dynamic of corporate engagement with social, environmental and legal responsibility. Typically, this takes place through the phases of: (1) the commitment to respond via self-regulation; (2) the acquisition of specialised skills and knowledge for self-regulation; and (3) the institutionalisation of purpose in self-regulation. Each of the three phases represents a decision point at which external influences can transform corporate practice and decision-making; but continuing interaction with external stakeholders and regulators at the next decision point is necessary to ensure an appropriate management response. Ultimately, external stakeholders and regulators must prompt self-critique and continuous improvement through accountability and meta-evaluation, which keeps the cycle of engagement moving forward (see Figure 4.2).

Both responsive regulation and my meta-regulation of the open corporation are predicated on the need for strong governments and strong public interest-oriented civil society. Both theories also assume markets and businesses with the capacity to do the right thing and which can be forced to do the right thing with a judicious combination of sticks, carrots and, crucially, corporate capital punishment (or de-licensing). Yet these elements are often lacking in the way in which 'responsive regulation' and 'meta-regulation' are adopted in either scholarly literature or regulatory practice.

They are frequently narrowed down by conceptions of what is required either by the rule of law (see Yeung 2004; Westerman 2013) or to avoid interfering 'too much' in markets (see Haines and Parker 2018). Meta-regulation is often discussed in a way that is narrowed back down to a dyadic relationship between a single regulator and regulatee with no democratic participation and no vision of the overall embeddedness of business activity in social democracy (contrast Braithwaite 2008; Parker 2002). It becomes merely meta-governance of risk management in which the government regulator places responsibility on the regulated enterprises themselves (usually large organisations) to submit their plans to the regulator

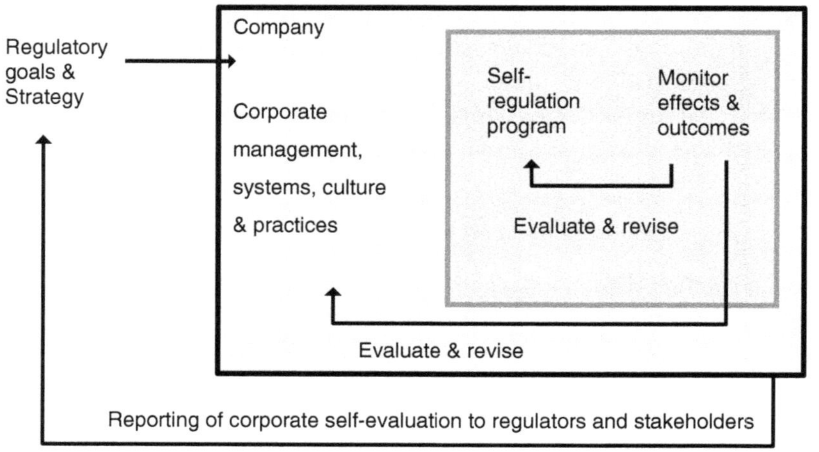

FIGURE 4.2 Meta-regulation
Source: Taken directly from Parker 2002, but re-drawn.

for approval, with the regulator's role being to 'risk-manage' those individual enterprises (see Gilad 2010; Coglianese and Lazer 2003 for overviews of different uses of the term). The application of responsive regulation and responsive compliance in scholarship and practice has often failed to sufficiently highlight the need to bring business activity (and also regulatory activity) inside democratic accountability and social and environmental responsibility. Instead, regulation has often become a means of legitimating further exploitation and commodification and without sufficient responsibility (Shamir and Weiss 2012). Section 4.4 turns to the existential challenge of social and ecological systems and introduces the notions of ecological regulation and ecological compliance as developments in responsive regulation and responsive compliance.

4.4 ECOLOGICAL REGULATION AND ECOLOGICAL COMPLIANCE

4.4.1 *Failure of Business Regulation and Compliance in the Anthropocene*

The challenge of ensuring corporate compliance with public interest-oriented business regulation is increasingly urgent in light of the existential social, environmental and economic threats facing the inhabitants of planet Earth. The 'planetary boundaries' concept is one conceptualisation of how human activity is dangerously disrupting the way in which Earth systems operate (e.g., Steffen et al. 2015). According to this model, climate disruption is not the only looming ecological disaster. Other dire threats to the social, political and economic conditions of human life include biodiversity loss, the disruption of the global nitrogen and phosphorous cycles, and the accumulation of plastics and other novel human-made materials in places where they never previously existed (especially the ocean). Ecological disruption will also further cement pre-existing global social and economic inequalities (Gough 2017), not to mention its impact on other species.

The production of both ecological crisis and social inequality is to a large degree tied to the way in which capitalism and business activity are organised and governed (see Raworth 2017; Sjåfjell and Taylor 2019). They are driven by commercial activities for which one of the important drivers is financial profit-oriented business activity. These firms and their major share-owners, directors and senior managers have profited enormously from these extractive and destructive activities. They will be the first to be able to afford protection from the ravages of climate change and the like. Meanwhile, those who have benefitted least from economic growth – those in the global South and the precariat in Western industrialised countries – are already the first to suffer the burdens. Hence the argument of some that instead of calling the current geologically disrupted era the 'Anthropocene', we should call it the 'Capitalocene' (see Haraway 2015). This is a problem of how whole markets operate to create and perpetuate over-production and over-consumption, a 'consumptogenic' system (see Parker and Johnson 2019 following Dixon and Banwell 2012).

As Levi-Faur (2017: 289) observes in his theory of regulatory capitalism, 'regulation made, nurtured and constrained the capitalist system' through the creation and enforcement of concepts such as private property, companies, stock markets, competition law and insurance. Law and regulation thus helped create the Anthropocene. Fiona Haines and I have therefore posed the challenge of 'ecological regulation', that is, the regulatory challenge of re-embedding business activity inside socio-ecological systems (Haines and Parker 2018; Parker and Haines 2018). We see this as an expansion and development from the social embeddedness recognised by responsive regulation to the need for regulatory governance of all human activity (including business activity) to operate within *ecological* limits while also still responding to social and economic tensions and crises.

If ecological regulation is necessary then so too is ecological compliance, that is, the capacity for business entities to open out their own governance not just to meet social and legal responsibilities but also to comprehend our human embeddedness within ecological systems. This challenges the very frontiers of capitalism, that is, what can be allowed to count as 'business as usual' and what must become no longer thinkable as legitimate commercial activity. It also challenges current conceptions of regulation by law, requiring a much greater prominence to ensuring the protection, enhancement and regeneration of socio-ecological systems and non-capitalist economic activity. What then does the challenge of ecological compliance mean for regulatory compliance scholarship and practice?

4.4.2 *Studying Ecological Compliance*

'Ecological compliance' extends beyond individual business decisions in relation to particular rules and regulators to businesses' responses to ecologies of regulation or 'regulatory space' (Scott 2001) across whole markets.

Much of the regulatory compliance literature asks the question: When is regulation effective at achieving compliance with a particular rule or regulatory objective? This implies that the question is about how regulatory interventions influence otherwise stable firms and markets at particular points in time. Traditional compliance studies therefore often start with a particular rule or instrument that a particular governmental regulatory agency or self-regulatory body seeks to implement, monitor and enforce. This approach has produced many valuable results. However, it can also encourage a narrow focus on technique, procedures and dyadic relationships at the expense of broader-ranging inquiries into the overall regulatory politics of markets. Ecological compliance studies would ask how different rules and regulatory objectives interact, and how unsustainable production and consumption are created and legitimated across a whole market despite specific attempts to regulate them and rein them in.

An ecological compliance approach suggests that compliance scholars and practitioners should critically examine business activity more holistically, that is, ecologically, in terms of a set of changing relations inside the firm, between the firm's activities, the market (broadly conceived as customers, competitors, supply chain partners, service providers and so on) and civil society in which public and private standards are continually being created, adjusted, solidified or destroyed. The developing area of regulatory studies of hybrid public and private governance interactions or 'regulatory networks' in transnational business regulation is a useful resource for this task (see Abbott and Snidal 2009; Bartley 2018; Braithwaite and Drahos 2000; Cashore et al. 2011; Eberlein et al. 2014; Perez 2011; Rodriguez-Garavito 2017). Regulatory network analysis recognises that the important regulatory question is not whether some issue, such as whether hens should be kept in conventional cages, is or is not regulated. The question is how is it governed, by whom and to what effect? Regulatory network analysis draws attention to the way that the regulatory governance of any particular area at any particular time is the result of ongoing interactions (contests, conflicts, alliances, modelling and mimicry) by multiple actors (government, industry and civil society) at multiple levels (local, national and global) each seeking to exercise power legitimately and effectively (Scott 2001). It is important to understand the dynamics of regulatory governance networks because markets and regulation (by which we mean business-government-NGO regulatory interactions) continually constitute one another. In my own recent work on food system governance in relation to the factory farming of animals, I use this methodological approach to understand how the dynamics of regulation and compliance influence what products are available, how they are produced and sold, with what impact on humans (workers, local communities), animals and ecologies (see, e.g., Parker et al. 2017; Parker and Johnson 2019).

'Ecological compliance' is also ecological in the sense that it must be concerned with responsiveness not just to regulators and traditional civil society actors but also to social and ecological actors, and regardless of legal jurisdiction and national boundaries. How does business interact with the 'core' economy that is households in which the vulnerable are cared for and children are nurtured and educated, the gift economy, volunteer and activist work (Gough 2017)? And how does business activity interact with the forests, oceans, waterways, atmosphere? Is the need for embeddedness, respect and reciprocity recognised and responded to with integrity? Although responsively rational regulation demonstrates that plural voices can in fact impact on regulating capitalism and normatively proposes responsive procedures for these voices, we are only just beginning to develop ways – in scholarship and policy – to pay attention to ecology itself and to the most basic forms of human interdependence on one another within ecologies. Fiona Haines and I have previously analysed ways in which social movements are seeking to progress this agenda in one direction through the naming and shaming of fossil fuel corporations who have contributed the most to global warming (the 'carbon majors') and to name their behaviour as totally unacceptable 'ecocide' (Haines and Parker 2018). We argue that this might have an impact on overall compliance by changing the very baseline for what counts as acceptable business conduct by reference to its interaction with the global climate (an ecological actor). Other researchers are seeking to reconceptualise and validate conceptions of commercial activity that take their meaning and purpose from how they sit within basic social relationships (Morgan and Kuch 2015), and that might also change the overall ecological compliance of a market. These are important developments that deserve more attention.

4.5 CONCLUSION

Compliance scholarship and practice often get narrowed down to measuring and demonstrating sufficient compliance with particular rules and regulations. In this chapter I have suggested that the spirit of responsive regulation should be expanded to ecological compliance in which the main concern is the overall dynamic of the degree to which regulation and governance systems are able to continually and dynamically embed business activity inside social and ecological systems. This is not just deliberative democracy (as in Braithwaite's vision of responsive regulation) but also ecological democracy, as befits the social and ecological crisis of the Anthropocene.

REFERENCES

Abbott, Kenneth, and Duncan Snidal. 2009. 'Strengthening International Regulation through Transnational New Governance: Overcoming the Orchestration Deficit'. *Vanderbilt Journal of Transnational Law* 42: 501–78.

Ayres, Ian, and John Braithwaite. 1992. *Responsive Regulation: Transcending the Deregulation Debate*. New York: Oxford University Press.

Bartley, Tim. 2018. *Rules Without Rights: Land, Labor, and Private Authority in the Global Economy*. New York: Oxford University Press.

Black, Julia. 2003. 'Enrolling Actors in Regulatory Processes: Examples from UK Financial Services Regulation'. *Public Law* (Spring): 63–91.

Braithwaite, John. 2002. *Restorative Justice and Responsive Regulation*. Oxford University Press.

2008. *Regulatory Capitalism: How It Works, Ideas for Making It Work Better*. Cheltenham, UK: Edward Elgar.

Braithwaite, John, and Peter Drahos. 2000. *Global Business Regulation*. Cambridge University Press.

Braithwaite, Valerie. 2009. *Defiance in Taxation and Governance: Resisting and Dismissing Authority in a Democracy*. Cheltenham, UK: Edward Elgar.

Cashore, Benjamin, Graeme Auld and Stefan Renckens. 2011. 'The Impact of Private, Industry and Transnational Civil Society Regulation and Their Interaction with Official Regulation'. In *Explaining Compliance: Business Responses to Regulation*, edited by Christine Parker and Vibeke Nielsen, 343–70. Cheltenham, UK: Edward Elgar.

Coglianese, Cary, and David Lazer. 2003. 'Management-Based Regulation: Prescribing Private Management to Achieve Public Goals'. *Law & Society Review* 37: 691–730.

Dixon, Jane, and Cathy Banwell. 2012. 'Choice Editing for the Environment: Managing Corporate Risks'. In *Risk and Social Theory in Environmental Management*, edited by Thomas Measham and Stewart Lockie, 175–85. Melbourne: CSIRO.

Eberlein, Burkard, Kenneth W. Abbott, Julia Black, Errol Meidinger and Stepan Wood. 2014. 'Transnational Business Governance Interactions: Conceptualization and Framework for Analysis'. *Regulation & Governance* 8: 1–21.

Edelman, Lauren. 2016. *Working Law: Courts, Corporations, and Symbolic Civil Rights*. Chicago: University of Chicago Press.

Gilad, Sharon. 2010. 'It Runs in the Family: Meta-regulation and Its Siblings'. *Regulation & Governance* 4: 485–506.

Gough, Ian. 2017. *Heat, Greed and Human Need: Climate Change, Capitalism and Sustainable Wellbeing*. Cheltenham, UK: Edward Elgar.

Grabosky, Peter. 2013. 'Beyond Responsive Regulation: The Expanding Role of Non-state Actors in the Regulatory Process'. *Regulation & Governance* 7: 114–23.

Gray, Garry C., and Susan Silbey. 2011. 'The Other Side of the Compliance Relationship'. In *Explaining Compliance: Business Responses to Regulation*, edited by Christine Parker and Vibeke Nielsen, 123–38. Cheltenham, UK: Edward Elgar.

Gunningham, Neil, and Peter Grabosky. 1998. *Smart Regulation: Designing Environmental Policy*. Oxford: Clarendon Press.

Gunningham, Neil, Robert Kagan and Dorothy Thornton. 2003. *Shades of Green: Business, Regulation and Environment*. Palo Alto, CA: Stanford University Press.

Haines, Fiona, and Christine Parker. 2018. 'Moving Towards Ecological Regulation'. In *Criminology and the Anthropocene*, edited by Cameron Holley and Clifford Shearing, 81–108. New York and London: Routledge.

Hall, Peter, and David Soskice. 2001. *Varieties of Capitalism: The Institutional Foundations of Comparative Advantage*. Oxford: Oxford University Press.

Haraway, Donna. 2015. 'Anthropocene, Capitalocene, Plantationocene, Chthulucene: Making Kin'. *Environmental Humanities* 6: 159–65.

Heimer, Carol A. 2013. 'Resilience in the Middle: Contributions of Regulated Organizations to Regulatory Success'. *Annals of the American Academy of Political and Social Science* 649: 139–56.

Hutter, Bridget. 1997. *Compliance: Regulation and Environment*. Oxford: Oxford University Press.

Levi-Faur, David. 2006. 'Varieties of Regulatory Capitalism: Getting the Most out of the Comparative Method'. *Governance* 19: 367–82.

2017. 'Regulatory Capitalism' In *Regulatory Theory: Foundations and Applications*, edited by Peter Drahos, 289–302. Canberra: ANU Press.

Morgan, Bronwen, and Declan Kuch. 2015. 'Radical Transactionalism: Legal Consciousness, Diverse Economies, and the Sharing Economy'. *Journal of Law & Society* 42: 556–87.

Nielsen, Vibeke Lehmann, and Christine Parker. 2008. 'To What Extent Do Third Parties Influence Business Compliance?'. *Journal of Law and Society* 35: 309–40.

2009. 'Testing Responsive Regulation in Regulatory Enforcement'. *Regulation & Governance* 3: 376–400.

2012. 'Mixed Motives: Economic, Social and Normative Motivations in Business Compliance'. *Law & Policy* 34: 428–62.

Parker, Christine. 2002. *The Open Corporation: Effective Self-Regulation and Democracy*. Cambridge University Press.

Parker, Christine, and Fiona Haines. 2018. 'An Ecological Approach to Regulatory Studies?' *Journal of Law and Society* 45: 136–55.

Parker, Christine, and Hope Johnson. 2019. 'From Food Chains to Food Webs: Regulating Capitalist Production and Consumption in the Food System'. *Annual Review of Law and Social Sciences* 15: 205–25.

Parker, Christine, and Vibeke Lehmann Nielsen (eds.). 2011. *Explaining Compliance: Business Responses to Regulation*. Cheltenham, UK: Edward Elgar Publications.

Parker, Christine, Rachel Carey, Josephine De Costa, and Gyorgy Scrinis. 2017. 'Can the Hidden Hand of the Market Be an Effective and Legitimate Regulator? The Case of Animal Welfare under a Labeling for Consumer Choice Policy Approach'. *Regulation & Governance* 11: 368–87.

Perez, Oren. 2011. 'Private Environmental Governance as Ensemble Regulation: A Critical Exploration of Sustainability Indexes and the New Ensemble Politics'. *Theoretical Inquiries in Law* 12: 543–79.

Pettit, Philip. 1997. *Republicanism: A Theory of Freedom and Government*. Oxford: Oxford University Press.

Raworth, Kate. 2017. *Doughnut Economics: Seven Ways to Think Like a 21st Century Economist*. Hartford, CT: Chelsea Green.

Rees, Joseph. 1997. 'Development of Communitarian Regulation in the Chemical Industry'. *Law & Policy* 19: 477–528.

Rodriguez-Garavito, César (ed.). 2017. *Business and Human Rights: Beyond the End of the Beginning*. New York: Cambridge University Press.

Scott, Colin. 2001. 'Analysing Regulatory Space: Fragmented Resources and Institutional Design'. *Public Law* (Summer): 283–305.

Shamir, Ronen, and Dana Weiss. 2012. 'Semiotics of Indicators: The Case of Corporate Human Rights Responsibility'. *Governance* 46: 4.
Simpson, Sally. 2002. *Corporate Crime, Law and Social Control*. Cambridge: Cambridge University Press.
Sjåfjell, Beate, and Mark B. Taylor. 2019. 'Clash of Norms: Shareholder Primacy vs. Sustainable Corporate Purpose'. *International and Comparative Corporate Law Journal* 13: 40–66.
Steffen, Will, Katherine Richardson, Johan Rockström, Sarah E. Cornell, Ingo Fetzer, Elena M. Bennett, Reinette Biggs et al. 2015. 'Planetary Boundaries: Guiding Human Development on a Changing Planet'. *Science* 347(6223): 1259855.
Tombs, Steve, and David Whyte. 2013. 'Transcending the Deregulation Debate? Regulation, Risk, and the Enforcement of Health and Safety Law in the UK'. *Regulation & Governance* 7: 61–79.
Tyler, Tom R. 2006. *Why People Obey the Law*. Princeton, NJ: Princeton University Press.
Van Erp, Judith. 2011. 'Naming and Shaming in Regulatory Enforcement'. In *Explaining Compliance: Business Responses to Regulation*, edited by Christine Parker and Vibeke Nielsen, 322–42. Cheltenham, UK: Edward Elgar.
Westerman, Pauline. 2013. 'Pyramids and the Value of Generality'. *Regulation & Governance* 7: 80–94.
Winter, Søren C., and Peter J. May. 2001. 'Motivation for Compliance with Environmental Regulations'. *Journal of Policy Analysis and Management* 20: 675–98.
Yeung, Karen. 2004. *Securing Compliance – A Principled Approach*. Oxford: Hart Publishing.

5

Behavioral Ethics as Compliance

Yuval Feldman and Yotam Kaplan

Abstract: This chapter studies the implications of behavioral ethics research to questions of legal compliance. Behavioral ethics emphasizes the concept of bounded ethicality, referring to a long list of biases and cognitive limitations that prevent people from making a full and candid evaluation of the ethicality of their own actions. In other words, people often act unethically not because they made a conscious choice to behave badly but because they were able to ignore, downplay, or justify their own misconduct. This chapter explores the meaning of behavioral ethics findings for questions of compliance with the law. That is, if people often ignore or downplay their own unethical choices, how can lawmakers and regulators act to improve compliance with the law? The chapter describes the central relevant findings of behavioral ethics research and the challenges these findings pose for legal compliance, and outlines possible solutions. In particular, we advocate a novel regulatory approach utilizing ethical nudges: regulatory interventions that are designed to improve ethical deliberations by potential wrongdoers.

5.1 INTRODUCTION

Research in behavioral ethics aims to study the cognitive processes involved in ethical decision-making. One of the key findings of this emerging field of study is the phenomenon of bounded ethicality, a board term used to capture the wide variety of psychological biases that people encounter in their ethical deliberations. Research shows that people often fail to make an objective and candid evaluation of the ethicality of their own actions (Feldman 2018), and that a long list of cognitive biases causes them to ignore or downplay their own unethical conduct. Very often people do not make an explicit decision to act unethically but instead act in this way while convincing themselves that there is nothing wrong with their conduct.

The current chapter describes the implications of behavioral ethics research for questions of legal compliance. It is important to note that the behavioral ethics literature typically speaks of unethicality and unethical behavior, and does not explicitly address issues of illegality or legal compliance. Thus, research in behavioral ethics typically studies people's willingness to lie, cheat, or act in ways that are generally considered to clash with conventional morality, and does not focus on compliance with specific legal norms. Existing literature, for the most part, also does not explicate the connections between behavioral ethics' experimental findings and the rich literature on compliance. Therefore, the challenge for the current chapter is to make the transition from the ethical realm to the legal arena, and to showcase the implications of behavioral ethics findings for the decision to comply with legal, as opposed to ethical, norms. The successful application of behavioral insights to the legal setting necessitates careful consideration of the particular features of legal regimes, which differ in important ways from moral conventions and nonlegal ethical commitments. In particular, the challenge here is to account for the interrelations between social norms, the cognitive aspects of ethical deliberations, legal institutions, and legal sanctions. Legal settings present a unique mixture of motivations, relating to expressive moral functions, the threat of punishment, and self-identification with state and government authorities. This complexity adds an additional layer to the ethical decision-making process described in behavioral ethics research and experimental works.

With these caveats in mind, the core insights of behavioral ethics research are highly relevant for questions of legal compliance. The decision whether or not to comply with the law bears important similarities to the more abstract ethical dilemmas studied by behavioral experimentalists. Existing experimental work in behavioral ethics often structures a semilegal environment, in which participants are able to choose whether or not to comply with the explicit "rules of the game" presented by the researchers. Such a setting can be reasonably compared to compliance with the law, where rules are provided by the state. More generally, the same cognitive biases that seem to influence people's ethical decisions in the lab might be instructive in forming a better understanding of questions of legal compliance. If people can indeed ignore or downplay their own unethical choices, as suggested by behavioral studies, this has far-reaching implications for any policy designed to improve compliance and curb misconduct. In other words, if wrongdoers often convince themselves that they are in fact committing no wrong, how should the law act to prevent wrongdoing? This question stands at the core of this chapter.

5.2 THREE MODES OF UNETHICALITY

This section lays the groundwork for our analysis by distinguishing three cognitive sources of wrongdoing: calculated, self-justified, and self-blinded wrongdoing. Each mode describes a different mindset with regard to ethical decision-making and compliance (Jacobsen, Fosgaard, and Pascual-Ezama 2018).

5.2.1 *Calculated Wrongdoing*

The first mode of behavior is calculative wrongdoing, referring to instances in which wrongdoers act as a result of a deliberative cognitive process. A wrongdoer might decide not to comply with the law because the benefit of doing so outweighs the risk of sanction, or because the benefit of wrongdoing is so great that it overcomes any moral inhibitions.[1] Alternatively, the wrongdoer may decide that a specific legal order does not merit obedience. We would say that wrongdoing is calculated in such cases if it originates with a deliberative cognitive process by the perpetrator, who weighs several options and makes a conscious choice between them. This means that the wrongdoer conducts some type of objective moral

[1] Note that calculated wrongdoing does not necessarily mean that the wrongdoer is completely egoistic or devoid of morality. Thus, a calculated wrongdoer may hold altruistic preferences and value the welfare of others, or hold beliefs regarding the independent value of compliance with the law or with moral convention; nevertheless, in some instances the calculated wrongdoer will decide that these moral preferences would withdraw before some other value (typically personal gain).

deliberation, and arrives at a decision that is more-or-less coherent with her general moral commitments. This mode of wrongdoing is often the standard (typically implicit) assumption behind much of the existing scholarship in criminology, law, and law and economics in particular. Accordingly, existing strands of study tend to emphasize punishment and sanction as the main means of improving compliance. Supposedly, these tools can most effectively alter the calculus potential that perpetrators would face, making sure that misconduct is not worthwhile from a cost–benefit perspective.

Behavioral ethics research challenges these familiar assumptions by highlighting the concept of bounded ethicality, as well as other mechanisms which establish individuals' limited ability to conduct a fully objective assessment of their own ethical behavior. Thus, behavioral ethics research shows that, while calculated wrongdoing is possible, in many instances misconduct originates from less-than-fully deliberative processes of decision-making. In many cases, wrongdoers have trouble recognizing their own unethicality, meaning that they act wrongly not because they are willing to pay some external or internal price but, rather, because they have a biased assessment of what it is that they are doing. Many people tend to think of themselves as "good people" and value their positive self-image (Mazar, Amir, and Ariely 2008: 633); they therefore rarely make a deliberate decision to behave "badly." Rather, people will act unethically as long as they can do so while still maintaining a moral self-image. This can be achieved through a series of cognitive and motivational biases that lead people to ignore, justify, or excuse their own wrongful conduct in a way that often diverges significantly from an objective and candid deliberative process. We distinguish two types of biased process: self-justified wrongdoing and self-blinded wrongdoing.

5.2.2 *Self-Justified Noncompliance*

Self-justified wrongdoing, as opposed to calculated wrongdoing, involves biased ethical reasoning. In particular, under this mode of wrongdoing the perpetrator may understand that they are facing a moral dilemma, but their self-interest prevents them from conducting a fair and objective assessment of the situation. This is similar to calculated wrongdoing in the sense that some deliberative or semi-deliberative process may be taking place, but different in the fact that this process is biased, rather than objective. More specifically, since people typically value a positive self-image, they will tend to distort ethical deliberations in a way that presents them in a positive light. Self-justified noncompliance can therefore be defined as semiconscious, in the following sense: the wrongdoer is aware of the ethical dilemma but is unaware of the fact that their self-interest is distorting their ethical judgment. Many behavioral studies highlight such effects of objectivity biases, leading people to think that they are more objective than they actually are. Similar findings relate to the concept of moral disengagement, by which people tend to excuse their own unethical conduct even when aware of it (Bandura 1999: 204; Tenbrunsel and Messick 2004: 228). Thus, studies find that people are more likely to cheat when the experimental setting is changed so that their lies seem less blatant (Shalvi, Eldar, and Bereby-Meyer 2012: 1264); this means that wrongdoing is more prevalent when perpetrators can find creative ways to justify it to themselves (Shalvi, Eldar, and Bereby-Meyer 2012: 1264). Wrongdoers similarly engage in moral licensing, relying on a previously established image of a moral self to justify minor deviations from ethical conduct. Even people who place high value on compliance with the law can violate it, because their self-interest may cause them, for instance, to underappreciate the harmfulness of their own actions, thereby distorting their ethical calculation.

5.2.3 *Self-Blinded Noncompliance*

The third mode of wrongdoing is self-blinded wrongdoing, in which perpetrators' self-interest generates self-serving biases that prevent them from recognizing a moral dilemma at all. Unlike self-justified wrongdoing, in this mode of wrongdoing ethical biases do not distort the deliberative process of ethical decision-making but, rather, prevent it from taking place. Behavioral ethics literature describes several mechanisms that prevent ethical deliberation (Gino 2015: 107–8). For example, this can result from motivated reasoning, a process by which individuals ignore some facts and emphasize others in a way that helps them support a perception of a moral self (Kunda 1990: 480). This concept highlights the various ways by which self-interest unconsciously shapes people's understanding of reality, as individuals tend to interpret situations in ways that serve them best (Merritt, Effron, and Monin 2010: 344). Thus, through motivated reasoning, wrongdoers can interpret situations in a way that eliminates ethical dilemmas. Consequently, perpetrators often adopt a biased perception of reality that prevents them from seeing their own wrongdoing (Kunda 1990: 480). The concept of self-blinded unethicality can be illustrated through empirical findings for motivated seeing, referring to the influence of self-interest on people's ability to process visual stimuli (Balcetis and Dunning 2006: 612). Thus, it has been shown that cognitive processes involved in the recognition and interpretation of information (written signs, for instance) are not fully objective, but that people indeed tend to see different things, depending on what better serves their interest (Balcetis and Dunning 2006: 615, 617). The concept of moral forgetting provides another such example for self-blinded unethicality, as researchers have demonstrated that people are more likely to forget facts that contradict their self-interest or that will portray them in a bad light (Shu, Gino, and Bazerman 2011: 339–41; Chugh, Bazerman, and Banaji 2005: 74–95). This means that pertinent facts, necessary for candid ethical deliberation, will often be less available to potential perpetrators, thus distorting the result of the ethical calculus, or subverting it completely. Therefore, even law-abiding citizens, who value the law, can act illegally if their self-interest prevents them from recognizing that they are doing so.

Recognition of the varied cognitive sources of wrongdoing has deep implications for compliance. Thus, if wrongdoing is calculated and deliberate, the most effective regulatory means would be to introduce sanctions in order to alter the deliberative process by potential wrongdoers. However, if unethicality originates without full and objective deliberation, such interventions might be less effective, and it would be more important to introduce enforcement tools designed to enhance ethical deliberation, and to make it more difficult for individuals to ignore, misrepresent, and misinterpret moral dilemmas.

5.3 SITUATIONAL WRONGDOING

Behavioral ethics research shows that wrongdoing often originates with nondeliberative choice and with automated cognitive processes. This insight not only challenges received wisdom regarding the cognitive sources of wrongdoing but also helps generate useful predictions regarding expected patterns of socially harmful behavior. Thus, behavioral ethics research shows that self-justified and self-blinded wrongdoing are highly predictable based on situational factors (Feldman and Kaplan 2019). In particular, wrongdoing will be more common when people can find ways to excuse and justify their own misconduct. These insights are closely related to the concept of ethical blind spots associated with the work of

Bazerman and Tenbrunsel (2011: 1–3). Ethical blind spots are described as situations in which ethical deliberation is hindered, and in which wrongdoing therefore proliferates.

Many commonplace situational factors contribute to self-justified wrongdoing. For instance, research shows that people find it easier to lie and cheat when they can justify their cheating as beneficial to others, and not (just) to themselves. This understandable tendency has devastating consequences in the context of corporations and other large organizations. Corporate misconduct is extremely common; behavioral research shows that the prevalence of corporate misconduct can be at least partially attributed to the fact that people find it easier to act unethically when they can tell themselves they are doing so in the name of the corporation and for its interests, and not for their own personal goals.[2] Research similarly shows that employee misconduct increases when profits from wrongdoing go to the employer and not to employees (Kouchaki 2013). This insight leads to the counterintuitive result according to which altruism can in fact increase corruption and misconduct: people's misbehavior increases when they think they can benefit others through their misbehavior (Gino, Ayal, and Ariely 2013: 291–2). These findings challenge the prediction of the familiar model of calculated wrongdoing, which would hold that people will tend to cheat more when they stand to benefit personally from doing so. Research similarly shows that people are more likely to behave unethically when they share the benefits of their wrongdoing with others, rather than enjoy those benefits exclusively (Wiltermuth 2011: 168). This again demonstrates the idea that people do not cheat when this is worthwhile based on objective calculated analysis but, rather, when they can justify their misconduct to themselves.

Research indicates that self-blinded unethicality is more common in situations where the identity of specific victims is less clear to wrongdoers. Where the harms of their actions are less clearly visible to wrongdoers, it is easier for them to ignore the harmfulness of their actions and avoid ethical dilemmas. Self-blinded wrongdoing is also prevalent in situations in which wrongdoers' decisions could be attributed to both legitimate and illegitimate reasons, as, in such situations, it is often difficult for people to recognize ethical dilemmas. For example, research on motivated reasoning and objectivity bias (Pronin, Gilovich, and Ross 2004: 781) suggests that when choosing a contractor for public works, a municipal officeholder might fail to recognize potential conflicts of interests, and would be convinced that their choice is based solely on legitimate reason relating to the good of the city, and is not affected by earlier familiarity with participants.

Ambiguity in legal norms is another antecedent of self-blinded unethicality, as ambiguous norms are easier to ignore, thereby hindering wrongdoers' ability to recognize ethical and legal dilemmas (Feldman and Smith 2014: 137–59). Legal ambiguity can similarly contribute to self-justified wrongdoing, as it is easier for perpetrators to interpret such rules in a way that will justify their wrongful actions. For instance, people find it easier to lie when the truth is complex or unclear, and find it easier to cheat when the moral code of conduct is ambiguous or poorly defined. Thus, for instance, unethicality is more prevalent against the background of oral contracts (as opposed to written contracts) since oral contracts less commonly define a clear and comprehensive set of legal obligations. Similarly, misrepresentation by commercial parties is more common in verbal communication, where the specific content of the misleading communication is vaguer.

[2] Yuval Feldman, Adi Leibson, and Gideon Porchomovski, "Corporate Law for 'Good' People," forthcoming, *Northwestern Law Review*, 2021.

All these findings not only challenge existing understanding of the sources of wrongdoing but also help produce new predictions regarding the focal points of noncompliance. Behavioral ethics research provides a growing number of findings regarding the situational antecedents of unethicality, offering increasingly nuanced accounts of factors that can hinder ethical deliberations. To improve compliance, policymakers should develop ways to identify such moral blind spots and then focus enforcement efforts on those situations that are shown to breed misconduct.

5.4 REVISITING TRADITIONAL LAW ENFORCEMENT

This section discusses some of the underlying assumptions characterizing existing law enforcement approaches in light of the insights of behavioral ethics research. Findings regarding self-justified, self-blinded, and situational unethicality carry far-reaching implications for efforts to improve compliance with the law. In particular, if people systematically ignore, excuse, or justify their own wrongdoing, many current tools designed to improve compliance may be ineffective.

5.4.1 *Deterrence and Its Limits*

One of the central themes of contemporary literature on law enforcement is the focus on deterrence as a main tool to improve behavior and prevent misconduct (Tittle 1980; Zimring, Hawkins, and Vorenberg 1973: 189–90). Scholars in this tradition study different rules and enforcement mechanisms as ways to effect private cost–benefit analysis by wrongdoers, thereby altering their behavior and curbing wrongdoing (Coase 1960; Shapiro and Pearse 2012: 1489). The issue with this standard framework is that it too often assumes calculative wrongdoing as the one and only source of unethicality. That is, the analysis typically views legal sanctions as explicit prices, assuming that wrongdoers will consider these sanctions as part of their decision-making process (Landes and Posner 1987: 4; Hirsch 1998; Shavell 2002: 227; Miceli 2004).

Findings regarding self-justified and self-blinded unethicality challenge this basic premise. If wrongdoers behave unethically only when they can convince themselves of the ethicality of their choices, this means that they systematically tend to think of their actions as not violating legal norms. Therefore, wrongdoers will fail to accurately assess the probability of being sanctioned and will not react to deterrence in the same way predicted under an assumption of calculated wrongdoing. Similarly, if perception biases prevent wrongdoers from at all recognizing the harmfulness of their own conduct, they will by the same token fail to give any consideration to the possibility of breaking the law and being sanctioned. This means that current deterrence theory must be recalibrated in light of behavioral ethics findings (Nagin 1998: 13; Feldman 2018: 69). To improve compliance, it is not enough to set effective sanctions, but it is equally important to consider the way in which these sanctions affect ethical deliberation and awareness by wrongdoers in real time, in light of the ability of perpetrators to understand their own misconduct in the face of a varied selection of ethical blind spots. Punishments and sanctions might be, in some circumstances, effective means to improve ethical deliberations (Kajackaite and Gneezy 2017; Gneezy, Kajackaite, and Sobel 2018), but this depends less on the sanction itself and more on the situational antecedents of unethicality in specific cases, and on the ways that the possibility of sanction is brought to the attention of potential perpetrators to effectively improve their moral deliberation.

5.4.2 *Fairness and Its Limits*

A second major theme in contemporary compliance research is that of procedural fairness as a main mechanism to improve ethical conduct and respect for the law. This rich theoretical and experimental literature suggests that people comply with the law if they generally perceive it to be just and fair, and that this perception of fairness is enhanced if the legal norm is produced in a procedurally legitimate manner (Kahneman, Knetsch, and Thaler 1986: s285, s299; Tyler 1990: 5). Thus, in experimental settings, researchers have found improvement in compliance when participants were given information regarding the procedural fairness of state laws and organizational rules in a variety of contexts (Feldman and Tyler 2012: 46; Feldman and Perez 2012: 405; Feldman and Lobel 2009: 1151–2).

Behavioral ethics research suggests that the current approach to procedural fairness suffers from the same issues discussed already in the context of deterrence. That is, in the framework of calculated and deliberative decision-making, it may very well be true that a perception of procedural legitimacy operates to improve compliance; however, when unethicality is self-blinded or self-justified, it is less clear how perceptions of legal legitimacy are incorporated into the decision-making process, if at all. Thus, we lack significant evidence regarding wrongdoers' knowledge and perception of legal legitimacy generally and their effect on real-time ethical deliberation more specifically. These issues are not sufficiently addressed in the mainstream of the research on compliance and legitimacy, which mostly adopts a deliberative framework as its baseline for ethical decision-making (Feldman 2018: 16–17). Experimental literature in particular tends to clearly present participants with a moral dilemma (Feldman 2018: 16–17), thereby disregarding the possibility that wrongdoers will fail to recognize the dilemma in the first place. Thus, researchers typically structure their experiments as an explicit choice between a "good" option and a "bad" one (Fischbacher, Gächter, and Fehr 2001: 398–9), bypassing a multitude of psychological mechanisms that might blur this distinction for potential wrongdoers in real-world situations. In fact, behavioral research shows that processes of motivated reasoning as well as of perspective-taking can hinder this type of decision-making by leading individuals to identify whichever choice benefits them most as ethically superior (Underwood and Moore 1982: 143; Kunda 1990: 480). In a similar way to the case of deterrence theory, these insights call for a reorientation of procedural justice research. Thus, it is not enough to assure the procedural fairness of legal norms in order to improve compliance; instead, it is more important to understand how these factors affect people's moral awareness (if at all) and improve ethical deliberation and wrongdoers' understanding of their own actions. Of course, procedural fairness may yet prove crucial for compliance; but this would require current theory to be fine-tuned to account for behavioral findings regarding the limited cognitive resources often dedicated to real-world compliance decisions.

5.4.3 *The Need to Prevent Ordinary Unethicality*

Finally, current approaches to law enforcement and compliance tend to focus on "smoking guns" and extreme violations of the law as the core case and as the ultimate manifestation of the problem of illegality. This tendency is understandable, as it would seem most important to prevent wrongdoing in those cases where it produces the most harm. However, behavioral ethics findings challenge this prevailing wisdom. While devastating in their effects, extreme violations of the law are relatively rare as they are difficult for most people to ignore or justify.

On the other hand, most people can, and very often do, ignore and justify "minor" violations, or acts of "ordinary unethicality": supposedly small deviations from legal and ethical norms common in day-to-day activities. This means that acts of ordinary unethicality can be by far more common, and therefore by far more harmful in the aggregate. Ordinary unethicality can be found in all areas of the law, from contract breach and disregard for the property of others, to corruption in administrative law, corporate misconduct, or insensitive interpersonal behavior. Behavioral ethics research suggests that "minor" wrongs are endemic, widespread, and difficult to regulate and prevent.

The reason that ordinary unethicality is so common, and so difficult to deal with, is that it is easier for perpetrators to ignore, justify, and excuse to themselves. For instance, current legal practices single out monetary bribes as the more blameworthy case, compared to the supposedly more "innocent" one of nonmonetary bribes; indeed, monetary bribes seem more harmful as they represent a more blatant violation of anticorruption norms. Yet, behavioral ethics insights would suggest that nonmonetary bribes, supposedly the less severe case, are in fact by far more dangerous, and more deserving of policymakers' attention. The reason for this is that nonmonetary bribes are easier for perpetrators to excuse, ignore, and justify to themselves, and therefore present a larger danger of noncompliance. To take another example, few people will steal cash from their employer, even a small sum; yet, many more can justify to themselves stealing small items from the workplace (Hollinger and Clark 1983: 398). The reason for this is, of course, that this type of violation is much easier to ignore or disregard as harmless. This shows how self-justified and self-blinded unethicality crucially contribute to the ubiquity of noncompliance and illegal conduct. This effect is important, as the aggregate result of small violations leads to a staggering costs of hundreds of billions a year to employers as a result of employee misconduct (Banning 1988: 80; Lipman and McGraw 1988: 51; Niehoff and Paul 2000: 51). Importantly, the reason that unethical behavior by employees, employee theft in particular, is so costly is because it is prone to the ethical traps and blind spots that are characteristic antecedents of unethical behavior. Since it is easy to disregard, ignore, or justify, employee theft is extremely common, and a great majority of ordinary normative people in fact participate in it. Thus, some studies show that close to 50 percent of employees steal from their employer (Niehoff and Paul 2000: 51; Thoms et al. 2001: 562). These findings can be stated in a more general way to create the counterintuitive conclusion according to which those violations that appear more "innocent" or "mundane" are in fact the more harmful in the aggregate, because they are easier for ordinary people to ignore or justify, and are therefore commonly practiced by the majority of individuals. On the other hand, "severe" crimes and extreme violations of the law are more difficult to ignore and justify, requiring a unique antisocial temperament, and therefore will not typically become the norm. Thus, mundane practices such as "wardrobing" (buying an item, using it, and then returning it for a full refund) can cost billions of dollars annually (Mazar, Amir, and Ariely 2008: 633). To put these numbers into perspective, the harms of wardrobing seem to at least double (if not triple) those of more serious crimes such as car theft or burglary.[3] Such findings, backed by behavioral theory, call for a reorientation of law enforcement efforts, in order to focus on the prevailing forms of unethical conduct, instead of on extreme cases.

3 See "2016 Crime in the United States," FBI Uniform Crime Report, https://ucr.fbi.gov/crime-in-the-u.s/2016/crime-in-the-u.s.-2016/topic-pages/property-crime.

The prevalence of self-blinded and self-justified unethicality can spell disaster to interpersonal trust and to levels of social capital (Putnam 1995: 65–6). Due to the prevalence of wrongdoing, originating with people's tendencies to ignore and justify their own unethicality, dishonest or harmful behavior can become the norm rather than the exception, thus further threatening societal codes of conduct (Gillespie and Hurley 2013: 177). A behavioral approach to compliance therefore emphasizes the need to depart from the traditional approach to law enforcement, with its focus on big cases and extreme violations, in favor of a broader regulatory perspective, accounting for the constant stream of more subtle violations that continuously erode societal norms of conduct.

5.5 A NEW BEHAVIORALLY INFORMED RESPONSIVE REGULATION

The analysis in the previous sections demonstrates the need for a new regulatory approach, one that incorporates behavioral ethics findings into a comprehensive framework aimed to improve compliance. Such an approach must account for the need to engage effectively with the awareness of potential perpetrators and attempt to improve ethical deliberation and defuse ethical blind spots. Such an approach should also aim to identify the situational antecedents of unethicality, and to tailor specific regulatory responses to specific situations. The new regulatory approach will also give account to the prevalence of ordinary unethicality and to the need to regulate common cases of routine violations, rather than focusing primarily on extreme cases of crude antisocial behavior.

In order to improve compliance, it is not enough to impose sanctions or to assure that legal regimes are created in a procedurally fair way. Rather, it is by far more important to find ways to improve ethical deliberations and help people overcome the cognitive biases that generate noncompliance. The key to effective legal intervention is in enhancing people's ability to evaluate their own actions in light of the relevant legal and ethical standards. Such regulatory interventions can be termed ethical nudges, legal mechanisms designed to push potential perpetrators toward a more candid evaluation of their own actions, aiming to decrease the chances of them harming other people or violating the law. Deployed appropriately, ethical nudges can be highly effective. In some circumstances, a measure as simple as making people sign an ethical code of conduct before making an important decision was found to reduce wrongdoing significantly, or even eliminate it (Shu, Gino, and Bazerman 2011: 330; Shu et al. 2012). Despite their potential effectiveness, ethical nudges also present some unique challenges for law-enforcers. Ethical nudges differ from traditional nudges in at least one important way: traditional nudges (as popularized by Thaler and Sunstein (2009)) are designed to help people make decisions that better serve their own self-interest; in contrast, ethical nudges are supposed to help people make decisions that more candidly consider the interests of others. This means that it would typically be more difficult to design and implement effective ethical nudges, compared to traditional nudges, so that they will successfully alter behavior. The legal standing of ethical nudges and the ability to back them with sanctions (when appropriate) can serve this purpose.

5.5.1 *Ethical Reminders*

Ethical nudges can come in the form of alerts and reminders, aimed to directly improve ethical deliberations. Wrongdoing often originates with motivated reasoning and other cognitive biases that push potential perpetrators to ignore or disregard pertinent facts such as the identity of potential victims, the harm of certain actions, or a certain legal standard (Kunda

1999c). Ethical reminders can bring specific facts to the attention of wrongdoers at crucial junctures of decision-making, to make sure that they are more difficult to ignore (Mazar, Amir, and Ariely 2008: 635). To be effective, such reminders must stand out so that they are not easy to brush off. Reminders may therefore also include references to legal or social sanctions, when appropriate (Koessler et al. 2016; Feldman and Halali 2019). Importantly, ethical alerts have been proven effective not only in prompting deliberative decision-making but also in improving the ethical outcomes of nondeliberative choices. That is, a statement of commitment to a moral code, as well as other ethical reminders, can help people reach more ethical outcomes even in their nondeliberative decision-making (Bandura 1999: 203).

5.5.2 *De-biasing Tools*

Ethical nudges do not have to be limited to reminding perpetrators of specific facts. Instead, they can serve to prompt individuals to pause and dedicate more cognitive resources to important compliance decisions (Mazar, Amir, and Ariely 2008: 635–6). Since wrongdoing is often closely connected with nondeliberative decision-making, prompting perpetrators to engage in a more deliberative process can help to reduce misconduct (Ayal et al. 2015: 739–40). A wide variety of de-biasing tools can be used to overcome biased thinking and nondeliberative choices, thus allowing people to engage in more candid ethical deliberation (Jolls and Sunstein 2006; Feldman 2018: 58). De-biasing measures can be designed, for instance, to prompt wrongdoers to consider the implications of their behavior or to look at a situation from the perspective of other parties. Ethical declarations, prompting individuals to declare their commitment to a legal or ethical norm of conduct, have been shown to be used effectively to improve ethical deliberations in a wide variety of contexts (Feldman 2018: 199). Declarations or pledges are currently used in business contexts, where officeholders are sometimes required to state their commitment to detailed ethical codes before participating in important votes or decisions (Feldman 2018: 200).

5.5.3 *Situational Design*

Another form of ethical nudges can aim to improve behavior indirectly, through situational design. Since unethicality has strong situational antecedents and since ethical blind spots greatly contribute to the prevalence of wrongdoing (Feldman 2018: 2, 16, 48–9), a key mechanism to curb unethical conduct is to act to eliminate those situations that have been shown to breed unethicality. Thus, instead of deploying ethical reminders, regulators can work to nudge people toward more ethical conduct by redesigning problematic situations in order to ensure that ethical blind spots and traps are less common. For instance, regulators should work to reduce ambiguity, both situational and legal, as ambiguity has been shown to breed self-justified and self-blinded wrongdoing in many contexts (Feldman and Teichman 2009). More generally, regulators should work to identify those situations in which it is easy for ordinary people to justify or ignore their own unethicality, and then seek ways to alter these situations.

5.6 CONCLUSION

A wide variety of ethical nudges can help regulators improve compliance with the law. Behavioral ethics research offers many such tools, suitable for use under different circumstances and for different types of wrongdoing. Importantly, this nudge approach is not a substitute to current law enforcement mechanisms (such as sanctions and deterrence); rather, it is a complementary perspective to law enforcement. Any legal measure has a nudge effect, and legal interventions must be evaluated based on their behavioral effect and their influence on real-time decision-making by wrongdoers and on the ability to defuse ethical biases. In reality, wrongdoing can be calculated, self-blinded, or self-justified, or move on a spectrum between these ideal types. Regulators therefore must be responsive and offer a combination of regulatory approaches and address the possibility of the multiple cognitive sources of wrongdoing Ayres & Braithwaite (1992). This approach can be explained with President Roosevelt's adage: "Speak softly and carry a big stick." Thus, on many occasions, speaking softly should suffice to improve ethical awareness, as most people need only a gentle reminder in order to recognize their own unethicality and refrain from it; yet, these reminders should be accompanied by a potential threat, in order to prevent people from finding self-serving justifications which will allow them to feel that their behavior is tolerable or does not violate any major principle. When law is effectively engaging people's ethical deliberation, and is also backed by sanctions, it can send a clear message about accountability, when self-serving interpretations of reality would otherwise present a problem.

REFERENCES

Ayal, Shahar, Francesca Gino, Rachel Barkan, and Dan Ariely. 2015. "Three Principles to REVISE People's Unethical Behavior." *Perspectives on Psychology Science* 10, no. 6: 738–41.

Ayres, Ian, and John Braithwaite. Responsive regulation: Transcending the deregulation debate. Oxford University Press, USA, 1992.

Balcetis, Emily E., and David Dunning. 2006. "See What You Want to See: Motivational Influences on Visual Perception." *Journal of Personality and Social Psychology* 91, no. 4: 612–25.

Bandura, Albert. 1999. "Moral Disengagement in the Perpetration of Inhumanities." *Personality and Social Psychology Review* 3, no. 3: 193–209.

Banning, Lary K. 1988. "Thievery on the Inside." *Security Management* 32, no. 5: 79–84.

Bazerman, Max H., and Ann E. Tenbrunsel. 2011. *Blind Spots: Why We Fail to Do What's Right and What to Do About It*. Princeton, NJ: Princeton University Press.

Chugh, Dolly, Max H. Bazerman, and Mahzarin R. Banaji. 2005. "Bounded Ethicality as a Psychological Barrier to Recognizing Conflicts of Interest" in *Conflicts of Interest: Challenges and Solutions in Business, Law, Medicine, and Public Policy*, ed. Don A. Moore, Daylian M. Cain, George Loewenstein, and Max H. Bazerman, 74–95. New York: Cambridge University Press.

Coase, Ronald. 1960. "The Problem of Social Cost." *Journal of Law and Economics* 3: 1–44.

Feldman, Yuval. 2018. *The Law of Good People*. Cambridge: Cambridge University Press.

Feldman, Yuval, and Eliran Halali. 2019. "Regulating 'Good' People in Subtle Conflicts of Interest Situations." *Journal of Business Ethics* 154, no. 1: 65–83.

Feldman, Yuval, and Yotam Kaplan. 2019. "Bounded Ethicality and Big Data." *Cornell Journal of Law and Public Policy*.

Feldman, Yuval, and Orly Lobel. 2009. "The Incentives Matrix: The Comparative Effectiveness of Rewards, Liabilities, Duties, and Protections for Reporting Illegality." *Texas Law Review* 88, no. 6: 1151–1212.

Feldman, Yuval, and Oren Perez. 2012. "Motivating Environmental Action in a Pluralistic Regulatory Environment: An Experimental Study of Framing, Crowding Out, and Institutional Effects in the Context of Recycling Policies." *Law & Society Review* 46, no. 2: 405–42.

Feldman, Yuval, and Henry E. Smith. 2014. "Behavioral Equity." *Journal of Institutional and Theoretical Economics (JITE)* 170, no. 1: 137–59.

Feldman, Yuval, and Doron Teichman. 2009. "Are All Legal Probabilities Created Equal?" *NYU Law Review* 84: 980–1022.

Feldman, Yuval, and Tom R. Tyler. 2012. "Mandated Justice: The Potential Promise and Possible Pitfalls of Mandating Procedural Justice in the Workplace." *Regulation & Governance* 6, no. 1: 46–65.

Fischbacher, Urs, Simon Gächter, and Ernst Fehr. 2001. "Are People Conditionally Cooperative? Evidence from a Public Goods Experiment." *Economics Letters* 71, no. 3: 397–404.

Gillespie, Nicole, and Robert Hurley. 2013. "Trust and the Global Financial Crisis" in *Handbook of Advances in Trust Research*, ed. Reinhard Bachmann and Akbar Zaheer, 177–204. Cheltenham, UK: Edward Elgar Publishing.

Gino, Francesca. 2015. "Understanding Ordinary Unethical Behavior: Why People Who Value Morality Act Immorally." *Current Opinion in Behavioral Science* 3: 107–11.

Gino, Francesca, Shahar Ayal, and Dan Ariely. 2013. "Self-Serving Altruism? The Lure of Unethical Actions that Benefit Others." *Journal of Economic Behavior & Organization* 93: 291–2.

Gneezy, Uri, Agne Kajackaite, and Joel Sobel. 2018. "Lying Aversion and the Size of the Lie." *American Economic Review* 108, no. 2: 419–53.

Hirsch, Werner Z. 1998. *Law and Economics: An Introductory Analysis*. San Diego, CA: Academic Press.

Hollinger, Richard C., and John P. Clark. 1983. "Deterrence in the Workplace: Perceived Certainty, Perceived Severity, and Employee Theft." *Social Forces* 62, no. 2: 398–418.

Jacobsen, Catrine, Toke Reinholt Fosgaard, and David Pascual-Ezama. 2018. "Why Do We Lie? A Practical Guide to the Dishonesty Literature." *Journal of Economic Surveys* 32, no. 2: 357–87.

Jolls, Christine, and Cass R. Sunstein. 2006. "Debiasing through Law." *Journal of Legal Studies* 35, no. 1: 199–242.

Kahneman, Daniel, Jack L. Knetsch, and Richard H. Thaler. 1986. "Fairness and the Assumptions of Economics." *Journal of Business*: S285–S230.

Kajackaite, Agne, and Uri Gneezy. 2017. "Incentives and Cheating." *Games and Economic Behavior* 102: 433–44.

Koessler, Ann-Kathrin, Benno Torgler, Lars P. Feld, and Bruno S. Frey. 2016. "Commitment to Pay Taxes: A Field Experiment on the Importance of Promise." Tax and Transfer Policy Institute-Working Paper 10.

Kouchaki, Maryam. 2013. "Professionalism and Moral Behavior: Does a Professional Self-Conception Make One More Unethical?" *Edmond J. Safra Working Papers* 4. https://dx.doi.org/10.2139/ssrn.2243811.

Kunda, Ziva. 1990. "The Case for Motivated Reasoning." *Psychology Bulletin* 108: 480–98.

Landes, William M., and Richard Posner. 1987. *The Economic Structure of Tort Law*. Cambridge, MA: Harvard University Press.

Lipman, Mark, and W. R. McGraw. 1988. "Employee Theft: A $40 Billion Industry." *Annals of the American Academy of Political and Social Science* 498, no. 1: 51–9.

Mazar, Nina, On Amir, and Dan Ariely. 2008. "The Dishonesty of Honest People: A Theory of Self-Concept Maintenance." *Journal of Marketing Research* 45, no. 6: 633–44.

Merritt, Anna C., Daniel A. Effron, and Benoît Monin. 2010. "Moral Self-Licensing: When Being Good Frees Us to Be Bad." *Social and Personality Psychology Compass* 4, no. 5: 344–57.

Miceli, Thomas J. 2004. *The Economic Approach to Law*. California: Stanford University Press.

Nagin, Daniel S. 1998. "Criminal Deterrence Research at the Outset of the Twenty-First Century." *Crime and Justice* 23: 1–42.

Niehoff, Brian P., and Robert J. Paul. 2000. "Causes of Employee Theft and Strategies that HR Managers Can Use for Prevention." *Human Resource Management* 39, no. 1: 51–64.

Pronin, Emily, Thomas Gilovich, and Lee Ross. 2004. "Objectivity in the Eye of the Beholder: Divergent Perceptions of Bias in Self Versus Others." *Psychological Review* 111, no. 3: 781–99.

Putnam, Robert D. 1995. "Bowling Alone: America's Declining Social Capital." *Journal of Democracy* 6, no. 1: 65–78.

Shalvi, Shaul, Ori Eldar, and Yoella Bereby-Meyer. 2012. "Honesty Requires Time (and Lack of Justifications)." *Psychology Science* 23, no. 10: 1264–70.

Shapiro, Fred R., and Michelle Pearse. 2012. "The Most Cited Law Review Articles of All Times." *Michigan Law Review* 110, no. 8: 1483–1520.

Shavell, Steven. 2002. "Law Versus Morality as Regulators of Conduct." *American Law and Economics Review* 4, no. 2: 227–57.

Shu, Lisa L., Francesca Gino, and Max H Bazerman. 2011. "Dishonest Deed, Clear Conscience: When Cheating Leads to Moral Disengagement and Motivated Forgetting." *Personality and Social Psychology Bulletin* 37, no. 3: 330–49.

Shu, Lisa L., Nina Mazar, Francesca Gino, Dan Ariely, and Max H. Bazerman. 2012. "Signing at the Beginning Makes Ethics Salient and Decreases Dishonest Self-Reports in Comparison to Signing at the End." *Proceedings of the National Academy of Sciences* 109, no. 38: 15197–200.

Tenbrunsel, Ann E., and David M. Messick. 2004. "Ethical Fading: The Role of Self-Deception in Unethical Behavior." *Social Justice Research* 17, no. 2: 223–36.

Thaler, Richard H., and Cass R. Sunstein. 2009. *Nudge: Improving Decisions about Health, Wealth, and Happiness*. New York: Penguin.

Thoms, Peg, Paula Wolper, Kimberly S. Scott, and Dave Jones. 2001. "The Relationship between Immediate Turnover and Employee Theft in the Restaurant Industry." *Journal of Business and Psychology* 15, no. 4: 561–77.

Tittle, Charles R. 1980. *Sanctions and Social Deviance: The Question of Deterrence*. Connecticut: Praeger Publishers.

Tyler, Tom R. 1990. *Why People Obey the Law*. Connecticut: Yale University.

Underwood, Bill, and Bert Moore. 1982. "Perspective-Taking and Altruism." *Psychological Bulletin* 91, no. 1: 143–73.

Wiltermuth, Scott S. 2011. "Cheating More When the Spoils Are Split." *Organizational Behavior and Human Decision Processes* 115, no. 2: 157–68.

Zimring, Franklin E., Gordon J. Hawkins, and James Vorenberg. 1973. *Deterrence: The Legal Threat in Crime Control*. Chicago: University of Chicago Press.

6

Constructing the Content and Meaning of Law and Compliance

Shauhin A. Talesh

Abstract: This chapter argues that organizational compliance is best illustrated not by a compliance versus noncompliance dichotomy but by a processual model in which organizations construct the meaning of both compliance and law. I argue that organizations must be understood as social actors that are influenced by widely institutionalized beliefs about legality, morality, politics, and rationality. I review the empirical research in this vein and show how institutionalized conceptions of law and compliance first become widely accepted within the business community and eventually come to be seen as rational and legitimate by public legal actors and institutions and thus influence the very meaning of law. Through two distinct waves of research, I offer a theoretical framework for understanding compliance as a process and by specifying the institutional and political mechanisms through which organizations shape the content and meaning of law. First wave studies laid out the initial framework for how to understand organizations as constructers of legal meaning while second wave studies refined and extended the theory in multiple ways. I suggest that the increasing complexity and ambiguity of legal rules provides legal intermediaries greater opportunities to influence what compliance means by filtering what law means through nonlegal logics. I conclude by discussing the implications of organizational construction of law and compliance for studies of law, business, and the state and suggest directions for a third wave of research.

6.1 INTRODUCTION

Typically, studies of compliance, especially by businesses, view law as top-down. Under this perspective, law is defined as exogenous or outside of organizations and the role of organizations is limited to reacting to law by either complying or not complying with law. The basis for complying or not complying is often due to rational, strategic considerations and motivations (Simpson 1992, 1998), and moral (Tyler 1990), social, and normative concerns (Parker and Nielsen 2011). The majority of compliance research falls within two categories: objectivist and interpretative research. Using objectivist, theory-testing frames, research in this vein maps and measures compliance and noncompliance and builds and tests theories that provide explanations for the associations among various concepts relating to the compliant and noncompliant behavior of institutions. The conceptual themes of interest in these studies include explaining motives, organizational characteristics and capacities, modes of regulation and enforcement, and social and economic environments. Under a more interpretative frame, scholars attempt to understand how and why businesses comply with law, fail to comply with law, go beyond compliance in some instances (Kagan, Gunningham, and Thornton 2003), or interact with regulatory enforcement officials and the regulatory process (Haines 1997; Parker and Nielsen 2011). Under these distinct approaches, law is an exogenous force which organizations react to by either complying or not complying. The chapters in this book explore not just how to measure and evaluate compliance but also how to articulate the various incentives, social norms, legitimacy, capacity, management processes, and unconscious influences that play a role in organizational compliance behavior.

Whereas most accounts in this book seek to specify the conditions under which organizations do or do not comply with legal regulations, I argue that organizations influence and shape the content and meaning of law and compliance. The nature of compliance is best explained not by a compliance/noncompliance dichotomy but by a model in which organizations construct the meaning of law and compliance. Organizations are social actors that are influenced by institutionalized norms and beliefs about rationality, legality, and morality. Largely drawing from new institutional theories of law and organizations, a body of research has developed over the past thirty years that articulates how institutionalized conceptions of law and compliance initially become widely accepted within organizations and eventually institutionalized as they come to be seen as legitimate and rational by public legal institutions like courts, legislatures, and administrative agencies. Unlike an exogenous approach, law is seen as part of an *endogenous* process in which the content and meaning of law and compliance is shaped by private organizations, the very group that such laws are designed to regulate.

I articulate this framework for understanding compliance as socially constructed by organizations as undergoing two "waves" or phases. Deriving largely from empirical work in the civil rights context, first wave legal endogeneity studies articulated a theoretical framework for understanding compliance as a process and specified the institutional mechanisms through which organizations shape the content and meaning of law. In particular, empirical research highlights how ambiguous civil rights laws led employers to develop a number of symbolic forms of compliance that were more attentive to managerial ideals and preferences than to legal ideals. These symbolic forms of compliance were eventually incorporated into judicial decisions interpreting civil rights laws (Edelman 2016). Empirical research identified a series of mechanisms including how organizations legalize themselves through the creation of formal policies and procedures, how managerial notions of what constitutes compliance influence the manner in which organizations understand law and compliance, and how forms of compliance developed and were institutionalized within organizational fields and eventually incorporated into judicial conceptions of compliance.

Next, I turn to second wave studies that have taken the original framework and refined and expanded it into other legal settings beyond the civil rights context. Second wave studies have not just moved legal endogeneity to new areas like consumer protection, insurance, and prisons, to name but a few; they have elaborated the theoretical framework to explain how organizations can shape the content and meaning of legislation and regulation through institutional *and* political mechanisms. Empirical research in the second wave also reveals how other logics beyond managerial values such as consumer, risk, and penal logics can influence the way in which actors within organizational fields understand law and compliance. The final section discusses the implications of organizational construction of law and compliance research and briefly offers suggestions for a third wave of research.

6.2 FIRST WAVE LEGAL ENDOGENEITY STUDIES

The organizational construction of the law and compliance theoretical framework is largely derived from a strand of organizational sociology called new institutional theory. Early work in this area focused on exploring organizational influence on civil rights laws. Lauren Edelman, a sociology of law and organizations scholar, conducted a series of empirical studies in the 1990s and 2000s that explored how law is endogenous, that is, how employers shape the way that courts understand law and compliance. She was part of a movement of organizational theorists exploring how organizational structures form and spread within organizational fields. The following synthesizes the key mechanisms through which first wave studies showed how organizations construct the meaning of compliance and uses examples from studies of the civil rights context to illustrate the theory.

New institutionalists challenge the idea that organizations simply resist, obey, or avoid law in a way that yields the most rational or cost-benefit outcome (Vaughan 1998). New institutionalists argue that rationality is socially constructed by nonmarket factors such as widely accepted norms and patterns of behavior that become taken for granted and institutionalized among the community of organizations that make up an organizational field (Meyer and Rowan 1977; DiMaggio and Powell 1983; Scott 2001). An "organizational field" refers to the subset of the environment that is most closely relevant to a given organization, including suppliers, competitors, and customers, as well as flows of influence, communication, and innovation (DiMaggio and Powell 1983). Just as organizations exist within broader organizational fields, legal organizations such as courts, legislatures, and administrative agencies exist within legal fields (Edelman 2007). Legal fields are institutional environments within which ideas about law evolve, are exchanged, and become institutionalized. Ideas about rational legal behavior, including how to respond to legal regulation, tend to evolve and, in some cases, become institutionalized within legal fields (Edelman and Talesh 2011).

New institutionalists studying the relationship between law and organizations often start with a basic premise that there is nearly always some degree of legal ambiguity in laws regulating organizations. Title VII of the Civil Rights Act of 1964 codified strong protections against employment discrimination but failed to specify the meaning of discrimination (Edelman 1990, 1992). The ambiguity in legal regulation leaves a space for the social construction of the meaning of law through a blending of, and sometimes contest between, the logics of legal and organizational fields (Edelman 2007). In particular, organizations often turn to their legal environments or law-related aspects of organizational fields for ideas on how to respond to legal regulations. An organization's legal environment is the broad set of rules, norms, practices, and routines that shape not only an organization's understandings of law and compliance but also its notion of what is fair and right (Edelman 1990, 1992).

In response to anti-discrimination laws that alter the legal environment, organizations respond by creating written rules, policies, and procedures that fill in law's meaning and adopt many legal practices and structures because their cultural environment constructs adoption as the legitimate or natural thing to do. For example, Edelman (1990, 1992) shows how organizations responded to new laws by creating new offices and developing written policies, rules, and procedures in an attempt to achieve legal legitimacy, while simultaneously curbing law's impact on managerial power and unfettered discretion over employment decisions. In a sample of 346 organizations, only 30 had created anti-discrimination guidelines by 1969, 118 instituted guidelines in the 1970s and 75 more did so in the 1980s. There was also a noticeable increase in other forms of legalization in the 1970s. This included the spread of special offices devoted solely to civil rights issues and special procedures for processing discrimination complaints. Initially, early movers or first-adopters created these structures, but eventually it spread through organizational fields (Edelman 1990, 1992; Dobbin et al. 1993; Sutton et al. 1994; Edelman and Peterson 1999).

Civil rights offices, grievance procedures, and other anti-discrimination rules serve as visible indicators of attention to law and give the appearance of legitimacy. However, these structures often serve to allow for compliance in form, but do not require or lead to substantive change in the workplace environment. As more and more organizations adopt such structures into practice and they become the taken-for-granted norm, these structures come to be seen as "rational" forms of compliance (Edelman, Uggen, and Erlanger 1999). Once these symbolic structures are established within organizations, they become locations in which the requirements and the meaning of compliance are encountered and negotiated in the context of daily organizational events.

As organizations legalize themselves, managerial and business values such as rationality, efficiency, and discretion come to influence the way in which organizations understand law and compliance. That is, organizations struggle to find rational modes of response to legal ambiguity and devise strategies to preserve managerial discretion and authority while at the same time maximizing the appearance of compliance with legal principles (Edelman, Fuller, and Mara-Drita 2001). When legal ideals conflict with business goals and agendas, compliance officers often interpret law and compliance in a way that tilts toward business values. The meaning of compliance is understood in ways that incorporate managerial values, logics, and ways of understanding the world derived from organizational fields. As this process takes place, law becomes managerialized or infused with managerial values and interests, which in turn leads to symbolic structures or structures less likely to further social justice goals.

Prior new institutional research shows that business, management, and legal professionals are key carriers of ideas among and across organizational fields. In particular, human resource officials, personnel managers, management consultants, and in-house lawyers communicate ideas about law as they move among organizations; participate in conferences, workshops, training sessions, and professional networking meetings; and publish professional personnel literature (Jacoby 1985; Baron, Dobbin, and Jennings 1986; Edelman, Erlanger, and Lande 1993). Existing empirical research reveals that when organizations attempt to comply with laws, managerial conceptions of law transform sexual harassment claims into personality conflicts (Edelman, Erlanger, and Lande 1993), deflect or discourage complaints rather than offering informal resolution (Marshall 2005), and broaden the term "diversity" in a way that disassociates it from its original goal of protecting civil rights (Edelman, Fuller, and Mara-Drita 2001).

A study of internal grievance officers for ten large organizations reveals that complaint handlers were quite often unconcerned with actual formal legal rights and outcomes, were not fully informed of the law, and chose not to invoke legal principles when addressing employee legal complaints. In lieu of formal legal solutions, complaint managers often chose to address employee grievances with managerial solutions, including using training programs, transferring the grievant and providing counseling rather than formal recognition of legal rights violations (Edelman, Erlanger, and Lande 1993; Edelman and Cahill 1998; Edelman and Suchman 1999; Albiston 2005). Another study reveals that ideas about civil rights were transformed in the context of managerial rhetoric about diversity that reframed legal values in terms of traditional managerial goals. In particular, the term "diversity" was transformed through managerial rhetoric during the 1980s and 1990s such that it became detached or disassociated from the legal ideal of equitable racial and gender representation and, instead, transformed into a managerial ideal in which varying backgrounds and viewpoints in a workforce could be mobilized for constructive purposes (Edelman, Fuller, and Mara-Drita 2001). Similarly, in France, managerial rhetoric transformed principles of discrimination into managerial categories such as diversity (Bereni 2009) and recast concerns of psychological bullying (Bastard, Cardia-Vonèche, and Gonik 2003). Thus, managerialization occurs through decoupling legal rules from organizational activities, rhetorically reframing legal ideals, and internalizing dispute resolution (Edelman 2016)

The infusion of managerial logics into law is not limited to organizations or organizational fields. The managerialization of law affects the construction of law in legal fields. New institutionalists show how law becomes endogenous as legal rules derived from court cases come to be determined by organizations – the very group that such laws are designed to regulate (Edelman 2016). Similar to employers, employees, compliance professionals, and lawyers, judges over time end up equating the symbolic structures that organizations create in response to civil rights law with the achievement of civil rights on organizations. For example, empirical work in the civil rights context shows how ambiguous civil rights legislation led employers to create a variety of symbolic forms of compliance that, despite being more attentive to managerial prerogatives than to legal ideas, were incorporated into judicial opinions interpreting civil rights law (Edelman, Uggen, and Erlanger 1999). Judges in employment cases increasingly defer to the presence of organizational structures as evidence of nondiscriminatory treatment without paying attention to evidence that suggests that these structures fail to protect employees' legal rights or evaluating whether these structures do anything substantively to curb discrimination (Edelman et al. 2011; Edelman 2016).

In sum, through a series of empirical studies, first wave research on the interaction between organizations and law laid out a series of mechanisms through which we understand how organizations do not just comply or not comply with laws but shape the content and meaning of laws that are designed to regulate them. Organizations do not resist or avoid ambiguous laws when they are passed but, instead, respond by often creating law-like structures that are designed to symbolize their attention to law. Organizations essentially "legalize" themselves through the structures they create. Once these processes are in place, they trigger struggles among professionals and other organizational field actors over the meaning of compliance. Through conferences, professional networking, and professional written and marketing materials, these institutionalized structures diffuse across the organizational field and become the taken-for-granted norm of acceptable behavior. However, because of their training, experience, or professional socialization and perspective, organizational field actors often construct law in ways that are consistent with managerial values and goals. Thus, as organizations legalize themselves, managerial values seep into the way that organizations understand law and compliance. As these constructions of what law and compliance mean become institutionalized over time, they subtly impact how courts and eventually larger society understand law and compliance and what constitutes rational compliance with law.

6.3 SECOND WAVE LEGAL ENDOGENEITY STUDIES

First wave research on organizational constructions of law laid a foundation upon which scholars could continue elaborating the relationship between law and organizational compliance. Scholars have moved in different directions and are exploring various aspects of how organizations construct legal meaning and compliance. Both within and outside the United

States, scholars are exploring the ways in which organizations construct the content and meaning of laws that are designed to regulate them in consumer regulation (Talesh 2009, 2012, 2013, 2014; Talesh and Alter 2020); insurance (Schneiberg 2005; Talesh 2015a, 2015b); welfare regulation (Covaleski, Dirsmith, and Weiss 2013); insider trader laws (Bozanic, Dirsmith, and Huddart 2012); prison rape regulation (Jenness and Smyth 2011); school sexual harassment policies (Short 2006); restaurant hygiene regulation (Lehma, Kovacs, and Carroll 2014); privacy (Pandy 2013); cybersecurity (Talesh 2018); the medical education field (Dunn and Jones 2010); employers' use of criminal background checks (Lageson, Vuolo, and Uggen 2014); financial derivatives (Krawiec 2003, 2005; Holder-Webb and Cohen 2012; Funk and Hirschman 2014); antitrust in the film industry (Mezias and Boyle 2005); tax incentives for employer-sponsored childcare (Kelly 2003); international environmental management standards (Delmas and Montes-Sancho 2011); tax regulation (Mulligan and Oats 2005); Canadian wrongful dismissal doctrine (Nierobisz 2010); Australian labor law (Frazer 2014); and British financial services regulation (Gilad 2014). I refer to these as second wave studies because they build upon the framework laid out by first wave studies. For the most part, studies of organizational construction of law have explored particular aspects of legal endogeneity theory. In particular, many of these studies analyze particular aspects of legal endogeneity, such as the development of symbolic compliance or the manner in which legal institutions follow norms and practices developed within organizations. However, others have explored the entire cycle of legal endogeneity and, in doing so, extended and refined the theory of legal endogeneity to go beyond how organizations influence the meaning of judicial decisions as demonstrated in the equal employment opportunity context (Talesh 2009, 2012, 2014, 2015a, 2015b). The following highlights how legal endogeneity theory has been expanded and extended theoretically and methodologically. Second wave studies broaden the range of mechanisms through which organizations shape legal meaning. In doing so, second wave studies of legal endogeneity expand the web of scholars that can potentially use and apply the theory across multiple disciplines beyond the original framework.

6.3.1 *How Organizations Shape the Content and Meaning of Legislation and Administrative Agencies*

As opposed to the judicial context, recent research explores the process through which legislation and administrative law are constructed by organizations. Most extant work on the relationships among business organizations, legislators, and regulators understands organizations as rational actors. Analyses of interest group politics, mostly in political science, suggest that business interests often coopt the legislative process through tactics such as lobbying, agenda setting, and venue shopping (Bernstein 1955; Stigler 1971; Baumgartner and Jones 1993; Ayres and Braithwaite 2001). With respect to administrative agencies, work in this vein points to the role of strategic organizations in "capturing" regulatory agencies (Bernstein 1955; Stigler 1971). In general, the extant literature envisions regulation as a top-down process, whereby regulators try to coerce or in some cases encourage organizations to comply, while organizations engage in rational, strategic choices as to whether to comply (Braithwaite 2008). In this view, law is exogenous to organizations in that it is imposed upon them, although it is open to their influence.

More recent empirical research demonstrates how institutionalized logics operating among organizations play an important role in determining the form and structure of legislation and regulation. Research in this vein brings together sociology and political science to help better explain how organizations shape the meaning of law within organizational fields but also how those constructions of law bubble up into what ends up being codified into legislation and regulations (Barnes and Burke 2006; Talesh 2009, 2014). Scholars have refined legal endogeneity theory to account for politics and power in the interaction that organizations have with public legal institutions. As organizations struggle to define the meaning of compliance, the process through which organizational ideas about compliance evolve may be contested as the logics of organizational and legal fields come into conflict (Talesh 2012, 2014, 2015c; Edelman and Stryker 2005; Heimer 1999; Schneiberg and Soule 2005; Edelman et al. 2011). In particular, although political mobilization and contestation remain prevalent in the legislative process, the political frames used by organizations lobbying the legislature reflect logics that are derived from institutionalized norms and structures developed by these same organizations. Contests over the meaning of compliance are particularly likely where multiple interest groups have stakes in the meaning of compliance (Talesh 2014, 2015c). Political battles over legal meaning are particularly salient in the legislative and administrative contexts, where interest groups engage in overt battles regarding the meaning of compliance (Pedriana and Stryker 1997, 2004; Talesh 2014). In sum, through some combination of institutional logics and political contestation, private organizations are able to shape the content and meaning of laws that are designed to regulate them.

Through a quantitative coding and qualitative content analysis of twenty-five years of legislative history and interviews with legislative analysts involved in crafting laws in both California and Vermont, Talesh highlights how businesses influence legislation in some, but not all, circumstances based on various political alliances that are mobilized during the legislative process. Specifically, automobile manufacturers, who were initially subject to a powerful but ambiguous consumer warranty law in California in 1971 that created powerful rights and remedies in court such as full restitution, attorneys' fees and civil penalties, transformed and ultimately weakened the impact of this law by creating their own dispute-resolution arbitration forums and eventually convinced the legislature to adopt them into law. These legalized structures diffused among the majority of automobile manufacturers and automotive dealers and became institutionalized among the organizational field. Eventually, automobile manufacturers gave control over these arbitration programs to third-party organizational surrogates with whom they contracted. As this process of legalization by manufacturers took place, manufacturers infused managerial and business values into California legislation in varying degrees and reshaped the meaning of law and compliance not just among organizations but also in the legislature. At first glance, one might infer that institutionalized business structures may in fact serve as a useful mechanism for resolving these statutory rights. However, deference to organizational construction of the California "lemon law" made powerful consumer rights and remedies contingent on first using manufacturer dispute resolution procedures, where rights and remedies equivalent to those available in court, such as civil penalties and attorneys' fees, do not exist (Talesh, 2009, 2014).

Once organizational logic as to the meaning of compliance became formally codified into law, legislative amendments had less to do with protecting consumer rights and more to do with giving legal legitimacy to organizational dispute resolution venues through soft, passive regulatory monitoring and oversight, and enhancing the degree to which consumers, manufacturers, legislators, and regulators defer to institutional venues designed and funded by manufacturers (Talesh 2009, 2014). Thus, as businesses "legalized" their domains with law-like structures, business logics – anchored in informality, efficiency, discretion, and problem solving – flowed back into core public legal institutions through the efforts of advocacy coalitions, who reframed the meaning of consumer protection for legislators and regulators. In a multilayered level of deference, court cases interpreting California's consumer warranty laws and the lemon law in particular, reflect deference to these quasi-private dispute resolution structures in a manner consistent with the legislature's codification of manufacturers' preference for informal, private resolution of statutory rights (Talesh 2009). The content and meaning of consumer protection legislation, judicial decisions, and regulatory rules are determined by manufacturers, the very group that such laws were designed to regulate.

As was the case in California, the Vermont legislature in 1984 reached consensus that alternative dispute resolution (ADR) forums as opposed to courts were the proper place to resolve legal disputes. However, the contested and varying political alliances in Vermont, as well as a different developmental path (cf. Pierson 2004), led to a different dispute-resolution structure being codified into law. Unlike California, Vermont did not create a court-based option for consumers in the 1970s. Thus, when Vermont created a lemon law in the 1980s, Vermont considered both court and ADR options. In particular, different interest groups, namely consumer advocates and automotive dealers, dominated the Vermont legislative process. A political trade-off ensued among key stakeholders such as automotive dealers, manufacturers, consumer advocates, and the state attorney general, whereby a court option was eliminated from consideration in return for permitting the state of Vermont to administer a public arbitration board in addition to allowing the private dispute-resolution process to operate. Thus, by comparing two states that developed two different institutional processes with varying degrees of business control and participation in the dispute-resolution structures, Talesh (2014) shows under what conditions business and managerial conceptions of law reshape the meaning of public legal rights and the conditions under which they do not.

The consumer protection example in California highlights why a compliance versus noncompliance dichotomy fails to capture the relationship between business and law. Manufacturers did not strategically choose to "comply" or "not comply" with consumer warranty laws. Instead, manufacturers were able to reshape the meaning of compliance with consumer warranty laws and transform public rights attainable in court into private rights to dispute resolution (Talesh 2009, 2014). As in the employment context (Edelman, Erlanger, and Lande 1993), dispute resolution processes provided a means through which manufacturers' values and norms influenced the structure and content of the organizational field far more than did consumers' interests. However, unlike legal endogeneity in the judicial context, political mobilization in the form of manufacturer advocacy coalitions influenced the legislative process by claiming that the legal value of these dispute-resolution structures lay in their efficiency and informality. Because private dispute-resolution structures created and institutionalized within the organizational field ultimately shaped the legislative facet of the legal environment, the politics of consumer protection policy were at least partially rooted within the logic of organizational fields. Vermont provides an actual counterfactual that highlights how different political alliances can shape legislative and regulatory rules in a different manner. Either way, political contestation is a critical factor in determining which legal principles, structures, and rules come to dominate the meaning of law as organizational and legal field logics overlap.

The interdisciplinary interaction of sociology, new institutionalism, and political science augments the reach of legal endogeneity research. Second wave studies of legal endogeneity do not negate political, cultural, instrumental, or normative approaches of law and organizations that have been previously explored. Strategic political action, lobbying, political mobilization, cultural reframing, decoupling, diffusion, and other mechanisms developed in prior work by sociologists and political scientists are crucial to understanding the way in which intermediaries impact law and social change. But more recent scholarship on organizational constructions of law and compliance suggest that these political, cultural, instrumental, and even normative processes are often derived from and influenced by the increasing professionalization of law by nonlegal actors in organizational fields and how nonlegal actors encounter and filter what law means through nonlegal logics in their institutional environments. Thus, organizations' lobbying choices, political mobilization agendas, strategic considerations, and cultural and cognitive scripts are often drawn from and shaped by the nonlegal logics operating in an organizational field and the intermediary's professional experience. This blending of political science and sociology scholarship gives this theoretical approach more empirical reach.

6.3.2 *Filtering Law and Compliance through Nonlegal Logics*

Scholars are also increasingly focusing on how rule or legal intermediaries shape organizational construction of law. Rule or legal intermediaries are state, business, and civil society actors that affect, control, or monitor how legal rules are interpreted, implemented, or constructed. Legal intermediaries influence the way that organizations understand law and compliance by filtering what law means through nonlegal logics emanating from various organizational fields (Talesh and Pélisse 2019).

This focus led second wave scholars to broaden the framework beyond managerialization and explore how other nonmanagerial logics influence the way that organizations understand the meaning of law and, in particular, the role of intermediaries who are not legal professionals (Pélisse 2014, 2016). Unlike first wave studies, second wave studies of legal endogeneity more precisely tease out how organizational field actors can filter law and compliance through *multiple* field logics. Consumer, risk, science, and prison logics emanating in various organizational fields can influence the way that organizations understand the meaning of law (Stryker, Docka-Filipek, and Wald 2012; Verma, 2015; Talesh, 2012, 2014, 2015a, 2015c). Although managerial logics are prevalent among businesses, second wave studies highlight how there can be multiple field logics operating and how field actors can have cohesion or settlement among some logics and contestation around others (Talesh 2015a).

For example, Talesh continued his analysis by studying the present-day lemon law field by attending lemon law conferences, interviewing field actors from across the United States, and participating and observing arbitration training programs that arbitrators undergo in two states (California and Vermont) (Talesh 2012, 2015c). Rather than a single managerial logic dominating an organizational field, as first wave studies highlight, Talesh (2015c) demonstrates how there can be multiple logics operating in an organizational field. Talesh's fieldwork revealed that private actors mediate the purpose of lemon laws and the value of informal dispute-resolution forums through business logics of efficiency, cost-effectiveness, managerial discretion, and productivity whereas public actors, such as consumer advocates and state regulators, anchor their discourse in a consumer logic that emphasizes consumer rights, public safety, transparency, and following formal law.

Unlike the organizational field examined in the civil rights context, the lemon law field was simultaneously settled in some areas and contested in others. While field actors from across the United States recognize the inherent ambiguity in lemon laws and share a logic that favors ADR forums over courts for resolving lemon law disputes, they contest the meaning and implementation of lemon laws and consumer rights in powerful ways. Thus, compliance is a socially and organizationally constructed concept and the legal rules that organizations are tasked with implementing are evaluated through various filters (in this case, business and consumer logics) (Talesh 2015c). This is important because law is interpreted and implemented by rule-intermediaries that are tasked with implementing lemon law arbitration programs through two distinct logics.

To that end, Talesh (2012) continued his analysis by comparing how two different ADR forums (one created and administered by private organizations in California, and the other administered and run by the state of Vermont) operating outside the court system resolve consumer disputes. Unlike the single-arbitrator system in the private arbitration programs, Vermont uses an arbitration board consisting of a five-person panel of arbitrators (three citizens, an automotive dealer representative, and a technical expert). Talesh finds that the institutional design of dispute resolution, and how business and consumer values and perspectives are translated by field actors in different dispute-resolution systems, leads to two different meanings of law operating in private and state-run dispute-resolution forums. Managerial and business values of rationality, efficiency, and discretion flow into law operating in California's private dispute-resolution structures primarily through an arbitration training and socialization process conducted by third-party administrators hired by automobile manufacturers to run their lemon law arbitration program (Talesh 2012). The institutional context socializes arbitrators to ignore consumer emotion and narrows the fact-finding role of arbitrators to that of a passive arbiter reliant on parties to present facts. As a result, arbitrators are taught to adjudicate cases not in the shadow of the formal lemon law on the books but in the shadow of a managerialized lemon law filled with its *own* rules, procedures, and construction of law that changes the meaning of consumer protection. Moreover, as business values flow through the disputing structure, organizational repeat players gain subtle opportunities for advantages through the operation of California dispute-resolution structures.

Vermont's vastly different dispute resolution system has far less tendency than the process in California to introduce business values into the meaning and operation of lemon laws. To the extent that business values are introduced into the process by the presence of dealer and technical expert board members, they are balanced with competing consumer logics by the presence of citizen panel members and a state administrator. Rather than emphasizing professional training and socialization, Vermont's structure illustrates how participatory representation, an inquisitorial fact-finding approach, and balancing consumer and business perspectives in the decision-making process can help curb repeat player advantages. In terms of consumer outcomes in these hearings, consumers do far worse in private than in state-run disputing structures (Talesh 2012).

Thus, in contrast to prior studies (Edelman, Erlanger, and Lande 1993; Edelman, Fuller, and Mara-Drita 2001; Marshall 2005), comparing distinct lemon law arbitration programs within the same organizational field allows one to explore the *variation* in how managerial values flow into the compliance behavior of businesses. In particular, such qualitative empirical studies of the processes and mechanisms through which managerial values seep into the design of legal institutions in varying degrees give us great insight into the subtle ways in which managerial values flow into understandings of compliance in some but not all instances. Moreover, where prior studies focused on how managerial values influence written policies and internal legal structures (Edelman, Erlanger, and Lande 1993; Marshall 2005), managerial logics flow into *third-party* organizations that train arbitrators on the meaning of lemon laws. This is a critical way that organizational repeat players gain structural advantages through seemingly neutral dispute-resolution processes.

Second wave legal endogeneity scholars who focus on how organizations construct the meaning of law note that it is not only the ambiguity of legal rules and regulations that make organizations likely to influence legal meaning. Rather, the variety of second wave studies in different regulatory arenas mentioned earlier in this section emerged in part due to the global shift from government to governance, the inherent ambiguity in legal rules, and the increasing complexity of legal rules (Talesh and Pélisse 2019; Abbott, Levi-Faur, and Snidal 2017). The interaction of these three elements has created greater space for nontraditional actors to emerge and influence law. In this era of coregulation and public–private partnerships, state, business, and civil society actors act as rule-intermediaries that affect, control, and monitor relations between rule-takers and rule-makers (Abbott, Levi-Faur, and Snidal 2017). In particular, a wide variety of legal and nonlegal actors among and within organizations that come into contact with law have increasing discretion in their legal environments. In a world where private actors are increasingly involved in handling functions traditionally run by the government such as lemon law dispute resolution, organizations no longer simply play for favorable rules in the public arena (cf. Galanter 1974). Rather, they play for removing the entire disputing game from the public arena into the private arena, actively creating the terms of legal compliance and reshaping the meaning of rights and remedies through business and consumer logics operating in the organizational field.

Scholars writing about prisons highlight how penal field logics operating within the field shaped penal policy among legislators and courts (Verma 2015; Jenness and Smyth 2011). There is some variance among scholars on whether prisons complied with reform efforts substantively or merely symbolically. A mixture of judicial activism and deference drives substantive reform with varying degrees of success. On the one hand, legal deference devised by the corrections professionals and adopted by prisons, coupled with careful monitoring to ensure that the standards are met, influenced law and compliance in the prison context (Feeley and Rubin 1999). On the other hand, compliance by prisons with prison overcrowding and conditions in solitary confinement that was mandated by courts and legislatures has been shown to be large symbolic in many instances (Schoenfeld 2010; Geutzkow and Schoon 2015). Others show that the prison grievance process, although used extensively, only rarely results in substantive relief and a meaningful change in the authority of correctional officials (Calavita and Jenness 2015).

Second wave scholars in the new institutionalist tradition show how institutional and political mechanisms mobilized by intermediaries are not just driven by managerial logics. There have also been a series of studies concerning the way that risk logics and risk management principles operating within a field can mediate the meaning of law and compliance. Different professions are anchored in different logics and these logics shape the prism through which law is interpreted. The insurance industry, as an active intermediary for organizations, uses the logic of risk to shape the way in which organizations that purchase certain lines of insurance understand law.

Specifically, the insurance field (insurance companies, agents, brokers, and risk management consultants), through Employment Practice Liability Insurance (EPLI) and the accompanying risk management services that the insurance field offers, construct the threat of employment law and influence the nature of civil rights compliance (Talesh 2015a). Insurers began offering EPLI in response to perceived threats of employment discrimination lawsuits. Unlike other insurance policies, EPLI policies provide defense and indemnification coverage to employers for claims of discrimination and other employment-related allegations made by employees, former employees, or potential employees. Insurers increasingly offer EPLI and employers increasingly purchase this insurance. Insurers play a role in trying to nudge employers to avert such risk and act as a regulatory intermediary because employers have an incentive to avoid discrimination. But insurers do so in a way that avoids litigation rather than fostering fair governance, due process, and equality in the workplace.

Drawing from participant observation and interviews at EPLI conferences across the country as well as content analysis of EPLI policies, loss-prevention manuals, EPLI industry guidelines, and webinars, Talesh (2015a, 2015b) shows how insurance companies and institutions use a risk-based logic and institutionalize a way of thinking centered on risk management and reduction. Faced with uncertain and unpredictable legal risk concerning potential discrimination violations, insurance institutions elevate the risk and threat in the legal environment and offer a series of risk management services that they argue will avert risk for employers that purchase EPLI. Insurers use policy language to build discretion into legal rules and often reframe legal rules and principles around a nonlegal risk logic that focuses on avoiding risk and making discrimination claims more defensible (Talesh 2015a, 2015b).

By framing employers' legal environment in these terms, the insurance industry creates a space to encourage employers to engage in managerialized responses and develop formalized policies and procedures by using the various risk-management services offered by insurers to help reduce these risks. Thus, in this instance, risk and managerial values work in a complementary manner and allow insurers as rule-intermediaries greater influence over compliance issues concerning employers (Talesh 2015a, 2015b).

The institutionalized practice of EPLI ultimately leads to public legal institutions affording considerable deference to EPLI. In addition to courts expanding coverage afforded to those insured under EPLI when interpreting coverage questions, federal, state, and municipal governments adopt the logics of EPLI insurers and encourage, and in some instances require, public organizations and governmental institutions to purchase EPLI (Talesh 2015b).

Insurers also mediate the meaning of privacy law and compliance in the cybersecurity context through cyber insurance. Recent research suggests that insurance companies and institutions, through cyber liability insurance, do not simply pool and transfer an insured's risk to an insurance company or provide defense and indemnification services to an insured (Talesh 2018). In addition to transferring risk, cyber insurers provide a series of risk management services that actively shape the way in which an organization's various departments tasked with dealing with data breach, such as in-house counsel, information technology, compliance, public relations, and other organizational units, respond to data breach. Cyber insurers frame the legal environment in terms of risk and then encourage corporations to use their risk management services to avoid data breaches and privacy law violations. Although it is too early to tell how successful cyber insurers are, they are acting as compliance regulators and trying to prevent, detect, and respond to data breaches and trying to help organizations comply with various privacy laws (Talesh 2018).

Risk logics do not just influence the insurance field or actors that interact with insurance companies. Risk reduction and risk management principles shape the way that professional safety officers interpret and implement a variety of environmental, health, and safety rules (Silbey 2017). Anchored in risk values and risk management principles, safety officers implement surveillance technology and databases to manage hazards (Silbey and Agrawal 2011), develop "relational regulation practices" in science laboratories (Huising and Silbey 2011), and use legal rules to manage risks, influence safe practices, and build good working conditions (Borelle and Pélisse 2017; Talesh and Pélisse 2019).

While a deep analysis of each second wave study drawing on legal endogeneity is beyond the scope of this chapter, the theory is clearly moving forward in exciting ways. Second wave studies of how organizations shape the content and meaning of laws designed to regulate them have not just replicated the entire cycle of legal endogeneity theory; they extend, refine, and broaden the reach and applicability of the theory to multiple subject areas. Whereas first wave studies focused on how organizations shape the meaning of law in the judicial context, second wave studies have demonstrated how organizations shape the meaning of legislation and the applicability of administrative regulations. In doing so, they have brought political science studies of business influence over public legal institutions into conversation with organizational sociologists. Second wave studies have moved outside the employment law context and shown how organizations mediate law's meaning in a variety of other areas. Second wave studies have shown how organizational fields do not filter law through a managerial logic; rather, the logic operating in each field is an empirical question unique to each field that is studied. In addition to managerial logics, organizational field actors filter law's meaning through risk, penal, and consumer logics, among others. Not only can multiple logics operate, but fields can be simultaneously contested and cohesive, which leads to multiple compliance frameworks emerging. Each of these additional dimensions provides nuance into how organizations influence the meaning of law and compliance and sets the stage for a third wave of studies to follow.

6.4 IMPLICATIONS AND THOUGHTS ON A THIRD WAVE OF LEGAL ENDOGENEITY STUDIES

This chapter challenges the ambition of compliance research to explain what organizations do to comply or not comply with legal regulations. In doing so, new institutional theories of organizational constructions of law and compliance turn traditional understandings of regulation and compliance inside out by focusing on the processes and mechanisms through which organizations create their own meanings for regulation and, therefore, compliance. Thus, research about what motivates compliance and noncompliance often asks the wrong question, since organizations possess the capacity to influence the meaning of compliance. Scholars writing in this tradition do not contend that organizations never respond rationally to top-down mandates. Rather, they argue that studies of compliance that focus only on organizations as rational actors miss a big part of the compliance picture.

Because laws regulating organizations are usually complex, broad, uncoercive, and vague as to how to comply, they motivate a process through which organizations collectively seek to construct legal meaning. First and second wave legal endogeneity studies demonstrate that this process is shaped by institutionalized logics that evolve over time through the processes of organizational life. This process also involves politics as organizations and their employees, customers, and competitors compete for legal constructions that favor their interests. Through the ongoing overlap of organizational and legal fields and interaction among legal and organizational field actors, the meaning of compliance evolves and takes shape. Legal and nonlegal actors act as intermediaries of law and shape organizational constructions of law by filtering law through nonlegal logics emanating in organizational fields. Understanding law as shaped through a process of institutionalization and political mobilization that takes place within and at the intersection of organizational and legal fields reveals the ways that organizations reshape the meaning of compliance.

In sum, first wave studies laid out the initial framework for how to understand organizations as constructers of legal meaning. Second wave studies refined and extended legal endogeneity theory. There is tremendous opportunity for a third wave of studies to emerge in the next decade. Continued inquiry into the subtle processes through which organizations shape the meaning of compliance is important and ripe for further exploration because countries across the world are increasingly moving toward more coregulatory frameworks. The private role in public governance across virtually all sectors of society is real. Because private organizations are not merely influencing governmental institutions but, rather, performing many traditional government functions with government approval, organizations have greater opportunity than ever before to shape what constitutes the meaning of legal regulations and compliance itself. Although there are potential benefits to self-regulatory and collaborative governance arrangements, studies of how organizations influence the meaning of compliance that I highlighted in this chapter suggest that there is great potential for organizations to inhibit legal ideals through symbolic or ineffective structures and policies.

I briefly outline a few directions for further research. Third wave studies should explore the institutional and political mechanisms through which organizations shape the meaning of compliance in normatively undesirable *and* desirable ways. Whereas first and second wave studies often show how organizational constructions of compliance weaken law's meaning (cf. Talesh 2012), future studies should explore the conditions under which organizational policies, procedures, and practices lead to greater compliance or are consistent with the goals of legislation and regulatory rules. Across a wide variety of regulatory settings, closer focus is needed on the ways that legal and nonlegal actors filter law's meaning through nonlegal logics. Comparing cases in regulatory settings, or even across common law and civil law societies, might give us insight into the ways to prevent organizational structures from becoming symbolic (cf. Talesh 2012, 2014). Finally, research should explore what legal reforms or interventions by public legal institutions might limit or prevent legal endogeneity from occurring. Each of these suggestions could expand the research arc in new directions theoretically and methodologically. At a minimum, further research in this manner will move thinking about compliance away from focusing on when organizations do or do not comply with law, and toward asking, rather, how organizations construct the meaning of law and compliance.

REFERENCES

Abbott, K., D. Levi-Faur, and D. Snidal. 2017. "Regulatory Intermediaries in the Age of Governance." *Annals of the American Academy of Political and Social Science* 670:1–288.

Albiston, Catherine. 2005. "Bargaining in the Shadow of the Social Institutions: Competing Discourses and Social Change in Workplace Mobilization of Civil Rights." *Law & Society Review* 39:11–50.

Ayres, Ian, and John Braithwaite. 2001. "Tripartism: Regulatory Capture and Empowerment." *Law & Social Inquiry* 16:435–96.

Barnes, Jeb, and Thomas Burke. 2006. "The Diffusion of Rights: From Law on the Books to Organizational Practices." *Law & Society Review* 40(3):493–524.

Baron, James N., Frank R. Dobbin, and P. Devereaux Jennings. 1986. "War and Peace: The Evolution of Modern Personnel Administration in U.S. Industry." *American Journal of Sociology* 92(2):350–83.

Bastard, B., L. Cardia-Vonèche, and V. Gonik. 2003. "Judiciarisation et déformalisation. Le 'Groupe H' et le traitement institutionnel du harcèlement psychologique." *Droit et société* 53(1):185–208.

Baumgartner, Frank R., and Bryan D. Jones. 1993. *Agendas and Instability in American Politics*. Chicago: University of Chicago Press.

Bereni, Laure. 2009. "'Faire de la diversité une richesse pour l'entreprise'. La transformation d'une contrainte juridique en catégorie managériale." *Raisons Politiques* 35:87–106.

Bernstein, Marver H. 1955. *Regulating Business by Independent Commission*. Princeton: Princeton University Press.

Borelle, Celine, and Jérôme Pélisse. 2017. "Ca sent bizarre, ici': la sécurité dans les laboratoires de nanomédecine (France-Etats-Unis)." *Sociologie du travail* [En ligne] 59(3): http://sdt.revues.org/934.

Bozanic, Zahn, Mark W. Dirsmith, and Steven Huddart. 2012. "The Social Constitution of Regulation: The Endogenization of Insider Trading Laws." *Accounting, Organizations and Society* 37 (7):461–81.

Braithwaite, John. 2008. *Regulatory Capitalism: How It Works, Ideas for Making It Work Better*. Cheltenham, UK: Edward Elgar Publishing.

Calavita, Kitty, and Valerie Jenness. 2015. *Appealing to Justice: Prisoner Grievances, Rights, and Carceral Logic*. Oakland: University of California Press.

Covaleski, Mark A., Mark W. Dirsmith, and Jane M. Weiss. 2013. "The Social Construction, Challenge and Transformation of a Budgetary Regime: The Endogenization of Welfare Regulation by Institutional Entrepreneurs." *Accounting, Organizations and Society* 38(5):333–64.

Delmas, Magali A., and Maria J. Montes-Sancho. 2011. "An Institutional Perspective on the Diffusion of International Management System Standards." *Business Ethics Quarterly* 21(1):103–32.

DiMaggio, Paul J., and Walter Powell. 1983. "The Iron Cage Revisited: Institutional Isomorphism and Collective Rationality in Organizational Fields." *American Sociological Review* 48:147–60.

Dobbin, Frank, John Sutton, John Meyer, and Richard Scott. 1993. "Equal Employment Opportunity Law and the Construction of Internal Labor Markets." *American Journal of Sociology* 99:396–427.

Dunn, Mary B., and Candace Jones. 2010. "Institutional Logics and Institutional Pluralism: The Contestation and Science Logics in Medical Education." *Administrative Science Quarterly* 55 (1):114–49.

Edelman, Lauren B. 1990. "Legal Environments and Organizational Governance: The Expansion of Due Process in the American Workplace." *American Journal of Sociology* 95:1401–40.

1992. "Legal Ambiguity and Symbolic Structures: Organizational Mediation of Civil Rights Law." *American Journal of Sociology* 97:1531–76.

2007. "Overlapping Fields and Constructed Legalities: The Endogeneity of Law." In *Private Equity, Corporate Governance and the Dynamics of Capital Market Regulation*, edited by Justin O'Brien, 55–90. London: Imperial College Press.

2016. *Working Law: Courts, Corporations, and Symbolic Civil Rights*. Chicago: University of Chicago Press.

Edelman, Lauren B., and Mia Cahill. 1998. "How Law Matters in Disputing and Dispute Processing (or the Contingency of Legal Matter in Informal Dispute Process)." In *How Law Matters?* edited by Bryant Garth and Austin Sarat, 15–44. Evanston, IL: Northwestern University Press.

Edelman, Lauren B., and Stephen Peterson. 1999. "Symbols and Substance in Organizational Response to Civil Rights Law." *Research in Social Stratification and Mobility* 17:107–35.

Edelman, Lauren B., and Robin Stryker. 2005. "A Sociological Approach to Law and the Economy." In *The Handbook of Economic Sociology*, edited by Neil Smelser and Richard Swedberg, 527–51. Princeton: Princeton University Press.

Edelman, Lauren B., and Mark Suchman. 1999. "When the 'Haves' Hold Court: Speculations on the Organizational Internalization of Law." *Law & Society Review* 33:941–91.

Edelman, Lauren B., and Shauhin Talesh. 2011. "To Comply or Not to Comply – That Isn't the Question: How Organizations Construct the Meaning of Compliance." In *Explaining Compliance: Business Responses to Regulation*, edited by Christine Parker and Vibeke Lehmann Nielsen, 103–22. Cheltenham, UK: Edward Elgar.

Edelman, Lauren B., Howard Erlanger, and John Lande. 1993. "Internal Dispute Resolution: The Transformation of Civil Rights in the Workplace." *Law & Society Review* 27:497–534.

Edelman, Lauren B., Christopher Uggen, and Howard Erlanger. 1999. "The Endogeneity of Legal Regulation: Grievance Procedures as Rational Myth." *American Journal of Sociology* 105:406–54.

Edelman, Lauren B., Sally Riggs Fuller, and Iona Mara-Drita. 2001. "Diversity Rhetoric and the Managerialization of Law." *American Journal of Sociology* 106:1589–641.

Edelman, Lauren B., Linda Krieger, Scott Eliason, Catherine Albiston, and Virgina Mellema. 2011. "When Organizations Rule: Judicial Deference to Institutionalized Employment Structures." *American Journal of Sociology* 117(3):888–954.

Feeley, Malcolm, and Edward L. Rubin. 1999. *Judicial Policy Making and the Modern State: How the Courts Reformed America's Prisons*. New York: Cambridge University Press.

Frazer, Andrew. 2014. "Labour Law, Institutionalist Regulation and the Employing Organisation." *International Employment Relations Review* 20(1):4–26.

Funk, Russell J., and Daniel Hirschman. 2014. "Derivatives and Deregulation Financial Innovation and the Demise of Glass-Steagall." *Administrative Science Quarterly* 59(4):669–704.

Galanter, Marc. 1974. "Why the 'Haves' Come Out Ahead: Speculations on the Limits of Legal Change." *Law & Society Review* 9:95–160.

Gilad, Sharon. 2014. "Beyond Endogeneity: How Firms and Regulators Construct the Meaning of Regulation." *Law & Policy* 36(2):134–64.

Guetzkow, Joshua, and Eric W. Schoon. 2015. "If You Build It, They Will Fill It: The Consequences of Prison Overcrowding Litigation." *Law & Society Review* 49(2):401–32.

Haines, Fiona. 1997. *Corporate Regulation: Beyond "Punish or Persuade."* New York: Oxford University Press.

Heimer, Carol. 1999. "Competing Institutions: Law, Medicine, and Family in Neonatal Intensive Care." *Law & Society Review* 33:17–67.

Holder-Webb, Lori, and Jeffrey Cohen. 2012. "The Cut and Paste Society: Isomorphism in Codes of Ethics." *Journal of Business Ethics* 107(4):485–509.

Huising, R., and Susan Silbey. 2011. "Governing the Gap: Forging Safe Science through Relational Regulation." *Regulation & Governance* 5:14–42.

Jacoby, Sandford. 1985. *Employing Bureaucracy: Managers, Unions, and the Transformation of Work in American Industry 1900–45*. New York: Columbia University Press.

Jenness, Valerie, and Michael Smyth. 2011. "The Passage of the Prison Rape Elimination Act: Legal Endogeneity and the Uncertain Road from Symbolic Law to Instrumental Effects." *Stanford Law & Policy Review* 22(2):489–518.

Kagan, Robert A., Neil Gunningham, and Dorothy Thornton. 2003. "Explaining Corporate Environmental Performance: How Does Regulation Matter" *Law & Society Review* 37:51–90.

Kelly, Erin L. 2003. "The Strange History of Employer-Sponsored Child Care: Interested Actors, Uncertainty, and the Transformation of Law in Organizational Fields." *American Journal of Sociology* 109(3):606–49.

Krawiec, Kimberly D. 2003. "Cosmetic Compliance and the Failure of Negotiated Governance." *Washington University Law Quarterly* 81(2):487–544.

2005. "Organizational Misconduct: Beyond the Principal-Agent Model." *Florida State University Law Review* 32(2):571–616.

Lageson, Sarah Esther, Mike Vuolo, and Christopher Uggen. 2014. "Legal Ambiguity in Managerial Assessments of Criminal Records." *Law & Social Inquiry* 40(1):175–204.

Lehman, David W., Balázs Kovács, and Glenn R. Carroll. 2014. "Conflicting Social Codes and Organizations: Hygiene and the Authenticity in Consumer Evaluations of Restaurants." *Management Science* 60(10):2602–17.

Marshall, Anna-Maria. 2005. "Idle Rights: Employees' Rights Consciousness and the Construction of Sexual Harassment Policies." *Law & Society Review* 39:83–124.

Meyer, John, and Brian Rowan. 1977. "Institutionalized Organizations: Formal Structure as Myth and Ceremony." *American Journal of Sociology* 83:340–63.

Mezias, Stephen J., and Elizabeth Boyle. 2005. "Blind Trust: Market Control, Legal Environments, and the Dynamics of Competitive Intensity in the Early American Film Industry, 1893–1920." *Administrative Science Quarterly* 50(1):1–34.

Mulligan, Emer and Lynne M. Oats. 2005. "Movers and Shakers: The Secret Lives of In-House Tax Professionals." *Critical Perspectives on Accounting Conference* (July).

Nierobisz, Annette. 2010. "Wrestling with the New Economy: Judicial Rhetoric in Canadian Wrongful Dismissal Claims." *Law & Social Inquiry* 35(2):403–49.

Pandy, Susan M. 2013. "An Examination of the Privacy Impact Assessment as a Vehicle for Privacy Policy Implementation in U.S. Federal Agencies." PhD dissertation, Virginia Polytechnic and State University.

Parker, Christine, and Vibeke Lehmann Nielsen. 2011. *Explaining Business Compliance: Business Responses to Regulation*. Cheltenham, UK: Edward Elgar.

Pedriana, Nicholas, and Robin Stryker. 1997. "Political Culture Wars, 1960s Style: Equal Opportunity-Affirmative Action Law and the Philadelphia Plan." *American Journal of Sociology* 103:633–91.

2004. "The Strength of a Weak Agency: Enforcement of Title VII of the 1964 Civil Rights Act and the Expansion of State Capacity, 1965–1971." *American Journal of Sociology* 110:709–60.

Pélisse, Jérôme. 2014. "Le travail du droit. Trois essais sur la légalité ordinaire, mémoire d'Habilitation à diriger les recherches." *Sciences Po Paris*:244.

2016. "Legal Intermediaries as Moral Actors." Communication at the SASE's Meeting, Berkeley:24.

Pierson, Paul. 2004. *Politics in Time: History, Institutions and Social Analysis*. Princeton, NJ: Princeton University Press.

Scott, W. Richard. 2001. *Institutions and Organizations: Foundations for Organizations Science*. London: SAGE Publications.

Schneiberg, Marc. 2005. "Combining New Institutionalisms: Explaining Institutional Change in American Property Insurance." *Sociological Forum* 2(1):93–137.

Schneiberg, Marc, and Sara A. Soule. 2005. "Institutionalization as a Contested, Multilevel Process: The Case of Rate Regulation in American Fire Insurance." In *Social Movements and Organization Theory*, edited by Gerald F. Davis et al., 122–60. Cambridge: Cambridge University Press.

Schoenfeld, Heather. 2010. "Mass Incarceration and the Paradox of Prison Conditions Litigation." *Law & Society Review* 44(3–4):1750–843.

Short, Jodi L. 2006. "Creating Peer Sexual Harassment: Mobilizing Schools to Throw the Book at Themselves." Law and Policy 28(1):31–59.

Silbey, Susan. 2017. "Governing Green Laboratories: How Scientific Authority and Expertise Mediate Institutional Pressures for Organizational Change." Unpublished paper.

Silbey, Susan., and T. Agrawal. 2011. "The Illusion of Accountability: Information Management and Organizational Culture." *Droit et société* 77(1):69–86.

Simpson, Sally S. 1992. "Corporate-Crime Deterrence and Corporate-Control Policies: Views from the Inside." In *White-Collar Crime Reconsidered*, edited by Kip Schlegel and David Weisburd, 289–308. Boston: Northeastern University Press.

1998. *Why Corporations Obey the Law*, New York: Cambridge University Press.

Stigler, Goerge J. 1971. "The Theory of Economic Regulation." *Bell Journal of Economics and Management Science* 2(1):3–21.

Stryker, R., D. Docka-Filipek, and P. Wald. 2012. "Employment Discrimination Law and Industrial Psychology: Social Science as Social Authority and the Co-production of Law and Science." *Law & Social Inquiry* 37:777–914.

Sutton, John, Frank Dobbin, John Meyer, and Richard Scott. 1994. "The Legalization of the Workplace." *American Journal of Sociology* 99:944–71.

Talesh, Shauhin. 2009. "The Privatization of Public Legal Rights: How Manufacturers Construct the Meaning of Consumer Law." *Law & Society Review* 43:527–62.

2012. "How Dispute Resolution System Design Matters: An Organizational Analysis of Dispute Resolution Structures and Consumer Lemon Laws." *Law & Society Review* 46(3):463–9.

2013. "How the 'Haves' Come Out Ahead in the Twenty-First Century." *DePaul Law Review* 62: 519–54.

2014. "Institutional and Political Sources of Legislative Change: Explaining How Private Organizations Influence the Form and Content of Consumer Protection Legislation." *Law & Soc. Inquiry* 39(4):973–1005.

2015a. "Legal Intermediaries: How Insurance Companies Construct the Meaning of Compliance with Antidiscrimination Law." *Law & Policy* 37(3):209–39.
2015b. "A New Institutional Theory of Insurance." *UC Irvine Law Review* 5(3):617–50.
2015c. "Rule-Intermediaries in Action: How State and Business Stakeholders Influence the Meaning of Consumer Rights in Regulatory Governance Arrangements." *Law & Policy* 37(1–2):1–31.
2018. "Data Breach, Privacy, and Cyber Insurance: How Insurance Companies Act as 'Compliance Managers' for Businesses." *Law and Social Inquiry* 43(2):417–40.
Talesh, Shauhin, and Peter Alter. 2020. "The Devil Is in the Details: How Arbitration System Design and Training Facilitate and Inhibit Repeat Player Advantages in Private and State-Run Arbitration Hearings." *Law & Policy* 42: 315–43.
Talesh, Shauhin, and Jérôme Pélisse. 2019. "How Legal Intermediaries Facilitate or Inhibit Social Change." *Studies in Law, Politics, and Society* 79:111–45.
Tyler, Tom R. 1990. *Why People Obey the Law*. New Haven: Yale University Press.
Vaughan, Diane. 1998. "Rational Choice, Situated Action, and the Social Control of Organizations." *Law & Society Review* 32(1):23–61.
Verma, Anjuli. 2015. "The Law-Before: Legacies and Gaps in Penal Reform." *Law & Society Review* 49 (4):847–82.

7

Compliance as Operations Management

Saed Alizamir, Sang-Hyun Kim, Suresh Muthulingam

Abstract: In this chapter we review the body of operations management (OM) literature that studies compliance issues. Researchers in OM focus on how operational-level decisions (such as process improvement, capacity, quality, and risk mitigation) impact performance outcomes in business and society. In recent years there has been growing interest among OM scholars in compliance issues, mostly in the context of environmental regulation and corporate social responsibility (CSR). The focus on operations casts new light and brings novel insights to compliance issues, and in some cases provides guidance for implementable solutions.

7.1 INTRODUCTION

Compliance issues have received increased attention in the field of operations management (OM) in recent years, coinciding with the emergence of sustainable operations as a major subdiscipline within OM. Researchers in OM focus on how operational-level decisions (such as process improvement, capacity, quality, and risk mitigation) impact performance outcomes in business and society. Traditionally, OM studies have been conducted in manufacturing and service settings, with a goal of identifying strategies and tactics that enable cost-effective delivery of goods and services within enterprises as well as across different levels of supply chains. The predominant focus of academic studies in OM has been on reducing costs or improving profitability for a firm or a collection of firms within a supply chain. This emphasis started to change in the 1990s as researchers recognized the impact of operational decisions on stakeholders beyond firm boundaries, such as the environment and the society, which led to the establishment of the sustainable operations subdiscipline. In this context, operating under government regulations and influencing regulatory actions through informed decision-making in production and service settings have emerged as important considerations. At the same time, another major thrust of research has been to understand how firms can drive compliance adherence in supply chains. In this chapter we review the literature in these streams of research. While the studies discussed are primarily sourced from OM journals, since the subject is fairly new to the OM community, we also discuss related influential papers from other disciplines, such as environmental economics and organizational science. It is not the goal of this review to be exhaustive; instead, we aim to demonstrate OM researchers' approaches to addressing some of the key issues that arise when firms' day-to-day operations are shaped by compliance considerations.

7.2 REGULATORY COMPLIANCE IN PRODUCTION AND SERVICE SETTINGS

The subject that has received particular attention in the OM literature is the regulatory bodies' actions to enforce environmental standards and the effect of such actions on firms' decisions, especially in production and service delivery settings. While much has been written about this subject in the environmental economics literature from a policy design perspective, many OM scholars have instead focused on the *process* of compliance enforcement in order to highlight how day-to-day activities performed at the firm level influence compliance. This naturally led to numerous studies on regulators' inspection activities, a key mechanism that enables implementation of the enforcement policies.

Inspections are performed for the purpose of verifying whether operations adhere to accepted norms and regulations. At the same time, they influence profit-conscious firms' operational decisions, creating dynamics that may or may not result in the outcomes intended by regulators. Investigating inspection activity and operational dynamics, several scholars document the link between inspections and compliance outcomes for firms. Using data from manufacturing operations in California, Levine et al. (2012) study the US Occupational Safety and Health Administration's (OSHA) inspection program that monitors worker safety in manufacturing facilities. They find that OSHA inspections had the beneficial effect of reducing annual injuries by 9.4 percent in the year the manufacturing establishment was inspected. In another study, Anand et al. (2012) examine whether inspections by the US Food and Drug Administration (FDA) influence pharmaceutical firms to adhere to manufacturing processes approved by the FDA, concluding that a tendency for manufacturing processes to deviate from those approved by the FDA is reversed in the presence of FDA inspections. In other words, inspections serve as a mechanism that resets the production processes to adhere with what was approved by the FDA. In contrast to these examples, select instances have documented the opposite effect, namely that, under certain conditions, inspections can be detrimental to compliance. For instance, Ball et al. (2017), in their examination of the relationship between FDA inspections and product recalls in the medical equipment industry, illustrate that inspections could result in increased product recalls if the same inspectors repeatedly inspect a specific plant. Use of technology that replaces the need for inspections has been examined as well. Staats et al. (2017) study whether the introduction of a radio frequency identification (RFID)-based system designed to monitor the hand hygiene compliance of healthcare workers had a significant impact on actual compliance, and they find that compliance rates, indeed, improved by over 24 percent.

Researchers have also sought to understand the mechanisms that enable inspections to foster compliance. An important theme that emerged from this effort is the role of institutional learning. Anand et al. (2012) argue that inspections provide information feedback on the departures from accepted norms and regulations, thereby heightening the importance of minimizing deviations in manufacturing practices. Mani and Muthulingam (2019a), in their investigation of the environmental performance of oil and gas wells in Pennsylvania, find that operators of unconventional wells improve their environmental compliance performance by learning from the inspection experience of other unconventional wells, especially when such inspections identify compliance violations rather than when the inspections confirm compliance. In an illustration of the benefits from inspection activities reaching beyond improved regulatory compliance, Mani and Muthulingam (2019b) find that unconventional wells reduce the amount of waste in their operations as they gain experience with environmental inspections.

In many regulatory settings, an inspection program has to be coupled with sanctions or financial incentives in order for it to be an effective compliance enforcement mechanism. One of the early efforts that illustrated the importance of sanctions and penalties is King and Lenox (2000), who studied the Chemical Manufacturers Association's Responsible Care Program, which relied on manufacturers' voluntary self-regulation of toxic chemical emissions at their facilities. Their analysis reveals that, due to the absence of a credible sanction mechanism under the Responsible Care Program, manufacturing facilities with a poor history of environmental compliance performance failed to reduce their toxic emissions. Given the important role of penalties, scholars have sought to understand how penalties can be structured to improve operational outcomes. Gawande and Bohara (2005) explore these issues in the context of oil spill prevention activities by the US Coast Guard. They highlight that the optimal approach for the regulator would be to utilize a mix of penalties based on both the expected and the actual amounts of pollution. Along similar lines, Dhanorkar et al. (2017) point out the need for complementing penalties with supportive tactics such as technical assistance or recommendations. They identify the timing of applying punitive versus supportive tactics as a key determinant of operational improvements; while supportive tactics are more effective if they are applied immediately after the imposition of penalty, their impact is limited if the sequence is reversed. Handley and Gray (2013), in their study of buyer firms' interactions with contract manufacturers (CMs), find that quality audits and penalties complement each other because together they serve to improve the CMs' quality performance.

A number of studies further examine how inspections, coupled with penalties, impact firms' voluntary disclosure decisions and the environmental outcomes. Kim (2015), inspired by works such as Harrington (1988), Kaplow and Shavell (1994), Innes (1999), Livernois and McKenna (1999), Friesen (2006), Pfaff and Sanchirico (2000), Short and Toffel (2007), and Toffel and Short (2011), built a theoretical model that combines the elements of reliability theory and law enforcement economics to reveal the insights that can be obtained only by a detailed description of stochastic processes that govern random compliance failures as well as inspection activities. In the context of environmental standard enforcement, Kim (2015) focuses on a contrast between "periodic inspections" under which inspections are performed at fixed intervals (capturing timing certainty of announced inspection visits) and "random inspections," highlighting how inspection timing uncertainty impacts a firm's decision on whether to voluntarily disclose compliance violations. While intuition suggests that random inspections will lead to better environmental outcome since they suppress a firm's opportunistic nondisclosure, Kim (2015) identifies situations in which periodic inspections are actually better for the environment, which arises from the stochastic nature of compliance failure and inspection processes. A follow-up study by Wang et al. (2016) analyzes a similar problem using the continuous-time dynamic mechanism design framework, deriving the optimal inspection policy under which a regulator will alternate between increasing inspection intensity and providing more financial incentive over time. Alizamir and Kim (2019) extend Kim (2015) by considering firms' self-inspections, which arise in settings where a firm does not have complete visibility to its compliance status at all times and therefore has to exert costly effort to discover the status and apply a remedy if needed.

Other factors of inspection processes have been examined by researchers. Using information on code-of-conduct audits done at suppliers across the world, Short et al. (2016) find that audit teams with inspectors who have had prior experience with the facility under audit are likely to find fewer violations. By contrast, audit teams with diverse gender, or with only women, or with trained inspectors are likely to find more violations. Ibanez and Toffel (2019) explore the impact of schedules on inspection outcomes. They analyze data from food-safety inspections and find that inspectors identify more violations at a focal establishment if they had previously visited an establishment with worse compliance levels. Additionally, they find that inspectors identify fewer violations in inspections that are done at the end of the day.

Another theme that received attention in the OM literature is the role of third-party inspection services. Regulators often outsource the inspection or monitoring process, in many settings such as vehicle emissions testing and factory pollution recording. Bennett et al. (2013) examine the role of competition in the context of vehicle emissions testing and find that increased competition can compromise the efficiency of the inspection activities. This is because third-party inspectors are tempted to provide lenient inspections in the hope of generating customer loyalty that can garner future business by providing cross-selling opportunities. So how can regulators overcome this detrimental effect of competition? Research indicates two potential options. The first option relates to the characteristics of the third-party inspectors as illustrated by Pierce and Toffel (2013). They find that, for vehicle emissions testing, organizational units that do not have the opportunity for cross-selling, or subsidiary units in a larger organization, or units that are affiliated with multi-location brands are unlikely to exhibit inspection leniency. The second option relates to use of supplementary audits and incentive alignment. Duflo et al. (2013) illustrate this idea using a field experiment in India. They find that third-party auditors can be made to report their results more accurately if their reports are audited by other firms in a supplementary audit and if their future business is tied to the results of the supplementary audits. In other words, if third-party auditors are subject to sanctions for lenient audits then their audit performance improves.

A number of papers study how inspection activities can improve the organization of operations. Gray et al. (2011), using FDA inspections to study the quality performance of domestic and offshore plants, conclude that offshore plants tend to have poorer quality performance than domestic plants. From a regulator's perspective, these results indicate the need for more intensified scrutiny of offshore units. In a similar vein, Gray et al. (2015a) explore the quality implications of collocating manufacturing with research and development (R&D). By examining the outcomes of FDA inspections, they infer that firms with collocated manufacturing and R&D achieve better conformance quality, and that these benefits persist even in the presence of technological and communication advances that might mitigate the impact of geographical distance. These results illustrate that physical proximity between manufacturing activities and R&D is valuable to achieve improved quality compliance, especially in settings that require high knowledge interdependence. In a related study, Gray et al. (2015b) explore the process compliance of medical device firms certified to the ISO 9000 standards. By examining the outcomes of FDA inspections, they infer that firms that got certified early to the ISO 9000 standard have better compliance than firms that got certified later. Moreover, the results indicate that process compliance deteriorates over time, which suggests the need for continued vigilance within organizations to maintain process compliance. Overall, this stream of work indicates that greater coordination and continued monitoring are important to maintain compliance.

Aside from the topic of inspections, a number of OM scholars have studied environmental compliance issues that arose from the enactment of legislations such as Waste Electronic and Electrical Equipment, Restriction of Hazardous Substances, and Extended Producer

Responsibility (EPR). Many of these studies are in the context of managing electronics waste (e-waste). Atasu and Van Wassenhove (2012) draw on the learnings from e-waste laws passed across nations and geographies to point out that the choices of consumers and manufacturers play an important role in compliance with the requirements of e-waste legislations. Ferguson and Toktay (2006) support this notion by illustrating that, in some circumstances, policies designed to reduce e-waste may have adverse effects because of the incentive misalignments across stakeholders. Building on this theme, Atasu et al. (2013) discuss how stakeholders' preferences can influence and enable the success of e-waste laws. Other researchers have delved deeper to explore the operational challenges of involving consumers or holding producers responsible for managing e-waste. Plambeck and Wang (2009) show that "fee-upon-sale" e-waste legislations that focus more on consumers can produce behavioral changes not only in consumers but also in manufacturers, to reduce e-waste. Gui et al. (2013) show that mechanisms such as EPR, which holds producers accountable for the post-usage stage of their products, can run into implementation challenges because of diverging preferences of the involved stakeholders. At the extreme, Gui et al. (2015) show that EPR schemes such as weight-based proportional allocation of cost among multiple producers may in fact discourage the participation of some producers.

Another topic that OM scholars have investigated in the context of regulatory compliance is product recalls. Firms undertake product recalls when products fail to comply with safety expectations or regulations. This is inherently an operational problem, since product recalls are triggered by inadequate quality assurance or process failures within a firm's operations. Haunschild and Rhee (2004) were among the early scholars to recognize this view. In their study of product recalls in the automotive industry, they find that firms learn to reduce future product recalls as they gain more experience with recalls, and that voluntary recalls contribute more to the learning effect than mandated recalls do. Thirumalai and Sinha (2011), in their study of product recalls in the medical device industry, find that firms with R&D focus and with a broader product portfolio experience higher incidence of recalls. Along similar lines, Hora et al. (2011) explore product recalls in the toy industry and find that product recalls due to manufacturing defects get initiated faster than product recalls that can be traced to design defects. Shah et al. (2017) attempt to identify the drivers of product recalls in the automotive industry, showing that product variety and plant utilizations have significant effect on product recalls, but the same cannot be said about plant variety. Colak and Bray (2016) formulate the joint recall decision by a manufacturer and a regulator as a dynamic discrete choice game to find evidence from data as to whether, among others, the manufacturer's voluntary recall decision serves to preempt the government's future recalls. Overall, this stream of research provides a deeper understanding of the operational factors that can influence product recalls.

7.3 COMPLIANCE IN SUPPLY CHAINS

A substantial body of research in the OM literature has focused on compliance issues that arise in supply chain management, especially in the context of sourcing management. Papers in this domain typically deal with compliance of environmental and labor standards by the suppliers of multinational firms. Suppliers are often located in developing countries with weak regulations, which makes legal enforcement of such obligations difficult. Downstream buyers, however, face significant reputational and financial risks if violations committed by their suppliers are detected and revealed to their customers. To enforce compliance, the buyers in these situations resort to a variety of measures ranging from punitive means such as penalty and threat of business termination to supportive mechanisms such as preemptive audits and investment in suppliers' compliance enhancement. Since the supplier's decision in exerting compliance efforts is endogenous and unobservable to the buyer, such measures are adopted to influence the supplier's incentive and encourage internal monitoring.

The first stream of research in this literature examines how an incentive contract can elicit responsible behavior by the suppliers. Using a large data set from contract manufacturers regulated by the FDA, Handley and Gray (2013) empirically investigate the relationship between quality audits and penalties levied for contractual failures, finding that the two enforcement mechanisms substitute one another but are complementary in improving overall compliance. Lee and Li (2018) illustrate how a buyer organization in a supply chain could utilize investment, inspections, and financial incentives in an optimal sourcing contract depending on whether the efforts by the buyer and the supplier are substitutable or complementary. In a similar vein, Chen and Lee (2017) study the complementary roles of supplier certification, process audits, and contingency payments in influencing a supplier's adherence to environmental and labor norms. Cho et al. (2019) propose that a well-crafted combination of inspections and pricing strategies can be used to combat child labor in global supply chains. The authors also allude to the role of nongovernmental organizations (NGOs) and recommend their efforts to be directed toward increasing a buyer's goodwill cost (e.g., by further publicizing the incidence of a violation) rather than reducing the buyer's inspection cost. Babich and Tang (2012) consider a combination of supplier inspections and deferred payments as a deterrence against product adulteration. Bondareva and Pinker (2018) apply a repeated game framework to capture the interaction between a buyer and a supplier, characterizing the optimal relational contract designed to mitigate the risks of quality or compliance failures. The structure of contracts has also been investigated in connection with the enforcement of antitrust laws. Jain et al. (2018) characterize market conditions that are more conducive to antitrust violations in supply chains, and demonstrate the implications of a court case ruling on supply chain members' behavior as dependent on contract type, for example wholesale price, revenue-sharing, two-part tariff, or slotting fee contract.

A supplier's incentive to improve its compliance practices can also be influenced by a buyer's voluntary disclosure of information to the public. Chen et al. (2018) study a buyer firm's disclosure of its supplier list, which in turn drives the NGO's perception of the supplier's behavior and the level of scrutiny it exercises. The revelation of the supplier list is always beneficial from a social standpoint, but the buyer's incentive to do so may be impaired if its reputational/financial burden upon a violation detection is too high. When there is limited visibility into the supplier's practices, the buyer can manage the supplier's incentive by optimally investing in the supplier's social responsibility capabilities and disclosing the available social responsibility information to the customers, as analyzed by Kraft et al. (2017). Regulatory mandate for disclosing the social and environmental risks in a firm's supply chain, however, may discourage the firm from measuring these risks. Kalkanci et al. (2016) underline the impact of such mandatory disclosures in reducing the firm's expected gain in market share and investors' valuation. Similarly, Kalkanci and Plambeck (2020) investigate whether or not a manager should learn about supply chain compliance risks, when they need to be reduced through investment in the supply chain, and whether they have to be reported to the investors.

Another topic that has received substantial attention among OM researchers is designing an efficient contract that incentivizes the compliance of a large population of small suppliers with limited bargaining power. Lewis et al. (2017) propose a partnership agreement between a big retailer and multiple weak suppliers in the presence of asymmetric information and moral hazard. This agreement differs from other widely adopted approaches that rely on external auditing and violation penalty, in that it is based on a sustainability index that measures each supplier's current compliance state. Motivated by field research in Indonesia's palm oil industry, de Zegher et al. (2018) address illegal deforestation of rainforests by smallholders who produce a global commodity. The authors conclude that deforestation can be halted if the buyers eliminate payment delay, and adopt a village-level incentive in which all farmers in a village are rewarded when no violation occurs in their surrounding lands.

In contrast to the works cited above, a number of papers demonstrate the unintended consequences of enforcement mechanisms that are commonly used in practice. Guo et al. (2016) study the role of consumer activism and show that, by engaging in actions to punish a buyer organization for any violation committed by its suppliers, socially conscious consumers may in fact contribute to less responsible sourcing practices in equilibrium. Similarly, Guo et al. (2017) show that having a larger population of socially conscious consumers may make the responsible firms worse off, recommending that efforts be first directed toward creating transparency in firms' practices. Plambeck and Taylor (2015) identify the conditions under which intensifying the pressure on a supplier by increasing auditing frequency, violation penalty, and publicizing negative outcomes may backfire for a buyer firm, driven by the supplier's incentive to engage in evasive activities (e.g., hiding information, second booking, etc.). Zhang et al. (2017), in their analysis of conflict minerals supply chains, caution that while penalizing manufacturers for their use of conflict minerals may induce more of them to become compliance-prone, doing so simultaneously drives up the price of certified metals to the extent that the opposite of the intended outcome may arise.

Designing the right supply chain structure for an organization is one of the traditional research topics in OM, and it has received renewed interest among scholars as a compliance enforcement mechanism. Litizia and Hendrikse (2016) introduce the notion of utilizing supply chain structure (e.g., the distribution of ownership rights and vertical/horizontal alliances) as an instrumental incentive for fostering compliance enhancement initiatives. They find that the structure that performs best in achieving this goal depends on factors such as vertical synergy, free-riding, and countervailing power in the supply chain. Orsdemir et al. (2019) suggest that vertical integration may help improve adherence to compliance standards, but caution that the effectiveness of this measure depends on whether horizontal sourcing is feasible and whether the demand externality between the competing buyers is positive or negative. Supply chain structure has also been examined in connection with its dispersion and traceability. Levi et al. (2019) specify adulteration in farming supply chain as a threat to public health, and show that farmers' incentive to preemptively or reactively adulterate depends, among other things, on how fragmented the supply chain is and, hence, how traceable violations are. Building on this insight, the authors argue that relying on end-product inspection is not sufficient for deterring adulteration.

Interactions among multiple firms in a complex supply network present nontrivial challenges related to compliance. Chen et al. (2019) develop a stylized model that captures such intricacies to discuss shared liability among buyers of a noncompliant supplier using a cooperative game framework. Specifically, they show that competing downstream firms' tendency to prioritize suppliers with lower degree centrality for their enforcement efforts, despite its detrimental impact on the entire supply chain, can be mitigated if a stable coalition is formed among buyers for joint auditing and sharing of auditing cost. Huang et al. (2017), in their study of a three-tier supply chain, observe that monitoring efforts by multiple downstream firms often substitute one another while they complement the most upstream firm's compliance effort. Their finding indicates that the equilibrium strategy always takes an extreme form in which only one of the two downstream firms (or none of them) exerts monitoring effort, and that sometimes the pressure from external stakeholders (e.g., NGOs) may backfire and reduce the overall responsibility level in the supply chain. Kim and Lim (2017) also study a three-tier supply chain, examining the possibility of collusion between the two upstream firms. They discuss "carrot-and-stick" strategies by downstream firms as a possible means to overcome this challenge and improve compliance, finding that the carrot strategy is more effective in incentivizing the supplier to act responsibly, while the stick strategy is better at preventing collusion.

Another group of papers focuses on the role of auditing in supply chain settings. Aral et al. (2014) consider the value of audits by third-party agencies in resolving the uncertainty about price-bidding suppliers that have unknown compliance performances. The authors show that selective auditing (as opposed to all or none) may be the preferred strategy even if suppliers are *ex ante* symmetric, as doing so impacts the level of competition in the supply network. Zhang et al. (2019) propose a dynamic auditing strategy that specifies the sequence in which suppliers have to be audited by the buyer and whether a supplier has to be dropped or rectified if poor practices are revealed. Chen et al. (2017) raise the possibility of a noncompliant supplier colluding with the auditor (e.g., through bribery) and thereby hindering the reliability of the auditing results. This paper elaborates on the implications of supplier–auditor collusion and suggests contracting strategies for the buyer that alleviate this risk. Auditing has also been viewed as an instrument for encouraging cooperation among competing firms. Fang and Cho (2019) develop a cooperative game analysis and propose joint auditing and information sharing (of independent audits) as two possible cooperative approaches to enhancing compliance. Similarly, Caro et al. (2019) address the inefficiencies of independent auditing, which is still the common practice in many industries. In particular, they show that buyers can improve responsibility in their supply chain and hence reduce the risk of public backlash if they form a buyer consortium. Caro et al. (2018) further add shared auditing as another alternative where audits are conducted independently but the results are shared among buyers. They characterize conditions under which either joint or shared auditing is preferred by buyers.

While the majority of papers cited in the last paragraph present analyses based on theoretical models of auditing, empirical investigations into various aspects of compliance audits have also appeared in the OM literature. Drawing on a large data set from a major auditor, Short et al. (2018) empirically analyze multinational firms' monitoring of their suppliers' labor conditions and show that suppliers are more likely to comply with codes of conduct when the auditing process is indicative of a cooperative approach, the auditors are well trained, and the suppliers face greater exposure risk. Short et al. (2016) underscore human biases in the auditing process, finding evidence that auditors report fewer violations of labor rights when they have visited the factory before, when they are less trained, when they are all male, and when the audits are paid for by the supplier. Using data from apparel industry, Caro et al. (in press) identify factors that increase the likelihood of a supplier outsourcing all or part of its production to other suppliers without the buyer's consent. The use of blockchain technology by the buyer has been suggested by Benjaafar et al. (2018) as a means to reduce the cost of auditing and record-keeping, and to address information problems such as moral hazard and adverse selection.

Finally, a number of OM scholars have shed light on other governance issues that potentially impact compliance in supply chains. Lee et al. (2020) propose collaborative governance as an alternative to bilateral coercion and cooperation mechanisms, where a coalition of competing buyers collectively addresses labor issues in the garment industry. Porteous et al. (2015) analyze a data set of survey responses from practitioner participants across different industries, and identify incentives that are attributable to reductions in social/environmental violations in supply chains. This includes, for instance, the promise of increased business in the future as well as training and information sharing initiatives. Toffel et al. (2015) empirically show that adherence of supply chain factories to codes of conduct imposed by multinational buyers is influenced by various international and domestic institutions. In particular, they highlight the correlation between the supplier's compliance and the attributes of the states in which the supplier and the buyer are located.

To summarize, in this chapter we provided a survey of works by researchers in OM who have studied compliance issues arising in the context of managing intra-firm and inter-firm operations. As discussed in the chapter, many of them shed new light on how to evaluate and design policies aimed at enhancing compliance.

REFERENCES

Alizamir, Saed and Kim, Sang-Hyun. 2019. "Competing to Discover Compliance Violations: Self-Inspections and Enforcement Policies." Working paper, Yale University.

Anand, Gopesh, John Gray, and Enno Siemsen. 2012. "Decay, Shock, and Renewal: Operational Routines and Process Entropy in the Pharmaceutical Industry." *Organization Science* 23(6): 1700–16.

Aral, Karca D., Damian R. Beil, and Luk N. Van Wassenhove. 2014. "Total-Cost Procurement Auctions with Sustainability Audits to Inform Bid Markups." Working paper, INSEAD.

Atasu, Atalay, and Luke N. Van Wassenhove. 2012. "An Operations Perspective on Product Take-Back Legislation for E-waste: Theory, Practice, and Research Needs." *Production and Operations Management* 21(3): 407–22.

Atasu, Atalay, Özner Özdemir, and Luke N. Van Wassenhove. 2013. "Stakeholder Perspectives on E-waste Take-Back Legislation." *Production and Operations Management* 22(2): 382–96.

Babich, Volodymyr, and Christopher S. Tang. 2012. "Managing Opportunistic Supplier Product Adulteration: Deferred Payments, Inspection, and Combined Mechanisms." *Manufacturing and Service Operations Management* 14(2): 301–14.

Ball, George, Enno Siemsen, and Rachna Shah. 2017. "Do Plant Inspections Predict Future Quality? The Role of Investigator Experience." *Manufacturing & Service Operations Management* 19(4): 534–50.

Benjaafar, Saif, Xi Chen, Niyazi Taneri, and Guangyu Wan. 2018. "A Permissioned Blockchain Business Model for Green Sourcing." Working paper, University of Minnesota.

Bennett, Victor M., Lamar Pierce, Jason A. Snyder, and Michael W. Toffel. 2013. "Customer-Driven Misconduct: How Competition Corrupts Business Practices." *Management Science* 59(8):1725–42.

Bondareva, Mariya, and Edieal Pinker. 2018. "Dynamic Relational Contracts for Quality Enforcement in Supply Chains." *Management Science* 65(3): 1305–21.

Caro, Felipe, Prashant Chintapalli, Kumar Rajaram, and Chris S. Tang. 2018. "Improving Supplier Compliance through Joint and Shared Audits with Collective Penalty." *Manufacturing & Service Operations Management* 20(2): 363–80.

Caro, Felipe, Leonard Lane, and Anna Saez De Tejada Cuenca. in press. "Can Brands Claim Ignorance? Unauthorized Subcontracting in Apparel Supply Chains (April 10, 2020)."

Management Science. IESE Business School Working Paper No. 74851, https://ssrn.com/abstract=3621141 or http://dx.doi.org/10.2139/ssrn.3621141.

Caro, Felipe, Prashant Chintapalli, Kumar Rajaram, and Christopher S. Tang. 2019. "Can Buyer Consortiums Improve Supplier Compliance?" In *Revisiting Supply Chain Risk*, eds. George Zsidisin and Michael Henke, 189–208. Cham: Springer.

Chen, Li, and Hau L. Lee. 2017. "Sourcing under Supplier Responsibility Risk: The Effects of Certification, Audit, and Contingency Payment." *Management Science* 63(9): 2795–2812.

Chen, Li, Shiqing Yao, and Kaijie Zhu. 2017. "Responsible Sourcing under Supplier-Auditor Collusion." Working paper, Cornell University.

Chen, Shi, Qinqin Zhang, and Yong-Pin Zhou. 2018. "Impact of Supply Chain Transparency on Sustainability under NGO Scrutiny (October 2, 2018)." Forthcoming in *Production and Operations Management*, https://ssrn.com/abstract=2590152.

Chen, Jiayu, Anyan Qi, and Milind Dawande. 2019. "Supplier Centrality and Auditing Priority in Socially-Responsible Supply Chains (February 14, 2019)." Forthcoming in *Manufacturing & Service Operations Management*, https://ssrn.com/abstract=2889889.

Cho, Soo-Haeng, Xin Fang, Sridhar Tayur, and Ying Xu. 2019. "Combating Child Labor: Incentives and Information Disclosure in Global Supply Chains." *Manufacturing & Service Operations Management* 21(3): 692–711.

Colak, Ahmet, and Robert L. Bray. 2016. "Why Do Automakers Initiate Recalls? A Structural Econometric Game" Working paper, Northwestern University.

de Zegher, Joanne, Dan A. Iancu, and E. Plambeck. 2018. "Sustaining Smallholders and Rainforests by Eliminating Payment Delay in a Commodity Supply Chain – It Takes a Village." Working paper, Stanford University.

Dhanorkar, Suvrat, Enno Siemsen, and Kevin W. Linderman. 2017. "Promoting Change from the Outside: Directing Managerial Attention in the Implementation of Environmental Improvements." *Management Science* 64(6): 2535–56.

Duflo, Esther, Michael Greenstone, Rohini Pande, and Nicholas Ryan. 2013. "Truth-Telling by Third-Party Auditors and the Response of Polluting Firms: Experimental Evidence from India." *Quarterly Journal of Economics* 128(4): 1499–1545.

Fang, Xin and Soo-Haeng Cho. 2019. "Cooperative Approaches to Managing Social Responsibility in a Market with Externalities." Working paper, Carnegie Mellon University.

Ferguson, Mark E., and L. Beril Toktay. 2006. "The Effect of Competition on Recovery Strategies." *Production and Operations Management* 15(3): 351–68.

Friesen, Lana. 2006. "The Social Welfare Implications of Industry Self-auditing." *Journal of Environmental Economics and Management* 51(3): 280–94.

Gawande, Kishore, and Alok K. Bohara. 2005. "Agency Problems in Law Enforcement: Theory and Application to the US Coast Guard." *Management Science* 51(11): 1593–1609.

Gray, John V., Aleda V. Roth, and Michael J. Leiblein, 2011. "Quality Risk in Offshore Manufacturing: Evidence from the Pharmaceutical Industry." *Journal of Operations Management* 29(7–8): 737–52.

Gray, John V., Gopesh Anand, and Aleda V. Roth. 2015a. "The Influence of ISO 9000 Certification on Process Compliance." *Production and Operations Management* 24(3): 369–82.

Gray, John V., Enno Siemsen, and Gurneeta Vasudeva, 2015b. "Colocation Still Matters: Conformance Quality and the Interdependence of R&D and Manufacturing in the Pharmaceutical Industry." *Management Science* 61(11): 2760–81.

Gui, Luyi, Atalay Atasu, Özlem Ergun, and L. Beril Toktay. 2013. "Implementing Extended Producer Responsibility Legislation: A Multi-stakeholder Case Analysis." *Journal of Industrial Ecology* 17(2): 262–76.

2015. "Efficient Implementation of Collective Extended Producer Responsibility Legislation." *Management Science* 62(4): 1098–1123.

Guo, Ruixue, Hau L. Lee, and Robert Swinney. 2016. "Responsible Sourcing in Supply Chains." *Management Science* 62(9): 2722–44.

Guo, Xiaomeng, Guang Xiao, and Fuqiang Zhang. 2017. "Effect of Consumer Awareness on Corporate Social Responsibility under Asymmetric Information." Working paper, Washington University.

Handley, Sean M., and John V. Gray. 2013. "Inter-organizational Quality Management: The Use of Contractual Incentives and Monitoring Mechanisms with Outsourced Manufacturing." *Production and Operations Management* 22(6): 1540–56.

Haunschild, Pamela R., and Mooweon Rhee. 2004. "The Role of Volition in Organizational Learning: The Case of Automotive Product Recalls." *Management Science* 50(11): 1545–60.

Harrington, Winston. 1988. "Enforcement Leverage When Penalties Are Restricted." *Journal of Public Economics* 37(1): 29–53.

Hora, Manpreet, Hari Bapuji, and Aleda V. Roth. 2011. "Safety Hazard and Time to Recall: The Role of Recall Strategy, Product Defect Type, and Supply Chain Player in the U.S. Toy Industry." *Journal of Operations Management* 29(7): 766–77.

Huang, Lu, Jing-Sheng J. Song, and Robert Swinney. 2017. "Managing Social Responsibility in Multitier Supply Chains." Working paper, Duke University.

Ibanez, Maria, and Michael W. Toffel. 2019. "How Scheduling Can Bias Quality Assessment: Evidence from Food Safety Inspections (February 11, 2019)." Forthcoming in *Management Science*, Harvard Business School Technology & Operations Mgt. Unit Working Paper No. 17-090, https://ssrn.com/abstract=2953142.

Innes, Robert. 1999. "Remediation and Self-Reporting in Optimal Law Enforcement." *Journal of Public Economics* 72(3): 379–93.

Jain, Nitish, Sameer Hasija, and Serguei Netessine. 2018. "Supply Chains and Antitrust Governance." Working paper, London Business School.

Kalkanci, Basak, and Erica L. Plambeck. 2020. "Managing Supplier Social and Environmental Impacts with Voluntary versus Mandatory Disclosure to Investors." *Management Science* 66(8): 3311–28. https://pubsonline.informs.org/doi/10.1287/mnsc.2019.3382.

Kalkanci, Basak, Erjie Ang, and Erica L. Plambeck. 2016. "Strategic Disclosure of Social and Environmental Impacts in a Supply Chain." In *Environmentally Responsible Supply Chains*, ed. Atalay Atasu, 223–39. Cham: Springer.

Kaplow, Louis, and Steven Shavell. 1994. "Optimal Law Enforcement with Self-Reporting of Behavior." *Journal of Political Economy* 102(3): 583–606.

Kim, Sang-Hyun. 2015. "Time to Come Clean? Disclosure and Inspection Policies for Green Production." *Operations Research*. 63(1): 1–20.

Kim, KiHyung, and Heejong Lim. 2017. "Carrot and Stick Strategy for Regulatory Compliance in Multilevel Supply Chains." Working paper, University of Missouri.

King, Andrew, and M. Lenox. 2000. "Industry Self-Regulation without Sanctions: The Chemical Industry's Responsible Care program." *Academy of Management Journal* 43(4): 698–716.

Kraft, Tim, León Valdés, and Yanchong Zheng. 2017. "Improving Supplier Social Responsibility under Incomplete Visibility." Working paper, MIT.

Lee, Hsiao-Hui, and Cuihong Li. 2018. "Supplier Quality Management: Investment, Inspection, and Incentives." *Production and Operations Management* 27(2): 304–22.

Lee, Sun Hye, Kamel Mellahi, Michael J. Mol, and Vijay Pereira. 2020. "No-Size-Fits-All: Collaborative Governance as an Alternative for Addressing Labour Issues in Global Supply Chains." *Journal of Business Ethics* 162(2): 1–15.

Letizia, Paolo, and George Hendrikse. 2016. "Supply Chain Structure Incentives for Corporate Social Responsibility: An Incomplete Contracting Analysis." *Production and Operations Management* 25 (11): 1919–41.

Levi, Retsef, Somya Singhvi, and Yanchong Zheng. 2019. "Economically Motivated Adulteration in Farming Supply Chains." *Management Science* 66(1): 209–26.

Levine, David I., Michael W. Toffel, and Matthew S. Johnson. 2012. "Randomized Government Safety Inspections Reduce Worker Injuries with No Detectable Job Loss." *Science* 336(6083): 907–11.

Livernois, John, and C. J. McKenna. 1999. "Truth or Consequences: Enforcing Pollution Standards with Self-Reporting." *Journal of Public Economics* 71(3): 415–40.

Lewis, Tracy, Fang Liu, and Jing-Sheng J. Song. 2017. "Developing Long-Term Voluntary Partnerships with Suppliers to Achieve Sustainable Quality." Working paper, Duke University.

Mani, Vidya, and Suresh Muthulingam. 2019a. "Does Learning from Inspections Affect Environmental Performance? Evidence from Unconventional Well Development in Pennsylvania." *Manufacturing & Service Operations Management* 21(1): 177–97.

2019b. "Reducing Waste by Learning from Environmental Inspections: Empirical Evidence from Unconventional Wells in Pennsylvania." Working paper, Pennsylvania State University.

Orsdemir, Adem, Bin Hu, and Vinayak Deshpande. 2019. "Ensuring Corporate Social and Environmental Responsibility through Vertical Integration and Horizontal Sourcing." *Manufacturing & Service Operations Management* 21(2): 417–34.

Pfaff, Alexander S. P., and Chris W. Sanchirico, 2000. "Environmental Self-Auditing: Setting the Proper Incentives for Discovery and Correction of Environmental Harm." *Journal of Law, Economics, and Organization* 16(1): 189–208.

Pierce, Lamar, and Michael W. Toffel. 2013. "The Role of Organizational Scope and Governance in Strengthening Private Monitoring." *Organization Science* 24(5): 1558–84.

Plambeck, Erica L., and Terry A. Taylor. 2015. "Supplier Evasion of a Buyer's Audit: Implications for Motivating Supplier Social and Environmental Responsibility." *Manufacturing & Service Operations Management* 18(2): 184–97.

Plambeck Erica L., and Qiong Wang. 2009. "Effects of E-waste Regulation on New Product Introduction." *Management Science* 55(3): 333–47.

Porteous, Angharad H., Sonali V. Rammohan, and Hau L. Lee. 2015. "Carrots or Sticks? Improving Social and Environmental Compliance at Suppliers through Incentives and Penalties." *Production and Operations Management* 24(9): 1402–13.

Shah, Rachna, George Ball, and Serguei Netessine. 2017. "Plant Operations and Product Recalls in the Automotive Industry: An Empirical Investigation." *Management Science* 63(8): 2439–59.

Short, Jodi L., and Michael W. Toffel. 2007. "Coerced Confessions: Self-Policing in the Shadow of the Regulator." *Journal of Law, Economics, and Organization* 24(1): 5–71.

Short, Jodi L., Michael W. Toffel, and A. R. Hugill. 2016. "Monitoring Global Supply Chains." *Strategic Management Journal* 27: 1878–97.

Short, Jodi L., Michael W. Toffel, and Andrea Hugill. 2018. "Beyond Symbolic Responses to Private Politics: Codes of Conduct and Improvement in Global Supply Chain Working Conditions." Working paper, Harvard University.

Staats, Bradley R., Hengchen Dai, David Hofmann, and Katherine L. Milkman. 2017. "Motivating Process Compliance through Individual Electronic Monitoring: An Empirical Examination of Hand Hygiene in Healthcare." *Management Science* 63(5): 1563–85.

Thirumalai, Sriram and Kingshuk Sinha. 2011. "Product Recalls in the Medical Device Industry: An Empirical Exploration of the Sources and Financial Consequences." *Management Science* 57(2): 376–92.

Toffel, Michael W., and Jodi L. Short. 2011. "Coming Clean and Cleaning Up: Does Voluntary Self-Reporting Indicate Effective Self-Policing?" *Journal of Law and Economics* 54(3): 609–49.

Toffel, Michael W., Jodi L. Short, and Melissa Ouellet. 2015. "Codes in Context: How States, Markets, and Civil Society Shape Adherence to Global Labor Standards." *Regulation & Governance* 9(3): 205–23.

Wang, Shouqiang, Peng Sun, and Francis de Vericourt. 2016. "Inducing Environmental Disclosures: A Dynamic Mechanism Design Approach." *Operations Research* 64(2): 371–89.

Zhang, Han, Goker Aydin, and H. Sebastian Heese. 2017. "Curbing the Usage of Conflict Minerals: A Supply Network Perspective." Working paper, Indiana University.

Zhang, Han, Goker Aydin, and Rodney P. Parker. 2019. "Social Responsibility Auditing in Supply Chain Networks." Working paper, Indiana University.

8

Compliance and Contestation

Fiona Haines

Abstract: The study of compliance is enriched when it is analysed as part of a contested landscape over the rules governing business conduct. This analysis requires going beyond the assumed connection between compliance and specific regulatory obligations, authorised actors or legal rules to interrogate its entanglement with multiple economic, social and political goals. The contours of this entanglement are often shaped by the tension between and within economic and social goals, tension that can be resolved either by supporting or challenging the status quo. Governments, and state authorities more broadly, bear primary responsibility for the management of the tension between economic and social demands. By modulating compliance obligations, these authorities can achieve temporary resolution of this tension, modulation that often, but not always, retains existing power relations. The chapter then focuses on which actors can challenge the status quo governing business behaviour by authoritatively calling attention to that behaviour as either compliant or non-compliant with legal obligations. Finally, the chapter explores the phenomenon of compliance independent from any connection to hard law, state-based regulatory regimes or courts and instances where acceptable behaviour, or a state of compliance, is not determined by regulators, laws or courts. Being able to define compliance independently from governments or law provides an alternative means to challenge the status quo governing business obligations. Here the chapter looks to international efforts to hold multinational businesses accountable for the harm they cause across borders. Efforts by local communities to demand that business meet social and not just legal expectations, namely that they comply with a social licence, provide a second example of compliance expectations beyond the law. Ultimately compliance, unmoored from a specific regulatory regime, actor or type of rule, becomes part of a fluid contested political landscape aimed at determining the rules governing business and commerce rather than a technocratic and restricted policy dilemma.

8.1 INTRODUCTION

This chapter sets out how the study of compliance can be used to provide significant insight into the political and social tensions that shape the rules governing business conduct. With this purpose in mind, the study of compliance needs to extend beyond three assumptions or purposes that are often associated with compliance scholarship. Firstly, compliance needs to be untethered from legislative or regulatory intent and interrogated as a separate phenomenon able to be used for multiple purposes in defining what the obligations of business should be. These purposes include, importantly, government modulating compliance expectations to manage tensions arising from public demands that businesses do more to reduce their social and environmental impact and business demands to reduce those obligations. Secondly, the study of compliance in the context of contestation involves identifying who, beyond the regulators themselves, succeeds in demonstrating or authorising behaviour as compliant or non-compliant with laws or regulations. Finally, compliance needs to be separated from its connection to a legal or regulatory obligation to identify who else succeeds in demanding that businesses comply with their desired standard of behaviour. When viewed through the lens of contestation, compliance emerges as a semi-autonomous tool used within a field of struggle over the social and political expectations placed on business activity.

The chapter is organised in the following way. Section 8.2 highlights aspects of the compliance scholarship that point to the importance of exploring compliance as a phenomenon independent from regulatory intent. Section 8.3 explores how different actors succeed in shaping the obligations on business by authoritatively calling out behaviour as non-compliant with legal obligations. These actors are enabled either where regulatory authority is explicitly extended to third parties, or where actors specifically take on that role, for example, through the creative use of civil litigation. Finally, Section 8.4 explores compliance as a phenomenon independent from a legal or regulatory obligation. Examples are given of this at both the international and the local level. At the international level, it is examined through international initiatives aimed at pushing compliance by multinational businesses with a range of developing, but still contested, expectations of multinational business conduct. At the local level, it is examined in communities demanding business compliance with a social licence, independently from any legal obligations that business may owe.

8.2 INTERROGATING COMPLIANCE TO UNDERSTAND CONTESTATION

Much regulatory scholarship is centred on bridging the gap between the intent of the law or regulation and the level and character of compliance. Substantive acceptance of regulatory goals is compared favourably with non-compliance or ritualistic adherence that may achieve only a semblance of compliance without a significant change in organisational behaviour (Braithwaite, Makkai and Braithwaite 2007). Possible ways to ensure such compliance – from responsive regulation (Ayres and Braithwaite 1992) and smart regulation (Gunningham and Grabosky 1998) to new governance (Simon 2004; de Búrca, Keohane and Sabel 2013) and self-regulation 'beyond compliance' (Coglianese 2003) – accept the goals of a regime as normatively desirable, with regulatory strategies providing a wide variety of means to reach those goals. Regulatory enforcement strategies are designed to overcome defiance (Braithwaite 2009), undercut material benefits from non-compliance and establish human connections that can educate businesses on the benefits of compliance (Braithwaite 2009). Sources of contestation between regulators and regulated entities tend to be premised on the assumed integrity of the intent of the regulatory regime where committed regulatees join with regulators in ensuring substantive improvements in outcome. Defiance, resistance and creative compliance are problems to be overcome.

However, compliance scholarship points to a more complex picture, one where compliance is used for a range of purposes beyond an evaluation of the nature of compliance with a given regulatory obligation. These other purposes can be specific – to call out non-compliance to reach a goal unrelated to the specific obligation (such as sanctioning illegal businesses or mobsters for tax evasion rather than extortion (Richman and Stuntz 2005)[1]) – or general – to frame compliance as a 'burden' and economically inefficient in order to push for deregulation. Debates and practices related to compliance can be used to prioritise economic interests over social concerns or to emphasise one social value at the expense of another. This facet of compliance as a window into contestation deserves attention.

Long-standing compliance scholarship demonstrates how the binary of compliance/non-compliance itself can also be used strategically to pursue a range of goals unrelated to the specific regulatory regime that invokes the obligation. Multiple laws pertaining to different regulatory regimes can be beneficial, providing diverse means to reaching an outcome not intended by the regime itself. In the context of research into how government agencies pursued consumer protection, Silbey and Bittner (1982) showed that regulators explored a broad range of legal avenues, beyond those specifically concerned with consumer protection. They concluded that 'a specific law may be invoked not only in pursuit of its own ends, but also for such other uses as law enforcement or private interests may demand in pursuit of other ends' (Silbey and Bittner 1982: 400). Interrogation of these other 'ends', or goals, is central to understanding the dynamics of contestation that may lie behind compliance.

Compliance scholarship also reveals the way in which economic interests can be prioritised over social concerns, or one social concern prioritised over another. Yeung (2004), for example, draws attention to 'overcompliance', a term that denotes a state of affairs where compliance efforts detract from what is economically desirable. The promotion of a goal of economic efficiency can often be embedded within ideological assumptions of the importance of free markets and the removal of social obligations from businesses (Chen and Hanson 2004). But this ideological orientation should not be assumed. Social goals can also be in conflict. Carol Heimer's (2008) work, for example, traces the challenge of when too much attention to complying with one regulatory requirement (in this case compliance with funding rules or concerns about research integrity) distracted from the social goals (HIV treatment and prevention) at the heart of the development program itself. In this case, the intent of social programs was undermined by well-resourced compliance regimes whose goals were tangential – or even counterproductive – to those social goals.

Ultimately, invoking compliance obligations on businesses is part of institutionalising specific values within a given society (Haines 2011). This can be messy, with the values and goals that underpin regulatory regimes coming into conflict (e.g. protection of human life [and whose life] vs environmental protection) either simultaneously or over time. In cases of conflict, compliance with one obligation takes precedence over another or compliance with one undermines the regulatory goals of the another (Haines and Sutton 2003; Haines and Gurney 2003).

How conflict is resolved in favour of one form of compliance over another provides an important insight into the rules governing business in a given place. Certainly, an explicit hierarchy of obligations may exist, for example in federal systems where constitutional rules determine precedence, or where there is some other mechanism of determining whose compliance demands take priority. However, such rules may not be present and even when they are, they are unlikely to resolve the contested nature of public value (Haines 2011). Regulators themselves may enter the fray vying not only for the attention of regulated entities but for a larger share of resources and support from governments to provide them with greater regulatory authority (Reichman 1998). As a result, regulated

[1] Note that Richman and Stuntz (2005) are critiquing the use of prosecution in this way.

entities may be pushed and pulled in multiple directions when called to comply with different regimes.

This messiness should not divert attention from the way that businesses shape the rules governing commerce, and hence what the compliance obligations on businesses are and what they look like in practice. As highlighted above, complaints about the excessive burden of compliance and demands to cut 'red' or 'green' tape (Chen and Hanson 2004; Haines 2011) aim to change the rules governing competition by removing regulations through, in Browne's (2020) words, obtaining a 'regulatory gift' (or perhaps more accurately a 'deregulatory gift') from government. Pointing to the burden of compliance can be part of a strategy by business to reduce their overall obligations to society. But this is not the only way in which businesses shape and use compliance obligations for economic gain. Compliance obligations can also be used by businesses to outcompete each other. A business may point out the non-compliance of their competitors to the regulator, for example calling attention to a competitor's lack of compliance with product safety standards (see also Chapter 5 in this volume) to argue that this allows competing businesses to gain an unfair advantage. Such accusations can be an important aspect of gaining commercial advantage. Business can also shape what constitutes compliant behaviour. Edelman and Talesh (2011) draw on an institutionalist perspective to show the way that symbolic compliance that is legally effective but substantively problematic emerges from interaction between the institutional field of business and that of politics and law.

Interrogation of compliance reveals much about which political constituents require appeasing at any particular time and place. To maintain their legitimacy, governments must manage the tension between responding to the demands of business for a 'more conducive' environment for investment and responding to public demands for greater protection from the harms that businesses generate. Bold legal reforms to curb business harms that appeal to one audience (the public) can be combined with weak enforcement to ensure political support from elites leading to the ambiguous nature of regulatory controls (Carson 1974). Non-enforcement has long been understood as part of a 'trade-off' with governments in their relationship to industry (Aubert 1952). The beneficiaries of selective enforcement, though, can vary with the audience whose political loyalty is needed to maintain power. In the context of poverty and the licensing of street vendors, Alisha Holland (2015, 2017) points to selective enforcement or enforcement as 'forbearance' in her terms, acts of political generosity aimed at assisting local constituents and responding to local needs. Strict rules around the need for a licence to run a business (to appease middle-class [or more authoritarian] concerns with social order) could be met in poor neighbourhoods with lax enforcement to support street sellers. It also allowed mayors in those neighbourhoods to retain popularity. Securing political legitimacy through the practice of enforcement and compliance is patterned and needs to be understood in context.

8.3 COMPLIANCE IN A CONTESTED LANDSCAPE: WHO DECIDES WHAT IS COMPLIANT?

8.3.1 *Calling Out Non-compliance*

Who can and who does bring non-compliance to the attention of the regulator and the law forms part of the arena where different actors can contest incumbent power and harmful business practices. Certainly, many regimes explicitly draw on a range of third parties – local communities, health and safety representatives, for example – to bring non-compliance to regulatory attention. The political challenges in enabling what Ayres and Braithwaite (1992) coined a 'tripartite' focus of regulatory enforcement attests to the underlying struggle for regulatory influence. This can be a powerful tool in enhancing the obligations of business (Haines 1997).

Not surprisingly, extending regulatory authority to a wider range of actors can be met with resistance. The strategies involved in resisting this extension include casting doubt on the motives of those so included. There can be some truth to these accusations. Indeed, regulatory regimes can be designed to appeal to multiple motives specifically to enhance the enforcement capacity of third parties. This can include a greater or lesser component of private gain (including compensation) alongside a concern with the specific goals of a regime. This includes Qui Tam provisions (Braithwaite 2008; Engstrom 2012), where the enforcement involves returning revenue to government together with the provision of a bounty. Yet, there is hypocrisy too. The financial motives of third parties can form a large part of the debate about the desirability or otherwise of these private enforcement methods (Engstrom 2012), even as an underlying profit motive for commerce itself remains unquestioned.

Civil litigation more generally is important in exploring the way that non-compliance comes to legal and regulatory attention through actors, in this case plaintiff lawyers, taking legal action against business. Certainly, the reasons behind such action are not simply regulatory (see Chapter 24) yet have gained a significant place in regulatory scholarship. Civil litigation covers a wide range of goals from being purely compensatory to being viewed as a primary deterrent against a wide variety of business harms. Indeed, both Qui Tam and civil litigation more broadly are part of diverse struggles aimed at increasing business accountability for a wide variety of social and environmental harms, notably tobacco (McCann, Haltom and Fisher 2013), carbon pollution (Haines and Parker 2018) and animal cruelty (Welty 2007).

Civil litigation takes contestation of whether compliance is required, and what comprises compliant behaviour, securely into the territory of social and political struggle. Litigation against tobacco, asbestos and, more recently, fossil fuel companies can reframe what compliance obligations are owed by business and under which legislative or regulatory regime. Governments can respond to such litigation by enhancing and bolstering these new obligations, by changing the status quo, or by curbing the capacity to sue and retaining it (Cummings 2007). McCann et al.'s (2011) analysis of tobacco litigation in the United States parses the various strands at play as the litigation against tobacco shifted from liability and compensation to conspiracy and criminality. From a compliance perspective, multiple efforts at litigation can be seen to shift the rules governing responsibility for tobacco harm from the individual affected through to civil corporate liability and finally corporate criminality. In this case the 'regulators' move from individual plaintiffs and class actions to state governments and health departments.

8.3.2 *Using State Law to Call Out Non-compliance beyond State Borders*

A focus on civil litigation as part of the compliance and contestation canvas brings the behaviour of multinational business into view. Here, accusations and findings of non-compliance are used not only to control multinational business behaviour but to extend the responsibilities of a specific state for corporate harm that takes place outside of its national borders. The intensely contested nature of non-compliance, not just the reality of harm or damage, resonates with the socially constructed nature of compliance referred to earlier. Here, the emphasis is on the social and legal construction of the harm caused by multinational corporate behaviour as 'non-compliant' with a legal regime that had not previously been construed as relevant in this context.

One prominent example of this dynamic is cases brought under the Alien Torts Claims Act of the United States. Litigation brought under this statute positioned the USA as an exemplary global citizen in terms of binding it not only to US law but to customary international norms firstly, with respect to torture and then, following this, to a range of serious social and environmental traumas wrought both by governments and by companies (Seibert-Fohr 2018). The narrowing of the statute's remit to require a direct connection to the United States in proving liability points to a reverse dynamic in compliance where findings of non-compliance are responded to by narrowing the pool of responsible actors. The successful construction of non-compliance through litigation in the international context is best understood as the successful creation of a new means to contest multinational corporate behaviour, with an overall goal of reshaping global rules and responsibilities pertaining to multinational business conduct.

8.4 COMPLIANCE IN A CONTESTED LANDSCAPE: COMPLIANCE OBLIGATIONS BEYOND (STATE) LEGAL AUTHORITY

This final section explores compliance and contestation by analysing how compliance obligations can be owed to institutions other than those enshrined in law and authorised by a state (at whatever level, national, provincial or local). These compliance obligations can provide some leverage in shaping the rules governing business conduct at both the international and the local level.

8.4.1 *Compliance with International Obligations: The Case of the United Nations Guidelines on Business and Human Rights*

In the international context, the leverage that can be provided by a successful claim of non-compliance, in the absence of enforceable legal obligations, is replaced by the leverage made available under codes of conduct – such as the United Nations Global Compact, the OECD Guidelines for Multinational Enterprises and the United Nations Guidelines for Business and Human Rights. This functional role-based account of compliance might not fit a purist definition, yet when understood as a means to an end within the context of the struggle over acceptable business conduct, the multiplicity of these regimes and actors that shape these regimes must be part of our understanding of the dynamic work that compliance and non-compliance are doing.

From a contestation perspective, the analysis so far has highlighted how a state-based regulatory regime intended for one purpose may be used to pursue multiple goals, some narrow, some broad. Demonstrating non-compliance can be how incumbent power, shaping the obligations on business, can be challenged. A similar process in challenging the status quo of international business conduct can be seen through utilising the compliance obligations owed under international codes and guidelines and hence is not restricted to state borders. There are three aspects to this challenge: through the ongoing interaction between compliance expected under these guidelines and reform to enable or resist stricter standards; through the strategic use of the tools enabled through these codes and standards to push for greater change, and finally by the reformulation of jurisdiction. Each of these three is iterative and dynamic.

In the first case, the efforts to increase the responsibilities of multinational businesses are met by resistance by those businesses and states that benefit from the status quo. Compromises are then found. The shortcomings of compromise then spur further demands for change. The ongoing negotiations around the Treaty for Business and Human Rights demonstrate this dynamic. The Guidelines resulted from the failure of the initial treaty negotiations and arose as a compromise solution (Ruggie 2014); the failures of the Guidelines have revitalised the treaty negotiations.

Secondly, despite the weakness of the Guidelines as a solution to multinational business harm, their existence does provide some strategic opportunities for leverage by affected communities and their supporters. Non-judicial mechanisms of redress called for under the Guidelines are designed to provide some accountability for non-compliance by multinationals to the Guiding Principles. Such mechanisms include the Compliance Advisor Ombudsman associated with the lending to private actors by the World Bank (that includes the International Finance Corporation (IFC)) and the national contact points required of OECD (Organisation for Economic Co-operation and Development) member countries. The character of these mechanisms can be diverse, with specific processes, procedures and rules. Nonetheless, the tools are more commonly shared – namely mediation and negotiation 'problem solving' strategies to provide redress on the one hand and shaming and condemnation of the activities of a multinational business on the other. Shaming and condemnation are facilitated through the publication of compliance findings in a 'Compliance Report' undertaken by the relevant mechanism. Mediation and negotiation can see some redress forthcoming (Balaton-Chrimes and Macdonald 2015; Haines and Macdonald 2019) whilst also allowing multinational businesses' non-compliance with human rights obligations to go unsanctioned. For communities, the limited avenues for redress may mean that mediation is the only option available to them. A damning report of non-compliance by a non-judicial redress mechanism against a multinational business can also be used by civil society activists to push for third parties such as investors to take their capital elsewhere (Macdonald, Marshall and Balaton-Chrimes 2017).

The third dynamic is that of extending and rewriting jurisdictional boundaries. Non-judicial mechanisms transform jurisdiction away from a state-based governance regime to one established by membership or through some obligation owed as a condition of finance. Examples of this include multinational businesses domiciled in an OECD member country in the case of the national contact points or, in the case of the Compliance Advisor Ombudsman, by virtue of being the recipient of IFC loans. Access to the leverage provided by non-judicial mechanisms and their compliance mechanisms depends on the reach or jurisdiction covered by that mechanism. Strategies extending or narrowing jurisdiction are common. One example that extends jurisdiction relates to a recent decision that communities can access a national contact point even where the business domiciled in the member state is only a minority investor in the business that has breached human rights (Balaton-Chrimes and Haines 2016). In contrast, multinational businesses can exit a jurisdiction and avoid scrutiny by, in the case of the Compliance Advisory Ombudsman, paying back their loans to the IFC (Balaton-Chrimes and Macdonald 2015).

8.4.2 *Compliance with Community Obligations: The Social Licence*

In the local context, the leverage that can be provided by a successful claim of non-compliance, in the absence of enforceable legal obligations, can be replaced by demands that businesses comply with their social, and not just their legal, licence. Compliance in the context of the social licence is interesting because it shifts attention to who has the authority to demand compliance as well as what the purpose is behind claiming compliance or non-compliance. To explore this dynamic requires attention beyond the dominant understanding of the social licence within compliance scholarship.

Predominantly, within compliance scholarship, the social licence is hierarchically organised underneath an obligation to comply with legal requirements. Social pressure in the form of a social licence enhances regulatory compliance, leading to companies going 'beyond compliance' (Gunningham, Kagan and Thornton 2004; Kagan, Gunningham and Thornton 2003). Compliance is tied to regulation, and the purpose of compliance with social demands or a social licence is measured by its impact on legal compliance. From a contestation perspective, this orientation to a social licence can overlook the way it is used to contest inequities that may be enshrined in law.

Contestation is prominent when the need for a company to gain a social licence and to meet community expectations is separated from – and potentially a challenge to – the obligations owed by business to law. Research demonstrates that vehement claims can be made by a community that a company does not have a social licence, even when that behaviour is legally approved. Here, the social licence to operate is claimed as social property (Curran 2017). Power is vested in the community to determine whether a social licence has, or has not, been awarded. The obligation of compliance with expectations is owed to the community, not to the state.

However, this assertion of an obligation owed to the community can be both shaped and contested by the businesses concerned. Invocation of the need for business to gain a social licence can be used to deepen the obligations of the business to the community (Boutilier and Thomson 2011). Enlightened self-interest of the company may result in robust and fair communication with local communities that can result in mutual benefit (Moffat and Zhang 2014; Parsons, Lacey, and Moffat 2014). However, this is not necessarily the outcome. Others highlight how businesses invoke the need for a social licence as a method of dividing and disciplining communities in order to justify their current business activities. This can involve classifying community members as either mature or immature depending on their orientation towards the business concerned, in favour or against, respectively (Mayes 2015). This latter dynamic resonates with Edelman and Talesh's (2011) work in looking at how (in this case) the social licence is constructed and framed to secure the legitimacy of business activity within a community yet at the same time not necessarily reducing the harms produced by that activity. In this case, the social licence legitimates the status quo.

In each of these three iterations, power and authority shifts and with it the significance of compliance with a social licence. In the first traditional compliance-oriented approach, authority is vested in the law with the aim of the social licence to secure greater adherence to the law. Compliance remains tied to conventional regulatory territory. In the second, power and authority over compliance are claimed by the community that seeks to exert pressure over business behaviour and often to expel business activity (e.g. mining) in its entirety. In the final orientation, power shifts dynamically between business compliance with a community's interests and community's compliance with business interests. A determination of business compliance with their social licence shifts in like manner, determined not by a state-based regulatory authority but alternately by the community or by the business itself.

8.5 CONCLUSION

This chapter has explored compliance through the lens of contestation. In doing so, compliance can be understood as a multi-faceted and flexible tool with many purposes. This chapter has outlined three ways to extend compliance scholarship in order to understand the nature of contestation and how it can either retain or challenge the status quo regarding the social obligations on business conduct. These three extensions involve untethering compliance from regulatory intent, extending the purview of who has or can successfully claim the authority to determine compliance or non-compliance and finally exploring compliance obligations on businesses beyond the purview of law and state-based regulation. When these lines of enquiry are pursued, it becomes clear that compliance can be put to multiple uses. Pursing compliance or demonstrating non-compliance can be used as tools to achieve goals and enshrine new norms governing business obligations that may only be tangentially related to the specific regulatory regime. Alternatively, pointing to a compliance burden and its consequences for economic inefficiency can be a way of reducing obligations placed on business. New actors who can determine what is and what is not compliant also bring opportunities to shape business obligations. Finally, interrogation of compliance with a view to understanding contestation involves an appreciation of the diverse range of 'authorities' to which an obligation for compliance is owed both at the international and at the local level. Ultimately, attention to compliance in the context of contestation brings rich rewards, not as a replacement for scholarship aimed at enhancing compliance but as a necessary corollary to it.

REFERENCES

Aubert, Wilhelm. 1952. 'White Collar Crime and Social Structure'. *American Journal of Sociology* 58: 263–71.

Ayres, Ian, and John Braithwaite. 1992. *Responsive Regulation: Transcending the Deregulation Debate.* New York: Oxford University Press.

Balaton-Chrimes, Samantha, and Fiona Haines. 2016. 'Redress and Corporate Human Rights Harms: An Analysis of New Governance and the POSCO Odisha Project'. *Globalizations* 1–15. https://doi.org/10.1080/14747731.2016.1223958.

Balaton-Chrimes, Samantha, and Kate Macdonald. 2015. 'Wilmar'. Corporate Accountability Research. http://corporateaccountabilityresearch.net/njm-report-viii-wilmar.

Boutilier, Robert G., and Ian Thomson. 2011. 'Modelling and Measuring the Social License to Operate: Fruits of a Dialogue between Theory and Practice'. https://socialicense.com/publications/Modelling_and_Measuring_the_SLO.pdf.

Braithwaite, John. 2008. *Regulatory Capitalism: How It Works, Ideas for Making It Work Better.* Cheltenham, UK: Edward Elgar.

Braithwaite, Valerie. 2009. *Defiance in Taxation and Governance: Resisting and Dismissing Authority in a Democracy*. Cheltenham, UK: Edward Elgar.

Braithwaite, John, Toni Makkai and Valerie A. Braithwaite. 2007. *Regulating Aged Care: Ritualism and the New Pyramid.* Cheltenham, UK: Edward Elgar Publishing.

Browne, Jude. 2020. 'The Regulatory Gift: Politics, Regulation and Governance'. *Regulation and Governance* 14 (2): 203–218. https://doi.org/10.1111/rego.12194.

Carson, W. G. 1974. 'Symbolic and Instrumental Dimensions of Early Factory Legislation: A Case Study in the Social Origins of Criminal Law'. In *Crime, Criminology and Public Policy: Essays in Honour of Sir Leon Radnowicz*, edited by Roger Hood, 107–38. London: Heinemann.

Chen, Ronald, and Jon Hanson. 2004. 'The Illusion of Law: The Legitimating Scripts of Modern Policy and Corporate Law'. *Michigan Law Review* 103 (1): 1–149. https://repository.law.umich.edu/mlr/vol103/iss1/1/.

Coglianese, Cary. 2003. 'Management-Based Regulation: Prescribing Private Management to Achieve Public Goals'. *Law and Society Review* 37 (4): 691–730. https://doi.org/10.1046/j.0023–9216.2003.03703001.x.

Cummings, Scott L. 2007. 'Law in the Labor Movement's Challenge to Wal-Mart: A Case Study of the Inglewood Site Fight. *California Law Review* 95 (5): 1927–98. https://doi.org/10.2307/20439128.

Curran, Giorel. 2017. 'Social Licence, Corporate Social Responsibility and Coal Seam Gas: Framing the New Political Dynamics of Contestation'. *Energy Policy* 101 (February): 427–35. https://doi.org/10.1016/j.enpol.2016.10.042.

de Búrca, Gráinne, Robert O. Keohane and Charles F. Sabel. 2013. 'New Modes of Pluralist Global Governance'. *New York University Journal of International Law and Politics* 45: 723–86. www.cambridge.org/core/journals/british-journal-of-political-science/article/global-experimentalist-governance/58CA5F5F83C954A22B2465FC3BE52A10.

Edelman, Lauren B., and Shauhin A. Talesh. 2011. 'To Comply or Not to Comply – That Isn't the Question: How Organizations Construct the Meaning of Compliance'. In *Explaining Compliance: Business Responses to Regulation*, edited by Christine Parker and Vibeke Lehmann Nielsen, 103–22. Cheltenham, UK: Edward Elgar.

Engstrom, David Freeman. 2012. 'Harnessing the Private Attorney General: Evidence from Qui Tam Litigation'. *Columbia Law Review* 112 (6): 1244–1325 https://columbialawreview.org/content/private-enforcements-pathways-lessons-from-qui-tam-litigation/.

Gunningham, Neil, and Peter Grabosky. 1998. *Smart Regulation: Designing Environmental Policy*. Oxford: Clarendon Press.

Gunningham, Neil, Robert A. Kagan and Dorothy Thornton. 2004. 'Social License and Environmental Protection: Why Businesses Go beyond Compliance'. *Law & Social Inquiry* 29 (2): 307–41. https://doi.org/10.1111/j.1747–4469.2004.tb00338.x.

Haines, Fiona. 1997. *Corporate Regulation: Beyond 'Punish or Persuade'*. Oxford Socio-Legal Studies Series on Regulation. Oxford: Clarendon Press.

2011. *Paradox of Regulation: What Regulation Can Achieve and What It Cannot*. Cheltenham, UK: Edward Elgar.

Haines, Fiona, and David Gurney. 2003. 'The Shadows of the Law: Contemporary Approaches to Regulation and the Problem of Regulatory Conflict'. *Law & Policy* 25 (4): 353–80. https://doi.org/10.1111/j.0265–8240.2003.00154.x.

Haines, Fiona, and Kate Macdonald. 2019. 'Nonjudicial Business Regulation and Community Access to Remedy'. *Regulation & Governance* online early. https://doi.org/10.1111/rego.12279.

Haines, Fiona, and Christine Parker. 2018. 'Moving towards Ecological Regulation: The Role of Criminalisation'. In *Criminology and the Anthropocene*, edited by Cameron Holley and Clifford Shearing, 81–108. Criminology at the Edge. Abingdon, UK: Routledge.

Haines, Fiona, and Adam Sutton. 2003. 'The Engineers Dilemma: A Sociological Perspective on the Juridification of Regulation'. *Crime, Law & Social Change* 39 (1): 1–22. https://doi.org/10.1023/A:1022499020874.

Heimer, Carol A. 2008. 'Thinking About How to Avoid Thought: Deep Norms, Shallow Rules, and the Structure of Attention'. *Regulation and Governance* 2 (1): 30–47. https://doi.org/10.1111/j.1748–5991.2007.00026.x.

Holland, Alisha C. 2015. 'The Distributive Politics of Enforcement'. *American Journal of Political Science* 59 (2): 357–71. https://doi.org/10.1111/ajps.12125.

2017. *Forbearance as Redistribution: The Politics of Informal Welfare in Latin America*. Cambridge: Cambridge University Press. https://doi.org/10.1017/9781316795613.

Kagan, Robert A., Neil Gunningham and Dorothy Thornton. 2003. 'Explaining Corporate Environmental Performance: How Does Regulation Matter?' *Law and Society Review* 37 (1): 51–90. https://doi.org/10.1111/1540–5893.3701002.

Macdonald, Kate, Shelley Marshall and Samantha Balaton-Chrimes. 2017. 'Demanding Rights in Company-Community Resource Extraction Conflicts: Examining the Cases of Vedanta and

POSCO in Odisha, India'. In *Demanding Justice in the Global South: Claiming Rights*, edited by Jean Grugel, Jewellord Nem Singh, Lorenza Fontana, and Anders Uhlin, 43–67. Development, Justice and Citizenship. Cham: Springer International. https://doi.org/10.1007/978-3-319-38821-2_3.

Mayes, Robyn. 2015. 'A Social Licence to Operate: Corporate Social Responsibility, Local Communities and the Constitution of Global Production Networks'. *Global Networks* 15 (s1): S109–28. https://doi.org/10.1111/glob.12090.

McCann, Michael, William Haltom and Shauna Fisher. 2013. 'Criminalizing Big Tobacco: Legal Mobilization and the Politics of Responsibility for Health Risks in the United States'. *Law & Social Inquiry* 38 (2): 288–321. https://doi.org/10.1111/j.1747-4469.2011.01270.x.

Moffat, Kieren, and Airong Zhang. 2014. 'The Paths to Social Licence to Operate: An Integrative Model Explaining Community Acceptance of Mining'. *Resources Policy* 39 (March): 61–70. https://doi.org/10.1016/j.resourpol.2013.11.003.

Parsons, Richard, Justine Lacey and Kieren Moffat. 2014. 'Maintaining Legitimacy of a Contested Practice: How the Minerals Industry Understands Its "Social Licence to Operate"'. *Resources Policy* 41 (September): 83–90. https://doi.org/10.1016/j.resourpol.2014.04.002.

Reichman, Nancy. 1998. 'Moving Backstage: Uncovering the Role of Compliance Practices in Shaping Regulatory Policies'. In *A Reader on Regulation*, edited by Robert Baldwin, Colin Scott, and Christopher Hood, 325–46. Oxford: Oxford University Press.

Richman, Daniel C., and William J. Stuntz. 2005. 'Al Capone's Revenge: An Essay on the Political Economy of Pretextual Prosecution Essay'. *Columbia Law Review* 105 (2): 583–640.

Ruggie, John. 2014. 'A UN Business and Human Rights Treaty?' Harvard Kennedy School. www.business-humanrights.org/sites/default/files/media/documents/ruggie-on-un-business-human-rights-treaty-jan-2014.pdf.

Seibert-Fohr, Anja. 2018. 'Transnational Labour Litigation: The Ups and Downs Under the Alien Tort Statute'. In *Labour Standards in International Economic Law*, edited by Henner Gött, 341–54. Cham: Springer International. https://doi.org/10.1007/978-3-319-69447-4_16.

Silbey, Susan S., and Egon Bittner. 1982. 'The Availability of Law'. *Law & Policy Quarterly* 4 (4): 399–434. https://doi.org/10.1111/j.1467-9930.1982.tb00284.x.

Simon, William H. 2004. 'Solving Problems vs. Claiming Rights: The Pragmatist Challenge to Legal Liberalism'. *William & Mary Law Review* 46: 127–212.

Welty, Jeff. 2007. 'Foreword: Animal Law: Thinking about the Future'. *Law and Contemporary Problems* 70 (1): 1–8 https://scholarship.law.duke.edu/lcp/vol70/iss1/1.

Yeung, Karen. 2004. *Securing Compliance: A Principled Approach*. Oxford: Hart.

9

Compliance as Management

J. S. Nelson

Abstract: Compliance – from the root "to comply" – is "the set of rules, principles, controls, authorities, offices, and practices designed to ensure that the organization conforms to external and internal norms." But toward what ends does management use an organization's compliance system? Compliance ideally has aspirational goals to at least discourage outright violations of the law, if not to encourage ethical behavior more generally. The methods through which management enforces compliance, however, can increase unethical behavior within the corporation and, in some cases, have incubated and helped perpetuate illegal behavior. As with all other tools, the tools of compliance can be abused. This chapter explores management abuse of corporate compliance systems, and it provides a caution about the dark side of compliance.

What is right in the corporation is not what is right in a man's home or in his church. *What is right in the corporation is what the guy above you wants from you.* That's what morality is in the corporation.

— a former vice-president of a large firm, as quoted in Robert Jackall, *Moral Mazes: The World of Corporate Managers* (Jackall 1988: 6).

9.1 DIFFERENT IMAGES OF COMPLIANCE

A common image of compliance often held by lawyers is a layer of checks that lies on top of a stack of other, more substantive sources of guidance such as laws, regulations, control, standards, and policy. In this view, compliance is merely the implementation of the established substance that businesses need to pay attention to. A full-color double-page stock image in the June 2019 issue of the D.C. Bar's *Washington Lawyer* magazine, for example, depicts compliance as a last red Lego on the stack of core building blocks with the labels above (Leon 2019). Compliance laid on top of this pile is similar to icing on a cake: good to have, sweet to the taste, and surprising to people when not there.

But this image both misunderstands compliance and epitomizes the blindness that lawyers often exhibit to the much more pervasive – and sometimes very dangerous – power of compliance within organizations. Compliance is not merely the aspirational implementation of rules and guidelines set forth elsewhere: it is an important tool for managers to exert control over the organization and the behavior that takes place within it. This control often has its own agenda and its own impacts. Moreover, the method by which the control is implemented has its own effects and messages. Lost in the lawyer's image of compliance is the dynamism of the push and feedback of compliance mechanisms. These processes have impacts. The more we learn about the intended or unintended effects of compliance, the more we should be careful about how we use its tools. For example, "[r]esearch suggests that when companies monitor an employee's every move, they signal distrust, which can lead to employee disengagement" (Filabi and Hurley 2019). Thus, "[m]onitoring employees can have benefits, but it can also decimate employee morale and, paradoxically, weaken ethical behavior" (Ibid.).

9.2 COMPLIANCE FOR WHAT PURPOSE?

Compliance, like every exercise of power and direction in organizations (Foucault 1975), conveys the messages that those in power seek to propagate. It also collects information for management. A better mental image of compliance might then be a vine that climbs through and binds the various layers of organizations. The tentacles of the vine may have been developed to transport guidance to stay on the legitimate side of laws, regulations, control, standards, and policy (to cite the D.C. Bar magazine's two-page spread again) (Leon 2019), but once those tentacles are established throughout an organization, they carry information in both directions. Management uses the network of tentacles both to push messages to the ends of the vine and to collect data on the behavior, thoughts, and even emotions of individuals in the layers through which the tentacles travel.

Compliance systems then can be abused. The fact that the positive image of compliance justifies the establishment of tentacles throughout an organization, for example, enables surveillance and invasive monitoring of the workforce. It also allows management to push employees to cut corners, thereby creating conditions ripe for widespread corporate wrongdoing. Tools are merely tools. We cannot be surprised when a tool ostensibly developed for one purpose is used for others. Despite the fact, for example, that the Internet may have been funded by the U.S. government to enable communication among computers for war planning (Cerf 2019), the invention has evolved to be dominated by shopping, cat videos, and misanthropic diatribes (Cerf 2019; Johnston 2017; Marshall 2015; Myrick 2015).[1] Similarly, compliance systems, even those idealistically intended, contain powerful sets of tools for control that, as applied, can have very different effects.

9.3 HOW MANAGEMENT MAY USE COMPLIANCE

Into this complicated landscape arrives management. In the corporate world, pressure to make profit typically incentivizes behavior at all levels of business organizations (Jensen and Meckling 1976: 307). Managers often understand their jobs to be pushing employees toward the goal of making such profits (ibid.: 308). Management is commonly defined, of course, as the "process of dealing with or controlling things or people" (Oxford English Dictionary n.d.). How to control people is the core of agency theory:[2] as taught in business schools, to align people within an organization and bind them to pursue the organization's purpose (Jensen and Meckling 1976; Jensen 1994; Shapiro 2005). Agency costs flow from people not doing

[1] Myrick (2015) notes that "[a]s of 2014 there were more than 2 million cat videos posted on YouTube.com with nearly 26 billion total views. That is an average of 12,000 views for each cat video – more views-per-video than any other category of YouTube content" (citing Marshall 2015). Johnston (2017), meanwhile, reports how "a Microsoft chatbot called Tay was given its own Twitter account and allowed to interact with the public. It turned into a racist, pro-Hitler troll with a penchant for bizarre conspiracy theories in just 24 hours."

[2] Merely to emphasize the point, "agency theory" as taught in business schools is not the same as "agency law" as taught in law schools.

what their superiors tell them to do in the way that the superiors want them to do it (Jensen and Meckling 1976; Jensen 1994).[3]

As we will see, the primary way compliance systems and incentives may be abused is to push employees to make profits at the expense of framing issues as ethical choices and engaging in more ethical behavior.[4] As Professor Lynn Stout has explained, "[b]eginning with obedience, corporations are hierarchical social environments in which employees are explicitly instructed by those above them in the chain of command"; and "[t]ypically these instructions are some variation on 'increase profits'" (Stout 2011: 169).

The following chapter will more closely examine examples of how different compliance systems have been abused, almost always to make profits. The chapter also examines in some detail recent situations in which compliance systems have been abused to the point of becoming oppressive to the employee experience, particularly in the fraudulent accounts and related scandals at Wells Fargo. It ends by describing recent push-back by employees at valuable technology, accounting, and consulting corporations, and with a reminder for management to consider how compliance initiatives may be experienced by employees.

9.4 THE RANGE OF COMPLIANCE TOOLS

The intended purpose of many compliance systems may certainly be to encourage lawful behavior. The American Law Institute (ALI)'s *Principles of the Law* draft on "Compliance, Enforcement, and Risk Management for Corporations, Nonprofits, and Other Organizations" describes the "nature of the compliance function" as "the set of rules, principles, controls, authorities, offices, and practices designed to ensure that the organization conforms to external and internal norms" (American Law Institute 2018: §5.01). The ALI's *Principles* describe among the major goals of the compliance function "[d]eterring misconduct by employees, agents, or others who[se] actions can be attributed to the organization"; "[e]nforcing the organization's code of ethics"; and "[i]dentifying violations of the law" (ibid.: §5.02).

When compliance works well, it may check the poor impulses of select employees or units and allow management to set a better tone for the organization. Compliance can be the conscience of the organization and help it to adopt best practices. Certainly, this is what compliance officers want to believe they can contribute to the organization's overall health (Nocero 2015).

In terms of how compliance initiatives may be implemented, compliance may have many goals and take many forms. Compliance literature now often starts with how best to execute a company's mission or vision statement of the type that Johnson & Johnson has literally carved into stone in the lobby of its headquarters (American Law Institute 2018: §5.02; Janes 2018; Zimmerman 2018). Compliance departments may also be more narrowly charged with ensuring that the company does not run afoul of laws governing its behavior and industry. Compliance departments, which are often staffed with lawyers but which may include data scientists, organizational psychologists, and specialists from other behavioral disciplines,

[3] Agency theory and its associated study of how to reduce agency costs have "had a significant impact on the intellectual agenda of the academy, spawning a massive empirical literature in management and organizational behavior. Agency theory has become a cottage industry that explores every permutation and combination of agency experience in the corporate form" (Shapiro 2005: 269).

[4] The author is not saying that this phenomenon happens in all business settings, only that this phenomenon can happen in business settings and needs to be discussed. Managers, lawyers, employees, and anyone interested in the welfare of organizations and the public should be aware of this potential.

apply their interpretation of guiding statements, however, for the rest of the organization through a range of methods from highly specific directives to very broad initiatives.[5] Specific directives tend to be procedural, such as to follow rules, regulations, policies, guidelines, checklists, etc. (Dwaraganath 2018). Broader initiatives may include nudges, rewards, pronouncements, the realignment of incentive systems, and other techniques to shape culture (Darcy and Hanley 2014). Companies may use a mix of specific directives and broader initiatives to achieve results (Sandford 2015). Additionally, as information about the behavioral reaction to compliance initiatives is fed back to compliance departments, their compliance methods and mix may be adjusted, sometimes as fast as on a real-time computer dashboard (see, e.g., LogicGate n.d.).

It is too simple to describe compliance efforts as merely fixed on a spectrum from specific directives to cultural change. A specific directive may have cultural impact and vice versa. Consider, for example, that the washing of hands in a hospital may start as a checklist item, but the directive may grow into a culture of safety in which employees will not allow a person to omit washing his or her hands before interacting with patients. Similarly, espousing a culture of safety may manifest itself in an entire team buying and wearing hardhats, which management eventually learns to incorporate into a workplace checklist.

9.5 SURVEILLANCE COMPONENTS OF COMPLIANCE

Surveillance to enforce compliance may have interesting effects of its own. There may be casual ways of checking on worksites, for example to confirm that workers are wearing their hardhats. This data may be initially collected with a human touch and involve a degree of human interaction. But the same data – and much more of it – could be more efficiently and perhaps more objectively collected through cameras and artificial intelligence (AI) programs scanning workers at each site for hardhat use. In a sense, introducing technology into surveillance techniques may start as a difference of quantity and quality rather than in the kind of data being collected. But once an employer possesses and analyzes significant amounts of data, having access to such data starts to change impacts as well. Increasingly, AI may scan for larger numbers of issues and put together clues that would evade human beings tasked with similarly observing groups of people. Meta-analysis of network data, facial recognition systems, and location tracking can all be used, for example, to map employees' social exchanges with astonishing accuracy in discovering who may revolt against a management initiative or soon leave the company (Scott 2019).

With the evolution of methods including technology, corporations are becoming increasingly good at implementing compliance systems in the shape of managing their employees and measuring output for conformity with sets of goals. But in our push to further increase management control of human behavior, we have not as often discussed when the tools of compliance may either be abused and/or actually push larger organizational behavior toward unethical ends.

9.6 THE DARK SIDE OF ATTEMPTS AT CONTROL

Compliance programs contain tools that managers can use to enforce objectives, both those set externally and those set internally. Control that is too intrusive, however, may push

5 See, e.g., Deloitte's paid advertisement to look like an article in the *Wall Street Journal* touting the company's expertise and description of compliance (Sandford 2015).

employees toward unethical behavior, and deprives business enterprises of the warning voices they may need to avoid large-scale wrongdoing (Nelson 2019, 2020, in press). Management has used compliance rationales both to invasively surveil employees and to push them through metrics such as quotas to reach company goals without thinking about the consequences of such pressure.

That compliance could have a dark side is suggested even by the word's origin, from the root "to comply" (Cambridge English Dictionary n.d.a).[6] Merriam-Webster Dictionary defines to comply as "to conform, submit, or adapt (as to a regulation or to another's wishes) as required or requested" (Merriam-Webster Dictionary n.d.a). To force people to comply is to exert control over them with the ultimate threat of punishment, as shown by the Merriam-Webster example of the verb in a sentence: "There will be penalties against individuals who fail to comply" (ibid.).

Regulators are part of the problem as well.[7] They may overly require companies to prove that management knows what is happening inside organizations, providing excuse and muscle for management ironically to develop the same mechanisms that can push wrongdoing. Especially within the financial industry, regulators have been insisting that companies collect and keep more and more data on employee behavior because they can (Noone 2019; Paul 2019). Regulators (and at times prosecutors who may effectively be regulating a company under a deferred or non-prosecution agreement) may justify encouraging such abuses of employee personal privacy on the ground that the company is monitoring for insider trading and other illegal or unethical behavior (see Barkow and Barkow 2011). And when something goes wrong within the company, regulators may interpret a company's decision not to have collected and monitored this information as a weak system of controls that invites liability (see Chapter 10 in this volume). Lost in this discussion between regulators and the company is any conversation about the impact that such invasive and constant monitoring has on employee morale, investment in the workplace, and concern about the overall ethical direction of the company.

9.7 MANAGERS' POTENTIAL NEED FOR CONTROL

It is a particularly toxic combination that surveillance may both satisfy regulators and feed a need for managers. As Brian Beeghly, founder and CEO of informed360, explains, "[b]usinesses need something tangible that they can latch onto and implement."[8] Indeed, as heard often in management settings, "[d]ata is the new oil": valuable for all kinds of reasons and helpful for running the world.[9] Surveillance becomes another part of management, defined as the "process of dealing with or controlling things or people" (*Oxford English Dictionary* n.d.: "Management"). Surveillance, however, by managers who "want to control decisions, and ... concentrate[] resources in their [own] hands" is "problematic because it is a self-perpetuating strategy" (Tyler 2014: 286). Additionally, surveillance over the long term "crowds out" other possibly pro-social motivations in shaping employee behavior (ibid.).

6 To comply is "to obey an order, rule, or request" (Cambridge English Dictionary n.d.a).
7 This was a point nicely made recently by Rosemarie Paul (2019).
8 Conference call on February 14, 2019.
9 The quote is commonly attributed to Clive Humby, a British mathematician and architect of Tesco grocery store's Clubcard. Although attributed to Mr. Humby in 2006, the words have been requoted many times since (Haupt 2019).

Meanwhile, a booming economic industry built around the monitoring and control of employees within organizations advertises itself for intertwined productivity and compliance purposes. As one website reviewing technology products detailed, "[t]he most comprehensive programs keep detailed logs of your employees' visited websites and applications, emails and online chats, keystrokes, created and downloaded files, print jobs, inserted devices, and even their physical locations when they have company devices" (Uzialko 2019). Additionally, the technology "should provide regular reports (at the intervals you choose) with easy-to-read statistics and visual breakdowns of employee habits" (ibid.). Managers can detail and customize their notification options for all types of situation, including "alert[s] if an employee downloads a document online or tries to access a forbidden website" (ibid.). Alerts and overview statistics can be used "in tandem" to provide an even more detailed picture of employee activities (ibid.). A product called "Humanyze™ asks employees to wear sociometric badges that use a combination of microphones, infrared sensors, accelerometers and Bluetooth to measure worker movements, [face-to-face] encounters, speech patterns, vocal intonations and posture to create data about how workers interact" (Ella 2016: 2).

The main U.S. corporate law cases out of Delaware are set up with this blindness as well. Under the landmark *Caremark* decision[10] and progeny (*Stone* v. *Ritter* 2006[11]; *Marchand* v. *Barnhill* 2019[12]), monitoring and procedures matter – the more the better – but the sincerity of ethical investment in the shaping of compliance programs may not. Thus, court decisions such as *Caremark* may in fact send a "'just do something' message invit[ing] a check-the-box mentality" (Langevoort 2017: 941). Furthermore, compliance programs may be used merely as "window dressing" for companies that have to respond, but do not want to substantially reexamine the pressure they create to reach profit-driven goals (Khanna 2003: 1231).

9.8 HOW DIFFERENT TOOLS OF COMPLIANCE MAY BACKFIRE

With this background in mind, we examine why certain types of compliance become problematic and why certain compliance initiatives go wrong. Starting first with versions of compliance that rely on specific directives, such directives often backfire, and in predictable ways.

There must be control and obedience to rules. But, as we discover from social science literature, adherence to rules may actually be counterproductive in encouraging pro-social behavior. Ethics defined more broadly as doing the right thing by others can be at odds with control and measurement. A notorious example of this distinction between compliance as obedience versus ethical behavior is the German universities' compliance with the Nazi "Law for the Reconstruction of the Professional Civil Service," which set the stage to remove ethnically Jewish and other professors from faculties (Schleunes 1970: 102–3; Chen 2019; Falk n.d.). As one historian documents,

> the dismissals of professors at German universities began in earnest with the academic year of 1934–35. In that year, 1,145 professors were dismissed or pensioned early. These constituted 14.3% of the previous year's faculty at all German universities. By the beginning of the following fall semester, 16% of the original 1934–35 faculty had been dismissed. By 1938 this figure had risen to 33% and by 1939 to 45% (Falk n.d.).

10 In re Caremark Int'l Deriv. Litig., 698 A.2d 959 (Del. Ch. 1996).
11 Stone ex rel. AmSouth Bancorporation v. Ritter, 911 A.2d 362 (Del. 2006).
12 Marchand v. Barnhill, 212 A.3d 805 (Del. 2019).

These numbers demonstrate excellent compliance. But the same numbers are also testament to terrible ethical decisions and dangerous results.

As Professor Gary Weaver (2014: 294) explains, within legal frameworks, "[i]nitiatives with 'compliance' orientations strongly incorporate and rely upon 'command and control' features." Enforcement messages through the Federal Sentencing Guidelines (U.S. Sentencing Commission 2018), as well as the Department of Justice's memorandum on the prosecution of organizations (U.S. Department of Justice 2019), and the requirements of the Sarbanes-Oxley legislation (Sarbanes-Oxley Act of 2002 (SOX)) all "focus heavily on 'command-and control' or 'compliance' activities, [by] emphasizing employee direction through formal policies and training, detection of wrongdoing through monitoring and reporting systems, and discipline and incentive policies to encourage proper behavior" (Weaver 2014: 293). He calls their approach "direction, detection, and discipline" (ibid.: 294). The approach is a product of the legal system's emphasis on "prevention through detection and punishment," as well as the need for "businesses, judicial systems, and political actors to demonstrate that they are doing their job by being able to show something concrete to the other social actors on whom their legitimacy depends" (ibid.).

There are myriad legal compliance rules and directives. As Professor Donald Langevoort (2017: 940) describes, "[i]n some fields (like securities regulation), statutes or rules impose duties to monitor or supervise, thereby making compliance an affirmative legal obligation." Under Section 404(a) of SOX, for example, the U.S. Securities and Exchange Commission prescribes rules both to "state the responsibility of management for establishing and maintaining an adequate internal control structure and procedures for financial reporting," and to require regular "assessment ... of the effectiveness of the internal control structure and procedure of the issuer for financial reporting." There are so many such legal directives that they can become numbing.

9.8.1 *Accounting and Training Procedures*

Another method of rule-based compliance in which companies often invest is accounting training and procedures, which are typically lauded as a way to keep enterprises from misbehavior (Complete Controller 2020). Yet relying on accounting rules may have negative impacts too. Accounting research confirms that the more that a manager in power has an auditing background and is incentivized with stock options, the more likely that there will be misstatements of financial results – a proxy for compliance misconduct – under his or her tenure (Albrecht, Mauldin, and Newton 2018; Shumsky 2018). A "combination of audit-firm experience and excess pay" appears to bring out the "'dark side' of accounting competence and raise[] the risk of misstatements" (Shumsky 2018). As Professor Anne Albrecht explains, "[a]ccounting competence is good because [these executives are] able to generate more reliable financial statements .... But it's bad because the knowledge of accounting procedures allows them to make the misstatements in the first place, and their knowledge of the auditing process allows them to hide it" (ibid.).

9.8.2 *Legal-Rule-Based Compliance*

Similarly, in the law-review literature, Professor Todd Haugh has noted how the rule-based compliance program at computer-chip maker Intel became an instrument of managerial abuse (Haugh 2017: 1217). Intel had developed an advanced system to monitor and report misconduct based on actively training its staff to understand legal rules and to think like the lawyers who would regulate the company (Yoffie and Kwak 2001). That legalistic approach drummed out the individual ethical compasses of employees. In suing the company, the New York Attorney General (NYAG) asserted that "not only was Intel's compliance program ineffective, but that it contributed to the company's illegal behavior" (Haugh 2017: 1217). According to the NYAG complaint, "[w]hatever the intention, … the actual effect of the program was to school Intel executives in coverup, rather than compliance" as otherwise understood as seeking to encourage legal behavior.[13]

9.8.3 *Culture-Based Compliance*

Because specific-directive-based compliance seems to engender these problems, there is a new interest in broader tools of culture. Psychologists and criminologists have discovered that this second level of compliance – cultural control – can be far more important and pervasive in shaping human behavior than solely rule-based deterrence. As Professor Tom Tyler (2014: 270) writes, traditional rule-based "deterrence is found to have, at best, a small influence on people's behavior." Research concludes that "the relationship between risk judgements and crime is 'modest to negligible' and that the 'perceived certainly [of punishment] plays virtually no role in explaining deviant/criminal conduct" (Paternoster 1987: 191; Pratt et al. 2006: 383; Tyler 2014: 270). Even in the corporate context, whether a law (or rule) is followed is "not related to perceptions of the likelihood of being caught and punished for breaking the law" (Braithwaite and Makkai 1991: 35; Tyler 2014: 271). Point-blank, studies find "minimal deterrence effects on employees' rule-following behavior" (Tyler 2014: 271). Instead, a better explanation than traditional deterrence for much of employees' behavior within organizations is an "intrinsic[] motivat[ion] to follow organizational rules" (Tyler 2014: 276).

But culture as part of compliance, if not tethered to explicitly ethical goals, can also be dangerous. Indeed, compliance, with its roots in "comply" can have an even more insidious implication to it in a cultural context. As cultural compliance is even more powerful at controlling behavior within groups than rule-based compliance, the danger of it suppressing and punishing non-conforming but helpful individual contributions may be greater. A broad and pervasive threat from cultural punishment emerges from compliance that applies "penalties against individuals who fail to comply" (Merriam-Webster n.d.a: "Comply").

To illustrate the socialization power of cultural compliance, consider that the secondary and obsolete Merriam-Webster Dictionary definition of comply is "to be ceremoniously courteous" (ibid.). To be courteous can mean "marked by respect for and consideration of others" (Merriam-Webster n.d.b: "Courteous"), which might be thought of as pro-social behavior, but it has a darker connotation too as merely "having or showing good manners; polite" (Dictionary.com n.d.: "Courteous"). Polite can mean "socially correct rather than friendly" (Cambridge English Dictionary n.d.b).[14] "Groupthink," as "tendency for cohesive groups to avoid a realistic appraisal of alternative courses of action in favor of unanimity," is politeness run amok – for the sake of social conformity, we may agree to actions with terrible consequences (Bazerman and Tenbrunsel 2011: 16).

13 Complaint at 20, *New York* v. *Intel Corp.*, No. 09-827 (D. Del., Nov. 4, 2009).

14 As the Cambridge English Dictionary (n.d.b) further provides as an example, "[t]hey're very polite in your presence, but you get the feeling they're laughing up their sleeves."

Professors Max Bazerman and Ann Tenbrunsel (2011) describe both "groupthink" and "ethical fading" in their landmark work *Blind Spots*. Their research into choices leading to the *Challenger* shuttle explosion exposes that a different mental framework may come into place for individuals within organizations when profits are at stake. Ethical choices may be reframed as "management decision[s]" (Bazerman and Tenbrunsel 2011: 16). "Groupthink" tends to prevent individuals from asking important questions. "Ethical fading" allows individuals to "fade the ethical dimensions of the problem from consideration" – even when human lives are very much at stake – by framing it solely as a business decision (ibid.: 16, 31).

With the use of cultural tools, the morals themselves of people within a company may shift dramatically from pressure to produce profit. As one executive reflects on his involvement in Ford's decision to place the gas tanks in Pinto cars where the company knew they would explode and kill occupants, in "two short years" within the company, he "engaged in a decision process that appeared to violate [his] own strong values" (Gioia 2017: 101). He describes the "socialization processes and the overriding influence of organizational culture, [which] provide a strong, if generally subtle, context for defining appropriate ways of seeing and understanding" information and making decisions in the business world (ibid.: 102). His own "personal identity [became] heavily influenced by corporation identity" (ibid.: 103).

9.9 SPECIFIC EXAMPLES OF DEHUMANIZING COMPLIANCE

When a highly competitive culture and the type of information being gathered for compliance programs are combined in the workplace, the impact on decisions can be especially dehumanizing. Examples show the increasing degree of control that businesses are exercising over the thoughts and actions of workers.[15] For the Uber driving platform, code developers laughingly describe techniques to "'trick[]" drivers "into working longer hours" for company profit (Fowler 2018). They "compare[] the drivers to animals: 'You need to dangle the carrot right in front of their face'" (ibid.). As the *New York Times* has reported, Uber "[e]mploy[s] hundreds of social scientists and data scientists ... [to] experiment[] with video game techniques, graphics and non cash rewards of little value that can prod drivers into working longer and harder – and sometimes at hours and locations that are less lucrative for them" (Scheiber 2017).

Inside the Disneyland Resort Hotel, "[e]ach laundry machine ... monitor[s] the rate of worker input, and flash[es] red and yellow lights at the workers directly if they slow[] down" (Gabrielle 2018). On scoreboards all around the facility, "every worker's name [is] compared with the names of coworkers, each one colour-coded like traffic signals" (ibid.).

The retailer Target "track[s] and score[s] the speed of minimum-wage checkout clerks" through its point-of-sale Checkout Game (ibid.). "[C]lerks [can] see themselves scored in real time on their point-of-sale computers" (ibid.). Amazon, of course, is famous for implementing similar systems in its warehouses, including personal tracking systems on the horizon to monitor workers' movements at all times (Yeginsu 2018). New technology in wristbands could "track where an employee's hands were in relation to inventory bins, and provide 'haptic feedback' to steer the worker toward the correct bin" (ibid.).

[15] Even when managers are aware of this issue, their actions can belie their words. At Facebook, for example, "[f]ormer employees describe a top-down approach where major decisions are made by the company's leadership, and employees are discouraged from voicing dissent – in direct contradiction to one of [Chief Operating Officer] Sandberg's mantras, [of allowing expression for the] 'authentic self'" (Rodriguez 2019).

Merely selecting one set of tools over others does not solve the problem. Primarily culture-based techniques even without data can be equally, if not more, dehumanizing for workers' ethical systems. For example, among its white collar workforce, Amazon "is conducting a little-known experiment in how far it can push white-collar workers, redrawing the boundaries of what is acceptable" (Kantor and Streitfeld 2015). Using culture-based systems, the company insists that employees in its headquarters be "guided by the leadership principles, 14 rules inscribed on handy laminated cards" (ibid.). Its secret feedback system "is frequently used to sabotage others" in an experiment labeled "purposeful Darwinism" (ibid.).

And cultural tools are rarely used in isolation. For example, to supplement the company's cultural expectations, "Amazon employees are held accountable for a staggering array of metrics" (ibid.). Before their business reviews, "employees receive printouts, sometimes up to 50 or 60 pages long .... At the reviews, employees are cold-called and pop-quizzed on any one of those thousands of numbers" (ibid.). As an employee summed up the experience of working at the company, "[n]early every person I worked with, I saw cry at their desk" (ibid.).

The net impact of these controls systematically pushes worker behavior at key points to enhance profits for the company, even as it takes away from workers' ability to engage their own ethical systems to prevent abuses or even consider their own interests. For example, a longitudinal study of changes in a UK manufacturing plant undergoing profit-driven transformation to "lean production" found "negative effects on employee outcomes after the implementation of 3 lean production practices: lean teams, assembly lines, and workflow formalization. Employees in all lean production groups were negatively affected, but those in assembly lines fared the worst, with reduced organizational commitment and role breadth self-efficacy and increased job depression" (Parker 2003: 620; Bulgarella 2018). The "negative effects of lean production were at least partly attributable to declines in perceived work characteristics (job autonomy, skill utilization, and participation in decision making)" (Parker 2003: 620; Bulgarella 2018).

9.10 CASE EXAMPLE OF WELLS FARGO

Finally, for an in-depth example of how the combined tools of compliance systems may actually drive the development and spread of large-scale corporate wrongdoing, consider what has been revealed about the 2015–18 scandal at Wells Fargo. At Wells Fargo, the full spectrum of compliance tools – specific directives, cultural norms, incentive systems, and information feedback – were combined by management to drive the shape and spread of misconduct within the organization. The tip of the iceberg of the 2015–18 Wells Fargo scandal was that the bank had pressured employees to open millions of fraudulent accounts. Wells Fargo now admits that it created 3.5 million fraudulent accounts that cost retail banking customers money and impacted their credit ratings (Bloomberg.com 2017). These fraudulent accounts, however, were not the only result of management abusing the organization's compliance methods to enhance profits on a broad scale. The bank also allegedly falsified mortgage documents to charge more on mortgages and to foreclose houses; improperly repossessed veterans' cars; charged customers for insurance that they did not need; charged mortgage payers late fees that were the company's fault; overcharged small merchants for credit card processing fees; and sold customers dangerous investments that the company did not understand (Wattles, Geier, and Egan 2018). The bank fired 5,300 employees for conduct it pressured them to engage in, and it admits that it may have systematically retaliated against whistleblowers (ibid.). The bank has settled some of these cases, while regulatory actions and litigation in others are on-going (ibid.).

Misconduct on this scale was not merely an oversight missed by the bank's compliance systems. Reporting reveals that compliance mechanisms were intimately involved in driving these behaviors within the bank. A former employee explained that "[t]raining in 'questionable sales practices was required or you were to be fired'" (Colvin 2017). As a former branch manager related "[w]e were constantly told we would end up working for McDonald's" for not meeting quotas (Reckard 2013). "Regional bosses required hourly conferences on ... [a] branch's progress toward daily quotas for opening accounts and selling customers extras such as overdraft protection. Employees who lagged behind had to stay late and work weekends to meet goals" (ibid.).

The bank's management tracked the activity it wanted to promote carefully through monitoring programs it had allegedly created to keep the bank on the proper side of the law. As the *Los Angeles Times* reports in detail,

> [t]he tracking starts each morning. Managers are asked not only to meet but to exceed daily quotas passed down by regional bosses. Branch managers are expected to commit to 120% of the daily quotas ... [and] results were reviewed at day's end on a conference call with managers from across the region .... [According to a former branch manager, if] you do not make your goal, you are severely chastised and embarrassed in front of 60-plus managers in your area by the community banking president ....
>
> Internal documents ... show how carefully Wells Fargo tracks account openings and lucrative add-ons .... The documents, dated from 2011 through October, include a 10-page report tracking sales of overdraft protection at more than 300 [California] Southland branches from Ventura to Victorville; a spreadsheet of daily performance by personal bankers in 21 sales categories; and widely distributed emails urging laggard branches to boost sales and require employees to stay after hours for telemarketing sessions .... A report this spring from a district in the Southwest provided a count of direct-deposit accounts opened by each of 11 branches during a 15-day period, also with the percentage of customers who signed up for overdraft protection (ibid.).

Under this type of constant pressure to satisfy company goals and cultural expectations, managers inside Wells Fargo pushed their employees to lie, cheat, and steal, and to bend rules to satisfy sales goals and make a profit. Employees were told to sign up their mothers, siblings, and friends (Glazer 2016); instructed to hunt for sales at bus stops and retirement homes (ibid.); and often targeted elderly clients and people who did not speak English well (Cowley 2017).

When employees protested that "This doesn't make sense" and "Where are you getting these sales goals?," managers would answer, "No, you can do it," or "You're negative," or "Oh, you're not a team player" (ibid.). Low-level ethical employees who reported to hotlines and through the chain of command were fired for insubordination (Glazer 2016). Wells Fargo human resources personnel admit that the bank had a playbook for watching employees who reported and then finding ways to fire them for other reasons (Egan 2016).

Harnessing the data-gathering and cultural tools of compliance to push such unethical behavior made sense from the bank management's point of view. There was money to be made in these violations, far in excess of fines the bank might have to pay. There were too many profits to be made from widespread wrongdoing for the corporation as a whole, and for top management in the form of stock incentives, for management not to rationally attempt to use tools this way.

Subsequent events demonstrate that the bank's management was correct, certainly in its stock price calculations. After revelations that Wells Fargo had created over two million fraudulent accounts (later revised up to 3.5 million such accounts), "[i]nvestors merely yawned" (Colvin 2017). On the day that news of the fraud broke, Wells Fargo's stock actually rose (ibid.). It had little impact on stock price that the Consumer Financial Protection Bureau (CFPB) identified the creation of the fraudulent accounts as a "widespread illegal practice," and that the bank paid a $100 million fine to the CFPB, as well as another "$85 million to settle with the Los Angeles City Attorney and the Office of the Comptroller of the Currency" (ibid.).[16] Despite these pieces of bad regulatory news, "Wall Street analysts were as nonplussed as investors; none of the 30-plus sages who cover the company – [number] 25 on [2017's] Fortune 500 – issued any urgent reassessments. Even three weeks later, with little break in the scalding headlines, John Stumpf, then Wells Fargo's CEO, was calmly telling a House committee that the scandal was 'absolutely immaterial'" (ibid.). Indeed, although Stumpf and then his successor Tim Sloan have since resigned, many critics remain skeptical that the bank itself has actually changed directions (Ensign 2019).

In financial terms, Wells Fargo's CEO and the banking analysts were also correct to push for profit. "The company would go on to earn $5.3 billion in the quarter following the scandal – and another $5.5 billion in the most recent period, ending in March [2017]" (Colvin 2017).[17] Wells Fargo's "earnings streak . . . now runs to 18 consecutive quarters of profit above $5 billion, a feat achieved only by one other company in recent history: Apple" (ibid.). Even in 2016, "Wells Fargo was the fourth-most-profitable company [in the public market] overall, trailing only Apple, JPMorgan Chase, and Berkshire Hathaway" (ibid.).

In the Wells Fargo example, one might merely claim that the bank had the wrong metrics in place and attempt to excuse management's broader effort to control behavior within the organization. But evidence from the banking industry points the finger squarely at problems with banking culture as well. All parts of compliance systems were suspect. Management research on identity theory shows that bankers' cultural identity qua bankers has an important impact on behavior (Cohn, Fehr, and Maréchal 2014: 86–9). Without the triggering of their professional identities, "bank employees behave honestly on average in the control condition" (ibid.: 88). The moment that bankers' "professional identity as bank employees is rendered salient"[18] during experimentation, "a significant portion of them become dishonest" (ibid.: 86).[19] Moreover, bank "employees in core business units [become] more dishonest than those in support units" (ibid.: 87). These results are particular to industry culture because the triggers did not hold outside of banking (ibid.: 88).[20] As the authors of the study suggest, banks may then have to undertake a far larger ethical initiative to "encourage

16 Settlements for $65 million with the State of New York and for $575 million with state attorneys general were announced in December 2018 (Cowley and Flitter 2018). The bank is additionally planning to pay $480 million to settle a shareholder class-action suit (Ibid.).

17 Additional disciplinary actions by the Federal Reserve limiting Wells Fargo's growth and forcing the company to replace three directors were imposed in February 2018, and it is unclear what the effects from those actions will be (U.S. Federal Reserve 2018).

18 Specifically, "[t]he frequency of bank-related words in the professional identity condition was increased by 40%, from 26% in the control to 36% (P= 0.035, rank-sum test), indicating that our manipulation [to trigger the bankers' professional identities] was successful" (Cohn, Fehr, and Maréchal 2014: 87).

19 As a group, the bank employees whose professional identities had been triggered reported "58.2% successful coin flips, which is significantly above chance (95% confidence interval: 53%, 63%) and significantly higher than the success rate reported by the control group" (Cohn, Fehr, and Maréchal 2014: 87).

20 "[T]he professional identity condition had no significant influence on dishonest behavior in non-banking employees (P = 0.123, rank-sum test; Fig. 3a and Extended Data Fig. 3)" (Cohn, Fehr, and Maréchal 2014: 88).

honest behaviors by changing the norms associated with their workers' professional identity" (ibid.).

9.11 WHAT WE SHOULD LEARN FROM THESE EXAMPLES AND DISCUSSION

So what cautions should we keep in mind from these examples of compliance systems either going off the rails or being systematically abused to achieve higher profits at the expense of ethical behavior? Compliance is powerful. And it can be dangerous. As we increase compliance – "the set of rules, principles, controls, authorities, offices, and practices designed to ensure that the organization conforms to external and internal norms" (American Law Institute 2018: § 5.01) – we risk losing the ethical engagement of workers that keeps organizations from veering toward the large-scale wrongdoing we have seen at Wells Fargo and other businesses.

Workers should not merely be sent the message that they are to enhance management's profits. Changing why that message is sent within corporations will have to be part of a broader movement to reconceive corporate purpose as more focused on creating social value and respecting corporate stakeholders (Mayer 2012, 2018: 2). Such changes may slowly be coming.[21] Meanwhile, within compliance systems that will interpret these new statements of corporate purpose, there must be mechanisms to engage employees' ethical systems. With the increasing sophistication of management techniques, including harnessing the tools of compliance, we are becoming ever better at manipulating human behavior within groups. We need to confront how we use those tools and what ethical checks there should be on these systems.

9.11.1 *Revolts Against Control Techniques*

Interestingly, revolts against some of these control techniques are coming from amongst the most highly paid and valued of employees, including those who design many of the surveillance and control systems: tech and knowledge workers.[22] In August 2018, 1,400 Google employees signed a letter protesting the use of their work without their consent on a search engine for China that allegedly blocked specific searches and linked searches to users' phone numbers for monitoring by the Chinese government (Menegus 2018; Smith 2018). Employees were concerned that the secret project known as "Dragonfly" would make Google and its employees complicit in human rights abuses in China (Robertson 2018). In November 2018, employees signed an additional letter pushing the company to cancel the project (ibid.).

Similarly, in October 2018, Amazon and Microsoft employees published open letters protesting U.S. military application of their work (Cuthbertson 2018). Further employee protests have sparked at the software firm Salesforce, the management consulting firm McKinsey, and the accounting firm Deloitte over those companies' involvement in helping the U.S. government separate immigrant children from their families (MacLellan 2018).

[21] In August 2019, the U.S. Business Roundtable, for example, released a new statement of corporate purpose that, according to the group's own press release "[r]edefines the [p]urpose of a [c]orporation to [p]romote '[a]n [e]conomy [t]hat [s]erves [a]ll Americans." The new joint statement "[m]oves [a]way from [s]hareholder [p]rimacy," and "[i]ncludes [a] [c]ommitment to [a]ll [of a businesses' s]takeholders[:]" "customers, employees, suppliers, communities and shareholders" (U.S. Business Roundtable 2019).

[22] These highly paid and valued workers are the group that one of the fathers of modern management, Peter Drucker, wrote "will be the group that gives the emerging knowledge society its character, its leadership, its social profile" (Drucker 2001: 307).

McKinsey employees have pressured management over revelations that McKinsey enabled corruption and worked for dictators around the world (Bogdanich and Forsythe 2018a, 2018b; Breland 2018).

Protests at Google over Dragonfly and Project Maven, Google's own U.S. Department of Defense project, sparked the resignation of dozens of key scientists and academics who are difficult to replace given publicity surrounding the company's choices (Shane, Metz, and Wakabayashi 2018). Accordingly, Google, whose company mantra used to be "Don't Be Evil," may be listening more to its employees' ethical warnings, as those systems are meant to function (ibid.). Google has announced that it will end its involvement with Project Maven by 2019 and not take on more military contracts (Wakabayashi and Shane 2018).

Throughout compliance runs an inevitable tension between two strong forces: management's desire for control on the one hand, and a need for productive employee engagement on the other. Social psychologists and organizational behaviorists in management departments and elsewhere have written that "without a values or ethics base to crowd out excessive legalism in compliance, compliance programs would predictably fall short" (Langevoort 2017: 942). In order to achieve more pro-social outcomes within organizations, cultures must be more "values-based" and "anti-command and control" (ibid.: 946). The best motivators are when the rules of an organization comport with employees' own values, bestowing "legitimacy, morality, and the general role of fairness in shaping social behavior" (Tyler 2014: 276).

9.11.2 *Hearing the Voice of Employee Ethical Engagement*

At its best, management's desire for control is tempered to hear the individual voices of employees and encourage their ethical engagement in their work. Similarly, employee engagement energizes employees to think broadly about their jobs, consider how to improve the work they do for the benefit of the company, and bring their best personal qualities and judgment to their work. Indeed, some companies emphasize that "[g]ood leaders establish standards and guidelines and then give their employees the autonomy and independence to work the way they work best within those guidelines" (Haden 2019). In evaluating the quality of its managers as leaders, Google, for example, administers a survey asking the manager's employees how much they agree with statements such as "[m]y manager does not 'micro-manage' (get involved in details that should be handled at other levels)"; "[m]y manager shows consideration for me as a person"; and "[t]he actions of my manager show that he/she values the perspective I bring to the team, even if it is different from his/her own" (ibid.).

In creating compliance programs, then, the best results for a company occur when a program values not only conformity and efficiency but also the contributions and ethical engagement of employees at all levels (Nelson in press). There is otherwise a moral dissonance for employees that hinders their work,[23] and which corporations need to listen to as a sign of larger-scale ethical trouble ahead (ibid.). Ideally, there should not be a significant gap for employees between "what is right in the corporation [as] what the guy above you wants from you" versus "what is right in a man's home or in his church" (Jackall 1988: 6).

[23] Employees who receive an unethical order perform worse on cognitive tasks, suffer increased anxiety, and lose intrinsic job motivation (Nelson and Stout in press; Smith, Kouchaki, and Wareham 2013).

9.12 CONCLUSION

In sum, ensuring that employees remain ethically engaged and listening to employees' ethical warnings should be central to a new model of compliance. Instead of being based in legal top-down obedience, ethical compliance should be rooted in employee engagement to keep the organization thinking about its purpose and the social implications of its behavior. With the tech and knowledge workers of the future leading the way, the hope is that more workers can safely preserve their moral engagement against invasive management control to remain central to compliance, and to keep it as it should ideally be: part of the conscience of the places in which they work.

REFERENCES

Albrecht, A., Mauldin, E., and Newton, N. 2018. "Do Auditors Recognize the Potential Dark Side of Executives' Accounting Competence?" *Accounting Review* (January 25), https://doi.org/10.2308/accr-52028.

American Law Institute 2018. *Principles of the Law: Compliance, Enforcement, and Risk Management for Corporations, Nonprofits, and Other Organizations*, Council Draft No. 1.

Barkow, A., and Barkow, R. 2011. "Introduction," in *Prosecutors in the Boardroom: Using Criminal Law to Regulate Corporate Conduct*. New York University Press, 1–10.

Bazerman, M. D. and Tenbrunsel, A. 2011. *Blind Spots: Why We Fail to Do What's Right and What to Do about It*. Princeton University Press.

Bloomberg.com 2017. "Wells Fargo Boosts Fake-Account Estimate 67% to 3.5 Million" (August 31), www.bloomberg.com/news/articles/2017–08-31/wells-fargo-increases-fake-account-estimate-67-to-3–5-million.

Bogdanich, W., and Forsythe, M. 2018a. "How McKinsey Has Helped Raise the Stature of Authoritarian Governments," *New York Times* (December 15), www.nytimes.com/2018/12/15/world/asia/mckinsey-china-russia.html.

2018b. "'Exhibit A': How McKinsey Got Entangled in a Bribery Case," *New York Times* (December 30), www.nytimes.com/2018/12/30/world/mckinsey-bribes-boeing-firtash-extradition.html.

Braithwaite, J., and Makkai, T. 1991. "Testing an Expected Utility Model of Corporate Deterrence." *Law and Society Review* 25(1): 7–40.

Breland, A. 2018. "Accenture Workers Join Tech Protests of Contracts with US Border Enforcement," *The Hill* (November 15), https://thehill.com/policy/technology/417061-accenture-workers-join-tech-protests-of-contracts-with-us-border (describing actions at various companies as a result of employee unrest).

Bulgarella, C. 2018. "Why Companies Should Resist Data Chaining Themselves and Their Employees," LinkedIn (March 15), www.linkedin.com/pulse/why-companies-should-resist-data-chaining-themselves-bulgarella.

Cambridge English Dictionary, n.d.a. "Comply" (accessed December 5, 2018), https://dictionary.cambridge.org/us/dictionary/english/comply.

n.d.b. "Polite" (accessed December 5, 2018), https://dictionary.cambridge.org/us/dictionary/english/polite.

Cerf, V. n.d. "A Brief History of the Internet & Related Networks," *The Internet Society.Org* (accessed September 1, 2019), www.internetsociety.org/internet/history-internet/brief-history-internet-related-networks.

Chen, H. (Hui Chen Ethics) 2019. "Designing Wise & Ethical Limits to Speech Panel," Ethical Systems Conference, New York (March 15).

Cohn, A., Fehr, E., and Maréchal, M.E. 2014. "Business Culture and Dishonesty in the Banking Industry." *Nature* 516(7529) (December), https://doi.org/10.1038/nature13977.

Colvin, G. 2017. "Inside Wells Fargo's Plan to Fix Its Culture Post-Scandal," *Fortune* (June 11), http://fortune.com/2017/06/11/wells-fargo-scandal-culture/.

Complete Controller 2020. "Ensuring Compliance with Accounting Standards – The No Go Area for Business" (March 16), www.completecontroller.com/ensuring-compliance-with-accounting-standards-the-no-go-area-for-business/.

Cowley, S. 2017. "Wells Fargo Workers Claim Retaliation for Playing by the Rules," *New York Times* (December 21), www.nytimes.com/2016/09/27/business/dealbook/wells-fargo-workers-claim-retaliation-for-playing-by-the-rules.html.

Cowley, S., and Flitter, E. 2018. "Wells Fargo Agrees to Pay $575 Million to Resolve State Investigations," *New York Times* (December 29), www.nytimes.com/2018/12/28/business/wells-fargo-settlement.html.

Cuthbertson, A. 2018. "Microsoft and Amazon Workers Are Questioning Their Firms' Morality," *The Independent* (October 18), www.independent.co.uk/life-style/gadgets-and-tech/news/microsoft-amazon-military-ai-protest-workers-jedi-rekognition-contract-pentagon-a8590016.html.

Darcy, K., and Hanley, G. (for Deloitte) 2014. "Ethics and Compliance Programs: Moving from 'Good Enough' to 'Great'," *Risk and Compliance Journal* (a publication of the *Wall Street Journal*) (April 14), https://deloitte.wsj.com/riskandcompliance/2014/04/14/ethics-and-compliance-programs-moving-from-good-enough-to-great/.

Dictionary.com n.d. "Courteous" (accessed December 5, 2018), www.dictionary.com/browse/courteous.

Drucker, P. 2001. "A Century of Social Transformation–Emergence of Knowledge Society." In *The Essential Drucker* (Collins Business Essentials). Butterworth-Heinemann.

Dwaraganath, S. 2018. "Creating a Culture of Ethics & Compliance in the Workplace," *Corporate Compliance Insights* (October 5), www.corporatecomplianceinsights.com/creating-a-culture-of-ethics-compliance-in-the-workplace/.

Egan, M. 2016. "Wells Fargo Workers: I Called the Ethics Line and Was Fired," *CNN Money* (September 21), https://money.cnn.com/2016/09/21/investing/wells-fargo-fired-workers-retaliation-fake-accounts.

Ella, J. V. 2016. "Employee Monitoring and Workplace Privacy Law," *American Bar Association, Section on Labor and Employment Law* (April).

Ensign, R. 2019. "Wells Fargo CEO Tim Sloan Steps Down," *Wall Street Journal* (March 28), www.wsj.com/articles/wells-fargo-said-ceo-timothy-sloan-will-step-down–11553804261.

Falk, G. n.d. "The Expulsion of the Professors from the Universities in Nazi Germany, 1933–1941," *JBuff.com* (accessed April 5, 2019), http://jbuff.com/c013102.htm.

Filabi, A., and Hurley, R. 2019. "The Paradox of Employee Surveillance," *Behavioral Scientist* (February 18), https://behavioralscientist.org/the-paradox-of-employee-surveillance/.

Foucault, M. 1975. *Discipline & Punish: The Birth of the Prison*, Alan Sheridan trans. 1995, Vintage Books.

Fowler, S. 2018. "'What Have We Done?': Silicon Valley Engineers Fear They've Created a Monster," *Vanity Fair* (September), www.vanityfair.com/news/2018/08/silicon-valley-engineers-fear-they-created-a-monster.

Gabrielle, V. 2018. "How Employers Have Gamified Work for Maximum Profit," *Aeon* (October 10), https://aeon.co/essays/how-employers-have-gamified-work-for-maximum-profit.

Gioia, D. 2017. "Reflections on the Pinto Fires Case," as republished in L. Treviño and K. Nelson, *Managing Business Ethics: Straight Talk about How to Do It Right*, 7th ed. Wiley.

Glazer, E. 2016. "How Wells Fargo's High-Pressure Sales Culture Spiraled Out of Control," *Wall Street Journal* (September 16), www.wsj.com/articles/how-wells-fargos-high-pressure-sales-culture-spiraled-out-of-control–1474053044.

Haden, J. 2019. "Here's How Google Knows in Less Than 5 Minutes If Someone Is a Great Leader," *Inc. Com* (April 19), https://www.inc.com/jeff-haden/heres-how-google-knows-in-less-than-5-minutes-if-someone-is-a-great-leader.html.

Haugh, T. 2017. "The Criminalization of Compliance," *Notre Dame Law Review* 92(3): 1215–69.

Haupt, M. 2019. "Who Should Get Credit for the Quote 'Data Is the New Oil'?," *Quora* (November 4), www.quora.com/Who-should-get-credit-for-the-quote-data-is-the-new-oil.

Jackall, R. 1988. *Moral Mazes: The World of Corporate Managers*. Oxford University Press.

James, E. 2018. "8 Fun Facts About Our Credo – Johnson & Johnson's Mission Statement," *Johnson & Johnson (jnj.com)*, (February 5), www.jnj.com/our-heritage/8-fun-facts-about-the-johnson-johnson-credo.

Jensen, M. 1994. "Self-Interest, Altruism, Incentives, and Agency Theory." *Journal of Applied Corporate Finance* 7(2): 40–5.
Jensen, M., and Meckling, W. 1976. "Theory of the Firm: Managerial Behavior, Agency Costs and Ownership Structure." *Journal of Financial Economics* 3(4), https://doi.org/10.1016/0304-405X(76)90026-X.
Johnston, I. 2017. "AI Robots Learning Racism, Sexism and Other Prejudices from Humans, Study Finds," *The Independent* (April 14), www.independent.co.uk/life-style/gadgets-and-tech/news/ai-robots-artificial-intelligence-racism-sexism-prejudice-bias-language-learn-from-humans-a7683161.html.
Kantor, J. and Streitfeld, D. 2015. "Inside Amazon: Wrestling Big Ideas in a Bruising Workplace," *New York Times* (August 15), www.nytimes.com/2015/08/16/technology/inside-amazon-wrestling-big-ideas-in-a-bruising-workplace.html.
Khanna, V. S. 2003. "Should the Behavior of Top Management Matter?" *Georgetown Law Journal* 91(6): 1215–56.
Langevoort, D. 2017. "Cultures of Compliance," *American Criminal Law Review* 54(4): 933–78.
Leon, J. 2019. "The D.C. Bar Regulation Counsel: Helping Members Meet the Highest Ethical Standards." *Washington Lawyer: The District of Columbia Bar Magazine* (June).
LogicGate n.d. "Regulatory Compliance Software with LogicGate," *LogicGate* (accessed September 8, 2019), www.logicgate.com/google-compliance-software/ (advertising how compliance can be tracked from one control panel).
MacLellan, L. 2018. "McKinsey & Co. Will No Longer Work with ICE," *Quartz at Work* (July 10), https://qz.com/work/1325101/mckinsey-company-employees-forced-the-company-to-stop-working-with-ice/ (describing similar unrest at Salesforce and Deloitte).
Marshall, C. 2015. "How Many Views Does a YouTube Video Get? Average Views by Category," *Tubular* (February 2), https://tubularlabs.com/blog/average-youtube-views/.
Mayer, C. 2012. *Firm Commitment: Why the Corporation Is Failing Us and How to Restore Trust in It.* Oxford University Press.
2018. *Prosperity: Better Business Makes the Greater Good.* Oxford University Press.
Menegus, B. 2018. "Here's the Letter 1,400 Google Workers Sent Leadership in Protest of Censored Search Engine for China," *Gizmodo* (August 16), https://gizmodo.com/heres-the-letter-1–400-google-workers-sent-leadership-i–1828393599.
Merriam-Webster Dictionary n.d.a. "Comply" (accessed December 5, 2018), www.merriam-webster.com/dictionary/comply.
"Courteous" (accessed December 5, 2018), www.merriam-webster.com/dictionary/courteous.
Myrick, Jessica Gall. 2015. "Emotion Regulation, Procrastination, and Watching Cat Videos Online: Who Watches Internet Cats, Why, and to What Effect?" *Computers in Human Behavior* 52 (November): 168.
Nelson, J. S. 2019. "Disclosure-Driven Crime," *UC Davis Law Review* 52(3): 1487–1583.
2020. "Management Culture and Surveillance," *Seattle University Law Review* 43(2): 631–82.
in press. "Engaging Middle Management."
Nelson, J. S. and Stout, L. in press. *Business Ethics: What Everyone Needs to Know*, Oxford University Press.
Nocero, J. 2015. "Love Always, Your Compliance Conscience," *The Compliance and Ethics Blog* (November 30), http://complianceandethics.org/love-always-your-compliance-conscience/.
Noone, T. (counsel and assistant vice president, Federal Reserve Bank of New York) 2019. Presentation to the Berle XI Symposium on Corporate Culture, Seattle University Law School (May 17).
Oxford English Dictionary, n.d. "Management" (accessed December 28, 2018), https://en.oxforddictionaries.com/definition/management.
Parker, S. 2003. "Longitudinal Effects of Lean Production on Employee Outcomes and the Mediating Role of Work Characteristics." *Journal of Applied Psychology* 88(4): 620–34.
Paternoster, R. 1987. "The Deterrent Effect of the Perceived Certainty and Severity of Punishment: A Review of the Evidence and Issues." *Justice Quarterly* 4(2): 173–217.
Paul, R. (partner, Ropes & Gray, London) 2019. "The Ethics of Workplace Surveillance & Monitoring Panel," Ethical Systems Conference, New York (March 15).

Pratt, T., Cullen, F. T., Blevins, K. R., Daigle, L. E., and Madensen, T. D. 2006. "The Empirical Status of Deterrence Theory: A Meta-analysis." In *Taking Stock: The Status of Criminological Theory*, edited by F. T. Cullen, J. P. Wright, and K. R. Blevins. Transaction.

Reckard, E. S. 2013. "Wells Fargo's Pressure-Cooker Sales Culture Comes at a Cost," *Los Angeles Times* (December 21), www.latimes.com/business/la-fi-wells-fargo-sale-pressure-20131222-story.html.

Robertson, A. 2018. "Google Employees Push to Cancel Chinese Search Engine in New Letter," *The Verge* (November 27), www.theverge.com/2018/11/27/18114285/google-employee-china-censorship-protest-project-dragonfly-search-engine-letter.

Rodriguez, S. 2019. "Facebook Culture Described as 'Cult-Like', Review Process Blamed" (January 8), www.cnbc.com/2019/01/08/facebook-culture-cult-performance-review-process-blamed.html.

Sandford, N. 2015. "Corporate Culture: The Center of Strong Ethics and Compliance," *Risk and Compliance Journal* (a publication of the *Wall Street Journal*) (January 20), https://deloitte.wsj.com/riskandcompliance/2015/01/20/corporate-culture-the-center-of-strong-ethics-and-compliance/.

Scheiber, N. 2017. "How Uber Uses Psychological Tricks to Push Its Drivers' Buttons," *New York Times* (April 2), www.nytimes.com/interactive/2017/04/02/technology/uber-drivers-psychological-tricks.html.

Schleunes, K. 1970. *The Twisted Road to Auschwitz: Nazi Policy toward German Jews, 1933–39*, University of Illinois Press, re-issued 1990.

Scott, S. (partner, Starling Trust) 2019. "Trust & Technology: A New Paradigm for Culture & Conduct in Risk Management." Presentation to the Berle XI Symposium on Corporate Culture, Seattle University Law School (May 17).

Shane, S., Metz, C., and Wakabayashi, D. 2018. "How a Pentagon Contract Became an Identity Crisis for Google," *New York Times* (May 30), www.nytimes.com/2018/05/30/technology/google-project-maven-pentagon.html.

Shapiro, S. 2005. "Agency Theory." *Annual Review of Sociology* 31(1): 263–84, https://doi.org/10.1146/annurev.soc.31.041304.122159.

Shumsky, T. 2018. "The 'Dark Side' of Managers With Audit Background," *WSJ* (blog) (November 1), https://blogs.wsj.com/cfo/2018/11/01/the-dark-side-of-managers-with-audit-background/.

Smith, I., Kouchaki, M., and Wareham, J. 2013. "Be Careful What You Wish For: The Performance Consequences of Unethical Requests at Work," *Academy of Management Proceedings*.

Smith, N. 2018. "Google's Prototype Chinese Search Engine Links Searches to Phone Numbers," *The Guardian* (September 18), www.theguardian.com/technology/2018/sep/18/google-china-dragonfly-search-engine.

Stout, L. 2011. *Cultivating Conscience: How Good Laws Make Good People*. Princeton University Press.

Tyler, T. 2014. "Reducing Corporate Criminality: The Role of Values," *American Criminal Law Review* 51: 267–92

U.S. Business Roundtable 2019. "Business Roundtable Redefines the Purpose of a Corporation to Promote 'An Economy That Serves All Americans'," *BusinessRoundtable.org* (August 19), www.businessroundtable.org/business-roundtable-redefines-the-purpose-of-a-corporation-to-promote-an-economy-that-serves-all-americans. The full revised statement on corporate purpose may be found here: https://opportunity.businessroundtable.org/wp-content/uploads/2019/09/BRT-Statement-on-the-Purpose-of-a-Corporation-with-Signatures-1.pdf.

U.S. Department of Justice 2019. *U.S. Attorney's Manual*, § 9–28.000 (July).

U.S. Federal Reserve 2018. "Responding to Widespread Consumer Abuses and Compliance Breakdowns by Wells Fargo, Federal Reserve Restricts Wells' Growth until Firm Improves Governance and Controls. Concurrent with Fed Action, Wells to Replace Three Directors by April, One by Year End" (February 2), www.federalreserve.gov/newsevents/pressreleases/enforcement20180202a.htm.

U.S. Sentencing Commission 2018. *U.S. Sentencing Guidelines Manual*.

Uzialko, A. 2019. "The Best Employee Monitoring Software for 2019," *Business.com*.

Wakabayashi, D., and Shane, S. 2018. "Google Will Not Renew Pentagon Contract That Upset Employees," *New York Times* (June 1), www.nytimes.com/2018/06/01/technology/google-pentagon-project-maven.html.

Wattles, J., Geier, B., and Egan, M. 2018. "Wells Fargo's 17-Month Nightmare," *CNNMoney* (February 5), https://money.cnn.com/2018/02/05/news/companies/wells-fargo-timeline/index.html.

Weaver, G. 2014. "Encouraging Ethics in Organizations: A Review of Some Key Research Findings," *American Criminal Law Review* 51(1): 293–316.

Yeginsu, C. 2018. "If Workers Slack Off, the Wristband Will Know. (And Amazon Has a Patent for It.)," *New York Times* (February 1), www.nytimes.com/2018/02/01/technology/amazon-wristband-tracking-privacy.html.

Yoffie, D., and Kwak, M. 2001. "Playing by the Rules: How Intel Avoids Antitrust Litigation," *Harvard Business Review* (June), https://hbr.org/2001/06/playing-by-the-rules-how-intel-avoids-antitrust-litigation.

Zimmerman, J. 2018. "Set in Stone: 30,000 Pounds of Purpose," *Brand Purpose* (August 30), www.brandpurposellc.com/brand-purpose-blog/set-in-stone-johnson-and-johnson.

10

Compliance as Liability Risk Management

Donald C. Langevoort

Abstract: It is natural to think of compliance in terms of liability risk management. In the face of potentially massive liability exposure, it behooves boards of directors and senior executives to take costly steps to reduce these risks for the sake of the firm and its shareholders, akin to other serious enterprise risks. The liability risk management perspective treats compliance as a matter of business judgment rather than a moral or cultural imperative, which has important consequences. The prevailing idea is that firms are expected to invest in precaution (i.e., compliance investments) up to a level where the marginal benefits in terms of diminished liability risk to the firm equal the marginal costs associated with such efforts. This chapter explores from a multidisciplinary perspective the consequences of adopting a liability risk management perspective along three dimensions: the agency cost problem (i.e., whose risk is being managed); the social construct invoked as a result (the problem of cultural legitimacy); and the clash between a company's own assessment of liability risk and sound public policy.

10.1 LIABILITY RISK MANAGEMENT IN THE FACE OF UNCERTAINTY

Of the many ways of thinking about corporate compliance as a sociolegal phenomenon and field of practice, the idea that it performs a liability risk management role is particularly compelling. In the United States, corporations face potentially harsh vicarious liability for crimes and civil wrongdoing by their agents acting within the scope of their authority, whether or not there is any upper management complicity. In the face of that and related liability exposure, it behooves boards of directors and senior executives to take costly steps to reduce these risks for the sake of the firm and its shareholders, akin to other serious enterprise risks. Hence, the creation of elaborate compliance programs, which have grown significantly in size and sophistication in the last few decades (Baer 2009; Griffith 2016a).

The liability risk management perspective treats compliance as a matter of business judgment rather than a moral or cultural imperative, which has important consequences. That is not to say that corporations are expected to break the law with impunity so long as the expected economic payoff is positive (for a discussion, see Pollman 2019). Rather, the prevailing idea is that firms are expected to invest in precaution (i.e., compliance investments) up to a level where the marginal benefits in terms of diminished liability risk to the firm equal the marginal costs associated with such efforts (Miller 2018). The Delaware courts' *Caremark* standard for board-level attention to compliance famously endorses this business judgment framework, albeit in a form that imposes little serious threat of director liability for later-discovered compliance deficiencies because it makes liability turn on proof of the directors' bad faith (Armour et al. 2020; Langevoort 2018b).

This chapter addresses the challenges and consequences, intended and not, of adopting this kind of business judgment perspective for the design and assessment of corporate compliance programs. There are many to consider, starting with the important qualifier that *liability* risk management is surely too narrow a description. Firms face reputational risks as well as the possibility of legal sanctions from managerial or employee wrongdoing, with serious economic consequences regardless of how, or even whether, the matter is ultimately resolved by law enforcers – consequences that reverberate through product markets, labor markets, capital markets, governmental relations and the like. These effects can sometimes dwarf the actual fines and penalties imposed. That by itself complicates the business judgment calculus, because reputational risks are especially contingent on how the company handles the crisis and hence impossible to estimate *ex ante*.

Some of the challenges in managing liability risk derive from the way in which the law imposes vicarious corporate liability. The American *respondeat superior* standard can discourage good compliance to the extent that a strong program will inevitably identify and expose some instances of wrongdoing that have already occurred, and thus make it more likely that the corporation will suffer liability than if the matter was left buried somewhere in the organization. The federal Organizational Sentencing Guidelines seek to moderate this effect by giving credit for good compliance at the sentencing stage (and the Department of Justice does the same in charging decisions), but the assessment challenge remains vexing (Arlen 2012). For those regulatory regimes like some scienter-based fraud statutes where the knowledge or awareness of senior managers does determine whether there is corporate liability or not, there can be the incentive to block the upward flow of information about potential wrongdoing in order to reduce the likelihood of culpable intent and hence liability at all (Langevoort 2019).

To begin with, however, I will assume that the firm has an incentive and capacity to optimize its compliance efforts along the lines mentioned earlier: investing in compliance to the point where benefits equal costs, with prevention being the dominant business strategy. I also assume a fairly capacious commitment to what compliance generally involves in this effort to optimize: a sizable mix of strategies to deter legally problematic behavior via efforts to identify, interdict and remediate it. Among other things, this involves tonal messages; education and training; audit and surveillance; investigation of suspicious activity; whistleblower encouragement; and prompt and proper remediation, internally and externally, when wrongdoing happens (e.g., Root 2018). The state-of-the-art on these techniques has evolved rapidly, along with ever-increasing costs associated with the best available strategies, especially in terms of technology and staffing.

It is neither original nor surprising to say that making the optimality assessment about exactly how much compliance to "buy" involves an immense level of guesswork. Consider the task even if we ignore the reputational risks and concentrate solely on legal ones. There must be an assessment of all the many kinds of legal wrongdoing – large and small – that might happen and the incentives throughout the organization to engage in it.[1] Because the law is so often uncertain as applied (an important but often ignored point discussed more fully later in this chapter), the calculation becomes all the more contingent, especially as to low-

[1] As many point out, the incentive structures, cultural influences and the like will vary field to field, so that one size by no means fits all in addressing the aggregate of different subject-matter risks. On the unique features of price-fixing in antitrust, for example, see Sokol (2013); on broker-dealer regulation, see Fanto (2014).

probability, high-impact risks. The risks of law violations are endogenous, moreover, insofar as one begets another so that wrongdoing can be viral, spreading epidemiologically in ways that can produce recidivism (Root 2017) or even legal catastrophe (Haugh 2018).

Then, of course, there is the assessment of likelihood of detection and sanction. Substantial evidence exists that enforcers are woefully underresourced, so that the penalties imposed when illegality is detected are below what is socially optimal in terms of deterrence. Karpoff et al. (2017) make an estimate of Foreign Corrupt Practices Act (FCPA) enforcement wherein the level of sanctioning is eight times less than it should be to make the crime not pay. Enforcement intensity drops off predictably when times are good, moreover, creating a problematic cyclicality. And there is plenty of evidence that firms can reduce their legal risks by lobbying and other influence activities, which may be less costly than vigorous internal compliance efforts (Correia 2014). So the variables multiply, endlessly.

The cost function is somewhat different. The operational costs in terms of human resources and technology expenditures are amply measurable; no doubt the recent rate of cost increase has, to corporate executives, been frustratingly large. There are also opportunity costs – profitable activities forgone in the name of compliance. While most business people do not regard patently illegal profits that are forgone as costs to the firm, aggressive compliance does have a chilling effect with regard to questionable behavior that might be lawful if tested in court but is nixed by legal or compliance personnel. There are many other indirect costs that we examine in more detail later, relating to motivation and morale.

Based on all this, it should be blindingly obvious that the business judgment associated with optimal firm-level investment in compliance is subjective to the level of guesswork. To be sure, there is a core list of what should be done that is clear enough. But out toward the margins, rigor is lost. Griffith (2016a: 2106) quotes a frustrated compliance officer as conceding as much: "In the end do we know if we have an effective program? We haven't figured that out yet. We do know we have a program in size. We just don't know if it works."

A number of important consequences follow from this. One is that compliance decisions can readily become mimetic across (and within – see Root 2017) firms, with benchmarking and "best practices" emerging from what is essentially a herd instinct rather than solid empirical evidence. Firms fear being identified as an outlier on the downside with respect to compliance investments. On the other hand, compliance faces challenges in the internal contest for budget and resources precisely because there are often no tangible revenue-related payoffs to the investment – the biggest benefits come in the form of bad things that do not happen. Since no compliance program achieves a zero failure-rate, there will always be small or moderate failures to call into question whether the investments are paying off.

When there is less than optimal government enforcement on average, moreover, the doubters will often appear to be right in downplaying liability threats. They may gain power as a result, leading to a decline in the firm's commitment to compliance. The lack of negative feedback to such legally aggressive strategic behavior rewards firms that limit their expenditures, thus contributing in the short run to the firm's bottom line. This may explain why high-impact enforcement often comes as such a shock to the firm and its leaders (Haugh 2018).

10.2 AGENCY COSTS AND LIABILITY RISK MANAGEMENT

A familiar challenge to prompting optimal investments in liability risk management becomes vivid if we shift our focus from the anthropomorphic perspective of the firm itself to the one that agency cost adherents prefer: looking at the compliance function in terms of the individual and group interests of those natural persons charged with making the choices as to the architecture and operation of the firm's internal compliance investment – directors, officers and compliance personnel.

Agency cost theory has come to dominate corporate legal scholarship, with insights that are readily applied to the compliance function. This perspective proceeds from the simplifying assumption that corporate governance arrangements exist to constrain – but never entirely eliminate – the pursuit of self-interest by those able to exercise power in the firm ("opportunism with guile," to use a famous phrase by Oliver Williamson). Among those who take this economics-driven approach, the fault lines are about how well, relatively, strategies like fiduciary responsibility, shareholder voting and disclosure requirements work in reducing agency costs to a tolerable level to attract and allocate equity capital. We must tread gently here, because many other scholars, especially those trained in or influenced by sociology and anthropology, regard the agency cost perspective as a gross misreading of human nature that has the unfortunate effect of being self-fulfilling – normalizing the pursuit of self-interest inside the firm and thereby legitimating a particular normative approach to corporate law and governance (shareholder primacy) as supposedly necessary to counter it (e.g., Jung and Dobbin 2016). This disagreement has important implications for thinking about compliance, which we take up in Section 10.3.

The agency cost approach asks how a powerful corporate actor makes decisions in light of their likely effect on his or her career and wealth.[2] For our purposes, the decision is how much to invest in compliance, perhaps coupled with how much pressure to exert on subordinate managers to meet high performance goals, which might create heightened pressure to break the law. Under US law, for the most part, a chief executive officer (CEO) does not face much risk of criminal (or even civil) liability either for preferring underinvestment in compliance or for creating high performance expectations, though there may be some regulatory settings where failure to supervise risk is present (Fanto 2014). So the risk of individual enforcement against the (individually nonculpable) CEO is far less than the risk of sanction against the firm, which itself may be less than optimal. If so, we turn to the other costs and benefits to the CEO from such a strategy. If the firm is sanctioned, the CEO may suffer reputationally to some extent, and if his or her wealth is heavily invested in issuer stock or unexercised options, the CEO may suffer as well from the stock price drop accompanying the charges of wrongdoing. These instances of suffering can bring considerable pain, to be sure, creating some incentive to invest in good compliance. But there will be many situations where even that incentive fails short. If the CEO fears that he or she will lose the job if performance does not improve markedly, for example, that negative career risk could easily override concern about the enforcement risk to the firm.

What if primary responsibility for liability risk management is shifted to less conflicted actors like the independent members of the board of directors, or the chief legal officer (CLO)? As to directors, there are informational impediments to exercising effective control over compliance, though they clearly can and should play some proactive role (Langevoort 2018b). There is some data suggesting that greater board independence is correlated with lesser compliance risk. However, as Armour et al. (2020) show, the increasing tendency to pay

[2] To be clear, this is separate from the incentives for such high-ranking persons to themselves violate the law, which can also be addressed from an agency cost perspective (Arlen and Kahan 2017). My own view is that many violations of law are motivated not by personal greed but, rather, by a desire to protect or further the value of the enterprise over which they exercise a controlling influence.

directors fees in stock and options can frustrate optimal investment in liability risk management. This is because such investments are likely to pay off only in the long run, whereas stock and options may well be cashed out in a shorter time frame. They recommend a move back to fixed director fees. This cautionary note about time horizons and incentive compensation extends to other important gatekeepers, such as CLOs. Morse et al. (2016) provide evidence that CLOs can be very effective at limiting unlawful behavior but that this effectiveness diminishes if the pay package of the CLO is structured like that of other high-ranking executives in the firm in terms of options and other stock-based incentives for strategic behavior.

This suggests another discouraging fact about liability risk management in public companies. In theory, an efficient stock market should reward firms that invest optimally, and punish those that underinvest or fail to control agency costs that lead managers to make self-serving compliance choices. That, in turn, would provide some incentive for officers and directors to move closer to the optimal from a firm perspective. But investors, no matter how sophisticated, have a hard time valuing compliance expenditures which are not subject to standardized disclosure requirements (Griffith 2016a).[3] The market thus gives less weight to them, lessening the discipline that market pressure might otherwise produce (Armour et al. 2020).

10.3 LIABILITY RISK MANAGEMENT AS A SOCIAL CONSTRUCT

The predictive uncertainty discussed in Section 10.1 poses a legitimacy challenge for those who pursue strong compliance efforts inside the firm, felt noticeably on a day-to-day basis by compliance personnel (Trevino et al. 2014). To find legitimacy and a secure place at the corporate high table, the compliance function needs to make a better impression than that. This shifts the focus of compliance from rational choice to social construction: sense-making in the face of pervasive uncertainty. Liability risk management becomes a cultural exercise in assessing the firm's taste for legal risk, the perception of risk at any given time, and the legitimate means of managing it in accordance with the established distribution of power and challenges to it. One long-standing fear is that compliance inevitably loses out to the doubters given such uncertainty and becomes entirely cosmetic as a result, designed to manage external impressions simply by checking a long list of inconsequential boxes (Krawiec 2003). Money is spent and work is done, but not in a way that interferes much with the prime objective (subjectively construed) of competitive survival and success. Procedures and routines come to dominate, decoupled from anything resembling optimal risk management (Meyer and Rowan 1979).

But this may be overly pessimistic; external pressures for more compliance may be strong enough to push back against such radical devolution and actually seek to accomplish something. As noted earlier, fear of both the reputational and the legal consequences of a legal scandal can be empowering – advocates for more serious compliance can emerge (lawyers, independent directors, managers concerned about overaggressive peers, consultants and, of course, compliance personnel themselves), invoking some combination of fear and appeals to social legitimacy to reduce liability risks. Regulators and prosecutors will be their

3 A similar effect may arise with respect to investments in ethical corporate cultures (see Guiso et al. 2015), suggesting that integrity might be stronger when there is less public shareholder influence.

allies, amplifying liability threats so as to get firms to internalize more of the real work of preventive law.

To the extent that compliance gains power, compliance personnel may instinctively adopt a "command and control" stance (Haugh 2017), employing more intense supervision and monitoring to overcome perceived self-serving resistance to the compliance message. There are many critics of this aggressive form of liability risk management, however, who argue that the resulting combination of high routinization and command and control initiatives is not only empirically ungrounded but actually counterproductive (see Hess 2016; Weaver 2014; Tyler 2018). Fundamentally, they question agency theory as a useful descriptive or normative account based in part on the more optimistic belief that human beings have natural prosocial inclinations (and are influenced by prosocial cultural norms), so that law-abidingness within corporations does not have to be induced via threats of enforcement or strict compliance mandates. Indeed, such heavy-handed strategies crowd out ethicality by making liability risk management a purely strategic choice (Langevoort 2002; Hess 2016). Even the framing of compliance as liability risk *management* no doubt contributes to the impression that the directive stance is normatively appropriate.

In this view, good compliance initiatives should instead directly and forcefully speak to both healthy and unhealthy beliefs and values, nudging the community of agents toward the former and away from the latter (van Rooij and Fine 2018).[4] Prominent experts in organizational behavior thus offer lists of compliance initiatives that work, and believe that as metrics to measure organizational culture and climate improve (Trevino et al. 2017; Chen and Soltes 2018), the case for a savvy, values-based compliance design will strengthen.

The reaction of many to this (economists in particular) is skepticism and doubt that softer compliance is somehow the route to better liability risk management. Some of this pushback is just a more cynical view of human nature, coupled with the conviction that situational pressures in highly competitive firms usually point in the opposite direction from virtue. To this, proponents respond that these doubts are artifacts from the agency-cost-driven view of the task of business management, a naïve and often self-serving cynicism more the product of motivated inference than tested observation. As Tom Tyler (2018: 26) writes, for those in power these cynical models "support illusions of competence, moral superiority, and enhanced security, all of which provide important psychological benefits to authorities and give them a reason to continue to embrace coercive methods."

This argument is probably unresolvable from current knowledge. It does seem to be true that firms where senior managers are seen to have integrity are both better places to work and long-term sustainable, without necessarily attributing integrity to a heavy deployment of carrots and sticks. I am agnostic on all this, hoping (with some reason) that the case for a more trust-based system proves worthy, but fearing that it may not (Langevoort 2017). After all, the same research that shows people's inclination to cheat less than they can get away with

[4] Rigorously assessing these alternative ways of thinking about compliance is hard. Social scientists are divided methodologically as to whether these impulses are at work in individual cognition and decision-making (as psychologists assume) or at a higher level of cultural beliefs (the assumption in sociology and anthropology). Each faces challenges in exploring organizational behavior. But, gradually, progress is being made in both psychology and sociology (and anthropology), bolstered by a cadre of economists who have rejected that field's natural skepticism about both culture and psychology (e.g., Guiso et al. 2015). A burgeoning subject of inquiry in financial economics, for example, seeks out correlations and causal inferences running from senior executive traits and beliefs – like extreme risk-taking (Davidson et al. 2015) or religious commitment (Baxamusa and Jalal 2016) – to outcomes such as stock price performance or, importantly to those interested in compliance, litigation and other liability threats. The psychological perspective is taken up in other chapters in this volume; for my discussion, see Langevoort 2018a).

also shows that they still cheat more than they should. And so many of the situational enablers that have been shown by psychologists to increase the incidence of cheating are baked into the prevailing cultures of competitive businesses – the tournaments for status, power and compensation; the deep-seated dread that any reduction in competitive zeal can result in a sudden decline in marketplace standing, and potential oblivion. These beliefs may be myths, but they are deeply believed and potent nonetheless.

The command and control attitude would at least seem to indicate a commitment to strict compliance. However, it is simply a form of compliance design, not a measure of compliance intensity. As noted earlier, proponents of heightened intensity face a rough road simply because of the subjectivity of risk estimates. Whether as a matter of culture or of cognition, potent beliefs can emerge in firms (especially among the powerful and power-seeking) that diminish intensity as well. The optimistic view of prosociality inside organizations is that people are inclined to obey the law even with diminished enforcement threats, but this turns crucially on the extent to which legal and regulatory demands are perceived as fair and legitimate (Tyler 2014). And internal beliefs can emerge that denigrate such liability threats. Characterizing potential enforcement as bureaucratic, politically motivated, or backwards and out of touch with the spirit of entrepreneurial innovation can readily promote rationalizations that justify opportunistic behaviors.

Fortunately, the opposite can also happen. Firms can come to embrace legal compliance even above the efficient level in terms of firm risk. As noted, this can be the product of agents within the firm (e.g., from compliance or human resources) who accept the values embedded in legal mandates as valuable and seek to spread that gospel throughout the firm (Edelman and Suchman 1997), or who seek profitable alliances with stakeholders who espouse those values and can help the firm succeed (Gunningham et al. 2004; Henisz et al. 2014). As noted earlier, there are personal, political and religious traits among corporate leaders that appear to correlate with greater law-abidingness.

In the end, the social constructionist perspective on liability risk management is largely indeterminate. Different firms, at different times, will develop their preferred construals of the likelihood and magnitude of liability risks, and of the soundness and legitimacy of different strategic investments in response. This produces a scattered diversity of outcomes, with constraints often coming more from the immediate feedback or the inclination to follow what peers are doing than anything approaching scientific rationality.

10.4 LIABILITY RISK MANAGEMENT AS PUBLIC POLICY

Liability risk management is firm and industry specific – the size, strategy and deployment of compliance investments are such that one size (or style) does not suit all. From the firm's standpoint, it makes sense to treat the necessary choices as a business judgment, though surely influenced by what peer firms seem to be doing to address similar problems. Thus far we have examined some of the many consequences of adopting such a business judgment stance to compliance, largely flowing from the massive ambiguity associated with strategic compliance planning and efficient resource allocation. As we saw, this invites other interests (managerial self-interest in particular) to come into play even when there is a seemingly genuine commitment to optimality.

From a public policy standpoint, however, leaving compliance judgment to these economic and social forces in the name of business judgment is wrong. That is because the *regulatory* objective is not to incentivize compliance investments that satisfy the best interests of the firm or its managers from a liability risk standpoint but, rather, to gain socially optimal investments in compliance (Miller 2018). Usually, that will be more of an investment than firms would make on their own. Over the last few decades, regulators and public enforcers have tried to up these incentives by making both prosecutorial choices and penalties being sought vary depending on how genuinely and effectively they have undertaken the business of compliance, thereby introducing good or bad compliance as itself a variable in the liability risk assessment.

There are many critics of this regulatory/enforcement stance, both in academia and in practice. Regulators likely lack expertise in *ex ante* risk management generally or in the firm-specific issues associated with its application, and thus err in their assessments of how well or poorly the firm has done and what good remedial reforms might be. And they face strong political pressures as well as their own career interests. As a result, the compliance changes they seek might not pass a rigorous cost–benefit test in terms of the social good they actually produce (Arlen and Kahan 2017; Griffith 2016a; Cunningham 2014.) There are spillovers to this as well. Any compliance-related enforcement initiative that is perceived by business-people inside firms as incompetent, unfair or excessively punitive will generate reactance, not respect (Haugh 2017). This plays into the already strong inclination to view compliance demands as illegitimate, diminishing their normative force and enabling a greater amount of rationalization for risky behaviors.

So the liability risk management perspective puts regulators and enforcers in a bind. They want and need to outsource work to well-meaning compliance and legal officers inside firms so as to promote social welfare, not competitive success. If they push too hard at this, it may backfire and be costly; push too little and the internal forces in the firm that lead toward underinvestment might overwhelm their meager efforts (Langevoort 2017). All this in the often-distorted glare associated with the politics of public litigation. So regulators have to make decisions similar to boards of directors in firms: in the face of uncertainty, and with the suspicion that the cultural and cognitive impulses that drive liability risk-taking are not entirely manageable no matter what strategies they try.

10.5 CONCLUSION

The characterization of compliance as liability risk management carries with it multiple possible implications. One is that compliance is an exercise in scientific rationality. This is surely not so, although there are underutilized quantitative tools and metrics that could improve compliance quality (Soltes 2018). The technology of compliance is also rapidly evolving, so that more in-depth monitoring and surveillance is becoming possible, to assess the ebbs and flows of perceived integrity at the moment, and real-time surveillance data analytics can be used to develop predictive algorithms for legally risky behaviors (Fanto 2014; Griffith 2016b; Walsh 2017).

But increasing monitoring intensity is itself risky, maybe even scary. Recall the belief of the prosocial optimists mentioned earlier that the regulatory task as to compliance is one of encouraging trust and values-based initiatives, presumably by dialing back their command and control threats. By most accounts, the conventional framework of compliance as liability risk management implies that people are expected to respond to economic incentives (carrots and sticks) by making calculative choices. And as social scientists have long claimed, we usually get what we expect and normalize. That arguably "crowds out" the inclination to do what is right because it is right in terms of personal moral judgment or broader cultural norms.

Avoiding this is the main tenet of virtue and ethics-based compliance, which, as we have seen, faces substantial opposition from cynics and others heavily invested in and privileged by the risk management status quo. It takes a brave regulatory enforcer to be willing to risk charges of hopeless naïveté to dial back liability threats and insist on the commitments to ethics, fairness and reordering of the internal corporate incentive structure necessary to nurture that alternative vision of corporate prosociality. And the cynics may be right, even as the cynicism becomes a self-fulfilling prophecy. We just don't know enough for sure about human nature or organizational behavior.

So there is still much to learn. The social science of compliance – the work of sociologists, anthropologists, psychologists and economists – is still expanding as a research subject, promising a greater understanding of what works in compliance, and what hurts. Eventually, neuroscientists may be able to provide a better sense of how innate nature, nurture and situational forces interact to produce prosocial or antisocial beliefs and behaviors. Someday, in other words, liability risks may be managed in a more rigorous sense than they are today, hopefully for the better.

REFERENCES

Arlen, Jennifer. 2012. "The Failure of the Organizational Sentencing Guidelines." *University of Miami Law Review* 66: 321–62.

Arlen, Jennifer and Marcel Kahan. 2017. "Corporate Governance Regulation through Non-prosecution." *University of Chicago Law Review* 84: 323–86.

Armour, John, Jeffrey Gordon and Geeyoung Min. 2020. "Taking Compliance Seriously." *Yale Journal of Regulation* 37: 1–66.

Baer, Miriam Hechler. 2009. "Governing Corporate Compliance." *Boston College Law Review* 50: 949–1020.

Baxamusa, Muffala, and Abu Jalal. 2016. "CEO's Religious Affiliation and Managerial Conservatism." *Financial Management* 45: 67–104.

Chen, Hui and Eugene Soltes. 2018. "Why Compliance Programs Fail and How to Fix Them." *Harvard Business Review* March–April: 117–25.

Correia, Maria M. 2014. "Political Connections and SEC Enforcement." *Journal of Accounting and Economics* 57: 241–62.

Cunningham, Lawrence A. 2014. "Deferred Prosecutions and Corporate Governance: An Integrated Approach to Investigations and Reform." *Florida Law Review* 66: 1–85.

Davidson, Robert, Aiyesha Dye and Abbie J. Smith. 2015. "Executives' Off the Job Behavior, Corporate Culture and Financial Reporting Risk." *Journal of Financial Economics* 117: 5–28.

Edelman, Lauren D., and Mark Suchman. 1997. "The Legal Environment of Organizations." *Annual Review of Sociology* 23: 479–515.

Fanto, James. 2014. "Surveilant and Counsellor: A Reorientation of Compliance for Broker-Dealers." *Brigham Young University Law Review* 2014: 1121–84.

Griffith, Sean J. 2016a. "Corporate Governance in an Era of Compliance." *William & Mary Law Review* 57: 2075–2140.

Griffith, Sean J. 2016b. "The Question Concerning Technology in Compliance." *Brooklyn Journal of Corporate, Financial and Commercial Law* 11: 25–38.

Guiso, Luigi, Paolo Sapienza and Luigi Zingales. 2015. "The Value of Corporate Culture." *Journal of Financial Economics* 117: 60–76.

Gunningham, Neal, Robert A. Kagan and Dorothy Thornton. 2004. "Social License and Environmental Protection: Why Businesses Go Beyond Compliance." *Law and Social Inquiry* 29: 301–41.

Haugh, Todd. 2017. "The Criminalization of Compliance." *Notre Dame Law Review* 92: 1215–69.

Haugh, Todd. 2018. "The Power Few of Corporate Compliance." *Georgia Law Review* 53: 1–67.

Henisz, Witold J., Sinziana Dorobantu and Lite Nartey. 2014. "Spinning Gold: The Financial Returns to Stakeholder Engagement." *Strategic Management Journal* 35: 1727–48.

Hess, David. 2016. "Ethical Infrastructure and Evidence-Based Corporate Compliance and Ethics Programs: Policy Implications from Empirical Evidence." *NYU Journal of Law & Business* 12: 317–68.

Jung, Jiwook, and Frank Dobbin. 2016. "Agency Theory as Prophecy." *Seattle University Law Review* 39: 291–320.

Karpoff, Jonathan M., D. Scott Lee and Gerald Martin. 2017. "The Value of Foreign Bribery to Bribe Paying Firms." Working Paper, https://ssrn.com/abstract=1573222.

Krawiec, Kimberly D. 2003. "Cosmetic Compliance and the Failure of Negotiated Governance." *Washington University Law Quarterly* 81: 487–544.

Langevoort, Donald C. 2002. "Monitoring: The Behavioral Economics of Corporate Compliance with Law." *Columbia Business Law Review* 71: 74–118.

Langevoort, Donald C. 2017. "Cultures of Compliance." *American Criminal Law Review* 54: 933–77.

Langevoort, Donald C. 2018a. "Behavioral Ethics, Behavioral Compliance." In Jennifer Arlen, ed., *Research Handbook on Corporate Crime and Financial Misdealing*, 263–81. Cheltenham, UK: Edward Elgar.

Langevoort, Donald C. 2018b. "Caremark and Compliance: A Twenty-Year Lookback." *Temple Law Review* 90: 727–42.

Langevoort, Donald C. 2019. "Disasters and Disclosures." *Georgetown Law Journal* 107: 967–1016.

Meyer, John W., and Brian Rowan. 1979. "Institutionalized Organizations: Formal Structure as Myth and Ceremony." *American Journal of Sociology* 83: 340–63.

Miller, Geoffrey P. 2018. "An Economic Analysis of Effective Compliance Programs." In Jennifer Arlen, ed., *Research Handbook on Corporate Crime and Financial Misdealing*, 247–62. Cheltenham, UK: Edward Elgar.

Morse, Adair, Wei Wang and Serena Wu. 2016. "Executive Lawyers: Gatekeepers or Strategic Officers?" *Journal of Law and Economics* 59: 847–88.

Pollman, Elizabeth. 2019. "Corporate Disobedience." *Duke Law Journal* 68: 709–65.

Root, Veronica. 2017. "Coordinating Compliance Incentives." *Cornell Law Review* 102: 1003–86.

Root, Veronica. 2018. "The Compliance Process." *Indiana Law Journal* 94: 203–51.

Sokol, D. Daniel. 2013. "Policing the Firm." *Notre Dame Law Review* 85: 785–848.

Soltes, Eugene. 2018. "Evaluating the Effectiveness of Corporate Compliance Programs: Establishing a Model for Prosecutors, Courts and Firms." *NYU Journal of Law & Business* 14: 965–1011.

Trevino, Linda Klebe, Glen E. Kreiner and Derron Bishop. 2014. "Legitimating the Legitimate: A Grounded Theory Study of Legitimacy Work among Ethics and Compliance Officers." *Organizational Behavior & Human Decision Processes* 123: 186–204.

Trevino, Linda Klebe, Jonathan Haidt and Azish Filabi. 2017. "Regulating for Ethical Culture." *Behavioral Science and Policy* 3(2): 57–61.

Tyler, Tom R. 2014. "Reducing Corporate Criminality: The Role of Values." *American Criminal Law Review* 51: 267–92.

Tyler, Tom R. 2018. "Psychology and the Deterrence of Corporate Crime." In Jennifer Arlen, ed. *Research Handbook on Corporate Crime and Financial Misdealing*, 11-39. Cheltenham, UK: Edward Elgar.

Van Rooij, Benjamin, and Adam Fine. 2018. "Toxic Corporate Culture: Assessing Organizational Processes of Deviancy." *Administrative Sciences* 8: 23–61.

Walsh, John H. 2017. "Compliance in the Age of Complexity." *Rutgers University Law Review* 69: 533.

Weaver, Gary R. 2014. "Encouraging Ethics in Organizations: A Review of Some Key Research Findings." *American Criminal Law Review* 51: 293–316.

11

Criminalized Compliance

Todd Haugh

Abstract: Corporate compliance programs have become increasingly criminalized. In the truest of ironies, companies have adopted compliance protocols that are motivated by and mimic application of the law they seek to avoid most. This approach to compliance – using the precepts of criminal enforcement and adjudication to govern employee conduct – is inherently flawed, however, and can never be fully effective in abating corporate wrongdoing. Criminalized compliance programs impose unintended behavioral consequences on employees, specifically by fostering rationalizations that allow would-be offenders to square their self-perception as "good people" with the unethical or illegal behavior they are contemplating, thereby allowing wrongdoing to go forward. By importing into the corporation many of the criminal law's delegitimizing features, criminalized compliance encourages rationalizations and creates the necessary precursors to the commission of corporate crime. Once this dynamic is understood, it provides a new way of conceptualizing corporate compliance and explains the ineffectiveness of many "leading" compliance programs. It also suggests that companies committed to making gains in ethics and compliance should often ignore the practices of their peers and the regulators that influence them, and instead design behaviorally cognizant strategies aimed at combating individual and organizational rationalizations.

11.1 INTRODUCTION

There is an older lady in my neighborhood who walks her dog religiously. Three times a day they can be seen strolling the same loop around the few blocks of our subdivision. Although we haven't had much interaction, only nodding hello occasionally if we happen to walk past each other, she appears to be a perfectly fine person. The dog seems fine too, a Standard Poodle mix that regards me with a practiced air of indifference.

None of this is remarkable, of course, or even worth mentioning, as pet owners are pretty common in my area. Except for one thing: this woman and her dog bear a striking resemblance. More than striking, really, it's *uncanny*. They are human–canine doppelgangers, doubles, twins; bipartite in their angular facial features, frizzy dark hair, and round brown eyes. They walk at the same pace, tense at the same time, and generally appear to have morphed into some semblance of one another, a state of being my kids find equal parts fascinating and hilarious. I chide them to be respectful, but I have to admit I'm a little fascinated myself.

Turns out there is a surprising amount of research on the similarities between pets and their owners. Suffice it to say, humans tend to prefer pets that look like them,[1] pets and owners usually have similar body types,[2] and the two often share dispositions.[3] Whether it's a matter of selection or transference, I don't know, but pet owners like my neighbor seem intent on propagating their own image through their animals. They want Fido to look and act just like them.

A similar thing is happening in corporate America, at least in the corner of it occupied by legal and compliance. Corporate compliance programs are being – or, in most cases, have already been – remade in their owner's image. That would make perfect sense if their owners were the larger corporations to which the compliance apparatus belonged. Problem is, the *true* owner of most compliance programs is not the company itself but the government regulator or prosecutor's office that oversees it. Regulators own modern compliance because they frame its mission, determine its priorities, and write the rules and guidance documents that compliance officers have adopted as their set of de facto operating procedures. In some cases, regulators are doing all this from inside the company as part of a deferred or non-prosecution agreement. To put it in direct terms, regulators "have found their way deep into America's corporations through compliance" and they are remaking it in their image. To put it in the terms above, regulators are the ones holding compliance's leash.[4]

But also like the story above, this might not be all that notable on its own. Corporate law and governance scholars have been calling attention to this regulator–compliance relationship for some time.[5] Companies are certainly aware of it; at this point, their acquiescence might almost be deemed an invitation. Yet what haven't received much attention, and what are indeed notable, are the behavioral effects of the relationship. In this chapter, I'd like to explore two interrelated ways in which the government's ownership of corporate compliance is impacting companies and the behaviors of the employees within them. First is that compliance has become criminalized, meaning it mimics the criminal law by using the precepts of criminal enforcement and adjudication to govern employee conduct. Second is that criminalized compliance actually fosters the very wrongdoing that compliance is aimed at preventing by allowing employees to more easily rationalize their unethical conduct. Put simply, when companies allow government to remake compliance in its image, we all end up walking in circles.

1 Stanley Coren, *Do People Look Like Their Dogs?*, 12 ANTHROZOÖS 111, 113 (1999) (study of 261 participants finding that "we have some preference for dogs that have a general likeness that is somewhat reminiscent of the appearance of our own faces"). [www.tandfonline.com/doi/pdf/10.2752/089279399787000336?needAccess=true]

2 Michael M. Roy & J.S. Christenfeld Nicholas, *Do Dogs Resemble Their Owners?*, 15 PSYCHOLOGICAL SCIENCE 361, 362 (2004). [https://journals.sagepub.com/doi/pdf/10.1111/j.0956–7976.2004.00684.x]; Marieke L. Nijland, Frank Stam & Jacob C. Seidell, *Overweight in Dogs, But Not in Cats, Is Related to Overweight in Their Owners*, 13 PUBLIC HEALTH NUTRITION 102, 104 (2009) (demonstrating a positive relationship between overweight dogs and the body mass index of their owners; no such finding for cats and their owners). [http://citeseerx.ist.psu.edu/viewdoc/download?doi=10.1.1.896.6796&rep=rep1&type=pdf]

3 William J. Chopik & Jonathan R. Weaver, *Old Dog, New Tricks: Age Differences in Dog Personality Traits, Associations with Human Personality Traits, and Links to Important Outcomes*, 79 J. RESEARCH PERSONALITY 94, 104 (2019) (finding many dog personality dimensions that correlate with owner personality dimensions). [https://reader.elsevier.com/reader/sd/pii/S0092656618301661?token=FFC5DDBE622A2BB6B09956AE3DD1DB5E9FBB5FB8AF9B0E0D943DA22FC09D160D8C859621B7AEFE921AEA76D4CB733330]

4 Todd Haugh, *The Criminalization of Compliance*, 92 NOTRE DAME L. REV. 1215, 1240 (2017). Portions of this chapter are adopted, with permission, from this article, as well as Todd Haugh, *"Cadillac Compliance" Breakdown*, 69 STAN. L. REV. ONLINE 198 (2017).

5 *See e.g.*, Sean J. Griffith, *Corporate Governance in an Era of Compliance*, 57 WM. & MARY L. REV. 2075, 2092 (2016) (contending that the government, specifically federal prosecutors, have been "the leading force in the development of compliance").

11.2 THE PATH TO CRIMINALIZED COMPLIANCE

Let's start by unpacking the idea of criminalized compliance. The compliance function in most corporations has evolved pursuant to a reoccurring cycle – a corporate scandal hits, public outcry and governmental investigation follow, next is sweeping criminal legislation, and finally there is a compliance increase. This cycle is perpetuated by minimal *mens rea* requirements for most white-collar offenses coupled with expansive *respondeat superior* liability, allowing almost any crime committed by an employee to be imputed to the corporation. Government agents leverage these features of white-collar and corporate criminal law to enter companies; their goal – a laudable one – is to change corporate culture for the better. In response, companies preemptively ratchet up their compliance functions, ostensibly to keep regulators at bay. However, companies have done so in a way that transfers ownership of compliance to the government by adopting its rhetoric, tools, and even its former personnel – elements of the very thing companies say they wish to keep *out* of the firm. The result is that corporate compliance programs in many organizations now look like they were torn from a page of the Justice Manual – they are "criminalized" because they mimic the criminal law by using the precepts of criminal enforcement and adjudication to govern employee conduct. That's criminalized compliance.

But to understand the concept more deeply, we have to consider compliance's past. How compliance came to be owned by government regulators, which results in its current criminalized nature, is an historical tale that manifests itself in the very recent example of antitrust compliance. First the historical background.

For the roughly fifty years between 1909, when the Supreme Court recognized that companies can be held vicariously liable for the criminal acts of their agents,[6] and the 1961 "electrical cases" that implicated dozens of prominent US companies in a price-fixing scandal,[7] compliance was mostly a matter of business regulating itself. During this time, companies created their own internal rules to "maintain an orderly way of life by regulating the conduct of members."[8] Some of this was in reaction to society's distrust of corporations after the market crash of 1929, a concerted effort to rebuild the image of businessmen in their local communities. But it also served the purpose of forestalling regulation that may have otherwise been more onerous: better for business to regulate itself than have the government do it. Self-regulation within and across industry was eventually codified and filtered into the formal codes and governing principles of individual companies.

This self-governance model of compliance, which had offered a tenuous but largely stable balance between government- and industry-initiated regulation, changed drastically in the three decades after the electrical cases. There is something about learning your favorite companies (giants such as GE and Allis-Chalmers) are colluding to rip off the US military in order to maintain their manufacturing monopolies that has a way of souring the public on the concept of self-regulation.[9] So does watching it happen twice more over the next two decades, as prominent companies became embroiled in foreign bribery and insider trading scandals.[10]

6 New York Central R. Co. v. United States, 212 U.S. 481 (1909).

7 *See* Jed S. Rakoff & Jonathan S. Sack, Federal Corporate Sentencing: Compliance and Mitigation § 5.02[1][a] (10th ed. 2012) (describing that companies including General Electric, Westinghouse, and Allis-Chalmers agreed to divvy up markets, fix prices, and rig bids to secure their manufacturing monopolies).

8 Harvey L. Pitt & Karl A. Groskaufmanis, *Minimizing Corporate Civil and Criminal Liability: A Second Look at Corporate Codes of Conduct*, 78 Geo. L.J. 1559, 1576 (1990) (internal footnotes omitted).

9 Richard Smith, *The Incredible Electrical Conspiracy (Part I)*, Fortune, Apr. 1961, at 132.

10 *See* Pitt & Groskaufmanis, *supra* note 8, at 1582–90 (detailing how in the mid-1970s, in response to corporate disclosures revealing that approximately 400 companies had collectively made $300 million in illegal payments to secure corporate benefits, Congress passed the FCPA; and how in 1988, after a series of prosecutions regarding

In a fairly short span, then, large areas of the economy were subject to very public corporate criminal investigations, some of which resulted in previously unseen prison sentences for business executives.[11] Broad legislation aimed at curbing corporate wrongdoing followed, which in turn caused businesses around the country to add crime-specific rules to their codes of conduct and employee trainings.[12] This was the beginning of the "modern era" of compliance, a period dominated by a paradigmatic cycle – corporate scandal, public outcry, sweeping legislation, and a regulation-specific compliance increase.[13]

But the true "watershed" moment in compliance came in 1991 with the advent of the Organizational Sentencing Guidelines.[14] The innovation of the Organizational Guidelines was to shift the focus of punishment from a post-crime additive process, as it operates with individual wrongdoers who are given increasing sentences based primarily on characteristics of the committed offense, to one that is pre-crime focused and decremental. A company subject to the Organizational Guidelines starts with an offense-based fine, but that amount may be reduced by up to 95 percent if the company had an effective compliance program operating *prior to* the wrongdoing.[15] Under this "duty-based" approach, companies are incentivized to preemptively police the criminal conduct of their employees, arguably converting firms from "passive bystanders ... hop[ing] their employees would behave well to active advocates for ethical conduct on the job."[16]

What makes a compliance program "effective" in both preventing criminal conduct and promoting ethical culture, thereby justifying a steep sentencing reduction (particularly given the program has obviously failed in at least one of those regards), has always been the central question.[17] According to the Sentencing Commission, effective compliance is judged on the following criteria:

(1) Standards and procedures to prevent and detect criminal conduct;
(2) Responsibility at all levels of the program, together with adequate program resources and authority for its managers;
(3) Due diligence in hiring and assigning personnel to positions with substantial authority;
(4) Communicating standards and procedures, including a specific requirement for training at all levels;
(5) Monitoring, auditing, and non-retaliatory internal guidance/reporting systems, including periodic evaluation of program effectiveness;
(6) Promotion and enforcement of compliance and ethical conduct; and

insider trading at prominent banks, including that of Ivan Boesky and Michael Milken, Congress passed the Insider Trading and Securities Fraud Enforcement Act).

11 For example, in the electrical cases, almost $2 million in fines were levied against executives and seven individuals were sentenced to jail – that was unheard of at the time. RAKOFF & SACK, *supra* note 7, at § 5.02[1][a].

12 Pitt & Groskaufmanis, *supra* note 8, at 1578.

13 Haugh, *Criminalization*, *supra* note 4, at 113.

14 Robert C. Bird & Stephen Kim Park, *The Domains of Corporate Counsel in an Era of Compliance*, 53 AM. BUS. L. J. 203, 212 (2016); *see also* Cristie Ford & David Hess, *Can Corporate Monitorships Improve Corporate Compliance?*, 34 J. CORP. L. 679, 690 (2008) (stating that the Organizational Sentencing Guidelines are "the most important influence" in compliance).

15 Under this "composite liability system," companies are held strictly liable for their employees' illegal acts, but that liability is mitigated upon a showing that compliance efforts were made. Miriam H. Baer, *Governing Corporate Compliance*, 50 B.C. L. REV. 949, 964 (2009) (citing Jennifer Arlen & Reinier Kraakman, *Controlling Corporate Misconduct: An Analysis of Corporate Liability Regimes*, 72 N.Y.U. L. REV. 687, 692 (1997)).

16 ETHICS RES. CTR., THE FEDERAL SENTENCING GUIDELINES FOR ORGANIZATIONS AT TWENTY YEARS 16, 22 (2012), www.theagc.org/docs/f12.10.pdf.

17 UNITED STATES SENTENCING GUIDELINES MANUAL § 8B2.1(a)–(b) (2018).

(7) Taking reasonable steps to respond appropriately and prevent further misconduct upon detecting a violation.[18]

Exactly how all this operates in practice is – and remains – quite fuzzy, but that is almost beside the point. These pronouncements spurred a massive increase in compliance because companies now had a clear (or at least clearer) sense of what they could do to mitigate *respondeat superior* liability. Rather than compliance focusing on a particular industry or regulation, it was now a vehicle for lessening culpability for *any* potential corporate wrongdoing.

While the Organizational Guidelines and the compliance boom they initiated have been a net positive, one by-product was to vastly increase the role of regulators in companies through compliance. Although only about 150 companies are found guilty of crimes each year,[19] the guidelines are "foundational" for all things related to corporate wrongdoing.[20] If a company is actually convicted, the guidelines become the formal measure of culpability. But even short of an indictment, because the elements of an effective compliance program have been incorporated into the Justice Manual, they guide prosecutors as to whether a deferred or non-prosecution agreement is appropriate.[21] Ultimately, every Justice Department memo on corporate investigation and prosecution, every SEC (Securities and Exchange Commission) or other alphabet agency's report on determining fraudulent corporate behavior, and even most SRO (self-regulatory organization) guidance is heavily influenced by the Organizational Guidelines.[22] As one would expect, the compliance community studies these materials closely to "divine clues about how to proceed," and then alters their compliance policies to follow suit.[23]

Such practices only increased beginning in the early 2000s and throughout the financial crisis era when major pieces of legislation – the Sarbanes-Oxley Act of 2002 and the Dodd-Frank Act of 2010 – criminalized the lack of compliance protocols within companies.[24] Now, simply not doing compliance correctly could be a substantive violation in and of itself. These

[18] *Id.*; Phillip A. Wellner, *Effective Compliance Programs and Corporate Criminal Prosecutions*, 27 Cardozo L. Rev. 497, 500–02 (2005). In addition to these core indicators of effectiveness, the guidelines now also require that companies periodically assess the risk of the occurrence of criminal conduct. § 8B2.1(c).

[19] U.S. Sent. Comm'n, *No. of Organizational Offenders over Time*, (Jan. 24, 2021), https://www.ussc.gov/sites/default/files/pdf/research-and-publications/annual-reports-and-sourcebooks/2019/FigureO2.pdf (yearly total corporate sentencings between 217 and 131 from 2006 to 2017). Another thirty or so are subject to deferred or non-prosecution agreements. Gibson Dunn, 2018 Mid-Year Update on Corporate Non-Prosecution Agreements and Deferred Prosecution Agreements 2 chart 1 (2018), https://www.gibsondunn.com/wp-content/uploads/2019/01/2018-year-end-npa-dpa-update.pdf (showing that aside from 2015, the total number of yearly agreements averaged approximately thirty from 2016 to 2018).

[20] Griffith, *supra* note 5, at 2086.

[21] Baer, *supra* note 15, at 966.

[22] *See, e.g.*, Diana E. Murphy, *The Federal Sentencing Guidelines for Organizations: A Decade of Promoting Compliance and Ethics*, 87 Iowa L. Rev. 697, 712 (2002); Report of Investigation Pursuant to Section 21(a) of the Securities Exchange Act of 1934 and Commission Statement on the Relationship of Cooperation to Agency Enforcement Decisions, Exchange Act Release No. 44,969, 76 SEC Docket 220 (Oct. 23, 2001), www.sec.gov/litigation/investreport/34–44969.htm; William A. Birdthistle & M. Todd Henderson, *Becoming a Fifth Branch*, 99 Cornell L. Rev. 1, 5 (2013).

[23] Matt Kelly, *Deregulation News: Calm Yourselves*, Radical Compliance Blog (Oct. 9, 2019), www.radicalcompliance.com/2019/10/09/deregulation-news-calm-yourselves/.

[24] Rakoff & Sack, *supra* note 7, at § 5.02[1][f] (Sarbanes-Oxley made adoption of codes of conduct compulsory; no additional substantive violations are necessary); Rebecca Walker, *The Evolution of the Law of Corporate Compliance in the United States: A Brief Overview (March 2014)*, *in* Corporate Compliance and Ethics Institute 2014, at 117 (Theodore L. Banks & Rebecca Walker eds. 2014). In conjunction, the Sentencing Commission raised penalties for corporate offenders and further clarified what constituted an effective compliance program. *See* Baer, *supra* note 15, at 965 (explaining that the Sentencing Commission explicitly included

compliance-related expansions of the law coincided with expansions of the criminal law more generally. There are now more than 5,000 federal criminal statutes on the books.[25] Add to that approximately 300,000 federal administrative regulations that can be enforced criminally, many of which are targeted at business-related conduct.[26] No surprise, then, that white-collar and corporate crime underwent the biggest expansion of federal law in three of the past five decades.[27] This is largely a product of the cycle discussed above – each new corporate scandal results in the passage of criminal legislation meant to combat it.

The result for compliance has been almost exponential growth, as evidenced by companies hiring thousands of compliance personnel at a time and at a cost of millions of dollars per year.[28] Although things have leveled out since the financial crisis, the compliance industry is expected to reach $65 billion by 2025, up from $30 billion in 2012 and much less a decade prior.[29]

But more important than raw numbers are how – and on whom – companies are spending their compliance dollars. Although there is no formal educational requirement to work in compliance, sought-after hires tend to be attorneys and those with regulatory backgrounds.[30] This makes sense given that compliance officers must keep up with increasingly complex regulatory systems in order to train on, monitor, and enforce those systems. For senior compliance positions, hires are not only lawyers but former high-ranking prosecutors and regulatory agents.[31]

While that makes sense given the arguably necessary skillset for compliance work, it also means compliance groups within companies take on the sheen of the agencies whence they came. If a company is faced with the reality of broad *respondeat superior* liability for the acts of its employees, yet wants to avoid the risk that comes from it, that company might reasonably seek to beef up its compliance function. The most obvious way is to get a bunch of people in the company's compliance ranks that understand the criminal law and procedure that create some of that risk. Naturally, these folks formulate a compliance approach that tends to shape

provisions for board oversight and for compliance programs to educate employees on the importance of corporate ethics, all with the intention of improving corporate culture).

25 *See* John S. Baker, Jr., *Revisiting the Explosive Growth of Federal Crimes*, 26 Legal Memo. 1, 1–2 (2008) (finding that Congress creates approximately five hundred crimes per decade). Between 2002 and 2007, Congress created, on average, one new crime per week, for each week of each year. *Id.* at 1.

26 Ellen S. Podgor, *Introduction: Overcriminalization: New Approaches to a Growing Problem*, 102 J. Crim. L. & Criminology 529, 531 n.10 (2012).

27 William J. Stuntz, *The Pathological Politics of Criminal Law*, 100 Mich. L. Rev. 505, 525 (2001).

28 *See* Anthony Effinger, *The Rise of the Compliance Guru – and Banker Ire*, Bloomberg (June 25, 2015), www.bloomberg.com/news/features/2015-06-25/compliance-is-now-calling-the-shots-and-bankers-are-bristling (giving example of JPMorgan hiring 8,000 compliance personnel since the financial crisis); Robert Bird & Stephen Park, *An Efficient Investment-Risk Model of Compliance*, Colum. Blue Sky Blog, Nov. 30, 2016, http://clsbluesky.law.columbia.edu/2016/11/30/an-efficient-investment-risk-model-of-corporate-compliance/ (citing study finding costs associated with compliance to be almost $10,000 per employee).

29 Report, Enterprise Governance, Risk & Compliance Market Worth $64.62 Billion by 2025, Grand View Research (May 2019), www.grandviewresearch.com/press-release/global-enterprise-governance-risk-compliance-egrc-market;Dov Seidman, *Why Companies Shouldn't 'Do' Compliance*, Forbes (May 4, 2012).

30 Effinger, *supra* note 28; Aruna Viswanatha & Brett Wolf, *Wall Street's Hot Hire: Anti-Money Laundering Compliance Officers*, Reuters (Oct. 14, 2013), http://blogs.reuters.com/financial-regulatory-forum/2013/10/14/wall-streets-hot-hire-anti-money-laundering-compliance-officers/.

31 Nicole Sandford, *Building World-Class Ethics and Compliance Programs: Making a Good Program Great*, Deloitte (2015), www2.deloitte.com/content/dam/Deloitte/no/Documents/risk/Building-world-class-ethics-and-compliance-programs.pdf ("Because a visible number of the CCO roles originated in response to enforcement activities, and because many of the more modern ethics and compliance functions evolved from regulatory compliance departments, many of the first CCOs came from legal backgrounds.").

their programs toward a focus on preventing unlawful conduct, "primarily by increasing surveillance and control and by imposing penalties for wrongdoers" – just as they would have done in their prior professional roles.[32] The result is often "over-compliance," something both regulators and most corporate leaders advocate for – it gives regulators more opportunity to influence corporate culture and companies more support for arguing that their compliance programs are effective.[33]

How this dynamic among regulator, company, and compliance plays out can be seen in the current sphere of antitrust compliance. For many years, the US Department of Justice's (DOJ) Antitrust Division had a hard and fast rule regarding criminal cases: the first company to self-report and cooperate received immunity.[34] There was no credit given to other companies involved in the collusive behavior regardless of their antitrust compliance programs. However, just recently, the policy was changed to allow for leniency in both sentencing and charging decisions for all companies having an "effective" Organizational Guidelines-style program.[35] Although it is too early to know exactly how companies will respond, all signs point to a ratcheting up of antitrust compliance across firms.[36] This will necessitate more compliance hires, undoubtedly drawn from the antitrust regulator ranks, who will remake antitrust compliance as they know it – thus, it will become an increasingly criminalized endeavor.

Take the example of Intel from a few years ago. In the early 2000s, the company pioneered what it termed the "active approach" to antitrust compliance. Intel lawyers devised a program where they would periodically "swoop in" and search through papers, disks, and emails of senior executives, seizing anything that might be demanded by the DOJ during an actual antitrust investigation.[37] If any irregularities were found, the seized materials would be used in hour-long, public mock depositions of the offending executives to establish that criminal regulations had been violated. Intel's general counsel explained that these role-playing exercises served as a dramatic wake-up call, giving lax executives the experience of being in the government's crosshairs. He boasted at the time that Intel's approach to compliance – what was essentially a standing criminal investigation of its executives – was "the world's best."[38]

Intel's approach is far from unique. In fact, many compliance programs still follow a similar approach today. And when companies are required to go from "zero to sixty" to

32 *See* Lynn S. Paine, *Managing for Organizational Integrity*, HARV. BUS. REV., Mar.–Apr. 1994, at 106, 109.

33 Ashlee Vance, *Over-Compliance Is the New Compliance, Says Former SEC Chairman*, REGISTER (May 18, 2005), www.theregister.co.uk/2005/05/18/pitt_sec_kalorama/ (describing how Harvey Pitt, former SEC Chairman and CEO of a compliance and regulatory risk management firm, approaches the design of compliance programs).

34 *See* Bruce H. Kobayashi, *Antitrust, Agency, and Amnesty: An Economic Analysis of the Criminal Enforcement of the Antitrust Laws Against Corporations*, 69 GEO. WASH. L. REV. 715, 719 (2000) (explaining operation and changes to Division's corporate amnesty program); Jeffrey Kaplan, *Assessing Antitrust Compliance Programs*, CEP MAG. (Oct. 2019), https://compliancecosmos.org/assessing-antitrust-compliance-programs?authkey=4e14318491865810 73a9c3a7ad92dd1df77202e606faeef778593419193a5ffd.

35 Remarks of Assistant Attorney General Makan Delrahim, *Wind of Change: A New Model for Incentivizing Antitrust Compliance Program*, York University School of Law Program on Corporate Compliance and Enforcement (July 11, 2019), www.justice.gov/opa/speech/assistant-attorney-general-makan-delrahim-delivers-remarks-new-york-university-school-l-0.

36 *See* Kaplan, *supra* note 34 (arguing that companies should "rise to the occasion and implement strong antitrust compliance programs").

37 Complaint at 19, New York v. Intel Corp., No. 09-827 (D. Del. Nov. 4, 2009).

38 David B. Yoffie & Mary Kwak, *Playing by the Rules: How Intel Avoids Antitrust Litigation*, 79 HARV. BUS. REV. 119, 120–21 (2001).

conform to new government edicts that are grounded in the Organizational Guidelines, they are likely to adopt what they know – criminal law-driven compliance then cedes ownership of their programs' structure and tenor to regulators.[39]

11.3 THE BEHAVIORAL EFFECTS OF CRIMINALIZED COMPLIANCE

When companies adopt criminalized compliance practices, it leads to an additional, and more problematic, impact. As compliance programs become more criminalized, they impose negative behavioral consequences on corporate employees. Both regulators and the companies they have so deeply influenced are creating environments within them that actually *foster* employee wrongdoing. This occurs because criminalized compliance regimes provide employees with opportunities to rationalize their unethical and illegal conduct. Rationalizations are at the heart of white-collar crime and corporate wrongdoing, yet the process by which they are created is seldom understood by companies, and even less so by regulators. By adopting compliance measures that mimic the criminal law, criminalized compliance programs are helping to create the very conditions that will ensure their compliance efforts will never be fully effective. In other words, by allowing compliance to become more like its regulatory master, companies are not only ignoring the behavioral science explanations as to why employees act unethically, they are actually helping to thwart the goal of compliance – lessening wrongdoing within the firm.

Why and how this occurs is a product of behavioral mechanisms operating on corporate employees subject to criminalized compliance. One is the rationalization process. Since the work of criminologist Donald Cressey in the 1950s, we have understood that the commission of white-collar crime and unethical behavior within organizations is a three-step process. For an individual to commit wrongdoing, they must have *pressure*, what Cressey called a "non-sharable financial problem"; *opportunity*, or the ability to solve that non-sharable problem by violating a trust conferred upon them by the organization; and *rationalization*, a way to verbalize the trust violation so as to make the behavior acceptable in their own mind.[40] Because the first two steps are often a given for those offenders within a corporate hierarchy – after all, most employees face periodic personal or professional financial pressures, and all employees hold positions of trust to some degree as agents of the firm – the "crux of the problem" of white-collar crime and unethical acts in business is rationalizations.[41]

Rationalizations do something quite amazing. They allow a wrongdoer to essentially hold two opposing notions constant in their mind – that they are a good person deserving of society's respect, but also that they are knowingly taking an action that violates society's laws or norms. In this way, by "pacify[ing] the morality of the situation and dissuad[ing] the feelings of guilt that may occur,"[42] rationalizations allow behavior to go forward that would otherwise be psychologically unavailable or unacceptable to an offender.[43] Cressey saw these "conversations" the offender held with themselves as "actually the most important elements in the

39 Kaplan, *supra* note 34.

40 Donald R. Cressey, *The Respectable Criminal: Why Some of Our Best Friends Are Crooks*, CRIMINOLOGICA, May 1965, at 13, 15.

41 *Id.* at 14-15.

42 Paul M. Klenowski, *"Learning the Good with the Bad": Are Occupational White-Collar Offenders Taught How to Neutralize Their Crimes?*, 37 CRIM. JUSTICE REV. 461, 471 (2012).

43 DONALD R. CRESSEY, OTHER PEOPLE'S MONEY: A STUDY IN THE SOCIAL PSYCHOLOGY OF EMBEZZLEMENT 153 (1973). *See also*, Gresham M. Sykes & David Matza, *Techniques of Neutralization: A Theory of Delinquency*, 22 AM. SOC. REV. 664, 666 (1957).

process which gets [them] into trouble, or keeps [them] out of trouble."[44] Rationalizations are the bridge between unethical thoughts and unethical action.

This insight hints at one of the critical features of rationalizations: they are not just excuses that offenders cook up after-the-fact to absolve themselves of culpability; instead, they are "vocabularies of motive," words and phrases that exist as group definitions labeling their deviant behavior as appropriate.[45] Put another way, rationalizations are created not on the "spur of the moment" but, rather, prior to the unethical action being taken.[46] Thus, a rationalization is properly understood as motivation – it not only justifies the wrongdoer's behavior to others, it makes that behavior intelligible to oneself and therefore actionable.[47]

Rationalizations as a behavioral concept are so important for compliance because they explain how an employee with a history of rule-following behavior might come to act unethically or illegally. One aspect of this is theoretical. Rationalization theory is especially applicable to corporate crime because "almost by definition white-collar offenders are more strongly committed to the central normative structure," and therefore they must rationalize their behavior through "elaborate ... processes prior to their offenses."[48] Because they are able to navigate a normative hierarchical society, have benefited from it, and have a greater stake in maintaining their status in it, they necessarily must use a rationalizing mechanism to psychologically operate outside of it.

The other aspect is relational. A key question regarding rationalizations is how they develop. Cressey believed that rationalizations originate from "popular ideologies that sanction [wrongdoing] in our culture" – they are, in essence swirling around in society, waiting to be assimilated and internalized by those considering violating a trust.[49] Recent research confirms that but also a more specific delivery mechanism: rationalizations are funneled primarily through either family and friends or coworkers.[50] Paul Klenwoski, in a follow-up to Cressey's landmark study, found that the most common source of justifications for white-collar crime were "coworkers or others peers in their industry."[51] White-collar offenders in Klenowski's study identified common mindsets and verbalizations that "taught [them] early in [their] career[s] that [they] should do whatever it takes" to succeed in business, including using deceit.[52] Like the commonplace sayings that Cressey found suggesting that wrongdoing was acceptable in certain situations (*e.g.*, "[a]ll people steal when they get in a tight spot" and "[h]onesty is the best policy, but business is business"),[53] Klenowski found that similar rationalizations (*e.g.*, "in order to level the playing field, some rules need to be bent") were part of the organizational learning process.[54]

44 Cressey, *supra* note 43, at 153.
45 Cressey, *supra* note 40, at 15.
46 *Id.*
47 Cressey, *supra* note 43, at 94, 95.
48 Michael L. Benson, *Denying the Guilty Mind: Accounting for Involvement in a White-Collar Crime*, 23 Criminology 583, 587 (1985). White collar offenders are older, more educated, better employed, and have more assets than other offenders. Michael L. Benson & Sally S. Simpson, White-Collar Crime: An Opportunity Perspective 51–52 (2009).
49 Cressey, *supra* note 40, at 15.
50 Klenowski, *Learning*, *supra* note 42, at 471.
51 *Id.*
52 *Id.*
53 Cressey, *supra* note 40, at 15.
54 Klenowski, *Learning*, *supra* note 42, at 473.

TABLE 11.1 *White-collar rationalizations*

Rationalization	Description	Example of verbalization
Denial of responsibility	The actors engaging in corrupt behaviors perceive that they have no other choice than to participate in such activities.	*"I didn't do anything wrong; it was an accident" or "It was an emergency, I needed it"*
Denial of injury	The actors are convinced that no one is harmed by their actions; hence, the actions are not really corrupt.	*"Nobody got hurt" or "I didn't steal, I just borrowed"*
Denial of the victim	The actors counter any blame for their actions by arguing that the violated party deserved whatever happened.	*"I'm the real victim here" or "They got what they deserved"*
Condemning the condemners	The actors shift attention away from their conduct onto the motives of other persons or groups that may be enforcing rules or standards applied to the actors.	*"This place is unfair or corrupt" or "The rules are unjust anyway"*
Appeal to higher loyalties	The actors argue that their violation of norms is due to their attempt to realize a higher-order value.	*"I did it for the company" or "I had to put my family first"*
Metaphor of the ledger	The actors contend that they are entitled to indulge in deviant behaviors because of their accrued credits (time and effort) in their jobs.	*"I've done way more good than bad in my life" or "For all I've done for this place, this is nothing"*
Claim of entitlement	The actors justify their conduct on the grounds that they deserve the fruits of their wrongful behavior.	*"I deserve this" or "I've earned the right to have this"*
Claim of relative acceptability/ normality	The actors justify their conduct by comparing it to others, whom they believe are committing actions that are worse.	*"There are people way worse than me"* or *"Everybody does it"*

Table 11.1 lists the most common white-collar rationalizations, a description of how they work, and examples of ways in which they might be verbalized.[55]

Understanding rationalizations and how they allow unethical and illegal behavior to go forward is essential to understanding effective corporate compliance, but we haven't yet connected that to criminalized compliance. This is easy enough if you consider the setting in which rationalizations originate: if rationalizations are drawn from an offender's work environment, that would include the compliance regime under which that individual operates. Which in turn means that a compliance program itself can be a source of criminogenic rationalizations under the right conditions–unfortunately, criminalized compliance regimes create those conditions.

Legal scholar William Stuntz recognized nearly two decades ago that the expansion of the criminal law had caused it to become uncoordinated and illogical.[56] Stuntz described the process by which the "depth and breadth" of the criminal law consolidates power in prosecutors and government agents, shifting lawmaking from legislatures to those who

[55] Descriptions adapted from Vikas Anad et. al, *Business as Usual: The Acceptance and Perpetuation of Corruption in Organizations*, 18 ACAD. MGMT. EXEC. 39, 40–43 (2004). Verbalizations drawn from Paul Michael Klenowski, "Other People's Money": An Empirical Examination of the Motivational Differences between Male and Female White Collar Offenders 56, 67 (May 2008) (unpublished Ph.D. dissertation, Indiana University of Pennsylvania).

[56] *See* Stuntz, *supra note* 27, at 519–20.

inevitably enforce the law in inconsistent or arbitrary ways.[57] It's not that the "law enforcers" mean to act arbitrarily; it's a feature of the system. Yet the result is the same. A society faced with criminal justice enforcement it perceives to be arbitrary or unjust will question the criminal law's legitimacy as a whole. This erosion of legitimacy fosters rationalizations because it provides space for verbalizations to develop. In essence, would-be offenders are able to create more "defenses" to the law that allow them to see their unethical and lawbreaking behavior as something other than illegal.[58]

This same thing happens in companies with criminalized compliance programs. Because compliance has come to mimic the criminal law by adopting many of its precepts, it suffers from the same lack of legitimacy in the eyes of corporate employees as white-collar and corporate criminal law does in the eyes of the public. This is especially true for those programs run as if they were designed by regulators (and many *were* designed by former regulators) with the primary goal of catching corporate criminals. "'[C]ommand-and-control' oriented [compliance] programs ... [provide] [t]he explicit message [that] is the same as the message from law enforcement: follow the rules or pay the penalty."[59] This results in employee reactions "rang[ing] from resentment, to an 'us-versus-them' attitude towards management,"[60] that cause the "legitimacy of the program [to be] slowly chipped away."[61] This erosion of legitimacy in compliance programs that share the features of the criminal law has been well documented.[62]

To provide some context, let's return to Intel. By all accounts, the company's active approach to compliance may have been the world's best. It was rigorous and state-of-the-art for its time – certainly effective according to the Organizational Guidelines and industry best practices. Despite that, the program failed to prevent the antitrust wrongdoing it was designed to stop. And, more importantly, it likely fueled that very same behavior among Intel employees.

Since 2001, when the company's CEO and general counsel touted the criminalized compliance program, Intel spent the next decade in antitrust litigation. In what became one of the largest antitrust sagas in history, AMD sued Intel for engaging in wide-ranging anticompetitive behavior related to microprocessor sales. Intel ended the litigation in 2009 by agreeing to pay AMD over a billion dollars.[63] A year later, Intel signed a consent decree with the FTC to settle allegations that the company "waged a 'systematic campaign'" to cut off rivals' access to markets.[64] And four years after that, Intel lost its appeal of a $1.44 billion fine imposed by the European Commission, the largest antitrust penalty

57 *Id. See also* Sara Sun Beale, *The Many Faces of Overcriminalization: From Morals and Mattress Tags to Overfederalization*, 54 Am. U. L. Rev. 747, 757 (2005).

58 Sykes & Matza, *supra* note 43, at 666 (finding that much anti-normative behavior is based on "what is essentially an unrecognized extension of [legal] defenses to crimes, in the form of justifications for deviance that are seen as valid by the delinquent but not by the legal system or society at large").

59 Scott Killingsworth, *Modeling the Message: Communicating Compliance Through Organizational Values and Culture*, 25 Geo. J. Legal Ethics 961, 966 (2012).

60 *Id.* at 968.

61 David Hess, *Ethical Infrastructures and Evidence-Based Corporate Compliance and Ethics Programs: Policy Implications from the Empirical Evidence*, 12 N.Y.U. J.L. & Bus. 317, 364 (2016).

62 *See, e.g.*, Donald C. Langevoort, *Monitoring: The Behavioral Economics of Corporate Compliance with the Law*, 2002 Colum. Bus. Rev. 71, 97–98; Killingsworth, *supra* note 59, at 968; Paine, *supra note* 32, at 111.

63 Steve Lohr & James Kanter, *A.M.D.-Intel Settlement Won't End Their Woes*, N.Y. Times (Nov. 12, 2009), www.nytimes.com/2009/11/13/technology/companies/13chip.html?_r=0.

64 Grant Gross, *US FTC Files Formal Antitrust Complaint Against Intel*, PCWorld (Dec. 16, 2009), www.pcworld.com/article/184822/article.html.

levied on a single company.[65] Not a great return on its investment in criminalized compliance.

Even more telling, though, was the 2009 complaint filed by the New York Attorney General alleging that Intel's antitrust compliance program actually contributed to the company's illegal behavior.[66] As detailed in the complaint, Intel employees repeatedly discussed kicking competitors out of other companies and markets, while also warning against using language that might "come under anti-trust scrutiny."[67] In other words, employees taught each other to continue the illegal behavior but make sure to not get caught by the compliance program. "Whatever the intention," the complaint stated, "the actual effect of the program was to school Intel executives in cover-up, rather than compliance."[68]

This result occurred because the mock raids at the heart of the company's compliance efforts communicated to employees that the goal of antitrust compliance was to limit mention of antitrust behavior, rather than to eliminate the behavior itself. When compliance is seen as only a legal requirement, and one that can be obviated by shrewd communication strategies, employees view the underlying conduct as harmless. This facilitates a host of rationalizations, including denial of the injury caused and denial of the potential victims. In addition, if anticompetitive practices are seen as part of doing business, employees may more easily deny their responsibility, another rationalization, when using such tactics. Moreover, Intel's approach generally delegitimized corporate compliance in the eyes of its employees, which created space for all rationalizations to take hold. And once that happens, there is very little stopping a white-collar crime from becoming a reality – one that the company will be compelled to face.

11.4 CONCLUSION

It certainly is odd – and often fascinating – this thing corporate compliance. What began as self-regulation has morphed into a regulator-dominated process that has largely been remade in the regulator's image, all within the firm and usually with the company's enthusiastic help. The problem is, this is bad for compliance, companies, employees, and ultimately society, if we intend to meaningfully reduce the instances of corporate wrongdoing. When companies adopt compliance practices that mimic the criminal law, they import its many faults. This includes the legitimacy concerns that foster rationalizations, the critical component of white-collar crime and unethical actions that allows wrongful conduct to go forward. Instead of blindly following the Organizational Guidelines-based edicts of regulators, companies need to regain control of compliance – they need to grab the leash – and remake it once again, this time focusing on what matters most: the employee decision-making that leads to ethical conduct. This approach has less to do with the criminal law and more to do with the behaviors that companies want to foster. While this is a significant reconceptualization of compliance as it currently operates, it is the only way that corporate compliance programs will actually achieve what we all expect of them. Otherwise, we should all just keep strolling, passing one another with a respectful nod while waiting for something bad to happen.

65 James Kanter, *European Court Upholds $1.44 Billion Fine Against Intel*, N.Y. Times (June 12, 2014), www.nytimes.com/2014/06/13/business/international/european-court-upholds-1-06-billion-fine-against-intel.html. In total, at least six government regulatory bodies representing thirty nations found that Intel engaged in anticompetitive behavior to preserve its market share. *See* Roger Parloff, *An Insider's View of AMD's War with Intel*, Fortune (May 2, 2013), http://fortune.com/2013/05/02/an-insiders-view-of-amds-war-with-intel/.

66 Complaint, *supra* note 37, at 19.

67 *Id.*

68 *Id.*

12

Supply Chain Compliance

Li Chen and Hau L. Lee

Abstract: Responsible supply chain is about ensuring that members of the supply chain act responsibly for the well-being of all people and Mother Earth. It involves both the environmental responsibility side and the social responsibility side. On top of this, responsibility also entails ensuring that products sold to consumers are authentic without having been adulterated, and that the processes throughout the supply chain are run in an ethical manner. Although interests in and concerns over responsibility by the general public, governments, and companies have continued to increase, the problems of controlling violations and noncompliance with responsibility standards remain daunting. This chapter uses a "sense" and "respond" lens to look at how such problems can be addressed. We describe some of the innovative ways that some leading companies have used to make progress.

12.1 INTRODUCTION

Globalization has led to the world's manufacturing and service supply chain spanning multiple continents. The footprint includes both developed as well as emerging and developing economies. Global enterprises have leveraged the cost and abundant labor supply afforded by the emerging economies, as well as the potential of resources such as minerals in such economies. In more recent times, there has also been an escalation of trade frictions, notably between the United States and China but extended to other countries (such as between Japan and South Korea). The tariff increases and trade restrictions among some countries might induce certain manufacturing companies to reshore their operations back to the countries where the home markets are located (Chen and Hu 2017; Cohen et al. 2018); at the same time, though, the global footprint might actually be extended even more, as some manufacturers look beyond China as their main manufacturing site. China is no longer the only Factory of the World. We have seen companies extending their manufacturing footprint to other developing economies such as Vietnam, Cambodia, East Africa, Bangladesh, Sri Lanka, etc. This extension to developing economies has not been purely due to trade frictions, however, as some companies have already been faced with the pressure of increasing costs of manufacture and the migration from low-value manufacturing to high-value design and manufacturing in mature production-based countries like China. In addition, major policy initiatives such as China's Belt and Road initiative have helped the significant economic development of many developing economies. The overall trend is that we are seeing greater and greater globalization of the supply chain.

Understandably, this globalization of the supply chain comes with many challenges. Besides the logistic inefficiencies caused by insufficient infrastructure in roads, ports, and communications, the extended supply chain could make it harder for executives to have visibility of potential production problems such as quality, yield, and potential violations at remote locations. In this chapter, we focus on how to ensure that the supply chain complies with government, industry, and corporate standards in labor practices, work conditions, environmental responsibility, and ethical treatment of people and processes.

The challenge of ensuring supply chain compliance is huge, especially with a globally distributed supply chain. In the supply chain literature, a supply chain is vulnerable to the so-called bullwhip effect when it involves many entities (Lee et al. 1997). The bullwhip effect is about information distortion. It applies to information related to sustainability and responsibility performance, making it more difficult to have true visibility of the working conditions and environmental performances of factories and operations, as well as whether products shipped out are genuine and without having been adulterated. Weak law enforcement, corruption, and lack of cross-cultural knowledge in some developing countries have also contributed to such challenges (Lee and Tang 2017).

Brands as customers have learned that violations in any of the above problems could have severe negative impacts on the brands – losing consumer confidence, reducing sales, making it difficult to recruit and retain talent, and also causing drops in market values. In this chapter, we describe how companies have begun to gain control over noncompliance problems, and how some innovative approaches have emerged.

12.2 COMPLIANCE RISKS AND MOTIVATIONS

In 2016, O'Marah and Chen surveyed global supply chain executives and asked them about the key supply chain risk concerns that they had. The traditional, expected concerns related to supply chain operational performances naturally came up, such as shipping and logistic disruptions, supply shortages, financial failures of critical suppliers, natural disasters, etc. Interestingly, though, some less well-recognized concerns had been in the minds of the supply chain executives, too. High on the list were breach of intellectual property rights, counterfeit products, and unsatisfactory supplier ethical standards. These are concerns related to how supply chains observe property rights, behave ethically, and produce genuine products that have not been tampered with (Figure 12.1).

Hence, violations in sustainability, labor practices, and ethical treatment of products and processes have become major risk concerns for supply chain managers. Although the motivations for supply chain executives to pay attention to the risk of violations may stem from the immediate costs such as possible penalty by governments, legal actions by stakeholders for violations, and disruptions or loss in productivity as a result of violation discoveries, there are other motivations. Indirect costs include negative media coverage, and the subsequent increased scrutiny by customers, governments, or other stakeholders. On the other hand, having well-recognized sustainability practices can sometimes allow the firm to command premium pricing. Cotte and Trudel (2009) reviewed over 1,700 academic and practitioner reports and found that a typical premium paid for a product manufactured with sustainable practices is 10 percent, and that consumers demand a discount for "unsustainability."

O'Marah and Chen (2017)'s follow-up survey was also quite revealing about how a company board's motivations relating to sustainability (environmental and social) investments can change

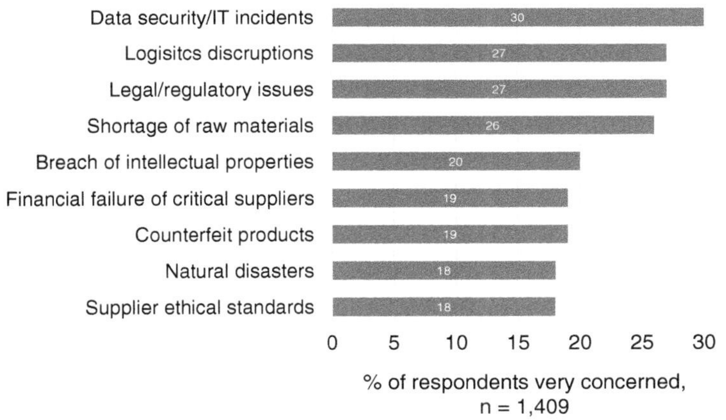

FIGURE 12.1 Key supply chain risk concerns
Source: O'Marah and Chen (2016).

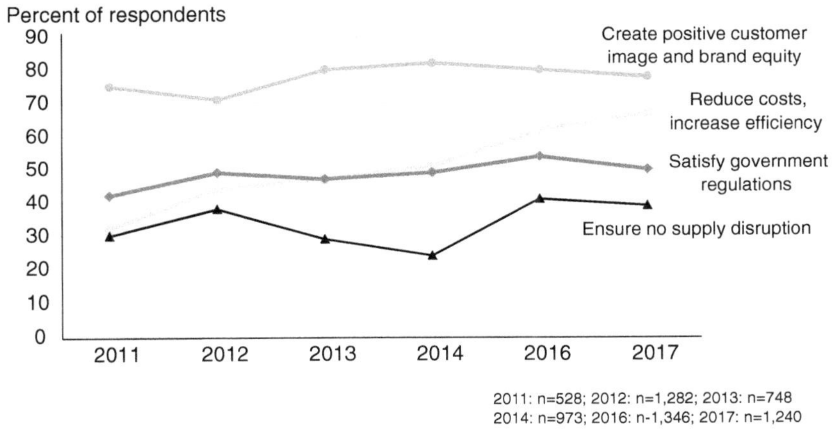

FIGURE 12.2 Motivations for sustainability investment
Sources: SCM World Chief Supply Chain Officer surveys 2011–14; Future of Supply Chain surveys 2016–17.

over a six-year period. As shown in Figure 12.2, throughout the last six years, around 80 percent of respondents claimed that the need to invest was to create a positive customer image and enhance brand equity. Interestingly, the motivation of increased sales revenue has grown from just over 30 percent in 2011 to more than double that in 2017. Hence, there is now strong indication that supply chain sustainability has significant positive value-add benefits to companies. The third most cited reason is a more defensive one – between 40 percent and 50 percent wanted to satisfy government regulations. We believe that the focus on sustainability, responsibility, and integrity is no longer a cost-containment concern. World-class companies need to look at this as a way to enhance company values, a revenue-generating proposition, and a way to create long-term equity values through stronger brand values.

12.3 SENSE AND RESPOND

Supply chain compliance can be viewed as a quality problem. Here, quality is not just limited to physical product quality but also includes process quality, for example, how raw materials are sourced from suppliers, how finished products are made and packaged in manufacturing facilities, and how products are distributed to end customers (see Chen and Lee 2017 for a detailed discussion). From this perspective, we can borrow ideas from the classic quality control literature to tackle the supply chain compliance problem.

As a starting point, companies need to employ a solid "Sense and Respond" approach to have a better handle on supply chain compliance. This is similar to the well-known Six Sigma Process for quality improvement. Quality management must start with having the right and timely measures to identify potential issues or out-of-control problems. This is what we label "Sense." For example, companies can do more inspection of the supply chain processes, and leverage new technologies to monitor and track the processes in real time.

Then, we must continue with deep analysis to see what are real out-of-control conditions and what the root causes of the problems are, and then follow up with swift actions to rectify the problems and correct the out-of-control conditions. This is what we call "Respond." Once that is done, we must continue to measure and observe again; thus, the process continues. Furthermore, companies can adopt the Kaizen principle of the Toyota Production System (TPS) (Mishina and Takeda 1995) to empower all stakeholders along the supply chain to address the compliance problem as a joint continuous improvement effort.

Management of sustainability requires a similar approach, such as that laid out in Lee and Rammohan (2017); we outline the key points here. First, we must ensure that we are able to "sense" the pulse of the supply chain, that is, we must have visibility of what is going on in the supply chain. This involves:

- traceability – being able to trace the points of origin of materials used in a product;
- visibility – knowing the social, environmental, and ethical performance of suppliers; and
- monitoring – examining supplier performance.

Once we have a "sense" of the supply chain, there are various ways to "respond." The following are typical practices commonly used in industry:

- reacting to violations once they have occurred (e.g., undertaking root cause analysis, and imposing penalties such as fines, supplier warnings, reduced business, contract termination)
- offering incentives (e.g., preferred supplier status, increased business, price premiums)
- building supplier capacity (e.g., productivity improvement, capability expansion)
- implementing proactive product and/or process design (e.g., design for the environment)
- adopting shared value strategies (e.g., creating value through community development)
- cascading responsible practices to the supplier network (e.g., training and motivating suppliers to adopt incentives, building capacity, sharing design principles to improve the sustainability of suppliers' own supply networks).

At its core, supply chain compliance is also a people problem. Process quality defects are often the result of actions committed by economic agents in a supply chain. So how do we prevent and deter the potential individuals from committing organizational violations in a complex global supply chain? "Sense" helps establish the supply chain visibility and

	Sense	*Respond*
Reactive Actions	Visibility of violations	Actions to violations
Proactive Actions	Visibility of monitoring performances	Actions & incentives for improvements

FIGURE 12.3 "Sense and Respond" for managing sustainability

accountability that are needed to tackle this challenge. Having full visibility of who does what in the supplier network can enable companies to install accountability for all parties involved in the supply chain. Companies should also "respond" by collaborating with local governments and social activists to detect and take actions against all the possible noncomplying activities along the supply chain. Yet one also needs to realize that there will always be loopholes and misaligned incentives in the supply chain that people and businesses can take advantage of. Besides vigilantly watching out for noncompliance activities, companies should also view exposed incidents as valuable learning opportunities. As the Kaizen principle suggests, after identifying the root cause of the problem, companies should be willing to make efforts to realign the existing incentive structures and/or redesign the supply chain process for continuous improvement. Figure 12.3 summarizes the Sense and Respond approach.

12.3.1 *"Sense" Challenges and Approaches*

Sensing violations and sustainability performances of the supply chain turns out to be a very difficult and challenging problem. In a survey by Lee et al. (2012), supply chain executives reported having fairly limited visibility of environmental and social sustainability violations at various levels in the supply network. For example, only 39 percent of respondents reported having visibility of environmental violations within internal operations. The percentage declined when considering operations outside of the firm, with 28 percent of respondents reporting having visibility of immediate suppliers and 25 percent reporting having visibility of the extended supply network. Finally, 8 percent reported having no visibility at all.

Without good visibility of the supply chain, it is a daunting job to ensure that the supply chain is compliant and responsible. In a supply chain, unauthorized subcontracting can often occur. Suppliers may outsource part of their production to third parties without their buyers' knowledge or authorization. This practice could be a result of the suppliers desiring to save costs as unauthorized subcontractors might not have the same production and labor standards as the suppliers, who are under the close monitoring of the buyers. It could also be a way for suppliers to respond to unexpected demand surges. Such subcontractors would thus fall outside the radar of the buyer, and would not be monitored. The product's origin can thus become untraceable, and the production environment of these subcontractors is unknown to the buyer, let alone the public. Indeed, Caro et al. (in press) found that, in a global apparel supply chain, 36 percent of production was subcontracted without authorization.

To improve visibility and accountability, companies often rely on supplier screening and monitoring instruments such as certification to identify risky suppliers and/or conduct process audits to detect potential violations. However, the availability of these instruments varies in industries. For example, when special minerals are used in production, supplier violations could be things like sourcing the minerals from conflict or sanctioned regions. Because minerals are often mixed by smelters, rendering traceability almost impossible, it is thus difficult to conduct either certification or audit. In agricultural produce such as coffee, a large number of small farms are scattered all over the world in difficult-to-access regions, rendering frequent audits cost-prohibitive. In this case, the buyers choose one-time certification such as Fairtrade certification or Starbucks's Coffee and Farmer Equity (C.A.F.E.) Practices certification. On the other hand, in the electronics manufacturing industry, where there is a limited pool of qualified suppliers, one-time certification is not useful and it is the ongoing process that the buyers are concerned with. Thus, companies (such as Apple) are stepping up their efforts on audits of factory work conditions. Finally, in the apparel manufacturing industry, the factories are not as small as farms but not as big as electronic manufacturers (e.g., Foxconn). In this case, both certification and audits are feasible for the buyers (e.g., Li & Fung and Nike). Figure 12.4 provides an illustration of these four scenarios.

Adding to the challenge of supplier audit and certification, it is often difficult for global brands to carry out audit work by themselves for the large number of small suppliers scattered in remote regions. As a result, audit work is often delegated to local audit agencies. In regions with lax law enforcement such as the "Higher Risk" countries specified by Walmart (2018), however, this could breed corruption. An unethical, noncomplying supplier seeking a lucrative production contract may very well bribe an unethical auditor to pass the audit. Such supplier–auditor collusion compromises the integrity of the audit and weakens its effectiveness in ensuring compliance. Chen et al. (2020) showed that addressing the threat of supplier–auditor collusion calls for higher process quality requirement for suppliers located in high–risk countries. Moreover, it is important for global brands to collaborate with local governments to increase the penalty for collusion and to promote the ethical level of the third-party auditors located in high-risk countries. Apart from the potential corruption and/or financial conflicts of interest between the auditor and the supplier, Short et al. (2016) found in an empirical study that audit results could sometimes be significantly biased due to the influence of social factors such as the auditors' experience and professional training, and

Process Audit	Supplier Certification: *Unavailable*	Supplier Certification: *Available*
Unavailable	Difficult to do certification or audit due to little traceability, e.g., mining of special (conflict) minerals	Difficult to do frequent audits, one-time certification possible, e.g., farm produce such as Starbucks' C.A.F.E.
Available	Difficult to do certification due to limited pool of suppliers, frequent audits possible, e.g., electronic manufacturing such as Apple	Effective certification and frequent audits possible, e.g., apparel manufacturing such as Li & Fung and Nike

FIGURE 12.4 Supplier audit and certification

the social characteristics of the audit team as well as their repeated interactions with those being audited.

Gaining visibility of violations or improved sustainability performance often requires firms to carefully establish mechanisms to detect them. Such mechanisms can include (1) suppliers sharing data with the buyer, which requires a high degree of trust and a collaborative relationship; (2) direct monitoring by buyers or buyer-designated agencies, and (3) reporting from interested parties. Supplier self-reporting is a low-cost way of getting "Sense." According to Starbucks's C.A.F.E. program, the first step is for the farmers to fill out a lengthy questionnaire that serves as a self-reporting tool, and then this is followed by more detailed audits for certification. Toffel and Short (2011) found that self-reporting of violations can be a useful tool for identifying the self-policing efforts of firms, so as to improve compliance and environmental performance. Of course, self-reporting can be imperfect and often insufficient to "sense" all violations. Crowd-sourcing is another low-cost way of getting "Sense." One example is the nongovernmental group called the Institute of Public and Environmental Affairs (IPE) (Plambeck et al., 2012), which uses a vast volunteer network to collect extensive data and reports environmental violations throughout China on a public website. Other examples of reporting make use of third-party companies, often social enterprises, such as Labor Link (Schwartz 2013) and Labor Voices (Lahiri 2012), which utilize information technologies such as mobile phones for workers to directly report to global brands information on violations, working conditions, worker well-being, job satisfaction, and more.

12.3.2 *"Respond" Challenges and Approaches*

As discussed earlier, "Respond" includes both actions to address violations after they have been identified or exposed and actions to prevent or reduce the chance of future violations. Increasingly, global companies are intolerant of violations in sustainability and labor compliance. Many companies have a "zero tolerance" policy for serious issues such as child labor, and will terminate business relationships if such issues are detected. In their study of supply chain executives, Lee et al. (2012) found that, out of 1,228 respondents, 32 percent would not issue a warning but instead would immediately invoke an action like immediate termination of the business relationship (47 percent of the 32 percent), reduced business plus monetary fines (13 percent of the 32 percent), or reduced business (40 percent of the 32 percent). For the other 68 percent of respondents, they would be given warning first, and the follow-on actions for continual violations would be termination of business relationship (42 percent of the 68 percent), reduced business plus monetary fines (14 percent of the 68 percent), or reduced business (44 percent of the 68 percent).

What about actions to improve compliance? Based on a study of 763 factories' audit results on compliance ratings, Locke et al. (2007) found little change in factories' compliance performance after Nike started monitoring them. Every twelve to eighteen months, Nike scored each factory on a variety of labor standards (such as wages, working hours, and disciplinary actions) as well as health, safety, and environmental standards (such as access to emergency exits and safe storage of hazardous chemicals). The resulting grades in the two compliance areas ranged from A and B ratings for factories with good workplace conditions to C and D ratings for factories demonstrating serious violations. Over time, with close monitoring, one might expect compliance performance to improve. The Locke et al. (2007) study found little such evidence. In fact, one might say that performance actually deteriorated: 42 percent of the sample saw no change in grades, 22 percent improved, while 36 percent deteriorated in grades. This showed the limitation of pure monitoring. Hence, monitoring is only an imperfect means to gain "Sense," and it may not be a sufficiently effective means to make improvements or "Respond."

Distelhorst et al. (2017) found that introducing lean[1] production practices to factories supplying to Nike significantly improved labor compliance. The study, based on labor compliance data from 2009 and 2013 at 300 factories 2 years prior to and 2 years after the 2011 introduction of lean practices, suggests that stronger performance can enable a factory to be more compliant. Those factories that had adopted 100 percent lean practices saw their compliance grade improve over half a letter. Overall, the authors estimated that lean factories reduced the probability of serious labor violations by 15 percent, and that it could be by as much as 33 percent.

The success of lean practices demonstrates the power of *incentive alignment* (the incentives of productivity improvement and compliance are aligned) and *capacity building* (factories can achieve greater efficiency through lean practices without having to cut corners).

Nike has continued its journey in managing compliance by moving from "lean manufacturing" to "equitable manufacturing" (Barrientos 2019). The idea of equitable manufacturing is that, in addition to focusing on productivity improvement at the factory floor level, we must also extend our attention to the well-being of the workers and their families. The premise is that a valued workforce leads to better business, benefiting the worker, the factory, and Nike. Hence, Nike aims to build such a manufacturing environment at its factories for all its workers.

The focus on workers' well-being has led to Nike investing in upskilling workers and developing their multiskills. This can lead to productivity increase and, at the same time, higher take-home pay for workers. To enable workers to be able to address production problems better, problem-solving training was provided. The lean concept of Kaizen was extended to well-being development. Management was asked to have a mindset change to encourage worker engagement. Surveys were undertaken periodically with workers to learn about their views and needs. Capacity-building investment included the setting up of integrated teams, boot camps, better training documents, and training centers. To do all this, Nike involved outside new ventures such as Micro Benefits, to help build the right tools and services, including smart phone apps and digital learning platforms. Pilots were successfully completed in Indonesia and China.

The early results from the pilots have been encouraging. The initiative has resulted in improvements in production efficiency, reduction of direct labor cost per piece of product (either apparel or footwear), improvement of quality, and increases in effective capacity as a result. At the same time, surveys have shown that workers feel more energized, valued, and supported by management. The increase in morale has led to reduction of worker turnover.

The Nike experiments with lean production and equitable manufacturing aimed at improving the productivity and well-being of workers, with the premise that these efforts would then lead to compliance and sustainability improvement. This is a positive "Respond" action, as it creates incentives for factory owners and workers to improve compliance and sustainability. As Lee et al. (2012) found, positive incentives have increasingly been used by global companies to address compliance problems. Figure 12.5 shows how various incentive schemes have been deployed by companies.

1 The lean production process was championed by Toyota, and has been widely adopted by companies as a way to eliminate waste, improve productivity, and increase the efficiency of production systems.

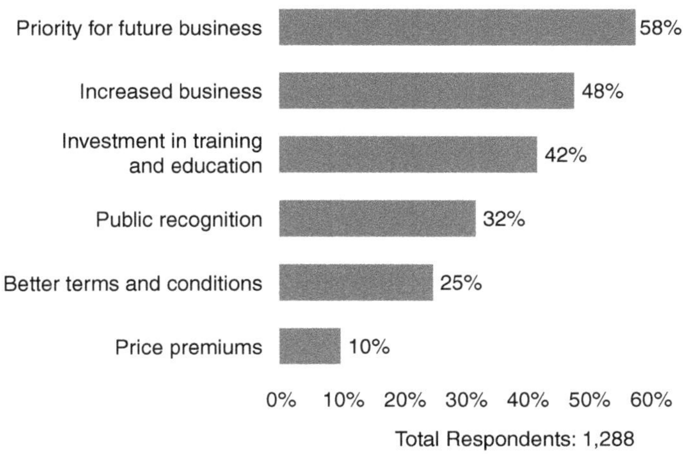

FIGURE 12.5 Incentives used
Source: Lee et al. (2012).

It is worth elaborating a bit on what incentives are used by leading companies. Very few companies use price premiums as a reward; more common is to give suppliers special status, increased business, more recognition, and better terms and conditions. Of these companies, 47 percent also invested in training and education of suppliers. Babich and Tang (2012) found that the deferred payment mechanism can help deter suppliers from product adulteration. Chen and Lee (2017) showed that incentives such as contingency payments, used in combination with supplier certification and process audit instruments, can help reduce supplier violations and improve supply chain compliance. Furthermore, Bondareva and Pinker (2019) showed that a dynamic relational contract that postpones the supplier's opportunity for profit can be used to create incentives for suppliers to exert effort to achieve quality compliance in supply chains.

12.3.3 *A Case Example*

A case in point of using "Sense and Respond" to improve supply chain compliance is Starbucks. As a major coffee retailer, Starbucks sources coffee beans from all over the world, including developing regions such as East Africa, Central America, and Indonesia. The supply chain of coffee involves coffee farmers, cooperatives, processors, importers, exporters, and eventually brand owners and retailers. Along the supply chain, violations relating to environmental practices – e.g. water pollution, use of abrasive fertilizers, extended use of pesticides and insecticides – treatment of labor – e.g. low wages, poor work conditions – and even ethical financial management or corruption could occur. Starbucks seeks a stable supply of high-quality coffee from farmers who grow it in environmentally sound ways, and from farm owners who avoid unsafe or exploitative labor practices. In the early 2000s, Starbucks initiated a program called Coffee and Farmer Equity (C.A.F.E.) Practices to develop a sustainable coffee supply chain (Lee et al. 2007).

C.A.F.E. could be viewed as a code of conduct or compliance standard for suppliers. It includes coffee quality and economic transparency (suppliers are expected to disclose the amount of money that is ultimately paid to farmers). It is a major step toward "Sense" and allows clear guidelines for monitoring. Suppliers are graded based on a set of environmental and social criteria, then audited by an independent verifier, before being licensed by Scientific Certification Systems.

As part of the "Respond" strategy, Starbucks put in place some incentive schemes. Farmers are rewarded for coffee growing and processing practices that contribute positively to the conservation of soil, water, energy, and biological diversity, and have minimal impact on the environment. A supplier qualifies as a preferred supplier and gains preferential treatment in future purchases if it scores at least 60 percent of the available points in the certification process – Starbucks would buy from the supplier first and then offer preferential contract terms. Suppliers who earn scores above 80 percent qualify as strategic suppliers and earn a premium of $0.05 per pound of coffee for one year. To encourage continuous improvement, the company also offers an additional sustainability performance premium of $0.05 per pound of coffee to suppliers who are able to achieve a 10-point increase above 80 percent over the course of a year. In addition to monetary incentives, Starbucks's "Respond" strategy also includes capacity-building investment. Farmer support centers were set up in coffee-growing regions to give technical support and training to improve the farmers' cultivation and production methods. Micro-financing loans were given to help farmers in making the necessary investments in tools.

C.A.F.E. has become the cornerstone of both "Sense" and "Respond" practices for Starbucks. C.A.F.E. delivers benefits to both Starbucks and suppliers. The company enjoys a more stable supply base, and has gained more direct access to farmers. Based on a study in Costa Rica by Earthwatch (2007), C.A.F.E. implementation resulted in annual cost savings of $243 per hectare, which translated to an increase of $1,200 in the annual income of a small farmer; there was a 25 percent increase in yield, which was equivalent to an average annual revenue increase of $2,875 per farmer; and coffee quality improved as a result of stronger plant health and increased farm productivity.

12.4 INNOVATIONS AND OPPORTUNITIES

Innovations in products and processes, aided by technological advances, can also be important means to respond to the problems of compliance in a positive way. Of course, innovations should not be solely the responsibility of the global enterprise buyer. It is true that, sometimes, a global enterprise may have the resources and knowhow to take a leadership position to drive innovations across the supply chain. The Starbucks and Nike cases we described earlier are such examples. But innovations can also occur in all parts of the supply chain, as Lee and Schmidt (2017) showed. Thus, it is important that we leverage the full supply chain ecosystem as sources and enablers of innovations, particularly in the area of improving compliance and sustainability performance. Such leverage is not just about learning who can innovate but also about creating a collaborative relationship to encourage such innovations to occur.

As the Nike case also demonstrated, innovations that drive compliance and sustainability improvements are often ones that improve productivity and efficiency, and vice versa. Hence, we should view such innovations not just as for the sake of avoiding violations or as costs but as opportunities, too. Product design is another area where innovations can occur; it can have an impact on manufacturing cost, quality, and product performance, but it can also affect compliance and sustainability. Designing products with the right choice of materials, for example, may reduce the chance or extent of water or environmental pollution. Designing products and their associated production processes in a certain way could lead to less hazardous impacts on worker health and work-related injuries.

The rapid advances of technologies have offered great opportunities to develop responsible and integral supply chains. In "Sense," the extensive information networks that now exist even in developing economies allow connectivity among the different nodes in a supply chain to be easy and reliable. The tremendous advances in Internet of Things (IoT) enable much easier sensing of products and the environment, and it is also increasingly possible to have "smart" sensors connected. All these devices contribute to transparency, that is, better "Sense" of the supply chain, which in turn could have great value toward achieving supply chain compliance.

Another "Sense" innovation is the use of satellite monitoring of geomaps. This is what Unilever, Nestlé, and Mondelez use regularly to check on whether palm oil farmers are complying with industry agreements regarding deforestation (Meyer 2019). Global Fishing Watch, a nonprofit organization, has been using an onboard automatic identification system created by satellite technology consultancy SkyTruth and Google to sense illegal transshipment, which is often linked to illegal or unregulated fishing, as well as illegal labor practices (Ship Technology 2018).

As for "Respond," we have described how Nike uses smart phone apps in its equitable manufacturing initiative. Another example is Li & Fung, which has created a special Workers App to allow management to engage workers through surveys, announcements, and educational content about health, safety, and productivity (Fung Academy 2018). In a soft-launch in 2018 at 10 suppliers in Vietnam, it reached 15,000 workers.

At the very early stage, microbe and DNA technologies may also be of potential value in monitoring factory origin, factory workers' composition (like the possibility of child labor being used), or exposure to chemicals and hazardous materials. An example of such early use of technology was the bio-monitoring of DNA damage of workers in Pakistan (Khisroon et al. 2018). These are just some of the potential opportunities for innovation in managing supply chain compliance that are being created by technological advancements. Opportunities exist in three main thrusts of technological advance – visibility and connectivity, AI and data analytics, and process advances – to directly improve product integrity, to be able to trace the origins of products, to ensure the authenticity of supply chain flows, to detect any problems and diagnose their root causes, to prevent product adulteration, and to enable fast contingency action to be taken when problem occur.

Technological advances such as IoT and digitization have given rise to data being more transparent and accessible, which should create enormous opportunities for research on how to improve compliance (see Sodhi and Tang 2019). At the same time, we want to mention that there are still challenges. For example, IPE's database (Plambeck et al. 2012) has tracked environmental violations in China, and the information has been used by corporations and even consumers to track the responsibility performances of factories and suppliers. But, as we know, these were data based on violations (reported by local governments, or discovered by NGOs, etc.); many incidences went undetected and therefore were not reported. Hence, we face the problem of incompleteness. For reported violations, there could also be two potential caveats. One is that cross-sectional data analysis may encounter difficulties with violations measurement data being inconsistent, which is due to different countries sometimes assessing and categorizing violations differently. Second is that data on the degree of violations (e.g., "excessive overtime" is used to describe two hours' overtime *and* twenty hours' overtime, which are very different) are often just not there.

To do a thorough job requires deep collaboration with a company (such as Distelhorst et al. 2017 managed with Nike, or Caro et al. in press with Li & Fung) to get comprehensive and full data, or longitudinal data. Such data records – for example, the full incidences of noncompliance, with specifics on where, who, and what (the nature of the noncompliance) – are necessary to do a rigorous investigation, and to learn about potential causal effects. We need more of such successful deep collaboration with companies.

Furthermore, the hardest part is to measure the impact of companies' investments into improvements. It is not easy to differentiate how companies' investments have helped in the compliance dimension, as they often have parallel effects on many fronts. In addition, although it would be great to have quantitative data sets for statistical analysis, we should not discount the value of deep case-based field studies, which can be useful to supplement quantitative data. They can also be used to help formulate hypotheses or explain phenomena and management actions.

In summary, although the challenges of creating a supply chain that is free from violations and compliance problems are huge, by having the right "Sense and Respond" strategies in place, engaging with the extended supply chain partners in a collaborative way, and making use of technological innovations, we can make big steps forward.

REFERENCES

Barrientos, S. 2019. *Gender and Work in Global Value Chains: Capturing the Gains?* Cambridge: Cambridge University Press.

Babich, V., and C. S. Tang. 2012. "Managing Opportunistic Supplier Product Adulteration: Deferred Payments, Inspection, and Combined Mechanisms." *Manufacturing & Service Operations Management* 14, 2, 301–14.

Bondareva, M., and E. Pinker. 2019."Dynamic Relational Contracts for Quality Enforcement in Supply Chains." *Management Science* 65, 3, 955–1453.

Caro, F., L. Lane, and A. Sáez De Tejada Cuenca. in press. "Can Brands Claim Ignorance? Unauthorized Subcontracting in Apparel Supply Chains." *Management Science*.

Chen, L., and B. Hu. 2017. "Is Reshoring Better than Offshoring? The Effect of Offshore Supply Dependence." *Manufacturing & Service Operations Management* 19, 2, 166–84.

Chen, L., and H. L. Lee. 2017. "Sourcing under Supplier Responsibility Risk: The Effects of Certification, Audit and Contingency Payment." *Management Science* 63, 9, 2795–2812.

Chen, L., S. Yao, and K. Zhu, 2020. "Responsible Sourcing under Supplier-Auditor Collusion." *Manufacturing & Service Operations Management* 22, 6, 1234–50.

Cohen, M. A., S. Cui, R. Ernst, A. Huchzermeier, P. Kouvelis, H. L. Lee, H. Matsuo, M. Steuber, and A. A. Tsay. 2018. "OM Forum – Benchmarking Global Production Sourcing Decisions: Where and Why Firms Offshore and Reshore." *Manufacturing & Service Operations Management* 20, 3, 389–402.

Cotte, J., and R. Trudel. 2009. "Socially Conscious Consumerism: A Systematic Review of the Body of Knowledge." *Network for Business Sustainability*.

Distelhorst, G., J. Haimnueller, and R. M. Locke. 2017. "Does Lean Improve Labor Standards? Management and Social Performance in the Nike Supply Chain." *Management Science* 63, 3, 707–28.

Earthwatch. 2007. https://earthwatch.org/Corporate-Partnerships/Corporate-Partnership-Case-Studies/STARBUCKS, accessed August 8, 2019.

Fung Academy. 2018 (March 12). www.fungacademy.com/news/news-1/, accessed August 8, 2019.

Khisroon, M., A. Khan, F. Zaidi, and Ahmadullah. 2018, "Bio-monitoring of DNA Damage in Matchstick Industry Workers from Peshawar Khyber Pakhtunkhwa, Pakistan." *International Journal of Occupational and Environmental Health*, 24, 3–4, 126–33.
Lahiri, T. 2012. "Can Mobile Phones Improve Factory Safety?" *Wall Street Journal India*, December 24.
Lee, H. L., and S. V. Rammohan. 2017. "Improving Social and Environmental Performance in Global Supply Chains." In *Sustainable Supply Chains*, edited by Y. Bouchery, C. J. Corbett, J. C. Fransoo, and T. Tan. Springer Series in Supply Chain Management. Switzerland: Springer Nature, 439–64.
Lee, H. L., and G. Schmidt. 2017. "Using Value Chains to Enhance Innovation." *Production and Operations Management* 26, 4, 617–32.
Lee, H. L., and C. S. Tang. 2017. "Socially and Environmentally Responsible Value Chain Innovations: New Operations Management Research Opportunities." *Management Science* 64, 3, 983–96.
Lee, H. L., V. Padmanabhan, and S. Whang. 1997. "The Bullwhip Effect in Supply Chains." *Sloan Management Review* 38, 3, 93–102.
Lee, H. L., K. O'Marah, and G. John. 2012. "The Chief Supply Chain Officer Report." SCM World Research Report.
Lee, H. L., S. Duda, L. James, Z. Mackwani, R. Munoz, and D. Volk. 2007. "Building a Sustainable Supply Chain: Starbucks' Coffee and Farm Equity Program." In *Building Supply Chain Excellence in Emerging Economies*, edited by H. L. Lee and C. Y. Lee. New York: Springer, 391–405.
Locke, R. M., F. Qin, and A. Brause. 2007. "Does Monitoring Improve Labor Standards? Lessons from Nike." *Industrial and Labor Relations Review* 61, 3–31.
Meyer, C. 2019. "With Satellites and Supply Chains, Global Brands Take Aim at Deforestation." The Fourth Wave of Environmental Innovation, https://medium.com/the-fourth-wave/with-satellites-and-supply-chains-global-brands-take-aim-at-deforestation-ecb6282cce99, accessed August 8, 2019.
Mishina, K., and K. Takeda. 1995. "Toyota Motor Manufacturing, U.S.A., Inc." Harvard Business School, Case 9–693-019.
O'Marah, K., and X. Chen. 2016. "Future of Supply Chain 2016." SCM World Research Report.
2017. "Future of Supply Chain 2017." SCM World Research Report.
Plambeck, E., H. L. Lee, and P. Yatsko. 2012. "Improving Environmental Performance in Your Chinese Supply Chain." *Sloan Management Review* Winter, 43–51.
Schwartz, A. 2013. "Can Mobile Phones Prevent More Factory Deaths?" *Fast Company*, January 9.
Ship Technology. 2018 (August 20). www.ship-technology.com/features/global-fishing-watch/, accessed on 8 August, 2019.
Short, J. L., M. W. Toffel, and A. R. Hugill. 2016. "Monitoring Global Supply Chains." *Strategic Management Journal* 37, 9, 1878–97.
Sodhi, M. S., and C. S. Tang. 2019. "Research Opportunities in Supply Chain Transparency." *Production and Operations Management* 28, 12, 2946–59.
Toffel, M. W., and J. L. Short. 2011. "Coming Clean and Cleaning Up: Does Voluntary Self-Reporting Indicate Effective Self-Policing?" *Journal of Law & Economics* 54, 3, 609–49.
Walmart. 2018. "Audit and Assessment Policy & Guidance." https://corporate.walmart.com/media-library/document/audit-and-assessment-policy-guidance-april-2018/_proxyDocument?id=00000162-cf62-d3f6-a7f7-ef6b7cfe0000, accessed August 27, 2019.

13

Regulatory Compliance in a Global Perspective: Developing Countries, Emerging Markets and the Role of International Development Institutions

Florentin Blanc and Giuseppa Ottimofiore

Abstract: Regulatory compliance is crucial to ensure that regulation and related public policies achieve their intended public outcomes – that is, safeguarding key elements of public welfare in a given country, while supporting economic and social development. Although this often remains implicit, promoting regulatory compliance is an important aspect of international development work. Nonetheless, the need to treat "compliance" or behavior change as a specific object has taken time to emerge, as has the understanding of the entire process between inputs (regulations, resources) and outcome (compliance or behavior change, or the absence thereof). Research shows that compliance is not an automatic consequence of regulations, that it does not always produce the desired outcomes, and that the "volume" and severity of enforcement do not necessarily correlate with compliance and regulatory outcomes. Significant evidence also suggests that poorly designed regulation, regulatory administration, procedures and systems can be both a hindrance to economic growth and a source of corruption.

This chapter looks at the specific aspects and challenges of regulatory compliance in a broad "development" context – characterized by a vast informal sector or significant "gray economy," regulatory burden and barriers, and overall insufficient regulatory compliance (and thus effectiveness). In this context, "regulatory delivery" – that is, how the whole range of state activities aiming at improving or securing compliance is designed, structured, resourced and implemented – particularly matters. A more risk-based, focused, responsive regulatory delivery helps to maintain institutional integrity while taking into account actual issues and demands and can also support good governance and the rule of law.

13.1 INTRODUCTION

This chapter looks at regulatory compliance (i.e. compliance by economic operators in a broad range of matters, from e.g. taxes and duties through health and safety to environment or consumer protection) in an international development context. This means that it considers both how international development institutions conceive regulatory compliance as part of development work, and address it within their programs, and what can be said of compliance issues *specifically* in a development context (i.e. beyond all the general aspects covered in other chapters, and which generally remain valid).

13.1.1 *Compliance and "International Development Institutions"*

Considering compliance from an "international development institutions" perspective requires us to "unpack" a series of concepts and terms. First, "development," broadly understood, is a "challenged" concept – for example because of what is seen as an inherent value judgment in using the word, which gives precedence to certain goals and priorities for human societies, and is largely aligned with dominant cultures. Thus, referring to "developing" or "emerging" countries is simultaneously convenient and problematic. "Development" remains, however, an important notion, in terms, for example, of its impact on public policies. This influence on public policy, in turn, stems first from the demands of large swathes of most countries' populations, who strive for higher incomes, greater access to health care and modern comforts, but also from other aspects of development such as a well-functioning public administration, or a safeguarded environment. It also derives from the objectives of national governments – regardless of whether they arise from self-interest or from more altruistic views, but also from the work and influence of international institutions explicitly set up for the purpose of fostering (economic or broader) development. Second, "development" can be seen as primarily economic (meaning not only GDP growth but also an economy that is not overly dependent on a very narrow base of extractive or agricultural, export-oriented sectors, and thus is more resilient in the face of economic downturns)[1] – or in a broader perspective (including limiting inequality, addressing poverty, protecting the environment, promoting health, etc.). While these considerations were rarely absent from narrower "economic" perspectives (as they all, in turn, influence longer-term economic performance) (Rodrik 2003), they are much more central to broader development approaches, for example "sustainable development."

It is far beyond the scope of this chapter to enter into discussions of whether, indeed, "development" can be made a fully workable and/or coherent context – and of which factors are the most important in achieving economic growth and broader development (Rodrik 2006, 2012). Similarly beyond our scope is a discussion of which types of intervention really "work" (Duflo and Banerjee 2011) and/or what can be the role of development interventions versus other factors in actually achieving "development."[2] What we shall limit ourselves to is to see, within a given perspective that is the one of "international development institutions," what the role and views of compliance are – and how they are trying to address compliance issues within their interventions.

The "international development institutions" that this chapter refers to are essentially the World Bank Group (the International Bank for Reconstruction and Development, together with the International Development Association, the International Finance Corporation and the Multilateral Investment Guarantee Agency), the regional development institutions (the Inter-American Development Bank, the African Development Bank, the Asian Development Bank and the European Bank for Reconstruction and Development), and the OECD (Organisation for Economic Co-operation and Development). Most of these organizations have "development" in their names, and all their mission statements emphasize a broad approach to social and economic "sustainable" development. All provide (directly or through contractors) advice to governments (and, for the OECD, it is its primary mission), and most of them provide loans to states or private investors in developing countries (and it is the primary mission of the "development banks"). We do not cover here other institutions of the United

[1] On the downside risks of overreliance on a narrow economic basis, see Blattman et al. 2007.

[2] See e.g. for critical views Easterly and Williamson 2011.

Nations family, because compliance issues are usually far more peripheral to their work (with the partial exception of the UN WHO (World Health Organization) and the UN FAO (Food and Agriculture Organization)), and we also do not cover other regional institutions – or entities, like the European Union, that are more a "meta-state" than an "international organization."

Promoting regulatory compliance, in aspects as diverse as taxes or environmental protection, is an important priority of international development work – though one that is not always stated as such, or indeed conceived properly at all. It often remains implicit, with the stated objective of development interventions being to improve a given outcome (say, tax revenue, or protection of forests and other natural reserves), and the instruments including new or improved laws and regulations, and "strengthened" public administration (through investment in equipment or training, internal restructuring, etc.). The need to treat "compliance" (or, more broadly, behavior change) as a specific object has taken time to emerge, with the whole process between the inputs (regulations, resources) and the outcome (compliance or behavior change, or the absence thereof) being long treated as a kind of "black box."

The first projects of international development institutions focusing on regulatory compliance issues, in terms of either research and/or implementation, seem to date to the late 1990s and early 2000s. The OECD commissioned some work on enforcement of regulations, commissioning papers from 1993, for example by Braithwaite (1993), and set up the Forum on Tax Administration in 2002 (see www.oecd.org/tax/administration/). The World Bank Group started a project focusing on inspections reform in Uzbekistan and Tajikistan in 2003 (Blanc 2011), following some earlier work on inspections in Latvia in the late 1990s (Coolidge et al. 2003). The OECD work on tax administration stemmed from the strong findings in the tax field that the overall level of compliance[3] varied not only due to tax rates or to the "intensity" of controls but also in connection with other factors (complexity of administration, ways of dealing with taxpayers, risk analysis, etc.), and that "stricter" enforcement efforts may in fact result in *lower* compliance. The World Bank Group projects were responding to the findings that regulatory inspections and enforcement in a number of countries were major sources of barriers and burden, limiting business entry and growth, and major channels of corruption – with little (if any) benefit in terms of health, safety or other public goods (Blanc 2012b).[4]

Increasing research showed not only that compliance was not a consequence outcome of regulations, that even compliance did not always produce the desired outcomes, and that the "volume" and severity of enforcement did not necessarily produce compliance (or regulatory outcomes) either (Kirchler 2007; Gunningham et al. 2003). There was also significant evidence that regulation, and more specifically regulatory administration, procedures and systems, could be both a hindrance to economic growth (at least in some cases) (Djankov at al. 2006) and a source of corruption (Djankov et al. 2002; Ogus 2004).

Confronted with this situation, and with only limited experience to draw from in terms of successful reforms and transformations, the World Bank Group initially largely focused on getting framework legislation adopted. Such legislation aimed to cancel excessive permits and licenses, cap inspections frequency (which, with up to fifteen inspections per year even

3 Compliance level in tax is more easily measurable than in other fields, since economic modeling allows for estimation of the theoretical tax revenue, which can then be compared with actual tax revenue – the lower the actual tax revenue as a percentage of the theoretical tax revenue, the lower the compliance.

4 This conclusion was already explicit since the early 2000s in OECD and WBG papers: see e.g. Coolidge 2006; World Bank 2006b.

for the smallest businesses e.g. in Tajikistan, was really vastly excessive), and "coerce" further reforms in methods and practices through binding legal requirements. Transformation of practices often did not happen, because the underlying forces that drove abuse of power or corruption were not affected, and because more legislation generally cannot solve problems stemming from inadequate or improper enforcement of existing legislation (an apparently obvious point that many anti-corruption laws seem to miss). In addition, because international development projects are under constant pressure to deliver outcomes as soon as possible, they tend to be too focused on formal results (adopting laws) and constrained by short time frames (a couple of years at most, in general).[5] Drawing on the research of "good practices" done in the framework of the reform projects, and on the lessons of experience, the World Bank Group prepared successive manuals and handbooks on regulatory inspections that largely articulate what it deemed most important for improving regulatory systems so as to decrease barriers and burdens and simultaneously improve compliance (World Bank Group 2011). In cases where sufficiently constant efforts were put on supporting "on the ground" changes in culture and practices, and where government commitment was similarly constant enough, tangible reforms were achieved in how the public administration works on inspections and enforcement. These appear to lead to some improvements in compliance or at least in attitude toward compliance (e.g. in Mongolia) (Dugeree et al. 2019).

In the same period, awareness of regulatory inspections, enforcement and compliance issues increased and spread in OECD countries,[6] with the most high-profile analytical piece and reform program being the 2005 Hampton Review in the UK (Hampton 2005). It was followed by efforts (still ongoing) to make inspections more risk-based, compliance-promoting, growth-friendly, coherent and consistent, etc.[7] While some research work on inspections and enforcement has been carried out/commissioned by the OECD since the late 1990s, the first OECD research program on this subject started in 2012 (Blanc 2012b). The *Good Practice Principles* were published 2014 (OECD 2014a), followed by the *Toolkit* in 2018 (OECD 2018). These set forth a vision of a "good practice" inspections and enforcement system as being evidence- and risk-based, compliance-supporting more than punitive, and based on professional competence, data management, transparent procedures and processes, etc It articulates compliance as something that is to be supported and helped by regulators, and not only controlled and enforced. It broadly corresponds to what is increasingly called in the UK "better regulatory delivery" (Russell and Hodges 2019).

13.1.2 *Compliance and Regulatory Delivery in a Developing or Emerging Context*

In the "development" and/or "emerging" context, we find broadly two types of situation in respect of the level of (in)formality, leading to two sets of somewhat different issues. The first situation corresponds to the existence of a vast informal sector (i.e. enterprises which are not legally established, or which are registered only in a "semi-formal" way) – in particular in Latin America, Africa and South/South-East Asia. The second situation is often found in

5 Issues mostly documented in internal reviews and assessments. A recent evaluation of World Bank "investment climate" interventions (Independent Evaluation Group 2015), in spite of serious shortcomings and limitations, rightly points out the "implementation" gap.

6 Such as Italy in 2002 ("Directive on Inspection Activities" from the Civil Service Department, see www.funzionepubblica.gov.it/sites/funzionepubblica.gov.it/files/16870.pdf) or the Netherlands in 2005 with the official cabinet vision "More Effect, Less Burden" for inspections (https://zoek.officielebekendmakingen.nl/kst-29362–107-b1.pdf).

7 Structured by legislation such as the 2008 Code of Conduct for Regulators and the 2015 Regulators Code.

former Communist countries (Former Soviet Union, Mongolia), and "informality" there is rather in the form of a (significant) share of revenue and labor force/wages being undeclared ("gray economy"), whereas fully unregistered businesses tend to be rare. Where informal economy is ubiquitous, there is a subsequent impact on inspections and enforcement – as businesses that operate "outside of the law" are, supposedly, also outside regulatory supervision. However, de facto, economic operators still undergo controls, more often by police forces and law enforcement, whereas formal businesses undergo more inspections by regulatory delivery agencies. This has an obvious effect on how compliance is shaped, understood and implemented. Conversely, the burdens created by regulatory enforcement have been found to contribute to creating disincentives to formalization, as informal businesses judged that they were relatively less "exposed" by staying "under the radar."

Furthermore, in the import/export sector, compliance (and regulatory controls) can often be organized and structured differently because of the complementarity between "regular" regulatory inspections and private certification or inspections carried out by third parties – with even, in some cases, the preponderance of the latter over the former. Third-party systems are complex and their discussion would go far beyond this chapter's scope, but it is important to note that they play a significant role in enabling access to foreign markets for countries with limited regulatory capacity (see e.g. Chapter 66 in this volume). They can also be used for imports, and outsourced pre-shipment inspections (PSIs) are widely used, for example in many sub-Saharan countries in Africa – usually with approaches that impose excessive, non-risk-based controls and significant costs.

However, distinctions need to be made between groups of countries and types of product, with differences between food and non-food, and between both exporting and importing countries.[8] In terms of access to the food market, products presenting more significant risks (live animals, products of animal origin, plants and plant products) are often required to be checked by means of "official"/regulatory inspections. Certain import markets (e.g. the EU) will not accept imports (particularly of higher-risk products, as listed above) if the only guarantee of compliance and safety is third-party (private) certification (but they may do so for lower-risk products, e.g. fruits).[9] Third-party certification anyway can have an important role especially where there is insufficient interstate regulatory alignment and enforcement (Cafaggi et al. 2013).

In any case, more enforcement unfortunately does not automatically result in better/increased compliance, nor in higher level of safety – but too often, rather, in excessive burden borne by economic operators (especially when checks are applied systematically). This relates, on the one hand, to rules not being intrinsically optimal (Baldwin 1990, 1995), and therefore compliance not being translated into effective management of risks (Gunningham 2015). On the other hand, this is a context where economic operators actually struggle to comply with (too) high standards that in many cases cannot be met, where technical norms are confused with standards that have an excessive scope, and subsequent informal payments are not rare.

[8] See Chapter 66 in this volume, and in particular the role (a) of international standards set by various international organizations (*Codex Alimentarius* in particular), (b) of proprietary standards applied at the "meta-market" level that supersede national and even *Codex* standards, and (c) of the Global Food Safety Initiative (GFSI) in trying to supersede even these – https://mygfsi.com/.

[9] See in particular the European Commission webpage on official controls on imported products and relevant regulations at https://ec.europa.eu/food/safety/official_controls/legislation/imports_en.

Turning to the situation and specific aspects and challenges of regulatory compliance in a broad "development" context, we look both at "emerging markets," that is, mostly middle-income countries, with significant achievements in terms of living standards, GDP (gross domestic product), etc. but still major challenges of inequality, public welfare, state administration, etc. – and at "developing countries," that is, mostly low-income countries with poverty and low productivity remaining major constraints, and even lower public/state capacity and effectiveness. In both cases, the importance of *regulatory delivery* is central. Indeed, in a number of cases at least, there has been a growing degree of regulatory alignment internationally in terms of what are the substantive norms that need to be complied with, but this does not mean that the administrative procedures and processes that exist to (supposedly) ensure compliance are similar.[10] The question, often, may not be to know which substantive norms are more difficult or costly to comply with but to know how likely it is that regulatory enforcement ends up being "unreasonable" (Bardach and Kagan 1982) and leads to major costs or even, possibly, closure of operations. As evidenced by the many closures of dairy and meat processing plants post EU-entry in Poland and other Eastern European countries, EU rules on food safety may well be substantially more demanding than older, Communist-time rules (which, however, are/were more specific and detailed, and hence more constraining for technological innovation). On the other hand, however, procedures to obtain permits for such plants in non-EU Eastern European states have often remained particularly complex, burdensome and arcane – and inspections and enforcement have likewise remained often excessively punitive and often arbitrary (or downright corrupt). This means that, in terms of investment and growth barriers, the "less stringent" regulations may in fact end up being worse because of the "regulatory delivery" side.

Successive studies and surveys in particular conducted by the World Bank Group (2006a, 2007, 2010b, 2017) have shown the importance of "delivery" issues in creating regulatory burden and barriers, and overall decreasing regulatory compliance (and thus effectiveness). Exceedingly numerous and complex approval procedures, obscure (or outright corrupt) decision-making, lack of risk-focus in controls and enforcement, lack of proportionality and fairness, all lead to a decrease in perceived procedural fairness (Tyler 2003, 2011), increased resistance to regulatory demands and "evasion" of rules (Hofmann et al. 2008; Kirchler and Hoelzl 2006). This all contributes to undermining further the rule of law (Blanc 2012a). This was particularly in evidence in countries of the Former Soviet Union and post-Communist countries more broadly, but was also strongly visible in other developing and emerging countries.[11] Similar issues, in fact, were also found in a number of developed (including OECD) countries, particularly those where regional inequality, social and economic structures, corruption and/or public administration problems are significant.[12]

The conclusion of this analytical work, and of the lessons learned from successive reform projects, is that "regulatory delivery" – that is, how the whole range of state activities aiming (notionally) at improving or securing compliance is designed, structured, resourced and implemented – matters. Because "regulatory delivery" is a new word, there could be

10 On the importance of procedures, enforcement etc. relative to actual content of rules in explaining international divergences in regulatory impact, see Blanc 2018: 121–9.

11 See some examples covering Kenya, Ethiopia, Peru, etc. in World Bank notes on tax compliance work: Coolidge 2010; Coolidge and Yilmaz 2016; Yesegat et al. 2015; and on inspections in Jordan: Aranki and Shalan 2012 (this chapter also draws on unpublished survey results from Kenya in 2010 covering licensing and inspections).

12 E.g. in Greece – most assessments led by World Bank et al. are unpublished but see: (a) Richter et al. 2015 and (b) OECD 2017. Similar issues are present in Italy (unpublished survey by the *Dipartimento Funzione Pubblica* and ISTAT in 2012, ongoing OECD work, not yet published).

a perception that this is something of a "luxury" that could be desirable for advanced economies and regulatory systems but that would not belong to the basic building blocks of economic development, to the fundamental institutions that enable it. This would be a mistake, and it would likewise be wrong to think that "better regulatory delivery" is not important for developing countries or "emerging" economies. Just as regulatory compliance matters in terms of its direct domestic outcomes (improved safety, health etc.), it also matters for participation in international trade.[13]

First, because regulatory delivery includes processes, procedures and institutions that have their first roots in the distant past, and often have grown to be considered fundamental functions of the state, there are only very rare countries where they are not significant in terms of staff employed, as well as citizens, consumers and businesses affected. Research shows that structures specifically created to control and enforce definite rules started early on in history – and the nineteenth and twentieth centuries have seen larger structures gradually being set up in an increasing number of countries to check compliance with rules, but also in charge of issuing authorizations needed to start a certain activity (Blanc 2018: ch. 1).

In fact, though there are some countries where regulatory delivery institutions ("regulators," "inspectorates" or any other name) function on very limited resources due to ongoing or recent conflict, most countries in the world tend to have a significant part of their government staff and procedures pertaining to regulatory delivery. The authors' experience working in over forty countries suggests that the size of the regulatory delivery system is generally only partially related to the income level of countries, and even fragile and post-conflict states such as Mozambique or Côte d'Ivoire have substantial resources and a number of structures devoted to regulatory inspections, customs, licensing and so on.

Furthermore, having a regulatory delivery system that lacks effectiveness (in terms of protection of key elements of the public welfare) does not necessarily exclude this from being highly burdensome to regulated subjects in many other ways. In many developing countries and emerging economies, the number of licenses and permits that apply to businesses, the number of approvals needed to trade, the frequency of controls, etc. tends to be very high – at least in some sectors or for some types of business (World Bank Group 2006a, 2007, 2010, 2017).[14] In others, limited resources may constrain the number of controls, but very heavy procedures mean that the number of formal businesses is small, and most operate at varying degrees of informality, which in turn limits access to credit, growth potential etc. There is also a widespread relationship between excessively burdensome regulatory delivery procedures and corruption. This has been evidenced in a number of reports by international organizations (World Bank Group 2008: 14, 20–5, Annex 11, Annex 12; World Bank Group 2010c: Table 16; IFC 2009: 6, 141–66, Attachment 6.1; World Bank Group 2010; World Bank Group 2011: 7, 9, 16–25, 37, 44–5, 59, Annex 2; World Bank Group 2013a; World Bank Group 2013b: 4, 14–19, 29–30, 36, 50, 57; Putnina 2005; OECD 2014c, 2015), as well as in academic research (Ogus and Zhang 2005; Ogus 2004). Much of this work has focused on "frontline" corruption linked to specific regulatory procedures, but there is evidence that corruption linked to regulatory delivery issues goes all the way up to avoid

13 See e.g. "Introduction" in World Bank 2014 (focusing on food safety regulation).

14 See also the whole World Bank *Investment Climate Assessments* series available at: http://documents.worldbank.org/curated/en/docsearch/document-type/904594 – see e.g. the specific example of Georgia at www.doingbusiness.org/content/dam/doingBusiness/media/Reforms/Case-Studies/2007/Georgia-Permits-2007.pdf.

problems during on-site visits, obtain licenses more rapidly, or get "outsourced" regulatory delivery such as PSI contracts[15].

The relevance of "good regulatory delivery" as an approach to promoting compliance is particularly strong in many (if not necessarily all) fragile and post-conflict countries, as more effective and transparent public administration, and higher compliance, can help create/foster trust, and "bad" regulatory delivery can harm recovery and create additional tensions.

13.2 REGULATORY COMPLIANCE AND DELIVERY: AN OVERVIEW OF DIFFERENCES IN INSTITUTIONS AND PRACTICES IN DIFFERENT REGIONS

As defined in this chapter, regulatory delivery covers a broad range of government activities and regulatory domains. While, in some countries and regions, regulatory delivery institutions and processes will be significant across most or all of these, states with fewer resources will tend to have them more concentrated in a few fields – typically border control, supervision of trade, and a few salient risks. The size of regulatory delivery institutions, the number of procedures and controls, the extent of the spread of regulatory delivery activities across different sectors and domains – all tend to be to a degree linked to the level of government resources (and thus of GDP), but also depend strongly on the institutional and legal heritage of the country. In other words, there is a strong path dependency, which largely explains differences in terms of methods, practice, or the exact split of institutional mandates among governmental agencies tasked with the verification and enforcement of regulatory compliance. While these aspects influence the regulatory delivery system, they do not necessarily prevent the transformations – for example the introduction of a risk-based and compliance-supporting approach (Blanc 2018).

Many developing countries and emerging economies can, from the perspective of regulatory path dependency, be classified in three groups, within which of course variations are significant but some important common characteristics can be observed:

(i) long-independent former Spanish colonies of Latin America (to some extent, Brazil can be linked to this group, with strong similarities between Portuguese and Spanish colonial administrative cultures);
(ii) former colonies of Africa and South/South-East Asia (a group that in turn has some common features, and others that require differentiation of several sub-groups);
(iii) former Communist countries of Eastern Europe and Northern Asia (with China significantly different from countries that were influenced by or part of the Former Soviet Union).

While being an obvious oversimplification, both the concise description and Table 13.1 lay out a summary of features of these groups that helps in understanding the differences in their context and needs.

15 PSI companies are typically large certification companies based in high-income countries that get developing countries' governments to engage in multi-year contracts with them, with the PSI contractors doing customs valuation verification, technical compliance checks, or both. They get paid a percentage of the shipment. The costs tend to be significantly higher than the cost of entry procedures in non-PSI countries, effectiveness (at least for technical compliance) is dubious, revenue is lost by the developing countries, there is mostly no capacity building, and controls tend to be done on a 100 percent basis rather than being risk-based (again, leading to far higher burden). Corruption is deemed to be considerable in the award of PSI contracts (source: unpublished World Bank Group note – published World Bank notes on this topic covered only customs-valuation PSI, and, though cautious, did highlight many limitations and weaknesses – see e.g. Cadot et al. 2003).

TABLE 13.1 *Summary of key features by groups of countries*

	Licensing	Enforcement	General features	Specific features (by area etc.)
Latin America (long-independent former Spanish colonies)	Most countries show: - a "universal" approach to licensing (generic operational license); and - a number of specialized, specific licenses, approvals etc.	- Inspection structures often fragmented, with limited resources etc. - Heavy focus on the more formal, "visible" firms – far less on informal sector – strengthens barriers to formalization, growth	Recent events show that low effectiveness can become a serious problem for the more advanced economies, e.g. Brazil food exports and inspection scandals	
Post-colonial states in Africa, South and South-East Asia	Large number of licenses/approvals needed, including generic "operational licenses" for most businesses	- Limited ability (staff, resources) to supervise/inspect all firms – but heavy controls on the more formal ones – reinforcing the barrier to formalization - Non-risk-based border controls in a number of countries, "outsourced" partly or wholly to PSI contractors	- Technical norms often underdeveloped - Sector regulations giving very large powers to regulatory delivery institutions, but often without any precise norms to refer to. When they do exist: very restrictive, mandatory standards	**Organization at national or local level** (linked to metropolis's institutional model) - Former British colonies tend to have more "municipal-level" inspections etc. - Former French colonies are rather organized at "national level" - Other former colonies present a mix of both models – e.g. Mozambique mostly

national, but some municipal – also true to an extent even in former French colonies

Former British India

- Tendency toward a particularly high level of bureaucracy
- Significant size of regulatory delivery bodies – higher probably than in most of Africa, and in SE Asia (regardless of former colonial power). Linked to population levels, pre-colonial history, specific features of colonial regime, etc.
- Reforms in India e.g. have reduced some features (licensing), but far from "across the board"

(continued)

TABLE 13.1 *(continued)*

	Licensing	Enforcement	General features	Specific features (by area etc.)
Post-Communist countries	High number and coverage of licenses, approvals, etc. (but not "universal" operational license)	- Heavily resourced inspectorates, with a high coverage of inspections "across the board" - Generally heavy import/export controls (more-or-less reformed in EU Member States, but not in most others)	- Heavy burden "across the board" - Relatively less discrimination between different categories of businesses – larger, more "established" ones (legal entities vs. sole traders) bear somewhat heavier burden in general, but less of a gap than in "formal vs. informal" contexts. Fewer possibilities to "fly under the radar" - Very detailed, numerous technical norms – making operations difficult (outdated, excessive, contradictory, impossible to know of, etc.), with inspectors having wide possibilities for (negative) discretion and abuse	- "Heavier" system in post-Soviet than in Eastern Europe - "Heavier" system in Eastern Europe (former COMECON) than in former-Yugoslavia. - China is a special case: • due to the size of economy, controlling resources tend to be smaller in comparison • different approach to trade • serious problems of effectiveness nonetheless

13.2.1 *Latin America (Long-Independent Former Spanish and Portuguese Colonies)*

Recent research shows that many governments have been working on improving regulatory policy, and that bodies for regulatory quality are thus increasingly being established, but not always with clear oversight functions (Querbach and Arndt 2017; OECD 2008; 2014b).

A defining feature in terms of procedures aiming at verifying and enforcing compliance is the reliance on *ex ante* controls including both a generic operational license (Independent Evaluation Group 2013)[16] and a number of specialized, specific licenses, approvals, authorizations, etc. With regards to *ex post* enforcement, inspection structures are often fragmented with limited resources focusing heavily on the more formal, "visible" firms and far less on businesses operating informally. In addition, systems are generally not based on risk assessment and risk-focus. Despite some recent efforts to develop compliance promotion strategies and actions in countries like Colombia (especially at a local level) and Mexico (e.g. in the energy sector), these remain relatively rare.

The existing approach to licensing and inspections systems tends to strengthen barriers to formalization of economic operators and to growth in general. As evidenced during a number of recent crises (e.g. Brazil with regards to food exports and inspection scandals[17]), the low effectiveness of inspections can become a serious issue for public welfare and economic performance.

13.2.2 *Post-Colonial States in Africa and South and South-East Asia*

In general, post-colonial states in Africa, South and South-East Asia are often characterized by underdeveloped technical norms[18] (which makes compliance verification and enforcement all the more difficult to conduct and/or arbitrary). While sector-specific laws and regulations give broad powers to regulatory delivery institutions, there is often a lack of precise norms to refer to. When such norms do exist, these tend to be very restrictive, mandatory standards (e.g. excessively burdensome norms on translation and approval of labels for foodstuffs in Mozambique).[19] Limited ability (in terms of staff and resources) to carry out enforcement activities means that these are heavily focused on formal businesses, reinforcing barriers to formalization. In a number of countries, non-risk-based border controls aiming at controlling all shipments, "outsourced" partly or wholly to PSI contractors (mostly European firms, charging a fee on each shipment for customs valuation checks, technical checks, or both), involve major costs for businesses, and as a result also for consumers, who indirectly bear these costs. This practice also harms the competitiveness of formal imports.[20] Finally, in

16 However, some countries (e.g. Colombia) have made effort toward abolishing such license, in particular to facilitate access to formal economy.

17 See in particular the commentary by Sylvain Charlebois published by the Atlantic Institute for Market Studies in 2017, available at www.aims.ca/op-ed/brazil-mother-food-fraud-cases/.

18 "Technical norms" mean technical requirements and mandatory standards. A definition can be as follows: mandatory regulations provided for by international documents (in particular SPS and TBT Agreements, and *Codex Alimentarius*) and legislation, adopted in conformity with the constitution and applicable laws of a given country, that prescribe specific requirements and/or characteristics that food and non-food products are required to have, in particular in relation to safety of products and operations (particularly pertaining to the production, transportation, storage and sale of those products).

19 Source: authors' direct observations and discussion (unpublished World Bank Group assessment).

20 This practice challenges priorities emphasized in particular in Benno et al. 2007, which underlines the importance of "strengthening capabilities for taking advantage of the rapid growth in the global markets, and improving the investment climate," "scaling up and diversifying exports" – concluding that "enhanced competitiveness and reduced barriers to trade are the two critical areas of action."

addition to the burdens they often create for trade, PSI contracts imply transferring resources from lower-income countries to richest ones.

With regards to the licensing system, the number of approvals, authorizations etc. needed to start a business activity is habitually exceedingly large, and these often come on top of generic "operational licenses" for most businesses.

Regulatory delivery institutional and territorial organization in this group of countries is also substantially shaped by colonial heritage. This means that, for instance, in former British colonies, inspections and enforcement tend to be organized at a municipal – or at least local – level, whilst former French colonies present a more centralized (but not *entirely* centralized) system. Often, there is a mix of both approaches – for example, in Mozambique regulatory delivery structures are mostly national, but a number of operations (often overlapping with those carried out by central authorities) are performed at the municipal level.

For their part, countries that were part of former British India are characterized by a particularly high level of bureaucracy[21] in addition to the relatively larger size of regulatory delivery bodies – again linked to longer-term historical features. Reforms in India have reduced some particularly burdensome features of the licensing regime, but procedures and processes focused on regulatory compliance remain burdensome.

13.2.3 *Post-Communist Countries*

In spite of different levels of evolution since 1990 depending on political choices,[22] international integration resulting in far more changes in EU Member States or accession countries, etc., many post-Communist countries still present a number of common features regarding regulatory delivery and compliance institutions. In general, there is a high number and level of coverage of licenses, approvals, etc. (with, however, no "universal" operational license), inspectorates being heavily resourced (resulting in a high coverage of inspections of all businesses), and generally heavy import/export controls (more or less fully reformed only in EU Member States). The system tends to be more burdensome in terms of requirements to be complied with and frequency of controls in post-Soviet countries than in Eastern Europe, and heavier in Eastern Europe (former COMECON) than in former Yugoslavia[23]. Despite serious problems of effectiveness, China is a particular case that would have to be studied on its own: given the size of the economy, and the relatively recent rise in income level, the resources devoted to enforcement overall are smaller in comparison with other post-Communist countries. The level of technical competence and development of methods is also quite different (and overall may be lagging). By contrast, trade-focused controls may be somewhat lighter.

Given the large resources devoted to enforcement in post-Communist countries – compared to other groups of countries mentioned in this chapter – a significant regulatory burden is usually borne by businesses in post-Communist countries. Although larger and more "established" establishments (legal entities vs. sole traders) tend to bear a heavier somewhat burden, there are relatively fewer differences among categories of businesses than in the other

21 See e.g. on Bangladesh Rahmat et al. 2019.

22 Countries such as Georgia or Mongolia have been among the most reformist ones so far (see World Bank Group reports).

23 In a number of countries – in particular Russia, and most of the former Soviet Union – "inspectors" have a more preeminent cultural and political role in the society and in the market than in other emerging countries due to historical legacy. See in this respect Nikolai Gogol's work *The Inspector General* (1842).

two groups of countries. As "flying under the radar" entirely is difficult, enforcement-related activities are usually carried out more uniformly.

The very detailed and numerous technical norms in force provide wide opportunities for inspectors to abuse their authority and power and to act arbitrarily because they are outdated, excessive, contradictory, opaque, etc. and thus are in practice "impossible to comply with."

13.3 IMPACT OF PREVAILING PRACTICES IN COMPLIANCE ENFORCEMENT AND REGULATORY DELIVERY IN DEVELOPING AND EMERGING COUNTRIES

Features of the different regulatory delivery systems in the regions indicated throughout Section 13.2 are known to greater or lesser extent based on available research (in particular World Bank Group reports and studies, OECD reviews) and reform projects carried out with external technical assistance. These are mostly unpublished, hence the lack of references for some sections, which rely on the authors' direct involvement in the different countries discussed. Evidence shows that, in most cases, the approach to supervision and inspections tends to be punitive rather than preventative, not based on (and not fostering) trust among the different actors involved, and that as a result it creates significant opportunities for abuses. There also tends to be a high level of focus on formal compliance (holding the right approvals, documents, certificates, etc.), and on the physical condition of the controlled establishments (often verified in a superficial way), and low capacity (or lack of attention) to substantive compliance (in particular in terms of staff knowledge, effective implementation of internal control/safety systems etc.).

Regulatory delivery activities create real problems in most if not all of these countries: they create significant burden and barriers to economic activities, with a negative impact on growth, employment and incomes (and also lead to price increases through barriers to trade). The excessive administrative and regulatory burden is especially borne by enterprises involving more significant investments, which are therefore more "visible" to state authorities, but SMEs and small traders are not immune to this issue either. There are also insidious gender effects from burdensome and heavy-handed regulatory practices. A number of studies show that women are more affected than men by informality, as they "face a more hostile environment including discrimination in various markets, which [in turn] explains the presence of gender bias in the informal sector" (Sethuraman 1998). In developing and emerging economies, the share of women in the informal sector is higher than their share in total labor force. As informality is reinforced by inadequate regulatory delivery regimes, this also has a gender effect. There is generally an increased awareness of the gender dimension of trade policies (UNCTAD 2017).

Most crucially from the compliance perspective, these systems are not creating burden as a trade-off for effectiveness – they are also ineffective at promoting/securing compliance; in some cases they may even actively lead to *reduced* compliance. Lack of responsive regulatory enforcement (to the conduct of regulated subjects) results in lower effectiveness – and efficiency – of the regulatory delivery system (Braithwaite 2006) and of its outcomes – with compliance as the first step toward securing public welfare in fields such as environment, health, safety, etc. As evidenced through many studies, excessively burdensome and "hostile" compliance approaches can lead not only to disappointing results in terms of efficiency (very little increase in compliance compared to the costs) but even to actual decreases in compliance because excessive burden, perceived as unfair, leads to a *decrease* in voluntary compliance (Kirchler and Hoelzl 2006; Hodges 2015; Blanc 2018). This is even truer in countries where corruption is important and thus enforcement is seen as thoroughly unfair. The issue is further compounded if the competence of regulatory staff is low, and/or when procedures are seen as being primarily formalistic and disconnected from real risks. These situations feed a vicious circle of ineffectiveness of regulation, growing disrespect for public authorities, lower compliance, even greater ineffectiveness, etc.

A number of descriptions of regulatory systems in developing countries, and of recommendations, have been based on an assumption than "more is better." This is not only incorrect *in general* (Kirchler and Hoelzl 2006) but even more so in the contexts we are describing here, as has been made clear in the many country-specific publications already referenced. By contrast, a more risk-based, focused, responsive regulatory delivery is also a means of securing good governance and democracy, as it allows institutions "to maintain . . . integrity while taking into account new problems, new forces in the environment, new demands, and expectations" (Selznick 1992). Risk-based regulatory delivery involves not only focusing regulatory delivery institutions' efforts on higher risks but also e.g. choosing the adequate regulatory tools and tailoring the instruments used for regulation and control based on the level of risk and the characteristics of regulated subjects. It also means supporting risk management at all levels in a manner that is proportionate to the potential danger, understanding barriers to compliance and supporting regulated subjects' growth.

13.4 PROPOSED SOLUTIONS AND CONCLUSION

A variety of solutions, [24] remedies, good practices, tools and methods can be, and have been, considered to improve regulatory systems and institutions in charge of compliance verification and enforcement, that is, "regulatory delivery." Because there are large differences in capacity, priorities, legal systems, institutions and cultures, direct *copying* of regulatory systems and institutions as they are from one setting to another will not necessarily be easy or advisable. Of course, countries can draw inspiration from practices elsewhere, but always by taking into account, and adapting possible solutions to, the actual context (World Bank Group pending publication).

Apart from discretion, where the strongest difference may exist between different contexts, the other tools built on the OECD 2014 *Good Practice Principles for Regulatory Inspections and Enforcement* (OECD 2014a) appear broadly relevant for many developing/emerging contexts, and indeed were developed taking into account around fifteen years of diagnostic and reform experiences in such countries. However, their respective importance – and relevance – will vary depending on what are the most salient problems in a given country – for example whether it is more about competence and effectiveness, corruption, excessive burden, lack of planning, overlaps and duplication, etc. The relevant cost and benefit, or the sequencing, of some of the *Good Practice Principles* (which are rather broad by nature) will have to be considered, as some of them may be more relevant or "urgent" in a given situation. It will also depend on the context in terms of legal framework – what level of discretion is normally granted to officials, whether the court system is independent, trusted and accessible, etc.

Regulatory compliance and regulatory delivery are of global relevance. More work should be done to consolidate, analyze, draw lessons from the many experiences around the world –

[24] On the different solutions that can be considered, see in particular OECD 2014a; Wille and Blanc 2013; World Bank 2006; 2011.

and to understand better what is relevant everywhere, what is only relevant to certain contexts, and how priorities and ways of achieving certain outcomes can differ.

The most significant constraints on the use of certain reform elements or tools can be the capacities (i.e. professionalism, resources) available but also the existing legal instruments and the institutional organization of regulatory delivery systems. The adoption and use of a number of tools (risk-based planning, responsive and proportional enforcement, information systems integration (Wille and Blanc 2013), etc.) imply being able to answer the question "how far can this be done?" For some other aspects, such as regulatory discretion, the relevant question is rather "what is the right approach at this stage of development of the system?"

The greatest common challenge that remains, however, and is difficult to address, is how to change *culture*, since this is necessary to move from a "policing system" to a "trust-based system," or from a system that focuses on punishment of violations to one that aims at maximizing public welfare outcomes. The general consensus seems to be that this may result only from many complementary and sustained efforts, and requires resources, time and perseverance. Nonetheless, there have been examples of more radical change that have yielded quite positive results in terms of paradigm shift. These range from Bosnia and Herzegovina (with the setup of a new enforcement institution, the selective rehiring of staff, and the establishment of completely new administrative and information systems) (World Bank Group 2010a) to Georgia (World Bank Group 2012) (the more radical example, mostly doing away with regulatory delivery institutions and practices for some time before gradually rebuilding some of them from scratch). Much, however, remains to be done to try to understand what approaches work best to transform culture and reach a trust-based equilibrium – and this cannot happen without a clear understanding of the specific context, the actual opportunities for change and scope of movement.

REFERENCES

Aranki, W. M. E., and Shalan, A. K. (2012), *Jordan Inspection Reform: Lessons and Reflections*, Washington, DC: World Bank Group: http://documents.worldbank.org/curated/en/243721493197647965/Jordan-inspection-reform-lessons-and-reflections.

Baldwin, R. (1990), "Why Rules Don't Work," *Modern Law Review*, 53, 321–37.

(1995), *Rules and Government*, Oxford: Clarendon Press.

Bardach, E., and Kagan, R. A. (1982), *Going by the Book. The Problem of Regulatory Unreasonableness*, Philadelphia: Temple University Press.

Benno, N. et al. (2007), *Challenges of African Growth: Opportunities, Constraints and Strategic Directions*, Washington, DC: World Bank Group.

Blanc, F. (2011), "Moving Away from Total Control: What the Experiences of Former Soviet Countries Can Tell Us about Risk and Regulation," in van Tol, J., Helsloot, I., and Mertens, F. J. H. (eds.), *Veiligheid boven alles? Essays over oorzaken en gevolgen van de risico-regelreflex*, pp. 137–46, Den Haag: Boom Lemma.

(2012a), "Moving Away from Total Control in Former Communist Countries – The RRR in Inspections, and Lessons Learned from Reforming Them," *European Journal of Risk Regulation*, 3, 327–41.

(2012b), *Reforming Inspections: Why, How and with What Results?*, Paris: OECD: www.oecd.org/regreform/Inspection%20reforms%20-%20web%20-F.%20Blanc.pdf.

(2018), *From Chasing Violations to Managing Risks: Origins, Challenges and Evolutions in Regulatory Inspections*, Elgar Studies in Law and Regulation, Cheltenham, UK: Edward Elgar.

Blattman, C., Hwang, J., and Williamson, J. (2007), "Winners and Losers in the Commodity Lottery: The Impact of Terms of Trade Growth and Volatility in the Periphery, 1870–1939," *Journal of*

Development Economics, 82, 156–79: https://chrisblattman.com/documents/research/2007.Winners&Losers.JDE.pdf.
Braithwaite, J. (1993), *Improving Regulatory Compliance: Strategies and Practical Applications in OECD Countries*, Paris: OECD.
(2006), "Responsive Regulation and Developing Economy," *World Development*, 24(5), 884–98.
Cadot, O., Anson, J., and Olarreaga, M. (2003). *Tariff Evasion and Customs Corruption: Does Pre-shipment Inspection Help?*, Policy, Research Working Paper No. WPS 3156, Washington, DC: World Bank Group: http://documents.worldbank.org/curated/en/803371468762590738/Tariff-evasion-and-customs-corruption-does-pre-shipment-inspection-help.
Cafaggi, F., Renda, A., and Schmidt, R. (2013), "Transnational Private Regulation", in *International Regulatory Co-operation: Case Studies, Vol. 3: Transnational Private Regulation and Water Management*, Paris: OECD: https://doi.org/10.1787/9789264200524–3-en.
Coolidge, J. (2006), *Reforming Inspections*, Public Policy for the Private Sector, Note No. 308, Washington, DC: World Bank Group: http://documents.worldbank.org/curated/en/921331468315289997/Reforming-inspections.
(2010), *Tax Compliance Cost Surveys: Using Data to Design Targeted Reforms*, Investment Climate in Practice, No. 8, Business Taxation Note, Washington, DC: World Bank Group: http://documents.worldbank.org/curated/en/371871468295501537/Tax-compliance-cost-surveys-using-data-to-design-targeted-reforms.
Coolidge, J., Grava, L., and Putnina, S. (2003), *Case Study: Inspectorate Reform in Latvia 1999–2003*, Washington, DC: World Bank Group: http://documents.worldbank.org/curated/en/2003/12/5598512/case-study-inspectorate-reform-latvia–1999–2003.
Coolidge, J., and Yilmaz, F. (2016), *Small Business Tax Regimes*, Viewpoint, No. 34, Washington, DC: World Bank Group: https://openknowledge.worldbank.org/handle/10986/24250.
Djankov, S., La Porta, R., Lopez-De-Silanes, F., and Shleifer, A. (2002), "The Regulation of Entry," *Quarterly Journal of Economics*, 117(1), 1–37.
Djankov, S., McLiesh, C., and Ramalho, R. M. (2006), *Regulation and Growth*, Washington, DC: World Bank Group: http://ssrn.com/abstract=893321.
Duflo. E., and Banerjee, A. (2011), *Poor Economics. A Radical Rethinking of the Way to Fight Global Poverty*, New York: Public Affairs.
Dugeree, J., Cola, G., Blanc, F., and Ottimofiore, G. (2019), "Lessons from Creating a Consolidated Inspection Agency in Mongolia", in Russell, G. and Hodges, C. (eds.), *Regulatory Delivery*, London: Hart/Beck.
Easterly, W., and Williamson, C. (2011), "Rhetoric versus Reality: The Best and Worst of Aid Agency Practices," *World Development*, 39(11), 1930–49.
Gunningham, N. (2015), "Compliance, Deterrence and Beyond", forthcoming in Paddock, L. (ed.), *Compliance and Enforcement in Environmental Law*, Cheltenham, UK: Edward Elgar. SSRN RegNet Research Paper No. 2015/87, https://ssrn.com/abstract=2646427.
Gunningham, N., Kagan, R. A., and Thornton, D. (2003), *Shades of Green: Business, Regulation and Environment*, Stanford: Stanford University Press.
Hampton, P. (2005), *Reducing Administrative Burdens: Effective Inspection and Enforcement*, London: HM Treasury: https://webarchive.nationalarchives.gov.uk/+/http:/www.bis.gov.uk/policies/better-regulation/improving-regulatory-delivery/assessing-our-regulatory-system.
Hodges, C. (2015), *Law and Corporate Behaviour*, London: Hart/Beck.
Hofmann, E., Hoelzl, E., and Kirchler, E. (2008), "Preconditions of Voluntary Tax Compliance: Knowledge and Evaluation of Taxation, Norms, Fairness, and Motivation to Cooperate," *Zeitschrift Fur Psychologie* 216(4), 209–17, doi:10.1027/0044-3409.216.4.209.
Independent Evaluation Group (2013), *Impact Evaluation of Business License Simplification in Peru: An Independent and International Finance Corporation-Supported Project*, Washington, DC: World Bank Group.
(2015), *Investment Climate Reforms: An Independent Evaluation of World Bank Group Support to Reforms of Business Regulations*, Washington, DC: World Bank Group: https://openknowledge.worldbank.org/handle/10986/22724.
International Finance Corporation (2009), *Business Environment in Tajikistan as Seen by Small and Medium Enterprises*, IFC.

(2010), *Business Inspections in Mongolia*, IFC.

(2011), *Investment Climate in Ukraine as Seen by Private Businesses*, IFC.

(2013a), *Inspection Reform Coordination and Implementation Process Review Report – Armenia*, IFC.

(2013b), *Investment Climate in the Kyrgyz Republic as Seen by Businesses*, IFC.

Kirchler, E. (2007), *The Economic Psychology of Tax Behaviour*, Cambridge: Cambridge University Press.

Kirchler, E., and Hoelzl, E. (2006), "Modelling Taxpayers' Behaviour as a Function of Interaction between Tax Authorities and Taxpayers," in Elffers, H., Verboon, P., and Huisman, W. (eds.), *Managing and Maintaining Compliance*, Den Haag: Boom Legal, pp. 1–23.

OECD (2008), *Brazil: Strengthening Governance for Growth*, OECD Reviews of Regulatory Reform, Paris: OECD.

(2014a), *Regulatory Enforcement and Inspections*, OECD Best Practice Principles for Regulatory Policy, Paris: OECD: https://doi.org/10.1787/9789264208117-en.

(2014b), *Regulatory Policy in Mexico: Towards a Whole-of-Government Perspective to Regulatory Improvement*, OECD Reviews of Regulatory Reform, Paris: OECD.

(2014c), *OECD Review of Regulatory Policy in Kazakhstan: Towards Improved Implementation*, OECD: https://dx.doi.org/10.1787/9789264214255-en.

(2015), *Regulatory Policy in Lithuania: Focusing on the Delivery Side*, OCDE Reviews of Regulatory Reform, OECD: http://dx.doi.org/.

(2017), *OECD Competition Assessment Reviews: Greece 2017*, Paris: OECD: https://doi.org/10.1787/9789264088276-en.

(2018), *OECD Regulatory Enforcement and Inspections Toolkit*, Paris: OECD: https://doi.org/10.1787/9789264303959-en.

Ogus, A. (2004), "Corruption and Regulatory Structures," *Law & Policy*, 26(3–4),329–46; abstract available at: http://ssrn.com/abstract=591563.

Ogus, A., and Zhang, Q. (2005), "Licensing Regimes East and West," *International Review of Law and Economics*, 25(1), 124–42.

Putnina, S. (2005), *Review of International Practice in Inspections Reform*, IFC.

Querbach, T., and Arndt, C. (2017), *Regulatory Policy in Latin America: An Analysis of the State of Play*, OECD Regulatory Policy Working Paper, No. 7, Paris: OECD: http://dx.doi.org/10.1787/2cb29d8c-en.

Rahmat, A., Grava L., and Masrur, R. (2019), *Agile Regulatory Delivery for Improved Investment Competitiveness in Bangladesh*, Washington, DC: World Bank Group: www.ifc.org/wps/wcm/connect/aa810dcf-7f07-40c0-b9e4-e2ea7515c89a/Bangladesh+Competitiveness+Publication.pdf?MOD=AJPERES&CVID=mR7ZTaN.

Richter, K., Giudice, G., and Cozzi, A. (2015), "Product Market Reforms in Greece: Unblocking Investments and Exports," *Vierteljahrshefte zur Wirtschaftsforschung*, 84(3), 107–27, ISSN 1861–1559, http://dx.doi.org/10.3790/vjh.84.3.107.

Rodrik, D. (2003), *In Search of Prosperity: Analytic Narratives on Economic Growth*, Princeton: Princeton University Press.

(2006), "An African Growth Miracle?" *Journal of African Economies*, 1–18: https://drodrik.scholar.harvard.edu/files/dani-rodrik/files/an_african_growth_miracle_01.pdf.

(2012), "Do We Need to Rethink Growth Policies?" in Blanchard, O., Romer, D., Spence, M., and Stiglitz, J. (eds.), *In the Wake of the Crisis: Leading Economists Reassess Economic Policy*, pp. 157–67, Cambridge: MIT Press: https://drodrik.scholar.harvard.edu/files/dani-rodrik/files/do-we-need-to-rethink-growth-policies_0.pdf.

Russell, G., and Hodges, C. (eds.) (2019), *Regulatory Delivery*, London: Hart/Beck.

Selznick, P. (1992), *The Moral Commonwealth: Social Theory and the Promise of Community*, Berkeley: University of California Press.

Sethuraman, S. V. (1998), *Gender, Informality and Poverty: A Global Review Gender Bias in Female Informal Employment and Incomes in Developing Countries*, Women in Informal Employment Globalizing and Organizing (WIEGO).

Tyler, T. R. (2003), "Procedural Justice, Legitimacy, and the Effective Rule of Law," *Crime and Justice*, 30, 283–357.

(2011), "Chapter 4: The Psychology of Self-Regulation: Normative Motivations for Compliance," in Parker, C., and Nielsen, V. L. (eds.), *Explaining Compliance: Business Responses to Regulation*, Cheltenham, UK: Edward Elgar, http://dx.doi.org/10.4337/9780857938732.

UNCTAD (2017), *The New Way of Addressing Gender Equality Issues on Trade Agreements: Is It a True Revolution?*, Policy Brief No. 53: http://unctad.org/en/PublicationsLibrary/presspb2017d2_en.pdf.

Wille, J., and Blanc, F. (2013), *Implementing a Shared Inspection Management System: Insights from Recent International Experience*, Washington, DC; World Bank Group: http://documents.worldbank.org/curated/en/190851468152706158/Implementing-a-shared-inspection-management-system-insights-from-recent-international-experience.

World Bank Group (2006a), *Business Environment in Tajikistan as Seen by Small and Medium Enterprises*, Washington, DC: World Bank Group: http://documents.worldbank.org/curated/en/875701468173954834/Business-environment-in-Tajikistan-as-seen-by-small-and-medium-enterprises–2006.

(2006b), *Good Practices for Business Inspections: Guidelines for Reformers*, Washington, DC: World Bank Group: http://documents.worldbank.org/curated/en/286811468329950178/Good-practices-for-business-inspections-guidelines-for-reformers.

(2007), *Business Environment in Ukraine*, Washington, DC: World Bank Group: http://documents.worldbank.org/curated/en/138251468171870911/Business-environment-in-Ukraine.

(2008), *Ukraine – Technical Regulations : Ensuring Economic Development and Consumer Protection*, Washington, DC: World Bank Group: http://documents.worldbank.org/curated/en/884721468316454988/Ukraine-Technical-regulations-ensuring-economic-development-and-consumer-protection.

(2010a), *Inspections Reform: Do Models Exist?*, Washington, DC: World Bank Group: http://documents.worldbank.org/curated/en/216181471587685722/pdf/107899-WP-PUBLIC-TAG-TO-Investment-Climate-inspection-reforms-paper.pdf.

(2010b), *Investment Climate in the Kyrgyz Republic as Seen by Small and Medium Enterprises*, Washington, DC: World Bank Group: http://documents.worldbank.org/curated/en/405241501159231994/Investment-climate-in-the-Kyrgyz-Republic-as-seen-by-small-and-medium-enterprises.

(2010c), *Business Environment in Belarus 2010: Survey of Small and Medium-Sized Businesses Analytical Report*, Washington, DC: World Bank Group: http://documents.worldbank.org/curated/en/998781468201277048/Business-environment-in-Belarus-2010-survey-of-small-and-medium-sized-businesses-analytical-report.

(2011), *How to Reform Business Inspections: Design, Implementation, Challenges*, Washington, DC: World Bank Group: https://elibrary.worldbank.org/doi/abs/10.1596/25076.

(2012), *Fighting Corruption in Public Services: Chronicling Georgia's Reforms*, Washington, DC: World Bank Group: http://documents.worldbank.org/curated/en/518301468256183463/Fighting-corruption-in-public-services-chronicling-Georgias-reforms.

(2014), *Food Safety Toolkit: Introduction and Quick Start Guide*, Washington, DC: World Bank Group: http://documents.worldbank.org/curated/en/995191474485316487/Food-safety-toolkit-introduction-and-quick-start-guide.

(2017), *Assessment of Tax Compliance Costs for Businesses in the Kyrgyz Republic*, Washington, DC: World Bank Group: http://documents.worldbank.org/curated/en/690711540541894216/Assessment-of-Tax-Compliance-Costs-for-Businesses-in-the-Kyrgyz-Republic.

(pending publication), *Assessment of Institutional and Technological Models Supporting Integrated Inspection Functions*.

Yesegat, W., Vorontsov, D. E., Coolidge, J., and Corthay, L. O. (2015), *Tax Compliance Cost Burden and Tax Perceptions Survey in Ethiopia*, Washington, DC: World Bank Group: http://documents.worldbank.org/curated/en/761151467995397531/Tax-compliance-cost-burden-and-tax-perceptions-survey-in-Ethiopia.

PART II

Deterrence and Incapacitation

14

Deterrence Theory: Key Findings and Challenges

Alex Raskolnikov

Abstract: This chapter reviews the key findings of the optimal deterrence theory and discusses the remaining challenges. Some of these challenges reflect current modeling choices and limitations. These include the treatment of the offender's gains in the social welfare function; the design of the damages multiplier in a realistic, multi-period framework; the effects of different types of uncertainty on behavior; and the study of optional, imperfectly enforced, threshold-based regimes – that is, regimes that reflect the most common real-world regulatory setting. Other challenges arise because several key regulatory features and enforcement outcomes are inconsistent with the deterrence theory's predictions and prescriptions. These inconsistencies include the "abnormally" high levels of compliance, the pervasiveness of gain-based (rather than harm-based) sanctions, the widespread use of offense history in sanctions design, the variation of sanctions based on legal aggressiveness, and the significance of the offender's mental state in the determinations of both liability and sanctions. The chapter discusses how the recent optimal deterrence scholarship has addressed – but has not fully resolved – all these challenges.

14.1 INTRODUCTION

Governments regulate for many reasons, and deterring future undesirable acts is surely one of them. Economists have much to offer to deterrence-minded regulators. Economics studies how people respond to incentives, so economists can tell regulators *how* to deter. Economics also aspires to offer a rigorous definition of desirable behavior, so economists aim to tell regulators *what* to deter and *why*.

This chapter focuses on the economic analysis of deterrence. This analysis is not tied to any particular body of law. If we consider voluntary agreements among individuals – the subject of contract law – deterrence aims to induce efficient contracting, including efficient breach. If we focus on accidental harms governed by tort law, deterrence refers to assuring efficient levels of care and activity by tortfeasors and victims. And if we consider public enforcement of law – government enforcement of rules ranging from criminal law to banking, securities, competition, tax, environmental, labor, and safety regulation among others – deterrence refers to preventing future socially harmful conduct.

Each area just mentioned has been extensively studied, and comprehensive reviews are available for each (Hermalin, Katz, and Craswell 2007 for contracts, Shavell 2007 for accidents, Polinsky and Shavell 2007 for public enforcement of law). Given the space constraints as well as the continuous growth and importance of government regulation, this chapter focuses on public enforcement of law.

No attempt is made here to replicate Polinsky and Shavell's (2007) masterful review of the economic theory of public enforcement of law, also known as the theory of optimal deterrence. That review excels in presenting a cohesive theoretical framework that answers many basic questions of law enforcement. Rather, this chapter outlines the key findings of the deterrence theory and highlights the remaining challenges.

The theory of optimal deterrence investigates how the government may achieve its objective given the individual decision-making strategy. The government objective is to maximize what deterrence scholars often refer to as social welfare. The meaning of that term, however, is typically restricted to efficiency or just to net gains. Thus, Polinsky and Shavell (2007) define social welfare as "the benefits that individuals obtain from their behavior, less the costs that they incur to avoid causing harm, the harm that they do cause, the cost of catching violators, and the costs of imposing sanctions on them (including any costs associated with risk aversion)" (Polinsky and Shavell 2007:406). As for the individual decision-making strategy, the theory generally assumes informed, rational agents who act if their actions yield private benefits (certain or expected) in excess of all costs of acting (certain or expected). Some privately beneficial acts, however, give rise not only to private costs and benefits but also to external harms – harms (net of external gains) that individuals do not take into account absent government intervention. The deterrence theory posits that when the act's external harm exceeds its private gain, the act is socially undesirable and should be deterred at the lowest social cost.

The government deters individuals by imposing sanctions. In the basic setup, sanctions take the form of either fines (viewed as costless for the government to impose) or imprisonment (viewed as costly for the government to impose). Whatever the sanction's form, the regulator must choose its magnitude. And given that most violations are not detected with certainty, the regulator must also choose the probability with which the sanction will be imposed. Moreover, the regulator must decide whether to sanction all individuals causing external harm (by setting up a strict liability regime) or only those whose actions cross some government-determined threshold (by enacting what is often called a fault-based or negligence regime).[1] The theory of optimal deterrence has made much progress in explaining how the government should make all these choices. Yet conceptual issues remain, as do challenges of reconciling theoretical prescriptions and predictions with real-world enforcement regimes and individual behavior.

14.2 THE TREATMENT OF OFFENDERS' GAINS

To start, recall the most basic proposition of the optimal deterrence theory: the government should deter private acts producing external harms in excess of private gains while allowing private acts for which the gains exceed the harms.[2] This point, articulated in Becker's (1968) seminal article, was immediately challenged by Stigler (1970). The two Nobel laureates

[1] Threshold-based regimes are typically referred to as fault-based (Polinsky and Shavell 2007) or negligence (Craswell 1999:2215–18) regimes. The latter definition is less than ideal because it confuses an economic concept of a socially optimal threshold that may exist in any area of the law with a legal concept in tort law. The former definition is unfortunate because the term fault implies blameworthiness based on one's mental state. No such connection between government-set thresholds and the offender's mental state exists as a general matter. Threshold simply means a (socially optimal) line separating behavior subject to sanctions from that not subject to sanctions. Moreover, as will be discussed, the deterrence theory has had very limited success in accounting for the offender's mental state.

[2] Some of the discussion in Sections 14.2–14.4 overlaps with Raskolnikov (2020).

disagreed about whose gains ought to count. Becker's answer was "everyone's." Stigler's view was "certainly not!" "What evidence is there that society sets a positive value upon the utility derived from a murder, rape, or arson?," he asked incredulously (Stigler 1970:527). The "society has branded the utility derived from such activities as illicit," Stigler added, without offering any evidence that society as much as recognizes the concept of utility, let alone brands some kinds of utility different from others.

Adopting Becker's view leads to the inescapable conclusion that society should allow efficient crimes (as well as efficient torts) – the result that at least in some cases economists find to be distasteful (Curry and Doyle 2016; Dharmapala and Garoupa 2004). Adopting Stigler's view leads to an uncomfortable realization that society's "branding" of "illicit utility" is quite contingent. Acts that society "branded . . . as illicit" and criminalized just a few short decades ago are now constitutionally protected fundamental rights (same-sex relationships, interracial marriages, and so on). Likewise, acts that society brands as "illicit" and criminalizes today used to be acceptable not long ago (for example, marital rape (Bennice and Resick 2003; Hasday 2000)).

The Becker–Stigler debate has not been resolved, but scholars have found ways to advance the theory while avoiding the issue. Curry and Doyle (2016) formalize Posner's (1985) suggestion that criminal law aims to induce putative criminals to achieve their objectives through voluntary market exchanges – a notion that is easier to accept for some crimes (property theft) than others (rape or battery). When market exchange is added to the choice between committing a crime or doing nothing, Curry and Doyle (2016) show, maximizing social welfare becomes equivalent to minimizing the cost of crime. Because the offender's gain is not part of this cost, there is no need to decide whether gains of some offenders should count or not. Curry and Doyle's (2016) analysis explains several features of criminal law such as the use of criminal history in sentencing and the necessity defense.

Raskolnikov (2014) avoids the same question by focusing on a subset of socially undesirable acts where the offender's gain is always equal to the victim's harm. These acts – ranging from price fixing to market manipulation, securities churning, and insider trading – are all intentional, nonconsensual transfers of money; they are quasi-theft. While the transfer itself neither adds nor detracts from social welfare, victims incur defensive costs to prevent these transfers while offenders incur costs to carry them out. These costs make all such quasi-theft acts unambiguously inefficient whether or not the social welfare function includes the offender's gain. Focusing on these acts allows Raskolnikov (2014) to evaluate the efficiency of some common penalty structures and mental state inquiries, as will be discussed.

While some scholars deal with the "illicit gain" problem by narrowing the acts under consideration, others deal with the same issue by considering both alternatives. Mungan (2019) builds a case for rewarding individuals who abstain from engaging in criminal acts while either including the utility of criminals in the social welfare function or ignoring it. The results, it turns out, do not depend on the inclusion of the offender's gains (Mungan 2019:11). Mungan (2014) follows the same strategy with the same indifference result in his analysis of escalating sanctions. Miceli and Bucci (2005) also consider both alternatives in their study of escalating penalties, but their result holds only if the offenders' gains are excluded (Miceli and Bucci 2005:77–8). Finally, one can avoid the "illicit gain" problem by switching from normative to positive analysis and focusing on how society can deter offenses without asking what offenses should be deterred, as discussed at the end of this chapter.

14.3 THE DESIGN OF SANCTION MULTIPLIERS

Both positive and normative analyses of deterrence take account of the obvious fact that many offenses are not observed by the regulators. *Ex ante*, the probability of facing sanctions – which is often called the "probability of detection" as a shortcut – is less than one.[3] The standard response to the problem of imperfect detection is to increase the nominal (that is, statutory) sanction by the so-called multiplier, making sure that the expected sanction equals the act's external harm. If the offender's gain is not available to pay the fine (that is, if the offender keeps the gain even if he is caught and convicted), the multiplier is simply the inverse of the probability of detection, p, or $\frac{1}{p}$ (Polinsky and Shavell 2007). If the fine includes the gain (as is the case, for example, for tax fines), the multiplier is $\frac{1-p}{p}$ (Leung 1991).

In principle, the government can choose both the nominal sanction and the probability of detection. So one of the key payoffs of the optimal deterrence theory is identifying the optimal combination of the two. That combination depends on many factors, including the wealth of offenders, their risk preferences, errors in determination of liability, the cost of imposing fines, whether sanctions are based on risky acts or actual harms, and other considerations (Craswell 1996; Polinsky and Shavell 2007). But whatever the case, the basic approach remains the same: set the expected sanction to equal the external harm (possibly adjusted, most often downwards, to account for a number of factors), determine the probability of detection, and then set the optimal nominal (statutory) sanction using the multiplier.

While much of the deterrence literature follows this logic, this approach faces long-known challenges. The standard approach is static – it is based on a one-period model. In reality, offenses happen over time. Leung's (1991) adaptation of the standard deterrence model to infinite horizon yields multipliers where the probability of detection is replaced by the hazard rate of detection, which may or may not be constant over time.[4] Moreover, Craswell (1999) notes that the simple multiplier formula relies on three critical assumptions. First, sanctions are based on the external harm. Second, sanctions are set on a case-by-case basis. And third, the offender's behavior does not affect the likelihood of detection – egregious violations are as likely to be punished as minor transgressions are.[5]

In reality, law enforcement agencies often target particularly egregious behavior, sanction multipliers are set at the same level for all offenses of a given type, and sanctions take the form of schedule-based fines rather than of damages based on external harms. Craswell (1999) shows that all these real-world deviations from the basic model make the multiplier approach "useful, and [possibly] even dominat[ing] the alternatives, in a fairly small set of cases. In other cases, however, the balance of advantages and disadvantages is harder to assess" (Craswell 1999:2189). The analysis of multipliers has seen little progress since Craswell's (1999) contribution.

3 The probability of facing sanctions is a compound probability that the offense is detected, that the enforcement agents decide to litigate/prosecute the case (rather than to ignore it in order to focus on other, more severe violations), and that the parties do not resolve the controversy through settlement which may or may not include a payment.

4 While the hazard rate, strictly speaking, is neither a probability nor a density function, it may be understood as the probability that an event occurs in a particular infinitesimally small time period given that the event has not happened prior to that period (Kim 1996).

5 What terms like "egregious" mean is more complicated than it appears, as discussed later. In Craswell's (1999) analysis, egregious means producing a great external harm.

14.4 OPTIMAL DETERRENCE IN OPTIONAL REGIMES

The optimal deterrence theory separates all legal regimes into strict liability and threshold-based types. The theory reveals many differences between the two. Each type has some theoretical advantages,[6] but, in practice, threshold-based regimes are much more pervasive.[7]

Much of the optimal deterrence analysis focuses on creating incentives for potential offenders to make efficient decisions about whether or not to offend. Yet behavior in most threshold-based regimes varies along another margin as well. In addition to choosing whether to comply with the regime's requirements (the margin typically referred to as the level of care, precaution, or compliance), individuals also choose whether to participate in the regime at all (the margin often referred to as the level of activity or participation).

One of the key insights of the optimal deterrence theory is that threshold-based regimes lead to excessive participation while strict liability regimes do not. If a threshold-based regime is perfectly enforced, individuals who comply with the threshold face no risk of legal liability even though their actions give rise to some risk of external harm (albeit the risk viewed as acceptable by the threshold-setting regulator). Rational individuals ignore this risk, leading to excessive participation. In a strict liability regime, in contrast, all individuals causing harm face sanctions, so they take account of all risks that they create.

Perfect enforcement, however, does not exist in the real world. Enforcement errors are inevitable, and Png (1986) showed that they have two effects. First, not only mistaken exonerations (mistaken failures to impose liability) reduce deterrence; mistaken impositions of liability do as well.[8] Second, a mistaken imposition of liability chills socially desirable behavior. Individuals who would have complied with the threshold if enforcement were perfect abstain from engaging in the activity for fear of being found mistakenly liable. Png (1986) showed that regulators should increase sanctions to counter the first effect and introduce subsidies to counter the second.

Kaplow (2011a) extended Png's (1986) inquiry by considering a population of agents with varying benefits. Kaplow (2011a) focused on the implications of deterrence and chilling for the socially optimal burden of proof. He showed that the preponderance-of-the-evidence and other familiar proof thresholds are optimal only by chance, and that the optimal threshold depends on multiple factors in a complex way.[9]

6 Strict liability regimes require less information than threshold-based ones to determine liability. While the enforcer in both regimes needs to determine the external harm, the enforcer does not need to ascertain the private gain in a strict liability regime while such determination is necessary in a threshold-based one. Moreover, strict liability regimes lead to optimal incentives along two margins of behavior (typically referred to as the levels of activity and care) while threshold-based regimes do not. On the other hand, threshold-based regimes have an advantage over strict liability ones if sanctions are costly to impose. This advantage arises because if one assumes that the threshold is set optimally, enforcement is perfect, and all individuals know the law, no one would ever violate the threshold, so the sanctioning costs would never arise. In reality, of course, none of these assumptions hold, so the advantage of threshold-based regimes over strict liability ones is theoretical.

7 Even legal regimes that are called "strict liability" are often threshold-based as these terms are used in the optimal deterrence theory. For example, strict liability for products with design defects really turns on the threshold of whether the design is unreasonably dangerous (Craswell 1999). A "strict liability" tax penalty for transactions lacking economic substance (Thomas 2011) really turns on the threshold of whether the transaction has economic substance. And a "strict liability wrong" of copyright infringement arises only if the defendant produced something that is a copy, and, in addition, if the defendant did so wrongfully (Balganesh 2018:492).

8 A mistaken imposition of liability reduces the expected benefit of complying with the threshold. This benefit reduction diminishes the difference in the payoffs from complying and violating, making violating less costly relative to complying.

9 In related work, Kaplow showed how the burden of proof interacts with the optimal choices of sanctions and enforcement effort, and how changes to that burden affect participation by would-be-compliers and would-be-

Dari-Mattiacci and Raskolnikov (in press) investigate the interplay between deterrence and chilling more broadly, and they discover that neither higher sanctions nor a greater probability of detection unambiguously increases deterrence. The interaction of the deterrence and the chilling effects is the reason. Higher expected sanctions induce some agents participating in the regime to switch from violations to compliance – the standard Becker (1968) result. However, higher expected sanctions also induce some previously complying agents to abstain from participation altogether. Depending on the relative magnitudes of the two shifts, higher sanctions may end up reducing both the number of compliers and their share of all participants. Given that individuals facing most real-world regulatory regimes do face both the choice of whether or not to participate and the choice of whether or not to comply, Dari-Mattiacci and Raskolnikov's (in press) findings raise new questions about the optimal design of optional regulatory systems.

14.5 UNCERTAINTY ABOUT UNCERTAINTY

These new questions add to another long-standing challenge. When Png (1986) considered the effects of mistaken exonerations and mistaken liability, he assumed that individual behavior is binary: "the motorist drives either with due care or does not" (Png 1986:102). Speed, of course, is a continuous variable, and as it increases from zero to the maximum possible, the chances of both types of enforcement error change continuously. A mistaken liability for speeding is virtually impossible if a vehicle moves at 10mph; the same is true of a mistaken exoneration if the vehicle's speed exceeds 150mph.

Craswell and Calfee (1986) and Shavell (1987) showed that in threshold-based regimes where gradual changes in behavior lead to gradual changes in error rates, the magnitude of enforcement errors has an ambiguous effect on deterrence. If the enforcement uncertainty is not too great (error rates are not too high), overdeterrence results; otherwise Png's (1986) underdeterrence result holds. Craswell and Calfee (1986) and Kahan (1989) explained that overdeterrence occurs only if crossing the threshold leads to a discontinuous increase in sanctions – something that may not be the case in contract law or in tort law given the operation of its causation requirement. But in many regulatory regimes ranging from environmental protection to tax and securities regulation, sanctions are indeed discontinuous, so the uncertain conclusion about the effect of enforcement uncertainty remains.

Baker and Raskolnikov (2017) point out that at least some effects of enforcement uncertainty become clear if the basic model is modified to account for a very common feature of numerous enforcement regimes – targeted enforcement. Enforcement agents have limited resources, and they often focus their efforts on the most egregious violators while ignoring minor transgressions (Baker and Raskolnikov 2017:283 and sources cited therein). When such targeting takes place, legal and factual uncertainty are unambiguously harmful even for risk-neutral agents. Whether the same two types of uncertainty reduce social welfare remains to be discovered.

Until now, the discussion has highlighted some of the main results of the optimal deterrence theory and the challenges of deriving clear takeaways while modeling realistically complex legal regimes. We now turn to a different set of challenges. Many key features of

violators (Kaplow 2011b, 2012). Mungan (2011) considered the same interactions and found that a heightened burden of proof is efficient in criminal but not civil settings. In contrast, Demougin and Fluet (2006) showed that when unbiased decision-makers (who initially presume that the likelihood of the defendant's guilt is 50 percent) determine liability in threshold-based regimes, a more-likely-than-not burden of proof maximizes deterrence.

actual legal regimes are inconsistent either with the deterrence theory's predictions or with its prescriptions.

14.6 THE COMPLIANCE PUZZLE AND COMPLIANCE BEHAVIOR

The first such feature is the abnormally high levels of compliance with anything from drunk driving (Ross 1992:61–2), to burglary and corporate misconduct (Polinsky and Shavell 2007), to environmental regulation (Bose 1995). Perhaps the starkest example of this so-called compliance puzzle is tax. Setting aside the types of income subject to withholding or information reporting, compliance rates with tax obligations that may be enforced only during a highly unlikely audit are much higher than the deterrence theory would predict. Nominal civil tax penalties are low; criminal tax penalties are extremely rare and can be avoided while taking very questionable positions (Raskolnikov 2017), so taxpayers earning income not reported to the government by third parties should pay almost no tax (Weisbach 2002). Yet this is not the case.

Granted, the deterrence model shows that risk-averse agents are more likely to comply than risk-neutral agents are, and it is plausible to assume that taxpayers are risk-averse. But the levels of risk aversion necessary to explain the observed levels of tax compliance are wholly implausible (Hashimzade, Myles, and Tran-Nam 2013; Luttmer and Singhal 2014). It is also true that the probability of detection that determines behavior is the perceived rather than the actual one. But while evidence suggests that taxpayers generally overestimate audit probabilities, it also suggests that taxpayers with a greater opportunity to evade have a more realistic view of audit coverage (Andreoni, Erard, and Feinstein 1998; DeBacker et al. 2018; Scholz and Pinney 1995). The findings are similar with respect to other offenses (Apel 2013; Nagin 2013).

There have been a number of recent efforts to modify the basic deterrence model in a way that would resolve the compliance puzzle. These efforts extend the workhorse expected utility model to include social interactions, replace that basic model with more complex behavioral variants (including those with rank-dependent expected utility, ambiguity, regret and disappointment, first- and second-order risk aversion, and so on), or both. Some of the results do show that, in theory, these models can predict the realistic level of compliance for reasonable parameter values (Hashimzade, Myles, and Tran-Nam 2013). The problem, however, is that these models do so either at a cost of great complexity that makes empirical testing all but impossible or by relying on a parameter (such as the psychic cost of noncompliance or a reputational loss from it) that is both unobservable and drives the results (Hashimzade, Myles, and Tran-Nam 2013).

The compliance puzzle aside, a vast empirical literature investigates whether sanctions and detection probabilities affect behavior as predicted by the basic deterrence model. The short answer is "yes, but." Econometric studies of real-world effects of certainty and severity of sanctions do show that both instruments affect behavior as predicted by the model. But the relevant elasticities are small and their estimation is difficult (Chalfin and McCrary 2017). Moreover, there is some evidence that swiftness (or celerity) of punishment But this evidence is strongly contested (Raskolnikov 2020) has a noticeable effect on behavior as well (Hawken and Kleiman 2009). Evidence also suggests that certainty and severity of sanctions are not (always) interchangeable – people respond to probabilities more than to the magnitudes of sanctions (Durlauf and Nagin 2011; Nagin 2013). The reasons for this differential responsiveness remain unclear (Mungan and Klick 2016).

Extensions of the basic deterrence model explain the differential reactions to probabilities and magnitudes by turning the model from a static into a dynamic one and introducing myopic agents (Chalfin and McCrary 2017), by incorporating informal sanctions (Nagin 2013), or by introducing discounting of the future disutility of sanctions (Polinsky and Shavell 1999). Further extensions – developed mostly in accounting and finance literatures – introduce agency costs into the basic model and explore their implications. These range from the effect of corporate governance on (tax) compliance (Desai and Dharmapala 2006; Slemrod 2004) to the impact of unions on (tax) aggressiveness (Chyz et al. 2013; Hanlon and Heitzman 2010). Overall, the basic deterrence model clearly captures the essence of the incentive effects of sanctions, and the model's extensions bring theoretical predictions closer to observed behavior. At the same time, the compliance puzzle is only the tip of the iceberg in terms of matching the key takeaways of the deterrence theory to real-world outcomes.

14.7 WHY GAIN-BASED SANCTIONS?

The second pervasive feature of real-world regimes that is at odds with the basic deterrence model is the form of sanctions. Recall that the deterrence theory instructs the government to prevent socially undesirable behavior by forcing individuals to fully account for the external harms resulting from their acts. Naturally, sanctions in that theory are based on the external harm. But while harm-based sanctions exist in tort law, contract law, and in some modern regulatory schemes, vastly more widespread are sanctions based on the offender's gain. Gain-based sanctions are imposed for violations of securities laws, environmental laws, financial regulation, many forms of white-collar crime, and tax laws among others (Polinsky and Shavell 1994; Raskolnikov 2014), not to mention the disgorgement remedy in torts and contracts (Huang 2016).

The divergence between theory and reality of sanctioning regimes has not escaped deterrence theorists. Polinsky and Shavell (1994) acknowledge it, but highlight the inferiority of gain-based sanctions. A small underestimation of the offender's gain, they show, may lead to a misguided failure to deter an act producing the external harm greatly in excess of the offender's gain if sanctions are gain-based. In contrast, a small underestimation of the external harm will not lead to similar underdeterrence under harm-based sanctions. This is an intuitive and appealing argument. But its rigorous proof does not extend to realistic regulatory threshold-based regimes where legality thresholds are not set on a case-by-case basis (Polinsky and Shavell 1994:436). Moreover, enforcement costs may favor gain-based liability, with sanctions set to equal the offender's gain "plus an additional amount sufficient to ensure that deterrence will occur with a high probability even if the gain is underestimated" (Polinsky and Shavell 1994:436). Real-world sanctions calculated as multiples of the offender's gain reflect this approach (Raskolnikov 2014:1175 for examples).

Hylton (2005) explains gain-based sanctions by relying on Posner's (1985) conceptualization of criminal law as a system deterring market-bypassing transactions. Under this view, if a potential offender may purchase an item legally, obtaining the same item through a coercive transfer is a crime. Notably, it makes no difference in this case whether the offender's gain happens to exceed the victim's loss. The only certain way to induce the offender to use legal means is to impose a sanction that would deny the offender any gain from the coercive transfer.

Hylton (2005) argues that such gain-based sanctions are preferable to harm-internalizing sanctions "whenever the cost of transacting with respect to some entitlement is less than the cost of enforcing the right to that entitlement" (Hylton 2005:175). This explanation, however, does not apply to any crime for which no market-equivalent transaction is readily available. Moreover, gain-based fines are widely used to deter noncriminal regulatory violations not subject to Posner's (1985) market bypass theory. And in any case, the realism of that theory is left to the reader's own judgment.

Huang (2016) explains how gain-based sanctions may achieve optimal deterrence. He points out that substituting gain-based sanctions for harm-based sanctions "part of the time can emulate the incentive effect of using [harm-based sanctions] all of the time" (Huang 2016:1595). Notably, the party doing the substituting must be the court or a public-minded enforcement agency. If, in contrast, victims are allowed to choose between harm- and gain-based sanctions, the result would be complete rather than optimal deterrence. While several real-world regimes allow victims such choice, few, if any, give that choice to a neutral (or public-minded) arbiter that Huang (2016) recommends. So just like the compliance puzzle, the pervasive use of gain-based sanctions presents a continuing challenge for the optimal deterrence theory.

The difficulty of explaining real-world sanctioning regimes goes beyond rationalizing gain-based sanctions. The deterrence theory offers no general explanation as to why many sanctions depend on the offense history and on the legal aggressiveness of the act.

14.8 THE ROLE OF OFFENSE HISTORY

The dependence of sanctions on the offense history has puzzled economists for some time. "At *the very best* the literature ... has shown that under *rather special circumstances* escalating penalty schemes *may be* optimal" (Emons 2003: 254, emphasis added). Researchers have offered multiple explanations for higher sanctions for repeat offenders.

Mungan (2014) identifies three main types of explanation: the stigmatization effect of the first penalty, the variation in the offender's propensity for crime, and the offender's learning how to escape punishment (Mungan 2014:190–1 citing sources). Curry and Doyle (2016) show that higher sanctions for repeat offenders are optimal if these offenders have a market alternative to achieving their criminal objectives, and if criminal history reveals that the offender cannot be cheaply deterred. Miceli and Bucci (2005) show that if the criminals' opportunities to earn income legally decline as they commit more crimes, sanctions should be higher for repeat offenders under some restrictive assumptions. Mungan (2014) offers a behavioral justification for escalating penalties based on the assumption that potential offenders are "weak-willed ... [meaning that they] ordinarily possess self-control, but [] may lapse into committing crime" (Mungan 2014:190). These individuals may rationally abstain from committing a profitable offense in order to avoid a higher penalty for a future offense which they may commit in their weak-willed state. Other recent efficiency-based justifications of escalating penalties for repeat offenders include Endres and Rundshagen (2016) and Müller and Schmitz (2015). Although none of these contributions offer a general theory, it appears that higher sanctions for repeat offenders may be efficient in many different, albeit specific, cases.

14.9 WHY GREATER SANCTIONS FOR MORE AGGRESSIVE VIOLATIONS?

Aggressiveness-based graduation of sanctions presents a tougher challenge for the deterrence theory. Not only is it not well explained, it is poorly recognized in the literature. The likely culprit of this inattention is the assumption that aggressiveness is equivalent to harmfulness. Sometimes it is. Faster driving is a more aggressive violation of the "reasonable speed" threshold, in the sense that it is a greater deviation from the line separating legal and illegal conduct. Faster driving also gives rise to a greater expected harm both because it makes accidents more likely and because it makes damages from accidents more severe. So, for speeding, it appears to make perfect sense that more aggressive (or egregious) violations are subject to higher sanctions.

This highly intuitive explanation runs into two problems. First, a more aggressive (in a legal sense) behavior is more likely to trigger an enforcement action. Very aggressive speeding is easier to detect. A patrol officer is more likely to pursue an egregious speeder upon detection. And a court is more likely to convict an offender whose actions deviated greatly from the legal norm. A greater likelihood of sanctions for any of these reasons leads to higher expected sanctions for more aggressive speed limit violators even if the statutory fines do not vary with speed. So why do they?

Raskolnikov (2014) offers two possible explanations. Perhaps, as the conduct becomes increasingly aggressive, the external harm increases faster than the probability of sanction does. It is also possible that that the external harm continues to increase after the probability of sanction approaches its upper bound. In both scenarios, higher nominal sanctions for more aggressive violations may reflect optimal deterrence. However, the empirical validity of these conjectures has never been tested.

The second and more challenging problem is that in some areas such as tax, aggressiveness is not equivalent to the magnitude of harm (Raskolnikov 2016). A barely plausible (very aggressive) tax position may involve a trivial dollar amount; a plausible though not unassailable (moderately aggressive) position may involve billions. The former would be sanctioned; the latter would not. Given that the social harm of tax noncompliance is the cost of raising the lost revenue elsewhere, variations in the external harm do not explain this structure of sanctions. The deterrence theory is still searching for a general explanation of aggressiveness-based sanctions graduation.

14.10 THE PERPLEXING IMPORTANCE OF THE OFFENDER'S MENTAL STATE

The theory's next challenge is to explain the relevance of another legal distinction that is both pervasive and important – the offender's mental state. From the *mens rea* requirement in criminal law, to the willful breach doctrine in contract law, to tests based on knowledge, purpose, and good faith in environmental regulation, securities regulation, corporate governance, and taxation, the offender's mental state determines both the existence of liability and the severity of sanctions (Raskolnikov 2016). Yet "economic analysis of law has expressed puzzlement at the intent rules in the law .... Under the standard economic approach, which focused on internalization of external costs, the actor's intent would appear to be irrelevant" (Hylton 2010:1242). It is revealing that Polinsky and Shavell's (2007) comprehensive review of the optimal deterrence theory makes no mention of the offender's mental state despite discussing such subjects as social norms and fairness.

Deterrence theorists have offered several explanations for the role of the offender's state of mind, all limited to certain doctrinal areas and all lacking rigorous empirical support. Posner (1985) suggests that the intent requirement in criminal law is a proxy for the probability of apprehension and conviction, a proxy for the offender's responsiveness to punishment, or a means of identifying what he calls pure coercive transfers. Shavell (1985) links the same requirement to the probability of harm and the likelihood of escaping from sanctions. Parker (1993) argues that the *mens rea* requirement in criminal law relates to a putative offender's cost of acquiring information about the nature and consequences of his actions. Hylton (2010) posits that intent requirements in tort law contribute to cost internalization and reduce transaction costs.

Raskolnikov (2014) identifies cases where the intent requirement is not limited to criminal or tort law and has a direct and obvious connection to both efficiency and legality. He points out that inefficient and illegal acts ranging from insider trading to naked price fixing, securities churning, embezzlement, and others all have efficient and legal counterparts that differ from their illegal "twins" only in the actor's mental state. If companies in the same industry raise prices because raw materials have become more expensive, the act is both efficient and legal. If the same companies raise prices collusively, the act is both inefficient and illegal. If someone takes twenty dollars out of my wallet without my knowledge while thinking that I owe him twenty dollars, there are no negative consequences in terms of either efficiency or legality. If someone does the same while thinking that the money is mine, the act is both inefficient and a crime. The role of the offender's mental state in identifying and deterring all these inefficient and illegal forms of quasi-theft is obvious and intuitive. But while Raskolnikov (2014) offers many examples of quasi-theft, and Raskolnikov (2020) shows that the quasi-theft analysis applies to a large portion of all crimes, it surely does not cover all possible illegal acts. Deterrence theorists are yet to offer a general explanation of why the offender's state of mind matters in so many legal regimes.

14.11 DETERRENCE VERSUS COMPLIANCE

This chapter's final point addresses neither the findings nor the challenges of the deterrence theory but rather its limitations. Optimal deterrence aims at maximizing efficiency or, if distributional and some other considerations are ignored, social welfare. But many real-world regulatory regimes – both the substantive rules and the enforcement provisions – cannot be plausibly viewed as efficiency-maximizing. Tax is the most obvious example (Raskolnikov 2013), but hardly the only one. Optimal deterrence theory does not have much to say in the analysis of all those decidedly nonoptimal regimes.

But economic theory certainly does. Whatever the merits of a particular rule or sanction, economics studies how rational agents respond to incentives, including those created by law. So law-and-economics can and does shed light on compliance decisions even with laws that the optimal deterrence theory can neither endorse nor explain. Deterrence theorists often use the terms compliance and deterrence interchangeably. But, in general, the two terms have very different meanings. Deterrence (meaning optimal deterrence) is an economic concept referring to welfare (or efficiency) maximization. Compliance is a legal concept referring to actions that do not violate legal commands, however efficient or inefficient these commands happen to be.

The same question may produce different answers from the deterrence and compliance perspectives, as Raskolnikov (2017) demonstrates in his study of legal uncertainty. Reproducing and expanding Craswell and Calfee's (1986) simulations, he shows that while lower uncertainty has an ambiguous effect on behavior (such as the speed of drivers facing an uncertain "reasonable speed" standard), lower uncertainty leads rational actors to take increasingly less aggressive positions (meaning positions with a greater likelihood of success) in a great majority of realistic scenarios. Lower legal uncertainty may or may not be good for deterrence, but it is good for compliance. More generally, any time a deterrence analyst studies individual's responses to rules or sanctions while taking the law as given (or, equivalently but somewhat misleadingly, assuming that the law is socially optimal), the analyst undertakes the economic analysis of compliance rather than deterrence.

Part I of this handbook makes it plain that, compared to deterrence, compliance is a much broader concept. The theory of deterrence is not the only approach to the study of compliance decisions. Nevertheless, it is an important and insightful approach. So while the deterrence theory faces some persistent challenges, as discussed in this chapter, it has, over the past several decades, produced numerous findings of great value for policymakers who design, reform, and enforce legal regimes.

REFERENCES

Andreoni, James, Brian Erard, and Jonathan Feinstein. 1998. "Tax Compliance." *Journal of Economic Literature* 36:818–60.

Apel, Robert. 2013. "Sanctions, Perceptions, and Crime: Implications for Criminal Deterrence." *Journal of Quantitative Criminology* 29:67–101.

Baker, Scott, and Alex Raskolnikov. 2017. "Harmful, Harmless, and Beneficial Uncertainty in Law." *Journal of Legal Studies* 46:281–307.

Balganesh, Shyamkrishna. 2018. "Copyright as Market Prospect." *University of Pennsylvania Law Review* 166:443–513.

Becker, Gary S. 1968. "Crime and Punishment: An Economic Approach." *Journal of Political Economy* 76:169–217.

Bennice, Jennifer A., and Patricia A. Resick. 2003. "Marital Rape." *Trauma, Violence and Abuse* 4:228–46.

Bose, Pinaki. 1995. "Anticipatory Compliance and Effective Regulatory Activity." *International Review of Law and Economics* 15:1551–9.

Chalfin, Aaron, and Justin McCrary. 2017. "Criminal Deterrence: A Review of the Literature." *Journal of Economic Literature* 55:5–48.

Chyz, James A., Winnie Siu Ching Leung, Oliver Zhen Li, and Oliver Meng Rui. 2013. "Labor Unions and Tax Aggressiveness." *Journal of Financial Economics* 108: 675–98.

Craswell, Richard. 1996. "Damage Multipliers in Market Relationships." *Journal of Legal Studies* 25:463–92.

1999. "Deterrence and Damages: The Multiplier Principle and Its Alternatives." *Michigan Law Review* 97:2185–2238.

Craswell, Richard, and John E. Calfee. 1986. "Deterrence and Uncertain Legal Standards." *Journal of Law, Economics, and Organization* 2:279–303.

Curry, Philip A., and Matthew Doyle. 2016. "Integrating Market Alternatives into the Economic Theory of Optimal Deterrence." *Economic Inquiry* 54:1873–83.

Dari-Mattiacci, Giuseppe, and Alex Raskolnikov. in press. "Unexpected Effects of Expected Sanctions." *Journal of Legal Studies*.

DeBacker, Jason, Bradley T. Heim, Anh Tran, and Alexander Yuskavage. 2018. "Once Bitten, Twice Shy? The Lasting Impact of Enforcement on Tax Compliance." *Journal of Law and Economics* 61:1–35.

Dharmapala, Dhammika, and Nuno Garoupa. 2004. "Penalty Enhancements for Hate Crimes: An Economic Analysis." *American Law and Economics Review* 6:185–207.

Demougin, Dominique, and Claude Fluet. 2006. "Preponderance of Evidence." *European Economic Review* 50:963–76.

Desai, Mihir A., and Dhammika Dharmapala. 2006. "Corporate Tax Avoidance and High-Powered Incentives." *Journal of Financial Economics* 79:145–79.

Durlauf, Steven N., and Daniel S. Nagin. 2011. "Imprisonment and Crime: Can Both Be Reduced?" *Criminology and Public Policy* 10:13–54.

Emons, Winand. 2003. "A Note on the Optimal Punishment for Repeat Offenders." *International Review of Law and Economics* 23:253–9.

Endres, Alfred, and Bianca Rundshagen. 2016. "Optimal Penalties for Repeat Offenders – The Role of Offense History." *BE Journal of Theoretical Economics* 16:545–78.

Hanlon, Michelle, and Shane Heitzman. 2010. "A Review of Tax Research." *Journal of Accounting and Economics* 50:127–78.

Hasday, Jill Elaine. 2000. "Contest and Consent: A Legal History of Marital Rape." *California Law Review* 88:1373–1505.

Hashimzade, Nigar, Gareth D. Myles, and Binh Tran-Nam. 2013. "Applications of Behavioural Economics to Tax Evasion." *Journal of Economic Surveys* 27:941–77.

Hawken, Angela, and Mark A. R. Kleiman. 2009. "Managing Drug Involved Probationers with Swift and Certain Sanctions: Evaluating Hawaii's HOPE." Washington, DC: National Criminal Justice Reference Service.

Hermalin, Benjamin E., Avery W. Katz, and Richard Craswell. 2007. "Contract Law." In *Handbook of Law and Economics*, ed. A. Mitchell Polinsky and Steven Shavell, 403–54. Amsterdam: Elsevier.

Huang, Bert. 2016. "Equipoise Effect." *Columbia Law Review* 116:1595–1638.

Hylton, Keith N. 2005. "The Theory of Penalties and the Economics of Criminal Law." *Review of Law and Economics* 1:175–201.

2010. "Intent in Tort Law." *Valparaiso University Law Review* 44:1217–42.

Kahan, Marcel. 1989. "Causation and Incentives to Take Care under the Negligence Rule." *Journal of Legal Studies* 18:427–47.

Kaplow, Louis. 2011a. "Optimal Proof Burdens, Deterrence, and the Chilling of Desirable Behavior." *American Economic Review: Papers and Proceedings* 101:277–80.

2011b. "On the Optimal Burden of Proof." *Journal of Political Economy* 119:1104–40.

2012. "Burden of Proof." *Yale Law Journal* 121:738–859.

Kim, Yungsan. 1996. "Long-Term Firm Performance and Chief Executive Turnover: An Empirical Study of the Dynamics." *Journal of Law, Economics and Organization* 12:480–96.

Leung, Siu F. 1991. "How to Make the Fine Fit the Corporate Crime? And Analysis of Static and Dynamic Optimal Punishment Theories." *Journal of Public Economics* 45:243–56.

Luttmer, Erzo F. P., and Monica Singhal. 2014. "Tax Morale." *Journal of Economic Perspectives* 28:149–68.

Miceli, Thomas J., and Catherine Bucci. 2005. "A Simple Theory of Increasing Penalties for Repeat Offenders." *Review of Law and Economics* 1:70–9.

Miller, Daniel, and Patrick W. Schmitz. 2015. "Overdeterrence of Repeat Offenders When Penalties for Frist-Time Offenders Are Restricted." *Economic Letters* 129:116–20.

Mungan, Murat 2011. "A Utilitarian Justification for Heightened Standards of Proof in Criminal Trials." *Journal of Institutional and Theoretical Economics* 167:352–70.

2014. "Behavioral Justification for Escalating Punishment Schemes." *International Review of Law and Economics* 37:189–97.

2019. "Positive Sanctions versus Imprisonment." *George Mason University Law and Economics Research Paper* 19–03.

Mungan, Murat, and Jonathan Klick. 2016. "Identifying Criminals' Risk Preferences." *Indiana Law Journal* 91:791–821.

Nagin, Daniel S. 2013. "Deterrence: A Review of the Evidence by a Criminologist for Economists." *Annual Review of Economics* 5:83–105.

Parker, Jeffrey S. 1993. "The Economics of Mens Rea." *Virginia Law Review* 79:741–811.

Png, Ivan P. L. 1986. "Optimal Subsidies and Damages in the Presence of Judicial Error." *International Review of Law and Economics* 6:101–5.

Polinsky, A. Mitchell, and Steven Shavell. 1994. "Should Liability Be Based on the Harm to the Victim or the Gain to the Injurer?" *Journal of Law, Economics and Organization* 10:427–37.

1999. "On the Disutility and Discounting of Imprisonment and the Theory of Deterrence." *Journal of Legal Studies* 28:1–16.

2007. "The Theory of Public Enforcement of Law." In *Handbook of Law and Economics*, ed. A. Mitchell Polinsky and Steven Shavell, 403–54. Amsterdam: Elsevier.

Posner, Richard A. 1985. "An Economic Theory of the Criminal Law." *Columbia Law Review* 85:1193–1231.

Raskolnikov, Alex. 2013. "Accepting the Limits of Tax Law and Economics." *Cornell Law Review* 98:523–90.

2014. "Irredeemably Inefficient Acts: A Threat to Markets, Firms, and the Fisc." *Georgetown Law Journal* 102:1133–89.
2016. "Six Degrees of Graduation: Law and Economics of Variable Sanctions." *Florida State Law Review* 43:1015–42.
2017. "Probabilistic Compliance." *Yale Journal on Regulation* 34:491–544.
2020. "Criminal Deterrence: A Review of the Missing Literature." *Supreme Court Economic Review* 28:1–59.
Ross, Laurence H. 1992. *Confronting Drunk Driving: Social Policy for Saving Lives.* New Haven, CT: Yale University Press.
Scholz, John T., and Neil Pinney. 1995. "Duty, Fear, and Tax Compliance: The Heuristic Basis of Citizenship Behavior." *American Journal of Political Science* 39:490–512.
Shavell, Steven. 1985. "Criminal Law and the Optimal Use of Nonmonetary Sanctions as a Deterrent." *Columbia Law Review* 85:1232–62.
1987. *Economic Analysis of Accident Law.* Cambridge, MA: Harvard University Press.
2007. "Liability for Accidents." In *Handbook of Law and Economics*, ed. A. Mitchell Polinsky and Steven Shavell, 139–82. Amsterdam: Elsevier.
Slemrod, Joel. 2004. "The Economics of Corporate Selfishness." *National Tax Journal* 57:877–99.
Stigler, George J. 1970. "The Optimum Enforcement of Laws." *Journal of Political Economy* 78:526–36.
Thomas, Kathleen DeLaney. 2011. "The Case Against a Strict Liability Economic Substance Penalty." *University of Pennsylvania Journal of Business Law* 13:445–97.
Weisbach, David A. 2002. "Ten Truths about Tax Shelters." *Tax Law Review* 55:215–53.

15

General Deterrence: Review with Commentary on Decision-Making

Greg Pogarsky

Abstract: Abundant research has investigated general deterrence, a process whereby threats of punishment reduce crime rates. This chapter has several purposes: 1) to briefly explain the rational choice perspective on deterrence; 2) to highlight several empirical challenges to the causal estimation of deterrent effects; 3) to evaluate the evidence for general deterrence from research that takes these challenges to causal estimation most seriously; and 4) to explain how additional perspectives are needed from behavioral economics and psychology to fully understand deterrence, and in particular the empirical regularity that the deterrent capacity of the certainty of punishment far exceeds that of sanction severity.

15.1 INTRODUCTION

The criminal justice system promotes compliance with the law through general deterrence, a notion that traces to the Enlightenment philosophers Beccaria and Bentham. But those works were not theories about why people commit crimes. Instead, the priorities of that time were maintaining civil order while transitioning from monotheism and authoritarianism to secularism and free will. The Enlightenment writings constituted principles of rationality and fairness around which to organize society. Foremost among those principles was that to minimize state overreach and legitimize governmental institutions, punishments should only be certain, severe, and celeritous enough to deter crime (Paternoster, 2010). These ideas helped structure some empirical research on deterrence up to the middle 1900s. However, that work lacked the requisite theoretical and empirical depth to reliably influence policy. This changed with Becker's (1968) economic theory of crime.

15.2 BACKGROUND CONCEPTS

15.2.1 *The Crime Decision*

Becker (1968) drew from Expected Utility theory (von Neumann and Morgenstern, 1944; Savage 1954) to develop an economic model of crime control. Ironically, the normative implications of the economic model, which assumes that individuals maximize their self-interests, coincide with Enlightenment prescriptions for a fair and just society. Figure 15.1 presents an oversimplified version of the crime decision. Economic actors assess their

Rational Choice Model of Crime Decision

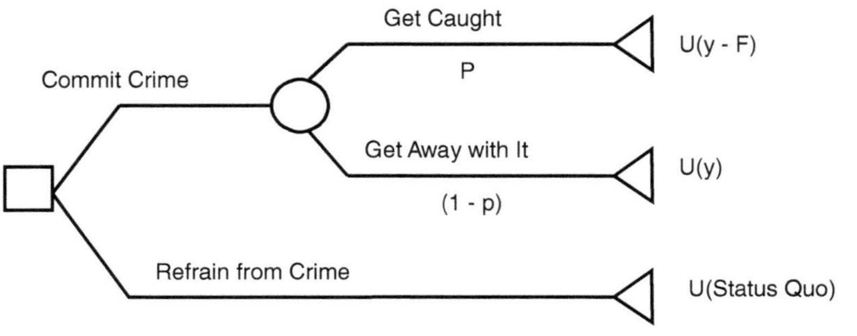

FIGURE 15.1 Rational choice model of crime decision

well-being with a *Utility Function*, U(*), which recalibrates dissimilar consequences (e.g. jail vs. money) into like units (*utiles*) for decision-making purposes. Refraining from crime yields U(status quo). The consequences to an actor from offending are uncertain. Three variables are central: p, the probability of detection *and* punishment;[1] y, the benefits the actor anticipates from committing the offense; and f, the punishment if caught. With probability (1-p), the actor will evade capture and experience U(y). With probability p, the actor will be caught and punished. In this case, a punishment of f is subtracted from the benefits from offending, y. The actor will therefore experience U(Y-f). The Expected Utility from crime is a global assessment of the risks and consequences.

An individual should offend if

$$EU_{crime} = pU(Y - f) + (1 - p)U(Y) > U(\text{status quo}) \quad (1)$$

Among other things, this expression formalizes the propositions of Beccaria and Bentham that crime should decrease with actors' perceptions of higher certainty and severity of punishment.[2] This approach also generalizes to include other decision-making dynamics, such as guilt and stigma, issues of future orientation and self-regulation, and sanction celerity.

Although the ensuing review addresses crime rates in places rather than offending by individuals, the operative deterrence principles apply at both levels (Matsueda, 2013). If crime rates decrease following a policy that elevates the probability of apprehension, the deterrence explanation is grounded in individual behavior. Enough individuals are assumed to have refrained from crimes they otherwise would have committed, to reduce the crime rate.

1 Nagin (2013a: 207–9) shows how the construct of "perceived certainty" in deterrence research is routinely oversimplified to obscure a series of separate and conditional probabilities, relating to successfully completing the act, apprehension by the police for noncompliance, and conviction if apprehended.

2 Reasoning through this expression shows that the expected utility, and therefore the attractiveness of crime, decreases with increases in p and f. This is confirmed mathematically as the partial derivatives with respect to each are negative.

15.2.2 *Empirical Challenges*

Estimating causal models of real-world phenomena requires considerable thought, and crime is no exception. Randomized experiments are often considered the "gold standard" for causal inference in crime research (Nagin and Sampson, 2019). Such research has investigated the prevalence and determinants of transgression by participants, usually college students, in laboratory experiments. Transgressions in these settings involved behaviors such as cheating when grading one's own exercise or playing computer games (e.g. Tittle and Rowe, 1973; Ward et al., 1986). Building on these literatures, Nagin and Pogarsky (2003) and Pogarsky (2004) gave college students a survey which included a trivia quiz on which they could cheat in order to improve their chances of a monetary bonus for quiz performance. They found that cheating was less likely among participants who were supervised more frequently and for whom the punishment was consequently more certain. Cheating was unaffected by the magnitude of the penalty for getting caught. Well-executed studies of this type can produce sound causal inference. However, rather than serious crime, these experiments involve low-stakes laboratory rule-breaking by persons with little to no criminal experience.

Recognizing this, there have been more naturalistic randomized experiments embedded in the criminal justice system. For example, Weisburd, Einat, and Kowalski (2008) found that among offenders in New Jersey sentenced to probation, those randomly assigned to more vigorous supervision with higher risk of incarceration for nonpayment of fines were more likely to pay their fines than were less vigorously supervised control respondents. A related empirical paradigm involves "hot spots" policing, which is addressed in Section 15.3.1. This approach focuses disproportionate policing resources in high-crime areas to enhance overall prospects for deterrence. The advantage of randomization is retained, but in a more naturalistic setting than in the laboratory experiments, and with actual offenders. Still, this approach has drawbacks. Estimation depends on the assumption that the intervention, which in this case is enhanced policing, is localized onto the target with no spillover impacts on untreated control areas. Yet this assumption has been called into question. Hot spots researchers assert that there is diffusion of benefits. This refers to a positive externality whereby deterrent effects may occur in untreated areas if citizens in these other areas learn about the hot spot intervention. Opposite spillover effects are also possible since the hot spot intervention leaves fewer remaining resources to deploy elsewhere if needed. Finally, as Nagin and Sampson (2019) observed, examining slices of a system in this way may not produce adequate counterfactuals needed to assess systemwide impacts from the intervention.

Therefore, triangulation across other empirical paradigms is necessary, and crime researchers have also analyzed ecological data on arrest, crime, adjudication, sentencing and other facets of the criminal justice process. Although this empirical orientation has the advantage of being grounded in actual, real-world criminal justice, these very strengths raise unique challenges for causal inference. Many of these challenges arise because causation between predictors and outcome variables in deterrence is simultaneous and reciprocal. That is, whether it is reflected by arrests, sentences, or policing resources, law enforcement strength potentially deters crime. Over time, however, crime rates also influence public safety efforts. This means that key predictors in deterrence models are often reciprocally influenced by crime levels. Even more, variables omitted from these models may influence both predictors and outcomes. Absent some remediation on these matters, causal estimation is threatened.

Bias resulting from omitted variables, reciprocal causation, or other sources of endogeneity has been addressed in several ways. One approach involves instrumental variables. The idea is to identify a proxy for the endogenously caused predictor, which only influences the outcome through its association with the predictor but is otherwise unrelated to the outcome or some consequential omitted variable. Consider estimating the impact of smoking on health. Even if smoking adversely affects health, smoking may well be a consequence of health outcomes, or also omitted variables such as emotional state or intelligence. It is therefore worthwhile to locate an instrumental variable that affects the key predictor, smoking, but is not reciprocally caused by smoking. In this case, the tax rate for cigarettes is a logical candidate because while it too affects cigarette consumption, it is defensibly assumed to be unrelated to health outcomes (see Angrist and Krueger, 2001; Leigh and Schembri, 2004).

Several other approaches have been taken for causal estimation of deterrence effects in administrative or archival data. Nagin (2013a, 2013b) discussed research on "abrupt changes" in law enforcement that in rare cases can mimic some dynamics of a natural experiment. An example might be a change in law or policing strategy that naturally generates treated and untreated data over time. Another approach, termed "Granger causality" involves some penetrating logic. If, in a multivariate model, significantly more variance in the outcome is explained by *both* past values of the outcome *and* past values of the predictors than is explained simply by past values of the outcome, then causation is presumed (Granger, 2001). However, while this approach may mitigate simultaneity bias, as Chalfin and McCrary (2017) observe, potential bias from omitted variables remains.

Thus, each of these empirical strategies has strengths and weaknesses, but each reflects considerable thought on matters of crime causation. The ensuing review will concentrate on research that, with one or more of these or related techniques, thoughtfully addresses threats to causal inference in deterrence research. A final issue pertains to distinguishing the crime reduction impacts of deterrence versus incapacitation. That is, even if a period of confinement does causally reduce offending, is this because high rate offenders are out of circulation, an *incapacitation effect*, or because the period of incarceration experienced by each offender contributes to the general public impression that crime is risky and costly and should be avoided, *a deterrent effect* (Durlauf and Nagin, 2011b)? Approaches will be highlighted in the rest of this chapter that also address this challenge to generating causal deterrent effects.

15.3 GENERAL DETERRENCE FINDINGS

15.3.1 *Police and Deterrence*

The criminal justice process includes various possible levers for deterrence. A number of these involve policing. As Lum and Nagin (2017) note, police apprehend criminals, but they also serve as sentinels to discourage crime. This distinction is essential for policy. Arresting criminal perpetrators invariably increases the correctional population, whereas preventing crime decreases it (Durlauf and Nagin, 2011a). Research has investigated the general deterrent capacity of several aspects of policing.

Police Resources and Strength. One approach estimates the relationship between crime rates and indicators of policing intensity in a time and place. Marvell and Moody (1996) analyzed two panel data sets, one on crime and police per capita for forty-nine states from 1968 to 1973, and another with comparable information on fifty-six large cities from 1971 to

1992. Using Granger causality methods, the authors found that more police per capita reduced crime (see also Corman and Mocan, 2000).

Levitt (1997) used the political cycle as an instrumental variable for police staffing. Elections are regularly scheduled and thereby unresponsive to crime rates, whereas public safety expenditures increase near elections. Although Levitt (1997) produced evidence for deterrence with this approach, McCrary (2002) reported errors in these analyses. In response, Levitt (2002) instrumented with the number of civil service workers and firefighters. Evans and Owens (2007) instrumented for number of police with federal expenditures to states under the Community Oriented Policing Services (COPS) program of 1994, which funded state and local hiring of new police officers. These studies generally find that more police results in less crime. Chalfin and McCrary (2018) showed how measurement error in data on police staffing and personnel has biased estimates of the causal relationship between police and crime downwards.[3]

Another way to isolate the causal effect of police on crime is to exploit exogenous changes to policing strength that are not responsive to changes in crime, through "abrupt change" studies (Nagin, 2013a, 2013b). For example, Shi (2009) found that crime increased in Cincinnati after a white police officer killed an unarmed black man, civil unrest ensued, and officers were indicted. Presumably, the public climate increased the consequences to officers from transgressing, prompting them to police less vigorously (see also DeAngelo and Hansen, 2014; Heaton, 2010). Klick and Tabarrok (2005) found that higher terror alert levels in Washington, DC from 2002 to 2003 corresponded with greater police presence on city streets, and less crime. This last series of studies, then, also provides evidence for a general deterrent effect from policing.

Police Deployment. Beyond ebbs and flows in staffing and public enforcement climate, research has also evaluated specific policing techniques. Sherman (1990: 1) assessed the crime control impacts of "police crackdowns," defined as "sudden increases in officer presence, sanctions, and threats of apprehension either for specific offenses or for all offenses in specific places." While a strong majority of the eighteen crackdowns evaluated produced initial deterrent effects, some of these effects decayed, and only persisted after the crackdown had subsided in a subset of cases.

Contemporary "hot spots" research ensued (e.g. Braga et al., 2019; Braga et al., 2014; Weisburd, 2018). This perspective follows from long-standing empirical regularities in the spatial and temporal distribution of crime within places. In general, crime clusters at specific locations, and these patterns tend to persist over time (Braga et al., 2017; Brantingham and Brantingham, 1999; Weisburd, 2015; Weisburd et al., 2012). Deterrence principles, then, suggest that elevating the police presence in a hot spot should reduce the crime rate.

Subject to these qualifications, there is some evidence that hot spots policing successfully reduces crime (Berk and MacDonald, 2010; Braga, 2008; Braga et al., 2014; Lum et al., 2011; National Research Council, 2004; Weisburd and Majmundar, 2018). One caveat is that the durability of these impacts over time is unclear. A related intervention is Problem Oriented Policing, in which law enforcement and community members convene to identify specific problems and, based on this consultation, fashion a plan (Goldstein, 1990). A prominent success in this regard was Operation Ceasefire in Boston, a multidimensional approach to reducing the number of guns in the city (Braga and Weisburd, 2010; Kennedy et al., 2001).

[3] The authors reported "error-corrected elasticities" (% change in crime/% change in police) of -.27 for murder, -.19 for car theft, and -.18 for robbery.

15.3.2 *Sanctions*

In addition to policing the general population, the criminal justice system also punishes wrongdoers. General deterrence can come from actual punishments given, under the notion that these punishments should elevate perceptions of the severity of punishment in an area and reduce crime. Also relevant are the sanctions *authorized* by law, particularly when these authorized sanctions change (see Apel et al., 2006). Several aspects of criminal justice sanctioning have been studied to provide information on general deterrence.

Prison Population One approach focuses on prison populations as broad indicators of punishment strength. More incarcerated individuals are presumed to reflect more severe punishments, which should generally deter crime. Marvell and Moody (1994) investigated this problem as well, again with Granger causality techniques. As with estimates regarding police staffing or funding, this approach uses state-level data over time. Although the authors found a modest negative correlation between imprisonment and crime, the magnitude was smaller than for police. Other studies have used a similar approach to estimate the elasticity of crime with respect to the prison population (Besci, 1999; Liedka et al., 2006; Spelman, 2000, 2005). In a recent review, Donohue (2009) concluded that estimates varied considerably. Moreover, Nagin (2013a) and Chalfin and McCrary (2017) observed that the benefits from Granger's (1969) techniques in bolstering causal inference may be overstated.

Research has used instrumental variable methods to address endogenous variability in this literature as well. In a seminal paper, Levitt (1996) instrumented for changes in the prison population with court orders to reduce that population, theorizing that the latter should be somewhat random with respect to crime. Levitt (1996) produced large negative estimates of the deterrent effect of the prison population on crime. That said, questions have been raised about the suitability of court orders as an instrumental variable (see Durlauf and Nagin, 2011b; Johnson and Raphael, 2012; Liedka et al., 2006).

Moreover, this approach has at least two additional limitations. First, Durlauf and Nagin (2011a) question the degree to which variation in the size of prison populations reflects coordinated policy activity. Also, although the prison population reflects the sanctioning rather than the policing side of the criminal justice equation, the number of prisoners may still also affect the perceived certainty of punishment. Nagin (2013a) shows that sanction certainty is often treated monolithically, whereas it actually reflects a series of compound probabilities – of detection, conviction given detection, incarceration given conviction, and so on. Beyond reflecting the severity of punishment, the number of prisoners may also reflect the perceived probability of incarceration, given conviction. Thus, this empirical approach does not map as directly as do others onto the theoretical framework it aims to test.

Authorized Sanctions Research has also exploited variation in criminal laws across jurisdictions, or changes in those laws within jurisdictions (or both) to investigate general deterrence. A well-developed literature on the deterrent effect of capital punishment finds little to no relationship between executions and murders across states and over time (Grogger, 1991; Hjalmarsson, 2012; Land et al., 2009; Stolzenberg and D'Alessio, 2004; Zimring et al., 2010). A related literature testing for general deterrence in states and at times where capital punishment was possible has produced mixed findings (Berk 2005; Dezhbakhsh et al., 2003; Donohue and Wolfers 2005, 2009; Katz et al., 2003; Mocan and Gittings 2003; Zimmerman

2006). But as publicly salient as executions are, only a small fraction of cases are even death penalty eligible.

Several additional approaches have been taken to estimate the effect of sanctions on crime. *Age of majority* studies begin from the premise that for comparable criminal conduct, an adult is more likely to go to jail, and for longer, than is a juvenile. This leaves two logical comparison groups – individuals just below the age of majority (eighteen mostly) versus individuals just above that age. Recent adults, who are otherwise mostly comparable to juveniles who are almost adults, should be more deterred by the possibility of harsher sanctions. Yet the several econometric investigations of this type find little evidence for the hypothesized deterrent effect (Lee and McCrary, 2017; Hjalmarsson, 2009). As Chalfin and McCrary (2017) observe, it is difficult to know whether either group has sufficient awareness of the sentencing discrepancy, thus leaving the full import of these findings unclear.

Quasi-experimental comparison groups to estimate the deterrent effect of sanctions have also been identified using sentence enhancements. For example, beginning in the late 1970s, jurisdictions started adopting mandatory minimum sentences for qualifying gun crimes. Yet several studies found little evidence for deterrent effects from these policies (Loftin and McDowall, 1981, 1984). Research has also investigated the deterrent effects of "three-strikes" legislation. Although Helland and Tabarrok (2007) found modest deterrent effects from three-strikes laws in California, Zimring et al. (2001) found none.

Instead of retroactively identifying useful comparison groups in archival data, there have been natural experiments on the deterrent impact of sanctions. A study by Weisburd et al. (2008) was addressed earlier in the general context of causal estimation. Recall that these authors found that probationers in New Jersey who were randomly assigned to an elevated risk of incarceration for nonpayment of fines paid their fines at far higher rates than the others. Similar logic underlies *swift and certain* (SAC) sanctioning. The idea is that certainty and swiftness have more deterrent potential than severity does, and SAC sanctioning is needed to deter relatively present oriented individuals who do not respond to the length of punishments anyway. Hawken and Kleiman (2009) found that Hawaii's Project Hope, which included SAC punishment strategies, deterred rearrest for all crimes including drug use (see also Kilmer et al., 2013). In a comprehensive follow-up, however, Lattimore et al. (2016) found little to no deterrent effects from SAC policies across four geographically diverse sites, in Arkansas, Massachusetts, Oregon, and Texas.

Finally, additional evidence for the role of authorized sanctions in compliance comes from research on corporate crime. Although Schell-Busey et al. (2016: 409) recognize the "need for more complete and methodologically rigorous studies," their meta-analysis uncovers some suggestions for general deterrence. Consistent with the preponderance of findings from the larger literature on criminal deterrence, the most promising possibilities emerging from this analysis in the corporate arena involve monitoring, inspections, and the administrative policies that tend to influence these (see also Simpson et al., 2014).

15.4 DISCUSSION OF FINDINGS

Thus, research that seriously engages with fundamental conceptual challenges, such as distinguishing deterrence from incapacitation or issues of endogenous causation, tends to find evidence for general deterrence. The findings coalesce around a comparable empirical regularity as in individual-level research – elevating the certainty of punishment produces larger deterrent effects than does elevating the severity of punishment. But if rational choice and deterrence principles postulate independent certainty and severity effects, why does empirical research only identify certainty effects?

15.4.1 *Offenders Are Different*

Under the deterrence and rational choice perspectives, all persons share a fundamental attribute. They each seek to maximize their self-interests.[4] Crimes trace to perceptions of the risks, costs, and incentives corresponding to a given offending opportunity. That said, the rational choice model does generalize to account for two individual differences, the preferences for risk and time.

Risk preference is generally conceived in terms of a choice between a gamble and a sure thing. As Pogarsky et al. (2018: 43–4) explain, consider "flipping a fair coin and receiving $10,000 if it lands heads, but nothing if it lands tails. Or alternatively, the actor can receive the average outcome of the gamble for sure: 0.5($10,000) + 0.5(0) = $5,000." An actor is risk averse if "he or she would accept an amount less than the average monetary value of a gamble rather than take that gamble." Conversely, that individual is risk seeking if they "would prefer a gamble over an amount equal to the expected dollar value of that gamble."

The rational choice model predicts that certainty effects should exceed severity effects, *if offenders are assumed to be more risk seeking than nonoffenders are.* While this may seem uncontroversial and empirically supported (Block and Gerety, 1995; Mungan and Klick, 2016), the assumption is an oversimplification. In behavioral economics, risk preference is neither situationally nor temporally stable. Instead, it depends on whether the actor views the potential outcome as a gain or a loss. People tend to be risk averse for perceived gains, but risk seeking for perceived losses (Kahneman and Tversky, 1979). Thus, rather than attaching to the person, risk preference varies according to the perceived valence of the *situation*. This means that risk preference alone cannot account for the preeminence of certainty effects over severity effects.

Another relevant extension of rational choice theory involves issues of intertemporal choice and time preference. Although the benefits from offending, whether psychic or tangible, tend to be immediate, the legal and extralegal costs are mostly delayed. Nagin and Pogarsky (2001) modified expression (1) to account for these intertemporal considerations as follows:

$$\mathrm{EU_{crime}} = \delta_i \mathrm{pU(Y - f) + (1 - p)U(Y) > U(status\ quo)} \tag{2}$$

where

$$\delta_i = \frac{1}{(1 + r_i)^t} \tag{3}$$

is a discount factor varying from 0 to 1 which scales down the perceived costs of crime with increases in two parameters: t, the length of the expected delay (also objective sanction celerity) and r_i, each person's *discount rate*, reflecting the degree of devaluation for a given delay.[5] Consistent with Gottfredson and Hirschi's (1990) assertion that offenders have "here and now" temporal orientations, offenders should also have higher discount rates for future consequences.

[4] Using ultimatum and dictator game experiments from economics, Jaynes and Loughran (2019) found that the perceived impact of one's behavior on others can indeed impact crime decisions.

[5] An exponential discount function is assumed for simplicity. However, more advanced conceptions of intertemporal choice employ a hyperbolic discounting functioning, which allows the impact of a given discount rate to vary over different possible delays (Loughran et al., 2012).

But, as with the risk preference explanation, attributing the paramountcy of certainty effects to temporally and situationally stable time preferences entails some empirically questionable assumptions. One is that individuals even have a global time preference that transcends the different types of situation they encounter (Frederick et al., 2002). Another is the exponential form of the discounting function. Recent findings suggest that the role of time preference in offending decision may conform to a hyperbolic function implying a nonconstant discount rate for a given delay depending on how far into the future the delay period is contemplated (Laibson, 1997; Loughran et al., 2012) in which the discount rate for a given period of delay can actually vary according to how far off in the future the period of delay is assessed. Finally, the discounting perspective tends to ignore situational variation in time perspective – based on hurriedness or visceral activation, for example – that predictably if only contemporaneously affects temporal orientation. For these reasons, why certainty effects tend to be larger and more dependable than severity effects merits further scrutiny.

15.4.2 *Behavioral Economic Considerations*

Cognitive Nature of Certainty and Severity Determinations. Crime research has increasingly appealed to advancements in behavioral economics (Loughran, 2019; Pogarsky et al., 2017, 2018), which is "based on realistic assumptions and descriptions of human behavior. It is just economics with more explanatory power because the models are a better fit with the data" (Thaler, 2015: 23). Various behavioral economic notions also help explain why sanction certainty deters crime more strongly than sanction severity does. Expression (1) abstractly implies that the independent crime-reduction effects of variation in perceived certainty (p) and perceived severity (f) are comparable. Yet this obscures any cognitive differences between certainty and severity determinations.

The certainty consideration is immediate. It involves getting caught, the threshold requisite for punishment. Perceived certainty is often conceived probabilistically, in terms of *what is the probability that I will be caught?* But people often have difficulty quantifying judgments, particularly emotional or intuitive ones (Joel and Putnam, 2015; Sunstein et al., 1998). Moreover, rather than probability, people tend to prefer blunter, less finely calibrated means of expressing uncertainty, such as Likert-type characterizations like *unlikely* or *somewhat likely* (Roche and Pickett, 2017). Even for an explicit response scale, people *question-substitute*, by mentally transforming a cognitively taxing task into a more manageable one (Kahneman and Frederick, 2002). Given the exigencies in crime opportunities, like time pressure, visceral arousal, and incomplete information, a workable shorthand representation of the certainty determination is *will I be caught?* This coincides with the concept of threshold probability highlighted by Nagin et al. (2015). Certainly, each actor's estimated probability of detection for a given crime is central, but so too is p*, a tolerance threshold. Offending results from the binary determination that the perceived probability of detection for a given act is below their personal threshold.

The severity determination is fundamentally different. It is iterative and contingent. Contemplating perceived severity is a less direct perceptual exercise since one must first envision being caught for punishment to be relevant. The severity judgment thus distills to two steps. First, imagine being caught, and if this likelihood feels minimally consequential, then evaluate the potential consequences. The severity judgment is also contingent; if the actor does not expect to be caught, the severity of punishment is irrelevant.

The dual process nature of behavioral economics underscores why these cognitive differences lend themselves to the paramountcy of certainty over severity in deterring crime. According to Kahneman and Frederick (2002: 51), "cognitive processes can be partitioned into two main families – traditionally called intuition and reason." System 2 processes are controlled, effortful, slow, self-aware, rule-following, and effable. In contrast, system 1 processes are intuitive, automatic, effortless, fast, unconscious, and ineffable (Kahneman, 2011; Thaler and Sunstein, 2009). Pogarsky and Herman (2019: 824) explain that "system 1 instinctual processes run continuously, whereas system 2 stays in 'low effort mode.' System 2 often remains unengaged; involvement takes effort and is thus reserved for times when system 1 encounters difficulty or dissonance." Certainty judgments are better positioned cognitively to impact offending decisions than severity judgments are. The nature of severity perceptions places them squarely within the province of system 2. But real-world decision-making often requires quick, minimally effortful assessments. It is easy to see how attention is drawn to an immediate, perhaps cognitively simplified certainty assessment, whereas focus is led away from the secondary and contingent aspects of the decision, involving *future* consequences, *if caught*.

Future and Past Selves. Even assuming that the actor had perfect factual information regarding the consequences from offending if caught, the severity evaluation still requires them to forecast *how they will feel* about a possible future occurrence. A threshold issue concerns the degree to which the contemporaneous evaluator of sanction severity *identifies with* the version of their *self* that would experience the future sanction. Frederick (2003: 94) highlighted the contemporary implications of Parfit (1971, 1984), namely that "a person is nothing more than a succession of overlapping selves related to varying degrees by physical continuities, memories, and similarities of character and interests. On this view, the separation between selves may be just as significant as the separation between persons ...." This helps explain why "people exaggerate the degree to which their future tastes will resemble their current tastes" (Loewenstein et al., 2003: 1209). Van Gelder et al. (2015) found that people who imagine a more vivid future self commit less delinquency (see also Brezina et al., 2009).

Retrospectively evaluating a past consequence is also nontrivial. If severity perceptions are at all rationally grounded, then as with the Bayesian Updating of sanction certainty perceptions (Anwar and Loughran, 2011), the experienced severity of past sanctions provides highly relevant information for present decision-making. But on this score, crime research and policy at least implicitly conflate the *global* determination of sanction severity with one of its *inputs*, length or duration. This neglects findings by Kahneman et al. (1993) on the pervasiveness of *duration neglect* in retrospective evaluation. Kahneman et al. (1993) instructed all subjects in an experiment to submerge their hands in ice-cold water and thereafter rate the painfulness of this experience. Those assigned to the experimental manipulation immersed their hands in the water for the precise length of time and coldness of temperature that the control subjects did. However, they also immersed their hands for thirty additional seconds at a slightly warmer and less (but still) painful temperature. Clearly subjects receiving the experimental manipulation endured a longer period of pain than the remaining subjects did. Nonetheless, treated respondents rated the *longer* period of submersion as *less* and *not more* painful than those in the control condition. Rather than retrospectively rate the aversiveness of the experience by its length, Kahneman et al. (1993) find that such evaluations instead conform to a "peak-end heuristic." The global evaluation of aversiveness is a function of how bad the experience was at two points: its peak and its end.

There is strong evidence for duration neglect in crime research. In a sample of 4,683 adult Dutch offenders, Snodgrass et al. (2011) found little evidence for the expected deterrence relationship between the length of incarceration ("dosage") and reoffending within the next three years. Similarly, Loughran et al. (2009) found no relationship in a large US sample of serious juvenile offenders between the length of institutional placement and recidivism. A recent study by Raaijmakers et al. (2017) tested the impact of *experienced* sanction severity on recidivism. Interestingly, while there is some evidence that higher perceived severity ("my stay is severe" or "this detention is hard") three weeks after entering a pretrial detention facility was associated with less recidivism, the relationship was ultimately nullified with the introduction of control variables.

The theoretical conception of the severity dimension of deterrence is thin, and not well linked with relevant psychological research or the exigencies of real-world decision-making. Further insights could be gained from research that tests duration, intensity, and other possible determinants of experienced severity such as decision heuristics and biases, and that leverages repeated measures of these factors at several points during the sanction period.

15.5 CONCLUSION

General deterrence research that addresses the considerable empirical challenges in estimating causal effects continues to find that deterrence strategies can reduce crime. Two broad forms of deterrence research were examined – that pertaining to police activities versus deterrence attempted through downstream punishment and sanctioning. Consistent deterrent effects are attributable to police activities, such as staffing and deployment, but not to the sanctions given to convicted offenders, and threatened to all. General deterrence research thus coalesces around a comparable conclusion to that generated by offender decision-making research: deterrent effects are more readily achievable by manipulating the certainty rather than the severity of punishment. Moreover, the evidence is unclear as to whether there is a severity effect at all.

Discussion then turned to how well standard economic extensions to the rational choice model account for these findings. The preeminence of certainty effects over severity effects is plausibly because offenders are more risk seeking and discount the future at a higher rate than nonoffenders do. However, such explanations are invariably incomplete due to untenable assumptions that time and risk preference are temporally and situationally stable within persons. Behavioral economic research establishes that they are not.

Thus, prevailing criminological theories of deterrence do not align as well as they might with the more nuanced principles of behavioral economics. This has resulted from an overly antiseptic application of the economic principles in expression (1) (Section 15.2.1). But the purposes of economic theory were always normative rather than descriptive (Thaler, 2015). Dhami (2016: 2) observed that "economics provides a coherent and internally consistent body of theory that offers rigorous, parsimonious, and falsifiable models of human behavior." The falsifiability objective is key. Economic models are explicit and amenable to empirical testing for this very reason; so that disconfirming findings can form the basis for improved theories.

The remainder of the chapter analyzed the preeminence of certainty effects from a decision-making and behavioral economic standpoint. Prevailing theoretical treatments of this problem do not adequately capture the perceptual differences between the certainty and the severity determinations. The certainty perception is an immediate prerequisite for potential consequences. Also, it is cognitively reducible to a binary determination (*will I be caught?*), which can be useful under the exigencies of real-world offending decisions. Research has also found no duration or length effects from periods of incarceration. However, it seems premature to deny that severity effects exist absent a more nuanced conception of severity that recognizes multiple dimensions beyond length of confinement, and which captures sequences (rather than just one) of impressions over the entire period of confinement.

This leads to several implications for compliance. Pretty clearly, variations in the duration of penalties, or adverse consequences that ensue only after a period of delay, have little impact on deterrence. Instead, attention should focus on more immediate issues related to *detecting* noncompliance. As Nagin et al. (2015) noted, preventing transgression from occurring in the first place can be far preferable to addressing wrongs once they have already occurred. Moreover, interventions to promote compliance should appeal to the burgeoning literature on "nudging" (Thaler and Sunstein, 2009) which emerges from the dual process conception of behavioral economics discussed earlier (Kahneman, 2011). If theories of compliance rely too much on familiar paradigms, opportunities can be missed to deter crime more creatively – for example by "temperance contracts" as a precondition for legal cannabis use, or by reentry checklists that simplify and routinize compliance following a sanction.

As Matsueda (2013) underscores, a complete understanding of deterrence requires simultaneous attention to both aggregate and individual-level determinants of crime. Ultimately, principles of risks, costs, and incentives provide the key intellectual currency for deterrence thinking at either unit of observation. Thus, pushing knowledge on individual-level decision-making and crime should provide further context and insights into both crime patterns in places and general deterrence. Insights from psychology and behavioral economics hold great promise for advancing the Becker (1968) and deterrence framework to provide a more descriptively accurate understanding of crime that can better assist policymakers.

REFERENCES

Angrist, Joshua D., and Alan B. Krueger 2001. "Instrumental Variables and the Search for Identification." *Journal of Economic Perspectives* 15: 69–85.

Anwar, Shamina, and Thomas A. Loughran. 2011. "Testing a Bayesian Learning Theory of Deterrence among Serious Juvenile Offenders." *Criminology* 49: 667–98.

Apel, Robert, Greg Pogarsky, and Leigh Bates. 2009. "The Sanctions-Perceptions Link in a Model of School-Based Deterrence." *Journal of Quantitative Criminology* 25: 201–26.

Becker, Gary S. 1968. "Crime and Punishment: An Economic Approach. *Journal of Political Economy* 76: 169–217.

Becsi, Zsolt. 1999. "Economics and Crime in the States." *Federal Reserve Bank of Atlanta Economic Review* Q1: 38–56.

Berk, Richard. 2005. "New Claims about Executions and General Deterrence: Deja Vu All Over Again?" *Journal of Empirical Legal Studies* 2: 303–30.

Berk, Richard, and John MacDonald. 2010. "Policing the Homeless: An Evaluation of Efforts to Reduce Homeless-Related Crime." *Criminology and Public Policy* 9: 813–40.

Block, Michael K., and Vernon E. Gerety. 1995. "Some Experimental Evidence on Differences between Student and Prisoner Reactions to Monetary Penalties and Risk." *Journal of Legal Studies* 24(1): 123–38.

Braga, Anthony A. 2008. "Police Enforcement Strategies to Prevent Crime in Hot Spot Areas." Washington, DC: US Department of Justice Office of Community Oriented Policing Services.

Braga, Anthony A., and David Weisburd. 2010. *Policing Problem Places: Crime Hot Spots and Effective Prevention*. New York: Oxford University Press.

Braga, Anthony A., Andrew V. Papachristos, and David Hureau. 2014. "The Effects of Hot Spots Policing on Crime: An Updated Systematic Review and Meta-Analysis." *Justice Quarterly* 31:633–63.

Braga, Anthony A., Martin A. Andersen, and Brian Lawton. 2017. "The Law of Crime Concentration at Places: Editors' Introduction." *Journal of Quantitative Criminology* 33: 421–6.
Braga, Anthony A., Brandon Turchan, Andrew V. Papachristos, and David M. Hureau. 2019. "Hot Spots Policing of Small Geographic Areas Effects on Crime." *Campbell Systematic Reviews* 15: 1–88.
Brantingham, Patricia L., and Paul J. Brantingham. 1999. "A Theoretical Model of Crime Hot Spot Generation." *Studies on Crime & Crime Prevention* 8: 7–26.
Brezina, Timothy, Erdal Tekin, and Volkan Topalli. 2009. "Might Not Be a Tomorrow: A Multimethods Approach to Anticipated Early Death and Youth Crime." *Criminology* 47: 1091–1129.
Chalfin, Aaron, and Justin McCrary. 2017. "Criminal Deterrence: A Review of the Literature." *Journal of Economic Literature* 55: 5–48.
2018. "Are U.S. Cities Underpoliced? Theory and Evidence." *Review of Economics and Statistics* 100: 167–86.
Corman, Hope, and Naci Mocan. 2005. "Carrots, Sticks, and Broken Windows." *Journal of Law and Economics* 48: 235–66.
DeAngelo, Gregory, and Benjamin Hansen. 2014. "Life and Death in the Fast Lane: Police Enforcement and Traffic Fatalities." *American Economic Journal: Economic Policy* 6: 231–57.
Dezhbakhsh, Hashem, Paul H. Rubin, and Joanna M. Shepherd. 2003. "Does Capital Punishment Have a Deterrent Effect? New Evidence from Postmoratorium Panel Data." *American Law and Economics Review* 5(2): 344–76.
Dhami, Sanjit. 2016. *Behavioral Economics*. Oxford: Oxford University Press.
Donohue, John J. 2009. "Assessing the Relative Benefits of Incarceration: Overall Changes and the Benefits on the Margin." In *Do Prisons Make Us Safer? The Benefits and Costs of the Prison Boom*, eds. Stephen Raphael and Michael A. Stoll, 269–341. New York: Russell Sage Foundation.
Donohue, John J., and Justin Wolfers. 2005. "Uses and Abuses of Empirical Evidence in the Death Penalty Debate." *Stanford Law Review* 58(3): 791–846.
2009. "Estimating the Impact of the Death Penalty on Murder." *American Law and Economics Review* 11(2): 249–309.
Durlauf, Steven N., and Daniel S. Nagin. 2011a. "The Deterrent Effect of Imprisonment." In *Controlling Crime: Strategies and Tradeoffs*, ed. Philip Cook, Jens Ludwig, and Justin McCrary, 43–94. Chicago: University of Chicago Press.
2011b. "Imprisonment and Crime: Can Both Be Reduced?" *Criminology Public Policy* 10: 9–54.
Evans, William N., and Emily G. Owens. 2007. "COPS and Crime." *Journal of Public Economics* 91 1–2): 181–201.
Frederick, Shane. 2003. "Time Preference and Personal Identity" in *Time and Decision*, eds. G. Loewenstein, D. Read, and R. Baumeister, pp. 89–113. New York: Russell Sage Press.
Frederick, Shane, Loewenstein, George, and Ted O'Donoghue. 2002. "Time Discounting and Time Preference: A Critical Review." *Journal of Economic Literature* 40: 351–401.
Goldstein, H. (1990). *Problem-Oriented Policing*. Philadelphia, PA: Temple University Press.
Gottfredson, Michael R., and Travis Hirschi. 1990. *A General Theory of Crime*. Stanford, CA: Stanford University Press.
Granger, Clive W. 1969. "Investigating Causal Relationships by Econometric Models and Cross Spectral Models." *Econometrica* 37: 424–38.
2001. *Essays in Econometrics: The Collected Papers of Clive W.J. Granger*. Cambridge: Cambridge University Press.
Grogger, Jeffrey. 1991. "Certainty vs. Severity of Punishment." *Economic Inquiry* 29(2): 297–309.
Hawken, Angela, and Mark A. R. Kleiman. 2009. "Managing Drug Involved Probationers with Swift and Certain Sanctions: Evaluating Hawaii's HOPE." Washington, DC: National Criminal Justice Reference Service.
Heaton, Paul. 2010. "Understanding the Effects of Anti-profiling Policies." *Journal of Law and Economics*, 53(1): 29–64.
Helland, Eric, and Alexander Tabarrok. 2007. "Does Three Strikes Deter? A Nonparametric Estimation." *Journal of Human Resources* 42(2): 309–30.
Hjalmarsson, Randi. 2009. "Juvenile Jails: A Path to the Straight and Narrow or to Hardened Criminality?" *Journal of Law and Economics* 52(4): 779–809.

2012. "Can Executions Have a Short-Term Deterrence Effect on Non-felony Homicides?" *Criminology and Public Policy* 11(3): 565–71.
Jaynes, Chae M., and Thomas A. Loughran. 2019. "Social Preferences as an Individual Difference in Offender Decision-Making." *Journal of Research in Crime and Delinquency* 56(1): 129–69.
Joel, Jeffrey H., and Anthony O. Putman. 2015. "Subjective Probability in Behavioral Economics and Finance: A Radical Reformulation." *Journal of Behavioral Finance* 16: 231–49.
Johnson, Rucker, and Steven Raphael. 2012. "How Much Crime Reduction Does the Marginal Prisoner Buy?" *Journal of Law and Economics* 55(2): 275–310.
Kahneman, Daniel. 2011. *Thinking, Fast and Slow*. New York: Macmillan.
Kahneman, Daniel, and Amos Tversky. 1979. "Prospect Theory: An Analysis of Decision Making under Risk." *Econometrica* 47: 263–92.
Kahneman, Daniel, and Shane Frederick. 2002. "Representativeness Revisited: Attribute Substitution in Intuitive Judgment." In *Heuristics and Biases: The Psychology of Intuitive Judgment*, eds. T. Gilovich, D. Griffin, and D. Kahneman, pp. 49–81. New York: Cambridge University Press.
Kahneman, Daniel, Barbara L. Fredrickson, Charles A. Schreiber, and Donald A. Redelmeier. 1993. "When More Pain Is Preferred to Less: Adding a Better End. *Psychological Science* 4: 401–5.
Katz, Lawrence, Steven D. Levitt, and Ellen Shustorovich. 2003. "Prison Conditions, Capital Punishment, and Deterrence." *American Law and Economics Review* 5(2): 318–43.
Kennedy, David M., Anthony A. Braga, Ann M. Piehl, and Elen J. Waring. 2001. "Reducing Gun Violence: The Boston Gun Project's Operation Ceasefire." Research Report, US National Institute of Justice, Washington, DC.
Kilmer, Beau, Nancy Nicosia, Paul Heaton, and Greg Midgette. 2013. "Efficacy of Frequent Monitoring with Swift, Certain, and Modest Sanctions for Violations: Insights from South Dakota's 24/7 Sobriety Project." *American Journal of Public Health* 103(1): 37–43.
Klick, Jonathan, and Alexander Tabarrok. 2005. "Using Terror Alert Levels to Estimate the Effect of Police on Crime." *Journal of Law and Economics* 48(1): 267–79.
Laibson, David I. 1997. "Golden Eggs and Hyperbolic Discounting." *Quarterly Journal of Economics* 112: 443–77.
Land, Kenneth C., Raymond H. C. Teske, Jr., and Hui Zheng. 2009. "The Short-Term Effects of Executions on Homicides: Deterrence, Displacement, or Both?" *Criminology* 47(4): 1009–43.
Lattimore, Pamela K., Doris Layton Mackenzie, Gary Zajac, Debbie Dawes, Elaine Arsenault, and Stephen J. Tueller. 2016. "Outcome Findings from the HOPE Demonstration Field Experiment: Is Swift, Certain, and Fair an Effective Supervision Strategy?" *Criminology and Public Policy* 15: 1103–41.
Lee, David S., and Justin McCrary. 2017. "The Deterrence Effect of Prison: Dynamic Theory and Evidence." Advances in Econometrics. In Regression Discontinuity Designs, vol. 38, eds. Matias D. Cattaneo and Juan Carlos Escanciano, pp. 73–146. Bingley, UK: Emerald Group Publishing.
Leigh, John P., and Daryl Schembri. 2004. "Instrumental Variable Technique: Cigarette Price Provided Better Estimate of Effects of Smoking." *Journal of Clinical Epidemiology* 57: 284–93.
Levitt, Steven D. 1996. "The Effect of Prison Population Size on Crime Rates: Evidence from Prison Overcrowding Litigation." *Quarterly Journal of Economics* 111(2): 319–51.
1997. "Using Electoral Cycles in Police Hiring to Estimate the Effects of Police on Crime." *American Economic Review* 87(3): 270–90.
2002. "Using Electoral Cycles in Police Hiring to Estimate the Effects of Police on Crime: Reply." *American Economic Review* 92(4): 1244–50.
Liedka, Raymond V., Anne Morrison Piehl, and Bert Useem. 2006. "The Crime-Control Effect of Incarceration: Does Scale Matter?" Criminology and Public Policy 5(2): 245–76.
Loewenstein, George, Ted O'Donoghue, and Matthew Rabin. 2003. "Projection Bias in Predicting Future Utility." *Quarterly Journal of Economics* 118: 1209–48.
Loftin, Colin, and David McDowall. 1981. "'One with a Gun Gets You Two': Mandatory Sentencing and Firearms Violence in Detroit." *Annals of the American Academy of Political and Social Science* 455: 150–67.
1984. "The Deterrent Effects of the Florida Felony Firearm Law." *Journal of Criminal Law and Criminology* 75(1): 250–9.
Loughran, Thomas A. 2019. "Behavioral Criminology and Public Policy." *Criminology and Public Policy* 18(4): 737–58.

Loughran T. A., R. Paternoster, and D. Weiss. 2012. "Hyperbolic Time Discounting, Offender Time Preferences and Deterrence." *Journal of Quantitative Criminology* 28: 607–28.

Loughran, Thomas A., Edward P. Mulvey, Carol A. Schubert, Jeffrey Fagan, Alex R. Piquero, and Sandra H. Losoya. 2009. "Estimating a Dose-Response Relationship between Length of Stay and Future Recidivism in Serious Juvenile Offenders." *Criminology* 47(3): 699–740.

Lum, Cynthia, and Daniel Nagin. 2017. "Reinventing American Policing: A Seven-Point Blueprint for the 21st Century." *Crime and Justice* 46: 339–93.

Lum, Cynthia, Christopher S. Koper, and Cody W. Telep. 2011. "The Evidence-Based Policing Matrix." *Journal of Experimental Criminology* 7(1): 3–26.

Marvell, Thomas B., and Carlisle E. Moody, Jr. 1994. "Prison Population Growth and Crime Reduction." *Journal of Quantitative Criminology* 10(2): 109–40.

1996. "Specification Problems, Police Levels, and Crime Rates." *Criminology* 34(4): 609–46.

Matsueda, Ross L. 2013. "Rational Choice Research in Criminology: A Multi-level Framework." In *Handbook of Rational Choice Social Research*, ed. R. Wittek, T. Snijders, and V. Nee, pp. 283–321. Palo Alto, CA: Stanford University Press.

McCrary, Justin. 2002. "Using Electoral Cycles in Police Hiring to Estimate the Effect of Police on Crime: Comment." *American Economic Review* 92(4): 1236–43.

Mocan, H. Naci, and R. Kaj Gittings. 2003. "Getting Off Death Row: Commuted Sentences and the Deterrent Effect of Capital Punishment." *Journal of Law and Economics* 46(2): 453–78.

Mungan, Murat C., and Jonathan Klick. 2016. "Identifying Criminals' Risk Preferences." *Indiana Law Journal* 91: 791–851.

Nagin, Daniel S. 2013a. "Deterrence in the 21st Century: A Review of the Evidence." In *Crime and Justice: An Annual Review of Research*, Vol. 42, ed. M. Tonry, pp. 199–263. Chicago: University of Chicago Press.

2013b. "Deterrence: A Review of the Evidence by a Criminologist for Economists." *Annual Review of Economics* 5: 83–105.

Nagin, Daniel S., and Greg Pogarsky. 2001. "Integrating Celerity, Impulsivity, and Extralegal Sanction Threats into a Model of General Deterrence: Theory and Evidence." *Criminology* 39: 865–92.

2003. "An Experimental Investigation of Deterrence: Cheating, Self-Serving Bias, and Impulsivity." *Criminology* 41: 501–27.

Nagin, Daniel S., and Robert J. Sampson. 2019. "The Real Gold Standard: Measuring Counterfactual Worlds That Matter Most to Social Science and Policy." *Annual Review of Criminology* 2: 123–45.

Nagin, Daniel S., Robert M. Solow, and Cynthia Lum. 2015. "Deterrence, Criminal Opportunities, and the Police." *Criminology* 53: 74–100.

National Research Council (NRC). 2004. *Fairness and Effectiveness in Policing: The Evidence*. Committee to Review Research on Police Policy and Practices. Committee on Law and Justice, Division of Behavioral and Social Sciences and Education. Ed. Wesley Skogan and Kathleen Frydl. Washington, DC: National Academies Press.

Paternoster, Raymond. 2010. "How Much Do We Really Know about Criminal Deterrence?" *Journal of Criminal Law and Criminology* 10: 765–823.

Parfit, Derek. 1971. "Personal Identity." *Philosophical Review* 80: 3–27.

1984. "Rationality and Time." *Proceedings of the Aristotelian Society* 84: 47–82.

Pogarsky, Greg. 2004. "Projected Offending and Contemporaneous Rule Violation: Implications for Heterotypic Continuity." *Criminology* 42: 111–35.

Pogarsky, Greg, and Shaina Herman. 2019. "Nudging and the Choice Architecture of Offending Decisions." *Criminology and Public Policy* 18(4): 823–39.

Pogarsky, Greg, Sean P. Roche, and Justin T. Pickett. 2017. "Heuristics and Biases, Rational Choice, and Sanction Perceptions." *Criminology* 55: 85–111.

2018. "Offender Decision-Making in Criminology: Contributions from Behavioral Economics." *Annual Review of Criminology* 1: 379–400.

Raaijmakers, Ellen, Thomas A. Loughran, Jan W. de Keijser, Anja J. E. Dirkzwager, and Paul Nieuwbeerta. 2017. "Exploring the Relationship between Subjectively Experienced Severity of Imprisonment and Recidivism: A Neglected Element in Testing Perceptual Deterrence Theory." *Journal of Research in Crime and Delinquency* 54(1): 3–28.

Roche, Sean Patrick, and Justin T. Pickett. 2017. "Evidence on How Individuals Consider Sanction Risk." Unpublished working paper.

Savage L. J. 1954. *The Foundations of Statistics*. New York: John Wiley.

Schell-Busey, Natalie, Sally S. Simpson, Melissa Rorie, and Mariel Alper. 2016. "What Works? A Systematic Review of Corporate Crime Deterrence." *Criminology & Public Policy* 15(2): 387–416.

Sherman, Lawrence W. 1990. "Police Crackdowns: Initial and Residual Deterrence." *Crime and Justice* 12: 1–48.

Shi, Lan. 2009. "The Limit of Oversight in Policing: Evidence from the 2001 Cincinnati Riot." *Journal of Public Economics* 93(1–2): 99–113.

Simpson, Sally, Melissa Rorie, Mariel Elise Alper, Natalie Schell-Busey, William Laufer, and N. Craig Smith. 2014. "Corporate Crime Deterrence: A Systematic Review." *Campbell Systematic Reviews* 10(4): 5–88.

Snodgrass, Matthew G., Amelia Haviland, Arjan A. J. Blokland, Paul Nieuwbeerta, and Daniel S. Nagin. 2011. "Does the Time Cause the Crime? An Examination of the Relationship between Time Served and Reoffending in the Netherlands." *Criminology* 49: 1149–94.

Spelman, William. 2000. "What Recent Studies Do (and Don't) Tell Us about Imprisonment and Crime." *Crime and Justice: A Review of Research* 27: 419–94.

2005. "Jobs or Jails? The Crime Drop in Texas." *Journal of Policy Analysis and Management* 24(1): 133–65.

Stolzenberg, Lisa, and Stewart J. D'Alessio. 2004. "Capital Punishment, Execution Publicity and Murder in Houston, Texas." *Journal of Criminal Law and Criminology* 94(2): 351–80.

Sunstein, Cass R., Daniel Kahneman, and David Schkade. 1998. "Assessing Punitive Damages (with Notes on Cognition and Valuation in Law)." *Yale Law Journal* 107: 2071–153.

Thaler, Richard H. 2015. *Misbehaving: The Making of Behavioral Economics*. New York: WW Norton & Company.

Thaler, Richard H., and Cass R. Sunstein. 2009. *Nudge: Improving Decisions about Health, Wealth, and Happiness*. London: Penguin.

Tittle, Charles R., and Alan R. Rowe. 1973. "Moral Appeal, Sanction Threat, and Deviance: An Experimental Test." *Social Problems* 20: 488–98.

von Neumann, John, and Oscar Morgenstern. 1944. *Theory of Games and Economic Behavior*. Princeton, NJ: Princeton University Press.

Ward, David A., Ben A. Menke, Louis N. Gray, and Mark C. Stafford. 1986. "Sanctions, Modeling and Deviant Behavior." *Journal of Criminal Justice* 14: 501–8.

Weisburd, David. 2015. "The Law of Crime Concentration and the Criminology of Place." *Criminology* 53: 133–57.

2018. "Hot Spots of Crime and Place-Based Prevention." *Criminology and Public Policy* 17: 5–25.

Weisburd, D., and Majmundar, M. K. (eds.). 2018. *Proactive Policing: Effects on Crime and Communities*. Committee on Proactive Policing: Effects on Crime, Communities, and Civil Liberties. Washington, DC: National Academies Press.

Weisburd, David, Tomar Einat, and Martin Kowalski. 2008. "The Miracle of the Cells: An Experimental Study of Interventions to Increase Payment of Court-Ordered Financial Obligations." *Criminology Public Policy* 7: 9–36.

Weisburd, David, Elizabeth R. Groff, and Sue-Ming Yang. 2012. *The Criminology of Place: Street Segments and Our Understanding of the Crime Problem*. New York: Oxford University Press.

Van Gelder, J. L., E. C. Luciano, M. Weulen Kranenbarg, and H. E. Hershfield. 2015. "Friends with My Future Self: A Longitudinal Vividness Intervention Reduces Delinquency." *Criminology* 53(2): 158–79.

Zimmerman, Paul R. 2006. "Estimates of the Deterrent Effect of Alternative Execution Methods in the United States: 1978–2000." *American Journal of Economics and Sociology* 65 4): 909–41.

Zimring, Franklin E., Gordon Hawkins, and Sam Kamin. 2001. *Punishment and Democracy: Three Strikes and You're Out in California*. Oxford/New York: Oxford University Press.

Zimring, Franklin E., Jeffrey Fagan, and David T. Johnson. 2010. "Executions, Deterrence, and Homicide: A Tale of Two Cities." *Journal of Empirical Legal Studies* 7(1): 1–29.

16

Incarceration and Crime

Alex R. Piquero

Abstract: The relationship between incarceration and crime has had a long and contentious history in criminology, with answers about the extent to which incarceration has general and/or specific deterrent effects on the crime rate and offending somewhat elusive. This chapter provides a broad overview of the literature in this area with a specific focus on how knowledge gained from research on criminal careers can help inform policy decisions regarding the use of incarceration not just in the aggregate but in particular at the individual level. The conclusion is reached that incarceration does not have a very strong anti-crime effect at the individual level, and in some cases may actually exacerbate criminal offending.

16.1 INTRODUCTION

Between 1925 and the mid to late 1970s, the United States had a very low and surprisingly stable rate of incarceration, hovering at around 200,000 incarcerated persons (Blumstein and Cohen, 1973). That changed dramatically, as many readers know, throughout the 1980s and 1990s when the US incarceration rate soared, peaking at almost 1.6 million persons incarcerated in state and federal prison facilities by 2010 (The Sentencing Project, 2018). Although the trend since then has been declining slightly, there are still about 1.5 million persons incarcerated in the USA, and many hundreds of thousands more locked up in jails. The USA holds the distinction of having the highest incarceration rate in the world, per 100,000 persons, at about 670, with the next closest country, Rwanda, at 434 per 100,000 (Walmsley, 2018).

To the extent that incarceration is hypothesized to serve the general and specific deterrent effect of preventing criminal behavior, a key policy question is the extent to which incarceration does produce lower crime at both the aggregate and the individual levels of analysis (Blumstein et al., 1986; Spelman, 1994). Or, another way to think about the effect of incarceration on crime rates is through general deterrence and incapacitation (Piquero and Blumstein, 2007, pp. 278–9). The former is a measure of the broad effect of a custodial sanction on offending while the latter focuses on individual offending frequency and the effect of a custodial sanction upon it.

Although there have been several narrative and empirical reviews of the literature on incarceration and crime (Cullen et al., 2011; Durlauf and Nagin, 2011; Nagin et al., 2009; National Research Council, 2014), the purpose of this chapter is to provide a broad review of this literature with a critical eye. One additional aspect of this chapter will be a discussion of how knowledge gained from criminal career research can be very helpful in informing policy decisions regarding the use of incarceration. To presuppose the chapter's summary conclusion: incarceration does not have much of an incapacitative effect – and in some cases may produce a criminogenic effect – and the cost associated with the extensive use of incarceration may actually be doing more harm than good.

16.2 KEY FINDINGS FROM PAST RESEARCH

The argument for incapacitation is twofold. First, it is believed that incapacitation sends a message to the general public and would-be offenders in particular that their continued offending will result in detection, arrest, and potentially an incarceration stint. This can be inferred as a type of general deterrence. Second, it is hypothesized that incapacitating an offender will prevent a certain amount of their criminal offending because they are in custody and will prevent future offending upon release because of the pains of imprisonment the offender was exposed to. Therefore, incapacitating an offender somehow not only reduces some number of offenses that would be committed by an offender if s/he were free but also reduces some sub-number of offenses upon release and/or shortens the amount of time that an offender would keep offending (Blumstein et al., 1986). To the extent that incapacitation serves one or both of these ends at the individual level of analysis, then, this can be inferred as a type of specific deterrence.

As noted by Piquero and Blumstein (2007, p. 268), there have been two main approaches in developing estimates concerning the effect that incarceration may have on crime. The first more general deterrence/economics-based approach uses aggregate-level data (county, state, nation) to examine the effect of incarceration on crime (e.g., Marvell and Moody, 1994). Here, the focus lies on calculating the "elasticity" of crime rates with respect to changes in imprisonment rates. The second more criminological approach lies in examining individual offending rates, with a focus on trying to calculate the number of crimes averted by removing an offender from the general population (Avi-Itzhak and Shinnar, 1973) and calculating some estimate of the amount of time an individual has remaining in their criminal career.

Numerous studies have attempted to calculate the crime-reduction potential of incarceration from a general deterrence perspective, yet the results are so heterogeneous because of the different data sources, differences in how crime and incarceration are modeled, and important differences in the values of model parameters used. In fact, elasticity estimates range from -0.05 to -0.70, and just about everywhere in between. A reasonably safe conclusion would be that the prison population needs to be increased quite a bit to attain even the slightest of crime reductions (i.e., about a 5 percent increase for about a 1 percent decrease; Piquero and Blumstein, 2007, p. 270). This notwithstanding, Durlauf and Nagin (2011, pp. 24–5) caution that the aggregate-based literature on the effects of imprisonment on crime is flawed both statistically and theoretically, for reasons including: (1) failure to evaluate how alternative policies affect both crime and imprisonment; (2) difficulty in establishing a causal relationship between the two; and (3) failure to deal with basic statistical problems such as assumptions of model specification and inclusion of control variables. Because "a high level of scientific certainty about the effects of increased incarceration rates is elusive" (National Research Council, 2014, p. 336), and because of the "concerns about the validity of the computed elasticity [due to] the many explicit and implicit assumptions on which it is based" (Piquero and Blumstein, 2007, p. 279), more attention (and comfort) tends to be given to the individual-level studies that focus on how many crimes are averted by incapacitating an offender and what effect (if any) the custodial sanction has on the remainder of their offending career and offenses committed upon release.

Here, there is a need to estimate a key parameter of the criminal career paradigm (to be discussed in greater detail in Section 16.3) referred to as lambda, or an individual's rate of offending while active. Lambda is a key input into the incapacitation model because it can provide some sense of the potential number of crimes averted should the offender not be incapacitated. Space precludes a detailed discussion about the various estimates of lambda that have been reported in the literature, such variations due, in large part, to how estimates of offending are obtained (self-report versus arrest versus conviction), what time window they are collected for (weekly, monthly, yearly), and for what type of sample (prisoner, active offender, general population). Regardless of whether the lambda estimates indicate three crimes per person per year, or fourteen crimes per person per year, or even almost two hundred crimes per person per year (Chaiken and Chaiken, 1982; Cohen, 1983; Zedlewski, 1985), it is the case that some unknown number of crimes are averted due to likely offenders being incapacitated. Moreover, it is also the case that a small number of individuals evidence a very high rate of offending, while active, and especially prior to being arrested/incarcerated (Canela-Cacho et al., 1997). The question, of course, is the extent to which these high lambdas are curtailed to a short-term window or constant over time, matters which speak to both theory and policy within criminology more generally (Blumstein, 2005; Piquero et al., 2010). As noted by Piquero and Blumstein (2007, pp. 273–4),

> [m]easuring the distribution of the frequency of offending among active offenders is a key need in estimating the incapacitative implications of various incarceration policies. That measurement is complicated by the selection biases introduced when the samples are drawn from criminal justice populations that have passed through the filter of arrest. The problem of selection effects is particularly important in studies that focus on the effectiveness of incapacitation. Differential selection of offenders arising stochastically from variation in individual offending frequencies will result in measurement bias if one applies this biased estimate of offending frequency to all offenders and not just those offenders processed through the same stage of the system; the bias is larger the further into the system the samples are drawn (Canela-Cacho et al. 1997, p. 135).[1]

With this backdrop of lambda in hand, the majority of incapacitation-focused studies uncover higher – not lower – recidivism rates among individuals who are incapacitated compared to those who are not, "even with extensive statistical controls for potentially confounding factors" (Durlauf and Nagin, 2011, p. 23). And while the literature is sprinkled with some studies providing evidence of an incapacitative effect, it is the case that most results are either null or criminogenic. Since publication of several contemporary reviews on the effects of incapacitation on crime, a few studies using methodological sound, rigorous, and rather clever designs have emerged and are described next in an illustrative manner to provide some context for the conclusion noted earlier.

Recognizing that the offending population hides important variability in the frequency and duration of offending and criminal careers (Nagin and Land, 1993; Piquero, 2008), which, in turn, provides support for turning attention away from a measurement of lambda for each individual offender and instead toward estimating the distribution of lambda among various populations, Bhati and Piquero (2008) examined the extent to which incarceration has

[1] To be sure, each offense does not generate an arrest, much less a custodial sanction. Potentially more useful would be calibrating an estimate of the frequency of offending (or arrest if using official records) divided by the probability of arrest given crime commission. Blumstein et al. (2010) have referred to this quantity as q.

variable effects (deterrent, criminogenic, or null) for some categories of offenders who have specific offending patterns. Using arrest histories from the Bureau of Justice Statistics (BJS), a 1994 recidivism study of a sample of prisoners followed in fifteen states for three years post-release, along with a comparison of the counterfactual and actual offending patterns of these releases,[2] they found that most releases were either deterred from future offending or merely incapacitated, while only about 4 percent experienced a criminogenic effect (i.e., returned to trajectories of offending higher than prior to being incarcerated). Other notable findings revealed that there was little variability across the states, the average false positive rate was 38 percent (while the average false negative rate was 27 percent), and those prisoners with higher numbers of prior arrests were more likely to experience criminogenic effects, while older parolees were less likely to experience criminogenic effects.

Using a large sample of 79,000 felons sentenced to state prisons in Florida alongside a sample of 65,000 offenders sentenced to a prison diversion program, Bales and Piquero (2012) examined the effect of imprisonment on recidivism using three different statistical approaches (logistic regression, precision matching,[3] and propensity score matching[4]) with one-, two-, and three-year follow-up periods. Their results showed that, across all three statistical methods, imprisonment exerted a criminogenic – and not deterrent – effect on recidivism.

Nagin and Snodgrass (2013) were able to leverage the county-level randomization of cases to judges in order to estimate the effect of incarceration on post-release offending. Using data from convicted Pennsylvania offenders, employing judge as an instrumental variable, and examining re-arrest rates at one, two, five, and ten years, produced results that provide little support for the notion that incarceration reduces future reoffending rates.

In a recent and exemplary analysis, Harding et al. (2017) leveraged a natural experiment using random assignment of judges with different propensities for sentencing offenders to prison in the state of Michigan in order to examine whether being sentenced to prison itself has a causal effect on the probability of a new return to prison or on criminal behavior. Compared to being sentenced to probation, being sentenced to prison increased the probability of imprisonment in the first three years after release. In other words, the authors were able to identify a true causal relationship: sentencing an individual to prison has a criminogenic effect and this effect is not due to any preexisting difference between prisoners and probationers. Two additional findings are noteworthy. First, the effects differed little between whites and nonwhites. Second, these returns to prison were due more to technical violations than to new felony convictions.

[2] The authors' goal was to "estimate and compare a releasee's actual post-prison offending trajectory with his or her criminal history-based counterfactual offending trajectory for the purpose of answering the question: 'How, if at all, has this incarceration experience deflected the trajectory the offender was on?'" (Bhati and Piquero, 2008: 218). A key parameter in the model, of course, is lambda, or the offending rate while active. As this is a key criminal career parameter and a focus of Section 16.3, we reserve extended discussion until appropriate.

[3] Precision matching refers to case-by-case matching on a range of variables including sex, race, ethnicity, age, current offense, prior criminal history, etc.

[4] Propensity score matching has emerged as a technique that attempts to approximate a randomized experiment. In particular, this approach attempts to deal with selection problems by matching techniques which attempt to "identify, for each individual in a treatment condition, at least one other individual in a comparison condition that 'looks like' the treated individual on the basis of a vector of measured characteristics that may be relevant to the treatment and response in question" (Apel and Sweeten, 2010, p. 543). It is the case, of course, that persons who are sentenced to prison (and incarcerated) may be different from those persons who are not sentenced to prison (and incarcerated) such that these "unobservable factors" that lead to being incarcerated somehow are related to future offending.

One key input into estimating the effect that incapacitation may have on current or future criminal behavior is the extent to which an offender's current level of crime would somehow be altered (decrease) while incapacitated. In other words, if the offender had not been incapacitated, what would his/her criminal activity look like? It is the case that just prior to arrest and incapacitation, the offending activity of offenders is quite high (Canela-Cacho et al., 1997). So, incapacitating these offenders would avert some of this offending activity, but it is difficult to discern precisely how much of that activity would be averted. Relatedly, upon release offenders likely have some non-zero probability of offending, especially immediately upon release. Therefore, it is of interest to see how much crime is averted during incarceration and then due to incapacitation upon release, that is, how much a custodial sanction affects the offender's rate of offending upon release. Section 16.3 provides an overview of the criminal career paradigm and how it offers a useful framework for understanding a criminal career, from its beginning to its end.

16.3 USE OF CRIMINAL CAREER RESEARCH TO INFORM INCARCERATION POLICY

The study of criminal careers is concerned with charting an individual's longitudinal sequence of offending, from its onset to its eventual desistance. The framework within which one studies criminal careers, the criminal career paradigm, was the result of a 1986 National Academy of Sciences Panel led by Alfred Blumstein and his colleagues (Blumstein et al., 1986). This paradigm presented a conceptual framework for understanding an individual's criminal career, from its onset to its eventual desistance. As well, the paradigm offered a variety of informative parameters associated with criminal offending. These include the following: (1) prevalence, or the proportion of any given sample that has offended; (2) onset age, or the age at which an individual first begins to offend; (3) frequency, the number of offenses committed by those who offend (sometimes referred to as lambda); (4) co-offending, the extent to which individuals offend with other persons; (5) specialization, or the extent to which offenders specialize in particular crimes or crime types; (6) escalation, the extent to which offenders escalate from less to more serious offenses over the course of their criminal career; (7) career length, or the amount of time between an individual's onset of offending and their last offense; and (8) desistance, or the end of the criminal career. A key expectation within the criminal career paradigm is that there may be heterogeneity within the population of offenders across many of these domains and the theoretical variables that are related to one dimension may be similar to – or different from – those related to another dimension.

From a policy perspective, an incarceration spell may have an effect on many of these parameters. For example, because a custodial sanction removes the offender from society, hence eliminating the chance that they could offend in public, being incapacitated may alter their criminal offending upon release. The pains of imprisonment may cause the offender to reevaluate their life trajectory, or may alter their risk/reward calculus such that their release may be associated with reductions – or eliminations – in offending. This, of course, is what the criminal justice system would hope for with the use of incarceration. On the other hand, the custodial sanction could backfire and lead to more offending upon release. In this scenario, an offender may learn more skills while in prison or may meet other like-minded persons who may offer offending opportunities upon release. Or the offender may have viewed the custodial sanction as a "hazard of the trade" associated with a criminal career and simply pick up where they left off offending-wise when released. Thus, studying how incapacitation affects individual offending frequency and, most important, potential desistance is critical.

Unfortunately, while it is easier to study individual offending patterns, it is harder to empirically study desistance. This is true for both operational definitions (Bushway et al., 2001) and empirical confirmation that desistance has in fact occurred (Blumstein et al., 1986). After all, true desistance is probably never realized until the death of an offender, but, practically speaking, this is not very helpful to criminologists or, especially, to policymakers. To help circumvent this limitation, researchers have turned toward studying the residual career length (RCL) and residual number of offenses (RNO). Although they represent the least explored of all criminal career dimensions (Blumstein, 2005), they are critical pieces of information that are necessary to form smarter incarceration policies because lengthy criminal careers would support longer sentences while shorter criminal careers would support shorter sentences. A mismatch of long custodial sentences where the majority of offenders evince a short criminal career would be an inefficient use of scarce correctional resources and result in wasted bed space allocation (Blumstein, 2016; Blumstein and Piquero, 2007).

According to Kazemian and Farrington (2006, 2018), who are among the leading researchers working on RCL and RNO, the former "refers to the remaining number of years in criminal careers until the last offense" while the latter "is defined as the remaining number of offenses in criminal careers" (Kazemian and Farrington, 2018, p. 1). Knowledge gained from studying distributions of RCL and RNO sheds insight into decisions surrounding sentencing/incapacitation and, thereafter, the parole decision. When not under some mandatory or otherwise proscriptive sentencing guideline, judges decide both whether to incarcerate someone and, if so, for how long. To the extent that RCLs are on the short side, then absent some sort of retributive rationale (i.e., a heinous act) judges could mete out sentences on the shorter rather than longer end of the continuum. With respect to parole, officials need to have some sense of the individual's likelihood of recidivism. And while recidivism studies tend to show that failure is the mode, a strong subset of offenders do not recidivate. Thus, providing parole officials with information regarding RCLs can help them make decisions about how much longer an offender is likely to remain active and committing crime.[5]

Due to heavy data requirements, there have only been a handful of empirical investigations on RCL and RNO. The pioneering investigation on this topic was undertaken by Blumstein et al. (1982) in a precursor to the 1986 National Academy of Sciences report on criminal careers. Using data on arrests in Washington, DC in the early 1970s, these authors identified three periods in the criminal career: (1) the break-in period, where rates of desistance from crime decline steadily; (2) the stable period, marked by low dropout rates and average RCL peaking at around age thirty with average time remaining in a career at ten years; and (3) the wear-out period, occurring at around age forty where greater dropout rates and declining RCLs are observed. The three phases observed by Blumstein and his colleagues, therefore, showed an increase in RCL to age thirty, a stable RCL between ages thirty and forty, and then a declining RCL after age forty. The latter observation is important because it suggests that

[5] As noted earlier, it is important, at the time of the sentencing decision, to make as good a prediction as possible about the frequency of offending of the individual. Ideally, high-rate offenders would be incapacitated during their most active period of offending, while low-rate offenders would likely be diverted from custodial sanctions. Research does show high-rate offending peaks just prior to an incarceration stint, suggesting that those offenders who have been recently incapacitated are likely among the highest-rate offenders, what Canela-Cacho et al. (1997) refer to as stochastic selectivity. The larger issue is not the decision to incarcerate but the length of time of incarceration. This is precisely where knowledge about RCL is critical.

incapacitating individuals into their forties and especially into their fifties and beyond will likely waste prison resources.

Kazemian and Farrington conducted two analyses of RCL and RNO in the Cambridge Study in Delinquent Development, a longitudinal study of 411 males from South London followed into middle adulthood (thus far). In the first study (2006), the authors analyzed career offending through age forty of the main study sample and up to age forty for the fathers of the males. Of all their reported findings, the most important were that both RCL and RNO steadily declined with age for both the study sample and their fathers, yet RCL declined more consistently than RNO suggesting variability in paths of offending as well as desistance from offending. In their follow-up investigation of the study sample through age fifty-six (2018), they once again found that both RCL and RNO steadily declined with age, with both RCL and RNO showing the most substantial declines after five years of a crime-free life. This observation of substantial declines in RCL (and RNO) after five years since the previous crime is an important point that deserves additional attention, especially in light of other research efforts investigating the notion of redemption.

In two related studies, Kurlycheck et al. (2006, 2007) were interested in determining how long an individual needed to be crime-free in order to approximate the risk of offending among those with no criminal record at all. The first (2006) study, using data from the 1958 Philadelphia Birth Cohort Study, revealed that the risk of new offending among those whose last arrest was between six and seven years prior begins to look like (but does not perfectly match) the risk of offending among those individuals without any criminal record. In their second (2007) study with data from the 1942 Racine (WI) birth cohort study, they found a substantively similar finding. That is, "the more distant the last evidence of criminal activity is in the past, the less likely there is to be a meaningful elevation in the hazard rate for new offenses" (Kurlycheck et al. 2007, pp. 72–3). Although the number of years may be one or two longer or shorter, substantively similar findings have now been observed in studies of New York offenders (Blumstein and Nakamura, 2009), adjudicated French-Canadian males (Kazemian et al., 2007), as well as convicts from England and Wales (Soothill and Francis, 2009) and parolees from California (Piquero et al., 2004) – though they had a slighter longer average career length.

It should be obvious by now that knowledge gained about crime risks since the time of the last offense as well as RCL and RNO offers useful information to policymakers with respect to making more informed (and hopefully better) decisions surrounding the length of incarceration as well as parole decisions and supervisions. As shown, if the total time remaining in the career is expected to be less than the total time served, the time served after the career would have terminated represents a waste of prison space from an incapacitation perspective (Blumstein et al., 1986, p. 128; Piquero et al., 2003). This is exactly the kind of knowledge that policymakers need in order to design more cost-effective incapacitation policies. And while this information may not be easily obtainable for each single individual, they can be calculated with existing data from databases in many jurisdictions and provided as information at the sentencing and parole decision stages. To be sure, however, as in any criminal justice decision, there will be both false positives and false negatives. But the point remains that improved estimates of the effect of incapacitation on crime will emerge through greater, more expansive, and longitudinal information gleaned from the criminal activity of offenders (Piquero and Blumstein, 2007, p. 276). In particular, cohort studies that track individuals from birth to death, ideally, and that contain self-reported and official offending information as well as incapacitation information are necessary to provide more precise estimates of the number of crimes averted by incapacitating an offender (Piquero et al., 2003). This will permit investigating the extent to which incapacitation changes the expected length of the remaining criminal career (and offenses committed throughout the remaining career). That is, to the extent that incapacitation offers a viable crime prevention strategy, knowledge on lambda and residual career length is critical.

16.4 CONCLUSION

The aforementioned review of the research evidence on incapacitation and crime should not be construed as an outright dismissal of using this type of sanction. To be sure, there is no doubt that some types of offenders who commit certain types of crime should be removed from the general population and placed in custody. Moreover, there is little doubt that doing so would avert some potential criminal offending, but this potential alleviation in offending is not expected to be great and, in some cases, may actually backfire. The key policy question in this space, as Cullen et al. (2011, p. 51S) so aptly noted, is "not whether some offenders need to be incapacitated, but rather how many and for how long." The US prison experience over the past forty years has been to place more offenders in prison and for longer periods of time. The weight of the evidence suggests that this policy approach has not yielded significant reductions in crime but has had the adverse effect of straining economic resources across the USA because of the need to build more prisons, with more beds, with more staff to oversee a population of offenders who have been incarcerated for lengthy periods of time due to sentencing policies that conferred long sentences, that is, that were based on mandatory minimums, three strikes legislation, etc. And in some individual offender cases, it may actually have a criminogenic effect.

Fortunately, the declining crime trend observed in the USA over the past fifteen or so years has given some states the cover needed to temper the overreliance on incapacitation and to divert the expenditures associated with it to prevention, rehabilitation, and treatment programs. Whether through the Smart on Crime Movement and the experience of Texas, or the Justice Reinvestment experiences of many mid-western states, especially Ohio, the USA has made some traction in starting to ease the expanded use of incapacitation generally and lengthy incapacitation in particular.

Going forward, researchers and policymakers should redouble their efforts at using the knowledge gained from research on criminal careers (Farrington et al., 2016), especially with respect to time since last offense, residual career length, and residual number of offenses, to help guide policy decisions regarding sentences and parole decisions. Doing so would help to better allocate correctional resources by incapacitating only the highest-lambda offenders who have the longest time remaining in their criminal careers, to not waste prison bed space for offenders who have very little risk of offending – or very little time left in their criminal career – and to revert those monies toward prevention and intervention strategies early in the life course such that incapacitation becomes less and less the norm and more and more the exception.

On this score, the COVID-19 pandemic that ravaged the world also opened the door toward a rethinking of correctional strategies – especially with regard to limiting the kinds of offenders who are given custodial sanctions as well as releasing offenders earlier than the end of their custodial terms (Nowotny and Piquero, 2020). Going forward, it will be important to assess the effects of these decisions on the rate of offending among these two offender classifications.

REFERENCES

Apel, R. J., and Sweeten, G. 2010. "Propensity Score Matching in Criminology and Criminal Justice." In A. R. Piquero and D. Weisburd (eds.), *Handbook of Quantitative Criminology* (pp. 543–62). New York: Springer.
Avi-Itzhak, B., and Shinnar, R. 1973. "Quantitative Models in Crime Control." *Journal of Criminal Justice*, 1, 185–217.
Bales, W., and Piquero, A. R. 2012. "Assessing the Impact of Imprisonment on Recidivism." *Journal of Experimental Criminology*, 8, 71–101.
Bhati, A. S., and Piquero, A. R. 2008. "Estimating the Impact of Incarceration on Subsequent Offending Trajectories: Deterrent, Criminogenic, or Null Effect." *Journal of Criminal Law and Criminology*, 98, 207–54.
Blumstein, A. 2005. "An Overview of the Symposium and Some Next Steps." *Annals of the American Academy of Political and Social Sciences*, 602, 242–58.
2016. "From Incapacitation to Criminal Careers." *Journal of Research in Crime and Delinquency*, 53, 291–305.
Blumstein, A., and Cohen, J. 1973. "A Theory of Stability of Punishment." *Journal of Criminal Law and Criminology*, 64, 198–206.
Blumstein, A., and Nakamura, K. 2009. "Redemption in the Presence of Widespread Criminal Background Checks." *Criminology*, 47, 327–59.
Blumstein, Alfred, and Piquero, Alex R. 2007. "Restore Rationality to Sentencing Policy." *Criminology & Public Policy*, 6: 679–87.
Blumstein, A., Cohen, J., and Hsieh, P. 1982. "The Duration of Adult Criminal Careers." (Final report submitted to National Institute of Justice). Carnegie-Mellon University School of Urban and Public Affairs, Pittsburgh, PA.
Blumstein, A., Cohen, J., Roth, J. A., and Visher, C. A. (eds.). 1986. *Criminal Careers and Career Criminals*, vol 1. Washington, DC: National Academy Press.
Blumstein, A., Cohen, J., Piquero, A. R., and Visher, C. A. 2010. "Linking the Crime and Arrest Processes to Measure Variations in Individual Arrest Risk per Crime (Q)." *Journal of Quantitative Criminology*, 26, 533–48.
Bushway, S. D., Piquero, A. R., Broidy, L. M., Cauffman, E., and Mazerolle, P. 2001. "An Empirical Framework for Studying Desistance as a Process." *Criminology*, 39, 491–516.
Canela-Cacho, J. A., Blumstein, A., and Cohen, J. 1997. "Relationship between the Offending Frequency (k) of Imprisoned and Free Offenders." *Criminology*, 35, 133–76.
Chaiken, J. M., and Chaiken, M. R. 1982. *Varieties of Criminal Behavior*. Santa Monica, CA: Rand Corporation.
Cohen, J. 1983. "Incapacitation as a Strategy for Crime Control: Possibilities and Pitfalls." In M. Tonry and N. Morris (eds.), *Crime and Justice: An Annual Review of Research* (vol 5, pp. 1–84). Chicago: University of Chicago Press.
Cullen, F. T., Jonson, C. L., and Nagin, D. S. 2011. "Prisons Do Not Reduce Recidivism: The High Cost of Ignoring Science." *Prison Journal*, 91, 48S–65S.
Durlauf, S. N., and Nagin, D. S. 2011. "Imprisonment and Crime: Can Both Be Reduced?" *Criminology & Public Policy*, 10, 13–54.
Farrington, D. P., MacLeod, J. F., and Piquero, A. R. 2016. "Mathematical Models of Criminal Careers: Deriving and Testing Quantitative Predictions." *Journal of Research in Crime and Delinquency*, 53, 336–55.
Harding, D. J., Morenoff, J. D., Nguyen, A. P., and Bushway, S. D. 2017. "Short- and Long-Term Effects of Imprisonment on Future Felony Convictions and Prison Admissions." *PNAS*, 114, 11103–8.
Kazemian, L., and Farrington, D. P. 2006. "Exploring Residual Career Length and Residual Number of Offenses for Two Generations of Repeat Offenders." *Journal of Research in Crime and Delinquency*, 43, 89–113.
2018. "Advancing Knowledge about Residual Criminal Careers: A Follow-Up to Age 56 from the Cambridge Study in Delinquent Development." *Journal of Criminal Justice*, 57, 1–10.

Kazemian, L., Le Blanc, M., Farrington, D. P., and Pease, K. 2007. "Patterns of Residual Criminal Careers among a Sample of Adjudicated French-Canadian Males." *Canadian Journal of Criminology and Criminal Justice*, 49, 307–40.

Kurlychek, M. C., Brame, R., and Bushway, S. D. 2006. "Scarlet Letters and Recidivism: Does an Old Criminal Record Predict Future Offending." *Criminology & Public Policy*, 5, 483–504.

2007. "Enduring Risk? Old Criminal Records and Predictions of Future Criminal Involvement." *Crime & Delinquency*, 53, 64–83.

Marvell, T. B., and Moody, C. E., Jr. 1994. "Prison Population Growth and Crime Reduction." *Journal of Quantitative Criminology*, 10, 109–40.

Nagin, D. S., and Land, K. C. 1993. "Age, Criminal Careers, and Population Heterogeneity: Specification and Estimation of a Nonparametric, Mixed Poisson Model." *Criminology*, 31, 327–62.

Nagin, D. S., and Snodgrass, G. M. 2013. "The Effect of Incarceration on Re-offending: Evidence from a Natural Experiment in Pennsylvania." *Journal of Quantitative Criminology*, 29, 601–42.

Nagin, D. S., Cullen, F. T., and Jonson, C. L. 2009. "Imprisonment and Reoffending." In M. Tonry (ed.), *Crime and Justice: A Review of Research* (vol. 38, pp. 115–200). Chicago: University of Chicago Press.

National Research Council. 2014. "The Growth of Incarceration in the United States: Exploring Causes and Consequences. Committee on Causes and Consequences of High Rates of Incarceration." J. Travis, B. Western, and S. Redburn (eds.). Committee on Law and Justice, Division of Behavioral and Social Sciences and Education. Washington, DC: National Academies Press.

Nowotny, Kathryn M., and Piquero, Alex R. 2020. "The Global Impact of the Pandemic on Institutional and Community Corrections: Assessing Short-Term Crisis Management and Long-Term Change Strategies." *Victims & Offenders*, 17, 1–9.

Piquero, A. R. 2008. "Taking Stock of Developmental Trajectories of Criminal Activity over the Life Course." In A. Liberman (ed.), *The Long View of Crime: A Synthesis of Longitudinal Research* (pp. 23–78). New York: Springer.

Piquero, A. R., and Blumstein, A. 2007. "Does Incapacitation Reduce Crime?" *Journal of Quantitative Criminology*, 23, 267–85.

Piquero, A. R., Farrington, D. P., and Blumstein, A. 2003. "The Criminal Career Paradigm: Background and Recent Developments." In M. Tonry (ed.), *Crime and Justice: A Review of Research* (vol. 30, pp. 359–506). Chicago: University of Chicago Press.

Piquero, A. R., Brame, R., and Lynam, D. 2004. "Studying Criminal Career Length through Early Adulthood among Serious Offenders." *Crime & Delinquency*, 40, 412–35.

Piquero, A. R., Sullivan, C. J., and Farrington, D. P. 2010. "Assessing Differences between Short-Term, High-Rate Offenders and Long-Term, Low-Rate Offenders." *Criminal Justice and Behavior*, 37, 1309–29.

Soothill, K., and Francis, B. 2009. "When Do Ex-offenders Become like Non-offenders?" *Howard Journal of Criminal Justice*, 48, 373–87.

Spelman, W. 1994. *Criminal Incapacitation*. New York: Plenum.

The Sentencing Project. 2018. "Fact Sheet: Trends in U.S. Corrections." June 2018 update. Washington, DC: The Sentencing Project.

Walmsley, R. 2018. "World Prison Brief." London: Institute for Criminal Policy Research. www.prisonstudies.org/world-prison-brief.

Zedlewski, E. W. 1985. "When Have We Punished Enough?" *Public Administration Review*, November, 771–9.

17

Corporate Crime Deterrence

Melissa Rorie and Natalie Schell-Busey

Abstract: This chapter examines what is known about corporate crime deterrence in hopes of identifying legal strategies that can prevent such crimes and their often-immense harms against consumers, competitors, employees, creditors, and owners. In this chapter, we rely heavily on results from a meta-analytic study of corporate crime deterrence research but also examine the extant literature in an effort to summarize what formal mechanisms might be effective in promoting compliance. Despite increasing awareness of the frequency and consequences of these violations, research has produced almost no conclusive recommendations. We find that simply making new corporate crime laws is ineffective, while actual criminal justice sanctions (e.g., arrest, incarceration) seem to be inconsistently effective. There is some support for the use of fines and monetary sanctions (both civil and criminal) in producing compliance, but financial penalties seem to be effective only in the short term and only when they are very high. Furthermore, in our review, regulatory sanctions seem to be effective against individual-level offending, but these sanctions have wildly inconsistent impacts when leveled against corporations. We discuss the dire need for more research, offering specific suggestions for scholarship.

17.1 INTRODUCTION

Sutherland (1945) argued that while "white-collar" criminals (i.e., those offenders of high social status using legitimate occupational resources to commit crimes) typically avoid criminal stigma, white-collar offending should be criminalized because of the often-immense social injury that results from such malfeasance. In particular, he emphasized the harms caused by *corporate* malfeasance – in his seminal book *White Collar Crime* (1949), he documented the extensive deviant behavior of seventy eminent companies over a sixty-year period. Such behaviors have since been given their own label of "corporate crimes" and (due to the definitional ambiguity associated with the term white-collar crime[1] as well as the complex task of considering all of the subsets[2] included in that term) are the focus of the current review.

Corporate crime is a specific subset of the broader "white-collar crime" term; corporate crime specifically involves conduct by a corporation, or company representatives acting on behalf of the corporation, which is punishable by law (Braithwaite 1984). These acts can include crimes against consumers (such as price fixing and false advertising), crimes against

[1] For a more detailed discussion of this definitional ambiguity in the field of corporate crime, see Rorie et al. 2018.

[2] Including, as a few examples, financial crimes, professional crimes, state crimes, and avocational crimes.

competitors that include a range of monopolistic behaviors, crimes against labor (as with violations of the Occupational Safety and Health Act 1970 (hereafter OSHA)), and crimes against creditors and owners (e.g., accounting fraud). Violators of corporate crime can be pursued through criminal proceedings but are more often adjudicated in administrative or civil courts (Simpson 2002; Laufer 2006; Garrett 2014; Anderson and Waggoner 2014; Braithwaite 1984).

The economic and political consequences of corporate crime are vast. For example, the fraudulent actions by investment banks that contributed to the global subprime mortgage crisis resulted in over $3 trillion in government bailouts, around 3.2 million foreclosures, at least 4.8 million jobs lost, and the loss of $2 trillion in retirement savings in the United States alone (Brandon 2008; Bureau of Justice Assistance/Center for Court Innovation 2010; Collins 2015; Davis 2008; Isidore 2010; Montgomery and Cho 2009). However, the effects were not limited to the USA; banks around the globe failed in a domino effect, which required the influx of tens of billions of euros, pounds, and kronas. Further, the effects are still reverberating through the global economy as workers continue to suffer from an "income squeeze" – salaries that dropped during the Great Recession have not caught up with the rate of inflation, meaning that workers are becoming poorer as the cost of living increases and salaries remain lower than before the financial crisis (Ahmed 2018).

In addition to the monetary costs of corporate crime, there can be dire physical consequences as well, such as injury, sickness, and death from defective and unsafe products, toxic pollution, and poor working conditions. Victims of corporate crime also suffer emotional trauma that is similar to the trauma suffered by victims of street crime. Victims report anger, generalized anxiety disorder, and depressive episodes (Ganzini et al. 2001; Titus 2001). Further, Sutherland (1945) argued that the direst consequence of corporate criminal behavior is the erosion of trust. The violation of trust by respected people in society leads to cynicism toward our economic and political institutions, which then leads to widespread social disorganization.

Given the numerous costs of corporate crime, there is a pressing need to determine how to prevent it. The question being examined in this chapter is whether laws and penalties can effectively deter these violations. Legislators typically respond to prominent cases of corporate crime by enacting significant changes to laws regulating companies, as well as by increasing penalties for violating those laws. It is thought that greater regulation and harsher penalties will deter these (seemingly) rational offenders. However, there is mixed evidence on the impact of formal sanctions for corporate crime (Block et al. 1981; Simpson et al. 2013; Cohen 2000; Makkai and Braithwaite 1991; Simpson and Koper 1992). Additionally, other studies have found more support for the use of informal sanctions (Simpson 2002) or the strengthening of internal corporate controls, like ethics training (Waples et al. 2009) and codes of conduct (Schell-Busey 2009). Despite the mixed evidence, there are some things we can learn from the literature about controlling corporate crime. Before examining the literature on specific strategies in more depth, we turn to an overview of deterrence as it relates to corporate crime.

17.2 DETERRENCE

A central component of almost all criminal justice strategies is that crime can be "deterred" by increasing the costs of offending (Pratt et al. 2006; Nagin 2013). As detailed in previous chapters, two Enlightenment philosophers – Cesare Beccaria and Jeremy Bentham – posited that crime occurs when individuals seek to maximize their own pleasure and minimize their pain (Paternoster 2010; see Beccaria 1777; Bentham, 1789). Although the "costs" of crime can be informal (e.g., reputational damage, loss of financial income), the original deterrence scholars focused heavily on the ability of formal criminal justice mechanisms to prevent crime – and this is the focus of this chapter.[3] Specifically, those scholars noted that formal justice system sanctions need to be certain, swift, and severe (but not disproportionately severe in comparison to the offense) in order to prevent crimes from occurring (Kreager and Matsueda 2014). Simply, a potential offender needs to expect more pain than pleasure to result from offending – when they expect to be punished, they will opt not to offend (Paternoster 2010).

Deterrence theory is thought to be especially useful for explaining elite white-collar offending, as such crimes are generally committed under the guise of profit maximization – in other words, to obtain benefits and with little risk of being detected/punished. As opposed to expressive crimes (e.g., assault or homicide), offenses such as embezzlement, accounting fraud, or insider trading involve a clear cost–benefit calculus whereby the offender considers the monetary gain to be made versus the likelihood of sanctions (Paternoster and Simpson 1993; Shover and Hochstetler 2006; Weisburd et al. 1995). There is much evidence to support the deterrent impact of regulatory policies and criminal sanctions for potential white-collar offenders (e.g., Cardi et al. 2012; Pratt et al. 2006; Schell-Busey et al. 2016; Simpson et al. 2013), though deterrence is not always achieved. A recent study provided accurate arrest certainty statistics to members of the public and found that in doing so they *increased* people's intentions to commit white-collar crime (Pickett and Roche 2016). The authors argued that most people have inflated estimates of the likelihood of being arrested for white-collar crime, so when laypeople discover how unlikely it is that they will face formal criminal justice action, they are more likely to commit the crime. White-collar crime scholars commonly note that sanctioning for white-collar offenders is less likely to come from the criminal justice system than it is to come from administrative agencies (and therefore it is perceived as less severe)[4], and even punitive regulatory sanctions are rare due to the lack of staffing and resources for regulatory monitoring and detection of such crimes (McKendall et al. 2002; Payne 2017; Simpson 2002; see also Schoepfer et al. 2007). When sanctions such as fines are used, they are often insufficient deterrents as they are generally small compared to company's profits, easily absorbed into standard business costs, and do not result in more consequential reputational damages (Rodwin 2015; White 2017; Yeager 2016). White-collar offenders might be punished more harshly via informal mechanisms (e.g., reputational damage or internal company sanctions; Friedrichs 2009; Simpson 2002; Wheeler et al. 1988).

In this chapter, we focus specifically on the ability to deter "corporate crimes" as opposed to other forms of white-collar crime meant to benefit the individual offender. Deterrence of corporate crimes – while following a similar "rational choice" framework

3 For excellent reviews of informal deterrence strategies in the corporate crime domain, see Makkai and Brathwaite 1994; Moore 1987; Paternoster and Simpson 1993, 1996; Simpson 2002; Simpson et al. 2013.

4 Although administrative sanctions in the USA are commonly thought to be less severe than criminal justice sanctions, a helpful reviewer notes that European regulators (and in particular those monitoring the financial system) are able to sanction more punitively and are well-staffed as well as well-funded (see Lord and Levi 2015 as well as Walburg 2015 for discussions on the strength of European regulatory agencies).

for individually beneficial crimes – is more complex as both individual as well as company costs and benefits must be considered, as must informal as well as formal sanctions and rewards (Paternoster and Simpson 1993, 1996; Simpson 2002). In the next sections, we review the evidence (or lack thereof) for law enforcement agents to have an impact on such crimes and offer suggestions for improving enforcement efforts.

17.3 THE DETERRENCE OF CORPORATE CRIME

Current efforts to deter corporate crime can be described as twelve unique strategies, distinguished primarily by whether they occur in the criminal justice system or in the regulatory system. In the *criminal justice system*, it is important to examine the following approaches separately:

- laws themselves
- detection and arrest
- deferred prosecution or non-prosecution agreements
- financial sanctions (fines or restitution)
- carceral sanctions (probation, jail, prison).

In the *regulatory* system, deterrence efforts might involve:

- regulatory policies themselves
- self-regulation
- inspections and detection
- injunction orders
- financial sanctions (fines, restitution, civil actions)
- license revocations.

It is also possible that an agency uses more than one strategy to motivate compliance (e.g., the use of criminal fines as well as increased inspections). Such efforts call to mind the "*pulling levers*" strategy implemented by law enforcement agencies in Boston in order to reduce homicides. A key aspect of the pulling levers approach was to increase the perceived certainty of arrest and punishment, but the police also used informal mechanisms of control like church leader influence, support for youth who wanted to leave the gang, etc. (Kennedy 1997). One might see similarities between the *pulling levers* strategy in Gunningham, Grabosky, and Sinclair's (1998) recommendation for incorporating third parties in corporate control efforts (see also Grabosky 1997, 2013). The primary entreaty from both sets of scholarship is for the use of mixed approaches to better address heterogeneity in motives and offenders.

The current chapter relies heavily on a 2014 meta-analysis of research examining the impact of the above strategies on corporate crime (Simpson et al. 2014; see also Schell-Busey et al. 2016; Rorie et al. 2018), but we will also examine the extant empirical literature when appropriate. Note that the meta-analysis included studies of deterrence regardless of nationality, but did require them to be written in the English language. We also used offenses specific to the US legal system in our search criteria; it is perhaps not surprising that 78 percent of the effect sizes calculated for the meta-analysis came from that country (Simpson et al. 2014). As we describe the results below, we recognize that they reflect a US-centric perspective but will attempt to describe international differences where relevant.

17.3.1 *Criminal Justice System Sanctions*

17.3.1.1 Effectiveness Overall

The 2014 meta-analysis found that legal sanctions tended to have small deterrent effects on corporate offending, but these effects were not statistically significant so it is possible that they could be explained by another factor (i.e., they might not be due to the legal sanctions themselves). Laws in and of themselves, for example, had a small deterrent effect when examined using cross-sectional studies (an effect highly susceptible to publication biases), but then had a small counterintuitive impact on corporate crimes when studied longitudinally. This could occur if laws have a short-term impact on offending that then decays over time, but there are many other potential reasons for the finding (see also Schell-Busey et al. 2016).

The meta-analysis also examined "punitive sanctions" as an entire category – one that included any sort of legal sanction such as fines, carceral punishments, arrest, etc. Although we found a small deterrence effect at the individual and company levels, the finding could be due to chance as it was not statistically significant, it varied depending on study characteristics (i.e., whether studied cross-sectionally or longitudinally, using self-report data or official data, whether using behavioral intentions as opposed to actual behavior), and it was highly susceptible to publication biases (Simpson et al. 2014, Schell-Busey et al. 2016; Rorie et al. 2018). Importantly, we also found that there was a stronger deterrent effect for punitive sanctions studied outside of the United States (which implies that such strategies are more effective in other countries, although the moderator analyses are limited by small sample sizes; Simpson et al. 2014).

17.3.1.2 Effectiveness of Different Strategies

Laws Themselves. Similar to the meta-analysis findings, review articles note that the passage of laws seems to do little to quell corporate malfeasance, especially without concomitant resources to increase enforcement (Rockness and Rockness 2005; Szott-Moohr 2003, 2007). Scholars argue that laws targeting corporate crime fail to deter because they are vague and unclear about what behaviors *specifically* are illegal. Such ambiguity means that prosecutors can look at a behavior and classify it as a crime *after* it has been committed, while the offender (and often the victim) is not aware ahead of time that the behavior would constitute a criminal act (Szott-Moohr 2007); for example, a study of the Corporate Manslaughter and Corporate Homicide Act in the United Kingdom found that the act led to more corporate convictions but did not reduce the number of work-related deaths (Roper 2018). Furthermore, the more-proximal environment to the offender seems to matter more than distant laws – when in the workplace, decisions are made by groups and not by individuals, and considerations such as workplace loyalty and authority hierarchies might overwhelm ethical considerations governing the wider society (Szott-Moohr 2007). Although the creation of new laws might promote compliance for a little while, individuals (who likely view the large financial payoffs of crime as outweighing the low likelihood of being caught) will find ways to skirt the law in order to generate a profit (Rockness and Rockness 2005; Szott-Moohr 2003). Overall, legal scholars seem to believe that laws are only effective when they are seen as legitimate or when the law reinforces already-held beliefs about ethics (Rockness and Rockness 2005; Szott-Moohr 2003, 2007)

Detection and Arrest. Deterrence scholars generally argue that increasing the *certainty* of punishment is much more important than enhancing the *severity* of punishment, yet policymaking in the corporate crime domain has almost exclusively focused on the latter. Enhanced sentencing mechanisms have been put into place for corporate crimes (e.g., Sarbanes-Oxley, Sherman Antitrust Act), yet no policies have stipulated that corporate offenders will be more likely to face arrest or prosecution (analogous to "mandatory arrest" laws targeting domestic violence offenders). The Organizational Sentencing Guidelines provide rewards for self-regulatory compliance programs which (in theory) would increase the likelihood of a company detecting noncompliance among its own ranks, but – as far as we know – no law enforcement agencies have increased efforts to actively monitor corporations even after detecting noncompliance. Such monitoring and enforcement is often left to administrative/regulatory agencies (discussed in Section 17.3.2). This is perhaps why there is so little knowledge about the deterrent effects of arrest. Even when scholars directly measure the impact of arrest on the likelihood of committing crime (e.g., through the use of hypothetical vignettes; Paternoster and Simpson 1993, 1996; Simpson and Paternoster 1993; Simpson et al. 2013; Smith et al. 2007), those items are almost always combined with other questions asking about the chance of the firm being investigated by a regulatory agency or the chance that the individual would be sued. We were only able to find one empirical study in the *Journal of Corporate Finance* arguing that the "perp walks" common in white-collar crime arrests (in that study, the arrest of Adelphia's top executives) enhances the awareness that shareholders have about corporate crime, which then decreases share values. They postulate that the awareness–share value relationship would serve as a deterrent to corporate crime but do not directly test the relationship (Knoeber and Walker 2013).

Deferred Prosecution or Non-prosecution Agreements. Since 1997, the US Department of Justice has increasingly relied on the use of deferred prosecution agreements (DPAs) or non-prosecution agreements (NPAs) as an alternative to the often lengthy and resource-intensive criminal trials involved in prosecuting corporate crime (Alexander and Cohen 2015). DPAs and NPAs allow corporations to settle cases without having to formally plead guilty and are generally used only when the corporation has cooperated with investigations or disclosed malfeasance to prosecutors willingly (Alexander and Cohen 2015). This is not without controversy; people see such agreements (in which prosecution is avoided as long as the corporation meets certain conditions to improve compliance) as unfairly allowing corporations to avoid the stigma assigned to lower-status "traditional" offenders; circumventing the role of courts (i.e., judges and juries) in judging guilt and assigning sanctions according to the principles of restitution, rehabilitation, incapacitation, deterrence, and just deserts; and removing protections for the corporations allotted to criminal defendants (Steinzor 2014; Alexander and Cohen 2015).

Given the novelty of the DPA/NPA strategy, no empirical research has examined whether it has actually deterred corporate criminal behavior, though a few articles have assessed whether corporations have complied with the agreement conditions and the impact of DPAs/NPAs on individual prosecutions. In the United States, Kaal and Lacine (2014) found that between 1993 and 2013, 91 percent of the corporations complied fully with agreement requirements (e.g., changes to the board of directors, development of internal compliance programs, changes to top management). Koehler (2015) examined DPAs and NPAS specific to the Foreign Corrupt Practices Act and found that the increased use of agreements has correlated with a decrease in prosecutions against individual offenders. This is likely because the use of such agreements allows prosecutors to avoid proving individual liability. The authors argue that – with corporations taking responsibility for corruption allegations – deterrence may be reduced as individuals do not see themselves as likely targets of prosecution. Garrett (2014) found similar results more generally – the increased use of DPAs/NPAs between 2001 and 2014 correlated with fewer individual prosecutions, *despite* earlier DOJ sentiments arguing that individual prosecutions would be a better deterrent. DPAs and NPAs have also been used in Europe, yet research on their deterrence capabilities does not exist there either. Notably, the use of DPAs in England and Wales was partially motivated by fears that corporations would work with US authorities after offending and avoid harsher sanctions in the EU. However, DPAs are unlikely to serve as a deterrence mechanism in England and Wales simply because prosecution of corporations in those countries is rare generally (Lord and King 2018). Again, none of these articles directly measured how the use of such agreements impacted corporate crime directly. If changes to internal management programs (as a result of DPA/NPA mandates) help reduce crime, then we can say that such programs help deter future crimes by that corporation.

Financial Sanctions (Fines or Restitution). There have been more studies examining the use of fines as a deterrent than most of the other punitive sanctions discussed here. Results tend to be mixed about the deterrent impact of financial sanctions, with most studies offering conditional support for such punishments. For example, Blondiau et al. (2015) found that financial sanctions deter corporate crime but have more of an impact when these are criminal justice sanctions as opposed to administrative penalties; they argue that a combined law enforcement and regulatory approach might be most effective. Pierce (2018) also found a deterrent effect of financial sanctions on corporate crime, but noted that those sanctions must be high enough to impact the firm's market value *and* that any impact might actually be due to reputational damage – not the fine itself. On the other hand, studies of environmental crimes found that fines did not impact compliance, except in the very short term after the offense (Barrett et al. 2018) and possibly when fines were more than $10 million (Stretesky et al. 2013).

Carceral Sanctions (Probation, Jail, Prison). It is often noted that carceral sanctions are far less likely for corporate criminals than for "traditional offenders" (see Reiman and Leighton 2016), and when corporate offenders are given incarceration, they are more likely to receive probation, house arrest, and community service than being sentenced to serve time in a correctional facility (Payne 2017). As such, there is no real empirical basis on which to assess the deterrent impact of incarceration in and of itself. One article noted that prison sentences for international cartel cases did increase by 150 percent between 1990 and 2009 yet remains an underused option for sentencing in such cases (Connor 2011). This article did not, however, assess the impact of incarceration on corporate recidivism.

17.3.2 *Regulatory System Sanctions*

17.3.2.1 Effectiveness Overall

The 2014 meta-analysis also grouped all forms of regulatory strategies (e.g., inspections, fines, injunctive orders) into one category for analysis. Overall, the impact of regulatory approaches was inconsistent, and depended on the unit of analysis employed. At the individual level, regulatory approaches seemed to deter offending. At the company level, deterrence depended on which type of effect size was used; comparing group differences indicated a strong impact (and one *not* susceptible to publication bias), while using correlational measures implied an iatrogenic impact of regulation. It's possible that there's a "tipping point" of regulation after which it becomes less effective or even encourages resistance, but much more research is needed to test whether that's an accurate interpretation. It's also worth noting that the firm-level group-difference deterrence effect is found only in self-report data (using official data, we found an iatrogenic effect of regulatory strategies). When measuring deterrence at the macro-level (i.e., by geographic differences), regulatory strategies seem to have a small impact; however, the effect could be due to chance as it was not statistically significant (Simpson et al. 2014; Schell-Busey et al. 2016; Rorie et al. 2018).

17.3.2.2 Effectiveness of Different Strategies

Regulatory Policies Themselves. Individual studies on regulatory policies (i.e., stated, written regulatory priorities and plans for action; analogous to formal criminal law) imply that changes in these policies can have an impact, although with some caveats. Recent studies of financial crimes in the Netherlands (Baarsma et al. 2012) and internationally (Khalil et al. 2015) demonstrated that competition regulations and stricter financial reporting requirements produced lower offending. There is much scholarship generally supporting the idea that regulatory guidance is necessary and effective in deterring crimes, although the effectiveness of specific policies depends on the environment and industry being targeted (see, e.g., Ayres and Braithwaite 1992; Baldwin and Black 2008; Scholz 1984).

Self-Regulation. There has been increasing emphasis on self-regulation as a regulatory strategy (i.e., the mechanism for regulation – this can be the same as a stated regulatory policy but could also be an informal approach to motivating compliance) over the past thirty years, or what some might call the "governance turn," whereby the responsibility for monitoring corporations has come to rely more on third parties and the corporations themselves. Self-regulation occurs when regulatory agencies encourage the creation and implementation of internal compliance programs that are funded and monitored by the corporations themselves. This is thought to increase compliance while reducing government overhead – arguably, the corporations are better than regulatory agencies at monitoring internal processes and employees, creating practicable solutions, and will see the government as more legitimate (Braithwaite 1982; Tyler 2009). On the other hand, critics of this regulatory trend argue that corporations are likely to "turn a blind eye" to profitable behavior regardless of its ethicality and will adopt ineffective internal compliance programs as a symbolic gesture to enhance their reputation as well as to avoid costly fines when they are caught by government agencies (Braithwaite 1982; Short and Toffel 2010). Further, some critics argue that self-regulation in the form of corporate social responsibility (CSR) allows corporations to *deliberately* manipulate the public with fraudulent messaging under the guise of CSR. For example, Leon and Ken (2017) recently argued that the fast food industry coopted Michelle Obama's *Let's Move* initiative in an effort to deceive the public about the industry's commitment to public health. Evidence on the effectiveness of self-regulation is mixed, and it generally seems that self-regulation can be effective only when supported by strong government efforts – or "enforced self-regulation" (see, e.g., Hart 2010; Ojo 2011; Short and Toffel 2010).

Inspections and Detection. One of the most important duties of regulators is that of inspection, whereby noncompliance can be prevented, or detected and resolved. Deterrence can occur either through the threat of inspection or via actions taken once inspection has occurred. A systematic review of the occupational safety and health (OSH) literature found that inspections did not seem to have a "general deterrent" impact (i.e., differences in inspection risk across industries did not significantly impact relevant outcomes) but did find that inspections with accompanying penalties had a pretty clear "specific deterrence" effect on a wide range of outcomes. Inspections without penalties (note that this category included studies where it was unclear whether a sanction was given) produced inconsistent deterrent effects, rendering it uncertain whether inspections have a deterrent impact without the use of sanctions (Tompa et al. 2016). Surveys studying perceptual deterrence in the corporate crime domain do tend to find that the perceived likelihood of regulatory inspections decreases the likelihood of offending (e.g., Braithwaite and Makkai 1991; Elis and Simpson 1995), while interviews have demonstrated that inspections are effective if they are a sustained regulatory effort within the industry (e.g., Gunningham et al. 2004). For example, in a study on the effectiveness of three new regulatory policies created and enforced by Environment Canada, Krahn (1998) reported greater declines in pollution when the policies were backed by consistent inspections compared to the use of voluntary programs with no inspections. Similarly, Gerardu and Wasserman (1994) showed that standardized inspection checks and consistent follow-ups significantly reduced waste disposal licensing violations in the Netherlands.

Injunction Orders. Injunctions are used by regulatory agencies to immediately halt noncompliant behavior, especially behavior that can be expected to continue during criminal or civil procedures, or those behaviors that regulators can expect to occur more than once (Clinard and Yeager 1980). As such, "the injunction's purpose is to prevent, not to punish" (Yale Law Journal Editorial Board 1948: 1027). This might be why we were unable to find scholarship quantitatively investigating the deterrent impact of injunctive relief mechanisms. However, some scholars note that injunction orders might better serve deterrence goals when punitive sanctions are unlikely to change the ways in which corporations operate (Fisse 1982). The benefits of injunctions include the ease and efficiency of obtaining one (there are fewer protections for the alleged offender at this stage and most regulatory agencies have specific statutes protecting the process from judicial intervention). Furthermore, a defendant has to demonstrate a voluntary discontinuation of the activity under question *and* a credible commitment to future compliance to obtain injunctive relief. Such efforts often lead regulated entities and regulators to consent decrees in which the entity details how it will come into compliance. If such planning is sincere and regulators continue to monitor the entity, the remedial action plan (along with the fear of possible punishments should noncompliance continue) might serve an important deterrent function (Yale Law Journal Editorial Board 1948).

Financial Sanctions (Fines, Restitution, Civil Actions). Research on regulatory financial sanctions inconsistently supports their deterrent effect, and their impact seems to be outweighed by other considerations. Studies of bribery (Sampath et al. 2018), antitrust (Parker and Nielsen 2011), and waste disposal (van Wingerde 2015), for example, indicate that regulatory fines are less important than the risk of detection and reputational damage incurred by regulatory actions. As mentioned already, a 2016 systematic review of OSHA enforcement found that inspections with accompanying penalties had a pretty clear "specific deterrence" effect on a wide range of outcomes (Tompa et al. 2016) but did not break down their findings by the type of sanction meted out.

License Revocations. Regulatory agencies have at their disposal a critical, but seldom used, tool in their deterrence toolbox – license revocation. The threat of a license revocation is often considered to be necessary in promoting compliance even when using less punitive strategies – if the regulator has demonstrated a willingness to invoke the "corporate death penalty" (Ramirez 2005), they are in a position to promote change in the early stages of handling noncompliance (Ayres and Braithwaite 1992). Only one research endeavor could be found examining the potential deterrent effect of license revocations separately from other penalties. In their study of small nursing homes in Australia, Braithwaite and Makkai (1991; see also Makkai and Braithwaite 1994) found that the possibility of state license revocation did not significantly promote compliance.

17.3.3 *"Pulling Levers" Approaches: Effectiveness Overall*

In the meta-analysis, when studies incorporated multiple types of intervention, there was a small but statistically significant deterrent impact at both the individual and the company level. At the company level, half of the studies driving the significant effect were conducted outside of the United States (e.g., Hartman et al. 1995; Almutairi 2000), suggesting that combining regulatory monitoring, inspections, and enforcement may be effective across cultures. All of the studies included were cross-sectional, but these results indicate a potential benefit of exploring the use of multiple sanctions at one point in time (Simpson et al. 2014; Schell-Busey et al. 2016). An example of such an approach in the corporate crime literature is that of the "enforcement pyramid" as articulated by Ayres and Braithwaite (1992), in which regulatory agencies and agents are encouraged to start with more educative/persuasive responses (e.g., providing training, informal warning letters) to the initial violations by a company and then escalating to more deterrence-based sanctions (e.g., fines, prosecution) as noncompliance continues. Braithwaite (2016) reviews the extensive research on the pyramid as well as the more general research on using multiple sanctions in the regulatory domain. We refer the reader to this excellent monograph for more details, as well as to Mascini (2013) for a critique and review of the challenges associated with the strategy. Experimental evidence suggests that deterrence of cartel formation can be achieved by offering leniency to the first reporting party in an antitrust case, followed by high fines for the other parties involved (Bigoni et al. 2012).

17.4 DISCUSSION AND FUTURE DIRECTIONS

Generally, the research on corporate crime deterrence yields few consistent suggestions for policy but many questions for research. One of the consistent conclusions is that simply making new corporate crime laws is ineffective, while actual criminal justice sanctions seem to be inconsistently effective. Importantly, most of the research on sanctions focuses on the impact of sanction severity, ignoring the potential for increasing sanction *certainty* to have a deterrent impact. To that end, we suggest that additional research is needed that examines the impact of arrest certainty uniquely from other types of sanctions (e.g., through the study of "mandated arrest" strategies, "perp walks," or analyzing the impact of individual arrest likelihood separately from other potential punishments in hypothetical vignette surveys).

There is some support for the use of fines and monetary sanctions (both civil and criminal) in producing compliance, but financial penalties seem to be effective only in the short term and only when they are very high. It's also unclear whether financial penalties matter more or less than the accompanying reputational damages that come from such sanctions. One way to tease out the financial penalty impact from the impact of reputational damage might be to conduct research on NPAs/DPAs and compliance. NPAs/DPAs often entail financial compensation but do not carry reputational impacts to the same extent as criminal justice sentences.

Furthermore, it remains clear that law enforcement is not the primary mechanism acting to deter corporate crime – regulatory actions are the most common way in which governing bodies handle corporate noncompliance. Very little empirical research directly compares the perceived threat of regulatory sanctions to the threat of criminal sanctions, although we would expect criminal sanctions to carry more "weight" because of the moral stigma associated with being labeled a "criminal" as opposed to being labeled "out of compliance" (see Croall 2004; McCormick 1977; Simester and von Hirsch 2011; Yoder 1978). Yet, we do not have an empirical understanding of whether (and under what conditions) a corporate offender might see the two types of sanctions as different.

We found in our review that regulatory sanctions seem to be effective against individual-level offending, but these sanctions have wildly inconsistent impacts when leveled against corporations. Much more research needs to be done on the circumstances and conditions under which regulatory sanctions produce the desired outcome, including which specific sanctions are effective and for whom. Some support exists for regulatory inspections as a deterrent, but only when they are accompanied by sanction threats and are part of a sustained effort in an industry. There has been no empirical research (to our knowledge) on the impact of injunctive orders, and very little research on the impact of license revocation, despite theoretical reasons for thinking that these strategies might be effective.

It's important to recognize that we framed our discussion here around the use of formal deterrents (i.e., criminal and regulatory strategies) and only rarely distinguished between perceptual and objective deterrence. Also noteworthy is that most of the studies included in the meta-analysis relied on official statistics (although studies using self-report/perceptual data were more likely to support deterrence; Simpson et al. 2014). Clearly, laws and regulations cannot have an impact on corporate crime if the people making decisions are unaware of them and/or do not think that enforcement is likely (see Williams and Hawkins 1986). This is an especially important consideration in the domain of corporate crime, in which: companies increasingly operate in multiple jurisdictions (who have different legal/regulatory expectations), behavior is inconsistently defined as criminal, and uncertainty exists around the penalties that one might expect should their behavior be prosecuted criminally or administratively. Such considerations render a "simple" cost–benefit analysis into a very complicated equation. Although it is beyond the scope of this chapter to review the perceptual corporate crime deterrence literature in detail, we recommend Paternoster and Tibbets (2016) for an excellent review of this literature.

Before concluding, it is also important to recognize that deterrence-based approaches, even when they are shown to promote compliance, have their limitations. Scholars note that deterrence-based approaches (also known as the "punishment school" (e.g., Gray 2006) or "command-and-control strategies" (e.g., Sinclair 1997)) can impede otherwise socially productive behavior for the sake of patrolling relatively minor violations (Gray 2006); are too expensive for resource-strapped regulatory agencies to properly implement; are difficult to implement due to the complexity of regulations as well as the volatility of the regulatory environment; and promote adversarial relationships that squash information sharing that could otherwise have resulted in more compliance (Braithwaite 2011; Hawkins 2013; Kagan 2009; Potoski and Prakash 2004; Rorie 2015; Sinclair 1997). Thus, when reviewing the inconsistencies of the findings discussed here, future research should examine if and how deterrence can be made more effective while minimizing some of the unintended consequences – for example, by taking a more "responsive" approach that incorporates persuasive strategies (Ayres and Braithwaite 1992) or by incorporating considerations of procedural justice (Tyler 2006). There is some evidence that creating policies in cooperation with the regulated industries and educating businesses about compliance requirements can enhance the deterrent impact of those regulatory programs (Krahn 1998; GAO 1988; Nielsen and Parker 2005)

Overall, much more empirical work must be done that investigates law enforcement and regulatory strategies and *actual* compliance behaviors. Although empirical research in this domain is beset with obstacles, scholars must continue to ask for access to law enforcement and regulatory data, to corporate records, and to the individuals responsible for compliance – both within the companies and within the agencies monitoring them. Researchers also need to pursue more rigorous approaches to research, including the use of randomized experiments that will firmly establish the true causal impact of deterrent strategies. Without such efforts, we will continue to flounder in our attempts to inform policy and protect the billions of people impacted by corporate malfeasance.

REFERENCES

Ahmed, Kamal. 2018. "Is the Income Squeeze Coming to an End?" *BBC News* (March). www.bbc.com/news/business-43470288.

Alexander, Cindy R., and Mark A. Cohen. 2015. "The Evolution of Corporate Criminal Settlements: An Empirical Perspective on Non-prosecution, Deferred Prosecution, and Plea Agreements." *American Criminal Law Review* 52: 537.

Almutairi, Yousef M. 2000. Enforcing Budgetary and Legal Compliance in the Government Sector: An Assessment of Preauditing in the State of Kuwait. Unpublished doctoral dissertation, Florida Atlantic University.

Anderson, J. M., and I. Waggoner. 2014. *The Changing Role of Criminal Law in Controlling Corporate Behavior*. Santa Monica: Rand Corporation.

Ayres, I., and J. Braithwaite. 1992. *Responsive Regulation: Transcending the Deregulation Debate*. New York: Oxford University Press.

Baarsma, Barbara, Ron Kemp, Rob van der Noll, and Jo Seldeslachts. 2012. "Let's Not Stick Together: Anticipation of Cartel and Merger Control in The Netherlands." *De Economist* 160, no.4: 357–76.

Baldwin, Robert, and Julia Black. 2008. "Really Responsive Regulation." *Modern Law Review* 71, no.1: 59–94.

Barrett, Kimberly L., Michael J. Lynch, Michael A. Long, and Paul B. Stretesky. 2018. "Monetary Penalties and Noncompliance with Environmental Laws: A Mediation Analysis." *American Journal of Criminal Justice* 43: 1–21.

Beccaria, Cesare. 1777. *An Essay on Crimes and Punishments Translated from the Italian; with a Commentary, Attributed to Mons. de Voltaire, translated from the French* (5th ed.). Dublin: n.p.

Bentham, Jeremy. 1789. *An Introduction to the Principles of Morals and Legislation. Printed in the Year 1780, and Now First Published by Jeremy Bentham, of Lincoln's Inn, Esquire*. London: n.p.

Bigoni, Maria, Sven-Olof Fridolfsson, Chloe Le Coq, and Giancarlo Spagnolo. 2012. "Fines, Leniency, and Rewards in Antitrust." *RAND Journal of Economics* 43, no.2: 368–90.

Block, Michael K., Frederick C. Nold, and Joseph G. Sidak. 1981. "The Deterrent Effect of Antitrust Enforcement." *Journal of Political Economy* 89, no.3: 429–45.

Blondiau, Thomas, Carole M. Billiet, and Sandra Rousseau. 2015. "Comparison of Criminal and Administrative Penalties for Environmental Offenses." *European Journal of Law and Economics* 39, no.1: 11–35.

Braithwaite, John. 1982. "Enforced Self-Regulation: A New Strategy for Corporate Crime Control." *Michigan Law Review* 80, no.7: 1466–1507.

1984. *Corporate Crime in the Pharmaceutical Industry*. London: Routledge & Kegan Paul.

2011. "The Essence of Responsive Regulation." *University of British Columbia Law Review* 44: 475.

2016. "Restorative Justice and Responsive Regulation: The Question of Evidence." RegNet Research Papers, No. 51. Acton, AU: RegNet School of Regulation & Global Governance, Australia National University. http://regnet.anu.edu.au/sites/default/files/uploads/2016–10/SSRN_2016_updated_Braithwaite%20J.pdf.

Braithwaite, John, and Toni Makkai. 1991. "Testing an Expected Utility Model of Corporate Deterrence." *Law & Society Review* 25: 7.

Brandon, Emily. 2008. "Retirement Savers Lost $2 Trillion in the Stock Market." *US News and World Report* (October 8). https://money.usnews.com/money/blogs/planning-to-retire/2008/10/08/retirement-savers-lost-2-trillion-in-the-stock-market.

Bureau of Justice Assistance/Center for Court Innovation. 2010. "Addressing Foreclosed and Abandoned Properties." www.bja.gov/Publications/CCI_Abandoned_Property.pdf.

Cardi, W. Jonathan, Randall D. Penfield, and Albert H. Yoon. 2012. "Does Tort Law Deter Individuals? A Behavioral Science Study." *Journal of Empirical Legal Studies* 9, no.3: 567–603.

Clinard, Marshall B., and Peter C. Yeager. 1980. "Corporate Crime." *Michigan Law Review* 80, no.4: 978.

Cohen, Mark A. 2000. "The Economics of Crime and Punishment: Implications for Sentencing of Economic Crimes and New Technology Offenses." *George Mason Law Review* 9: 503.

Collins, Mike. 2015. "The Big Bank Bailout." *Forbes* (July 14). www.forbes.com/sites/mikecollins/2015/07/14/the-big-bank-bailout/#7daa866f2d83.

Connor, John M. 2011. "Problems with Prison in International Cartel Cases." *Antitrust Bulletin* 56, no.2: 311–44.

Croall, Hazel. 2004. "Combating Financial Crime: Regulatory versus Crime Control Approaches." *Journal of Financial Crime* 11, no.1: 45–55.

Davis, Julie Hirschfeld. 2008. "Retirement Accounts Have Lost $2 Trillion – So Far." *Fox News* (October). www.foxnews.com/printer_friendly_wires/2008Oct07/0,4675,MeltdownRetirement,00.html.

Elis, Lori A., and Simpson, Sally S. 1995. "Informal Sanction Threats and Corporate Crime: Additive versus Multiplicative Models." *Journal of Research in Crime and Delinquency* 32, no.4: 399–424.

Fisse, Brent. 1982. "Reconstructing Corporate Criminal Law: Deterrence, Retribution, Fault, and Sanctions." *Southern California Law Review* 56: 1141.

Friedrichs, David O. 2009. *Trusted Criminals: White Collar Crime in Contemporary Society*. Belmont, CA: Thomson-Wadsworth.

Ganzini, Linda, Bentson McFarland, and Joseph Bloom. 2001. "Victims of Fraud: Comparing Victims of White-Collar and Violent Crime." In *Crimes of Privilege*, edited by N. Shover and J. P. Wright, New York: Oxford University Press.

Garrett, Brandon. 2014. *Too Big to Jail: How Prosecutors Compromise with Corporations*. Cambridge, MA: Harvard University Press.

Gerardu, Jo and Cheryl Wasserman. 1994. Third International Conference on Environmental Enforcement: Conference Proceedings Volume 2: April 25–28, 1994, Oaxaca, México. Environmental Protection Agency.

Government Accountability Office. 1988. "Status of Implementing Employer Sanctions after Second Year." Report to Congress: Immigration Reform. www.gao.gov/assets/150/147204.pdf.

Grabosky, Peter N. 1997. "Discussion Paper: Inside the Pyramid: Towards a Conceptual Framework for the Analysis of Regulatory Systems." *International Journal of the Sociology of Law* 25, no.3: 195–201.

2013. "Beyond Responsive Regulation: The Expanding Role of Non-state Actors in the Regulatory Process." *Regulation & Governance* 7, no.1: 114–23.

Gray, G. C. 2006. "The Regulation of Corporate Violations: Punishment, Compliance, and the Blurring of Responsibility." *British Journal of Criminology* 46, no.5: 875–92.

Gunningham, Neil, Peter N. Grabosky, and Darren Sinclair. 1998. *Smart Regulation: Designing Environmental Policy*. Oxford: Clarendon Press.

Gunningham, Neil, Robert A. Kagan, and Dorothy Thornton. 2004. "Social License and Environmental Protection: Why Businesses Go Beyond Compliance." *Law & Social Inquiry* 29, no.2: 307–41.

Hart, Susan M. 2010. "Self-Regulation, Corporate Social Responsibility, and the Business Case: Do They Work in Achieving Workplace Equality and Safety?" *Journal of Business Ethics* 92, no.4: 585–600.

Hartman, Raymond S., Mainul Huq, and David Wheeler. 1995. *Why Paper Mills Clean Up: Determinants of Pollution Abatement in Four Asian Countries* (No. 1710). World Bank.

Hawkins, Keith. 2013. "Enforcing Regulation: Robert Kagan's Contribution – And Some Questions." *Law & Social Inquiry* 38, no.4: 950–72.

Isidore, Chris. 2010. "Poof: Another 800,000 Jobs Disappear." *CNN* (February). https://money.cnn.com/2010/02/04/news/economy/jobs_outlook/.

Kaal, Wulf A., and Timothy A. Lacine. 2014. "Effect of Deferred and Non-prosecution Agreements on Corporate Governance: Evidence from 1993–2013." *Business Law* 70: 61.

Kagan, Robert A. 2009. *Adversarial Legalism: The American Way of Law*. Cambridge, MA: Harvard University Press.

Kennedy, David M. 1997. "Pulling Levers: Chronic Offenders, High-Crime Settings, and a Theory of Prevention." *Valparaiso University Law Review* 31, no.1: 449–84.

Khalil, Samer, Walid Saffar, and Samir Trabelsi. 2015. "Disclosure Standards, Auditing Infrastructure, and Bribery Mitigation." *Journal of Business Ethics* 132, no.2: 379–99.

Knoeber, Charles R., and Mark D. Walker. 2013. "The Effect of Tougher Enforcement on Foreign Firms: Evidence from the Adelphia Perp Walk." *Journal of Corporate Finance* 23: 382–94.

Koehler, Mike. 2015. "Measuring the Impact of Non-prosecution and Deferred Prosecution Agreements on Foreign Corrupt Practices Act Enforcement." *University of California Davis Law Review* 49: 497–565.

Krahn, Peter K. 1998. Enforcement vs. Voluntary Compliance: An Examination of the Strategic Enforcement Initiatives Implemented by the Pacific and Yukon Regional Offices of Environment Canada 1983–1998. Fifth International Conference on Environmental Compliance and Enforcement, Monterey, CA.

Kreager, Derek A., and Ross L. Matsueda. 2014. "Bayesian Updating and Crime." In *Encyclopedia of Criminology and Criminal Justice*, New York: Springer New York. https://link.springer.com/referenceworkentry/10.1007%2F978-1-4614-5690-2_397.

Laufer, William S. 2006. "Illusions of Compliance and Governance." *Corporate Governance: The International Journal of Business in Society* 6, no.3: 239–49.

Leon, Kenneth S., and Ivy Ken. 2017. "Food Fraud and the Partnership for a 'Healthier' America: A Case Study in State-Corporate Crime." *Critical Criminology* 25, no.3: 393–410.

Lord, Nicholas, and Colin King. 2018. "Negotiating Non-contention: Civil Recovery and Deferred Prosecution in Response to Transnational Corporate Bribery." In *Corruption in Commercial Enterprise: Law, Theory and Practice*, edited by L. Campbell and N. Lord. London: Routledge.

Lord, Nicholas, and Michael Levi. 2015. "Determining the Adequate Enforcement of White-Collar and Corporate Crimes in Europe." In *Routledge Handbook of White-Collar and Corporate Crime in Europe*, edited by Judith van Erp, Wim Huisman, and Gudrun Vande Walle. Abingdon, UK/New York: Routledge.

Makkai, Toni, and John Braithwaite. 1991. "Criminological Theories and Regulatory Compliance." *Criminology* 29, no.2: 191–220.

1994. "Reintegrative Shaming and Compliance with Regulatory Standards." *Criminology* 32, no.3: 361–85.

Mascini, Peter. 2013. "Why Was the Enforcement Pyramid So Influential? And What Price Was Paid?" *Regulation & Governance* 7, no.1: 48–60.

McCormick Jr, Albert E. 1977. "Rule Enforcement and Moral Indignation: Some Observations on the Effects of Criminal Antitrust Convictions upon Societal Reaction Processes." *Social Problems* 25, no.1: 30–9.

McKendall, Maire, Beverly DeMarr, and Catherine Jones-Rikkers. 2002. "Ethical Compliance Programs and Corporate Illegality: Testing the Assumptions of the Corporate Sentencing Guidelines." *Journal of Business Ethics* 37, no.4: 367–83.

Montgomery, Lori, and Cho, David. 2008 (September). "Washington Readies Sea Change for Wall Street; Rescue Plan Grows to $700 Billion; Similar Measures Urged Overseas." www.sas.upenn.edu/~egme/econ252/news_files/Washington%20Readies%20Sea%20Change%20for%20Wall%20Street.pdf.

Moore, Charles A. 1987. "Taming the Giant Corporation? Some Cautionary Remarks on the Deterrability of Corporate Crime." *Crime & Delinquency* 33, no.3: 379–402.

Nagin, Daniel S. 2013. "Deterrence in the Twenty-First Century." *Crime and Justice* 42, no.1: 199–263.

Nielsen, Vibeke L. and Christine Parker. 2005. "The ACCC Enforcement and Compliance Survey: Report of Preliminary Findings." University of Melbourne Legal Studies Research Paper, 150.

Ojo, Marianne. 2011. "Co-operative and Competitive Enforced Self Regulation: The Role of Governments, Private Actors and Banks in Corporate Responsibility." *Journal of Financial Regulation and Compliance* 19, no.2: 139–55.

Parker, Christine, and Viebke L. Nielson. 2006. "Do Businesses Take Compliance Systems Seriously? An Empirical Study of the Implementation of Trade Practices Compliance Systems in Australia." *Melbourne University Law Review* 30, no.2: 441–94.

2011. *Explaining Compliance: Business Responses to Regulation*. Cheltenham, UK, and Northampton, MA: Edward Elgar.

Paternoster, Raymond. 2010. "How Much Do We Really Know about Criminal Deterrence?" *Journal of Criminal Law and Criminology* 100, no.3: 765–824.

Paternoster, Raymond, and Sally Simpson. 1993. "A Rational Choice Theory of Corporate Crime." *Routine Activity and Rational Choice* 5: 37.

1996. "Sanction Threats and Appeals to Morality: Testing a Rational Choice Model of Corporate Crime." *Law & Society Review* 30: 549.

Paternoster, Raymond, and Stephen G. Tibbets. 2016. "White-Collar Crime and Perceptual Deterrence." In *The Oxford Handbook of White-Collar Crime*, edited byShanna van Slyke, Michael L. Benson, and Francis T. Cullen. New York: Oxford University Press.

Payne, Brian K. 2017. *White-Collar Crime: The Essentials*, 2nd ed. Thousand Oaks, CA: Sage Publications.

Pickett, Justin T., and Sean Patrick Roche. 2016. "Arrested Development: Misguided Directions in Deterrence Theory and Policy." *Criminology & Public Policy* 15, no.3: 727–51.

Pierce, Jason R. 2018. "Reexamining the Cost of Corporate Criminal Prosecutions." *Journal of Management* 44, no.3: 892–918.

Potoski, Matthew, and Aseem Prakash. 2004. "The Regulation Dilemma: Cooperation and Conflict in Environmental Governance." *Public Administration Review* 64, no.2: 152–63.

Pratt, T., F. T. Cullen, K. R. Blevins, L. E. Daigle, and T. D. Madensen. 2006. *The Empirical Status of Deterrence Theory*. New Brunswick, NJ: Transaction.

Ramirez, Mary Kreiner. 2005. "The Science Fiction of Corporate Criminal Liability: Containing the Machine through the Corporate Death Penalty." *Arizona Law Review* 47: 933.

Reiman, J., and P. Leighton. 2016. *The Rich Get Richer and the Poor Get Prison: Ideology, Class, and Criminal Justice*. New York: Routledge/Taylor & Francis Group.

Rockness, Howard, and Joanne Rockness. 2005. "Legislated Ethics: From Enron to Sarbanes-Oxley, the Impact on Corporate America." *Journal of Business Ethics* 57, no.1: 31–54.

Rodwin, Marc A. 2015. "Do We Need Stronger Sanctions to Ensure Legal Compliance by Pharmaceutical Firms?" *Food & Drug Law Journal* 70, no.3: 435–52.

Roper, Victoria. 2018. "The Corporate Manslaughter and Corporate Homicide Act 2007 – A 10-Year Review." *The Journal of Criminal Law* 82, no.1: 48–75.

Rorie, M. L. 2015. "Responsive Regulation." Oxford Handbooks Online. http://dx.doi.org/10.1093/oxfordhb/9780199935383.013.109.

Rorie, Melissa, Mariel Alper, Natalie Schell-Busey, and Sally S. Simpson. 2018. "Using Meta-analysis under Conditions of Definitional Ambiguity: The Case of Corporate Crime." *Criminal Justice Studies* 31, no.1: 38–61.

Sampath, Vijay, Naomi Gardberg, and Noushi Rahman. 2018. "Corporate Reputation's Invisible Hand: Bribery, Rational Choice, and Market Penalties." *Journal of Business Ethics* 151, no.3: 743–60.

Schell-Busey, Natalie M. 2009. "The Deterrent Effects of Ethics Codes for Corporate Crime: A Meta-analysis." PhD dissertation, University of Maryland, College Park.

Schell-Busey, Natalie, Sally S. Simpson, Melissa Rorie, and Mariel Alper. 2016. "What Works? A Systematic Review of Corporate Crime Deterrence." *Criminology & Public Policy* 15, no.2: 387–416.

Schoepfer, Andrea, Stephanie Carmichael, and Nicole Leeper Piquero. 2007. "Do Perceptions of Punishment Vary between White-Collar and Street Crimes?" *Journal of Criminal Justice* 35, no.2: 151–63. doi:10.1016/j.jcrimjus.2007.01.003.

Scholz, John T. 1984. "Reliability, Responsiveness, and Regulatory Policy." *Public Administration Review* 44, no.2: 145–53.

Short, Jodi L., and Michael W. Toffel. 2010. "Making Self-Regulation More than Merely Symbolic: The Critical Role of the Legal Environment." *Administrative Science Quarterly* 55, no.3: 361–96.

Shover, N., and A. Hochstetler. 2005. *Choosing White-Collar Crime*. Cambridge: Cambridge University Press.

Simester, Andrew P., and Andreas von Hirsch. 2011. *Crimes, Harms, and Wrongs: On the Principles of Criminalisation*. London: Bloomsbury Publishing.

Simpson, Sally S. 2002. *Corporate Crime, Law, and Social Control*. Cambridge: Cambridge University Press.

Simpson, Sally S., and Christopher S. Koper. 1992. "Deterring Corporate Crime." *Criminology* 30, no.3: 347–76.

Simpson, Sally S., Carole Gibbs, Melissa Rorie, Lee A. Slocum, Mark A. Cohen, and Michael Vandenbergh. 2013. "An Empirical Assessment of Corporate Environmental Crime-Control Strategies." *Journal of Criminal Law and Criminology* 103: 231–78.

Simpson, Sally S., Melissa Rorie, Mariel E. Alper, Natalie Schell-Busey, William Laufer, and N. Craig Smith. 2014. "Corporate Crime Deterrence: A Systematic Review." *Campbell Systematic Reviews* 10, no.4.

Sinclair, Darren. 1997. "Self-Regulation versus Command and Control? Beyond False Dichotomies." *Law & Policy* 19, no.4: 529–59.

Smith, N. Craig, Sally S. Simpson, and Chun-Yao Huang. 2007. "Why Managers Fail to Do the Right Thing: An Empirical Study of Unethical and Illegal Conduct." *Business Ethics Quarterly* 17, no.4: 633–67.

Steinzor, Rena. 2014. *Why Not Jail? Industrial Catastrophes, Corporate Malfeasance, and Government Inaction*. Cambridge: Cambridge University Press.

Stretesky, Paul B., Michaela A. Long, and Michael J. Lynch. 2013. "Does Environmental Enforcement Slow the Treadmill of Production? The Relationship between Large Monetary Penalties, Ecological Disorganization and Toxic Releases within Offending Corporations." *Journal of Crime and Justice* 36, no.2: 233–47.

Sutherland, Edwin H. 1945. "Is 'White Collar Crime' Crime?" *American Sociological Review* 10, no.2: 132–9.

Szott-Moohr, Geraldine S. 2003. "An Enron Lesson: The Modest Role of Criminal Law in Preventing Corporate Crime." *Florida Law Review* 55: 937.

2007. "On the Prospects of Deterring Corporate Crime." *Journal of Business and Technology Law* 2: 25.

Titus, Richard M. 2001. "Personal Fraud and Its Victims." In *Crimes of Privilege: Readings in White-Collar Crime*, edited by N. Shover and J. P. Wright, 57–66. New York: Oxford University Press.

Tompa, Emile, Christina Kalcevich, Michael Foley, Chris McLeod, Sheilah Hogg-Johnson, Kim Cullen, Ellen MacEachen et al. 2016. "A Systematic Literature Review of the Effectiveness of Occupational Health and Safety Regulatory Enforcement." *American Journal of Industrial Medicine* 59, no.11: 919–33.

Tyler, Tom R. 2006. *Why People Obey the Law*. Princeton, NJ: Princeton University Press.

2009. "Self-Regulatory Approaches to White-Collar Crime: The Importance of Legitimacy and Procedural Justice." In *The Criminology of White-Collar Crime*, edited by S. S. Simpson and D. Weisburd, 195–216. New York: Springer New York.

van Wingerde, K. 2015. "The Limits of Environmental Regulation in a Globalized Economy." In *The Routledge Handbook of White-Collar and Corporate Crime in Europe*, edited by J. van Erp, W. Huisman, and G. Vande Walle. Abingdon, UK/New York: Routledge.

Walburg, Christian. 2015. "The Measurement of Corporate Crime: An Exercise in Futility?" In *Routledge Handbook of White-Collar and Corporate Crime in Europe*, edited by Judith van Erp, Wim Huisman, and Gudrun Vande Walle. Abingdon, UK/New York: Routledge.

Waples, Ethan P., Alison L. Antes, Stephen T. Murphy, Shane Connelly, and Michael D. Mumford. 2009. "A Meta-analytic Investigation of Business Ethics Instruction." *Journal of Business Ethics* 87, no.1: 133–51.

Weisburd, David, Elin Waring, and Ellen Chayet. 1995. "Specific Deterrence in a Sample of Offenders Convicted of White-Collar Crimes." *Criminology* 33, no.4: 587–607. doi:10.1111/j.1745-9125.1995.tb01191.x.

Wheeler, S., K. Mann, and A. Sarat. 1988. *Sitting in Judgment: The Sentencing of White-Collar Criminals*. New Haven, CT: Yale University Press.

White, Rob. 2017. "Reparative Justice, Environmental Crime and Penalties for the Powerful." *Crime, Law and Social Change* 67, no.2: 117–32.

Williams, Kirk R., and Richard Hawkins. 1986. "Perceptual Research on General Deterrence: A Critical Review." *Law & Society Review* 20: 545.

Yale Law Journal Editorial Board. 1948. "The Statutory Injunction as an Enforcement Weapon of Federal Agencies." *Yale Law Journal* 57: 1023.

Yeager, Peter Cleary. 2016. "The Elusive Deterrence of Corporate Crime." *Criminology & Public Policy* 15: 439.

Yoder, Stephen A. 1978. "Criminal Sanctions for Corporate Illegality." *Journal of Criminal Law and Criminology* 69, no. 1: 40–58.

18

Deterrence Perceptions

Robert J. Apel

Abstract: The perceptual features of criminal penalties are crucial to their capacity to deter, at least in theory. This chapter devotes attention to the accuracy of people's perceptions about criminal penalties. The empirical findings from so-called perceptual calibration studies are summarized, focused on people's understanding of the statutory applicability of criminal sanctions, as well as the certainty and severity of punishments applied in practice. While the average citizen is reasonably well informed about what criminal penalties are statutorily allowed, he or she does a poor job estimating the probability and magnitude of the penalties. On the other hand, studies which inquire about more common offenses (alcohol and marijuana use) from more crime-prone populations (young people, offenders) reveal that perceptions are consistently better calibrated to actual punishments.

18.1 INTRODUCTION

Criminology is a discipline that is uniquely concerned with the nature of the decision-making which underlies law-violating behavior. One prominent subfield inquires as to how people perceive the consequences of illegal behavior – its rewards but especially its legal risks (e.g., fine, arrest, prosecution) – and how these perceptions shape their choices about participation in illegal behavior relative to legal courses of action. Perceptions are therefore a central feature of modern crime decision-making models, with deterrence as the practical aim of many (but by no means all) criminal justice policies. Indeed, Nagin (1998:18) observes that "behavior is immune to policy manipulation" to the degree that there is no consistent link between policy and perceptions.

Interest in crime as choice, and in the prospect of deterring criminal choices in favor of noncriminal ones (or less seriously criminal ones, at the very least), is as old as the discipline of criminology, with its intellectual roots in the Age of Enlightenment. Cesare Beccaria's (1764) short treatise *On Crimes and Punishments* represents the first comprehensive treatment based on a set of more or less coherent principles of deterrence. The purpose of punishment (and, in particular, the law prescribing it), according to Beccaria, is to prevent a criminal from inflicting new injuries, as well as to prevent others from similar acts – what are today known as specific deterrence and general deterrence, respectively. Deterrence is best achieved when punishment makes a lasting impression on people's minds. A stronger such impression follows from punishment which is *promptly administered after the fact* (to strengthen relations of cause [crime] and effect [punishment] in a person's mind); punishment which is *delivered with a high degree of certainty* (the sign of the inevitability of punishment); and punishment which is *proportionate in severity to the nature of the offense* (an "excess of evil" whereby the pain inflicted from punishment just exceeds the advantage derived from crime). While Beccaria references other important properties of punishment (e.g., clarity, publicity, necessity, legitimacy, modifiability), these three properties of celerity, certainty, and severity constitute the cornerstone concepts in the theory and practice of criminal deterrence.

This chapter begins with a brief overview of rational choice, which is the predominant model of crime decision-making. It then turns to a review of research on the accuracy of people's perceptions of the certainty and severity of criminal penalties. To accomplish these objectives, I draw heavily from an earlier review (Apel 2013), which interested readers may consult for more detailed information.

18.2 ROLE OF SANCTION PERCEPTIONS IN CRIME DECISION-MAKING

Crime decision-making involves forming expectations about the future, which concern potential rewards (benefits, incentives) as well as potential punishments (costs, disincentives). Because these outcomes are uncertain, crime decisions also entail the corresponding probabilities of these rewards and punishments. A person therefore chooses to commit crime when the expected returns from illegal behavior, discounted by punishment risk, exceed the expected returns from law-abiding behavior such as legitimate employment (Becker 1968). These considerations give rise to the basic rational choice model of criminal behavior rooted in *expected utility*:

$$E(C) = (1 - \pi) \times \text{U(Reward)} - \pi \times \text{U(Punishment)} \times \delta$$

In this model, U(·) represents an individual's *utility function*, which refers to the (un) happiness or overall (dis)satisfaction that he or she achieves from a particular outcome. The rewards encompass the monetized benefits from the successful commission of a crime, including the "loot" but also the psychic benefits (e.g., thrill) as well as the reputational gains (e.g., peer approval). The punishments refer to the monetized costs of crime commission, for example, fines and lost wages due to court appearances but also psychic costs (e.g., shame), injury, and reputational losses. These collectively represent the disutility of crime. The probability parameter, π, denotes the likelihood that the individual will be caught and punished for the crime. The discount parameter, δ, devalues the disutility of crime as a function of the length of time that would elapse before punishment could be realized. A particular crime is therefore said to be deterred when the probability of punishment (i.e., punishment certainty), the magnitude of punishment (i.e., sentence severity), or the immediacy of punishment (i.e., punishment celerity) lowers the expected utility of that crime relative to the expected utility of noncriminal or less seriously criminal courses of action.

Implicit in the expected utility model is an assumption known as rational expectations, which requires that individuals contemplating a crime possess complete information about sanction risk such that, for example, π is objectively known. On the other hand, *subjective expected utility* allows individuals to have a subjective probability distribution, and the model substitutes an estimate in place of π, usually the expected value of the distribution (Piliavin et al. 1986). It therefore need not be the case that every person possesses objectively correct knowledge of punishment probabilities and magnitudes – merely the average person.

Perceptions about punishment are therefore critical components of the rational choice model. Criminologists regard deterrence, fundamentally, as a process of information transmission intended to discourage law violation, because it entails communicating the sanctions that will potentially ensue if individuals fail to conform to proscribed behavior (Geerken and Gove 1975; Gibbs 1975). Theoretical discourse about criminal deterrence therefore acknowledges that risk perceptions are an important intermediate link between sanctions and behavior (Nagin 1998; Waldo and Chiricos 1972), and that the success or failure of deterrence theory and deterrence-based policies hinge on the accuracy of those perceptions. It is to this question that the next section turns.

18.3 REVIEW OF RESEARCH FINDINGS ON PERCEPTUAL CALIBRATION

The *calibration study* is a description coined by Manski (2004) to characterize a design in which probabilistic expectations about events or eventualities are compared to objective outcomes. For example, subjective expectations with respect to job insecurity, income, investments, and voting behavior align to a respectable degree when those expectations can be calibrated against actual outcomes (Manski 2004). In criminology, a calibration study seeks to determine whether individual perceptions of the certainty and severity of criminal sanctions (e.g., the probability of arrest) are grounded in punishment actualities.

18.3.1 *How Accurate Are People's Perceptions of Penalties for Serious Street Crime?*

In the first study of its kind, the California State Assembly commissioned a study of the deterrent effectiveness of criminal penalties (Committee on Criminal Procedure 1968). The study explored how knowledgeable survey respondents were about statutory penalties for six criminal offenses – assault with a deadly weapon, second-degree burglary, first-degree robbery, forcible rape, joy riding, and fraudulent check writing. Across all offenses, the percentage of respondents who correctly identified the maximum penalty was only about 27 percent. The worst calibration was attained by noninstitutionalized adults (22 percent), while the best calibration was attained by institutionalized adults (62 percent). Interestingly, between 21 and 28 percent of noninstitutionalized adults did not feel knowledgeable enough to provide a maximum sentence at all. Among those who did but did so incorrectly, however, the predominant tendency was to underestimate the statutory maximum.

The committee also inquired about public knowledge concerning legislative activity for three offenses whose penalties had recently increased (rape, robbery, burglary), as well as two offenses whose penalties had not changed (marijuana possession, driving under the influence). The percentage of respondents who answered correctly about whether or not the penalties had recently changed was 28 percent. Again, the most knowledgeable subjects were institutionalized adults, among whom 52 percent responded correctly. Additionally, between 35 and 49 percent of noninstitutionalized adults reported that they did not know whether the legislature had acted on these offenses. Among those who responded and did so incorrectly, the universal pattern was to report that the severity of the penalty had decreased, contrary to reality. And among those who correctly responded that the penalty had increased, the overwhelming tendency was to understate the magnitude of the statutory change. Taking these findings into consideration, the committee's conclusion concerning recent legislative changes was uncharacteristically blunt: "While the Legislature had supposedly responded to public appeal and increased the penalties for crime of violence to victims, this was not known by the public" (Committee on Criminal Procedure 1968:14).

In a 1974 survey of Tucson residents, Erickson and Gibbs (1978) obtained self-reported estimates of the number of suspects arrested out of the last 100 offenses committed – a measure of perceived arrest certainty. The correlation of perceived arrest certainty with the actual arrest rate (number of arrests per 100,000 population) was 0.82, while its correlation with the clearance rate (proportion of crimes recorded that are cleared by arrest) was 0.55. Close inspection also revealed that perceived arrest certainty was systematically underestimated for crimes of an interpersonal and violent nature (e.g., homicide, rape, aggravated assault), whereas it was systematically overestimated for crimes that either do not involve face-to-face confrontation (e.g., burglary, grand theft, vehicle theft, petty theft) or largely involve face-to-face confrontation between strangers (e.g., unarmed robbery). Viewed differently, the perceived arrest certainty of offenses with a comparatively high clearance rate tended to be underestimated, while the perceived arrest certainty of offenses with a comparatively low clearance rate tended to be overestimated.

Williams et al. (1980) analyzed the Tucson data to study the calibration of perceived applicability of specific punishments to their statutory applicability (e.g., fine, probation, jail, prison, death penalty) for nineteen criminal offenses. They found that respondent perceptions were respectably accurate concerning the allowable criminal penalties for all but imprisonment. They also found that the perceived statutory maximum penalty overwhelmingly underestimated the maximum penalty allowed under Arizona law (see also Williams and Gibbs 1981). One interesting set of findings stemmed from a consideration of the death penalty. Williams et al.'s (1980) respondents were very well informed about the (in)applicability of the death penalty for virtually all of the nineteen criminal offenses that they considered. For example, well over 90 percent of the sample correctly reported that this penalty was not statutorily applicable for seventeen of the nineteen offenses. In light of these percentages, Tucson residents appeared to be very well informed about the inapplicability of the death penalty. Surprisingly, the single offense about which respondents were wildly misinformed was first-degree murder – the universal offense for which the death penalty is statutorily allowed in those states that have not abolished it, Arizona included. Only 20 percent of respondents accurately reported that the death penalty was statutorily allowed in cases of first-degree murder.

This last result is most surprising in light of the historical circumstances in which Williams et al. (1980) carried out their study. The surveys were conducted in 1974, during an era in which the US Supreme Court had been actively ruling on the constitutionality of the death penalty. In fact, it was during this time that the Court had issued a moratorium on the death penalty while procedural challenges were working their way through the lower courts (1972–6). Instead of being well informed in light of the legal activity surrounding this penalty, it is quite possible that respondents were simply confused. In any case, it serves as a caution against taking for granted how well calibrated the typical individual's perceptions are to the most severe penalty allowed under the law, even one that routinely receives publicity on the occasions in which sentences are handed down and executions are carried out.

Kleck et al. (2005) conducted a telephone survey in 1998 to inquire about perceptions of criminal punishment for four serious criminal offenses (homicide, robbery, burglary, aggravated assault). In their survey, they were able to operationalize perceived certainty (number of arrests per 100 offenses known to police, number of adults convicted per 100 arrests) and perceived severity (number of adults sentenced to prison per 100 convictions, maximum sentence imposed), and then merged county-level measures of objective punishments. Perceived certainty for homicide and assault systematically underestimated objective certainty, whereas perceived certainty for robbery and burglary overestimated objective certainty. Perceived severity, on the other hand, was consistently underestimated for all offenses, and considerably so.

18.3.2 *How Accurate Are People's Perceptions of Penalties for Drunk Driving?*

Ross (1973) reported on perceptions of the British Road Safety Act (BRSA) of 1967. The BRSA included a number of provisions: adoption of a fixed blood alcohol level, a required field breath test upon reasonable suspicion of drunkenness, and equivalent penalties as a failed test if a driver refused to submit upon request (e.g., loss of driver's license, arrest). In addition to widespread publicity generated by legislative deliberation, the British government embarked on a large-scale campaign to inform the public about the provisions of the BRSA, utilizing newspaper and television announcements as well as dissemination of brochures. A public opinion survey conducted before and after the law's passage indicated that the percentage of respondents who were aware of the blood alcohol limit increased from 22 to 39 percent. In the post-BRSA survey, well over 90 percent knew that a breath test was the basis for prosecution, and that refusal of a breath test could lead to arrest.

Grube and Kearney (1983) evaluated the Yakima (WA) Drinking and Driving Project, which in 1979 called for a mandatory two-day jail sentence for all individuals convicted of drinking and driving, and, like the BRSA, coincided with a large-scale public awareness campaign. Retrospective perceptions were collected in a telephone survey of licensed drivers, 60 percent of whom reported that they were aware of the new drunk driving policy and correctly identified the sanction as a mandatory jail sentence. The investigators also found that awareness of the policy was 68 percent among respondents who drank alcohol, compared to 44 percent among those who did not drink.

Ross and Voas (1990) evaluated the perceptual and behavioral impact of a strict sentencing policy adopted by a newly appointed judge in New Philadelphia, OH, for individuals convicted of drunk driving. The policy mandated a fifteen-day jail sentence accompanied by heavy fines and license revocation. Traffic surveys conducted in New Philadelphia and a city of similar size and composition under the jurisdiction of a different court indicated higher perceived certainty and severity of punishment for drunk driving, as intended. Specifically, New Philadelphia drivers perceived a higher chance of arrest for driving while over the legal limit (e.g., 64 vs. 57 percent reported a one in ten chance or higher). New Philadelphia drivers also perceived a higher likelihood of other penalties, including fines, loss of license, and being jailed.

18.3.3 *How Accurate Are People's Perceptions of Penalties for Marijuana Possession?*

Johnston et al. (1981) surveyed high school seniors from the classes of 1976–80, asking them to describe the law regarding marijuana possession of one ounce or less in their state. A comparison of responses from the classes of 1976 and 1980 demonstrated that, among students residing in states that decriminalized marijuana possession in the interim, the percentage reporting a possible jail sentence declined substantially from 58 to 18 percent, while the percentage reporting a fine increased substantially from 4 to 35 percent. About 22 percent of youths in each year reported not knowing the prescribed penalty.

MacCoun et al. (2009) compared perceived penalties to statutory penalties in a nationally representative survey of households. Respondents reported whether, to their knowledge, the maximum penalty in their state for first-time possession of an ounce or less of marijuana was a fine, probation, community service, possible prison sentence, or mandatory prison sentence. Residents of states that decriminalized marijuana possession, compared to residents of states in which marijuana possession was still criminalized, reported more lenient sanctions for violation, but the actual differences were modest. For example, among residents of states with a decriminalization policy, 44 percent still reported that the maximum penalty included the possibility of a jail or prison sentence, compared to 49 percent among residents of states without a decriminalization policy. Furthermore, almost one-third of both groups reported not knowing the maximum penalty.

18.3.4 *How Accurate Are People's Perceptions of Penalties for Firearm Violation?*

Barragan et al. (2017) interviewed Los Angeles County jail detainees accused of firearm violations about their knowledge of state and local firearm and ammunition laws. The respondents indicated familiarity with general facets of gun laws, but their knowledge fell short on many of the particulars. For example, the sample was very well informed about prohibitions on possession by certain classes of individuals (namely, those with a criminal record), and moderately well informed about licensing requirements for legal possession. By comparison, the sample expressed inaccurate and incomplete knowledge of ammunition regulations, although cross-jurisdictional variability or what the authors referred to as "unevenness of the legal landscape at the local level" might have understandably limited this kind of knowledge. When the investigators probed the sample's perceptions of the legal consequences of firearm violations, on the other hand, there was very accurate knowledge of the potential charges and the likelihood and duration of incarceration, as well as the salience of one's criminal history for these determinations.

18.3.5 *Summary of Perceptual Calibration Research*

The foregoing review of calibration studies indicates that survey respondents tend to either under- or overestimate the arrest likelihood (certainty) for different kinds of criminal offense but also to consistently underestimate, by a fairly large margin, maximum penalties (severity). Yet when respondents are asked about the statutory applicability of specific criminal penalties, there tends to be somewhat stronger correspondence between perception and reality. Therefore, while the average citizen is reasonably well informed about what criminal penalties are statutorily allowed, he or she does a poor job estimating the probability and magnitude of the penalties. To be sure, criminologists are probably not much better informed about the latter, simply because the use of discretion by police officers, prosecuting attorneys, judges, and correctional officials can inject a great deal of uncertainty into punishment practices.

This review also indicates that individuals with crime and arrest experience tend to have more accurate perceptions of criminal penalties than their uninvolved peers, often substantially so. For example, the sanction perceptions of adult offenders in California were particularly well calibrated to objective sanctions, at least compared to other subgroups (Committee on Criminal Procedure 1968). MacCoun et al. (2009) showed that past-year marijuana users were mildly better informed about their state's decriminalization policy compared to nonusers. This harmonizes with other survey research indicating that perceptions of punishment risk are significantly lower among individuals with delinquent or criminal experience compared to their noncriminal peers (Claster 1967; Jensen 1969). This could indicate either that criminally involved individuals have incentives to stay informed about punishment or that experiences with crime and punishment endow one with more realistic perceptions about sanction risk. The reality is that it is probably a combination of both.

18.4 DISCUSSION AND CONCLUDING THOUGHTS

One promising finding from the review provided in the chapter derives from evaluations of changes in the legislation or enforcement of drunk driving and marijuana possession. In these studies, survey respondents more consistently demonstrate awareness of the changes, especially those that are implemented with a great deal of publicity. One possible reason for stronger correspondence between perception and reality is that these are violations which concern offenses (alcohol and marijuana use) and populations (young people) that are actually "deterrable" in the sense that many individuals are on the margin for these kinds of behavior (Pogarsky 2002; Zimring and Hawkins 1968). Yet any enthusiasm must be tempered by the fact that public knowledge of the changes is still far from universal. Furthermore, whatever correspondence exists in the immediate aftermath of a change in legislation or enforcement is likely to be eroded in the long term once individuals learn, either through trial and error (i.e., personal experience) or through word of mouth (i.e., vicarious experience), that the true likelihood of detection for any single violation is exceedingly remote (Ross 1982, 1992). Sherman (1990), reviewing a different context, suggests that police crackdowns on crime deter because of a short-term increase in the objective risk of apprehension, but this initial deterrence is subject to decay when police back off.

Experience with changes in drunk-driving legislation or enforcement also highlights two related weaknesses in deterrence-based policies. First, many sanctions concern "downstream penalties" that modify sanction severity but leave sanction certainty unchanged. This distinction is important because deterrence scholarship uniformly suggests that would-be offenders are more strongly deterred by the certainty of punishment than by its severity, not to mention that downstream penalties can be heavily discounted because of inevitable delay in implementation. Second, the inability or failure of criminal justice officials to carry through on sanction threats can undermine deterrence. It is true that drunk-driving policies tend to have short-lived deterrent effects on outcomes associated with impaired driving (e.g., alcohol-related traffic fatalities). However, evaluations also demonstrate that, while downstream penalties are often harsher, as intended, "upstream enforcement" is largely unchanged (Ross 1973). Specifically, changes in drunk-driving policies do not materially alter police behavior, and thus result in little change in the objective risk of apprehension. These two observations suggest that, even when the public is knowledgeable about criminal penalties, the perceptual features of sanctions can be significantly corroded when crime detection remains ignorable, even when the penalties conditional on apprehension are quite severe.

One thing that is clear is that scholars ought not take for granted that perceptions about criminal sanctions are strongly calibrated to punishment actualities, or that there is otherwise a strong correlation between expectations and reality (Apel 2013). In calibration studies, for example, it is not uncommon for 20–30 percent of samples to report that they simply do not know the prescribed punishments, statutory maxima, arrest rates, clearance rates, prison sentence lengths, etc. And among those who opt to guess, there can be substantial slippage between their perceptions and actual punishments. Deterrence scholars thus have their work cut out for them if their theoretical models require a large share of the public to possess "rational expectations" about punishment. It seems that the observation made by Zimring and Hawkins (1973:149) is still relevant today: "The moment of truth in the life of a potential delinquent will seldom take place in a law library."

REFERENCES

Apel, Robert. 2013. "Sanctions, Perceptions, and Crime: Implications for Criminal Deterrence." *Journal of Quantitative Criminology* 29:67–101.

Barragan, Melissa, Kelsie Y. Chesnut, Jason Gravel, Natalie A. Pifer, Keramet Reiter, Nicole Sherman, and George Tita. 2017. "Prohibited Possessors and the Law: How Inmates in Los Angeles Jails Understand Firearm and Ammunition Regulations." *Russell Sage Foundation Journal of the Social Sciences* 3:141–63.

Beccaria, Cesare. [1764] 1963. *On Crimes and Punishments*. Translated by Henry Paolucci. New York: Macmillan.

Becker, Gary S. 1968. "Crime and Punishment: An Economic Approach. *Journal of Political Economy* 76: 169–217.

Claster, Daniel S. 1967. "Comparison of Risk Perception between Delinquents and Non-delinquents." *Journal of Criminal Law and Criminology* 58:80–6.

Committee on Criminal Procedure. 1968. *Deterrent Effects of Criminal Sanctions*. Sacramento: Assembly of the State of California.

Erickson, Maynard L., and Jack P. Gibbs. 1978. "Objective and Perceptual Properties of Legal Punishment and the Deterrence Doctrine." *Social Problems* 25:253–64.

Geerken, Michael R., and Walter R. Gove. 1975. "Deterrence: Some Theoretical Considerations." *Law and Society Review* 9:497–513.

Gibbs, Jack P. 1975. *Crime, Punishment, and Deterrence*. New York: Elsevier.

Grube, Joel W., and Kathleen A. Kearney. 1983. "A 'Mandatory' Jail Sentence for Drinking and Driving." *Evaluation Review* 7:235–46.

Jensen, Gary F. 1969. "Crime Doesn't Pay: Correlates of a Shared Misunderstanding." *Social Problems* 17:189–201.

Johnston, Lloyd D., Patrick M. O'Malley, and Jerald G. Bachman. 1981. "Cannabis Decriminalization: The Impact on Youth 1975–1980." Monitoring the Future Occasional Paper no. 13. Ann Arbor, MI: Institute for Social Research.

Kleck, Gary, Brion Sever, Spencer Li, and Marc Gertz. 2005. "The Missing Link in General Deterrence Research." *Criminology* 43:623–59.

MacCoun, Robert, Rosalie Liccardo Pacula, Jamie Chriqui, Katherine Harris, and Peter Reuter. 2009. "Do Citizens Know Whether Their State Has Decriminalized Marijuana? Assessing the Perceptual Component of Deterrence Theory." *Review of Law and Economics* 5:347–71.

Manski, Charles F. 2004. "Measuring Expectations." *Econometrica* 72:1329–76.

Nagin, Daniel S. 1998. "Criminal Deterrence Research at the Outset of the Twenty-First Century." In Michael Tonry (ed.), *Crime and Justice: A Review of Research*, vol. 23 (pp. 1–42). Chicago: University of Chicago Press.

Piliavin, Irving, Craig Thornton, Rosemary Gartner, and Ross L. Matsueda. 1986. "Crime, Deterrence, and Rational Choice." *American Sociological Review* 51:101–19.

Pogarsky, Greg. 2002. "Identifying 'Deterrable' Offenders: Implications for Research on Deterrence." *Justice Quarterly* 19:431–52.

Ross, H. Laurence. 1973. "Law, Science, and Accidents: The British Road Safety Act of 1967." *Journal of Legal Studies* 2:1–78.

1982. *Deterring the Drinking Driver: Legal Policy and Social Control*. Lexington, MA: Lexington Books.

1992. *Confronting Drunk Driving: Social Policies for Saving Lives*. New Haven, CT: Yale University Press.

Ross, H. Laurence, and Robert B. Voas. 1990. "The New Philadelphia Story: The Effects of Severe Punishment for Drunk Driving." *Law and Policy* 12:51–79.

Sherman, Lawrence W. 1990. "Police Crackdowns: Initial and Residual Deterrence." In Michael Tonry and Norval Morris (eds.), *Crime and Justice: A Review of Research*, vol. 12 (pp. 1–48). Chicago: University of Chicago Press.
Waldo, Gordon P., and Theodore G. Chiricos. 1972. "Perceived Penal Sanction and Self-Reported Criminality: A Neglected Approach to Deterrence Research." *Social Problems* 19:522–40.
Williams, Kirk R., and Jack P. Gibbs. 1981. "Deterrence and Knowledge of Statutory Penalties." *Sociological Quarterly* 22:591–606.
Williams, Kirk R., Jack P. Gibbs, and Maynard L. Erickson. 1980. "Public Knowledge of Statutory Penalties: The Extent and Basis of Accurate Perception." *Pacific Sociological Review* 23:105–28.
Zimring, Frank, and Gordon Hawkins. 1968. "Deterrence and Marginal Groups." *Journal of Research in Crime and Delinquency* 2:100–14.
Zimring, Franklin E., and Gordon J. Hawkins. 1973. *Deterrence: The Legal Threat in Crime Control*. Chicago: University of Chicago Press.

19

Reputational Effects of Noncompliance with Financial Market Regulations

Douglas Cumming, Robert Dannhauser, and Sofia Johan

Abstract: This chapter reviews recent research on the reputational consequences of different forms of financial market misconduct and potential agency conflicts and the impact of regulating financial market misconduct. We examine regulatory responses to financial market misconduct and highlight the presence of complementarities in financial market misconduct regulation and enforcement. We feature papers that make use of natural experiments, rule changes, and market design changes. Further, the interdisciplinary nature of financial market misconduct research is highlighted, and potential avenues for future research are discussed.

19.1 INTRODUCTION

Financial market misconduct and potential agency conflicts come in many forms. Insider trading (trading on material nonpublic information), financial restatements, and options backdating are some of the more common forms of misconduct. But the scope of misconduct is much wider, and includes various other types of manipulative trading. For instance, there is a variety of specific forms of insider trading other than insider tipping such as front-running (brokers trading on the information in and in advance of a client's trade), violation of client precedence, and trading ahead of research reports. There is a variety of forms of price manipulation, including marking the open, marking the close, portfolio pumping with misleading end of the month/quarter/year trades designed to influence marks to market, intraday ramping/gouging, market setting, prearranged trades, influencing or rewarding the employees of others, intimidation/coordination, and domination and control of market segments. Apart from price manipulation, volume can be manipulated through churning and wash trades. Further, market manipulators may engage in spoofing, which includes giving up priority, switches, and layering of bids/asks. Financial misconduct also encompasses false disclosure, which includes the dissemination of false and misleading information, and parking/warehousing (hiding the true ownership of securities). Other types of misconduct include broker-agency relationships such as improper trade through, improper execution, improper member use of exchange name, improper sales materials and telemarketing, and improper dealing with customers. Financial misconduct further includes numerous classes of agency problems, including, for example, conflicts of interest among investment banks in taking firms public, and more broadly a variety of conflicts between equity holders and bond holders. Lawsuits may mitigate the effect of some of these conflicts, but at other times they may exacerbate some of these conflicts.

Financial market misconduct is not merely an interesting scholarly area of study; it is also one with meaningful practical industry and public policy implications. Dyck, Morse, and Zingales (2010, 2014) and Karpoff, Lee, and Martin (2008a) show that fraud costs firms 20–38 percent of a firm's value, which aggregates to hundreds of billions in lost value per year in the USA. Dyck, Morse, and Zingales (2010, 2014) expect that up to 14 percent of firms engage in fraud. Cumming and Johan (2013a) report Securities and Exchange Commission (SEC) investigations among 2–5 percent of listed companies per year in the USA. A broad cross-section of investment practitioners surveyed by the CFA Institute (2014) cite market fraud the integrity of financial reporting, and mis-selling as significant ethical issues facing global markets. Financial market misconduct is therefore widely recognized as being both common and costly; hence, it is an important scholarly area of research in corporate governance and corporate finance, as well as microstructure, law and finance, and a number of related interdisciplinary fields.

The purpose of this chapter is to review recent research on the causes and consequence of different forms of financial market misconduct, and the impact of regulating financial market misconduct, and to suggest future directions of research. The review highlights the importance of papers that make use of natural experiments, rule changes, and market design changes to study the causes and consequences of financial market misconduct. Some insights drawn from the review include evidence that there are complementarities in different forms of manipulation, and evidence that there are complementarities in the regulation of different forms of manipulation. Further, the interdisciplinary nature of financial market misconduct research is highlighted herein, and we discuss how the array of interdisciplinary angles offers many interesting avenues for future financial market misconduct scholars.

This chapter proceeds as follows. Section 19.2 describes research on the presence and determinants of financial market misconduct. Section 19.3 reviews the consequences of financial market misconduct. Section 19.4 presents research on the regulation of financial market misconduct. Section 19.5 discusses interdisciplinary approaches to financial market misconduct work and offers suggestions for future research. Concluding remarks follow in Section 19.6.

19.2 THE PRESENCE AND CAUSES OF MARKET MISCONDUCT

19.2.1 *The Presence of Market Misconduct*

What constitutes financial market misconduct? Insider trading, accounting fraud, and dissemination of false information are commonly understood forms of misconduct. But there are many other types of misconduct that compromise the integrity of markets and that are formally banned in many countries and exchanges around the world (see Table 19.1, and Cumming, Johan, and Li, 2011). Authorities commonly use computer surveillance algorithms to search for this type of misconduct (Cumming and Johan, 2008).

It has long been understood that uninformed speculators/manipulators can make profits from insider trading or the release of false information, as long as other investors attach a positive probability to the manipulator being an informed trader (Allen and Gale, 1992). In equilibrium, therefore, we expect a positive amount of manipulation (Allen and Gorton, 1992). Early empirical work has established that there is significant stock-price run-up and an increase in trading volume before takeover bids (Jarrell and Poulsen, 1989). But the pre-announcement run-up is largely, but not exclusively, attributable to insider trading

TABLE 19.1 *Types of financial market misconduct*

Type of manipulation	Explanation
Insider trading	
Insider trading (general)	Trading on material nonpublic information.
Front-running	Buying/selling in a period shortly prior to significant buying/selling by a client.
Client precedence	Violating the time priority of client orders.
Trading ahead of research reports	Brokers with proprietary access to research reports trading ahead of the release of those reports.
Price manipulation	
Marking the open	Purchase orders at slightly higher prices or sale orders at lower prices to drive up/suppress the price of the securities when the market opens.
Marking the close	Buying/selling securities at the close of the market in an effort to alter the securities' closing price.
Misleading end of the month/ quarter/year trades	Executing transactions on a particular date to establish gains/losses or conceal portfolio losses/true positions in connection with end of the month/quarter/year.
Intraday ramping/gouging	Executing a series of trades over a short time period to generate unusual price movement over that period, given the trading history of the security.
Market setting	Market setting by crossing in the short term, high or low, e.g., to set the VWAP (volume weighted average price) or cross market (setting the price in one market to justify crossing in the follow-on market).
Prearranged trades	Prearranging trades within an extremely short time period where the client broker and another broker enter a bid and ask for the same volume and price, which then generates a trade between the two brokers for the whole of the volume. The volume of the order must be significant given the trading history of the security.
Domination and control	A broker/client generates significantly greater price changes in a security, possibly for corners (securing control of the bid/ demand-side of both the derivative and the underlying asset, so that the dominant position can be exploited to manipulate the price of the derivative and/or the asset), squeezes (taking advantage of a shortage in an asset by controlling the demand-side and exploiting market congestion during such shortages in such a way as to create artificial prices), or mini-manipulations (trading in the underlying security of an option in order to manipulate its price so that the options will become in-the-money).
Volume manipulation	
Churning	Explicitly prohibit excessive buying/selling of stocks by a trader such as a broker in order to generate large commission fees (in the case of churning client accounts) and/or the appearance of significant volume (in the case of churning house accounts and/or churning client accounts).
Wash trade	The same client reference on both sides of a trade.

(*continued*)

Spoofing rules	
Giving up priority	Brokers giving up priority, such as entering a bid/ask for a significant quantity at a price away from priority, then canceling this order as it approaches priority and re-entering the order shortly thereafter at a price level further away from priority.
Switch	Brokers entering fictitious orders, such as entering a significant quantity at or close to priority, then completing a trade on the opposite side of the market and thereafter deleting the original order shortly after the completion of the opposite order.
Layering of bids/asks	Brokers layering bids/asks, such as stagger orders from the same client reference at different price and volume levels, with the intent of giving a false or misleading appearance with respect to the market for the security.
False disclosure	
Dissemination of false and misleading information	A dummy variable equal to one if the trading rules explicitly prohibit the dissemination of false or misleading market information.
Parking or warehousing	A dummy variable equal to one if the trading rules explicitly prohibit hiding the true ownership of securities by creating a set of fictitious transactions and trades.
Broker-agency	
Trade through	Completing a client's order at a price inferior to the best posted bid or ask; e.g., the market maker who received the order is unable or unwilling to fill it at the best posted bid/ask price, so the trade is instead executed at the market maker's price.
Improper execution	Brokers charging fees for completing a client order which are unwarranted given the circumstances.
Restrictions on sales materials and telemarketing	Restrictions on exchange members' nature of sales and telemarketing.
Fair dealing with customers	The "know your client rule" requires brokerages not to make trades that do not fit within their clients' interests, not to delay the handling of client orders, and the like.
Influencing or rewarding employees of others	Relates to any means of influencing/rewarding employees of other members/member companies.
Anti-intimidation/coordination	Relates to any form of intimidation of or coordination with other members/member companies.

Sources: Cumming and Johan (2008); Cumming, Johan, and Li (2011).

(Meulbroek, 1992). It is difficult to sort out whether pre-announcement run-up is attributable to rational anticipation or to insider trading. King (2009) argues that insider trading is consistent with large abnormal turnover and abnormal returns on days when insiders are active, and there is limited reaction to the announcement due to the price discovery ahead of the announcement; market anticipation, by contrast, is consistent with abnormal trading ahead of returns with rising serial correlation closer to the announcement date, and a significant market reaction upon announcement. Cumming and Li (2011) further distinguish between abnormal returns and market anticipation by examining the number of acquisitions previously made by firms (firms with a history of takeovers are more likely to be in the market again), and toehold positions (toeholds are potentially signaling a future takeover). Cumming and Johan (2008) explain that, in practice, surveillance authorities look for patterns of activity that are otherwise difficult to explain by the manipulator. With a one-off manipulation, the manipulator likely has an alternative plausible explanation (or "APE," as it is often called in industry).

How often is financial market misconduct observed? Dyck, Morse, and Zingales (2010, 2014) estimate that on average one out of seven large publicly traded US firms engages in fraud, and destroys on average one-fifth of its value, giving rise to an estimated average cost of fraud in large corporations of $380 billion per year. Karpoff, Lee, and Martin (2008a) show that firms lose on average 38 percent of their value as a reputational penalty when fraud is revealed, well over 7.5 times the sum of all penalties imposed through the legal and regulatory system. Cumming and Johan (2013a) show that in the USA, detected fraud rates differ substantially by exchange, and yet investors have no way of discerning the different frequencies of fraud on each exchange's listings since there is no document available to investors that compares fraud cases on the New York Stock Exchange (NYSE) versus NASDAQ or other exchanges around the world.[1] Fraud litigation cases per year on average represent 1.9 percent of NYSE listings, but 4.5 percent of NASDAQ listings and 5.1 percent of Pink Sheet listings (see Table 19.2). Financial fraud, insider trading, and improper trading are more often litigated (relative to the number of listed companies) on NASDAQ than NYSE and the Pink Sheets. Pink Sheets, by contrast, are more often associated with illegal distributions and delinquencies in filing periodic reports with the Commission. Financial fraud cases involve reputational penalties on average amounting to 38 percent of a stock's value (Karpoff, Lee, and Martin, 2008b). The differences in the frequency of fraud across NYSE and NASDAQ thereby imply an expected cost of 3.2 percent of the value of a NASDAQ listing and 0.8 percent of the value of a NYSE listing. These costs are not trivial. Because fraud statistics are rarely reported by exchange (as far as we are aware, Cumming and Johan, 2013a, is the only source), investors do not have the opportunity to consider how differences in fraud across the listing exchange may affect their investment and/or pricing decisions.

In contrast to the USA, all types of detected fraud cases involving Toronto Stock Exchange (TSX) companies represent on average 0.3 percent of TSX listings and only 0.1 percent of TSX-V listings. In the UK, all types of detected fraud cases involving London Stock Exchange (LSE) companies represent 0.4 percent of LSE listings and 0.1 percent of AIM listings. Litigated frauds involving private (non-listed) companies sum to 2.2 percent of the total number of listed companies in Canada per year and 2.0 percent of the total number of listed companies in the UK per year. There is scant evidence that we are aware of on detected frauds by exchange from other countries around the world, with a few isolated exceptions. In China, detected fraud comprises 3.8 percent of listed companies per year. Brazil completed its first insider trading case ever in 2011. And the now defunct junior stock market in Germany, the Neur Markt, had merely four confirmed cases of fraud and twenty-five documented rumors of suspected fraud in its brief history.

19.2.2 *The Determinants of Financial Market Misconduct*

The determinants of financial market misconduct are best understood at a general level from the lens of Becker's (1968) economic model of crime: commit a crime if the expected benefits

[1] The detected fraud statistics in Table 19.2 are litigated cases. These statistics are not the proven cases with judgments. See Cumming and Johan (2013a) for further details.

TABLE 19.2 *Detected fraud in Canada, the United Kingdom, and the United States*

	Av. no. listed firms	Total cases January 2005 – June 2011		Financial fraud		Other fraudulent misrepre-sentation and disclosure		Illegal distribution		Bribery		Pump and dump		Wash / matched / improper trade / marking the close		Insider trading		Delinquent in its periodic filings with the Commission	
		#	%	#	%	#	%	#	%	#	%	#	%	#	%	#	%	#	%
(1) NYSE	2392	290	12.12	48	2.01	31	1.30	34	1.42	15	0.63	12	0.50	47	1.96	98	4.10	5	0.21
(2) NASDAQ	2953	867	29.36	230	7.79	142	4.81	47	1.59	13	0.44	31	1.05	82	2.78	301	10.19	21	0.71
(3) Pink Sheets	5667	1880	33.17	159	2.81	212	3.74	178	3.14	0	0.00	151	2.66	20	0.35	12	0.21	1148	20.26
(4) TSX	1560	33	2.12	6	0.38	23	1.47	3	0.19	0	0.00	0	0.00	0	0.00	1	0.06	0	0.00
(5) TSX-V	2333	15	0.64	4	0.17	2	0.09	9	0.39	0	0.00	0	0.00	0	0.00	0	0.00	0	0.00
(6) LSE	1549	40	2.58	4	0.26	11	0.71	6	0.39	0	0.00	4	0.26	5	0.32	8	0.52	2	0.13
(7) AIM	1452	9	0.62	0	0.00	1	0.07	0	0.00	0	0.00	0	0.00	1	0.07	7	0.48	0	0.00
(8) Private – US	5345	95	1.78	19	0.36	36	0.67	18	0.34	0	0.00	7	0.13	7	0.13	6	0.11	2	0.04
(9) Private – Can	3893	567	14.56	28	0.72	136	3.49	379	9.74	0	0.00	1	0.03	19	0.49	4	0.10	0	0.00
(10) Private – UK	3001	390	13.00	86	2.87	138	4.60	85	2.83	0	0.00	7	0.23	17	0.57	39	1.30	18	0.60

This table presents the number of listed firms on the NYSE, NASDAQ, Pink Sheets (including OTC and gray market stocks), TSX, TSX-V, LSE, and AIM, as well as the number of litigated securities cases in each jurisdiction, categorized into eight different types of fraud. "Private" cases in the USA comprise all cases where a fraud was carried out by a private company against an unidentified listed public company. "Private" cases in Canada and the UK comprise all cases where a fraud was carried out by a private company against an unidentified publicly listed company or private company. The data cover the years January 2005 to June 2011.
Source: Cumming and Johan (2013a).

exceed the costs.[2] There is a large and varied empirical literature on the factors that affect the expected benefits and the expected costs of committing financial market misconduct. A number of these papers are summarized in Table 19.3.

One collection of papers on the presence and determinants of financial market misconduct pertains to the opportunities to commit misconduct and the benefits from such misconduct. First, in their very interesting paper, Agrawal and Cooper (2015) show that frequently managers will engage in insider trading around the timing of accounting scandals. In other words, managers engage in a fraud that was made possible by a preexisting fraud. The benefits to the illegal misconduct with financial misreporting are heightened by the insider trading before news of the misconduct is made public. Second, a group of papers has shown that managers also engage in insider trading vis-à-vis options and equities markets. For example, insider trading often takes place in equity options prior to mergers and acquisitions (M&A) announcements (Jarrow, 1992, 1994; Augustin, Brenner, and Subrahmanyam, 2019). Trading in options and equities is often done in ways such that equity prices are manipulated to affect the value of options around the time of option expiry (Merrick, Naik, and Yadav, 2005; Ni, Pearson, and Poteshman, 2005; see also Pirrong, 1993, 1995a, 1995b). Third, there is a set of papers dealing with market manipulation in the presence of collusion. Noncompetitive pricing has been demonstrated in recent scandals such as that involving London Inter-Bank Offered Rate (LIBOR) manipulation (Gandhi et al., 2014). Atanasov, Davies, and Merrick (2015) show that collusion and noncompetitive pricing among small numbers of traders exacerbate market manipulation at the close. By contrast, factors that make markets more competitive and liquid, such as high frequency trading, mitigate the presence and severity of end-of-day manipulation (Aitken, Cumming, and Zhan, 2015b). Fourth, there are varied papers dealing with the benefits to fund management in terms of fundraising by financial misreporting, such as in the case of hedge funds (Bollen and Pool, 2009; Cumming, Dai, and Johan, 2013) and venture capital (VC) and private equity (PE) funds (Cumming and Walz, 2010).

Another collection of papers deals with internal governance factors that in some cases exacerbate and in other cases mitigate the ability to commit financial market misconduct. Internal corporate governance factors that exacerbate the potential to commit fraud pertain to managerial compensation, such as stock options which are correlated with a greater propensity of firm managers to engage in financial misreporting (Burns and Kedia, 2006). As well, in an interesting recent study, Hass, Muller, and Vergauwe (2015) show that promotion-based incentives within a firm, as proxied by the CEO pay gaps among other things, exacerbate the likelihood of fraud. Promotion-based incentives in fund management have been shown to mitigate the likelihood of fund managers making socially responsible investments (Cumming and Johan, 2013b). Internal corporate governance factors that mitigate the potential to commit fraud pertain to strong governance from the board. For example, there is work that shows that having more women on the board, which in turn reflects ethicality, diversity, risk aversion, and stronger oversight, mitigates the frequency and severity of financial market misconduct (Cumming, Leung, and Rui, 2015), even after controlling for endogeneity and propensity score matching, among other things.

2 Bhattacharya and Marshall (2012) provide evidence that insiders with greater wealth are more likely to engage in insider trading, which casts doubt on the economic motive for crime. However, strictly speaking, Becker's (1968) model of crime is based on the transaction value of a crime (probability of a benefit * value of benefit – probability of detection * cost of detection).

TABLE 19.3 *Overview of studies on the presence and causes of financial market misconduct*

Author(s)	Data source(s)	Country samples	Time period	Dependent variables	Main explanatory variables	Main findings
Jarrell and Poulsen (1989)	Securities and Exchange Commission (SEC)	526 Tender offer cases (US)	1963–86	Market activity in target stock before bids	Size, date	Significant stock-price run-up and increase in trading volume before bids. Presence of rumors in the news media as well as other legitimate sources contributes to the target's stock price run-up.
Meulbroek (1992)	Individual cases charged with insider trading by SEC	229 illegal insider trading cases related to 218 companies (US)	1980–9	Market activity in target stock before bids	Insider trading days and news days	Stock market detects the possibility of insider trading and transforms this information into stock price. Insider trading is an important contributor to the pre-announcement price run-up.
Burns and Kedia (2006)	ExecuComp; US General Accounting Office (GAO); LexisNexis	USA	1995–2001	Financial restatements and misreporting	Executive compensation	The sensitivity of the CEO's option portfolio to stock price is significantly positively related to the propensity to misreport. The sensitivity of other components of CEO compensation, i.e., equity, restricted stock, long-term incentive payouts and salary and bonus are not significantly related to the propensity to misreport. Relative to other components of compensation, stock options are associated with stronger incentives to misreport because convexity in CEO wealth introduced by stock options limits the downside risk on detection of the misreporting. Similar evidence is seen for accounting fraud (Erickson, Hanlon, and Maydew, 2006).
Bollen and Pool (2009)	Center for International Securities and Derivatives Markets (CISDM)	Many countries	1994–2005	Return discontinuity for marginally negative and marginally positive returns	Firm investment strategies, risk factors, audit periods, managerial skill	Significant discontinuity in the pooled distribution of reported hedge fund returns: the number of small gains far exceeds the number of small losses. The discontinuity is present in live funds, defunct funds, and funds of all ages, suggesting that it is not caused by database biases. The discontinuity is absent in the three months culminating in an audit, funds that invest in liquid assets, and hedge fund risk factors, suggesting that it is generated neither by the skill of managers to avoid losses nor by nonlinearities in hedge fund asset returns. A remaining explanation is that hedge fund managers avoid reporting losses to attract and retain investors.

Cumming and Walz (2010)	Center for Private Equity Research (CEPRES, Germany)	5,038 venture capital (VC) and private equity (PE)-backed companies in 39 countries	1971–2003	Severity of misreporting of unexited VC and PE returns	Country-level legal and accounting standards, various VC and PE governance proxies	Unexited VC and PE returns are severely overreported. The severity of overreporting is more pronounced in countries with worse legal and accounting standards, worse contractual governance, and among first-time fund managers who have pronounced incentives to overreport for fundraising reasons.
Dyck, Morse, and Zingales (2010)	Stanford Securities Class Action Clearinghouse (SSCAC) – and six filters applied to clean the data	USA	1996–2004	Detection of fraud	Employees, media, industry regulators (and effect of Sarbanes-Oxley (SOX))	Fraud detection does not rely on obvious actors (investors, SEC, auditors) but takes a village of several nontraditional players (employees, media, industry regulators). Having access to information or monetary rewards has a significant impact on the probability that a stakeholder will become a whistleblower. Reputational incentives in general seem to be weak, except for journalists in large cases.
Wang, Winton, and Yu (2010)	SEC's Accounting and Auditing Enforcement Releases (AAERs, www.sec.gov/litigation) and the SSCAC, http://securities.stanford.edu)	USA	1996–2007	Accounting fraud	Industry conditions, legal conditions (SOX), VC	The authors show that fraud propensity increases with the level of investor belief about industry prospects but decreases in the presence of extremely high belief (boom periods). The mechanisms at work include monitoring by investors and underwriters, and short-term executive compensation.
Cumming and Li (2011)	SDC Mergers and Acquisitions Database	736 acquisition announcements by Canadian listed companies, domestic and international public and private acquisitions	1991–2008	Market activity in acquirer stock before bids	Public versus private target, method of payment, financial variables, country variables, number of investors	Run-up Cumulative Abnormal Returns (CARs) are lower for acquisitions when the bidder has a higher Tobin's q and exhibits greater information asymmetry as measured by the standard deviation of the market model used. Run-up CARs are lower for foreign targets but higher for PE-backed private targets. For non-PE-backed acquisitions, run-up CARs are on average negative, but there is significant heterogeneity across quintiles. Finally, run-up CARs are lower for share payments, consistent with theory showing negative performance associated with signals from insiders that their equity is overvalued.

(*continued*)

TABLE 19.3 *(continued)*

Author(s)	Data source(s)	Country samples	Time period	Dependent variables	Main explanatory variables	Main findings
Yu and Yu (2011)	Senate's Office of Public Records (SOPR); Stanford Securities Class Actions Clearing House; Dyck, Morse, and Zingales (2010)	USA	1998–2004	Fraud detection	Lobbying firms versus non-lobbying firms	Compared to non-lobbying firms, firms that lobby on average have a significantly lower hazard rate of being detected for fraud, evade fraud detection 117 days longer, and are 38% less likely to be detected by regulators. Fraudulent firms on average spend 77% more on lobbying than non-fraudulent firms, and spend 29% more on lobbying during their fraud periods than during their non-fraud periods. The delay in detection allows managers to postpone the negative market reaction and to sell more of their shares.
Dyreng, Mayew, and Williams (2012)	Religious Congregations and Membership Study (RCMS); Glenmary Research Center, American Religion Data Archive (www.arda.com)	USA	1990–2008	Frequency of financial restatement	Regional-level religious adherence	Higher levels of religious adherence (for both Catholics and Protestants) in a region are associated with a lower likelihood of financial restatements.
Karpoff et al. (2012)	Karpoff, Lee, and Martin (2008a, 2008b)	USA	1988–2005	Earnings restatements, share price impacts	Short selling activity	Short sellers predict financial market misconduct and dampen the share price inflation of firms that misstate their earnings.

Chen et al. (2013)	China Center for Economic Research (CCER); China Securities Market & Accounting Research (GTA/CSMAR)	China	2001–8	Financial market misconduct	Auditors	Regarding the influence of auditors on corporate fraud in China, firms with lower-integrity executives are associated with higher propensity of regulatory enforcement actions against corporate fraud in the subsequent year. This effect is moderated by the issuance of the modified audit opinion report by the auditors. This finding implies that auditors can serve an early warning role to discourage low-integrity executives from engaging in corporate fraud.
Cumming and Johan (2013a)	SEC; Canadian Securities Association (CSA); Financial Services Authority (FSA); various other exchange data	Brazil, Canada, China, Germany, UK, USA	2005–11	Financial market misconduct (all types)	Exchange listing standards	Higher exchange listing standards in the USA (across NYSE, NASDAQ, and the Pink Sheets) are correlated with lower incidences of detected fraud. Outside the USA, such as in Canada and the UK, there is substantially less frequent detection of fraud, and the frequency of detected fraud is uncorrelated with listing standards. The authors note that fraud is never reported on an exchange-by-exchange basis, which implies that fraud risk is inefficiently priced and that capital is inefficiently allocated.
Augustin, Brenner, and Subrahmanyam (2019)	Thomson Reuters Securities Data Company Platinum Database (SDC); Center for Research in Securities Prices (CRSP) Database; OptionMetrics Database	1,859 transactions undertaken by 1,279 unique acquirers on 1,669 unique targets in the USA	1996–2012	Abnormal trading activity in equity options	News and rumors of M&A announcements	The authors document pervasive informed trading activity in equity options before M&A announcements. For targets, such activity is demonstrated by positive abnormal volumes, especially for out-of-the-money and short-dated calls, excess implied volatility, higher bid-ask spreads, and a decrease in the slope of the term structure of implied volatility. For acquirers, abnormal volume arises for at-the-money options and stock-financed deals that have a higher uncertainty of deal completion.
Dyck, Morse, and Zingales (2014)	SSCAC – and six filters applied to clean the data	USA	1996–2004	Frequency of fraud	Media, analysts, regulatory (post-SOX), various financial variables	On average one out of seven large publicly-traded US firms has engaged in fraud. This study obtains similar estimates using an alternative approach. Firms that engage in fraud destroy on average one-fifth of their value. These estimates set the average cost of fraud in large corporations to be $380 billion a year.

(continued)

TABLE 19.3 *(continued)*

Author(s)	Data source(s)	Country samples	Time period	Dependent variables	Main explanatory variables	Main findings
Gandhi, Golez, Jackwerth, and Plazzi (2014)	Bloomberg; British Bankers Association	Pooled panel of banks across four currencies (USD, GBP, JPY, and CHF)	1999–2012	LIBOR submissions	Sensitivity of banks' excess returns and risk to changes in the London Inter-Bank Offered Rate (LIBOR)	There is weak evidence that banks manipulate submissions to appear less risky, and strong evidence that banks manipulate LIBOR to generate higher cash flows.
Aitken, Cumming, and Zhan (2015b)	Capital Markets CRC; SMARTS Inc.; Thomson Reuters Datastream; Thompson Reuters Tick History	22 countries	2003–11	End-of-day price dislocation	Proxies for the start of high-frequency trading (HFT) by trade size, cancellation of orders, and co-location	The presence of HFT significantly mitigates the frequency and severity of end-of-day price dislocation. The effect of HFT is more pronounced on days when end-of-day price dislocation is more likely to be the result of market manipulation, such as on option expiry dates. Moreover, the effect of HFT is more pronounced than the role of trading rules, surveillance, enforcement, and legal conditions in curtailing the frequency and severity of end-of-day price dislocation.
Agrawal and Cooper (2015)	US GAO; SEC; CRSP	518 firms in the USA	1997–2002	Purchases, sales, and net sales of five groups of corporate insiders during the misstated period and a pre-misstated period	Firms that announce earnings-decreasing restatements	From a number of subsamples where insiders had greater incentives to sell before the revelation of accounting problems, there is strong evidence that top managers of restating firms sell substantially more stock during the misstated period.

Atanasov, Davies, and Merrick (2015)	CME DataMine; Bloomberg Financial	NYMEX (US) platinum and palladium futures contracts trades	Jul 2007–Jun 2008	Settlement price artificiality	Market-on-close trading	Fund managers manipulate platinum and palladium futures settlement prices. Traders operating in an environment with repeated interaction by a small number of participants extract significant rents from their noncompetitive pricing, and this behavior is consistent with tacit (implicit) collusion. The mechanism for determining the closing settlement price plays a central role in the overall impact of the alleged manipulation.
Bernile, Sulaeman, and Wang (2015)	Wall Street Journal's (WSJ's) "Options Backdating Scorecard" website; "Yellow Card Trend Alert: Stock-Option Backdating Scandal" report last updated by Glass, Lewis & Co.; Dow Jones News Service	3,133 unique firms, 157 of which are associated with firm-specific backdating news	Jan 2006–Dec 2007	Abnormal trading balances and abnormal trading profits	Backdating versus non-backdating firms	Unlike their inability to anticipate other corporate events, institutional investors as a group display negative abnormal trading imbalances in anticipation of firm-specific backdating exposures. Consistent with informed trading, the underlying trades earn positive abnormal short- and long-term profits. Moreover, the negative abnormal imbalances are larger in magnitude when backdating is likely a more severe issue and manifest earlier ahead of firm-specific exposures as the scope of the scandal broadens. Local institutions, in particular, display negative trading imbalances earlier in event-time and earn consistently higher trading profits than nonlocal institutions.
Black et al. (2015)	SEC; Center for Financial Reporting and Management at University of California, Berkeley	706 firms in the USA	1982–2012	Presence and duration of accounting fraud	Information in audited financial statements; presence of analysts	Information production by auditors and analysts reduces the duration of accounting fraud. The likelihood of fraud detection is significantly greater in the quarter following the issuance of audited financial statements. The presence of explanatory language in the audit report significantly strengthens the result, indicating that the content of the reports is important for reducing fraud duration. There is no evidence that Big N auditors matter for this relationship. In terms of the role of analysts, the presence of industry specialist analysts reduces the

(continued)

TABLE 19.3 *(continued)*

Author(s)	Data source(s)	Country samples	Time period	Dependent variables	Main explanatory variables	Main findings
Chen et al. (2016a)	CCER; GTA/CSMAR	China	2003–8	Share price response to fraud	Analyst coverage	The authors show a negative association between corporate fraud propensity and analyst coverage, and that this effect is more pronounced among non-state-owned enterprises (NSOEs), which are more reliant on the stock market for external funding.
Cumming, Leung, and Rui (2015)	China Securities Regulatory Commission (CSRC); China Securities Markets and Accounting Research (CSMAR)	China	2001–15	Fraud detection; cumulative abnormal returns response to fraud	Board of directors gender diversity	A more gender diverse board mitigates the frequency and severity of fraud. These effects are more pronounced in male-dominated industries.
Hass, Muller, and Vergauwe (2015)	Dyck, Morse, and Zingales (2010); SSCAC; ExecuComp; Compustat	USA	1996–2004	Fraud detection	CEO pay gap	Promotion-based incentives exacerbate the probability of fraud.
Parsons, Sulaeman, and Titman (2018)	Karpoff et al. (2012); various primary sources	USA	Not specified	Financial market misconduct	Demographic variables	Financial misconduct varies across cities and over time, and is highly correlated with corruption and variation in local enforcement. Financial misconduct is uncorrelated with economic and demographic variation, although financial misconduct is transmitted by peer effects such as a dominant industry in a city.

This table summarizes various papers that focus on the presence and causes of financial market misconduct. The main findings are largely paraphrased and/or copied from the abstracts of the papers to best and succinctly represent the authors' contributions, but they are not meant to exhaustively represent all of the findings from the papers.

A third stream of papers deals with external factors that govern the costs of committing financial market misconduct. Perhaps the most salient external factor is enforcement against misconduct, which limits incentives to engage in market misconduct (Aitken, Cumming, and Zhan, 2015a; Cumming, Knill, and Richardson, 2015). Relatedly, firms that engage in more lobbying activity are able to reduce the effect of enforcement, as there is a lower probability of detection, and there are delays with the prosecution of illegal activities for such firms (Yu and Yu, 2011). Dyck, Morse, and Zingales (2010) argue that "it takes a village" to detect fraud, and one cannot merely rely on financial regulators to catch all wrongful conduct. Other external factors include, for example, media, analysts, and auditors. Strong auditors and analysts have been shown to play an important role in mitigating the frequency and severity of fraud in China (Chen et al., 2013, 2016a), and in mitigating the presence and duration of fraud in the USA (Black et al., 2015). Short sellers can also play a strong role in the detection of fraudulent activity (Karpoff et al., 2012), as can industry and market conditions (Wang, Winton, and Yu, 2010). Institutional investors are informed traders, and their trades can predict corporate misconduct (Bernile, Sulaeman, and Wang, 2015), as they significantly profit from misconduct in both the short and the long run.

Within the set of external factors that govern financial market misconduct, there have been a few recent papers dealing with demographic variables. Two papers in this area are particularly noteworthy. Dyreng, Mayew, and Williams (2012) find that higher levels of Catholic and Protestant religious adherence in a region are associated with lower levels of financial restatements. Parsons, Sulaeman, and Titman (2018), by contrast, find that corporate misconduct is more closely linked to local corruption and enforcement, and less correlated with economic and demographic variables. Parsons, Sulaeman, and Titman (2018) also find that peer effects through dominant firms and industry play a large role in the transmission of financial market misconduct.

19.3 CONSEQUENCES OF FINANCIAL MARKET MISCONDUCT

Research on the consequences of financial market misconduct can be grouped into four types of paper, and these papers are summarized in Table 19.4. First, there are papers that examine the managerial consequences to financial market misconduct. Karpoff, Lee, and Martin (2008a) show that, among individuals identified as responsible for financial misrepresentation in the USA, 93 percent lose their jobs, 28 percent face criminal penalties, and jail sentences average 4.3 years. Bereskin, Campbell II, and Kedia (in press) show that there is a greater likelihood of CEO termination among US firms that have a culture of "doing good" as proxied by a firm's charitable giving. Aharony, Liu, and Yawson (2015) show that the likelihood of CEO turnover depends on the nature of the lawsuit against the company: contractual lawsuits are more likely to give rise to CEO turnover, unlike antitrust lawsuits, for example. Looking at management that do not face dismissal, Aharony, Liu, and Yawson (2015) show that CEO pay significantly declines.

Second, there are papers that examine financial market participation following financial market misconduct. Broadly at a country level, there is work that shows that having weak regulations and enforcement (and implicitly, based on Becker's (1968) model of crime, more financial market misconduct) is associated with lower financial market trading, lower participation, and lower economic values of firms (see, e.g., La Porta et al., 1997, 1998, 2002; La Porta, Lopez-de-Silanes, and Shleifer, 2006). At a state level, there is recent work that measures the direct participation of households in financial markets, which shows that greater

TABLE 19.4 *Overview of studies on the consequences of financial market misconduct*

Author(s)	Data source(s)	Country samples	Time period	Dependent variables (effect of financial market misconduct)	Main explanatory variables (type of financial market misconduct)	Main findings
Karpoff, Lee, and Martin (2008a)	Securities and Exchange Commission (SEC); Department of Justice (DOJ); LexisNexis	USA	1978–2006	CEO turnover, restrictions on future employment, criminal charges, jail	Cost of misconduct, fines, shareholdings, various governance variables	Among the individuals identified as responsible parties for DOJ enforcement actions for financial misrepresentation, 93% lose their jobs by the end of the regulatory enforcement period. The likelihood of ouster increases with the cost of the misconduct to shareholders and the quality of the firm's governance. A sizeable minority (28%) face criminal charges and penalties, including jail sentences that average 4.3 years.
Karpoff, Lee, and Martin (2008b)	SEC; DOJ; LexisNexis	USA	1978–2005	Abnormal returns	Legal penalties, other controls	The reputational penalty (the expected loss in the present value of future cash flows due to lower sales and higher contracting costs) is over 7.5 times the sum of all penalties imposed through the legal and regulatory system. For each dollar that a firm misleadingly inflates its market value by, on average, it loses that dollar when its misconduct is revealed, plus an additional \$3.08. Of this additional loss, \$0.36 is due to expected legal penalties and \$2.71 is due to lost reputation. In firms that survive the enforcement process, lost reputation is even greater at \$3.83. In the cross-section, the reputational penalty is positively related to measures of the firm's reliance on implicit contracts and repeat contracting.

Chapman-Davies, Parwada, and Tan (2013)	Center for Research in Securities Prices (CRSP) Survivor-Bias-Free US Mutual Fund Database; Form ADV; SEC	USA	2003–9	Fund performance, fund flows	Mutual fund fraud	Mutual fund fraud is punished by reduced fund inflows to affected funds. Underperformance and money outflows are more severe with higher monetary fines, regulatory actions initiated by the SEC, and the involvement of more than one regulatory body. Scandal funds reduce their expense ratios, possibly to retain and attract investors. This effort allows scandal funds to delay asset fire sales by up to a quarter. However, fund families reduce expenditure on marketing and distribution costs, likely to ameliorate the fallout from scandals by withdrawing affected funds from the limelight.
Bereskin, Campbell II, and Kedia (in press)	National Centre for Charitable Statistics (NCCS); Stanford Securities Class Action Clearinghouse (SSCAC); Compustat; CRSP; other sources	2,720 firm-years in the USA	1996–2011	CEO turnover	Class action lawsuits, charitable giving	The findings show that the culture arising from philanthropic activities is associated with greater employee whistle blowing and greater likelihood of forced CEO turnover after misconduct.
Giannetti and Wang (2016)	SEC and/or DOJ	1,099 hand-collected securities fraud cases in the USA	1978–2011	Household holdings of stock, in-state and out-of-state	In-state and out-of-state financial misrepresentation, family size, married status, portfolio return	Corporate fraud has a causal negative effect on household stock market participation. The effect holds for both fraud and non-fraud firms, due to a general lack of trust in the stock market.

(continued)

TABLE 19.4 *(continued)*

Author(s)	Data source(s)	Country samples	Time period	Dependent variables (effect of financial market misconduct)	Main explanatory variables (type of financial market misconduct)	Main findings
Aharony, Liu, and Yawson, (2015)	Public Access to Court Electronic Records (PACER) Database PACER; Compustat Executive Compensation ("Execucomp") Database	16,901 lawsuits filed against 1,653 unique companies in the USA	Jan 2000–Dec 2007	CEO turnover and CEO pay	Different types of lawsuit	Companies' response to lawsuits depends on the nature of the allegations. In particular, contractual lawsuits are followed by increased turnover of CEOs and inside directors, whereas following environmental and intellectual property (IP) lawsuits, only outside directors tend to depart. There is no evidence that antitrust lawsuits impact on executive turnover. Also, lawsuit merit and pecuniary demands for damages play a role in determining executive turnover. In addition, following IP lawsuits, CEO compensation tends to reduce.
Chen et al. (2016b)	China Center for Economic Research (CCER); China Stock Market and Accounting Research (CSMAR)	409 fraud cases	1999–2008	CEO turnover	Split share structure reform, state-owned enterprises (SOEs), other controls	Legislative reform that enables state shareholders to freely trade shares strengthens the incentives of SOEs to replace fraudulent management.
Vismara, Paleari, and Signori (2015)	Euripo prospectuses; Investext investment research	125 initial public offerings (IPOs) in France, Germany, and Italy	1999–2012	Long-run performance	Biased selection of peers by underwriters in IPO valuation	More biased selection of peers by underwriters worsens long-term IPO performance.

Zhou and Reesor (2015)	Not applicable – theoretical model	Not applicable	Not applicable	Valuation	Fraud and misrepresentation in securities class actions – theoretical model	A modified Merton framework is used to measure the impact of misrepresentation on the value of components (e.g., debt, warrants) of a firm's capital structure. Leverage affects the misrepresentation impact on the value of debt and warrants. Additionally, misrepresentation affects the value of subordinated debt much more than senior debt, with this effect increasing with firm leverage.

This table summarizes various papers that focus on the presence and consequences of financial market misconduct. The main findings are largely paraphrased and/or copied from the abstracts of the papers to best and succinctly represent the authors' contributions, but they are not meant to exhaustively represent all of the findings from the papers.

levels of financial market misconduct are associated with lower levels of financial market participation (Giannetti and Wang, 2016).

Third, there are papers that examine the fundraising loss to funds that engage in financial market misconduct. Chapman-Davies, Parwada, and Tan (2013) show that scandals in mutual funds significantly inhibit capital flows to mutual funds. Similarly, misreporting activity in general in the VC and PE industry inhibits institutional investors' willingness to contribute capital to VC and PE industry overall (Cumming and Johan, 2013b), although such activity enables some funds to benefit at the expense of other funds in the cross-section (Cumming and Walz, 2010).

Fourth, there are papers that examine the financial consequences of financial market misconduct in terms of legal penalties and lower share prices. Vismara, Paleari, and Signori (2015) show that a biased selection of peers by underwriters worsens long-term initial public offering (IPO) performance. Zhou and Reesor (2015) provide a model that enables calculation of the value decrease associated with financial misrepresentation; it incorporates the capital structure of the firm, and shows, among other things, how different investors such as the holders of subordinated debt are made worse off as a result of misrepresentation. Dyck, Morse, and Zingales (2010, 2014) estimate that firms lose on average 22 percent of their value when they are caught engaged in financial market misconduct, while Karpoff, Lee, and Martin (2008b) show that firm value declines by 38 percent on average, which is mainly due to reputational loss. The reputational penalty is larger for firms that more heavily rely on repeat contracts.

19.4 CONSEQUENCES OF REGULATING FINANCIAL MARKET MISCONDUCT

19.4.1 *Regulation of Insider Trading*

Regulations banning insider trading were adopted in many countries around the world from the 1960s through the 1990s, but they appear to have been ineffective. Early evidence from Seyhun (1992) shows that US regulations pertaining to insider trading had no impact on insider trading activities and profits, but enforcement activities were effective in reducing insider trading activities (see Table 19.5). Garfinkel (1997) looks into the effects of the 1988 Insider Trading and Securities Fraud Enforcement Act (ITSFEA) in the USA, which significantly increased penalties to insider trading and securities fraud, and finds that, following the ITSFEA, insiders postponed liquidity sales until after negative earnings surprises, and that there was less information-based trading in front of earnings announcements. More recent evidence from Cohen, Frazzini, and Malloy (2010) shows that Regulation Fair Disclosure (Regulation FD) in the USA appears to be effective in mitigating the ability to profit from insider trading, insofar as analysts' access to senior management through school ties is mitigated, which in turn makes it more difficult to profit on such analyst recommendations.

Early international evidence on introduction of laws banning insider trading around the world shows that such laws failed to reduce the number of cases, and even increased profits per case (Bris, 2005). There is much evidence that laws banning insider trading do more harm than good when they are not properly enforced (Beny, 2005, 2007; Bhattacharya and Daouk, 2002, 2009). The evidence in Aitken, Cumming, and Zhan (2015) is consistent with this view, but with a few salient differences. First, there are many different exchange trading rules specific to insider trading; that is, insider trading rules are not just a homogeneous ban on

TABLE 19.5 *Overview of studies on the consequences of regulating financial market misconduct: Regulation of insider trading*

Author(s)	Data source(s)	Country samples	Time period	Dependent variables	Financial market regulation and enforcement variables	Main findings
Seyhun (1992)	National archives	19,571 firms (US)	1975–89	Insiders' abnormal profits and share traded	Changes in insider trading regulation: (1) March 1980, when the Chiarella decision was announced; (2) August 1984, when ITSA was signed into law; (3) November 1988, when ITSFEA was signed into law	The increased statutory sanctions on corporate insider trading in the 1980s had no impact on corporate insider trading activities and profit. The enforcements by courts have negative impact on insider trading activities, especially around earning announcements and takeover information.
Garfinkel (1997)	PC-Compustat Plus; Institutional Brokers' Estimate System (IBES); Wall Street Journal (WSJ); Center for Research in Securities Prices (CRSP); Securities and Exchange Commission (SEC) Ownership and Reporting System	644 firms (US)	1984–91	Pre-announcement and post-announcement trades	Insider Trading and Securities Fraud Enforcement Act (ITSFEA) (1998)	The ITSFEA, which significantly increased penalties to insider trading and securities fraud, caused insiders to postpone liquidity sales until after negative earnings surprises, and mitigated information-based trading in front of earnings announcements.
Bhattacharya and Daouk (2002)	Morgan Stanley Capital International (MSCI); International Financial Corporation (IFC); International Monetary Fund (IMF) Datastream	103 countries	1969–98	Cost of equity	Survey approach [email, letter and fax to 103 stock exchanges and their regulator on whether or not the stock market has insider trading laws and on whether or not there has been a prosecution under the insider trading laws]	Introduction of insider trading laws has no impact on the cost of equity in a country, but the enforcement of insider trading laws is associated with a significant decrease in the cost of equity.

(continued)

TABLE 19.5 *(continued)*

Author(s)	Data source(s)	Country samples	Time period	Dependent variables	Financial market regulation and enforcement variables	Main findings
Bris (2005)	SDC Mergers and Acquisitions Database	4,541 acquisitions across 52 countries	1990–9	Insider trading profit	Insider trading laws and their enforcement: initial prosecution data are from Bhattacharya and Daouk (2002)	Insider trading law enforcement increases both the incidence and the profitability of insider trading. Harsher laws reduce the incidence of illegal insider trading.
Beny (2005, 2007)	La Porta et al. (1998); IFC	33 countries	Cross-section	Ownership dispersion, stock market turnover, stock price synchronicity	Insider trading law index – the sum of (1) tipping, (2) tippee, (3) damages, and (4) criminal, or, equivalently, the sum of (5) scope and (6) sanction – these six being the insider trading law variables (Gaillard, 1992; Stamp and Welsh, 1996); enforcement variables e (Bhattacharya and Daouk, 2002), public enforcement power (La Porta et al., 2002), and private right (Gaillard, 1992; Stamp and Welsh, 1996)	Countries with more prohibitive formal insider trading laws are associated with more dispersed equity ownership, more informative stock prices, and more liquidity stock markets. Both enforceability and formal insider trading laws have positive impact on stock market development.
Bhattacharya and Daouk (2009)	MSCI; IFC; IMF; Datastream; etc.	55 countries	1969–98	Cost of equity	Insider trading law and enforcement data (Bhattacharya and Daouk, 2002)	Sometimes no securities law may be better than a good securities law that is not enforced. The authors find that the cost of equity rises when some countries enact an insider trading law but do not enforce it.

(continued)

Cohen, Frazzini, and Malloy (2010)	IBES; Internet searches zoominfo.com, brokercheck. finra.org; CRSP; Compustat; others sources	USA	1992–2006	Cumulative abnormal returns	Regulation Fair Disclosure (Regulation FD), school ties	Regulation FD constrains the use of direct access to senior management, and weakens the effect of school ties and the ability of analysts with school ties to outperform on their stock recommendations.
Aitken, Cumming, and Zhan (2015a)	SMARTS, Inc.; Capital Markets CRC; Cumming and Johan's (2008) survey data; Cumming, Johan, and Li's (2011) exchange trading rules indices; La Porta et al.'s (1998, 2006) law and finance indices; Jackson and Roe's (2009) resource-based enforcement indices; Thompson Reuters Datastream	22 countries	2003–11	Frequency of suspected insider trading and trading value surrounding insider trading	Trading rules (Cumming, Johan, and Li, 2011); surveillance index – the principal component of both single-market and cross-market surveillance (Cumming and Johan, (2008); efficiency of the judiciary (La Porta, Lopez-de-Silanes, and Shleifer, 2006); staff per million (Jackson and Roe, 2009); public enforcement (Djankov et al., 2008)	More detailed exchange trading rules and surveillance over time and across markets significantly reduce the number of cases but increase the profits per case. There are complementarities across different trading rules and surveillance, and these complementarities are at least twice as important as stand-alone insider trading rules for predicting the frequency of insider trading cases; however, the complementarities are less economically important for predicting the trading value for surrounding the insider trading cases relative to stand-alone insider trading rules.

This table summarizes various papers that focus on regulating financial market misconduct. The main findings are largely paraphrased and/or copied from the abstracts of the papers to best and succinctly represent the authors' contributions, but they are not meant to exhaustively represent all of the findings from the papers.

insider trading in different countries. Second, other trading rules that do not deal with insider trading directly may indirectly influence the ability of an insider trader to engage in insider trading through rule complementarities. Third, instead of only examining enforcement, Aitken, Cumming, and Zhan (2015) also examine the intermediate step toward enforcement actions, namely surveillance. Surveillance refers to computer algorithms directed at detecting insider trading and other forms of market manipulation. Aitken, Cumming, and Zhan (2015) use a natural experiment of exchange trading rule changes in Europe and find that having more detailed exchange trading rules across countries and over time as well as surveillance mitigates the frequency of suspected insider trading cases but exacerbates the profits per case. Aitken, Cumming, and Zhan (2015) do not observe any material differences in stealth trading (which they proxy by trading activity around contaminated news announcements) as a result of such rule changes across counties and over time. However, other evidence is consistent with the view that exchange design can influence the transparency of insider trading; for example, evidence in Garfinkel and Nimalendran (2003) is consistent with the view that insider trades are more transparent on the NYSE specialist system relative to the NASDAQ dealer system.

19.4.2 *Regulation of Non-insider Trading Manipulative Trading Practices and Bribery*

Aggarwal and Wu (2006) show that stock price manipulation – not merely insider trading laws – affects volatility, liquidity, and returns.[3] As such, it is not surprising that there are many papers that connect securities laws and their enforcement to the efficiency of capital markets (see Table 19.6).

Substantial research has shown that more efficient securities laws have a positive impact on IPOs (La Porta, Lopez-de-Silanes, and Shleifer, 2006), and generally enhance stock market valuations (La Porta et al., 1997, 1998, 2002). More expenditures on enforcing securities regulation likewise improve fraud detection and facilitate more trading and stock market participation (Jackson and Roe, 2009; Cumming, Groh, and Johan, 2018). This evidence, however, has largely been examined at the aggregated level for all firms on an exchange (La Porta, Lopez-de-Silanes, and Shleifer, 2006; Jackson and Roe, 2009), and hence the benefit of public versus private enforcement of securities laws has been debated depending on which way the data are examined. Disaggregated data, by contrast, show that public enforcement facilitates small firm security issuance, while private enforcement benefits large firms more than small firms (Cumming, Knill, and Richardson, 2015); stronger public enforcement gives rise to larger firms raising capital internationally.

Other evidence has examined exogenous changes in exchange trading rules and enforcement pertaining to the different types of manipulation identified in Table 19.1. These exchange trading rule changes across countries and over time mitigate volatility and increase stock market liquidity (Cumming, Johan, and Li, 2011) and the trading location of cross-listed stocks (Cumming, Hou, and Wu, 2018). Relatedly, there is evidence that surveillance efforts to detect illegal market manipulation enhance market efficiency and trading activity (Comerton-Forde and Rydge, 2006; Cumming and Johan, 2008). By contrast, there is little evidence that accounting changes such as mandatory International Financial Reporting

[3] See also, e.g., Allen and Gale (1992), Allen and Gorton (1992), Comerton-Forde and Putnins (2011), Comerton-Forde and Rydge (2006), Daouk, Lee, and Ng (2006), Gerard and Nanda (1993), Hillion and Suominen (2004), Jarrow (1992, 1994), Merrick, Naik, and Yadav (2005), and Ni et al. (2005).

TABLE 19.6 *Overview of studies on the consequences of regulating financial market misconduct: Regulation of non-insider-trading manipulative trading practices and other types of illegal activity*

Author(s)	Data source(s)	Country samples	Time period	Dependent variables	Financial market regulation and enforcement variables	Main findings
La Porta, Lopez-de-Silanes, and Shleifer (2006)	Survey of attorneys in 49 countries; other sources in La Porta et al. (1998) and elsewhere	49 countries	1996–2000	Market, capitalization, number of firms, initial public offerings (IPOs), block premia, access to equity, ownership concentration, liquidity	Public enforcement, private enforcement, liability standards, efficiency of the judiciary, GDP per capita, others	The authors find little evidence that public enforcement benefits stock markets, but strong evidence that laws mandating disclosure and facilitating private enforcement through liability rules do benefit stock markets.
Comerton-Forde and Rydge (2006)	Australian Stock Exchange	Australia	1989–2002	Not applicable	Market surveillance and enforcement actions documented (not an econometric study)	More surveillance improves market integrity.
Cumming and Johan (2008)	Survey data from surveillance authorities in each jurisdiction; World Federation of Exchanges	25 exchanges	2005	Trading velocity, listings, market capitalization	Single-market surveillance – the sum of dummy variables equal to 1 where surveillance is carried out over each of the market manipulative practices identified (e.g., spoofing, painting the tape, wash sales, etc.) on a single-market basis; cross-market surveillance – the sum of dummy variables equal to 1 where surveillance is carried out over each of the market manipulative practices identified in the jurisdiction (e.g., spoofing, painting the tape, wash sales, etc.) on a cross-market basis (including cross-product, cross-exchange and international)	Relative to the scope of single-market surveillance, the scope of cross-market surveillance shows a stronger positive association with trading velocity, the number of listed companies, and market capitalization.
Jackson and Roe (2009)	Courtis (2006, 2007); La Porta, Lopez-de-Silanes, and Shleifer (2006); other sources	53 countries	2005	Stock market capitalization, trading volume, domestic firms, IPOs	Expenditures in dollars on enforcement, staffing per population, and other controls as in La Porta, Lopez-de-Silanes, and Shleifer (2006)	In horse races between these resource-based measures of public enforcement intensity and the most common measures of private enforcement, public enforcement is overall as important as disclosure in explaining financial market outcomes around the world and more important than private liability rules.

(continued)

TABLE 19.6 *(continued)*

Author(s)	Data source(s)	Country samples	Time period	Dependent variables	Financial market regulation and enforcement variables	Main findings
Cumming, Johan, and Li (2011)	SMARTS, Inc.; Capital Markets CRC; Cumming and Johan's (2008) survey data; Cumming, Johan, and Li's (2011) exchange trading rules indices; La Porta et al.'s (1998, 2006) law and finance indices; World Federation of Exchanges; Thompson Reuters Datastream	39 countries (42 exchanges)	2006–8	Various proxies for stock market liquidity: trading velocity, volatility, bid-ask spread	Trading rules: insider trading index – the sum of dummy variables for front-running, client precedence, trading ahead of research reports, separation of research and trading, broker ownership limit, restrictions on affiliation, restrictions on communications, investment company securities, influencing/rewarding the employees of others, and anti-intimidation/coordination; price manipulation rule index – the sum of dummy variables for marking the open, marking the close, misleading end of the month/quarter/year trades, intraday ramping/gouging, market setting, prearranged trades, and domination and control; volume manipulation rule index – the sum of dummy variables for churning and wash trade; spoofing rules index – the sum of dummy variables for giving up priority, switch and layering of bids/asks; false disclosure rules index – the sum of dummy variables for dissemination of false and misleading information, and parking or warehousing; market manipulation rules index – the sum of price manipulation rules index, volume manipulation rules index, spoofing rules index, and false disclosure rules index; broker-agency rules index – the sum of dummy variables for trade through, improper execution, restrictions on member use of exchange name, restrictions on sales materials and telemarketing, and fair dealing with customers; total trading rules index – the sum of insider trading index, market manipulation rules index, and broker-agency rules index (sourced from the trading rulebooks of each exchange) Enforcement: surveillance index (Cumming and Johan, 2008); various law and finance variables (La Porta et al., 1998, 2006).	Having more detailed trading rules across exchanges and over time increases trading liquidity.

(continued)

Zeume (2017)	London Stock Exchange	645 UK-listed firms from UK and various non-UK countries	2008–9	Cumulative abnormal returns	Corruption exposure with UK versus non-UK linkage	UK firms operating in high corruption regions of the world display negative abnormal returns since passage of the UK Bribery Act of 2010. Foreign firms subject to the Act because they have a UK subsidiary also exhibit negative abnormal returns. Relative to comparable continental European firms, UK firms expand their subsidiary network less into high corruption regions and their sales in these regions grow 6 percentage points more slowly.

This table summarizes various papers that focus on regulating financial market misconduct. The main findings are largely paraphrased and/or copied from the abstracts of the papers to best and succinctly represent the authors' contributions, but they are not meant to exhaustively represent all of the findings from the papers.

Standards (IFRS) have fostered significant changes in liquidity, unless there are commensurate changes in reporting enforcement (Christensen, Hail, and Leuz, 2013).

Financial market misconduct is not merely about manipulative trading activities; it may come in the form of bribery. In an interesting recent paper, Zeume (2017) shows that UK bribery regulation lowers firm value and growth, particularly among firms that have international operations and subsidiaries in high corruption regions around the world. Hence, while manipulative trading lowers firm value and stock market participation, (undetected) bribery enhances firm value, at least among firms that have incentives to engage in bribery.

19.5 FUTURE DIRECTIONS

Research on financial market misconduct is a growth area of research. Figure 19.1 clearly shows that research on "financial market manipulation" and "market manipulation" has grown at a faster rate in recent years relative to other topics such as "corporate finance" and "fraud." A strong divergence in these research streams is notable since the global financial crisis, which is widely recognized as having started in August 2007 and become more pronounced in 2008 and 2009. Research on financial market misconduct has taken off since that time, while research growth on benchmarked fields of market misconduct and corporate finance has been stable and even tapered off in recent years. The growth in datasets and the strong industry and public policy implications for research on financial market misconduct and corporate fraud suggest that the demand for high-quality research on corporate fraud and financial market misconduct will continue to grow significantly in the future.

A recent paper that has caught the attention of many scholars involves a critical assessment of the quality of datasets used in financial market misconduct research in the USA. Karpoff et al. (2012) show that near 100 published studies that use data from the Government Accountability Office (GAO) and Audit Analytics (AA) databases of restatement

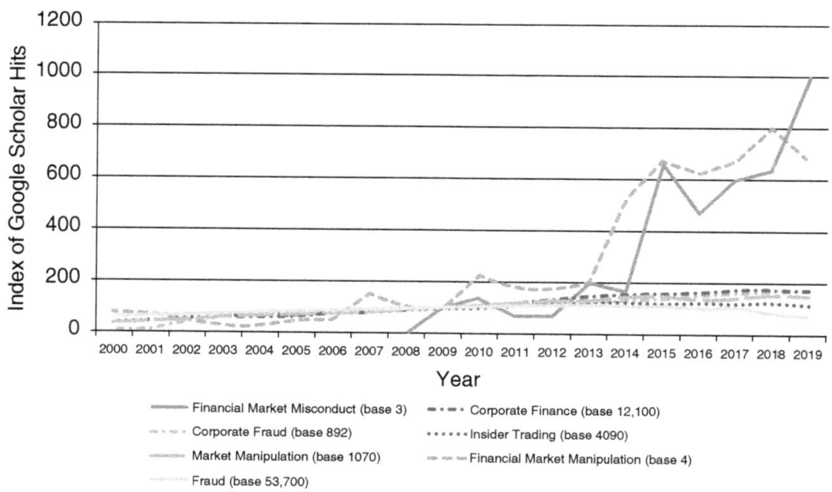

FIGURE 19.1 Google Scholar hits on various search terms for corporate finance, financial market misconduct, and fraud

This figure presents the number of Google Scholar hits on various search terms. The search was carried out on February 1, 2020. "Base" refers to the number of hits on the base year 2009.

announcements, the Securities Class Action Clearinghouse (SCAC) database of securities class action lawsuits, and the SEC's series of Accounting and Auditing Enforcement Releases (AAERs) have five types of problem that can affect the validity and interpretation of empirical findings. These problem types are misidentified event dates, missing value-relevant information, errors of omission, duplicate events for the same instance of misconduct, and inclusion of events unrelated to misconduct. This evidence on data quality implies that there is scope to reexamine prior studies to ascertain the implications of data corrections.

Outside the USA, there is a comparative dearth of research on the frequency, cause, and effects of financial market misconduct and fraud. While some evidence is available from select countries around the world, as documented earlier, clearly more studies are warranted so that we may better understand the legal, economic, sociological, organizational, demographic, and cultural conditions that give rise to financial market misconduct and fraud. A very interesting study by Parsons, Sulaeman, and Titman (2018) highlights the importance of these interdisciplinary forces that shape both the frequency and the consequences of fraud within the USA. Also, this evidence highlights the role of interdisciplinary work on financial market misconduct and fraud research so that we may better understand the causal mechanisms at work from an intermixing of fields outside of the traditional realm of finance.

Future research on fraud and financial market misconduct could also make use of new computer methods with text mining (and "big data"), including internet message boards, for example. Increased computing power gives rise to massive scope for new empirical studies in this area. This type of work could also be extended to studies of crowdfunding markets where there is a significant presence of information on the Internet and scant work on topic. For example, one such recent crowdfunding fraud involved a simple comparison between the production of "all Kobe beef" beef jerky and the worldwide production of Kobe beef.[4]

Fraud research could further extend into psychology and analyses of the brain. A small field in behavioral finance has begun to investigate issues involving mental activity around trading. This type of medical/psychological/behavioral work could likewise be extended toward analyses of financial market misconduct and fraud.

Finally, there could be more work on the real consequences of fraud in terms of investment activity. There has been some work done in the past (e.g., Bebchuk and Fershtman, 1994), but there is wide scope for more types of study in the future.

19.6 CONCLUSIONS

This chapter reviewed recent research on the causes and consequences of different forms of financial market misconduct. We also examined the impact of regulating financial market misconduct. We provided data from Google Scholar that clearly shows that financial market misconduct and fraud have been growth areas of research, particularly since the financial market crisis. Despite the massive growth in research in this area, however, we highlighted a large number of gaps in the literature and directions for future research.

[4] http://crowdfrauds.com/uncovered/biggest-crowdfunding-scam-yet/. See Cumming and Johan (2019).

REFERENCES

Aggarwal, R. K., and Wu, G., 2006. "Stock Market Manipulations." *Journal of Business* 79, 1915–53.
Agrawal, A., and Cooper, T., 2015. "Insider Trading before Accounting Scandals." *Journal of Corporate Finance* 34, 169–90.
Aharony, J., Liu, C., and Yawson, A., 2015. "Corporate Litigation and Executive Turnover." *Journal of Corporate Finance* 34, 268–92.
Aitken, M., Cumming, D. J., and Zhan, F. 2015a. "Exchange Trading Rules, Surveillance, and Insider Trading." *Journal of Corporate Finance* 34, 150–68.
2015b. "High Frequency Trading and End-of-Day Price Dislocation." *Journal of Banking and Finance* 59, 330–49.
Allen, F., and Gale, D., 1992. "Stock-Price Manipulation." *Review of Financial Studies* 5, 503–29.
Allen, F., and Gorton, G., 1992. "Stock Price Manipulation, Market Microstructure and Asymmetric Information." *European Economic Review* 36, 624–30.
Atanasov, V., Davies, R. J., and Merrick Jr., J. J., 2015. "Financial Intermediaries in the Midst of Market Manipulation: Did They Protect the Fool or Help the Knave?" *Journal of Corporate Finance* 34, 210–34.
Augustin, P., Brenner, M., and Subrahmanyam, M. G., 2019. "Informed Options Trading Prior to Takeover Announcements: Insider Trading?" *Management Science* 65, 5449–5956.
Bebchuk, L. A., and Fershtman, C., 1994. "Insider Trading and the Managerial Choice among Risky Projects." *Journal of Financial and Quantitative Analysis* 29, 1–14.
Becker, G., 1968. "Crime and Punishment: An Economic Approach." *Journal of Political Economy* 76, 169–217.
Beny, L. N., 2005. "Do Insider Trading Laws Matter? Some Preliminary Comparative Evidence." *American Law and Economics Review* 7, 144–83.
2007. "Insider Trading Laws and Stock Markets around the World: An Empirical Contribution to the Theoretical Law and Economics Debate." *Journal of Corporation Law* 32, 237–300.
Bereskin, F., Campbell II, T., and Kedia, S., in press. "Whistle Blowing, Forced CEO Turnover and Misconduct: The Role of Socially Minded Employees and Directors." Management Science.
Bernile, G., Sulaeman, J., and Wang, Q., 2015. "Institutional Trading during a Wave of Corporate Scandals: 'Perfect Payday'?" *Journal of Corporate Finance* 34, 191–209.
Bhattacharya, U., and Daouk, H., 2002. "The World Price of Insider Trading." *Journal of Finance* 57, 75–108.
2009. "When No Law Is Better than a Good Law." *Review of Finance* 13, 577–627.
Bhattacharya, U., and Marshall, C., 2012. "Do They Do It for the Money?" *Journal of Corporate Finance* 18, 92–104.
Black, J., Nilsson, M., Pinheiro, R., and da Silva, M. B., 2015. "Information Production and the Duration of Accounting Fraud." Working Paper, University of Colorado.
Bollen, N. P. B., and Pool, V. K., 2009. "Do Hedge Fund Managers Misreport Returns? Evidence from the Pooled Distribution." *Journal of Finance* 64, 2257–88.
Bris, A., 2005. "Do Insider Trading Laws Work?" *European Financial Management* 11, 267–312.
Burns, N., and Kedia, S., 2006. "The Impact of Performance-Based Compensation on Misreporting." *Journal of Financial Economics* 79, 35–67.
CFA Institute (2014). "Global Market Sentiment Survey 2015: Detailed Survey Results." www.cfainstitute.org/Survey/gmss_2015_detailed_results.pdf.
Chapman-Davies, A., Parwada, J. T., and Tan, K. M., 2013. "The Impact of Scandals on Mutual Fund Performance, Money Flows and Fees." UNSW Business School Research Paper.
Chen, J., Cumming, D. J., Hou, W., and Lee, E., 2013. "Executive Integrity, Audit Opinion, and Fraud in Chinese Listed Firms." *Emerging Markets Review* 15, 72–91.
2016a. "Does the External Monitoring Effect of Analysts Deter Corporate Fraud in China?" *Journal of Business Ethics* 134, 727–42.
2016b. "Corporate Fraud, CEO Turnover, and State Ownership in China." *Journal of Business Ethics* 138, 787–806.
Christensen, H., Hail, L., and Leuz, C., 2013. "Mandatory IFRS Reporting and Changes in Enforcement." *Journal of Accounting and Economics* 56, 147–77.

Cohen, L., Frazzini, A., and Malloy, C., 2010. "Sell Side School Ties." *Journal of Finance* 65, 1409–37.
Comerton-Forde, C., and Putnins, T. J., 2011. "Measuring Closing Price Manipulation." *Journal of Financial Intermediation* 20, 135–58.
Comerton-Forde, C., and Rydge, J., 2006. "Market Integrity and Surveillance Effort." *Journal of Financial Services Research* 29, 149–72.
Courtis, N., ed., 2006, 2007. *How Countries Supervise Their Banks, Insurers, and Securities Markets*. London: Central Banking Publications.
Cumming, D., and Johan, S. A., 2008. "Global Market Surveillance." *American Law and Economics Review* 10, 454–506.
Cumming, D. J., and Johan, S., 2013a. "Listing Standards and Fraud." *Managerial and Decision Economics* 34, 451–70.
Cumming, D. J., and Johan, S. A., 2013b. *Venture Capital and Private Equity Contracting: An International Perspective*, 2nd ed. London: Elsevier Science Academic Press.
2019. *Crowdfunding: Fundamental Cases, Facts, and Insights*. London: Elsevier Science Academic Press.
Cumming, D. J., and Li, D., 2011. "Run-Up of Acquirer Stock in Public and Private Acquisitions." *Corporate Governance: An International Review* 19(3), 210–39.
Cumming, D. J., and Walz, U., 2010. "Private Equity Returns and Disclosure around the World." *Journal of International Business Studies* 41, 727–54.
Cumming, D. J., Johan, S. A., and Li, D., 2011. "Exchange Trading Rules and Stock Market Liquidity." *Journal of Financial Economics* 99(3), 651–71.
Cumming, D. J., Dai, N., and Johan, S. A., 2013. *Hedge Fund Structure, Regulation and Performance around the World*. Oxford: Oxford University Press.
Cumming, D. J., Knill, A., and Richardson, N., 2015. "Firm Size, Institutional Quality and the Impact of Securities Regulation." *Journal of Comparative Economics* 43, 417–42.
Cumming, D. J., Leung, T. Y., and Rui, O. M., 2015. "Gender Diversity and Securities Fraud." *Academy of Management Journal* 58, 1572–93.
Cumming, D., Groh, A., and Johan, S. A., 2018. "Same Rules, Different Enforcement: Market Abuse in Europe." *Journal of International Financial Markets, Institutions, and Money* 54, 130–51.
Cumming, D. J., Hou, W., and Wu, E., 2018. "Exchange Trading Rules, Governance, and the Trading Location of Cross-Listed Stocks." *European Journal of Finance* 24, 1453–84.
Daouk, H., Lee, C. M. C., and Ng, D. 2006. "Capital Market Governance: How Do Security Laws Affect Market Performance?" *Journal of Corporate Finance* 12, 560–93.
Djankov, S., La Porta, R., Lopez-de-Silanes, F., and Shleifer, A., 2008. "The Law and Economics of Self-Dealing." *Journal of Financial Economics* 88, 430–65.
Dyck, A., Morse, A., and Zingales, L., 2010. "Who Blows the Whistle on Corporate Fraud?" *Journal of Finance* 65, 2063–2253.
2014. "How Pervasive Is Corporate Fraud?" Working Paper, University of Chicago.
Dyreng, S., Mayew, W., and Williams, C., 2012. "Religious Social Norms and Corporate Financial Reporting." *Journal of Business Finance and Accounting* 39, 845–75.
Erickson, M., Hanlon, M., and Maydew, E., 2006. "Is There a Link between Executive Equity Incentives and Accounting Fraud?" *Journal of Accounting Research* 44, 113–43.
Gaillard, E., ed. 1992. *Insider Trading: The Laws of Europe, the United States, and Japan*. Boston: Kluwer Law and Taxation Publishers.
Gandhi, P., Golez, B., Jackwerth, J. C., and Plazzi, A., 2014. "Libor Manipulation: Cui Bono?" Working Paper, University of Notre Dame.
Garfinkel, J. A. 1997. "New Evidence on the Effects of Federal Regulations on Insider Trading: The Insider Trading and Securities Fraud Enforcement Act (ITSFEA)." *Journal of Corporate Finance* 3, 89–111.
Garfinkel, J. A., and Nimalendran, M., 2003, "Market Structure and Trader Anonymity: An Analysis of Insider Trading." *Journal of Financial and Quantitative Analysis* 38, 591–610.
Gerard, B., and Nanda, V., 1993. "Trading and Manipulation around Seasoned Equity Offerings." *Journal of Finance* 48, 213–45.
Giannetti, M., and Wang, T. Y., 2016. "Corporate Scandals and Household Stock Market Participation." *Journal of Finance* 71(6), 2591–636.

Hass, L. H., Muller, M. A., and Vergauwe, S., 2015. "Tournament Incentives and Corporate Fraud." *Journal of Corporate Finance* 34, 251–67.

Hillion, P., and Suominen, M., 2004. "The Manipulation of Closing Prices." *Journal of Financial Markets* 7, 351–75.

Jackson, H. E., and Roe, M. J., 2009. "Public and Private Enforcement of Securities Laws: Resource-Based Evidence." *Journal of Financial Economics* 93, 207–38.

Jarrell, G. A., and Poulsen, A. B., 1989. "Stock Trading before the Announcement of Tender Offers: Insider Trading or Market Anticipation?" *Journal of Law, Economics and Organization* 5, 225–48.

Jarrow, R. A., 1992. "Market Manipulation, Bubbles, Corners and Short Squeezes." *Journal of Financial and Quantitative Analysis* 27, 311–36.

1994. "Derivative Security Markets, Market Manipulation and Option Pricing Theory." *Journal of Financial and Quantitative Analysis* 29, 241–61.

Karpoff, J., Koester, A., Lee, D. S., and Martin, G. S., 2012. "A Critical Analysis of Databases Used in Financial Misconduct Research." Mays Business School Research Paper No. 2012–73.

Karpoff, J., Lee, D. S., and Martin, G. S., 2008a. "The Consequences to Managers for Cooking the Books." *Journal of Financial Economics* 88, 193–215.

Karpoff, J. M., Lee, D. S., and Martin, G. S., 2008b. "The Consequences to Managers for Financial Misrepresentation." *Journal of Financial Economics* 85, 66–101.

King, M., 2009. "Pre-bid Run-Ups ahead of Canadian Takeovers: How Big Is the Problem?" *Financial Management* 38, 699–726.

La Porta, R., Lopez-de-Silanes, F., Shleifer, A., and Vishny, R., 1997. "Legal Determinants of External Finance." *Journal of Finance* 52, 1131–50.

1998. "Law and Finance." *Journal of Political Economy* 106, 1113–55.

2002. "Investor Protection and Corporate Valuation." *Journal of Finance* 57, 1147–70.

La Porta, R., Lopez-de-Silanes, F., and Shleifer, A., 2006. "What Works in Securities Laws?" *Journal of Finance* 61, 1–32.

Merrick Jr,. J. J., Naik, N. Y., and Yadav, P. K., 2005. "Strategic Trading Behavior and Price Distortion in a Manipulated Market: Anatomy of a Squeeze." *Journal of Financial Economics* 77, 171–218.

Meulbroek, L. K., 1992. "An Empirical Analysis of Illegal Insider Trading." *Journal of Finance* 47, 1661–99.

Ni, S. X., Pearson, N. D., and Poteshman, A. M., 2005. "Stock Price Clustering on Option Expiration Dates." *Journal of Financial Economics* 78, 49–87.

Parsons, C. A., Sulaeman, J., and Titman, S. 2018. "The Geography of Financial Misconduct." *Journal of Finance* 73(5), 2087–2137.

Pirrong, S. C., 1993. "Manipulation of the Commodity Futures Market Delivery Process." *Journal of Business* 15, 335–70.

1995a. "The Self-Regulation of Commodity Exchanges: The Case of Market Manipulation." *Journal of Law and Economics* 38, 141–206.

1995b. "Mixed Manipulation Strategies in Commodity Futures Markets." *Journal of Futures Markets* 15, 13–38.

Seyhun, H. N. 1992. "The Effectiveness of the Insider-Trading Sanctions." *Journal of Law & Economics* 35(1), 149–82.

Stamp, M., and Welsh, C., eds. 1996. *International Insider Dealing*. London: FT Law & Tax.

Vismara, S., Paleari, S., and Signori, A., 2015. "Changes in Underwriters' Selection of Comparable Firms Pre- and Post-IPO: Same Bank, Same Company, Different Peers." *Journal of Corporate Finance*, 34, 235–50.

Wang, T., Winton, A., and Yu, X. 2010. "Corporate Fraud and Business Conditions: Evidence from IPOs." *Journal of Finance* 65, 2255–92.

Yu, F., and Yu, X., 2011. "Corporate Lobbying and Fraud Detection." Journal of Financial and Quantitative Analysis 46, 1865–91.

Zeume, S. 2017. "Bribes and Firm Value." *Review of Financial Studies* 30(5), 1457–89.

Zhou, X., and Reesor, R. M., 2015. "Misrepresentation and Capital Structure: Quantifying the Impact on Corporate Security Value in a Modified Merton Framework." Journal of Corporate Finance 34, 293–310.

20

Deterrability and Moral Judgment

Arynn A. Infante and Adam D. Fine

Abstract: Crime control policies of the latter half of the twentieth century were largely grounded in the notion that punishment effectively deters crime and increases compliance. The inherent assumption is that offenders rationally weigh the costs and benefits of their actions before acting, and then act if and only if the benefits outweigh the costs. In retrospect, the policies informed by this "deterrence" perspective have done little to answer the age-old question of what deters crime and increases compliance, and instead have left us in an era of mass incarceration in which the US prison population has inflated by over 500 percent since the 1970s. However, rather than halt deterrence research wholesale, researchers have shifted to identifying *for whom* deterrence threats actually work. While the literature is in its nascent stages, studies indicate that individual differences may underlie who may be more or less susceptible to deterrence threats, and support a number of different mechanisms. For instance, emerging research suggests that individuals high in the obligation to obey the law and low in moral disengagement may be more responsive to deterrence threats. This chapter reports the findings of a developing body of research that focuses on identifying key individual differences that may underlie susceptibility to deterrence threats.

20.1 INTRODUCTION

Deterrence theory is grounded in the assumption that when the benefits of crime outweigh the costs, crime is likely to occur. Deterrence theory is not only intuitive but also appears simplistic to implement: increase the costs of crime because people will not engage in crime if the punishment is harsh enough. Unfortunately, as this chapter details, empirical support for the deterrence–crime relationship is, at best, weak. As a result, scholars have shifted from asking *whether* deterrence works to asking *for whom* deterrence might work. From this literature, self-control has emerged as a potential determinant of who might be more deterrable, yet considerably less research has examined additional determinants such as one's morality and the extent to which one perceives a general obligation to obey the law. Section 20.2 provides an overview of deterrence theory and Section 20.3 discusses the recent shift towards studying perceptual deterrence. Section 20.4 focuses on differential susceptibility to deterrence, paying particular attention to morality and the obligation to obey the law, before Section 20.5 concludes.

20.2 OVERVIEW OF DETERRENCE THEORY

Originating from the classical school of criminology, in which rational choice decision-making is the hallmark of human behavior (Beccaria [1764] 1986), deterrence theory offers an intuitively appealing view of crime (Pratt et al. 2008). The underlying assumption is that people are rational actors who pursue behavior that maximizes pleasure and minimizes pain (Bentham [1789] 1988). The central premise is that individuals calculate the benefits and the costs of crime before engaging in a particular behavior, and crime specifically occurs when the benefits of committing the crime outweigh the anticipated costs of legal or social sanctions. Simply, people engage in crime when crime "pays."

According to deterrence theory, crime can be prevented through increasing the perceived risk of the certainty, celerity, and severity of punishment (Nagin 1998; Braga et al. 2018). Indeed, punishment that is swift, certain, and severe is theorized to deter not only the future offending of the individual receiving the punishment (i.e., specific deterrence) but also the future offending of others (i.e., general deterrence). That is, deterrence purportedly impacts not just the behavior of a particular would-be offender or reoffender but that of other would-be offenders.

Unsurprisingly, provided its alluring simplicity, deterrence theory gained traction among lawmakers as a viable crime-prevention framework. Most notably, the deterrence-based model informed the War on Drugs campaign in the 1980s, mobilizing strict law enforcement and sentencing polices to incarcerate drug offenders. Unfortunately, these "tough on crime" policies resulted in an unprecedented era of mass incarceration in which the USA became the world leader in incarcerating its people (Sawyer and Wagner 2019). As a result of these policies, there are now 2.3 million people under some form of correctional supervision in the American criminal justice system, which is more than a 500 percent increase in rates since the 1970s (Sawyer and Wagner 2019). In light of the decades-long implementation of harsh criminal justice sanctioning largely informed by the deterrence model, scientists began to question whether increasing the costs of crime actually reduced crime and made society safer. The answer: it depends.

Originally, deterrence scholars focused on examining whether objective, macro-level indicators of deterrence (e.g., police force size, arrest ratios, and harsh sentencing policies) were associated with crime rates aggregated at the city, county, and/or state level (Pratt and Cullen 2005; Paternoster 2018). A recent meta-analysis of these studies, however, indicated that such aggregate-level measures of deterrence were actually among the weakest predictors of crime (Pratt and Cullen 2005). Subsequent reviews of studies that utilize this macro-level approach also tended to find little support, if any, for a general deterrent effect (Chalfin and McCrary 2017; Nagin 2018; Tonry 2018).

Provided the underwhelming evidence for any general deterrent effects, scholarship has begun to focus on whether particular aspects of deterrence are more effective. In particular, researchers focused on three dimensions: certainty, severity, and celerity. Certainty typically refers to the probability of being caught and/or punished, severity typically refers to the magnitude of the punishment, and celerity typically refers to how quickly the individual actually receives the punishment after being caught. While it may be intuitive to think that increasing the severity of the punishment might be the most effective way to impact crime, findings largely support the notion that the certainty of punishment, particularly the certainty of apprehension, is a more effective deterrent (Nagin 2018). Indeed, as Beccaria ([1764] 1986: 58) noted centuries ago, "One of the greatest curbs on crime is not the cruelty of punishments, but their infallibility . . . The certainty of punishment even if moderate will always make a stronger impression."

In reality, the typical way in which officials seek to improve the certainty of apprehension is through increasing law enforcement presence or capacity. In support of this practice, studies do suggest that investments in law enforcement, versus investments in incarceration, are more conducive to crime control (Chalfin and McCrary 2017; Kaplan and Chalfin 2019). Another fascinating effect of improving the certainty of apprehension through increasing law enforcement presence is that it has the potential to yield a "double dividend" by reducing crime rates and decreasing prison populations (Durlauf and Nagin 2011; Kaplan and Chalfin 2019). In fact, preliminary evidence suggests that there is a negative association between increases in police resources and prison commitments (Kaplan and Chalfin 2019). Specifically, for every officer hired, there appears to be a 19 percent reduction in commitments (Kaplan and Chalfin 2019: 187).

Altogether, research is largely unsupportive of an association between the severity of punishment (e.g., mandatory minimum sentences and lengthy prison terms) and crime (Tonry 2018). However, this is not to say that deterrence is ineffective. The modern deterrence literature demonstrates that of the three core components of deterrence, the certainty of apprehension provides the most promising crime reduction strategy and also has the greatest potential to alleviate overwhelmed and overcrowded prison systems through reducing commitment rates (Durlauf and Nagin 2011; Nagin 2018; Kaplan and Chalfin 2019).

20.3 PERCEPTUAL DETERRENCE

Recall that the underlying assumption of deterrence theory is that individuals calculate the benefits and the costs of crime before engaging in a particular behavior, and crime specifically occurs when the anticipated benefits outweigh the costs. Yet when the system attempts to reduce crime through deterrence (e.g., hiring more police to increase the certainty of apprehension), there is often an inherent assumption that individuals process the deterrence threat similarly, and further that they are even similarly aware of the deterrence threat in the first place. Indeed, for the objective risk to influence behavior, it must inform an individual's subjective assessment of risk (Pickett and Roche 2016).

Unfortunately, a recent state-of-the-art review of perceptual deterrence literature found that the association between actual sanctioning and perceived sanction risk is weak (Apel and Nagin 2017). Individuals' views of the costs of a crime are actually largely unrelated to the actual deterrence threats (Pickett and Roche 2016). That finding poses fundamental challenges for deterrence theory and for deterrence research; researchers must shift from studying objective deterrence to subjective (i.e., perceptual) deterrence on an individual level. Indeed, this shift is one of the most significant developments in deterrence research and has enormous implications for both policy and practice (Paternoster 2018).

The question then becomes to what extent does perceptual deterrence actually deter crime? Studies do suggest that the perceived risk of sanctions can deter crime; however, this finding is typically only found among cross-sectional and scenario-based studies (Nagin 1998). Indeed, meta-analytic evidence suggests that the effects of perceptual deterrence on crime vary by the rigorousness of the study's methodology (Pratt et al. 2008). Problematically, as the methodological rigor increases, the strength of the relationship between deterrence and crime actually *weakens*. However, even though the effects are modest at best, this body of research also tends to find that perceived certainty is more robustly associated with crime than is the perceived severity of punishment (Paternoster 1987; Nagin 1998; Pratt et al. 2008). Thus, much like macro-level indicators of deterrence, perceptual deterrence also demonstrates relatively weak effects on crime, yet the most strongly associated aspect would be the perceived certainty versus perceived severity.

In light of these disappointing findings, some in the deterrence field have called attention to the fact that deterrence might actually be more impactful for certain individuals. In response, the field has started shifting from studying *whether* deterrence works to *for whom* deterrence works (Piquero et al. 2011) and this pursuit is considered to be one of the most promising avenues for the deterrence field (Loughran et al. 2018). Indeed, Pratt et al. (2008: 386) called for research to assess "how individual differences . . . determine when – and for whom – deterrence 'works,'" which they argue is a necessary avenue to "save" the deterrence field.

20.4 DIFFERENTIAL SUSCEPTIBILITY TO DETERRENCE

In their review, Piquero et al. (2011) argued for a "kinds-of-people" approach to deterrence that focuses on individual differences in social and psychological factors that condition their susceptibility to deterrence threats. Since then, a body of literature has emerged that focuses on identifying the individual-level factors that might influence variation in susceptibility to deterrence threats (Jacobs 2010; Piquero et al. 2011; Thomas et al. 2013; Loughran et al. 2018). While we have made significant advances in this direction, most of this research has focused on the moderating effects of self-control, impulsivity, and time discounting in the deterrence–crime relationship (Nagin and Paternoster 1993, 1994; Piquero and Tibbetts 1996; Nagin and Pogarsky 2001, 2003, 2004; Pogarsky 2007). While evidence is mixed, studies often find that individuals who are more present-oriented or who are less able to exhibit self-control tend to be comparatively less impacted by deterrence threats (e.g., Piquero et al. 2011; Fine and van Rooij 2017). In addition to self-control, researchers have started identifying other factors that may promote differential susceptibility to deterrence. We begin with morality.

20.4.1 *Morality and Deterrence*

Compared with self-control, much less attention has been given to differences in morality as a factor influencing individual susceptibility to deterrence threats. However, this is an important oversight in light of the strength of the theoretical argument. The morality literature suggests that an individual's decision to commit crime is bound not only by the threat of punishment (i.e., deterrence) but also by their own conception of what is right and what is wrong (i.e., morality). Some individuals do not even consider engaging in crime due to their own strict moral code. Considering these individuals do not even enter the secondary stage of weighing the possible costs and benefits of crime because they do not consider engaging in crime in the first place, deterrence threats for these individuals may be entirely irrelevant (Zimring 1971; Wikström 2006). That is, deterrence threats might operate only for those whose levels of moral condemnation of crime are low to moderate and who would consider engaging in crime to begin with (Grasmick and Green 1981). Consequently, if we do not account for individual differences in morality or remove from our analysis individuals who have a strict moral code, the effect of deterrence threats on crime may actually be *underestimated*.

Beyond this simplistic notion, two more robust theoretical frameworks have been applied to explain the morality, deterrence, and crime relationships: Wikström's (2006) situational action theory and Bandura's (1991) mechanisms of moral disengagement. The next sections introduce each framework before discussing their relevance to the differential susceptibility to deterrence threats.

20.4.1.1 Situational Action Theory

The situational action theory (SAT) of crime considers how individual morality and criminogenic settings interact to produce criminal behavior (Wikström 2006). Specifically, it argues that crime is a moral action determined by a set of internalized rules of conduct. According to SAT, morality is conceptualized as "value-based rules about what is the right or wrong thing to do (or not to do) in particular circumstances" (Wikström 2014: 76). Thus, the key individual characteristic that governs whether an individual perceives crime as an action alternative is his/her "moral categories," which are "expressed in the making of moral judgment or the execution of moral habits" (Wikström and Treiber 2007: 245). In addition, differences in individual levels of self-control determine their process of choice (i.e., their ability to "act in accordance with [their] morality when faced with morally conflicting temptations or provocations" (p. 243)). Thus, within this framework, self-control is also a key conditional factor in the morality–deterrence relationship.

The expression of morality, however, is also dependent on characteristics of the environment. This is where concepts of deterrence come into play, as settings will also vary in the extent to which deterrent qualities are present. According to SAT, the degree to which deterrence threats influence crime depends on an individual's commitment to a moral code. Individuals who do not see crime as an action alternative due to their high moral standards will likely not deliberate the costs of crime because criminality does not enter their repertoire of action choices. Thus, deterrence threats should have no effect on individuals who maintain a high moral standard. On the other hand, deterrence threats should matter most among individuals who see crime as an action alternative (i.e., have low morality) and subsequently deliberate whether to commit a crime or not. Therefore, it is only under conditions in which individuals are low in morality *and* are actively deliberating crime as a choice of action that they will be most influenced by sanction threats. Repeat offenders, for example, are likely creatures of habit and engage in criminal activity out of routine; thus, sanction threats do not enter as a factor that influences their action choices as morality and self-control are likely low, and crime as a tried and true alternative is an accepted action regardless of the risks. Thus, according to SAT, morality can be viewed as the lens through which sanction threats are evaluated, and individuals with low levels of morality (who deliberate the costs of crime) are hypothesized to be most influenced by deterrence threats (Wikström 2006, 2014).

20.4.1.2 Moral Disengagement

By contrast, instead of conceptualizing morality as a value-based set of behaviors deemed right or wrong, Bandura (1991) introduced a concept of moral disengagement that focuses on the mechanisms that govern self-regulation. Mechanisms of moral disengagement capture the cognitive process by which individuals effectively disengage from their morality to engage in unethical behavior free from personal distress (i.e., internal sanctioning). Bandura (1991) posits that an individual's level of morality is best assessed by their engagement in mechanisms that justify or rationalize immoral behavior. Specifically, Bandura et al. (1996: 364–6) posit that individuals engage in the following four cognitive mechanisms as a means to moral disengagement: 1) reconstruing conduct via moral justifications, palliative comparisons, and euphemistic language; 2) obscuring causal agency through displacement and diffusion of responsibility; 3) disregarding or misrepresenting injurious consequences by distorting the consequences; and 4) blaming and devaluing victims via dehumanization techniques and the attribution of blame. Bandura (1991) argues that as opposed to focusing on value-based judgments regarding the moral wrongness of certain behaviors, we should be focusing on the cognitive processes that enable these judgments. The more these mechanisms are employed, the greater the chances that the individual will disengage from the threats associated with self-sanctioning (i.e., shame, guilt, stress), which frees them to commit crime.

Within the context of deterrence threats, individuals who have low morality (i.e., who are more morally disengaged) are less deterred by self-sanctioning, and thus might also be less deterred by threats of legal sanctioning. Stated differently, individuals who employ mechanisms to disengage from the immorality of their actions will likely engage in crime regardless of the threat of legal sanction because they have already excused themselves from self-sanctioning (i.e., personal distress). These individuals are more likely to reframe their actions as morally just, obscure their own personal agency, distort the consequences of their actions, and shift the blame onto someone else; all of which inhibit self-censure (Bandura et al. 1996). Individuals who are high in morality, on the other hand, might be more influenced by sanction threats. This is because these individuals likely feel greater distress at the thought of committing an immoral act, and thus, combined with the threat of legal sanction, might cause greater anticipatory distress.

Taken together, Wikström's (2006) SAT argues that those low in morality (who also deliberate the costs of crime) will be most susceptible to deterrence threats, whereas Bandura's (1991) mechanisms of moral disengagement would suggest that it is those who are highest in morality that are most susceptible to deterrence threats because these individuals are influenced by both internal (i.e., personal distress) and external sanction threats (i.e., threat of punishment). What both perspectives seem to agree on, however, is that deterrence threats matter least among those on the extreme lowest end of the morality spectrum in which crime has likely become a habit (i.e., repeat offenders). These individuals have likely internally excused themselves from the personal ramifications of their immoral actions and thus external factors, like the costs of legal sanctions, might no longer bear any consequence.

20.4.1.3 Mixed Findings in Research on Morality and Deterrence

There is a growing body of research that supports the notion that the effects of deterrence are dependent on an individual's level of morality; however, the findings are largely inconclusive with regard to the directionality of this effect – much like the mixed hypotheses surrounding how these relationships should work. While some studies have found that the effects of deterrence on crime are most pronounced when levels of morality are low (Bachman et al. 1992; Paternoster and Simpson 1996; Svensson 2015), others show that these effects matter most when levels of morality are high (Pauwels et al. 2011; Gallupe and Baron 2014; Fine and Van Rooij 2017), with the remainder of studies reporting no interaction effect at all (Jensen et al. 1978; Grasmick and Green 1981). For instance, Bachman et al. (1992) found that deterrence was effective in predicting intentions to commit a sexual assault for males, but only among those with low morality. When predicting business graduate students' intentions to commit corporate crime, Paternoster and Simpson (1996) similarly found that deterrence threats matter most for those with lower moral inhibitions. More recently, several studies have emerged that contradict these findings regarding the directionality of these effects. Using a sample of street youth, Gallupe and Baron (2014) found that while morality was the strongest predictor of drug use overall, the effect of deterrence on soft drug use was stronger among those with higher morality. Similarly, Piquero et al. (2016) used a sample of incarcerated individuals and found that the effect of sanction certainty on intentions to drive drunk was most pronounced for individuals who reported high levels of morality. Most recently, Fine and van Rooij (2017) found that deterrence threats against cheating were most effective among respondents who were high in morality. That is, the last three studies found that respondents who tended to engage in moral questions were most susceptible to the threat of legal sanctions. Yet, as a whole, the mixed findings regarding morality are difficult to interpret given the considerable variation in the measurement of key constructs, the type of sample used, as well as the operationalization of crime/deviance across studies. Consequently, more research is needed on morality and deterrence.

20.4.2 *Deterrence and the Obligation to Obey the Law*

In addition to morality, Fine et al. (2016) argued that the obligation to obey the law may play a critical role in differential susceptibility to deterrence. The inherent premise of their argument is that individuals vary in the extent to which they feel obligated to obey the law, which raises the question of how to define the obligation to obey the law. In the procedural justice literature, Tyler (1997, 2006) originally posited that the obligation to obey the law derives in part from an individual's perceptions of the legitimacy of the legal system and procedural justice. Yet, there is reason to believe that the system's functioning is not the sole determinant of how much one feels obligated to obey the law. In developing their "rule orientation" measure, Fine et al. (2016, 2020) posited that there are a variety of reasons why an individual may feel less obligated to obey the law beyond the procedural justness of the system, including when the law is not enforced, when it has not been publicized, if one's friends or colleagues violate the law or approve of violating the law, or if the law violates one's morality. While Fine et al. (2016) called their construct "rule orientation" in light of the original conceptualization of the "perceived obligation to obey the law" (Tyler 1997), rule orientation can reasonably be conceptualized as being synonymous with the perceived obligation to obey the law if one takes a literal interpretation of the phrase "perceived obligation to obey the law."

Returning to the discussion of deterrence, it is reasonable to believe that the obligation to obey the law (OOL) influences deterrability. Specifically, individuals who feel more OOL should theoretically be more influenced by a perceived deterrence threat whereas individuals who feel less OOL should be more prone to offending regardless of perceived deterrence threats. To date, only two studies have examined the impact of OOL on the deterrence–crime relationship. The first study found that individuals with low OOL are better able to justify offending regardless of whether a system explicitly declares an enforcement campaign (Fine et al. 2016). Thus, individuals who are already low in rule orientation will likely engage in deviant behaviors regardless of external factors (i.e., deterrence threat). Those high in rule orientation, on the other hand, appear to be more susceptible to deterrence threats. These individuals, by nature of feeling more obligated to obey the law, may take the deterrence threat to be a manifestation of the law, and consequently may feel more obligated to behave according to what it demands. It is reasonable to conclude that these individuals, who are more concerned with the rules, may also anticipate greater personal distress when faced with the prospect of violating rules in contexts in which sanction threats are made explicit.

The second study utilized an experimental approach to examine cheating behavior (Fine and van Rooij 2017). The study found that individuals who are low in OOL cheat the same amount regardless of the presence of a deterrence threat. However, individuals who feel moderate or high OOL cheat comparatively less when a deterrence threat is present. Thus, the experiment provided additional evidence that deterrence threats may be more effective for individuals who feel more obligated to obey the law, yet such threats may be less effective – or even ineffective –for individuals who feel less obligated to obey the law. Taken together, these two studies highlight the potential importance of the perceived obligation to obey the law in understanding differential deterrence. However, considering that there are few studies on the topic, more research is clearly necessary and such effects must be parsed out in future studies with more diverse samples.

20.5 CONCLUSION

Rooted in the assumption that people are relatively hedonistic and choose to avoid behaviors that cause them pain, deterrence theory appears relatively parsimonious and simplistic to implement: increase the costs of crime, and if the punishment is harsh enough, people will not engage in crime. The intuitively appealing nature of this theory is part of the reason it gained so much traction among criminal justice policymakers in the 1970s. Unfortunately, research has shown that the process is not that simple and the literature routinely finds that empirical support for the deterrence–crime relationship is weak at best (Nagin 1998; Pratt and Cullen 2005; Pratt et al. 2008). Thus, it should come as no surprise that the tough on crime legislation of the late twentieth century did not yield appreciable effects on crime but instead resulted in the greatest imprisonment binge the world has ever seen (Sawyer and Wagner 2019). While emerging research suggests that focusing on the certainty of apprehension through the mobilization of law enforcement resources could prove promising for reducing crime and imprisonment rates (Durlauf and Nagin 2011; Nagin 2018; Kaplan and Chalfin 2019), more research needs to be done in this area before making more conclusive claims about the deterrent effects of apprehension certainty.

Overall, as a field, scholars have shifted away from asking *whether* deterrence works to asking *for whom* deterrence might work. Transitioning to this "kinds-of-people" approach to deterrence has yielded promising results (Piquero et al. 2011). A number of studies have identified individual differences in social and psychological factors that condition an individual's susceptibility to deterrence threats. The majority of this research, however, has focused solely on factors related to self-control (Nagin and Paternoster 1993, 1994; Piquero and Tibbetts 1996; Nagin and Pogarsky 2001, 2003, 2004; Pogarsky 2007); to this day, much less research examines morality and the perceived obligation to obey the law. Morality could render deterrence threats irrelevant if those high in morality do not even consider crime as a possibility in the first place (Zimring 1971; Wikström 2006). The problem, however, is that there is a mixed body of findings and the evidence is inconclusive. More research is needed to shed light on the directionality of morality in the deterrence–crime relationship.

The obligation to obey the law (OOL) is another individual-level factor that has recently received attention in deterrence literature. According to this framework, individuals who feel less OOL should be less influenced by deterrence threats because they feel less obligated to obey the law, and a deterrence threat may be perceived as a manifestation of the law. Those who feel more OOL, on the other hand, will be more susceptible to deterrence threats given that they are more attuned to the law and also likely feel greater personal distress when faced with the prospect of violating the rules. While two recent studies found support for these notions (Fine et al. 2016; Fine and van Rooij 2017), the literature to date is far too nascent to be conclusive.

Altogether, research on individual differences in deterrability is still in its infancy. For instance, evidence is beginning to accumulate on the roles of emotion such as perceived fear (Pickett et al. 2018) and developmental level (Loughran et al. 2012; Shulman et al. 2017) in determining differential susceptibility to deterrence. The field continues to make advancements in the way of exploring differences in deterrence susceptibility, yet, in light of how recent the shift has been toward studying individual differences, more research is needed to parse out these effects using more diverse samples and more consistent measures.

REFERENCES

Apel, Robert, and Daniel S. Nagin. 2017. "Perceptual Deterrence." In *The Oxford Handbook of Offender Decision Making*, edited by Wim Bernasco, Jean-Louis Van Gelder, and Henk Elffers, 121–40. New York: Oxford University Press.

Bachman, Ronet, Raymond Paternoster, and Sally Ward. 1992. "The Rationality of Sexual Offending: Testing a Deterrence/Rational Choice Conception of Sexual Assault." *Law & Society Review* 26: 343–72.

Bandura, Albert. 1991. "Social Cognitive Theory of Moral Thought and Action." In *Handbook of Moral Behavior and Development, Volume 1: Theory*, edited by William M. Kurtines and Jacob L. Gewirtz, 45–103. New Jersey: Psychology Press.

Bandura, Albert, Claudio Barbaranelli, Gian Vittorio Caprara, and Concetta Pastorelli. 1996. "Mechanisms of Moral Disengagement in the Exercise of Moral Agency." *Journal of Personality and Social Psychology* 71: 364–74.

Beccaria, Cesare. [1764] 1986. *On Crimes and Punishments*. Transaction Press.

Bentham, Jeremy. [1879] 1988. *An Introduction to the Principles of Morals and Legislation*. Clarendon Press.

Braga, Anthony A., David Weisburd, and Brandon Turchan. 2018. "Focused Deterrence Strategies and Crime Control: An Updated Systematic Review and Meta-analysis of the Empirical Evidence." *Criminology & Public Policy* 17(1): 205–50.

Chalfin, Aaron, and Justin McCrary. 2017. "Criminal Deterrence: A Review of the Literature." *Journal of Economic Literature* 55(1): 5–48.

Durlauf, Steven N., and Daniel S. Nagin. 2011. "Imprisonment and Crime: Can Both Be Reduced?" *Criminology & Public Policy* 10(1): 13–54.

Fine, Adam, and Benjamin van Rooij. 2017. "For Whom Does Deterrence Affect Behavior? Identifying Key Individual Differences." *Law and Human Behavior* 41(4): 354–60.

Fine, Adam, Benjamin Van Rooij, Yuval Feldman, Shaul Shalvi, Eline Scheper, Margarita Leib, and Elizabeth Cauffman. 2016. "Rule Orientation and Behavior: Development and Validation of a Scale Measuring Individual Acceptance of Rule Violation." *Psychology, Public Policy, and Law* 22 (3): 314–29.

Fine, A., A. Thomas, B. van Rooij, and E. Cauffman. 2020. "Age-Graded Differences and Parental Influences on Adolescents' Obligation to Obey the Law." *Journal of Developmental and Life-Course Criminology* 6(1): 25–42. https://doi.org/10.1007/s40865-020-00134-8.

Gallupe, Owen, and Stephen W. Baron. 2014. "Morality, Self-Control, Deterrence, and Drug Use: Street Youths and Situational Action Theory." *Crime & Delinquency* 60(2): 284–305.

Grasmick, Harold G., and Donald E. Green. 1981. "Deterrence and the Morally Committed." *Sociological Quarterly* 22(1): 1–14.

Jacobs, Bruce A. 2010. "Deterrence and Deterrability." *Criminology* 48(2): 417–41.

Jensen, Gary F., Maynard L. Erickson, and Jack P. Gibbs. 1978. "Perceived Risk of Punishment and Self-Reported Delinquency." *Social Forces* 57(1): 57–78.

Kaplan, Jacob, and Aaron Chalfin. 2019. "More Cops, Fewer Prisoners?" *Criminology & Public Policy* 18 (1): 171–200.

Loughran, Thomas A., Alex R. Piquero, Jeffrey Fagan, and Edward P. Mulvey. 2012. "Differential Deterrence: Studying Heterogeneity and Changes in Perceptual Deterrence among Serious Youthful Offenders." *Crime & Delinquency* 58(1): 3–27.

Loughran, Thomas A., Raymond Paternoster, and Alex R. Piquero. 2018. "Individual Difference and Deterrence." In *Deterrence, Choice, and Crime*, edited by Daniel S Nagin, Francis T. Cullen, and Cheryl L. Jonson, vol. 23, 211–38. New York: Routledge.

Nagin, Daniel S. 1998. "Criminal Deterrence Research at the Outset of the Twenty-First Century." In *Crime and Justice: A Review of Research*, edited by Michael Tonry, vol. 23, 1–42. Chicago: University of Chicago Press.

2018. "Deterrent Effects of the Certainty and Severity of Punishment." In *Deterrence, Choice, and Crime*, edited by Daniel S Nagin, Francis T. Cullen, and Cheryl L. Jonson, vol. 23, 157–86. New York: Routledge.

Nagin, Daniel S., and Raymond Paternoster. 1993. "Enduring Individual Differences and Rational Choice Theories of Crime." *Law & Society Review* 27(3): 467–96.

1994. "Personal Capital and Social Control: The Deterrence Implications of a Theory of Individual Differences in Criminal Offending." *Criminology* 32(4): 581–606.

Nagin, Daniel S., and Greg Pogarsky. 2001. "Integrating Celerity, Impulsivity, and Extralegal Sanction Threats into a Model of General Deterrence: Theory and Evidence." *Criminology* 39(4): 865–92.

2003. "An Experimental Investigation of Deterrence: Cheating, Self-Serving Bias, and Impulsivity." *Criminology* 41(1): 167–94.

2004. "Time and Punishment: Delayed Consequences and Criminal Behavior." *Journal of Quantitative Criminology* 20(4): 295–317.

Paternoster, Raymond. 1987. "The Deterrent Effect of the Perceived Certainty and Severity of Punishment: A Review of the Evidence and Issues." *Justice Quarterly* 4(2): 173–217.

2018. "Perceptual Deterrence Theory." In *Deterrence, Choice, and Crime*, edited by Daniel S. Nagin, Francis T. Cullen, and Cheryl L. Jonson, vol. 23, 81–106. New York: Routledge.

Paternoster, Raymond, and Sally Simpson. 1996. "Sanction Threats and Appeals to Morality: Testing a Rational Choice Model of Corporate Crime." *Law & Society Review* 30(3): 549–83.

Pauwels, Lieven, Frank Weerman, Gerben Bruinsma, and Wim Bernasco. 2011. "Perceived Sanction Risk, Individual Propensity and Adolescent Offending: Assessing Key Findings from the Deterrence Literature in a Dutch Sample." *European Journal of Criminology* 8(5): 386–400.

Pickett, Justin T., and Sean Patrick Roche. 2016. "Arrested Development: Misguided Directions in Deterrence Theory and Policy." *Criminology & Public Policy* 15(3): 727–51.

Pickett, Justin T., Sean Patrick Roche, and Greg Pogarsky. 2018. "Toward a Bifurcated Theory of Emotional Deterrence." *Criminology* 56(1): 27–58.

Piquero, Alex, and Stephen Tibbetts. 1996. "Specifying the Direct and Indirect Effects of Low Self-Control and Situational Factors in Offenders' Decision Making: Toward a More Complete Model of Rational Offending." *Justice Quarterly* 13(3): 481–510.

Piquero, Alex R., Raymond Paternoster, Greg Pogarsky, and Thomas Loughran. 2011. "Elaborating the Individual Difference Component in Deterrence Theory." *Annual Review of Law and Social Science* 7: 335–60.

Pogarsky, Greg. 2007. "Deterrence and Individual Differences among Convicted Offenders." *Journal of Quantitative Criminology* 23(1): 59–74.

Pratt, Travis C., and Francis T. Cullen. 2005. "Assessing Macro-Level Predictors and Theories of Crime: A Meta-analysis." *Crime and Justice* 32: 373–450.

Pratt, Travis C., Francis T. Cullen, Kristie R. Blevins, Leah E. Daigle, and Tamara D. Madensen. 2008. "The Empirical Status of Deterrence Theory: A Meta-analysis." In *Taking Stock: The Status of Criminological Theory*, edited by Francis T. Cullen, John P. Wright, and Kristie R. Blevins, vol. 15, 367–96. New York: Routledge.

Sawyer, W., and Wagner, P. 2019. "Mass Incarceration: The Whole Pie 2019." *Prison Policy Initiative*. www.prisonpolicy.org/reports/pie2019.html.

Shulman, Elizabeth P., Kathryn C. Monahan, and Laurence Steinberg. 2017. "Severe Violence during Adolescence and Early Adulthood and Its Relation to Anticipated Rewards and Costs." *Child Development* 88(1): 16–26.

Svensson, Robert. 2015. "An Examination of the Interaction between Morality and Deterrence in Offending: A Research Note." *Crime & Delinquency* 61(1): 3–18.

Thomas, Kyle J., Thomas A. Loughran, and Alex R. Piquero. 2013. "Do Individual Characteristics Explain Variation in Sanction Risk Updating among Serious Juvenile Offenders? Advancing the Logic of Differential Deterrence." *Law and Human Behavior* 37(1): 10–21.

Tonry, Michael. 2018. "An Honest Politician's Guide to Deterrence: Certainty, Severity, Celerity, and Parsimony." In *Deterrence, Choice, and Crime*, edited by Daniel S Nagin, Francis T. Cullen, and Cheryl L. Jonson, vol. 23, 365–92. New York: Routledge.

Tyler, T. 1997. "Procedural Fairness and Compliance with the Law." *Swiss Journal of Economics and Statistics* 133: 219–40.

Tyler, Tom R. 2006. *Why People Obey the Law*. Princeton, NJ: Princeton University Press.

Wikström, Per-Olof H. 2006. "Individuals, Settings, and Acts of Crime: Situational Mechanisms and the Explanation of Crime." In *The Explanation of Crime: Contexts, Mechanisms, and Development*, edited by Per-Olof H. Wikström and Robert J. Sampson, 61–107. Cambridge: Cambridge University Press.

2014. "Why Crime Happens: A Situational Action Theory." In *Analytical Sociology: Actions and Networks*, edited by Gianluca Manzo, 74–94. Chester, UK: John Wiley & Sons, Ltd.

Wikström, Per-Olof H., and Kyle Treiber. 2007. "The Role of Self-Control in Crime Causation: Beyond Gottfredson and Hirschi's General Theory of Crime." *European Journal of criminology* 4(2): 237–64.

Zimring, Franklin E. 1971. *Perspectives on Deterrence*, vol. 2. National Institute of Mental Health, Center for Studies of Crime and Delinquency.

21

US Debarment: An Introduction

John Pachter, Christopher Yukins, and Jessica Tillipman

Abstract: This chapter, cowritten by senior members of the bar who teach in the leading public procurement law program in the United States, discusses corruption, compliance, and debarment in government procurement. When a government procures goods or services, it must decide questions of price and quality, and – equally importantly – whether the contractor is qualified ("responsible" in US federal contracting), that is, whether the contractor possesses the requisite physical and financial capability, a record of satisfactory performance, and integrity. For the government buyer, the question is whether the prospective contractor poses disqualifying performance or reputational risks to the government. When those risks are severe, suspension (temporary exclusion) and debarment (exclusion for a term of years) are tools that a government can use to exclude nonqualified individuals and companies from competing for public contracts. Suspension and debarment can be economically devastating – a "death sentence" for contractors. As this chapter reflects, remedial corporate compliance efforts – "self-cleaning," as it is termed in European procurement law – play a central role in a government's decision on whether to debar or suspend a contractor. For US federal contractors, the basic requirements for compliance efforts match the emerging worldwide standards for compliance systems. This chapter focuses on suspensions and debarments under the US federal system, while drawing on illustrative comparative examples from other procurement systems.

21.1 INTRODUCTION

When a government procures goods or services, it must decide questions of price and quality, and – equally importantly – whether the contractor is qualified ("responsible" in US federal contracting), that is, whether the contractor possesses the requisite physical and financial capability, a record of satisfactory performance, and integrity. Stated otherwise, the question is whether the prospective contractor poses disqualifying performance or reputational risks to the government. When those risks are severe, suspension (temporary exclusion) and debarment (exclusion for a term of years) are tools that a government can use to exclude nonqualified individuals and companies from competing for public contracts. Suspension and debarment can be economically devastating – a "death sentence." When a government agency or institution suspends or debars a firm or individual, other public entities may follow in what is known as a "cross-debarment" (Yukins 2013).

A number of prominent companies have been suspended or debarred over the years – or have narrowly avoided being excluded, despite extensive evidence of corruption or poor performance. Units of the Boeing Company, for example, were suspended from sales to the US government as a result of corruption and fraud, and the World Bank debarred many units of the Canadian construction services firm SNC-Lavalin, as a result of reported misconduct. While the causes of and approaches to debarment have varied enormously, the affected firm's response – typically intensive compliance efforts – is often the same, and the basic approach to compliance has remained relatively constant and uniform, as was acknowledged in the publication *A Resource Guide to the Foreign Corrupt Practices Act*, published by the US Justice Department and the US Securities and Exchange Commission, and as was reflected in the US Justice Department's Criminal Division's 2019 revised guidelines for corporate compliance programs.

Procurement systems take different approaches to excluding contractors. In the US federal procurement system, suspension and debarment are treated as extensions of a contracting officer's responsibility determination in an individual procurement (FAR 2019, §9.4). Suspension and debarment, in contrast, involve blanket exclusions from bidding for all federal agency procurements, grants, and other forms of assistance, with the likelihood of exclusion from state and local procurements and other impairments, including creditworthiness. Suspension and debarment can be imposed when a suspension and debarment official ("SDO") concludes that, based on a review of the administrative record, the contractor should be suspended or debarred for a variety of reasons, including commission of a punishable offense or other conduct indicating lack of integrity. The overall test is whether the contractor possesses "present responsibility."

Other systems, such as the World Bank sanctions regime (Dubois, Ezzeddin, and Swan 2016), take an approach more narrowly based on a principle of sanctioning contractors that have engaged in fraudulent, corrupt, or collusive behavior, or that have acted obstructively or coercively (in the context of an ongoing investigation, for example) (World Bank 2019).

As the discussion below reflects, remedial corporate compliance efforts – "self-cleaning," as it is termed in European procurement law – play a central role in US debarment. For federal contractors, the basic requirements for compliance efforts match the emerging worldwide standards for compliance systems.[1] While most federal contractors in general are required to have compliance systems in place, those compliance efforts are especially critical to contractors facing potential suspension or debarment. For those contractors, which must prove their "present responsibility" to suspension and debarment officials, it is critical to demonstrate that their compliance systems are in place and reliable. As is further discussed later, compliance efforts may be a central element in a negotiated administrative agreement between a contractor and a debarring official, and those efforts may be bolstered by additional measures to ensure present responsibility, such as a corporate monitor.

This chapter will focus on suspensions and debarments under the US federal system, while drawing on illustrative comparative examples from other procurement systems (Yukins and Kania 2019). Section 21.2 will introduce federal suspension and debarment, and discuss recent trends in the federal government. Because compliance systems are an integral part of an SDO's investigation, contractors are advised to implement and maintain a state-of-the-art system, to guard against improper conduct. In any case, a contractor under scrutiny will need to institute remedial compliance measures to convince the SDO that the risk of reoccurrence of improper conduct is minimized. Section 21.3 reviews the compliance systems required of

1 Compare FAR 2019, § 52.203–13 (clause describing federal contractors' compliance requirements) with DOJ SEC 2019: 56, n.309 (noting emerging common international standards for compliance systems).

federal contractors, and draws parallels between federal compliance requirements and those under the laws of other nations and international institutions. Section 21.4 discusses mandatory disclosures, and Section 21.5 addresses past performance in evaluation and award. Section 21.6 considers the nature of debarment in the federal system, including how agencies coordinate their debarment efforts. Section 21.7 discusses the effects of suspension and debarment, including current and prospective contracting efforts. Section 21.8 reviews "statutory" or "mandatory" suspensions and debarments, driven by statutory requirements such as labeling requirements under the Buy American Act. Section 21.9 discusses whether, and how, corporate affiliates may be suspended or debarred. Section 21.10 gives a detailed description of debarment proceedings, and Section 21.11 describes suspension proceedings. Section 21.12 discusses other suspensions and debarments under US federal law, and Section 21.13 concludes by suggesting that the US model, which is relatively well established and administratively flexible, may be a useful model for other nations.

21.2 US FEDERAL SUSPENSION AND DEBARMENT

In recent years, the emphasis on detecting fraud in government procurement has yielded an increase in the number of suspension and debarment actions in the US government. Several factors have contributed, among them the following:

(1) The Inspector General Act of 1978 and its 1988 amendments (codified at 5 USC Appendix) established federal Inspectors General ("IGs") as permanent, nonpartisan, and independent offices in more than seventy federal agencies (USPS OIG 2012).
(2) Recurring scandals, beginning with Operation Ill Wind in 1988 (FBI n.d.), a major multiagency investigation into defense procurement fraud which resulted in prosecutions of more than sixty contractors, consultants, and government officials, including a high-ranking Pentagon assistant secretary and a deputy assistant secretary of the Navy. The operation resulted in a total of $622 million worth of fines, recoveries, restitutions, and forfeitures, giving credence to the notion of widespread procurement fraud. Other incidents, including a multinational bribery scandal involving Siemens and the BP oil spill in the Gulf of Mexico, have played a significant role in drawing public attention to debarment. The most recent major example is the notorious "Fat Leonard" scandal, involving extensive corruption within the Navy's 7th Fleet (at least nineteen guilty pleas, including fourteen Navy officials, five courts martial and five admirals admonished and disciplined, and one admiral sentenced to eighteen months in prison and a $150,000 fine) (Whitlock and Uhrmacher 2018).
(3) Qui tam "whistleblower" suits, which have resulted in huge Civil False Claims Act judgments and settlements, putting pressure on companies to enter into alternative arrangements (deferred prosecution agreements ("DPAs") and nonprosecution agreements ("NPAs")) rather than face years of potentially ruinous litigation.
(4) Additional federal resources applied to fraud investigation and enforcement, which, in cooperation with Department of Justice prosecutors, have resulted in a formidable capability to investigate, prosecute, and debar individuals and companies.
(5) An increase in debarment of individuals, often contractor employees and other individuals identified in internal investigations disclosed to SDOs.
(6) Concern from Congress and others that debarment is too seldom employed has focused attention on the effectiveness of agencies' debarment systems. (GAO 2013).

Discretionary debarment remains a flexible tool for managing the government's perceived reputational and performance risks – but not for punishment. The Federal Acquisition Regulation ("FAR") states: "The serious nature of debarment and suspension requires that these sanctions be imposed only in the public interest for the Government's protection and *not for purposes of punishment*" (FAR 2019, § 9.402(b) (emphasis added)). Even where a cause for debarment exists, exclusion may not be in the government's interest. A company accused of improper conduct may be able to avoid debarment by demonstrating understanding of the seriousness of the situation and instituting remedial measures to prevent reoccurrence. This would include a showing that the company eradicated the circumstances that gave rise to the conduct, strengthened its ethics and compliance program, and provided assurance that the questioned conduct will not reoccur.

Government contractors live under a regime of ever-increasing stringency. Federal rules require contractors to adopt and implement an ethics and compliance program, including the education and training of employees. Federal contractors have added responsibility to discover and disclose instances of improper conduct in connection with government contracts. The result is that contractors must ensure that they already have an effective program in place *before* the government initiates debarment proceedings. These steps will also help a company make a convincing case that any improper conduct occurred despite the company's vigorous efforts to prevent it from happening. The same measures form a critical affirmative defense under anti-corruption laws around the world, such as the UK Bribery Act.[2] Accordingly, contractors have much at stake in maintaining a sound system of compliance, business integrity and ethics, along with a solid contract performance history.

21.3 CONTRACTOR COMPLIANCE SYSTEMS

Any consideration of debarment and suspension should begin with an understanding of the government's requirement for a Contractor Code of Business Ethics and Conduct – the cornerstone of a contractor's internal controls in a compliance system.[3] The FAR requires that "[g]overnment contractors must conduct themselves with the highest degree of integrity and honesty" and that they have a written code of business ethics and conduct (FAR 2019, § 3.1002(a)–(b)). In addition, contractors "should have an employee business ethics and compliance training program and an internal control system" that (1) are "suitable to the size of the company and extent of its involvement in Government contracting"; (2) "[f]acilitate timely discovery and disclosure of improper conduct in connection with Government contracts"; and (3) "[e]nsure corrective measures are promptly instituted and carried out" (FAR 2019, § 3.1002(b)).

While this policy applies as guidance to *all* federal contracts, two FAR clauses – (FAR 2019, § 52.203–13), Contractor Code of Business Ethics and Conduct, and (FAR 2019, § 52.203–14), Display of Hotline Poster(s) – are mandatory if the contract meets certain conditions, as follows:

2 Bribery Act of 2010, c. 23, Sec. 7 (Eng.), www.legislation.gov.uk/ukpga/2010/23/contents (discussing the "adequate procedures" defense).

3 In October 2018, the Justice Department announced new directions in compliance and monitoring. In a speech by Assistant Attorney General Brian Benczkowski and new guidance, the Justice Department indicated that it would place less emphasis on corporate monitors when assessing corporate controls, and that the Department would assess company compliance efforts with a recognition that compliance systems may vary substantially from industry to industry (DOJ 2018; DOJ Benczkowski 2018).

- FAR 52.203–13, Contractor Code of Business Ethics and Conduct is mandatory if the value of the contract is expected to exceed $5.5 million and the performance period is 120 days or more (FAR 2019, § 3.1004(a)).
- FAR 52.203–14, Display of Hotline Poster(s) is mandatory unless the contract is for the acquisition of a commercial item or will be performed entirely outside the United States if –
  - The contract exceeds $5.5 million or a lesser amount established by the agency; and
  - The agency has a fraud hotline poster; or
  - The contract is funded with disaster assistance funds (FAR 2019, § 3.1004(b)(1)).

21.4 MANDATORY DISCLOSURES

These requirements for a compliance system are bolstered by a separate requirement for mandatory disclosure if a federal contractor discovers certain misconduct (ABA PCLS 2010; Yukins 2015). Even if the clause at FAR 52.203–13, Contractor Code of Business Ethics and Conduct, is inapplicable, a contractor may be suspended or debarred for a "knowing failure" by a principal to timely disclose to the government, in connection with the award, performance, or closeout of a government contract performed by the contractor or a subcontract, "credible evidence" of a violation of federal criminal law involving fraud, conflict of interest, bribery, or gratuity violations in Title 18 of the United States Code or a violation of the Civil False Claims Act (FAR 2019, § 3.1003(a)(2)). Knowing failure to timely disclose credible evidence of any of the above violations remains a cause for suspension or debarment until three years after final payment (§ 3.1003(a)(2)).

The Payment clauses at FAR 2019 §§ 52.212–4(i)(5), 52.232–25(d), 52.232–26(c), and 52.232–27(l) require that, if the contractor becomes aware that the government has overpaid on a contract financing or invoice payment, the contractor shall remit the overpayment amount to the government. A contractor may be suspended or debarred for "knowing failure" by a principal to timely disclose "credible evidence" of a "significant overpayment," other than overpayments resulting from contract financing payments as defined in FAR 32.001(FAR 2019, § 3.1003(a)(3)).

It is a mistake to assume that these disclosure obligations limit the contractor's duty to the reasons enumerated. The FAR debarment mitigation standards discussed later contain an additional backward-looking disclosure obligation: the contractor is asked to address, among other things, whether "[t]he contractor timely brought the activity to the attention of the Government agency" (FAR 2019, § 9.406–1(a)). In this instance "timely" means before receiving notice from the Suspension and Debarment Official ("SDO").[4]

21.5 PAST PERFORMANCE: EVALUATION FACTOR AND RESPONSIBILITY DETERMINATION

The FAR states that "[p]urchases shall be made from, and contracts shall be awarded to, responsible prospective contractors only" (FAR 2019, §§ 9.103(a), 9.402(a)).[5] One element of "responsibility" requires the prospective contractor to "[h]ave a satisfactory record of integrity

[4] A short note on titles: in the US Department of Defense, these officials are referred to as "Suspending and Debarring Officials" (Grandon 2016).

[5] Special rules apply if the prospective contractor is a small business concern (FAR 2019, §§ 19.6, 19.8).

and business ethics" (FAR 2019, § 9.104–1(d)). A serious integrity-based failure thus can be a ground for denial of award of a single contract.

Corrupt actions or shoddy performance also can affect a contractor's past performance evaluation. With limited exceptions, past performance is included as an evaluation factor "in all source selections for negotiated competitive acquisitions expected to exceed the simplified acquisition threshold" (FAR 2019, § 15.304(c)(3)(i)). Agencies compile past performance information, to include, among other things, the contractor's record of "[r]easonable and cooperative behavior and commitment to customer satisfaction" (FAR 2019, § 42.1501(a)(4)); "[i]ntegrity and business ethics"(§ 42.1501(a)(6)); and "[b]usiness-like concern for the interest of the customer" (§ 42.1501(a)(7)). In addition to the separate evaluation factor in FAR Part 15 negotiated competitive acquisitions, another element of the general standards of responsibility is that a prospective contractor "[h]ave a satisfactory performance record" (FAR 2019, § 9.104–1(c)).

That past performance information and record of integrity and business ethics are compiled and relied upon by agencies in making award decisions. Agencies "use the Contractor Performance Assessment Reporting System (CPARS) and Past Performance Information Retrieval System (PPIRS) metric tools to measure the quality and timely reporting of past performance information" (FAR 2019, § 42.1501(b)). Past performance evaluations are entered into CPARS, the government-wide evaluation reporting tool for past performance reports on contracts and orders (FAR 2019, § 42.1502(a); GSA 2019a).

In summary, negative past performance assessments and an unsatisfactory record of integrity and business ethics can result in a determination of nonresponsibility for a single contract award. Suspension and debarment, in contrast, involve an agency's blanket disqualification of a contractor from award of *any* contract for a period of time. In addition, a succession of nonresponsibility determinations may constitute a de facto debarment.

21.6 NATURE OF DEBARMENT

Courts have recognized that debarment and suspension are draconian measures with a stigmatizing effect that can put "the very economic life of the contractor ... in jeopardy."[6] In addition to cutting off eligibility for federal contracts, grants, and other forms of assistance, debarment can mean loss of ability to bid on state and local government contracts, and can lead to "sudden contraction of bank credit, adverse impact on market price of shares of listed stock, if any, and critical uneasiness of creditors generally, to say nothing of 'loss of face' in the business community."[7] The stigmatizing effect of these sanctions gives a powerful weapon to aggressive competitors, especially in other public markets (e.g., state and local government procurements) as well as commercial markets. Thus, even contractors with a relatively small dollar value of federal government contracts can face dire consequences from debarment.

A seminal opinion of the US Court of Appeals for the DC Circuit in 1964 mandated regulations providing due process protections for contractors subjected to debarment.[8]

6 *Old Dominion Dairy Prods., Inc.* v. *Sec'y of Def.*, 631 F. 2d 953, 968 (D.C. Cir. 1980).

7 *Gonzalez* v. *Freeman*, 344 F.2d 570, 574 (D.C. Cir. 1964).

8 Ibid. at 578 ("Considerations of basic fairness require administrative regulations establishing standards for debarment and procedures which will include notice of specific charges, opportunity to present evidence and to cross-examine adverse witnesses, all culminating in administrative findings and conclusions based upon the record so made."). Contractors enjoy similar protections under the European Union's procurement directive (EU 2014), which in Article 57, paragraph 6 requires a "statement of the reasons" when a procuring entity chooses *not* to

Nevertheless, whether the contractor receives notice of specific charges and is granted an opportunity to be heard *before* imposition of suspension or debarment is in the hands of agency debarment officials. SDOs may, but are not required to, issue show cause letters or requests for information to afford the contractor an opportunity to give reasons why it should not be suspended or debarred.

There have also been instances of de facto debarment or suspension: successive determinations of nonresponsibility, amounting to a blanket disqualification. This type of action implicates due process "liberty interests," requiring notice and an opportunity to be heard.[9]

Since debarment and suspension are "discretionary actions" (FAR 2019, § 9.402(a)), the existence of a cause for debarment or suspension does not mandate imposition of the sanction. Moreover, as noted, the FAR states: "The serious nature of debarment and suspension requires that these sanctions be imposed *only in the public interest for the Government's protection and not for purposes of punishment.* Agencies shall impose debarment or suspension to protect the Government's interest and only for the causes and in accordance with the procedures set forth in this subpart" (FAR 2019, § 9.402(b), emphasis added).[10] Finally, a contractor is entitled to seek judicial review of an agency's decision to suspend or debar (Block 2018).

21.6.1 *Relationship to the "Common Rule"*

The FAR suspension and debarment rules apply to federal agency procurements. The Nonprocurement Common Rule, on the other hand, governs debarment and suspension regarding matters such as "grants, cooperative agreements, scholarships, fellowships, contracts of assistance, loans, loan guarantees, subsidies, insurance, payments for specified use, and donation agreements" under Executive Order 12549 (FAR 2019, § 9.403).[11] Debarment or suspension under the FAR or the Common Rule excludes entities from eligibility under the other (FAR 2019, § 9.401).

Unlike the FAR, which gives a notice of proposed debarment the same immediate effect as a suspension or debarment, the Common Rule provides for exclusion only upon suspension or debarment. The Common Rule nevertheless gives immediate preclusive effect to notices of proposals to debar issued under the FAR (OMB 2019).

21.6.2 *The Interagency Committee on Debarment and Suspension*

The Interagency Suspension and Debarment Committee (ISDC)[12] ensures that executive departments and agencies "[p]articipate in a government-wide system for debarment and

admit a excluded contractor to a procurement because the contractor's remedial ("self-cleaning") measures regarding past misconduct have been determined inadequate.

9 *Old Dominion Dairy*, 631 F.2d at 961, 963, 966.

10 For a comparison to the World Bank sanctions system, which approaches contractor exclusion using a system of calibrated sanctions for misconduct, through a highly structured adjudicative process, see, e.g., Dubois 2012.

11 Cf. Meunier and Nelson 2017; ISDC 2018: 3 ("The ISDC is exploring the development of a consistent set of procedures for both procurement and nonprocurement suspensions and debarments, including pre-notice tools and the application of exclusion concerning notices of proposed debarment.").

12 Established pursuant to Section 4 of Executive Order 12549 on Debarment and Suspension. 51 Fed. Reg. 6370 (Feb. 21, 1986).

suspension from programs and activities involving Federal financial and nonfinancial assistance and benefits." Federal agency SDOs are listed with contact information at www.acquisition.gov/isdc-debarring-officials.

The ISDC plays a coordinating and leadership role in the suspension and debarment process. When more than one agency has an interest in debarring or suspending a contractor, agencies will usually defer to the "lead agency" – generally the one with the highest dollar value of contracts with the company. The ISDC resolves any lead agency issue and coordinates among interested agencies before any agency initiates suspension, debarment, or related administrative action (FAR 2019, § 9.402(d)).

In addition to assisting agencies with suspension and debarment, the ISDC annual report for fiscal year 2016 (Jan. 12, 2017) noted that the ISDC works with agencies "to identify other practices that protect the government's interest by promoting contractor and program participant responsibility without the need to impose an exclusion through suspension or debarment." Alternative tools identified in the report "include the use of pre-notice engagements that allow the agency to develop information to better assess the risk to government programs and determine what measures are necessary to protect the government's interest without immediately imposing an exclusion. As a result, agencies again reported significant use of Show Cause letters, Requests for Information, or other pre-notice investigative engagement letters." The report also noted continued use of administrative agreements as an alternative to suspension and debarment. These administrative agreements "typically mandate the implementation of several provisions to improve the ethical culture and corporate governance processes of a respondent, often with the use of independent third party monitors."

21.6.3 *The System for Award Management (SAM)*

Names of companies and individuals debarred or suspended under the FAR and the Common Rule are entered into the web-based System for Award Management ("SAM"), administered by the General Services Administration ("GSA") (FAR 2019, § 9.404; GSA 2019b). This element of the SAM, previously known as the Excluded Parties List System, is used by contracting agencies and also by prime contractors in evaluation of prospective contractors and subcontractors.

21.7 EFFECT OF DEBARMENT AND SUSPENSION

Contractors that are "debarred, suspended, *or proposed for debarment*" are ineligible to receive contracts (FAR 2019, § 9.405(a), emphasis added). An unusual feature is that, as noted in Section 21.6.1, "proposed for debarment" under the FAR has the same practical effect as debarred (Meunier and Nelson 2017: 574) (discussing history of preclusive rule). Agencies may not solicit offers from, award contracts to, or consent to subcontracts with these contractors, unless the agency head determines that there is a compelling reason (FAR 2019, §§ 9.405–1(b), 9.405–2, 9.406–1(c), 9.407–1(d), 23.506(e)). Listed contractors "are also excluded from conducting business with the Government as agents or representatives of other contractors" (FAR 2019, § 9.405(a)). As noted, and as discussed in more detail later, agencies may not consent to subcontracts with listed contractors. (FAR 2019, § 9.405(b)). Nor may listed concerns act as individual sureties (FAR 2019, § 9.405(c)).

If a contractor's period of ineligibility expires or is terminated before award, the contracting officer "may, but is not required to, consider such proposals, quotations, or offers" from the contractor (FAR 2019, § 9.405(c)(3)).

As to existing contracts, the FAR states that "agencies may continue contracts or subcontracts in existence at the time the contractor was debarred, suspended, or proposed for debarment unless the agency head directs otherwise" (FAR 2019, § 9.405–1(a)). However, for excluded contractors, agencies may not (1) place orders exceeding the guaranteed minimum under indefinite quantity contracts, (2) place orders under Federal Supply Schedule contracts, blanket purchase agreements, or basic ordering agreements, or (3) add new work, exercise options, or otherwise extend the duration of current contracts or orders (FAR 2019, § 9.405–1(b)).

In some instances, government consent to subcontracting is required (FAR 2019, § 44.2). When a contractor that is debarred, suspended, or proposed for debarment is proposed as a subcontractor for any subcontract subject to government consent, consent will be withheld unless the agency head states in writing the compelling reasons for approval action (FAR 2019, §§ 9.405–2(a), 9.405–2(b)).

In the standard contract clause titled "Protecting the Government's Interests When Subcontracting with Contractors Debarred, Suspended or Proposed for Debarment," the FAR (2019, § 52.209–6) provides that contractors shall not enter into any subcontract in excess of $35,000, other than a subcontract for a commercially available off-the-shelf item, with a contractor that has been debarred, suspended, or proposed for debarment unless there is a compelling reason to do so. If a contractor intends to enter into a subcontract in excess of $35,000, other than a subcontract for a commercially available off-the-shelf item, with a party that has been listed as excluded in SAM, a corporate officer or designee of the contractor must notify the contracting officer, in writing, before entering into the subcontract. The notice must include, among other information, the compelling reasons for doing business with the subcontractor notwithstanding its listing. For contracts for the acquisition of commercial items, the notification requirement applies only for first-tier subcontracts. For all other contracts, the notification requirement applies to subcontracts at any tier.

21.8 STATUTORY DEBARMENTS

The bulk of our discussion has focused on discretionary debarments, undertaken to protect the government from undue performance or reputational risk. A separate class of exclusions (sometimes called "statutory" or "mandatory" suspensions and debarments) stems from statutes that mandate suspension or debarment in the event of a conviction for violation of certain statutes, or formal agency determinations of certain types of wrongdoing. Statutes that contain their own debarment provisions include, for example, the Buy American Act, the Service Contract Act, the Davis-Bacon Act, the Walsh-Healey Act, the Clean Air Act and the Clean Water Act. Some statutes mandating exclusion allow agencies to waive the suspension or debarment; some, however, do not.[13]

21.9 SCOPE OF DEBARMENT: AFFILIATES

Debarment constitutes debarment of all divisions or other organizational elements of the contractor, unless the debarment decision is limited by its terms to specific divisions,

[13] For a more complete listing of statutory debarments, see, e.g., Manuel 2008: 2–5.

organizational elements, or commodities (FAR 2019, § 9.406–1(b)). The SDO may extend the debarment decision to include any affiliates of the contractor if they are specifically named and given written notice and an opportunity to be heard. Business concerns, organizations, or individuals are affiliates of each other if, directly or indirectly, (1) either one controls or has the power to control the other, or (2) a third party controls or has the power to control both.[14]

The "fraudulent, criminal, or other seriously improper conduct" of an officer, director, shareholder, partner, employee, or other individual associated with a contractor may be imputed to the contractor when the conduct occurred "in connection with the individual's performance of duties for or on behalf of the contractor, or with the contractor's knowledge, approval, or acquiescence" (FAR 2019, § 9.406–5(a)). Conversely, the conduct of a contractor may be imputed to any officer, director, shareholder, partner, employee, or other individual associated with the contractor "who participated in, knew of, or had reason to know of the contractor's conduct" (FAR 2019, § 9.406–5(b)). Similar imputation rules apply to participants in a joint venture or similar arrangement (FAR 2019, § 9.406–5(c)).

Debarment and proposed debarment are effective throughout the executive branch of the government unless an agency head or designee states in writing compelling reasons justifying continued business dealings between that agency and the contractor (FAR 2019, § 9.406–1 (c)). Debarment from procurement contracts may extend to disqualification from contracts for the purchase of federal personal property pursuant to the Federal Property Management Regulations (FPMR) 101–45.6 (FAR 2019, § 9.406–1(d)).

21.10 DEBARMENT PROCEEDINGS

21.10.1 *General*

Above all, the SDO must "determine whether debarment is in the Government's interest." The mere finding of a cause for debarment does not require imposition of the sanction. Rather, the debarring official must consider "the seriousness of the contractor's acts or omissions and any remedial measures or mitigating factors" (FAR 2019, § 9.406–1(a)).

The contractor has the burden of demonstrating, to the satisfaction of the debarring official, its present responsibility and that debarment is not necessary.[15]

21.10.2 *Causes for Debarment*

The listed causes for suspension and debarment are essentially the same. In summary, the causes include:

- Commission of fraud, embezzlement, theft, forgery, bribery, falsification or destruction of records, making false statements, tax evasion, violating Federal criminal laws, receiving stolen property, an unfair trade practice
- Violation of antitrust statutes

[14] Indicia of control include, but are not limited to, interlocking management or ownership, identity of interests among family members, shared facilities and equipment, common use of employees, or a business entity organized following the debarment, suspension, or proposed debarment of a contractor which has the same or similar management, ownership, or principal employees as the contractor that was debarred, suspended, or proposed for debarment (FAR 2019, § 9.403).

[15] Procedures for debarment and suspension in the US Department of Defense are described in Appendix H to the Defense Federal Acquisition Regulation Supplement.

- Willful failure to perform a contract, or a history of failure to perform
- Violation of the Drug-Free Workplace Act
- Delinquent Federal taxes (more than $3,000)
- Knowing failure to disclose "credible evidence" of a violation of criminal law or the Civil False Claims Act, or significant overpayments on a contract
- Any other cause of so serious or compelling a nature that it affects present responsibility (FAR 2019, §§ 9.406–2, 9.407–2).

As noted, a contractor may be also be suspended or debarred for "knowing failure" by a principal to timely disclose "credible evidence" of a "significant overpayment," other than overpayments resulting from contract financing payments as defined in FAR 32.001(FAR 2019, § 3.1003(a)(3); see Section 21.4).

In addition, the government contracting officer must notify the SDO of credible evidence that:

(i) a contractor, contractor employee, subcontractor, subcontractor employee, or agent engages in severe forms of trafficking in persons or procures a commercial sex act during the period of performance of a contract;
(ii) a contractor, contractor employee, subcontractor, subcontractor employee, or agent uses forced labor in the performance of the contract; or
(iii) the contractor fails to comply with contractual responsibilities to combat human trafficking in FAR (2019, § 52.222–50).

21.10.3 *Mitigating Factors*

Mitigating factors to be considered by the SDO include, under the FAR (2019, § 9.406–1(a)), whether:

(1) The contractor had effective standards of conduct and internal control systems in place or had adopted procedures before the Government investigation began.
(2) The contractor timely brought the activity to the attention of the Government agency.
(3) The contractor fully investigated the circumstances and made the result available to the debarring official.
(4) The contractor cooperated fully with Government agencies during the investigation and any court or administrative action.
(5) The contractor paid or agreed to pay criminal, civil, and administrative liability for the improper activity, including investigative or administrative costs incurred by the Government, and has made or agreed to make restitution.
(6) The contractor has taken appropriate disciplinary action against the responsible individuals.
(7) The contractor implemented or agreed to implement remedial measures.
(8) The contractor instituted or agreed to institute new or revised review and control procedures and ethics training programs.
(9) The contractor has had adequate time to eliminate the circumstances within the contractor's organization that led to the cause for debarment.
(10) The contractor's management recognizes and understands the seriousness of the misconduct and has implemented programs to prevent recurrence.

As a practical matter, the mitigating factors listed in the regulation may help frame a contractor's response to a threatened debarment. In preparing to respond to a potential debarment, for example, the contractor may gather evidence to demonstrate mitigating efforts regarding some or all of these regulatory factors.

Note that these mitigation standards are designed for companies. There are no separate mitigation standards for individuals. As a result, individuals who are noticed for debarment must tailor their response to the facts of their situation, borrowing as much as possible from the mitigation standards in the regulation (Sacilotto 2018). This would include, for example, any role that the individual played in enhancing the company's culture of ethics and compliance.

21.10.4 *Administrative Procedures*

Debarment procedures are informal, giving the contractor "an opportunity to submit, in person, in writing, or through a representative, information and argument in opposition to the proposed debarment" (FAR 2019, § 9.406–3(b)(1)). If the debarment action is based on a conviction or plea agreement, or a civil judgment, the contractor will not be allowed to challenge the facts found by the tribunal or recited in the plea agreement. In other cases, in contrast, the contractor will be allowed to show that there is a "genuine dispute over facts material to the proposed debarment" (FAR 2019, § 9.406–3(b)(2)). In that case, the contractor will have the opportunity to "appear with counsel, submit documentary evidence, present witnesses, and confront any person the agency presents" (FAR 2019,§ 9.406–3(b)(2)(i)).

A notice of proposed debarment should, among other things, inform the contractor and any named affiliates that "debarment is being considered"; the reasons for the proposed debarment "in terms sufficient to put the contractor on notice" of the causes relied upon; the effect of the issuance of the notice of proposed debarment; the potential effect of an actual debarment; and that within thirty days after receipt the contractor may submit "information and argument in opposition, including any additional specific information that raises a genuine dispute over the material facts" (FAR 2019, § 9.406–3(c)). Because a notice of proposed debarment automatically results in listing of the contractor in the online SAM (GSA 2019b; FAR 2019, § 9.405(b)), the phrase required by the FAR in the notice that "debarment is being considered" is misleading. To avoid the unfairness in the process, some SDOs instead send show cause letters or requests for information, stating the agency's perceived grounds for debarment and asking the contractor to provide any reasons why debarment should not be imposed.

If the debarment is based on a conviction or civil judgment, or there is no genuine dispute over material facts, "the debarring official shall make a decision on the basis of all the information in the administrative record, including any submission made by the contractor" (FAR 2019, § 9.406–3(d)(1)). "If no suspension is in effect, the decision shall be made within 30 working days after receipt of any information and argument submitted by the contractor, unless the debarring official extends this period for good cause." (§ 9.406–3(d)).

If the matter involves disputed material facts, the debarring official will prepare written findings of fact (FAR 2019, § 9.406–3(d)(2)(i)). If the debarment is not based on a conviction or civil judgment, "the cause for debarment must be established by a preponderance of the evidence" (§ 9.406–3(d)(3)).

21.10.5 *Administrative Agreements*

In some instances, as an alternative to debarment, the SDO may agree to enter into an administrative agreement, usually for three years, to permit the company to continue to bid on government contracts, subject to fulfillment of the requirements of the administrative agreement. These agreements typically require the appointment of an independent monitor who supervises the company's remedial steps and the strengthening of its ethics and compliance program (Pachter 2013). While the FAR does not expressly authorize the use of administrative agreements, it acknowledges them by requiring the SDO to enter information relating to an administrative agreement in the Federal Awardee Performance and Integrity Information System ("FAPIIS"), at www.cpars.gov/fapiismain.htm (FAR 2019, §§ 9.406–3(f), 9.407–3(e)).

In other instances, a US attorney may enter into an alternative agreement (DPA or NPA) that requires the appointment of an independent monitor. The debarring official of the procuring agency (or lead agency) is not bound by the Justice Department's agreement but may recognize the appointment of the monitor and withhold debarment for the same period.

21.10.6 *Period of Debarment*

Debarments generally should not exceed three years (FAR 2019, § 9.406–4(a)(1)). Debarments for violations of the provisions of the Drug-Free Workplace Act of 1988 may be for a period not to exceed five years (FAR 2019, § 23.506).

If the Secretary of Homeland Security or the Attorney General of the United States determines that a contractor is not in compliance with Immigration and Nationality Act employment provisions (Clinton 1994),[16] that determination is not reviewable in the debarment proceeding that is to result from that violation (FAR 2019, § 9.406–2 (b)(2)). The period of debarment is one year, but it may be extended for additional periods of one year if the Secretary of Homeland Security or the Attorney General determines that the contractor continues to be in violation of the employment provisions of the Immigration and Nationality Act (FAR 2019, § 9.406–4(b)).

If the contractor is already subject to suspension, the SDO will consider the period of suspension in determining the term of debarment (FAR 2019, § 9.406–4(a)(2)).

The SDO may extend the debarment for an additional period if the SDO determines that an extension is "necessary to protect the Government's interest." However, the extension may not be based "solely on the basis of the facts and circumstances upon which the initial debarment action was based" (FAR 2019, § 9.406–4(b)).

The SDO may reduce the period or extent of debarment upon the contractor's request, based on (1) newly discovered material evidence; (2) reversal of the conviction or civil judgment on which the debarment was based; (3) bona fide change in ownership or management; (4) elimination of other causes for which the debarment was imposed; or (5) other reasons that the SDO deems appropriate (FAR 2019, § 9.406–4(c)).

[16] See Exec. Order No. 12989, 59 Fed. Reg. 7629 (Feb. 16, 1994) *as amended by* Exec. Order No. 3286, 68 Fed. Reg. 10619 (Mar. 5, 2003).

21.11 SUSPENSION PROCEEDINGS

Suspension is a "serious action" to be imposed on the basis of "adequate evidence,"[17] pending the completion of investigation or legal proceedings, when immediate action is necessary to protect the government's interest. In assessing the adequacy of evidence, agencies should consider how much information is available, the credibility of the evidence, whether important allegations are corroborated, and what inferences can reasonably be drawn. This assessment should include an examination of basic documents such as contracts, inspection reports, and correspondence (FAR 2019, § 9.407–1(b)(1)).

As is true for debarments, the existence of a cause for suspension does not require the SDO to suspend the contractor. The SDO should consider the seriousness of the contractor's acts or omissions and may, but is not required to, consider remedial measures or mitigating factors. Another disclosure obligation is contained in the following FAR language: "A contractor has the burden of promptly presenting to the suspending official evidence of remedial measures or mitigating factors *when it has reason to know that a cause for suspension exists*" (emphasis added). The existence or nonexistence of any remedial measures or mitigating factors does not necessarily determine a contractor's present responsibility (FAR 2019, § 9.407–1(b)(2)).

As in the case of debarment, suspension includes all divisions or other organizational elements of the contractor, unless the suspension decision is limited by its terms to specific divisions, organizational elements, or commodities. The same rules as in debarment apply to affiliates of the contractor (FAR 2019, § 9.407–1(c)). Similarly, suspension is effective throughout the executive branch unless the agency head or designee states in writing the compelling reasons justifying continued business dealings between that agency and the contractor (FAR 2019, § 9.407–1(d)). Suspension may also extend to contracts for the purchase of federal property (FAR 2019, § 9.407–1(e)).

21.11.1 *Causes for Suspension*

The causes for suspension are the same as the causes for debarment, except that the standard is "adequate evidence" (FAR 2019, § 9.407–2 (a)). Indictment for any of the causes in FAR 9.407–2(a) "constitutes adequate evidence for suspension" (FAR 2019, § 9.407–2(b)). A prosecutor obtains an indictment by presenting witnesses, selected by the prosecutor, to a grand jury, asking the grand jury to concur that there is probable cause to proceed in court. No judge is present in the grand jury proceeding, and the accused has no right to participate.

Nevertheless, a contractor may be suspended as soon as the prosecutor obtains the indictment. The FAR states that the agency "shall afford the contractor (and any specifically named affiliates) an opportunity *following the imposition of suspension* to submit, in person, in writing, or through a representative, information and argument in opposition to the suspension" (FAR 2019, § 9.407–3(b)(1) (emphasis added)). In the case of an indictment, the contractor is not allowed to raise disputed issues of fact.

If the suspension is not based on an indictment, the contractor may raise disputed issues of fact. However, the agency may ask the Department of Justice to advise whether "substantial

17 In *Horne Brothers, Inc.* v. *Laird*, 463 F.2d 1268, 1271 (D.C. Cir. 1972), the court stated that "'adequate evidence' … need not be the kind necessary for a successful criminal prosecution or a formal debarment. The matter may be likened to the probable cause necessary for an arrest, a search warrant, or a preliminary hearing. This is less than must be shown at the trial, but it must be more than uncorroborated suspicion or accusation."

interests of the Government in pending or contemplated legal proceedings based on the same facts as the suspension would be prejudiced" by the presentation of facts (FAR 2019, § 9.407–3 (b)(2)). If the agency makes no such determination based on Department of Justice advice, the agency will "[a]fford the contractor an opportunity to appear with counsel, submit documentary evidence, present witnesses, and confront any person the agency presents" (FAR 2019, § 9.407–3(b)(2)).

21.11.2 *Notice of Suspension*

The agency's notice of suspension will inform the contractor and any named affiliates that they have been suspended based on an indictment or other adequate evidence of irregularities of a serious nature in business dealings with the government or seriously reflecting on the propriety of further government dealings with the contractor. The notice should state:

- The suspension is for a temporary period pending the completion of investigation and ensuing legal proceedings "in terms sufficient to place the contractor on notice without disclosing the Government's evidence";
- The causes relied upon;
- The effect of the suspension;
- That the contractor may, within 30 days after receipt of notice, submit "in writing, or through a representative, information and argument in opposition to the suspension, including any additional specific information that raises a genuine dispute over the material facts"; and,
- That additional proceedings to determine disputed material facts will be conducted unless the action is based on an indictment or "[a] determination is made, on the basis of Department of Justice advice, that the substantial interests of the Government in pending or contemplated legal proceedings based on the same facts as the suspension would be prejudiced" (FAR 2019, § 9.407–3(c)).

21.11.3 *Administrative Procedures: Suspension*

The SDO's decision on suspension will be made on the administrative record, including any submission by the contractor, where the action is based on an indictment, or the contractor's submission does not raise a genuine dispute of material fact, or additional proceedings are denied based on Department of Justice advice (FAR 2019, § 9.407–3(1)). In actions where additional proceedings are conducted to resolve disputed material facts, the SDO will prepare written findings of fact (FAR 2019, § 9.407–3(2)). The SDO may modify or terminate the suspension or leave it in force, without prejudice to suspension or debarment by another agency (FAR 2019, § 9.407–3(3)). If the contractor enters into an administrative agreement to resolve the suspension proceedings, the SDO will enter the information into FAPIIS at www.cpars.csd.disa.mil (FAR 2019, § 9.407.3(e)(1)).

21.11.4 *Period of Suspension*

Suspension is for a temporary period pending the completion of investigation and any ensuing legal proceedings, unless the SDO terminates the suspension sooner (FAR 2019, § 9.407–4(a)). If no legal proceedings are initiated within twelve months after the suspension notice, the suspension will be terminated unless an Assistant Attorney General requests its extension. In that case the suspension may be extended for an additional six months. In no event may a suspension extend beyond eighteen months, unless legal proceedings are initiated within that period (FAR 2019, § 9.407–4 (b)). If legal proceedings are initiated, the suspension may continue for as long as it takes to complete the proceedings.

The SDO will notify the Department of Justice of the proposed termination of the suspension at least thirty days before the twelve-month period expires, to give that Department an opportunity to request an extension (FAR 2019, § 9.407–4 (c)).

21.12 ADDITIONAL EXCLUSIONS IN US FEDERAL PROCUREMENT

Beyond the discretionary and mandatory suspensions and debarments discussed so far, US law provides for additional potential grounds of exclusion; some of the most commonly encountered are discussed later.

21.12.1 *Vetting of Non-US Contractors in Contingency Operations*

Congress and the US Department of Defense (DOD) have established a system of vetting non-US contractors seeking or performing work in Afghanistan, designed to prevent dollars from flowing to the insurgents the US military is fighting in contingency operations. The program extends to other combatant commands.[18] Each combatant command has a program to identify persons or entities that directly or indirectly provide funds from DOD contracts to a person or entity activity opposing US or coalition forces in a contingency operation. The program also identifies persons or entities that fail to exercise due diligence to prevent persons or entities so identified from receiving contract funds. In Afghanistan the vetting program is conducted in secret, so that a contractor may not be informed that it is barred from contract award eligibility.

The Court of Federal Claims has acknowledged that this vetting program constitutes a de facto debarment without the normal due process rights accorded contractors. The court ruled, however, that national security interests take priority, and that traditional due process of notice and opportunity to be heard could "compromise national security" because it could "endanger military intelligence sources" and "provide information to entities that pose a potential threat to the United States, thereby placing United States forces at risk."[19]

21.12.2 *Government Corporations*

Government corporations, which are not subject to the FAR or the NCR, may have their own suspension and debarment procedures. For example, the US Postal Service ("USPS") has its own debarment regulation and maintains its own list (USPS 2019, § 601.113). Contractors excluded by the USPS will be reported to the government-wide SAM database (USPS 2019, § 601.113(c)(3)). The USPS Vice President of Supply Management makes

18 National Defense Authorization Act ("NDAA") for Fiscal Year (FY) 2015, sections 814–43, "Never Contract with the Enemy"; NDAA for FY 2012, section 841 "Prohibition on Contracting with the Enemy in the United States Central Command Theater of Operations"; NDAA for FY 2014, section 831. See Sander and Romero 2015; Cook, Roberson, and Knowles 2017.

19 *MG Altus Apache Co.* v. *United States*, 111 Fed. Cl. 425, 445 (2013); see also *NCL Logistics* v. *United States*, 109 Fed. Cl. 596 (2012); *Ettefzq-Meliat-Hai-Afghan Consulting, Inc.* v. *United States*, 106 Fed. Cl. 429 (2012).

debarment determinations in conjunction with the USPS General Counsel. The Vice President of Supply Management may also request that the Judicial Officer hold a fact-finding hearing, but the Vice President of Supply Management retains authority to accept or reject the Judicial Officer's findings of fact if such findings are clearly erroneous (USPS 2019, § 601.113(k)(2)). Rules of Practice before the Judicial Officer in proceedings for debarment have been published (USPS 2019, § 957.1–957.18).

There is limited case law involving challenges to USPS debarments. *Myers & Myers, Inc.* v. *United* States *Postal Service*[20] addressed allegations that the USPS refused to renew contracts based on debarment actions that lacked sufficient notice. The US Court of Appeals for the Second Circuit held that the USPS action constituted a claim for wrongful act or omission under the Federal Tort Claims Act.[21]

The USPS (2019) debarment regulation at 601.113 does not cite the "present responsibility" standard. Older USPS administrative decisions adopt the "present responsibility" standard from the USPS Procurement Manual (USPS 1995).[22] However, the USPS has replaced the Procurement Manual with various iterations of the Supplying Principles and Practices ("SPPs"). The current SPPs do not reference the "present responsibility" standard or proscribe debarment as a form of additional punishment (USPS 2018, § 409–413).

Effective November 14, 2007, the USPS issued revised procurement regulations, revoking and superseding all previous postal purchasing regulations, including the Postal Contracting Manual and the Procurement Manual (USPS 2019, § 601.102). Accordingly, the SPPs are "advisory and illustrative of approaches that may generally be used by Postal Service employees to conduct SCM activities, but are intended to provide for flexibility and discretion in their application to specific business situations. They are designed to supplement the Postal Service's purchasing regulations contained in 39 CFR Part 601" (USPS 2018, 1).

The USPS establishes business relationships with suppliers based on quality of service and overall professionalism. The USPS has discretion not to engage suppliers that exhibit unacceptable conduct or business practices, including "questionable or unprofessional conduct or business practices." The regulations do not include eligibility procedures (or a determination of responsibility) prior to awarding a supplier contract (USPS 2019, § 601.105 "Business Relationships").

As noted, the USPS debarment regulation does not include a present responsibility standard. However, the USPS relies upon debarment determinations from federal agencies to refuse awards to "ineligible" suppliers (USPS 2019, § 601.113(b)(5)). In USPS's own determinations, causes for debarment include topics such as offenses "indicating a lack of business integrity or business honesty" (USPS 2019, § 601.113(h)(1)(v)). USPS also considers contractors' written standards of conduct and agreements to institute or revise ethics programs as mitigating factors in the discretionary debarment decision (USPS 2019, § 601.113(i)(1)(i), (viii)).

While the SPPs do not include requirements for responsibility determinations of suppliers or a description of the purpose of debarment, the SPPs reference supplier professionalism, integrity, and ethics. The SPPs also discuss contracting with ineligible suppliers if in the USPS's best interest as integral to USPS procurement policy.

The SPPs provide an introduction to supplier relations that highlight the goals of sound business practices and professional conduct (USPS 2018, 9–10) ("Relations between the Postal

20 527 F.2d 1252 (2d Cir. 1975).

21 Ibid. at 1258-61.

22 See, e.g., *In the Matter of the Suspension of David K. Gillett Majestic Airlines*, 1995 WL 18241261 (Jan. 20, 1995).

Service and its suppliers will be strong, mutually beneficial, and based upon sound business practices, respect and trust, with both parties working toward a common goal. Within the relationship, both parties – Postal Service supplying professionals and suppliers – are expected to act ethically. . . .").

For evaluation of suppliers, USPS defines contract performance metrics, including "integrity and ethics" within the USPS–supplier relationship (USPS 2018,§ 152–53). USPS also considers past performance and responsibility topics when developing proposal evaluation strategies (USPS 2018, § 161) ("All past performance evaluations should consider the following factors: . . . Business relations (a history of being reasonable and cooperative with customers; commitment to customer satisfaction; integrity and ethics)."). To evaluate supplier capability, USPS considers whether the supplier has "a sound record on integrity and business ethics" (USPS 2018, 162).

In the SPP section on Supplier Suspension, Debarment, and Ineligibility, USPS considers the agency's "best interest" in determining whether to continue performance with a debarred supplier (USPS 2018, 410, 412) (suspension and debarment requests should include

> [a] detailed written explanation why suspension and debarment is in the Postal Service's best interest. . . . If the supplier presents a significant risk to the Postal Service in completing the existing contract, the Contracting Officer must determine whether termination for convenience or otherwise is in the Postal Service's best interest. In making this determination, the Contracting Officer must consult with assigned counsel and consider the following factors: . . . Availability of other safeguards to protect the Postal Service's interest until completion of the contract. . . . In certain circumstances, soliciting or awarding a contract to a suspended, debarred, and ineligible supplier may be in the best interest of the Postal Service.).

21.13 CONCLUSION

Suspension and debarment are well-established tools for combating corruption, compliance and integrity-based concerns, and poor performance in public procurement. By excluding contractors that pose unacceptable risk, governments foster compliance, discourage corruption, and reinforce public confidence in the procurement system. While suspension and debarment systems continue to evolve around the world, the US government has a relatively mature, flexible system that affords due process protections to contractors, and that emphasizes reliance upon contractors' own compliance efforts to reduce risk to the US government customer. Companies working with the federal government should recognize the seriousness of suspension and debarment in the US system, and other nations building their own systems of contractor exclusion may wish to draw lessons from the US model (Yukins and Schnitzer 2016).

REFERENCES

ABA PCLS (American Bar Association, Public Contract Law Section). 2010. Guide to the Mandatory Disclosure Rule: Issues, Guidelines, and Best Practices. Washington, DC.

Block, Samantha. 2018. "Defying Debarment: Judicial Review of Agency Suspension and Debarment Actions." *George Washington University Law Review* 86: 1316. www.gwlr.org/wp-content/uploads/2018/10/86-Geo.-Wash.-L.-Rev.-1316.pdf.

Clinton, William J., Executive Order 12989 (1996), amended by Executive Order 13286 (2003).

Cook, Daniel, Eric P. Roberson, and Sam Knowles. 2017. "Prime Contractor Found Nonresponsible Based on Undisclosed Vendor-Vetting Process – Contingency Contractors Beware." *Westlaw Journal on Government Contracts* 31(1).

DOJ (US Department of Justice). 2018. Assistant Attorney General Brian A. Benczkowski Delivers Remarks at NYU School of Law Program on Corporate Compliance and Enforcement Conference on Achieving Effective Compliance. www.justice.gov/opa/speech/assistant-attorney-general-brian-benczkowski-delivers-remarks-nyu-school-law-program.

DOJ Benczkowski (US Department of Justice), Criminal Division, Office of the Assistant Attorney General Brian Benczkowski. 2018. Memorandum: Selection of Monitors in Criminal Division Matters. Washington, DC. www.justice.gov/opa/speech/file/1100531/download.

DOJ SEC (US Department of Justice and US Securities and Exchange Commission). 2019. A Resource Guide to the U.S. Foreign Corrupt Practices Act. Washington, DC. www.justice.gov/sites/default/files/criminal-fraud/legacy/2015/01/16/guide.pdf.

Dubois, Pascale. 2012. "Domestic and International Administrative Tools to Combat Fraud and Corruption: A Comparison of US Suspension and Debarment with the World Bank's Sanctions System." *University of Chicago Legal Forum* 2012(1): 195–235. https://chicagounbound.uchicago.edu/cgi/viewcontent.cgi?article=1497&context=uclf.

Dubois, Pascale, Paul Ezzeddin, and Collin D. Swan. 2016. "Suspension and Debarment on the International Stage: Experience in the World Bank's Sanctions System." *Public Procurement Law Review* 25(61). https://ssrn.com/abstract=2792137.

EU (European Parliament and Council of the European Union). 2014. "Directive 2014/24/EU." *Official Journal of the European Union*. Article 57. https://eur-lex.europa.eu/legalcontent/EN/TXT/PDF/?uri=CELEX:32014L0024&from=EN.

FAR (Federal Acquisition Regulation). 2019. "*Code of Federal Regulation* (CFR). Title 48. www.acquisition.gov.

FBI (Federal Bureau of Investigation). n.d. "Operation Illwind." Accessed July 21, 2019. www.fbi.gov/history/famous-cases/operation-illwind.

GAO (Government Accountability Office). 2013. Suspension and Debarment: Characteristics of Active Agency Programs and Governmentwide Oversight Efforts (GAO-13-707 T, June 12), www.gao.gov/products/GAO-13-707T.

Grandon, Rodney A. 2016. *DoD Suspension and Debarment: Protecting the Government and Promoting Contractor Responsibility*. Washington, DC: Department of the Air Force. www.safgc.hq.af.mil/Portals/80/documents/AFD-160729-001.pdf?ver=2016–08-05-104750–383.

GSA (General Services Administration). 2019a. "Contractor Performance Assessment Reporting System (CPARS)." http://www.cpars.gov/.

2019b. "System for Award Management (SAM)." www.sam.gov/SAM/.

ISDC (Interagency Suspension and Debarment Committee). 2018. "Annual Report to Congress on the Status of the Federal Suspension and Debarment System." Washington, DC. 3. https://acquisition.gov/sites/default/files/page_file_uploads/Control%20ISDC%20FY%202017%20Report_Final_07_31_2018%20–2.pdf.

Manuel, Kate M. 2008. *Debarment and Suspension of Government Contractors: An Overview of the Law Including Recently Enacted and Proposed Amendments*. Washington, DC. Congressional Research Service. 2–5. https://fas.org/sgp/crs/misc/RL34753.pdf.

Meunier, Robert F. and Trevor B. A. Nelson. 2017. "Is It Time for a Single Federal Suspension and Debarment Rule?" *Public Contracts Law Journal* 46: 553.

OMB (Office of Management and Budget). 2019. "Does an Exclusion under the Federal Procurement System Affect a Person's Eligibility to Participate in Nonprocurement Transactions?" *Code of Federal Regulation* (CFR). Title 2: 180.145.

Pachter, John S. 2013. "Independent Monitors: What They Do and How to Avoid the Need for Them." *Federal Contracts Report* 100 FCR 637. www.smithpachter.com/post-detail.php?id=11654.

Sacilotto, Kara. 2018. "One Is the Loneliest Number: A Case for Changing Suspension and Debarment Regulations to Better Address Potential Exclusion of Individuals." *Public Contracts Law Journal* 47: 479.

Sander, Brett, and Joe Romero. 2015. "Vendor Vetting of Non-US Contractors in Afghanistan." *ABA PCLS Procurement Law Newsletter*. 50(4).

USPS (US Postal Service). 1995. "USPS Procurement Manual." Washington, DC. http://about.usps.com/publications/pub41/pub41toc.htm.

2018. "Supplying Principles and Practices." Washington, DC. 409–13. https://about.usps.com/manuals/spp/html/welcome.htm.
2019. "Postal Service." *Code of Federal Regulation* (CFR). Title 39.
USPS OIG (Office of the Inspector General, US Postal Service). 2012. Suspension and Debarment Program Audit Report. Report Number CA-AR-12-002. Arlington, VA. www.uspsoig.gov/sites/default/files/document-library-files/2015/CA-AR-12-002.pdf.
Whitlock, Craig and Kevin Uhrmacher. 2018. "Investigations: Prostitutes, Vacations and Cash: The Navy Officials 'Fat Leonard' Took Down." *Washington Post*, www.washingtonpost.com/graphics/investigations/seducing-the-seventh-fleet/.
World Bank. 2019. World Bank Sanctions Regime. www.worldbank.org/content/dam/documents/sanctions/other-documents/osd/The_World_Bank_ Group_Sanctions_Regime.pdf.
Yukins, Christopher R. 2013. "Cross-Debarment: A Stakeholder Analysis." *The George Washington International Law Review* 45:219. http://ssrn.com/abstract=2316252
2015. *Mandatory Disclosure: A Case Study in How Anti-corruption Measures Can Affect Competition in Defense Markets*. Philadelphia, PA: Center for Ethics and the Rule of Law, University of Pennsylvania Law School. https://papers.ssrn.com/sol3/papers.cfm?abstract_id=2600676.
Yukins, Christopher R., and Michal Kania. 2019. "Suspension and Debarment in the U.S. Government: Comparative Lessons for the EU's Next Steps in Procurement." *Upphandlingsrättslig Tidskrift* (UrT) 19(2): 47–73. https://papers.ssrn.com/sol3/papers.cfm?abstract_id=3422499.
Yukins, Christopher R., and Johannes Schnitzer. 2016. "Combating Corruption in Procurement: Debarment Present and Future, in UNOPS, Future-Proofing Procurement." *Future-Proofing Procurement*. Copenhagen, DNK. United Nations Office of Project Services. 26. https://content.unops.org/publications/ASR/ASR-supplement-2015_EN.pdf?mtime=20171214185135.

PART III

Incentives

22

Does Tort Deter? Inconclusive Empirical Evidence about the Effect of Liability in Preventing Harmful Behaviour

Benjamin van Rooij and Megan Brownlee

The tort system is a mouse with an other-worldly roar.

—Saks 1992: 1287

Abstract: This chapter assesses whether tort liability can have a deterrent effect and reduce risky and harmful behaviour. It discusses insights from key reviews of empirical work across regulatory domains. These reviews show that this body of empirical work, in all but one of the domains (corporate director liability towards shareholders) studied, does not find conclusive evidence that tort deters or that it does not deter. Studies do find some indication of negative side effects of tort regimes, such as lowering necessary services, enhancing unnecessary legal defensive practices and raising costs. The chapter concludes that common assumptions about the role that tort can play in compliance require a more solid empirical basis. The chapter presents directions for future tort and deterrence research with a focus on better understanding the causal processes through which liability rules may shape human and organizational conduct.

22.1 INTRODUCTION

In August 2019, a judge in Oklahoma ruled that Johnson and Johnson had breached a public nuisance law when it had intentionally downplayed the risks and overstated the benefits of prescription painkillers containing opioids. The drug company was ordered to pay the plaintiff, the state of Oklahoma, $572 million in compensation. This massive award was well below the $17 billion Oklahoma had claimed that Johnson and Johnson should have paid for addiction treatment, drug courts and other necessary services from the fallout of the opioid crisis that the state would otherwise have to bear. This was the first major ruling about liability in the aftermath of the opioid crisis. The case, with its massive claim about the immense amount of social harm directly attributable to major corporations, bears a resemblance to the cases against big tobacco companies in the late 1990s, which ended in the Tobacco Master Settlement Agreement where the tobacco companies agreed to pay a minimum of $206 billion over the first twenty-five years of the agreement.

These are highly newsworthy cases. They attract attention because of the large awards. They offer the spectacle of the legal battle, with lawyers on both sides, with testimony,

This research was made possible through a generous grant from the European Research Council (ERC-2018-CoG - HomoJuridicus - 817680).

sometimes with juries and finally a verdict or a mass settlement. What gets lost in the reporting is whether these cases actually serve to reduce harm. These two cases are telling. Rather than focus on the verdicts here, we should have asked a different set of questions: Did the mass settlement in the tobacco cases scare other corporations away from misleading the public about how their products may cause harm and addiction? Did drug companies ever think of the dangers of liability when they pushed opioid prescription painkillers? In other words, did instituting a high liability help to prevent future harm, and not just compensate for harm in the past?

For economists, this is the core function of the tort liability system; such systems should exist only if they have utility in that they can reduce more harm than the tort system itself costs. As Judge Posner put it: 'If ... the benefits in accident avoidance exceed the cost of prevention, society is better off if those costs are incurred and the accident averted [by adopting] precautions in order to avoid a greater cost in tort judgments' (Posner 1972: 33).

The key assumption here is that instituting a liability will somehow come to change future conduct, and often this is summarized in what we shall call *the tort deterrence thesis*, namely that tort can deter people and organizations from causing harm (cf. Landes and Posner 1987; Roisman, Judy and Stein 2004; Popper 2011). As Goldberg summarizes this idea: 'the most obvious function tort might play is to send a message to powerful actors that they must give due consideration to the well-being of others' (Goldberg 2010: 326).

Tort liability can be a major mechanism through which law can shape behaviour and measure compliance. Rather than changing behaviour through criminal law sanctions or regulatory law, tort law could provide a private law incentive to improve behaviour and reduce misconduct.

The question is whether tort liability in practice can achieve such an effect and whether it can improve behaviour. This chapter will discuss the empirical knowledge about the deterrent effect of tort. As such, it will explicitly not focus on the rich economic literature that models deterrent effects of tort and that discusses this in light of tort utility and debates about tort reform; rather, it will focus on what is known and still unclear about the empirical reality in which tort may influence human and organizational decision-making and prevent risk and harm.

This chapter will assess leading reviews of this body of empirical work. It will show how in all but one domain (corporate director liability towards shareholders), the empirical studies do not offer conclusive evidence that tort deters or that it does not deter. Reviewed studies do find some indication of negative side effects of tort regimes, such as lowering necessary services, enhancing unnecessary legal defensive practices and raising costs. The paper concludes by considering what this means for compliance and for future research on tort and deterrence.

22.2 REVIEWED EMPIRICAL WORK: AN OVERVIEW

The present chapter focuses on empirical work on the deterrent effect of tort as discussed in English language review papers. Much of the English-language work that is reviewed focuses on the US jurisdiction, while there is also some work from other Western jurisdictions. The body of work found in the reviews is still fragmented, with reviews for different types of damages. Here the largest reviews cover medical malpractice liability. This body of work has been the most systematic, the most up to date, and also the best systematically reviewed (Mello and Brennan 2001; Agarwal, Gupta and Gupta 2019). Another large body of work for which we have reviews is about corporate director and officer liability in relation to liability insurance. And the third largest reviewed body of work assesses the effect of liability in preventing car accident damages. This is a well-developed body of work that allows an insight into how insurance features in the deterrent effect of tort. There is only one review that assesses the deterrent effect across different domains of liability covering medical malpractice and car incidents, as well as product liability, workplace injuries and environmental damages, but unfortunately it is from 1992.

Most of the work the reviews cover uses larger sets of available data with indicators (or proxies) for damages, and with indicators for the tort liability system. Such studies use statistical analysis to find associations between trends in liability and trends in damages. Most of the studies that are reviewed look at how different forms of tort reform affect risky or harmful behaviour. These studies focus on reforms that lower liability, for instance through instituting caps on damages, allowing tortfeasors to have insurance for liability, or by instituting a no-fault insurance (where victims get paid through insurance and not through liability claims). If the tort deterrence thesis holds true, these reforms that lower liability would result in riskier behaviour and higher damages than jurisdictions with higher liability.

As such, most of these studies try to establish a rather linear relationship between a form of tort on the one hand and a form of risky behaviour on the other. When the law changes and lowers liability, these studies test whether it will result in the hypothesized increase in risky and damaging behaviour. However, it is also recognized that the relationship between tort and risky behaviour is not as clear-cut and that the process can be more differentiated (cf. Havinga 2012). A core issue in tort here is the mediating effect of liability insurance. Such insurance, as we just discussed, can on the one hand reduce liability and create moral hazard with those insured from liability engaging in riskier behaviour more frequently. However, when insurance exists, the insurance company gets a stake in the insured behaviour and may try to reduce risk through monitoring the insured client (Baker and Griffith 2010; Baker and Swedloff 2012; Boyer and Tennyson 2015). Amongst the reviews discussed here, one focuses on this issue and looks at shareholder liability insurance for corporate directors and officers and its effect on their risky decision-making. This body of work is different from some of the other work reviewed in that its data are not solely aggregate data (such as insurance coverage, share prices, management earnings and mergers and acquisitions decisions (see Boyer and Tennyson 2015)) but also include interviews with corporate risk managers and insurance professionals (i.e. Baker and Griffith 2010; Baker and Swedloff 2012).

Some studies covered in the reviews also assess the side effects of tort on regulated behaviour, or mediating influences on the effect of tort and risky behaviour. This has been most prominent in medical malpractice studies where a range of scholars have looked at how changes in tort law have affected the provision of care, specifically at whether stricter liability created lower availability of medical services that may lead to liability (for a review of earlier work see Mello 2006 and for recent work see Agarwal, Gupta and Gupta 2019). Reviewed studies have also looked at other side effects of liability such as the influence it has on the costs of insurance, administrative overheads, litigation rates, access to claims for victims and the amount of funds spent to reduce liability (for instance through so-called defensive medicine where doctors order unnecessary tests and referrals).

Table 22.1 below provides an overview of the review studies covered in this chapter.

The body of work reviewed here does not represent all empirical work on tort but, rather, gives a picture of several larger bodies of work that have been reviewed separately in the past and that are now assessed together for the first time. As such, it covers work on medical malpractice, director liability towards shareholders and car accidents. For other areas of damages, reviews are less readily available and the reviews we have are older and less robust in

TABLE 22.1 *Review studies on the deterrent effect of tort*

Review studies	Type of damages	Type of review	# studies reviewed	Mediating or side effects
Agarwal, Gupta and Gupta 2019	Medical malpractice	Systematic	37	Supply of medical services
Kachalia and Mello 2011; Mello and Kachalia 2010	Medical malpractice	Systematic	64/201	Supply of medical services, insurance costs, overhead costs, costs of defensive medicine
Boyer and Tennyson 2015	Corporate misconduct and risk	Regular literature review	25	Liability insurance, premium levels, firm value
Engstrom 2011	Automobile accidents	Regular literature review	11	Effects on insurance premiums
Anderson, Heaton and Carroll 2010	Automobile accidents	Regular literature review	8	Costs, access to claims for victims, litigation rates
Dewees and Trebilcock 1992	Automobile accidents, medical malpractice, product damages, environmental damages, workplace injuries	Regular literature review (only partly empirical aggregate-level data studies)	20	Premium levels, defensive medicine, physician activity levels, innovation

terms of numbers and studies discussed. Most reviews focus on studies using aggregate data, and some older reviews also include less formal analysis of historical patterns of liability and damages. The present chapter does not cover studies using survey and laboratory methods (of which there have been a few).

22.3 EMPIRICAL EVIDENCE ABOUT THE DETERRENT EFFECT OF TORT

22.3.1 *Medical Malpractice*

In theory, liability for medical malpractice should have a deterrent effect and improve the quality of care for patients. If doctors become liable for damages their work causes patients, they may use a higher standard of care and work to reduce medical errors. At the same time, instituting such liability might have negative side effects, as it may reduce the willingness of doctors to work in high-risk practice areas (or in jurisdictions with higher liability) and it may increase the so-called defensive medicine (where care specialists provide services that are not strictly necessary but serve to reduce potential liability).

There are two major reviews of the deterrent and other effects of medical malpractice. The first, and most recent, is by Agarwal, Gupta and Gupta (2019). Their study reviewed thirty-seven previous empirical studies that were selected through a systemic method. These included studies that looked at the effects of caps on non-economic damages, and of caps on punitive damages.

Of these studies, eight papers evaluated the impact of caps of non-economic damages on a range of quality of care outcomes (Klick and Stratmann 2007; Currie and MacLeod 2008; Frakes 2012; Iizuka 2013; Avraham and Schanzenbach 2015; Frakes and Jena 2016; Bilimoria et al. 2017; Minami et al. 2017). Such studies look at whether when the potential amount of damages awarded is lowered, the quality of care given on a number of different issues (such as inpatient mortality, preventable delivery complications or certain kinds of other medical complications) is affected. As such, these studies provide an assessment of whether liability reduces risk, and thus about whether tort deters. If the deterrence thesis is correct, lower liability (through caps on damages) will result in lower quality of care.

Most studies did not find evidence that there was such a deterrent effect and that lowering the caps resulted in a lower level of care. Exceptions were Avraham and Schanzenbach (2015) who found that caps on non-economic damages were associated with a decrease in mortality for those aged forty-five to sixty-five but not for those older. Another exception was a study by Currie and MacLeod (2008), which found that caps of non-economic damages led to a decrease (6 per cent) in preventable labour complications. None of the other six studies found an association between caps on damages and care benefits across a wide range of patient safety indicators including those of acute care, inpatient mortality, avoidable hospitalizations, preventable delivery complications, medical errors related to birth or obstetric trauma, infant mortality and postoperative complications.

Seven studies reviewed by Agarwal, Gupta and Gupta (2019) (i.e. Kessler and McClellan 1996, 2002; Currie and MacLeod 2008; Sloan and Shadle 2009; Frakes 2012; Iizuka 2013; Frakes and Jena 2016) looked at whether the introduction of caps on punitive damages affected the quality of care. And as such, they looked at whether reducing the severity of expected punishment would lead to more damaging behaviour and thus a reduced deterrence.

Again, just as with the studies of caps on economic damages, the studies of caps on punitive damages mostly do not find the hypothesized link between lower damages and lower patient care. Frakes and Jena (2016) report mixed findings, with a significant reduction in the rate of maternal trauma but no effects of the caps on punitive damages on 'mortality, avoidable hospitalizations, delivery complications, or cancer screening' (Agarwal, Gupta and Gupta 2019: 6). The rest of the studies showed 'no association with preventable complications of labour, APGAR scores, medical errors related to birth or obstetric trauma, mortality, or readmissions' (Agarwal, Gupta and Gupta 2019: 6).

Finally, six studies reviewed by Agarwal, Gupta and Gupta (2019) (i.e. Kessler and McClellan 1996, 2002; Konety et al. 2005; Klick and Stratmann 2007; Sloan and Shadle 2009; Yang et al. 2012) studied whether the introduction of caps on total damages would affect the quality of care. And again, the expected link between lower damages and lower care was not clearly found. Of these six studies, only Konety et al. (2005: 2086) found an effect, seeing a significant 13 per cent reduction in mortality probabilities among patients with bladder cancer, while the rest of the studies found no association.

Agarwal, Gupta and Gupta (2019) have also looked at the side effects of medical malpractice. Here they concluded that liability did have negative side effects and 'that caps on non-economic damages were associated with a decrease in defensive medicine, an increase in physician supply and decreases in health-care spending' (Agarwal, Gupta and Gupta 2019: 1). In other words, they found that when there is less liability, there is less chance that doctors will engage in unnecessary medical practices to reduce liability, meaning that there are more doctors willing to practise in such areas and that overall it lessens medical costs. The overall conclusion here is thus that higher liability does not come with the expected benefits of higher patient care, but does come with the higher costs of having fewer doctors, and a higher cost in terms of performing more unnecessary tests and operations.

Kachalia and Mello have published two papers (Kachalia and Mello 2011; Mello and Kachalia 2010) reviewing empirical work about the effects of different types of tort reforms in the area of medical malpractice. Just like Agarwal, Gupta and Gupta (2019), they look both at the effects of liability on patient care (and thus on deterrence) and at several side effects, including physician supply and spending on defensive medicine. The work reviewed by Kachalia and Mello uses different types of tort reform to assess the effects of these medical malpractice liability systems. These include: setting caps on damages, putting limits on attorney fees, setting limits on the amounts that plaintiffs can get from defendants in relation to their overall fault in the case of joint liability (so-called joint and several liability reforms), eliminating double payment by defendants who could claim damages even if they have already been paid by other sources such as their health insurance (collateral-source rule reform), and introducing statutes of limitation. All tort reforms studied reduce the claims that plaintiffs can make and thus would in theory be expected to reduce deterrence and have a negative effect on the quality of care provided to patients.

However, similarly to Agarwal, Gupta and Gupta's (2019) review, Kachalia and Mello's (Kachalia and Mello 2011; Mello and Kachalia 2010) reviews report that there is no conclusive proof that these tort reforms have had an effect on the quality of care for patients. Table 22.2 contains a summary of their main findings about how different tort reforms have affected such quality of care. In contrast to Agarwal, Gupta and Gupta (2019), however, they do not find clearly that tort reform has side effects in terms of physician supply and defensive medical practices. As outlined in Table 22.2, they find mixed evidence that caps on damages lead to more physician supply and some evidence that they lead to less defensive practices, but they do not find this for all other tort reforms studied, including limits on attorney fees, joint and several liability reforms, and statutes of limitations.

TABLE 22.2 *Summary of key findings on medical liability, deterrence and side effects*

Type of tort reform	Core findings	Implications for deterrence	Side effects
Caps on damages	'Evidence on quality of care too limited to draw conclusions'[1]	No conclusive evidence	Mixed findings on physician supply, reduction of some defensive practices
Limits on attorney fees	'Effect on quality of care not studied'	No evidence	No effect on physician supply, limited evidence of no effect on defensive practices
Joint and several liability reform	'Evidence on quality of care too limited to draw conclusions'	No conclusive evidence	No effect on physician supply, mixed findings on defensive practices
Statutes of limitations and repose	'Evidence on quality of care too limited to draw conclusions"	No conclusive evidence	No conclusive evidence on physician supply and defensive medicine

Source: Drawn from Kachalia and Mello 2011: 1568.

[1] Quotes in this table are all from Kachalia and Mello 2011: 1568.

In sum, the studies of medical malpractice do not find conclusive evidence for the deterrent effect of tort, as they do not find that reducing liability also leads to lowering of patient care and safety, as the tort deterrence thesis would expect. And they provide some indication that medical malpractice liability can have negative side effects in limiting the supply of doctors in higher liability jurisdictions and areas of work, enhancing defensive medicine practice and increasing overall costs of health care.

22.3.2 *Liability of Corporate Directors and Officers towards Shareholders*

If directors and officers make decisions that damage the interest of their corporation, they can face liability towards the corporate shareholders. In some jurisdictions, such directors and officers can buy insurance to reduce their liability towards shareholders. There has been a large body of empirical work about how such insurance will affect risky corporate decision-making. If the tort deterrence thesis holds true, the more directors and officers purchase insurance, the less liability they will face and the more likely it is that they will engage in risky corporate decision-making. There is an additional hypothesis at play here as well, namely the insurer monitoring hypothesis, where insurers have a stake in monitoring the risky behaviour of their clients and can thus counter the moral hazard that their insurance creates. Here we shall review this body of work through a recent paper by Boyer and Tennyson (2015).

Their review discusses seven studies that find 'significant moral hazard effects' in corporations whose directors and officers have purchased liability insurance. One study by Chalmers, Dann and Harford (2002) looks at seventy-two initial public offering (IPO) firms that went public between 1992 and 1996, and finds, for instance, that there is a negative relationship between the three-year post-IPO stock price performance and the insurance coverage in relation to the IPO. From this they deduce that managers in cases where there is insurance are more likely to act opportunistically by taking the companies public when they are overvalued (Chalmers, Dann and Harford 2002: 609). Another study discussed in the review finds that firms are more likely to overpay for firms they acquire when their directors have liability insurance (Lin, Officer and Zou 2011). And several studies found that firms with liability insurance for directors and officers were more likely to engage in restatements of earnings (DuCharme, Malatesta and Sefcik 2004; Boyer and Hanon 2009; Cao and Narayanamoorthy 2011; Gillan and Panasian 2015; Kim 2015).

As such, this body of work finds that when there is more insurance for directors and officers to protect them from lawsuits from shareholders, they will be more likely to engage in risky behaviour for the corporation. In other words, when they face less liability, corporate executives will take more risk-prone decisions. In sum, this body of work finds that, in contrast to the research about medical malpractice, there is support for the tort deterrence thesis in that lower liability can result in riskier and potentially more damaging behaviour.

Reviewing another six studies, Boyer and Tennyson (2015) did not find that such moral hazard is mitigated by the insurance companies. As such, their research finds that although the premiums do seem to respond to the risk of directors getting sued by shareholders, it is not clear that such higher premiums reduce risky corporate decisions by directors or officers (Core 2000; Boyer and Stern 2012). In-depth qualitative work by Baker and Griffith (2007, 2010) further concludes that insurers who provide corporate executives with insurance against shareholder liability do not monitor corporate behaviour.

22.3.3 *Liability for Car Accidents*

A third, larger body of work on tort and deterrence is about car accidents. Here, again, the tort deterrence thesis would hold that where there is a higher liability for automotive accidents, risky driving will decrease and there should be fewer such accidents. Several jurisdictions have adopted so-called no-fault insurance systems, where victims have a direct right to partial compensation for their damages through insurance. In these systems, drivers causing accidents are no longer liable for the damages (Engstrom 2011:304). Thus, when jurisdictions adopt such no-fault insurance systems, they provide an ideal natural experimental setting in which to study the deterrent effect of tort. Under the tort deterrence thesis, we would expect there to be riskier behaviour when there is less liability, and thus with no-fault insurance systems we would expect more accidents.

A range of scholars have taken this opportunity and looked at how no-fault liability has affected car accidents. Such studies have also looked at potential side effects.

Two very similar papers, one by Engstrom (2011) and one by Anderson, Heaton and Carroll (2010), have reviewed this body of work: Engstrom reviewed ten studies, both about the USA as well as about Quebec and New Zealand, and Anderson and colleagues reviewed nine studies, all in the USA.

The reviews both found that the scientific findings were split. Six of the studies reviewed (Landes 1982; McEwin 1989; Devlin 1992; Sloan, Reilly and Schenzler 1994; Cummins, Phillips and Weiss 2001; Cohen and Dehejia 2004) found that with the no-fault insurance, and thus the reduction of driver liability, there were more fatal accidents (ranging from 2 per cent to 15 per cent). However, five of the studies reviewed did not find any effect of no-fault insurance on fatal accidents (Kochanowski and Young 1985; Zador and Lund 1986; Loughran 2001; Derrig et al. 2002; Heaton and Helland 2008).

In sum, both reviews conclude that the evidence is mixed and that there is no clear conclusion. As Anderson, Heaton and Carroll (2010: 82) conclude: '[A]lthough there are some theoretical reasons that no-fault coverage may raise costs by inducing less careful driving, the empirical evidence is mixed.' The study examining the broadest range of accident types (Heaton and Helland 2008) finds 'no evidence of an effect of no-fault on accident rates' (Anderson, Heaton and Carroll 2010: 82). Or, as Engstrom (2011: 333) puts it, '[a]ll told, roughly half of the studies published thus far claim that no-fault coverage increases fatal accidents, while the other half find no effect, and the notion that no-fault reduces fatalities has been seemingly put to rest. The proposition that no-fault may be associated with a greater number of accidents thus lingers.'

The reviews have also looked at side effects of the no-fault regimes. Anderson, Heaton and Carroll (2010), for instance, find that the no-fault regimes have led to higher insurance premiums, but this cannot be explained be a higher rate of claims per accident in jurisdictions with the no-fault rule. They also report that claimants in no-fault systems do get a higher percentage of their economic losses and get paid faster (Anderson, Heaton and Carroll 2010). Engstrom (2011: 337) concludes that the adoption of no-fault insurance systems is associated with higher premiums and overall costs than an ordinary liability system, and that between 2000 and 2004 the gap in premium levels between the two systems grew.

22.3.4 *Other Forms of Tort*

To understand whether tort deters in other domains, a cross-sectional review is important. Dewees and Trebilcock (1992) compared findings from nineteen studies about the deterrent

TABLE 22.3 *Summary of key findings in Dewees and Trebilcock's 1992 review*

Type of damages	Number of studies	Findings on deterrence	Findings on side effects
Automobile accidents	7	Mixed and inconclusive	None studied
Medical malpractice	2	Studies are fragmented and findings are inconclusive	Indications of more defensive medicine and reduction in physician services
Product damages	2	Mixed findings. No useful conclusions can be drawn from available aggregate data	Inconclusive findings on negative effects on innovation and development of socially desirable products
Environmental damages	4	No conclusive evidence of deterrence	Tort action may have given rise to legislative or regulatory action
Worker damages	5	Contradictory findings and limited sound empirical evidence	None studied

effect of tort across five different areas of tort: automobile accidents, medical malpractice, product damages, environmental damages and worker damages. The studies they reviewed were not all purely empirical studies with aggregate data but also included sources that sketched the history of both tort rules and the development of damages that were used to support ideas about causality between the two without testing this through statistical analysis. Table 22.3 presents an overview of their key findings.

As we can see from this summary, just like the work on medical malpractice and automobile accidents, and in contrast to the work on director liability towards shareholders, other fields of tort do not yield conclusive evidence that tort deters and reduces the harms it seeks to reduce. This is the case for product liability tort regimes, for environmental torts and for worker damage compensation torts. And although this body of work is not of the same size and quality as the work reviewed in medical malpractice and automobile accidents, it does show that older findings in other fields do not clearly show either that tort does deter or that it does not.

22.4 DISCUSSION AND CONCLUSION

Across the seven domains of tort reviewed here, in six there is no conclusive evidence that changes in tort systems have a clear effect on risk-taking and damaging behaviour. The exception is corporate director and officer liability towards shareholders, where empirical studies do find clearly that when liability is reduced because of insurance, executives will make riskier and more damaging decisions. For other domains, the body of empirical work does not show clear evidence that higher tort liability creates more deterrence and lowers risk, or that lower tort liability creates less deterrence and heightens risk. As the evidence is mixed and inconclusive, neither can we say that the literature proves that tort deters or that it does not deter. The best we can conclude right now, based on this body of work, is that we do not know.

The work discussed here is limited. Each review discussed here is limited by its own focus, its own selection of studies and also the year it was developed. This means that we get a fairly good picture of medical malpractice tort studies up to 2019, corporate director liability up to 2015 and automobile accidents up to 2011 or so, but for other forms of tort the reviews we have are old and also cover a rather limited body of work. The focus in these reviews is also mostly on aggregate studies that compare outcomes in terms of damages before and after changes in or between tort law systems. And most of these studies have looked empirically at what will happen when liability is lowered, but not at what will happen when liability increases.

For compliance generally, this body of work shows that we cannot clearly say that adopting a liability regime will enable an effective legal influence on human and organizational conduct. The findings from these reviews are an important warning that what is often taken for granted about the impact of law on behaviour, whether it is that higher punishment reduces crime (cf. Nagin and Pepper 2012; Nagin 2012, 2013; Simpson et al. 2014; Schell-Busey et al. 2016) or, as discussed here, that higher liability reduces risky behaviour, may not be empirical fact. It shows the importance of developing more and better empirical work and taking such work seriously in how we design and discuss legal systems and rules that seek to alter behaviour.

Part of the problem is that the existing body of work reviewed here has tried to assess the effects in a sort of direct cause and effect manner. As such, it has focused on the type of liability on the one hand and the type of behaviour on the other. In reality, there will be a complex causal set of processes that combine the two. And it is exactly that chain that is vital to understand to come up with meaningful data about how existing liability systems may become more effective and less costly in improving behaviour.

Another problem is that the existing work has not really tried to assess why sometimes (as in the case of shareholder liability) tort is effective, and in other cases such an effect is not clearly found. When it is unclear whether tort works to deter, we should try to understand how tort actually can deter and what conditions are at play in effectuating tort deterrence, and also what costs such deterrence may bring.

Here, there is much to learn from other areas of compliance studies, as also discussed in this handbook. A first lesson from other compliance work is that there are two key aspects of deterrence that are relevant for affecting behaviour: the certainty of punishment and the severity of punishment (Beccaria 1764; Bentham 1789; Becker 1968). Such certainty of punishment consists of the chances that offending behaviour will be detected and the probability that, upon detection, action will be undertaken that will result in such punishment (Nagin 2013). The study of criminal punishment has found that the certainty of punishment matters more than its severity (Nagin 2013). Scholars have found that punishment starts to deter only when there is a certain threshold level of certainty, ranging between 25 per cent and 40 per cent depending on the type of crime (Brown 1978; Chamlin 1991). As such, research on tort and deterrence should come to look more closely at what the certainty of getting sued, losing in litigation and ultimately having to pay damages, legal fees and other fees is, and of course how people perceive such certainty.

One study, using a laboratory experiment where students playing a public goods game could claim damages when harmed by other players, assessed the certainty and severity of liability (Eisenberg and Engel 2014). The experiment manipulated the height of such damages as well as the probability that such claims could be made. They found that 'a damages rule analogous to the most common measure of damages in contract and tort litigation, the harm to the aggrieved party, is insufficient to deter serious deterioration in co-operation over time' (Eisenberg and Engel 2014: 331). Only when the probability was high enough or when a very high liability (treble the normal rate) was introduced did such liability have a positive effect on co-operation. In other words, better insight into the relative weight that certainty and severity of liability play in shaping behaviour is crucial to designing systems with more effective forms of tort.

Once we focus on the certainty of liability as a core aspect of tort liability, the crucial issue is what the chances are that victims of damages will sue and how likely it is that they will be successful in such litigation. For medical malpractice it is striking, for instance, that victims of negligent medical errors are very rarely (in only 2–3 per cent of cases) likely to file a claim, and when they do so only 50 per cent will be awarded money, and in a quarter of the cases there is no connection between the merit of the claim and the outcome (Kachalia and Mello 2011: 1564–5). Here the empirical study of the effects of tort on behaviour can draw on the well-developed body of socio-legal scholarship on access to justice and the chances of success in litigation (Galanter 1974; Cappelletti and Garth 1978; Curran 1978; Felstiner, Abel and Sarat 1980–1; Genn and Beinart 1999; Talesh 2012).

Further understanding of how tort may influence behaviour starts with recognizing that people develop a subjective view of the law and how it is enforced. Chapter 32 in this volume shows how low the level of legal knowledge and understanding often is, both for laypersons and for professionals. Here, interestingly, one study found a surprising link between liability and legal knowledge, as it showed that doctors in Texas were much more afraid of legal liability and engaged much more in defensive medicine than doctors in Denmark, yet the doctors in Texas also had far worse knowledge of the law than their Danish colleagues (Van McCrary and Swanson 1999). If people do not know exactly when they are going to be liable and what for, how can such liability come to shape their behaviour? A key question in the study of tort and deterrence should thus be about the legal knowledge of potential tortfeasors.

Deterrence scholarship from other fields, notably criminology and regulatory studies, has also found that people have subjective views on how the law is enforced. This body of work has shown that people are not at all aware of the exact chances of getting caught and punished or what punishment they should then expect (Gunningham, Thornton and Kagan 2005; Apel 2013; Van Rooij 2016). Thus, potential offenders often do not see punishment as it exists in reality. This means that deterrence must be studied from the subjective perspective of the potential offender, as it is this perception that will shape how they see the punishment and thus whether it deters them from offending (Decker, Wright and Logie 1993; Nagin 2013; Van Rooij 2016). We have also learned from these studies that the severity of punishment is relative: what may be severe for some may not be for others.

This means that to understand how tort may deter risky and damaging behaviour, we must first understand the subjective view of those whose behaviour the liability system addresses. To do so requires adopting methods beyond aggregate studies testing the effects of different liability regimes, that is, studies that get into the minds of potential tortfeasors. To get a subjective understanding of the law and its enforcement requires using surveys, focus groups or other forms of interviewing. An example of a simple survey analysis of tort was a survey that presented 700 first-year law students with a series of vignettes, and asked respondents to rate the likelihood of their participation in tortious behaviour under differing legal conditions of criminal and tort liability (Cardi, Penfield and Yoon 2012). But to truly get to the pertinent issues here, surveys should develop instruments to test legal knowledge (without shaping it), and similarly test views on the certainty and severity of liability, and they should do so amongst subjects whose tortious behaviour really matters.

Once such subjective views about the legal rules of liability and the way they are enforced and invoked are clear, the final part of the research on tort liability should be about how these views then play a role in how people engage in or refrain from risky and harmful behaviour. This may well be the hardest part to capture in empirical research. One approach might be to use laboratory experiments where such behaviour can be directly observed and where influences on the decision-making can be tightly controlled (e.g. Eisenberg and Engel 2014). The next step will be to take these sorts of studies from the students in the laboratory to doctors in hospitals, directors in boardrooms and drivers in their cars.

REFERENCES

Agarwal, R., A. Gupta and S. Gupta, 2019. "The Impact of Tort Reform on Defensive Medicine, Quality of Care, and Physician Supply: A Systematic Review." *Health Services Research* 54(4): 851–9.

Anderson, J. M., P. Heaton and S. J. Carroll. 2010. *The US Experience with No-Fault Automobile Insurance: A Retrospective*. Santa Monica, CA: RAND Corporation.

Apel, Robert. 2013. "Sanctions, Perceptions, and Crime: Implications for Criminal Deterrence." *Journal of Quantitative Criminology* 29(1): 67–101.

Avraham, Ronen, and Max Schanzenbach. 2015. "The Impact of Tort Reform on Intensity of Treatment: Evidence from Heart Patients." *Journal of Health Economics* 39: 273–88.

Baker, Tom, and Sean J. Griffith. 2007. "Predicting Corporate Governance Risk: Evidence from the Directors'& (and) Officers' Liability Insurance Market." *University of Chicago Law Review* 74: 865.

2010. *Ensuring Corporate Misconduct: How Liability Insurance Undermines Shareholder Litigation*. Chicago: University of Chicago Press.

Baker, Tom, and Rick Swedloff. 2012. "Regulation by Liability Insurance: From Auto to Lawyers Professional Liability." *UCLA Law Review* 60: 1412.

Beccaria, Cesare. 1764 (reprinted in 1985). *On Crime and Punishment*. Indianapolis, IN: Hackett Publishing.

Becker, Gary S. 1968. "Crime and Punishment, An Economic Approach." *Journal of Political Economy* 76: 169–217.

Bentham, Jeremy. 1789 (reprinted in 1973). "An Introduction to the Principles and Morals of Legislation." In *The Utilitarians*. Report.Garden City, NY: Anchor Books.

Bilimoria, Karl Y., Jeanette W. Chung, Christina A. Minami, Min-Woong Sohn, Emily S. Pavey, Jane L. Holl and Michelle M. Mello. 2017. "Relationship between State Malpractice Environment and Quality of Health Care in the United States." *Joint Commission Journal on Quality and Patient Safety* 43(5): 241–50.

Boyer, M. M., and Amandine Hanon. 2009. "Protecting Directors and Officers from Liability Arising from Aggressive Earnings Management." CIRANO-Scientific Publications 2009s-35. https://cirano.qc.ca/files/publications/2009s-35.pdf.

Boyer, M. Martin, and Léa H. Stern. 2012. "Is Corporate Governance Risk Valued? Evidence from Directors' and Officers' Insurance." *Journal of Corporate Finance* 18(2): 349–72.

Boyer, M. Martin, and Sharon Tennyson. 2015. "Directors' and Officers' Liability Insurance, Corporate Risk and Risk Taking: New Panel Data Evidence on the Role of Directors' and Officers' Liability Insurance." *Journal of Risk and Insurance* 82(4): 753–91.

Brown, Don W. 1978. "Arrest Rates and Crime Rates: When Does a Tipping Effect Occur?" *Social Forces* 57(2): 671–82.

Cao, Zhiyan, and Ganapathi S Narayanamoorthy. 2011. "The Effect of Litigation Risk on Management Earnings Forecasts." *Contemporary Accounting Research* 28(1): 125–73.

Cappelletti, M., and B. Garth, eds. 1978. *Access to Justice, Vol. I: A World Survey*. Alphen a/d Rijn: Sijthoff and Noordhoff.

Cardi, W. Jonathan, Randall D. Penfield and Albert H. Yoon. 2012. "Does Tort Law Deter Individuals? A Behavioral Science Study." *Journal of Empirical Legal Studies* 9(3): 567–603.

Chalmers, John M. R., Larry Y. Dann and Jarrad Harford. 2002. "Managerial Opportunism? Evidence from Directors' and Officers' Insurance Purchases." *Journal of Finance* 57(2): 609–36.

Chamlin, Mitchell B. 1991. "A Longitudinal Analysis of the Arrest–Crime Relationship: A Further Examination of the Tipping Effect." *Justice Quarterly* 8(2): 187–99.

Cohen, Alma, and Rajeev Dehejia. 2004. "The Effect of Automobile Insurance and Accident Liability Laws on Traffic Fatalities." *Journal of Law and Economics* 47(2): 357–93.

Core, John E. 2000. "The Directors' and Officers' Insurance Premium: An Outside Assessment of the Quality of Corporate Governance." *Journal of Law, Economics, and Organization* 16(2): 449–77.

Cummins, J. David, Richard D. Phillips and Mary A. Weiss. 2001. "The Incentive Effects of No-Fault Automobile Insurance." *Journal of Law and Economics* 44(2): 427–64.

Curran, Barbara A. 1978. "Survey of the Public's Legal Needs." *American Bar Association Journal* 64: 848–52.

Currie, Janet, and W. Bentley MacLeod. 2008. "First Do No Harm? Tort Reform and Birth Outcomes." *Quarterly Journal of Economics* 123(2): 795–830.

Decker, Scott H., Richard Wright and Robert Logie. 1993. "Perceptual Deterrence among Active Residential Burglars: A Research Note." *Criminology* 31: 135–47.

Derrig, Richard A., Maria Segui-Gomez, Ali Abtahi, and Ling-Ling Liu. 2002. "The Effect of Population Safety Belt Usage Rates on Motor Vehicle-Related Fatalities." *Accident Analysis & Prevention* 34(1): 101–10.

Devlin, Rose Anne. 1992. "Liability Versus No-Fault Automobile Insurance Regimes: An Analysis of the Experience in Quebec." In *Contributions to Insurance Economics*, edited by Georges Dionne, 499–520. Dordrecht: Springer.

Dewees, Don, and Michael Trebilcock. 1992. "The Efficacy of the Tort System and Its Alternatives: A Review of Empirical Evidence." *Osgoode Hall Law Journal* 30: 57.

DuCharme, Larry L, Paul H Malatesta and Stephan E Sefcik. 2004. "Earnings Management, Stock Issues, and Shareholder Lawsuits." *Journal of Financial Economics* 71(1): 27–49.

Eisenberg, Theodore, and Christoph Engel. 2014. "Assuring Civil Damages Adequately Deter: A Public Good Experiment." *Journal of Empirical Legal Studies* 11(2): 301–49.

Engstrom, Nora Freeman. 2011. "An Alternative Explanation for No-Fault's Demise." *DePaul Law Review* 61: 303.

Felstiner, W., R. Abel and A. Sarat. 1980–1. "The Emergence and Transformation of Disputes: Naming, Blaming, Claiming." *Law and Society Review* 15: 631.

Frakes, Michael. 2012. "Defensive Medicine and Obstetric Practices." *Journal of Empirical Legal Studies* 9(3): 457–81.

Frakes, Michael, and Anupam B. Jena. 2016. "Does Medical Malpractice Law Improve Health Care Quality?" *Journal of Public Economics* 143: 142–58.

Galanter, M. 1974. "Why the 'Haves' Come Out Ahead: Speculations on the Limits of Legal Change." *Law and Society* 9(1): 95–160.

Genn, H., and S. Beinart. 1999. *Paths to Justice: What People Do and Think about Going to the Law*. Oxford: Hart.

Gillan, Stuart L., and Christine A. Panasian. 2015. "On Lawsuits, Corporate Governance, and Directors' and Officers' Liability Insurance." *Journal of Risk and Insurance* 82(4): 793–822.

Goldberg, John C. P. 2010. "Tort in Three Dimensions." *Pepperdine Law Review* 38:321.

Gunningham, Neil, Dorothy Thornton and Robert A. Kagan. 2005. "Motivating Management: Corporate Compliance in Environmental Protection." *Law & Policy* 27(2): 289–316.

Havinga, Tetty. 2012. "The Influence of Liability Law on Food Safety on Preventive Effects of Liability Claims and Liability Insurance." Nijmegen Sociology of Law Working Paper (2010/02).

Heaton, P., and Helland, E. 2008. No-Fault Insurance and Automobile Accidents. Rand Institute for Justice Working Paper, WR-551-ICJ, 1–35.

Iizuka, Toshiaki. 2013. "Does Higher Malpractice Pressure Deter Medical Errors?" *Journal of Law and Economics* 56(1): 161–88.

Kachalia, A., and M. M. Mello. 2011. "New Directions in Medical Liability Reform." *New England Journal of Medicine* 364(16): 1564.

Kessler, Daniel, and Mark McClellan. 1996. "Do Doctors Practice Defensive Medicine?" *Quarterly Journal of Economics* 111(2): 353–90.

2002. "Malpractice Law and Health Care Reform: Optimal Liability Policy in an Era of Managed Care." *Journal of Public Economics* 84(2): 175–97.

Kim, Irene. 2015. "Directors' and Officers' Insurance and Opportunism in Accounting Choice." *Accounting & Taxation* 7(1): 51–65.
Klick, Jonathan, and Thomas Stratmann. 2007. "Medical Malpractice Reform and Physicians in High-Risk Specialties." *Journal of Legal Studies* 36(S2): S121–S142.
Kochanowski, Paul S., and Madelyn V. Young. 1985. "Deterrent Aspects of No-Fault Automobile Insurance: Some Empirical Findings." *Journal of Risk and Insurance* 52(2): 269–88.
Konety, Badrinath R, Vibhu Dhawan, Veersathpurush Allareddy and Sue A. Joslyn. 2005. "Impact of Malpractice Caps on Use and Outcomes of Radical Cystectomy for Bladder Cancer: Data from the surveillance, Epidemiology, and End Results Program." *Journal of Urology* 173(6): 2085–9.
Landes, Elisabeth M. 1982. "Insurance, Liability, and Accidents: A Theoretical and Empirical Investigation of the Effect of No-Fault Accidents." *Journal of Law and Economics* 25(1): 49–65.
Landes, William M., and Richard A. Posner. 1987. *The Economic Structure of Tort Law*. Cambridge, MA: Harvard University Press.
Lin, Chen, Micah S. Officer and Hong Zou. 2011. "Directors' and Officers' Liability Insurance and Acquisition Outcomes." *Journal of Financial Economics* 102(3): 507–25.
Loughran, D. S. 2001. The Effect of No-Fault Automobile Insurance on Driver Behavior and Automobile Accidents in the United States. Rand Institute for Justice Working Paper.
McEwin, R. Ian. 1989. "No-Fault and Road Accidents: Some Australasian Evidence." *International Review of Law and Economics* 9(1): 13–24.
Mello, M. M. (2006). Medical Malpractice: Impact of the Crisis and Effect of State Tort Reforms. Robert Wood Johnson Foundation Research Synthesis Report No. 10.
Mello, Michelle M., and Troyen A. Brennan. 2001. "Deterrence of Medical Errors: Theory and Evidence for Malpractice Reform." *Texas Law Review* 80: 1595.
Mello, Michelle M., and Allen Kachalia. 2010. "Evaluation of Options for Medical Malpractice System Reform." A Report to the Medicare Payment Advisory Commission (MedPAC) No. 10–2.
Minami, Christina A., Catherine R. Sheils, Emily Pavey, Jeanette W. Chung, Jonah J. Stulberg, David D. Odell, Anthony D. Yang, David J. Bentrem and Karl Y. Bilimoria. 2017. "Association between State Medical Malpractice Environment and Postoperative Outcomes in the United States." *Journal of the American College of Surgeons* 224(3): 310–18. e2.
Nagin, Daniel S. 2012. "Imprisonment and Crime Control: Building Evidence-Based Policy." In *Contemporary Issues in Criminological Theory and Research: The Role of Social Institutions*, edited by R. Rosenfeld, K. Quinet, and C. A. Garcia, 309–17. Belmont, CA: Wadsworth.
2013. "Deterrence in the Twenty-First Century." *Crime and Justice* 42(1): 199–263.
Nagin, Daniel S., and John V. Pepper, eds. 2012. *Deterrence and the Death Penalty*. Washington, DC: National Academies Press.
Popper, Andrew F. 2011. "In Defense of Deterrence." *Albany Law Review* 75: 181.
Posner, Richard A. 1972. "A Theory of Negligence." *Journal of Legal Studies* 1(1): 29–96.
Roisman, Anthony Z., Martha L. Judy and Daniel Stein. 2004. "Preserving Justice: Defending Toxic Tort Litigation." *Fordham Environmental Law Review* 15: 191.
Saks, Michael J. 1992. "Do We Really Know Anything about the Behavior of the Tort Litigation System. And Why Not?" *University of Pennsylvania Law Review* 140(4): 1147–1292.
Schell-Busey, Natalie, Sally S. Simpson, Melissa Rorie and Mariel Alper. 2016. "What Works? A Systematic Review of Corporate Crime Deterrence." *Criminology & Public Policy* 15(2): 387–416.
Simpson, Sally, Melissa Rorie, Mariel Elise Alper, Natalie Schell-Busey, William Laufer and N. Craig Smith. 2014. "Corporate Crime Deterrence: A Systematic Review." *Campbell Systematic Reviews* 10(4): 5–88.
Sloan, Frank A., Bridget A. Reilly and Christoph M. Schenzler. 1994. "Tort Liability versus Other Approaches for Deterring Careless Driving." *International Review of Law and Economics* 14(1): 53–71.
Sloan, Frank A., and John H. Shadle. 2009. "Is There Empirical Evidence for 'Defensive Medicine'? A Reassessment." *Journal of Health Economics* 28(2): 481–91.
Talesh, Shauhin. 2012. "How the Haves Come out Ahead in the Twenty-First Century." *DePaul Law Review* 62: 519.
Van McCrary, S., and Jeffrey W. Swanson. 1999. "Physicians' Legal Defensiveness and Knowledge of Medical Law: Comparing Denmark and the USA." *Scandinavian Journal of Public Health* 27(1): 18–21.

Van Rooij, Benjamin. 2016. "Weak Enforcement, Strong Deterrence: Dialogues with Chinese Lawyers about Tax Evasion and Compliance." *Law and Social Inquiry* 41(2): 288–310.

Yang, Y. Tony, David M. Studdert, S. V. Subramanian and Michelle M. Mello. 2012. "Does Tort Law Improve the Health of Newborns, or Miscarry? A Longitudinal Analysis of the Effect of Liability Pressure on Birth Outcomes." *Journal of Empirical Legal Studies* 9(2): 217–45.

Zador, Paul, and Adrian Lund. 1986. "Re-analyses of the Effects of No-Fault Auto Insurance on Fatal Crashes." *Journal of Risk and Insurance (1986–1998)* 53(2): 226.

23

Crowding-Out Effects of Laws, Policies and Incentives on Compliant Behaviour

Christopher P. Reinders Folmer

Abstract: Laws, policies, and incentives provide people with extrinsic reasons to engage in desired behaviours. But by doing so, they may attenuate or displace people's intrinsic reasons for complying. In this chapter, I review theorising and empirical evidence on such *crowding-out effects*. I outline perspectives from psychology and economics on how laws, policies, and incentives may undermine people's intrinsic motivation. Moreover, I describe how such insights have been applied to explain why laws, policies, and incentives may fail to increase compliance – or may even undermine it. The chapter then reviews the empirical evidence on these processes in environmental, organisational, and other legal settings. Although it is plausible that laws, policies, and incentives affect intrinsic motivation to comply, I conclude that empirical evidence of these processes is still modest. I end the chapter by outlining some important directions for future research and some (tentative) recommendations for policy.

23.1 INTRODUCTION

Regulators, organisations, and other authorities all frequently rely on rules, affirmative duties, and incentives to shape behaviour and promote compliance. Consider the use of fines to punish tax violations (Listokin and Schizer 2012), or the use of duties to report whistleblowing (Feldman and Lobel 2010): in these and many other cases, authorities provide external reasons for citizens to show good or refrain from bad behaviour. But do these instruments effectively promote compliance? Behavioural evidence suggests that this is not so straightforward. The reason for this is that laws and policies may change the meaning of the behaviours that they seek to influence, and thereby people's willingness to perform them (Feldman 2011; Underhill 2016).

Consider the example of day-care centres, which are often faced with the problem that parents arrive late to pick up their children. This necessitates that staff remain after closing time, which is costly and inconvenient. In response, these businesses often use a sanctioning system, such that parents who arrive late receive a monetary fine. The reasoning is that increasing the cost of tardiness will increase parents' motivation to arrive on time. However, behavioural evidence has suggested the opposite: introducing a sanctioning system actually *increased* late arrivals (Gneezy and Rustichini 2000). By setting a price, it reframed after-hours

This research was made possible through a generous grant from the European Research Council (ERC-2018-CoG - HomoJuridicus - 817680).

pick-up into a buyable service, rather than a violation or inconvenience. Incentives thereby *crowded out* intrinsic reasons to not be late.

As this example illustrates, using laws and policies to shape good and bad behaviour may be ineffective, or may even have consequences that are diametrically opposed to their intention. According to motivational crowding theory (Frey and Jegen 2001), this occurs because providing extrinsic reasons to comply: 1) crowds out from the equation people's intrinsic motivations to comply; 2) makes decisions to comply (exclusively) contingent on extrinsic reasons (e.g., laws and policies); and 3) may ultimately result in a decline in compliance (e.g., when people become desensitised to the impact of these instruments, or they are abolished).

In this chapter, I will explain crowding-out effects and illustrate how they may impact compliance. To do so, I will review theories from psychology and economics, to illuminate how laws and policies may affect intrinsic motivation and behaviour. I will then review empirical evidence on how these processes affect compliance in environmental, organisational, and other legal settings. I conclude by outlining some important directions for future research and by providing (tentative) recommendations for policy, based on the existing (preliminary) evidence.

23.2 CROWDING-OUT EFFECTS: THEORY AND HISTORY

Theorising on crowding-out effects originates from research on blood donation. As with many public goods or noble causes, medical stocks of blood for transfusion depend on voluntary donations by individual citizens – for whom this act is costly (in terms of time, inconvenience, and pain). To increase donations, programmes may offer monetary rewards that aim to compensate donors for these costs. Titmuss (1970) argued, however, that providing such incentives may, in fact, be detrimental to this outcome. He hypothesised that providing rewards would undermine donors' intrinsic motivation, reducing or even displacing their altruistic motives with extrinsic reasons for doing so (i.e., earning rewards). In this way, providing incentives could be detrimental to blood donations by driving away donors who would give out of altruistic or moral reasons, and attracting donors who are extrinsically motivated (which, according to Titmuss, could include persons with infectious diseases or drug addictions).

As this example illustrates, crowding-out effects may occur when incentives (rewards, punishments) are provided to promote good (or reduce bad) behaviour. These incentives aim to make it more profitable for individuals to comply, which is in line with the economic assumption that greater rewards will increase behaviour (i.e., the relative price effect; the 'strongest predictive statement a social scientist can make with regard to human behavior' (McKenzie and Tullock 1985, p. 15). However, by doing so, these incentives may alter how people perceive the act, the reasons for performing it, and, ultimately, their willingness to perform it (often in different ways from those intended).

While crowding-out effects were originally linked mainly to monetary incentives (payments, bonuses, fines), they have since been expanded to encompass a broad range of laws and policies – including rules, affirmative duties, torts, and criminal sanctions (e.g., Feldman 2011; Frey and Jegen 2001; Underhill 2016). Like incentives, such instruments provide extrinsic reasons to comply, which thereby may crowd out individuals' intrinsic reasons for doing so. However, the reverse is also possible. Laws, policies, and incentives also proscribe which behaviours are permissible (or not) and express social norms. In these ways, these instruments may also produce crowding-in effects and strengthen people's intrinsic reasons to comply (Bowles and Polanía-Reyes 2012; Frey 1997a; McAdams and Nadler 2005).

Crowding-out effects are ambiguous in that different fields focus on different outcomes when referring to them (e.g., in psychology: intrinsic motivation and task persistence; in economics: behaviours that oppose the relative price effect). Moreover, they are ambiguous because much evidence shows that incentives can have favourable effects on behaviour (see, e.g., Part III of this volume). In truth, however, crowding-out effects may occur even when the effects on behaviour seem favourable (e.g., when those behaviours become exclusively contingent on external rewards; Gneezy, Meier, and Rey-Biel 2011) but their harmful effects may nevertheless be considerable (Frey 1997a). And, alarmingly, people generally seem to be oblivious to this possibility: for example, they remain convinced that incentives are effective (Murayama et al. 2016).

23.2.1 *Processes that Explain Crowding-Out Effects*

Several related processes have been suggested to underlie crowding-out effects (see Bowles and Polanía-Reyes 2012; Feldman 2011; Rode, Gómez-Baggethun, and Krause 2015; Underhill 2016), as discussed now.

23.2.1.1 Effects on Intrinsic Motivation

In the absence of extrinsic reasons to do so, individuals who show good behaviour (or refrain from showing bad behaviour) may do so primarily for intrinsic reasons; that is, because they regard it as moral or legitimate, they want to help others, or they want to feel good about themselves (Bénabou and Tirole 2006; Feld and Frey 2007). Laws, policies, and incentives introduce additional, extrinsic reasons for doing so. Although such instruments mainly serve to motivate those who are *not* (sufficiently) motivated, their introduction may also undermine intrinsic motivation (Deci, Koestner, and Ryan 1999; Frey 1997a). Several processes may contribute to this.

A first process is that these instruments may be experienced as controlling (Deci et al. 1999; Frey 1997a). According to this explanation, people may experience laws, policies, and incentives as attempts to control or manipulate their behaviour, reducing their intrinsic motivation to comply. Evidence on monitoring also suggests that control may crowd out intrinsic motivation: although monitoring people's behaviour can increase compliance and reduce dishonesty, it simultaneously undermines their intrinsic motivation to do so (e.g., Frey 1993; Schulze and Frank 2003).

A second process is that these instruments may lead people to misattribute the reasons for complying. According to this explanation, laws, policies, and incentives may lead people to misattribute their reasons for acting to these extrinsic forces, and to neglect the role of their intrinsic motives (i.e., the over-justification effect; Lepper, Greene, and Nisbett 1973; Tang and Hall 1995).

23.2.1.2 Effects on the Meaning of Behaviour

In the absence of extrinsic reasons, decisions to comply may be understood as a question of norms or morals (Gneezy and Rustichini 2000). However, when compliance is proscribed by laws, policies, or incentives, this may alter how such decisions are interpreted – both by the actors and by those who observe them. This involves several related processes:

Firstly, these instruments may change the frame from which people understand good (or bad) behaviour. This is illustrated by the example of the day-care centre: here, the introduction of a sanctioning system reframed the issue from a moral question into one of economic exchange, where a 'market ethic' is appropriate (Gneezy and Rustichini 2000; Heyman and Ariely 2004).

Secondly, these instruments may change how compliance reflects upon oneself. When proscribed or rewarded, good behaviours may no longer seem like moral or pro-social acts but rather like self-interested behaviours. For people who comply for intrinsic reasons, this may be highly objectionable and irreconcilable with their self-image. Laws, policies, and incentives may thus reduce the satisfaction or 'warm glow' that people receive from performing such behaviours (Andreoni 1990; Bowles and Polonía-Reyes 2012). Furthermore, when good behaviours are proscribed or rewarded, they also lose their meaning as a signal to others (i.e., image spoiling; Bénabou and Tirole 2006; Janssen and Mendys-Kamphorst 2004). Accordingly, people may also be less inclined to comply in order to gain a favourable image.

23.2.1.3 Laws, Policies, and Incentives as Signals

A third reason is that people may interpret laws, policies, and incentives as signals – signals that provide information on what behaviour is appropriate, on what others do, and on how the authority perceives them.

To begin with, people may interpret laws, policies, and incentives as normative signals. They interpret from these instruments what behaviours are appropriate or not. For example, punishment may be regarded as a signal that the authority disapproves of non-compliance, while rewards may do the opposite (Bowles and Polonía-Reyes 2012; Gneezy and Rustichini 2000). In this way, these instruments may strengthen people's intrinsic motivations to comply (i.e., a crowding-in effect; Bowles and Polanía-Reyes 2012; Frey 1997a; McAdams and Nadler 2005). Such interpretations may depend not only on the instrument itself (e.g., whether an act is prohibited) but also on how it is implemented. For example, if rewards are low, people may interpret that compliance is not highly valued by the authority (Bénabou and Tirole 2006; Gneezy and Rustichini 2000).

In addition, people may interpret laws, policies, and incentives as an indication of how frequently others comply. When authorities introduce such instruments to promote compliance, people may interpret from this that non-compliance must be widespread (Kahan 2001). If so, these instruments may reduce, rather than increase, their willingness to comply by suggesting that non-compliance is the norm (Underhill 2016).

Lastly, people may interpret such instruments as signals that the authority does not trust them to comply spontaneously (see Bénabou and Tirole 2006; Cerasoli, Nicklin, and Ford 2014; Frey 1997b). If so, people may experience this as demeaning, undermining their intrinsic motivation to comply.

23.3 HOW CROWDING-OUT EFFECTS MAY IMPACT BEHAVIOUR

How may crowding-out effects be reflected in people's behaviour? This is not self-evident. Although there is an extensive (psychological) literature that demonstrates that incentives may reduce intrinsic motivation (e.g., Cerasoli et al. 2014; Deci et al. 1999), this does not mean that laws, policies, and incentives will necessarily reduce compliance. The reason is that such instruments simultaneously increase extrinsic motivation – and it is their combination that determines their impact on behaviour.

According to economic theory, incentives make the target behaviour more attractive by increasing its payoff (i.e., the relative price effect). However, incentives may simultaneously decrease intrinsic motivation, reducing their net effect on behaviour. If people's extrinsic motivation from incentives exceeds the loss to their intrinsic motivation, they are likely to comply more. Conversely, if the loss to their intrinsic motivation is greater, they are likely to comply less. If intrinsic and extrinsic motivations are both affected in equal terms, their behaviour will be unaffected (Bowles and Polonía-Reyes 2012). As such, the impact of crowding-out effects will not always be directly visible in the target behaviour. Rather, this impact may be concealed (e.g., by changing the reasons why people display it), visible in other behaviours (e.g., by supplanting one undesirable behaviour with another; Thøgersen 1994), or visible in the future (e.g., when the instruments lose their draw on people, or, ultimately, are abolished; Funk 2007; Gneezy and Rustichini 2000).

23.4 EVIDENCE OF CROWDING-OUT EFFECTS IN COMPLIANCE

In terms of their impact on behaviour, crowding-out effects have particularly been related to (academic) performance (e.g., Cerasoli et al. 2014; Deci et al. 1999), co-operation (Bowles and Polonía-Reyes 2012), health behaviours (Promberger and Marteau 2013), and pro-social behaviour (Bénabou and Tirole 2006). However, laws, policies, and incentives are similarly used to shape behaviour in the domain of compliance. If we apply the insights from the literatures in psychology and economics, then there are strong theoretical reasons to assume that these instruments may crowd out intrinsic motivation and thereby undermine compliance. However, in the domain of law, policies and incentives also have a strong expressive function, by signalling what behaviour is appropriate (Funk 2007; Sunstein 1996). For this reason, it is not clear how these instruments may impact intrinsic motivation and compliance. To provide insight into this question, I will now review evidence on crowding-out effects in compliance in theorising and empirical research. To do so, I will integrate insights from laboratory studies and field research on compliance in environmental, organisational, and other legal settings.

23.4.1 *Laboratory Experiments*

Experimental studies on crowding-out effects in compliance examine these processes in the context of experimental games that are designed to model real-life principal–agent relationships (see Bowles and Polanía-Reyes 2012). In these types of game, participants either do or do not receive incentives (rewards, fines) to comply with requests to engage in behaviours that are costly to themselves but beneficial to the principal. By systematically manipulating these factors, and by controlling the variability that characterises principal–agent relationships in real life, these studies are well suited for demonstrating how incentives impact compliance levels – and for uncovering the mechanisms that contribute to this (Bowles and Polanía-Reyes 2012). Furthermore, because experiments are not limited by the constraints that exist in real life, they can also be used to explore how incentives could be shaped to prevent crowding-out effects – and to more effectively promote compliance.

As a case in point, Fehr and Rockenbach (2003) examined agents' compliance with requests from the principal in the context of a trust game. In this game, agents could return valuable endowments that had been transferred to them by the principal, who could specify their desired amount. Agents were less, rather than more, inclined to return the requested amount if the principal fined them for non-compliance. Conversely, they returned more when principals chose not to fine them, despite having the opportunity to do so.

The finding that fines reduce compliance was replicated by Henrich et al. (2001) in a study that spanned fifteen different societies. Across many of these societies, participants reduced (rather than increased) their transfers to a powerless recipient in the dictator game when a third party could fine them for low transfers.

Xiao and Houser (2011) examined how these processes operated in more complex situations that involved multiple actors. They did so by studying a public-good game, in which multiple players must donate in order to achieve a public good. Their findings showed that punishment for low contributions reduced, rather than increased, players' contributions when punishment was private and not visible to others. In contrast, when punishment was public, it did effectively increase their donations.

In sum, experimental studies have demonstrated that incentives can reduce compliance (or fail to affect it) in line with the idea of a crowding-out effect. The processes through which crowding out occurs remain nebulous, however, and are mostly based on inferences rather than direct measures (Bowles and Polanía-Reyes 2012). Also, it is important to note that these processes are likely to be more complex in real-life settings – where they unfold over longer time frames, where moral and legal implications will be stronger, and where the scope for tailoring incentives may be more limited (see Feldman 2011; Underhill 2016).

23.4.2 *Environmental Compliance*

Crowding-out effects have been strongly related to compliance with environmental policy. In particular, Frey (1999) has theorised that environmental policy may produce crowding-out effects, by being experienced as controlling, and by reframing pollution as an economic (rather than a moral) question.

To illustrate this process, Frey (1999) singled out emission rights; that is, measures that limit the amount that polluters are licensed to pollute. The reasoning behind such instruments is that they will make it costlier for actors to pollute, and thereby will reduce their tendency to do so. However, Frey (1999) argued that their effects may often be opposed. By reframing pollution as a buyable right (a 'licence to pollute'), such instruments instead may legitimise pollution and crowd out moral considerations. Similar concerns may arise over emission taxes, which impose a cost on polluters for harming the environment. However, relative to emission rights, taxes may more clearly express that pollution is undesirable, and, accordingly, their impact on moral considerations may be more limited. Instead, Frey (1999) argued that taxes may undermine intrinsic motivation by being perceived as controlling. These processes have also been applied to understand (non-)compliance with other environmental policies, such as the European Landing Obligation for fisheries (Kraak and Hart 2019).

A number of studies have followed up on such theorising by empirically studying crowding-out effects in environmental compliance. These studies examine whether fines or rewards for behaviours that harm (or conserve) the environment may have unintended consequences by affecting people's intrinsic motivation to comply. Rode et al. (2015) reviewed a set of eighteen empirical studies that examine these questions in the context of actual (Greiner and Gregg 2011, Sommerville et al. 2010) or simulated (e.g., Jack 2009; Velez, Murphy, and Stranlund 2010) environmental behaviours among rural populations in (mostly) developing countries. These studies included the effects of regulation and tax incentives on conservation behaviours among cattle farmers in Australia (Greiner and Gregg 2011) and the effects of rewards on compliance with forest management plans (prohibiting agricultural expansion and hunting) in Madagascar (Sommerville et al. 2010). Across the various studies, Rode et al. (2015) observed indications that fines and rewards fail to promote, or even undermine, people's compliance with conservation goals (e.g., Jack 2009). However, such findings mostly failed to reach significance, or occurred only in part of the sample (e.g., Sommerville et al. 2010; Velez et al. 2010). Conversely, other studies reported favourable effects of fines and rewards (e.g., Velez et al. 2010).

A more direct indication of crowding-out effects in environmental compliance was provided by Feldman and Perez (2012), who studied such processes in the domain of recycling. Legislature employs a range of instruments to encourage people to recycle, including deposits and fines. In an experimental study, Feldman and Perez (2012) demonstrated that (especially high) deposits and fines may undermine intrinsic motivation and compliance for people who are intrinsically motivated to recycle. Conversely, a low fine, or an ethical code to promote recycling, did seem to increase their compliance. These effects were opposed for people who were not intrinsically motivated to recycle: here, especially high fines and deposits enhanced compliance.

Importantly, Feldman and Perez (2009) also demonstrated that environmental regulation may produce crowding-out effects in observers. Participants reported lower condemnation of environmental offences if the offending company would be charged a tax or a fine. Conversely, they reported greater condemnation if the violation was prohibited (without penalties), would invoke a high sanction (fine and imprisonment), or occurred despite community-negotiated standards or permission to self-report. Furthermore, they were least inclined to take civic action when pollution was taxed (and most if it violated community standards or self-reporting). Feldman and Perez (2009) interpreted this as a crowding-out effect, such that putting a price on pollution may reduce moral considerations. Interestingly, they observed no indications that criminal sanctions (fines, imprisonment) could crowd in and evoke greater condemnation.

That incentives may have effects beyond the individuals or behaviours that they target is also suggested by a field study reported by Thøgersen (1994). Here, the introduction of a pay-by-weight scheme effectively reduced the volume of household waste (as intended) – but simultaneously increased illegal waste burning. These findings show that crowding-out effects may also manifest themselves in outcomes other than those that the policy targets (i.e., spillover effects).

23.4.3 *Health-Related Behaviours*

Following the seminal work of Titmuss (1970), a wealth of research has examined crowding-out effects in health-related behaviours (for a review, see Promberger and Marteau 2013). While fewer studies have focused on compliance, crowding-out effects may also be prominent in this domain. An important area is that of vaccination against infectious diseases.

Vaccination against infectious diseases is critical for public health, and many countries require citizens to inoculate children. Nevertheless, many citizens refuse to comply with such requests out of fears that vaccines may have harmful side-effects. To increase compliance, institutions have utilised rewards and fines, as well as legislation that makes vaccination compulsory. Research suggests that incentives may indeed promote compliance with vaccination obligations (for a meta-analysis, see Stone et al. 2002). Nevertheless, scholars have also expressed concern that such measures may produce crowding-out effects (e.g., Fiske et al. 2015; Promberger and Marteau 2013). In particular, such measures may be experienced as controlling and thus be believed to undermine voluntary compliance. Firm evidence on these processes is lacking, however, as studies generally do not directly assess how these instruments impact extrinsic and intrinsic motivation. As such, it remains unclear to what extent the greater compliance levels that they produce are at the expense of voluntary cooperation.

23.4.4 *Tax Compliance (and Evasion)*

Crowding-out effects have also been linked to tax compliance (and evasion). Authorities rely on monitoring, sanctions, and rewards to ensure citizens' tax compliance. Scholars have predicted, however, that doing so may undermine intrinsic motivation to comply – and thereby undermine, rather than promote, tax compliance (e.g., Listokin and Schizer 2012; Feld and Frey 2007).

In this vein, a considerable body of research has examined how fines may impact tax compliance (for an overview, see Feld and Frey 2007). The results are mixed, however. Some studies report that fines promote tax compliance (e.g., Alm, Sanchez, and De Juan 1995), while others suggest that fines may even reduce it (e.g., Lubell and Scholz 2001). Feld and Frey (2007) suggested that the effect of fines may differ from that of monitoring, such that fines may promote compliance, while monitoring may reduce it. Other studies have suggested that monitoring, too, may display both positive and negative effects on tax compliance. They have demonstrated that audits may strongly increase tax compliance by increasing deterrence (Beer et al. 2019) – but also may decrease it by reducing intrinsic motivation (Gangl et al. 2014).

Other scholars have argued that tax compliance results from perceptions of legitimacy. For example, Frey (1997b) has argued that tax morale may be promoted by fair laws and policies that express trust in citizens, which may crowd in civic virtue. Conversely, laws that convey distrust may do the opposite. In line with this idea, Frey demonstrated that tax morale is lower in Swiss Cantons where opportunities for political participation are lower (and those policies, thus, are less fair and inclusive). In an experimental study, Hofmann et al. (2014) demonstrated that greater legitimacy may counter the detrimental effects of strict audits and fines. Thus, it seems that tax compliance may result from both coercion and legitimacy, which may crowd motivation in opposing directions. It is the relative strength of these processes that is likely to determine whether compliance increases or decreases – which may explain the differing effects that are observed in the literature.

23.4.5 *Contract Breach*

Researchers have also related crowding-out effects to the enforcement of contracts. In order to stimulate compliance with contracts, the law provides affirmative duties and sanctions for breaking them. Jurisdictions may vary in their enforcement of such sanctions, however, and the level of enforcement may produce crowding-out effects.

As a case in point, Bohnet, Frey, and Huck (2001) conducted an experiment using a contract enforcement game, in which the level of enforcement was varied. They observed greater compliance with contract terms not only in case of high enforcement but also in case of low enforcement. In contrast, contract breaches were more common in case of intermediate enforcement. Their findings are in line with the idea that greater enforcement may crowd out trustworthiness. This may be countered by its effect on extrinsic motivation, which high enforcement may simultaneously increase. However, trustworthiness may be crowded in at low enforcement levels in which contracts may be performed for intrinsic reasons.

23.4.6 *Bribery*

Crowding-out effects have also been linked to bribery (e.g., Schulze and Frank 2003; Serra 2011). In an experimental study using a bribery game, Serra (2011) examined how monitoring affected the tendency of 'officials' to ask for bribes. A conventional, top-down auditing system (in which the chances of being caught were low) was ineffective for reducing bribery: instead, 'officials' asked for larger bribes. However, a whistleblowing system, where 'citizens' could report corrupt 'officials' to the 'authorities', did effectively reduce bribery – even though the chances that doing so would effectively result in punishment were stated to be equally low. Bowles and Polanía-Reyes (2012) suggested that being accountable towards one's peers may crowd in social preferences against corruption. As noted earlier, monitoring may operate in the opposite direction, by evoking resistance and strategic behaviour (Frey 1993; Schulze and Frank 2003).

23.4.7 *Civic Duty*

Crowding-out effects have also been related to compliance with civic duties such as voting (Funk 2007) and jury duty (Seamone 2002). In particular, this concerns the use of legislation or incentives to increase citizen compliance with civic duties. On the one hand, there is concern that such measures may reduce voluntary compliance. On the other hand, there are also suggestions that such measures may have beneficial effects by underlining the importance of these duties (i.e., crowding-in effects).

In several countries (e.g., Belgium, Australia), voting is compulsory, instead of citizens being free to decide whether or not to vote. Other countries have relied on fines or rewards in order to encourage voting (e.g., Switzerland). Some researchers have voiced concern that such measures may crowd out intrinsic motivation (e.g., Chapman 2019). However, there are also indications of the opposite: for example, Funk (2007) observed that the voting turnout decreased, rather than increased, when a (symbolic) fine for not voting was abolished. This implies that fines (or rewards) may also express the importance of voting, and thereby crowd in intrinsic motivation.

23.4.8 *Compliance in Organisational Settings*

In organisational settings, researchers have referred to crowding-out effects to understand how compliance is affected by organisational reward structures (e.g., Frey and Jegen 2001; Stout 2014) or monitoring (e.g., Ramaswami 1996). Specifically, there is concern that these instruments may undermine compliance by evoking opportunistic and unethical behaviours.

23.4.8.1 Opportunistic Behaviour

A case in point is the meta-analysis by Crosno and Brown (2015), which examined the effects of monitoring in marketing exchange relationships; that is, in interactions between companies and the agents that act on their behalf (e.g., employees, franchisees, contractors, or intermediaries). Across sixty-five studies, they found that monitoring improved agent performance but could also increase harmful, guileful opportunism. According to the authors, monitoring may have such effects because it undermines agents' sense of control, and thereby crowds out trust and voluntary cooperation (Ramaswami 1996). However, it seems that this impact can vary, as opportunism differed depending on what was being monitored (processes or outcomes) and in which relationship (within or between organisations).

23.4.8.2 Performance-Based Pay

At present, direct evidence that links performance-based pay to crowding-out effects is still limited. However, several scholars theorise that these reward structures may have such an impact and may (for example) crowd out moral considerations (e.g., Frey and Jegen 2001; Stout 2014). Although there is no direct evidence of these processes yet, several empirical studies have shown that compensation indeed may predict organisational misbehaviour (e.g., Harris and Bromiley 2007).

23.4.8.3 Whistleblowing

Crowding-out effects have been related not only to organisational deviance but also to the willingness to report it, known as whistleblowing. Because misbehaviour is often difficult for outsiders to detect, authorities are strongly dependent on whistleblowing by insiders. However, insiders often fail to report transgressions because doing so may have harmful consequences for themselves (e.g., dismissal, sanctions). For this reason, authorities use a range of instruments to promote whistleblowing, including incentives, legal protection, and duties to report. But because whistleblowing may normally arise from intrinsic reasons, scholars have argued that such instruments may lead to crowding-out effects (e.g., Feldman and Lobel 2010; Lobel 2012). Feldman and Lobel (2010) demonstrated this in an experimental study in which they tested how several laws and policies (rewards, fines, whistleblower protection, and/or affirmative duties to report) affected people's willingness to report misbehaviour. Participants generally reported strong intentions to blow the whistle across affirmative duties, legal protection, fines, or (high) rewards. Their intentions were the strongest when there was a duty to report misbehaviour and doing so would earn a high reward. Conversely, their willingness declined when reporting was not obligatory and earned only a low reward. Interestingly, participants did not seem to appreciate how influential (high) rewards were for their own intentions to report, and condemned others who reported misbehavior in order to gain a reward.

To understand how these processes relate to intrinsic motivation, the authors also separated participants by their tolerance for misbehaviour (which they regarded as a proxy for intrinsic motivation). Those with low intrinsic motivation were more willing to report misbehaviour when doing so was obligatory, would prevent a fine, or earned a high reward. Conversely, those with high intrinsic motivation reported regardless of the policy. Feldman and Lobel (2010) concluded that rewards may encourage people to report less severe misbehaviours – but may crowd out intrinsic motives for doing so, and give the impression that whistleblowing is motivated by greed. In contrast, a duty to report, fines, or whistleblower protection may encourage whistleblowing while simultaneously conserving intrinsic, moral motivations.

23.5 SYNTHESIS

Crowding-out effects refer to a diverse range of processes that may occur when authorities incentivise, control, or oblige compliant behaviour. They generally concern processes that undermine people's intrinsic motivation to comply (crowding-out effects), although the reverse is also possible (crowding-in effects). The impact of these effects on behaviour may often not be apparent, owing to the notion that such instruments simultaneously increase extrinsic motivation to comply; also, their impact may spill over to different outcomes from the target behaviour. Nevertheless, there are considerable indications that laws and policies may have unanticipated, detrimental (side-)effects because of crowding-out effects – particularly by supplanting valuable, intrinsic reasons to comply.

Evidence of crowding-out (and crowding-in) effects on compliance is relatively modest compared to that on (academic) performance (e.g., Deci et al. 1999) and co-operation (e.g., Bowles and Polanía-Reyes 2012). Crowding-out effects are frequently linked to compliance in theorising; however, empirical evidence of these effects is more limited and shows mixed results. The strongest evidence comes from (laboratory) experiments (e.g., Bowles and Polanía-Reyes 2012). Evidence from field experiments is more variable. Some studies report considerable detrimental effects on compliance (e.g., Gneezy and Rustichini 2000 on fines in day-care), while in other studies and settings, these effects are (at best) limited (e.g., Rode et al. 2015 on incentives for environmental conservation).

As a consequence of this variability, it is difficult to draw firm conclusions on the impact of crowding-out (and crowding-in) effects in the domain of compliance. One major limitation especially accounts for this: although many studies refer to crowding-out effects to explain their findings, few studies directly examine the processes that comprise them. Generally, studies do not measure intrinsic and extrinsic motivation, impaired control, or salience of moral or economic frames. Because these processes may work in opposing directions (and potentially may cancel each other out), their impact may not always be visible in (non-) compliant behaviour. As such, it is possible that similar processes (but in different proportions) are at work behind the differing effects on compliance.

If we want to understand their impact on compliance, an important question therefore remains: namely, how do crowding-out (and crowding-in) effects operate to shape people's decisions to comply (or not)? Future research should directly examine this question. On the one hand, this could be done through quantitative measures of intrinsic and extrinsic motivation, which can be used to predict (non-)compliant behaviour in structural models. On the other hand, much could be learned from qualitative research that asks the actors themselves to describe the reasons for their actions. Through either approach, we may come to understand the mixed picture that we observe in the present literature.

To understand crowding-out effects on compliance, it is also imperative that future research focuses more on rules, affirmative duties, and prohibitions, and less on incentives and monitoring. By proscribing which behaviours are or are not permissible, such laws and policies are arguably especially relevant for compliance; however, only a few studies have explored their impact (e.g., Feldman and Lobel 2010; Feldman and Perez 2009). Doing so may also shed more light on crowding-in effects and how these may contribute to greater compliance. The existing literature has mostly focused on how incentives and monitoring may produce crowding-out effects and thereby undermine compliance. However, laws, rules, and duties have a strong expressive function, signalling what behaviour is appropriate (Funk 2007; Sunstein 1996). In this fashion, such instruments may also evoke or strengthen intrinsic, moral motivations and thereby contribute to greater compliance (Bowles and Polanía-Reyes 2012; Frey 1997a; McAdams and Nadler 2005). By focusing more on these instruments and processes, future research may provide a more comprehensive picture of how law and policy shape compliance – and how this may be hurt or helped by crowding-out and crowding-in effects.

23.6 PRACTICAL IMPLICATIONS: HOW TO SHAPE LAW AND POLICY TO AVOID CROWDING-OUT EFFECTS

Although current research leaves some important questions unanswered, it is clear that crowding-out effects can potentially be very costly, whereas crowding-in effects may enhance compliance. As such, it is important to ask how law and policy should be shaped to harness these effects. More research is needed to fully understand this. Nevertheless, some (preliminary) recommendations can be derived from the work of Underhill (2016) and Feldman (2011), who provided a comprehensive analysis of how the existing work on crowding-out effects applies to law. I recount some of their recommendations below. Please note that these should be treated as preliminary because most of these processes have not directly been tested in the domain of law and policy or in relation to compliance.

23.6.1 *Setting Incentives*

Authorities frequently rely on incentives, yet (as noted) these may especially risk crowding-out effects. Underhill (2016) provided several recommendations on how incentives should be used to prevent this.

To begin with, she concluded that crowding-out effects may be reduced by relying on non-financial rewards, such as in-kind rewards or praise. These may be less likely to recast compliance as an economic transaction and more likely to conserve intrinsic motivation.

When setting financial incentives, Underhill (2016) observed that it is crucial that they be proportional to the requested behaviour and not too small. Small incentives may be ineffective. large incentives may undermine intrinsic motivation but may still ensure compliance for extrinsic reasons. Rewards that reflect mastery or quality may be less likely to crowd out intrinsic motives. In every case, if incentives are introduced, it is essential that they are continued, and not abolished. The reason for this is that incentives may fundamentally alter people's reasons for complying (e.g., Funk 2007) - such that their willingness to do so may strongly decline once the incentives are withdrawn.

To address concerns related to (self- or public) image, an intriguing recommendation is to allow recipients to indicate a beneficiary other than themselves (e.g., a charity; see Beretti, Figuières, and Grolleau 2019). This would enable decisions to comply to retain a moral character in spite of the reward.

For expressing disapproval, fines may be more effective (Bowles and Polonía-Reyes 2012). As such, they may be more suitable for misbehaviours where public disapproval is strong. Underhill (2016) noted that public punishment may be especially effective – but may also especially crowd out intrinsic motivation.

23.6.2 *Conserving Self-Determination and Control*

To prevent crowding-out effects that result from impaired self-determination or autonomy, Underhill (2016) suggested that authorities could consult recipients in the design of laws and policies. Citizens may feel more compelled to comply with fair policies and may be more willing to relinquish their autonomy to them (see Frey 1997b). Furthermore, policies that give them space in terms of *how* they comply (i.e., outcome control rather than process control) may invoke less resistance (Crosno and Brown 2015).

23.6.3 *Using Uniform or Targeted Policies*

Feldman (2011) recommended that when designing policies, authorities should consider which recipients and outcomes they target. Targeted policies, focusing specifically on people with low intrinsic motivation, should be used in cases where any violation can be critical (e.g., divulging trade secrets). If the goal is to achieve high compliance, regardless of people's motives for complying (e.g., recycling), then uniform incentives may be suitable. Conversely, if only a few individuals are needed to comply (e.g., whistleblowing), uniform incentives are excessive and may do more harm than good.

REFERENCES

Alm, James, Isabel Sanchez and Ana De Juan. 1995. 'Economic and Noneconomic Factors in Tax Compliance.' *Kyklos* 48: 1–18.

Andreoni, James. 1990. 'Impure Altruism and Donations to Public Goods: A Theory of Warm-Glow Giving'. *Economic Journal* 100: 464–77.

Beer, Sebastian, Matthias Kasper, Erich Kirchler and Brian Erard. 2019. 'Do Audits Deter or Provoke Future Tax Noncompliance? Evidence on Self-Employed Taxpayers'. IMF Working Paper WP/19/223. www.imf.org/~/media/Files/Publications/WP/2019/wpiea2019223-print-pdf.ashx.

Bénabou, Roland, and Jean Tirole. 2006. 'Incentives and Prosocial Behavior'. *American Economic Review* 96: 1652–78.

Beretti, Antoine, Charles Figuières and Gilles Grolleau. 2019. 'How to Turn Crowding-Out into Crowding-In? An Innovative Instrument and Some Law-Related Examples'. *European Journal of Law and Economics* 48: 417–38.

Bohnet, Iris, Bruno S. Frey and Steffen Huck. 2001. 'More Order with Less Law: On Contract Enforcement, Trust, and Crowding'. *American Political Science Review* 95: 131–44.

Bowles, Samuel, and Sandra Polanía-Reyes. 2012. 'Economic Incentives and Social Preferences: Substitutes or Complements?' *Journal of Economic Literature* 50: 368–425.

Cerasoli, Christopher P., Jessica M. Nicklin and Michael T. Ford. 2014. 'Intrinsic Motivation and Extrinsic Incentives Jointly Predict Performance: A 40-Year Meta-analysis'. *Psychological Bulletin* 140: 980–1008.

Chapman, Emilee Booth. 2019. 'The Distinctive Value of Elections and the Case for Compulsory Voting'. *American Journal of Political Science* 63: 101–12.

Crosno, Jody L., and James R. Brown. 2015. 'A Meta-analytic Review of the Effects of Organizational Control in Marketing Exchange Relationships'. *Journal of the Academy of Marketing Science* 43: 297–314.

Deci, Edward L., Richard Koestner and Richard M. Ryan. 1999. 'A Meta-analytic Review of Experiments Examining the Effects of Extrinsic Rewards on Intrinsic Motivation'. *Psychological Bulletin* 125: 627–68.

Fehr, Ernst, and Bettina Rockenbach. 2003. 'Detrimental Effects of Sanctions on Human Altruism'. *Nature* 422: 137–40.

Feld, Lars P., and Bruno S. Frey. 2007. 'Tax Compliance as the Result of a Psychological Tax Contract: The Role of Incentives and Responsive Regulation'. *Law and Policy* 29: 102–20.

Feldman, Yuval. 2011. 'The Complexity of Disentangling Intrinsic and Extrinsic Compliance Motivations: Theoretical and Empirical Insights From the Behavioral Analysis of Law.' Washington University Journal of Law and Policy 35: 11–51.

Feldman, Yuval, and Orly Lobel. 2010. 'The Incentives Matrix: The Comparative Effectiveness of Rewards, Liabilities, Duties, and Protections for Reporting Illegality'. *Texas Law Review* 88: 1151–1211.

Feldman, Yuval, and Oren Perez. 2009. 'How Law Changes the Environmental Mind: An Experimental Study of the Effect of Legal Norms on Moral Perceptions and Civic Enforcement'. *Journal of Law and Society* 36: 501–35.

2012. 'Motivating Environmental Action in a Pluralistic Regulatory Environment: An Experimental Study of Framing, Crowding Out, and Institutional Effects in the Context of Recycling Policies'. *Law and Society Review* 46: 405–42.

Fiske, S. T., C. Betsch, R. Böhm and G. B. Chapman. 2015. 'Using Behavioral Insights to Increase Vaccination Policy Effectiveness'. *Behavioral and Brain Sciences* 2: 61–73.

Frey, Bruno S. 1993. 'Does Monitoring Increase Work Effort? The Rivalry with Trust and Loyalty'. *Economic Inquiry* 31: 663–70.

1997a. *Not Just for the Money: An Economic Theory of Personal Motivation*. Cheltenham: Edward Elgar.

1997b. 'A Constitution for Knaves Crowds Out Civic Virtues'. *Economic Journal* 107: 1043–53.

1999. 'Morality and Rationality in Environmental Policy'. *Journal of Consumer Policy* 22: 395–417.

Frey, Bruno S., and Reto Jegen. 2001. 'Motivation Crowding Theory'. *Journal of Economic Surveys* 15: 589–611.

Funk, Patricia. 2007. 'Is There an Expressive Function of Law? An Empirical Analysis of Voting Laws with Symbolic Fines'. *American Law and Economics Review* 9: 135–59.

Gangl, Katharina, Benno Torgler, Erich Kirchler and Eva Hofmann. 2014. 'Effects of Supervision on Tax Compliance: Evidence from a Field Experiment in Austria'. *Economics Letters* 123: 378–82.

Gneezy, Uri, Stephan Meier and Pedro Rey-Biel. 2011. 'When and Why Incentives (Don't) Work to Modify Behavior'. *Journal of Economic Perspectives* 25: 191–210.

Gneezy, Uri, and Aldo Rustichini. 2000. 'A Fine Is a Price'. *Journal of Legal Studies* 29: 1–17.

Greiner, Romy, and Daniel Gregg. 2011. 'Farmers' Intrinsic Motivations, Barriers to the Adoption of Conservation Practices and Effectiveness of Policy Instruments: Empirical Evidence from Northern Australia'. *Land Use Policy* 28: 257–65.

Harris, Jared, and Philip Bromiley. 2007. 'Incentives to Cheat: The Influence of Executive Compensation and Firm Performance on Financial Misrepresentation'. *Organization Science* 18: 350–67.

Henrich, Joseph, Robert Boyd, Samuel Bowles, Colin Camerer, Ernst Fehr, Herbert Gintis and Richard McElreath. 2001. 'Cooperation, Reciprocity and Punishment in Fifteen Small-Scale Societies'. *American Economic Review* 91: 73–8.

Heyman, James, and Dan Ariely. 2004. 'Effort for Payment: A Tale of Two Markets'. *Psychological Science* 15: 787–93.

Hofmann, Eva B., Katharina Gangl, Erich Kirchler and Jennifer Stark. 2014. 'Enhancing Tax Compliance through Coercive and Legitimate Power of Tax Authorities by Concurrently Diminishing or Facilitating Trust in Tax Authorities'. *Law and Policy* 36: 290–313.

Jack, B. Kelsey. 2009. 'Upstream–Downstream Transactions and Watershed Externalities: Experimental Evidence from Kenya'. *Ecological Economics* 68: 1813–24.

Janssen, Maarten C., and Ewa Mendys-Kamphorst. 2004. 'The Price of a Price: On the Crowding Out and In of Social Norms'. *Journal of Economic Behavior and Organization* 55: 377–95.

Kahan, Dan M. 2001. 'Trust, Collective Action, and Law'. *Boston University Law Review* 81: 333–45.

Kraak, Sarah B. M., and Paul J. B. Hart. 2019. 'Creating a Breeding Ground for Compliance and Honest Reporting under the Landing Obligation: Insights from Behavioural Science'. In *The European Landing Obligation*, edited by Sven Sebastian Uhlmann, Clara Ulrich and Steven J. Kennelly, 219–36. Cham: Springer.

Lepper, Mark R., David Greene and Richard E. Nisbett. 1973. 'Undermining Children's Intrinsic Interest with Extrinsic Reward: A Test of the "Overjustification" Hypothesis'. *Journal of Personality and Social Psychology* 28: 129–37.

Listokin, Yair, and David M. Schizer. 2012. 'I Like to Pay Taxes: Taxpayer Support for Government Spending and the Efficiency of the Tax System'. *Tax Law Review* 66: 179–215.

Lobel, Orly. 2012. 'Linking Prevention, Detection, and Whistleblowing: Principles for Designing Effective Reporting Systems'. *South Texas Law Review* 54: 37–52.

Lubell, Mark, and John T. Scholz. 2001. 'Cooperation, Reciprocity, and the Collective-Action Heuristic'. *American Journal of Political Science* 45: 160–78.

McAdams, Richard H., and Janice Nadler. 2005. 'Testing the Focal Point Theory of Legal Compliance: The Effect of Third-Party Expression in an Experimental Hawk/Dove Game'. *Journal of Empirical Legal Studies* 2: 87–123.

McKenzie, Richard, and Gordon Tullock. 1985. *The New World of Economics* (4th revised edition). Homewood, IL: Irwin.

Murayama, Kou, Shinji Kitagami, Ayumi Tanaka and Jasmine A. Raw. 2016. 'People's Naiveté about How Extrinsic Rewards Influence Intrinsic Motivation'. *Motivation Science* 2: 138–42.

Promberger, Marianne, and Theresa M. Marteau. 2013. 'When Do Financial Incentives Reduce Intrinsic Motivation? Comparing Behaviors Studied in Psychological and Economic Literatures'. *Health Psychology* 32: 950–7.

Ramaswami, Sridhar N. 1996. 'Marketing Controls and Dysfunctional Employee Behaviors: A Test of Traditional and Contingency Theory Postulates'. *Journal of Marketing* 60: 105–20.

Rode, Julian, Erik Gómez-Baggethun, and Torsten Krause. 2015. 'Motivation Crowding by Economic Incentives in Conservation Policy: A Review of the Empirical Evidence'. *Ecological Economics* 117: 270–82.

Schulze, Günther G., and Björn Frank. 2003. 'Deterrence versus Intrinsic Motivation: Experimental Evidence on the Determinants of Corruptibility'. *Economics of Governance* 4: 143–60.

Seamone, Evan R. 2002. 'A Refreshing Jury Cola: Fulfilling the Duty to Compensate Jurors Adequately'. *New York University Journal of Legislation and Public Policy* 5: 289–417.

Serra, Danila. 2011. 'Combining Top-Down and Bottom-Up Accountability: Evidence from a Bribery Experiment'. *Journal of Law, Economics, and Organization* 28: 569–87.

Sommerville, Matthew, Julia P. G. Jones, Michael Rahajaharison and E. J. Milner-Gulland. 2010. 'The Role of Fairness and Benefit Distribution in Community-Based Payment for Environmental Services Interventions: A Case Study from Menabe, Madagascar'. *Ecological Economics* 69: 1262–71.

Stone, Erin G., Sally C. Morton, Marlies E. Hulscher, Margaret A. Maglione, Elizabeth A. Roth, Jeremy M. Grimshaw, Brian S. Mittman, Lisa V. Rubenstein, Laurence Z. Rubenstein and Paul G. Shekelle. 2002. 'Interventions that Increase Use of Adult Immunization and Cancer Screening Services: A Meta-analysis'. *Annals of Internal Medicine* 136: 641–51.

Stout, Lynn A. 2014. 'Killing Conscience: The Unintended Behavioral Consequences of Pay for Performance.' *Journal of Corporation Law* 39: 525–61.

Sunstein, Cass R. 1996. 'On the Expressive Function of Law'. *University of Pennsylvania Law Review* 144: 2021–53.

Tang, Shu-Hua, and Vernon C. Hall. 1995. 'The Overjustification Effect: A Meta-analysis'. *Applied Cognitive Psychology* 9: 365–404.

Thøgersen, John. 1994. 'Monetary Incentives and Environmental Concern: Effects of a Differentiated Garbage Fee'. *Journal of Consumer Policy* 17: 407–42.

Titmuss, Richard M. 1970. *The Gift Relationship*. London: Allen and Unwin.

Underhill, Kristen. 2016. 'When Extrinsic Incentives Displace Intrinsic Motivation: Designing Legal Carrots and Sticks to Confront the Challenge of Motivational Crowding-Out.' *Yale Journal on Regulation* 33: 213–79.

Velez, Maria Alejandra, James J. Murphy and John K. Stranlund. 2010. 'Centralized and Decentralized Management of Local Common Pool Resources in the Developing World: Experimental Evidence from Fishing Communities in Colombia'. *Economic Inquiry* 48: 254–65.

Xiao, Erte, and Daniel Houser. 2011. 'Punish in Public'. *Journal of Public Economics* 95: 1006–17.

24

Financial Incentives for Whistleblowers: A Short Survey

Giancarlo Spagnolo and Theo Nyreröd*

Abstract: Whistleblower reward programmes, or 'bounty regimes', are increasingly used in the United States. The effectiveness of these programmes has been questioned, and empirical evidence on their effectiveness has been scarce likely due to their relatively recent introduction. In recent years, however, empirical and experimental evidence on their effectiveness has become more available and robust. We review the (rather encouraging) evidence on whistleblower reward programmes, in terms of amount of additional information generated, deterrence effects, and administration costs, and consider the possibility of extending them to accomplice witnesses in antitrust cases.

24.1 INTRODUCTION

Although whistleblower reward programmes have existed in different forms since at least the Middle Ages, the United States is the only country that has experimented extensively with them in recent decades. The U.S. False Claims Act (FCA) is the most well-known whistleblower reward programme and was originally signed into law in 1863 under President Lincoln to curb fraud in military procurement for the Union Army. The Internal Revenue Office's (IRS) whistleblower reward programme was established with the enactment of the Tax Relief and Health Care Act in 2006. The Securities and Exchange Commission's (SEC) whistleblower programme was established with the enactment of the Dodd-Frank Act in 2010. In Canada, the Ontario Securities Commission (OSC) also implemented a bounty programme in 2016 inspired by that of the SEC, although with fundamental differences.

Whistleblowers are typically employees at the organization they blow the whistle on. Rewards can be considered a counterweight to the large retaliation costs usually associated with whistleblowing, such as reallocation, demotion, firing, blacklisting from the industry, and even physical harassment (see, e.g., Rothschild and Miethe 1999). We should indeed think of rewards as compensation for unquantifiable damages, as courts often find it difficult to establish causation between a person blowing the whistle and the retaliatory measures that follow, and therefore to award adequate compensation for damages caused by retaliation (see, e.g., Moberly 2007; Modesitt 2013).[1]

* We would like to acknowledge funding from Vetenskapsrådet Project number: 2014: 03770.

[1] Retaliating employers often argue that the whistleblower is a disgruntled or poorly performing employee, and therefore that any retaliatory measure was justified on other grounds. Confidentiality is also typically insufficient to protect whistleblowers from retaliation. The wrongdoing firm can typically figure out the identity of the whistleblower, especially as most whistleblowers first raise their concerns within the organization before reporting externally, and access to information on a certain organizational wrongdoing is often limited to a few individuals.

TABLE 24.1 *Whistleblower reward programmes*

Private litigation	FCA Yes	IRS No	SEC No	OSC No
Reward %	15%–30%	15%–30%	10%–30%	5%–15%
Ineligible if ...	Criminal conduct	Criminal conduct	Criminal conduct	Criminal conduct
Threshold	None	2 million USD (7623b*)	1 million USD	1 million CAD
Cap	No cap	No cap	No cap	5 million CAD
Confidentiality	No	Yes	Yes	Yes

* The IRS law has two sections, 7623a and 7623b. Under the former, there is no threshold and rewards are discretionary. Under the latter, the threshold is 2 million USD and rewards are non-discretionary.

Reward programmes differ along a set of design dimensions. The FCA allows individuals to litigate privately if the Department of Justice (DOJ) does not deem the information brought sufficient for litigation (see 'Private litigation' in Table 24.1). The reward size is determined as a percentage of the fine paid by the wrongdoing organization, plus the illegal gains recovered thanks to the whistleblower's information ('Reward %' in Table 24.1). Eligibility requirements for rewards appear to differ in practice (see, e.g., Pacella 2015), but whistleblowers who planned and initiated the wrongdoing they report on are not eligible for a reward ('Ineligible if ...' in Table 24.1). Some of the programmes have a monetary threshold for a claim to be considered – to reduce the administrative burden of having to look through meritless claims ('Threshold' in Table 24.1). Some programmes also put a monetary cap on the size of the reward ('Cap' in Table 24.1), and some programmes allow for confidentiality while others do not ('Confidentiality' in Table 24.1).

There is an ongoing debate about the viability of programmes like these for detecting and deterring crimes in a cost-efficient way. If they work, then these programmes could be effectively applied and used *mutatis mutandis* in other areas of law enforcement.[2] One such area, it has been suggested, is antitrust, and some countries other than the United States have started experimenting in that direction. In this chapter, we review the increasing amount of rigorous empirical and experimental evidence available on the performance of whistleblower reward programmes, in terms of their ability to help agencies detect corporate crimes and to deter firms from undertaking them in the first place. We also look at their administrative costs relative to recovered funds and discuss the proposal to extend them to accomplice witnesses in the field of antitrust law.

24.2 EMPIRICAL AND EXPERIMENTAL EVIDENCE

In this section we review the empirical and experimental evidence on how reward programmes affect the number of reports from employees and the sanctions awarded to wrongdoers (Section 2.1), on their deterrence effects on corporate crime (Section 2.2), and on administration costs relative to recovered funds (Section 2.3).

24.2.1 *Numbers and Sanctions*

In a seminal study, Dyck et al. (2010) compared whistleblowing in the healthcare sector, where rewards are available to employees blowing the whistle through the FCA, with

[2] Engstrom (2016: 5) provides an overview of regulatory areas that have been suggested as being fit for a bounty approach.

whistleblowing in nonhealthcare sectors, where they are not. The authors found that 41 per cent of fraud cases are detected by employees in the healthcare sector. This number is only 14 per cent for other sectors, a highly statistically significant difference (at the 1 per cent level) despite a small sample size (Dyck et al. 2010: 2247). They also found that, in comparison, 'classic' watchdogs emphasized in corporate finance (directors, auditors) play a negligible role in detecting fraud.

More recently, Call et al. (2018) studied a dataset of employee whistleblowing allegations and the universe of enforcement actions for financial misrepresentation in the United States. They found that whistleblower involvement in enforcement actions was correlated with higher monetary sanctions for the wrongdoing firms, that there was increased jail time for culpable executives, and that enforcement proceedings in which whistleblowers were involved began more quickly. This suggests that whistleblowers bring highly valuable additional information to law enforcement agencies.

On the experimental side, Breuer (2013) studied the effects of rewards on tax compliance. He found that monetary rewards led to a significant increase in whistleblowing frequency, and the larger the reward, the more pronounced the increase in whistleblowing and the resulting detection probability of tax evasion.

More recently, Butler et al. (in press) investigated experimentally whether and, if so, how monetary incentives and expectations of social approval or disapproval, and their interactions, affect an employee's decision to blow the whistle when the social damages from the reported misbehaviour are more or less salient. They found that rewards had a substantial and statistically significant effect on whistleblowing. This effect is stronger (weaker) when the negative externalities are (are not) visible to the public and the whistleblower is subject to public scrutiny.

Overall, this evidence suggests that important additional information is obtained by law enforcement agencies thanks to whistleblower reward programmes. However, it does not tell us if and how firms react. A primary objective of reward programmes is indeed to prevent corporate crime, but evidence on deterrence is difficult to obtain, and has been scarce until recently.

24.2.2 *Deterrence*

Amir et al. (2018) studied the effects of the introduction of a whistleblower hotline in Israel in February 2013, together with a reward programme. The introduction of the hotline was concurrent with a large media campaign attracting attention to the hotline, in an attempt to increase deterrence. They found a significant increase in tax collections in sectors where there is a high risk of tax avoidance. The authors attribute this increase in tax collections to the deterrence effects of the hotline in conjunction with the large media campaign, as the tax money returned through the hotline itself was insignificant (in 2013, around 250 events were processed by the Tax Authority of Israel, and 2 rewards paid (Amir et al. 2018: 953)).

Wiedman and Zhu (2018) studied the deterrent effects of Dodd-Frank by examining its impact on aggressive financial reporting in US firms. They measured aggressive reporting using the absolute value of abnormal accruals and found a significant reduction in abnormal accruals (approximately 11 per cent) following the introduction of Dodd-Frank.

Most recently, Berger and Lee (2019) tested the causal impact of state and federal whistleblower laws on reducing fraud probability (state-level FCA laws and Dodd-Frank). They looked at what happened when a state introduced an FCA. When firm shares are invested in by a state pension fund from a state with a general FCA, that firm becomes subject to the FCA and hence claims can be filed against it. Berger and Lee (2019: 41) found that when firms become exposed to FCAs, the probability of fraud decreases by 5 per cent to 9 per cent.

Berger and Lee (2019: 7) also predicted that exposure to a higher risk of whistleblowing under the FCAs will reduce audit fees because of a lower risk of fraud, and they found that audit fees were 4.5 per cent to 6 per cent lower after a firm was exposed to a state FCA relative to the firm-years not treated by FCA exposure. They thus found that both state-level whistleblower laws and Dodd-Frank have a deterrent effect.

Other empirical studies on whistleblowing – absent rewards – are also relevant, as they show how whistleblowers can have a significant effect on deterrence, which, coupled with the evidence in Section 2.1 on increasing whistleblowing, implies a robust deterrence effect of these schemes.

Wilde (2017) studied a dataset of retaliation complaints filed with the Organizational Safety and Health Administration (OSHA) between 2003 and 2010 on violations of the Sarbanes-Oxley Act paragraph 806, which prohibits retaliation against employees who provide evidence of fraud. He found that in the period prior to retaliation allegations, whistleblower firms exhibited higher incidence of financial misreporting compared with control firms, and that, following whistleblower allegations, whistleblower firms were significantly more likely to experience a decrease in the incidence of accounting irregularities and a decrease in tax aggressiveness compared with control firms (Wilde 2017: 3). The effect persisted for at least two years after the allegations.

Johannesen and Stolper (2017) studied the deterrence effects of whistleblowing in the offshore banking sector. They studied the stock market reaction before and after the whistleblower Heinrich Kieber leaked important tax documents from the Liechtenstein-based LGT Bank, and found abnormal stock returns in the period after the leak and that the market value of banks known to derive some of their revenues from offshore activities decreased. The authors interpreted their results as follows: 'Our preferred interpretation is that the leak induced a shock to the detection risk as perceived by offshore account holders and banks, which curbed the use of offshore bank accounts and ultimately lowered the expected future profits of banks providing access to such tax evasion technologies' (Johannesen and Stolper 2017: 21–2).

As for experimental evidence, Abbink and Wu (2017) experimentally studied collusive bribery, corruption, and the effects of whistleblower rewards on deterrence. They found that amnesty for whistleblowers and rewards strongly deterred illegal transactions in a one-shot setting, but that in repeated interactions the deterrence effect was reduced, so that higher rewards may be needed.

24.2.3 *Administration Costs*

Some observers have expressed concerns over the administration costs of these schemes (Ebersole 2011; Bank of England 2014). This concern, however, is unsubstantiated and, to our knowledge, no serious cost–benefit analysis has been carried out to support this objection.[3] Attempted evaluations of this kind are often defective in several respects.

[3] One cost–benefit evaluation we know of does not substantiate this concern either. Carson et al. (2008) estimate the ratio of benefits to costs to be between 14:1 and 52:1 for recoveries under the FCA between 1997 and 2001.

Consider, for example, Filler and Markham's (2018: 335–6) attempt to put the alleged success of the SEC's whistleblower programme into perspective, arguing that between 2012 and 2016 recoveries linked to whistleblowers were only about 5 per cent of the overall recoveries from the SEC's enforcement programme. However, they failed to compare this with the resources required to generate these enforcement benefits. The SEC whistleblower office has about 30 employees, which, compared to the rest of the SEC (in 2015 the SEC had a total of 4,301 employees (SEC 2017: 14)), is a meagre 0.83 per cent of SEC's employees.

More generally, a serious evaluation would require a thorough cost-benefit analysis, including personal costs and benefits to whistleblowers, deterrence effects, costs to firms, and any other costs and benefits. That is well beyond what has been done until now and the scope of this chapter. We can, however, do a much more down-to-earth – back-of-the-envelope – calculation, based on an estimation of *only* administrative costs and benefits, to shed light on the claim that these programmes may be costly to administer. The IRS and SEC programmes are suitable for this purpose since the agencies provide annual reports with enough information on their administration and net benefits. The IRS has received about 117,400 claims (7623(a) and (b)) since the introduction of the programme up until 2017, and information submitted by whistleblowers has assisted the IRS in collecting $3.6 billion since the introduction of the programme up until 2017 (IRS 2017: 3). If we divide $3.6 billion by 117 400, we get that the average whistleblower claim at the IRS generates **$30,664** dollars in returned tax money.

The SEC has received about 28,100 claims since the programme's introduction (SEC 2018: 20). The successful sanctions due to merited whistleblower claims amount to $1.7 billion since the programme's introduction. If we divide $1.7 billion by 28,100, we get that on average a whistleblower claim is worth **$60,498** dollars in sanctions.

The IRS Office of the Whistleblower (OWB) has thirty-six full-time employees (IRS 2018: 5). The SEC report from 2018 contains suggestive information on its staffing levels at its own OWB: it appears to have more than fifteen employees but fewer than thirty (SEC 2018: 6).

According to PayScale.com,[4] the average annual salary at the IRS is $74,000 and the highest is around $175,000. Taking the highest annual salary, we have 36 × $175,000 = $6,300,000. So, the annual cost of staffing at the IRS OWB amounts to approximately $6,300,000. Now we extend this over the years 2006–17, that is $6,300,000 × 12 = $75,600,000. We then divide this cost by the total number of claims to get the average cost per claim, $75,600,000/117,400 = **$643** per claim. According to PayScale.com,[5] the average annual salary at the SEC is $146,000 and the highest is $265,000 annually. Taking the highest annual salary, we have 30 × $265,000 = $7,950,000. Extending that over the years and then dividing that figure by the total number of claims gives: $7,950,000 × 8 (2011–18) = $63,600,000/28,100 = **$2,263** per claim.

This back-of-the-envelope calculation does not take deterrence effects into account, nor the fact that, although we have the number of claims submitted in recent years, it often takes several years until a reward is paid out. This means that while we have the total number of claims submitted to the IRS and the SEC, we do not yet have the total number of rewards paid out due to these claims. Of course, some of these wrongdoings may have come to the attention of enforcement agencies even without the aid of whistleblowers. But even if we assume that 90 per cent of recoveries linked to whistleblower rewards would be obtained even

4 www.payscale.com/research/US/Employer=U.S._Internal_Revenue_Service_(IRS)/Salary.
5 www.payscale.com/research/US/Employer=United_States_Government%2C_Securities_and_Exchange_Commission_(SEC)/Salary.

in their absence, these programmes would still fully pay for themselves in terms of pure administrative costs and benefits (abstracting from the improved detection and deterrence).

24.3 ANTITRUST ENFORCEMENT AND ACCOMPLICE WITNESSES

Some countries have started to experiment with whistleblower rewards in antitrust cartel enforcement. Antitrust reward programmes with different designs have been introduced in the United Kingdom, Hungary, South Korea, Slovakia, Pakistan, and, most recently, Peru. They typically involve very small rewards, however, at least compared with those under the FCA,[6] and they are too recent to have generated enough data for an empirical evaluation[7] (in any case some agencies do not disclose the few available data, as in the UK).[8] Table 24.2 summarizes current reward programmes in antitrust enforcement, and illustrates how they differ from the US programmes along the design dimensions.

A glaring difference between these programmes and those in the United States is the reward size. It is uncertain whether the small reward size of these programmes will incentivize any increase in reporting, given the huge retaliation costs usually associated with whistleblowing. Rewards are further discretionary in Pakistan, South Korea, and the UK, which makes blowing the whistle even more of a gamble. There is no reason, however, why the

TABLE 24.2 *Antitrust reward programmes*

	South Korea	Hungary	Pakistan	United Kingdom	Slovakia
Private litigation	No	No	No	No	No
Reward %	Discretionary	1% (of fine)	Discretionary	Discretionary	1% (of fine)
Ineligible if . . .	Criminal conduct**	Criminal conduct	Unknown/ none	Direct involvement***	Criminal conduct
Threshold	None	None	None	None	None
Cap*	2,800,000 USD	160,000 EUR	10,000 EUR	100,000 GBP	100,000 EUR
Confidentiality	Yes	Yes	Yes	Yes	Yes

* The monetary amounts stated in the 'Cap' row are approximations based on currency rates at August 19, 2019.
** The wording 'criminal conduct' is more precisely defined in the laws; we omit details due to space constraints.
*** Although this usually disqualifies a whistleblower from receiving a reward, it does not always do so. 'The CMA does not consider that an individual in such circumstances [direct involvement in cartel activity] should ordinarily also gain a financial reward' CMA (2014).

[6] The UK cap is £100,000 (Competition and Markets Authority (CMA) 2014). The cap in Pakistan is 2,000,000 rupees (approx. 10,000 euros; Reward Payment to Informants 2014). Hungary employs a 1 per cent statutory reward, capped at 50,000,000 Hungarian forints (approx. 160,000 euros; – Competition Act Article 79/A). The Slovak programme cap is 100,000 euros (Act No. 136/2001, paragraph 38g). The upper bound in South Korea is 3 billion won (approx. $2.8 million).

[7] The South Korean programme was adopted in 2002, the UK programme in 2008, the Hungarian programme in 2010, and the Slovak and Pakistani programmes in 2014.

[8] The CMA does not release data on its programme, citing public interest concerns over the confidentiality of those who report cartels (CMA 2018). This is contrary to most other agencies, who provide generic meta-data on their programmes, such as number of rewards granted, number of claims received, and average size of reward. One could argue, contrary to the CMA, that the public interest is better served by releasing these data, both for transparency reasons and for scholars who are interested in assessing the merits of these programmes. Marvão and Spagnolo (2016: 27) also argue that '[t]he development of meaningful research on leniency would be facilitated if competition authorities or agencies in charge of supervising them start[ed] to implement more consistent data collection and data disclosure policies'.

evidence outlined in Section 24.2 would not apply to these antitrust programmes as well, were the size of the rewards scaled up to the levels of the FCA or the SEC.

There has been discussion among antitrust scholars on whether to introduce rewards for accomplice witnesses, that is, as an extension of current leniency programmes offering immunity to the first cartel member who self-reports and collaborates with antitrust enforcers (Kovacic 1996). Theory suggests that paying rewards to the first self-reporting cartel member (or individual) could considerably increase detection and deterrence (Spagnolo 2004; Aubert et al. 2006). Bounties could be financed from a fraction of the fines paid by other cartel participants. Spagnolo (2004) shows that, contrary to standard results in the law and economic literature, a reward for the first spontaneously self-reporting party that is a fraction of other firms' fines can lead to the first best outcome – full deterrence with no inspection costs – if fines are sufficiently large (but still finite).

Although providing leniency for self-reporting of cartel participation appears to have been a success (Marvão and Spagnolo 2016), and leniency for self-reporting cartel members has become common practice in cartel enforcement in most jurisdictions, rewards have never been implemented in the field.[9] Nevertheless, there is some experimental evidence that gives us an idea of their likely effectiveness.

Apesteguia et al. (2007) pioneered the study of leniency and rewards for accomplice witnesses who report their cartel to the antitrust authority. They used a one-shot homogeneous Bertrand oligopoly model, where convicted firms faced fines equivalent to 10 per cent of their revenue. This implied, however, that subjects did not play repeatedly, and that no fines were imposed when a partner cartel member deviated from collusive strategies (in a Bertrand game, firm revenue is unrealistically zero because of the Bertrand paradox). The results of these pioneering experiments do not lend clear support for leniency or rewards, although they are difficult to interpret and relate to real-world law enforcement.

A second experimental study by Hamaguchi et al. (2009) considered the effects of cartel size (in terms of the number of members), the fine schedule, and the degree of leniency (partial reduction, immunity, or rewards) on the likelihood that a cartel is reported. They found that the possibility of reporters receiving a reward had a large positive impact on dissolving cartel activity.

Bigoni et al. (2012) experimentally studied leniency policies and rewards as tools with which to fight cartel formation in an environment that more closely resembles real-world antitrust enforcement and found that rewards financed by the fines imposed on the other cartel participants, after subjects had time to learn the game, had a much stronger negative effect on cartel formation and average price than leniency alone (returning prices to a competitive level). The results confirm Spagnolo's (2004) theoretical result that – if well implemented and sufficiently large – rewards can have a dramatic deterring and desisting effect on cartel formation.

In general, however, all types of reward in the antitrust context are more controversial than in the whistleblower context. In a report by the U.S. Government Accountability Office (GAO 2011: 36–50), enforcement agencies did not support the proposal of

[9] One difference between whistleblower reward programmes and corporate leniency programmes in antitrust is that the baseline case in the latter will be a culpable undertaking. There has been discussion over whether and to what extent to reward culpable whistleblowers (see, e.g., Pacella 2015), and there may be ethical obstacles to rewarding culpable people as the baseline case, as in antitrust (see also Buccirossi and Spagnolo 2006: 1282). That said, the practice of offering personal incentives for culpable persons is widespread in judicial systems (consider plea bargaining) and does not constitute a compelling prima facie case against their introduction.

introducing rewards, though it is not clear whether the object of inquiry was rewards for innocent witnesses, rewards for accomplice witnesses, or both. The predominant concern voiced appeared to be about the possibility that monetary rewards could diminish the credibility of whistleblowers as witnesses. However, if many firms and individuals are involved in a crime, as is typically the case for cartels, this concern could be easily remedied by rewarding the first firm or individual to report the cartel, providing only leniency or immunity to a second firm or individual that collaborates, and then having this second firm or individual that did not receive financial rewards testify in court. In the light of this, and of the evidence on other reward programmes discussed earlier, it is not clear why antitrust enforcers expressed a negative opinion in conflict with the opinion of the academics.

To be sure, the GAO report suggests that other concerns were present, such that antitrust rewards would undermine internal reporting, generate claims without merit, and require additional resources (GAO 2011: 36). All these concerns have been brought up before against whistleblower rewards, and the available evidence suggests that they have been grossly overstated (see, e.g., Nyreröd and Spagnolo 2019).

24.4 CONCLUSIONS

We surveyed the available empirical and experimental evidence from rigorous and independent academic studies on the effects of whistleblower reward programmes. The evidence shows that – if competently designed and properly administered – these programmes are very effective at increasing detection and sanctions against corporate fraud, and most importantly at deterring firms from engaging in fraudulent behaviour in the first place. In terms of administration costs, a simple back-of-the-envelope calculation suggests that these programmes are also largely self-financing, thereby also saving law enforcement costs. Experimental studies of rewards for accomplice witnesses who self-report first in antitrust frameworks suggest that these rewards can lead to much better enforcement outcomes than current policies offering leniency alone. Needless to say, poor design or negligent implementation can prevent these policies – as with any other ones – from delivering these positive effects.

REFERENCES

Abbink, K., and Wu, K. 2017. 'Reward Self-Reporting to Deter Corruption: An Experiment on Mitigating Collusive Bribery'. *Journal of Economic Behavior & Organization* 133: 256–72.

Amir, E., Lazar, A., and Levi, S. 2018. 'The Deterrent Effect of Whistleblowing on Tax Collections'. *European Accounting Review* 27, no. 5: 939–54.

Apesteguia, J., Dufwenberg, M., and Selten, R. 2007. 'Blowing the Whistle'. *Economic Theory* 31: 143–66.

Aubert, C., Rey, P., and Kovacic, W. 2006. 'The Impact of Leniency and Whistle-Blowing Programs on Cartels'. *International Journal of Industrial Organization* 24: 1241–66.

Bank of England. 2014. 'Financial Incentives for Whistleblowers'. Prudential Regulation Authority and Financial Conduct Authority, www.fca.org.uk/publication/financial-incentives-for-whistleblowers.pdf.

Berger, P., and Lee, H. 2019. 'Do Corporate Whistleblower Laws Deter Accounting Fraud?' Unpublished manuscript, https://papers.ssrn.com/sol3/papers.cfm?abstract_id=3059231.

Bigoni, M., Le Coq, C., Fridolfsson, S., and Spagnolo, G. 2012. 'Fines, Leniency and Rewards in Antitrust'. *RAND Journal of Economics* 43, no. 2: 368–90.

Breuer, L. 2013. 'Tax Compliance and Whistleblowing: The Role of Incentives'. *Bonn Journal of Economics* 2, no. 2: 7–44.

Buccirossi, P., and Spagnolo, G. 2006. 'Leniency Programs and Illegal Transactions'. *Journal of Public Economics* 90, no. 6–7: 1281–97.

Butler, J., Serra, D., and Spagnolo, G. in press. 'Motivating Whistleblowers'. *Management Science*, https://pubsonline.informs.org/doi/pdf/10.1287/mnsc.2018.3240.

Call, A., Martin, G., Nathan, S., and Wilde, J. 2018. 'Whistleblowers and Outcomes of Financial Misrepresentation Enforcement Actions'. Unpublished Manuscript, https://papers.ssrn.com/sol3/papers.cfm?abstract_id=2506418.

Carson, T., Verdu, M., and Wokutch, R. 2008. 'Whistle-Blowing for Profit: An Ethical Analysis of the Federal False Claims Act'. *Journal of Business Ethics* 77, no. 3: 361–76.

Competition and Markets Authority (CMA). 2014. 'Informant Rewards Policy'. www.gov.uk/government/publications/cartels-informant-rewards-policy.

2018. 'Reference Request Number: IAT/FOIA/509'. https://assets.publishing.service.gov.uk/government/uploads/system/uploads/attachment_data/file/774831/Cartel_Reward_FOIA_Request.pdf.

Dyck, A., Morse, A., and Zingales, L. 2010. 'Who Blows the Whistle on Corporate Fraud?' *Journal of Finance* 65, no. 6: 2213–53.

Ebersole, D. 2011. 'Blowing the Whistle on the Dodd-Frank Whistleblower Provisions'. *Ohio State Entrepreneurial Business Law Journal* 6, no.1: 123–74.

Engstrom, D. 2016. 'Bounty Regimes'. In J. Arlen (ed.), *Research Handbook on Corporate Criminal Enforcement and Financial Misdealing*, 334–63. Northampton, MA: Edward Elgar.

Filler, R., and Markham, J. 2018. 'Whistleblowers – A Case Study in the Regulatory Cycle for Financial Services'. *Brooklyn Journal of Corporate, Financial & Commercial Law* 12, no. 2: 311–40.

Government Accountability Office (GAO). 2011. 'Criminal Cartel Enforcement: Stakeholder Views on Impact of 2004 Antitrust Reform Are Mixed, but Support Whistleblower Protection'. www.hsdl.org/?abstract&did=682276.

Hamaguchi, Y., Kawagoe, T., and Shibata, A. 2009. 'Group Size Effects on Cartel Formation and the Enforcement Power of Leniency Programs'. *International Journal of Industrial Organization* 27: 145–65.

Internal Revenue Service (IRS). 2017. 'Annual Report to Congress'. www.irs.gov/compliance/whistleblower-office-annual-reports.

2018. 'Annual Report to Congress'. www.irs.gov/compliance/whistleblower-office-annual-reports.

Johannesen, N., and Stolper, T. 2017. 'The Deterrence Effect of Whistleblowing – An Event Study of Leaked Customer Information from Banks in Tax Havens'. Working paper of the Max Planck Institute for Tax Law and Public Finance No. 2017–4, https://ssrn.com/abstract=2976321.

Kovacic, W. 1996. 'Whistleblower Bounty Lawsuits as Monitoring Devices in Government Contracting.' *Loyola of Los Angeles Law Review* 29: 1799–1858.

Marvão, C., and Spagnolo, G. 2016. 'Cartels and Leniency: Taking Stock of What We Learnt'. Stockholm Institute of Transition Economics, working paper No.39, https://swopec.hhs.se/hasite/papers/hasite0039.pdf?_ga=2.195741548.1523066161.1567577039-350847113.1567577039.

Moberly, R. 2007. 'Unfulfilled Expectations: An Empirical Analysis of Why Sarbanes-Oxley Whistleblowers Rarely Win'. *William & Mary Law Review* 49, no. 1: 65–155.

Modesitt, N. 2013. 'Why Whistleblowers Lose: An Empirical and Qualitative Analysis'. *Sociological Inquiry* 64: 322–47.

Nyreröd, T., and Spagnolo, G. 2019. 'Myths and Numbers on Whistleblower Rewards'. *Regulation and Governance*, early view available at https://onlinelibrary.wiley.com/doi/abs/10.1111/rego.12267.

Pacella, J. 2015. 'Bounties for Bad Behavior: Rewarding Culpable Whistleblowers under the Dodd-Frank Act and Internal Revenue Code'. *University of Pennsylvania Journal of Business Law* 17, no.2: 345–92.

Rothschild, J., and Miethe, T. 1999. 'Whistle-Blower Disclosures and Management Retaliation'. *Work and Occupation* 26, no.1: 107–28.

Spagnolo, G. 2004. 'Divide et Impera: Optimal Leniency Programs'. CEPR Discussion Paper No. 4840, Center for Economic and Policy Research, Washington, DC.

Securities and Exchange Commission (SEC). 2017. 'Congressional Budget Justification'. www.sec.gov/about/reports/secfy17congbudgjust.pdf.

2018. 'Annual Report to Congress 2018'. www.sec.gov/sec-2018-annual-report-whistleblower-program.pdf.

Wiedman, C., and Zhu C. 2018. 'Do the SEC Whistleblower Provisions of Dodd-Frank Deter Aggressive Financial Reporting?' 2018 Canadian Academic Accounting Association (CAAA) Annual Conference (September). https://ssrn.com/abstract=3081174 or http://dx.doi.org/10.2139/ssrn.3081174.

Wilde, J. 2017. 'The Deterrent Effect of Employee Whistleblowing on Firms' Financial Misreporting and Tax Aggressiveness'. *Accounting Review* 92, no. 5: 247–80.

25

Designing Corporate Leniency Programs

*Miriam H. Baer**

Abstract: Corporate leniency programs promise putative offenders reduced punishment and fewer regulatory interventions in exchange for the corporation's credible and authentic commitment to remedy wrongdoing and promptly report future violations of law to the requisite authorities. Because these programs have been devised with multiple goals in mind – that is, deterring wrongdoing and punishing corporate executives, improving corporate cultural norms and extending the government's regulatory reach – it is all but impossible to gauge their success objectively. We know that corporations invest significant resources in compliance-related activity and that they do so in order to take advantage of the various benefits promised by leniency regimes. We cannot definitively say, however, how valuable this activity has been in reducing either the incidence or the severity of harms associated with corporate misconduct.

Notwithstanding these blind spots, recent developments in the US Department of Justice's stance toward corporate offenders provide valuable insight into the structural design of a leniency program. Message framing, precision of benefit, and the scope and centralization of the entity that administers a leniency program play important roles in how well the program is received by its intended targets and how long it survives. If the program's popularity and longevity say something about its success, then these design factors merit closer attention.

Using the Department of Justice's Yates Memo and FCPA Pilot Program as demonstrative examples, this chapter excavates the framing and design factors that influence a leniency program's performance. Carrots seemingly work better than sticks; and centralization of authority appears to better facilitate relationships between government enforcers and corporate representatives.

But that is not the end of the story. To the outside world, flexible leniency programs can appear clubby, weak and under-effective. The very design elements that generate trust between corporate targets and government enforcers may simultaneously sow credibility problems with the greater public. This conundrum will remain a core issue for policymakers as they continue to implement, shape and tinker with corporate leniency programs.

* Many thanks to those whose feedback enhanced this chapter, including commentators and panelists at the Law and Society Annual Meeting in Washington, DC in June 2019, as well as Daniel Sokol and Benjamin van Rooij, the editors of this volume. Comments and feedback are very much welcome.

25.1 INTRODUCTION

In September 2015, Sally Yates, the Deputy Attorney General of the US Department of Justice (DOJ), announced an ostensible change in the federal government's charging policies for corporate offenders. Nominally entitled "Individual Accountability for Corporate Wrongdoing," the policy instantaneously became known as the eponymous "Yates Memo" (Henning 2017).[1] The memo sought to clarify, for government prosecutors and the general public, the US government's leniency policy for corporate offenders.

Although not explicitly labeling it a "leniency" policy, the DOJ has long adhered to a multifactor rubric that accords lenient treatment to corporations whose employees violate the law. Provided these offenders cooperate fully in the government's investigation and take pains to remediate the conditions that caused or promoted the underlying wrongdoing in the first place, they can expect a less punitive outcome (Arlen and Kahan 2017).[2].For years, the government's policy has featured an open-ended, holistic approach whereby prosecutors analyze a mix of factors (the severity of the crime, the pervasiveness of wrongdoing, the voluntariness of the disclosure), but it has provided little guidance on how it will weigh these factors (Garrett 2014).

The Yates Memo was notable because it drew attention to a specific factor, the corporation's disclosure of its employees' wrongdoing. It explicitly warned corporations that they would receive *no* credit for cooperation if they withheld any information that tended to implicate any employee in the underlying misconduct. Issued in the wake of a financial crisis that had ruined the economy but had otherwise resulted in few prosecutions (Rakoff 2014; Haugh 2015), the Memo sought to assure the general public that the Department prioritized the punishment of responsible corporate executives.

The Yates Memo was even more notable because it unwittingly affirmed the narrative – increasingly popular in some quarters – that the government's previous leniency approach had amounted to a partial failure (Garrett 2014; Eisinger 2015). Despite a series of settlements with financial institutions (announced, of course, with much hullabaloo), the government had failed to identify (much less prosecute) the executives most responsible for the 2008 financial crisis. Thus, critics argued, the government had accorded corporations *too much* leniency for their cooperation (Garrett 2014; Uhlmann 2013). Moreover, the dearth of individual prosecutions made little sense. If corporations were receiving leniency because they were so cooperative, what was the government doing with the fruits of that cooperation (Garrett 2014)?

Positioned as a corrective measure, the Yates Memo all but conceded that the government's critics were right; prosecutors *had* been too lenient, and now Main Justice was going to fix that. The Memo's message was simple: Whereas corporations might once have received partial credit for disclosing some evidence of wrongdoing, now they would be left with *no* credit unless they dutifully handed over *all* information in their possession. Half-measures and sliding scales would no longer play any role in the Department's calculations (Joh and Joo 2015a). The Memo's "stick" was unmistakable: withhold evidence from the government, and a corporation could risk its ability to secure a settlement with the government. That, in turn, might risk a corporation's future existence.

[1] Deputy Attorney General Sally Quillian Yates Delivers Remarks at New York University School of Law, September 10, 2015, at www.justice.gov/opa/speech/deputy-attorneygeneral-sally-quillian-yates-delivers-remarks-new-york-university-school; Sally Quillian Yates, Memorandum, *Individual Accountability for Wrongdoing*, September 9, 2015, at www.justice.gov/dag/file/769036/download.

[2] This chapter focuses solely on leniency programs geared toward corporate violations of federal law. It does not focus on diversion programs for individual offenders or the program that the DOJ's Antitrust Division employs to address illegal cartel activity.

Meanwhile, a mere six months later, the DOJ's Fraud Section announced the creation of a new "pilot" enforcement program designed solely for cases involving violations of the Foreign Corrupt Practices Act (FCPA), the statute that prohibits and punishes the bribery of foreign officials.[3] Like the Yates Memo, the FCPA Pilot Program was aimed at corporations whose employees had violated federal law; also like the Yates Memo, it aimed to induce corporations to disclose wrongdoing in exchange for prosecutorial leniency. (The offenders were also required to disgorge their ill-gotten profits.)

The Department insisted that the Pilot Program was intended as a clarification of previous policies, including (presumably) the Yates Memo. Nevertheless, the Pilot Program's tone and content represented a significant departure from the Yates Memo and the policies that preceded it.

Under the Pilot Program, voluntary disclosure of an FCPA violation could secure a qualifying corporation a full declination of charges or a reduction in recommended fines by as much as 50 percent. On the other hand, the corporation's failure to disclose such behavior – even if the corporation subsequently cooperated in the government's investigation – would render the corporation eligible for a benefit of no more than 25 percent off the fine recommended by the US Sentencing Guidelines. Thus, in a clear and salient manner, the Pilot Program dramatically altered the relative costs and benefits of disclosing FCPA violations to federal authorities. Moreover, the Program differed from previous guidance in that it elevated the importance of voluntary disclosure relative to other enumerated factors that traditionally impacted the DOJ's analysis (Low and Prelogar 2020).

Judged solely by its longevity, the Pilot Program has been an unqualified success. Created and announced during the final years of the Obama administration, it was first extended through November 2017 and then eventually memorialized as a permanent enforcement policy,[4] with additional emphasis on declinations for corporations who promptly disclose FCPA violations.[5] More importantly, under the Trump administration, it became "nonbinding guidance" for corporate disclosures of *other* crimes (Garrett 2020).[6]

At the same time, the Program has borne tangible fruit. Self-reported FCPA violations increased significantly in the months following the DOJ Fraud Section's announcement of the Pilot Program and in fact doubled during its eighteen months as an experimental program (Koehler 2018; Oded 2018). As promised, the government rewarded self-reporting firms with declinations and lesser punishments (provided they were also cooperative, willing to disgorge their gains and had not been punished for the same violations previously), and it prominently announced these declinations on the DOJ's website. As it was extending leniency to self-disclosing offenders, the government continued to aggressively pursue firms who elected *not* to disclose their foreign bribery violations (Koehler 2018). From these facts, one might conclude that

[3] *The Fraud Section's Foreign Corrupt Practices Act Enforcement Plan and Guidance* (April 5, 2016), www.justice.gov/archives/opa/blog-entry/file/838386/download ("FCPA Pilot Program"); see also Press Release, *Criminal Division Launches New FCPA Pilot Program* (April 5, 2016), www.justice.gov/archives/opa/blog/criminal-division-launches-new-fcpa-pilot-program.

[4] Deputy Attorney General Rod Rosenstein Delivers Remarks at the 34th International Conference on the Foreign Corrupt Practices Act, November 29, 2017; *Foreign Corrupt Practices Act Corporate Enforcement Policy*, www.justice.gov/criminal-fraud/file/838416/download (November 29, 2017). See also Justice Manual, 9–47.120, at www.justice.gov/jm/jm-9–47000-foreign-corrupt-practices-act-1977#9–47.110.

[5] The declinations can be easily searched and analyzed on the Department's website, www.justice.gov/criminal-fraud/corporate-enforcement-policy/declinations.

[6] John F. Savarese et. al., *DOJ Applies Principles of FCPA Corporate Enforcement Policy in Other White-Collar Investigations, Increasing Opportunities for Corporate Declinations*, NYU Compliance and Enforcement Blog, at https://wp.nyu.edu/compliance_enforcement/2018/03/07/doj-applies-principles-of-fcpa-corporate-enforcement-policy-in-other-white-collar-investigations-increasing-opportunity-for-corporate-declinations/.

the Pilot Program and its successor program improved deterrence by enabling prosecutors and investigators to focus on recalcitrant firms who failed to self-report, while effectively leveraging the internal investigative resources of firms who wisely sought leniency's benefits.

The Yates Memo, by contrast, has performed poorly – according to *all* metrics. Almost immediately upon its announcement, it drew criticism from multiple parties. Skeptics worried that it was little more than political theater (Yockey 2016; Henning 2017). Others argued that it would impose unintended costs on low- and mid-level employees (Joh and Joo 2015b; Kelly and Mandelbaum 2016).

In the end, the skeptics' concerns were vindicated. Government prosecutions of corporate executives did *not* magically increase in the months following its announcement (Werle 2019), in part because it applied only prospectively to new investigations (Garrett 2020). Moreover, by the time the Yates Memo was formally incorporated into the US Attorney's Manual (now known as the "Justice Manual"), its language had softened considerably (Baer 2016). Finally, on November 29, 2018, Deputy Attorney General Rod Rosenstein announced that the Department would eliminate the requirement that corporations disclose *all* known wrongdoing to government prosecutors. Rather, it would be sufficient for corporations to disclose information identifying individuals "substantially involved or responsible for" violations of law.[7] This further softening of one of the Memo's core components all but suggested its extinction.

Examined in tandem, these two programs yield useful insights on how leniency programs contribute to the government's enforcement mission. Although corporate leniency programs have become pervasive components of criminal and civil enforcement regimes (Ford and Hess 2011), empirical evidence establishing their effectiveness remains thin, in part because policymakers have yet to reach consensus on their purpose, and corporations themselves have little obligation to reveal the fine details of their compliance programs (Griffith 2016).

Theory nevertheless supports leniency's persistence in corporate enforcement. Economists frequently cite its utilitarian benefits. A well-designed program preserves limited government resources, encourages earlier detection of wrongdoing, aids in more effective remediation and improves the government's record in identifying and punishing individual wrongdoers (Alexander and Cohen 2015; Alexander and Arlen 2018; Arlen and Kahan 2017).

Behavioral scholars embrace leniency programs because they induce corporations to staff, invest in and build out internal compliance programs, thereby improving the company's ethical infrastructure (Hess 2016). The compliance function, in turn, relieves the government of some of its enforcement responsibility and simultaneously strengthens social and self-interested arguments for complying with the law (Miller 2018a, b; Griffith 2016). If you are a *good* person (Feldman 2018), you will obey the law because the company's compliance program has set up systems designed to reinforce your intentions to behave ethically. And if you are a Machiavellian *bad* person, you'll desist from misconduct because the same compliance systems have reduced your opportunities to violate rules without consequence (Fanto 2014).

Leniency programs also expand the government's regulatory envelope. Employing the corporate settlement agreement as a sort of template, prosecutors can effectively regulate corporate offenders and related industries without burning through the political and social capital necessary to promulgate rules under conventional methods (Arlen 2016).

7 www.justice.gov/opa/speech/deputy-attorney-general-rod-j-rosenstein-delivers-remarks-american-conference-institute-0.

To perform *any* of the above functions, a program must engage the support of a wide variety of constituents; otherwise, it cannot survive. Accordingly, so long as leniency's empirical success remains inconclusive, policymakers would do well to compare programs that have flourished with ones that have withered away. A leniency program's design features can help predict its political longevity and practical success. Recent experience with the Yates Memo and FCPA Pilot Program provides an excellent opportunity for excavating and examining leniency law's relevant design elements.

The remainder of this chapter unfolds as follows. Section 25.2 reviews the standard justifications for leniency programs. Section 25.3 surveys the extant literature on program effectiveness. Section 25.4 extracts several lessons in institutional design from the divergent paths of the Yates Memo and Pilot Program. Section 25.5 concludes with a discussion of the implications for future programs and considers the broader social import of government leniency programs.

25.2 THE WHY AND HOW OF CORPORATE LENIENCY

25.2.1 *Leniency as a Means of Smoothing Strict Liability Regimes*

Under the doctrine of *respondeat superior*, a corporation can be held criminally liable in the United States for violations of federal law by *any of* its employees, provided they act within the scope of their employment and with "an" intention to aid their company.[8] Thus, the formal rule of corporate criminal liability in the United States is one of strict, vicarious liability (Laufer 1999). A corporation is legally responsible for its employee's violation of law, regardless of the employee's managerial level within the organization, whether he or she acted at the behest of a supervisor, or whether he or she acted in direct contravention of the company's policies or directives.[9] Moreover, the partial intention to aid the company need not be particularly convincing or robust. A desire to prop up the company's stock price, avoid detection by government enforcers or keep bad news from reaching the general public easily satisfies the partial intention requirement (Gruner 2004, collecting cases).

Criminal liability for crimes such as fraud, obstruction of justice, and bribery can thus be imputed quite easily to corporate entities, provided the government has proof of the underlying offense. This proof is often the sticking point for government prosecutors. In many cases, it is quite difficult for the government to collect sufficient proof of an underlying offense, particularly if that offense features a highly technical regulatory backdrop or an ambiguous set of facts. Corporate businesses, by nature, compartmentalize and diffuse responsibility across departments and units (Buell 2007). Corporate crime can therefore develop and spread, undetected, unless the corporation itself aggressively monitors and remediates workplace misconduct.

Corporate investigators enjoy an ease of access to their employees' work product and communications that government investigators lack (Baer 2018). The corporation can review its employees' emails, question its employees (and threaten said employees with termination if they refuse to cooperate) and even perpetrate undercover stings. The corporation's internal

8 *N.Y. Cent. & Hudson River R.R.* v. *United States*, 212 U.S. 481, 491–5 (1909).

9 *United States* v. *Automated Medical Laboratories*, 770 F.2d. 399, 407 (4th Cir. 1985) (fact that employees were acting contrary to policy does not absolve corporation of criminal liability); *United States* v. *Basic Construction Co.*, 711 F.2d 570 (4th Cir. 1983)(criminal behavior by low-level employees imputable to corporation so long as they were acting within the scope of their authority and with *an* intention to benefit the corporation).

investigative activity is less constrained by the Constitution than government activities such as searches and seizures (Arlen and Buell 2020).

The corporation may be better situated to detect its own crimes, but it is not well incentivized to do so. Doctrines such as *respondeat superior* impose on corporations vicarious criminal liability, regardless of their efforts to prevent or detect violations of law. Were government enforcers to leave the law exactly as is, corporations would be, as Professor Jennifer Arlen pointed out decades ago, perversely incentivized to ignore or bury violations of law that have already occurred (Arlen 1994). Unless the corporation could reliably *prevent* the crime from occurring at all, its monitoring effort would easily increase the corporation's overall costs, represented first by the cost of its detection program and second by the cost of the sanctions that would result from its disclosures (Arlen 1994).

Were we to leave this state of affairs as is, we would also place the government in an intolerable position: With too few resources to enforce the law, it would be forced to wait for crimes to grow visible and serious enough to enable its intervention and prosecution. Under such a system, employees would feel fairly free to violate the law, knowing their corporate employers would never willingly report to authorities (Arlen and Kraakman 1997).

Leniency programs ameliorate the foregoing problem. By promising a reduced sanction in exchange for the corporation's self-reporting and monitoring, the typical leniency program induces corporate monitoring of criminal violations. Moreover, it (theoretically) induces disclosure of nascent conspiracies before they become noticeably large or harmful. Put simply, leniency accelerates detection. Moreover, it improves corporate culture and forges a relationship between corporate officers and government prosecutors. Corporations report crimes because they expect the government's response to self-reported crimes to be far less severe than its response to government-detected crimes (cf. Arlen and Kraakman 1997, laying out the theory of "composite liability"). Government agencies, in turn, reward corporate self-policing because monitoring reduces the overall costs of enforcement (Innes 2001, 1999).

25.2.2 *Leniency Cascades and Corporate Compliance*

The way in which a corporation prevents and detects wrongdoing is by implementing a series of activities designed to educate, monitor and discipline wayward employees. This activity is collectively referred to as "compliance" (Baer 2009). The well-designed corporate compliance program enables the firm to relay information to government enforcers. This, in turn, permits government enforcers to improve and refine their own enforcement programs. Notice the virtuous circle: Leniency begets corporate compliance; corporate compliance improves external enforcement's efficacy; and enforcers publicize and celebrate leniency's perceived benefits.

Once a leniency program goes into effect, it can induce a healthy compliance cascade among initially skeptical regulated entities. For example, if 20 percent of a pool of regulated entities initially responds to the government's leniency program by monitoring and reporting wrongdoing, the government can apply its enforcement resources across a smaller group of potential offenders (Innes 2001, summarizing literature). This, in turn, ought to improve detection, which in turn should also improve deterrence. (This is doubly true if the self-reporting companies provide information not just about themselves but also about their competitors.) Finally, self-reporting is valuable when it persuades corporate offenders to avoid socially undesirable "avoidance activities" (e.g., covering up the crimes they have committed) (Innes 2001). In sum, self-reporting saves the government the cost of identifying underlying illegality *and* resulting cover-ups.

Thus, a credible and well-designed leniency program can induce a healthful compliance cascade among corporations (cf. Lemos and Stein 2011, on legal regimes and behavioral cascades). For this healthy herding effect to occur, however, a sufficient number of corporations must take seriously: (a) the threat of government detection; (b) the threat of post-apprehension sanctions; and (c) the promise of leniency if the corporation engages in voluntary disclosure.

25.2.3 *Leniency and Deceptive Misconduct*

In theory, an effective compliance program ought to reduce the incidence of fraud and other crimes of deception. Criminologists have attempted to explain fraud by employing a well-known (if somewhat overused) triangle metaphor that envisions a noxious combination of opportunity, pressure and internal rationalization (Cressey 1953; McGrath 2020, situating Cressey's within the criminological field's explanation of fraud). For example, within a corporation, mid-level managers might report false revenue figures because: (a) they believe they will be fired or demoted if they fail to meet a quarterly quota ("pressure"); (b) the firm's lax reporting channels have made it relatively easy to report false figures ("opportunity"); and (c) from the manager's vantage point, "everyone" seems to be violating one rule or another ("rationalization").

Effective compliance programs reduce fraud by working on all three of the fraud triangle's components. Through the deployment of internal policing measures, they reduce the *opportunities* for cheating. Through educative activities, they persuade managers to reconsider the wisdom of imposing undue *pressure*. And finally, through high-level emphasis on values, they persuade employees to replace empty *rationalizations* with ethical reasoning.

The foregoing paints the leniency program in its best light. In the sections that follow, I explain how and why a leniency program might fail to procure these benefits.

25.2.4 *When Leniency Goes Awry*

The previous sections explained why both a government enforcer and a corporate manager might find a leniency program beneficial. For an enforcement agency with limited resources, it reduces the agency's overall enforcement costs and hastens detection of harmful schemes. For the regulated entity, it offers the entity a means of reducing the overall penalties that accrue as a result of doctrines such as *respondeat superior*.

Despite these benefits, several factors undermine the leniency program's success. Before discussing these factors, a preliminary point is in order. One should be careful not to conflate the overall success of a *program* with that of a *single company*. The fact that one or several companies maintain bad compliance programs says fairly little about how well a government's leniency program has fared with an entire industry. The challenge for enforcers is not to induce *universal* compliance activity. Nor is it to necessarily induce *maximal* compliance activity, since such activity might well crowd out valuable behaviors or inflict unnecessary harms on employees. Rather, the most defensible level of compliance activity is the *optimal* level, the level at which compliance's social benefits exceed its social costs.

If compliance activity were completely transparent, reasonable people would still disagree on the level at which compliance activity is optimal, in part because costs and benefits are partially subjective. The question is academic, however, because corporate compliance activity is overwhelmingly *non*transparent. Much of the compliance effort that occurs within a company takes place out of the public's sight (Griffith 2016). Accordingly, the government agency extending leniency to self-disclosing firms must determine the authenticity of a given firm's compliance effort. Although much ink has been spilled on advising government investigators on how best to distinguish real compliance programs from sham ones (e.g., Soltes 2018), the process of verifying compliance effort is both costly and contextualized.

Beyond these challenges, additional pathologies challenge the implementation of leniency programs, namely agency costs and information asymmetries, firms being "too big to fail or jail," credibility and lemons markets, and there being leniency for firms but not employees. These are discussed next.

25.2.4.1 Agency Costs and Information Asymmetries

Leniency programs depend on corporate entities to develop internal monitoring and self-reporting systems. *Corporations* may harbor good reasons for monitoring and developing robust compliance channels, but corporate *managers* (including executives and board directors) have personal interests that diverge from those of the firm and managers possess better information about the corporation's compliance efforts (and its compliance failures) than do other constituents.

Jennifer Arlen and Marcel Kahan helpfully label the foregoing problem a "policing agency cost" (Arlen and Kahan 2017). Ordinary agency costs arise whenever an agent (in this case, corporate management) fails to act in the best interests of its principal (the corporation and arguably its shareholders). *Policing* agency costs are the costs that arise when an agent fails to undertake the amount of policing the principal would prefer the agent to do if the principals undertook the policing themselves. In Arlen and Kahan's account, deferred prosecution agreements – the settlement agreements that government prosecutors strike with corporate offenders after wrongdoing has been detected – are most valuable when they identify and address policing agency costs (Arlen and Kahan 2017).

A potential source of policing agency costs is the firm's compensation structure (Armour et al. 2020a). When the corporate board pays the executive for current or recent performance, and wrongdoing is unlikely to be detected until a later time period, a rational executive will decide to forgo costly investments in compliance. Armour and others contend that clawbacks and similar mechanisms can alleviate this problem without inducing overcompliance (Armour et al. 2020a).

25.2.4.2 Firms Too Big to Fail or Jail

Some firms are so large or systemically important that the government effectively cannot indict them due to the substantial collateral effects of criminal prosecution (Garrett 2014). For example, notwithstanding *respondeat superior*'s breadth of application, it seems highly unlikely that the government would choose a course of action that would place JP Morgan Chase or Pfizer at risk of failure. In the wake of the 2008 financial crisis, Eric Holder all but affirmed this belief in testimony before Congress in 2013 (Henning 2017). Moreover, scholars have long argued that whole categories of firms cannot be indicted without causing major economic aftershocks (Gilchrist 2014, citing financial institutions).

Scholars have rightfully worried that a firm's too big to fail (TBTF) status permits it to relax its compliance program. After all, what's the point of expending resources on monitoring and self-reporting (both expensive endeavors in and of themselves) when the firm knows it will receive leniency regardless of its efforts (Garrett 2014; Werle 2019)?

The concern is warranted, but the argument glosses over several points. First, although prosecutors may avoid indicting the company's parent, they can indict one or more of the company's subsidiaries (Golumbic and Lichy 2014). Second, prosecutors can build more expensive and vexatious terms into a deferred prosecution agreement (DPA) or corporate settlement agreement when it appears that the corporation has made no effort to police itself (Kaal and Lacine 2014). Third, the government can intentionally lengthen the DPA process, during which time the company's reputation and stock price may take hits, thereby leading the corporation's board to replace high-level managers. Moreover, when the government strings along a corporate target, it can become extremely costly for a firm to investigate itself and prove to government prosecutors that it is acting in good faith. In sum, even if a firm is too big to saddle with criminal charges, it presumably prefers a shorter lag time from announcement to resolution, as well as less intrusive and expensive settlement.

25.2.4.3 Credibility and Lemons Markets

Leniency programs succeed when corporations trust the government's promises of leniency *and* when government prosecutors believe in the authenticity of corporate compliance. When either of these beliefs weakens, transaction costs increase and a "lemons" market develops. The lemons reference is drawn from Professor Akerlof's seminal study of the used car market (Akerlof 1970). When buyers are unable to distinguish the difference between healthy used cars and lemons, they underbid the price of all used cars. Owners of used cars that are in good shape drop out of the market because buyers are unwilling to pay what their cars are worth. Adverse selection thus results in an unraveling market whereby only the worst actors (the sellers of lemons) are willing to play.

Scholars have applied Akerlof's teachings across a variety of contexts. It is not too difficult to see how adverse selection hampers the already inefficient "market" for leniency and corporate compliance (Baer 2018). Just as information asymmetries prevent buyers from distinguishing worthy and unworthy used cars, so too do these asymmetries undermine the government leniency mechanism.

Consider a typical government prosecutor. Voluntary self-reporting of foreign bribery violations has become relatively common (Koehler 2018). When a corporation's defense counsel contacts that prosecutor and advises her that it has identified FCPA violations, the prosecutor must decide whether the corporation's disclosure is prompt and complete. This, in turn, requires a fair amount of verification. The prosecutor might ask the corporation's counsel for a list of employees who have already been interviewed, for documents that have already been searched, and so on. The government might subpoena documents independently to corroborate the information it has received or engage its own interviews of relevant witnesses.

Verification is costly. The more time and energy the prosecutor expends testing the corporation's claims, the less valuable the government's leniency program becomes in the first place – to both the firm and the prosecutor. Thus, at some point, the government might decide to limit its verification efforts and offer less than full payment (i.e., less than full leniency). To a prosecutor, this leniency "discount" is useful for several reasons in the event that additional misconduct surfaces. It allows her to save face with her supervisors; it limits her office's reputational risk with the general public; and it relieves her of further verification efforts.

But there is a downside to leniency discounts, which is that they reduce a corporation's incentive to voluntarily monitor and disclose wrongdoing in the first place. When a government agency discounts the amount of leniency it confers in response to corporate disclosures, it inadvertently causes some firms to conclude that leniency's benefits aren't worth its costs (Baer 2018). Much like Akerlof's used car example, the exchange unravels due to adverse selection. "Good" corporations decide that disclosure isn't worth the trouble, while "bad" corporations continue to attempt to secure leniency with inauthentic cooperation. In less technical terms: "A climate of doubt and distrust between the regulatory and the firm imposes losses on both parties and society at large" (Bird and Park 2017: 288).

25.2.4.4 Leniency for Firms but Not Employees

A program that extends leniency to *firms* does not necessarily extend leniency to its *employees*. If the firm believes that government leniency will be forthcoming only if it demonstrates no tolerance for wrongdoing, its compliance efforts may be targeted more toward discipline (i.e., firing employees who break even relatively minor rules) and less toward coaching and improving mistakes (Baer 2016, 2009). Thus, one of the dilemmas for leniency programs is that for a *firm* to receive the prosecutor's forbearance, it may have to adopt an unforgiving stance with its employees (Baer 2009).

A strong zero tolerance approach to wrongdoing unleashes disparate reactions. Those who have yet to engage in any wrongdoing may decide to toe the line – and then some. They may also take advantage of channels the firm has put in place for reporting on wayward peers or supervisors, perhaps too precipitously. When employees inundate the whistleblower hotline, investigators become *less* effective as they have to expend greater efforts sorting through noise (Casey and Niblett 2014).

Other employees, however, may conclude that crime still pays, provided they take steps to avoid detection (Sanchirico 2006). And finally, an additional group of employees – notably, those already in the midst of carrying out frauds when the company implements a revved-up compliance program – may conclude that *additional* wrongdoing is necessary to cover up the crimes they have already committed (Baer 2008). Consider it a doubling-down effect: the manager who has been lying about his factory's toxic emissions for years isn't going to suddenly tell the truth on *this* month's report because telling the truth would undoubtedly cause auditors to question *last* month's report and the month before that and so on. So instead of fessing up or doing nothing, he will choose a far worse option, namely, doubling down and engaging in further wrongdoing, such as destroying evidence, bribing or intimidating colleagues, or layering new deceptions onto old ones.

25.3 TESTING LENIENCY PROGRAMS: INPUTS AND OUTCOMES

The first of the Department's charging policies, the so-called Holder Memo, which encapsulated the government's general principles for deciding whether to charge a corporate entity, is now two decades old. Since that time, the Justice Department has revised its primary leniency doctrine numerous times, has renamed it the Federal

Principles of Prosecution of Business Organizations ("Federal Principles") and has enshrined it in the Department's Justice Manual.

The Department's Federal Principles policy is just that; it vests no rights in any individual or entity. Nevertheless, the open-ended framework has attained the status of a "norm" among prosecutors, corporate defense attorneys and compliance officers (Buell 2018). Whenever a corporation has transgressed a given set of federal laws, one expects the government to consult and refer to the Federal Principles' multifactor rubric. Defense attorneys routinely consult its language, as do scholars and jurists. It is a "leniency program," in all respects, even if the Department declines to call it that.

That the Justice Department's leniency program has become an established and well-known framework for understanding government approaches to wrongdoing tells us fairly little about how well the program has achieved its goals. To judge a leniency program's success – assuming one defines success in the familiar economic terms of reducing the combined costs of crime and its detection (Miller 2018a) – one must know something about compliance inputs and outcomes across firms. As the following sections demonstrate, these inputs and outcomes remain difficult to quantify.

25.3.1 *Uncertainty in Inputs: Corporate Compliance's Black Box*

Corporate compliance has become a billion-dollar industry. Compliance budgets within publicly held firms have become sizable, and CEOs and directors routinely promote compliance mandates as essential to their company's respective missions (Bird and Park 2017; Laufer 2017). An eager industry of consultants stands ready to provide technical and infrastructural advice to compliance officers seeking to build out their programs (Bird and Park 2017). Prestigious law firms devote significant time and effort to developing "corporate investigation" and "white-collar" units (Weisselberg and Li 2011). However one feels about the compliance function writ large, it is difficult to write off these activities as mere window dressing. (But see Krawiec 2005.) To the contrary, most observers today accept the maxim that compliance "is an essential internal control activity at corporations and other complex organizations" (Miller 2018b: 981).

It's difficult to say how robustly compliance programs operate or whether, in the aggregate, they bear sufficient fruit in reducing wrongdoing (Garrett and Mitchell 2020; Bird and Park 2017; Krawiec 2005). Because compliance is largely a matter of business judgment, corporate managers have little obligation to announce how extensive or effective their compliance programs actually are (Griffith 2016). Nor do most corporate *boards*, who are vested with a fiduciary oversight obligation on behalf of the firm's shareholders, disclose significant compliance expenditures. Indeed, as Armour and his co-authors found, very few boards appear to host stand-alone compliance committees; instead, they allocate the company's compliance obligation to the audit committee or the company's general counsel (Armour et al. 2020b). Compliance accordingly occupies a corporate black box.

Because the corporation's compliance function remains shielded from public research (Garrett and Mitchell 2020), its inputs remain largely unknown, until and unless a given company's scandal explodes into the limelight. Even then, the company's subsequent investment may be known only to the prosecutor or third-party monitor overseeing the corporation's DPA. Accordingly, across industries, compliance inputs are heterogeneous, and the efficacy and long-term value of an industry's compliance effort remains unverified and "unvalidated" (Garrett and Mitchell 2020). One could imagine a government regime mandating standardized disclosures of expenditures, choices of technology and governance structures, and specific types of compliance testing, complete with publication and sharing of results. Notwithstanding free-rider issues, such a regime arguably would enable greater oversight of individual firms, create stronger accountability for companies that provided false compliance information, and enable researchers to better assess the efficacy of different compliance approaches. (Garrett and Mitchell 2020: 32–3, proposing a mandatory reporting framework that would privilege corporations' reports from subsequent enforcement actions). That is not the regime we currently have, however. Instead, the government tends to offer abstract, high-level advice that neither restrains nor substantially enlightens its regulatory targets (Laufer 2017). Thus, for the time being, corporate compliance efforts are likely to remain untested and underexamined.

25.3.2 *Uncertainty in Outcomes: Surveys and Proxies*

Although the DOJ has periodically deemed its leniency approach a great success in inducing detection and deterrence of wrongdoing, commentators rightfully challenge this claim. There certainly is no direct evidence of deterrence, in part because the incidence of white-collar crimes such as fraud and bribery is extremely difficult to measure. Moreover, excessive emphasis on one type of offense can overshadow equally important, but less policed, laws (Martinez 2019). Finally, it may be the case that the firm's compliance effort is less important than other factors. When one reviews the history of fraud in the United States, its schemes seem to follow their own trajectory, waxing and waning in response to broader political and socioeconomic forces (Balleisen 2017).

The data tracking the incidence of workplace misconduct is incomplete but still indicative of fraud and bribery's intractable nature. Annual surveys conducted by top accounting companies such as Ernst & Young[10] and PricewaterhouseCoopers[11] continue to report that employees observe on-the-job fraud and corruption within the workplace. Compliance *effort* is thus at an all-time high, but compliance *failure* nevertheless persists.

In sum, the compound assertion that leniency regimes promote better compliance *and* that compliance programs reduce the incidence of wrongdoing is far from a foregone conclusion. It is certainly the case that leniency programs have induced firms to build up their compliance programs. Even if one accepts these claims, however, there appears to be a limit to how much even a good faith compliance effort can accomplish, particularly in regard to difficult-to-detect crimes such as fraud and bribery. Moreover, for multinational corporations, the risk of foreign bribery is particularly heightened (Oded 2018). Indeed, one might argue that this heightened risk explains the DOJ's creation of an FCPA-specific leniency policy that appears to emphasize disclosure above all other factors.

25.4 LENIENCY PROGRAMS AND INSTITUTIONAL DESIGN

Despite their popularity, leniency programs have yet to demonstrate their conclusive ability to reduce wrongdoing. Nevertheless, leniency programs almost certainly have played a role in the corporate compliance industry's domestic and global growth. They also have

10 Ernst & Young 15th Global Fraud Survey, 2018, at https://assets.ey.com/content/dam/ey-sites/ey-com/en_gl/topics/assurance/assurance-pdfs/ey-integrity-in-spotlight.pdf.

11 PricewaterhouseCoopers' 2018 Global Economic Crime and Fraud Survey: US Perspectives, at www.pwc.com/us/en/forensic-services/assets/2018-global-economic-fraud-survey.pdf.

permanently altered the government's stance toward wayward companies. Prosecutors widely accept the Department's mission to be broader, more rehabilitative and more regulatory where corporations are concerned (Buell 2018). Finally, leniency programs have altered corporate officers' views of internal monitoring and self-reporting. Once viewed as either a naïve or a last-option move, corporate monitoring and self-reporting have become components of a viable and often indispensable strategy.

In this section, I consider several institutional design components of a leniency program. The Yates Memo and the FCPA Pilot Program provide a useful contrast because they were initiated in roughly the same time period and by the same presidential administration, that of President Obama. As described in the Introduction (Section 25.1), the Yates Memo was styled deliberately as a stick, while the FCPA Pilot Program adopted a more positive tone, advertising the benefits a corporation might attain through prompt self-reporting of newly detected violations of law. In the intervening years, one policy has all but fallen by the wayside, while the other has become a permanent program, poised to expand beyond its initial borders.

Taken together, the two programs yield fruitful insights into how institutional design impacts a program's political longevity and success. They also demonstrate several of the pitfalls inherent in crafting leniency policies. The typical policy reaches two major audiences: regulated actors and the general public. The policy that resonates well with one group might not resonate so well with the other. I discuss both of these issues in the subsections that follow.

25.4.1 *Message Framing*

An enforcement program communicates information to its intended targets. Over the years, the DOJ has tweaked its corporate leniency approach. Depending on how it chooses to communicate these changes, the Department can either emphasize cooperation's benefits or instead threaten sanctions for failing to disclose misconduct. By definition, the typical program rests upon a complex bundle of carrots *and* sticks. A program succeeds when it induces corporations to seek the enforcement agency's carrots (leniency) and avoid its sticks (more severe sanctions).

Were individuals perfectly rational, we might not need to say anything more on this topic. The rational actor would take notice of both elements and maximize her well-being. Behavioral research indicates, however, that people respond to positive and negative messages differently. Messages that emphasize the positive aspects of a given program might be more salient than ones that emphasize the negative. They may be perceived as more credible than sticks – or they may be more effective *when* they are perceived as more credible than sticks. Finally, carrots such as the Department's Pilot Program may play a role in shaping the social processes that underlie corporate compliance systems. That is, the carrot that a leniency program holds out, namely the distinct and credible promise of better treatment, may be incorporated into a broader narrative script that guides decision-making throughout the firm.

The Yates Memo was self-consciously styled as a stick. But it wasn't a particularly credible stick. Yates's announcement employed harsher language than the Memo itself, and the Memo appeared more unforgiving than the policy that was ultimately encoded within the US Attorney's Manual (Baer 2016). Moreover, the Memo never bore any noticeable fruit. There was no particularly salient moment, post-Yates, in which prosecutors refused a corporation a DPA on account of its officers' failure to turn over information. Nor was there any noticeable increase in the Department's prosecution of corporate executives (Garrett 2020). The Memo therefore was perceived first as an empty threat and later as a bureaucratic impediment to concluding an investigation. As such, it lacked a constituency to defend it. Corporate critics discounted it, and corporate defenders contended that it was too draconian. It came as no surprise to anyone that the Trump administration eventually shelved it.

In contrast, the FCPA Pilot Program emphasized its carrot-like qualities, and the Department demonstrated its commitment to delivering on those carrots by posting its declinations on an easily accessible website. This, in turn, enabled corporate lawyers and compliance officers to demonstrate to their clients the practical and social benefits of self-reporting (Low and Prelogar 2020). Self-reporting by corporate offenders increased (Oded 2018), but it did not stand in the way of the Department prosecuting those offenders who elected *not* to self-report. Although corporate criminal sanctions fell considerably during the Trump administration's first three years (Garrett 2020), it is difficult to discern a connection between this decrease and the Pilot Program, which not only covered a small fraction of the Department's corporate "docket" but also originated during the waning days of the Obama administration.

The reason the FCPA Pilot Program was popular – and eventually became permanent – is that it helped to forge some level of trust between government prosecutors and the corporate defense bar. Corporate lawyers and chief compliance officers could confidently assure their companies' highest authorities that self-reporting was a viable, and in most instances smart, strategy. Nondisclosure carried costs (presumably greater costs if one believed that the Department's enforcement effectiveness had improved), but voluntary disclosure promised tangible benefits.

The Program's nonbinding pledge to decline criminal charges in qualifying cases also succeeded because it allowed corporate actors to maintain their self-perceptions as law-abiding people, and to maintain perception of the firm as a "good corporate citizen." To be sure, their companies had made mistakes and their employees had crossed lines; but, by reporting these mistakes, disgorging any ill-gotten profits and shoring up internal controls, these firms could credibly argue that they had put the bad behavior behind them. (Although, under the permanent version of the program, they also had to avoid becoming recidivists, since repeat offenders were ineligible to participate in the program (Oded 2018).) To put it another way, the companies still had to pay penalties, but their executives were permitted to possess relatively positive views of themselves.

Psychologists have long posited that individuals *want* to believe they are more ethical and morally upright than they actually are (Langevoort 2018, citing Tenbrunsel and Messick 2003). Few people conceptualize themselves as opportunists or cheaters. Accordingly, a program that stressed a tangible benefit in exchange for reporting – namely, the benefit of avoiding any charges at all – attracted the support of multiple corporate constituencies because it also imbued those constituencies with a valuable *intangible* benefit, which was the government's imprimatur of good corporate citizenship.

Finally, as a practical matter, because it required corporations to invest resources in internal monitoring, detection and remediation, the Pilot Program and its successor also benefited the compliance industry. It encouraged corporate executives to spend more on preventive and defensive compliance activities, although it did so not on the basis of fear (as was the case with the Yates Memo) but on the basis of a promise of a salient, easy-to-grasp benefit: declination (in most cases) and drastically reduced fines if declination was deemed inappropriate.

Thus, the FCPA corporate enforcement program developed multiple constituencies of support. Prosecutors, corporate defense attorneys, compliance professionals and corporate boards could all derive tangible benefits from the program, and those benefits in turn encouraged prosecutors to promote and expand the program beyond its original limits.

25.4.2 *Precision of Benefit, Salience of a Specific Factor*

Prior to the implementation of the FCPA Pilot Program, the Department had always stressed the benefits of its flexible and open-ended charging principles. No single factor was dispositive, prosecutors liked to say. What a company lost in one factor, it might make up in the other. Although this might have inspired hope in some corporate offenders, it appeared to fuel frustration and uncertainty in the corporate defense bar. If no single factor mattered, lawyers lacked the tools to predict the costs of nondisclosure, much less the benefits of voluntary disclosure. Prosecutors held all the cards.

Indeed, the Holder Memo and the various memos that followed it never quite spelled out the payoff a corporation would receive in exchange for its cooperation and compliance efforts. To the contrary, they stressed that the ultimate decision fell within the discretion of the prosecutor. Accordingly, the corporation whose compliance officials assisted prosecutors in good faith *could* be rewarded with a DPA or something less onerous, but it also *might* be charged in a criminal indictment if the circumstances warranted its prosecution.

This lack of precision – and lack of public commitment on the Department's end – vested the individual prosecutor (not to mention the prosecutor's office) with maximal discretion. It also contributed to the trust issues outlined in Section 25.3. Why should a corporation voluntarily come forward with information if the benefits of doing so remained so uncertain? Moreover, if prosecutors were to depend on multiple factors in reaching their charging decision, why should a company rely so much on *self-reporting* (as opposed to any other factor) to obtain some unspecified benefit?

By placing a definitive price on self-disclosure, the Pilot Program noticeably changed the Department's open-ended multifactor approach and ameliorated its credibility problem with corporate executives and defense counsel. Particularly after the program became permanent, it effectively committed its prosecutors to a precise and salient benefit: declination of charges. By publicly announcing that benefit in a written policy (even a nonbinding one), the Department signaled to corporate executives that its promise was more than just cheap talk. To the contrary, the government's commitment to decline charges and publish those declinations online represented a costly concession on its part, one which left it vulnerable to political attack and which effectively restrained its prosecutors' discretion. At the same time, by narrowing the group of corporations who could compete for that benefit – namely, corporations who had not violated the FCPA previously – the Department created a cost for corporations whose compliance efforts were insincere. Self-reporting could garner cooperative corporations a valuable credit, but it would be only a one-time credit.

25.4.3 *Centralization of Enforcement*

Like the Department's charging policies, the Yates Memo was intended for all corporate crimes (except antitrust cartels, which are covered by a different policy), and was further intended to apply to all federal prosecutors within the ninety-four US Attorneys' Offices.

Across the federal system, prosecutorial decision-making is highly decentralized (Arffa 2019; Richman 1999; Kahan 1996). Although decentralization can be a benefit in some instances, it can be a curse in others, leading to a lack of uniformity among decision-makers and weaker social norms inducing compliance (Werle 2019: 1424, contending that decentralization "stymies institutional learning").

The Yates Memo's rollout suggested that some of the nation's federal prosecutors (although not all) had wrongfully accorded corporate offenders partial credit for less than fulsome cooperation. Sally Yates's announcement appeared to confirm previously stated concerns (Garrett 2014) that prosecutors were contenting themselves with corporate settlements at the expense of more complex, and ultimately more useful, prosecutions of high-level corporate offenders. Indeed, one of the less discussed aspects of the Yates Memo was that it required prosecutors to write closing memos for each corporate criminal case explaining why there had been no individual prosecution.

In sum, the Yates Memo reminded its audience in an unfortunate way that federal law enforcement was decentralized, that prosecutorial practice sometimes diverged from Department policy and that, to the extent that the Department sought a more unified approach, it would be less favorable to corporate defendants. The problem with this narrative is that it instantiated critics' concerns about the DOJ, reminded corporate defendants that the government was highly decentralized (and therefore unpredictable) and antagonized prosecutors in local offices. If leniency relies on trust and a belief that all parties are acting in good faith, the Yates Memo seemed to highlight the many reasons why prosecutors and the corporate defense bar should *distrust* each other.

By contrast, the FCPA Pilot Program fell solely within the jurisdiction of the Department's Fraud Section, in part because Main Justice has exercised exclusive control over FCPA prosecutions (Garrett 2020). To the extent that the Fraud Section is smaller and more centralized than the sprawling US Attorneys' Offices, its policy announcement may have been more trusted by regulated entities and their representatives. The Fraud Section's prosecutors may have been perceived as repeat players, with strong incentives to adhere to their own policies and cooperate with criminal defense attorneys. Centralization in the FCPA context thus promised tangible benefits that corporate offenders and their counsel could trust in making fateful decisions to self-disclose wrongdoing.

25.4.4 *Altering the Social Meaning of Compliance*

One of the more popular trade magazines, *Compliance Week*, rhetorically inquired in its January/February 2019 print edition whether 2019 might be remembered as "the year of the compliance officer."[12] The article focused primarily on the Department's announcement that the Pilot Program had become permanent and was now known as the "FCPA Corporate Enforcement Program."

The permanent Corporate Enforcement Program was, in some ways, more corporate-friendly than its predecessor, as it explicitly stated that declination would become a *presumption* provided the company voluntarily disclosed its foreign bribery, disgorged all gains, remediated the misconduct and fully cooperated in any subsequent investigation. Moreover, under the now-permanent policy, self-disclosing companies would continue to

[12] For the online edition, see Jaclyn Jaeger, "How Compliance Officers Can Shape Enforcement in 2019," *Compliance Week* (December 27, 2018), at www.complianceweek.com/regulatory-enforcement/how-compliance-officers-can-shape-enforcement-in-2019/24711.article.

escape the imposition of an outside third-party monitor, a provision that firms had long complained of. To qualify for these benefits, the company had to cooperate in the identification of individual offenders (an echo of the Yates Memo), perform a root cause analysis of what had led to the wrongful conduct and preserve relevant business records. Most importantly, it could not be eligible for declination if the Department determined it to be a "recidivist" (see Oded 2018, critiquing this bar), although the policy left that term undefined.

In its discussion of the now-permanent program, *Compliance Week* quoted a number of law partners whose practices covered corporate investigations. Unsurprisingly, all were rather complimentary. One law partner explained that the program made his job "easier" by altering the "cost-benefit analysis of self-disclosure."[13] Another explained that the program effectively incentivized internal investments in compliance. Whatever the cost of pumping up one's compliance program, it apparently cost far less than an outside monitor, whose presence would invariably lead to revelations of *other* violations of law (*Compliance Week* 2019).

The article concluded by advising that "compliance officers and in-house counsel will increasingly be expected to play a leading role in the Department's efforts to combat fraud in all areas, and thus can have a significant impact on shaping enforcement efforts to their benefit in 2019 and beyond" (*Compliance Week* 2019). In other words, compliance officers (and in-house counsel) should expect to enjoy a symbiotic partnership with DOJ enforcement personnel.

The vision of a company's internal investigators acting in partnership with government enforcers is hardly new (First 2010), but it has yet to be fully achieved, in part because the law would never really countenance a true partnership. Lawyers owe fiduciary duties, duties of zealous representation and duties of confidentiality to their *clients* – and certainly not to government prosecutors (Henning 2016, describing potential conflict). Prosecutors, in turn, owe duties to the general public – and not specifically to corporate shareholders (Michaels 2020, describing concerns that arose when it appeared that government enforcers and regulators grew too close to corporate executives). The DOJ's Corporate Enforcement Policy may *appear* to have created a lay "partnership" between external enforcers and internal corporate investigators, but this model is inherently unstable. Moreover, as Laufer's work emphasizes, the government has yet to make the investment in corporate enforcement that private companies have made in terms of headcount and technology (Laufer 2017). Until it does, it is difficult to think of the two as partners.

Although it will continue to please the compliance industry, the Corporate Enforcement Policy may eventually incite the general public's disdain. The Pilot Program and its successor have been received enthusiastically by corporate defense counsel because they allow corporate targets to adopt a positive narrative and they reduce the uncertainty that accompanies self-disclosure. These very characteristics will make the government appear overly forgiving of serious violations of criminal law. Those who conceptualize DPAs as instantiations of either a "rehabilitative" or a "restorative" model of criminal justice (Diamantis 2018; Spalding 2015) may find it increasingly difficult to cling to these ideals when the leniency program in question evinces a crude exchange of disclosure for declination. When the government's criminal justice system devolves into little more than a market platform through which to trade reduced punishment for voluntary disclosure, the system's moral authority erodes. It is

[13] See *Compliance Week* article, *supra* note 13.

difficult to say that one is committed to doing "the right thing" when one is willing to sell the right thing for just the right bundle of information. And this problem grows even more profound if the government sells itself short, offering leniency to companies whose voluntary self-disclosures are less impressive than they at first seem.

Thus, a program that has garnered positive attention from corporate defense attorneys and internal compliance officers risks a backlash from scholars and reformers. This is particularly the case among those who believe that corporate and white-collar crime is pervasively underpoliced. For those who already believe that the "game is rigged," the Department's Corporate Enforcement Policy will simply look like a stronger, more robust version of cheating-and-confessing.

Nevertheless, one can say that the government's policy appears to have played a role in changing how corporate compliance personnel see themselves and pitch their services. An enforcement policy that dangles a valuable carrot (a presumption of declination) allows the corporate compliance function to portray itself to corporate managers as a valuable investment opportunity and not just a "cost center." So long as the government adheres to its Corporate Enforcement Policy, its marketing pitch may succeed in changing the social meaning of compliance among compliance personnel, defense attorneys and corporate executives. Under this new policy, compliance may morph from a negative, cost-minimizing model to a more positive, long-term investment model. At the same time, the Department would do well to continue its aggressive enforcement of violations among firms that *fail* to report or that otherwise appear to be recidivists. Otherwise, it risks losing the general public's support, as well as the support of those political actors (and jurists too) who believe that the government's enforcement apparatus has been captured.

25.5 FUTURE CONCERNS: GENERALIZABILITY AND SOCIAL MEANING

The FCPA Pilot Program is no longer a pilot. It has instead become the permanent corporate enforcement program for FCPA violations and appears poised to become a model for future leniency programs.

Given several of the design elements described earlier, it is questionable whether the expansion of this program beyond the FCPA context will net the government the gains it expects in terms of increased self-reporting and individual deterrence. First, if applied to crimes other than the FCPA, the program will lose its centralized group of repeat players, the Department's Fraud Section. Moreover, if expanded beyond the FCPA context, the bar against recidivists (corporations who have been charged with or have settled other investigations in the past) will become more significant and potentially more difficult to implement. If defined too broadly, the bar against recidivists may reduce the pool of eligible corporations so greatly that the policy loses its effectiveness in incentivizing voluntary disclosures.

Moreover, the FCPA Pilot has hardly been an unqualified success. Corporate advisors like it; likewise, federal prosecutors have touted its contributions to government enforcement efforts. But progressive critics have panned it for allowing corporations to write off bribery as just a cost of business (Woody 2018). They have worried as well that policies like it allow government enforcers to become too dependent on corporate investigations and forgo more effective techniques such as the use of wiretaps and undercover stings (Werle 2019).

These concerns are real and ought not to be dismissed. Nevertheless, if it is true that self-disclosure programs reduce the government's utilization of wiretaps and stings, the government's critics have yet to document this claim empirically. More likely, the government refrains from employing these controversial methods because it lacks the evidence or – in the case of undercover stings – the practical ability to introduce an undercover investigator into the corporate context. In any event, the Department *has* occasionally used wiretaps and undercover stings in the corporate context, although admittedly not to the same degree that it has used them in street crime and narcotics cases (Barkow 2014). This should surprise no one. Given the prevalence of in-house attorneys and outside legal counsel (and, therefore, the many attorney–client privilege and professional responsibility issues that arise from government contacts with represented parties), it is hardly cause for concern that the government has limited the introduction of "moles" into the corporate workplace.

Leniency can mean many things to different people. In the context of corporate crime, it has come to mean "no prosecution" among progressives, and "no prosecutorial constraints" among corporate defenders. For many academics, it has long suggested a flawed, yet plausible approach to an intractable problem. Business organizations will forever play host to crimes of deceit, such as fraud and bribery, in part because the performance standards they set for their employees are often too difficult to achieve legitimately. Employees who fear the loss of their jobs will, in at least some instances, choose self-preservation over adherence to the law (Arlen and Carney 1992). At the same time, regardless of how business organizations evolve, their organizational processes will always serve as a partial shield for individual wrongdoing. Even when armed with strong subpoena powers, formidable search warrants and enticing bounties for whistleblowers, the prosecutor can learn only so much.

Accordingly, the government will always be in search of tools best designed to extract information, deter wrongdoing and induce the creation of a law-abiding culture within the workplace. Leniency policies are here to stay, whether we like them or not. Institutional design cannot solve all of leniency's most pressing challenges, but it can illuminate the factors that render some programs more viable than others. A leniency program that makes little dent in on-the-ground practices and all but disappears only a few years after its introduction can hardly be deemed a success. Survival, however, is only the beginning of the story. For a leniency program to produce *real* gains in deterrence and regulation, it has to alter our understanding of why it is appropriate to behave in a certain manner, even when we find ourselves coming under the most pernicious of pressures. Has the DOJ's leniency approach successfully altered the psychology of the workplace? Better yet, has it reduced the incidence of fraud and corruption across the private sector? Suffice it to say that the jury is still out on these questions.

REFERENCES

Akerlof, George. 1970. "The Market for 'Lemons': Quality Uncertainty and the Market Mechanism." *Quarterly Journal of Economics* 84: 488–500.

Alexander, Cindy A., and Jennifer Arlen. 2018. "Does Conviction Matter? The Reputational and Collateral Consequences of Corporate Crime." In Jennifer Arlen (ed.), *Research Handbook on Corporate Crime and Financial Misdealing*. Northampton, MA: Edward Elgar, 87–150.

Alexander, Cindy A., and Mark Cohen. 2015. "The Evolution of Corporate Criminal Settlements: An Empirical Perspective on Deferred Prosecution, Non-Prosecution and Plea Agreements." *American Criminal Law Review* 52: 537–91.

Arffa, Leslie B. 2019. "Separation of Prosecutors." *Yale Law Journal* 128: 1078–1129.

Arlen, Jennifer. 2016. "Prosecuting Beyond the Rule of Law: Corporate Mandates Imposed through Deferred Prosecution Agreements." *Journal of Legal Analysis* 8: 191–234.

1994. "The Potentially Perverse Effects of Corporate Criminal Liability." *Journal of Legal Studies* 23: 833–67.
Arlen, Jennifer, and Samuel W. Buell. 2020. "The Law of Corporate Investigations and the Global Expansion of Corporate Criminal Enforcement." *Southern California Law Review* 93: 697–761.
Arlen, Jennifer, and William Carney. 1992. "Vicarious Liability for Fraud on the Market: Theory and Evidence." *Illinois Law Review* 1992: 691–734.
Arlen, Jennifer, and Marcel Kahan. 2017. "Corporate Governance Regulation through Non-prosecution." *University of Chicago Law Review* 84: 323–87.
Arlen, Jennifer, and Reinier Kraakman. 1997. "Controlling Corporate Misconduct: An Analysis of Corporate Liability Regimes." *New York University Law Review* 72: 687–779.
Armour, John, Jeffrey Gordon and Geeyoung Min. 2020a. "Taking Compliance Seriously." *Yale Journal on Regulation* 37: 1–66.
Armour, John, Brandon L. Garrett, Jeffrey N. Gordon and Geeyoung Min. 2020b. "Board Compliance." *Minnesota Law Review* 104: 1191–1273.
Baer, Miriam H. 2018. "When the Corporation Investigates Itself." In Jennifer Arlen (ed.), *Research Handbook on Corporate Crime and Financial Misdealing*. Northampton, MA: Edward Elgar, 308–33.
2016. "The Stick That Never Was: Parsing the Yates Memo and the Revised Principles of Federal Prosecution of Business Organizations." NYU Corporate Enforcement and Compliance Blog.
2009. "Governing Corporate Compliance." *Boston College Law Review* 52: 949–1019.
2008. "Linkage and the Deterrence of Corporate Fraud." *Virginia Law Review* 94: 1295–1365.
Balleisen, Edward J. 2017. *Fraud: An American History from Barnum to Madoff*. Princeton, NJ: Princeton University Press.
Barkow, Rachel. 2014. "The New Policing of Business Crime." *Seattle University Law Review* 37: 435–73.
Bird, Robert C., and Stephen Kim Park. 2017. "Turning Compliance into Competitive Advantage." *University of Pennsylvania Journal of Business Law* 19: 285–338.
Buell, Samuel W., 2018. "Why Do Prosecutors Say Anything? The Case of Corporate Crime." *North Carolina Law Review* 96: 823–58.
2007. "Criminal Procedure Within the Firm." *Stanford Law Review* 59: 1613–70.
Casey, Anthony J., and Anthony Niblett. 2014. "Noise Reduction: The Screening Value of Qui Tam." *Washington University Law Review* 91: 1169–1217.
Cressey, Donald Ray. 1953. *Other People's Money: A Study in the Social Psychology of Embezzlement*. New York: Free Press.
Diamantis, Mihailis E. 2018. "Clockwork Corporations: A Character Theory of Corporate Punishment." *Iowa Law Review*: 507–69.
Eisinger, Jesse. 2015. *The Chickenshit Club: Why the Justice Department Fails to Prosecute Executives*. New York: Simon & Schuster.
Fanto, James A. 2014. "Surveillant and Counselor: A Reorientation in Compliance for Broker-Dealers." *Brigham Young University Law Review* 2014: 1121–83.
Feldman, Yuval. 2018. *The Law of Good People: Challenging States' Ability to Regulate Human Behavior*. Cambridge: Cambridge University Press.
First, Harry. 2010. "Branch Office of the Prosecutor: The New Role of Corporations in Business Crime Prosecutions." *North Carolina Law Review* 89: 23.
Ford, Cristie, and David Hess. 2011. "Corporate Monitorships and New Governance Regulation: In Theory, In Practice and In Context." *Law and Policy* 33: 509–41.
Garrett, Brandon L. 2020. "Declining Corporate Prosecutions." *American Criminal Law Review* 57: 109–55.
2014. *Too Big to Jail*. Cambridge, MA: Belknap/Harvard University Press.
Garrett, Brandon L., and Gregory Mitchell. 2020. "Testing Compliance." *Law and Contemporary Problems*, https://papers.ssrn.com/sol3/papers.cfm?abstract_id=3535913.
Gilchrist, Gregory M. 2014. "The Special Problem of Banks and Crime." *University of Colorado Law Review* 85: 1–52.
Golumbic, Court E., and Albert D. Lichy. 2014. "The 'Too Big to Jail' Effect and the Impact on the Justice's Department's Corporate Charging Policy." *Hastings Law Journal* 65: 1293–1344.
Griffith, Sean J. 2016. "Corporate Governance in an Era of Compliance." *William and Mary Law Review* 57: 2075–2140.

Gruner, Richard S. 2004. *Corporate Criminal Liability and Prevention*. New York: Law Journal Press.

Haugh, Todd. 2015. "The Most Senior Wall Street Official: Evaluating the State of Financial Crises Prosecutions." *Virginia Business Law Review* 9: 153–99.

Henning, Peter. 2017. "Why Is It Getting Harder to Prosecute Executives for Corporate Misconduct?" *Vermont Law Review* 41: 503–21.

2016. "The New Corporate Gatekeeper." *Wayne Law Review* 62: 29–52.

Hess, David. 2016. "Ethical Infrastructures and Evidence-Based Corporate Compliance and Ethics Programs: Policy Implications from the Empirical Evidence." *New York University Journal of Law and Business* 12: 317–68.

Innes, Robert. 2001. "Violator Avoidance Activities and Self-Reporting in Optimal Law Enforcement." *Journal of Law, Economics and Organization* 17: 239–56.

1999. "Remediation and Self-Reporting in Optimal Law Enforcement." *Journal of Public Economics* 72: 379–93.

Joh, Elizabeth E., and Thomas W. Joo. 2015a. "The Corporation as Snitch: The New DOJ Guidelines on Prosecuting White Collar Crime." *Virginia Law Review Online* 101: 51–9.

2015b. "Third Party Harms in Undercover Police Operations." *Southern California Law Review* 88: 1309–55.

Kaal, Wolf A., and Timothy Lacine. 2014. "The Effect of Deferred and Non-prosecution Agreements on Corporate Governance: Evidence from 1993–2003." *Business Lawyer* 70: 61–119.

Kahan, Dan M. 1996. "Is Chevron Relevant to Federal Criminal Law?" *Harvard Law Review* 110: 469–521.

Kelly, Michael P., and Ruth E. Mandelbaum. 2016. "Are the Yates Memorandum and the Federal Judiciary's Concerns about Over-Criminalization Destined to Collide?" *American Criminal Law Review* 53: 899–937.

Koehler, Mike. 2018. "The FCPA's Record-Breaking Year." *Connecticut Law Review* 50: 91–160.

Krawiec, Kimberley D. 2005. "Organizational Misconduct: Beyond the Principal–Agent Model." *Florida State Law Review* 32: 571–615.

Langevoort, Donald C. 2018. "Behavioral Ethics, Behavioral Compliance." In Jennifer Arlen (ed.), *Research Handbook on Corporate Crime and Financial Misdealing*. Northampton, MA: Edward Elgar, 263–81.

Laufer, William S. 2017. "A Very Special Regulatory Milestone." *Journal of Business Law* 20: 392–428.

1999. "Corporate Liability, Risk Shifting and the Paradox of Compliance." *Vanderbilt Law Review* 52: 1343–1420.

Lemos, Margaret H., and Alex Stein. 2011. "Strategic Enforcement." *Minnesota Law Review* 95: 9–58.

Low, Lucinda A., and Brittany Prelogar. 2020. "Incentives for Self-Reporting and Cooperation." In Tina Soreide and Abiola Makinwa (eds.), *Negotiated Settlements in Bribery Cases: A Principled Approach*. Northampton, MA: Edward Elgar, 200–27.

Martinez, Veronica Root. 2019. "The Outsize Influence of the FCPA?" *University of Illinois Law Review* 2019: 1205–25.

McGrath, Joe. 2020. "Why Do Good People Do Bad Things? A Multi-Level Analysis of Individual, Organizational, and Structural Causes of White-Collar Crime." *Seattle Law Review* 43: 525–53.

Michaels, Jon D. 2020. "We the Shareholders: Government Market Participation in the Postliberal U.S. Political Economy." *Columbia Law Review* 120: 465.

Miller, Geoffrey. 2018a. "An Economic Analysis of Effective Compliance Programs." In Jennifer Arlen (ed.), *Research Handbook on Corporate Crime and Financial Misdealing*. Northampton, MA: Edward Elgar, 247–62.

2018b. "The Compliance Function: An Overview." In Jeffrey N. Gordon and Wolf-Georg Ringe (eds.), *Oxford Handbook of Corporate Law and Governance*. Oxford: Oxford University Press, 981–1002.

Oded, Sharon. 2018. "Trumping Recidivism: Assessing the FCPA Corporate Enforcement Policy." *Columbia Law Review Online* 118: 135–52.

Rakoff, Jed S. 2014. "The Financial Crisis: Why Have No High-Level Executives Been Prosecuted?" *New York Review of Books* Jan. 9. www.nybooks.com/articles/2014/01/09/financial-crisis-why-no-executive-prosecutions/.

Richman, Daniel C. 1999. "Federal Criminal Law, Congressional Delegation and Enforcement Discretion." *UCLA Law Review* 46: 757–814.

Sanchirico, Chris William. 2006. "Detection Avoidance." *New York University Law Review* 81: 1331–99.

Soltes, Eugene. 2018. "Evaluating the Effectiveness of Corporate Compliance Programs: Establishing a Model for Prosecutors, Courts and Firms." *NYU Journal of Law and Business* 14: 965–1011.

Spalding, Andrew. 2015. "Restorative Justice for Multinational Corporations." *Ohio State Law Journal* 76: 357–408.

Tenbrunsel, Ann, and David Messick. 2004. "Ethical Fading: The Role of Self-Deception in Unethical Behavior." *Social Justice Research* 17: 223–36.

Uhlmann, David M. 2013. "Deferred Prosecution and Non-prosecution Agreements and the Erosion of Corporate Criminal Liability." *Maryland Law Review* 72: 1295–1344.

Weisselberg, Charles D., and Su Li. 2011."Big Law's Sixth Amendment: The Rise of Corporate White-Collar Practices in Large U.S. Law Firms." *Arizona Law Review* 53: 1221–98.

Werle, Nick. 2019. "Prosecuting Corporate Crime When Firms Are Too Big to Jail: Investigation, Deterrence, and Judicial Review." *Yale Law Journal* 128: 1366–1427.

Woody, Karen. 2018. "'Declinations with Disgorgement' in FCPA Enforcement." *University of Michigan Journal of Law Reform* 51: 269–311.

Yockey, Joseph W. 2016. "Beyond Yates: From Engagement to Accountability in Corporate Crime." *New York University Journal of Law and Business* 12: 409–23.

26

Incentive Contracts

Jesse Bull[*]

Abstract: This chapter explores the importance of verifiability to contractual provision of incentives for contract performance or compliance. The crucial role of evidence and evidence-disclosure decisions is highlighted. Parties to a contract dispute convey information to the court by disclosing evidence. Actions taken by the parties in the productive phase (or primary activity) of their relationship influence the evidence that is available should a dispute arise. These considerations are important for practitioners in that 1) the lack of evidence to prove one's claim may lead to some productive relationships being avoided or undertaken at a less than optimal level, and 2) the primary activity of the parties may involve steps to ensure relevant evidence should a breach occur. Many practical examples are discussed.

26.1 INTRODUCTION

A critical feature of a contract is to shape incentives. A contract is an agreement that is intended to be enforced. My focus in this chapter is on externally or court-enforced contracts, as opposed to relational contracting. My primary aim is to present some practical insights that are meaningful for a wide range of disciplines and practitioners. I'll focus on hard evidence and verifiability as I believe these to be important concepts that may not receive enough attention. I should note, for full disclosure, that these are areas on which my research has focused.

There is a rich economics literature on contract theory and game-theoretic models of information transmission and provision of incentives. This has resulted in many insights. These include the now familiar concepts of adverse selection, moral hazard, and signaling. These are commonly taught, in some form, in undergraduate game theory courses. The implications of these models provide powerful insights for many practical situations. Price discrimination is often studied by a monopolist, offering a menu of contracts, with one intended for a buyer with a particular valuation. Laffont and Martimort (2009) and Bolton and Dewatripont (2005) provide thorough coverage of many aspects of economic contract theory. Many of these models are well known outside of economics and there are many texts that address them in depth; these are not covered here.

The chapter is organized as follows. In Section 26.2, we'll consider some practical examples that highlight the importance of verifiability and incentives in evidence disclosure for

* I thank Daniel Sokol and Benjamin van Rooij for asking me to write this chapter and for their helpful comments. I also thank participants at the Compliance Handbook chapter conference, which Daniel and Benjamin organized for the authors of the various chapters to get feedback on their contributions. I'm especially indebted to Joel Watson as much of this chapter draws on our joint work over the years.

contracts. This will help illustrate how the evidence environment and incentives in evidence disclosure impact the scope for inducing incentives with a contract. In Section 26.3, we'll turn to some results in the literature. Much of this will be in the context of the practical examples already discussed. Finally, Section 26.4 contains a brief discussion of the scope for empirical work.

26.2 SOME PRACTICAL MOTIVATION

Consider a transaction in which a buyer buys an object from a seller. Suppose the object is already made and the exchange of money and the object can occur simultaneously. An example might be a store selling a pencil to a consumer in a cash sale. If the consumer has exact change, they could hand the money to the clerk at roughly the same time that the clerk hands them the pencil. So, there is little need for an externally enforced contract or to verify performance to a third party such as a court.

However, most transactions that create economic value or gains to the parties are not so simple, and require performance after the parties have reached an agreement. Most of these require some kind of external enforcement to shape incentives for parties to perform. Refer to the activity the parties take prior to the external enforcement as primary or productive activity. This is to make a distinction between that activity and activity during the enforcement phase of the interaction. In order for a contract to provide incentives to a party, there must potentially be a different court action following some productive activities than following others.

In order for the court to be able to take a different action following one productive activity, say outcome a, and another, say outcome b, it must be that the court has information that allows it to make a distinction between the outcomes a and b. Obviously, not all contract disputes go to trial. However, the anticipated outcome, should it go to trial, can influence the outcome of other resolutions, such as negotiation.

Parties to the contract convey this information to the court through the disclosure of evidence. So, the incentives to disclose evidence are critical in understanding what incentives a contract can provide for productive or primary activity. In the context of the outcomes a and b example, the court cannot take a different action following a than following b if it does not have information about which has occurred. Naturally, this depends on the incentives of the parties to provide evidence. This is a key idea that we will explore later in this section and Section 26.3, but first let's consider some practical examples.

Consider a seller of a good who contracts for a delivery service to deliver the good to the buyer of the good. Suppose that timely delivery is of primary concern for the seller and the contract specifies that the delivery service is to ensure delivery by date x. If the delivery service requires a signature from the buyer upon delivery and this is done in a way that documents the date, it is easy to verify that the delivery service has performed. One may be concerned about the scenario in which the delivery service attempts to deliver, and the buyer is not at home or at their place of business to receive the good. This could be dealt with by the delivery service taking a time-dated (and perhaps even location-marked) photo of the attempted delivery.

Naturally, there are examples where it may be difficult to verify performance. Suppose someone hires a piano teacher. The student and the teacher agree that successful performance by the teacher is defined as the student learning to play a particular song well. Since the student's improvement will depend on how much she practices and the instructor will not be present for all of that, there is the possibility that the student meets the standard but acts as though she doesn't. That is because someone who can play the piano well can also play it badly.[1] Of course, this involves the student behaving in a disingenuous manner and, in practice, piano teachers do not usually offer contracts of this type. Further, most music lessons have an ongoing nature to them and there is likely to be some form of relational contracting in addition to externally enforced contracting.

There are other contractual situations where it is difficult to verify performance. These include construction or architectural contracts. Someone having a building built may not be able to verify whether the procedures used satisfy those specified. It is common for an engineering firm to be used to verify performance while construction is ongoing.[2]

Imagine a homeowner who needs to have the glass for an "impact window" replaced in his home. Impact windows are commonly used in hurricane-prone areas such as Miami, Florida. They are designed to withstand strong winds and flying debris. The standards in Miami-Dade County, Florida are quite stringent, and acceptance of a window design for use as an impact window requires that the manufacturer submit testing and engineering documentation to the county.[3] Although the "impact glass" in such windows may crack, it is designed to not shatter so as to keep those inside the dwelling safe. The glass is typically of a laminate construction and is made by the window manufacturer using polyvinyl butyral (PVB) interlayer. A homeowner who contracts with a window installer to replace a cracked glass in an impact window would not have a way of telling simply by looking at the glass whether it is suitable for the window. However, the installer could, potentially, provide documentation that suggests that the glass was manufactured by the original manufacturer of the window and is similar to the glass that was originally in the window. One may view this as making it more likely that the glass is suitable.

So far, we've considered a series of examples that emphasize the importance of verifiability, using some sort of hard evidence, of either contract performance or lack of performance. Implicit to these examples is need for the party who possesses the critical evidence to have the incentive to disclose it. In most of these examples, this is the case. In the delivery of the good example, the delivery service certainly has the incentive to disclose the signature of the buyer indicating acceptance. Similarly, in the impact window example, the window installer clearly has the incentive to disclose the documentation on the replacement glass when it is suitable for the window. However, in the piano lesson example, the student may not have the incentive to demonstrate that she can play the particular song well, at least in the narrower version of the example, so as to avoid paying for the lessons.

This suggests constraints that go beyond whether there is potentially evidence to prove performance or nonperformance, and suggests the importance of considering incentives in disclosing evidence. We explore this further in Section 26.3. Next, we consider the role of evidence and the importance of verifiability of productive actions in more complicated situations.

The band Van Halen was known for requiring that M&M candy, with no brown ones, be provided for them backstage at their concerts. This was not a rock band making outrageous

1 This example is based on an example in Lipman and Seppi (1995) that was originally suggested by Michael Peters.

2 Chakravarty and MacLeod (2009) provide analysis of standard architectural contracts.

3 This is obviously not intended to be a complete description of the details or standards one would want in purchasing or installing impact windows. As someone who lives in Miami-Dade County and who has had to navigate some of these issues for replacement of the glass in an impact window, I'm basing my discussion here on information from the Miami-Dade County Notices of Acceptance for various window manufacturers.

demands; it actually had a verifiability component to it. As explained in Roth (2012) and Zeveloff (2016), the band had a very elaborate lighting and stage setup that was also specified in their contract.[4] If brown M&Ms were present, it was quite likely that the details of the lighting and staging had been missed, which potentially posed serious safety issues. The band's concert rider contained a clause specifying that if there were brown M&Ms, the promoter would "forfeit the entire show at full price." David Lee Roth, the lead singer of Van Halen at the time, explained: "Van Halen was the first to take 850 par lamp lights – huge lights – around the country. At the time, it was the biggest production ever. If I came backstage, having been one of the architects of this lighting and staging design, and I saw brown M&Ms on the catering table, then I [could] guarantee the promoter had not read the contract rider, and we would have to do a serious line check."

While the focus in the explanation for the brown M&Ms clause is on knowing whether a serious line check was needed prior to the concert, I suspect it also made it much easier to enforce should the situation end up in litigation. It's quite easy to document that there were brown M&Ms, but it may be likely that the technical details of the lighting and staging would have been difficult to argue in court. There could potentially be some issue with how some evidence that may be presented would be interpreted by a jury. So the clause helped ensure verifiable evidence both prior to the concert when the deficiencies in the lighting and staging could be dealt with and also for litigation, should it come to that. One might note that the liquidated damage amount for failure to provide M&Ms with no brown ones is quite extreme, which could pose an issue for a court actually enforcing it. In conjunction with a lighting or staging issue, the presence of brown M&Ms may provide a more convincing argument that the promoter had not read the concert rider in its entirety, which would make it more likely that the technical lighting and staging features had not been given adequate attention.

In a similar way, employers might specify some minimum performance standards that are easily verifiable, where failure to meet those may go along with failure to meet other standards that are more difficult to verify. For example, a university may specify that faculty are to attend departmental meetings and seminars as part of its requirements for "service." While an academic department would typically expect much more than this for service, a faculty member who is unengaged and not participating in their department is likely to not attend meetings or seminars. This is quite easy to document, whereas documenting that someone is not making a good effort on committee assignments or other tasks may be more difficult.[5]

It's worth noting that in some of these examples we have tended to focus on the case where evidence either exists or doesn't. In reality, evidence typically exists with different probabilities in different contingencies and rarely provides definitive proof that some set of contingencies occurred. Many of the previous examples have this aspect. As another example, a personal trainer being diligent in her work may make it more likely that her client will lose weight, but there is some positive probability, although lower, that her client will lose weight even if the trainer is not diligent. Refer to this type of evidence as *statistical evidence*. In these sorts of situation, the fact-finder, which could be a jury, will weigh the evidence to update its belief that a party performed or did not perform.

4 See also Mikkelson (2001).

5 Others have pointed out the difficulty of fully describing standards in other areas of university and faculty contracts. The standard for tenure has received considerable attention. See, for example, Hart (1995). Cater et al. (2009) suggest that faculty research may be a proxy for knowledge.

26.3 CONTRACTS AND VERIFIABILITY

I now present the previous ideas in the context of some economic models, continuing with an emphasis on practical ideas. Incentives can be provided through either a reward or a punishment – the so called "carrot" or "stick." We typically assume that economic agents weigh expected benefits against expected costs in determining how to behave; in this case, whether to perform as specified in the contract. This view fits with a Becker-type calculation by the parties to a contract.[6] Of course, this requires that the expected payoff differs following some productive actions. Since we are considering contracts, we would typically think of monetary transfers differing following some productive actions/outcomes.

For a contract to condition on some action or outcome requires verifiability. Many economic models of contract assume that some things are verifiable and others are not. See, for example, general moral hazard models, and team-production models such as those studied in Holmstrom (1982). Often this amounts to assuming that verifiability is given by a partition of the action space of a production game. See, for example, Holmstrom (1982), Legros and Matthews (1993), Miller (1997), and Bernheim and Whinston (1999).

Importantly, the availability of hard evidence is a function of primary activity. Hard evidence can include physical objects such as documents, recordings, etc. These could also include witness testimony. These are possessed by an individual and disclosure decisions are inalienable. So an individual who possesses a particular document chooses whether to disclose it. This makes incentives to disclose evidence critical for being able to provide incentives in productive activity.

Let's begin with the case where evidence is realized deterministically. Here, the "state," which we use to refer to the profile of productive activity for each party to the contract, determines, with no randomness, the evidence that is available to each party. Thus, the available documents imply a subset of the states that may have occurred. The ideas here are from Bull and Watson (2004). Importantly, we assume that the court action is a transfer between the parties to the contract, and we assume that this must be "balanced" in that monetary resources cannot be added to or removed from the contractual relationship.

Consider the following simple example as in Bull and Watson (2004). Suppose there are two states or possible productive outcomes: a and b. For simplicity, assume that the state is the result of only person 1's choice of productive action. Further, assume that the only hard evidence is the following. In state a person 1 possesses document d, and in state b person 1 possesses no documents. Person 2, the other party to the contract, never possesses any documents. This is represented below, with $\oslash$ denoting when someone possesses no document.

State	1's evidence	2's evidence
a	d	$\oslash$
b	$\oslash$	$\oslash$

Following Bull and Watson (2004), we would say that disclosure of d is *positive evidence* of state a, and nondisclosure of d is *negative evidence* of state b. Further, we say that person 1 can *positively distinguish* state a from state b. We say this because she has a document in state a that she does not have in b.

6 Becker (1968) modeled a potential criminal as weighing the expected benefits against the expected costs of committing a crime. The expected punishment could be used to deter criminal activity.

If we wish to have a different transfer following *a* than following *b*, we need for person 1 to have the incentive to disclose *d* when she possesses it. This requires that person 1's transfer following disclosure of *d* be higher than her transfer following nondisclosure of *d*. So this implies that person 1 must receive a higher transfer following *a* than she does following *b*. Note that this implies constraints on the transfers or court action that go beyond just the "partition" or those outcomes that evidence can distinguish between. If person 1 must undertake more effort so that *b* is realized, there is not a contract that can induce *b*.

Now suppose instead that both parties have the following similar evidence. In state *a* person 1 possesses document d_1 and person 2 possesses d_2, and in state *b* person 1 possesses document d_1' and person 2 possesses document d_2'. This is represented like this:

State	1's evidence	2's evidence
a	d_1	d_2
b	d_1'	d_2'

Here, Bull and Watson (2004) say that each person (1 and 2) can *fully distinguish a* from *b* since each has a document in state *a* that they do not have in *b*, and vice versa.

In this case, there are not the kinds of restrictions discussed in the previous example. To see this, suppose we wish to have a transfer that favors one of the parties in state *a* relative to that in state *b*. As the transfer must be balanced, if it favors person 1 in state *a*, person 1 will disclose the document she possesses d_1 and in state *b* person 2 will disclose the document he possesses d_2'. A similar logic applies if the transfer favors person 2 in state *a*. Here we also see that verifiability depends on the existence and nonexistence of documents.

Since it nicely summarizes this point, I'll briefly describe the setup and main result, in a two-party version, from Bull and Watson (2004). They assume complete information between the parties to the contract implying that each party knows the state. The timing is the following:

1. The parties contract – specify an externally enforced contract that specifies the transfer as a function of evidence disclosed.
2. The parties take their productive actions, which determines the state.
3. The parties simultaneously and independently make evidence disclosure decisions.
4. The court imposes a transfer, given the evidence that is disclosed.

A "transfer function" describes the transfer between the parties as a function of the state (not the evidence disclosed). If the parties can work out what incentives they need in primary activity, they would then like to be able to assess whether those incentives can be induced given the evidence environment. Theorem 1 in Bull and Watson (2004) provides guidance on this. It states that a transfer function is implementable if and only if, for all possible states *a* and *b*, the transfer to person 1 in *a* specified by the transfer function is strictly greater than the transfer to person 1 in *b* specified by the transfer function implies to that person 1 can positively distinguish *a* from *b*, or that person 2 can positively distinguish *b* from *a*, or both.[7] Returning to the first example in which only person 1 potentially has a document following *a*, the result implies that we could not incentivize person 1 to exert effort to induce *b*.

[7] They also provide a version of this result for $n > 2$ players when an impervious to side contracting condition holds.

This result relies on the court's action being transfers that are specified by the court. Being able to specify the transfers as a function of evidence fits with the mechanism design approach, and can be viewed as liquidated damages. In reality, the legal system imposes some constraints on this – both in terms of evidentiary rules and for the application of the legal rules to the facts of the case. However, I suggest that the ideas concerning the roles of positive and negative evidence and incentives in disclosure fit in a more realistic setting. For example, in *State* v. *Simons* the court based its decision on negative evidence. In that case, Simons was accused of selling spirits without a license. Simons' failure to present a license, although the state provided no evidence of a lack of the license, was held to be sufficient to conclude that Simons possessed no license.

Considering models that do not assume the ability of the parties to commit to transfers as a function of documents *ex ante* also allows us to see the importance of incentives in disclosure. It is common to model the fact-finder or jury as updating its belief about the true state when we do not allow for the *ex ante* commitment to how evidence will lead to court action. Typically, it's assumed that the fact-finder wishes to choose the most appropriate action, given its updated beliefs, that is, that the fact-finder behaves in line with society's interest. Economists typically use Bayesian updating.[8]

Let's now focus on statistical evidence. Focusing on just one party to a contract, that person may have unverifiable private information in addition to potentially having evidence. This private information corresponds to a person's *type*. At one extreme, this could be knowing the true state, which typically will not be the case as, although someone may know her own actions, she may not know the legal standard or the actions of others. It's also possible that the private information is not fully informative but provides some information. This private information is considered unverifiable because there is no hard evidence that allows it to be conveyed. The basic idea is that someone may not be able to prove everything she knows. A person's private information can influence her choice of whether to disclose a document that she possesses. Bull and Watson (2019) study the potential for evidence to be misleading in a single-litigant setting where the litigant has private information. The discussion here follows from that and focuses on their case where the litigant potentially possesses a single document.[9] This scope for evidence to be misleading can occur in other situations as well.

One way to view the different types, in a contractual setting, is that people may have different propensities to perform according to the contract. This litigant's behavior and, perhaps, some exogenous random forces lead to an outcome of preliminary activity, which can include whether breach occurred, relevant evidence, and whether the case goes to trial. It's possible that the litigant is at trial and did not breach the contract, and it's also possible that she did breach the contract. The two types of litigant are different people in society and their personal backgrounds, to the extent not observable to the court, are represented by their types.

Since the litigant has private information, her disclosure decision has two channels of information. The first is a *face-value signal* based only on the statistical properties of the evidence (and not on the disclosure behavior of the litigant). The second is a signal of the litigant's private information since her disclosure decision is a function of her private

8 There is a large literature on Bayesian decision-makers, divided between two main approaches. One approach treats evidence as statistical in nature but assumes that it exogenously makes its way to the court, so it does not address individual incentives in the disclosure of evidence. The other approach models individuals' evidence-disclosure decisions but assumes that the evidence can provide definitive proof of a subset of states. Shin (1994) is a classic example of this.

9 The multiple document case gets quite complicated and the main point can be made in a relatively simple model.

information. As members of a jury do not regularly engage in fact-finding activity, the jury may not correctly anticipate the litigant's behavior as a function of her private information (the litigant's strategy in game-theoretic terms).[10] This means that, in some cases, the jury may misinterpret the disclosure or nondisclosure of the document, and update its belief in the wrong way. There is scope for this happening when the litigant's private information is informative relative to the hard evidence. However, when the hard evidence is strong relative to the litigant's private information, there is no scope for evidence to be misleading. These ideas are important for contracting parties to consider as they suggest limitations on the incentives that a contract can provide that go beyond just positive and negative evidence.

To get some intuition about the result, let's consider a criminal litigation example from the Bull and Watson (2019) paper. It has a defendant who is accused of robbing a store at 10 p.m. on a particular night. The hard evidence in question is a video recording of him on a security camera at a sports stadium across town that is time-stamped as 9:20 p.m. on the same night. Suppose that traffic was such that the accused could have left the stadium by 9:25 p.m. and sped across town to have arrived at the store by 10 p.m. Perhaps the defendant being on the security camera video is more likely when he is innocent. This would suggest that the face-value signal implies the jury should update so as to put more weight on the defendant being innocent. If this face-value signal is strong relative to any private information the defendant might have, when the recording is disclosed, the jury should always update so as to put more weight on the defendant being innocent, and, thus, the defendant will always disclose the recording when he has it.

However, imagine a scenario in which a sophisticated criminal goes to the sports stadium and makes sure to get on the security camera before robbing the store. If the jury thinks this type of criminal would disclose the recording and the innocent type would not, it will update so as to put less weight on the defendant being innocent when the recording is disclosed. If the jury does this, but the innocent defendant always discloses the recording and the guilty one never does, the jury updates in exactly the opposite direction from that which the behavior of the defendant suggests.

This idea suggests that in contract situations, the parties should think carefully about the scope for misleading evidence should a dispute arise. Let's return to two of the practical examples from Section 26.2. Consider the example of a university faculty member who is accused of not performing adequate service for his department. If the document provided by the university is an email in which the faculty member declined to serve as chair of a particular committee, there may be multiple interpretations of this. It may be that the faculty member declined because the role was not a good fit for him, perhaps because he has had some conflict with others who are on the committee, and he is engaged in other ways. However, it may be that the faculty member is just unengaged in service to his department. The jury, should it get to that, might think that the university is presenting this as evidence because it doesn't have a very strong case. However, it could also be that the faculty member is unengaged, but this is the only hard evidence that the university has. So, this could be interpreted in two different directions. It's worth noting that this document by itself isn't that strong a piece of evidence.[11] As noted in Section 26.2, this may be a reason for a university to

[10] As such, the coordination of beliefs and strategies needed for equilibrium is not likely to be attained. So Bull and Watson (2019) use the solution concept of rationalizability; see their paper for the formal details.

[11] It's also worth noting that, fortunately, most faculty members understand the importance of service to the institution.

specify some easy-to-prove things, the failure of which is strongly correlated with a lack of service, as required for service.

Returning to the Van Halen brown M&Ms example, suppose that such a clause was not in the contract, and during a concert there was a significantly disruptive lighting malfunction. Further suppose that the dispute over this went to litigation. Assuming that the malfunction did not cause injury, it's likely that the setup would be torn down to move to the next show and that the venue would also prepare for its next act, rendering testing of the electrical system made available for the lighting for Van Halen's show unfeasible. Per Mr. Roth's statements, the band's rider contained very specific details about the amperage of outlets available. One sort of hard evidence that might be available would be an expert's testimony about whether failure to follow the specifications in the rider was likely to have caused the malfunction. This sort of testimony would likely also contain a lot of technical details about the lighting requirements. There's the possibility for the jury to misinterpret this. Potentially, the jury could think that when it's likely that the issue was caused by the band's lighting equipment, instead of the venue not being properly prepared, the band would present such hard evidence. The presence of brown M&Ms would strengthen the likelihood that the promoter didn't read the rider, and hence the venue wasn't properly prepared. Bull and Watson (2019) also study the requirement for multiple documents to be disclosed together so as to avoid the jury being misled by evidence with a weak face-value. This example fits. In addition to protecting the band and its people from potential safety issues and providing scope to fix problems before the concert, it may also have helped with potential litigation issues.

Much of the economics literature that models a cost of evidence focuses on the costly search for evidence once the dispute proceeds to litigation. I would suggest, instead, that a focus on primary activity that makes it more likely that hard evidence is available may be more useful for practitioners.[12] Additionally, there is scope for catching some issues that arise and having them corrected while there is still scope for joint gains being realized. This would fit with the building contracts and Van Halen examples.

There is quite a bit of work on sequential disclosure. See, for example, Bull and Watson (2007), Deneckere and Severinov (2008), and Lipman and Seppi (1995). Additionally, there has been recent work on cross-examination by Fluet and Lanzi (2018).[13]

26.4 EMPIRICAL WORK

It's natural to wonder what empirical research there is in this direction or what empirical work could be done. A challenge in this direction of research is that, typically, there are no data available that allow us to know whether someone has breached a contract (or, similarly, is guilty in a criminal setting). This poses a challenge. As a researcher who has focused on game-theoretic models of these issues, I will suggest that this limitation makes theoretical study quite important. However, as one who advocates updating beliefs based on hard evidence, I would like to do some empirical work in this direction. Experimental studies, where subjects are presented with situations and incentives are created, are likely to provide some important insights and some scope for testing some of the theoretical findings. My own research agenda includes some of these studies with coauthors. Certainly, the legal psychology literature has made good use of studies in this direction.

12 My research plans include this sort of analysis. Some of my previous work has considered scope for the suppression of evidence and also a moderate cost of disclosure. See Bull (2008a), Bull (2008b) and Bull (2009).

13 Fluet and Lanzi's (2018) model has scope for two channels of information.

One potential source of data is contracts that must be filed and are publicly available. While these will generally not provide information about any disputes arising from them, they may provide insights about how the parties structure their contracts. Several papers have made use of contracts filed with the Securities and Exchange Commission (SEC) as part of the filings required for publicly traded companies. These obtain contracts from the SEC's Electronic Data Gathering, Analysis, and Retrieval (EDGAR) system. Then an application can be used to count or analyze keywords in the contract, and the data can be used in regression analysis. See Schwartz and Watson (2013) and Moszoro et al. (2016).

REFERENCES

Becker, Gary. 1968. "Crime and Punishment: An Economic Approach." *Journal of Political Economy* 76: 169–217.

Bernheim, B. Douglas, and Michael Whinston. 1999. "Incomplete Contracts and Strategic Ambiguity." *American Economic Review* 88: 902–32.

Bolton, Patrick, and Mathias Dewatripont. 2005. *Contract Theory*. Cambridge, MA: MIT Press.

Bull, Jesse. 2008a. "Mechanism Design with Moderate Evidence Cost." *B.E. Journal of Theoretical Economics* 8(1): article 15.

2008b. "Costly Evidence Production and the Limits of Verifiability." *B.E. Journal of Theoretical Economics* 8(1): article 18.

2009. "Costly Evidence and Systems of Fact-Finding." *Bulletin of Economic Research* 61: 103–25.

Bull, Jesse, and Joel Watson. 2004. "Evidence Disclosure and Verifiability." *Journal of Economic Theory* 118: 1–31.

2007. "Hard Evidence and Mechanism Design." *Games and Economic Behavior* 58: 75–93.

2019. "Statistical Evidence and the Problem of Robust Litigation." *RAND Journal of Economics* 50(4): 974–1003.

Cater, Bruce, Byron Lew, and Marcus Pivato. 2009. "Why Tenure?" Working paper.

Chakravarty, Surajeet, and W. Bentley MacLeod. 2009. "Contracting in the Shadow of the Law." *RAND Journal of Economics* 40(3): 533–57.

Deneckere, Raymond, and Sergei Severinov. 2008. "Mechanism Design with Partial State Verifiability." *Games and Economic Behavior* 64: 487–513.

Fluet, Claude, and Thomas Lanzi. 2018. "Adversarial Persuasion with Cross-Examination." Working paper.

Hart, Oliver. 1995. *Firms, Contracts, and Financial Structure*. Oxford. Oxford University Press.

Holmstrom, Bengt. 1982. "Moral Hazard in Teams." *Bell Journal of Economics* 13(2): 324–40.

Laffont, Jean-Jacques, and David Martimort. 2009. *The Theory of Incentives: The Principal-Agent Model*. Princeton, NJ: Princeton University Press.

Legros, Patrick, and Steven Matthews. 1993. "Efficient and Nearly-Efficient Partnerships." *Review of Economic Studies* 68: 599–611.

Lipman, Barton, and Duane Seppi. 1995. "Robust Inference in Communication Games with Partial Provability." *Journal of Economic Theory* 66: 370–405.

Mikkelson, David. 2001. "Did Van Halen's Concert Contract Require the Removal of Brown M&Ms?" *Snopes*, www.snopes.com/fact-check/brown-out/.

Miller, Nolan. 1997. "Efficiency in Partnerships with Joint Monitoring." *Journal of Economic Theory* 77: 285–99.

Moszoro, Marian, Pablo T. Spiller, and Sebastian Stolorz. 2016. "Rigidity of Public Contracts." *Journal of Empirical Legal Studies* 13(3): 396–427.

Roth, David Lee. 2012. "Brown M&Ms." Vimeo, https://vimeo.com/36615187.

Schwartz, Alan, and Joel Watson. 2013. "Conceptualizing Contractual Interpretation." *Journal of Legal Studies* 42: 1–34.

Shin, Hyun Song. 1994. "The Burden of Proof in a Game of Persuasion." *Journal of Economic Theory* 64: 253–64.

Zeveloff, Julie. 2016, "There's a Brilliant Reason Why Van Halen Asked for a Bowl of M&Ms with All the Brown Candies Removed before Every Show." Business Insider, September 7.

PART IV

Legitimacy and Social Norms

27

Procedural Justice and Legal Compliance

Daniel S. Nagin and Cody W. Telep

Abstract: This chapter reviews the evidence on whether procedurally just treatment of citizens by agents of the criminal justice system (CJS), usually the police, has the effect of increasing the citizen's compliance with the law. There are many operational definitions of procedurally just treatment, but all share the common characteristics of CJS agents treating citizens with respect and affording them the opportunity to explain themselves. In brief, we find that perceptions-based studies consistently show that citizen perceptions of procedurally just treatment are closely tied to perceptions of legitimacy of the police, and that, with only a few exceptions, perceptions of legitimacy are strongly associated with legal compliance. Perceptions, however, cannot be directly manipulated. What can be manipulated are policies designed to improve procedurally just treatment of citizens. What has not yet been established is the necessary requirement for such policies to be effective in improving compliance, namely that policy changes are effective in changing procedurally just treatment of citizens by police and other CJS agents and that such changes are effective in triggering the causal chain underlying the theory of procedural justice: improvements in actual treatment lead to improved perceptions of procedurally just treatment, which in turn leads to improved perceptions of legitimacy, which in turn increases legal compliance. In light of this conclusion, policy implications and suggestions for future research are discussed.

27.1 INTRODUCTION

The landmark work of Tom Tyler and colleagues (Tyler 1988, 1990, 2003, 2006; Tyler and Huo 2002) on procedural justice (PJ) has received prominent attention in wide-ranging literature related to the willingness of individuals to comply with organizational rules and procedures, regulations, and criminal laws. There are many operational definitions of procedurally just treatment (see Lind and Tyler 1988), but all share the common characteristics of authority figures treating subordinates to their authority with respect and affording them the opportunity to explain themselves. Tyler and colleagues argue that procedurally just treatment has the effect of increasing subordinate's compliance with the behavioral prescriptions the authority figure is seeking to enforce.

This chapter reviews the evidence on whether procedurally just treatment of citizens by agents of the criminal justice system (CJS), usually the police, has the effect of increasing the citizen's compliance with the criminal law. The foundational premise of Tyler's (1990:4) seminal book *Why People Obey the Law? Procedural Justice, Legitimacy and Compliance* is:

"[I]f [citizens] regard legal authorities as more legitimate, they are less likely to break any laws, for they believe that they ought to follow them, regardless of potential for punishment."

This premise is echoed in the report of the President's Task Force on 21st Century Policing (2015:5): "People are more likely to obey the law when they believe those who are enforcing it have the right – the legitimate authority – to tell them what to do." The report goes on to state: "Research demonstrates that [the] principles [of procedural justice] lead to relationships in which the community trusts that officers are honest, unbiased, benevolent, and lawful. *The community therefore feels obligated to follow the law . . .*" (emphasis added, 10).

This chapter is organized as follows: We first summarize evidence on the theory of PJ. Here we synthesize the findings of an earlier review (Nagin and Telep, 2017) with a large body of research that has appeared since then. Our updated review of available evidence shows that there is still doubt about the full causal chain between procedurally just treatment and legal compliance. We do, however, note greater optimism about the impacts of interventions on actual officer behavior. We close with a discussion of policy implications and suggestions for future research.

27.2 REVIEW AND UPDATE OF THE EVIDENCE

Figure 27.1 is a schematic representation of Tyler's (1990) theory of PJ as we understand it. The causal chain begins with agents of the CJS acting in a trustworthy and neutral manner, treating citizens with dignity and respect, and providing citizens the opportunity to explain their actions (voice). The other three stages in the causal sequence pertain to the citizens who were the subject of the agent's attention. The theory assumes that if citizens are treated in procedurally just ways, they will recognize their fair treatment. Such perceptions in turn increase the citizen's perceptions of the legitimacy of CJS agents, which in turn increases compliance with the law.

In this section we review the research evidence for each stage of this causal chain. We build upon our prior review (Nagin and Telep 2017) with new evidence that has appeared since its publication.

27.2.1 *The Linkage between Actual and Perceived Treatment*

The first arrow in Figure 27.1 predicts that procedurally just treatment by police will translate into improved citizen perceptions of fair treatment. This is the key first step in the causal chain, because the theory depends upon perceptions of fair treatment being grounded in the fairness of actual treatment. There is surprisingly little work examining this relationship. This is partly because of the difficulty of assembling both survey data on

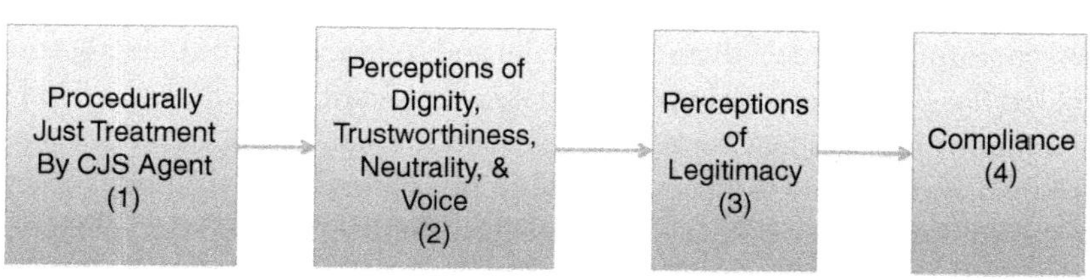

FIGURE 27.1 A schematic of the theory of procedural justice

citizen perceptions of interactions with police and independent assessment of actual treatment received.

Worden and McLean (2017) completed the only study we know of where citizen perceptions of PJ from surveys can be compared to independent assessments of police behavior from researcher coding of in-car camera footage. Trained observers coded 539 police–citizen interactions in Schenectady, NY for indicators of officers acting in both a procedurally just and a procedurally unjust (e.g., not considering the citizen's views, interrupting the citizen, insulting the citizen) fashion. They found that objective and subjective measures of PJ were only weakly correlated (.16) and the degree of PJ received accounted for a small amount of the variability in citizen assessments of the encounter. Citizens tended to overestimate the degree of PJ they received, but were, however, more sensitive to negative treatment. Procedural injustice was more highly negatively correlated with citizen perceptions of PJ (-.31). Worden and McLean (2017:148) conclude: "Police can detract somewhat from the subjective experience of citizens through procedural injustice, but they do not add substantially to subjective experience through procedural justice" (see Skogan 2006 for a similar finding). While this is just one study, the poor correlation between actual and perceived treatment could reflect the fact that citizen views are likely based on an accumulation of interactions and vicarious interactions (Augustyn 2016; Pickett et al. 2018; Rosenbaum et al. 2005) in addition to a plethora of historical, community, and family influences, which may limit the impact of any particular encounter.

27.2.2 *The Linkage of Perceptions of Procedurally Just Treatment to Legitimacy*

There is a far larger evidence base assessing the relationship between citizen perceptions of PJ and their perceptions of legitimacy (the relationship between boxes 2 and 3). These studies are generally based on surveys of individuals about overall police fairness or the fairness of recent police interactions. These studies typically create a PJ scale. Less work has considered the individual contributions of dignity, trustworthiness, neutrality, and voice to legitimacy perceptions, because the components tend to be highly correlated in responses.

Several recent studies find a link between perceptions about general PJ and police legitimacy (e.g., Hinds 2007; Jonathan-Zamir and Weisburd 2013; Reisig and Lloyd 2009). Wolfe et al. (2016), for example, found a strong association between perceived PJ and perceived legitimacy. There was also no evidence that this relationship varied based on demographic or neighborhood factors, providing evidence for the invariance of the PJ–legitimacy relationship. This relationship even seems to hold among offender or delinquent populations (Piquero et al. 2005; White et al. 2016).

A smaller number of studies have examined the link between PJ and legitimacy based on particular encounters. Gau (2014), for example, examined citizens' overall perceptions of PJ and views of specific police interactions, finding that both mattered but that global PJ impacted trust more than particular encounters. Similar results have been found in recent survey experiments. Maguire et al. (2017), for example, found that students watching a clip of an officer behaving with PJ were more likely to report trust in the officer and an obligation to obey, while those watching a clip with procedural injustice reported the opposite. Impacts on more global views about the police were less consistent (see Johnson et al. 2017).

27.2.3 *The Linkage of Perceived Legitimacy to Legal Compliance*

There is also a large body of survey-based work supportive of the relationship between boxes 3 and 4. Perceptions of police legitimacy are correlated with greater compliance with the law, at least based on self-reported behavior (e.g., Fagan and Tyler 2005; Reisig et al. 2007; Jackson et al. 2012). Tyler's (1990) initial test of the theory, using a two-wave survey of Chicagoans, showed a positive relationship between legitimacy and legal compliance, even when controlling for a variety of factors (i.e., peer disapproval, personal morality, demographics). Tyler and Huo (2002) and Sunshine and Tyler (2003) reached similar conclusions in studies in Oakland, Los Angeles, and New York. There is somewhat less consensus here than in the work linking boxes 2 and 3, with some recent studies raising questions about the model and in particular whether legitimacy perceptions impact offending (see Augustyn 2015; Kaiser and Reisig 2019; Slocum et al. 2016).

A meta-analysis by Walters and Bolger (2019) examined correlations between PJ, legitimacy, and compliance from sixty-four studies. They found significant associations between procedural justice and legitimacy and legitimacy and compliance, and a weaker direct relationship between PJ and compliance. While this is promising evidence for the model, the authors also note the overall heterogeneity in effect sizes across studies and the relatively small number of studies (five) that assessed all three components using longitudinal data.

27.2.4 *Other Linkages*

There is also a small body of research using observers of police–citizen encounters to examine the link between boxes 1 and 4, or at least on-scene compliance behavior. These third-party observer studies use trained observers conducting ride-alongs with officers to carefully document police–citizen interactions. While they can code police behavior and assess how citizens respond on the scene, these studies cannot measure citizen attitudes about police fairness or legitimacy and thus generally do not account for boxes 2 and 3.

Findings here are somewhat mixed. In observations in Richmond, Virginia, Mastrofski et al. (1996) found that police disrespect significantly decreased compliance, but police making an effort to show respect had no significant effect. McCluskey et al. (1999) analyzed encounters in two cities, also finding less compliance when officers showed disrespect. Efforts by officers to show respect did significantly increase compliance. Dai et al. (2011) found that officers giving citizens a voice in encounters in Cincinnati significantly reduced noncompliance, but providing assistance, showing disrespect, and force were unrelated to compliance.

Jonathan-Zamir et al. (2015) attempt to examine the link between PJ and legitimacy in an observer study. They found that PJ and citizen satisfaction were correlated but that citizens only overtly indicated their satisfaction with the officer in half of encounters. They also found a low correlation between each element of PJ. Officers were not necessarily displaying all components of PJ simultaneously. This raises concerns about the validity of citizen subjective assessments of PJ, which generally show high correlations between elements. These findings suggest that those views may not match "objective" reality (see Worden and McLean 2017).

27.2.5 *Interventions to Improve Procedural Justice*

In recent years, a growing, but still fairly small body of work has examined different approaches to impact box 1. These studies use training, scripts, or policy change to try to impact officer PJ, with the hope that more PJ will lead to benefits in legitimacy and compliance. We review these studies in this section.

We identified ten sets of quasi-experimental or experimental studies of the effectiveness of PJ training. Quasi-experimental pre-post studies in Chicago (Skogan et al. 2015) and Louisville (Schaefer and Hughes 2016) suggest one-day trainings can improve officer attitudes about using PJ. Studies examining the impact of lengthier PJ training in Chicago (Rosenbaum and Lawrence 2017) and Scotland (Robertson et al. 2014) show mixed effects on officer attitudes and performance in scenarios.

More recently, a multifaceted evaluation of the National Initiative for Building Community Trust and Justice showed impacts of training on officer attitudes, but more mixed results for other outcomes (La Vigne et al. 2019). The six-city study included two days of training on PJ and legitimacy and one on implicit bias. Officer attitudes toward PJ improved post-training. There was no direct assessment of officer behavior, but, across the sites, there were mixed results in terms of impacts on crime. Resident survey data also showed variability across sites in post-initiative police legitimacy, but did offer some indication of improvements in trust in police among minority residents of high-crime communities.

Wolfe et al. (2020) report on findings from a two-department evaluation of T3 (Tact, Tactics, and Trust) training. The program is focused more broadly on deescalation, but emphasizes the value of PJ in interactions. The training was associated with officers placing more priority on PJ and less on physical control in hypothetical citizen encounters. Wolfe and colleagues (2020) emphasize the value of a "deliberate practice framework," where officers can repeatedly practice a task and get immediate feedback. This stands in contrast to most PJ training programs, which are short in duration and provide limited opportunities to practice.

Wood et al. (2020) used the random and longitudinal nature of the rollout of Chicago's one-day training to the entire agency to examine impacts on officer activity in the field. They found that the training was associated with reductions in police complaints, use of force, and settlement agreements (used as a proxy for misconduct).

None of these studies directly examined officer behavior in the field. Four recent randomized trials do so. In England, Wheller et al. (2013) found mixed effects of PJ training on officer attitudes, more positive effects on behavior in scenarios, and inconsistent impacts on officer fairness in the field. In Seattle, Owens et al. (2018) found that supervisors focusing on PJ in individual officer meetings was associated with these officers being less likely to make arrests and use force.

Antrobus et al. (2019) tested the impact of a day and a half PJ training integrated into academy training in Queensland. Field training officers rated the level of PJ used by new officers during citizen interactions. The twenty-eight treatment officers had overall higher ratings on PJ in the field, particularly in suspect interactions. Impacts on officer attitudes were less consistent, but treatment group officers were more likely to view procedural justice as effective.

An ongoing study on PJ in hot spots policing uses systematic observation to assess impacts of a forty-hour training. In the initial project site, trained officers were more likely to be active listeners, show neutrality, and be respectful in citizen encounters. There was less impact on officers showing care and concern. Results were similar in the second project site, although trained officers here also demonstrated more care and concern. These results are based on observations in just the first two of four experimental sites (Telep et al. in progress).

While these later studies provide some promising evidence for the impact of training on behavior, there is no strong evidence on the appropriate content, dosage, or method of delivery for PJ training. Additionally, much of this work focuses on small-scale studies and less is known about the long-term impacts of such programs and the extent to which such training is reinforced by supervisors.

Four randomized field experiments involving traffic stops and airport screening test the linkage between PJ policy and perceptions of legitimacy (see Bennett et al. 2019). We review these studies in more detail in Nagin and Telep (2017), but provide brief summaries here and note that we are aware of multiple in-progress trials that will add to the limited policy study evidence base. We note that these are all studies of infusing PJ into more routine police contacts. While we recognize the high potential danger of traffic stops, these interventions all cover areas where citizens are generally compliant.

The first of these, the Queensland Community Engagement Trial (QCET), involved an experimental condition where officers used a script that explicitly incorporated PJ in road-blocks administering a random breathalyzer test for drunk driving. Mazerolle et al. (2012) found that drivers receiving the experimental treatment reported higher levels of perceived PJ. Mazerolle et al. (2013) found that the PJ script also impacted more general views of how procedurally fair the police are.

Langley (2014) adapted the QCET protocol to the airport security setting. Passengers were randomly assigned to receive a PJ-based checklist or an experienced utility treatment that involved providing incentives to passengers. While those receiving the PJ treatment were more likely to report that the officer listened to them, they did not report higher overall levels of PJ. Sahin et al. (2017) adapted the QCET protocol for stops for speeding in Adana, Turkey. Drivers in the PJ treatment group reported higher levels of perceived PJ, trust, and satisfaction. The experimental group drivers did not, however, report higher levels of overall PJ in the police.

The closest replication of QCET was conducted by MacQueen and Bradford (2015) in Scotland. The main difference was that officers did not use scripts but instead were given a series of key messages to deliver to the driver, which offered greater flexibility. Results offered no support for the efficacy of the flexible PJ script. If anything, the intervention had backfire effects on citizen perceptions of police legitimacy.

MacQueen and Bradford's (2017) autopsy of the trial failures provides key insight into why the experiment's findings were almost directly the opposite of those from QCET. Based on group interviews with fifty-five officers involved in project implementation, MacQueen and Bradford (2017) identify a series of issues, including poor communication from management about the project and lack of officer buy-in, which threatened consistent implementation. Officers resisted using the messages because of concerns that they made them look inept to the public. Additionally, officers felt as though the project was sprung on them by management and was not grounded in their experience. This lack of organizational justice (Trinkner et al. 2016), in conjunction with overall poor communication of the process, led to weak implementation and even the resentment of project officers.

This autopsy illustrates a larger point that field trials focused on procedural justice are complex and challenging. PJ is not a well-defined treatment such as an inoculation. Instead, its effectiveness will depend on how it is used by individual officers and also how its use is monitored by their superiors. These complexities make it difficult to parse out how much the results of this and other replications of QCET are driven by application of the principles of PJ versus implementation issues (see also Antrobus, Alpert and Rojek n.d.).

We know of no study that provides a direct test of whether PJ on its own can affect legal compliance. But we discuss here studies that provide an indirect test relying on some mechanism to infuse PJ into policy other than training. These studies are important because of their focus on how PJ is administered in the field, but they are also limited either because PJ was not part of the manipulated treatment or because it is just one part of a multifaceted intervention. This makes it challenging to disentangle the impact of infusing treatment with PJ from other substantive elements of the intervention that are also focused on compliance as an outcome (e.g., deterrence).

We focus on studies of four general types: PJ in arrests, PJ as part of a meeting or forum for those who have engaged in crime or delinquency, PJ as part of a more general community-oriented meeting or program, and PJ as a by-product of body-worn camera (BWC) implementation. We devote particular attention to recent work on BWCs, which we did not discuss in Nagin and Telep (2017).

Paternoster at al. (1997) coded domestic violence arrest incidents for their level of PJ as perceived by the arrestee. Arrest in general increased recidivism relative to offenders who received only a warning, but high levels of perceived levels of PJ during an arrest negated this criminogenic impact. PJ, however, was not part of the original intervention and thus was not directly manipulated.

Wallace et al. (2016) examined the impact of a Chicago offender meeting program infused with PJ on recidivism. The one-hour forums for parolees were explicitly designed to focus not just on deterrence but also on respect and fairness. The Wallace at al. analysis built on an earlier study by Papachristos, Meares, and Fagan (2007) which concluded that the forums were effective in reducing crime. Wallace et al. found that parolees attending a forum had a longer time out of prison, on average, than nonattendees. Effects for violent crime overall and violent property crime were less consistent.

Wallace et al. (2016) and Papachristos et al. (2007) are both important because they analyze the impact of an actual policy intervention addressing a serious crime problem that was directed at individuals with extensive criminal histories (in contrast to the script studies reviewed earlier). The difficulty of interpretation involves measuring the contribution of PJ to a multipronged intervention involving focused deterrence and access to social service components. Most recently, Trinkner (2019) tried to parse out the impacts of the forums more directly, finding that PJ and legitimacy perceptions were higher among parolees who took a survey after the forums compared to those who took a pre-forum survey. While only a small group of questions assessed these perceptions, this is evidence that a fairly brief interaction can have impacts on perceptions.

More recently, Clark-Moorman et al. (2019) evaluated a similar program in Rockford, IL, where parolees attended forums that delivered a strong deterrent message, alongside a PJ-infused message regarding service provision. The evaluation suggested that crime declined following the start of the forums, but did not focus on individual-level outcomes. Importantly, more than 70 percent of forum participants declined services. This raises questions about whether such combined approaches are more dependent on deterrence or whether any PJ benefits come from how authority figures deliver messages at these meetings.

A recent policy experiment similarly integrated PJ into a meeting format. Mazerolle et al. (2017, 2019) evaluated a truancy reduction program involving schools and police collaborating to deliver a message regarding the importance of school attendance. A facilitator, school personnel, and police worked together to create a dialogue with parents that emphasized creating trust, allowing parents to have voice, and treating parents with respect. Findings suggest that the program led to declines in antisocial behavior for two years following the intervention, as well as criminal offending in the year after the program (Bennett et al. 2018).

This is promising evidence for a link between PJ and compliance, but the experiment includes a small sample (102 youths total) and also included elements of restorative justice and deterrence.

Several recent studies have focused on community policing programs that incorporate PJ into police meetings or engagement strategies. The focus of these studies is the impact of PJ-infused contacts on nonenforcement interactions. While community policing programs generally focus on building trust (Gill et al. 2014), these particular strategies focus on police using PJ in direct meetings or forums with residents. They cannot be defined solely as PJ interventions, since they incorporate other elements, but we review them here because of the emphasis across these programs on how police communicate with the public.

In Brooklyn Park, MN, a focus on police building collective efficacy in crime hotspots through positive communication and PJ led to more collective actions and collaboration but did not impact resident legitimacy perceptions (Weisburd et al. in press). These findings are consistent with those from a mail survey of Portland, OR hotspot residents. A police program focused on community engagement patrols did lead to respondents reporting more positive police contacts, but it did not impact legitimacy perceptions (Kahn et al. 2019). Results from these two US studies are also similar to those from a Liberian experiment testing the impact of confidence patrols (Blair et al. 2019). Police focused on town hall meetings, answering questions and engaging with youth during multiple visits to rural communities. While not a PJ intervention per se, the treatment did focus on treating citizens with respect and giving citizens voice. The patrols were associated with increased knowledge about police and reductions in some types of crime, but did not improve trust in the Liberian National Police.

Conversely, two studies show greater impacts of police engagement on trust, although they do not assess compliance. Fine et al. (2019) found that Team Kids Challenge, a five-week program where police engage with youth in community service projects, positively impacted juvenile views about police. While this is not exclusively a PJ program, it does emphasize participation and respect. In the post-program survey, ten to eleven-year-old respondents from six schools showed improvements in their perceptions of police. In contrast to this lengthier program with repeated police–youth interaction, Peyton et al. (2019) report on the impacts of a single, ten minute police–resident encounter in New Haven, CT. During these unannounced visits to homes, officers emphasized respectful treatment and gave residents voice and an opportunity to provide feedback on the police and problems in the neighborhood. Officers ended the interaction by providing their contact information and cell phone number. Survey results showed that visited residents had significantly more positive perceptions of police legitimacy and were more willing to cooperate with police both three and twenty-one days after the interaction.

These PJ in community policing studies show varying results, which suggests the need for further research. The issue could be partly methodological; the Peyton et al. (2019) study, for example, was designed to ensure that the respondent had recent police contact, while surveys of hotspot residents by Weisburd et al. (in press) and Kahn et al. (2019) may not have reached the individuals who had been most engaged in the program. The salience of the interaction could also be relevant. Perhaps an unexpected home visit by an officer was so memorable that it had greater impacts than repeated contacts with police in the context of a long-term hotspots project.

It could also be that some police activities were more likely to be seen as reconciliatory gestures designed to repair past harm, which O'Brien et al. (2020) argue can be impactful in building trust. Peyton et al. (2019) do find that racial minorities and those with lower trust in police at baseline were most impacted by the intervention. This is consistent with work by Murphy et al. (2019), who argue that those who feel most excluded from society (in their study, the focus was on Muslim Australians) react most positively to being treated fairly by police.

27.2.6 *Body-Worn Cameras and Procedural Justice*

Finally, we discuss the potential for BWCs to serve as an important accountability mechanism for increasing PJ. BWCs also have the potential to enhance monitoring of officer compliance with training or other policies regarding the use of PJ (see Mell 2016). BWCs, however, will likely only be effective in this regard if they are regularly used as an accountability tool by supervisors. Body cameras and research assessing them have diffused rapidly across American policing. A recent review by Lum et al. (2019) found seventy empirical studies examining a host of questions about effects. We did not discuss BWCs in Nagin and Telep (2017), but a small number of recent studies have examined the relationship between BWCs and citizen perceptions of the police.

Demir et al. (2020) assess the impact of BWCs on citizen perceptions of PJ and legitimacy in a quasi-experiment in Turkey. Using 624 surveys of drivers who had just been in a traffic stop, they find that citizens who interacted with an officer wearing a BWC viewed those interactions as being more procedurally just, which was also associated with enhanced views about legitimacy. This was the case, even though officers did not receive any special training on PJ.

White et al. (2017) saw similar effects in Spokane, with body camera awareness associated with increased perceptions of PJ. But just 28 percent of their respondents accurately recalled the presence of a BWC. Thus, it remains unclear whether any positive effects of BWCs require citizens to recognize that the interaction is being filmed. Ariel et al. (2020) also report similar findings in a trial in Uruguay, where respondents who interacted with an officer with a BWC perceived more PJ from the officer, particularly when it came to participation (Ariel et al. 2020). Unlike most US BWC studies, this intervention used cameras with a front-facing screen, so that members of the public could see a live feed of what the camera captured, and thus were more likely to be aware of its presence.

McCluskey et al. (2019) provide an important addition to this literature with one of the first systematic social observation studies to examine police PJ in conjunction with a "treatment." In this case, they observed 555 police–citizen interactions in Los Angeles through ride-alongs that occurred before and after the adoption of BWCs in two districts. They found a direct relationship between BWC adoption and increased PJ; officers were coded as using elements of PJ more frequently in observations conducted after BWC adoption. This occurred without any training or explicit emphasis on officers using more PJ. It could be that BWCs on their own help build trust. It could also be that officers wearing a camera are more likely to engage in procedurally just actions, because they are aware that they are being filmed.

These findings overall suggest some promise for policy efforts to enhance PJ, but work in this area remains limited, particularly in respect of full tests of the PJ–compliance model. We know little about how officers make decisions to use PJ in the field. This is in part because officers have a great deal of discretion in their interactions with citizens, and, as Mastrofski et al. (2016:121) note, "police organizations do little to learn when officers produce higher levels of PJ, much less reward it. Consequently, one might expect that the prediction of PJ levels would be sensitive to influences other than the law and policies."

Thus, more work is needed to understand how training or other policies can be effectively monitored and reinforced to have long-term impacts on behavior. As Worden and McLean (2018:151) argue, the "procedural justice model is long on the forms that procedurally just policing takes at the street level, but rather short on the managerial steps that police departments should take to implement the model." And, as our review makes clear, increases in PJ in the field may still go unnoticed by citizens.

27.3 SUMMARY AND INTERPRETATION OF THE EVIDENCE

So, what is the bottom line of our review of the evidence on PJ? Concerning the linkage between PJ and legal compliance, our conclusion is that no study has credibly established a causal linkage between procedurally just treatment and legal compliance, but with the more optimistic qualification that the rapid growth in the literature offers some encouraging evidence on the effectiveness of PJ training in affecting officers' attitudes and the effectiveness of some community policing programs infused with elements of PJ in improving citizen perceptions of police. Research on BWCs also provides indirect support that respectful police–citizen interactions have salutary impacts.

Some, including Tyler (2017), have interpreted the conclusion of our earlier review as a methodological critique, namely, suggesting that there is no experimental evidence demonstrating a causal linkage. That was not our point. Rather, our conclusion is grounded in fundamental substantive issues, as depicted in Figure 27.2 (see Thacher 2019). Figure 27.2 is a schematic that overlays the schematic in Figure 27.1 of the theory of PJ's two social forces – third common causes and reverse causality – that confound a causal interpretation of the research evidence and also point to major gaps in the theory of PJ as depicted in Figure 27.1. The former is indeed methodological, albeit fundamental, but the latter is substantive and also fundamental.

The problem of reverse causality is most concretely reflected in the third-party observer studies (see also Trinkner et al. 2019). Interpretation of these studies is complicated by deep

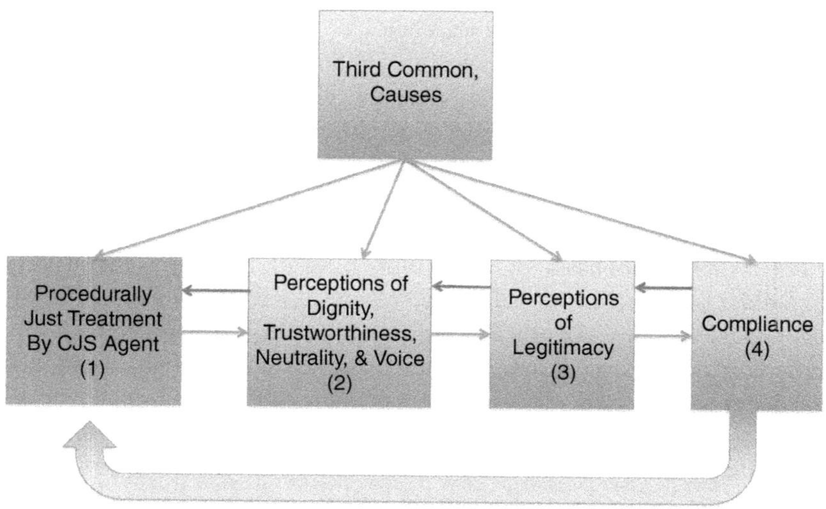

FIGURE 27.2 A schematic of the challenge of making causal inferences about the theory's predictions with observational data

uncertainties about the parsing of cause from effect. Human interactions are bidirectional (Bottoms and Tankebe 2012; Dai et al. 2011; Reisig et al. 2004). Just as the citizen's response to a police officer's order depends on the manner in which the order is made, so, too, does the manner in which the police officer makes the order depend on the actions and demeanor of the citizen (Reiss 1971). Still another explanation for left-pointing arrows is the concept of neutralization that is central to Sykes and Matza's (1957) theory of delinquency. The left-pointing arrows might reflect the post hoc rationalization that legal noncompliance is justified because the legal authorities are not legitimate and do not treat citizens fairly (see Nettler 1974).

More broadly, the problem of reverse causality may play itself out at the community level where police–citizen interactions may be seen as a two-sided game in which the police and citizens are anticipating the behavior of the other party and responding accordingly. The resulting equilibrium, whether involving cooperative or oppositional behavior on each side, is a reminder of the difficulty of inferring causality in bidirectional interactions, even those in which one party has more authority than the other.

Viewed in the form of a bidirectional interaction played out at the level of individuals or at the community level, reverse causality is more than a methodological obstacle; it is reflective of an important gap in theorizing about PJ. While police can and should be held accountable for the form and demeanor of their interactions with citizens, they must also respond to the form and demeanor of the citizen response to them. The theory of PJ is, thus, incomplete without a component on the bidirectional relationship of police–citizen interactions and its impact on the form of procedurally just interactions between police and citizens.

Concerning the third common cause interpretation, one possibility is that persons with higher "stakes in conformity" (Toby 1957) or investments in conventional social bonds as defined by Hirschi (1969) not only are more legally compliant but also perceive fairer treatment by and greater legitimacy of the agents responsible for enforcing legal compliance. After all, these enforcement agents are the officially anointed guardians of the social structure that legally compliant citizens are so invested in.

Another source of third common causes is community, political, and historical context (see Mehozay and Factor 2017; Roché and Roux 2017). An enormous body of historical research, exemplified most recently by Alexander's (2010) *The New Jim Crow* and research on legal cynicism (Kirk and Papachristos 2011; Sampson and Bartusch 1998), documents the enduring negative impact of ill treatment of disadvantaged minorities, particularly African-Americans, by the police and other agents of the CJS on their perceptions of the legitimacy of legal institutions. Community context also matters (see Braga et al. 2014). The residential segregation by race may reinforce, probably powerfully, perceptions of the legitimacy of legal institutions independent of personal experience with the police due to a shared cultural and social narrative about the legitimacy of legal institutions.

Recent survey work by White et al. (2018) exemplifies the enduring quality of perceptions of the police, whether positive or negative. In longitudinal individual-level survey data, they found little change in respondent attitudes about police legitimacy before and after the death of Freddie Gray while being transported by the Baltimore police in 2015. These findings reflect the possibility that even significant single police events may do little to change long-held views about police fairness. These historical and social forces may also explain the lack of correlation between actual treatment and perceived treatment found in Worden and McLean (2017) – deeply held perceptions grounded in history and powerful community forces may overwhelm the actual actions of police officers in specific one-on-one interactions.

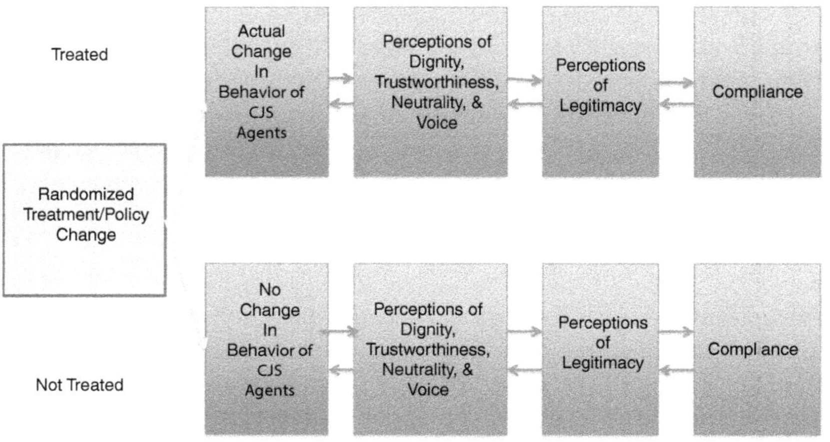

FIGURE 27.3 Identifying the causal impact of procedurally just treatment

The lack of correlation between actual and perceived procedurally just treatment also brings us back to an argument that was foundational to our earlier contention – perceptions of procedurally just treatment and legitimacy cannot be directly altered. What can potentially be manipulated is the way in which agents of the CJS interact with citizens. This point is fundamental for both inferences about causality and conclusions about policy. Figure 27.3 is a revised version of Figure 27.1. It includes two arms, one depicting improved procedurally just treatment and another depicting no change in such treatment. It also bifurcates the first stage of Figure 27.1 with two stages. The first is labeled "Randomized treatment/policy change," referring to a treatment or change in policy designed to improve procedurally just treatment of citizens by CJS actors. The second stage highlights the importance of the effectiveness of stage 1. There is no possibility for the treatment/policy to change citizen perceptions and behavior unless it is successful in actually changing the behavior of CJS agents.

If treatment is successful in altering CJS agent behavior, the stage is set for testing the predictions of the theory in terms of effects on citizen perceptions and behavior. This is done by comparing perceptions of procedurally just treatment, perceptions of legitimacy, and compliance with the law between the treated in the upper arm and the controls in the lower arm of Figure 27.3. The differences measure the causal effects of improved procedurally just treatment. Also included in Figure 27.3 are bidirectional arrows between the second and third, third and fourth, and fourth and fifth stages in both arms. Even if such bidirectionality is present, it would not compromise evidence showing that exogenous manipulation of procedurally just treatment positively affected perceptions of legitimacy and/or compliance. Instead, the bidirectionality of the arrow would imply only that the underlying mechanism of the change is complex.

27.4 POLICY IMPLICATIONS AND CONCLUSIONS

Since the death of Michael Brown at the hand of a Ferguson, MO police officer in 2014, instances of police use of lethal force have triggered mass protests and spawned social movements such as Black Lives Matter, demanding fundamental changes in the way in which the police interact with citizens, particularly in disadvantaged minority communities. The concepts underlying procedurally just treatment of citizens are understandably attractive to those on the frontlines of responding to demands for reform. PJ is grounded on the principle that treating citizens with dignity should be the rule, not the exception, in police interactions with the public. It is ironic, therefore, that the case for PJ has often been framed in terms of crime prevention, not in terms of the quality of police–citizen interaction. Tyler et al. (2015), for example, note that compliance alone has traditionally been the main concern of police and policy leaders. They point to more recent emphases on cooperation and community engagement, which suggest broader roles for PJ, but even these concepts are frequently measured in relation to crime control (e.g., citizen cooperation in identifying criminals or community involvement in crime prevention).

Concerning the crime prevention effectiveness of procedurally just treatment of citizens, our earlier conclusion in Nagin and Telep (2017) remains largely unchanged: there is no credible evidence that procedurally just treatment of citizens increases their compliance with the law. We are not alone in this assessment. The National Academies of Sciences' Committee on Proactive Policing (2017) reached the same conclusion.

Our critical assessment of the evidence on the crime prevention efficacy of procedurally just treatment does not, however, mean that PJ should be relegated to a secondary status in policy discussion about effective policing. On the contrary, procedurally just treatment of citizens has social value independent of its impact on crime. Yet those benefits are still to be demonstrated. The National Academies' report (2017:248) also concluded that "the research base [on procedural justice] is currently insufficient to draw conclusions about whether procedurally just policing causally influences either perceived legitimacy or cooperation." The Committee report, however, went on to conclude that studies of PJ outside of policing suggest that PJ concepts have promise in the policing domain.

In our view, for those potential benefits to be realized, important changes need to be made in how policy analysis is conducted and even more fundamentally in police management. Concerning policy analysis, the scope of the analysis must be broadened to include more than crime prevention benefits. It must also include the social cost of confrontational policing tactics (Manski and Nagin 2017) and the social benefits arising from the many other activities that police regularly perform. Fundamental changes in the management of police organizations must also be made to elevate the status of procedurally just treatment of citizens. Since the appearance of Nagin and Telep (2017) and the National Academies report (2017), which both concluded that evidence is scant that PJ training is effective in changing officer behavior, there have been some encouraging signs of effectiveness. Still, the situation is not much different from 2015 when Skogan et al. (2015:321) observed: "[V]irtually no research of any flavor has been done on procedural justice training, despite this being a necessary precursor to turning the theory into practice." To reverse the dearth of evidence on the effectiveness not only of PJ training but also of training in general, the culture of police executives checking off boxes on training received must shift to their insisting on demonstrations of the effectiveness of that training.

More than training, however, is required. Systems for monitoring and rewarding procedurally just treatment of citizens are required. Nearly fifty years ago, Reiss (1971:220–1) observed: "Continual review of the behavior of all police in all encounters with citizens is an ideal mechanism to insure that officers meet standards of practice." Recent evidence suggesting that BWCs are effective in improving the civility of police–citizen interactions (McCluskey et al. 2019) supports Reiss's recommendation.

When Reiss made this observation, such monitoring was technologically infeasible. That has changed. Modern computerized audio-visual recognition systems now make it possible to use artificial intelligence-based technologies to review feed from BWCs and other monitoring devices to create systems for measuring the quality of police–citizen interactions. What still remains lacking fifty years after Reiss's recommendation for monitoring systems are the management systems for incorporating measurements of the quality of police–citizen interactions into systems of rewards and sanctions, not only of individual officers but also of those responsible for the management of higher organizational aggregates from the police station to the precinct to the entire police organization (Lum and Nagin 2017; Worden and McLean 2017).

It is our view that the role of scientists in the policy process is to provide policymakers with an objective and balanced assessment of the *present* state of scientific knowledge as it relates to the policy dilemma that policymakers are facing, which in the context of this chapter is how to respond to demands for reforms in the way in which police interact with the public. Policymakers must still make decisions even in the face of weak science relevant to those decisions. Those decisions should not, however, be based on mistaken premises about the state of relevant science. If the evidence is weak, policymakers should be told that. The state of current knowledge about the effectiveness of policing based on the concepts of PJ does not preclude its implementation into police practice, but expectations about impact should be realistic. As we have emphasized, the prescription of PJ advocates about the manner in which police should strive to interact with citizens has substantial normative merit. Police executives should, however, be cognizant that the effectiveness of this approach to policing should be closely monitored.

REFERENCES

Alexander, Michelle. 2010. *The New Jim Crow: Mass Incarceration in the Age of Colorblindness*. New York: The New Press.

Antrobus, Emma, Geoff Alpert, and Jeff Rojek. n.d. "Replicating Experiments in Criminology: Lessons Learned from a Replication of the Queensland Community Engagement Trial (QCET)." Unpublished manuscript.

Antrobus, Emma, Ian Thompson, and Barak Ariel. 2019. "Procedural Justice Training for Police Recruits: Results of a Randomized Controlled Trial." *Journal of Experimental Criminology* 15:29–53.

Ariel, Barak, Renée J. Mitchell, Justice Tankebe, Maria Emilia Firpo, Ricardo Fraiman, and Jordan M. Hyatt. 2020. "Using Wearable Technology to Increase Police Legitimacy in Uruguay: The Case of Body-Worn Cameras." *Law & Social Inquiry* 45:52–80.

Augustyn, Megan B. 2015. "The (Ir)relevance of Procedural Justice in the Pathways to Crime." *Law and Human Behavior* 39:388–401.

2016. "Updating Perceptions of (In)justice." *Journal of Research in Crime and Delinquency* 53:255–86.

Bennett, Sarah, Lorraine Mazerolle, Emma Antrobus, Elizabeth Eggins, and Alex R. Piquero. 2018. "Truancy Intervention Reduces Crime: Results from a Randomized Field Trial." *Justice Quarterly* 35:309–29.

Bennett, Sarah, Lorraine Mazerolle, Emma Antrobus, Peter Martin, and Lorelei Hine. 2019. "The Trials and Tribulations of Evidence Based Procedural Justice." In *Evidence Based Policing: An Introduction*, edited by Renee J. Mitchell and Laura Huey, 145–60. Bristol, UK: Policy Press.

Blair, Robert A., Sabrina M. Karim, and Benjamin S. Morse. "Establishing the Rule of Law in Weak and War-Torn States: Evidence from a Field Experiment with the Liberian National Police." *American Political Science Review* 113:641–57.

Bottoms, Anthony, and Justice Tankebe. 2012. "Beyond Procedural Justice: A Dialogic Approach to Legitimacy in Criminal Justice." *Journal of Criminal Law & Criminology* 102:119–70.

Braga, Anthony A., Christopher Winship, Tom R. Tyler, Jeffrey Fagan, and Tracey L. Meares. 2014. "The Salience of Social Contextual Factors in Appraisals of Police Interactions with Citizens: A Randomized Factorial Experiment." *Journal of Quantitative Criminology* 30:599–627.

Clark-Moorman, Kyleigh, Jason Rydberg, and Edmund F. McGarrell. 2019. "Impact Evaluation of a Parolee-Based Focused Deterrence Program on Community-Level Violence." *Criminal Justice Policy Review*. 30:1408–30.

Dai, Mengyan, James Frank, and Ivan Sun. 2011. "Procedural Justice During Police-Citizen Encounters: The Effects of Process Based Policing on Citizen Compliance and Demeanor." *Journal of Criminal Justice* 39:159–68.

Demir, Mustafa, Robert Apel, Anthony A. Braga, Rod K. Brunson, and Barak Ariel. 2020. "Body Worn Cameras, Procedural Justice, and Police Legitimacy: A Controlled Experimental Evaluation of Traffic Stops." *Justice Quarterly* 37:53–84.

Fagan, Jeffrey, and Tom R. Tyler 2005. "Legal Socialization of Children and Adolescents." *Social Science Research* 18:217–41.

Fine, Adam D., Kathleen E. Padilla, and Julie Tapp. 2019. "Can Youths' Perceptions of the Police Be Improved? Results of a School-Based Field Evaluation in Three Jurisdictions." *Psychology, Public Policy, and Law* 25:303–14.

Gau, Jacinta M. 2014. "Procedural Justice and Police Legitimacy: A Test of Measurement and Structure." *American Journal of Criminal Justice* 39:187–205.

Gill, Charlotte, David Weisburd, Cody W. Telep, Zoe Vitter, and Trevor Bennett. 2014. "Community-Oriented Policing to Reduce Crime, Disorder and Fear and Increase Satisfaction and Legitimacy Among Citizens: A Systematic Review." *Journal of Experimental Criminology* 10:399–428.

Hinds, Lyn. 2007. "Building Police–Youth Relationships: The Importance of Procedural Justice." *Youth Justice* 7:195–209.

Hirschi, Travis. 1969. *Causes of Delinquency*. Berkeley: University of California Press.

Jackson, Jonathan, Ben Bradford, Mike Hough, Andy Myhill, Paul Quinton, and Tom R. Tyler. 2012. "Why Do People Comply with the Law? Legitimacy and the Influence of Legal Institutions." *British Journal of Criminology* 52:1051–71.

Johnson, Devon, David B. Wilson, Edward R. Maguire, and Belén V. Lowrey-Kinberg. 2017. "Race and Perceptions of Police: Experimental Results on the Impact of Procedural (In)justice." *Justice Quarterly* 34:1184–1212.

Jonathan-Zamir, Tal, Stephen D. Mastrofski, and Shomron Moyal. 2015. "Measuring Procedural Justice in Police-Citizen Encounters." *Justice Quarterly* 32:845–71.

Jonathan-Zamir, Tal and David Weisburd. 2013. "The Effects of Security Threats on Antecedents of Police Legitimacy: Findings from a Quasi-Experiment in Israel." *Journal of Research in Crime and Delinquency* 50:3–32.

Kahn, Kimberly Barsamian, Kris Henning, Greg Stewart, Brian C. Renauer, Christian Peterson, Renée Jean Mitchell, Yves Labissiere, and Sean Sothern. 2019. "Public Response to Community Engagement Patrols in High Crime Areas." *Policing: An International Journal* 42:917–30.

Kaiser, Kimberly, and Michael D. Reisig. 2019. "Legal Socialization and Self-Reported Criminal Offending: The Role of Procedural Justice and Legal Orientations." *Journal of Quantitative Criminology* 35:135–54.

Kirk, David S., and Andrew V. Papachristos. 2011. "Cultural Mechanisms and the Persistence of Neighborhood Violence." *American Journal of Sociology* 116:1190–1233.

Langley, Brandon R. 2014. *A Randomised Control Trial Comparing the Effects of Procedural Justice to Experienced Utility Theories in Airport Security Stops*. Master's thesis. Cambridge, UK: University of Cambridge.

La Vigne, Nancy, Jesse Jannetta, Jocelyn Fontaine, Daniel S. Lawrence, and Sino Esthappan. 2019. *The National Initiative for Building Community Trust and Justice: Key Process and Outcome Evaluation Findings*. Washington, DC: Urban Institute.

Lind, E. Allan, and Tom R. Tyler. 1988. *The Social Psychology of Procedural Justice*. New York: Plenum Press.

Lum, Cynthia, and Daniel S. Nagin. 2017. "Reinventing American Policing." In *Reinventing American Criminal Justice: Crime and Justice: A Review of Research*, vol. 46, edited by Michael Tonry and Daniel S. Nagin, 339–93. Chicago: University of Chicago Press.

Lum, Cynthia, Megan Stoltz, Christopher S. Koper, and J. Amber Scherer. 2019. "Research on Body-Worn Cameras: What We Know, What We Need to Know." *Criminology & Public Policy* 18: 93–118.

MacQueen, Sarah and Ben Bradford. 2015. "Enhancing Public Trust and Police Legitimacy During Road Traffic Encounters: Results from a Randomized Controlled Trial in Scotland." *Journal of Experimental Criminology* 11:419–43.

2017. "Where Did It All Go Wrong? Implementation Failure – and More – in a Field Experiment of Procedural Justice Policing." *Journal of Experimental Criminology* 13:321–45.

Maguire, Edward R., Belén V. Lowrey, and Devon Johnson. 2017. "Evaluating the Relative Impact of Positive and Negative Encounters with Police: A Randomized Experiment." *Journal of Experimental Criminology* 13:367–91.

Manski, Charles F., and Daniel S. Nagin. 2017. "Assessing Benefits, Costs, and Disparate Racial Impacts of Confrontational Proactive Policing." *Proceedings of the National Academy of Sciences* 114:9308–13.

Mastrofski, Stephen D., Jeffrey B. Snipes, and Anne E. Supina. 1996. "Compliance on Demand: The Public's Response to Specific Police Requests." *Journal of Research in Crime and Delinquency* 33:269–305.

Mastrofski, Stephen D., Tal Jonathan-Zamir, Shomron Moyal, and James J. Willis. 2016. "Predicting Procedural Justice in Police-Citizen Encounters." *Criminal Justice and Behavior* 43:119–39.

Mazerolle, Lorraine, Sarah Bennett, Emma Antrobus, and Elizabeth Eggins. 2012. "Procedural Justice, Routine Activities and Citizen Perceptions of Police: Main Findings from the Queensland Community Engagement Trial." *Journal of Experimental Criminology* 8:343–67.

Mazerolle, Lorraine, Emma Antrobus, Sarah Bennett, and Tom R. Tyler. 2013. "Shaping Citizen Perceptions of Police Legitimacy: A Randomized Field Trial of Procedural Justice." *Criminology* 51:33–64.

Mazerolle, Lorraine, Sarah Bennett, Emma Antrobus, and Elizabeth Eggins. 2017. "The Coproduction of Truancy Control: Results from a Randomized Trial of a Police-Schools Partnership Program." *Journal of Research in Crime and Delinquency* 54:791–823.

Mazerolle, Lorraine, Sarah Bennett, Emma Antrobus, Stephanie M. Cardwell, Elizabeth Eggins, and Alex R. Piquero. 2019. "Disrupting the Pathway from Truancy to Delinquency: A Randomized Field Trial Test of the Longitudinal Impact of a School Engagement Program." *Journal of Quantitative Criminology*. 35:663–89.

McCluskey John D., Stephen D. Mastrofski, and Roger B. Parks. 1999. "To Acquiesce or Rebel: Predicting Citizen Compliance with Police Requests." *Police Quarterly* 2:389–416.

McCluskey, John D., Craig D. Uchida, Shellie E. Solomon, Alese Wooditch, Christine Connor, and Lauren Revier. 2019. "Assessing the Effects of Body-Worn Cameras on Procedural Justice in the Los Angeles Police Department." *Criminology* 57.

Mehozay, Yoav, and Roni Factor. 2017. "Deeply Embedded Core Normative Values and Legitimacy of Law Enforcement Authorities." *Journal of Research in Crime and Delinquency* 54:151–80.

Mell, Shana M. 2016. *The Role of Procedural Justice within Police-Citizen Contacts in Explaining Citizen Behaviors and Other Outcomes*. Doctoral dissertation. Richmond: Virginia Commonwealth University.

Murphy, Kristina, Adrian Cherney, and Marcus Teston. 2019. "Promoting Muslims' Willingness to Report Terror Threats to Police: Testing Competing Theories of Procedural Justice." *Justice Quarterly* 36:594–619.

Nagin, Daniel S., and Cody W. Telep. 2017. "Procedural Justice and Legal Compliance." *Annual Review of Law and Social Science* 13:5–28.

National Academies of Sciences, Engineering, and Medicine. 2017. *Proactive Policing: Effects on Crime and Communities*, edited by David Weisburd and Malay K. Majmundar. Washington, DC: National Academies Press.

Nettler, Gwynn. 1974. "Embezzlement without Problems." *British Journal of Criminology* 14:70–7.

O'Brien, Thomas C., Tom R. Tyler, and Tracey L. Meares. 2020. "Building Popular Legitimacy with Reconciliatory Gestures and Participation: A Community-Level Model of Authority." *Regulation & Governance* 14:821–39.

Owens, Emily, David Weisburd, Karen L. Amendola, and Geoffrey P. Alpert. 2018. "Can You Build a Better Cop? Experimental Evidence on Supervision, Training, and Policing in the Community." *Criminology & Public Policy* 17:41–87.

Papachristos, Andrew V., Tracey L. Meares, and Jeffrey Fagan. 2007. "Attention Felons: Evaluating Project Safe Neighborhoods in Chicago." *Journal of Empirical Legal Studies* 4:223–72.

Paternoster, Raymond, Ronet Bachman, Robert Brame, and Lawrence W. Sherman. 1997. "Do Fair Procedures Matter? The Effect of Procedural Justice on Spouse Assault." *Law & Society Review* 31:163–204.

Peyton, Kyle, Michael Sierra-Arévalo, and David G. Rand. 2019. "A Field Experiment on Community Policing and Police Legitimacy." *Proceedings of the National Academy of Sciences* 116:19894–8.

Pickett, Justin T., Justin Nix, and Sean Patrick Roche. 2018. "Testing a Social Schematic Model of Procedural Justice." *Social Psychology Quarterly* 81:97–125.

Piquero, Alex R., Jeffrey Fagan, Edward P. Mulvey, Laurence Steinberg, and Candice Odgers. 2005. "Developmental Trajectories of Legal Socialization among Serious Adolescent Offenders." *Journal of Criminal Law and Criminology* 96:267–98.

President's Task Force on 21st Century Policing. 2015. *Final Report of the President's Task Force on 21st Century Policing*. Washington, DC: Office of Community Oriented Policing Services, US Department of Justice.

Reisig, Michael D. and Camille Lloyd. 2009. "Procedural Justice, Police Legitimacy, and Helping the Police Fight Crime: Results from a Survey of Jamaican Adolescents." *Police Quarterly* 12:42–62.

Reisig, Michael D., John D. McCluskey, Stephen D. Mastrofski, and William Terrill. 2004. "Suspect Disrespect Toward the Police." *Justice Quarterly* 21:241–68.

Reisig, Michael D., Jason Bratton, and Marc G. Gertz. 2007. "The Construct Validity and Refinement of Process-Based Policing Measures." *Criminal Justice and Behavior* 34:1005–28.

Reiss, Albert J. Jr. 1971. *The Police and the Public*. New Haven, CT: Yale University Press.

Robertson, Annette, Lesley McMillan, Jon Godwin, and Ross Deuchar. 2014. *The Scottish Police and Citizen Engagement (SPACE) Trial: Final Report*. Glasgow, UK: Glasgow Caledonian University.

Roché, Sebastian, and Guillaume Roux. 2017. "The 'Silver Bullet' to Good Policing: A Mirage: An Analysis of the Effects of Political Ideology and Ethnic Identity on Procedural Justice." *Policing: An International Journal* 40:514–28.

Rosenbaum, Dennis P. and Daniel S. Lawrence. 2017. "Teaching Procedural Justice and Communication Skills During Police-Community Encounters: Results of a Randomized Control Trial with Police Recruits." *Journal of Experimental Criminology* 13:293–319.

Rosenbaum, Dennis P., Amie M. Schuck, Sandra K. Costello, Darnell F. Hawkins, and Marianne K. Ring. 2005. "Attitudes Toward the Police: The Effects of Direct and Vicarious Experience." *Police Quarterly* 8:343–65.

Sahin, Nusret, Anthony A. Braga, Robert Apel, and Rod K. Brunson. 2017. "The Impact of Procedurally-Just Policing on Citizen Perceptions of Police During Traffic Stops: The Adana Randomized Controlled Trial." *Journal of Quantitative Criminology* 33:701–26.

Sampson, Robert J., and Dawn J. Bartusch. 1998. "Legal Cynicism and (Subcultural?) Tolerance of Deviance: The Neighborhood Context of Racial Differences. *Law & Society Review* 32:777–804.

Schaefer, Brian, and Thomas Hughes. 2016. *Honing Interpersonal Necessary Tactics (H.I.N.T.): An Evaluation of Procedural Justice Training*. Louisville, KY: Southern Police Institute, University of Louisville.

Skogan, Wesley G. 2006. "Asymmetry in the Impact of Encounters with Police." *Policing & Society* 16:99–126.

Skogan, Wesley G., Maarten Van Craen, and Cari Hennessy. 2015. "Training Police for Procedural Justice." *Journal of Experimental Criminology* 11:319–34.

Slocum, Lee A., Stephanie A. Wiley, and Finn-Aage Esbensen. 2016. "The Importance of Being Satisfied: A Longitudinal Exploration of Police Contact, Procedural Injustice, and Subsequent Delinquency." *Criminal Justice and Behavior* 43:7–26.

Sunshine, Jason, and Tom R. Tyler. 2003. "The Role of Procedural Justice and Legitimacy in Shaping Public Support for Policing." *Law & Society Review* 27:513–48.

Sykes, Gresham M. and David Matza. 1957. "Techniques of Neutralization: A Theory of Delinquency." *American Sociological Review* 22:664–70.

Telep, Cody W., David Weisburd, Anthony A. Braga, Heather Vovak, Brandon Turchan, and Tal Jonathan-Zamir. in progress. "Can Police Training Be Used to Advance Evidence-Based Policing? Evidence from a Randomized Experiment in Procedural Justice." *Cambridge Elements in Criminology*. New York: Cambridge University Press.

Thacher, David. 2019. "Critic: The Limits of Procedural Justice." In *Police Innovation: Contrasting Perspectives*. 2nd edition, edited by David Weisburd and Anthony A. Braga, 95–118. New York: Cambridge University Press.

Toby, Jackson. 1957. "Social Disorganization and Stake in Conformity: Complementary Factors in the Predatory Behavior of Hoodlums." *Journal of Criminal Law, Criminology, and Police Science* 48:12–17.

Trinkner, Rick. 2019. "Addressing the 'Black Box' of Focused Deterrence: An Examination of the Mechanisms of Change in Chicago's Project Safe Neighborhoods." *Journal of Experimental Criminology* 15:673–83.

Trinkner, Rick, Tom R. Tyler, and Phillip A. Goff. 2016. "Justice from Within: The Relations Between a Procedurally Just Organizational Climate and Police Organizational Efficiency, Endorsement of Democratic Policing, and Officer Well-Being." *Psychology, Public Policy, and Law* 22:158–72.

Trinkner, Rick D., Ryan D. Mays, Ellen S. Cohn, Karen T. Van Gundy, and Cesar J. Rebellon. 2019. "Turning the Corner on Procedural Justice Theory: Exploring Reverse Causality with an Experimental Vignette in a Longitudinal Survey." *Journal of Experimental Criminology* 15:661–71.

Tyler, Tom R. 1988. "What Is Procedural Justice? Criteria Used by Citizens to Assess the Fairness of Legal Procedures." *Law & Society Review* 22:103–36.

1990. *Why People Obey the Law? Procedural Justice, Legitimacy, and Compliance*. New Haven, CT: Yale University Press.

2003. "Procedural Justice, Legitimacy, and the Effective Rule of Law." In *Crime and Justice: A Review of Research*, vol. 30, edited by Michael Tonry, 283–357. Chicago: University of Chicago Press.

2006. "Psychological Perspectives on Legitimacy and Legitimation." *Annual Review of Psychology* 57:375–400.

2017. "Procedural Justice and Policing: A Rush to Judgment?" *Annual Review of Law and Social Science* 13:29–53.

Tyler, Tom R., and Yuen J. Huo. 2002. *Trust in the Law: Encouraging Public Cooperation with the Police and Courts*. New York: Russell Sage Foundation.

Tyler, Tom R., Phillip A. Goff, and Robert J. MacCoun. 2015. "The Impact of Psychological Science on Policing in the United States: Procedural Justice, Legitimacy and Effective Law Enforcement." *Psychological Science in the Public Interest* 16:75–109.

Wallace, Danielle, Andrew V. Papachristos, Tracey Meares, and Jeffrey Fagan. 2016. "Desistance and Legitimacy: The Impact of Offender Notification Meetings on Recidivism among High Risk Offenders." *Justice Quarterly* 33:1237–64.

Walters, Glenn D., and P. Colin Bolger. 2019. "Procedural Justice Perceptions, Legitimacy Beliefs, and Compliance with the Law: A Meta-analysis." *Journal of Experimental Criminology* 15:341–72.

Weisburd, David, Charlotte Gill, Alese Wooditch, William Barritt, and Jody Murphy. in press. "Building Collective Action at Crime Hot Spots: Findings from a Randomized Field Experiment." *Journal of Experimental Criminology*.

Wheller, Levin, Paul Quinton, Alistair Fildes, and Andy Mills. 2013. *The Greater Manchester Police Procedural Justice Training Experiment*. Coventry, UK: College of Policing.

White, Michael D., Philip Mulvey, and Lisa M. Dario. 2016. "Arrestees' Perceptions of the Police: Exploring Procedural Justice, Legitimacy, and Willingness to Cooperate with Police across Offender Types." *Criminal Justice and Behavior* 43:343–64.

White, Michael D., Janne E. Gaub, and Natalie Todak. 2017. "Exploring the Potential for Body-Worn Cameras to Reduce Violence in Police–Citizen Encounters." *Policing: A Journal of Policy and Practice* 12:66–76.

White, Clair, David Weisburd, and Sean Wire. 2018. "Examining the Impact of the Freddie Gray Unrest on Perceptions of the Police." *Criminology & Public Policy* 17:829–58.

Wolfe, Scott E., Justin Nix, Robert Kaminski, and Jeff Rojek. 2016. "Is the Effect of Procedural Justice on Police Legitimacy Invariant? Testing the Generality of Procedural Justice and Competing Antecedents of Legitimacy." *Journal of Quantitative Criminology* 32:253–82.

Wolfe, Scott, Jeff Rojek, Kyle McLean, and Geoffrey Alpert. 2020. "Social Interaction Training to Reduce Police Use of Force." *ANNALS of the American Academy of Political and Social Science*, 687.

Wood, George, Tom Tyler, and Andrew Papachristos. 2020. "Procedural Justice Training Reduces Police Use of Force and Complaints Against Officers." Proceedings of the National Academy of Sciences 117:9815–21

Worden, Robert E., and Sarah J. McLean. 2017. *Mirage of Police Reform*. Berkeley: University of California Press.

2018. "Measuring, Managing, and Enhancing Procedural Justice in Policing: Promise and Pitfalls." *Criminal Justice Policy Review* 29:149–71.

28

Social Norms and Persuasion

Jessica M. Nolan and Kenneth E. Wallen

Abstract: Social norms, what most people do or approve of, can be leveraged as a powerful tool for gaining compliance. This chapter reviews the behavioral intervention literature to describe and summarize the different ways that social norms can be operationalized to obtain compliance, the underlying motivations and mechanisms driving these effects, and possible delivery mechanisms. Best practices are highlighted for ensuring maximum compliance. The chapter also explores theoretical and empirical literature to review and characterize the behavioral domains in which social norm techniques are effectively implemented, including large-scale applications. The chapter concludes with a general discussion of research findings and suggestions for future research.

28.1 INTRODUCTION: GAINING COMPLIANCE WITHOUT ASKING

A college student using the bathroom learns from a sign on the back of the stall door that 62.5 percent of women and 56.3 percent of men had between zero and three alcoholic drinks the last time they socialized and decides to have one fewer drink at a party that night. A homeowner opens their electricity bill and sees that they are using more energy than their "most efficient neighbors" and decides to take steps to conserve energy. A registered voter opens their Facebook account on election day and sees that many of their friends have voted and decides to head to the polls. What each of these scenarios has in common is that social norms are being leveraged to promote beneficial behaviors.

The term *social norm* is commonly used interchangeably to refer to behaviors enacted or approved of by others and to the beliefs or perceptions that support conformity to those behaviors (Schultz et al. 2008). However, it is helpful to distinguish between behavior and belief and is suggested that the term social norm be used in reference to actual behavior and normative beliefs in reference to beliefs (Farrow et al. 2017; Wallen and Romulo 2017). In practice, the distinction between behavior and belief is helpful as social norm interventions do not necessarily require direct observation or interaction with others or their behavior to be persuasive. That is, when properly operationalized, the normative information used as part of an intervention implies that a behavior or belief is the social norm. Here, we use social norm interchangeably but distinguish between behaviors and normative beliefs when applicable.

Sherif (1936: 3) defined social norms as "criteria of conduct which are standardized as a consequence of the contact of individuals." Pepitone (1976: 642) suggested that "social behavior is more characteristic of some sociocultural collective unit than of individuals observed at random." Though formative, these abstract definitions do not provide useful operational guidance toward empirical measurement and application. A more useful definition comes from Cialdini and Trost (1998: 152): "rules and standards that are understood by members of a group, and that guide and/or constrain social behavior without the force of laws." A variant from van Kleef et al. (2019: 1) suggests "implicit or explicit rules or principles that are understood by members of a group and that guide and/or constrain behavior without the force of laws to engender proper conduct." More simply, Paluck and Ball (2010) define a social norm as the perception that certain attitudes and behaviors are considered *typical* or *desirable* in a person's community. A synthesis of these from Nolan (2017: 148) offers some necessary specificity: "rules and standards that are understood by members of a group, and that guide morally relevant social behavior by way of social sanctions, instead of the force of laws."

These definitions highlight a common dimensionality associated with social norms, that is, *typical* and *desirable*, and the importance of social sanctions. The two-dimensional social norm framework distinguishes between informational (typical) and normative (desirable) influence – the *is* and *ought* (Deutsch and Gerard 1955). In the 1990s, Cialdini et al. (1990) mainstreamed these dimensions, which they termed descriptive (typical) and injunctive (desirable). The descriptive norm provides information on what *is* typical, common, or normal, that is, what most people do, while descriptive normative *beliefs* refer to what one thinks most people do. The injunctive norm provides information on what *ought* to be done, referring to a social rule that proscribes or prescribes (un)desirable behavior, while injunctive normative *beliefs* refer to the perception that a behavior is approved or disapproved of.

Since the 1990s, social norm research and interventions have been predominately based on the descriptive/injunctive framework. More recently, Bicchieri (2017) suggests an operationalization based on the ideas of social expectations and preferences (see also Mackie et al. 2015). Here, a social norm is defined as a pattern of behavior such that an individual prefers to conform to it on the condition that they believe that most people in the relevant social network conform to it and/or that most people in the relevant social network believe that they ought to conform to it. Said another way, you are most likely to be persuaded to behave in a certain way if you hold the expectations that (1) enough people conform to the behavioral rule (*empirical expectation*; typical/descriptive), (2) enough people think that you should conform to the rule and will sanction you for nonconformity (*normative expectation*; desirable/injunctive), and (3) you prefer to conform to the rule based on those empirical and normative expectations (*conditional preference*). In this framework, two orders of normative beliefs/expectations exist; a first-order belief about what others do and what others should do and a second-order belief about what others believe I/others do and what others believe I/others should do, the latter of which is assumed to be most persuasive. In general, the idea that we hold beliefs about others' expectations of a typical or desirable behavior or belief is the predominant principle.

With social norms defined, there are a few things that are worth noting about social norms interventions. First, unlike other popular compliance techniques such as the door-in-the-face (Cialdini et al. 1975), the foot-in-the-door (Freedman and Fraser 1966), and the even-a-penny techniques (Cialdini and Schroeder 1976), social norms interventions do not require a face-to-face interaction or that an explicit request is made of the target. Instead, the request is implied by the normative information "everyone is (not) doing X, so you should (not) do it too." Although some interventions do attach a specific request to the normative information, such requests are not required for social norms interventions to be effective.

In this chapter we focus on experimental research conducted in the past two decades that investigated deliberate attempts to leverage social norms to promote beneficial attitudes and behaviors. While naturally existing social norms can also be a source of persuasion, investigations of such norms are typically correlational and do not allow for conclusions to be drawn about social norms as a causal influence. In the remainder of the chapter, we discuss the behavioral domains that have utilized and tested social norms interventions, how social norms have been operationalized and delivered across these domains, best practices for ensuring an effective intervention as well as discussion of the underlying motivations and mechanisms driving these effects.

28.2 EVIDENCE FOR EFFECTIVENESS ACROSS BEHAVIORAL DOMAINS

Social norms interventions have been used successfully to change a wide variety of behaviors including health-related behaviors such as problematic drinking and eating, proenvironmental behaviors such as energy and water conservation, and prosocial behaviors such as donating to charities.

Problematic Drinking. Research on social norms marketing began in the 1980s with interventions designed to reduce problematic drinking on college campuses (Perkins and Berkowitz 1986; Perkins 2003). Since then, the field has seen a surge in research exploring social norms as a tool for reducing both the rate and the frequency of alcohol consumption among college students, particularly those high users who are most at risk for alcohol-related problems such as blacking out. The typical intervention advertises that alcohol consumption by peers is less than many people expect. A recent meta-analysis of 44 studies comprising 17,445 participants found that social norms interventions targeting alcohol consumption produce substantial changes in normative beliefs (in the direction of the advertised norm) which then led to smaller, but not insignificant, changes in behaviors such as alcohol intake and binge drinking (Prestwich et al. 2016). These results are especially impressive given that most of the social norms interventions were brief single-exposure communications that were not delivered face-to-face. Importantly, social norms interventions were found to be more effective than social influence interventions that relied on other techniques, such as social support.

The effectiveness of social norms marketing campaigns to address problematic drinking is not limited to college campuses. A statewide social norms marketing campaign targeting young adults in Montana successfully changed normative beliefs about drinking and driving (Perkins et al. 2010). The social norms campaign included TV, radio, and print ads that advertised that most young adults in Montana (four out of five) do not drink and drive and portrayed designating a driver as a normative activity. Following the intervention, young adults in counties exposed to the social norms campaign reported a 2 percent decrease in driving after drinking, while those in the control condition saw a 12 percent *increase*.

Healthy Eating. While most research on social norms marketing for problematic drinking has been conducted in field settings, research on social norms interventions for healthy eating has been primarily conducted in the laboratory. Although conducted in what might be considered an artificial setting, a strength of this research is that it typically measures actual eating behavior, operationalized either as choice or as quantity of one or more target foods. A meta-analysis of interventions that manipulated eating norms showed that participants who were led to believe that past participants had eaten a lot of cookies (or other unhealthy food) consumed more of the high-calorie food themselves, compared to a control condition, while the reverse was true when participants were told that most previous participants had consumed a small quantity of the food (Robinson et al. 2014). Descriptive normative information can also be used successfully to promote healthy food options, such as eating fruits and vegetables, but seem to be more effective among low consumers of such healthy snacks (Stok et al. 2016).

Other Health Behaviors. Other health-related behaviors, such as indoor tanning and sedentary behavior, may be suitable targets for social norms interventions. Office workers reported walking more, sitting less, and using the stairs more after receiving an email telling them that other employees were more active than they were during the workday (Priebe and Spink 2015). Similarly, providing students who engage in indoor tanning with a personalized feedback message highlighting their self-reported indoor tanning behavior, their estimate of the norm for indoor tanning, and the actual norm reduced future tanning intentions, particularly among high-frequency tanners who grossly overestimated the norm (Carcioppolo et al. 2019). Though promising, this study did not include a control group and so further research is required to increase confidence in the results.

Social norms interventions can influence private as well as public behaviors. College students were more likely to wash their hands after using the restroom when they saw signs indicating that members of their in-group washed their hands (Lapinski et al. 2013). The normative messages were more effective than a control message both when a confederate was present in the bathroom *and* when the student was alone.

Most recently, the social norms approach has been adopted by researchers and practitioners working in the field of adolescent and youth sexual and reproductive health. This work is carried out globally to address problems such as child marriage, teen pregnancy, and condom use. Addressing many of these behaviors requires a multi-component approach that incorporates but does not rely solely on social norms interventions (Bingenheimer 2019).

Energy and Water Conservation. In a recent review of the literature on social norms and proenvironmental behavior, most studies targeted water and energy conservation or related behaviors such as reusing towels and turning off unused lights (Farrow et al. 2017). Results showed that social norms interventions are an effective way to motivate proenvironmental behavior. For example, bathroom goers in Poland were over three times as likely to turn the light off when leaving a public restroom when they saw a descriptive norm sign above the light fixture that read "the vast majority of people turn off the light when leaving a restroom." They were over eight times as likely when they saw an injunctive norm sign that read "it is commonly approved that the light should be turned off when leaving a restroom," compared to a no-sign control (Leoniak and Cwalina 2019: 3). These effects were even more pronounced when the lights were initially off when the participant entered the single stall bathroom and, thus, the contextual cues affirmed the message in the sign.

Attempts to reduce energy and water consumption lend themselves well to the social norms approach: households can be provided with regular feedback about their consumption via utility bills, and information about aggregate energy usage for a given area is readily available to the utility. Perhaps the best-known large-scale application of the social norms approach is via the Opower program. Opower has partnered with more than 100 utility districts to provide households with customized reports about how their energy consumption compares to their neighbors'. Over a six-month period these reports were found to reduce home energy consumption by an average of 1 to 2 percent (Allcott 2011). In a large-scale field experiment,

Ferraro et al. (2011) found that even a single "dose" of comparative normative feedback reduced home water consumption by approximately 4.8 percent compared to the control group in the summer following treatment. Importantly, social norms interventions to reduce both energy (Allcott and Rogers 2014) and water (Ferraro and Price 2013) consumption have effects that last beyond the life of the intervention.

It is worth noting that the social norms approach has worked to reduce energy consumption where more traditional approaches have failed. For example, in a study that provided participants in southern California with doorhangers once a week for four weeks, only those who saw messages indicating that a majority of their neighbors did things to conserve energy (e.g., taking shorter showers, using fans instead of air-conditioning) reduced their energy consumption in the weeks following the intervention (Nolan et al. 2008). Interestingly, those who received appeals to "save money," "protect the environment," and "do your part for future generations" perceived these messages to be more motivating than those in the social norms condition, even though they failed to actually conserve energy. Similarly, hotel guests who were told that 75 percent of guests participated in the hotel's towel reuse program were significantly more likely to reuse their towels compared to those who received the standard environmental message imploring them to "help save the environment" (Goldstein et al. 2008). Follow-up research showed that the social norms message was especially effective when it referenced "other guests who stayed in this room." This was true even though guests identified other tested reference groups, such as "citizens" or "men and women," as being more important to their identities.

While most research has focused on adoption of curtailment behaviors, social norms interventions may also be used to promote uptake of efficiency behaviors such as purchase of energy-efficient home appliances. In both a scenario study measuring hypothetical consumer choices and a survey study that asked homeowners about their intentions to purchase an efficient home heating pump, providing normative information indicating that a majority of neighbors had installed the efficient heat pump increased choices and intentions in that direction, compared to a control condition (Hafner et al. 2019). Similarly, households who received a social norms message were almost twice as likely to sign up for a utility sponsored program to install water-saving devices compared to those who received a standard appeal (Lede et al. 2019).

Other Environmental Behaviors. Surprisingly, only one study has looked at intervening with social norms to promote recycling behavior. Schultz (1999) found that providing normative feedback about the recycling behavior of neighbors increased both the frequency of participation in the curbside recycling program and the amount recycled.

Social norms interventions can also be designed to promote proenvironmental behaviors that are not yet descriptively normative. For example, Sparkmann and Walton (2017) used *dynamic norms* to reduce meat consumption. Specifically, they emphasized how three in ten people were making an effort to eat less meat in recent years and found that this decreased the likelihood of the participant ordering a meal with meat for their lunch, compared to a control group that read about changes in people's hobbies.

When designing a social norms message, it may be more powerful to provide people with information about what a majority of people *don't* do. For example, participants in a simulated online shopping environment were more likely to choose (reject) an organic (low-priced) peanut butter jar when told "other people avoid" the low-priced peanut butter versus "want" the organic version (Bergquist and Nilsson 2019).

Donating to Charity. Individuals are more likely to donate to charitable causes when given social proof that those who have previously been approached have complied with the request. This social proof can be provided via written information (e.g., Agerström et al. 2016) or a visual display. For example, store customers in France were more likely to donate money to build a school in the Congo when the experimenter making the request carried a transparent collection box that contained twelve coins versus one that contained no coins (Jacob et al. 2018). Similar results were found in a bakery setting when the request was made passively via a sign on the collection box located next to the register. Providing visual proof of previous donations also worked to increase donations of clothing in a door-to-door campaign.

When only a minority of people donate to charity, trending norms can be used to increase donations (Mortenson et al. 2017). Participants who were told that a minority of previous participants (48 percent) had donated to a charitable group in the past year, but that this represented a 17 percent increase, expected more participants to make a financial contribution in the coming years, and were more likely to donate their time to help the organization compared to those provided only with the minority norm or no normative information.

Other Prosocial Behaviors. Participants were more willing to sign a series of six online petitions related to international issues, such as climate change and whaling, when they believed that a large number of others (>1 million people) had already signed (Margetts et al. 2011). Additional research has shown that information about the absolute number of people who have engaged in a given behavior can be further enhanced by showing them that this number includes some of their close friends. For example, in a massive online experiment on Facebook, users who saw a message reporting how many people on Facebook voted that included profile pictures of their friends were more likely to self-report voting, to search for their polling place, and to *actually* vote (Bond et al. 2012). Furthermore, this increase in voting behavior then spread to close friends and close friends of close friends, showing that social norms interventions can have powerful ripple effects across social networks.

28.3 THE OPERATIONALIZATION OF SOCIAL NORMS

Experimental research has operationalized social norms along several lines of inquiry: descriptive and injunctive, prescriptive and proscriptive, reference group, dynamic and trending.

28.3.1 *Descriptive and Injunctive*

Descriptive norms are perhaps the most common way in which social norms are operationalized to persuade compliance. In this form, the social norm is quantified, which stems from the idea that if a person knows a belief or behavior is common, it provides social proof that an action or thought is adaptive or beneficial. Operationalization is achieved via (a) a reference to the majority of others (not) doing the target behavior or holding the belief, (b) highlighting how frequently others (do not) do the target behavior, or (c) emphasizing in some manner that (not) doing the target behavior is common. For example, Agerström et al. (2016: 149) operationalized the descriptive norm with a majority percentage to encourage prosocial behavior by stating that "73% of [students] who were asked for a contribution have donated," whereas Demarque et al. (2015: 169), to nudge proenvironmental behavior, used the statement "70% bought at least one ecological product." Others have simply used a majority descriptor: "[T]he majority of the people who used this soap helped the environment by turning off the tap while soaping hands" (Richetin et al. 2014: 7). The use of a percentage, frequency, average, or amount is a standard operationalization of a descriptive norm (see also Goldstein et al. 2008).

Experiments operationalize the descriptive norm by manipulating the physical and social environment, real or imagined, in which a target behavior occurs. For instance, to make salient a pro-litter or anti-litter descriptive norm, Cialdini et al. (1990) varied the amount of litter that participants were exposed to and observed if participants littered or not in the manipulated environment. Relatedly, Heywood and Murdock (2002) manipulated the descriptive norm, that is, the amount of litter within a park, using digitally altered images to measure participants' responses to the perceived social norm.

The injunctive norm, as complementary to the descriptive norm, has a similar operationalization within the experimental research literature. Semantically, that tends to include the words or phrases: should, ought, accept, approve, endorse, expect, will, believe, support, certify, must, would. For example, "[S]hoppers in this store believe that re-using shopping bags is a useful way to help the environment" (de Groot et al. 2013: 1837); "[Most] students indicated that participants should be willing to stay for the full hour and complete extra surveys" (Jacobson et al. 2011: 440); "[Texans] expect you to clean, drain, dry [your boat]" (Wallen and Kyle 2018: 7).

28.3.2 *Aligned Descriptive and Injunctive*

Though distinct, the interplay between descriptive and injunctive norms can affect how norms influence behavior, and the two dimensions can have a greater impact together than either alone. The combination of descriptive and injunctive is also crucial to assure congruence between the normative information communicated – for example, a behavior is common and approved by others (Smith et al. 2012). Experimental research has operationalized descriptive and injunctive alignment to increase efficacy, prevent unintended behavior, and as a component of comparative feedback. In contrast, the misalignment of descriptive and injunctive norms may actually lead to spillover from one undesirable behavior to another (see also Chapter 29 in this volume)

In practice, to improve efficacy, an operationalized alignment of descriptive and injunctive norms follows individual formats. For example, in the context of conservation and proenvironmental behavior, Schultz et al. (2008: 8) used the combined message "Many of our hotel guests have expressed to us their approval of conserving energy. When given the opportunity, nearly 75% of hotel guests choose to reuse their towels each day" to significantly increase the target behavior, above and beyond individual norm messages. Similarly, Smith et al. (2012: 355) combined "82% of the student sample engaged in energy conservation" with "85% of the student sample approved of other students who engaged in energy conservation" to significant effect, as well.

The alignment of descriptive and injunctive norms has also been operationalized to serve as a stopgap to prevent unintended behavior. Cialdini (2003: 1) explains the need for alignment by suggesting that "within the statement 'many people are doing this undesirable thing' lurks the powerful and undercutting normative message 'many people are doing this.'" That is, drawing attention to an undesirable behavior – littering, heavy drinking, unhealthy eating, etc. – as common only serves to reinforce its normativeness and cause an increase in the undesirable behavior. In cases where the desirable behavior is uncommon and an undesirable one "regrettably frequent," the addition of a supportive injunctive norm is beneficial (Blanton et al. 2001). For example, Schultz et al. (2007) found that households given normative feedback showing below-average energy usage (i.e., they consumed less energy compared to their neighbors) increased their energy consumption in subsequent weeks. To increase compliance with the well-intended descriptive norm, a supportive injunctive norm was added to doorhangers – a smiley-face for below-average use, which indicates approval, and a frowny-face communicating disapproval for above-average use. This operationalization, in addition to aligning descriptive and injunctive norms, is a form of personalized social norm feedback (Burchell et al. 2013; Schultz 1999; Schultz et al. 2014).

28.3.3 *Prescriptive and Proscriptive*

Another useful operationalization is to alter the prescriptive, positive (what should be done, e.g., please turn off the lights) or the proscriptive, negative (what should not be done; e.g., do not leave the lights on) framing of the social norm, typically the injunctive norm. Experimental evidence suggests, in general, that proscriptive or negative frames are more effective (Farrow et al. 2017). For example, in a prosocial health behavior context, Blanton et al. (2001) found that people were more concerned with avoiding negative social consequences of not using condoms than attaining positive social consequences of using them. In the context of proenvironmental behavior, Cialdini et al. (2006) found negative framing – "Don't remove the petrified wood from the park" – to be more effective than positive "Leave petrified wood in the park." A common explanation for these results is that proscriptions tend to attract more cognitive attention as people attend more readily to information that will help them avoid social disapproval (Bergquist and Nilsson 2019).

28.3.4 *Reference Groups*

The expectations of others are a primary mechanism that contributes to the persuasiveness of social norms. By operationalizing social norms to reference a social group relevant to or that influences the target audience, behavioral interventions leverage the phenomenon that people are more likely to adhere to the expectations of others like themselves. This approach to social norms has many operationalizations: subjective (Ajzen 1991), group or in-group (Smith and Louis 2008), peer (van de Bongardt et al. 2014), local or provincial (Agerström et al. 2016; Goldstein et al. 2008), and proximal (Borsari and Carey 2003). The purpose is to operationalize normative information in reference to a relevant social group (not) doing, (dis) approving, and/or punishing/rewarding the (un)desired behavior or belief. For instance, a subjective norm would reference "close friends," "family members" (Ajzen 1991), local norms "fellow guests" or "guests stayed in this room" (Goldstein et al. 2008), and group norms "students at your university" (Smith and Louis 2008).

28.3.5 *Dynamic and Trending*

A recent development in social norm operationalization is the use of dynamic and trending norms. A dynamic social norm references information about how others' behavior is changing over time. A recent application used the statement "[I]n the last 5 years, 30% of Americans have now started to make an effort to limit their meat consumption. That means that, in recent years, 3 in 10 people have changed their behavior and begun to eat less meat than they otherwise would" and found that participants expressed significantly more interest in reducing meat consumption compared to a standard descriptive norm statement (Sparkman and Walton 2017: 3). Relatedly, a trending norm is used to emphasize that a behavior or belief that a minority of people engaged in previously is currently becoming more common. For example, Mortensen et al. (2017: 204) used "In July [previous year], 48% of the MTurk workers who took our surveys donated funds to the SEAA. This increased from 17% in July (2 years previous). Please help if you can" and found that it performed significantly better than a minority norm statement and control.

28.4 COMMON NORM DELIVERY MECHANISMS

The delivery of social norms interventions primarily occurs via written and verbal communication modes and print, digital/technological, or confederate media. These include the use of signage (viz. flyers, billboards, etc.), vignettes, print ads, commercials, mailers, and billing statements, which can vary in their degree of active or passive interaction with participants. In addition to analog methods, digital mass and social media are also widespread delivery mechanisms. More direct and active forms of social norm delivery include face-to-face interaction, the use of confederates, and real-time feedback.

Many of the examples in Section 28.3 are representative of interventions that use signage or print delivery methods. For example, Schultz et al. (2007) printed their social norm messages on doorhangers, Cialdini et al. (2006) placed signage in the area in which the desired behavior was to be enacted, and de Groot et al. (2013) printed social norm messages on grocery bags used by participants. In the context of proenvironmental and conservation behavior, the efficacy of these and other delivery methods has been extensively reviewed and critiqued (see Abrahamse et al. 2005; Abrahamse and Steg 2013; Miller and Prentice 2016). In the context of health behavior, interventions use similar communication methods. Examples of these include many of the signs, brochures, and posters designed to reduce problematic drinking on college campuses (i.e., Perkins and Berkowitz 1986; Perkins 2003).

The development of digital and technological delivery mechanisms has been a boon for social norm interventions. For example, as health and medical fields tend to incorporate technology more readily (e.g., tele-medicine), digital delivery is becoming more common. Thus, remote interactions among providers, caregivers, and patients are becoming more common wherein impersonal computer-delivered interventions occur more often at a patient's home, health care facilities, or other settings. In these contexts, though, the efficacy of social norm interventions has been mixed (see Rodriguez et al. 2015). Another interesting use of digital delivery and technology is for real- or relatively real-time feedback. For instance, in the age of social media networks, interventions can use Facebook, Instagram, and Snapchat as tools to enact social transmission of the norm. For example, Bond et al. (2012) used the Facebook News Feed to encourage voting with an intervention that provided local polling station information, an "I Voted" button, a counter of the number of other users who reported voting, and profile pictures of the participant's friends who clicked the "I Voted" button. Another example of technological delivery is the use of smart meters, which provide real-time feedback of users' energy and water consumption (e.g., Schultz et al. 2015).

A less common delivery mode is via confederates. With this method, experiments use individuals who seem to be participants but are actual research team members. For example, Cialdini et al. (1990) instructed confederates to litter or not as actual participants witnessed their action and whose subsequent actions were observed by researchers as the dependent variable (see also Aronson and O'Leary 1983). Jacob et al. (2018) similarly used social proof, as it is a chief mechanism of compliance, to increase the salience of the social norm in real-time. In two experiments – one using a passive method, a transparent monetary donation collection box, and the other an active method, a face-to-face interaction with partially filled clothing donation bags – researchers found that providing real-time evidence that the desired target behavior is common is efficacious. In health behavior contexts, a variation called a remote confederate design has been used to persuade healthy eating. Here, as participants enter the research setting, they are told that prior participants did or did not engage in a certain level of a behavior, for example "ate X amount of food" (Robinson et al. 2014; see also Asch 1955). Examples of a confederate design being used in a real-world social norm intervention are those that employ active, face-to-face interactions using influencers or block leaders (see Abrahamse and Steg 2013). These delivery modes use a significant or influential other as an active deliverer of the social norm, which can provide descriptive and injunctive normative information, comparative feedback, and an appropriate reference group.

28.5 LARGE-SCALE IMPLEMENTATION EXEMPLARS

The relatively small-scale and cross-sectional examples of the previous sections beg the question: can the persuasion and compliance proffered by social norm interventions be scaled up (see review in Nguyen et al. 2019)? To that end, various large-scale initiatives have been implemented over the past two decades. Prominent examples are found in the domains of problematic drinking, various prosocial behaviors, and energy and water conservation.

Under the social norms approach framework, several large-scale problematic drinking interventions have been implemented across the USA. For example, Perkins et al. (2010) implemented a statewide social norms media marketing campaign over an eighteen-month period. Their findings suggest that a social norm intervention can reduce normative misperceptions, increase use of designated drivers, and decrease drink-driving among target audiences. Though many large-scale interventions to reduce alcohol consumption have noted success, others have not (Wechsler et al. 2003) and a meta-analysis by Foxcroft et al. (2015) cautions that several large-scale social norm interventions yield limited benefits for the prevention of alcohol misuse among target audiences.

In the context of prosocial behavior, large-scale interventions become more common. For example, Paluck (2009) implemented a countrywide social norm intervention in Rwanda using radio programs designed to successfully encourage more frequent prosocial behaviors, such as, intra- and intergroup cooperation and communicating with others about traumatic or sensitive issues. Similar mass-media methods are developed and implemented at large scales by organizations like the Population Media Center. From radio to today's interconnected world of social media, interventions have become broader in scope and reach. For instance, Bond et al. (2012) implemented a large-scale randomized controlled trial (RCT) of 61 million participants in the USA to encourage voting behavior. Their finding showed the social norm treatment to perform significantly better than one without. Similar large-scale persuasion and compliance interventions are likely to continue being developed, particularly with social media and big data facilitating implementation.

Modern challenges of environmental sustainability have ushered in large-scale social norm campaigns to conserve energy and water. A well-known example from Allcott (2011) examined the effect of a social norm intervention – a personalized comparative social norm feedback message – on 600,000 participant households receiving energy utilities from the company Opower (see also Ayres et al. 2012). Similar to Schultz et al. (2007), this study examined the effect that an aligned descriptive and injunctive norm can have on persuading households to reduce their energy usage or continue their below-average usage. Results suggest a small but significant effect of the social norm intervention. In another large-scale example, Jachimowicz et al. (2018) synthesized the results of 211 independent Opower RCTs in twenty-seven states from 16 million participants to examine the effect of social norm feedback on energy conservation behavior. Their work observed second-order normative beliefs – that is, their belief that their neighbors or community approved of energy conservation – to have a significant effect on energy conservation behavior (see also Bicchieri 2017). In the context of water conservation, Ferraro et al. (2013) conducted a countywide intervention encompassing 100,000 water utility customers. Those results found that a social norm intervention can have a significant effect on behavior, particularly on high-use customers, but that the effectiveness of the intervention wanes over time.

Overall, these large-scale examples have implemented social norm interventions using similar conceptual and operational foundations, which, likewise, have similar underlying motivations and mechanisms. Yet, many of the above examples, in general, have scaled up their social norm interventions spatially (geographically) rather than temporally (over time), with results highlighting that the long-term robustness of social norm interventions varies.

28.6 UNDERLYING MOTIVATIONS AND MECHANISMS

Social norms interventions harness the power of people's tendency to conform to social norms. Conformity that is motivated by a desire to be accurate was labeled as informational social influence by Deutsch and Gerard (1955) and is most strongly connected to descriptive norms (i.e., norms of "is"), while conformity that is motivated by a desire to receive approval or to avoid disapproval is referred to as normative social influence and is most strongly connected to injunctive norms (i.e., norms of "ought"). However, in order to be motivating, social norms must be made salient and/or must correct a misperception about the prevalence of the behavior (descriptive norms) or the extent to which it is approved (injunctive norms). In addition, according to goal-framing theory, when a normative goal is activated it "creates feelings of obligation to act appropriately" (Chapter 29 in this volume). Furthermore, goal-framing theory proposes that the felt obligation to comply with norms increases when rule-following is widespread, and decreases when norms are disrespected, particularly by in-group members.

Several mechanisms have been proposed for how the need for accuracy and the need for approval work to persuade people to conform to social norms (e.g., Nolan et al. 2021). First, it is possible that people use social norms in a heuristic fashion, assuming that what most people do is both what is right (accurate) and what will earn them the approval of the group, or at least allow them to avoid disapproval. Evidence for the heuristic nature of conformity to social norms comes from research showing that participants are more likely to conform to a descriptive norm message when under cognitive load (Jacobson et al. 2011) and less likely to conform when they are encouraged to elaborate on the message (Kredentser et al. 2012) or are personally involved with the target behavior (Göckeritz et al. 2010).

Alternatively, social norms may change behavior by first changing individuals' normative beliefs. For example, in their meta-analysis of social norms marketing, Prestwich et al. (2016) found that normative beliefs mediate the relationship between social norms interventions and changes in problematic drinking. Interestingly, other research shows that social norms interventions can have a "cognitive ripple effect" whereby communicating descriptive normative information about one behavior and one referent group can spill over to change normative beliefs about both more proximal and more distal referents as well as related behaviors (Nolan 2011).

Most recently, research in social neuroscience has explored the neural mechanisms underlying conformity to the behavior of others. For example, individuals who showed greater activation of the nucleus accumbens (a reward center) when told that their judgments agreed with those of the group were more likely to make conforming judgments in a subsequent task (Nook and Zaki 2015). The posterior medial frontal cortex (pMFC) has also been implicated. Experimental research using transcranial magnetic stimulation (TMS) shows that individuals are less likely to conform when the pMFC has been downregulated via TMS (Klucharev et al. 2011). Other areas of the brain, such as the right lateral prefrontal cortex (rLPFC) are involved in regulating compliance to social norms when there is a clear threat of punishment for norm violations (Ruff et al. 2013).

28.7 BEST PRACTICES

As our review of the recent literature suggests, social norms interventions can be a relatively low-cost, adaptable, scalable, and highly effective way to change behavior. Here we offer four best practices for optimizing success:

1) ***Use a credible source and data***. Like most persuasive messages, social norms communications will be most effective when the source of the message is perceived to be credible and the information presented is believable. Message sources that are perceived as having a vested interest or that convey false information may arouse doubt, suspicion, or even reactance in the target audience. For example, social norms messages promoting purchase of sustainable seafood failed in Norwegian supermarkets and backfired in German supermarkets (Richter et al. 2018). This could be because the supermarket was perceived as having a vested interest in the customer purchasing a more expensive seafood option (Germany) or because they became aware that the social norms messages did not convey accurate information about the local norm (signs conveying seven different percentages were rotated each day in the same supermarket).
2) ***Know your audience***. Social norms interventions tend to be more effective at changing the behavior of those who engage in more of an undesired behavior (e.g., problem drinking) or less of a desired behavior (e.g., recycling). If possible, it is helpful to establish baseline behavior among a target audience so that high users/low adopters can be targeted. When it is not possible to target only those whose behavior needs to change then care should be taken in how descriptive norms are operationalized. For example, households that received normative feedback indicating that they were below-average energy consumers actually *increased* their daily energy consumption (Schultz et al. 2007). This is because people conform to social norms, regardless of whether the norm is helpful or harmful.
3) ***Know your context***. Practitioners should be mindful of the context in which social norms messages are delivered. Social norms messages promoting desirable behaviors

can be undermined by contextual cues that suggest the opposite. For example, a sign suggesting that most people don't litter in an area that is heavily littered or that most students drink responsibly on a campus with plentiful alcohol outlets are likely to have little to no effect on behavior (e.g., Scribner et al. 2011). After all, normative beliefs are constructed from observed behavior (or traces of behavior) as well as explicit communications about how common or approved a behavior is.

4) ***Keep it subtle***. Recall that social norms interventions work via a heuristic mechanism, providing social proof of what constitutes appropriate or desirable behavior. The success of the social norms approach, like other "wise" interventions, may be due, in part, to the fact that it is "minimally directive" (Walton and Wilson 2018). That is, normative messages can often appear to simply be providing information, thus minimizing feelings of coercion. Conversely, social norms, and injunctive norms in particular, that are communicated too forcefully (e.g., suggesting that peers think that one should eat healthier) may backfire if they are construed as an attempt to restrict freedom (Stok et al. 2016). The minimally directive nature of social norms interventions may also help to explain why they are underestimated, even by experts (Nolan et al. 2011).

28.8 FUTURE DIRECTIONS

Providing people with information about the behaviors and beliefs of others is an increasingly common strategy to gain compliance. As our review highlights, the effect that social norms interventions have on a suite of prosocial, health, and proenvironmental behaviors is robust. Yet, within these contexts, a needed future direction is to further substantiate the magnitude and persistence of compliance – behavior change – generated by social norm interventions, particularly as interventions attempt to scale up (Bingenheimer 2019). There is also a need to better understand the interplay between descriptive and injunctive norms and the extent to which one norm inherently communicates the other.

While these contexts covered in our review are not inclusive of all the social norm intervention contexts (e.g., regulatory or tax compliance), a positive trajectory for social norm research would include broadening the scope of behavioral domains, delivery modes, and scales of implementation. This would also facilitate researchers' ability to "give psychology away" and put the persuasive power of social norms to leverage compliance in the hands of people who can use it for positive social change (Nolan et al. 2011). Broadening the contexts in which social norms are applied would also alleviate and disabuse faulty commonsense psychology of persuasion assumptions that lead to erroneous or suboptimal intervention techniques. Future research should continue to investigate how best to transfer knowledge to those positioned to use it, so that they are armed with the best tools available.

A final consideration for the future of social norms and persuasion is to better understand and investigate interactions with policy. That is, how do policies impact social norm interventions in the real world, and how do preexisting or intended changes to social norms impact policy outcomes? These interactions will likely have tremendous impact on both the magnitude and the persistence of compliance that social norm interventions are able to generate. Better linking the academic research that predominates the social norm intervention domain to real-world scenarios and policy instruments via our research questions and experimental designs is an essential first step.

REFERENCES

Abrahamse, Wokje, and Linda Steg. 2013. "Social Influence Approaches to Encourage Resource Conservation: A Meta-analysis." *Global Environmental Change* 23: 1773–85.

Abrahamse, Wokje, Linda Steg, Charles Vlek, and Talib Rothengatter. 2005. "A Review of Intervention Studies Aimed at Household Energy Conservation." *Journal of Environmental Psychology* 25: 273–91.

Agerström, Jens, Rickard Carlsson, Linda Nicklasson, and Linda Guntell. 2016. "Using Descriptive Social Norms to Increase Charitable Giving: The Power of Local Norms." *Journal of Economic Psychology* 52: 147–53.

Allcott, Hunt. 2011. "Social Norms and Energy Conservation." *Journal of Public Economics*, 95: 1082–95.

Allcott, Hunt, and Todd Rogers. 2014. "The Short-Run and Long-Run Effects of Behavioral Interventions: Experimental Evidence from Energy Conservation." *American Economic Review* 104: 3003–37.

Ajzen, Icek. 1991. "The Theory of Planned Behavior." *Organizational Behavior and Human Decision Processes* 50: 179–211.

Aronson, Elliot, and Michael O'Leary. 1983. "The Relative Effectiveness of Models and Prompts on Energy Conservation: A Field Experiment in a Shower Room." *Journal of Environmental Systems* 12: 219–24.

Asch, Solomon. 1955. "Opinions and Social Pressure." *Scientific American* 193: 31–5.

Ayres, Ian, Sophie Raseman, and Alice Shih. 2012. "Evidence from Two Large Field Experiments that Peer Comparison Feedback Can Reduce Residential Energy Usage." *Journal of Law, Economics, and Organization* 29: 992–1022.

Bergquist, Magnus, and Andreas Nilsson. 2019. The DOs and DON'Ts in Social Norms: A Descriptive Don't-Norm Increases Conformity." *Journal of Theoretical Social Psychology* 3: 158–66.

Bicchieri, Cristina. 2017. *Norms in the Wild*. Oxford: Oxford University Press.

Bingenheimer, Jeffery. 2019. "Veering from a Narrow Path: The Second Decade of Social Norms Research." *Journal of Adolescent Health* 64: S1–S3.

Blanton, Hart, Anne Stuart, and Regina van den Eijnden. 2001. "An Introduction to Deviance-Regulation Theory: The Effect of Behavioral Norms on Message Framing." *Personality and Social Psychology Bulletin* 27: 848–58.

Bond, Robert, Christopher Fariss, Jason Jones, Adam Kramer, Cameron Marlow, Jaime Settle, and James Fowler. 2012. "A 61-Million-Person Experiment in Social Influence and Political Mobilization." *Nature* 489: 295–8.

Borsari, Brian, and Kate Carey. 2003. "Descriptive and Injunctive Norms in College Drinking: A Meta-analytic Integration." *Journal of Studies on Alcohol* 64: 331–41.

Burchell, Kevin, Ruth Rettie, and Kavita Patel. 2013. "Marketing Social Norms: Social Marketing and the Social Norm Approach." *Journal of Consumer Behaviour* 12: 1–9.

Carcioppolo, Nick, Wei Peng, Du Lun, and Aurora Occa. 2019. "Can a Social Norms Appeal Reduce Indoor Tanning? Preliminary Findings from a Tailored Messaging Intervention." *Health Education and Behavior* 46: 818–23.

Cialdini, Robert. 2003. "Crafting Normative Messages to Protect the Environment." *Current Directions in Psychological Science* 12: 105–9.

Cialdini, Robert B., and David A. Schroeder. 1976. "Increasing Compliance by Legitimizing Paltry Contributions: When Even a Penny Helps." *Journal of Personality and Social Psychology* 34: 599–604.

Cialdini, Robert, and Melanie Trost. 1998. "Social Influence: Social Norms, Conformity and Compliance." In *The Handbook of Social Psychology*, edited by Daniel Gilbert, Susan Fiske, and Gardner Lindzey, 151–92. New York: McGraw–Hill.

Cialdini, Robert B., Joyce E. Vincent, Stephen K. Lewis, Jose Catalan, Diane Wheeler, and Betty Lee Darby. 1975. "Reciprocal Concessions Procedure for Inducing Compliance: The Door-in-the-Face Technique." *Journal of personality and Social Psychology* 31: 206–15.

Cialdini, Robert, Raymond Reno, and Carl Kallgren. 1990. "A Focus Theory of Normative Conduct: Recycling the Concept of Norms to Reduce Littering in Public Places." *Journal of Personality and Social Psychology* 58: 1015–26.

Cialdini, Robert, Linda Demain, Brad Sagarin, Daniel Barrett, Kelton Rhoads, and Patricia Winters. 2006. "Managing Social Norms for Persuasive Impact." *Social Influence* 1: 3–15.

de Groot, Judith, Wojke Abrahamse, and Kayleigh Jones. 2013. "Persuasive Normative Messages: The Influence of Injunctive and Personal Norms on Using Free Plastic Bags." *Sustainability* 5: 1829–44.

Demarque, Christophe, Laetitia Charalambides, Denis Hilton, and Laurent Waroquier. 2015. "Nudging Sustainable Consumption: The Use of Descriptive Norms to Promote a Minority Behavior in a Realistic Online Shopping Environment." *Journal of Environmental Psychology* 43: 166–74.

Deutsch, Morton and Harold Gerard. 1955. "A Study of Normative and Informational Social Influences upon Individual Judgment." *Journal of Abnormal and Social Psychology* 51: 629–36.

Farrow, K., G. Grolleau, and L. Ibanez. (2017). "Social Norms and Pro–environmental Behavior: A Review of the Evidence." *Ecological Economics* 140: 1–13.

Ferraro, Paul, Juan Miranda, and Michael Price. 2011. "The Persistence of Treatment Effects with Norm-Based Policy Instruments: Evidence from a Randomized Environmental Policy Experiment." *American Economic Review* 101: 318–22.

Ferraro, Paul, and Michael Price. 2013. "Using Nonpecuniary Strategies to Influence Behavior: Evidence from a Large-Scale Field Experiment." *Review of Economics and Statistics* 95: 64–73.

Foxcroft, David, Maria Moreira, Nerissa Almeida Santimano, and Lesley Smith. 2015. "Social Norms Information for Alcohol Misuse in University and College Students." *Cochrane Database of Systematic Reviews* 1: doi:10.1002/14651858.CD006748.pub4.

Freedman, Jonathan L., and Scott C. Fraser. 1966. "Compliance without Pressure: The Foot-in-the-Door Technique." *Journal of Personality and Social Psychology* 4: 195–202.

Göckeritz, Suzanne, P. Wesley Schultz, Tania Rendón, Robert Cialdini, Noah Goldstein, and Vlad Griskevicius. 2010. "Descriptive Normative Beliefs and Conservation Behavior: The Moderating Roles of Personal Involvement and Injunctive Normative Beliefs." *European Journal of Social Psychology* 40: 514–23.

Goldstein, Noah, Robert Cialdini, and Vlad Griskevicius. 2008. "A Room with a Viewpoint: Using Social Norms to Motivate Environmental Conservation in Hotels." *Journal of Consumer Research* 35: 472–82.

Hafner, Rebecca, David Elmes, Daniel Read, and Mathew White. 2019. "Exploring the Role of Normative, Financial and Environmental Information in Promoting Uptake of Energy Efficient Technologies." *Journal of Environmental Psychology* 63: 26–35.

Heywood, John, and William Murdock. 2002. "Social Norms in Outdoor Recreation: Searching for the Behavior–Condition Link." *Leisure Sciences* 24: 283–95.

Jachimowicz, Jon, Oliver Hauser, Julia O'Brien, Erin Sherman, and Adam Galinsky. 2018. "The Critical Role of Second-Order Normative Beliefs in Predicting Energy Conservation." *Nature Human Behaviour* 2: 757–64.

Jacob, Céline, Nicolas Guéguen, and Gaëlle Boulbry. 2018. "How Proof of Previous Donations Influences Compliance with a Donation Request: Three Field Experiments." *International Review on Public and Nonprofit Marketing* 15: 1–8.

Jacobson, Ryan, Chad Mortensen, and Robert Cialdini. 2011. "Bodies Obliged and Unbound: Differentiated Response Tendencies for Injunctive and Descriptive Social Norms." *Journal of Personality and Social Psychology* 100: 433–48.

Klucharev, Vasily, Moniek Munneke, Ale Smidts, and Guillén Fernández. 2011. "Downregulation of the Posterior Medial Frontal Cortex Prevents Social Conformity." *Journal of Neuroscience* 31: 11934–40.

Kredentser, Maia, Leandre Fabrigar, Steven Smith, and Kimberly Fulton. 2012. "Following What People Think We Should Do versus What People Actually Do: Elaboration as a Moderator of the Impact of Descriptive and Injunctive Norms." *Social Psychological and Personality Science* 3: 341–7.

Lapinski, Maria, Erin Maloney, Mary Braz, and Hillary Shulman. 2013. "Testing the Effects of Social Norms and Behavioral Privacy on Hand Washing: A Field Experiment." *Human Communication Research* 39: 21–46.

Lede, Ellin, Rose Meleady, and Charles Seger. 2019. "Optimizing the Influence of Social Norms Interventions: Applying Social Identity Insights to Motivate Residential Water Conservation." *Journal of Environmental Psychology* 62: 105–14.

Leoniak, Krzysztof, and Wojciech Cwalina. 2019. "The Role of Normative Prompts and Norm Support Cues in Promoting Light-Switching Behavior: A Field Study." *Journal of Environmental Psychology* 64: 1–11.

Mackie, Gerry, Francesca Moneti, Holly Shakya, and Elaine Denny. 2015. *What Are Social Norms? How Are They Measured?* San Diego: UNICEF and University of California–San Diego, Center on Global Justice.

Margetts, Helen, Peter John, Tobias Escher, and Stéphane Reissfelder. 2011. "Social Information and Political Participation on the Internet: An Experiment." *European Political Science Review* 3: 321–44.

Miller, Daniel, and Deborah Prentice. 2016. "Changing Norms to Change Behavior." *Annual Review of Psychology* 67: 339–61.

Mortensen, Chad, Rebecca Neel, Robert Cialdini, Christine Jaeger, Ryan Jacobson, and Megan Ringel. 2017. "Trending Norms: A Lever for Encouraging Behaviors Performed by the Minority." *Social Psychological and Personality Science* 10: 201–10.

Nguyen, Gabrielle, Elizabeth Costenbader, Kate Plourde, Brad Kerner, and Susan Igras. 2019. "Scaling-Up Normative Change Interventions for Adolescent and Youth Reproductive Health: An Examination of the Evidence." *Journal of Adolescent Health* 64: S16–S30.

Nolan, Jessica. 2011. "The Cognitive Ripple of Social Norms Communications." *Group Processes and Intergroup Relations* 14: 689–702.

2017. "Social Norms and Their Enforcement." In *The Oxford Handbook of Social Influence*, edited by Stephen Harkins, Kipling Williams, and Jerry Burger, 147–64. Oxford: Oxford University Press.

Nolan, Jessica, P., Wesley Schultz, Robert Cialdini, Noah Goldstein, and Vlad Griskevicius. 2008. "Normative Social Influence Is Underdetected." *Personality and Social Psychology Bulletin* 34: 913–23.

Nolan, Jessica, Jessica Kenefick, and P. Wesley Schultz. 2011. "Normative Messages Promoting Energy Conservation Will Be Underestimated by Experts … Unless You Show Them the Data." *Social Influence* 6: 169–80.

Nolan, Jessica, P. Wesley Schultz, Robert Cialdini, and Noah Goldstein. 2021. "The Social Norms Approach: A Wise Intervention for Solving Social and Environmental Problems." In *Handbook of Wise Interventions: How Social-Psychological Insights Can Help Solve Problems*, edited by Gregory Walto n and Alia Crum. New York: Guilford.

Nook, Eric, and Jamil Zaki. 2015. "Social Norms Shift Behavioral and Neural Responses to Foods." *Journal of Cognitive Neuroscience* 27: 1412–26.

Paluck, Elizabeth. 2009. "Reducing Intergroup Prejudice and Conflict Using the Media: A Field Experiment in Rwanda." *Journal of Personality and Social Psychology* 96: 574–87.

Paluck, Elizabeth, and Laurie Ball. 2010. *Social Norms Marketing Aimed at Gender–Based Violence: A Literature Review and Critical Assessment*. New York: International Rescue Committee.

Pepitone, Albert. 1976. "Toward a Normative and Comparative Biocultural Social Psychology." *Journal of Personality and Social Psychology* 34: 641–53.

Perkins, H. Wesley. 2003 "The Emergence and Evolution of the Social Norms Approach to Substance Abuse Prevention." In *The Social Norms Approach to Preventing School and College Age Substance Abuse: A Handbook for Educators, Counselors, and Clinicians*, edited by H. Wesley Perkins, 3–17. San Francisco: Jossey–Bass.

Perkins, H. Wesley, and Alan Berkowitz. 1986. "Perceiving the Community Norms of Alcohol Use among Students: Some Research Implications for Campus Alcohol Education Programming." *International Journal of the Addictions* 21: 961–76.

Perkins, H. Wesley, Jeffrey Linkenbach, Melissa Lewis, and Clayton Neighbors. 2010. "Effectiveness of Social Norms Media Marketing in Reducing Drinking and Driving: A Statewide Campaign." *Addictive Behaviors* 35: 866–74.

Prestwich, Andrew, Ian Kellar, Mark Conner, Rebecca Lawton, Peter Gardner, and Liz Turgut. 2016. "Does Changing Social Influence Engender Changes in Alcohol Intake? A Meta-analysis." *Journal of Consulting and Clinical Psychology* 84: 845–60.

Priebe, Carly, and Kevin Spink. 2015. "Less Sitting and More Moving in the Office: Using Descriptive Norm Messages to Decrease Sedentary Behavior and Increase Light Physical Activity at Work." *Psychology of Sport and Exercise* 19: 76–84.

Richetin, Juliette, Marco Perugini, Denny Mondini, and Robert Hurling. 2014. "Conserving Water While Washing Hands: The Immediate and Durable Impacts of Descriptive Norms." *Environment and Behavior* 48: 343–64.

Richter, Isabal, John Thøgersen, and Christian Klöckner. 2018. "A Social Norms Intervention Going Wrong: Boomerang Effects from Descriptive Norms Information." *Sustainability* 10: 2848.

Robinson, Eric, Jason Thomas, Paul Aveyard, and Suzanna Higgs. 2014. "What Everyone Else Is Eating: A Systematic Review and Meta-analysis of the Effect of Informational Eating Norms on Eating Behavior." *Journal of the Academy of Nutrition and Dietetics* 114: 414–29.

Rodriguez, Lindsey, Clayton Neighbors, Dipali Rinker, Melissa Lewis, Brenda Lazorwitz, Rubi Gonzales, and Mary Larimer. 2015. "Remote versus In-Lab Computer-Delivered Personalized Normative Feedback Interventions for College Student Drinking." *Journal of Consulting and Clinical Psychology* 83: 455.

Ruff, Christian, Giuseppe Ugazio, and Ernst Fehr. 2013. "Changing Social Norm Compliance with Noninvasive Brain Stimulation." *Science* 342: 482–4.

Schultz, P. Wesley. 1999. "Changing Behavior with Normative Feedback Interventions: A Field Experiment on Curbside Recycling." *Basic and Applied Social Psychology* 21: 25–36.

Schultz, P. Wesley, Jessica Nolan, Robert Cialdini, Noah Goldstein, and Vlad Griskevicius. 2007. "The Constructive, Destructive, and Reconstructive Power of Social Norms." *Psychological Science* 18: 429–33.

Schultz, P. Wesley, Azar Khazian, and Adam Zaleski. 2008. "Using Normative Social Influence to Promote Conservation among Hotel Guests." *Social Influence* 3: 4–23.

Schultz, P. Wesley, Alyssa Messina, Giuseppe Tronu, Eleuterio Limas, Rupanwita Gupta, and Mica Estrada. 2014. "Personalized Normative Feedback and the Moderating Role of Personal Norms: A Field Experiment to Reduce Residential Water Consumption." *Environment and Behavior* 48: 686–710.

Schultz, P. Wesley, Mica Estrada, Joseph Schmitta, Rebecca Sokoloski, and Nilmini Silva-Send. 2015. "Using In–Home Displays to Provide Smart Meter Feedback about Household Electricity Consumption: A Randomized Control Trial Comparing Kilowatts, Cost, and Social Norms." *Energy* 90: 351–8.

Scribner, Robert, Katherine Theall, Karen Mason, Neal Simonsen, Shari Schneider, Laura Towvim, and William DeJong. 2011. "Alcohol Prevention on College Campuses: The Moderating Effect of the Alcohol Environment on the Effectiveness of Social Norms Marketing Campaigns." *Journal of Studies on Alcohol and Drugs* 72: 232–9.

Sherif, Muzafer. 1936. *The Psychology of Social Norms*. New York: Harper.

Smith, J. Russell, and Winnifred Louis. 2008. "Do As We Say and As We Do: The Interplay of Descriptive and Injunctive Group Norms in the Attitude–Behaviour Relationship." *British Journal of Social Psychology* 47: 647–66.

Smith, J. Russell, Winnifred Louis, Deborah Terry, Katharine Greenaway, Miranda Clarke, and Xiaoliang Cheng. 2012. "Congruent or Conflicted? The Impact of Injunctive and Descriptive Norms on Environmental Intentions." *Journal of Environmental Psychology* 32: 353–61.

Sparkman, Gregg, and Gregory Walton. 2017. "Dynamic Norms Promote Sustainable Behavior, even if It Is Counternormative." *Psychological Science* 28: 1663–74.

Stok, F. Marijn, Emely de Vet, Denise de Ridder, and John de Wit. (2016). "The Potential of Peer Social Norms to Shape Food Intake in Adolescents and Young Adults: A Systematic Review of Effects and Moderators." *Health Psychology Review* 10: 326–40.

van Kleef, Gerben, Florian Wanders, Eftychia Stamkou, and Astrid Homan. 2019. "The Social Dynamics of Breaking the Rules: Antecedents and Consequences of Norm–Violating Behavior." *Current Opinion in Psychology* 6: 25–31.

van de Bongardt, Daphne, Ellen Reitz, Theo Sandfort, and Maja Deković. 2014. "A Meta-analysis of the Relations between Three Types of Peer Norms and Adolescent Sexual Behavior." *Personality and Social Psychology Review* 19: 203–34.

Wallen, Kenneth E., and Gerard Kyle. 2018. "The Efficacy of Message Frames on Recreational Boaters' Aquatic Invasive Species Mitigation Behavioral Intentions." *Human Dimensions of Wildlife*, 23: 297–312.

Wallen, Kenneth E., and Chelsie Romulo. 2017. "Social Norms: More Details, Please." *Proceedings of the National Academy of Sciences* USA, 117: E5283–E5284.

Walton, Gregory, and Timothy Wilson. 2018. "Wise Interventions: Psychological Remedies for Social and Personal Problems." *Psychological Review* 125: 617–55.

Wechsler, Henry, Toben Nelson, Jae Lee, Mark Seibring, Catherine Lewis, and Richard Keeling. 2003. "Perception and Reality: A National Evaluation of Social Norms Marketing Interventions to Reduce College Students' Heavy Alcohol Use." *Journal of Studies on Alcohol and Drugs* 64: 484–94.

29

Social Contagion and Goal Framing: The Sustainability of Rule Compliance

Siegwart Lindenberg, Frédérique Six and Kees Keizer

Abstract: Rule compliance (in organizations or society at large) may be strengthened or weakened by social contagion processes. Observing others' (non-)compliance with rules influences one's own likelihood of compliance. Extant literature shows two social contagion theories that can explain this phenomenon. First, the theory of normative conduct (TNC) (Cialdini et al. 1990) suggests that people interpret the observed behaviour of others (i.e. the descriptive norm) as adaptive for that context, resulting in rational imitation. Second, Goal Framing Theory (GFT) (Lindenberg and Steg 2007) suggests that we should look not just at the contagion of concrete behaviour but at the process that governs the contagion of the very goal to comply with norms and legitimate rules. This is particularly important because it predicts that observed (non-) compliance regarding one rule also affects (non-)compliance with other rules ('cross-norm effects'). Because the goal to comply tends to decay, it needs continuous support from the observation of other people's respect for norms and legitimate rules. Compliance and non-compliance are thus both self-reinforcing mechanisms. This has clear implications for policy which are discussed in this chapter, most notably the importance of a focus on legitimizing rules, so that they are interpreted as norms by the general public.

29.1 INTRODUCTION

Compliance requires that people are both willing and able to act in line with the organizational or state regulatory rules. Whether people comply with rules may be influenced by many different factors such as deterrence and sanctions, monitoring, rewards and bonuses, peer pressure and shaming, and technical and legal knowledge (see Chapters 12–15, 17, 23, 35, 39, 40 in this volume). In this chapter we focus on the social contagion of rule compliance. By social contagion of rule compliance, we mean that the level of rule compliance of a person is influenced by the level of rule compliance of one or more others. This kind of contagion is a particular kind of social influence process.

Two main theories of social contagion processes related to rule compliance may be distinguished: the theory of normative conduct (TNC; see Cialdini et al. 1990) and Goal Framing Theory (GFT; see Lindenberg and Steg 2007). Both are based on so-called shifting 'salience' effects: observing or surmising other people's behaviour or beliefs influences the activation (i.e. the 'salience') of a norm (TNC) or the goal to comply with a norm (GFT). There are two kinds of social contagion. First, there is what may be called 'imitative contagion' where people are more likely to do X if they see others do X. TNC is mainly concerned with this type of social contagion. In economics, this phenomenon is often called 'conditional cooperation' (Gächter 2007). Second, GFT deals with what may be called 'compliance contagion', where people are more (less) likely to comply with rule X if they see others (not) complying with rule Y. We argue that, when dealing with the contagion of compliance with rules, GFT is especially interesting compared to TNC because GFT's processes for social contagion in rule compliance predict that (non-)compliance itself is contagious and that it can thus spread across different rules. The major theoretical difference between the theories is that, contrary to TNC, GFT deals explicitly with the goal to comply with norms and legitimate rules. In this way, GFT is able to consider the influence of other goals that weaken or strengthen the goal to comply with norms and rules (Etienne 2011), and it is able to specify the conditions under which social contagion of compliance with rules is likely to take place or not to take place. Most importantly, because of the tendency of the goal to comply with norms and legitimate rules to decay, its sustainability depends on an ongoing process of contagion. As we will argue, people's compliance signals respect for norms and legitimate rules and thus 'infects' other people's goal to comply. In turn, one's own goal to comply needs to be infected by exposure to signals of others' respect for norms and legitimate rules. The central message of this chapter is thus that the sustainability of compliance depends to a large extent on the ongoing contagion of the goal to comply.

This chapter focuses mainly on these GFT-based social contagion processes and how they may influence rule compliance. We start by briefly introducing the foundations of both theories and then elaborate on GFT's perspective on social contagion processes of rule compliance. We conclude with some outstanding research questions and implications for policy (be that for organizations or governments).

29.2 THE THEORY OF NORMATIVE CONDUCT (TNC)

The theory by Cialdini and colleagues explains how social norms affect behaviour. The main propositions of the theory are (a) that there is a distinction between the two types of social norms (injunctive and descriptive; see also Chapter 32 in this volume), that it is their salience that determines their impact, and (b) that their salience can be influenced by the situation (Cialdini et al. 1990). *Injunctive social norms* are the behaviours (perceived as) commonly (dis)approved of. The violation of rules prohibiting behaviour will generally be disapproved of, and as such these rules typically serve as injunctive norms. Not littering, speeding, embezzling money or scratching the car of your manager after not getting a raise are all injunctive norms in our kind of society. There is in TNC no particular difference between norms (informal) and rules (formal). Not serving alcohol to minors is a formal rule, and not coming late for work is an informal norm by a company, and not stealing is both a formal rule and a norm. Injunctive norms can also describe the approved-of behaviour in a certain situation. It is an injunctive norm to help someone in need, hold the door or greet your colleagues in the morning. Injunctive norms regulate behaviour by the social sanctions and appraisal we associate with (not) complying with them. Holding the door will probably result in a 'thank you' while *not* holding the door will likely result in a less pleasant remark. In TNC, injunctive norms have no direct effect on the social contagion of rule compliance; rather, it is descriptive norms that affect contagion.

Descriptive norms refer to the behaviour perceived to be common in a specific situation, and they are the major vehicle of social contagion. They indicate what the majority of people are doing. Descriptive norms influence behaviour by telling us that 'if a lot of people are doing this, it's probably a wise thing to do' (Cialdini 2007). Examples are the most bought book, the very crowded restaurant next to an empty one, and the behaviour of others in traffic. People copy this behaviour because if so many others are doing it, it will most likely result in the best outcome. This leads to an imitative contagion of compliance with a norm that is defined by 'what others are seen as doing'. A littered environment suggests that many have littered here, which, in the light of Cialdini's work, signals littering as adaptive behaviour for that context, thereby making the behaviour more likely (Cialdini et al. 1990). Conversely, seeing a person litter in a litter-free environment focuses attention on a descriptive norm that signals 'almost nobody litters here' and which therefore reduces littering, as shown by Reno et al. (1993). In this approach, rules exert their contagious influence on compliance indirectly via behavioural regularities that are perceived and imitated.

TNC does consider that descriptive norms should also be seen in the context of injunctive norms, because the two can be in conflict. However, TNC does not specify exactly how descriptive and injunctive norms interact, other than that the most salient of the two will influence behaviour. Would it matter if people's behaviour were seen as disrespect for an injunctive norm, or as a norm contradicting an injunctive norm? Would it matter whether it were one or the other? There is no room in TNC to consider such questions.

29.3 GOAL FRAMING THEORY (GFT)

The second theory of social contagion processes is Goal Framing Theory (GFT) (Lindenberg and Steg 2007). It provides explanations for the motivational dynamics of behaviour and how compliant behaviour may be stimulated or thwarted, including processes of contagion. GFT posits that the likelihood of a behaviour is determined by the goals that people pursue. In turn, the salience of these goals is influenced by the observed or surmised behaviour of others. Thus, rule compliance depends on the salience of an overarching goal, and this salience depends to a large extent on what others do, creating contagion effects. GFT distinguishes three overarching goals: hedonic, gain and normative. Overarching goals determine the playing field of what is considered relevant (including what are the relevant alternatives to choose from). When people pursue a hedonic goal, they focus on immediate gratification, aiming 'to feel good right now' and avoid unpleasurable effort or discomfort. It is strongly linked to people's fundamental needs and automatic decision-making. When people pursue a gain goal, they are more future-oriented, aiming 'to preserve and improve their resources'. In a gain goal, decision-making is more deliberate and calculative. People pursuing a normative goal focus on 'acting appropriately', on what they believe they ought to do. They are then highly sensitive to social norms; social norms specify what behaviour is appropriate in a given situation (e.g. Keizer et al. 2011; Lindenberg 2006).

For a goal to influence behaviour, it must be activated ('salient') to some degree. All three overarching goals are activated to some degree at the same time, but their relative salience varies. At any one moment, one goal is the most salient and thus frames the decision-making, while the other goals are present in the background. The most salient overarching goal determines what information is attended to and how that information is used in decision-making processes, thus making people focus on certain alternatives, neglecting others (Steg et al. 2015). Goals in the cognitive background may either support or weaken the salient goal. When a background goal points decision-making in the same direction as the salient goal, the salient goal is strengthened and the likelihood that people choose options that realize this focal goal is increased (Steg et al. 2015). Think, for example, of a warm glow (a hedonic goal effect in the background) when complying with the norm to help somebody in need. When, on the other hand, the background goal conflicts with the salient goal and points decision-making in the opposite direction, the salient goal is weakened. Think, for example, of having to spend quite a bit of money (a gain goal effect in the background) to help somebody in need.

Rule compliance can be motivated by any of the overarching goals. When rule compliance is pleasurable and does not require much effort, compliance is possible even with a salient hedonic goal. This does not offer a stable basis for rule compliance. When the gain goal is salient and compliance is profitable, people are likely to comply because it is prudent to do so (which is often called 'instrumental' compliance (Tyler 2006)). This type of compliance is likely to lead to a strategic use of compliance (or what McBarnet (2002) has called 'creative' compliance aimed at bending rules to one's own advantage). Rules, however, are usually introduced to create a stable basis for compliance and to make people behave in ways that are deemed desirable by society. Rule-compliant behaviour is usually beneficial for others but not pleasurable, effortless or profitable for the individual. For this very reason, we see in the literature a heavy emphasis on the importance of 'normative compliance' (Tyler 2006; McBarnet 2002). However, in the literature, normative compliance is, by and large, seen as an attitude rather than a dynamic process of contagion. Paying attention to the shifting salience of overarching goals, the precariousness of the normative goal, and the concomitant importance that a rule is clearly seen as a social norm, that is, that it safeguards the values and needs of the collective (Lindenberg 2017; Steg et al. 2015), allows us to put the searchlight on the dynamic nature of compliance which is rooted in the contagion of the very goal to comply.

In GFT, an activated normative goal creates feelings of obligation to act appropriately, that is, to comply with norms and legitimate rules in general. By contrast, in TNC what is activated is not a goal but a particular norm, and people comply with this norm because it seems wise (descriptive norm) or prudent (injunctive norm) to do so. Feelings of obligation don't play a role in TNC. We contend that to understand the dynamics of rule compliance and its contagion necessitates understanding not just the activation of norms but also the activation of the very goal to comply with norms, and when and how rules are taken to be norms.

The a priori likelihood of being salient is not the same for each of the three overarching goals. The hedonic goal is a priori most likely to be salient as it focuses on fundamental needs; the gain goal is a priori *less likely to be salient* than the hedonic goal, because it deals only with secondary needs (resources); finally, the normative goal is a priori the most precarious. It is least likely to be salient because it deals only with the tertiary needs of collectivity (Lindenberg and Steg 2007). This implies that for the normative goal to be more salient than the hedonic or gain goals requires much support from the context within which people act. This support may help develop habits and thus foster a self-identity as a moral and/or law-abiding person (Verplanken and Sui 2019), which can stabilize the normative goal and make it less susceptible to the contrary influences of the hedonic and gain goals. But when this support wanes, even a salient normative goal and a moral self-identity will become less salient over time and give way to increasing salience of gain and hedonic goals (Aquino et al. 2009). It is these kinds of context effects on the salience of normative goals that create social contagion of rule compliance, and, at the same time, make the sustainability of compliance dependent on an ongoing process of positive contagion. How this works will be explained in the following sections.

29.4 GFT-BASED SOCIAL CONTAGION PROCESSES OF COMPLIANCE

For social contagion processes concerning rule compliance, two aspects are most important (from the point of view of GFT). First, the salience of the normative goal is particularly strongly influenced by the signal that relevant others respect or disrespect shared norms. Thus (non-)compliance is relevant not only because a norm is followed or not followed but also because, for others, it is a signal of (dis)respect for norms in general. Thus, for social contagion of *norm* compliance, we must look closer at these influences.

Second, rules are covered by the normative goal only if they are seen as norms. For this to happen, rules must be seen as legitimate. Thus, in order to transfer what we know about the contagion of norm compliance to the contagion of rule compliance, we must deal with processes of legitimation (of rules and of authority). In the following, we will first deal with processes of legitimation and then discuss the contagion of rule compliance (i.e. compliance with norms or with rules that are legitimate and thus are treated like norms).

29.4.1 *From Rules to Social Norms: Legitimacy of Rules*

The normative goal focuses on serving a particular collective by acting appropriately and having a sense of obligation to do so. However: what is 'acting appropriately'? One answer is: doing whatever helps the achievement of the goals of the collective, such as helping one's team to win. Yet, collectives also develop directives that indicate what would be good for the collective: norms. There are some basic norms that are virtually universal because they are adaptive for any collective. These are norms that have to do with the achievement of solidarity with the collective: cooperation, sharing, helping, efforts to understand and be understood, trustworthiness and considerateness (see Lindenberg 2006, 2014a). In addition, there are norms that are specific to a collective by defining and protecting the identity of the collective (such as honouring the flag and the core values of the collective). Both kinds of norms are shared and generally highly internalized in participants of a collective. We assume that they form the 'hard core' of the normative goal. Additional norms (such as 'be honest', 'be silent in the library') can become part of the normative goal by becoming ways in which core norms are 'operationalized'.

Formal rules, be they from the organization people work in or the country they live in, are not necessarily congruent with these norms. Thus, many collectives impose rules that are not intuitively linked to norms that are covered by the normative goal. For example, a hotel may have a rule for room service personnel that loose-hanging curtains may be repaired only by using a ladder rather than a chair. For such a rule to acquire a sense of obligation in the hotel personnel, it must be 'legitimized'. If it is not legitimized in this sense, the rule may be linked to a gain goal (for example 'it is advantageous to comply with the rule when one is monitored') or to a hedonic goal (for example 'I follow it only if it is little effort').

Legitimacy is the major link between institutional systems (with their formal rules) and the normative goal (Lindenberg 2017; Tyler 2006). How do rules become legitimized, that is, become social norms that are part of the normative goal of those who have to comply with them (the regulated actors)? We propose three conditions that need to be met so that organizational and regulatory rules may become part of the normative goal. First, the regulating actor who imposes the rule needs to be seen as a legitimate authority; and the regulating actor should not be seen to be violating their own rule. Second, regulated actors need to perceive that the rule has widespread support among those who have to comply with the rule. Third, the rule must 'make sense' for those who are supposed to comply with it. Given that these conditions are fulfilled, the regulated actors are likely to see the rule as a norm that is part of the normative goal. We return to legitimation processes when discussing ways to increase contagion of rule compliance.

29.4.2 *Respect or Disrespect for a Norm and Cross-Norm Effects*

As the normative goal, being a priori the weakest, needs much support to become and remain salient, the behaviour of others showing respect (active support) or disrespect (lack of active support) of a norm (or a legitimate rule) has a large effect on the salience of the normative goal. This is not a 'descriptive norm' effect. From the perspective of TNC, littering in a setting tells us that littering is an adaptive behaviour in that setting, and therefore I will do it too. Littering thus creates an imitative contagion. From the perspective of GFT, in our society people know that littering is transgressing a norm, so that seeing litter is a cue indicating that many pursued the hedonic goal and therefore showed disrespect not just for the anti-litter norm itself but also for the need to interpret the situation as relevant for the normative goal itself. We argue that this cue will therefore lower the salience of one's own normative goal. In the literature, it has been found that when a descriptive norm contradicts an injunctive norm, it lowers the degree of compliance to the injunctive norm (cf. Smith et al. 2012). A less salient normative goal, however, will not only make it more likely that one litters (rather than making the effort of carrying that empty soda can to a trashcan); it will also make it more likely that one will transgress other norms. This 'cross-norm effect' makes social contagion of rule compliance particularly relevant because it spreads across contexts, as a variety of field experiments shows (Keizer et al. 2008). This creates, for example, a curious effect of prohibition signs. Graffiti in Dutch cities is forbidden by presumably legitimate rules. A study on littering (Keizer et al. 2011) showed not only a cross-norm effect (that when there was graffiti on a wall, people were more likely to litter) but also that this effect was even stronger when there was also a sign that explicitly prohibited graffiti. Thus, disrespect for norm A (graffiti) created a contagion effect across behavioural domains to disrespect for norm B (littering). The sign against graffiti activates the anti-litter norm, so that perceived disrespect for this norm is even more obvious and the salience of the normative goal is lowered even more.[1] For legitimate rules, the implication is that they have to be seen as being enforced (or, if not, abandoned), because unenforced rules will make disrespect highly visible and thus create negative cross-norm effects on compliance. In the informal sphere, enforcement depends on people's negative reactions to others' disrespect for a social norm. However, even the very willingness to sanction others is caught up in the dynamics of cross-norm effects: people are less willing to sanction others if they believe that many others disrespect the norm or legitimate rule (Traxler and Winter 2012). In this way, non-compliance is likely to occur in cascades. For example, in organizations this is observed in studies of problematic 'climates' (Peterson 2002).

If this mechanism is indeed operative, then it should also be the case that observed respect for norm A increases the likelihood that the observer complies with norm B (assuming there is no ceiling effect). This was indeed found in field experiments. For example, people are more likely to adhere to the pro-social norm of helping others in need (by picking up dropped

[1] Notice that for TNC, a sign prohibiting graffiti should increase the strength of the injunctive norm and thereby weaken the influence of the conflicting descriptive norm, leading to exactly the opposite prediction from what is expected on the basis of GFT.

groceries) after observing someone sweeping the pavement in front of his or her house (Keizer et al. 2013). It is important to note that, in these experiments, the 'behaviour of others' is only the behaviour of one person. This also holds for compliance cascades (see Appelbaum et al. 2007). The most important effect of other people on the contagion of compliance with norms and legitimate rules thus comes not from imitation of what most people do, but from the effects of observed respect or disrespect for norms, even if only one person is observed. These mechanisms affect not just concrete behaviour but the very goal to comply with a norm or legitimate rule.

29.4.3 *The Effect of Outgroups*

In a recent meta-analysis of experiments using social norms to promote pro-environmental behaviours, Bergquist et al. (2019) found that the strongest effect on activating norms came from direct or indirect cues of the behaviour of others. However, there is also another important mechanism that may block or even reverse social contagion based on perceived or surmised (dis)respect for norms. GFT assumes that it matters who shows (dis)respect. If I observe or surmise disrespect for a norm that I endorse by people like you and me (my 'in-group'), the salience of my normative goal will be lowered. However, if I observe or surmise disrespect for a norm that I endorse by people who represent a 'dissociative' out-group (a group I don't want to be identified with, see White and Dahl 2007), the salience of my normative goal will increase, and I will even more likely comply with the norm. An out-group is also dissociative if it is known that its members don't disrespect my norms. For example, an experiment in the main train station of Berlin (see Lindenberg & Keizer in press) showed that people who pass other 'normal' Berliners who smoke where it is not allowed are more likely to smoke as well where it is not allowed, compared to a control group. However, people who pass Punk-Goths (in black robes with a mohawk hairdo, taken to be dissociative) smoking where it is not allowed, are less likely to smoke where it is not allowed than people in a control group. Thus, disrespect for my norms by a dissociative out-group makes the norms of my in-group and my obligation to comply with them (i.e. the normative goal) more salient. The irony is that dissociative out-groups thereby help contagion of norm compliance within the in-group. Another illustration of this effect is provided by research done on car sharing (Schaefers et al. 2016). Cars in such sharing groups are supposed to be returned in a clean state. If a car is returned in a messy state by an anonymous previous user, the new user is more inclined to leave the car messy for the next user, a clear sign of compliance contagion. However, when the car brand is 'high-brow' (versus 'low-brow'), this contagious effect almost vanishes. Presumably, the highbrow brand is taken as an indication that 'good' people would not leave the car messy, so that customers who do leave it messy are seen as belonging to a dissociative out-group.

All these effects on the social contagion of compliance with norms and legitimate rules are summarized in Figure 29.1. This figure also suggests that social contagion of compliance is a self-reinforcing mechanism if the goal to comply with norms is salient, and, for the same reason, that non-compliance is also a self-reinforcing mechanism.

The cross-norm effect is crucial here. For example, Ariely and Garcia-Rada (2019: 64) conclude that their contagion of dishonesty experiments 'suggest that receiving a bribe request erodes individuals' moral character, prompting them to behave more dishonestly in subsequent ethical decisions'. Thus, the dishonesty can spread to many other kinds of ethical decision. Yet,

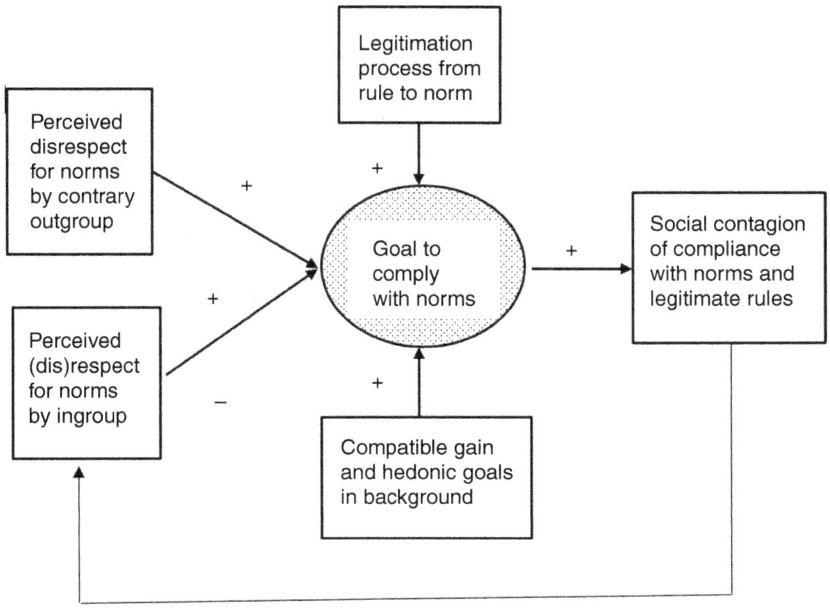

FIGURE 29.1 Social contagion of compliance with norms and legitimate rules

the authors have no real explanation for the cross-norm effect itself. For this effect, we need to pay attention to the dynamics of the overarching goals, as shown in Figure 29.1.

29.4.4 *The Influence of Others When the Goal to Comply with Norms Is Already Salient*

Behaviour that Informs about a Norm: The Injunctive Norm Search Effect. Given that the goal to comply with norms is already salient, other people may still have an effect on the social contagion process. Attention to this possibility also helps to clarify the possible interaction between injunctive and descriptive norms in TNC. When people are motivated to comply with norms, they often seem to actively look to what others are doing in order to find out what the concrete injunctive norms in a particular situation are. Imagine you come to a foreign country for the first time. Then you might want to comply with their norms (say about greeting, about driving, about voice level, about waiting at traffic lights for pedestrians, etc.) but you are not sure what the norms are. In that case, you do have a salient normative goal which makes you search for information on what the local injunctive norms are. You infer the injunctive norms from the behaviour you observe. The behaviour of others is then highly relevant as a cue to what the injunctive norms are, but its relevance comes from the link with the activated goal to comply with norms (see Panel A in Figure 29.2). This effect can be called 'injunctive norm search effect', which can be distinguished from a 'descriptive norm search effect' that comes about when people search for rational alternatives ways to act (see Panel B in Figure 29.2). In the literature, these two effects are often confused.

Behaviour that Fine-Tunes or Operationalizes a Norm. Another kind of injunctive norm search effect is looking to others for fine-tuning one's injunctive norm. Imagine that there is a rule

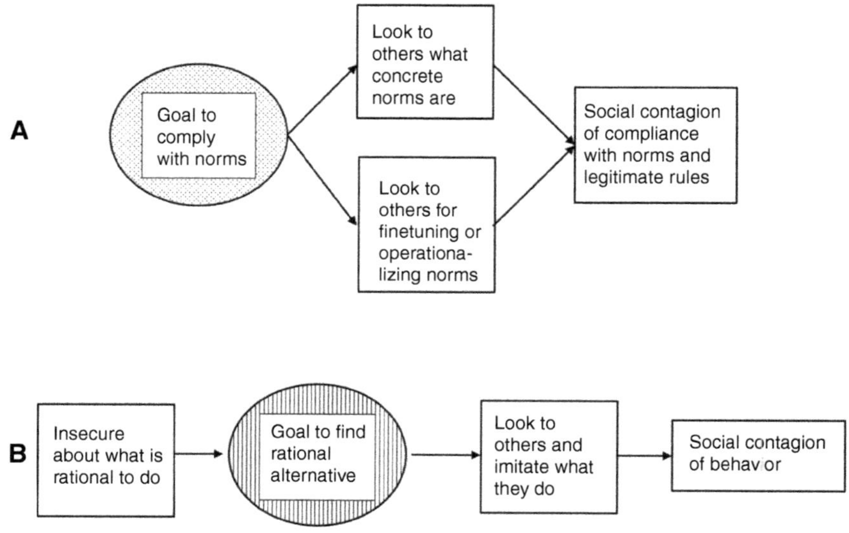

FIGURE 29.2 Norm search effects: Panel A: injunctive; Panel B: descriptive

in an organization that every employee should come on time and that this rule is legitimate for the employees. There is no time stamp clock. Then, for a newcomer who also finds this norm legitimate, there is still the question: what is 'on time'? Is it on the dot, or may I be a few minutes late? How many minutes? In short, for the newcomer, the norm 'to be on time' needs to be fine-tuned, and the easiest way to do it is to see what experienced colleagues are doing. In this way, the fine-tuned norm will spread. A sense-making narrative for the particular fine-tuning is likely to increase compliance. Observe that even though people seemingly imitate others, it is not an imitative descriptive norm effect.

Given that close monitoring without a time stamp clock is unlikely, having a salient normative goal is important for compliance. Employees who have a chronically salient hedonic goal may still often fail to conform. And people who have a chronically salient gain goal and time constraints will be 'on time' only when they expect some advantage from doing so. The fine-tuning effect of others' behaviour on norm compliance thus requires a salient normative goal for contagion effects. Another example concerns electricity use. A study showed that information on the electricity use of others had an effect on one's own electricity use. But the same study also showed that this effect worked especially for people who have environmentally conscious social networks and who are already concerned about the environment through their political identification (Costa and Kahn 2013). For those with a salient normative goal regarding the environment, information on others' use fine-tuned their own norms about electricity use. Similar effects have been found in many other studies, for example for so-called productivity spillover and peer effects (Mas and Moretti 2009; Thöni and Gächter 2015), even though the explanations for the effects vary widely in the literature.

The same can be said about 'operationalizing' a norm by information on how one can best comply with a somewhat abstract norm.[2] For example, given that I want to comply with the norm to protect the environment, should I recycle household waste? To answer this question,

[2] Scientific research and education are highly important for the basis that ultimately leads to the operationalization of abstract norms via contagion effects (Lindenberg 2008). Thus, given a widespread abstract norm, its operationalization emerges from the flow of scientific arguments and education to early adaptors, and from there to the

one may get informed about what science says about it, but very likely the strongest influence comes from looking at what significant others and what neighbours do (Fornara et al. 2011). Because doing is a stronger indicator of respect for a norm than expecting others to comply, Fornara et al. (2011) and many other studies find a stronger effect of injunctive norm search information on compliance compared to messages about other people's expectations. Similarly, if we want to protect the environment and get the message in a hotel room 'You can join your fellow guests in this programme to help save the environment by reusing your towels during your stay', we are more apt to comply with the norm to save the environment by also reusing our hotel towel (Goldstein, Cialdini and Griskevicius 2008). Note that the information on what others do is linked to the normative appeal 'help save the environment'. With the normative goal being salient, the information on how others help to save the environment is much more influential than the information that other people expect us to reuse our towels. Operationalization of norms can even be achieved by injunctive norm search information about what only a few people do, if the information contains a trend, that is, information suggesting that the number of people who show respect for this operationalization is growing (Mortensen et al. 2019).

Behaviour That Is Taken to Indicate What Is Most Adaptive to Do in a Particular Situation: The 'Imitative' Descriptive Norm Search Effect. Remember, according to Cialdini (2007), a descriptive norm tells us that 'if a lot of people are doing this, it's probably a wise thing to do'. When looking for a restaurant in a foreign city, not knowing which one is good and which one is not, one searches for a descriptive norm, and one will go to the restaurant that is well populated with seemingly local people, who supposedly know the restaurants around here. This is rational imitation, which is not linked to signals of respect or disrespect for an injunctive norm and thus does not presuppose a salient normative goal. This 'pure' descriptive norm effect is important in its own right (for example for fads), but it is not really relevant for the contagion of compliance to rules. For the latter to happen, the normative goal needs to be involved.

29.5 STRENGTHENING SOCIAL CONTAGION OF RULE COMPLIANCE

GFT's perspective on social contagion processes provides policy guidance on how to strengthen the social contagion of rule compliance. Figure 29.1 outlines the major components of possible interventions: strengthening legitimacy; increasing visibility of respect for norms and the invisibility of disrespect for norms; and aligning gain and hedonic goals in the background with the normative goal.

29.5.1 *Strengthening Legitimacy*

Maybe the most important step to increase the contagion of rule compliance is to increase the legitimacy of the rule as addressed in Section 29.4.1. Because this process is so vital for the contagion of rule compliance, we discuss it in more detail than the other components.

broader processes of operationalization in daily interactions, a mechanism described long ago as the 'two step flow of communication' (Katz and Lazarsfeld 1955)

29.5.1.1 Rule-Legitimating Authority

Much has been written about the bases of legitimacy for authority, mostly based on Weber's (1978) classification of types of authority: charismatic, traditional, and rational-legal. Important for our purposes is that in charismatic and traditional legitimacy, the authority is legitimate and thereby also the rules issued by the authority. Yet in the rational-legal type of present-day society, an authority may have the right to make rules and claim conformity, but that does not make every rule automatically legitimate in the sense of making it a norm that is covered by a sense of obligation. For example, the police have the right to set a speed limit, but for many people such a limit is kept only in order to avoid sanctions, without any sense of obligation. This implies that for the legitimacy of rules in our sense, the regulating actors (authority) must be legitimate, but, in addition, they need to be seen as treating their own rule as a norm by not showing disrespect for it. The literature on ethical leadership provides ample support for the strong negative effect of violating one's own rules (e.g. Brown and Treviño 2006; Sims and Brinkmann 2002). Leaders violating their own rules also don't consistently enforce their rules and, thus, create rule ambiguity among their followers, both of which lower the legitimacy of rules (Singh and Twalo 2015). Yet, for legitimizing rules, it is not enough that the regulating actors comply with their own rules. Because people are so sensitive to what other people are doing, rules also need widespread support in order to be seen as norms with a sense of obligation to comply.

29.5.1.2 Rule-Legitimating Widespread Support

The more that other people for whom a particular rule applies are seen (or are believed) to respect a particular rule, the more this rule is seen as a norm that should be complied with. To return to our example of the rule to use a ladder to fix a curtain, getting a ladder to fix a curtain takes effort. It is much easier to use a chair. If an employee sees (or hears) that other employees take the trouble to use a ladder for fixing a curtain even though there is nobody in authority monitoring it at that moment, the 'ladder rule' is seemingly a rule to respect. Respecting a rule also implies that not complying with it would meet with disapproval from others like me. Once a rule is seen to be respected by others like me, it is likely that it functions like a norm. This also means that seeing others respect a particular rule not only legitimizes that rule but also increases the salience of the goal to comply with it. Note that purely verbal messages about the mutual expectations of peers, such as 'we expect of each other that this rule will be complied with', are no signal of respect. In fact, such a message conveys that the rule might not be really serious and that compliance is not expected by the legitimizing authorities. Recent research (Kouchaki, Gino and Feldman 2019) showed that such messages convey 'warmth' rather than legitimacy and are likely to even increase non-compliance.

29.5.1.3 Legitimating Instrumentality of Rules

In contrast to traditional and charismatic bases of legitimacy, rational-legal legitimacy implies that in order to be get widespread support as being legitimate, rules must also make sense, that is, be rational in the sense of being instrumental for achieving a collectively valued result. Rules need to have a 'sense-making narrative' in which they are embedded. Take the example of the 'ladder rule'. Why should anybody take the trouble to use a ladder for fixing a curtain in a hotel? A sense-making narrative may include that there is the safety issue, since employees in the past have injured themselves using a chair for this purpose. In addition, the insurance may not pay in case of an accident, if no ladder was used, meaning that the hotel will also not cover injuries that arise from not having used a ladder. The more convincing the narrative, the greater the legitimizing effect. Non-compliance by an authority with its own rules or clearly manipulative intentions in the use of rules render any sense-making narrative unconvincing. Controversial scientific results can also undermine the narrative by allowing political issues to play a role in which side to believe (Stryker 1994).

Sanctions can also be crucial for establishing instrumentality. If the sense-making narrative is about protecting a collective value, then failure to comply with a rule threatens a collective value. It creates negative externalities and the collective value needs to be protected also by sanctions. Take the example of smoking. As long as smoking was seen as affecting only the smoker's own health, it was difficult to make an anti-smoking rule legitimate in the sense of becoming a norm. However, when it became widely known that smoking is bad for bystanders, a sense-making narrative for anti-smoking rules could be established. The health of bystanders needs to be protected by sanctioning violations of the anti-smoking rule. Sanctions that are seen as protecting the collective value contained in the narrative of a rule thus become a signal that authorities take the narrative seriously which, in turn, increases the legitimacy of the rule.

In sum, in order to be covered by the normative goal, a rule needs to be seen as a norm, that is, be legitimate. The likelihood that it is legitimate for a person increases if (a) the authority that issued the rule does not show disrespect for the rule; and (b) people who are expected by the authority to follow the rule show respect for it. Respect for a rule becomes more likely if it is embedded in a sense-making narrative, and if this narrative is accompanied by sanctions for failure to comply.

29.5.2 *Other Measures to Increase Social Contagion of Rule Compliance*

Contagion of rule compliance, as discussed in this chapter, relies on influences on the salience of the normative goal (which in turn creates cross-norm effects). There are many ways to achieve this (Lindenberg and Papies 2019). But there is one influence that may be most important for the salience of the very goal to comply with norms: *perceiving* other people's respect or disrespect for norms. Social contagion thus depends heavily on the visibility of respect for norms and the invisibility of disrespect for norms. For example, Brunner and Ostermaier (2019) showed that if respect for norms in organizations is not transparent, managers and employees will interpret what they see and hear in favour of their own interest ('others probably also don't stick to the rules'). But the authors warn that transparency will backfire if compliance is low. Thus, interventions can target visibility of compliance, for example by information campaigns about rule-compliant behaviour (avoiding publicizing complaints about people showing disrespect for norms). Importantly, rules should either be enforced or dropped, because if they are made salient, say by a non-parking sign, but not enforced, then people's non-compliance with them will be even more obvious a sign of disrespect, leading to a self-reinforcing social contagion of non-compliance (Keizer et al. 2011). The exception to this strategy, as illustrated in Section 29.4.3 with the study by Lindenberg & Keizer (in press), is information about the disrespect for in-group norms by 'dissociative' out-groups (i.e. by out-groups that are seen as being contrary to the norms and legitimate rules of the in-group). In this case, information of disrespect for in-group norms would actually increase the salience of the goal to conform among people of the in-group. Of course, there may be good reasons *not* to make use of this latter strategy because it may create other problems, such as discrimination against minorities, and possibly even an increase in violations by out-groups.

Social contagion of compliance may be hampered by gain and hedonic goals that lower the salience of the normative goal and bar cross-norm effects. For this reason, an important component of an intervention for the contagion of rule compliance is aligning gain and hedonic goals in the background with the normative goal. Sanctions that are embedded in a sense-making narrative can have this effect for the gain goal. When cues about respect for norms come from others with whom one is in face-to-face interaction, the personal character of the interaction adds a positive hedonic aspect to observed respect for norms, making the contagion more likely (Rogers et al. 2018). Public approval (including awards; see Frey and Gallus 2017) for behaviour that is targeted for encouragement aligns the hedonic goal (creating a warm glow for compliance) with the normative goal[3] (for other practical examples within organizations, see Lindenberg and Foss 2011).

29.6 CONCLUSION

Why is it important to deal with the contagion of compliance with rules? Our answer, based on GFT, is that the very goal to comply tends to decay in favour of personal concerns, unless it is subject to an ongoing process of social contagion in which observed respect for norms and legitimate rules by others increases the salience of one's own goal to comply. Thus, when it comes to social contagion of compliance, we need to look not just at the contagion of concrete behaviour (such as littering) by imitation but at the dynamics of overarching goals that affect contagion of the very goal to comply. The importance of dealing with such a goal is not just that it tends to decay if not supported but also its ability to create cross-norm effects, so that observed (non-)compliance regarding one rule also affects (non-)compliance with other rules. Here, a caveat is in order. It is at present not known how far the cross-norm effect stretches. Because behaviour is not just influenced by norms, there may be gain or hedonic reasons why the contagion of (non-)compliance may not happen even if a rule is legitimate. For example, Van Wijk and Six (2014) found Dutch pub owners who followed others by complying with food safety and hygiene rules, to consciously violate the smoking ban. Presumably, the goal to keep the loyalty of customers (a gain goal) prevented the normative goal from covering enforcing the no-smoking rule. Future research might particularly focus on the conditions that influence the range of cross-norm effects.

Other people's behaviour is the basis for contagion effects. However, it is useful to pay attention to the interpretation of other people's behaviour: does it indicate respect/disrespect for norms? Is it performed by members of the in-group or members of a 'dissociative' out-group? Is it taken to be a cue for injunctive norms or is it something that tells us what is rational to do and to imitate? These different interpretations can be distinguished on the basis of GFT and they inform us about different mechanisms of social contagion of compliance with norms and legitimate rules.[4] Neglecting these dynamics of overarching goals by naïve use of the concepts 'descriptive norm' and 'conditional cooperation' leads to highly incomplete policy advice about compliance.

[3] Awards for conformity to rules, however, can backfire when they convey the message that others are doing less (and thus don't support the rule), as was recently shown in a large field study (Robinson et al. 2019).

[4] Paying close attention to the role of overarching goals also seems important for interventions that are aimed at spreading certain kinds of behaviour (see Lindenberg and Papies 2019).

This approach has very practical consequences for making compliance with rules sustainable. The GFT of compliance contagion makes it clear that one cannot rely on a 'compliance culture' as a steady state (Burdon and Sorour 2018). The dynamics of sustainable compliance are at the same time the dynamics of an ongoing compliance contagion in the face of contrary influence from gain and hedonic goals and limited positive cross-norm effects (Lindenberg 2012b). Yet, there can be a number of measures that support an ongoing contagion of compliance. First, because the voluntary compliance mechanism is driven by a goal to comply with norms, rules must be legitimized so that they are psychologically interpreted as norms. Second, because the contagion of compliance runs via observed (dis)respect for norms and legitimate rules, tailoring the manner in which the public is informed about how others comply should be an important part of policy. Third, personal concerns (related to money, status and feeling good) should be moulded to support the goal of compliance, without becoming explicit goals themselves. Finally, for any situation, policy should aim at making it relatively easy to find out what the relevant legitimate rules that apply to this situation are. In short, policy directed at sustainable compliance should not just focus on incentives and persuasion but pay close attention to the dynamics of overarching goals.

REFERENCES

Appelbaum, Steven H., Giulio David Iaconi and Albert Matousek. 'Positive and Negative Deviant Workplace Behaviors: Causes, Impacts, and Solutions'. *Corporate Governance* 7, no. 5 (2007): 586–98.

Aquino, Karl, Dan Freeman, Americus Reed II and Vivien K. G. Lim. 'Testing a Social-Cognitive Model of Moral Behavior: The Interactive Influence of Situations and Moral Identity Centrality'. *Journal of Personality and Social Psychology* 97, no. 1 (2009): 123–41.

Ariely, Dan, and Ximena Garcia-Rada. 'Contagious Dishonesty'. *Scientific American* 321, no. 3 (2019): 62–6.

Bergquist, Magnus, Andreas Nilsson and Wesley P. Schultz. 'A Meta-analysis of Field-Experiments Using Social Norms to Promote Proenvironmental Behaviors'. *Global Environmental Change* 58 (2019).

Brown, Michael E., and Linda K. Treviño. 'Ethical Leadership: A Review and Future Directions'. *Leadership Quarterly* 17 (2006): 595–616.

Brunner, Markus, and Andreas Ostermaier. 'Peer Influence on Managerial Honesty: The Role of Transparency and Expectations'. *Journal of Business Ethics* 154 (2019): 127–45.

Burdon, W. M., and Mohamed Karim Sorour. 'Institutional Theory and Evolution of "A Legitimate" Compliance Culture: The Case of the UK Financial Service Sector'. *Journal of Business Ethics* (2018): doi.org/10.1007/s10551-018-3981-4.

Cialdini, Robert. 'Descriptive Social Norms as Underappreciated Sources of Social Control'. *Psychometrika* 72, no. 2 (2007): 263–8.

Cialdini, Robert, Raymond R. Reno and Carl A. Kallgren. 'A Focus Theory of Normative Conduct – Recycling the Concept of Norms to Reduce Littering in Public Places'. *Journal of Personality and Social Psychology* 58 (1990): 1015–26.

Costa, Dora L., and Matthew E. Kahn. 'Energy Conservation "Nudge" and Environmentalist Ideology: Evidence from a Randomized Residential Field Experiment'. *Journal of the. European Economic Association* 11, no. 3 (2013): 680–702.

Etienne, Julien. 'Compliance Theory: A Goal Framing Approach'. *Law and Policy* 33, no. 3 (2011): 305–33.

Fornara, Ferdinando, Giuseppe Carrus, Paola Passafaro and Mirilia Bonnes. 'Distinguishing the Sources of Normative Influence on Proenvironmental Behaviors: The Role of Local Norms in Household Waste Recycling'. *Group Processes and Intergroup Relations* 14 (2011): 623–35.

Frey, Bruno S., and Jana Gallus. 2017. *Honours versus Money: The Economics of Awards*. Oxford: Oxford University Press.

Gächter, Simon. 2007. 'Conditional Cooperation: Behavioral Regularities from the Lab and the Field and Their Policy Implications'. In *Psychology and Economics: A Promising New Cross-Disciplinary Field* (Cesinfo Seminar Series), edited by B. S. Frey and A. Stutzer, 19–50. Cambridge, MA: MIT Press.

Goldstein, Noah, Robert Cialdini and Vladas Griskevicius. 'A Room with a Viewpoint: Using Norm-Based Appeals to Motivate Conservation Behaviors in a Hotel Setting'. *Journal of Consumer Research* 35 (2008): 472–82.

Katz, Elihu, and Paul Lazarsfeld. 1955. *Personal Influence: The Part Played by People in the Flow of Mass Communication*.Glencoe, IL:Free Press

Keizer, Kees, Siegwart Lindenberg and Linda Steg. 'The Spreading of Disorder'. *Science* 322, no. 5908 (2008): 1681–5.

'The Reversal Effect of Prohibition Signs'. *Group Processes & Intergroup Relations* 14, no. 5 (2011): 681–8.

'The Importance of Demonstratively Restoring Order'. *PLOSone* 8, no. 6 (2013): e65137.

Kouchaki, Maryam, Francesca Gino and Yval Feldman. 'The Ethical Perils of Personal, Communal Relations: A Language Perspective'. *Psychological Science* (2019): DOI: 10.1177/0956797619882917.

Lindenberg, Siegwart & Kees Keizer. in press. 'The Good Side of Bad Examples: Deviance by Out-Groups Can Increase Conformity to One's Own Norms'.

Lindenberg, Siegwart. 2006. 'Prosocial Behavior, Solidarity, and Framing Processes'. In *Solidarity and Prosocial Behavior: An Integration of Sociological and Psychological Perspectives*, edited by Detlef Fetchenhauer, Andreas Flache, Abraham P. Buunk and Siegwart Lindenberg, 23–44. New York: Springer.

2008. 'Social Norms: What Happens When They Become More Abstract?' In *Rational Choice: Theoretische Analysen und empirische Resultate*, edited by Anadreas Diekmann, Klaus Eichner, Peter Schmidt and Thomas Voss, 63–82. Wiesbaden: VS Verlag.

2014a. 'Solidarity: Unpacking the Social Brain'. In *Solidarity – Theory and Practice*, edited by Arto Laitinen and Anne Birgitta Pessi, 30–54. Lanham, MD: Lexington Books.

'Sustainable Cooperation Needs Tinkering with Both Rules and Social Motivation'. *Journal of Bioeconomics* 16 (2014b): 71–81.

2017. 'The Dependence of Human Cognitive and Motivational Processes on Institutional Systems'. In *Social Dilemmas, Institutions, and the Evolution of Cooperation*, edited by Ben Jann and Wojtek Przepiorka, 85–106. Berlin: De Gruyter.

Lindenberg, Siegwart, and Nicolai Foss. 'Managing Joint Production Motivation: The Role of Goal-Framing and Governance Mechanisms'. *Academy of Management Review* 36, no. 3 (2011): 500–25.

Lindenberg, Siegwart, and Esther K. Papies. 'Two Kinds of Nudging and the Power of Cues: Shifting Salience of Alternatives and Shifting Salience of Goals'. *International Review of Environmental and Resource Economics* 13 (2019): 229–63.

Lindenberg, Siegwart, and Linda Steg. 'Normative, Gain and Hedonic Goal Frames Guiding Environmental Behavior'. *Journal of Social Issues* 63, no. 1 (2007): 117–37.

Mas, Alexander, and Enrico Moretti. 'Peers at Work'. *American Economic Review* 99, no. 1 (2009): 112–45.

McBarnet, Doreen. 2002. 'When Compliance Is Not the Solution but the Problem: From Changes in Law to Changes in Attitude'. In *Taxing Democracy*, edited by Valerie Braithwaite, 229–244. Aldershot: Ashgate.

Mortensen, Chad F., Rebecca Neel, Robert B. Cialdini, Christine M. Jaeger, Ryan P. Jacobson and Megan M. Ringel. 'Trending Norms: A Lever for Encouraging Behaviors Performed by the Minority'. *Social Psychological and Personality Science* 10, no. 2 (2019): 201–10.

Peterson, Dane K. 'Deviant Workplace Behavior and the Organization's Ethical Climate'. *Journal of Business and Psychology* 17, no. 1 (2002): 47–61.

Reno, Raymond R., Robert B. Cialdini and Carl A. Kallgren. 'The Transsituational Influence of Social Norms'. *Journal of Personality and Social Psychology* 64, no.1 (1993): 104–12.

Robinson, Carly, Jana Gallus, Monica Lee and Todd Rogers. 'The Demotivating Effect (and Unintended Message) of Awards'. HKS Working Paper No. RWP18-020 (2019): https://ssrn.com/abstract=3219502 or http://dx.doi.org/10.2139/ssrn.3219502.

Rogers, Todd., Noah J. Goldstein and Craig R. Fox. 'Social Mobilization'. *Annual Review of Psychology* 69 (2018): 357–81.

Schaefers, Tobias, Kristina Wittkowski, Sabine Benoit and Rosellina Ferraro. 'Contagious Effects of Customer Misbehavior in Access-Based Services'. *Journal of Service Research* 19, no. 1 (2016): 3–21.

Sims, Ronald R., and Johannes Brinkmann. 'Leaders as Moral Role Models: The Case of John Gutfreund at Salomon Brothers'. *Journal of Business Ethics* 35 (2002): 327–39.

Singh, Prakash, and Thembinkosi Twalo. 'Mismanaging Unethical Behaviour in the Workplace'. *Journal of Applied Business Research* 31, no. 2 (2015): 515–30.

Smith, Joanne R., Winnifred R. Louis, Deborah J. Terry, Katharine H. Greenaway, Miranda R. Clarke and Xiaoliang Cheng. 'Congruent or Conflicted? The Impact of Injunctive and Descriptive Norms on Environmental Intentions'. *Journal of Environmental Psychology* 32 (2012): 353–61.

Steg Linda, Siegwart Lindenberg and Kees Keizer. 'Intrinsic Motivation, Norms and Environmental Behaviour: The Dynamics of Overarching Goals'. *International Review of Environmental and Resource Economics* 9, no. 1–2 (2015): 179–207.

Stryker, Robin. 'Rules, Resources, and Legitimacy Processes: Some Implications for Social Conflict, Order, and Change'. *American Journal of Sociology* 99, no. 4 (1994): 847–910.

Thöni, Christian, and Simon Gächter. 'Peer Effects and Social Preferences in Voluntary Cooperation: A Theoretical and Experimental Analysis'. *Journal of Economic Psychology* 48 (2015): 72–88.

Traxler, Christian, and Joachim Winter. 'Survey Evidence on Conditional Norm Enforcement'. *European Journal of Political Economy* 28 (2012): 390–8.

Tyler, Tom R. 2006. *Why People Obey the Law*. Princeton, NJ: Princeton University Press.

Van Wijk, Eelco, and Frédérique E. Six. 2014. *De diversiteit van het willen, Een onderzoek naar de dynamiek van motivaties achter regelnaleving [Dynamics of Multiple Motivations]*. The Hague: Boom.

Verplanken, Bas, and Jie Sui, 'Habit and Identity: Behavioral, Cognitive, Affective, and Motivational Facets of an Integrated Self'. *Frontiers in Psychology* (2019): doi: 10.3389/fpsyg.2019.01504.

Weber, Max. 1978 [1922]. *Economy and Society*, edited by G. Roth and C. Wittich. Berkeley: University of California Press.

White, Katharine, and Darren W. Dahl. 'Are All Out-Groups Created Equal? Consumer Identity and Dissociative Influence'. *Journal of Consumer Research* 34 (2007): 525–36.

30

Shaming and Compliance

Judith van Erp

Abstract: Naming and shaming offenders is often considered an effective strategy to improve compliance. Shaming exposes an offender to condemnation by a community of stakeholders. The threat of negative publicity, reputational damage and social disapproval is perceived as a sanction, and can in theory be more powerful than a formal legal sanction. This chapter asks to what extent naming and shaming can improve compliance. It takes stock of extant empirical evidence on the effect of shaming policies on regulatory compliance and identifies conditions for shaming to affect compliance. The complex relationship between 'naming and shaming' and compliance makes it difficult to predict and control the various effects of shaming sanctions. The chapter concludes that the unpredictability of effects makes 'naming and shaming' a risky tool for regulators. A theory about naming and shaming should differentiate among types of offender, shaming agent and social context.

30.1 INTRODUCTION

Societies are governed by a multitude of rules and norms. Some of these are explicit and formal, but many are implicit and informal. These norms safeguard the stability, predictability and trust necessary for societies to function and for collective action problems to be overcome. Part of these norms are legal rules, enforced through the legal system. But compliance with social norms is induced through a much broader array of social control mechanisms than legal sanctions: socialization, rewards, nudges, and social sanctions. One important type of social sanctions is shaming: the exposure of a norm offender to public disapproval of his or her behaviour. The threat of being exposed to public disapproval prevents people from offending social norms in many situations.

We can observe a wide variety of forms of naming and shaming. Perhaps the most prominent is vigilante online shaming. Body-shaming for people whose bodies defy beauty 'standards' and counter-shaming of body-shamers; drought-shaming for people who water their lawns in dry areas; shaming of racists, white supremacists or alleged sex offenders: the availability of mobile cameras and social media allows transgressors of social norms to be exposed worldwide in minutes and results in spontaneous ostracism. Such shaming is a weapon of the powerless: it exposes people and holds them to account for behaviour that is seen as bad but is at the same time retaliatory and can ruin lives (Ronson 2015). But shaming sanctions have always also been part of the legal system: from the medieval pillory until current times, judges have imposed legal shaming sanctions. Examples include'warning' signs – 'Here lives a sex offender' -(McAlinden 2007), obligations for shoplifters to pose with signs reading 'I am a thief' (Schwarcz 2003) or punishments for Driving under the Influence (DUI) such as obliging offenders to wear T-shirts or put stickers on their cars. Also, public registries are maintained of parents who evade child support or white-collar offenders in public registries.[1]

A very different, but equally prominent category of shaming is non-governmental organization (NGO) shaming campaigns against global corporations. Such shaming can address corporate irresponsible and harmful behaviour in the grey area between national laws, and pose a significant threat to corporate reputations. In a closely related category is NGOs shaming states and international regulatory bodies, such as Transparency International's Corruption Perceptions Index which ranks countries by their perceived level of public sector corruption[2] and the Financial Action Task Force's public list of jurisdictions with weak measures to combat money laundering and terrorist financing.[3]

Shaming of individuals or businesses is also increasingly common in the regulatory process. Regulators issue blacklists of tax offenders; disclose health and safety violations, toxic emissions and offences of financial laws; and issue public warnings against schools or nursing homes with quality deficits. Although often justified as 'transparency' in the context of open government and freedom of information, such disclosure equally serves to warn potential clients, deter individuals and organizations from offending and stimulate compliance, and thus clearly has elements of shaming (van Erp 2010). This chapter therefore focuses on naming and shaming in the context of regulatory compliance as a modern information-based strategy for regulatory enforcement.

The chapter first defines 'naming and shaming' as a regulatory instrument (Section 30.2). Then, I discuss the theoretical relation between shaming and compliance, by describing the working mechanisms behind shaming (Section 30.3). As this chapter focuses on regulatory compliance, its focus is not primarily on the psychology of shaming (psychological and emotional individual reactions to shaming in interpersonal relationships; see Lewis 1971; Harris 2001, Tangney and Dearing 2002; Coontz 2015). Instead, it focuses on the more sociological aspects of the relationship between shame and compliance in organizations and groups. Section 30.4 reviews existing research on the impact of shaming on compliance. Finally, in Section 30.5, I compare legal and shaming sanctions, and review existing evidence on the effectiveness of shaming in comparison with law.

30.2 NAMING AND SHAMING: DEFINITION

'Naming and shaming' can be defined as publicly naming or otherwise identifying a person, group or organization that is guilty of some antisocial act so as to expose him, her or them to public shame, with the intention of embarrassing them into improving their behaviour (Braithwaite 1989). 'Public shame' is the emotion related to being (or feeling) exposed to disapproval. Extensive psychological research has evaluated differences between shame – the emotion of negative evaluation of the self – and guilt – the emotion of negative evaluation of something one *did* (Lewis 1971; Tangney and Dearing 2002). In other words, shame is much more fundamental to one's core identity than guilt, which relates to a specific act and can be

1 https://des.az.gov/services/child-and-family/child-support/wanted-child-support-evaders; www.utfraud.com/RegistryLists.

2 www.transparency.org/cpi2018.

3 www.fatf-gafi.org/publications/high-risk-and-other-monitored-jurisdictions/more/more-on-high-risk-and-non-cooperative-jurisdictions.html?hf=10&b=0&s=desc(fatf_releasedate).

repaired, whereas shame relates to one's identity in the eyes of others, and makes one want to disappear from the public eye (Tangney and Dearing 2002).

In line with this psychological scholarship, criminologists have developed the concepts of *stigmatizing* and *reintegrative shaming* (Braithwaite 1989; Harris and Maruna 2006). Stigmatizing shaming happens when elements of humiliation are added to the act of exposure – such as the obligation to wear visible signs – and the aim is to exclude the offender from participation in the community. Stigmatizing shaming, ostracism, humiliation or status degradation are all related to the labelling of shamed individuals or businesses which alienates them from communities and disqualifies them from social acceptance. Stigmatization can exclude and reject people from communities and thus withdraw opportunities for compliant behaviour, or even confirm offending behaviour when the stigma results in the offence becoming the master trait – equalling a person to the offence and thus making it impossible to change.

Reintegrative shaming, by contrast, condemns the offence but not the offender, and thus rejects the idea that stigmatization is a defining element of naming and shaming (Harris 2017). Reintegrative shaming means that public disapproval of the offence is combined with communicating trust in the offender's willingness to improve (Makkai and Braithwaite 1994). The offender is addressed as a good person who committed a bad act, from which restoration is possible. Reintegrative shaming should encourage offenders to become re-engaged with the substantial goals of the law of a community with shared social norms. Thus, reintegrative shaming strengthens the bond between the offender and the community. As shaming is most effective when people reform their behaviour and remain part of the group (Jacquet 2016), as a general principle reintegrative shaming should be preferred and stigmatizing shaming should be avoided – both from the perspective of justice and from the perspective of effectiveness.

Whether or not it is a punishment in the legal sense, sociologists – in particular sociologists in the tradition of Durkheim – regard shame as one of the most prominent social emotions underlying society (Scheff 2003). Shaming entails the breaking of social bonds, which obstructs participation in society; the anticipation of shame is what makes people comply with social norms. Shaming, thus, is a punishment in the sociological sense: it punishes through social disapproval and damage to reputation. In the same vein, legal scholars have argued that shaming should be seen as a sanction just as financial sanctions or imprisonment (Kahan and Posner 1999): they have identical goals but damage different assets: a prison sentence targets individual liberty; a financial sanction targets capital; and shaming targets the social status, reputation or esteem of stakeholders (Kahan and Posner 1999). Of course, these effects can be combined. However, the analytical difference is that the sanctioning power exercised by shaming is not coercive or hierarchical by a 'sovereign', as is the case with formal sanctions, but disciplinary in a Foucauldian sense. It is exercised within societies rather than from above, dispersed in networks and a variety of social settings. Rather than pressuring individuals to conform to 'normality' through external surveillance, shaming exercises pressure through internalized surveillance and self-monitoring.

In a regulatory context, the goal of releasing information about offenders is often more prominent than the goal of condemnation as in a criminal justice shaming setting. Regulatory shaming can be defined as 'any intentional publication, by regulatory agencies in the executive branch, of information regarding companies' misbehavior that is designed to convey a normatively negative message to the public, for a regulatory purpose' (Yadin 2019: 4). It invites stakeholders to apply pressure, to change the discourse, to alter behavioral patterns or ways of thinking about the shamed entity, and in appropriate circumstances to denounce, condemn or boycott it. Regulatory shaming is therefore more directed towards triggering the community to shame an offender by informing them than imposing shame on the offender directly. Yadin's definition distinguishes regulatory shaming from more general regulatory transparency and disclosure, such as regulatory agencies publicizing inspection reports or performance information about regulated entities. These are, at least analytically, more neutral, as their intention is not to convey a normatively negative message to the public but to inform the public about the activities of government, in the context of government accountability, freedom of information and citizen's 'right-to-know'.

Of course, the line between disclosure and shaming is blurred, as disclosure may, in reality, be directed more towards persuading than informing, and more to the disclosed party than to citizens or consumers (Cortez 2018; van Erp 2010). Negative information disclosed by regulators can be used for naming and shaming when specific actors single out firms and publicly express disapproval. Thus, the act of shaming can be performed both by the 'naming' regulatory authority and by a third party, such as the media, NGOs or politicians. For example, Food and Safety inspectorates regularly publish 'scores on the doors': shortened versions of inspection reports of food service providers visible on their premises. Although their intention was to inform the public about inspection results and to assist consumer choice, the media have often subsequently added a normative component by compiling highly publicized lists of 'filthy restaurants'.

30.3 WORKING MECHANISMS OF SHAMING

A theoretical 'ideal' model of naming and shaming distinguishes the causal steps of naming, blaming and shaming that result in compliance (cf. Felstiner et al. 1980, see Figure 30.1). 'Naming' means that an offence is detected, attributed to a certain actor and disclosed. 'Blaming' means that the disclosed information actually reaches an audience and is not overlooked. Naming going unnoticed is quite possible, given the information overload that audiences often experience (van Erp 2010). 'Shaming', subsequently, refers to the public condemnation of a person or corporation; its exclusion from social networks, loss of reputation and loss of opportunities. In each step in the model, distortions can occur which limit the impact of naming and shaming on compliance.

FIGURE 30.1 Naming, shaming, and compliance

Theories about shaming generally identify two working mechanisms through which shaming results in compliance: deterrence and moral education (Braithwaite 1989; Ayres and Braithwaite 1992). Naming and shaming may *deter* individuals, or firms, from offending, as they fear social disapproval and exclusion as punishments from the community they belong to. The punishment may also result in more material damage as shaming leads to loss of status and reputation and may thus be detrimental for business opportunities. Shaming damages reputations: by revealing negative information about someone's behaviour. Upon hearing about an offender's bad behaviour, stakeholders may re-evaluate how likely that offender is to keep his promises or deliver expected outcomes (Ellickson 1994; Fombrun and Van Riel 1997). The fear of being shamed is an important motivation for compliance – hence, shaming deters, just as financial sanctions or imprisonment are intended to (Kahan and Posner 1999). Shaming, however, sends a more powerful normative message: whereas formal punishment communicates that legal norms have been breached, shaming communicates the message that social or moral norms have been offended. It is an expressive instrument that works through emotions such as the wish to be respected and the fear of being humiliated (Murphy and Harris 2007). A financial sanction invokes a calculative cost–benefit analysis, whereas shaming appeals to an offender's conscience by indicating that behaviour is irresponsible and impressing on the offender that she or he did not take their responsibilities towards the community seriously. It shows that an offence is not just technical but damages the community.

This means that effective shaming therefore works best in a normative 'community of conscience', where members agree about the damaging nature of the offence (Karp 1998: 289) and offenders care about their reputations. When these conditions are absent, shaming will not always lead to actual shame. Offenders may not acknowledge the social norm; or may attempt to reason away their responsibility for the offence (Harris 2001; Murphy and Harris 2007). Communities may not respond. Thus, a crucial precondition is that the compliant party values being part of the community and senses that being subject to shaming will hurt the relation with the community. In such situations, shaming can even stimulate compliance even when the offender does not genuinely feel ashamed, when he or she acknowledges that a reputation for compliance is important for functioning in the community. However, in situations where public consensus about the inappropriateness of the behaviour and public support for shaming sanctions are missing, shaming may not result in public condemnation (Parker 2006) or, subsequently, in compliance.

As shaming serves to deter through moral condemnation of offending behaviour, it aims not only to improve the behaviour of the offender but also to educate the community about what is accepted, and thus reconfirm the social norms within a community and build consciences (Braithwaite 1989). This 'moral education' effect is the second mechanism through which shaming could function. By expressing what is wrong, the community also expresses what it considers right. Thus, shaming is a much more participatory form of social control than legal sanctions, requiring an audience (Jacquet 2016). Here, it becomes clear that shaming punishments do not serve to retaliate in the first place (as stigmatizing shaming would) but contribute to the internalization of norms and the reinforcement of the social order. Shaming communicates that offences are harmful and aims to strengthen communities' shared expectations about appropriate behaviour. Public exposure of the offender underlines that the conduct is unacceptable and is expected to evoke normative disapproval from the general public or the offender's peers (Braithwaite 1989; Parker 2006).

The deterrent and moral education effects of shaming combine, as shaming not only deters potential offenders but also influences perceptions of appropriate behaviour and thus also influences behaviour indirectly (Kahan and Posner 1999: 377). In sum, the preventative effect of shaming can be seen as a mix of reputational deterrence and moral education or, as Kahan expresses it, 'a magic cocktail of instrumental utility and social meaning' (Kahan 2006: 1).

30.4 RESEARCH INTO THE EFFECTS OF SHAMING ON COMPLIANCE

Given the high expectations generally held about the impact and effectiveness of shaming on compliance, a surprisingly limited amount of empirical research has been carried out. This section reviews evidence on tax shaming; on shaming of alcohol-related offences; and miscellaneous research on business offences.

30.4.1 *Tax Shaming*

One of the few areas that has been relatively extensively researched is disclosure of tax non-compliance and tax shaming. Many countries and states disclose information on taxpayers with debts. Half of the taxation agencies in the OECD have the power to publish the names of tax avoiders/dodgers and nearly 90 per cent have used this power, according to most recent data (OECD 2017). The introduction of such policies and differences in disclosure rules between countries have given scholars the opportunity to conduct natural experiments to evaluate their effects.

In Norway, information about income tax payments has been publicly available since the early twentieth century. Compliance is not an explicit goal of tax transparency: the rationale behind publication of tax payments is government transparency and freedom of information. In the past, pamphlets detailing how much local residents paid in tax were frequently sold to raise funds for local soccer teams or other charities. One can assume, then, that tax information was widely distributed. Since 2001, the Norwegian government has provided user-friendly, searchable online databases with individual tax information as part of its digitalization strategy. This has resulted in an average increase of reported income among business owners of 3 per cent, with compliance increasing more in municipalities where paper tax lists were not widely distributed before (Slemrod et al. 2013). Anecdotal evidence also suggests that Portugal and New Zealand have increased tax compliance after they began to publish lists of taxpayer debts. Greece, too, annually publishes information about tax evaders but has not seen the same improvement in tax compliance. Scholars attribute this to the low tax morale of the Greek population in general (Perez-Truglia and Troiano 2018).

Dwenger and Treber (2018) investigate the introduction of a tax naming-and-shaming policy in Slovenia in 2012, a policy which aimed to reduce corporate income tax debt among businesses and the self-employed. The Slovenian shaming list publishes online the names of taxpayers with debt of more than 5,000 euros. As this policy was quite controversial, the publication received wide media attention: 42 per cent of the Slovenian population visited the tax agency/department website the day it was published, April 15, 2013. Dwenger and Treber (2018) find that taxpayers reduced their tax debt by 8.5 per cent before the first list was published. Thus, the policy raised more than 50 million euros in previously uncollected taxes (approximately 9 per cent of annual collected corporate income taxes). The largest improvement was in industries where businesses are more concerned about their reputation: industries selling to end-consumers. Such businesses are highly dependent on domestic markets and are well known to consumers (Dwenger and Treber 2018). Presumably, they wanted to keep their names off the list to avoid being publicly shamed.

After the initial improvement, however, the shaming policy seems to be losing its impact. The study shows that 96 per cent of the businesses that were on the first shaming list also appear on the second list. The *threat* of shaming, then, is effective, but shaming itself isn't. On this basis, the authors recommend that tax collectors give offenders a clear, visible threat that they will be shamed – for example through a warning or announcement letter – and allow taxpayers some time to settle their debts before executing the shaming.

Another illustrative study is a field experiment in which a relatively mild form of shaming was applied to individuals with tax debts in three US states. The experiment aimed to make tax debtors believe that their debts were going to be exposed to their neighbours. The researchers hypothesized that this would make debtors more likely to pay out of fear for their reputation. The (real) tax debtors were informed by letter that their name and tax debts were publicly listed, along with the names and tax debts of nine other tax delinquents in their geographic area, and given a web address where their names could be found. The experimental group was informed that this information *would be* sent to neighbours unless they paid, whereas the control group did not receive this last message. The experiment showed that people with relatively low debts (up to $2,500) paid those debts after receiving the letter. For higher debts, however, this effect did not occur. The researchers suggest that large debt owners may simply not be able to pay, or are stubbornly unwilling to. Those with larger debts may also be less sensitive to shaming: 'being taken off the delinquency list may be worth paying a debt of $250, but may not be worth paying a debt of $150,000' (Perez-Truglio and Troiano 2018: 12). The researchers also tested the effect of alternative deterrent measures, such as frequent reminders of financial penalties, yet the effect was lower than the threat of shaming (Perez-Truglia and Troiano 2018).

Equally insightful is an Australian study into feelings of stigmatization of taxpayers who were charged with violation of tax regulations by the Australian Tax Authority. Even without their offences being published, those offenders who reported to have experienced feelings of stigmatization in the enforcement process were more likely to report tax evasion in comparison to offenders who had received a more respectful, reintegrative treatment. The study design does not allow for causal claims, but it does provide some support that a reintegrative approach of tax offenders leads to lower reoffending while stigmatization leads to greater reoffending (Murphy and Harris 2007).

30.4.2 *Anticipated Shame and Compliance among Youth*

Criminological studies find that shame is negatively related to offending (Svensson et al. 2013). One area of this research has investigated the relation between anticipated shame and compliance intentions among youth. This research asked young people if they would feel shame when their significant other (such as a parent) found out about an offence. Young people who answer that they would feel shame are more likely to report that they intend to follow the law (Svensson et al. 2013). The cross-sectional design of such studies has limitations, however, as it relates responses in the present to behaviour in the past. For example, a study among college students in the USA examined the effect of various formal and informal sanctions on intended violations of college alcohol policies. Most US colleges prohibit the use of alcohol by undergraduates on campus. The survey indicates that students are not easily deterred by the threat of punishment, including the threat of suspension. What does deter students is the threat of being shamed and feeling guilty, but only among students who are already sensitive to feelings of embarrassment and guilt (Kelley et al. 2009). Likewise, a study of learner drivers in Australia demonstrates that drivers who expect to feel shame and guilt when violations are detected are more likely to comply with extra road safety regulations. Thus, shame is a more effective deterrent than formal sanctions – for those sensitive to it (Allen et al. 2015).

30.4.3 *Business Regulatory Offences*

In addition to tax offences, an area of business compliance that has received considerable attention from scholars is food hygiene. A common practice for food vendors is to have 'scores on the doors' which indicate hygiene ratings to customers. Several empirical studies show a significant improvement in food hygiene after the introduction of 'scores on the doors' or similar forms of disclosure. Compliance is higher when businesses expect a negative rating to affect sales and when they feel embarrassed upon being put in negative light (Bavorova et al. 2017).

Various researchers have studied the effects of the US Environmental Protection Agency's Toxics Release Inventory (TRI), one of the first and most prominent information disclosure schemes. The TRI is designed to inform citizens about pollution by firms in their local environment. The TRI was initially very effective. Within ten years of its inception, toxic emissions had been reduced by half (Cortez 2011). This effect can be attributed to the massive publicity surrounding the disclosed information in its early years. Later research, however, shows a flattening of the compliance effects after the volume of information increased and attention dropped (Cortez 2011). An event-study (Campa 2018) shows that industrial plants which receive newspaper coverage of their emissions reduce those emissions by 29 per cent more than plants which are not covered. Further, plants located near a larger number of newspaper headquarters produce lower toxic emissions (although this effect is limited to plants operating in industries that produce consumer goods) (Campa 2018). Moreover, in Campa's study it became clear that disclosed information is not followed up by consumers; but the threat of reputational damage has an independent deterrent effect on polluting firms – a finding supported in other research on regulatory disclosure (van Erp 2010).

Similarly, Johnson (2020) has studied the impact of press releases by the US Occupational Safety and Health Administration (OSHA). He finds that peer companies located within 5 kilometres of an offending firm improve their compliance with health and safety regulations and experience fewer occupational injuries. In fact, being close to a company that gets negative press has two to three times the effect on peer company compliance than an actual OSHA inspection of their own facility. In other words, OSHA would have to conduct at least forty additional inspections to achieve the same improvement in compliance as that achieved with a single press release. Johnson (2020) suggests that this effect occurs because of pressure from workers. Workers read press releases about companies with poor health and safety records, and put pressure on their own employer to keep workers secure. In Johnson's (2020) analysis, facilities in areas where unions are strong substantially improve compliance following a press release about a peer, whereas those in areas where unions are relatively weak display no improvement.

This finding concurs with the much earlier, seminal Australian nursing home study by Makkai and Braithwaite (1994). They found that expectations of a scandal in the media *as such* do not seem to deter nursing home managers from breaking the law. Negative press only matters insofar as it matters to professional peers, family, neighbours and friends. Only through disapproval from these groups will negative press invoke a process of reintegrative shaming which is expected to stimulate compliance. Whereas Johnson (2020) suggests that employers concede to workers' demands to avoid future litigation cost, an alternative explanation could be that they do not want to alienate their employees.

In Brazil, the government has blacklisted districts with high deforestation rates to monitor and control illegal deforestation as a forest conservation policy strategy since 2007 (Cisneros et al. 2015). Cisneros et al. (2015) find that the average effect of blacklisting ranges between roughly 13 per cent and 36 per cent of reduction in deforestation, corresponding to an average 4,022 square kilometres of forest saved per year (2008–12). This effect may not be primarily attributable to shaming, though. Landowners in blacklisted districts face more administrative burdens from the Brazilian government in obtaining licences for deforestation and, surprisingly, attract more support from international NGOs to assist improvements (which may also explain the effect). These studies suggest that it may be difficult to disentangle the various mechanisms through which shaming can lead to improved compliance. Whether reputational pressures from shaming lead to compliance or whether shaming affects other kinds of incentive may not be clear or even possible to delineate.

To conclude, empirical studies in a variety of fields and among diverse populations have found that shaming has a positive effect on compliance. Although most studies do not explicitly address a working mechanism, they give support for both the deterrence and the morality thesis – although the moral education of a community is more difficult to investigate. Extant research also clearly indicates that the effects are limited to those sensitive to shaming and reputation, and to regulations that are perceived as legitimate.

30.5 CONDITIONS, COMPLICATIONS AND PROPORTIONALITY

Both shaming and legal sanctions can improve compliance through inflicting reputational and financial damage on offenders. Further, the threat of sanctions acts as an incentive for compliance. Scholars generally argue that legal sanctions and reputational sanctions can complement each other. Formal litigation may produce negative publicity, which triggers further negative reactions from customers or other stakeholders in a snowball effect (Shapira 2016; Iaccobucci 2014; Cortez 2011). Legal scholars have therefore argued that shaming is a punishment disproportionate to the crime: offenders that are shamed following a legal sanction are effectively punished twice. To avoid violations of the *ne bis in idem* principle, legal scholars argue, legal sanctions should somehow factor reputational damage into the size of the penalties (Shapira 2016; Iaccobucci 2014).

The interactions between reputational and legal sanctions have been amply discussed in terms of sanction severity. The severity of sanctions, however, does not necessarily predict compliance with a rule. The question of whether legal and shaming sanctions interact with regard to inducing *compliance* has received less attention in the literature. A key question – particularly in the case of regulatory shaming – is what triggers compliance? Is it the legal sanction, the subsequent publicity or their combination? Drawing on the 'naming – blaming – shaming – compliance' framework, one would assume that legal sanctions are the trigger. Sanctions against corporations inform the general public that an offence has been committed. This can induce negative reactions from stakeholders, who may in turn demand organizational change (compliance). Parella (2018) gives the example of FIFA. After the international football federation was accused of corruption, Visa, Adidas and Coca-Cola threatened to withdraw their sponsorship unless FIFA cleaned up its act. That is, after stakeholders of these companies exercised pressure on *themselves*.

A variety of research evidence provides us with insights into the complexity of this relationship. First, research indicates that not all regulatory 'naming' generates 'blaming' (negative publicity) or results in shaming. Press releases about administrative penalties for smaller offences often do not get picked up in the press, and the process that decides which offences and offenders get selected for media exposure is unpredictable (van Erp 2011). Media messages may also not unequivocally condemn business offences. White-collar crime is often depicted as 'victimless' or cunning rather than morally wrong (Levi 2002). Some corporations are 'unshamable', especially those less known to the general public. Some industries are successful despite being 'disreputable'. Tobacco, weapons, porn, gambling and offshore tax avoidance are examples of industries that are relatively insensitive to shaming. Their reputation with the general public is already tarnished, and their direct stakeholders couldn't care less about the industry's tainted brand as long as it is still profitable (Mahon 2002). Studies on the impact of regulatory sanctions on stock value show very mixed effects. Despite capital markets being 'hyper-responsive' (Cortez 2011: 1396), several economic event-studies demonstrate that stock rates decline after accounting fraud but not after unethical corporate behaviour, environmental offences or human rights violations (Carberry et al. 2018; Karpoff 2012). In other words, the market imposes a reputational sanction for offences that directly affect stockholders but not for behaviour that inflicts damage to third parties. Although 'reputation' is a more complex and multidimensional concept than the stock rate reflects, these findings indicate that we should not take the deterrent effect of reputational sanctions for granted. All in all, empirical research demonstrates that 'naming' does not always entail shaming, which makes the positive relation between naming and shaming, and compliance, less likely.

At the opposite end of the spectrum, another distortion of the shaming–compliance relationship can be observed. Shaming can cripple an organization so badly that it lacks the means to reform itself. After a shaming, clients and investors are likely to abandon the firm, and its poor reputation makes them harder to replace. Compliance, however, usually requires organizations to make investments: in safer equipment, training programmes, extra staff and so on. Thus, shaming could lock companies into non-compliant practices, rather than encouraging improvement. Another risk of shaming is that the information disclosed could turn out to be wrong; even despite retraction, this results in undeserved reputational damage that is hard to correct. This risk is increasingly real in the era of open data (Cortez 2011, 2018). Regulatory shaming therefore requires procedural safeguards similar to those applied to other forms of regulatory enforcement (Cortez 2011).

A third potential adverse effect may occur when deviant subgroups hold alternative norms and values from those of the general public. For members of these subgroups, *compliance* with 'mainstream' social norms is more likely to garner shame than non-compliance (as compliance would imply disloyalty to the subgroup). This phenomenon has widely been acknowledged within criminological research into deviant youth cultures, but it can also be observed within corporate elites. For example, in the area of disclosure of corporate executive payment, excessive executive payment may be judged negatively by the general public and the press but may be interpreted as a signal of status among corporate elites (Gopalan 2007). Also, deviance among Wall Street investment banks has been found to attract clients, as firms interpret the deviance as a signal of boldness or risk appetite (Roulet 2018). Finally, compliance can be symbolic and ceremonial, as when firms take action to positively alter impressions about the firm and deflect attention away from them, without truly changing behaviour (Zavyalova et al. 2012).

30.6 CONCLUSION

If the review of research in this chapter has demonstrated one thing, it is that the relationship between 'naming and shaming' and compliance is ambiguous. Research has only started to disentangle various effects. The process by which naming and shaming of offenders by legal actors translates to financial or immaterial reputation damage, and subsequently to improved compliance of the offender and other firms, is very complex. The type of business and market, the existing reputation of the offender, the type of offence, the authority and legitimacy of the shaming actor, and the intensity of media coverage all influence the effect. This conclusion counters the often taken-for-granted notion that shaming is effective and that reputational sanctions deter more than financial ones. All in all, the effects of shaming sanctions can be difficult to predict and control.

More research is necessary to uncover mechanisms, conditions and counter-effects of shaming on compliance. The natural experiments and effect studies discussed in this chapter give some insights into the effects of various shaming policies but provide little understanding of the underlying causal mechanisms. Future research should address this and in particular could explore the moral and educative aspects of shaming, which have been relatively under-researched.

The unpredictability of effects makes 'naming and shaming' a risky tool for regulators. Jacquet (2016) therefore argues that shaming should be used with caution, and only in situations where formal legal sanctions are ineffective. For regular individual offenders, the legal system offers sufficient means to punish their behaviour to fulfil goals of retribution and deterrence. That's why shaming sanctions for drunk drivers, sex offenders and shoplifters are disproportional. There are better alternatives. But for powerful actors who stand above the law, because of their financial power or because their behaviour is in the grey area that is difficult to control through law, shaming can stimulate compliance with social norms where the law is less effective. 'It's not that shaming is preferable; it's just that, in some cases, shaming is all we have' (Jacquet 2016: 106).

REFERENCES

Allen S., K. Murphy and L. Bates (2015). 'What Drives Compliance? The Effect of Deterrence and Shame Emotions on Young Drivers' Compliance with Road Laws'. *Policing and Society*: 1–15. 10.1080/10439463.2015.1115502.

Ayres and Braithwaite (1992). Responsive Regulation. Transcending the Deregulation Debate. Osford, Oxford University Press.

Bavorova M., A. Fietz and N. Hirschauer (2017). 'Does Disclosure of Food Inspections Affect Business Compliance? The Case of Berlin, Germany'. *British Food Journal* 119(1): 143–63.

Braithwaite, J. (1989). *Crime, Shame and Reintegration*. Cambridge: Cambridge University Press.

Campa, P. (2018). 'Press and Leaks: Do Newspapers Reduce Toxic Emissions?' *Journal of Environmental Economics and Management* 91(C): 184–202.

Carberry, E., P. Engelen and M. Van Essen (2018). 'Which Firms Get Punished for Unethical Behavior? Explaining Variation in Stock Market Reactions to Corporate Misconduct'. *Business Ethics Quarterly* 28(2): 119–51.

Cisneros, E., S. L. Zhou and J. Börner (2015). 'Naming and Shaming for Conservation: Evidence from the Brazilian Amazon'. *PLoS ONE* 10(9): e0136402.

Coontz, D. (2015). 'Beyond First Blush: The Utility of Shame as a Master Emotion in Criminal Sentencing'. *Michigan State Law Review* 2015: 415–54.

Cortez, N. (2011). 'Adverse Publicity by Administrative Agencies in the Internet Era'. *Brigham Young University Law Review* 2011(5): 1371–1454.

(2018). 'Regulation by Database'. University of Colorado Law Review 89(1): 1–91.

Dwenger, N., and L. Treber (2018). 'Shaming for Tax Enforcement: Evidence from a New Policy'. CEPR Discussion Paper No. DP13194. https://ssrn.com/abstract=3254229.

Ellickson, R. (1994). *Order without Law: How Neighbors Settle Disputes*. Cambridge, MA: Harvard University Press.

Felstiner, W., R. Abel and A. Sarat (1980). 'The Emergence and Transformation of Disputes: Naming, Blaming, Claiming . . .'. *Law & Society Review* 15(3/4): 631–54.

Fombrun, C., and C. Van Riel (1997). 'The Reputational Landscape'. *Corporate Reputational Review* 1 (1–2): 5–13.

Gopalan, S. (2007). 'Shame Sanctions and Excessive CEO Pay'. *Delaware Journal of Corporate Law* 32: 1–41.
Harris, N. (2001). 'Part II. Shaming and Shame: Regulating Drink Driving'. In E. Ahmed, N. Harris, J. Braithwaite, and V. Braithwaite (eds.), *Shame Management through Reintegration*. Melbourne: Cambridge University Press, 71–207.
(2017). 'Shame in Regulatory Settings'. In P. Drahos (ed.), *Regulatory Theory: Foundations and Applications*. Acton ACT, Australia: ANU Press, 59–76.
Harris, N., and S. Maruna (2006). 'Shame, Shaming and Restorative Justice: A Critical Appraisal'. In G. Johnstone and D. Van Ness (eds.), *Handbook of Restorative Justice*. Abingdon, UK: Routledge, 452–62.
Iacobucci, E. (2014). 'On the Interaction between Legal and Reputational Sanctions'. *Journal of Legal Studies* 43: 189–207.
Jacquet, J. (2016). *Is Shame Necessary? New Uses for an Old Tool*. Vintage.
Johnson, M. (2020). 'Regulation by Shaming: Deterrence Effects of Publicizing Violations of Workplace Safety and Health Laws'. *American Economic Review* 110(6): 1866–1904.
Kahan, D. M. (2006). 'What's Really Wrong with Shaming Sanctions', *Texas Law Review* 84: 2075–.
Kahan, D. M., and E. A. Posner (1999). 'Shaming White-Collar Criminals: A Proposal for Reform of the Federal Sentencing Guidelines'. *Journal of Law & Economics* 42(1): 365–91.
Karp, D. R. (1998). 'The Judicial and Judicious Use of Shame Penalties'. *Crime & Delinquency* 44(2): 277–94.
Karpoff, J. M. (2012). 'Does Reputation Work to Discipline Corporate Misconduct?' In T. G. Pollock and M. L. Barnett (eds.), *Oxford Handbook of Corporate Reputation*. Oxford: Oxford University Press, 361–82.
Kelley, M. S., M. Fukushima, A. L. Spivak and D. Payne (2009). 'Deterrence Theory and the Role of Shame in Projected Offending of College Students against a Ban on Alcohol'. *Journal of Drug Education* 39(4): 419–37.
Levi, M. (2002). 'Suite Justice or Sweet Charity? Some Explorations of Shaming and Incapacitating Business Fraudsters'. *Punishment & Society* 4(2): 147–63.
Lewis, H. B. (1971). 'Shame and Guilt in Neurosis'. *Psychoanalytic Review* 58(3): 419–38.
Mahon, J. F. (2002). 'Corporate Reputation: A Research Agenda Using Strategy and Stakeholder Literature'. *Business & Society* 41: 415–.
Makkai, T., and J. Braithwaite (1994). 'Reintegrative Shaming and Compliance with Regulatory Standards'. *Criminology* 32: 361–85.
McAlinden, A. (2007). *The Shaming of Sexual Offenders: Risk, Retribution and Reintegration*. Oxford: Hart Publishing.
Murphy, K., and N. Harris (2007). 'Shaming, Shame and Recidivism: A Test of Reintegrative Shaming Theory in the White-Collar Crime Context'. *British Journal of Criminology* 47(6): 900–17.
OECD Tax Administration (2017). *Comparative Information on OECD and Other Advanced and Emerging Economies*. Paris: OECD Publishing.
Perez-Truglia, R., and U. Troiano (2018). 'Shaming Tax Delinquents'. February 1. https://ssrn.com/abstract=2558115 or http://dx.doi.org/10.2139/ssrn.2558115.
Parella K. (2018). 'Reputational Regulation'. *Duke Law Journal* 67(5): 944–79.
Parker, C. (2006). 'The Compliance Trap: The Moral Message in Responsive Regulatory Enforcement'. *Law & Society Review* 40(3): 591–622.
Ronson J. (2015). *So You've Been Publicly Shamed*. London: Picador.
Roulet, T. J. (2018). 'Sins for Some, Virtues for Others: Media Coverage of Investment Banks' Misconduct and Adherence to Professional Norms during the Financial Crisis'. *Human Relations*. https://doi.org/10.1177/0018726718799404.
Scheff, T. J. (2003). 'Shame in Self and Society'. *Symbolic Interaction* 26(2): 239–62.
Schwarcz, D. (2003). 'Shame, Stigma, and Crime: Evaluating the Efficacy of Shaming Sanctions in Criminal Law'. *Harvard Law Review* 116: 2186.
Shapira, R. (2016). 'Reputation through Litigation: How the Legal System Shapes Behavior by Producing Information'. *Washington Law Review* 91: 1193–1251.

Slemrod, J. B., T. Thoresen and E. Bo (2013). 'Taxes on the Internet: Deterrence Effects of Public Disclosure'. CESifo Working Paper Series No. 4107. https://ssrn.com/abstract=2220132.

Svensson, R., F. M. Weerman, L. J. R. Pauwels, G. J. N. Bruinsma and W. Bernasco (2013). 'Moral Emotions and Offending: Do Feelings of Anticipated Shame and Guilt Mediate the Effect of Socialization on Offending?'. *European Journal of Criminology* 10(1): 22–39.

Tangney, J. P., and R. Dearing (2002). *Shame and Guilt*. New York: Guildford Publications.

Yadin S. (2019). 'Regulatory Shaming'. *Lewis & Clark Environmental Law Review* 49: 2019.

Zavyalova, A., M. Pfarrer, R. Reger and D. Shapiro (2012). 'Managing the Message: The Effects of Firm Actions and Industry Spillovers on Media Coverage Following Wrongdoing'. *Academy of Management Journal* 55: 1079–1101.

van Erp, J. G. (2010). 'Regulatory Disclosure of Offending Companies in the Dutch Financial Market: Consumer Protection or Enforcement Publicity?'. *Law & Policy*, 32: 407–33.

(2011). 'Naming without Shaming: The Publication of Sanctions in the Dutch Financial Market'. *Regulation and Governance* 5(3): 287–308.

31

Neutralization

Stephanie M. Cardwell and Heith Copes

Abstract: Neutralization theory helps explain how people overcome the negative emotions associated with engaging in crime. Developed by Gresham Sykes and David Matza (1957), neutralization theory proposes that people use linguistic devices (i.e., techniques of neutralizations) when presented with opportunities to engage in crime. Techniques of neutralization allow individuals to temporarily overcome the deterrent effects of negative emotions (e.g., shame and guilt), preserve their self-image, and reinterpret crime as acceptable. Research testing the theory shows that neutralizations play an important role in the decision to engage in crime and deviance. Evidence also shows that neutralization use can be nullified through a variety of crime prevention and intervention methods. However, there are theoretical issues surrounding the theory, especially in regards to understanding what factors may make people more or less likely to use neutralizations, whether neutralizations come before deviant behavior, whether neutralization use is stable over the life-course, and how neutralization use explains persistence and desistance in criminal behavior over the life-course.

31.1 INTRODUCTION

Those who contemplate deviant or criminal behavior are often constrained from committing it because of the potential negative emotions that emerge from engaging in such behaviors. Overcoming these internal controls is necessary for the successful commission of deviance and crime. Originally presented in 1957 by Gresham Sykes and David Matza, neutralization theory explains how people overcome the guilt associated with violating norms. The theory proposes that when individuals are presented with an opportunity to engage in crime, they use linguistic devices (i.e., techniques of neutralization) beforehand to overcome guilt and preserve their self-image. Neutralizations are hypothesized to explain both the onset and the continuation of deviance.

Despite empirical research providing mixed results for the effectiveness of the theory in explaining crime and deviance (Maruna and Copes 2005), it has remained a popular theory within criminology and related disciplines. Its propositions have been integrated into numerous other crime theories and adapted for crime control policies. Our aim with this chapter is to provide an overview of the origins and current state of the theory for audiences interested in law. We provide an overview of the core tenets of the theory, a review of empirical evaluations of it, a discussion of several conceptual issues that have been raised with the theory, and implications for potential crime control policy.

31.2 TECHNIQUES OF NEUTRALIZATION

Neutralization theory was developed in response to subcultural theories of crime and delinquency that were popular at the time (Cohen 1955). Subcultural theories broadly assume that lower-class young people turn to delinquency as a reaction to middle-class values. Cohen suggested that in response to their inability to gain social status through conventional means, those in delinquent subcultures actively resist and reject conventional standards and replace them with a delinquent value system. Delinquency was assumed to allow these youths a means to obtain social status. Sykes and Matza (1957) did not agree with the argument that delinquency was due to a delinquent value system that guides behavior. Rather, they argued that many young people who experience guilt or shame when they engage in delinquency have respect and maintain attachments to law-abiding persons, clearly distinguish between people who can and cannot be victimized, and participate in conventional activities in dominant society.

Sykes and Matza (1957) argued that these youths still have commitments to dominant society. These commitments can contribute to experiencing guilt or shame and negative self-images when young people are presented with opportunities to engage in delinquency. These emotions or threats to self-image are usually enough to prevent young people from engaging in delinquency. However, some youths are able to use techniques of neutralization to overcome the potential guilt or negative self-image associated with norm violations, to engage in crime and deviance. Techniques of neutralization are linguistic devices that allow individuals to temporarily overcome the deterrent effects of shame and guilt and preserve their self-image. It is in this manner that neutralizations allow people to retain commitments to conventional society and to reinterpret crime and delinquency as acceptable.

People have a range of neutralization techniques to call forth when making sense of their actions and seeking to minimize internal controls. Sykes and Matza (1957) outlined five techniques of neutralization that people use to remove guilt when committing crime. The first technique is *denial of responsibility*. People who deny responsibility say that their behaviors were accidental or out of their control. A second technique is *denial of injury*, which is used when people mitigate the wrongfulness of their behavior by arguing that no one was hurt by their actions or that they did not intend any harm. Sometimes people admit that their actions have harmed others, but they neutralize guilt by denying the victims of their actions. *Denying victims* occurs when people say that their victims acted improperly and were thus deserving of being victimized. In this sense, people believe that their actions are a form of just retaliation. People also deny victims when the victims are absent, unknown, or abstract, or when they are seen as willing participants in the crime.

A fourth technique is *condemnation of the condemner*. Those who use this technique emphasize that persons who condemn their actions are "deviants in disguise" or that their condemners' own motivations and behaviors are hypocritical (Sykes and Matza 1957: 668). This technique allows people to shift the focus to the actions of others and, thus, minimize the importance of their own actions (Sykes and Matza 1957). The final neutralization technique described by Sykes and Matza is *appeal to higher loyalties*. When using this technique, people acknowledge the conventional norms of society but justify their actions because "norms, held to be more pressing or involving a higher loyalty, are accorded precedence" (Sykes and Matza 1957: 669).

While Sykes and Matza outlined these five techniques, others have expanded on the variety of neutralizations. Through study of the neutralizing behaviors of other types of people (rather than just young people), new techniques have emerged, including the defense of necessity, the claim of normality, the claim of entitlement, the metaphor of the ledger, and justification by comparison (Cromwell and Thurman 2003; Klockars 1974). Undoubtedly, there are numerous other techniques that people use to make sense of their criminal actions (see Kaptein and van Helvoort 2019 for an overview). However, uncovering the full list of neutralizations may not be theoretically or empirically important. What is important is understanding the *function* of neutralization techniques, rather than detailing the specific varieties in which they come (Maruna and Copes 2005; see also Kaptein and van Helvoort 2019).

31.3 ORIGINS AND SIMILAR THEORETICAL PARADIGMS

Neutralization theory has had a remarkable impact on our understanding of crime and delinquency. While it began as a stand-alone theory, today scholars have incorporated aspects of it into other theories. When classifying the theory, people have included it as a component of control theories, psychological theories, learning theories, and subcultural theories (Copes and Maruna 2005). It has been incorporated into reintegrative shaming theory (Braithwaite 1989), rational choice theory (Clarke 1997; Clarke and Homel 1997), and life-course theory (Laub and Sampson 2001).

The theory that it is most often associated with is differential association. Sykes and Matza (1957) argued that juvenile delinquency is learned through social interactions and techniques of neutralization, an elaboration of how people learn and use neutralizations that extends Sutherland's (1955) differential association theory (see also Cressey 1953). Sutherland (1955) proposed that social interactions with individuals who engage in criminal behavior teach persons not only how they can engage in crime and delinquency but also "the motives, drives, rationalizations, and attitudes favorable" to crime and delinquency (Sykes and Matza 1957: 664). Sykes and Matza (1957) argued that techniques of neutralization are a mechanism for learning "definitions favorable to the violation of the law" (Sutherland 1955; Sykes and Matza 1957: 667).

Matza (1964) extended techniques of neutralization into drift theory, which follows that people use neutralizations to drift between conventional and unconventional value systems. Interestingly, Matza's work both helped separate the theory from differential association and connected the theory with control theories that began to be developed in the 1960s (Hirschi 1969; Reckless 1961). For instance, some classify neutralization theory as one component of containment theory (Reckless 1961). According to Reckless (1961), people with a strong inner containment (positive self-concept, moral values, orientation toward legitimate goals, and high self-control) and outer containment (legal rules, associations with law-abiding persons, and opportunities to engage in legitimate activities) are discouraged from engaging in crime and delinquency. Neutralizations are thought to be one way that internal containments (i.e., moral beliefs) are worn down or eroded, which allows for participation in crime.

Scholars have also incorporated neutralization theory into rational choice frameworks (Clarke 1997; Clarke and Homel 1997). Contemporary rational choice theorists have advocated for the importance of modeling decision-making. This includes modeling the decision to engage in crime and decisions on how to enact specific crimes. Those working within a rational choice framework often study the stages of criminal decision-making, which include initiation, continuance, and desistance. Neutralizations are important in all of these stages (Maruna and Copes 2005). That is, neutralizations are used to initiate participation in crime and to continue committing it. Giving up neutralizations may be instrumental in criminal desistance and is important in the study of criminal decision-making and the development of crime prevention programs.

In addition to being incorporated into other theories, neutralization theory has been used to formulate new theories of crime. Following the presentation of techniques of neutralization, Scott and Lyman (1968) expanded upon Sykes and Matza's (1957) arguments by developing their theory of accounts. Accounts are linguistic devices used by people to justify or excuse behavior that is viewed as deviant. Accounts take two forms: justifications and excuses. Justifications are used by people who acknowledge engaging in improper behavior but believe that the situation in which the act occurred warranted it. Some techniques of neutralization (e.g., denial of injury, denial of the victim, condemnation of condemners, and appeal to higher loyalties) are justifications used by individuals to neutralize crime and delinquency.

Excuses are used by people who have engaged in crime and delinquency and who acknowledge that the act itself was morally wrong but deny responsibility for it. Scott and Lyman (1968) initially proposed four types of excuse. First, there is the *appeal to accidents*, which is used by people who argue that their behavior occurred by accident or chance. Second, there are *appeals to defeasibility*. Individuals who use this excuse argue that their behavior was due to not being aware of all aspects of the situation. For example, someone may use this excuse if they were not aware that their behavior would result in a certain outcome or they did not intend to cause any harm. Third, there are *appeals to biological drives*. People who use these excuses attribute blame to inherent biological differences (e.g., impulsive behavior). Finally, there is *scapegoating*, where people will attribute their actions to another person or entity. There are numerous similarities between the accounts and the neutralizations, including some of the same linguistic techniques. The key difference between the two is that people use neutralizations to manage internal controls (e.g., personal guilt) whereas they use accounts to manage external controls (e.g., potential stigma or negative assessments from others).

A similar theory was developed by Bandura et al. (1996), who proposed that individuals use different cognitive mechanisms as a way to counter the negative emotions that result from engaging in crime and delinquency. The theory of moral disengagement includes eight mechanisms that allow individuals to thwart the deterrent effects of moral beliefs that normally would prevent someone from engaging in deviance. *Moral justification* can be used by individuals to reframe deviance as serving a higher purpose. People can also use *euphemistic language* as a means to make their behavior appear more "palatable" and soften the reality of their behavior. *Advantageous comparison* allows individuals to minimize their actions by comparing them to other behaviors that are perceived as more severe.

People can *displace responsibility* for their actions to external social pressures such as others who may have encouraged the behavior. The *diffusion of responsibility* allows individuals in group settings who engage in deviance to place blame on the others in the group who were also involved. People may also *disregard or distort the consequences* that result from their behaviors. Examples of this include denying that anyone was hurt by their actions or minimizing the severity of the behavior. Finally, people can justify their deviance by *dehumanizing victims*. For instance, people may say that the victims were deserving of the outcomes. Again, Bandura's moral disengagement is quite similar to neutralization theory. One of the main differences is that Sykes and Matza (1957) emphasize the social nature of learning neutralizations whereas Bandura emphasizes the psychological nature of moral disengagement. Walters (2020: 213) further argues that moral disengagement "is driven by a cognitive mechanism designed to excuse or justify future offending behavior and preemptively reduce or eliminate moral emotions like guilt before they have had a chance to affect behavior." In contrast, he proposes that neutralizations are used "when guilt is elicited by the presence or prospect of offending . . . and ends when the individual uses a cognitive mechanism to neutralize the guilt associated with real or imagined offending" (Walters 2020: 213).

31.4 EMPIRICAL FINDINGS

There is much research addressing the use of techniques of neutralization in a variety of populations and contexts (see Maruna and Copes 2005 for an overview). A large portion of research on the theory involves the use of qualitative research techniques, such as semi-structured interviews. Qualitative research on the theory provides in-depth understanding of the use of techniques of neutralization from the perspective of those using them. Researchers have used qualitative methods to study neutralizations in a wide range of samples including active street offenders (Rosenfeld, Jacobs, and Wright 2003; Topalli 2005), white-collar offenders (Copes and Vieraitis 2012), juvenile street taggers (Vasquez and Vieraitis 2016), and psychiatric facility security guards (Johnston and Kilty 2016). Overall, this research suggests that regardless of the subset of individuals, people do regularly use neutralizations to overcome the deterrent effects of internal and external social controls (Maruna and Copes 2005). Moreover, neutralizations are not just limited to offending populations. They are also used by nonoffenders as well (e.g., Copes and Williams 2007).

Quantitative tests of the theory often use cross-sectional designs and self-reported questionnaires. Typically, these questionnaires present respondents with a list of neutralizing statements and ask them to indicate the degree to which they agree with the statement. Researchers have employed such questionnaires to compare whether there are differences between offending and nonoffending populations (Ball 1966; Mitchell and Dodder 1983) or to assess the correlation between neutralizations and self-reported deviant outcomes in general populations (e.g., Chua and Holt 2016; Piquero, Tibbetts, and Blankenship 2005; Morris and Higgins 2009; Vieraitis et al. 2012). While quantitative studies show that there is a significant positive correlation between neutralization and deviant outcomes and that offenders, when compared to nonoffenders, report higher use of neutralizations, there is variability in these findings due to different neutralization measures and populations across studies.

Findings also vary between studies because most have measured neutralizations and outcomes at one time point (cross-sectionally) as opposed to over longer periods (longitudinally). However, the strength of the relationship between neutralizations and deviance has largely remained unclear until recently. Helmond et al. (2015) conducted a meta-analysis of the relationship between cognitive distortions (defined as either neutralizations or moral disengagement, or, in the context of Gibbs et al. (1995), work on cognitive distortions) and externalizing problem behavior (e.g., delinquency, crime, and aggression). Their meta-analysis included fifty-three studies and showed a moderate to large positive relationship between cognitive distortions and externalizing problem behavior. This suggests the importance of neutralization use for understanding crime.

31.5 CONCEPTUAL ISSUES

While there is a consensus that the use of neutralizations is related to participation in crime and delinquency, there are still theoretical gaps that limit a complete understanding of the theory. Scholars from varying fields have tested the basic theoretical propositions of the theory in a wide variety of populations and contexts. While there have been recent strides by researchers who have refined the theory, there are still theoretical shortcomings that remain. Some of these conceptual issues that need clarity include the role of societal commitments in the neutralization – the deviance relationship, whether neutralizations are used prior to engaging in deviance, the stability of neutralizations over the life-course, and the role of neutralizations in explaining the onset and continuation of and desistance from crime.

31.5.1 *Are Neutralizations Used by Everyone?*

A key question about the theory is whether the use of neutralizations is pathological. It is true that people who engage in deviance neutralize their behavior. Decades of qualitative research show this to be true (Maruna and Copes 2005). However, people do not neutralize in every situation, and understanding this is an important aspect to consider when studying techniques of neutralization. Sykes and Matza (1957) proposed that neutralization use varies between people partly as a result of their individual attachments to conventional society. The assumption is that attachments to conventional norms lead to guilt, which must be neutralized. They argued that persons who have strong attachments to conventional society will need to neutralize to overcome the internal and external controls that normally prohibit deviance. Conversely, those with weak attachments to conventional society have no need to neutralize when they violate conventional norms. If a person "[exhibits] no feelings of guilt or shame at detection or confinement" then they do not need to neutralize (Sykes and Matza 1957: 664).

Other researchers have proposed alternative hypotheses to explain the interrelationships among neutralizations, deviance, and attachments. Hirschi (1969) argued that a strong attachment to law-abiding persons or beliefs should be associated with less neutralization use. This is because persons with strong attachments will be less likely to engage in deviance in the first place; neutralizations simply are not strong enough to overcome the corresponding guilt of norm violations. Another hypothesis is that there is a curvilinear relationship between neutralizations and deviance (Copes 2003; Copes and Williams 2007). This argument follows that individuals with very strong or very weak attachments to conventional society are less likely to neutralize while those who are somewhere in the middle are more likely to neutralize. Specifically, neutralization use should be most often employed by persons "who are in a state of drift: partially committed to conventional values and to a certain lifestyle or set of behaviors labeled as deviant" (Copes and Williams 2007: 251). Neutralizations allow such persons to drift between conventional and deviant behaviors (see also Matza 1964). Persons "either hypercommitted to dominant moral values or else strongly committed to a subcultural frame of reference" should not need to use neutralizations (Copes and Williams 2007: 251).

Only a few studies have looked at the impact of societal attachments on the neutralization–deviance relationship, and findings from these studies are mixed. For example, Thurman (1984) found that the positive effect of neutralizations on antisocial behavior was strongest for respondents who had low levels of moral commitment (i.e., the threat of guilt). Using data from a sample of adolescents, Costello (2000) found that neutralizations were negatively associated with delinquency among young people who reported strong attachments to their parents. These two studies provide support for the argument made by Hirschi (1969). In contrast, Copes (2003) found that auto thieves with higher levels of attachment to conventional society were more likely to use neutralizations than those who were not. Similarly, Cardwell, Mazerolle, and Piquero (2020) studied the use of rationalizations before and after a truancy intervention. They found that the relationship between rationalizations after the intervention and antisocial behavior was stronger at higher levels of parental attachment for only those in the experiment relative to the control. The findings from these two studies support Sykes and Matza's (1957) hypothesis.

Much of the early work on neutralization theory focused on how people make sense of violating conventional norms. The implicit assumption of the theory was that it was violating mainstream norms that led to guilt, which had to be overcome. However, this is not the case. Topalli (2005) showed that people can experience negative self-images for violating any belief system, even subcultural belief systems. Specifically, Topalli (2005) showed that persistent street offenders (e.g., persistent robbers, drug dealers, and burglars) rarely experienced guilt when committing serious forms of street crime. Consequently, they did not need to use neutralizations to maintain a positive sense of self. They did, however, use neutralizations when they violated subcultural norms, such as when they snitched or failed to retaliate when wronged. Thus, the range of the theory can be expanded to included violations of all held values.

31.5.2 *Do Neutralizations Come before Deviance?*

Sykes and Matza (1957) argue that neutralization must be used before engaging in deviance. This is an important claim about the theory that is often ignored by researchers. Neutralizations are not argued to be used *after* engaging in deviance because guilt, shame, and the threat to self-concept often deter deviance. Thus, neutralizations must be used *before* engaging in deviance as a means to overcome the deterrent effects of these factors. Importantly, Sykes and Matza (1957) do not state that neutralizations are the cause of deviance and deterministic in and of themselves. Rather, neutralization techniques increase the likelihood of deviance and allow people to drift between competing value systems.

The majority of research on neutralizations has studied the concept at one point in time. There are only a handful of studies that have sought to assess the relationship between neutralizations and antisocial behavior over time. Early longitudinal research on the topic showed that neutralizations were associated with later various forms of deviance (Agnew 1994; Minor 1981; Shields and Whitehall 1994). However, these studies only addressed this association between two time points. It has only been more recently that researchers have attempted to understand the causal ordering of these two variables over longer periods of time during adolescence.

Using a longitudinal research design, Morris and Copes (2012) studied the causal relationships between neutralizations and delinquency over the course of five years. Their results showed that earlier neutralizations were better able to predict subsequent delinquency; however, findings were mixed on whether earlier delinquency was associated with subsequent neutralization use. In a similar study, Topalli, Higgins, and Copes (2014) assessed the causal links between neutralization and delinquency over five years in a sample of adolescents. Their results showed that there were reciprocal relationships between neutralizations and delinquency; that is, earlier neutralizations were related to later delinquency, which was then related to later neutralizations and so forth. Using the same data set as Topalli, Higgins and Copes (2014), Walters (2020) found that there were reciprocal relationships among experiencing guilt, neutralizations, and delinquency. That is, guilt predicted future neutralizations and subsequent delinquency, but neutralizations also predicted higher guilt and future delinquency.

While these studies provide support for the idea that neutralizations are a priori justifications for subsequent deviant behavior, they also provide some evidence of the hardening process as described by Hirschi (1969; see also Minor 1984). Hirschi (1969) acknowledged that while neutralizations can result in the initiation into crime and delinquency, the use of neutralizations should also be associated with future crime and delinquency and future neutralization use. This continuous cycle of neutralization and crime and delinquency is proposed to result in a neutralization belief system and may lead to long-term criminal behavior (Hirschi 1969; Minor 1984).

31.5.3 *Are Neutralizing Beliefs Stable?*

Longitudinal analyses of neutralization beliefs have been able to provide insight into the stability of this behavior. Morris and Copes (2012) found that there was moderate stability in neutralizing beliefs among people. Topalli, Higgins, and Copes (2014) also found that there was stability in neutralizations from ages twelve to sixteen. Further, their results indicated that there were different trajectories of neutralization beliefs: a very low-level group, a low-level group, a moderate-level group, and a high-level group. While there was variation among these groups in the level of neutralization, persons within these trajectories, regardless of membership, exhibited relative stability in their neutralization beliefs throughout the time period. Further, these trajectories were associated with delinquency during the same time period.

It is important to note that because these studies were conducted on samples of adolescents, it remains to be determined whether neutralizations remain stable past this time period into adulthood. The period of adolescence is when antisocial behavior is at its highest levels in the life-course (Piquero, Farrington, and Blumstein 2003). Considering the possibility of reciprocal relationships between rationalizations and delinquency (Shulman et al. 2011; Topalli, Higgins, and Copes 2014) it is possible that adolescence is also the period where neutralizations are at their pinnacle levels. It would be worthwhile for future research to assess the stability of neutralization use from adolescence into adulthood. For example, research on trajectories of moral disengagement shows that there is a decline in these behaviors from middle adolescence into early adulthood (Cardwell et al. 2015; Paciello et al. 2008; Shulman et al. 2011).

31.5.4 *How Do Neutralizations Explain Persistence and Desistance in Criminal Behavior?*

Considering the previous discussions of the role of neutralization in explaining criminal outcomes and its relative stability in adolescence, neutralization appears to play a role in both persistence and desistance from crime and delinquency (Maruna and Copes 2005). Maruna (2001) was one of the earliest to offer insight into the role that neutralizations play in both persistence in and desistance from crime in the Liverpool Desistance Study. This study used in-depth life history interviews with close to 100 justice system-involved persons who self-reported that they were either desisting from crime (i.e., "desisters") or still actively engaging in criminal behavior (i.e., "persisters") (Maruna 2001). Maruna then compared the life histories between these two groups to see how their narratives related to desistance and persistence in criminal behavior.

In describing their life histories, persisters used what Maruna (2001: 75) referred to as "condemnation scripts." Persisters explained that their life circumstances and continued involvement in crime were the result of negative life events that were out of their control. Further, many in this group "[saw] no real hope for change in their lives and ... generally accepted the fate that has been handed to them" (Maruna 2001: 76). Persisters would often attribute continued criminal behavior to negative internal, stable, or global forces (Maruna 2004). Attributing criminal behavior to negatively viewed forces was hypothesized to contribute to continued criminal involvement and prevent desistance from crime. Conversely, desisters in the study utilized what Maruna (2001) referred to as "redemption scripts." Desisters made clear distinctions between their past and present selves and emphasized that they were inherently good people who had become ensnared by other forces that had led to their criminal involvement and presently sought to "make good" for past actions. As opposed to persisters, desisters would use positive internal, stable, or global forces when attributing explanations to their past actions (Maruna 2004).

Other scholars also argue that neutralizations play a role in explaining desistance from crime. For instance, Hulley (2016) conducted interviews with fifteen former male sex offenders to study the relationship between neutralizations and desistance. She found that the men in her study would use various neutralizations to explain their past offending behavior. Some respondents denoted that their behavior was "out of character" and due to other forces, other people's fault, and the result of medical issues. She concluded that neutralizations "allowed respondents to negotiate the stigma assigned to those with a conviction for a sexual offence," which "provided for a positive sense of self," and to "distance themselves from their offending behavior" (Hulley 2016: 1785). However, she noted that the majority of respondents, while they "demonstrated cognitive transformations," reported that their "desistance journey was incomplete" (Hulley 2016: 1786). Of the fifteen respondents, only one provided evidence of a transformation and distinction from their past self.

Research is mixed on the role of neutralization use in the desistance process. Much scholarship indicates that the desistance process involves a convergence of a wide range of individual, familial, and social factors (Laub and Sampson 2001; LeBel et al. 2008; Serin and Lloyd 2009). Because of this, future research is needed to disentangle the effects of neutralization on desistance from other influences at play throughout this process. Specifically, such research could assist in creating a clearer picture of how neutralizations can both facilitate or hamper the desistance process among active or former offenders.

31.6 Policy Implications

Some crime reduction programs contain aspects that directly confront neutralization beliefs in participants. Because the theory assumes that neutralizations make way for subsequent crime and deviance, prevention efforts are frequently focused on "neutralizing the neutralizations" in both criminal justice and general populations (Maruna and Copes 2005; Kieffer and Sloan 2009). These include restorative justice practices, situational crime prevention, and cognitive restructuring programs (Maruna and Copes 2005).

Restorative justice broadly focuses on bringing victims and offenders together in an open forum (often facilitated by a third party) to discuss the harm that has been done and to seek resolutions and outcomes to repair the harm done (Daly 2002: 58). A primary goal of restorative justice interventions is to reintegrate offenders back into society and reduce the likelihood of recidivism (Braithwaite 1989; Sherman et al. 2015a, 2015b). Restorative justice conferences are well suited to confronting the use of neutralizations. This is because before many restorative justice conferences, offenders are required to accept responsibility for their behavior and any harm they have caused to victims (Sherman et al. 2015a). Further, because restorative justice practices require offenders to meet directly with victims, restorative justice practices are theorized to reduce the likelihood of neutralization use in such forums (Hayes 2006). While much research has been done on restorative practices in general (Daly 2002; Sherman et al. 2015a, 2015b; Strang et al. 2013), and restorative justice practices themselves are designed to encourage offenders to acknowledge and accept responsibility for their behavior, there is a paucity of evidence on whether they reduce neutralizations.

One exception is from Cardwell, Mazerolle, and Piquero (2020). They used data from the Ability School Engagement Program (ASEP), a truancy reduction experiment, to assess whether young people who participated in the ASEP had better outcomes relative to those in the control group. The ASEP utilizes a conference with truanting young people, their parent(s), a uniformed police officer, a school representative (e.g., teacher), and a third-party facilitator. The conference incorporates "restorative practices to elicit the 'affect' of the truanting behavior from all forum participants" (i.e., to aid the young person in understanding how their truancy affects others) (Mazerolle 2014: 356). Cardwell, Mazerolle, and Piquero's (2020) measure of rationalizations addressed the concepts of denial of responsibility (Sykes and Matza 1957) and cognitive restructuring (Bandura 2002). They found evidence that those in the experiment had a significant reduction in rationalizations after the intervention relative to those in the control (Cardwell, Mazerolle, and Piquero 2020). This provides evidence that interventions containing elements of restorative practices can reduce rationalizing behavior.

Situational crime prevention strategies are designed to reduce opportunities for crime (Clarke 1997; Clarke and Homel 1997). One way in which these strategies do this is through making opportunities for crime less excusable. Since neutralizations reduce the effectiveness of internal and external social controls (e.g., guilt or the threat of sanctions) that would typically deter crime and delinquency, situational crime prevention programs "[make] it harder to find excuses for criminal action" (Clarke 1997: 5). These prevention strategies are often focused on specific offense types. Examples of situational crime prevention strategies include drunk driving advertisement campaigns or signs in shops warning customers of prosecution if they are caught stealing merchandise. Importantly, these types of crime control and prevention strategy are designed to reduce neutralizations at the specific point at which people are presented with the opportunity to offend. What they are not able to do is lead to long-term change in neutralization use (Clarke 1997; Clarke and Homel 1997).

Finally, there are some interventions designed to reduce neutralizations, crime, and delinquency by changing participants' cognitive thinking processes. Programs like EQUIPping Youth to Help One Another (Gibbs et al. 1995) are designed to reduce the use of neutralizations. Such programs are based on cognitive behavioral therapy practices and seek to change participants' criminal thinking in order to reduce deviant behavior. There is good evidence that cognitive restructuring programs can lead to reductions in cognitive distortions. Helmond et al. (2015) conducted a meta-analysis of the relationship between cognitive distortions (including neutralizations) and externalizing problem behavior (e.g., crime and delinquency). Among a subset of eighteen intervention studies, they found that these types of intervention resulted in a small reduction in cognitive distortions. However, they also assessed a further subset of nine studies that were interventions designed to reduce cognitive distortions and subsequent externalizing problem behavior. The researchers did not find evidence that interventions could reduce the use of cognitive distortions or the externalizing of problem behaviors. The authors concluded that it is still undetermined whether "reducing cognitive distortions is an effective mediating mechanism for reducing externalizing behavior" (Helmond et al. 2015: 258).

31.7 CONCLUSIONS

Moral beliefs guide people's actions and act as internal regulators of behavior. People will typically not choose to engage in deviance due to the threat of experiencing negative emotions or the threat of punishment. Regardless, moral beliefs in and of themselves may not be enough to prevent a person from engaging in deviance. Sykes and Matza's (1957) techniques of neutralization theory offers insight into why people, regardless of their moral beliefs, choose to engage in deviance. They proposed that people can overcome the potential for negative emotions or threats of punishments by neutralizing their actions. They do this through a variety of techniques including placing responsibility on other entities, denying that anyone was harmed by their actions, blaming the victims of their behavior, arguing that what they did was not as bad as other deviant actions, or arguing that their behavior served a higher purpose.

In the sixty-plus years since Sykes and Matza's (1957) theory was first published, scholars from the social sciences have tested its basic theoretical propositions in a wide variety of populations and contexts. The broad consensus from this line of research shows that neutralizations play an important role in the decision to engage in crime and deviant behaviors. Importantly, this finding holds in both criminal justice and general population samples. There is also good evidence to show that neutralizations can effectively be nullified through a variety of crime prevention methods, including restorative justice, situational crime prevention, and cognitive behavioral programs. Regardless of its theoretical and crime control success, there are still theoretical gaps that limit our understanding of the theory and potentially limit the effectiveness of these programs and strategies. In this chapter, we highlighted four such questions that still remain about the theory: 1) are neutralizations used by everyone; 2) do neutralizations come before deviance; 3) are neutralization beliefs stable? and 4) how do neutralizations explain persistence and desistance in crime?

In regards to the first question, there is evidence to support that most people neutralize their behavior, regardless of whether they are involved in the criminal justice system. Whether individuals use neutralizations in all situations in which they are presented with an opportunity for crime, however, is partly dependent on their level of attachment to society (e.g., parents or legal rules) and their own context. For the second question, there is some longitudinal research to support the idea that neutralizations precede deviant behavior. However, these studies also show evidence for a reciprocal relationship between neutralization and deviance: neutralization use can lead to deviance but also to future neutralization use. Third, while there is evidence for relative stability in neutralizations, research from similar theoretical paradigms (e.g., moral disengagement) provides evidence that rationalizing behavior decreases from middle adolescence into adulthood.

Finally, while neutralizations play a role in the process of both persistence in and desistance from deviance, it is still important for future research to tease out the role of neutralization in these processes from other well-known factors related to persistence and desistance.

REFERENCES

Agnew, Robert. 1994. "The Techniques of Neutralization and Violence." *Criminology* 32: 555–80.

Ball, Richard A. 1966. "An Empirical Exploration of Neutralization Theory." *Criminology* 4: 22–32.

Bandura, A. 2002. "Selective Moral Disengagement in the Exercise of Moral Agency." *Journal of Moral Education* 31: 101–19.

Bandura, Albert, Claudio Barbaranelli, Gian V. Caprara, and Concetta Pastorelli. 1996. "Mechanisms of Moral Disengagement in the Exercise of Moral Agency." *Journal of Personality and Social Psychology* 71: 364–74.

Braithwaite, John. 1989. *Crime, Shame, and Reintegration*. Cambridge: Cambridge University Press.

Cardwell, Stephanie M., Alex R. Piquero, Wesley G. Jennings, Heith Copes, Carol A. Schubert, and Edward P. Mulvey. 2015. "Variability in Moral Disengagement and Its Relation to Offending in a Sample of Serious Adolescent Offenders." *Criminal Justice and Behavior* 42: 819–39.

Cardwell, Stephanie M., Lorraine Mazerolle, and Alex R. Piquero. 2020. "Parental Attachment and Truant Rationalizations of Antisocial Behavior: Findings from a Randomized Controlled Trial." *Journal of Crime and Justice* 43: 263–81.

Chua, Yi T., and Thomas J. Holt. 2016. "A Cross-National Examination of the Techniques of Neutralization to Account for Hacking Behaviors." *Victims & Offenders* 11: 534–55.

Clarke, Ronald V. 1997. *Situational Crime Prevention: Successful Cases*, 2nd ed. Albany, NY: Harroy and Heston Publishers.

Clarke, Ronald V., and Ross Homel. 1997. "A Revised Classification of Situational Crime Prevention Techniques." In *Crime Prevention at the Crossroads*, edited by Steven P. Lab, 17–27. Cincinnati, OH: Anderson.

Cohen, Albert K. 1955. *Delinquent Boys: The Culture of the Gang*. New York: Free Press.

Copes, Heith. 2003. "Societal Attachments, Offending Frequency, and Techniques of Neutralization." *Deviant Behavior* 24: 101–27.

Copes, Heith, and Lynne M. Vieraitis. 2012. *Identity Thieves: Motives and Methods*. Boston: Northeastern University Press.

Copes, Heith, and J. Patrick Williams. 2007. "Techniques of Affirmation: Deviant Behavior, Moral Commitment, and Subcultural Identity." *Deviant Behavior* 28: 247–72.

Costello, Barbara J. 2000. "Techniques of Neutralization and Self-Esteem: A Critical Test of Social Control and Neutralization Theory." *Deviant Behavior* 21: 307–29.

Cressey, Donald R. 1953. *Other People's Money: Study in the Social Psychology of Embezzlement*. New York: Free Press.

Cromwell, Paul, and Quint Thurman. 2003. "The Devil Made Me Do It: Use of Neutralizations by Shoplifters." *Deviant Behavior* 24: 535–50.

Daly, Kahleen. 2002. "Restorative Justice: The Real Story." *Punishment & Society* 4: 55–79.

Gibbs, John C., Granville B. Potter, and Arnold P. Goldstein. 1995. *The EQUIP Program: Teaching Youth to Think and Act Responsibly through a Peer-Helping Approach*. Champaign, IL: Research Press.

Hayes, Hennessey. 2006. "Apologies and Accounts in Youth Justice Conferencing: Reinterpreting Research Outcomes." *Contemporary Justice Review* 9: 369–85.

Helmond, Petra, G. Overbeek, Daniel Brugman, and John C. Gibbs. 2015. "A Meta-analysis on Cognitive Distortions and Externalizing Problem Behavior: Associations, Moderators, and Treatment Effects." *Criminal Justice and Behavior* 42: 245–62.

Hirschi, Travis. 1969. *Causes of Delinquency*. Berkeley: University of California Press.

Hulley, Joanne L. 2016. "'While This Does Not in Any Way Excuse My Conduct ...': The Role of Treatment and Neutralizations in Desistance from Sexual Offending." *International Journal of Offender Therapy and Comparative Criminology* 60: 1776–90.

Johnston, Matthew S., and Jennifer M. Kilty. 2016. "'It's for Their Own Good': Techniques of Neutralization and Security Guard Violence Against Psychiatric Patients." *Punishment & Society* 18: 177–97.

Kaptein, Muel, and Martien van Helvoort. 2019. "A Model of Neutralization Techniques." *Deviant Behavior* 40: 1260–85.

Kieffer, Scott M., and John J. Sloan III. 2009. "Overcoming Moral Hurdles: Using Techniques of Neutralization by White-Collar Suspects as an Interrogation Tool." *Security Journal* 22: 317–30.

Klockars, Carl B. 1974. *The Professional Fence*. New York: Free Press.

Laub, John H., and Robert J. Sampson. 2001. "Understanding Desistance from Crime." *Crime & Justice* 28: 1–69.

LeBel, Thomas P., Ros Burnett, Shadd Maruna, and Shawn Bushway. 2008. "The 'Chicken and Egg' of Subjective and Social Factors in Desistance from Crime." *European Journal of Criminology* 5(2): 131–59.

Maruna, Shadd. 2001. *Making Good: How Ex-convicts Reform and Rebuild Their Lives*. Washington, DC: American Psychological Association.

2004. "Desistance from Crime and Explanatory Style: A New Direction in the Psychology of Reform." *Journal of Contemporary Criminal Justice* 20: 184–200.

Maruna, Shadd, and Heith Copes. 2005. "What Have We Learned from Five Decades of Neutralization Research?" *Crime and Justice: A Review of Research* 32: 221–320.

Matza, David. 1964. *Delinquency and Drift*. New York: John Wiley & Sons.

Mazerolle, Lorraine. 2014. "The Power of Policing Partnerships: Sustaining the Gains." *Journal of Experimental Criminology* 10: 341–65.

Minor, W. William. 1981. "Techniques of Neutralization: A Reconceptualization and Empirical Examination." *Journal of Research in Crime and Delinquency* 18: 295–318.

1984. "Neutralization as a Hardening Process: Considerations in the Modeling of Change." *Social Forces* 62: 995–1019.

Mitchell, Jim, and Richard A. Dodder. 1983. "Types of Neutralization and Types of Delinquency." *Journal of Youth and Adolescence* 12: 307–18.

Morris, Robert G., and Heith Copes. 2012. "Exploring the Temporal Dynamics of the Neutralization/Delinquency Relationship." *Criminal Justice Review* 37: 442–60.

Morris, Robert G., and George E. Higgins. 2009. "Neutralizing Potential and Self-Reported Digital Piracy: A Multitheoretical Exploration among College Undergraduates." *Criminal Justice Review* 34: 173–95.

Paciello, Marinella, Roberta Fida, Carlo Tramontano, Catia Lupinetti, and Gian V. Caprara. 2008. "Stability and Change of Moral Disengagement and Its Impact on Aggression and Violence in Late Adolescence." *Child Development* 27: 1288–1309.

Piquero, Alex R., David P. Farrington, and Alfred Blumstein. 2003. "The Criminal Career Paradigm." *Crime and Justice* 30: 359–506.

Piquero, Nicole L., Stephen G. Tibbetts, and Michael B. Blankenship. 2005. "Examining the Role of Differential Association and Techniques of Neutralization in Explaining Corporate Crime." *Deviant Behavior* 26: 159–88.

Reckless, Walter C. 1961. "A New Theory of Delinquency and Crime." *Federal Probation* 25: 42–6.

Rosenfeld, Richard, Bruce A. Jacobs, and Richard Wright. 2003. "Snitching and the Code of the Street." *British Journal of Criminology* 43: 291–309.

Scott, Marvin B., and Stanford M. Lyman. 1968. "Accounts." *American Sociological Review* 33: 46–62.

Serin, Ralph C., and Caleb D. Lloyd. 2009. "Examining the Process of Offender Change: The Transition to Crime Desistance." *Psychology, Crime & Law* 15(4): 347–64.

Sherman, Lawrence W., Heather Strang, Geoffrey Barnes, Daniel J. Woods, Sarah Bennett, Nova Inkpen, Dorothy Newbury-Birch, Meredith Rossner, Caroline Angel, Malcom Mearns, and Molly Slothtower. 2015a. "Twelve Experiments in Restorative Justice: The Jerry Lee Program of Randomized Trials of Restorative Justice." *Journal of Experimental Criminology* 11: 501–40.

Sherman, Lawrence W., Heather Strang, Evan Mayo-Wilson, Daniel J. Woods, and Barak Ariel. 2015b. "Are Restorative Justice Conferences Effective in Reducing Repeat Offending? Findings from a Campbell Systematic Review." *Journal of Quantitative Criminology* 31: 1–24.

Shields, Ian W., and Georga C. Whitehall. 1994. "Neutralization and Delinquency among Teenagers." *Criminal Justice and Behavior* 21: 223–35.

Shulman, Elizabeth P., Elizabeth Cauffman, Alex R. Piquero, and Jeffrey Fagan. 2011. "Moral Disengagement among Serious Juvenile Offenders: A Longitudinal Study of the Relations between Morally Disengaged Attitudes and Offending." *Developmental Psychology* 47: 1619–32.

Strang, Heather, Lawrence W. Sherman, Evan Mayo-Wilson, Daniel Woods, and Barak Ariel. 2013. "Restorative Justice Conferencing (RJC) Using Face-to-Face Meetings of Offenders and Victims: Effects on Offender Recidivism and Victim Satisfaction. A Systematic Review." *Campbell Systematic Reviews* 9: 1–59.

Sutherland, Edwin H. 1955. *Principles of Criminology*, 5th ed., edited by Donald R. Cressey. Chicago, IL: J. B. Lippincott Company.

Sykes, Gresham M., and David Matza. 1957. "Techniques of Neutralization: A Theory of Delinquency." *American Sociological Review* 22: 664–70.

Thurman, Quint C. 1984. "Deviance and the Neutralization of Moral Commitment: An Empirical Analysis." *Deviant Behavior* 5: 291–304.

Topalli, Volkan. 2005. "When Being Good Is Bad: An Expansion of Neutralization Theory." *Criminology* 43: 797–835.

Topalli, Volkan, George E. Higgins, and Heith Copes. 2014. "A Causal Model of Neutralization Acceptance and Delinquency: Making the Case for an Individual Difference Model." *Criminal Justice and Behavior* 41: 553–73.

Vasquez, Arthur, and Lynne M. Vieraitis. 2016. "'It's Just Paint': Street Taggers' Use of Neutralization Techniques." *Deviant Behavior* 37: 1179–95.

Vieraitis, Lynne M., Nicole L. Piquero, Alex R. Piquero, Stephen G. Tibbetts, and Michael Blankenship. 2012. "Do Women and Men Differ in Their Neutralizations of Corporate Crime?" *Criminal Justice Review* 37: 478–93.

Walters, Glenn D. 2020. "Neutralization, Moral Disengagement, and Delinquency in Adolescence: Testing the Reciprocal Effects of Proactive Criminal Thinking and Guilt on Future Offending." *Justice Quarterly* 37: 210–230.

PART V

Capacity and Opportunity

32

Do People Know the Law? Empirical Evidence about Legal Knowledge and Its Implications for Compliance

Benjamin van Rooij

Abstract: Legal knowledge is a core aspect in compliance. For law to shape behaviour, people whose conduct the law tries to influence should know the law. This chapter reviews the body of existing empirical research about legal knowledge. It assesses the extent to which laypersons and professionals know and understand legal rules across various domains including employment, family affairs, criminal justice, education and health care. This body of work shows that ignorance and misunderstanding of the law are common across these domains. There is variation and for some laws, amongst some people and in some jurisdictions, there is more or less legal knowledge. Also, the review shows that there is evidence that people tend to equate their own norms with the rules of the law. The chapter concludes by discussing what these findings mean for compliance and the way our laws try to steer human and organisational conduct. Here it questions compliance approaches that view it as a linear process from rule to behaviour.

32.1 INTRODUCTION

Compliance, ultimately, is about how legal rules get to shape behaviour. The most common, yet often implicit, conception of compliance involves a linear process: lawmakers develop rules; such rules are made public and enforced; people learn about these rules and the way they are implemented; they weigh the costs and benefits of obeying or breaking the rules; and they decide how to respond.

Within this process, a core element is that people get to learn the rules. And, thus, legal knowledge, indicating that regulated subjects have knowledge and understanding of the rules that seek to influence their behaviour, is a core aspect of compliance. Yet, so far in the discussion on compliance, legal knowledge has not featured centrally. Darley, Carlsmith and Robinson are an important exception, as their study of people's knowledge of criminal law directly asks the question of what legal knowledge means for the so-called '*ex ante* function of law', where law, rather than responding to bad behaviour from the past (*ex post*), tries to alter future conduct (Darley, Carlsmith and Robinson 2001). It seems at first blush that the relationship between legal knowledge and compliance is crucial and quite simple. The less people know the law, the less likely they will follow such a law. And therefore it is vital to know whether people actually know the law.

This research was made possible through a generous grant from the European Research Council (ERC-2018-CoG - HomoJuridicus - 817680).

This chapter reviews the body of empirical work about whether people actually know and understand the law. In doing so, it will show that studies mostly find that neither laypersons nor specialists have sound legal knowledge, and also that knowledge of the law is weaker in some areas than in others. The chapter will also show what factors shape people's legal knowledge, and here it will highlight how important people's norms are in shaping what they think the law is. The chapter will conclude by drawing out the implications of these findings for compliance. Here it argues that the link between legal knowledge and compliance may not be as linear and simple as it may seem, as a lower level of legal knowledge does not automatically mean that there will be lower compliance.

32.2 THE EXISTING BODY OF EMPIRICAL WORK ON LEGAL KNOWLEDGE

Doing a search about legal knowledge does not easily yield empirical studies about whether people know the law. A first search using the term 'legal knowledge' will produce a range of influential literature that focuses on other questions. As such, there is socio-legal work using the term 'legal knowledge' that discusses legal consciousness and that focuses on how people see their relation to the legal system rather than on whether they know the law itself (i.e. Sarat and Felstiner 1989; Gallagher 2006). There is legal anthropological work, most importantly by Annelise Riles, on how legal knowledge relates to the hegemony of legal instrumentalism, especially in the context of human rights (Riles 2006). Similarly, there has been work from legal scholars in the critical legal studies and feminist legal studies traditions that focuses on how the complexity of the law and legal language makes legal knowledge a form of power that can exclude the weak and poor from the legal system (i.e. Kennedy 1982; Matsuda 1988). A third strand of work using the term 'legal knowledge' is technical in nature and focuses on how firms can develop systems to manage legal knowledge (e.g. Bench-Capon and Coenen 1992; Edwards and Mahling 1997; Bench-Capon 2015). Finally, there are some legal studies that have looked at the implications of empirical work on whether people know the law for protection of their rights, for instance in the sphere of employment law, without, however, providing new empirical data (i.e. Estlund 2002; Rudy 2002).

While these studies give important insights into what legal knowledge means for access to the legal system, power and inequality in relation to the law, the relationship between the law, society and the market, and how to design technical systems to manage complex legal knowledge, they do not provide us with empirical knowledge about whether people actually know the law.

Fortunately, there is a body of work that empirically assesses whether people know the law. This chapter focuses on English-language work and most of that work again studies legal knowledge in the United States and some in the United Kingdom. The oldest work reviewed here is from the late 1960s (Cortese 1966) and early 1970s (Williams and Hall 1972; Sarat 1975; Saunders 1975) and each decade has seen about five new papers since. So far, this body of work has remained quite fragmented and has largely not sought to draw out its implications for compliance (here an exception is Darley, Carlsmith and Robinson 2001). Within the body of work assessed here there are three review studies, an older one by Sarat reviewing five studies from the late 1960s and early 1970s (Sarat 1976/7), and two recent ones both on legal knowledge of education law, one reviewing twenty-eight empirical studies (Littleton 2008) and the other reviewing seventy-seven studies (Eberwein III 2008).

Most studies analyse legal knowledge in light of a particular legal domain and a particular issue (family law and divorce rights, labour law and worker rights, health law, criminal law and education law). There are some broader studies that assess legal knowledge across domains (Williams and Hall 1972; Sarat 1975; Albrecht and Green 1977; Denvir, Balmer and Buck 2012; Denvir, Balmer and Pleasence 2013). Also, we see that some studies have focused on the legal knowledge of particular experts (doctors, teachers, school principals) and laypersons. Moreover, we see that some studies focus on whether people know their rights (labour and family law) and others on whether they understand their duties and what is legally allowed (criminal law and education law).

While the review here does not pretend to be exhaustive, even for English-language studies on the USA, it does offer a variety of arenas and subjects where legal knowledge has been researched to allow insights to be gained into the extent of the legal knowledge that people have. Some of these studies also allow us to probe further and understand what explains the variation in legal knowledge amongst the populations and subjects studied.

Before we turn to the existing body of empirical work on whether people know the law, we shall briefly discuss issues related to the methods of such work and how they have sought to assess legal knowledge.

32.3 METHODS TO MEASURE LEGAL KNOWLEDGE

A scientific assessment of whether people know the law is no easy task. As Sarat in his classic article on the study of legal culture states, '[m]easurement of knowledge of the law is always problematic' (Sarat 1976/7: 450). There have been three broad approaches to assessing legal knowledge with varying degrees of limitations.

32.3.1 *General Self-Reports on the Level of Knowledge*

The first method seeks to ask subjects to self-report what they themselves think is the level of their knowledge. An example is Winter and May's study about how legal knowledge affects compliance motivations amongst Danish farmers (Winter and May 2001). Their measurement of legal knowledge, which they called 'knowledge of rules', consisted of respondents to a survey indicating their agreement with the following statement: 'I believe I am well informed about environmental rules that apply to farming.' The core problem with this approach is that it does not actually measure legal knowledge. It does not test whether people have legal knowledge. Instead it measures whether they think they have such knowledge. In other words, it measures the level of confidence they have in their legal knowledge. People may have a high level of confidence even though they have limited legal knowledge, and vice versa; some may know more about the law than others but still feel that they do not know much. Because of this fundamental problem with this method, this chapter does not discuss findings using such self-reported levels of knowledge. As well as Winter and May's study, the works by Denvir and colleagues (Denvir, Balmer and Buck 2012; Denvir, Balmer and Pleasence 2013) have also used this approach as one of their two methods for assessing legal knowledge.

32.3.2 *Open Questions about Legal Knowledge*

The second method uses open questions to ask people to report what sort of rights they have. As Denvir and colleagues, whose two papers reviewed here are the only studies that use this method, explain, 'in this study we explore how individuals with one or more civil or social justice problems respond when asked to briefly describe their rights/legal position in the context of a quantitative survey' (Denvir, Balmer and Buck 2012: 143). The advantage here is that the survey does not indicate that it is after legal knowledge and thus it is less likely to sway people's knowledge. In addition, it allows subjects to report what they think and, in that way, it gathers unexpected information that comes fully from the perspective of the subject studied. However, this approach has major downsides. It is very difficult to draw conclusions about the extent to which people do or do not know the law. Denvir and colleagues have an elaborate method of analysing the raw data they derive from their open questions. They code answers in seven categories that capture what sort of discourse people use to state their rights, including, for instance, a factual situation (stating what the problem was they faced), a value judgement (stating whether they were right or wrong about their rights), a broad notion of rights (referring to human rights, for instance), indicating a lack of knowledge, and finally framing it correctly or incorrectly in terms of legal rights. An assessment of legal knowledge should of course be about the last two categories, namely whether people are right or wrong in how they see their legal rights. The problem with the open-question approach is that when people frame their rights simply as something factual or something very broad related to human rights or as a value judgement, it is impossible to say whether they do or do not know the law. People who frame their answer in a factual or value judgement way might still have sound legal knowledge but just not frame their answer this way. And people who correctly make statements about human rights might still be wrong about the exact rights in consumer law, or they may still be correct about those. Because the open-question approach, then, does not provide a clear measure of legal knowledge, the present chapter will not review work that has used this approach.

32.3.3 *Factual Questions about the Law (with or without Vignettes)*

This leaves the third method. The third method asks factual questions about the law. There have been several approaches.

An early approach, as used, for instance, by Williams and Hall, would present subjects with law-like statements and ask them to indicate whether these were part of the relevant law being studied (Texas law in this case) (Williams and Hall 1972).

Another approach is to ask respondents to indicate whether particular hypothetical behaviours are lawful or not. Here a good example is Kim's work on people's knowledge about applicable employment-at-will rules (Kim 1999). She would present a scenario such as 'Company discharges employee in order to hire another person to do the same job at a lower wage. Employee's job performance has been satisfactory.' Subjects are then asked to indicate whether the discharge is lawful or unlawful. And the survey instructs the respondents to '[a] nswer each question according to whether you believe *a court of law* would find the discharge to be lawful or unlawful, NOT what you would like the result to be' (Kim 1999: 508).

Other studies similarly ask factual questions about how the law applies to particular scenarios, using vignettes. Some of them use more elaborate, longer vignettes. One example is Darley and colleagues' study of lay knowledge of state criminal law in different American states, which uses elaborate little stories of five to seven sentences complete with fictional characters engaging in what in some states would be and in other states would not be criminal behaviour (Darley, Carlsmith and Robinson 2001). Even more elaborate is Pleasence and Balmer's work on people's knowledge of family law. Their study provides a complex multi-step scenario that involves a couple's sequences of events: for instance, the couple (John and Sarah) break up before they have children, or, instead of breaking up, John dies without leaving a will. Respondents would then be asked specific questions in relation to the legal rights at play here, such as, for instance, whether in the case of the break-up Sarah would have a claim to financial support from John or in the case of John's death whether Sarah automatically stood to inherit his belongings or savings (Pleasence and Balmer 2012: 309).

Although asking these factual questions about what is in the law, or better how the law applies to particular circumstances, offers a better way to understand the amount of legal knowledge people have, there are still a number of issues. These issues are not as problematic as with the general self-reports or open questions since the studies do not really report on legal knowledge, but they have to be considered when reading the remainder of this chapter. A first issue is that asking people to indicate what is in the law or what is legal or illegal or what are people's rights or not may not just measure their knowledge but also shape their knowledge. Here a particular problem may be that people do not like to indicate that they do not know and, especially in survey formats that have a true/false or lawful/unlawful binary option, as frequently used here, it may lead to guessing rather than expressing knowledge (cf. Denvir, Balmer and Buck 2012).

A second issue is that asking factual questions automatically means limiting the questions to a few particular aspects, or articles, of the law. It is impossible to have legal knowledge of all the rules even within a particular area of law. Relatedly, as a third issue, this also means that the focus of the questions shapes the outcome of the study. As no one can be expected to know all the intricacies of any particular law, a study can be designed in such a way that most people would fail. A proper design should take account of this. Van McCrary et al.'s (1992) study of legal knowledge amongst physicians is explicit about how it sought to address this issue: 'We did not design the questions to be tricky or particularly difficult; nonetheless, accurate responses would require knowledge of specific provisions of Texas law pertinent to clinical practice' (Van McCrary et al. 1992: 365). Of course, a problem remains in how scholars can assess what 'tricky' or 'particularly difficult' entails. And also, the level of difficulty of the questions still influences the outcome of the study. So, a study using simpler questions is more likely to find higher levels of legal knowledge than a study that uses more difficult questions.

A third problem is how to verify whether the subject's legal information is correct or not. While some aspects of the law may seem simple and straightforward, much of the law is open to interpretation and often through a complex array of court case rulings, some of which may be conflicting. And here the specific context and facts of the case are important. As Sarat has argued, 'the content of legal rules is not determinable in the abstract but only in specific situations; thus knowledge of the law can never be precise since legal rights are always at the mercy of events' (Sarat 1976/7: 451).

A fourth problem here may be that laypersons, in contrast to lawyers, have a very different understanding of the meaning of basic legal terms that also exist in ordinary language. Here a series of studies on how juries apply criminal law terms for culpable mental states as outlined in the US Model Penal Code, including purpose, knowledge, recklessness and negligence, shows how lay interpretations of these terms do not necessarily align with proper legal interpretations (Shen et al. 2011; Ginther et al. 2014; Ginther et al. 2018). So, when non-lawyers report on questions about the law, their answers may have a different meaning from those of lawyers. This may mean that even when laypersons give an answer that is in line with the language of the law, it may have a different meaning for them from that of the law.

A fifth set of problems is general survey problems of subjects wishing to respond in a socially desirable way. This may shape what they report on surveys in ways that are hard to predict and be accounted for by researchers (cf. Denvir, Balmer and Buck 2012).

32.4 EMPIRICAL FINDINGS ABOUT LEGAL KNOWLEDGE

With all these limitations considered, this section will outline the key findings from empirical studies about legal knowledge. It will, as explained earlier, use only empirical studies that have used factual questions about the law, both those that do not and those that do use vignettes.

32.4.1 *Lay Knowledge of Employment Law*

Within the sample of studies this chapter reviews, only one author, Pauline Kim, has studied whether people know employment law using factual questions (Kim 1998, 1999). Work by Denvir and colleagues also has some information about how people view their labour rights, but it is not discussed here as it does not use factual questions.

Kim's study sought to understand whether American employees were aware of their legal protection under employment-at-will contracts. Her research first studies this in Missouri (n = 337) and later in California (n = 281) and New York (n = 303). The study presented respondents with eight statements each describing a particular reason for discharge and asking respondents to indicate for each whether the discharge was lawful or unlawful according to how a court would see it. Of these eight statements, six were diagnostic questions (which were used to assess the level of knowledge) and two questions were deemed too easy to be used to assess knowledge. The study found that Missouri respondents were able to answer 51 per cent of all eight questions correctly, and 40 per cent were able to answer the six diagnostic questions correctly. The study also found that respondents especially answered questions wrong by overestimating the amount of protection that workers have, so in cases where a particular discharge was lawful (for instance when the employer intended to hire someone else for the same job at a lower wage), many respondents were prone to indicate that it was not allowed legally. Error rates for these lawful discharges ranged between 79.2 per cent and 89.0 per cent (Kim 1999: 456). Moreover, Missouri respondents widely shared erroneous beliefs about the law: '[F]ewer than 10% were able to answer more than six diagnostic questions correctly' (Kim 1999: 456). Kim used another part of the survey to assess knowledge of particular circumstances under which a company discharges an employee in order to hire a lower-wage replacement. Here it has four statements all indicating either text in the company manual or correspondence from the company to the employee, including, for instance, that the company personnel manual states that the '[c]ompany will resort to dismissal for just and sufficient cause only'. Again, respondents were asked to indicate for each of the circumstances whether it was lawful for the company to discharge the employee in order to hire a cheaper replacement. Here again, the study finds that Missouri employees were mostly mistaken and overestimated their protection. Error rates here ranged from 62.6 per cent to 84.9 per cent (Kim 1999: 459).

Kim subsequently conducted the same survey in New York and California. In California she found that, similarly to Missouri, respondents were able to answer 40 per cent of the diagnostic questions correctly, whereas in New York the number was even lower, at 25.2 per cent. The study further found that in all three states the error rate was widespread and existed amongst a broad range of respondents in the samples.

As such, Kim concludes that 'the data from California and New York confirm findings from Missouri that workers are seriously mistaken about their protections under the law and that erroneous beliefs are widely shared' (Kim 1999: 459–60).

Kim also sought to understand what can explain the variation in the lack of legal knowledge. To do so, she first assessed whether differences in the details of the legal limits and exceptions to the at-will employment rule shaped error rates in respondents' responses. Here she found no clear evidence for such an effect. Furthermore, she did not find that the general sense of legal protection and political climate that may offer such protection as it differs in these three states was clearly related to error in reporting about legal protection. Nor did she find that legal knowledge varied for respondents with different ages, union affiliation or experiences in being fired. The only exception was that in Missouri, surprisingly, an employee that was fired would become *more* – not less (as would be expected) – likely to mistakenly overstate their legal protection against discharge. The only three person-related variables that did predict higher knowledge were education, income and race, with higher scores amongst more educated richer respondents and lower scores amongst black and Hispanic respondents.

Kim also provides information about how respondents develop their ideas about what is lawful and unlawful and thus how they come to be mistaken about employment law and overestimate their legal protection against discharges. Analysing her data in light of findings about norms, Kim argues that people may come to confuse the law and their own personal norms (what they hold that their rights should be).

A recent study of Welsh and English laypersons in relation to their employment rights found similar findings. Using data from the 2010–12 English and Welsh Civil and Social Justice Survey, the paper sought to analyse the extent to which citizens have sufficient knowledge of the law in these areas. The survey contained detailed scenarios presenting employment rights cases (as well as housing and consumer scenarios, to be discussed in Section 32.4.4). And for each scenario respondents were asked to answer a series of questions for particular elements of the scenario that involved either their rights or their duties. The study sample included 966 respondents who answered the scenario questions. The study found that 66 per cent of respondents answered four of the six questions correctly, 37 per cent answered five questions correctly and only 13 per cent got all six questions correct. The study also assessed whether people who worked as an employee and those that had also reported employment problems had greater knowledge. Here they found that being an employee did lead to higher knowledge, but having experience reporting employment problems did not (Pleasence, Balmer and Denvir 2017).

32.4.2 *Lay Knowledge of Criminal Law*

Several scholars have sought to understand how ordinary citizens know key aspects of both procedural and substantive criminal law.

The earliest study is by Sarat who, in 1975, sought to empirically assess popular support for the legal system. He conducted a study amongst citizens in Wisconsin ($n = 220$) in 1973. As part of the questionnaire, he included questions about legal knowledge. He asked respondents to indicate whether particular statements related to rules in the law were true or false or to indicate that they did not know. Of the ten statements, six concerned general aspects of criminal law. Statements included, for instance: 'If an innocent man is arrested, it is up to him to prove that he is not guilty' and 'A man who has committed a crime can be made to answer questions about the crime in court.' His findings show that there is variation in the legal knowledge of citizens. Even though, for all statements, more respondents answered correctly than not, rates of knowledge varied. As such, an overwhelming majority (96.4 per cent) of Wisconsin citizens in 1973 knew that the police had to inform them of their rights before questioning them. But only 47.7 per cent correctly knew that suspects cannot be forced to answer questions in court. And, thus, more than half of the respondents did not know one of the core principles of criminal procedure in the United States, the protection against self-incrimination (Sarat 1975).

In 1977, Albrecht and Green also studied people's legal knowledge of criminal law. They studied citizens from rural, semi-rural and urban (both poor and minority and non-poor and non-minority) populations in a Rocky Mountain state (n = 398). To test legal knowledge, respondents were asked to indicate whether statements indicating legal duties or rights were false or correct or that they did not know. Five of the ten statements concerned criminal law, such as: 'In a trial, the presumption of innocence means that an accused person must prove charges are false.' Similarly to Sarat's study, Albrecht and Green (1977) also found variation in legal knowledge about criminal law. Two of the five statements had a very high number of correct responses. These concerned people's right to an attorney in criminal trials (86 per cent correct) and the police's duty to inform suspects of their constitutional rights when they perform an arrest (93 per cent correct). On other key issues of criminal procedural law, citizens were, however, frequently mistaken. These included the right against self-incrimination (48 per cent correct), the presumption of innocence (40 per cent correct) and the protection against double jeopardy in criminal cases (55 per cent correct) (Albrecht and Green 1977).

Another study about laypersons' knowledge of criminal law concerns the knowledge of jurors and potential jurors. Reifman, Gusick and Ellsworth (1992) studied citizens in Michigan (n = 224) who had been called for jury duty. They compared answers to their questions between those citizens that ended up serving as jurors and those who were not selected. They asked the citizens twenty-nine questions about relevant Michigan criminal law for various crimes; ten questions concerned procedural duties for juries and nineteen questions concerned substantive criminal law. The statements were taken from the Michigan Criminal Jury Instructions and had, where necessary, been reformatted to reduce excessive legalistic text. Similarly to the earlier criminal legal knowledge studies, respondents were asked to indicate whether statements were true or false or that they did not know. Sample statements include: 'In reaching a decision, the jury may consider the consequences of their verdict' and 'A person who gives a bottle containing illegal drugs to another person without knowing what is in the bottle is not guilty of delivering a controlled substance' (Reifman, Gusick and Ellsworth 1992: 545). Their study found that for the ten questions about the duties and procedural rules for juries, on average respondents who had served on criminal juries (and who had received instructions) got 4.78 (or 48 per cent) correct, those that had sat on civil juries 4.18 (42 per cent) correct, and those who had not been selected as jurors and sat in trials got 3.81 (or 38 per cent) correct. So, the study concluded that receiving instructions and serving on a jury did improve legal knowledge significantly – however, and this is most important, not to a level of being able to answer even half of the questions correctly, or of being aware of one's own lack of knowledge, with only 10 per cent of the criminal jurors and 11 per cent of the civil jurors opting for the 'I don't know' option. The study found similar results for substantive law, where those that had served on criminal juries and had been instructed on relevant aspects of substantive criminal law (such as theft, sexual crimes, assault and armed robbery) were not knowledgeable about such crimes, answering on average only 41 per cent correctly, which was only marginally higher than those without instructions, who got 35 per cent correct, a difference that was found not to be statistically significant (Reifman, Gusick and Ellsworth 1992: 547–9).

Two further studies have sought to understand more deeply whether people understand their state's substantive criminal law. The first focused on whether people understand the different levels of criminal liability for different stages of attempts at crime. Darley, Sanderson and LaMantia (1996) presented a sample of local community members ($n = 20$) and undergraduate students ($n = 28$) in New Jersey with a survey that presented them with criminal attempt scenarios. These scenarios all described instances where someone had attempted either a murder or a robbery (six scenarios for each level of attempt from *thought only* through *substantial step* to *dangerous proximity* to finally *completed offence*). Respondents would have to indicate first what they thought would be an appropriate sentence and after that what sentence they thought the criminal codes of New Jersey would assign in each case. The study first of all found that respondents did not distinguish between what they themselves thought was the appropriate liability and what they held that the law would assign. And second, the study found that in so reporting what the law would assign, the respondents were largely mistaken. As the authors conclude, '[i]t is obvious that our subjects deeply misunderstand the New Jersey state codes' Darley, Sanderson and LaMantia 1996: 416). Similarly to what Kim argued about employment law knowledge, Darley and colleagues also found that there is a link between what people think is in the law and what they themselves hold to be right (their norms): 'Most citizens hold the (erroneous) belief that the legal code matches their moral intuitions about the liability levels that should be assigned to various attempts' (Darley, Sanderson and LaMantia 1996: 419). Their conclusion based on this is that the legal code should be reformed to more closely match such moral beliefs, rather than trying to educate people in the law and change such morals.

The fifth study about criminal legal knowledge, by Darley, Carlsmith and Robinson (2001), again studied whether people are aware of the criminal laws of their states. It studied this amongst participants from four states (Texas, Wisconsin, South Dakota, North Dakota) ($n = 203$). Participants were presented with elaborate scenarios of four potentially illegal behaviours, including violating a duty to assist a person in trouble, violating a duty to retreat prior to the use of force in self-defence, failing to report a known felon, and using deadly force in order to protect one's property. Respondents were asked to indicate for each scenario what they thought the appropriate punishment was, and then to indicate what their state would consider an appropriate punishment, both on a 13-point scale. The study found that although state law was markedly different for these four scenarios, for three of the four scenarios they did not find that citizens from the state that was the outlier (and that would criminalise behaviour that others would not) came to a different prediction about state punishment. The exception was that Texans do clearly know that their state allows the use of deadly force to protect property. The authors conclude from this that 'in three cases, state law does not appear to be a factor in how people come to "know" their state law', and that people do not seem to be aware of the laws of their state'(Darley, Carlsmith and Robinson 2001: 175). Moreover, their study finds that for the most part people do not clearly develop better knowledge of their state's criminal law if they are better educated or if they have lived longer in that state. Darley, Carlsmith and Robinson (2001) also found that there was a high correlation between what sentence people would assign themselves and what they predicted the state would assign. And thus, similarly to Kim's (1999) argument and Darley, Sanderson and LaMantia's (1996) earlier findings, people tend to conflate what they hold personally with what they think is the law: '[T]hey guess[ed] that the law of the state was what their personal opinion thought it should be' (Darley, Carlsmith and Robinson 2001: 181).

The final study reviewed here about criminal legal knowledge concerns whether mothers of youth offenders know the law (Cavanagh and Cauffman 2017). This study analysed 324 dyads of mothers and their sons, all first-time juvenile offenders (n = 648). The study built on earlier work that had found that youths do not have proper knowledge of criminal law and procedural rights (this work is not included in our review here, which focuses on adult legal knowledge, but see, for instance, Grisso et al. 2003; Goodwin-De Faria and Marinos 2012). It assessed the mothers' legal knowledge about criminal law by asking them to indicate the correctness of thirty-eight statements that relate to legal rights, roles and procedures in the juvenile criminal procedure, and to answer six multiple-choice questions in response to a short scenario. The study found that mothers on average got 66 per cent of the questions correct. Mothers were most mistaken about issues related to probation and plea bargaining, and least mistaken about basic courtroom procedures. The study found an association in that mothers with prior arrest experience had better knowledge than those without prior arrest experience. It also found that Latina women knew less than any other racial group, that black knew less than white, and that women born in the United States knew more than women born abroad.

32.4.3 *Lay Knowledge of Family Law*

The third and final body of work that assesses laypeople's knowledge of the law focuses on family law. As most people have familial relations and thus potentially face disputes or rights issues there, knowing their rights in such relations is vital. A first study about whether people know family law was conducted in 1973 amongst adult residents in two communities in Oregon State (n = 309). Respondents were asked to answer factual questions in relation to applicable family law issues such as the age of majority, the rights of welfare families to decide about birth control, the rights of illegitimate children, and minors' rights to birth control information and to medical treatment. The study overall found that knowledge of family law was underdeveloped. Respondents on average were able to answer just over half of the questions (4.3 out of 8). The study found that there was a big difference in their knowledge where for some issues (such as the age of majority and the rights of illegitimate children) people were far more knowledgeable (with 66 per cent answering correctly) and for others (such as minors' rights to information about birth control and to medical treatment) they provided mostly (also about 66 per cent of the sample) wrong answers (Saunders 1975: 71). The study also found that women were more knowledgeable than men, while no other demographic variables (age, occupation, education, religion) were associated statistically with the level of legal knowledge.

A more elaborate study of the legal knowledge of family law was conducted in the UK. In the article 'Ignorance in Bliss', Pleasence and Balmer set out to understand how well British adults know their own family law. The study uses data from a large nationally representative survey (n = 3,806). The survey used an elaborate scenario presenting four hypothetical major family-related events in the lives of a couple, John and Sarah. Respondents were asked for each event to indicate (yes, no, don't know) their answers to a series of questions about what legal rights or legal options Sarah had. The study also employed two experimental elements: first, it randomly assigned respondents scenarios where John and Sarah were married and where they were legally cohabiting; and second, it randomised the duration of such a marriage or cohabitation.

The study concluded that there is a large amount of error in how respondents see the legal rights and options in these instances of family law. One example is that 52 per cent of the respondents were wrong in believing that a financially dependent cohabitant has a good legal claim to financial support when separating after ten years; 48 per cent were wrong to believe that a married spouse will not automatically inherit their partner's property when there is no will; 47 per cent of the respondents were wrong that a cohabiting father who fails to meet the legal requirements for 'parental responsibility' has the right to decide on 'important medical treatment'; and 36 per cent were wrong to believe that a married father does not have such a right. As we have seen with criminal legal knowledge, there was variation, and there were issues where respondents' answers were more often correct: for instance, only 14 per cent were wrong in holding that a partner automatically inherits from a deceased cohabitant when there is no will, and 20 per cent were wrong in holding that a married father has no legal responsibility to provide financial support for a child after a break-up.

Just as we have seen in studies about employment law and criminal law, here again the study finds that there is a relation between what people think is the law and what their own beliefs and social attitudes are about the matters that family covers. As the authors conclude, 'in general, public legal understanding may be substantially driven by attitudes. Consequently, our findings also highlight additional obstacles that public legal education initiatives must overcome in order to be successful ... People's immersion in the social world and exposure to social attitudes therefore act as obstacles to being receptive to contradictory information about the law' (Pleasence and Balmer 2012: 325).

32.4.4 *Lay Knowledge of Housing and Consumer Rights*

A recent study by Pleasence, Balmer and Denvir (2017) sought to understand how English and Welsh citizens know basic rights and duties in relation to consumer and housing rights. Using data from the 2010–12 English and Welsh Civil and Social Justice Survey, the paper sought to analyse the extent to which citizens have sufficient knowledge of the law in these areas. The surveys contained detailed scenarios presenting housing and consumer rights cases (as well as employment scenarios, the findings of which we have already discussed). And for each scenario, respondents were asked to answer a series of questions on particular elements of the scenario that involved either their rights or their duties. The sample included 1,005 respondents who answered the questions about the housing scenario and 982 who focused on the consumer scenario. Overall, the study found that respondents did only slightly better than if they had guessed the right answer (as the study used a binary yes or no option), with an average percentage of correct scores of 59 per cent across the three scenarios studied. The study found that informants performed worst in consumer-related questions. For consumer law, only 20 per cent got three of the five questions correct, [illegible] per cent got four out of five correct and only 0.3 per cent got all correct. Housing law had higher scores, with 77 per cent getting four out of six correct, 49 per cent getting five out of six correct and 13 per cent answering all six correctly. What is interesting here is that respondents had indicated greater confidence in their consumer law knowledge than in their housing law knowledge. The study further analysed whether people who needed more knowledge of their rights had better knowledge. Here it looked in particular at different housing law knowledge levels between people who were renting their house and those that were not. The study found no significant knowledge difference here. So, people who needed to know more about their rights, that is, renters, were not more knowledgeable. The study concluded that citizens were not well informed; in fact, they had 'substantial deficits' in understanding their legal rights and responsibilities. The authors noted that such deficits exist even when such rights have a 'special bearing' for them (Pleasence, Balmer and Denvir 2017).

32.4.5 *Expert Legal Knowledge in the Educational Field*

Quite surprisingly, there has been a very large body of empirical work on knowledge about law related to primary and secondary education, mostly focusing on whether educators or educational managers, such as principals, know the law. The body of work is so large that we will not assess it study by study as we have done so far, but instead discuss its core findings across a range of studies. Fortunately, there are two review studies from 2008 that provide an overview of the state of the field up to that year. The first study by Littleton reviews twenty-eight previous studies (Littleton 2008), and the second by Eberwein reviews seventy-seven studies (Eberwein III 2008). Here we shall use these two reviews to get an overall picture of this large body of work that goes back to 1978. The studies reviewed were largely of a quantitative nature and used either factual questions about the law with yes/no/don't know options or vignettes, similarly to what we have seen in the studies discussed so far. Studies looked at the legal knowledge of different actors in the educational system, including administrators (principals and superintendents), teachers, staff, and also students and parents. And most studies reviewed were conducted within one state.

The studies reviewed show a clear legal knowledge deficit amongst educators and administrators. As Eberwein concludes, '[t]he [seventy-seven] studies reviewed indicate that educators do not have an acceptable level of public school law knowledge. While each researcher polled educators using a different set of survey questions and, even more problematically, established a level of competence that varied, most agreed that legal knowledge in all groups (teachers, principals and superintendents) was unacceptably low' (Eberwein III 2008: 49–50). All but one (Shaw 1984) of the reviewed studies of the legal literacy of principals concluded that principals lacked sufficient legal knowledge. The reviews similarly found that the legal knowledge of superintendents and general administrators was weak, with average correct scores on knowledge questions in one study of about 50 per cent (Abegglen 1986), while another study (Clark 1990) reported superintendents as being 'only marginally knowledgeable' (Eberwein III 2008: 51), and another study focusing on the knowledge of legal rules about teacher evaluations found that knowledge was no better than chance (Zirkel 1996). Similarly, studies concluded that teachers 'were unfamiliar with school law' (Eberwein III 2008: 52), and as Littleton found from surveys of the body of work on teachers' knowledge of law, 'teachers possess a dismal comprehension of education law and legal issues pertaining to their jobs' (Littleton 2008: 72). One large study of 1,300 teachers found, for instance, that on average they got 41 per cent of 12 questions about students' rights correct and 39 per cent of questions about teachers' rights and liabilities (Schimmel and Militello 2007). Studies reviewed characterised teachers' legal knowledge as insufficient to 'maintain a safe school environment and/or protect themselves from tort liability' (quote from Eberwein III 2008: 53, summarizing Moore 1997) and that teachers 'lacked basic knowledge on laws that affect children' (Eberwein III 2008: 545, summarizing Sametz, McLoughlin and Streib 1981).

The reviews of the large body of work on the legal knowledge amongst school educators and administrators also show what variation there is. Even though the general conclusion is that knowledge is weak, it is not equally so. There are clearly areas of the law where legal knowledge is relatively worse than in others. Weak areas of knowledge include the Bill of Rights, religious legal issues in education, most aspects of tort law (except liability for abuse) and Supreme Court decisions (relevant for education, such as due process rights for students, e.g. *Goss* v. *Lopez*). Teachers have a weak grasp of the legal rights of students and disciplinary procedures (and issues such as searches and seizures), while principals have a better understanding of such rights and procedures (Eberwein III 2008; Littleton 2008).

The studies reviewed have also tried to see whether variables related to the demographics of the respondent (educator or administrator) or the school were associated with the level of legal knowledge. Most studies reviewed did not find a significant correlation here. There are, for instance, mixed findings about whether principals, superintendents, teachers and staff have a better grasp of the relevant law, with comparative studies across these groups reporting different results. Similarly, the experience of educators and administrators was not found clearly across the reviewed studies to be associated with more or less legal knowledge. There seems to be some indication that secondary-level educators and administrators have a better level of legal knowledge than those at the elementary level, and also that older teachers have better legal knowledge (Eberwein III 2008; Littleton 2008).

32.4.6 *Expert Legal Knowledge in the Medical Profession*

There is also a body of studies about the legal knowledge of professionals in health-care services. The present contribution reviews eight such studies. There are two earlier studies from the 1980s about the legal knowledge of psychotherapists. One study by Shuman and Weiner assessed how well Texas therapists ($n = 84$) understood state rules on psychotherapist–patient privilege. It found that legal knowledge was lacking, as 55 per cent of the respondents did not know that there was a statute on such privilege, and, more importantly, only 22 per cent knew that legal confidentiality limits patients' disclosures (Shuman and Weiner 1981: 922). Their study concludes: 'The responses to the questionnaire from the group of psychiatrists surveyed indicated that the enactment of the psychotherapist–patient privilege statute in 1979 had little impact on the practice of psychotherapy. Undoubtedly, a major contributing factor was the therapists' ignorance of the enactment of the privilege statute' (Shuman and Weiner 1981: 922). A study by Givelber, Bowers and Blitch (1984) analysed how well therapists across the USA ($n = 2{,}875$) understood the duty of care toward third parties that a California Supreme Court decided (the Tarasoff decision).[1] The study found that while most psychotherapists had heard of the Tarasoff case, many did not have a proper understanding of the contents of its ruling. One in four had a partly mistaken understanding of when the Tarasoff duty of care applies. More importantly, the majority misunderstood what the duty of care entails exactly. It is also interesting to note that the majority of non-Californian therapists surveyed erroneously believed that they were bound by Tarasoff. The

[1] *Tarasoff* v. *Regents of the University of California*, 17 Cal. 3d 425, 551 P.2d 334, 131 Cal. Rptr. 14 (Cal. 1976).

study argues that the limited understanding of the legal rules on the duty of care as they arise out of the vital court case originates in the complexity of the legal reasoning that the California Supreme Court used here (Givelber, Bowers and Blitch 1984).

Van McCrary and colleagues conducted two studies to understand how legal knowledge plays a role in how physicians make end-of-life decisions with regard to terminally ill patients (Van McCrary et al. 1992; Van McCrary and Swanson 1999). The first study was conducted amongst hospital doctors in Texas (n = 750). The study administered a survey that included ten questions that tested knowledge on issues covered in a standard handbook in Texas medical law (*The Texas Medical Jurisprudence Examination*). The study found that on average respondents answered half of the questions correctly. And only about 23 per cent of doctors surveyed 'achieved a "passing" score of 70% or above' (Van McCrary et al. 1992: 368). And just like in other areas of law discussed earlier here, there was variation with some issues where doctors had a higher level of knowledge (for instance about how competent patients may legally refuse any treatment even if it results in their own death). The study found that internists had better legal knowledge than surgeons. And second, physicians who derived their legal knowledge mostly from colleagues scored lower in the test. In a second study, Van McCrary teamed up with Swanson to conduct a comparative study about legal knowledge and end-of-life decisions amongst patients in Texas (discussed in the study above) and Denmark (n = 62). The study found that Danish doctors had a much higher level of legal knowledge, as 74 per cent of the doctors answered 70 per cent of the questions correctly and passed the test, in contrast to the low 23 per cent in the USA. What is interesting about this comparison is that US doctors are less informed about the law, yet (as was also measured in these studies) they are more worried about the law's impact on their medical practice. Van McCrary and Swanson argue that 'legal defensiveness in the USA creates a climate of misinformation regarding medical law that is not present in Denmark' (Van McCrary and Swanson 1999: 20).

Saltstone, Saltstone and Rowe (1997) sought to assess the medical legal knowledge amongst Canadian family medicine residents (n = 45). Their findings were similar to those in the study amongst Texan doctors. They found that the residents answered about half the questions correctly. Also, there was variation, with all respondents answering some questions correctly (for instance whether comments might be construed as sexual abuse) and others with very low scores (for instance, only 11 per cent correctly answered a question about doctor–patient privilege, and 4 per cent answered correctly in relation to duties to report certain diseases). Respondents also indicated that knowledge of medical-legal issues was vital for providing good medical care and to avoid being sued, and they felt 'inadequately trained in and uncomfortable about dealing with these issues' (Saltstone, Saltstone and Rowe 1997: 669).

In 2008, Chate assessed the legal knowledge in relation to informed consent amongst orthodontists in England, Wales and Northern Ireland (n = 179). This study found that respondents provided correct answers about half the time (it found that scores varied for different issues). Orthodontists were least knowledgeable about aspects of consent such as what level of explanation they needed to give patients to get informed consent, and how to manage a patient who is unable to give consent. The study concluded that 'the results of this audit indicate certain key areas of deficiency in the knowledge and understanding of informed consent amongst consultant orthodontists' (Chate 2008: 665).

Finally, a recent study by White and colleagues (2014) looked at the legal knowledge amongst doctors practising end-of-life medicine in Australia (n = 867). On average, it found that the mean correct response rate was 3.26 out of a possible 7 questions. It found that only 42 per cent of the overall respondents were able to get four or more of the seven questions correct. The study found that there were differences within the sample, with doctors in some states (e.g. Queensland) scoring much lower (25.7 per cent) than those in others (e.g. New South Wales, with 55 per cent answering four or more correctly). It also found that certain specialisms scored significantly higher than others, while other demographics such as age, country of degree and years of practice were not associated with the level of legal knowledge. The study also found that doctors were aware of their level of legal knowledge as their self-reported perception of their knowledge correlated significantly with how they scored in the knowledge test. Other interesting findings are that the more decisions doctors made about withholding life-sustaining treatment, the more knowledgeable they became, and that those with recent training had better knowledge. Overall, the study concluded that there is a knowledge deficit amongst the doctors studied: 'Our results demonstrate critical gaps in the legal knowledge of many doctors who practise end-of-life medicine' (White et al. 2014: 3).

In sum, in health care there is a clear lack of knowledge of relevant law. Here again we see that there is variation among some health-care providers and in some contexts, and for some legal rules there are greater amounts of knowledge than for others.

32.4.7 *Synthesis of Findings*

As a quick overview, Table 32.1 outlines the findings across the different domains. Based on this we can draw several conclusions. First and foremost, there are major gaps in the legal knowledge amongst both laypersons and professionals. Such knowledge deficits concern vital legal rules that provide basic rights relating to employment, the criminal justice trial, and marriage and divorce. And the lack of knowledge also covers areas of core concern to the professionals interviewed, such as school principals and end-of-life doctors. Most of the studies note that there is variation and that not all aspects of the law are understood equally well or equally poorly. And studies have also unearthed variables that can explain variation, yet when taken together we do not see a clear pattern emerge where certain demographics or other conditions would consistently predict greater legal knowledge. The findings in comparing physicians' medical legal knowledge in the USA and Denmark are particularly striking. Doctors who worry more about the repercussions of the law (those in the USA) are less knowledgeable about such law than their colleagues who do not have such worries (those in Denmark).

An important finding is that across several studies there is an association between what people think the law should be and what they themselves hold to be right and correct (their norms), and this shapes what they think the law is. And thus their sense of what the law should be influences their misunderstanding of the actual law. As such, there seems to be a link between (social and personal) norms and legal knowledge.

32.5 DISCUSSION AND CONCLUSION

Despite the inherent challenges in measuring legal knowledge, the empirical studies reviewed here all show that across domains and populations there is a lack of legal knowledge. This means that the laws as they have been drafted and designed do not arrive at the people whose behaviour such laws seek to influence, or that, if they arrive, the understanding of such laws is not complete. This is a key, yet underappreciated, empirical insight in regard to

TABLE 32.1 *An overview of empirical studies about legal knowledge*[2]

Domain	Type of actor	Studies reviewed	Core findings
Employment law	Lay	Kim 1998; Kim 1999; Denvir, Balmer and Buck 2012; Denvir, Balmer and Pleasence 2013; Pleasence, Balmer and Denvir 2017	People have limited knowledge about their employment rights. The knowledge they do have originates from their own views and norms of what the rights should be.
Criminal law	Lay	Sarat 1975; Albrecht and Green 1977; Reifman, Gusick and Ellsworth 1992; Darley, Sanderson and LaMantia 1996; Darley, Carlsmith and Robinson 2001; Cavanagh and Cauffman 2017	People have limited knowledge of core aspects of substantive and procedural law. Knowledge does vary and is better and worse for different aspects. Legal knowledge tends to converge with people's own views and norms.
Family law	Lay	Saunders 1975; Pleasence and Balmer 2012	People have limited knowledge of their core rights and duties in family law. There is variation with more knowledge on some issues and less on others. Women have better knowledge than men. People's knowledge of the law is shaped by their own norms.
Consumer and housing rights	Lay	Pleasence, Balmer and Denvir 2017	Overall, there are substantial deficits in how citizens understand their rights and duties. This is especially so for consumer law. The more confident people are of their rights, the lower their knowledge. Also, the more there is at stake, the less knowledge they have.
Education	Lay, professional	Core reviews by Littleton 2008 (reviewing 28 studies) and Eberwein III 2008 (reviewing 77 studies); examples of individual studies: Bowal 1998; Schimmel and Militello 2007; Militello, Schimmel and Eberwein 2009	Educators and administrators have limited knowledge of core aspects of the law that applies to their jobs (including elements of tort law). There is variation in knowledge with some issues with better and other with worse knowledge. No clear findings on demographic variation and legal knowledge.
Health	Professional	Shuman and Weiner 1981; Givelber, Bowers and Blitch 1984; Van McCrary et al. 1992; Saltstone, Saltstone and Rowe 1997; Van McCrary and Swanson 1999; Chate 2008; White et al. 2012; White et al. 2014	Doctors, psychotherapists, and orthodontists lack knowledge about legal rules in relation to their practice. There is variation with better knowledge for some rules, some doctors, and some jurisdictions, and worse for others.

[2] We have excluded empirical studies about the legal knowledge of nonadults here. Examples include Saunders 1981; Grisso et al. 2003; and Goodwin-De Faria and Marinos 2012.

compliance. There is a large body in criminology about how objective punishment (the way the law is enforced) is not the same as subjective punishment (the way that potential rule-breakers perceive it) (Thornton, Gunningham and Kagan 2005; Apel 2013). Similarly, the way the law has been drafted and exists objectively and the way it is known and understood are not the same. Darley, Carlsmith and Robinson (2001) argued that the lack of legal knowledge undermines the *ex ante* function of law. And indeed, it seems that when people do not know the law, such law has trouble shaping their future behaviour. We will ponder three bigger questions here.

The first question is: Why do so many people lack legal knowledge? Here a first issue is the sheer size and complexity of the legal system and its myriad rules. In the early 1990s, it was estimated that in the USA 300,000 rules of corporate law exist that may be criminally enforced (see Coffee, Jr. 1991: 216[3]). This was over three decades ago, and these were just the criminally enforceable rules for corporations. Bear in mind that the California Vehicle Code is over 1,000 pages long. And the US Internal Revenue Code, which covers basic tax policies on things like income, gifts, estates and payrolls, is about 2,600 pages long.[4] And this does not even include the thousands of pages of federal tax regulations.[5] Or just go into any law school library and look at the giant halls with stacks and stacks of tomes with the primary sources of law, which is the applicable law that we're supposed to know.

An overwhelming amount of law is made less accessible because of the complexity of the legal language used in the legislation, and even more so by the complex legal reasoning that exists in relevant case law and judicial interpretations of statutes. A clear example of how this even undermines the legal knowledge of highly trained professionals was Givelber, Bowers and Blitch's (1984) study on how psychotherapists did not understand the intricacies of the California Supreme Court's Tarasoff decision about the duty of care that therapists have towards third parties.

Another reason why people have trouble knowing the law, which became clear in several of the studies, is that the law is often not aligned with people's own or the broader social norms. This makes it hard for people to trust their normative instincts in guesstimating what the law is. And all of this is made more problematic because most people do not have easy access to legal advice, let alone have such access on a daily basis for all rules that apply to their everyday existence. Even a CEO of a major Fortune 500 company cannot get legal advice that would cover all 300,000 criminally enforceable rules that their corporation must comply with.

A core underlying issue here, however, is that our legal system has been designed and operates with a look to the past, through an *ex post* perspective. The massive number of complex legal rules may operate perfectly well when they are applied to past cases. When bad behaviour has occurred, prosecutors and other lawyers can carry out legal research and in the massive body of legal rules and interpretations find those that apply to the case and develop their legal arguments about how to assign liability or in other ways respond to such facts from the past. This is how law is taught in law school and this is also how many people perceive the law to operate. However, if law truly is to prevent damaging behaviour and have an effective

3 Citing an estimate made by Stanley Arkin, a well-known practitioner in the field of white-collar crime, at the George Mason Conference in October 1990, which produced the symposium that Coffee's article came from (see also Leary 1990: 144 note 10).

4 www.slate.com/articles/news_and_politics/politics/2014/04/how_long_is_the_tax_code_it_is_far_shorter_than_70_000_pages.html.

5 CCH Tax Law Editors 2016.

ex ante function, it must somehow come to shape such behaviour before it happens and not just respond after the fact (cf. Darley, Carlsmith and Robinson 2001).

The second question is: Does less legal knowledge automatically mean that there will be less compliance? A linear view of the compliance process from legal rule to behavioural change would clearly answer this question in the affirmative: if people do not know the law, how can they make a decision to obey such law and conform their behaviour to the goals espoused in the law. This conclusion is too simple, however.

Firstly, the empirical work on legal knowledge has clearly shown that what people think is in the law is aligned with their own social norms and morals. This has two potential effects on compliance. If the social norms and morals happen to be aligned with the law, there can be compliance even if people do not have sound legal knowledge. And vice versa, the less the social norms are aligned with the law, the less such social norms can remedy the lack of legal knowledge.

A second reason why there can still be compliance even if people do not know the law is that people are part of organisations that have legal knowledge and that have translated relevant legal norms into the processes of such an organisation. Such organisational processes can steer behaviour to conform with the law without teaching people the exact contents of the law.

This, of course, does require the organisation to have sufficient legal knowledge and be able to develop practical, technological or normative interventions that effectively steer their members' behaviour. Here, recent work on regulatory, rule or legal intermediaries is extremely interesting. This body of work shows the importance of lawyers, managers, HR professionals and other organisational actors in transmitting, and also interpreting, the law into the organisational process. In doing so, they shape what the law means and as such construct the meaning of compliance (Talesh 2009, 2015; Edelman and Talesh 2011; Abbott, Levi-Faur and Snidal 2017; Gray and Pélisse 2019; Talesh and Pélisse 2019). Organisations may thus have intermediaries that can come to broker complex legal knowledge into lower levels of the organisation. This may help to decrease fundamental knowledge problems but it cannot fully alleviate them. A first problem is that there is so much law that not all of it can be transformed into understandable organisational rules and processes. And second, there may also be limited understanding of organisational rules. A third problem is that the existence of, and access to, such rule intermediaries is limited and unequal. Here Saunders' observation about the lack of legal knowledge in family law is telling:

> The process of acquiring knowledge of pertinent laws is perhaps more problematic in relation to family law than it is in any other area of law. The family, as the least centralized of all our social institutions (Putney 1972; Vincent 1966), lacks specialists, i.e. 'corporate attorneys', who may act as a direct line of communication between the legal institution and the nation's millions of families. In the absence of such spokesmen, what knowledge of family law is diffused to the nation's families usually comes as a result of unco-ordinated and sometimes unintended efforts (Saunders 1975: 69).

And as a third caveat, compliance does not just result from an individual, rational, conscious decision to respond to the law, but may very well be driven socially, and through unconscious (and what may seem irrational) processes, or in some cases not even be the result of a free choice at all but the result of a lack of opportunity to engage in legally banned behaviour. In such situations, which are covered in depth in other chapters here on social norms (Chapter 28), on heuristics and biases in criminal decision-making (Chapter 36), and on opportunity for crime (Chapter 35), knowing the law is never a prerequisite for compliance, as the process never occurs linearly from rule to behaviour with the learning of the rule as a vital step.

The third and final question is: What does all this mean for how to make laws and manage compliance? As we have just seen, the relationship between legal knowledge and compliance is not simple and clear-cut, that is, less knowledge, less compliance. This means that for areas of the law where we cannot expect there to be high levels of legal knowledge, there should be extra attention given to tapping into social and personal norms, as far as they exist, that can come to support the legal rules. It also means that in such instances, as much as possible, implementation of law should involve the use of factual and practical means that make rule-breaking harder and rule-obedience easier while not requiring actors to make a decision in response to specific rules of the law. Here we can think of interventions that sway people unconsciously or that take away options or choice, popularised as *nudges*.

However, there will be many instances where it is still important for law to change behaviour but where there will be a lack of supporting social norms or the ability or political will to use unconscious influences or reduce choice or opportunities. Here things will be much harder as the institutional problems that have caused the lack of legal knowledge need to be addressed. This means trying to align the law to social and personal norms (cf. Darley, Sanderson and LaMantia 1996), reducing the number of legal rules, and reducing the complexity of the law and its judicial interpretations. None of these interventions are easily possible in the current legal system we have, with the *ex post* perspective that is driving it. And, as such, the limited legal knowledge that empirical studies have found will remain a major challenge for compliance.

REFERENCES

Abbott, Kenneth W., David Levi-Faur and Duncan Snidal. 2017. 'Theorizing Regulatory Intermediaries: The RIT Model'. *Annals of the American Academy of Political and Social Science* 670 no. 1: 14–35.

Abegglen, W. P. (1986). 'Knowledge of United States Supreme Court Decisions Affecting Education Held by Selected Tennessee Public School Personnel (Law)'. PhD Thesis, East Tennessee State University. https://dc.etsu.edu/etd/2621.

Albrecht, Stan L., and Miles Green. 1977. 'Cognitive Barriers to Equal Justice before the Law'. *Journal of Research in Crime and Delinquency* 14 no. 2: 206–21.

Apel, Robert. 2013. 'Sanctions, Perceptions, and Crime: Implications for Criminal Deterrence'. *Journal of Quantitative Criminology* 29 no. 1: 67–101.

Bench-Capon, Trevor J. M. 2015. *Knowledge-Based Systems and Legal Applications*, Vol. 36. Brighton, UK: Academic Press.

Bench-Capon, Trevor J. M., and Frans P. Coenen. 1992. 'Isomorphism and Legal Knowledge-Based Systems'. *Artificial Intelligence and Law* 1 no. 1:65–86.

Bowal, Peter. 1998. 'A Study of Lay Knowledge of Law in Canada'. *Indiana International & Comparative Law Review* 9: 121.

Cavanagh, Caitlin, and Elizabeth Cauffman. 2017. 'What They Don't Know Can Hurt Them: Mothers' Legal Knowledge and Youth Re-offending'. *Psychology, Public Policy, and Law* 23 no. 2: 141.

CCH Tax Law Editors. 2016. *Internal Revenue Code: Income, Estate, Gift, Employment and Excise Taxes*. New York: Wolters Kluwer CCH.

Chate, R. A. C. 2008. 'An Audit of the Level of Knowledge and Understanding of Informed Consent amongst Consultant Orthodontists in England, Wales and Northern Ireland'. *British Dental Journal* 205 no. 12: 665.

Clark, T. R. 1990. 'Mississippi Superintendents' and Secondary Educators' Knowledge of School Law as It Relates to Student Rights in Selected Areas'. PhD Thesis, University of Southern Mississippi. https://aquila.usm.edu/theses_dissertations/2745/.

Coffee, Jr, John C. 1991. 'Does Unlawful Mean Criminal?: Reflections on the Disappearing Tort/Crime Distinction in American Law'. *Boston University Law Review* 71: 193.

Cortese, Charles. 1966. 'A Study in Knowledge and Attitudes toward the Law: The Legal Knowledge Inventory'. *Rocky Mountain Social Science Journal* 3: 192–204.

Darley, John M., Kevin M. Carlsmith and Paul H. Robinson. 2001. 'The Ex Ante Function of the Criminal Law'. *Law and Society Review*:165–90.

Darley, John M., Catherine A. Sanderson and Peter S. LaMantia. 1996. 'Community Standards for Defining Attempt Inconsistencies with the Model Penal Code'. *American Behavioral Scientist* 39 no. 4: 405–20.

Denvir, Catrina, Nigel J. Balmer and Alexy Buck. 2012. 'Informed Citizens? Knowledge of Rights and the Resolution of Civil Justice Problems'. *Journal of Social Policy* 41 no. 3: 591–614.

Denvir, Catrina, Nigel J. Balmer and Pascoe Pleasence. 2013. 'When Legal Rights Are Not a Reality: Do Individuals Know Their Rights and How Can We Tell?'. *Journal of Social Welfare and Family Law* 35 no.1: 139–60.

Eberwein III, Howard Jacob. 2008. *Raising Legal Literacy in Public Schools: A Call for Principal Leadership: A National Study of Secondary School Principals' Knowledge of Public School Law*. University of Massachusetts Amherst.

Edelman, Lauren B., and Shauhin A. Talesh. 2011. 'To Comply or Not to Comply – That Isn't the Question: How Organizations Construct the Meaning of Compliance'. *Explaining Compliance: Business Responses to Regulation*:103–22.

Edwards, Deborah L., and Dirk E. Mahling. 1997. 'Toward Knowledge Management Systems in the Legal Domain'. Proceedings of the International ACM SIGGROUP Conference on Supporting Group Work: The Integration Challenge.

Estlund, Cynthia L. 2002. 'How Wrong Are Employees about Their Rights, and Why Does It Matter?' *New York University Law Review* 77: 6.

Gallagher, Mary E. 2006. 'Mobilizing the Law in China: "Informed Disenchantment" and the Development of Legal Consciousness'. *Law & Society Review* 40 no. 4: 783–816.

Ginther, Matthew R., Francis X. Shen, Richard J. Bonnie and Morris B. Hoffman. 2014. 'The Language of Men's Rea'. *Vanderbilt Law Review* 67: 1327.

Ginther, Matthew R., Francis X. Shen, Richard J. Bonnie, Morris B. Hoffman, Owen D. Jones and Kenneth W. Simons. 2018. 'Decoding Guilty Minds: How Jurors Attribute Knowledge and Guilt'. *Vanderbilt Law Review* 71: 241.

Givelber, Daniel J., William J. Bowers and Carolyn L. Blitch. 1984. 'Tarasoff, Myth and Reality: An Empirical Study of Private Law in Action'. *Wisconsin Law Review*: 443.

Goodwin-De Faria, Christine, and Voula Marinos. 2012. 'Youth Understanding & Assertion of Legal Rights: Examining the Roles of Age and Power'. *International Journal of Children's Rights* 20 no. 3: 343–64.

Gray, G., and J. Pelisse. 2019. 'Frontline Workers and the Role of Legal and Regulatory Intermediaries'. Sciences Po LIEPP Working Paper, n°94, 2019–10–12.

Grisso, Thomas, Laurence Steinberg, Jennifer Woolard, Elizabeth Cauffman, Elizabeth Scott, Sandra Graham, Fran Lexcen, N. Dickon Reppucci and Robert Schwartz. 2003. 'Juveniles' Competence to Stand Trial: A Comparison of Adolescents' and Adults' Capacities as Trial Defendants'. *Law and Human Behavior* 27 no. 4: 333–63.

Kennedy, Duncan. 1982. 'Legal Education and the Reproduction of Hierarchy'. *Journal of Legal Education* 32: 591.

Kim, Pauline T. 1998. 'An Empirical Challenge to Employment at Will'. *New Zealand Journal of Employment Relations* 23 no. 2: 91.

1999. 'Norms, Learning and Law: Exploring the Influences of Workers' Legal Knowledge'. *University of Illinois Legal Review* 1999 no. 2: 447–516.

Leary, Thomas B. 1990. 'The Commission's New Option That Favors Judicial Discretion in Corporate Sentencing'. *Federal Sentencing Reporter* 3: 142.

Littleton, Mark. 2008. 'Teachers' Knowledge of Education Law'. *Action in Teacher Education* 30 no. 2: 71–8.

Matsuda, Mari. 1988. 'Affirmative Action and Legal Knowledge: Planting Seeds in Plowed-Up Ground'. *Harvard Women's Law Journal* 11: 1.

Militello, M., D. Schimmel and H. J. Eberwein. 2009. 'If They Knew, They Would Change: How Legal Knowledge Impacts Principals' Practice'. *NASSP Bulletin* 93 no. 1: 27–52.

Moore, S. J. 1997. 'An Assessment of Selected Knowledge of School Law from Public Educators in the State of Tennessee'. PhD Thesis, Tennessee State University. https://digitalscholarship.tnstate.edu/dissertations/AAI9806345/.

Pleasence, Pascoe, and Nigel J. Balmer. 2012. 'Ignorance in Bliss: Modeling Knowledge of Rights in Marriage and Cohabitation'. *Law & Society Review* 46 no. 2: 297–333.

Pleasence, Pascoe, Nigel J. Balmer and Catrina Denvir. 2017. 'Wrong about Rights: Public Knowledge of Key Areas of Consumer, Housing and Employment Law in England and Wales'. *Modern Law Review* 80 no. 5: 836–59.

Reifman, Alan, Spencer M. Gusick and Phoebe C. Ellsworth. 1992. 'Real Jurors' Understanding of the Law in Real Cases'. *Law and Human Behavior* 16 no. 5: 539–54.

Riles, Annelise. 2006. 'Anthropology, Human Rights, and Legal Knowledge: Culture in the Iron Cage'. *American Anthropologist* 108 no. 1: 52–65.

Rudy, Jesse. 2002. 'What They Don't Know Won't Hurt Them: Defending Employment-at-Will in Light of Findings That Employees Believe They Possess Just Cause Protection'. *Berkeley Journal of Employment & Labor Law* 23: 307.

Saltstone, Scot P., Robert Saltstone and Brian H. Rowe. 1997. 'Knowledge of Medical-Legal Issues: Survey of Ontario Family Medicine Residents'. *Canadian Family Physician* 43: 669.

Sametz, L., C. McLoughlin and V. Streib. 1981. 'Teacher's Survey of Knowledge of School Law and Child Abuse'. Kent, OH. ED218243.

Sarat, Austin. 1975. 'Support for the Legal System: An Analysis of Knowledge, Attitudes, and Behavior'. *American Politics Quarterly* 3 no. 1: 3–24.

1976/7. 'Studying American Legal Culture: An Assessment of Survey Evidence'. *Law & Society Review* 11: 427.

Sarat, Austin, and William L. F. Felstiner. 1989. 'Lawyers and Legal Consciousness: Law Talk in the Divorce Lawyer's Office'. *Yale Law Journal*: 1663–88.

Saunders, LaVell E. 1975. 'Collective Ignorance: Public Knowledge of Family Law'. *Family Coordinator*:69–74.

1981. 'Ignorance of the Law among Teenagers: Is It a Barrier to the Exertion of Their Rights as Citizens?' *Adolescence* 16 no. 63: 711.

Schimmel, David, and Matthew Militello. 2007. 'Legal Literacy for Teachers: A Neglected Responsibility'. *Harvard Educational Review* 77 no. 3: 257–84.

Shaw, F. W. I. 1984. 'Principals' Knowledge of the Law of Public Education and Its Relation to Job Satisfaction'. Dissertation, University of Utah.

Shen, Francis X., Morris B. Hoffman, Owen D. Jones and Joshua D. Greene. 2011. 'Sorting Guilty Minds'. *New York University Law Review* 86: 1306.

Shuman, Daniel W., and Myron S. Weiner. 1981. 'Privilege Study: An Empirical Examination of the Psychotherapist–Patient Privilege'. *North Carolina Law Review* 60: 893.

Talesh, Shauhin A. 2009. 'The Privatization of Public Legal Rights: How Manufacturers Construct the Meaning of Consumer Law'. *Law & Society Review* 43 no. 3: 527–62.

2015. 'Rule-Intermediaries in Action: How State and Business Stakeholders Influence the Meaning of Consumer Rights in Regulatory Governance Arrangements'. *Law & Policy* 37 nos. 1–2: 1–31.

Talesh, Shauhin, and Jérôme Pélisse. 2019. 'How Legal Intermediaries Facilitate or Inhibit Social Change'. *Studies in Law, Politics, and Society* 79: 111–45.

Thornton, Dorothy, Neil Gunningham and Robert A. Kagan. 2005. 'General Deterrence and Corporate Environmental Behavior'. *Law & Policy* 27 no. 2: 262–88.

Van McCrary, S., and Jeffrey W. Swanson. 1999. 'Physicians' Legal Defensiveness and Knowledge of Medical Law: Comparing Denmark and the USA'. *Scandinavian Journal of Public Health* 27 no. 1: 18–21.

Van McCrary, S., Jeffrey W. Swanson, Henry S. Perkins and William J. Winslade. 1992. 'Treatment Decisions for Terminally Ill Patients: Physicians' Legal Defensiveness and Knowledge of Medical Law'. *Law, Medicine and Health Care* 20 no. 4: 364–76.

White, Ben, Lindy Willmott, Colleen Cartwright, Malcolm H. Parker and Gail Williams. 2014. 'Doctors' Knowledge of the Law on Withholding and Withdrawing Life-Sustaining Medical Treatment'. *Medical Journal of Australia* 201 no. 4: 229–32.

White, Ben, Lindy Willmott, Malcolm Parker, Colleen Cartwright and Gail Williams. 2012. 'What Do Emergency Physicians Think of Law?' *Emergency Medicine Australasia* 24 no. 4: 355–6.

Williams, Martha, and Jay Hall. 1972. 'Knowledge of the Law in Texas: Socioeconomic and Ethnic Differences'. *Law & Society Review* 7 no. 1: 99–118.

Winter, S., and P. J. May. 2001. 'Motivation for Compliance with Environmental Regulations'. *Journal of Policy Analysis and Management* 20 no. 4: 675–98.

Zirkel, Perry A. 1996. 'The Law or the Lore?' *Phi Delta Kappan* 77 no. 8: 579.

33

Self-Control and Offending

Travis C. Pratt and Kristin M. Lloyd

Abstract: Over the last three decades, self-control theory has established itself as one of the leading explanations of criminal and deviant behavior. At its core, the theory asserts that those with low self-control will be less likely to comply with the law (as well as other social norms). This chapter reviews the self-control perspective in terms of: (1) its origin and development within criminology, (2) its empirical status with respect to how well the theory predicts compliance/failure to comply with the law, (3) recent theoretical and empirical developments in the self-control model, and (4) what future research would be most useful to continue to explore in this theoretical tradition.

33.1 INTRODUCTION

The bulk of criminological theory and research focuses on why people break the law; that is, what motivates them to offend? And there appears to be no shortage of potential answers to that question, including factors like associating with deviant peers (Warr 2002), the strains associated with the failure to meet one's goals in life (Agnew 2007), and frustrations induced by racism and economic stratification (Colvin 2000). There is, however, a long tradition in criminology that asks the question in a different way: why don't people break the law? The assumption here is that we are all capable of engaging in misbehavior, so what are the things that constrain us from doing so? While there is no shortage of potential answers to this question as well (e.g., criminal penalties, social bonds, situational constraints; see Hirschi 1969; Tittle 1980; Clarke 1995), the last few decades have seen considerable work devoted to one potential reason: self-control.

The problem is that, though the self-control theoretical tradition is well known within criminological circles, those in other academic disciplines (and outside of academia more broadly) may be less aware of it. Indeed, within the policy-making domain, for example, the deterrence perspective still dominates – one that views criminal behavior through the lens of the effectiveness of certain, swift, and severe punishments to control crime (Pratt 2008; Cullen et al. 2018; Pratt and Turanovic 2018). This focus is in large part responsible for why the American punishment apparatus – one that boasts the highest incarceration rate in the world – looks the way it does (Pratt 2019). As a result, individual differences concerning why only some people break the law – even when potentially faced with the same criminal "opportunity" as others and subject to the same legal penalties – are not well understood. The self-control perspective (Gottfredson and Hirschi 1990) is one that attempts to fill in that gap.

Accordingly, the plan of this chapter is to discuss self-control theory in terms of: (Section 33.2) its origins in criminology, (Section 33.3) its empirical status in the social science literature as an explanation of crime, (Section 33.4) recent theoretical and empirical developments in the self-control tradition, and (Section 33.5) what to look forward to in the future with respect to the role that self-control plays in predicting criminal behavior.

33.2 ORIGIN OF SELF-CONTROL THEORY IN CRIMINOLOGY

The hallmark difference between control theories and other theories of crime is the focus on answering questions about why people *do not* commit crime. All control theories assume that crime and deviance are attractive and enticing. As a result, social explanations of crime must focus on why individuals decide not to commit crime or engage in deviance (Kubrin et al. 2009). Self-control theory hypothesizes that individuals have internal controls or constraints that prevent them from committing crime or deviance (Gottfredson and Hirschi 1990; Gottfredson 2008). It is the failure to establish adequate levels of these internal controls – or self-control – that results in crime and deviance (Gottfredson and Hirschi 1990).

Self-control theory was born out of Gottfredson and Hirschi's discontent with the explanations of crime and deviance that existed within academic criminology in the 1980s. They asserted that other positivistic explanations of crime – particularly those coming out of the social learning and strain theoretical traditions – did not reflect the reality of crime itself (Gottfredson and Hirschi 1990). It was their observation that crime is not some complex phenomenon – that it is mundane, requires no expertise, is relatively easy and quick to commit, and provides immediate gratification – that was the foundation of the theory.

As Gottfredson (2008: 80) stated, their theory was "explicitly constructed with an appreciation of what the empirical literature depicts about crime and delinquency." Therefore, Gottfredson and Hirschi (1990) posited that those who commit crime will have similar characteristics to crime itself. That is, those who commit crime are likely to be those who are impulsive, who engage in risk-taking behavior, and who want immediate gratification from the benefits of crime. They defined self-control as "the tendency to forego acts that provide immediate or near-term pleasures, but that also have negative consequences for the actor, and as the tendency to act in favor of long-term interest" (Gottfredson and Hirschi 2019: 4).

Developed in a way that works backwards from crime, self-control theory is inductive in nature – a defining characteristic as most theories are developed using a top-down approach. And while self-control and the concept of internal constraints were new to criminology in the 1990s, they were not new to the broader social and behavioral sciences. Indeed, self-control is closely related to social psychological principles such as self-regulation and self-restraint (Baumeister and Heatherton 1996; Moffit et al. 2013). While Gottfredson and Hirschi's ideas were not necessarily novel in broader academia, they have changed the way criminologists think about and study the causes of crime.

One of the major criticisms that Gottfredson and Hirschi faced in the years immediately following the formulation of their theory was the failure to adequately define self-control (Akers 1991; Gibbs et al. 1998). However, they provided a clear definition of *low self-control* that emphasizes the certain behavioral characteristics related to individual criminal propensity (Gottfredson and Hirschi 1990). The theory begins with the assumption that individuals act in their self-interest. This assumption, known as the human nature assumption, emphasizes that crime is ubiquitous because humans are conscious, knowing actors who weigh perceived costs and benefits of their actions before making a decision between engaging in crime or not. From this line of thought, Gottfredson and Hirschi hypothesized that those with low self-control are more likely to engage in impulsive behavior toward the end of immediate gratification. In this instance, the decision between criminal and noncriminal behavior is weighed differently because the benefits of crime are not delayed.

At this point, it is imperative to note that levels of self-control are not predetermined or set at birth. Rather, Gottfredson and Hirschi (1990, 2019) explicitly state that levels of self-control continue to develop and change until approximately age ten and are a direct result of child-rearing. Many sources of influence affect the establishment and development of self-control over the life course, such as neighborhood characteristics (Pratt et al. 2004; Zimmerman et al. 2015), school contexts (Cullen et al. 2008), and deviant peers (Chapple 2007; McGloin and O'Neil Shermer 2009), but parenting provides the most direct influence on how much or how little self-control one has and how it may change over time (Hay and Forrest 2006; Meldrum and Hay 2012; Na and Paternoster 2012). To that end, "parental concern for the welfare or behavior of the child is a necessary condition for child-rearing" and establishing high levels of self-control (Gottfredson and Hirschi 1990: 98). But as Cullen et al. (2008) pointed out, simply taking care of a child does not mean that parents will effectively carry out their duties.

Indeed, Gottfredson and Hirschi (1990) outline three critical components of parenting to establish adequate levels of self-control: (1) monitoring the children, (2) recognition of deviant acts, and (3) disciplining the children when they engage in deviant behavior. When these three components are consistently met at earlier stages in the life course (before and up to approximately age eight to ten), adequate levels of self-control are established and there is an increased probability of exercising constraint when considering crime and deviance (Gottfredson and Hirschi 1990). More recently, Hirschi (2004) emphasized the importance of positive parental qualities, such as caring and warmth, adding that these are also necessary components in the parent–child relationship to establish adequate self-control.

There are four key propositions of self-control theory that warrant discussion. First, levels of self-control are strongly associated with all types of offending, including analogous behaviors (e.g., gambling, speeding, and binge drinking) (Pratt and Cullen 2000; Kubrin et al. 2009; Vazsonyi et al. 2017). Second, specialization in offending is the exception, not the rule. Most offenders are versatile in the types of crime and deviance they commit (Brame et al. 2004; Hirschi 2004), although some instances of specialization are anticipated in later stages of the life course (Gottfredson and Hirschi 1990; Piquero et al. 1999). Third, an overwhelming body of research has concluded that levels of self-control remain relatively stable across the life course. While absolute levels of self-control (i.e., within-person) may change, individual levels of self-control relative to others remain consistent (Gottfredson and Hirschi 2019). And finally, individuals with low self-control are less likely to select into prosocial institutions such as good marriages, prosocial peer groups, and employment. What is more, those with low self-control tend to self-select into deviant peer groups, unstable intimate relationships, and often face negative life outcomes such as victimization (Chapple 2007; Pratt et al. 2014; Turanovic et al. 2015).

33.3 THE EMPIRICAL STATUS OF SELF-CONTROL AND OFFENDING

Self-control theory is one of the most prominent and empirically tested theories in criminology. In the most general sense, self-control should predict all crimes and analogous behaviors at all times, among all individuals, and across all countries – hence the original specification as the general theory of crime (Gottfredson and Hirschi 1990; Gottfredson 2008). Overall, research finds this to be true. Self-control theory has withstood the test of time, as extant interdisciplinary research has consistently found support for the association between self-control and deviance, with the bulk of this research specifically focusing on juvenile delinquency (Pratt and Cullen 2000; Meldrum et al. 2009; Vazsonyi et al. 2017).

From meta-analyses and literature reviews (e.g., Pratt and Cullen 2000; Vazsonyi et al. 2017) to countless individual studies, there has been considerable support for a variety of outcomes including certain white-collar offenses such as fraud (Holtfreter et al. 2010a, 2010b), and violent crimes (Piquero et al. 2005). In their recent meta-analysis, Vazsonyi et al. (2017) found a strong association between low self-control and general deviance and physical violence, but a weak overall association between low self-control and substance use and organizational crimes. This finding reveals that, while the low self-control–deviance link is well established, there are still certain offenses that self-control theory does not predict as well, which runs contrary to Gottfredson and Hirschi's original assumptions.

Extant literature reveals that while low self-control may have influence on other forms of deviance, people commit most white-collar crimes for alternative reasons. For example, Schoepfer et al. (2013) conducted an empirical test to determine the effect of both low self-control and a desire for control on white-collar offenses and conventional crime. Their findings indicate that desire for control is a better predictor than low self-control for white-collar offenses but not for conventional street crimes. Further, Piquero et al. (2010) found that it is the desire for control, not low self-control, that is associated with corporate offending. Taken together, this body of research provides partial support for the theory. Therefore, we can say that low self-control is one of the most salient predictors of a wide variety of offenses, although there are some exceptions when it comes to white-collar offenses and substance use. In the same vein, the preponderance of evidence indicates that specialization in offending is not very common and offenders are more likely to be versatile than to commit only one type of crime or deviance.

Specialization is the extent to which an offender engages in only one form of crime and deviance, whereas versatility in offending is the extent to which they engage in varying forms of crime and deviance (Farrington 1986; Kempf 1987). Despite some lines of research that have revealed modest specialization within larger samples and with specific white-collar offenses (Benson and Moore 1992) and some violent offenses (Blumstein and Cohen 1979; Deane et al. 2005), studies repeatedly confirm that versatility in offending is more common (Cloward and Ohlin 1960; Mazerolle et al. 2000; Piquero 2000; Delisi 2003; McGloin et al. 2007). This assertion has been made consistently by both Hirschi (2004) and Gottfredson (2008) in the years following their seminal book.

Hirschi (2004: 538) provided what is perhaps the clearest statement regarding specialization when he said that those "committing any one crime are more likely to commit all other crimes – given opportunities to do so." And despite the development of specialty courts that are geared toward particular offenders of particular types of offense, this statement is supported even in studies examining crimes that may seem to be more specialized. In their examination of specialization among bias crime offenders, Messner et al. (2004) concluded that we cannot call bias crime offenders specialized because they engage in a host of other offenses – not just bias crimes. Further, Piquero et al. (1999) asserted that any specialization we may see is strongly correlated to age and the natural effect of age itself on crime (i.e., desistance) leading to less versatility, which was anticipated by Gottfredson and Hirschi (1990).

Another emphasis in Gottfredson and Hirschi's (1990) original articulation of their theory was the stability of self-control. In recent decades, scholars across disciplines have generally found support for the stability thesis (Pratt and Cullen 2000; Vazsonyi et al. 2017), although some mixed results (Turner and Piquero 2002) and even negative results (Burt et al. 2006; Hay and Forrest 2006) have been discovered. In their most recent text, Gottfredson and Hirschi (2019: 82) emphasized that research indicating unstable levels of self-control suffers from misspecifications of self-control, and that they never explicitly stated that it is "set in stone." In fact, they anticipate changes relative to others. And that is largely what scholars have found. Despite stable levels of self-control across the life course, there is more change than originally predicted (Burt et al. 2006, 2014; Hay and Forrest 2006). Specifically, levels of self-control are likely to change in relation to others. That is, there is not an absolute change in self-control but one that is relative given age and time.

Research has also revealed that those with low self-control tend to engage in lifestyles that increase their chances of victimization and choose peers and other intimate relationships that are unstable and antisocial in nature (Turanovic and Pratt 2014; Pratt and Turanovic 2015; Turanovic et al. 2018). These selection effects are well documented and are often responsible for why low self-control is so strongly associated with negative life outcomes (Pratt et al. 2016). Both theoretically and simply from a commonsense standpoint, this makes sense. Those who are around crime a lot or who put themselves in certain circumstances are likely those who have lower levels of self-control. Research supports this. In their meta-analysis observing the link between self-control and victimization, Pratt et al. (2014) established that the effect of self-control on victimization tends to be indirect. They concluded that self-control itself does not lead to victimization – it is the various risky lifestyles and activities that people engage in as a result of self-control that increases the odds of victimization. Again, this is theoretically expected given the well-documented history of selection effects of those who have low self-control.

The most substantial selection effects are found when studying the link between self-control, deviant peers, and unstable personal relationships. Specifically, scholars have generally concluded that those who have low levels of self-control are more likely to share social networks with deviant peers, and these peers are likely to have an additive effect on crime and deviance (McGloin et al. 2009; McGloin and Thomas 2019). Put simply, the old adage "birds of a feather flock together" has been proven true, as research indicates a reciprocal relationship between deviance and deviant peers, which is largely influenced by self-control.

Taken together, this body of literature largely supports the propositions presented by Gottfredson and Hirschi. We can say that, without a doubt, low self-control is a robust and salient predictor of a variety of crime and deviance, despite certain exceptions. Additionally, specialization in offending is not very common. When specialization does occur, it is usually at later stages in the life course and follows the natural progression of the effect of age on crime. We can also conclude that self-control remains stable across the life course, although it may be slightly more unstable than originally predicted. And finally, those with low self-control are far more likely to select into deviant peer groups, forgo prosocial institutions such as marriage and employment, and engage in risky lifestyles and activities that can lead to victimization and other negative outcomes.

33.4 RECENT THEORETICAL AND EMPIRICAL DEVELOPMENTS

Although it has been present in the criminological literature for three decades now, self-control theory been subject to some key critiques and revisions. In particular, two significant theoretical and empirical developments have occurred, the first of which concerns how the effects of self-control on offending can be conditioned by other criminogenic factors. This is stated most clearly in the form of "situational action theory" (SAT) by Wikstrom and colleagues (Wikstrom and Treiber 2007; Wikstrom and Svensson 2010; Wikstrom et al. 2012). SAT merges the self-control perspective with the importance of individual morality. Specifically, SAT argues that when someone has a strong set of moral beliefs against criminal behavior, the effect of self-control on crime is effectively reduced (i.e., a person does not really need their level of self-control to keep them in line because they already have strong attitudes that prohibit crime).

A similar pattern of results is found in studies that examine how the effect of self-control on crime varies by neighborhood context, where the effects of self-control tend to be reduced for those living in harsh neighborhood environments (Zimmerman 2010; Zimmerman et al. 2015; cf. Lynam et al. 2000). Recent work has also focused on how self-control can be viewed as a muscle – one that can "tire out" and needs rest to be replenished (Baumeister et al. 1998; Muraven and Baumeister 2000; Pratt 2015). The bottom line here is that this body of work shows that the link between self-control and crime is likely more complex than Gottfredson and Hirschi claimed that it was.

A second recent development has been the integration of self-control theory with the life-course perspective in criminology (Pratt 2016). In particular, Pratt (2016) noted that self-control changes within individuals as they age, and that self-control influences "selection" into both positive (e.g., employment, marriage) and negative (e.g., victimization, arrest and incarceration) life events, and that such selection effects are age-graded. Recent work testing Pratt's theory has been supportive (Crank and Brezina 2019). It therefore appears that the self-control tradition within criminology is still evolving, and that new theoretical and empirical territory has yet to be discovered.

33.5 LOOKING TOWARD THE FUTURE

These theoretical and empirical developments within the self-control tradition are certainly important, and they have uncovered a broad range of criminal and deviant behaviors that can be explained by – at least to some extent – the inability of some individuals to control themselves. There is, however, still a lot that we do not know and, as we look into the future, one significant gap still remains: we need to better understand how the sources and mechanisms of self-control change over time.

Some of this change can be traced to normal cognitive and developmental changes in brain function and physiology as we age, particularly with respect to "executive functioning" (i.e., the ability to evaluate the long-term consequences of our actions; see Beaver et al. 2007). Yet there are also likely social sources of self-control change as well, including significant life events like getting married, finding a good job, and having kids, that have the potential to enhance and reinforce the growth of one's level of self-control (Schmidt et al. 2007; Rocque 2015; cf. Lee et al. 2010). And finally, we are only beginning to understand the institutional sources of changes in self-control – specifically, those brought about through effective correctional interventions (Piquero et al. 2016). The key implication is that research devoted to understanding when and how self-control can be meaningfully changed should arguably represent the next generation of scholarship on self-control and crime. Because the bottom line is that, when it comes to all forms of misbehavior, self-control matters. A lot. It should therefore always be part of the conversation about why people break the law – whatever that particular law might be.

REFERENCES

Agnew, Robert. 2007. *Pressured into Crime: An Overview of General Strain Theory*. New York: Oxford University Press.

Akers, Ronald L. 1991. "Self-Control as a General Theory of Crime." *Journal of Quantitative* Criminology 7, no. 2 (June):201–11. doi: 0748.4518/91/0600-0201506.50/0.

Baumeister, R. F., and Todd F. Heatherton. 1996. "Self-Regulation Failure: An Overview." *Psychological Inquiry* 7, no. 1:1–15. doi: 10.1207/s15327965pli0701_1.

Baumeister, Roy F., Ellen Bratslavsky, Mark Muravin, and Dianne M. Tice. 1998. "Ego Depletion: Is the Active Self a Limited Resource?" *Journal of Personality and Social Psychology* 74:1252–65.

Beaver, Kevin M., John Paul Wright, and Matt Delisi. 2007. "Self-Control as an Executive Function: Reformulating Gottfredson and Hirschi's Parental Socialization Thesis." *Criminal Justice and Behavior* 34:1345–61.

Bensonl, Michael L., and Elizabeth Moore. 1992. "Are White-Collar and Common Offenders the Same? An Empirical and Theoretical Critique of a Recently Proposed General Theory of Crime." *Journal of Research in Crime and Delinquency* 29:251–72.

Blumstein, Alfred, and Jacquelyn Cohen. 1979. "Estimation of Individual Crime Rates from Arrest Records." *Journal of Criminal Law and Criminology* 70, no.4:561–85.

Brame, Robert, Raymond Paternoster, and Shawn D. Bushway. 2004. "Criminal Offending Frequency and Offense Switching." *Journal of Contemporary Criminal Justice* 20, no. 2 (May):201–14. doi: 10.1177/1043986204263779.

Burt, Callie H., Ronald L. Simons, and Leslie G. Simons. 2006. "A Longitudinal Test of the Effects of Parenting and the Stability of Self-Control: Negative Evidence for the General Theory of Crime." *Criminology* 44, no. 2 (June):353–96. doi: 10.1111/j.1745-9125.2006.00052.x.

Burt, Callie H., Gary Sweeten, and Ronald L. Simons. 2014. "Self-Control through Emerging Adulthood: Instability, Multidimensionality, and Criminological Significance." *Criminology* 52, no. 3:450–87. doi: 10.1111/1745-9125.12045.

Chapple, Constance L. 2007. "Self-Control, Peer Relations, and Delinquency." *Justice Quarterly* 22, no. 1:89–106. doi: 10.1080/07418820420003336 54.

Clarke, Ronald V. 1995. "Situational Crime Prevention." *Crime and Justice: A Review of Research* 19:91–150.

Cloward, Richard, and Lloyd Ohlin. 1960. *Delinquency and Opportunity: A Theory of Delinquent Gangs*. New York: Free Press.

Colvin, Mark. 2000. *Crime and Coercion: An Integrated Theory of Chronic Criminality*. New York: St. Martins.

Crank, Beverly Reece, and Timothy Brezina. 2019. "Self-Control, Emerging Adulthood, and Desistance from Crime: A Partial Test of Pratt's Integrated Self-Control/Life-Course Theory of Offending. *Journal of Developmental and Life-Course Criminology* 5:38–59.

Cullen, Francis T., James D. Unnever, John Paul Wright, and Kevin M. Beaver. 2008. "Parenting and Self-Control." In *Out of Control: Assessing the General Theory of Crime*, edited by Erich Goode, 61–74. Stanford, CA: Stanford University Press.

Cullen, Francis T., Travis C. Pratt, Jillian J. Turanovic, and Leah Butler. 2018. "When Bad News Arrives: Project HOPE in a Post-Factual World." *Journal of Contemporary Criminal Justice* 43:13–34.

Deane, Glenn, David P. Armstrong, and Richard B. Felson. 2005. "An Examination of Offense Specialization Using Marginal Logit Models." *Criminology* 43, no. 4:955–88. doi: 10.1111/j.1745-9125.2005.00030.x.

Delisi, Matt. 2003. "The Imprisoned Nonviolent Drug Offender: Specialized Martyr or Versatile Career Criminal?" *American Journal of Criminal Justice* 27, no. 2:167–82.

Farrington, David P. 1986. "Age and Crime." In *Crime and Justice: An Annual Review of Research*, edited by Michael Tonry and N. Morris, 189–250. Chicago, IL: University of Chicago Press.
Farrington, David P., Alex R. Piquero, and Wesley G. Jennings. *Offending from Childhood to Late Middle Age: Recent Results from the Cambridge Study in Delinquent Development*. New York: Springer.
Gibbs, John J., Dennis Giever, and Jamie S. Martin. 1998. "Parental Management and Self-Control: An Empirical Test of Gottfredson and Hirschi's General Theory." *Journal of Research in Crime and Delinquency* 35, no. 1:40–70. doi: 10.1177/0022427898035001002.
Gottfredson, Michael R. 2008. "The Empirical Status of Control Theory in Criminology." In *Taking Stock: The Status of Criminological Theory*, edited by Francis T. Cullen, John Paul Wright, and Kristie R. Blevins, 77–100. New Brunswick, NJ: Transaction Publishers.
Gottfredson, Michael R., and Travis Hirschi. 1990. *A General Theory of Crime*. Palo Alto, CA: Stanford University Press.
Gottfredson, Michael, and Travis Hirschi. 2019. *Modern Control Theory and the Limits of Criminal Justice*. New York: Oxford University Press.
Hay, Carter. and Walter Forrest. 2006. "The Development of Self-Control: Examining Self-Control Theory's Stability Thesis." *Criminology* 44, no. 4 (December):739–74. doi: 10.1111/j.1745-9125.2006.00062.x.
Hirschi, Travis. 1969. *Causes of Delinquency*. Berkeley, CA: University of California Press.
2004. "Self-Control and Crime." In *Handbook of Self-Regulation: Research, Theory, and Application*, edited by Roy F. Baumeister and Kathleen D. Vohs, 538–52. New York: Guilford Press.
Holtfreter, Kristy, Kevin M. Beaver, Michael D. Reisig, and Travis C. Pratt. 2010a. "Low Self-Control and Fraud Offending." *Journal of Financial Crime* 17, no. 3:295–307. doi: 10.1108/13590791011056264.
Holtfreter, Kristy, Michael D. Reisig, Nicole Leeper Piquero, and Alex R. Piquero. 2010b. "Low Self-Control and Fraud: Offending, Victimization, and Their Overlap." *Criminal Justice and Behavior* 37, no. 2 (February):188–203. doi: 10.1177/0093854809354977.
Kempf, Kimberly L. 1987. "Specialization and the Criminal Career." *Criminology* 25, no. 2 (May):399–420. doi: 10.1111/j.1745-9125.1987.tb00803.x.
Kubrin, Charis, E. Thomas, D. Stucky, and Marvin D. Krohn. 2009. *Researching Theories of Crime and Deviance*. New York: Oxford University Press.
Lee, Matthew R., Laurie Chassin, and David MacKinnon. 2010. "The Effect of Marriage on Young Adult Heavy Drinking and Its Mediators: Results from Two Methods of Adjusting for Selection into Marriage." *Psychology of Addictive Behaviors*, 24:712–18.
Lynam, Donald R., Avshalom Caspi, Terri E. Moffitt, Per-Olof Wikstrom, Rolf Loeber, and Scott Novak. 2000. "The Interaction between Impulsivity and Neighborhood Context on Offending: The Effects of Impulsivity Are Stronger in Poorer Neighborhoods." *Journal of Abnormal Psychology* 109:563–74.
Mazerolle, Paul, Robert Brame, Ray Paternoster, Alex Piquero, and Charles Dean. 2000. "Onset Age, Persistence, and Offending Versatility: Comparisons across Gender." *Criminology* 38, no. 4 (November):1143–72. doi: 10.1111/j.1745-9125.2000.tb01417.x.
McGloin, Jean Marie, and Lauren O'Neil Shermer. 2009. "Self-Control and Deviant Peer Network Structure." *Journal of Research on Crime and Delinquency* 46, no. 1 (February):35–72. doi: 10.1177/0022427808326585.
McGloin, Jean Marie, and Kyle J. Thomas. 2019. "Peer Influence and Delinquency." Annual Review of Criminology 2:241–264.
McGloin, Jean Marie, Christopher J. Sullivan, Alex R. Piquero, and Travis C. Pratt. 2007. "Local Life Circumstances and Offending Specialization/Versatility: Comparing Opportunity and Propensity." *Journal of Research in Crime and Delinquency* 44, no. 3 (August):321–46. doi: 10.1177/0022427807302664.
McGloin, Jean Marie, Christopher J. Sullivan, and Alex R. Piquero. 2009. "Aggregating to Versatility? Transitions among Offender Types in the Short Term." British Journal of Criminlogy 49:243–264.
Meldrum, Ryan C., and Carter Hay. 2012. "Do Peers Matter in the Development of Self-Control? Evidence from a Longitudinal Study of Youth. *Journal of Youth and Adolescence* 41:691–703. doi: 10.1007/s10964-011-9692-0.

Meldrum, Ryan C., Jacob T. N. Young, and Frank M. Weerman. 2009. "Reconsidering the Effect of Self-Control and Delinquent Peers: Implications of Measurement for Theoretical Significance." *Journal of Research in Crime and Delinquency* 46, no. 3 (May):353–76. doi: 10.1177/0022427809335171.

Messner, Steven F., Richard Rosenfeld, and Eric P. Baumer. 2004. "Dimensions of Social Capital and Rates of Criminal Homicide." *American Sociological Review* 69:882–903.

Moffitt, Terrie E., Richie Poulton, and Avshalom Caspi. 2013. "Lifelong Impact of Early Self-Control." *American Scientist*, 101 (July):352–9.

Muraven, Mark, and Roy F. Baumeister. 2000. "Self-Regulation and Depletion of Limited Resources: Does Self-Control Resemble a Muscle? *Psychological Bulletin* 126:247–59.

Na, Chongmin, and Raymond Paternoster. 2012. "Can Self-Control Change Substantially Over Time? Rethinking the Relationship between Self- and Social Control." *Criminology* 50, no. 2:427–62. doi: 10.1111/j.1745-9125.2011.00269.x.

Piquero, Alex R. 2000. "Frequency, Specialization, and Violence in Offending Careers." *Journal of Research in Crime and Delinquency* 37, no. 4 (November):392–418. doi: 10.1177/0022427800037004003.

Piquero, Alex. R., Raymond Paternoster, Paul Mazerolle, Robert Brame, and Charles W. Dean. 1999. "Onset Age and Offense Specialization." *Journal of Research in Crime and Delinquency* 36, no. 3 (August):275–99. doi: 10.1177/0022427899036003002.

Piquero, Alex R., John MacDonald, Adam Dobrin, Leah E. Daigle, and Francis T. Cullen. 2005. "Self-Control, Violent Offending, and Homicide Victimization: Assessing the General Theory of Crime." *Journal of Quantitative Criminology* 21, no. 1 (March):55–71. doi: 10.1007/s10940-004-1787-2.

Piquero, Nicole Leeper, Andrea Schoepfer, and Lynn Langton. 2010. "Completely Out of Control or the Desire to Be in Complete Control? How Low Self-Control and the Desire for Control Relate to Corporate Offending." *Crime & Delinquency* 56, no. 4:627–47. doi: 10.1177/0011128708325052.

Piquero, Alex R., Wesley G. Jennings, David P. Farrington, Brie Diamond, and Jennifer M. Reingle Gonzalez. 2016. "A Meta-analysis Update on the Effectiveness of Early Self-Control Improvement Programs to Improve Self-Control and Reduce Delinquency." *Journal of Experimental Criminology*, 12:249–64.

Pratt, Travis C. 2008. "Rational Choice Theory, Crime Control Policy, and Criminological Relevance." *Criminology and Public Policy* 7:43–52.

2015. "A Reconceptualized Model of Self-Control and Crime: Specifying the Role of Self-Control Variability." *Criminal Justice and Behavior* 42:662–79.

2016. "A Self-Control/Life-Course Theory of Criminal Behavior." *European Journal of Criminology* 13:129–46.

2019. *Addicted to Incarceration: Corrections Policy and the Politics of Misinformation in the United States*. 2nd ed. Thousand Oaks, CA: Sage.

Pratt, Travis C., and Francis T. Cullen. 2000. "The Empirical Status of Gottfredson and Hirschi's General Theory of Crime: A Meta-analysis." *Criminology* 38, no. 3 (August):931–64. doi: 10.1111/j.1745-9125.2000.tb00911.x.

Pratt, Travis C., and Jillian J. Turanovic. 2016. "Lifestyle and Routine Activity Theories Revisited: The Importance of 'Risk' to the Study of Victimization." *Victims and Offenders* 11:335–54.

2018. "Celerity and Deterrence." In *Deterrence, Choice, and Crime – Contemporary Perspectives, Advances in Criminological Theory*, vol. 23, edited by Daniel S. Nagin, Francis T. Cullen, and Cheryl Lero Jonson, 187–210. New Brunswick, NJ: Transaction.

Pratt, Travis C., Michael G. Turner, and Alex R. Piquero. 2004. "Parental Socialization and Community Context: A Longitudinal Analysis of the Structural Sources of Low Self-Control." *Journal of Research in Crime and Delinquency* 41, no. 3 (August):219–43. doi: 10.1177/0022427803260270.

Pratt, Travis C., Jillian J. Turanovic, Kathleen A. Fox, and Kevin A. Wright. 2014. "Self-Control and Victimization: A Meta-Analysis." Criminology 52:87–116.

Pratt, Travis C., J. C. Barnes, Francis T. Cullen, and Jillian J. Turanovic. 2016. "'I Suck at Everything': Crime, Arrest, and the Generality of Failure." *Deviant Behavior* 37:837–51.

Rocque, Michael. 2015. "The Lost Concept: The (Re) Emerging Link between Maturation and Desistance from Crime." *Criminology and Criminal Justice*, 15, 340–60.

Schmidt, Klaus-Helmut, Barbara Neubach, and Herbert Heuer. 2007. "Self-Control Demands, Cognitive Control Deficits, and Burnout." *Work and Stress*, 21, 142–54.

Schoepfer, Andrea, Nicole Leeper Piquero, and Lynn Langton. 2013. "Low Self-Control versus the Desire-For-Control: An Empirical Test of White-Collar Crime and Conventional Crime." *Deviant Behavior* 35, no. 3 (February):197–214. doi: 10.1080/01639625.2013.834758.

Tittle, Charles R. 1980. *Sanctions and Social Deviance: The Question of Deterrence*. Westport, CT: Praeger.

Turanovic, Jillian J., and Travis C. Pratt. 2014. "'Can't Stop, Won't Stop': Self-Control, Risky Lifestyles, and Repeat Victimization." *Journal of Quantitative Criminology* 30:29–56.

Turanovic, Jillian J., Michael D. Reisig, and Travis C. Pratt. 2015. "Risky Lifestyles, Low Self-Control, and Violent Victimization across Gendered Pathways." *Journal of Quantitative Criminology*, 31:183–206.

Turanovic, Jillian J., Travis C. Pratt, and Alex R. Piquero. 2018. "Structural Constraints, Risky Lifestyles, and Repeat Victimization." *Journal of Quantitative Criminology* 34:251–74.

Turner, Michael G., and Alex R. Piquero. 2002. "The Stability of Self-Control." *Journal of Criminal Justice* 30, no. 6 (November–December):457–71. doi: 10.1016/S0047-2352(02)00169-1.

Vazsonyi, Alexander T., Jakub Mikuska, and Erin L. Kelly. 2017. "It's Time: A Meta-analysis on the Self-Control-Deviance Link." *Journal of Criminal Justice* 48, (January):48–63. doi: 10.1016/j.jcrimjus.2016.10.001.

Warr, Mark. 2002. *Companions in Crime: The Social Aspects of Criminal Conduct*. New York: Cambridge University Press.

Wikstrom, Per-Olof, and Robert Svensson. 2010. "When Does Self-Control Matter? The Interaction between Morality and Self-Control in Crime Causation." *European Journal of Criminology* 7:395–410.

Wikstrom, Per-Olof, and Kyle Treiber. 2007. "The Role of Self-Control in Crime Causation: Beyond Gottfredson and Hirschi's General Theory of Crime." *European Journal of Criminology* 4:237–64.

Wikstrom, Per-Olof, Dietrich Oberwittler, Kyle Treiber, and Beth Hardi. 2012. *Breaking Rules: The Social and Situational Dynamics of Young People's Urban Crime*. New York: Oxford University Press.

Zimmerman, Gregory M. 2010. "Impulsivity, Offending, and Neighborhood: Investigating the Person-Context Nexus." *Journal of Quantitative Criminology* 26:301–32.

Zimmerman, Gregory M., Ekaterina V. Botchkovar, Olena Antonaccio, and Lorine A. Hughes. 2015. "Low Self-Control in 'Bad' Neighborhoods: Assessing the Role of Context on the Relationship between Self-Control and Crime." *Justice Quarterly*, 32, no. 1 (November):56–84. doi: 10.1080/07418825.2012.737472.

34

Substance Abuse, Self-Control and Crime

Emmeke B. Kooistra

Abstract: This chapter reviews whether substance abuse can reduce capacity for compliance. It examines scientific findings on the links among substance abuse, self-control and (criminal) behaviour. Research findings indicate that substance abuse may negatively affect levels of self-control and cause increases in impulsive behaviour. These increases in impulsivity can in turn be linked to criminal behaviour. Moreover, substance abuse is associated with increases in violent behaviour. However, there is variability among substance abusers, and situational factors such as social environment or criminal opportunity play a major role. Rather than merely focusing on people's personal guilt in substance abuse-related misconduct and crimes, the chapter advocates focusing on correcting future behaviour and recommends the implementation of treatment programmes aimed at improving self-control of substance-abusing offenders.

34.1 INTRODUCTION

Capacity is a central issue in compliance. People can only obey the law if they are able to do as the law demands. We can note many issues with regard to people's capacity to obey the law. A good example is the knowledge of the law (see Chapter 32): people who do not know the law will be less able to comply. Furthermore, we must consider people's socio-economic circumstances, as people with less access to employment, housing and education may come to have greater difficulties in leading a law-abiding life (Van Rooij and Fine in press). The present chapter focuses on a different – and in the study of compliance often overlooked – aspect of capacity for compliance. Namely, a factor that can reduce people's ability to comply: substance abuse.

A large body of scientific work points to the relationship between substance abuse and crime. A systematic review of the prevalence of substance abuse in prisoners found that 18–30 per cent of male prisoners and 10–24 per cent of female prisoners suffer from alcohol abuse or dependence upon reception into custody. For drug abuse or dependence, prevalence ranges from 10 per cent to 48 per cent for men, and rises to 30–60 per cent for women (Fazel et al. 2006). This shows that the prevalence of substance abuse within incarcerated populations is highly variant but much higher than within the general population (i.e., 2.38 per cent worldwide; Global Burden of Disease Collaborative Network 2018). Outside of the criminal justice system, substance abuse may also play a role in rule-breaking behaviour and non-compliance, as substance use in the workspace is not uncommon (Smith and Davidson 2015). A US survey study on alcohol use and impairment in the workspace found that alcohol use directly affected

This research was made possible through a generous grant from the European Research Council (ERC-2018-CoG - HomoJuridicus - 817680).

approximately 15 per cent of the US workforce (Frone 2006). These findings indicate that there is a relationship between substance abuse and illegal behaviour. In light of this, to understand compliance and to be able to direct future behaviour, it is important to consider the extent to which substance abuse may lead to illegal behaviour. Therefore, this chapter examines whether substance abuse reduces capacity for legal compliance.

The present chapter will look at available empirical evidence regarding the relationship between substance abuse and crime. Its purpose is not to suggest that substance abuse is an excuse for breaking the law but more practically to understand how such abuse can cause illegal behaviour. Such knowledge is a critical element in an overall strategy to enhance compliance and reduce crime. Furthermore, there are many ways in which substance abuse and illegal behaviour are related. In most jurisdictions, the use of substances such as drugs in itself constitutes illegal behaviour. In addition, substance abuse may have numerous social effects, such as loss of employment, social bonds or housing, which may well be causes of or catalysts for criminal behaviour (e.g., Henkel 2011; Mowen and Visher 2015; Schütz 2016). However, the present chapter's focus is not on substance-use crimes or the social effects of substance abuse but rather on how substance abuse impairs an individual's capacity for compliance. Therefore, this chapter focuses on how substance abuse affects self-control and impulsivity, two core aspects of the capacity to comply (see also, generally, Chapter 33).

Thus, this chapter focuses on the question of how substance abuse relates to self-control and how self-control relates to illegal behaviour. First, the chapter will discuss the methods and the limitations of this research, followed by a brief discussion of general theories on the substance abuse–crime relationship. Subsequently, the chapter will consider the factors that play a role in the development and maintenance of substance abuse, and whether a person is in control of becoming or remaining a substance abuser. Next, the chapter assesses whether someone who abuses licit or illicit substances is capable of controlling their behaviour and complying with legal rules, or whether the abuse incapacitates their compliance. Lastly, a specific section is dedicated to the relationship between substance abuse and violence.

34.2 TERMINOLOGICAL AND METHODOLOGICAL NOTIONS

Before addressing the chapter's main points, some methodological and terminological issues within this research are discussed. The first area of concern regards the conceptualization and measurement of substance abuse. "Substances" is a broad term that encompasses both licit (e.g., alcohol) and illicit (e.g., opioids, cocaine, amphetamines) intoxicants. Furthermore, for some substances, legal status differs between countries or states (e.g., cannabis; Chatwin 2017). This chapter attempts to provide a systemic overview of the effects of substances on illegal behaviour, with substance abuse referring to both drug and alcohol use-related disorders. However, different types of substances have different effects on behaviour. Where necessary and possible, a distinction is made between different types of substances.

Moreover, there is considerable variability in the terminology used in the substance abuse literature (Kelly 2004). Scholars generally refer to two distinct terms: substance abuse and substance dependence (also referred to as addiction; American Psychiatric Association 1994). Substance abuse comprises a maladaptive pattern of continued substance use, despite (for example) possible social and interpersonal problems related to use. Substance dependence can be described as a more severe and uncontrollable form of substance abuse, distinguished by withdrawal symptoms, tolerance to the substance and failed attempts to quit using (American Psychiatric Association 1994). However, in the current version of the Diagnostic and Statistical Manual (DSM-V) of the American Psychiatric Association (APA 2013), this distinction between substance abuse and dependence is no longer made, as the two have been combined as a single 'substance use disorder' (SUD). SUD is defined as 'a problematic pattern of [substance] use leading to clinically significant impairment or distress' (APA 2013:490). The diagnosis of an SUD requires that a person meets at least two out of eleven diagnostic criteria, occurring within a twelve-month period. The disorder exists on a continuum from mild to severe, and the level of severity is determined by the number of diagnostic criteria that are met (APA 2013). The preferred option is to use the term 'substance use disorder' in this chapter. However, the problem is that a significant part of the empirical literature does not clearly distinguish between substance use and SUD, uses outdated criteria (i.e., abuse or dependence), or does not use or report standard diagnostic criteria at all. Given that it cannot be determined that all subjects in the reviewed literature meet the requirements for a diagnosis, it would be incorrect to systematically refer to 'SUD'. To avoid this issue, one might even argue to refer to 'substance use' in general. However, as this chapter seeks to discuss the effects of problematic forms of substance use on behaviour, it will primarily use the term 'substance abuse'. To be specific, the term 'substance abuse' in this chapter does not equal the DSM-IV diagnosis (APA 1994) but is used as a general indicator for problematic forms of substance use, which may include DSM-diagnosed abuse, dependence and/or SUD. If the literature specifies the effects of dependence or SUD, the chapter will do so accordingly. However, if not specifically mentioned, the results or findings about substance abuse discussed in this review cannot unquestionably be generalised to dependence or SUD.

Additionally, substance abuse research is often cross-sectional. This means that the results show only correlational relationships and it is not possible to draw conclusions on causality. Moreover, experimental research examining the direct and causal effects of substance abuse on behaviour faces ethical concerns. Given that it is unethical to expose human participants to actual abusive amounts of a substance to test how it affects their behaviour, research is restricted to testing the effects of the general use of different substances, rather than abuse or SUD. When it is not possible to discuss findings specific to substance abuse, this chapter will therefore draw on the effects of general substance usage.

A core methodological issue in the criminological literature on substance abuse concerns the measurement of criminal behaviour. Data on criminal behaviour in research may not always reflect the actual field situation (Hunt 1990). For example, studies on the association between substance abuse and criminal behaviour may focus on the general population, resulting in data that are more representative of 'typical' behaviour, but may only include a small subset of people with serious substance abuse problems. Alternatively, studies may focus on a specific sample of substance abusers, which is useful in obtaining detailed information about seriously deviant behaviour but cannot be generalized to a broader sample (Chaiken and Chaiken 1990). Furthermore, scholars can examine a variety of factors to measure criminal behaviour, including criminal justice system data such as arrest rates, convictions or the prison population, or self-report data (Hunt 1990). All these may provide a slightly different view of the actual amount of criminal behaviour, but they may also all be inaccurate. For example, criminal justice system records may underestimate a subject's involvement in crime. Self-reports, however, can be distorted as subjects may conceal or exaggerate their illegal activities, have difficulty recalling past behaviour, or find it difficult to understand the questions asked (Chaiken and Chaiken 1990). This is especially true when focusing on substance abuse: data reflecting substance abuse and criminal behaviour can be somewhat distorted, as people who are abusing drugs when committing a crime may be apprehended more easily than people who are not (Hunt 1990). As phrased by Hunt: '[b]oth drug users and offenders are hidden populations; portions of both are inaccessible to research, and truly random samples are beyond the reach of most studies' (Hunt 1990:160). These methodological challenges should be taken into consideration throughout this chapter.

34.3 THEORIES ON SUBSTANCE ABUSE AND CRIME

Substance users are not a uniform group and many users do not commit crimes (Nordstrom and Dackis 2011). Criminally active substance users are not a uniform group, either: for some, substance abuse precedes crime; for others, it succeeds crime; and for still others, they occur simultaneously. This has resulted in three leading theories on the association between substance abuse and crime: 1) substance abuse leads to crime; 2) crime leads to substance abuse; and 3) substance abuse and crime have common causes (Nordstrom and Dackis 2011). Scholars have found evidence for each of these theories. For example, to earn money to obtain drugs, drug users may resort to robbery or other property crimes (McGlothlin et al. 1978). Additionally, criminally active adolescents may find themselves among deviant peers who introduce them to the world of illicit substances (Nordstrom and Dackis 2011). Moreover, family factors such as adverse childhood experiences are risk factors both for criminal behaviour and for the development of a substance use disorder (Dube et al. 2003; Andrews and Bonta 2010).

Goldstein (1985) has developed a conceptual tripartite framework on how substance abuse leads to crime, comprising three models: the economic-compulsive model, the psychopharmacological model and the systemic model. The economic-compulsive model entails the situation described above, in which a substance abuser commits a crime in order to sustain the expensive habit of substance use. To do so, the substance abuser may resort to predatory crimes, such as (violent) property crime, in which they steal either the substance itself or money or property to acquire the substance (Chaiken and Chaiken 1990). Other possible economic-compulsive crimes are consensual crimes, in which both the perpetrator and the 'victim' engage in criminal behaviour. One example is drug dealing, where the offender (dealer) and the 'victim' (buyer) both participate in an illegal act (Hunt 1990). It should be mentioned that the crimes committed in this model may serve not only to acquire the substance but also to support the substance abuser in other life necessities. According to the psychopharmacological model, substances directly affect behaviour by reducing inhibitions and prompting aggression, often leading to criminal infractions (Goldstein 1985). In the systemic model, the relationship between criminal behaviour and substance abuse can be explained by the traditionally violent nature of the drug market and trafficking industries (Goldstein 1985). Here one may imagine rival gang disputes, retaliations (for example for fake drug sales, failing to pay debts, or robberies of drug dealers) and the elimination of police witnesses. Many users become involved in drug dealing (e.g., economic-compulsive model) and may therefore also become involved in systemic violence (Hunt 1990).

Originally, the tripartite framework was developed to illustrate the relationship between violence and substance abuse, but it can be argued that other types of crime also fit into the models. For example, a property crime committed to obtain money to buy drugs (economic-compulsive model) does not necessarily have to be violent. Furthermore, not every type of substance fits within each separate model. For example, the relationship between the psychopharmacological effects of alcohol and violence is quite apparent (Boles and Miotto 2003), but for opioids the research findings are less clear. Likewise, for cocaine or opioids, the economic-compulsive model is evident, but it seems less obvious that someone would resort to crime to purchase alcohol, if only because alcohol is so much easier to obtain. Lastly, it is important to keep in mind that the models are not mutually exclusive and that multiple models may apply to a single situation. For example, a heroin addict who wants to commit a robbery to be able to procure drugs (economic-compulsive model) may first drink large amounts of alcohol to remove impulse control and thereby encourage themselves to do so (psychopharmacological model; Goldstein 1985).

These theories provide a solid theoretical background for this chapter. Next, the main part of this chapter focuses on 1) how substance abuse develops, and which risk factors play a role; 2) how substance abuse affects self-control; 3) how self-control affects criminal behaviour; and 4) how substance abuse relates to violence.

34.4 THE DEVELOPMENT OF SUBSTANCE ABUSE

Over the past century, many social and neurobiological scientists have researched the factors that predict and influence the onset of substance abuse. This section will discuss these risk factors under three broad categories: impulsivity, social influences and genetics. In addition, scholars have researched the factors that influence the persistence of substance abuse, and this section discusses how these factors may hinder someone from managing or overcoming their substance abuse.

34.4.1 *Impulsivity*

Impulsivity has received substantial interest as a contributing factor to the development of substance abuse (Hyman 2007; Hester et al. 2010; Coskunpinar et al. 2013; Smith et al. 2014). Psychologists view impulsivity as a multidimensional construct consisting of several independent, interactive processes, including lack of persistence, novelty-seeking, reward dependence, risk-taking, inattention and negative urgency (Evenden 1999; Coskunpinar et al. 2013). The two most commonly identified processes are impaired decision-making and impaired behavioural inhibitory control (De Wit 2009). In the DSM-V, impaired control is implicated in the criteria for the diagnosis of a substance use disorder by 'often taking the substance in larger amounts or over a longer period than was intended' and 'reporting multiple unsuccessful efforts to decrease or discontinue use' (APA 2013:483). Furthermore, research has found that impulsivity is a pre-existing marker of vulnerability for substance use disorders (Verdejo-García et al. 2008). Impulsivity contributes to the onset of drug use, as people with more impulsive traits are more likely to experiment with drugs, use drugs more regularly and develop a substance use disorder (De Wit 2009). A meta-analysis (a comprehensive statistical review of existing studies) by Coskunpinar et al. (2013) sought to examine the effects of different constructs of impulsivity (i.e., lack of perseverance, lack of planning, sensation-seeking, negative urgency and positive urgency) on alcohol use. For alcohol-related problems and dependence, the largest effects were found for lack of planning and negative urgency (the tendency to act rashly when experiencing extreme negative emotions). Overall, these findings show that impulsivity can be regarded as a risk factor for the development of substance abuse.

34.4.2 *Social Influences*

Research has found that substance abuse is also associated with social influences. Studies have for instance found a relationship between substance abuse and several negative childhood and familial circumstances, such as physical or sexual abuse (Kendall-Tackett et al. 1993; Heffernan et al. 2000; Kendler et al. 2000) and familial alcoholism (Chassin et al. 2004). Furthermore, a large study has found that adverse childhood experiences (e.g., childhood abuse, neglect or household dysfunction) have a strong and gradually increasing relationship with drug use problems, indicating that the greater the number of adverse experiences a child is involved in, the greater the likelihood of drug use problems (Dube et al. 2003). To illustrate, the authors found that when a person experiences five or more adverse childhood experiences (e.g., parental divorce, emotional or physical neglect and abuse, and having an incarcerated household member), they are seven to ten times more likely to report problems with illicit drug use, addiction and parenteral (injected) drug use compared to someone with no adverse childhood experiences. Significantly, 42 per cent of the respondents reported having two or more adverse experiences, illustrating that a large group of people has an increased risk of developing a drug use problem. Furthermore, Dube et al. (2003) have found that adverse childhood experiences are most strongly associated with initiation of drug use by the age of fourteen. This is a key point, as King and Chassin (2007) have found that early drug use increases the likelihood of drug dependence by young adulthood. Moreover, research indicates that the relationship between social influences and substance abuse can be both direct and indirect. For example, scholars have found that familial alcoholism may lead to increased impulsivity (Chassin et al. 2004). As impulsivity is a major contributor to the development of substance abuse, familial alcoholism may lead to substance abuse both directly and indirectly, mediated by impulsivity. Altogether, it can be concluded that social influences, particularly those pertaining to familial and household circumstances, can strongly increase the likelihood of developing problems related to substance abuse.

34.4.3 *Genetics*

Another factor that contributes to the risk of developing a substance use disorder is genetic heritability. Heritability is the proportion of the variance in the population that can be attributed to genes (Agrawal and Lynskey 2008). The other contributing factor is environmental variation, including shared environment and non-shared environment.[1] Numerous large studies have sought to assess heritability by comparing mono- and dizygotic twin pairs. Among both male and female twin pairs, scholars have found that heritability for alcoholism ranges from 50 per cent to 70 per cent (e.g., Heath 1995; Prescott and Kendler 1999; Tsuang et al. 2001). Furthermore, for cannabis (34–78 per cent; e.g., Agrawal and Lynskey 2006) and other illicit drugs (22–87 per cent; e.g., Tsuang et al. 1996; Kendler and Prescott 1998; Kendler et al. 1999), genetic influences can play a large role. Moreover, research has found that people who suffer from substance abuse or dependence are by nature less sensitive to natural rewards, which is associated with a genetic variant that causes a reduction of dopamine receptors and dopamine activity in the brain (Volkow et al. 2002; Franken et al. 2006; Lee et al. 2007). This is in turn linked to impulsivity (Lee et al. 2009; Ghahremani et al. 2012) and increased substance-seeking behaviour (Volkow et al. 2002).

Genes play a role not only in the initiation of drug use but also in the passage from substance use or abuse to addiction and relapse. Moreover, previously mentioned risk factors

[1] In this context, shared environment encompasses environmental factors that one has in common with another person (e.g., shared household circumstances between siblings). Non-shared environment includes all factors that make people different from each other (e.g., different social groups or education; Agrawal and Lynskey 2008).

such as impulsivity and risk-taking also have a partial genetic basis (Kreek et al. 2005). However, it should be noted that genetic vulnerability does not imply that a substance use disorder will always occur. Currently, research focuses on the interaction between genes and environment (Agrawal and Lynskey 2008). Scholars have found that some genetic predispositions are only expressed under certain circumstances. For example, marriage may be a safeguard for genetic predisposition to alcoholism (Heath et al. 1989). Additionally, a study by Rose et al. (2001) found that heritability for alcohol consumption frequency was higher for adolescent twins living in an urban versus a rural neighbourhood. The authors argue that this is most likely due to the greater degree of religiosity and social contact in rural neighbourhoods, thereby increasing the portion of shared environment in the variance and limiting the impact of heritability. Thus, it should be kept in mind that genes and environment do not act independently of each other (Agrawal and Lynskey 2008).

34.4.4 *Desisting From and Managing Substance Abuse*

From choice theorists' perspective, people continue to abuse substances to seek pleasure and to avoid the uncomfortable feeling of withdrawal (Kennett et al. 2015). Even though there are some clear risk factors for the development of substance abuse, some scholars argue that people are still capable of desisting from the substance or at least of managing their use (e.g., Heyman 2009; Morse 2011). Morse (2017) reasons that people who continue their substance use do so intentionally, despite the fact that it may result in criminal behaviour. Arguments to support this involve cases of people who abstain from drugs whenever the market price rises or police are present (Morse 2011), or who eventually quit their substance habit without treatment and were thus not incapable of controlling themselves and their behaviour (Heyman 2009). By contrast, Baumeister et al. (1998) have proposed that people indeed are able to regulate themselves, but that this self-control is a limited resource. Substance users may initially be able to control themselves and refrain from using a substance, but eventually the cognitive resource of self-control becomes exhausted (ego-depletion; Baumeister et al. 1998) and their powers of resistance become overwhelmed. Furthermore, although there may be people who abstain from drugs without any treatment, there is also a significant group of substance abusers who continue their use, despite severe physical, social and psychological consequences, knowing that it might even result in their death (Kennett et al. 2015). Thus, it seems that desisting from and managing substance abuse is not a matter of course for everyone.

The incapacity to manage substance abuse can be explained by neurobiology, specifically the brain reward system. The reward system consists of the brain parts that are responsible for the feeling of reward, motivational aspects, memory and control over the eventual behaviour (for the specific brain regions, see Goldstein and Volkow 2002). This system is responsible for the reinforcement of behaviour that promotes survival and reproduction (Bozarth 1994). Dopamine has an important function in the reward system (Baler and Volkow 2006). Dopamine is a neurotransmitter, an organic chemical substance that exists naturally in the brain. It plays a role in experiencing the feeling of pleasure and is also associated with the pleasurable effect of substances (Franken et al. 2005). Substances elicit very complex effects in many diverse brain areas, and the pharmacological mechanisms by which the reward system is affected differ for each class of substance (APA 2013).[2] Ultimately, however, all

[2] For a more detailed explanation of the effects of different types of substances on the brain reward system, see Baler and Volkow (2006).

substances influence the levels of dopamine that are present in the brain (Hyman 2007). This can lead to long-term effects on the brain, in the form of lasting neurological changes in the reward system (Baler and Volkow 2006). For example, Hyman (2007) has noted that, similar to natural rewards, substances can cause the release of dopamine into the brain, but on a larger scale. Hereby, the substances influence the brain's reward system so that every time the person takes the substance, the brain receives a signal that it is 'better than expected', resulting in increased motivation for substance-seeking behaviour. The large amounts of dopamine that are present in the brain due to the substance can result in a sensitization of the dopamine system (Berridge 2009). As a consequence, the intensity of 'wanting' the substance may exceed the expectations of how much someone will like the substance, and outlast all feelings of withdrawal. Therefore, even after the symptoms of physical withdrawal have passed, a person can still relapse (Kennett et al. 2015).

34.5 EFFECTS OF SUBSTANCE ABUSE ON SELF-CONTROL AND CRIMINAL BEHAVIOUR

The next question that this chapter addresses is whether substance abuse impairs human behaviour and one's capacity to comply with the law. This is a core question to understand the relationship between substance abuse and crime. This section focuses on how substance abuse affects people's ability to control themselves. The subsequent section will then link (lack of) self-control to criminal behaviour.

34.5.1 *Self-Control*

Following the law and self-managing one's behaviour require some form of self-control. Self-control can be defined as 'the overriding or inhibiting of automatic, habitual, or innate behaviours, urges, emotions or desires that would otherwise interfere with goal-directed behaviour' (Muraven et al. 2006:524). The prefrontal cortex (PFC), a brain area responsible for executive functions such as planning and decision-making, plays an important role in the exertion of self-control (Goldstein and Volkow 2011; Cohen et al. 2013). The chronic effects of substance abuse may lead to structural changes in the PFC (e.g., grey matter reductions) that result in impaired behavioural self-control (Goldstein and Volkow 2011).

An important component of the self-control of behaviour is impulsivity. Impulsivity may not only affect the development of substance abuse; it can also influence criminal behaviour as a consequence of substance abuse. Research has found that levels of impulsivity are high in individuals with a history of substance abuse, and that these individuals are impaired on tasks that require inhibitory control or decision-making (De Wit 2009). For example, on a delayed reward discounting task, scholars have found that, compared to controls, substance abusers have an increased tendency to prefer a smaller, more immediate reward over a larger but delayed reward, indicating impaired decision-making (for a meta-analysis of forty-six studies on several different substances, see MacKillop et al. 2011). Furthermore, research has found that substance abusers have greater difficulty in inhibiting a response that has already been initiated, while there is no impairment of their ability to execute responses in terms of speed and accuracy (e.g., the stop-signal task; Logan 1994). Smith et al. (2014) analysed ninety-seven studies on substance abuse and response inhibition and found that impairments in inhibitory control and substance use disorders for most substances are associated; only for cannabis and opioid use did the authors find no association with impairments in inhibitory control.

Within this research, it remains unclear whether the impulsivity traits were already present before the substance abuse, or whether they are a direct consequence of the substance. Several scholars have examined the acute effects of substances on impulsivity (see De Wit 2009). However, this research has limitations, as, due to the aforementioned ethical reasons, it is restricted to testing the effects of substance use, rather than abuse or SUD. Research has found that alcohol reduces inhibitory control even at doses that do not lead to an overall impairment in cognitive functioning (Field et al. 2010). Furthermore, moderate doses of alcohol have been found to impair performance on a response-inhibition task (i.e., the stop-signal task), by reducing the frequency of inhibiting responses and increasing the time needed to inhibit a response (Fillmore 2003). For cocaine, similar effects have been found (Fillmore and Rush 2002). Conversely, psychostimulants such as methylphenidate (Ritalin) or d-amphetamine have been found to improve response inhibition (De Wit et al. 2000), consistent with results found in children treated for attention-deficit/hyperactivity disorder (ADHD) with this class of drugs (De Wit 2009). However, these effects seem to be confined to a specific dose (amount) of the substance (Fillmore 2003). For delayed reward discounting tasks, scholars have failed to find effects of acute drug administration (De Wit 2009). It therefore seems that, of the impulsivity traits, behavioural inhibition is more sensitive to acute drug effects than impaired decision-making. However, as mentioned earlier, these studies are not specific to substance abuse. A different method by which to study the acute effects of substance abuse is to use animal studies. For example, a laboratory animal study has found that chronic drug use may lead to cognitive dysfunction in regions of the PFC that can result in incapacity in response inhibition (Jentsch and Taylor 1999). In another animal study, Logue et al. (1992) found that exposing rats to a prolonged period of cocaine use reduced their preference for later, but larger, rewards. Similar effects on delayed reward discounting have been found for alcohol (De Wit and Mitchell 2010). In conclusion, the findings are inconsistent across tasks and types of substances, and the effects of substance abuse on self-control may therefore differ among individuals. However, in general the scientific findings show that substance abuse can influence levels of self-control and may stimulate increases in impulsive behaviour (De Wit 2009).

34.5.2 *Criminal Behaviour*

Now that we know that there is a link between substance abuse and impulsivity and self-control, the next question addresses the connection between increased impulsivity and criminal behaviour. In criminology, the major theory on this subject is *A General Theory of Crime* by Gottfredson and Hirschi (1990). The authors propose that a lack of self-control – in combination with criminal opportunity – is the major cause of crime. Neither self-control nor opportunity is a standalone cause of crime. Rather, it is the interaction between the two that underlies criminality. Self-control, in the view of Gottfredson and Hirschi (1990), is a personality construct that is caused by early childhood family factors. Negative factors, such as deficient behavioural monitoring by one's parents, failure to detect deviant behaviour and a lack of punishment for such behaviour, underlie a lack of self-control (Grasmick et al. 1993). Following Gottfredson and Hirschi (1990), people with low self-control are more vulnerable to temptations of the moment; when their desires are at odds with their long-term goals, people with greater self-control will be able to restrain themselves, while those lacking self-control will choose immediate desires. Self-control comprises several factors, including impulsivity, risk-seeking and lack of perseverance. According to Gottfredson and

Hirschi (1990), these are not independent factors that separately explain self-control, but together they form the unidimensional construct of self-control.[3] This differs from the substance abuse literature, which has focused more on impulsivity by itself and the distinct, independent processes that underlie it (Evenden 1999). Moreover, in the substance abuse literature, aforementioned factors such as risk-seeking and lack of perseverance are regarded as part of the independent processes within impulsivity (Evenden 1999). Furthermore, increased impulsivity is not regarded as solely derived from a dysfunctional childhood education, as in Gottfredson and Hirschi's (1990) research, but as at least partly caused by genetic and neurobiological factors (Kreek et al. 2005; Goldstein and Volkow 2011). Lastly, self-control is regarded as a more dynamic and changeable trait (e.g., Baumeister and Vonasch 2015), compared to the relatively stable trait that is established in childhood in Gottfredson and Hirschi's (1990) theory. Nevertheless, *A General Theory of Crime* has proved useful in explaining the substance abuse–crime relationship through self-control and (different dimensions of) impulsivity.

Several researchers have empirically tested Gottfredson and Hirschi's (1990) theory and have found that low self-control is indeed an important factor in explaining criminal behaviour (for meta-analyses, see Pratt and Cullen 2000 or Vazsonyi et al. 2017).[4] Scholars have also examined the effects of the underlying processes of impulsivity. For example, Dahlbäck (1990) found criminality and risk-taking to be related, especially under circumstances where detection was more uncertain. More specifically, when detection was extremely likely (i.e., no opportunity) or very unlikely, the level of self-control did not affect criminal behaviour. This is in line with research by Grasmick et al. (1993), who found that although the interaction between self-control and opportunity indeed affected crime, opportunity also had an isolated effect. To summarize, in line with Gottfredson and Hirschi (1990), a lack of self-control can be an important explanatory factor for criminal behaviour (Pratt and Cullen 2000). Therefore, through its impairing effect on self-control, substance abuse may indirectly reduce one's capacity to comply, potentially leading to illegal behaviour.[5]

34.6 SUBSTANCE ABUSE AND VIOLENCE

Next to illegal behaviour in general, a significant number of researchers have specifically focused on the link between substance use (or abuse) and violent behaviour (see Duke et al. 2018). This relationship is pronounced: in many violent events, alcohol and drugs are present in both the offenders and the victims (Boles and Miotto 2003). Furthermore, specific forms of violence are illegal in themselves. Thus, through their potential effects on violence, substance abuse and (in)capacity for legal compliance are directly related.

Given that different substances have different effects on violent behaviour, most research discusses the effects separately by type of substance (e.g., Boles and Miotto 2003) and this

[3] For more detailed information on self-control theory, see Chapter 33 in this volume.

[4] Chapter 33 discusses the empirical status of Gottfredson and Hirschi's theory in more detail.

[5] Apart from how substance abuse leads to criminal behaviour through low self-control, scholars have also looked at how the effects of substance abuse can be linked to criminal behaviour through the impaired brain reward system. The excess of dopamine in the brain reward system that is present due to the substance causes the substance to become overvalued compared to other (rational) goals, such as family or work obligations, self-care and compliance with the law (Hyman 2007). Thus, when prolonged substance abuse alters the brain reward system, substance seeking becomes a primary motivator, despite its adverse consequences (Volkow and Li 2004). This may result in extreme compulsive behaviour to obtain the substance, such as committing an economic-compulsive or violent crime.

section will do so accordingly. Violent behaviour can occur during the various phases of substance use, such as acute intoxication, withdrawal, or substance-induced psychosis. Furthermore, violence may occur both in individuals who do and in those who do not suffer from a substance use disorder (Boles and Miotto 2003). Although this chapter focuses on substance abuse rather than use, it is difficult to make a clear distinction between the two when discussing the relationship with violence. Therefore, this section will discuss the psychopharmacological effects of the use of different types of substances in general.

When examining the acute effects of intoxication on violence, scholars have consistently found a complex relationship between the two (Fagan 1990). For example, the association between violence and substance use is mediated by shared common causes such as a negative family situation (e.g., harsh punishment, lack of parental supervision, aggression or substance abuse in the family), or psychopathology (such as anti-social personality disorder). Furthermore, it should be mentioned that the best predictor for future violence is a history of violent behaviour. Accordingly, few studies have found aggressive behaviour not to precede substance abuse (Fagan 1990). For instance, Warshaw and Messite (1996) have found that many people act violently when under the influence of substances, but this effect is more pronounced for people who already behave violently when sober. In addition, some scholars argue that substances such as alcohol merely serve as a triggering mechanism to prompt violent acts in people who already have a tendency to be violent, and find themselves in situations that may lead to aggression (e.g., fight-bars; Boles and Miotto 2003). Nevertheless, this section will discuss the substance–violence relationship to examine whether there is a direct connection between the substance and the violent behaviour that may affect one's capacity for legal compliance.

The most commonly cited substance related to violence is alcohol (Boles and Miotto 2003). When considering the specific effects of alcohol on violence, there is evidence that it reduces inhibitions of (for example) fear. As a result, the capacity to plan behaviour in response to threatening situations may decrease, potentially resulting in violent behaviour (Boles and Miotto 2003). Moreover, alcohol can influence neurochemical systems that mediate violent behaviour (Miczek et al. 1993).

The most pronounced link with violence and drugs has been found for stimulants such as (meth)amphetamines and cocaine (Boles and Miotto 2003). For methamphetamines in particular, scholars have found that chronic use can lead to prolonged and persistent psychosis, including paranoia, hallucinations and impaired reality testing (Fischman and Haney 1999). In a meta-analysis of 204 studies, Douglas et al. (2009) have found that psychosis is a risk factor for violence to others. The findings show that psychosis is associated with a 49–68 per cent increase in the likelihood of engaging in violence relative to the likelihood in the absence of psychosis. Specifically, the so-called 'positive symptoms' of psychosis, including paranoia and suspiciousness, are related to increased odds of violent behaviour (Douglas et al. 2009). Scholars have found that chronic amphetamine use can lead to frightening delusions, hypervigilance and hyperawareness, which are related to the positive symptoms of psychosis that can result in violence (Fischman and Haney 1999). Fischman and Haney (1999) have also examined the effects of cocaine on violence, finding that use or abuse of (intranasal) cocaine can lead to more short-duration psychosis, with similar characteristics to psychosis resulting from (meth)amphetamines, potentially also leading to violence. The association between crack cocaine and violence is greater than for intranasal cocaine, as the rapid onset and offset of the intoxication effects are expected to cause higher levels of irritation and aggression (Fischman and Haney 1999).

Contrary to stimulant drugs, marijuana or opioids tend to depress activity (Boles and Miotto 2003). With marijuana, there is some evidence that the substance can induce psychiatric symptoms, such as paranoia, anxiety, panic attacks and psychosis, but this has been found only in individuals who already have a predisposition to psychiatric illness (Gold and Tullis 1999). When taken in high doses, marijuana can have psychoactive effects, resulting in paranoia with suspiciousness and delusions that may lead to violence. However, marijuana use in small doses has been found to (temporarily) inhibit violent responses and, in general, scholars have concluded that marijuana use either reduces violent behaviour or leaves it unaffected (Reiss and Roth 1993). With opioids, there is no evidence of a link with violent behaviour, apart from the effects caused by withdrawal (Roth 1994). It is more likely that opioids temporarily inhibit such behaviour. During withdrawal, however, opioid-dependent individuals experience agitation, aggression, craving, irritability, anxiety and physical pain. This may result in overly defensive and aggressive responses to provocative situations (Roth 1994), and possibly violent attempts to obtain more drugs to reduce the withdrawal symptoms (Goldstein 1985).

Thus, the findings on different types of substances are ambiguous (Parker and Auerhahn 1998). However, Duke et al. (2018) have identified and statistically reviewed thirty-two meta-analyses, showing that the combined use of alcohol and illicit drugs increases the association between substance use and violence relative to alcohol use alone.[6] Moreover, with regard to substance abuse specifically, there is evidence that as drug and alcohol use becomes more abusive, the strength of the relationship between violence and substance use increases (Fagan 1990). Overall, research has shown that substance use and abuse (in particular of alcohol and stimulant drugs) are associated with increases in violent behaviour (Boles and Miotto 2003), although this effect is more pronounced in individuals who already have violent tendencies when sober (Fagan 1990). In general, these findings suggest that substances can influence the capacity for legal compliance and may cause violent (criminal) behaviour.

34.7 CONCLUSION AND RECOMMENDATIONS

This chapter has reviewed the existing evidence on whether substance abuse affects the capacity to control one's behaviour and comply with the law. Throughout the chapter, the impairment of self-control and impulsivity have played a major role, both as risk factors for the development of substance abuse and as consequences of substance abuse. The findings suggest that substance abuse impairs self-control and increases impulsivity. In doing so, substance abuse may cause people to become unable to control their behaviour and impair their capacity for legal compliance. Moreover, some substances can directly provoke violent and aggressive behaviour, which may lead to violent crimes.

The relationship between substance abuse and capacity for legal compliance requires some nuance. Specifically, if substances have a direct effect on the brain, why do individual responses to them vary? Here it is important to keep in mind that context is everything. Situational factors may explain the variability between substance abusers in their propensity to engage in criminal behaviour. For example, one's social environment has been found to be a much more powerful contributor to violent behaviour than pharmacological

6 Duke et al. (2018) used a combined measure of all types of illicit drugs, providing an overall image of the effects of combined alcohol and drug use. Conclusions regarding the specific effects of different types of illicit drugs in combination with alcohol use cannot be drawn from this study.

effects linked to both cocaine and alcohol (Parker and Auerhahn 1998). Furthermore, as mentioned earlier, criminal opportunity is an important factor in explaining the relationship between self-control and crime (Grasmick et al. 1993). This, in combination with individual susceptibility to impulsive and/or violent behaviour, has a major effect on one's propensity to engage in crime as well as the extent to which substance abuse affects the capacity to legally comply. Moreover, other theories on how substance abuse and crime are associated, such as the systemic or economic-compulsive model (Goldstein 1985), should not be disregarded when trying to find an explanation or resolution for the large numbers of substance-related crimes.

As mentioned at the beginning of this chapter, the goal here is not to propose that existing findings regarding capacity imply that substance abuse is an excuse for breaking the law. Among scholars of substance abuse and criminal behaviour, there exists a debate concerning whether offenders with a substance use disorder are responsible for their actions (Morse 2017) or not (Kennett et al. 2015). Scholars tend to assess this from an *ex post* viewpoint: how should we respond to the past criminal behaviour of the substance-abusing offender? By contrast, this contribution advocates taking an *ex ante* viewpoint and focusing on how legal incentives can be used to enhance future compliance with the law. In this regard, the main objective is not to determine whether a person is responsible for their actions or not but rather to increase their capacity to comply and prevent illegal behaviour in the future. The next question is thus how this can be achieved, and how we can direct and change future behaviour.

This chapter has illustrated that there is a relationship between substance abuse and crime. To change behaviour and facilitate compliance, it may therefore be useful to address substance abuse directly. A possible intervention is substance abuse treatment. Scholars have focused on the effects of substance abuse treatment on criminal behaviour, studying recidivism in particular (Weekes et al. 2013). Meta-analyses have revealed interesting insights regarding, for example, the effects of different types of treatment (Latimer et al. 2006; Mitchell et al. 2007) and mandated versus voluntary treatment (Parhar et al. 2008; Werb et al. 2016). Importantly, an effective programme should focus on the principles of risk, need and responsivity (RNR) from Andrews and Bonta's (2010) *The Psychology of Criminal Conduct* (Weekes et al. 2013). RNR programmes are tailored to offenders' risks of reoffending as well as their criminogenic needs (e.g., work, family, personal factors). Moreover, it is crucial to select a programme to which the offender is responsive. Personal factors such as stress and family dysfunction that may undermine the efficacy of the intervention should be taken into account (Volkow and Li 2004). Lastly, it is important to develop and administer programmes specifically focused on improving self-control, for example through incorporating medicinal interventions or behavioural training to control inhibition (Smith et al. 2014). In this manner, even if the offender is fully responsible for their behaviour, we can serve both offender and society best.

REFERENCES

Agrawal, A., and M. T. Lynskey. 2006. "The Genetic Epidemiology of Cannabis Use, Abuse and Dependence." *Addiction* 101 (6):801–12.

2008. "Are There Genetic Influences on Addiction [*sic*]: Evidence from Family, Adoption and Twin Studies." *Addiction* 103 (7): 1069–81.

American Psychiatric Association (APA). 1994. *Diagnostic and Statistical Manual of Mental Disorders* (4th ed.). Arlington, VA: American Psychiatric Association.

2013. "Substance-Related and Addictive Disorders." In *Diagnostic and Statistical Manual of Mental Disorders* (5th ed.). Arlington, VA: American Psychiatric Association.

Andrews, D. A., and J. Bonta. 2010. *The Psychology of Criminal Conduct* (5th ed.). New Providence, NJ: Matthew Bender and Company, Inc.

Baler, R. D., and N. D. Volkow. 2006. "Drug Addiction: The Neurobiology of Disrupted Self-Control." *Trend in Molecular Medicine* 12 (12):559–66.

Baumeister, R. F., and A. J. Vonasch. 2015. "Uses of Self-Regulation to Facilitate and Restrain Addictive Behavior." *Addictive Behaviors* 44:3–8.

Baumeister, R. F., E. Bratslavsky, M. Muraven, and D. M. Tice. 1998. "Ego Depletion: Is the Active Self a Limited Resource?" *Journal of Personality and Social Psychology* 74 (5):1252–65.

Berridge, K. C. 2009. "Wanting and Liking: Observations from the Neuroscience and Psychology Laboratory." *Inquiry* 52 (4):378–98.

Boles, S. M., and K. Miotto. 2003. "Substance Abuse and Violence: A Review of the Literature." *Aggression and Violent Behavior* 8 (2):155–74.

Bozarth, M. A. 1994. "Pleasure Systems in the Brain." In *Pleasure: The Politics and the Reality*, edited by D. M. Warburton, 5–14. New York: John Wiley and Sons.

Chaiken, J. M., and M. R. Chaiken. 1990. "Drugs and Predatory Crime." In *Drugs and Crime*, edited by M. Tonry and J. Q. Wilson, 203–40. Chicago: University of Chicago Press.

Chassin, L., D. B. Flora, and K. M. King. 2004. "Trajectories of Alcohol and Drug Use and Dependence from Adolescence to Adulthood: The Effects of Familial Alcoholism and Personality." *Journal of Abnormal Psychology* 113 (4):483–98.

Chatwin, C. 2017. "UNGASS 2016: Insights from Europe on the Development of Global Cannabis Policy and the Need for Reform of the Global Drug Policy Regime." *International Journal of Drug Policy* 49:80–5.

Cohen, J. R., E. T. Berkman, and M. D. Lieberman. 2013. "Intentional and Incidental Self-Control in Ventrolateral PFC." In *Principles of Frontal Lobe Function* (2nd ed.), edited by D. T. Stuss and R. T. Knight, 417–40. New York: Oxford University Press.

Coskunpinar, A., A. L. Dir, and M. A. Cyders. 2013. "Multidimensionality in Impulsivity and Alcohol Use: A Meta-analysis Using the UPPS Model of Impulsivity." *Alcoholism: Clinical and Experimental Research* 37 (9):1441–50.

Dahlbäck, O. 1990. "Criminality and Risk-Taking." *Personality and Individual Difference* 11 (3):265–72.

De Wit, H. 2009. "Impulsivity as a Determinant and Consequence of Drug Use: A Review of Underlying Processes." *Addiction Biology* 14 (1):22–31.

De Wit, H., and S. H. Mitchell. 2010. "Drug Effects on Delay Discounting." In *Impulsivity: Theory, Science and Neuroscience of Discounting*, edited by G. Madden, W. Bickel and T. Critchfield, 213–41. Washington, DC: American Psychological Association.

De Wit, H., J. Crean, and J. B. Richards. 2000. "Effects of D-Amphetamine and Ethanol on a Measure of Behavioral Inhibition in Humans." *Behavioral Neuroscience* 114 (4):830–7.

Douglas, K. S., L. S. Guy, and S. D. Hart. 2009. "Psychosis as a Risk Factor for Violence to Others: A Meta-analysis." *Psychological Bulletin* 135 (5):679–706.

Dube, S. R., V. J. Felitti, M. Dong, D. P. Chapman, W. H. Giles, and R. F. Anda. 2003. "Childhood Abuse, Neglect, and Household Dysfunction and the Risk of Illicit Drug Use: The Adverse Childhood Experiences Study." *Pediatrics* 111 (3):564–72.

Duke, A. A., K. M. Smith, L. Oberleitner, A. Westphal, and S. A. McKee. 2018. "Alcohol, Drugs, and Violence: A Meta-meta-analysis." *Psychology of Violence* 8 (2):238–49.

Evenden, J. L. 1999. "Varieties of Impulsivity." *Psychopharmacology* 146 (4):348–61.

Fagan, J. 1990. "Intoxication and Aggression." In *Drugs and Crime*, edited by M. Tonry and J. Q. Wilson, 241–320. Chigaco: University of Chicago Press.

Fazel, S., P. Bains, and H. Doll. 2006. "Substance Abuse and Dependence in Prisoners: A Systematic Review." *Addiction* 101 (2):181–91.

Field, M., R. W. Wiers, P. Christiansen, M. T. Fillmore, and J. C. Verster. 2010. "Acute Alcohol Effects on Inhibitory Control and Implicit Cognition: Implications for Loss of Control over Drinking." *Alcoholism: Clinical and Experimental Research* 34 (8):1346–52.

Fillmore, M. T. 2003. "Drug Abuse as a Problem of Impaired Control: Current Approaches and Findings." *Behavioral Cognitive Neuroscience Reviews* 2 (3):179–97.

Fillmore, M. T., and C. R. Rush. 2002. "Impaired Inhibitory Control of Behavior in Chronic Cocaine Users." *Drug and Alcohol Dependence* 66 (3):265–73.
Fischman, M., and M. Haney. 1999. "Neurobiology of Stimulants." In *Textbook of Substance Abuse Treatment* (2nd ed.), edited by M. Galanter and H. D. Kleber, 21–31. Washington, DC: American Psychiatric Press.
Franken, I. H. A., J. Booij, and W. van den Brink. 2005. "The Role of Dopamine in Human Addiction: From Reward to Motivated Attention." *European Journal of Pharmacology* 526 (1–3):199–206.
Franken, I. H. A., P. Muris, and I. Georgieva. 2006. "Gray's Model of Personality and Addiction." *Addictive Behaviors* 31 (3):399–403.
Frone, M. R. 2006. "Prevalence and Distribution of Alcohol Use and Impairment in the Workplace: A US National Survey." *Journal of Studies on Alcohol* 67 (1):147–56.
Ghahremani, D. G., B. Lee, C. L. Robertson, G. Tabibnia, A. T. Morgan, N. De Shetler, A. K. Brown, J. R. Monterosso, A. R. Aron, and M. A. Mandelkern. 2012. "Striatal Dopamine D2/D3 Receptors Mediate Response Inhibition and Related Activity in Frontostriatal Neural Circuitry in Humans." *Journal of Neuroscience* 32 (21):7316–24.
Global Burden of Disease Collaborative Network. 2018. *Global Burden of Disease Study 2017 (GBD 2017) Results*. Institute for Health Metrics and Evaluation (IHME). http://ghdx.healthdata.org/gbd-results-tool.
Gold, M. S., and M. Tullis. 1999. "Cannabis." In *Textbook of Substance Abuse Treatment* (2nd ed.), edited by M. Galanter and H. D. Kleber, 165–81. Washington, DC: American Psychiatric Press.
Goldstein, P. J. 1985. "The Drugs/Violence Nexus: A Tripartite Conceptual Framework." *Journal of Drug Issues* 15 (4):493–506.
Goldstein, R. Z., and N. D. Volkow. 2002. "Drug Addiction and Its Underlying Neurobiological Basis: Neuroimaging Evidence for the Involvement of the Frontal Cortex." *American Journal of Psychiatry* 159 (10):1642–52.
2011. "Dysfunction of the Prefrontal Cortex in Addiction: Neuroimaging Findings and Clinical Implications." *Nature Reviews Neuroscience* 12 (11):652–69.
Gottfredson, M., and T. Hirschi. 1990. *A General Theory of Crime*. Stanford, CA: Stanford University Press.
Grasmick, H. G., C. R. Tittle, R. J. Bursik, and B. J. Arneklev. 1993. "Testing the Core Empirical Implications of Gottfredson and Hirschi's General Theory of Crime." *Journal of Research in Crime Delinquency* 30 (1):5–29.
Heath, A. C. 1995. "Genetic Influences on Alcoholism Risk." *Alcohol Health and Research World* 19:166–71.
Heath, A. C., R. Jardine, and N. G. Martin. 1989. "Interactive Effects of Genotype and Social Environment on Alcohol Consumption in Female Twins." *Journal of Studies on Alcohol* 50 (1):38–48.
Heffernan, K., M. Cloitre, K. Tardiff, P. M. Marzuk, L. Portera, and A. C. Leon. 2000. "Childhood Trauma as a Correlate of Lifetime Opiate Use in Psychiatric Patients." *Addictive Behaviors* 25 (5):797–803.
Henkel, D. 2011. "Unemployment and Substance Use: A Review of the Literature (1990–2010)." *Current Drug Abuse Reviews* 4 (1):4–27.
Hester, R., D. I. Lubman, and M. Yücel. 2010. "The Role of Executive Control in Human Drug Addiction." In *Behavioral Neuroscience of Drug Addiction*, edited by D. W. Self and J. K. Staley Gottschalk, 301–18. Berlin/Heidelberg: Springer.
Heyman, G. M. 2009. *Addiction: A Disorder of Choice*. Cambridge, MA: Harvard University Press.
Hunt, D. E. 1990. "Drugs and Consensual Crimes: Drug Dealing and Prostitution." In *Drugs and Crime*, edited by M. Tonry and J. Q. Wilson, 159–202. Chicago: University of Chicago Press.
Hyman, S. E. 2007. "The Neurobiology of Addiction: Implications for Voluntary Control of Behavior." *American Journal of Bioethics* 7 (1):8–11.
Jentsch, J. D., and J. R. Taylor. 1999. "Impulsivity Resulting from Frontostriatal Dysfunction in Drug Abuse: Implications for the Control of Behavior by Reward-Related Stimuli." *Psychopharmacology* 146 (4):373–90.
Kelly, J. F. 2004. "Toward an Addictionary: A Proposal for More Precise Terminology." *Alcoholism Treatment Quarterly* 22 (2):79–87.
Kendall-Tackett, K. A., L. M. Williams, and D. Finkelhor. 1993. "Impact of Sexual Abuse on Children: A Review and Synthesis of Recent Empirical Studies." *Psychological Bulletin* 113 (1):164–80.

Kendler, K. S., and C. A. Prescott. 1998. "Cocaine Use, Abuse and Dependence in a Population-Based Sample of Female Twins." *British Journal of Psychiatry* 173 (4):345–50.

Kendler, K. S., L. Karkowski, and C. A. Prescott. 1999. "Hallucinogen, Opiate, Sedative and Stimulant Use and Abuse in a Population-Based Sample of Female Twins." *Acta Psychiatrica Scandinavica* 99 (5):368–76.

Kendler, K. S., C. M. Bulik, J. Silberg, J. M. Hettema, J. Myers, and C. A. Prescott. 2000. "Childhood Sexual Abuse and Adult Psychiatric and Substance Use Disorders in Women: An Epidemiological and Cotwin Control Analysis." *Archives of General Psychiatry* 57 (10):953–9.

Kennett, J., N. A. Vincent, and A. Snoek. 2015. "Drug Addiction and Criminal Responsibility." In *Handbook of Neuroethics*, edited by J. Clausen and N. Levy, 1065–83. Dordrecht, NL: Springer Science.

King, K. M., and L. Chassin. 2007. "A Prospective Study of the Effects of Age of Initiation of Alcohol and Drug Use on Young Adult Substance Dependence." *Journal of Studies on Alcohol and Drugs* 68 (2):256–65.

Kreek, M. J., D. A. Nielsen, E. R. Butelman, and K. S. LaForge. 2005. "Genetic Influences on Impulsivity, Risk Taking, Stress Responsivity and Vulnerability to Drug Abuse and Addiction." *Nature Neuroscience* 8 (11):1450–7.

Latimer, J., K. Morton-Bourgon, and J.-A. Chrétien. 2006. *A Meta-analytic Examination of Drug Treatment Courts: Do They Reduce Recidivism?* Ottowa: Department of Justice Canada, Research and Statistics Division.

Lee, S. H., B.-J. Ham, Y.-H. Cho, S.-M. Lee, and S. H. Shim. 2007. "Association Study of Dopamine Receptor D2TaqI A Polymorphism and Reward-Related Personality Traits in Healthy Korean Young Females." *Neuropsychobiology* 56 (2–3):146–51.

Lee, B., E. D. London, R. A. Poldrack, J. Farahi, A. Nacca, J. R. Monterosso, J. A. Mumford, A. V. Bokarius, M. Dahlbom, and J. Mukherjee. 2009. "Striatal Dopamine d2/d3 Receptor Availability Is Reduced in Methamphetamine Dependence and Is Linked to Impulsivity." *Journal of Neuroscience* 29 (47):14734–40.

Logan, G. D. 1994. "On the Ability to Inhibit Thought and Action: A Users' Guide to the Stop Signal Paradigm." In *Inhibitory Process in Attention, Memory and Language*, edited by D. Dagenbach and T. H. Carr, 189–239. San Diego, CA: Academic Press.

Logue, A., H. Tobin, J. J. Chelonis, R. Y. Wang, N. Geary, and S. Schachter. 1992. "Cocaine Decreases Self-Control in Rats: A Preliminary Report." *Psychopharmacology* 109 (1–2):245–7.

MacKillop, J., M. T. Amlung, L. R. Few, L. A. Ray, L. H. Sweet, and M. R. Munafò. 2011. "Delayed Reward Discounting and Addictive Behavior: A Meta-analysis." *Psychopharmacology* 216 (3):305–21.

McGlothlin, W. H., M. D. Anglin, and B. D. Wilson. 1978. "Narcotic Addiction and Crime." *Criminology* 16 (3):293–316.

Miczek, K. A., E. M. Weerts, and J. F. DeBold. 1993. "Alcohol, Aggression and Violence: Biobehavioral Determinants." In *Alcohol and Interpersonal Violence: Fostering Multidisciplinary Perspectives*, edited by S. Martin, 83–119. Rockville, MD: US Department of Health and Human Services, Public Health Service, National Institutes of Health, National Institute on Alcohol Abuse and Alcoholism.

Mitchell, O., D. B. Wilson, and D. L. MacKenzie. 2007. "Does Incarceration-Based Drug Treatment Reduce Recidivism? A Meta-analytic Synthesis of the Research." *Journal of Experimental Criminology* 3 (4):353–75.

Morse, S. J. 2011. "Addiction and Criminal Responsibility." In *Addiction and Responsibility*, edited by J. Poland and G. Graham, 159–99. Cambridge, MA: MIT Press.

2017. "The Science of Addiction and Criminal Law." *Harvard Review of Psychiatry* 25 (6):261–9.

Mowen, T. J., and C. A. Visher. 2015. "Drug Use and Crime after Incarceration: The Role of Family Support and Family Conflict." *Justice Quarterly* 32 (2):337–59.

Muraven, M., D. Shmueli, and E. Burkley. 2006. "Conserving Self-Control Strength." *Journal of Personality and Social Psychology* 91 (3):524–37.

Nordstrom, B. R., and C. A. Dackis. 2011. "Drugs and Crime." *Journal of Psychiatry and Law* 39 (4):663–87.

Parhar, K. K., J. S. Wormith, D. M. Derkzen, and A. M. Beauregard. 2008. "Offender Coercion in Treatment: A Meta-analysis of Effectiveness." *Criminal Justice and Behavior* 35 (9):1109–35.

Parker, R. N., and K. Auerhahn. 1998. "Alcohol, Drugs, and Violence." *Annual Review of Sociology* 24 (1):291–311.
Pratt, T. C., and F. T. Cullen. 2000. "The Empirical Status of Gottfredson and Hirschi's General Theory of Crime: A Meta-analysis." *Criminology* 38 (3):931–64.
Prescott, C. A., and K. S. Kendler. 1999. "Genetic and Environmental Contributions to Alcohol Abuse and Dependence in a Population-Based Sample of Male Twins." *American Journal of Psychiatry* 156 (1):34–40.
Reiss, A. J., and J. A. Roth. 1993. "Alcohol, Other Psychoactive Drugs and Violence." In *Understanding and Preventing Violence* (Vol. 1), edited by A. Reiss and J. Roth, 182–220. Washington, DC: National Academy Press.
Rose, R. J., D. M. Dick, R. J. Viken, and J. Kaprio. 2001. "Gene-Environment Interaction in Patterns of Adolescent Drinking: Regional Residency Moderates Longitudinal Influences on Alcohol Use." *Alcoholism: Clinical Experimental Research* 25 (5):637–43.
Roth, J. A. 1994. *Psychoactive Substances and Violence*. Washington, DC: National Institute of Justice, Office of Justice Programs (February).
Schütz, C. G. 2016. "Homelessness and Addiction: Causes, Consequences and Interventions." *Current Treatment Options in Psychiatry* 3 (3):306–13.
Smith, D. E., and L. D. Davidson. 2015. "Strategies of Drug Prevention in the Workplace: An International Perspective of Drug Testing and Employee Assistance Programs (EAPs)." In *Textbook of Addiction Treatment: International Perspectives*, edited by N. el-Guebaly, G. Carrà and M. Galanter, 1111–27. Milan: Springer.
Smith, J. L., R. P. Mattick, S. D. Jamadar, and J. M. Iredale. 2014. "Deficits in Behavioural Inhibition in Substance Abuse and Addiction: A Meta-analysis." *Drug and Alcohol Dependence* 145:1–33.
Tsuang, M. T., M. J. Lyons, S. A. Eisen, J. Goldberg, W. True, N. Lin, J. M. Meyer, R. Toomey, S. V. Faraone, and L. Eaves. 1996. "Genetic Influences on DSM-III-R Drug Abuse and Dependence: A Study of 3,372 Twin Pairs." *American Journal of Medical Genetics* 67 (5):473–77.
Tsuang, M. T., J. L. Bar, R. M. Harley, and M. J. Lyons. 2001. "The Harvard Twin Study of Substance Abuse: What We Have Learned." *Harvard Review of Psychiatry* 9 (6):267–79.
Van Rooij, B., and A. Fine. in press. *The Invisible Code: Why Law Fails to Improve Our Behaviour*. Boston: Beacon Press.
Vazsonyi, A. T., J. Mikuška, and E. L. Kelley. 2017. "It's Time: A Meta-analysis on the Self-Control-Deviance Link." *Journal of Criminal Justice* 48:48–63.
Verdejo-García, A., A. J. Lawrence, and L. Clark. 2008. "Impulsivity as a Vulnerability Marker for Substance-Use Disorders: Review of Findings from High-Risk Research, Problem Gamblers and Genetic Association Studies." *Neuroscience and Biobehavioral Reviews* 32 (4):777–810.
Volkow, N. D., and T.-K. Li. 2004. "Drug Addiction: The Neurobiology of Behaviour Gone Awry." *Nature Reviews Neuroscience* 5 (12):963–70.
Volkow, N. D., J. S. Fowler, G.-J. Wang, and R. Z. Goldstein. 2002. "Role of Dopamine, the Frontal Cortex and Memory Circuits in Drug Addiction: Insight from Imaging Studies." *Neurobiology of Learning and Memory* 78 (3):610–24.
Warshaw, L. J., and J. Messite. 1996. "Workplace Violence: Preventive and Interventive Strategies." *Journal of Occupational and Environmental Medicine* 36 (10):993–1006.
Weekes, J., A. Moser, M. Wheatley, and F. Matheson. 2013. "What Works in Reducing Substance-Related Offending?" In *What Works in Offender Rehabilitation: An Evidence-Based Approach to Assessment and Treatment*, edited by L. A. Craig, L. Dixon and T. A. Gannon, 237–54. West Sussex, UK: John Wiley and Sons, Ltd.
Werb, D., A. Kamarulzaman, M. C. Meacham, C. Rafful, B. Fischer, S. A. Strathdee, and E. Wood. 2016. "The Effectiveness of Compulsory Drug Treatment: A Systematic Review." *International Journal of Drug Policy* 28:1–9.

35

The Opportunity Approach to Compliance

*Benjamin van Rooij and Adam D. Fine**

Abstract: The opportunity approach to compliance focuses on understanding how rule-breaking behaviour takes place and then tries to reduce the factors that enable rule breaking. This chapter reviews two core criminological theories within the opportunity approach: routine activity theory and situational crime prevention. The chapter assesses empirical evidence as to whether policies based on these theories can reduce rule-violating behaviour. Moreover, it discusses the extent to which the opportunity approach can result in displacement and adaptation effects. And, finally, it explores potential downsides to the opportunity approach such as victim blaming and reductions in autonomy and freedom of choice.

35.1 INTRODUCTION

In 2006, British authorities averted a massive terrorist plot aimed at exploding ten passenger airliners. The London-based plotters had developed a new approach to blowing up planes that involved smuggling liquid explosives hidden in soft-drink bottles. In the aftermath of what became known as the 'liquid bomb plot', airport security rules changed and began preventing passengers from bringing large amounts of liquids aboard planes. The new rules seek to prevent terrorism by disabling the behaviour in the first place.[1]

Changing the airport security rules in the wake of the liquid bomb plot demonstrates a very different approach to compliance and to using legal rules to deal with harmful, rule-violating behaviour. Rather than use incentives to try to sway people's motivation and make them act better, we can make it harder – or even impossible – to misbehave in the first place. We call this the 'opportunity approach' to compliance, as it seeks to enhance compliance by reducing the opportunities for non-compliant conduct.

This chapter discusses such approaches as they have developed in criminology. It focuses in particular on routine activity theory and on situational crime prevention. Although not discussed here, similar ideas have also developed in behavioural ethics, finding that situational conditions shape people's ethicality and ethical behaviour (Feldman 2018; Feldman and Kaplan 2018). For the purpose of this handbook, the current chapter gives an overview of

This research was made possible through a generous grant from the European Research Council (ERC-2018-CoG - HomoJuridicus - 817680).

* This chapter is based on a chapter in a forthcoming popular science book about law and behaviour. The chapter draws directly on key analysis and writing about the relevant literature discussed there but has altered the text to fit the handbook format.

[1] See www.nytimes.com/2006/08/28/world/europe/28plot.html and www.independent.co.uk/travel/news-and-advice/liquids-ban-on-flights-10th-anniversary-do-we-still-need-it-a7181216.html and http://news.bbc.co.uk/2/hi/uk_news/8242479.stm.

the leading ideas in both these theories, presents some of the key insights and studies, covers some of the empirical evidence about their effectiveness and ends by examining some of the potential downsides of an opportunity approach to compliance.

35.2 ROUTINE ACTIVITIES, LIFESTYLES, VICTIMIZATION AND CRIME

In the 1960s, the American economy was booming and people's lives improved. There was more employment, more people graduated from high school, there were higher wages, and standards of living improved. Typically, when these things happen, people tend to think that crime rates will decrease. In fact, the state of empirical evidence about this is not clear-cut (Zimring 2006; Benson and Zimmerman 2010; Rocque, Saunoris and Marshall 2019; but see Kelly 2000 on the strong relationship between inequality and crime). In fact, during this period, as the economic circumstances improved, crime rates went up. For instance, between 1960 and 1975, burglary rose by 200 percent.

Two criminologists, Lawrence Cohen and Marcus Felson (1979), utilized two sources of data to examine how these two trends coincided. First, they examined crime statistics, including victimization data (age, gender, occupation, marital status), crime locations (home or elsewhere) and victim–offender relations (close or strangers). Second, they analyzed how people's lives and their everyday practices changed in this period. Their analysis covered a range of data, including women's employment and education statistics, vacation period data and consumer data (including the value and weight of products). By combining these sets of data, they unearthed patterns that linked the crime data to the data about people's everyday practices that could help explain why crime rose as the economy boomed.

Cohen and Felson (1979:598) found that in the period they studied, more women went to school and work. At the same time, the number of single households increased by 34 per cent. People also received and took more holidays (with a rise of 81 per cent between 1967 and 1972 alone). The result was that more American houses were empty, especially during the morning.

Moreover, the actual goods themselves in the houses had also fundamentally changed. Consumer electronics became smaller and lighter. The lightest TV in 1960 weighed 38 pounds, yet by 1970, this had reduced by more than 50 per cent to only 15 pounds (Cohen and Felson 1979:599). The result of the weight loss was that houses had products that had more value per pound. In 1975, for instance, a car tape player was worth $30 per pound, and a record player cartridge was valued at $5,000 per pound (Cohen and Felson 1979:596). And with the growth of the economy, Americans bought more of these lightweight and valuable products.

Cohen and Felson's conclusion was that these two trends explained the increase in theft. As women went out to work and study, and Americans took more holiday time, more houses were left unattended and unprotected. And with the drop in the weight of consumer electronics and the increased expendable income that people had to buy such goods, these unguarded homes had more valuable goods that had become easier to carry (Cohen and Felson 1979:596).

Cohen and Felson analysed these trends beyond theft and burglary to also explain crime trends more generally. They used a large-scale data set with crime rates (for homicide, rape, aggravated assault, robbery and burglary). They used statistical analysis to test whether the types of crime were related to what they theoretically considered to be daily activities deemed to cause a risk of victimization. They found a robust relationship between crime rates and daily activities, with certain daily activities leading to higher crime rates.

On the basis of this research, Cohen and Felson developed what they called 'routine activity theory'. This theory holds that people's daily activities – where they live, with whom they live, what they buy, whether they work, whether they take holidays – affect crime. And not just property crime but also violent crime, including rape and murder (Cohen and Felson 1979).

35.2.1 *The Core Theory and Its Expansion*

Cohen and Felson (1979) came to see three core elements that played a role in how routine activities led to crime. First, there has to be a **motivated offender**, someone willing to commit the criminal activity. Second, there has to be a **valuable target** that attracts the offender. Examples include lightweight valuable goods such as smaller-sized radios and new colour TVs, and the tiny but extremely expensive diamond turntable needles. Finally, there should be **no capable guardian present**. For burglaries in the 1960s, that would be homeowners who were away more often and also just lived alone more often, which left their valuables in their houses unguarded.

These three core elements are brought together by a fourth aspect that gave rise to the theory's name, the routine activities that influence the encounters between the offenders and the targets (Groff 2007). When routine activities change, as they did, for instance, when women went to work, the interactions between targets and offenders can change and affect crime rates. And as such, as Groff (2007:99) has summarized, 'if the frequency with which these elements converge in space and time increases, crime will also increase, even if the supply of offenders or targets remains constant within a city'. Scholars have further expanded Cohen and Felson's original ideas and also started to include people's lifestyle choices (for instance whether they use alcohol or drugs), incorporating the so-called 'lifestyle exposure theory' (Hindelang, Gottfredson and Garofalo 1978), as additional crime victimization risk factors (McNeeley 2015).

An important line of research has looked not just at the routine activities of the victim but also at those of the offender. Osgood et al. (1996) make a vital contribution here in showing that individuals who spend more time performing unstructured activities with peers and in the absence of authority figures are more likely to engage in illegal and deviant behaviour. Here they find that such unstructured routine activities give them more time for deviant behaviour (Osgood et al. 1996).

Another line of research springing from the original theory has looked at how routine activities can explain the geographical distribution of crime. An influential study published in 1989 by Sherman, Gartin and Buerger developed a database of crime locations based on the spatial distribution of calls made to the police, analysing 323,979 calls made from all 115,000 addresses and intersections in Minneapolis over a period of one year. It finds a clear non-random distribution of crimes at a very small number of places, so-called 'hot spots'. The results, the authors argue, support the basic premise of routine activity theory that suitable targets, motivated offenders and available guardians play a major role in crime patterns. However, its core conclusion is that we must not merely focus on these actors but also on the places where they converge and thus on the criminogenic nature of places, which may stimulate crime through their capacity to generate or host crime (Sherman, Gartin and Buerger 1989). We shall look in more depth at this when discussing situational crime prevention in the next section.

35.2.2 *Applications of the Theory across Forms of Deviance*

Routine activity theory has become a key field in criminology. The theory has been found to explain a range of illegal behaviours. Several studies, for instance, have looked at how routine activities can predict sexual crimes. An earlier paper by Joanne Belknap (1987) used data from the US National Crime Survey to obtain data about rape and attempted rape. She identified 762 cases of women and girls who had reported having been victims of rape or attempted rape in the ten-year period the study covered and compared them with a random sample of 2,532 women and girls who had not reported the same crimes in the same survey. To test the predictive value of routine activity theory, the study drew on a number of variables also reported in the same survey, including the time of day, the season and the place where the attack occurred, race, age, marital status, lifestyle activities and family income. The study found that most of the variables associated with routine activity theory, such as the time of day and the season of the attack, were indeed of influence in the rape and attempted rape cases. The study found that marital status, age and family income were the strongest predictors of victimization of sexual violence (Belknap 1987).

A different line of study has shown that routine activity theory applies not just to people's activities in the physical world but also to online activities and cybercrime (e.g. Holt and Bossler 2008; Bossler and Holt 2009; Pratt, Holtfreter and Reisig 2010). One study has looked at how routine activity theory can predict online fraud. Using survey data from a sample of adults in Florida (n = 922), the study sought to understand how their routine online activities (such as the amount of time they spent online and online shopping) as well as several demographics were related to online fraud victimization (Pratt, Holtfreter and Reisig 2010). The study found that when controlling for key demographics (including age, education, race, marital status, retirement and home ownership), the core predictors for online fraud victimization were hours spent online and online purchases, with more online activities and shopping leading to people experiencing more fraud (Pratt, Holtfreter and Reisig 2010:282) Another study has looked at the risk of becoming a victim of cyberbullying (Mesch 2009). This study, using survey data from a representative US youth population (n = 935), looked at how both adolescent online activities and their parents' role in mediating their activities affect the risk of becoming a victim of cyberbullying. The study found that the risk of victimization was higher for young people who were active on social networking platforms and who participated in chat rooms. However, they did not find a higher risk for children who played more online video games. The study found further that parents have only a limited influence here and that most attempts to mediate behaviour do not protect against cyberbullying. Only parents who restricted the websites their children visited were found to decrease cyberbullying victimization (Mesch 2009:391).

Where most studies of routine activity theory use either data sets of lifestyle patterns and crime rates or victimization surveys, some criminologists have sought to further explore the theory through using computer-aided simulated modelling techniques. One study by Elizabeth Groff (2007), for instance, used such an approach to look at whether the rate of street robbery is related to the amount of time people spend away from home. Her study sought to understand whether the theory that predicts that more time away from home will increase street robbery also holds true in different types of setting and of temporal and spatial pattern where people's activities take place. She tried to assess whether there are differences among people whose activities outside of their home are completely random in terms of time and space, whether they are guided according to a time schedule but geographically random, or whether they perform activities at set times and in set spaces. Using a software package called Agent Analyst and ArcGIS, Groff sought to test her hypothesis in simulated models, applying them to the land use and street network of Seattle, Washington. She ran five experiments in these models that each changed the routine activities of potential targets when away from home, while also changing the spatial and temporal constraints of people's activities outside of their homes. The study found a significant increase in the risk of robbery for people in more constrained temporal and spatial patterns. In simpler terms, the more routine the outside activities were, the more chance that targets might meet offenders and get robbed. However, when people's outside activities did not follow clear spatial patterns and when they moved randomly, routine activity theory did not predict a risk of robbery (Groff 2007). This study shows how work in routine activity theory has developed to consider highly particular patterns at play while also employing computer-simulated modelling.

Routine activity theory has also been applied to white-collar crime and forms of organizational misconduct. This is especially important for the present handbook as it shows that this line of thinking is not restricted to ordinary crime or individual behaviour and may be a key form of analysis for major corporate compliance issues. One study, for instance, explored how routine activities could play a role in medical fraud (Benson, Madensen and Eck 2009). Using insights from Cohen and Felson's (1979) original study, the paper focuses on what in a white-collar crime setting would constitute a common place where targets and committed offenders could meet. The study uses the case of hospitals overcharging patients' insurance companies for medical services, a common form of medical fraud. Here the hospital is the committed offender, the insurance company the victim and the system for submitting insurance claims is the common place where the two meet. What enhances the risk of fraud here is not so much the meeting of offender and target, as they are bound to meet at the source of any claim made; rather, it is the level of guardianship that exists in the claims process. The key form of guardianship here, the article argues, could exist through a claims reviewer at the insurance company, a whistle-blower protection system at the hospital, or an accreditation commission that oversees the hospital's claims process and conducts audits (Benson, Madensen and Eck 2009). Although the paper does not systematically study these issues, it shows the relevance of routine activity theory in analyzing fraud.

And as a last application of routine activity theory, again with a focus on corporate misconduct, a recent study by (Gibbs, Cassidy and Rivers III (2013) used the theory to analyze fraud within the European Emissions Trading System, the world's largest market for trading carbon emissions. It analysed the system for fraud opportunities looking at whether it allows for a convergence of offenders and targets without capable guardianship. They analysed the structure of the carbon market and how trading in it occurs. They also looked at how the market is regulated and how monitoring and enforcement against fraudulent practices have been set up. Through this analysis they mapped the opportunities in this system for entities that want to engage in fraudulent trade, showing where there are attractive targets and whether these are sufficiently guarded. In addition, they analysed cases of fraudulent practice in these markets to see whether such opportunities were at play in reality. Their conclusion was that routine activity theory could be applied here and that it can also account for rule breaking in legitimate business environments (Gibbs, Cassidy and Rivers III 2013). This last study is thus a major example of how routine activities can also play a role in corporate compliance problems and also of how they can be applied through combining legal analysis, interviews and case studies of fraudulent practices to uncover major weaknesses in existing economic and regulatory systems that enable fraud.

35.2.3 *An Overall Review of the Available Studies*

These diverse bodies of work thus show the application of the theory. A deep dive into the many studies about routine activity theory, which this chapter cannot do, would show the nuance where the theory applies and what its limitations are for different forms of crime, different types of activity and various lifestyles. What we can offer here is an overall picture of what we know based on existing studies through two reviews we have, one from 2009 and one from 2015. The first literature review is by Richard Spano and Joshua Freilich (2009: 305), who reviewed twenty-two studies published between 1995 and 2005 to assess 'the empirical validity and conceptualization of routine activity theory by reviewing individual-level multivariate studies'. They first assessed whether the four key elements in the routine activity and lifestyles theory are at play as risk or protective factors for criminal victimization. They found clear support for the theory that

> [t]he results show a clear pattern of support that is consistent with hypothesized effects for all four key concepts. Multivariate findings for: (1) guardianship are over five times more likely to be protective factors, (2) target attractiveness are 3.33 times more likely to be risk factors, (3) deviant lifestyles are 7.4 times more likely to be risk factors, and (4) exposure to potential offenders are 3.12 times more likely to be risk factors (Spano and Freilich 2009:308).

The review further looked at whether there was variation in the overall findings for different types of samples (including national, college students or high poverty, and different age groups), types of outcome variable (victimization versus crime/deviance), type of data collection (cross-sectional versus longitudinal) and geographical location (USA versus other). For each of these, it assessed whether the overall findings varied for different types of study. Overall it found that none of the variation in the study designs yielded results that were inconsistent with the original theory, but it did find that the theory was more robust in certain samples, including adolescents, college students and American samples (Spano and Freilich 2009:309).

The latest large-scale review we have of routine activity theory is from 2015. This review, by McNeeley (2015), looks at the overall theoretical development of the theory and its incorporation of lifestyle choices with the original Cohen and Felson routine activities. It reviews forty-seven studies published between 1986 and 2012. Unlike Spano and Freilich's (2009) earlier review, this later study is not a meta-analysis or even a systematic review but rather a discussion of the selected studies in light of individual victimization, individual offending, and the link between crime and place. It finds, overall, that the theory

> has been useful in explaining macro-level crime rates, individual-level victimization and offending, and the concentration of crime at micro-level places. Lifestyle routine activities theory [as the study calls it] is also especially beneficial in that it can be used to explain multiple types of crime, including property, personal, white-collar and online crimes. The empirical evidence testing the theory's applicability to multiple types of crime is generally supportive (McNeeley 2015:40).

Routine activity theory has thus produced a clear framework for analyzing and addressing illegal behaviour and compliance challenges. It shows that to reduce rule-breaking behaviour, an analysis should be made as to whether valuable (desirable) targets are guarded well enough from potential (motivated) offenders. Based on such analysis, the approach can be used either to improve guardianship or to reduce access to valuable targets. As such, this approach to compliance does not focus on understanding *why* people break rules and commit crime, or really on reducing the number of motivated offenders. Instead, it focuses on *how* crimes are committed in order to understand what key enabling factors are at play in order to eliminate these. Routine activity theory is all about reducing crime by taking away opportunities for bad behaviour. Routine activity theory focuses on the convergence of targets and offenders in the absence of capable guardians; its implications centre either on trying to get potential victims to better protect themselves or on enhancing guardianship of these targets. There are highly valuable applications here. People can learn that certain activities, such as walking in dark, deserted neighbourhoods or shopping online at websites they do not know, can come with greater risk. If people are offered more information about what such risks are, they can protect themselves and prevent crime. The same applies to guardianship in cases where self-protection is not possible or desirable. A good example is how our computers have ever better firewalls and anti-virus software as most people do not have the skills to protect themselves. But as Sherman, Gartin and Buerger (1989) have shown in their discussion on hot spots for crime, the focus on targets and guardians misses a broader analysis of how particular situations can give rise to deviant and criminal behaviour beyond what an analysis of routine activity theory would find.

35.3 SITUATIONAL PREVENTION

Soon after Cohen and Felson developed routine activity theory, a second closely related theory developed, so-called 'situational crime prevention theory'. This idea was developed by Ronald Clarke. He developed his original ideas together with Pat Mayhew in a study about the effects of a law in West Germany that required motorcyclists to wear helmets. This law, which was adopted in 1976, had an unexpected and important by-effect. Between 1976 and 1982, the law that required people to wear motorcycle helmets when riding surprisingly caused a reduction in motorcycle thefts. Clarke, Mayhew and colleagues found that the more strictly the law was enforced, the less theft there was. They found that the pattern held up even when they controlled for trends in demographics with a decline in theft-prone juveniles in the same period. They even found that although motorcycle thefts declined in this period, overall theft increased (Mayhew, Clarke and Elliott 1989). They found similar crime drops following helmet mandates in the Netherlands (a reduction of 36 percent) and the UK (a drop of 24 percent in London). Their analysis concluded that the helmet mandate had made it harder to steal a motorbike. In the past, once a thief had unlocked the motorcycle, they could just ride off and no one would know they had stolen the bike; they looked just like any other motorcycle rider. But after the helmet mandate was instituted, jacking a motorcycle and riding off bare-headed would attract police attention. So, unless thieves made the effort to bring their own helmet, stealing a motorcycle became harder.

Ronald Clarke drew on these motorcycle studies to develop a new approach to addressing crime. He called his approach 'situational crime prevention'. He argued that reducing crime involved more than addressing the offender (Clarke 1980). Instead, Clarke argued that what matters is the situation that enables illegal behaviour before it occurs. According to Clarke, it is much simpler and easier to manipulate the opportunities for offending than it is to change the actual offender (Clarke 1980).

Just like routine activity theory has argued, rule-breaking behaviour depends on opportunity. Clarke's approach is broader than that of routine activity theory, as he looks beyond reducing the attractiveness of targets and target hardening, where crime is prevented by ensuring that potential victims are better protected or learn to better protect themselves. Instead, he focuses on the broader set of situations that enable rule breaking.

35.3.1 *Changing the Physical Environment*

There are several other key examples where situations could change crime. One example Clarke mentions is street lights. When urban centres developed better street lighting, crime levels went down (Clarke 1980). In fact, a recent systematic review of eight American and five British studies about the effects of street lights on crime levels confirms this: improved street lights reduced crime on average by 20 percent (Farrington and Welsh 2002).

The same idea has been applied to reduce public urination in Amsterdam, where researchers experimented with how shining bright lights could help to reduce public urination at the Royal Palace in Amsterdam. Robert Dur and Ben Vollaard spent seven months analysing video footage of public urination, examining how urination patterns were affected by lights they installed at the Palace. Their study showed that light had a strong effect, cutting public urination by half.[2]

Another study similarly found that the location of where people park their cars affects car thefts and damages to cars. The study found that parking in a public car park makes theft nearly four times more likely than parking in the street outside one's home, more than ten times more likely than in one's driveway and over 200 times more likely than parking inside one's home garage (Clarke and Mayhew 1998).

Another line of research, which actually pre-dates both situational crime prevention theory and routine activity theory, uses the same line of thinking about how the physical environment can cause crime. It moves us further away from routine activities and more towards understanding the place where such activities occur. Similarly to the idea of criminogenic spaces that Sherman, Gartin and Buerger (1989) discussed in their study of crime hot spots, this approach looks at how architecture and urban planning relate to crime. Here Oscar Newman's (1972) work on the 'defensible space' has been most influential. He did an extensive study about crime patterns and disorder in different urban centres in the United States. Based on this, he found that architecture and urban planning affect crime: for instance, the development of high-rise buildings had stimulated crime, and the height and architecture of buildings affected crime. Higher buildings had less of what Newman calls 'defensible space'. In low-rises, residents could more easily defend and control their own spaces. In low-rise buildings there was a clearer demarcation of what space belonged to the community in the building and what they could thus claim and for which they had responsibility to ensure its safety. Newman also focused on physical aspects in the built environment that could enable or undermine opportunities for surveillance. High-rises simply offered many spaces that obstructed surveillance by blocking the view to the street and by having enclosed lobbies, elevators and stairways (Newman 1972).

Another example of how the physical environment can affect rule-breaking or rule-compliant behaviour is obvious to all and does not really require much study. It is also how we design our roads. The clearest examples here are speed bumps. If these obstacles are well designed, most cars simply cannot drive faster than the speed limit.

2 www.erasmusmagazine.nl/2016/12/22/het-is-heel-moeilijk-om-wildplassers-op-heterdaad-te-betrappen/.

35.3.2 *Reducing Access to Dangerous Items*

Situational crime prevention is more than just changing the physical environment. It has many different approaches. There are many applications of the idea that harmful or rule-breaking behaviour can be reduced by limiting access to enabling items. Think of restrictions on the sale of spray paint to prevent graffiti, or restricting access to guns and ammunition to reduce homicide and suicide. And as a 2010 report in the UK argued, a good way to reduce harm in bar fights is by giving customers polycarbonate instead of glass beer glasses so they can no longer break the bottles and use the glass shards as weapons (Design Council 2010).

35.3.3 *Strategies and Interventions of Situational Crime Prevention*

Over the years, Clarke and his co-authors have categorized situational crime prevention strategies across five overall strategies: (i) increase the effort that offenders must make to do harm and break rules; (ii) increase the situational risks of performing unwanted and illegal behaviour; (iii) reduce the situational rewards of unwanted behaviour; (iv) reduce situational provocations that may cause stress, temptation, peer pressure or imitation; and (v) remove situational excuses. Situational crime prevention has developed these five overall approaches into twenty-five types of intervention that all share a pragmatic view of how unwanted and criminal behaviour occurs in order to see what elements can be addressed to eliminate people's opportunity to engage in such behaviour.

To understand the importance of this approach, we do not need to look at academic studies. We can find examples all around us. In shops, the tags on merchandise will trigger alarms when a thief takes items without paying upon exiting the store, or, worse, labels may stain stolen items with non-washable ink, and reduce the value of stolen goods. CCTV cameras on the streets should make many types of criminal activity easier to detect. Authorities regularly clean graffiti to deny spray-painting youths the pleasure of displaying their art, and if that fails, they use graffiti-resistant paint. Car alarms and removable radios reduce car theft and damages. And criminal finance is disrupted by eradicating high-value bank notes like the 1,000-USD bill (which was taken out of circulation by President Nixon in 1969) and the 500-euro bill (which is no longer issued since April 2019). One million euros in 500-euro bills only weighs 2.2 kilograms (just under 5 lb) and can easily fit in a suitcase.[3]

35.4 WILL REDUCING OPPORTUNITIES SIMPLY DISPLACE WRONGDOING?

One of the core critiques of the opportunity approach to illegal behaviour is that it may displace crime and misconduct. Also, despite one opportunity being closed off, committed offenders may adapt their strategies and find other opportunities. And reducing opportunities for some may create opportunities for others. In other words, a potential downside of the opportunity approach is that it may result in displacement, adaptation or replacement.

Let us look at displacement first. Several studies have sought to measure empirically whether the opportunity approach results in a displacement effect, where closing off opportunities in one area increases crime in others. Guerette and Bowers (2009) recently published a review of the available work, covering 102 studies. In 26 per cent of the cases reviewed, they found some type of displacement effect. However, overall, they concluded that crime

[3] www.scmp.com/news/world/europe/article/2183801/death-500-euro-note-bill-favoured-criminals-and-germans.

reduction was greater than crime displacement. In other words, closing off criminal opportunities saves more crime than it displaces (Guerette and Bowers 2009).

Research about gated communities shows an interesting insight into the complexity of the displacement effect. With the extra protection of the gated community, we would assume that there would be more crime outside than inside these communities. The empirical evidence is less clear, however. Blakely and Snyder's (1997) book *Fortress America: Gated Communities in the United States* analyzed crime rates in and outside of American gated communities. The book found no evidence that people living within the gates suffered less crime than those outside (Blakely and Snyder 1997). Interestingly, one study of gated communities in South Africa even found that crime rates were greater inside the gated communities than outside. The explanation was simple: people who live inside gated communities are richer and therefore make more attractive targets. The extra effort and risk involved in getting inside these communities is lower than the higher value these communities present as targets (Breetzke and Cohn 2013).

There is some evidence of the opposite effect of displacement, a 'halo effect' (Scherdin 1986) where closing off opportunities for misconduct works beyond the area where the opportunities have been closed off. Studies of using technology to prevent theft, such as home security systems, CCTV cameras, neighbourhood street lighting improvements and electronic library book tags, appear to show such an effect (Clarke 2005:52). There is less theft in houses without security when they are in a neighbourhood where other houses do have security (Pease 1991). Streets with better lights also reduce crime in adjacent streets with normal lighting (Painter and Farrington 1997). CCTV cameras also reduce car crimes in adjacent car parks where they were not installed (Scherdin 1986). And electronic tags not only reduce book thefts but also result in less theft of untagged library items like video cassettes (Scherdin 1986).

The second problem with the opportunity approach is that it may cause offenders to switch their strategies and find a different opportunity for the same type of crime. A good example where this has been studied is credit card fraud. In the late 1980s, credit card fraud had become a major problem costing hundreds of millions of US dollars each year. To deal with this, companies took several steps to reduce opportunities for the most prevalent forms of fraud, such as false credit card applications, theft of cards in transit from credit card companies to customers, misuse by genuine cardholders, and the recycling and reuse of stolen or lost cards (Levi, Bissell and Richardson 1991:7). Banks created a joint registry for fraud that tracked all people involved in credit card-related fraud schemes. They used the scheme to filter out credit card applications by people involved in previous fraud. To reduce credit card mail theft, they asked customers to pick up their card in person at the bank, or informed them when it would arrive so they would take good care, and banks also started to issue the PIN that customers needed to activate their card via separate mail. While these interventions worked very well at first, that is, between 1991 and 1995, the effects did not last. Since 1995 there has been a rapid increase in credit card fraud, which has doubled compared to the previous record numbers of 1990. What happened is that fraud strategies changed. Fraudsters could make use of new technological opportunities with the advent of the Internet and online sales, which increasingly did not need physical cards. Moreover, they perfected the art of producing complete counterfeit cards (Clarke 2005).

Adaptation can undermine the effectiveness of the opportunity approach. Closing off one opportunity can set a sort of arms race in motion that spurs criminals to find another. By its very nature, this makes the opportunity approach reactive as it is essential to discover what new approach offenders use and find a way to close it off. This may well leave offenders one step ahead as they adapt, and adapt again.

At worst, this adaptation can come with escalation. The introduction of car security alarms has reduced ordinary car theft, where people break into parked cars and speed away. But, as Clarke explains, these same car alarms may have also led to an increase in carjackings, where car owners are forced to hand over their car at gunpoint (Clarke 2005). Similarly, one study found that the introduction of glass windows between tellers and customers in London post offices led to an increase in the use of firearms in post office robberies (Ekblom 1988).

Routine activity theory and situational crime prevention may be effective ways to reduce crime. But they are not foolproof and can at times have negative effects on crime and may displace it or result in a game of cat and mouse as offenders adapt their practices to create new opportunities.

35.5 CONCLUSION

Routine activity theory and situational crime prevention provide a very different approach to compliance. They show that rule-breaking and damaging behaviours can be addressed by reducing opportunities for them. This type of opportunity approach to compliance can be highly effective and also efficient. It does not require the law to shape people's motivations and as such it mostly does not depend on deterrence, social norms, legitimacy or the capacity to comply. Simply making non-compliance harder should mean that compliance itself increases.

Altogether, the opportunity approach to compliance asks a different question to most other approaches. It does not ask why people break the rules; it asks *how* they break them. And based on the answer to that question, it seeks a way to reduce rule breaking by closing off a vital element that enables illegal behaviour. As the chapter has shown, that can include supporting potential targets in better protecting themselves, improving guardianship of such targets, changing the physical or online environment to make it harder practically to reach targets or perform rule-breaking behaviour, and limiting access to items that can cause harm or break rules. The literature has developed a nice range of options that can be used here.

Clearly, the opportunity approach should be a major strategy to ensure compliance. For any problems of non-compliance, one of the first questions should be whether there is a way to make breaking the rules harder. At present, however, the opportunity approach seems to be more prevalent in some areas of compliance and crime strategies than others. We see it clearly, for instance, against terrorism (where authorities learn from each attack or attempt and then close off avenues) and theft.

However, the opportunity approach is used far less frequently – if at all – for a variety of other types of behaviour, including texting while driving. For years, there have been effective techniques and technologies aimed at making cell-phone usage impossible in the driver's seat, yet they are rarely implemented.[4] To understand why the opportunity approach is not more widely used, we must account for its normative downsides. Apart from potential displacement, adaptation and escalation effects that may undermine such crime prevention efforts, there are also moral and political reasons against it.

The first reason is that the opportunity approach, especially routine activity theory's focus on target hardening, may result in blaming the victim. If studies find that certain types of

[4] www.nytimes.com/2016/09/25/technology/phone-makers-could-cut-off-drivers-so-why-dont-they.html.

clothing make people more likely to fall victim to sexual assault, should we reduce the number of such assaults by asking potential victims to dress differently? The second reason is that the opportunity approach can result in inequality. Richer people and organizations will be more able to afford the expertise and costs required to protect themselves against crime than people with lower resources. A good example of this is that when in the 1970s the USA mandated that all new cars should have a steering lock to prevent theft, people who could not afford to buy a new car with the new technology became prime targets for auto theft (Clarke 1980). And the third and final reason is that the opportunity approach inherently limits freedom. The very reason why it is so effective, namely, because it takes away the opportunity, is also what makes it politically suspect, namely, it takes away choice and thus freedom. We may all want to reduce the thief's freedom to burgle our house by having a better alarm, but few would support rules that would mandate car manufacturers to install technology that makes it impossible to speed on the highway or to blow into an alcohol breathalyzer before starting the ignition. All these reasons mean that even if there is an effective way to manage compliance through the opportunity approach, it still requires a proper balancing of the different interests involved here.

It is clear that the opportunity approach developed in criminology should become more central in the study and practice of compliance. While there has been some work applying it to white-collar crime, and also some work on the usage of technology in compliance (i.e. Staats et al. 2016), we do not yet have a comprehensive and systematic understanding of the different ways in which routine activity theory and situational crime prevention, as well as adjacent theories in behavioural ethics and ecological criminology, can be applied to compliance more broadly.

REFERENCES

Belknap, Joanne. 1987. 'Routine Activity Theory and the Risk of Rape: Analyzing Ten Years of National Crime Survey Data'. *Criminal Justice Policy Review* 2 no. 4: 337–56.

Benson, Bruce, and Paul R. Zimmerman. 2010. *Handbook on the Economics of Crime*. New York: Edward Elgar Publishing.

Benson, Michael L., Tamara D. Madensen, and John E. Eck. 2009. 'White-Collar Crime from an Opportunity Perspective'. In *The Criminology of White Collar Crime*, edited by Sally Simpson and David Weisburd, 175–95. New York: Springer.

Blakely, Edward J., and Mary Gail Snyder. 1997. *Fortress America: Gated Communities in the United States*. Washington, DC: Brookings Institution Press.

Bossler, Adam M., and Thomas J. Holt. 2009. 'On-line Activities, Guardianship, and Malware Infection: An Examination of Routine Activities Theory'. *International Journal of Cyber Criminology* 3 no. 1: 400–20.

Breetzke, Gregory D., and Ellen G. Cohn. 2013. 'Burglary in Gated Communities: An Empirical Analysis Using Routine Activities Theory'. *International Criminal Justice Review* 23 no. 1: 56–74.

Clarke, Ronald V. 2005. 'Seven Misconceptions of Situational Crime Prevention'. In Nick Tilley (ed.) *Handbook of Crime Prevention and Community Safety*, 39–70. New York: Routledge.

Clarke, Ronald V., and Pat Mayhew. 1998. 'Preventing Crime in Parking Lots: What We Know and Need to Know'. In *Reducing Crime through Real Estate Development and Planning*. Washington, DC: Urban Land Institute 34:205–10.

Clarke, Ronald V. G. 1980. '"Situational" Crime Prevention: Theory and Practice'. *British Journal of Criminology* 20 no. 2: 136–47.

Cohen, Lawrence E., and Marcus Felson. 1979. 'Social Change and Crime Rate Trends: A Routine Activity Approach'. *American Sociological Review* 44 no. 4: 588–608.

Design Council. 2010. 'Design Out Crime, Using Design to Reduce Injuries from Alcohol-Related Violence in Pubs and Clubs'. www.designcouncil.org.uk/sites/default/files/asset/document/design-out-crime-alcohol.pdf.

Ekblom, Paul. 1988. 'Preventing Post Office Robberies in London: Effects and Side Effects'. *Journal of Security Administration* 11 no. 2: 36–43.

Farrington, D. P., and Welsh, B. C. (2002). 'Improved Street Lighting and Crime Prevention'. *Justice Quarterly* 19(2): 313–42.

Feldman, Yuval. 2018. *The Law of Good People: Challenging States' Ability to Regulate Human Behavior*. Cambridge: Cambridge University Press.

Feldman, Yuval, and Yotam Kaplan. 2018. 'Big Data & Bounded Ethicality'. *Bar Ilan University Faculty of Law Research Paper* (19–05).

Gibbs, Carole, Michael B. Cassidy, and Louie Rivers III. 2013. 'A Routine Activities Analysis of White-Collar Crime in Carbon Markets'. *Law & Policy* 35 no. 4: 341–74.

Groff, Elizabeth R. 2007. 'Simulation for Theory Testing and Experimentation: An Example Using Routine Activity Theory and Street Robbery'. *Journal of Quantitative Criminology* 23 no. 2: 75–103.

Guerette, Rob T. and Kate J. Bowers. 2009. 'Assessing the Extent of Crime Displacement and Diffusion of Benefits: A Review of Situational Crime Prevention Evaluations'. *Criminology* 47 no. 4: 1331–68.

Hindelang, Michael J., Michael R. Gottfredson and James Garofalo. 1978. *Victims of Personal Crime: An Empirical Foundation for a Theory of Personal Victimization*. Cambridge, MA: Ballinger.

Holt, Thomas J., and Adam M. Bossler. 2008. 'Examining the Applicability of Lifestyle-Routine Activities Theory for Cybercrime Victimization'. *Deviant Behavior* 30 no. 1: 1–25.

Kelly, Morgan. 2000. 'Inequality and Crime'. *Review of Economics and Statistics* 82 no. 4: 530–9.

Levi, Michael, Paul Bissell and Tony Richardson. 1991. *The Prevention of Cheque and Credit Card Fraud*. London: Home Office.

Mayhew, Pat, Ronald V. Clarke, and David Elliott. 1989. 'Motorcycle Theft, Helmet Legislation and Displacement'. *Howard Journal of Criminal Justice* 28 no. 1: 1–8.

McNeeley, Susan. 2015. 'Lifestyle-Routine Activities and Crime Events'. *Journal of Contemporary Criminal Justice* 31 no. 1: 30–52.

Mesch, Gustavo S. 2009. 'Parental Mediation, Online Activities, and Cyberbullying'. *CyberPsychology & Behavior* 12 no. 4: 387–93.

Newman, Oscar. 1972. *Defensible Space*. New York: Macmillan.

Osgood, D. Wayne, Janet K. Wilson, Patrick M. O'Malley, Jerald G. Bachman, and Lloyd D. Johnston. 1996. 'Routine Activities and Individual Deviant Behavior'. *American Sociological Review*: 635–55.

Painter, Kate, and David P. Farrington. 1997. 'The Crime-Reducing Effect of Improved Street Lighting: The Dudley Project'. *Situational Crime Prevention: Successful Case Studies* 2: 209–26.

Pease, Ken. 1991. 'The Kirkholt Project: Preventing Burglary on a British Public Housing Estate'. *Security Journal* 2 no. 2: 73–7.

Pratt, Travis C., Kristy Holtfreter and Michael D. Reisig. 2010. 'Routine Online Activity and Internet Fraud Targeting: Extending the Generality of Routine Activity Theory'. *Journal of Research in Crime and Delinquency* 47 no. 3: 267–96.

Rocque, Michael, James W. Saunoris, and Emily C. Marshall. 2019. 'Revisiting the Relationship between the Economy and Crime: The Role of the Shadow Economy'. *Justice Quarterly* 36 no. 4: 620–55.

Scherdin, Mary Jane. 1986. 'The Halo Effect: Psychological Deterrence of Electronic Security Systems'. *Information Technology and Libraries* 5 no. 3: 232–5.

Sherman, Lawrence W., Patrick R. Gartin and Michael E. Buerger. 1989. 'Hot Spots of Predatory Crime: Routine Activities and the Criminology of Place'. *Criminology* 27 no. 1: 27–56.

Spano, Richard, and Joshua D. Freilich. 2009. 'An Assessment of the Empirical Validity and Conceptualization of Individual Level Multivariate Studies of Lifestyle/Routine Activities Theory Published from 1995 to 2005'. *Journal of Criminal Justice* 37 no. 3: 305–14.

Staats, Bradley R., Hengchen Dai, David Hofmann, and Katherine L. Milkman. 2016. 'Motivating Process Compliance through Individual Electronic Monitoring: An Empirical Examination of Hand Hygiene in Healthcare'. *Management Science* 63. 10.1287/mnsc.2015.2400.

Zimring, Franklin E. 2006. *The Great American Crime Decline*. New York: Oxford University Press.

PART VI

Compliance and Cognition

36

Heuristics and Biases in the Criminology of Compliance

Greg Pogarsky

Abstract: In criminology, compliance is a central focus of the deterrence and rational choice perspectives on crime. In turn, these perspectives have been guided by traditional microeconomics. Behavioral economics, a recent branch of economics which pivots from and amplifies economic theories, has increasingly informed decision-making on a range of matters, including public health and finance. Criminologists have begun to marshal behavioral economic insights to better understand decisions surrounding crime and transgression. Prominent in behavioral economics are heuristics and biases in judgments under uncertainty. These involve shortcuts, rules of thumb, and other deviations from traditional economic norms, in how people navigate uncertainty. This chapter discusses how various biases and heuristics from behavioral economics research affect one of the most prominent decision-making constructs in criminology and compliance – perceptions about the likelihood of punishment for a contemplated transgression.

36.1 INTRODUCTION

Compliance with the law is a central concern of the deterrence and rational choice criminological perspectives. The core themes of these perspectives coincide with Enlightenment prescriptions for an equitable and orderly society (Beccaria, 1764; Bentham, 1789). In this classical view, criminal punishments should only be as certain, severe and celeritous as is needed to deter crime and preserve civil order. They should be no more so, however, out of an implied social contract where citizens cede sanctioning authority to the state in return for institutional protections against government overreach (Locke, 1690; Rousseau, 1974). Microeconomics elaborated these instincts into a theoretical framework of system-wide equilibria in the supply and demand for crime and law enforcement (Becker, 1968). In Chapter 15 of this volume, Pogarsky explained how this perspective treats compliance decisions under conditions of risk and uncertainty.

Several important junctures mark the criminological life course of this post-Becker literature (Laub, 2004). Early on, research estimated relationships between objective indicators of law enforcement, such as police and punishments, and crime rates. But even the most sophisticated causal estimates neglected something essential – direct information regarding offenders' perceptual decision-making processes. According to Gibbs (1975: 115–16), "there is every reason to suppose that deterrence depends on the perception of certainty rather than on objective certainty; indeed it is difficult to imagine otherwise" (see also Andenaes, 1974; Tittle, 1980). Nagin (1998: 5) underscored the critical importance of this for policy: "[T]he conclusion that crime decisions are affected by sanction risk perceptions is not a sufficient condition for concluding that policy can deter crime. Unless the perceptions themselves are manipulable by policy, the desired deterrent effect will not be achieved."

Another benchmark criminological development involves the contingent nature of compliance decisions (Tittle, 1980). The pertinent questions evolved from *whether* punishment deters crime, to *how*, *under what conditions*, and *for whom*? Thus, research turned to moderators and contingencies. Apel et al. (2009), for example, investigated the places where deterrence is attempted. They found that larger and/or more disordered schools were less able to deter student misconduct because the capacity for unambiguous deterrence messaging is compromised. Considerable research has also identified personal attributes, such as present orientation, identification with a future self, or thoughtfully reflective decision-making, that influence compliance decisions (Piquero et al., 2011).

Presently there is significant advancement on another front. This involves the economic conception of offender decision-making as primarily a deliberative, incentive-driven process. Behavioral economic models assume a more descriptively accurate central actor, with predictable departures from rational choice norms. Insights in this regard are embodied in prospect theory (Kahneman and Tversky, 1979; Pogarsky et al., 2018; Thomas and Loughran, 2015), but also in the dual process nature of behavioral economics. Two types of cognitive process contribute to judgments; some are fast and intuitive, whereas others are slow and deliberative. Real-world compliance decisions can entail inaccurate, incomplete and asymmetric information, urgency, disorganization, intoxication and visceral arousal. The confluence of these real-world vicissitudes with the two systems of cognition potentially invites *heuristics and biases* in perceptual judgments. This chapter examines the implications of several behavioral economic heuristics for one of the central constructs in criminological discourse – perceptions about the likelihood of punishment for a given crime.

36.2 SANCTION CERTAINTY PERCEPTIONS

Perceptions of sanction certainty were focal in Becker's (1968) economic model of crime (see Chapter 15 in this volume), and they remain central in scholarship on offender decision-making today. To fully appreciate behavioral economic insights into sanction certainty perceptions, I begin with the economic approach that the behavioral economic perspective pivots from. Anwar and Loughran's (2011) application of Bayesian Updating principles to the formation and modification of sanction certainty perceptions is highly instructive:

$$p_{i,t} = \alpha_{i,t}\theta_{i.t} + (1 - \alpha_{i.t})pi, t - 1 \qquad (1).$$

People begin with a *prior* perception of sanction certainty, $p_{i,\ t\text{-}1}$, which is the end product from the last instance of updating. The actor generates a *posterior* risk estimate, $p_{i,t}$, based on a *signal* received during the updating period, $\theta_{i,t}$. A weighting parameter, $\alpha_{i,t}$ å[0, 1], determines how much the posterior reflects the prior perception versus the signal.

What constitutes a signal for updating purposes is complex and empirically unknown (see Apel, 2013). Attention has focused on each actor's past experiences with offending and the consequences therefrom (Pogarsky et al., 2004). Moreover, Stafford and Warr (1993) observe that it is not just the actor's experiences with offending and consequences but also comparable information the actor becomes aware of regarding others, most notably coworkers, family and/or friends (Wilson et al., 2017). Anwar and Loughran (2011) model the composition of signals as a weighted function of two elements,

$$\theta_{i,t} = \delta_{i,t}\frac{A_{i,t}}{C_{i,t}} + (1 - \delta_{i,t})s_{i,t} \qquad (2).$$

The first, $\frac{A_{i,t}}{C_{i,t}}$, reflects the logic above about prior punishment experiences and consequences. This represents person i's arrest clearance ratio at time t of $A_{i,t}$, the number of arrests, to $C_{i,t}$, the number of crimes committed by person i during the reference period. This expression is readily generalized to capture comparable information the actor becomes aware of regarding others. Notice that this first component of the signal conveniently yields a probability, $\frac{A_{i,t}}{C_{i,t}}$ å [0, 1], that is readily combined with the prior to form a posterior. Anwar and Loughran (2011: 675) suggest that the balance of the signal, $s_{i,t}$, consists of "factors that might affect the perception of his or her arrest rate, such as family and friends' arrest experiences, the individual's ongoing maturity, and city-level trends in policing." It is unclear, however, how nonprobabilistic signals influence a probabilistic risk estimate.

As analytically tractable as the economic approach to sanction risk perception is, consequential gaps exist. An often misunderstood aspect of economic modeling is that its primary goals are normative rather than descriptive. Dhami (2016: 2) explained that "economics provides a coherent and internally consistent body of theory that offers rigorous, parsimonious, and falsifiable models of human behavior." Thaler (2015) emphasized that economic theories logically and precisely demonstrate how self-interested actors can maximize their well-being. The intellectual orientation of behavioral economics is to catalogue predictable departures from these norms, and generate more descriptively accurate theories.

Several aspects of the Bayesian Updating approach to risk perception merit scrutiny in this regard. As indicated earlier, the full range of items that qualify as a signal for updating purposes is unknown (see Apel, 2013). Another issue concerns $\alpha_{i,t}$, the relative weighting of signal and prior. This should depend on a range of factors, including the salience, availability to memory, reasonableness, and perhaps vividness of the signal, some of which may be manipulable by policy (Pogarsky and Herman, 2019). But first and foremost is the notion that decision-making is orderly, contemplative and dispassionate. Yet potential criminal involvement entails incomplete or inaccurate information, intoxication or visceral arousal, disorganization, stress and aggression. The dual process nature of behavioral economics is particularly well suited for decisions of this nature.

36.3 HEURISTICS AND BIASES: GENERAL NOTIONS

According to Kahneman and Frederick (2002: 51), "cognitive processes can be partitioned into two main families – traditionally called intuition and reason." Becker's (1968) model and much current discourse on offender decision-making concerns system 2, which is controlled, effortful, slow and self-aware. Yet behavioral economics includes a distinct system of mental processes. System 1 is intuitive, automatic, effortless, fast and unconscious (Kahneman, 2011).

Estimating the probability of detection for a given crime, or retrieving an existing estimate, often occurs under conditions of urgency, stress or visceral activation. These circumstances lend themselves to shortcuts or rules of thumb. Simon's (1990: 6) insights on Bounded Rationality are highly relevant: "If the game of chess ... is beyond exact [human] computation, then we may expect the same of almost any real-world problem, including almost any problem of everyday life. From this simple fact, we derive one of the most important laws of qualitative structure. . . . Because of the limits on their computing speeds and power, intelligent systems must use approximate methods to handle most tasks." Initial evidence suggests that sanction risk perceptions are indeed prone to heuristics and biases.

Gigerenzer and Gaissmaier (2011: 454) define a heuristic as "a strategy that ignores part of the information, with the goal of making decisions more quickly, frugally, and/or accurately than more complex methods." Normally there is a tradeoff between effort and accuracy. Residential burglars use heuristics – signs of occupancy, such as lighting or cars – to approximate the chance of apprehension and punishment from burglarizing the home. Additional effort, maybe surveilling the home to confirm that it is unoccupied, could improve the estimate. However, the situation does not call for it.

Behavioral economics has a unique conception of heuristics, which is reflected in the tendency to refer to heuristics and biases together. Bias can refer to any number of things in common parlance, such as an insidious prejudice or a miscalibrated device. In behavioral economics, biases are departures from traditional rational choice norms. This is why the ensuing discussion has been set within prevailing economic thinking – in this case, the Bayesian Updating model of risk perception. With this model as a point of departure, I next identify several behavioral economic heuristics that influence risk perception.

36.4 HEURISTICS AND BIASES IN SANCTION RISK PERCEPTION

36.4.1 *Anchoring*

Various forms of information are potentially relevant to evaluating the risk of detection and punishment for a crime (Geerken and Gove, 1975). Relevant information is often numerical, which is particularly useful when the ultimate judgment is also numerical, as with probability. Numerical cues in the decision environment, however, can also *anchor* subsequent judgments.

In a seminal demonstration, Tversky and Kahneman (1974) asked respondents to estimate the percentage of United Nations countries that are African. Before respondents answered, however, the experimenters spun a wheel numbered 1–100, which was rigged to land on 10 for half the subjects and 65 for the rest. Subjects for whom the wheel landed on 10 gave an average estimate of 25 percent, whereas subjects for whom the wheel landed on 65 gave an average estimate of 45 percent. Thus, even irrelevant numerical cues can nonetheless influence resultant judgments.

Kahneman (2011) outlined two viable but distinct mechanisms for anchoring. One is *anchoring by adjustment*. At its inception, behavioral economics was not a dual process theory. Decision-making was still somewhat contemplative and slow, but with predictable departures from expected utility theory it was considered "quasi-rational" (Thaler, 1994). In this view, the anchor provides a ready starting point, from which the actor can then adjust. Adjustments tend to be insufficient, however, thus biasing resultant judgments toward the anchor.

A distinct explanation, *anchoring by priming*, emerges from the contemporary explication of behavioral economics as a dual process theory of decision-making. Whereas adjustment is conscious and deliberate, and within the realm of system 2, priming comes within system 1. Kahneman (2011: 122) illustrated this with two questions: "Was Ghandi more or less than 144 years old when he died?" and "How old was Ghandi when he died?" Kahneman suggested that rather than have system 2 deliberately begin at 144 years old and "adjust" downward, "144 years old" may conjure a mental image of a 144-year-old man, thus priming the decision-maker to estimate an older age than they otherwise would have.

Anchoring appears to influence perceptions of sanction risk. Prior to having respondents estimate the probability of detection for various crimes, Thomas et al. (2018) presented them with an unrelated percentage ("32/71% of college students contract a sexually transmitted disease before graduating"). Respondents receiving the high, irrelevant anchor estimated far higher sanction risk perceptions than respondents who received the low irrelevant anchor did. Pogarsky et al. (2017) asked respondents to estimate the chances that they would be caught by the police if they left the scene of an automobile accident they were involved in. Before providing this estimate, however, they were queried as to whether their estimate was higher or lower than 19/79 percent. Respondents receiving the high anchor estimated the probability of apprehension at 49 percent, versus 32 percent in the low anchor condition.

36.4.2 *Availability*

This heuristic also relates directly to the characterization of deterrence as a process of information transmission designed to promote compliance by manipulating citizens' sanction risk perceptions (Geerken and Gove, 1975). Whether a signal is detected, and if so the ultimate weight it is given, should depend on the salience of that information to the actor. Behavioral economic research has established that judgments of frequency and probability are affected by the ease with which individuals can recall past instances of the event, and also the degree to which they can imagine the described event happening.

Criminologists have investigated how the availability heuristic influences sanction risk perception. Pogarsky et al. (2017) tested the availability heuristic with an experimental manipulation based on the fluency of recall. That is, before asking respondents to estimate the probability of detection and punishment for several crimes, some respondents were randomly assigned to receive a "punishment prime" (e.g., "Do you know of someone who was given a ticket or received a DUI?"), whereas the remaining respondents received an "avoidance" prime (e.g., "Do you know of someone who sped or drove drunk and avoided punishment?"). It was theorized that sanction risk perceptions should be higher for individuals asked to recall instances of punishment versus those instructed to recall instances of avoiding punishment. However, mean risk estimates were not statistically distinguishable across groups.

Pickett (2019) tested the availability heuristic with a manipulation aimed more at "imaginability." He presented respondents with hypothetical scenarios in which they were instructed to estimate how difficult it would be to steal a purse that was pictured. The experimental manipulation was whether the pictured purse was large or small. On average, respondents in fact rated the larger purse as far more difficult to steal, presumably because one can more readily imagine getting away with stealing a smaller purse.

36.4.3 *Affect*

The previous two heuristics involved, respectively, relying on an arbitrary item of information, and ease of recall or imaginability. System 1 can gravitate toward these features of the decision as a substitute for the comprehensive inquiry envisioned under the normative economic model. Kahneman and Frederick (2005: 269) call this general tendency *attribute substitution*: "When confronted with a difficult question, people may answer an easier one instead and are often unaware of the substitution." This is no less true concerning how people feel while making judgments. Kahneman (2011: 138) identifies this as an affect heuristic, where the actor replaces the cognitive judgment at hand with questions such as "How do I feel?" or "Do I (dis)like it?".

Decision-making and public opinion scholars have studied affect for quite some time (van Gelder et al., 2009). Zajonc (1980) advanced the strong position that *all* perception involves one type of affect or another. Ordinary, psychologically realistic humans do not perceive an object in a vacuum; rather, they perceive its features as well (is it big, bright, appealing?). Slovic et al. (2007: 1335–6) captured the psychological basis for the affect heuristic:

> [R]epresentations of objects ... are tagged ... with affect .... Just as imaginability, memorability, and similarity serve as cues for probability judgments ... affect may serve as a cue for many important judgments. Using an overall, readily available affective impression can be far easier – more efficient – than weighing the pros and cons or retrieving from memory many relevant examples, especially when the required judgment or decision is complex or mental resources are limited.

In relation to sanction risk perception, the notion is that if a person feels favorably toward an activity, they should judge the benefits as high and the risks as low. It's as if the cognitions rationalize a decision the actor is already happy to make, by shading the benefits a bit higher and the costs lower.

Pogarsky et al. (2017) recently tested these ideas by measuring various sanction risk perceptions of respondents, including those corresponding to being ticketed for texting while driving. Immediately prior to giving these estimates, however, respondents were randomly assigned to an affect manipulation. Some received information designed to induce negative affect ("a new study shows that texting while driving is a leading cause of death among teens"), whereas the remaining respondents received either neutral or positive information. As predicted, the estimated probability of detection was highest in the negative affect condition.

36.4.4 *Ambiguity*

A final area of interest concerns the clarity or ambiguity in the information giving rise to a risk estimate. Consider Ellsberg's (1961) two color problem in which you must draw one ball from an urn – if the ball is red, you win $50; if the ball is black, you win nothing. You must select from one of two possible urns: Urn #1 has 100 balls total; 50 red and 50 black, whereas Urn #2 has 100 balls total with red and black balls in unknown proportion. Even though the probability of winning is identical across urns, people prefer Urn #1, an illustration of *ambiguity aversion*. In this case, rather than the respondent's feelings, his or her level of assuredness in the information underlying the estimate can affect the estimate in predictable ways.

Casey and Scholz (1991a, 1991b) investigated these questions with several perceptual deterrence vignettes aimed at tax compliance. Respondents were randomly assigned to different punishment certainty and severity levels. The ambiguity of the information in the decision environment was communicated either vaguely or assuredly. Pogarsky (2009: 252) explained that the authors found evidence for a "boundary hypothesis," suggesting that "ambiguously held perceptions near a boundary – 0 or 1, in the case of a certainty estimate – are revised toward the middle, whereas ambiguity near the middle is inconsequential." If crime control is part information transmission to alter risk perception, these ideas may be leveraged for criminal deterrence. This underlies Sherman's (1990) call for rotating police crackdowns to maximize the extra deterrent capability that ambiguity aversion can provide.

Several recent studies have also investigated the role of ambiguity in sanction risk perception. Loughran et al. (2011a) found evidence for ambiguity aversion principles in two separate data sources, the Pathways to Desistance Study (e.g., Loughran et al., 2011b), and several perceptual deterrence vignettes to college students. However, Pickett and Bushway (2015) did not find evidence supporting ambiguity aversion, and also found that individual heterogeneity, regarding positive affect and the "tolerance for ambiguity," affects the assuredness with which people interpret information.

36.5 CONCLUSION

As in criminology beginning with Becker (1968), microeconomic principles also influenced various noncriminological lines of thinking. Behavioral economics has produced insights in these areas, which include finance and public health. Offending decisions entail at least comparable levels of complexity and uncertainty. Thus, behavioral economics should also enhance criminological conceptions of choice. A first phase of behavioral economics centered on prospect theory as an alternative to subjective expected utility theory. A second involved the explication of behavioral economics as a dual process theory of decision-making. This, and particularly the nature of intuitive system 1, leads to various heuristics and biases in sanction risk perception. This raises several implications for compliance.

One set of implications concerns individual heterogeneity in the proneness to transgress (Piquero et al., 2011). Consequential individual attributes have been identified throughout criminology, and several involve cognitive acumen and general decision-making capabilities. Two examples are Cognitive Reflection (Frederick, 2005) and Thoughtfully Reflective Decision Making (Paternoster and Pogarsky, 2009). If slower, more effective decision-making can be taught, then it may be possible to "de-bias" decisions. Indeed, research suggests that this may be more than mere conjecture. Heller et al. (2017: 2) recently studied the Becoming a Man Program in Chicago, which "helps youth slow down and reflect on whether their automatic thoughts and behaviors are well suited to the situation they are in, or whether the situation could be construed differently." The program successfully reduced arrests and increased graduation rates among middle and high school students over a six-year period. Herman and Pogarsky (in press) recently discussed whether some of the core lessons from this intervention could be applied to instill other consequential decision-making tendencies in children and adolescents, such as moral identity.

A distinct set of implications pertains to the manner in which compliance opportunities unfold. Indeed, heuristics have been marshaled for prosocial purposes. Pogarsky and Herman (2019) discuss several of these in the context of "prosocial nudging." For example, simplification nudges exist to streamline the cognitive pathway to compliance. This principle underlies prerelease or prisoner reentry handbooks with checklists that disaggregate and isolate key steps, such as managing money, promoting one's physical and emotional health, and rebuilding relationships. This intervention is designed to reduce the cognitive load necessary to comply with the law.

Rather than streamline the cognitive complexity of compliance decisions, heuristics have also been designed to guard against future failures of self-control. These techniques encourage future-oriented decision-making by having individuals make commitments in a cool, dispassionate state before a "point of no return." The United Kingdom has employed Acceptable Behavior Contracts (ABCs) for minor offenses, which involve a meeting between the offender, his or her parents (if applicable), and the police, at which all agree to what is and is not acceptable behavior (Evans et al., 2008). Iwry and Kleiman (2017) advocated for "nudges toward temperance." These involve voluntary personal monthly quantity limits as a precondition for legal recreational cannabis use.

The heuristics and biases outlined in this chapter were by no means collectively exhaustive. There is a good deal of consequential scholarship on heuristics that extends outside the realm of behavioral economics. However, behavioral economics pivots directly from traditional microeconomics. Since economic notions have such a sustained tradition influencing thinking about various forms of compliance, it stands to reason that these ideas can also produce insights for criminology, and related disciplines concerned with various forms of transgression and deviance. It indeed appears that the behavioral economic heuristics outlined in this chapter may improve our understanding of how perceptions of sanction risk develop and influence offending decisions.

REFERENCES

Andenaes, Johannes. 1974. *Punishment and Deterrence*. Ann Arbor: University of Michigan Press.

Anwar, Shamina, and Thomas A. Loughran. 2011. "Testing a Bayesian Learning Theory of Deterrence among Serious Juvenile Offenders." *Criminology* 49: 667–98.

Apel, Robert. 2013. "Sanctions, Perceptions, and Crime: Implications for Criminal Deterrence." *Journal of Quantitative Criminology* 29: 67–101.

Apel, Robert, Greg Pogarsky, and Leigh Bates. 2009. "The Sanctions-Perceptions Link in a Model of School-Based Deterrence." *Journal of Quantitative Criminology* 25: 201–26.

Beccaria, Cesare. [1764] 1986. *On Crimes and Punishment*. Indianapolis, IN: Hackett.

Becker, Gary S. 1968. "Crime and Punishment: An Economic Approach." *Journal of Political Economy* 76: 169–217.

Bentham, Jeremy. 1789. *An Introduction to the Principles of Morals and Legislation*. Oxford: Clarendon Press.

Casey, Jeff T., and John T. Scholz. 1991a. "Beyond Deterrence: Behavior Decision Theory and Tax Compliance." *Law and Society Review* 25: 821–43.

1991b. "Boundary Effects of Vague Risk Information on Taxpayer Decisions." *Organizational Behavior and Human Decision Processes* 50: 360–94.

Dhami, Sanjit. 2016. *Foundations of Behavioral Economic Analysis*. Oxford: Oxford University Press.

Ellsberg, Daniel. 1961. "Risk, Ambiguity, and the Savage Axioms." *Quarterly Journal of Economics* 75: 643–69.

Evans, L., L. Hall, and S. Wreford. 2008. "Education-Related Parenting Contracts Evaluation" (Research Report DCSFRR030). London: Department for Children, Schools and Families, TNS Social.

Frederick, Shane. 2005. "Cognitive Reflection and Decision-Making." *Journal of Economic Perspectives* 19(4): 25–42.

Geerken, Michael R., and Walter R. Gove. 1975. "Deterrence: Some Theoretical Considerations." *Law & Society Review* 9: 497–513.

Gibbs, Jack P. 1975. *Crime Punishment and Deterrence*. New York: Elsevier.

Gigerenzer, Gerd, and Wolfgang Gaissmaier. 2011. "Heuristic Decision-Making." *Annual Review of Psychology* 62: 451–82.

Heller, S. B., A. K. Shah, J. Guryan, J. Ludwig, S. Mullainathan, and H. A. Pollack. 2017. "Thinking, Fast and Slow? Some Field Experiments to Reduce Crime and Dropout in Chicago." *Quarterly Journal of Economics* 132(1): 1–54.
Herman, Sherman, and Greg Pogarsky. in press. "Morality, Acute Conformity, and Offender Decision Making." *Justice Quarterly*.
Iwry, J., and M. A. Kleiman. 2017. "A Nudge toward Temperance: User-Set Consumption Limits as an Element of Cannabis Policy." https://ssrn.com/abstract=3166307 or https://doi.org/10.2139/ssrn.3166307.
Kahneman, Daniel. 2011. *Thinking, Fast and Slow*. New York: Farrar Straus Giroux.
Kahneman, Daniel, and Shane Frederick. 2005. "A Model of Heuristic Judgment." In K. J. Holyoak and R. G. Morrison (eds.), *The Cambridge Handbook of Thinking and Reasoning*, 267–93. New York: Cambridge University Press.
2002. "Representativeness Revisited: Attribute Substitution in Intuitive Judgment." In T. Gilovich, D. Griffin, and D. Kahneman (eds.), *Heuristics and Biases: The Psychology of Intuitive Judgment*, 49–81. New York: Cambridge University Press.
Kahneman, Daniel, and Amos Tversky. 1979. "Prospect Theory: An Analysis of Decision under Risk." *Econometrica* 47: 263–92.
Laub, John H. 2004. "The Life Course of Criminology in the United States: The American Society of Criminology 2003 Presidential Address." *Criminology* 42(1): 1–26.
Locke, John. 1690. *An Essay Concerning Human Understanding*. London: Thomas Basset.
Loughran, Thomas A., Ray Paternoster, Alex R. Piquero, and Greg Pogarsky. 2011a. "On Ambiguity in Perceptions of Risk: Implications for Decision-Making and Deterrence." *Criminology* 49: 1029–61.
Loughran, Thomas A., Alex Piquero, Jeffrey Fagan, and Edward Mulvey. 2011b. "Deterring Serious and Chronic Offenders: Research Findings and Policy Thoughts from the Pathways to Desistance Study." In N. Dowd (ed.), *Justice for Kids: Keeping Kids out of the Juvenile Justice System*. New York: NYU Press.
Nagin, D. S. 1998. "Criminal Deterrence Research at the Outset of the Twenty-First Century." *Crime and Justice* 23: 1–42.
Paternoster, Raymond, and Greg Pogarsky. 2009. "Rational Choice, Agency, and Thoughtfully Reflective Decision Making: The Short and Long-Term Consequences of Making Good Choices." *Journal of Quantitative Criminology* 25: 103–27.
Pickett, Justin T. 2019. "Using Behavioral Economics to Advance Deterrence Research and Improve Crime Policy: Some Illustrative Experiments." *Crime and Delinquency* 64(12): 1636–59.
Pickett, Justin T., and Shawn Bushway. 2015. "Dispositional Sources of Sanction Perceptions: Emotionality, Cognitive Style, Intolerance of Ambiguity, and Self Efficacy." *Law and Human Behavior* 39(6): 624–40.
Piquero, Alex, Ray Paternoster, Greg Pogarsky, and Thomas A. Loughran. 2011. "Elaborating the Individual Difference Component of Deterrence Theory." *Annual Review of Law and Social Science* 7: 335–60.
Pogarsky, Greg. 2009. "Deterrence and Decision-Making: Research Questions and Theoretical Refinements." In M. D. Krohn, A. J. Lizotte, and G. P. Hall (eds.), *Handbook on Crime and Deviance*. New York: Springer.
Pogarsky, Greg, and Shaina Herman. 2019. "Nudging and the Choice Architecture of Offending Decisions." *Criminology & Public Policy*. https://doi.org/10.1111/1745–9133.12470.
Pogarsky, Greg, Alex R. Piquero, and Ray Paternoster. 2004. "Modeling Change in Perceptions about Sanction Threats: The Neglected Linkage in Deterrence Theory." *Journal of Quantitative Criminology* 20: 343–69.
Pogarsky, Greg, Sean Patrick Roche, and Justin T. Pickett. 2017. "Heuristics and Biases, Rational Choice and Sanction Perceptions." *Criminology* 55: 85–111.
2018. "Offender Decision Making in Criminology: Contributions from Behavioral Economics." *Annual Review of Criminology* 1: 379–400.
Rousseau, Jean-Jacques. [1712–78] 1974. *The Essential Rousseau: The Social Contract, Discourse on the Origin of Inequality, Discourse on the Arts and Sciences, The Creed of a Savoyard Priest*. New York: New American Library.
Sherman, Lawrence W., 1990. "Police Crackdowns: Initial and Residual Deterrence." In Michael Tonry and Norval Morris (eds.), *Crime and Justice: An Annual Review of Research*, Vol. 12, 1–48. Chicago: University of Chicago Press.

Simon, Herbert A. 1990. "Invariants of Human Behavior." *Annual Review of Psychology* 41: 1–20.
Slovic, Paul, Melissa L. Finucane, Ellen Peters, and Donald G. MacGregor. 2007. "The Affect Heuristic." *European Journal of Operational Research* 177: 1333–52.
Stafford, Mark C., and Mark Warr. 1993. "A Reconceptualization of General and Specific Deterrence." *Journal of Research in Crime and Delinquency* 30: 123–35.
Thaler, Richard H. 1994. *Quasi Rational Economics*. New York: Russell Sage Foundation.
2015. *Misbehaving: The Making of Behavioral Economics*. New York: WW Norton & Company.
Thomas, Kyle, and Thomas A. Loughran. 2015. "Rational Choice and Prospect Theory." In *Encyclopedia of Criminology and Criminal Justice*, eds. Gerben Bruinsma and David Weisburd. New York: Springer.
Thomas, Kyle J., Benjamin C. Hamilton, and Thomas A. Loughran. 2018. "Testing the Transitivity of Reported Risk Perceptions: Evidence of Coherent Arbitrariness." *Criminology* 56: 59–86 (published online in 2017, https://doi.org/10.1111/1745-9125.12154).
Tittle, Charles R. 1980. *Sanctions and Social Deviance*. New York: Praeger.
Tversky, Amos, and Daniel Kahneman. 1974. "Judgment under Uncertainty: Heuristics and Biases." *Science* 185: 1124–31.
van Gelder, Jean-Louis, Reinout E. de Vries, and Joop van der Plight. 2009. "Evaluating a Dual Process Model of Risk: Affect and Cognition as Determinants of Risky Choice." *Journal of Behavioral Decision Making* 22: 45–61.
Wilson, Theodore, Ray Paternoster, and Tom Loughran. 2017. "Direct and Indirect Experiential Effects in an Updating Model of Deterrence: A Research Note." *Journal of Research in Crime and Delinquency* 54(1): 63–77.
Zajonc, R. B. 1980. "Feeling and Thinking: Preferences Need No Inferences." *American Psychologist* 35(2): 151–75.

37

Prospect Theory and Tax Compliance

Stephan Muehlbacher

Abstract: This chapter discusses prospect theory as an alternative approach in explaining tax compliance behavior. (Non)Compliance is frequently modeled as the outcome of a decision under risk, that is, the choice between a safe option of being compliant and a risky option of not complying with the law. Noncompliance results in either a better or a worse outcome than compliance, depending on whether the behavior is audited and penalized. The most prominent descriptive model to explain risky decisions is prospect theory. Many of this theory's core ideas have been applied in theoretical and empirical studies of compliance. After a brief overview of prospect theory, this chapter summarizes empirical studies as examples for prospect theory inspired compliance research. It closes with a summary and critique of this approach.

37.1 INTRODUCTION

Since the seminal work by neoclassical economist Gary Becker (1968), criminal behavior and noncompliance with the law are frequently described as decisions under risk. In this tradition, the most prominent economic model on income tax compliance (Allingham and Sandmo 1972; Srinivasan 1973; Yitzhaki 1974) conceptualizes taxpayers' reporting decisions as a choice between a "sure" option of reporting the full income and a "risky" option of evading all or part of the tax due. The latter option has a good chance to yield a better outcome but bears the risk of an audit and a fine, which would lower the effective income even more than an honest tax report. According to the economic model (that follows the principles of expected utility theory by Von Neumann and Morgenstern 1944), a rational agent would always evade the full tax due, given that – mainly due to the low probability of an audit – the expected value of evading taxes is much higher than the net income in case of honest declaration. Although the model stimulated a bulk of empirical research and still seems to be quite prevalent in the compliance literature, it has often been criticized for assuming too much economic rationality and for its inability to explain the empirical data (for a review see Kirchler et al. 2010). Most importantly, it fails to explain the actual behavior of taxpayers in the real world. Though its theory predicts extreme levels of noncompliance, the opposite is the case: Most individuals are compliant (Alm 1991; Andreoni et al. 1998) – a fact that puts the original model into question. One of the attempts to overcome the shortcomings of the economic model (for an overview of theoretical approaches see Alm et al. 2012) is to draw on insights from prospect theory, a descriptive model for explaining decisions under risk.

37.2 A SUMMARY OF PROSPECT THEORY

Prospect theory (Kahneman and Tversky 1979; Tversky and Kahneman 1992) was developed in response to the overwhelming empirical evidence violating the assumptions of traditional decision theory (Von Neumann and Morgenstern 1944). Subjects of prospect theory are abstract lotteries with a small number of outcomes. Participants in a typical study are, for instance, asked for their preference between a sure outcome of $500 and a lottery that yields either a larger outcome of $1,000 with a given probability of $p = .5$ or nothing with the complementary probability.

The theory distinguishes two phases in the decision process: (i) an editing phase and (ii) a subsequent evaluation phase. In the editing phase, the decision problem is mentally organized, simplified and reformulated by the decision-maker. It is assumed, for instance, that, to facilitate choice, similar outcomes of a complex decision are combined, riskless components are segregated from risky components, and components that are shared by all decision outcomes are disregarded. Further, numbers are rounded, extremely unlikely outcomes are discarded, and if one alternative dominates the others, these are rejected without further evaluation. The most important process in the editing phase, however, is the coding of outcomes as gains and losses. Prospect theory assumes that individuals perceive the outcomes of a decision as deviations from a reference point rather than considering the final state of wealth that each outcome would bring. Hence, the same outcome may be perceived as a gain or as a loss, depending on which reference point is applied. Usually, the reference point is the individual status quo. However, it may easily be affected, for instance, by the formulation of the decision problem (the so-called framing effect, see Tversky and Kahneman 1981), or by expectations.

In the second phase of the decision process the outcomes are evaluated and their associated probabilities are transferred into decision weights. The evaluation is done by a value function that transforms the outcomes to their corresponding subjective value. Figure 37.1 shows a hypothetical value function conforming to the assumptions of prospect theory. A neutral reference point divides the function into a domain of gains and a domain of losses. The value function for gains is concave; for losses it is convex, representing diminishing sensitivity for larger outcomes. A change from $0 to $100, for instance, is perceived as more substantial than an increase from $10,000 to $10,100. Further, the value function is steeper for losses than for gains. Empirical estimates yielded a factor for this "loss aversion" of more than 2 (Fox and Poldrack 2009; Tversky and Kahneman 1992), hence the pain of a loss is assumed to be more than twice the pleasure of a gain of similar magnitude.

Just as the value function relates objective outcomes to subjective values, prospect theory's weighting function transforms the outcome probabilities to subjective decision weights. These reflect the impact of probabilities on the overall value of an option. Note that decision weights are not subjective probabilities; they merely quantify how the attractiveness of an outcome is altered by its associated probability. For instance, if the choice is between $100 for sure and tossing a fair coin with the potential outcomes of $200 for heads and $0 for tails, the subjective probability of winning in the risky option is most likely to be just as the objective probability: $p = .5$. The decision weight for $p = .5$, however, is assumed to be lower than .5, reflecting that a probable gain is less attractive than a sure gain (although the expected value is $100 for both options). Figure 37.2 depicts a hypothetical weighting function as assumed in prospect theory. In summary, the function is characterized by overweighting of low probabilities (i.e., rare events are taken

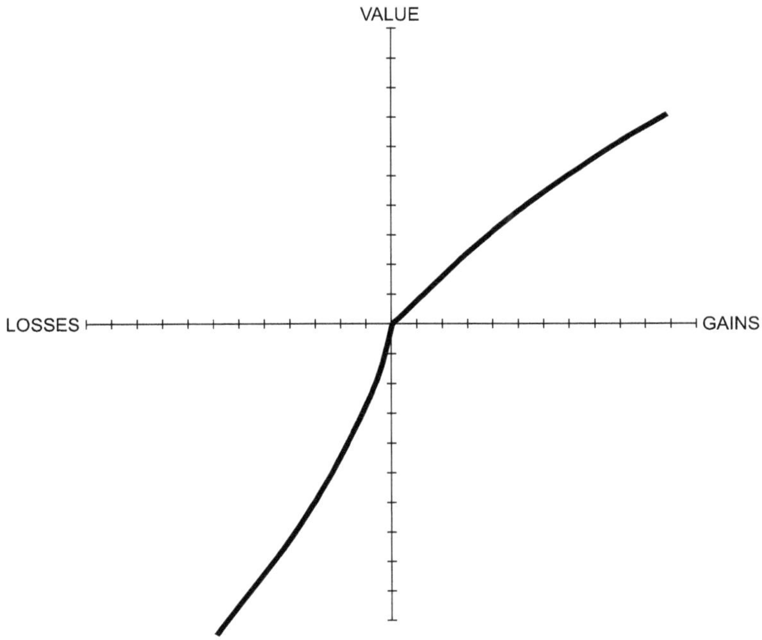

FIGURE 37.1 Prospect theory's value function

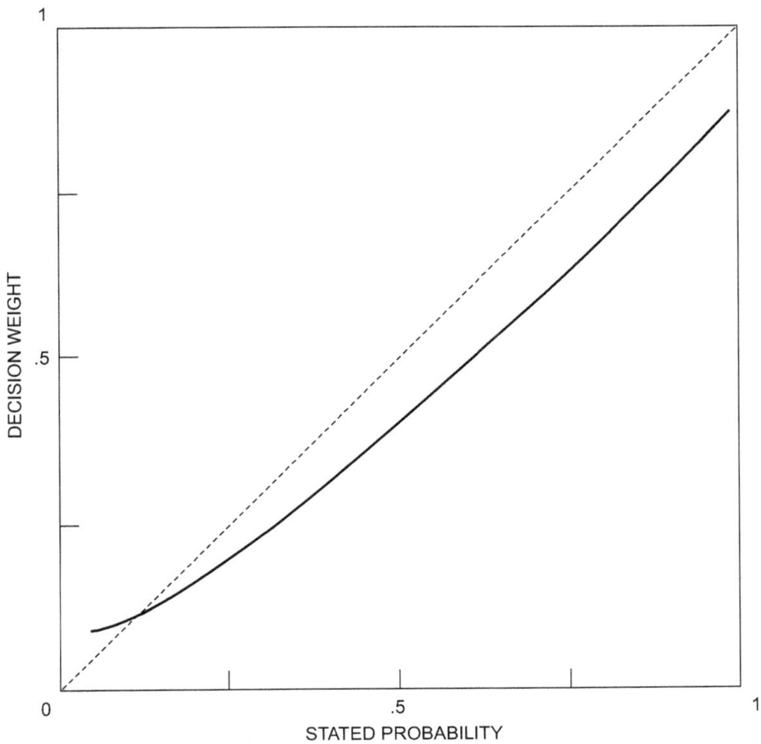

FIGURE 37.2 Prospect theory's weighting function

more into account than reasonable), underweighting of medium and high probabilities, subadditivity of low probabilities (e.g., the weight of $p = .002$ is larger than two times the weight of $p = .001$), and subcertainty (i.e., adding the weights for p to the weights for $(1 - p)$ yields a sum lower than 1 in most cases). Further, the function is assumed to be convex and not defined at its extreme endpoints.[1] The discontinuities of the weighting function reflect the subjective categorical distinction between certainty and uncertainty, and the discarding of extreme unlikely events (or – vice versa – the treatment of extremely likely events as if they were certain).

The decision process is completed by multiplying the subjective values with their decision weights and choosing the option with the highest overall value.

Outlined as a descriptive – rather than normative or prescriptive – theory of choice, prospect theory can explain a variety of empirical deviations from expected utility theory. Probably the most important is the so-called four-fold pattern of choice: Due to the shape of the value and the weighting function, choices between a gain with moderate or high probability and its expected value (e.g., a sure gain) typically are risk averse, and choices between a loss with moderate or high probability and its expected value (e.g., a sure loss) are risk-seeking. However, due to the overweighting of low probabilities, the opposite choice pattern is often found for gains and losses with low probability (i.e., risk-seeking for gains and risk aversion for losses, respectively), which explains why lottery tickets (i.e., small probability gains) and insurances against small probability losses are so popular.

37.3 PROSPECT THEORY AND TAX COMPLIANCE

Whereas the standard economic model predicts an extreme level of evasion for the audit and fine rates prevalent in the real world, an analysis on the basis of prospect theory is more complex and its predictions are ambiguous. Among other characteristics of the reporting decision, the level of compliance to be expected depends on which reference point is applied by taxpayers. Whether the gross income, the legal after-tax income, or the current asset position serves as reference makes a sharp difference. This and other issues of the analysis are discussed in the following.

37.3.1 *Coding of Outcomes in the Reporting Decision*

Probably the most prominent notion of prospect theory is that decision outcomes are coded as gains or losses relative to a neutral reference point. Although this issue is crucial in predicting choice, it is still an open question which reference point taxpayers apply in their reporting decisions. For self-employed taxpayers, mainly three possibilities of potential reference points are discussed in the literature: The gross income, the net income, and taxpayers' current asset position, that is, their financial status quo (e.g., Bernasconi et al. 2014; Copeland and Cuccia 2002; Dhami and Al-Nowaihi 2007; Kirchler and Maciejovsky 2001; Martinez-Vazquez et al. 1992; Piolatto and Rablen 2017; Schepanski and Shearer 1995).

Employing the gross income as reference point (i.e., the perception to pay taxes "out of pocket") frames the tax-paying situation as a decision in the loss domain. Then, the decision is

[1] The weighting function of cumulative prospect theory (Tversky and Kahneman 1992) differs from the original. There the function is fully defined for the whole range of probabilities, it is convex near its upper endpoint with $p = 1$, and concave near the lower endpoint with $p = 0$.

perceived as a choice between a sure loss by paying the full tax due and the risky option to evade all or part of the due, which – depending on whether the tax report is audited or not – results in either a smaller or a larger loss. Due to the convexity of the value function in the loss domain, prospect theory predicts a preference for evasion if the gross income serves as reference point. The second possibility being discussed as potential reference point is the expected legal after-tax income. Applying the net income as reference yields a so-called mixed gamble for the option to evade taxes. Then one potential outcome of the risky option occurs in the gain domain (in the case of undetected evasion) and the other in the loss domain (in the case of detected and fined evasion). In mixed gambles, loss aversion – that is, that losses loom larger than gains – is at full force, which leads to risk aversion and, thus, higher tax compliance. The third potential reference point, current asset position, is the taxpayers' financial status quo and depends on whether advance tax payments were made that led to over- or underwithholding of taxes. In the case of no tax prepayments, the current asset position equals the gross income earned and – equivalent to the case described above – yields more risk-seeking choices, that is, tax evasion. If tax prepayments were made during the year, but the sum of prepayments is lower than the actual tax due (i.e., underwithholding of taxes), then the expectation of an additional payment lets the reporting decision again occur in the loss domain and makes tax evasion more likely. Overwithholding (when the advance payments exceed the actual tax due), on the other hand, and the expectation of a tax refund frames the decision as a choice in the gain domain. Then the decision is between a sure gain (receiving the tax refund) and a potentially better outcome (a larger refund achieved by evading taxes) that bears the risk of an audit and a fine, which would result in a smaller gain than undercompliance. Due to the concavity of the value function in the gain domain and the underweighting of the probability of "successful" evasion, prospect theory predicts risk aversion and, thus, compliance in the case of overwitholding. In fact, prospect theory has often been applied to explain the so-called withholding phenomenon, that is, higher compliance if advance tax payments exceed the actual tax due and lower compliance otherwise (e.g., Engström et al. 2015; Martinez-Vazquez et al. 1992; Schepanski and Shearer 1995; Yaniv 1999).

Which of the three potential reference points are actually employed in reporting decisions is unclear, but the scarce empirical evidence suggests legal after-tax income (Copeland and Cuccia 2002; Kirchler et al. 2009) and current asset position (Kirchler and Maciejovsky 2001; Schepanski and Shearer 1995) as the most likely candidates. Note, however, that, as described just now, the current asset position without tax prepayments equals the gross income. Hence, all three options for reference points seem to be equally plausible and realistic theoretical assumptions in analyzing taxpayers' compliance.

A slightly different reference point effect than the ones outlined so far was reported from a recent experiment (Fochmann and Wolf 2019). In this study, participants had to declare a positive and a negative income and in consequence paid an income tax on the positive income and received a tax refund for the negative income. To maximize their experimental payoff, they had the possibility to either underreport the positive income (by declaring less than the actual income), to exaggerate the negative income (by deducting too much expenses), or to do both. The reference point in the first compliance decision was assumed to be the gross positive income, framing the tax payment as a loss. In the second decision, it was assumed to be the correct amount of negative income, framing the option to achieve a larger refund as a potential gain. In accordance with prospect theory, participants were less compliant in reporting the positive income than in reporting the negative income.

37.3.2 *Source Dependence in the Evaluation of Outcomes*

A phenomenon that has often been observed in empirical studies is source dependence in evaluation, that is, that the subjective value of an outcome depends on whether it was earned or obtained by luck (e.g., Arkes et al. 1994; Loewenstein and Issacharoff 1994). Source dependence violates the assumption of fungibility of money made in economics, that is, that money has no labels. In the prospect theory framework, it means that the value function is steeper for earned income than for "windfall" income, and that tax compliance decreases with the degree of effort invested to earn taxable income. A few empirical studies have tested this prediction. Whereas one experiment confirmed the hypothesis (Bühren and Kundt 2016), and two reported null results (Durham et al. 2014; Boylan and Sprinkle 2001), others have found the opposite effect: Hard earned income led to higher tax compliance than income earned without effort (Kirchler et al. 2009; Muehlbacher and Kirchler 2008; Muehlbacher et al. 2008). The latter finding was explained by a shift of the reference point due to the effort invested. Hard work might produce thoughts and expectations about the level of income that is aspired to as compensation. If this aspiration level serves as reference point and the effective net income satisfies the aspiration, then compliance is particularly strong. In this case, evading taxes would mean risking being audited and fined, falling beyond the aspiration level, and experiencing "the feeling of having worked for nothing" (Zeelenberg and van Dijk 1997: 682). Hence, compliance increases because "sometimes we have too much invested to gamble" (Zeelenberg and van Dijk 1997; 677).

37.3.3 *Mental Accounting of the Tax Due*

A theory strongly related with prospect theory is mental accounting, describing a "set of cognitive operations used by individuals and households to organize, evaluate, and keep track of financial activities" (Thaler 1999: 183). An interview study conducted with self-employed identified two types of taxpayer: a group that perceives the gross income as available funds for spending, as put into words by one of the interviewees: "I am not putting anything aside for paying my [income] tax per month, I simply take from the capital funds what I have to pay and book it as private withdrawal," and another group that mentally segregates the tax due from revenue to ensure liquidity when it comes to pay taxes: "Important as self-employed is that you do not look at money that comes with a project as your own, since you have to subtract a lot from it" (both statements from Muehlbacher and Kirchler 2013: 419). In the prospect theory framework, the first group, who are not mentally differentiating between net income and the tax due, is likely to use the gross income as reference point in their reporting decision and the latter group, mentally segregating the tax due from the gross income, uses the net income as reference point. In consequence, the first group is more prone to evasion than the latter, which was confirmed in three empirical studies (Duggan 2016; Muehlbacher et al. 2017; Muehlbacher and Kirchler 2013). A field study demonstrated that mental accounting practices of self-employed can be improved by a personalized training program on tax compliance and business outcomes (Nagel et al. 2019). A survey revealed that is easier for self-employed to mentally segregate the value added tax (VAT) from the net income than the income tax. However, no relation with tax compliance was observed in this study (Olsen et al. 2019).

A specific aspect of mental accounting regards the cognitive editing of multiple outcomes. According to the hedonic editing hypothesis (Thaler 1985; Thaler and Johnson 1990), gains and losses are mentally segregated or integrated with the rationale of maximizing the overall hedonic utility from experiencing the outcomes. On the basis of prospect theory's value function, the principles of hedonic editing suggest, for instance, that small gains are mentally segregated from larger losses (i.e., these outcomes are preferred to be experienced separately) and small losses are integrated into larger gains (i.e., the outcomes are preferred to be experienced jointly). By doing so it is ensured that, in the first case at least some utility can be derived from the small gain (the "silver lining principle") and that, in the latter case, the small loss is cancelled against the larger gain. The two hedonic editing principles exemplified here were tested in an experiment on tax compliance when completing multiple tax returns. In some states it is common that taxpayers report their income multiple times to different authorities, for example to complete a file for a federal income tax, and another for a state income tax. The experiment compared compliance when expecting either a refund (gain) or an additional payment (loss) in a single tax return, with expecting a refund for one tax and a smaller additional payment for another tax (gain and smaller loss) or an additional payment combined with a smaller refund in another tax (loss and smaller gain) in multiple tax returns. In the experimental conditions regarding the single return, a withholding phenomenon was observed, that is, higher compliance when expecting a tax refund than when expecting an additional payment. In line with the hedonic editing hypothesis, however, compliance decreased in comparison to the single refund condition when facing a large refund and smaller payment in multiple returns, although the total refund was the same in both conditions. The opposite, that is, an increase in compliance, was found when comparing the condition with a large payment and a small refund in multiple returns to the single payment condition. These findings demonstrate that observations made for single tax reports cannot be generalized to compliance in multiple reports, and that mental accounting theory is useful when explaining taxpayers' behavior.

37.3.4 *Subjective Probability of Audits*

Both the traditional economic model and alternative approaches drawing on prospect theory rely on the assumption that the exact outcome probabilities are known by the decision-maker. However, information about real audit probabilities is hardly available. Hence, taxpayers' compliance decisions are based on vague estimations about the likelihood that an attempt to evade taxes is detected by authorities during an audit (Fischer et al. 1992).

If taxpayers were aware of the extremely low audit probability (the U.S. Internal Revenue Service reports, for instance, that only 0.84 percent of the files from private taxpayers were audited in 2015; Internal Revenue Service 2016), the economic model would predict a compliance rate close to zero. The rather high compliance observed in the real world can in part be explained by overestimation of the true probability and the overweighting of low probabilities as postulated in prospect theory (Alm et al. 1992; Yaniv 1999). A survey study revealed, in fact, that estimates of the audit probability are higher among honest taxpayers than among tax evaders (Mason and Calvin 1978). Further, subjective probabilities are affected by the experience of an audit. In a laboratory experiment, compliance in later periods was positively correlated with the number of audits that occurred in previous rounds (Spicer and Hero 1985). This observation can be explained by the availability heuristic (Tversky and Kahneman 1974). According to this heuristic, the likelihood of an event is judged by how easily an instance or example of the event comes to mind. Having observed or experienced a similar event recently leads to overestimation of its probability. However, a recent audit can also have the opposite effect on compliance. In most laboratory experiments, a phenomenon is observed that is known as the "bomb crater" effect (Mittone 2006). As soldiers in the First World War tended to hide in bomb craters, because they assumed that a bomb would never hit the same place twice, participants in tax experiments seem to underestimate the probability of being audited twice in a row. In the experimental period after an audit took place, compliance is typically much lower than before.

37.4 SUMMARY AND DISCUSSION

Besides the economic model, prospect theory is frequently applied as alternative approach to describe taxpayers' compliance. Prospect theory can explain some of the puzzles in tax compliance research such as the withholding phenomenon, differences in compliance when declaring income vs. deducting business costs, and high compliance despite low audit probabilities. However, its application opens up further questions that need to be addressed in future research. Unclear, for instance, is which reference point taxpayers apply when it is not provided by the situation, as in the case of the withholding phenomenon. Research on mental accounting suggests that there are strong interindividual differences in whether the gross or the net income is employed as reference, but more research is needed to understand how mental accounting practices are developed and which mental processes determine which reference points are chosen. Another important field for research that is still in its infancy is regarding the formation of subjective probabilities and their linkage to objective probabilities; a problem that starts with the lack of a common definition for the audit (and detection) probability (Fischer et al. 1992). Further, whereas in the judgement and decision-making literature a distinction between decisions from description (where the likelihood of a risky outcome is stated in the problem formulation) and decisions from experience (where judgement of the likelihood of rare events is based on experience) has already been proposed (e.g., Hertwig et al. 2004), tax research still lacks such a differentiation. However, reporting decisions in the real world are most likely based on experienced and consequently subjective probabilities.

Although prospect theory is useful in explaining some of the observed behavior, it is not able to fully explain why people pay taxes. As the economic model for tax compliance, its approach still assumes a high degree of rationality and leaves noneconomic factors out of the equation. Psychological research emphasizes, for instance, the role of social norms and justice concerns, and differentiates between voluntary and enforced compliance (Kirchler 2007). Other research paradigms (for an overview see Alm et al. 2012) put the collective goals that are achieved by levying taxes into focus and suggest that tax compliance is the result of considering both: the egoistical goal of income maximization and the collective utility that is provided by the public goods financed by our taxes.

REFERENCES

Allingham, Michael G., and Agnar Sandmo. 1972. "Income Tax Evasion: A Theoretical Analysis." *Journal of Public Economics* 1 (3–4): 323–38.

Alm, James. 1991. "A Perspective on the Experimental Analysis of Taxpayer Reporting." *Accounting Review* 66 (3): 577–93.

Alm, James, Gary H. McClelland, and William D. Schulze. 1992. "Why Do People Pay Taxes?" *Journal of Public Economics* 48 (1): 21–38.

Alm, James, Erich Kirchler, and Stephan Muehlbacher. 2012. "Combining Psychology and Economics in the Analysis of Compliance: From Enforcement to Cooperation." *Economic Analysis & Policy* 42 (2): 133–51.

Andreoni, James, Brian Erard, and Jonathan Feinstein. 1998. "Tax Compliance." *Journal of Economic Literature* 36 (2): 818–60.

Arkes, Hal R., Cynthia A. Joyner, Mark V. Pezzo, Jane Gradwohl Nash, Karen Siegel-Jacobs, and Eric Stone. 1994. "The Psychology of Windfall Gains." *Organizational Behavior and Human Decision Processes* 59 (3): 331–47.

Becker, Gary S. 1968. "Crime and Punishment: An Economic Approach." *Journal of Political Economy* 76 (2): 169–217.

Bernasconi, Michele, Luca Corazzini, and Raffaello Seri. 2014. "Reference Dependent Preferences, Hedonic Adaptation and Tax Evasion: Does the Tax Burden Matter?" *Journal of Economic Psychology* 40 (0): 103–18.

Boylan, Scott J., and Geoffrey B Sprinkle. 2001. "Experimental Evidence on the Relation between Tax Rates and Compliance: The Effect of Earned vs. Endowed Income." *Journal of the American Taxation Association* 23 (1): 75–90.

Bühren, Christoph, and Thorben C. Kundt. 2016. "Does the Level of Work Effort Influence Tax Evasion? Experimental Evidence." *Review of Economics* 65 (2): 137–58.

Copeland, Phyllis V., and Andrew D. Cuccia. 2002. "Multiple Determinants of Framing Referents in Tax Reporting and Compliance." *Organizational Behavior and Human Decision Processes* 88 (1): 499–526.

Dhami, Sanjit, and Ali Al-Nowaihi. 2007. "Why Do People Pay Taxes? Prospect Theory versus Expected Utility Theory." *Journal of Economic Behavior & Organization* 64 (1): 171–92.

Duggan, Michael. 2016. "Thinking Tax: Mental [Tax] Accounting and Voluntary Compliance." Paper presented at 12th International Conference on Tax Administration, Sydney, Australia, March 31–April 1.

Durham, Yvonne, Tracy S. Manly, and Christina Ritsema. 2014. "The Effects of Income Source, Context, and Income Level on Tax Compliance Decisions in a Dynamic Experiment." *Journal of Economic Psychology* 40 (0): 220–33.

Engström, Per, Katarina Nordblom, Henry Ohlsson, and Annika Persson. 2015. "Tax Compliance and Loss Aversion." *American Economic Journal: Economic Policy* 7 (4): 132–64.

Fischer, Carol M., Martha Wartick, and Melvin M. Mark. 1992. "Detection Probability and Taxpayer Compliance: A Review of the Literature." *Journal of Accounting Literature* 11: 1–46.

Fochmann, Martin, and Nadja Wolf. 2019. "Framing and Salience Effects in Tax Evasion Decisions – An Experiment on Underreporting and Overdeducting." *Journal of Economic Psychology* 72: 260–77.

Fox, Craig R., and Russell A. Poldrack. 2009. "Chapter 11 – Prospect Theory and the Brain." In *Neuroeconomics*, edited by Paul W. Glimcher, Colin F. Camerer, Ernst Fehr, and Russell A. Poldrack, 145–73. London: Academic Press.

Hertwig, Ralph, Greg Barron, Elke U. Weber, and Ido Erev. 2004. "Decisions from Experience and the Effect of Rare Events in Risky Choice." *Psychological Science* 15 (8): 534–9.

Internal Revenue Service. 2016. *Data Book, 2015 (Publication 55B)*. Washington, DC. www.irs.gov/pub/irs-soi/15databk.pdf.

Kahneman, Daniel, and Amos Tversky. 1979. "Prospect Theory: An Analysis of Decision under Risk." *Econometrica* 47 (2): 263–92.

Kirchler, Erich. 2007. *The Economic Psychology of Tax Behaviour*. Cambridge: Cambridge University Press.

Kirchler, Erich, and Boris Maciejovsky. 2001. "Tax Compliance within the Context of Gain and Loss Situations, Expected and Current Asset Position, and Profession." *Journal of Economic Psychology* 22 (2): 179–94.

Kirchler, Erich, Stephan Muehlbacher, Erik Hoelzl, and P. Webley. 2009. "Effort and Aspirations in Tax Evasion: Experimental Evidence." *Applied Psychology: An International Review* 58 (3): 488–507.

Kirchler, Erich, Stephan Muehlbacher, Barbara Kastlunger, and Ingrid Wahl. 2010. "Why Pay Taxes? A Review of Tax Compliance Decisions." In *Developing Alternative Frameworks for Explaining Tax Compliance*, edited by James Alm, Jorge Martinez-Vazquez, and Benno Torgler, 15–31. Abingdon, UK: Routledge.

Loewenstein, George, and Samuel Issacharoff. 1994. "Source Dependence in the Valuation of Objects." *Journal of Behavioral Decision Making* 7 (3): 157–68.

Martinez-Vazquez, Jorge, Gordon B. Harwood, and Ernest R. Larkins. 1992. "Withholding Position and Income Tax Compliance: Some Experimental Evidence." *Public Finance Review* 20 (2): 152–74.
Mason, Robert, and Lyle D. Calvin. 1978. "Study of Admitted Income Tax Evasion." *Law & Society Review* 13: 73–89.
Mittone, Luigi. 2006. "Dynamic Behaviour in Tax Evasion: An Experimental Approach." *Journal of Socio-economics* 35 (5): 813–35.
Muehlbacher, Stephan, and Erich Kirchler. 2008. "Arbeitsaufwand, Anspruchsniveau Und Steuerehrlichkeit." *Zeitschrift Für Arbeits- Und Organisationspsychologie* 52 (2): 91–96.
2013. "Mental Accounting of Self-Employed Taxpayers: On the Mental Segregation of the Net Income and the Tax Due." *FinanzArchiv: Public Finance Analysis* 69 (4): 412–38.
Muehlbacher, Stephan, Erich Kirchler, Erik Hoelzl, J. Ashby, C. Berti, J. Job, S. Kemp, R. U. Peterlik, C. Roland-Levy, and K. Waldherr. 2008. "Hard-Earned Income and Tax Compliance: A Survey in Eight Nations." *European Psychologist* 13 (4): 298–304.
Muehlbacher, Stephan, Barbara Hartl, and Erich Kirchler. 2017. "Mental Accounting and Tax Compliance: Experimental Evidence for the Effect of Mental Segregation of Tax Due and Revenue on Compliance." *Public Finance Review* 45 (1): 118–39.
Nagel, Hanskje, Laura Rosendahl Huber, Mirjam Van Praag, and Sjoerd Goslinga. 2019. "The Effect of a Tax Training Program on Tax Compliance and Business Outcomes of Starting Entrepreneurs: Evidence from a Field Experiment." *Applying Experimental Methods to Advance Entrepreneurship Research* 34 (2): 261–83.
Olsen, Jerome, Matthias Kasper, Christoph Kogler, Stephan Muehlbacher, and Erich Kirchler. 2019. "Mental Accounting of Income Tax and Value Added Tax among Self-Employed Business Owners." *Journal of Economic Psychology* 70 (January): 125–39.
Piolatto, Amedeo, and Matthew D. Rablen. 2017. "Prospect Theory and Tax Evasion: A Reconsideration of the Yitzhaki Puzzle." *Theory and Decision* 82 (4): 543–65.
Schepanski, Albert, and Teri Shearer. 1995. "A Prospect Theory Account of the Income Tax Withholding Phenomenon." *Organizational Behavior and Human Decision Processes* 63 (2): 174–86.
Spicer, Michael W., and Rodney E. Hero. 1985. "Tax Evasion and Heuristics: A Research Note." *Journal of Public Economics* 26 (2): 263–7.
Srinivasan, Thirukodikaval N. 1973. "Tax Evasion: A Model." *Journal of Public Economics* 2 (4): 339–46.
Thaler, Richard H. 1985. "Mental Accounting and Consumer Choice." *Marketing Science* 4 (3): 199–217.
1999. "Mental Accounting Matters." *Journal of Behavioral Decision Making* 12 (3): 183–206.
Thaler, Richard H., and E. J. Johnson. 1990. "Gambling with the House Money and Trying to Break Even: The Effects of Prior Outcomes on Risky Choice." *Management Science* 36 (6): 643–60.
Tversky, Amos, and Daniel Kahneman. 1974. "Judgement under Uncertainty: Heuristics and Biases." *Science* 185 (4157): 1124–31.
1981. "The Framing of Decisions and the Psychology of Choice." *Science* 211 (4481): 453–8.
1992. "Advances in Prospect Theory: Cumulative Representation of Uncertainty." *Journal of Risk and Uncertainty* 5 (4): 297–323.
Von Neumann, John, and Oskar Morgenstern. 1944. *Theory of Games and Economic Behavior*. Princeton, NJ: Princeton University Press.
Yaniv, Gideon. 1999. "Tax Compliance and Advance Tax Payments: A Prospect Theory Analysis." *National Tax Journal* 52 (4): 753–64.
Yitzhaki, Shlomo. 1974. "A Note on Income Tax Evasion: A Theoretical Analysis." *Journal of Public Economics* 3: 201–2.
Zeelenberg, M., and E. van Dijk. 1997. "A Reverse Sunk Cost Effect in Risky Decision Making: Sometimes We Have Too Much Invested to Gamble." *Journal of Economic Psychology* 18 (6): 677–91.

38

Nudging Compliance

Elena Kantorowicz-Reznichenko and Liam Wells

Abstract: In recent decades, a new approach to regulations and compliance was developed to complement the traditional instruments, such as command-and-control and economic instruments. This approach is termed 'nudging' or 'choice architecture' as it proposes to design the environment in which individuals make choices, in order to promote welfare enhancing behaviour. By utilising insights from behavioural sciences, nudges direct people's behaviour without limiting their choices. In this chapter, we explain the concept of 'choice architecture' and review specific 'compliance nudges' in both the public and the private spheres. These include – amongst others – nudges that promote tax compliance, guideline-compliant drugs prescribing, and timely loan and fee repayments. The reviewed nudges include salience nudges, which emphasise certain aspects of a choice to make people focus on it; moral suasion nudges, which make more visible the moral consequences of people's decisions; and descriptive or injunctive social norms nudges, informing people what others are doing or believe should be done. Furthermore, we discuss the empirical literature demonstrating the effectiveness (or lack of it) of compliance nudges. Whilst it is not easy to compare the effectiveness and cost-effectiveness of these nudges across different fields of application, some conclusions are reached regarding the effectiveness of compliance nudges in general. Finally, we point out the limitations of nudging compliance, compared to the traditional tools, and present some thoughts on possible future developments. The area of nudging compliance has the potential to develop rapidly as technological advancements make compliance monitoring, and automated nudging, possible. Whilst nudging is a promising way forward in compliance, ethical questions remain about the proper extent of its use, and further research is required into the long-term effectiveness of this technique.

38.1 INTRODUCTION

The behavioural sciences were guiding private advertising firms in influencing people's choices decades ago, but only recently has the potential of such insights been explored for public regulation. As stated by the European Commission's Behavioural Insights Unit in 2016: 'The use of behavioural economics in the design and delivery of regulation is at the forefront of regulatory policy and governance' (Lourenço et al. 2016: 3). Prior to this approach, policies were mostly based on the assumption that people are rational and fully informed, and thus can be incentivised through different forms of regulation such as command-and-control and economic instruments. However, there is a growing body of evidence from psychology and behavioural economics that people have bounded rationality and a limited capacity to process available information. Therefore, in their seminal book, Thaler and Sunstein (2008) introduced the concept of 'nudging' and suggested that governmental institutions can utilise those findings in order to design legal rules that would direct people to behave in a welfare-enhancing manner.

Initially, nudges were proposed as instruments to benefit the individual himself. This can be derived from the term 'libertarian paternalism' which preceded the term 'nudges' (Thaler and Sunstein 2003). For example, using automatic enrolment (the default nudge) to increase the number of people enrolling in savings plans (Madrian and Shea 2001); rearranging food in a cafeteria to make healthy food more visible (salience nudge) thus reducing obesity (Rozin et al. 2011); or placing graphic warnings on cigarette packages (saliency and affect nudges) to deter people from smoking (Hammond et al. 2007).

However, with time the concept developed to include 'benevolent' nudges; namely, instruments to enhance *social* welfare. Examples of such nudges include: the use of social norm statements – stating the actual behaviour or normative beliefs of the majority of people – to promote energy-saving behaviour (Allcott 2011) or to increase tax compliance (Hallsworth et al. 2017); implementing automatic registration for post-mortem organ donation (default nudge) to increase available transplant organs (Johnson and Goldstein 2003); or setting an additional small default payment for a flight ticket to offset CO_2 emissions (Araña and Léon 2013). Different nudges use different psychological mechanisms to drive people's behaviour. They utilise, for example: people's inertia, their susceptibility to social influence, or their responsiveness to more salient events or objects.

Using people's psychology to design rules that shape behaviour might be a less intrusive approach than traditional policy instruments such as command-and-control regulation. Nudges are also often cheaper, and usually better accepted by the public (Reisch and Sunstein 2016; John 2018; Sunstein et al. 2018). High public approval can reduce the political costs of public policies.

Nudges (more precisely, the 'benevolent' nudges) can also be used in the context of compliance with different rules. In addition to the example of paying taxes, they may also be used to nudge truthful information reporting to various authorities, or compliance with internal corporate guidelines. However, the nudge instruments are fundamentally different from those which have traditionally been used to enhance compliance – the 'carrots and sticks' approach. These traditional tools are aimed at changing individuals' costs or benefits of actions. In such circumstances, a person faces either expected costs for violating a rule (punishment) or expected benefits for complying with it (incentives).

Nudges, on the other hand, are defined as 'any aspect of the choice architecture that alters people's behaviour in a predictable way *without forbidding any options or significantly changing their economic incentives*. To count as a mere nudge, the intervention must be easy and cheap to avoid' (Thaler and Sunstein 2008: 6).[1] Therefore, it is clear that a nudge should not increase the costs of any action. Nevertheless, one should note that in many cases where nudges are used as an instrument to enhance compliance, it is as a complementary tool rather than a substitution of the traditional method. For example, tax compliance nudges are implemented in addition to the regular sanctions for violation. This is not to say that nudges are always ineffective unless backed up by punishments.

In this chapter, we explain what choice architecture and nudges are, and how behavioural science can be used to design efficient rules and choice environments. Furthermore, we

[1] Emphasis added.

demonstrate the specific instruments used to enhance compliance in different fields. Finally, we discuss empirical studies relating to the effectiveness of nudging.

38.2 CHOICE ARCHITECTURE AND NUDGES

The idea of nudging and choice architecture began from the concept of 'libertarian paternalism'. Despite its initial contradiction – given that libertarians promote individual freedom and paternalists doubt it, endorsing intervention – this concept came to represent interventions that promote people's welfare (as defined by themselves, if fully informed: Sunstein 2015: 73) without limiting their freedom (Sunstein and Thaler 2003). The usual justification for these interventions is the bounded rationality and bounded willpower of individuals. As empirical evidence contradicting the predictions of rational choice theory grew, researchers understood that people might be unresponsive to regulations due to their cognitive or motivational biases (Sunstein 1997; Jolls et al. 1998; Korobkin and Ulen 2000). First, attempts to 'de-bias' people were made (Fischhoff 1982), but then a more promising approach was adopted: harnessing the behavioural biases in order to direct people's actions – that is, nudging.

The method to achieve this goal is 'architecting' the mental or physical environment in which a person makes his or her choices. In particular, by understanding the psychological mechanisms that drive the decisions of individuals, choice architects (e.g. government officials, advertisers, compliance officers) can influence people's decisions (Thaler and Sunstein 2008).

For example, defaults are a powerful tool to shape choices. This relies on the insight that people rarely deviate from a rule that is set to be triggered when no action is taken. To illustrate this, Johnson and Goldstein (2003) discussed the tremendous difference between countries' rates of organ donation registration. In countries that apply a default registration – an opt-out system, whereby individuals are registered as a donor unless otherwise stated – the rate of registered is almost 100 per cent. On the other hand, when the default rule is informed consent – an opt-in system, where only people who actively indicate their choice are registered as donors – the rate is very low. This is true even in countries where it is not expected, for example in Denmark in 2003, where only around 4 per cent of people were registered as donors. The psychological mechanisms explaining this phenomenon are: (1) reduced effort, (2) implied endorsement, (3) reference-dependence or endowment. In other words: (1) a default can be effective because it offers the option which requires the lowest effort; (2) the default option is perceived as chosen on its merit by a trusted designer of the choice; or (3) a default option can serve as a reference point in a way that causes the other options to be perceived as losses, or simply less attractive[2]. Which channel – or combination of psychological channels – is dominant depends on the situation (McKenzie et al. 2006; Dinner et al. 2011; Jachimowicz et al. 2019).

Another example of a nudge is the placing of food in cafeterias or supermarkets in order to promote healthy eating – that is, placing healthy food so as to be closer and more visible, and less healthy food farther away. This nudge relies on the fact that what is more salient to people – what is closer to them – will attract their attention. One potential explanation might be evolutionary – people generally try to minimise effort and physical energy to achieve any given goal. Therefore, closer items, which are easier to reach, would be selected

[2] Since, according to query theory, people focus on the advantages of the default option, see Weber and Johnson 2011.

more frequently. Alternatively, the effect might be simply a result of perceptual saliency. Closer items are more salient, and attract more attention (Rozin et al. 2011; Wansink 2016; Kroese et al. 2015). Finally, another explanation might come from query theory. According to this theory, people's constructed preferences are influenced by the order of the presented choices, in such a way that the first choice might be eventually perceived as more attractive. Hence, by placing healthy food closest to consumers, it becomes the first choice in the range of the available food items. Consequently, according to query theory, the consumer will focus on the advantages of this item, and this might increase the probability of choosing this item (Johnson et al. 2007; Weber and Johnson 2011; Dinner et al. 2011).

Nudging also attracted criticism voiced from different perspectives. Among others, concerns were raised about the limitation choice that architecture imposes on personal autonomy – given that people are 'tricked' to make certain choices rather than making them consciously. In addition, it is asserted that with the exploitation of people's biases, the government is no longer restricted by sufficient transparency and accountability.[3]

Nevertheless, despite the criticism, there has been a proliferation of governmental use of behavioural insights in designing different public policies. Already more than 150 governments around the world use nudges to shape consumers' choices (OECD 2017; Sunstein et al. 2018). Moreover, over the years many governments have institutionalised the use of those insights by establishing centralised or decentralised 'nudge units'. For instance, in the UK the Behavioural Insights Team was first established by the Cabinet Office in 2010 to inform policymakers on the many opportunities to utilise knowledge about people's behaviour for the advancement of different goals.[4] Many other countries have such units, some less centralised but still working towards the same objective (Sunstein 2016). Several large-scale international surveys demonstrate that the public, in many countries, generally support nudging (Reisch and Sunstein 2016; Sunstein et al. 2018). Furthermore, several studies on transparent default nudges demonstrated that even when people become aware of the utilised nudge, they tend to follow it (Loewenstein et al. 2015; Steffel et al. 2016; Bruns et al. 2018; Paunov et al. 2018).

38.3 EMPIRICAL EVIDENCE REGARDING THE EFFECTIVENESS OF COMPLIANCE NUDGES

This section focuses on nudges which specifically aim at increasing compliance with public or private rules and obligations. We discuss the nudges, their psychological mechanisms, and empirical findings concerning their effectiveness. By public nudges, we mean nudges which are applied to promote compliance with public legal rules, regulations and guidelines; and by private nudges, we refer to behavioural interventions adopted by private entities to enhance compliance with private obligations or common goals.

38.3.1 *Public Nudges*

38.3.1.1 Tax Compliance

The main nudges relevant for tax compliance are based upon social norms and moral suasion. Social norms are descriptions of what the majority of people do (descriptive

[3] For a good review of those and other lines of criticism, see Rebonato 2012.
[4] The Behavioral Insights Team www.bi.team/.

norms) or what people think should be done (injunctive norms). Descriptive norms are used as informational shortcuts, guiding individual choices in light of the belief that the majority would have an adaptive and efficient behaviour. Injunctive norms present the moral rules in society (or for certain groups) and can be followed by social rewards or punishments (Cialdini et al. 1990, 1991). Both types of social norm have the potential to influence people's choices, albeit due to different psychological mechanisms. Moral suasion, on the other hand, seeks to trigger individuals' sense of morality. This method purports to work by making statements which render salient, for example, the fairness of paying taxes, or the public benefits derived from it. This method assumes, of course, that people are intrinsically motivated to comply with tax rules (Ariel 2012: 32).

The first field experiment examining the effectiveness of social norms and moral suasion in enhancing tax compliance was conducted in the 1990s in the United States (Minnesota). The authors analysed the effects of two types of letter (containing a descriptive social norm and a moral suasion sentence, respectively) which were sent to randomly chosen taxpayers. The study measured the income reporting behaviour of those receiving the letters as compared to a group which did not receive any letter. The social norm letter stated that 'people who file tax returns report correctly and pay voluntarily 93 percent of the income taxes they owe'; and the moral suasion sentence stated that 'when taxpayers do not pay what they owe, the entire community suffers'. The authors did not find a statistically significant effect in either case (Blumenthal et al. 2001).

Descriptive social norms and moral suasion statements were also found to be ineffective in enhancing compliance with TV licence fee payment obligations in a field experiment in Austria (Fellner et al. 2013). Similarly, a study in Israel on corporation tax compliance did not find evidence for the effectiveness of moral suasion messages (Ariel 2012); and a study in Switzerland did not find strong evidence for the effectiveness of moral suasion on truthful reporting of wealth, income, or deductions (Torgler 2013).

By contrast, a more recent large-scale field experiment in the UK found that a descriptive social norm nudge had a significant effect upon timely payment of taxes (rather than honesty in income reporting). Hallsworth et al. (2017) examined data from more than 200,000 individuals who received reminders to pay their taxes. A group of randomly chosen individuals received – in addition to a standard reminder – a social norm message (descriptive or injunctive). The descriptive social norm (with moral implication) included the following sentences: 'Nine out of ten people in the UK pay their tax on time. You are currently in the very small minority of people who have not paid us yet.' This behavioural intervention increased tax payment by 5.1 per cent, which can be translated into £4.9 million during the testing period. Furthermore, it was demonstrated that a descriptive norm is more effective than an injunctive norm (Hallsworth et al. 2017). The positive effect of a descriptive social norm message, as well as a moral suasion message, was also found in other countries: in Norway, descriptive social norm and moral suasion (fairness and benefits to public goods) sentences increased self-reported foreign income (Bott et al. 2017); and in Guatemala, a descriptive social norm message was found to be effective in increasing tax payments (Kettle et al. 2016).

Even though nudges' effectiveness is less uniform than general methods of deterrence (Hallsworth 2014; Slemrod 2016), their costs are definitely lower than the administrative costs of monitoring and enforcement which are associated with the traditional approach. Therefore, the threat of punishment can be supplemented to good effect with different nudges – particularly descriptive social norm nudges – in order to enhance compliance.

38.3.1.2 Appointment Attendance

Another identified problem in the public sphere is missed appointments, including those occurring within the healthcare or justice systems. Missing doctors' appointments can be socially costly in a publicly funded system of healthcare. To resolve this problem, text messages were sent to remind patients of their appointment, in studies using randomised trials (Youssef et al. 2014; Robotham et al. 2016). Those messages utilised saliency in order to induce compliance, by focusing attention on the appointments. Furthermore, slightly changing the content of the message can have a significant effect. For example, in one study, the specific cost to the UK National Health Service of missing an appointment was clearly stated. This intervention significantly decreased the rate of people who missed their appointment (Hallsworth et al. 2015). In this case, a descriptive social norm message was also effective in inducing compliance, albeit less effective than the message which provided the specific cost.

Text messages sent to high-school graduates to remind them to enrol in college were also successful (Castleman and Page 2015). Simple reminders were not found effective in increasing compliance with court appointments for defendants, victims, or witnesses. However, it may be that problems with court record-keeping (of contact details) contributed to this null result (Chivers and Barnes 2018; Cumberbatch and Barnes 2018).

38.3.1.3 Drug Prescribing

Different studies also examined ways to increase compliance with medical guidelines, and in particular to reduce the prescription of unnecessary drugs. In one study, saliency and prior commitment were used as a nudge. The treatment group of doctors were exposed to a poster in their examination rooms reminding them about a commitment which they had previously made to avoid inappropriate prescription of antibiotics. This group prescribed significantly fewer antibiotics, as compared to a control group, during the intervention period (Meeker et al. 2014).

Another effective nudge to reduce inappropriate prescribing has been found in framing the choice. When doctors were presented with a menu of possible medications to prescribe, they prescribed fewer aggressive antibiotics when these were grouped together as one of the options, as compared to when they were presented as individual choices. This phenomenon is also termed 'equal allocation bias' (Tannenbaum et al. 2015).

Overall, the evidence on using social norms to induce compliance with drug prescription guidelines is, however, inconclusive. One randomised study found a descriptive social norm to be effective in reducing the rate of antibiotics prescribing to acute respiratory tract infection patients. The social norm statement stated that the practitioner is 'not a top performer', and was accompanied by the proportion of antibiotics they inappropriately prescribed as compared to the proportion prescribed by the 'top performers' (Meeker et al. 2016). On the other hand, in another randomised study, letters using a descriptive social norm to practitioners who overprescribed a range of risky drugs such as opioid pain relievers – informing them that they prescribed significantly more of the drug than other professionals in their field – were found to be ineffective in changing behaviour (Sacarny et al. 2016). Some notable differences between the studies were as follows. First, there was a much smaller sample in study one than in study two. Second, in study one, the doctors knew they were part of a study whereas in study two they were not informed of this. Third, in study two, the most 'problematic' group of doctors – in terms of over-prescription – was identified and examined as compared to a regular group of doctors in study one. Finally, the type of the drug prescribed in each study was different. These differences might shed some light on the reasons for the contradicting evidence.

38.3.1.4 Public Nudges in Other Policy Fields

One way to use nudges to reduce automobile speeding in places where it is especially dangerous is to use perceptual illusion. Thaler and Sunstein (2008)– in their seminal book *Nudge* – give the example of Chicago's Lake Shore Drive. The series of S-turns on this road puts drivers in danger if they speed. In light of the low level of compliance with the speed limit, the city placed a series of stripes on the road after the speed limit sign. As the drivers reach the most dangerous points, the white stripes get closer together. This gives the illusion that the driver is speeding, which automatically triggers the desire to slow down.

In a different public policy area, choice architects were interested in increasing compliance with the 'minimum distance-to-water rule' amongst German famers. The authors of the study implemented two nudges: saliency of the environmental damage caused by violating the rule (information and images); and an additional descriptive social norm informing participants that the majority of farmers in the region comply with the rule. They found that both nudges were equally effective in increasing compliance: the addition of the social norm did not increase the effect of the salience nudge.

Interestingly, the authors also found that for an especially unresponsive subgroup, the additional social norm message actually decreased compliance. There can be two potential explanations for this: 1) reactance to the regulation – if, for example, the rule is perceived as unfair; and 2) the problem of free riding – if most people comply with the rule, then a small number of non-compliers would not cause much damage (Peth et al. 2018). This finding is important when considering choice architecture because it demonstrates that some nudges can backfire.

38.3.2 *Private Nudges*

38.3.2.1 Insurance

One of the problems that insurance companies face is false information provided by customers. Different nudges were developed and tested to reduce such behaviour. In one of the most notable studies on dishonest behaviour, the authors suggested increasing the saliency of morality by requiring people to sign at the beginning of a form (rather than at the end) a declaration confirming the truthfulness of the information they provide. In their explanation, the authors suggest that signing at the end is too late if a person had already provided false information, as it was easier for the individual to justify this – thus maintaining the 'moral self'. On the other hand, signing at the beginning would make the obligation salient and relevant to the person's choice whether to misreport. In one of their experiments, the authors tested their suggested design in the context of reporting current mileage to a car insurance company. They found a significant increase in the reported number of miles (and thus increased compliance) as compared to participants who signed at the end of the form (Shu et al. 2012).

38.3.2.2 Loans and Fees

In the context of loan repayments, it was found that people with multiple debts tend to repay the small debt first, despite the higher interest rates attached to larger debts. This was termed 'debt account aversion', that is, individuals' desire to clear an account. In one study the saliency nudge was used to mitigate this problem. In particular, the authors focused people's attention on the interest rates by translating them into real amounts. In their experiments, the authors found that making the overall accumulated amount more salient increased optimal repayment of debt (Amar et al. 2011). Similar logic led to the introduction of the United States's 2009 Credit Card Accountability Responsibility and Disclosure (CARD) Act. In order to reduce the portion of people who choose the minimum repayment scheme (which is more costly in the long run), this Act requires credit providers to make salient the expected amount to be paid as a result of different repayment schemes (Agarwal et al. 2014).

Another study, which used saliency as a nudge, found that simple text message reminders were as effective as financial incentives in increasing the likelihood of timely debt repayment (Cadena and Schoar 2011). Finally, text message reminders were found to be particularly effective in increasing compliance with loan repayments when a personal element – the name of the loan officer who serviced the client – was included (Karlan et al. 2012).

In the context of late college tuition fee payment, one study used a descriptive social norm to enhance compliance. The message informed the recipients that 90 per cent of University College London students had already paid. The authors did not find evidence for the effectiveness of descriptive social norms in increasing timely payment of tuition fees (Silva and John 2017).

38.3.2.3 Comparing the Effectiveness of Compliance Nudges across Fields of Application

In Table 38.1, a summary of the literature discussed in this section is shown, grouped according to whether or not the nudge was found to be effective in changing behaviour. The studies are also separated according to the type of nudge employed, namely: salience nudges; moral suasion; descriptive social norms; and injunctive social norms.

Looking at the table, salience nudges seem to be the most effective of these four types. This type of nudge was only found *not* to be effective in the case of court attendance reminders (Chivers and Barnes 2018; Cumberbatch and Barnes 2018), which the authors of one study attributed to the likelihood that reminder messages were often sent to the incorrect number (Chivers and Barnes 2018: 18).

Perhaps we should not be too quick, however, to conclude that salience nudges are always superior. This form of nudging is broad in scope. In this review alone, it covered everything from simple reminders (e.g. Hallsworth et al. 2015), to the use of affective imagery (Peth et al. 2018), to the formatting of documents (Shu et al. 2012). In addition, manipulation of salience may be coupled with other psychological pathways in some studies but not in others. Compare, for example, salience through framing which harnessed 'equal allocation bias' (Tannenbaum et al. 2015) with salience through framing which obviated the problem of 'debt account aversion' (Amar et al. 2011). Both were effective, but this was not solely attributable to salience itself in either case.

Moreover, small changes to the method of increasing salience, or to the subject matter of that increase, seem to influence effectiveness. In one case, for example, stating the exact cost

TABLE 38.1 *Summary of nudges' effectiveness*

Salience	Moral suasion	Descriptive social norm	Injunctive social norm
Studies where nudge was found to be effective			
Drug prescribing: (Meeker et al. 2014) *salience of prior commitment.* **Drug prescribing:** (Tannenbaum et al. 2015) *salience through framing.* **Doctor's appointment attendance:** (Hallsworth et al. 2015) *salience through reminder texts.* **College enrolment:** (Castleman and Page 2015) *salience through reminder texts.* **Insurance claims:** (Shu et al. 2012) *salience of honesty: signing at beginning of form.* **Environmental compliance:** (Peth et al. 2018) *salience through affective imagery.* **Optimal loan repayment:** (Amar et al. 2011) *salience of total accumulated interest.* **Timely loan repayment:** (Cadena and Schoar 2011) *salience through reminder texts.* **Timely loan repayment:** (Karlan et al. 2012) *salience through reminder texts.*	**Tax reporting:** (Bott et al. 2017) *moral suasion coupled with descriptive social norm: effect upon foreign income reported in Norway.*	**Drug prescribing:** (Meeker et al. 2016) *effect of descriptive social norm message upon antibiotics prescribing.* **Doctor's appointment attendance:** (Hallsworth et al. 2015) *effect of descriptive social norm upon hospital appointment attendance (N.B. found to be less effective than salience message stating exact cost).* **Timely tax payment:** (Hallsworth et al. 2017) *effect of descriptive social norm upon timely payment of taxes in the UK.* **Tax reporting:** (Bott et al. 2017) *descriptive social norm coupled with moral suasion: effect upon foreign income reported in Norway.* **Tax reporting:** (Kettle et al. 2016) *effect of descriptive social norm upon income reporting in Guatemala.*	**Timely tax payment:** (Hallsworth et al. 2017) *effect of descriptive social norm upon timely payment of taxes in the UK (N.B. found to be less effective than descriptive social norm message).*
Studies where nudge was not found to be effective			
Salience	Moral suasion	Descriptive social norm	Injunctive social norm
Court appointment attendance: (Chivers and Barnes 2018) *salience through reminder texts.*	**Tax reporting:** (Blumenthal et al. 2001) *moral suasion: effect upon income reporting in Minnesota.*	**Drug prescribing:** (Sacarny et al. 2016) *effect of descriptive social norm upon prescribing of controlled substances.*	*n/a*

(continued)

TABLE 38.1 *(continued)*

Studies where nudge was not found to be effective			
Salience	Moral suasion	Descriptive social norm	Injunctive social norm
Court appointment attendance: (Cumberbatch and Barnes 2018) *salience through reminder texts.*	**Tax reporting:** (Ariel 2012) *moral suasion: effect upon corporate income reporting in Israel.* **Tax reporting:** (Torgler 2013) *moral suasion: effect upon income reporting and deductions in Switzerland.* **Fee payments:** (Fellner et al. 2013) *moral suasion: effect upon TV licence fee payments in Austria.*	**Environmental compliance:** (Peth et al. 2018) *descriptive social norm had no additional effect. In some cases, descriptive social norm had an adverse effect upon compliance.* **Tax reporting:** (Blumenthal et al. 2001) *descriptive social norm: effect upon income reporting in Minnesota.*	

of a missed doctor's appointment had a positive effect on the outcome relative to stating some unspecified cost (Hallsworth et al. 2015). In another, invoking a personal relationship – by stating the name of the loan officer with whom the message recipient had already dealt – had a positive impact upon effectiveness (Karlan et al. 2012). This potential to vary method and subject matter within the category of salience nudges suggests that it may be unfair to compare these with (say) the use of descriptive social norms nudges – a category which is much more specific.

It seems clear, however, that nudging through social norms (descriptive or injunctive) is more effective than nudging through moral suasion. In one field – tax compliance – it is also clear that descriptive social norms are more effective than injunctive social norms. However, for drug prescribing, evidence on the effectiveness of descriptive social norms messages is inconclusive;[5] and, in the case of fee payments, descriptive social norms messages appear to be ineffective (Fellner et al. 2013; Silva and John 2017). In the study concerning environmental compliance, descriptive social norms were even found to be counterproductive for a certain sub-population (Peth et al. 2018: 318).

Turning first to tax compliance: notwithstanding the conclusion reached in the previous paragraph regarding the effectiveness of descriptive social norms vis-à-vis moral suasion, the latter *was* found effective in the Norwegian study (Bott et al. 2017). Yet, neither moral suasion nor descriptive social norms were found effective in the (early) Minnesota study (Blumenthal et al. 2001). Perhaps the results of the Norway study were different from those of most of the other tax compliance studies due to foreign income reporting being measured.[6] It is also possible that the results were confused by the fact that the treatment message was a hybrid between moral appeal and descriptive social norm: it may have been

[5] See the discussion in Section 38.3.1.3.

[6] Whereas in the majority of the other studies it was domestic income reporting which was measured.

that the social norm alone accounted for the effect (Bott et al. 2017: 10).[7] Similarly, the differences between the Minnesota and the UK (Hallsworth et al. 2017) tax studies may be due to a difference in what was being measured. In the former, it was honesty in income reporting, but in the latter, it was timely payment of taxes already acknowledged to be owing. That explanation, however, would remain inconsistent with the Guatemala study – where a descriptive social norm message was found to be effective also in the case of income reporting (Kettle et al. 2016).

The anomalies and observations set out here shed light upon difficulties faced when comparing the effectiveness of types of nudges across fields of application, using (mostly) unconnected studies. Subtle differences in the substance of what is being measured, taken together with often major differences in the methodology used to perform the study,[8] can make seemingly similar studies inappropriate for comparison with each other. Because different fields (in which nudging may be applied) are more or less amenable to certain methods, that problem may become more pronounced as one seeks to draw comparisons across those fields.

More generally, measurement problems and methodological approaches may limit the reliability of the studies considered here. Most are field (or natural) experiments. Field experiments, due to their naturalistic settings, often produce results which are less specific than – and therefore difficult to compare with – laboratory experiments (see Bucher et al. 2016: 2261).[9] It also reduces the extent to which possible covariates can be examined (Bucher et al. 2016: 2260), making it difficult to understand who exactly is affected by nudging, and thus perhaps why. Moreover, experiments such as these fail to measure compensatory behaviour (Bucher et al. 2016: 2256): the individual nudged to honestly report their taxable income may fail to pay their loan debt on time the following day. The quality and consistency of methods used across this field of research may also be problematic. A meta-analysis undertaken in 2018 found that only 7 per cent of studies made use of power analysis (Szaszi et al. 2018: 17) and only 6 per cent made any attempt to estimate the necessary sample size (Szaszi et al. 2018: 27). The possibility of publication bias is another obstacle to obtaining an accurate picture of the effectiveness of nudging by surveying the literature (Szaszi et al. 2018: 28).

Returning to the difficulties posed when seeking to draw comparisons: in addition to problems with measurement and methodology, other practical issues may affect the ability of researchers to compare the results of different studies. These include: different levels of adherence to reporting conventions (Bucher et al. 2016: 2261); different use of nomenclature between studies – it has been remarked that often categories are 'redundant' or 'non-exhaustive' (Szaszi et al. 2018: 27);[10] and different extents to which the studies seek

7 The treatment message read: 'The great majority report information about their income and assets in Norway correctly and completely. In order to treat all taxpayers fairly, it is therefore important that foreign income and foreign assets are reported in the same manner.'

8 Contrast, for example, the two drug compliance studies discussed: Meeker et al. 2016 and Sacarny et al. 2016. The two studies seem remarkably similar at first blush, but several differences in methodology could easily account for their incongruous results.

9 Even so, difficulties in quantifying benefits may stand in the way of the researcher's ability to state that x amount spent on nudging will save the public purse amount y: how, for example, are we to monetise the benefits of reduced antibiotics prescription, when those benefits are derived from avoidance of a hypothetical scenario in which certain antibiotics become ineffective.

10 In addition to this, sometimes the researcher uses a term to refer to the mechanism through which the nudge is said to work, and other times they refer to the type of nudge intervention itself.

a theoretical explanation for the phenomena observed (Szaszi et al. 2018: 17)[11]. These difficulties, taken together, have made it difficult to build a theoretical framework robust enough to yield predictions capable of being tested (Szaszi et al. 2018: 17). Without a strong theoretical framework, this field of research will struggle to provide a reliable account of which types of nudges are likely to work best in various fields of application.

38.4 LONG-TERM EFFECTIVENESS AND COST-EFFECTIVENESS OF NUDGING

Without doubt, the popularity of nudging is partly due to it being cheap and effective. 'Effective' implies that nudging works, and that its effects are both persistent and welfare enhancing. 'Cheap' means cost-effective. In the review undertaken in this chapter, it was seen that some compliance nudges simply are not effective, and as such these nudges cannot be cost-effective. Other nudges were seen to produce the desired effects. In these cases, policy-makers must ask whether the effects persist in the long run and how the cost–benefit ratios of these nudge interventions compare to those of alternative methods. An explanation must also be sought for why, sometimes, nudging works, and sometimes it does not.

One successful and 'widely studied' nudge is the use of 'home energy reports' (HERs). In an influential study, Allcott (2011) found that monthly HERs reduced energy consumption by 1.9–2.0 per cent. Similarly, but in a different context, a meta-analysis undertaken by Arno and Thomas (2016) found that nudges led to an average 15.3 per cent increase in healthier eating. Other studies, however, have found nudging to be 'remarkable' in its lack of efficacy (Oreopoulos and Petronijevic 2019).

Cass Sunstein (2017) recognises that nudging can sometimes be ineffective. Writing in the context of 'default' nudges, he attributes this problem to two principal causes (Sunstein 2017: 8–13). The first (a) is the existence of 'strong contrary [and antecedent] preferences on the part of the chooser'; and the second (b) is the use of 'counter-nudges', meaning 'compensation behaviour on the part of those whose economic interest is at stake'. He also notes (c) that nudges may have only short-term effects. If (a) is proven, then a nudge is unlikely to have been the appropriate intervention in the first place. If (b) is the case then the counter-nudging itself may need to be targeted. However, if (c) is the culprit, and perpetual re-nudging is required, then nudging is neither truly effective nor likely to be cheap.

When nudges work, they can be cost-effective instruments to influence people's choices. A 2017 meta-analysis by Benartzi et al. (2017) scrutinised nudge interventions of several different types alongside traditional interventions such as tax incentives and coercive sanctions. In this case, the researchers were specifically addressing cost-effectiveness. Some nudges were found to be negligible in their effects, whilst others were found to be far more cost-effective than traditional interventions. In the case of energy conservation nudges (again), a billing information nudge (Asensio and Delmas 2015) led to only a 0.05 increase in kWh saved per $1 spent on the nudge, whilst the social norms nudge studied by Allcott (2011) led to a 27.3 increase (Benartzi et al. 2017: 1045). However, the cost-effectiveness of nudging vis-à-vis traditional tools was consistent across all areas, and seems well evidenced at this stage.

Even when a nudge is found to be effective in a study or in one context, its effectiveness in another context, or its persistency over time, is not guaranteed. In relation, specifically, to

[11] Szaszi et al. (2018) found that whilst 74 per cent of studies considered whether or not a particular nudge was effective, only 24 per cent discussed the psychological pathway through which this came to be the case.

long-term effectiveness, one should keep in mind that a large portion of insights which are used to design public nudges are based on one-shot experiments, many of them on very specific samples, like laboratory experiments on students. Not only may the external validity of such experiments be limited but the true power of those interventions to change behaviour is often unclear – even when tested in field experiments.

Nudges might be effective simply because they are novel and maybe surprising when presented for the first time. But it is possible that with time, once they become a routine, people stop responding to them, becoming numb to their effects. In such circumstances, the nudge did not really shape behaviour or change preferences but simply had a decaying effect. In order to design cost-effective policies, this aspect is of utmost importance. Is a one-time intervention enough, or should the nudge be repeated time after time? Can the same nudge be applied, or does it need to be changed every time in order to maintain the effect? Defaults often target a one-time decision (e.g. to enrol in a saving plan, to register as an organ donor). Therefore, they might have a long-term effect simply because once they are put in place, and people do not opt out, their effectiveness will endure. However, when the policy requires a repeated decision (e.g. to pay taxes every year, to recycle), repeated interventions are needed. Yet the majority of studies – and the used methodologies – which are currently measuring the effectiveness of different nudges do not capture the element of long-term effectiveness.

Nevertheless, exceptions exist. Some studies show what has been called 'high frequency action and backsliding' (Allcott and Rogers 2014). Initially, householders would take action, but as months passed the action taken would diminish, requiring a quarterly re-nudge (HER) to maintain the effect. It was found, however, that after two years of quarterly interventions, the effects were persistent to some extent. In a meta-analysis of energy conservation nudging, Brandon et al. (2017) identified that 35–55 per cent of effects persist after nudging ends, based on thirty-eight natural experiments reviewed. Of course, both papers considered energy conservation nudges only, thus limiting their generalisability, and so broader research is required. Having said this, it is noted that cost-effectiveness estimates of nudging have largely been based upon conservative assessments of persistence. Thus, the research overall indicates that nudging may be even more cost-effective than thought. It is also important to briefly consider the case in which one given nudge has heterogeneous effects across different social groups. Bronchetti et al. (2011) provide a good example of this. They consider the use of default nudging in retirement savings decisions. They found that low-income tax filers were much less likely to accept a default option to divert a tax refund to a US government savings bond. This, they concluded, was due to the fact that this social group had strong pre-existing plans to spend the tax refund. As such, the study provides support for Sunstein's view that the existence of strong contrary preferences on the part of the chooser may render a nudge ineffective (Sunstein 2017). However, it also stresses the limitation of relying on studies in one context or on a particular group, to design and implement behavioural interventions in another context.

38.5 CONCLUSIONS AND POSSIBLE FUTURE DEVELOPMENTS

In this chapter, we illustrated the different ways in which insights from behavioural science can be utilised, and are being used, in order to shape people's choices. One of the areas where *ex ante* compliance plays an important role is corporate compliance with regulatory obligations. Therefore, choice architecture is also a potential tool for enhancing corporate compliance. Given its cost-effectiveness, it can assist management in aligning employees' behaviour with the obligations of the firm, and reduce monitoring and enforcement costs. In recent years, some interventions have been developed in the field of 'ethics nudging' (Haugh 2017). For example, the saliency of morality can be used to increase compliance, for example, being reminded about ethical obligations through a signature on a certification, just before performing a task requiring ethical behaviour (Killingsworth 2017).

Another example involves a more covert behavioural intervention. One study measured the eye gaze of participants when making moral decisions. Unsurprisingly, they found that participants look longer at the option they eventually choose. The authors also demonstrated that manipulating the time at which participants looked at a certain (randomly chosen) option could determine their moral choice (Pärnamets et al. 2015). Such findings raise the possibility for corporations to use computer software that would manipulate the layout on the screen, to nudge employees to behave ethically just before they need to make a decision.

However, when considering the choice architecture for corporate compliance, one should note the type of misconduct which is usually addressed by nudges. Intentional and highly beneficial harmful behaviour is not expected to be effectively reduced by behavioural intervention. It is the spectrum of behaviours which are in the grey area, where people might be uncertain about the wrongfulness of their actions, or simply not paying due attention to the consequences of their actions. Tax compliance is a good example of such distinction. The underlying belief with respect to lack of compliance in this area, which can be in particular targeted by behavioural interventions, is that most people do have an intention to comply with tax rules but do not comply with them for different reasons other than intentional tax evasion, for instance, if the process is too complicated, or they simply forget to pay on time. This is not to say that there are no people who actively take actions to conceal their wealth and deceive the tax authorities. But those people are not expected to be influenced by nudges such as social norms.[12] Criminal sanctions are much more promising instruments against such behaviour. Similarly, the types of behaviour which are addressed with reminders (e.g. missing doctors' appointments) are not assumed to be malevolent and intentional. The underlying belief is that people have an intention to comply, but they forget, or are not properly aware of the costs of their lack of compliance. Nudges can also be effective when addressing small violations that people can justify to themselves. By undermining such justifications or making the moral obligation more salient (e.g. declarations or signatures prior to certain actions), minor violations can be reduced.

On the contrary, nudges are not expected to be effective in increasing compliance where the misconduct is clearly intentional, planned, and where people expect high benefits from the violation. For example, cases of bribery, violence, sexual violence, and fraud are clearly intentional, and require stricter measures to overcome them (such as punishment). This distinction goes to the core of the idea of nudges and choice architecture – they are not meant to change the incentives of the decision-makers, whereas with more traditional criminal behaviour, the goal is precisely to affect one's incentives (the costs and the benefits of the behaviour). Therefore, in order to prevent violations, or increase compliance, one must increase the costs of the conduct and cannot leave it to the goodwill of the violator.

A great deal can still be done in the sphere of nudging corporate compliance. Despite its limitations, choice architecture involving nudges seems to be a promising way forward to

12 One exception might be if people conceal just part of their income believing that most people are behaving the same way. For this group, a statement about the social norm (what most people do) might correct this perception, and enhance compliance with tax reporting rules.

enhance compliance with different rules. It is often effective, simple to implement, and less costly to enforce. Nevertheless, the ethical aspects and the practical questions (such as the persistence or the fitness to the conduct of the behavioural instruments) need to be further examined in this specific context.

REFERENCES

Agarwal, Sumit, Souphala Chomsisengphet, Neale Mahoney, and Johannes Stroebel. 2014. 'Regulating Consumer Financial Products: Evidence from Credit Cards'. *Quarterly Journal of Economics* 130(1): 111–64.

Allcott, Hunt. 2011. 'Social Norms and Energy Conservation.' *Journal of public Economics* 95(9–10): 1082–95.

Allcott, Hunt, and Todd Rogers. 2014. 'The Short-Run and Long-Run Effects of Behavioral Interventions: Experimental Evidence from Energy Conservation'. *American Economic Review* 104(10): 3003–37.

Amar, Moty, Dan Ariely, Shahar Ayal, Cynthia E. Cryder, and Scott I. Rick. 2011. 'Winning the Battle but Losing the War: The Psychology of Debt Management'. *Journal of Marketing Research* 48 (SPL): S38–S50.

Araña, Jorge E., and Carmelo J. León. 2013. 'Can Defaults Save the Climate? Evidence from a Field Experiment on Carbon Offsetting Programs'. *Environmental and Resource Economics* 54(4): 613–26.

Ariel, Barak. 2012. 'Deterrence and Moral Persuasion Effects on Corporate Tax Compliance: Findings from a Randomized Controlled Trial'. *Criminology* 50(1): 27–69.

Arno, Anneliese, and Steve Thomas. 2016. 'The Efficacy of Nudge Theory Strategies in Influencing Adult Dietary Behaviour: A Systematic Review and Meta-analysis'. *BMC public health* 16(1): 676.

Asensio, Omar I., and Magali A. Delmas. 2015. 'Nonprice Incentives and Energy Conservation'. *Proceedings of the National Academy of Sciences* 112(6): E510–E515.

Benartzi, Shlomo, John Beshears, Katherine L. Milkman, Cass R. Sunstein, Richard H. Thaler, Maya Shankar, Will Tucker-Ray, William J. Congdon, and Steven Galing. 2017. 'Should Governments Invest More in Nudging?' *Psychological science* 28(8): 1041–55.

Blumenthal, Marsha, Charles W. Christian, and Joel Slemrod. 2001. 'Do Normative Appeals Affect Tax Compliance? Evidence from a Controlled Experiment in Minnesota.' *National Tax Journal*. 54. 10.17310/ntj.2001.1.06.

Bott, Kristina Maria, Alexander W. Cappelen, Erik Sorensen, and Bertil Tungodden. 2017. 'You've Got Mail: A Randomised Field Experiment on Tax Evasion'. http://dx.doi.org/10.2139/ssrn.3033775.

Brandon, Alec, Paul J. Ferraro, John A. List, Robert D. Metcalfe, Michael K. Price, and Florian Rundhammer. 2017. 'Do the Effects of Social Nudges Persist? Theory and Evidence from 38 Natural Field Experiments.' *National Bureau of Economic Research* No. w23277.

Bronchetti, Erin Todd, Thomas S. Dee, David B. Huffman, and Ellen Magenheim. 2011. 'When a Nudge Isn't Enough: Defaults and Saving among Low-Income Tax Filers', National Bureau of Economic Research No. w16887.

Bruns, Hendrik, Elena Kantorowicz-Reznichenko, Katharina Klement, Marijane Jonsson Luistro, and Bilel Rahali. 2018. 'Can Nudges Be Transparent and yet Effective?' *Journal of Economic Psychology* 65(2018): 41–59.

Bucher, Tamara, Clare Collins, Megan E. Rollo, Tracy A. McCaffrey, Nienke de Vlieger, Daphne van der Bend, Helen Truby, and Federico J. A. Perez-Cueto. 2016. 'Nudging Consumers towards Healthier Choices: A Systematic Review of Positional Influences on Food Choice'. *British Journal of Nutrition* 115(12): 252–63.

Cadena, Ximena, and Antoinette Schoar. 2011. 'Remembering to Pay? Reminders vs. Financial Incentives for Loan Payments'. *National Bureau of Economic Research* No. w17020.

Castleman, Benjamin L., and Lindsay C. Page. 2015. 'Summer Nudging: Can Personalized Text Messages and Peer Mentor Outreach Increase College Going among Low-Income High School Graduates?' *Journal of Economic Behavior & Organization* 115(2015): 144–60.

Chivers, Ben, and Geoffrey Barnes. 2018. 'Sorry, Wrong Number: Tracking Court Attendance Targeting through Testing a "Nudge" Text'. *Cambridge Journal of Evidence-Based Policing* 2(1–2): 4–34.
Cialdini, Robert B., Raymond R. Reno, and Carl A Kallgren. 1990. 'A Focus Theory of Normative Conduct: Recycling the Concept of Norms to Reduce Littering in Public Places'. *Journal of Personality and Social Psychology* 58(6): 1015–26.
Cialdini, Robert B., Carl A. Kallgren, and Raymond R. Reno. 1991. 'A Focus Theory of Normative Conduct: A Theoretical Refinement and Reevaluation of the Role of Norms in Human Behavior' in *Advances in Experimental Social Psychology*, Vol. 24, edited by L. Berekowitz, 201–34. San Diego, CA: Academic Press.
Cumberbatch, Jonathan R., and Geoffrey C. Barnes. 2018. 'This Nudge Was Not Enough: A Randomised Trial of Text Message Reminders of Court Dates to Victims and Witnesses'. *Cambridge Journal of Evidence-Based Policing* 2(1–2): 35–51.
Dinner, Isaac, Eric J. Johnson, Daniel G. Goldstein, and Kaiya Liu. 2011. 'Partitioning Default Effects: Why People Choose Not to Choose'. *Journal of Experimental Psychology: Applied* 17(4): 332.
Fellner, Gerlinde, Rupert Sausgruber, and Christian Traxler. 2013. 'Testing Enforcement Strategies in the Field: Threat, Moral Appeal and Social Information'. *Journal of the European Economic Association* 11(3): 634–60.
Fischhoff, Baruch. 1982. 'Debiasing' in *Judgment under Uncertainty: Heuristics and Biases*, edited by Daniel Kahneman, Paul Slovic and Amos Tversky, 422–44. Harvard, MA: Cambridge University Press.
Hallsworth, Michael. 2014. 'The Use of Field Experiments to Increase Tax Compliance'. *Oxford Review of Economic Policy* 30(4): 658–79.
Hallsworth, Michael, Dan Berry, Michael Sanders, Anna Sallis, Dominic King, Ivo Vlaev, and Ara Darzi. 2015. 'Stating Appointment Costs in SMS Reminders Reduces Missed Hospital Appointments: Findings from Two Randomised Controlled Trials'. *PloS one* 10(9): e0137306.
Hallsworth, Michael, John A. List, Robert D. Metcalfe, and Ivo Vlaev. 2017. 'The Behavioralist as Tax Collector: Using Natural Field Experiments to Enhance Tax Compliance'. *Journal of Public Economics* 148: 14–31.
Hammond, David, Geoffrey T. Fong, Ron Borland, K. Michael Cummings, Ann McNeill, and Pete Driezen. 2007. 'Text and Graphic Warnings on Cigarette Packages: Findings from the International Tobacco Control Four Country Study'. *American Journal of Preventive Medicine* 32(3): 202–9.
Haugh, Todd. 2017. 'Nudging Corporate Compliance'. *American Business Law Journal* 54(4): 683–741.
Jachimowicz, Jon M., Shannon Duncan, Elke U. Weber, and Eric J. Johnson. 2019. 'When and Why Defaults Influence Decisions: A Meta-analysis of Default Effects'. *Behavioural Public Policy* 3(2): 1–28.
John, Peter. 2018. *How Far to Nudge? Assessing Behavioural Public Policy*. Cheltenham, UK: Edward Elgar.
Johnson, Eric J., and Daniel Goldstein. 2003. 'Do Defaults Save Lives?' *Science* 302(5649): 1338–9.
Johnson, Eric J., Gerald Häubl, and Anat Keinan. 2007. 'Aspects of Endowment: A Query Theory of Value Construction'. *Journal of Experimental Psychology: Learning, Memory, and Cognition* 33(3): 461.
Jolls, Christine, Cass R. Sunstein, and Richard Thaler. 1998. 'A Behavioral Approach to Law and Economics'. *Stanford Law Review* 50(5): 1471–1550.
Karlan, Dean, Melanie Morten, and Jonathan Zinman. 2012. 'A Personal Touch: Text Messaging for Loan Repayment.' National Bureau of Economic Research No. w17952.
Kettle, Stewart, Marco Hernandez, Simon Ruda, and Michael Sanders. 2016. 'Behavioral Interventions in Tax Compliance: Evidence from Guatemala'. World Bank Policy Research Working Paper 7690.
Killingsworth, Scott. 2017. 'Behavioral Ethics: From Nudges to Norms'. www.bclplaw.com/images/content/8/9/v2/89927/2017-01-jan-feb-ethikos-killingsworth.pdf.
Korobkin, Russell B., and Thomas S. Ulen. 2000. 'Law and Behavioral Science: Removing the Rationality Assumption from Law and Economics'. *California Law Review* 88(4): 1051–1144.
Kroese, Floor M., David R. Marchiori, and Denise T. D. de Ridder. 2015. 'Nudging Healthy Food Choices: A Field Experiment at the Train Station'. *Journal of Public Health* 38(2): e133–e137.

Lourenço, Joana Sousa, Emanuele Ciriolo, Sara Rafael Almeida, and Francois J. Dessart. 2016. 'Behavioural Insights Applied to Policy – Country Overviews 2016'. No. JRC100547. Joint Research Centre (Seville site).

Loewenstein, George, Cindy Bryce, David Hagmann, and Sachin Rajpal. 2015. 'Warning: You Are About to Be Nudged'. *Behavioral Science & Policy* 1(1): 35–42.

Madrian, Brigitte C., and Dennis F. Shea. 2001. 'The Power of Suggestion: Inertia in 401 (k) Participation and Savings Behavior'. *Quarterly Journal of Economics* 116(4): 1149–87.

McKenzie, Craig R. M., Michael J. Liersch, and Stacey R. Finkelstein. 2006. 'Recommendations Implicit in Policy Defaults'. *Psychological Science* 17(5): 414–20.

Meeker, Daniella, Tara K. Knight, Mark W. Friedberg, Jeffrey A. Linder, Noah J. Goldstein, Craig R. Fox, Alan Rothfeld, Guillermo Diaz, and Jason N. Doctor. 2014. 'Nudging Guideline-Concordant Antibiotic Prescribing: A Randomized Clinical Trial'. *JAMA internal medicine* 174(3): 425–31.

Meeker, Daniella, Jeffrey A. Linder, Craig R. Fox, Mark W. Friedberg, Stephen D. Persell, Noah J. Goldstein, Tara K. Knight, Joel W. Hay, and Jason N. Doctor. 2016. 'Effect of Behavioral Interventions on Inappropriate Antibiotic Prescribing among Primary Care Practices: A Randomized Clinical Trial'. *Jama* 315(6): 562–70.

OECD. 2017. 'Use of Behavioural Insights in Consumer Policy'. OECD Science, Technology and Industry Policy Papers No. 36. Paris: OECD Publishing. https://doi.org/10.1787/c2203c35-en.

Oreopoulos, Philip, and Uros Petronijevic. 2019. 'The Remarkable Unresponsiveness of College Students to Nudging and What We Can Learn from It'. National Bureau of Economic Research No. w26059.

Pärnamets, Philip, Petter Johansson, Lars Hall, Christian Balkenius, Michael J. Spivey, and Daniel C. Richardson. 2015. 'Biasing Moral Decisions by Exploiting the Dynamics of Eye Gaze'. *Proceedings of the National Academy of Sciences* 112(13): 4170–5.

Paunov, Yavor, Michaela Wänke, and Tobias Vogel. 2018. 'Transparency Effects on Policy Compliance: Disclosing How Defaults Work Can Enhance Their Effectiveness'. *Behavioural Public Policy*. doi:10.1017/bpp.2018.40.

Peth, Denise, Oliver Mußhoff, Katja Funke, and Norbert Hirschauer. 2018. 'Nudging Farmers to Comply with Water Protection Rules: Experimental Evidence from Germany'. *Ecological economics* 152 (2018): 310–21.

Rebonato, Riccardo. 2012. *Taking Liberties: A Critical Examination of Libertarian Paternalism*. New York: Palgrave Macmillan, pp. 89–248.

Reisch, L. A., and C. R. Sunstein. 2016. 'Do Europeans Like Nudges?' *Judgement and Decision Making* 11(4): 310–25.

Robotham, Dan, Safarina Satkunanathan, John Reynolds, Daniel Stahl, and Til Wykes. 2016. 'Using Digital Notifications to Improve Attendance in Clinic: Systematic Review and Meta-analysis'. *BMJ Open* 6(10): e012116.

Rozin, Paul, Sydney E. Scott, Megan Dingley, Joanna K. Urbanek, Hong Jiang, and Mark Kaltenbach. 2011. 'Nudge to Nobesity I: Minor Changes in Accessibility Decrease Food Intake'. *Judgment and Decision Making* 6(4): 323–32.

Sacarny, Adam, David Yokum, Amy Finkelstein, and Shantanu Agrawal. 2016. 'Medicare Letters to Curb Overprescribing of Controlled Substances Had No Detectable Effect on Providers'. *Health Affairs* 35(3): 471–9.

Shu, Lisa L., Nina Mazar, Francesca Gino, Dan Ariely, and Max H. Bazerman. 2012. 'Signing at the Beginning Makes Ethics Salient and Decreases Dishonest Self-Reports in Comparison to Signing at the End'. *Proceedings of the National Academy of Sciences* 109(38): 15197–200.

Silva, Antonio, and Peter John. 2017. 'Social Norms Don't Always Work: An Experiment to Encourage More Efficient Fees Collection for Students'. *PLoS One* 12(5). https://doi.org/10.1371/journal.pone.0177354.

Slemrod, Joel. 2016. 'Tax Compliance and Enforcement: New Research and Its Policy Implications'. Ross School of Business Working Paper No. 1302, January.

Steffel, Mary, Elanor F. Williams, and Ruth Pogacar. 2016. 'Ethically Deployed Defaults: Transparency and Consumer Protection through Disclosure and Preference Articulation'. *Journal of Marketing Research* 53(5): 865–80.

Sunstein, Cass R. 1997. 'Behavioral Analysis of Law'. *University of Chicago Law Review* 64(4): 1175–95.

2015. *Choosing Not to Choose: Understanding the Value of Choice*. New York: Oxford University Press.

2016. 'The Council of Psychological Advisers'. *Annual Review of Psychology* 67: 713–37.

2017. 'Nudges that Fail'. *Behavioural Public Policy* 1(1): 4–25.

Sunstein, Cass R., and Richard H. Thaler. 2003. 'Libertarian Paternalism Is Not an Oxymoron'. *University of Chicago Law Review* 70(4): 1159–1202.

Sunstein, Cass R., Lucia A. Reisch, and Julius Rauber. 2018. 'A Worldwide Consensus on Nudging? Not Quite, but Almost'. *Regulation & Governance* 12(1): 3–22.

Szaszi, Barnabas, Anna Palinkas, Bence Palfi, Aba Szollosi, and Balazs Aczel. 2018. 'A Systematic Scoping Review of the Choice Architecture Movement: Toward Understanding When and Why Nudges Work'. *Journal of Behavioral Decision Making* 31(3): 355–66.

Tannenbaum, David, Jason N. Doctor, Stephen D. Persell, Mark W. Friedberg, Daniella Meeker, Elisha M. Friesema, Noah J. Goldstein, Jeffrey A. Linder, and Craig R. Fox. 2015. 'Nudging Physician Prescription Decisions by Partitioning the Order Set: Results of a Vignette-Based Study'. *Journal of General Internal Medicine* 30(3): 298–304.

Thaler, Richard H., and Cass R. Sunstein. 2003. 'Libertarian Paternalism'. *American Economic Review* 93(2): 175–9.

2008. *Nudge: Improving Decisions about Health, Wealth, and Happiness*, ch. 5. New Haven, CT: Yale University Press.

Torgler, Benno. 2013. 'A Field Experiment in Moral Suasion and Tax Compliance Focusing on Underdeclaration and Overdeduction'. *FinanzArchiv: Public Finance Analysis* 69(4): 393–411.

Wansink, Brian. 2016. *Slim by Design: Mindless Eating Solutions for Everyday Life*. New York/London etc.: Hay House.

Weber, Elke U., and Eric J. Johnson. 2011. 'Query Theory: Knowing What We Want by Arguing with Ourselves'. *Behavioral and Brain Sciences* 34(2): 91–2.

Youssef, Adel, Hana Alharthi, Ohoud Al Khaldi, Fatima Alnaimi, Nujood Alsubaie, and Nada Alfariss. 2014. 'Effectiveness of Text Message Reminders on Nonattendance of Outpatient Clinic Appointments in Three Different Specialties: A Randomized Controlled Trial in a Saudi Hospital'. *Journal of Taibah University Medical Sciences* 9(1): 23–9.

PART VII

Management and Organizational Processes

39

Compliance Management Systems: Do They Make a Difference?

Cary Coglianese and Jennifer Nash *

Abstract: Regulatory compliance is vital for promoting the public values served by regulation. Yet many businesses remain out of compliance with at least some of the regulations that apply to them – not only presenting possible dangers to the public but also exposing themselves to potentially significant liability risk. Compliance management systems (CMSs) may help reduce the likelihood of noncompliance. In recent years, managers have begun using CMSs in an effort to address compliance issues in a variety of domains: environment, workplace health and safety, finance, health care, and aviation, among others. CMSs establish systematic, checklist-like processes by which managers seek to improve their organizations' compliance with government regulation. They can help managers identify compliance obligations, assign responsibility for meeting them, track progress, and take corrective action as needed. In effect, CMSs constitute and structure firms' own internal inspection and enforcement responsibilities. At least in theory, CMSs reduce noncompliance by increasing information available to employees and managers, facilitating internal incentives to correct instances of noncompliance once identified, and helping to foster a culture of compliance. Recognizing these potential benefits, some government policymakers and regulators have even started to require certain firms to adopt CMSs.

But do CMSs actually achieve their theoretical benefits? We review the available empirical research related to CMSs in an effort to discern how they work, paying particular attention to whether CMSs help firms fulfill both the letter as well as the spirit of the law. We also consider lessons that can be drawn from research on the effectiveness of still broader systems for risk management and corporate codes of ethics, as these systems either include regulatory compliance as one component or present comparable challenges in terms of internal monitoring and the shaping of organizational behavior. Overall, we find evidence that firms with certain types of CMSs in place experience fewer compliance violations and show improvements in risk management. But these effects also appear to be rather modest. Compliance in large organizations generally requires more than just a CMS; it also demands appropriate managerial attitudes, organizational cultures, and information technologies that extend beyond the systematic, checklist processes that are characteristic of CMSs. We address implications of what we find for policy and future research, especially about the conditions under which CMSs appear to work best, the types or features of CMSs that appear to work

* The authors are grateful for helpful comments on earlier versions of this chapter from John Hollway, Christine Parker, Jodi Short, Susan Silbey, Dan Sokol, Lauren Steinfeld, Mike Toffel, Rory Van Loo, and Benjamin van Rooij. In addition, Ben Meltzer and Emma Ronzetti provided helpful assistance with the manuscript.

better than others, and the possible value of regulatory mandates that firms implement CMSs.

39.1 INTRODUCTION

During the 1970s and 1980s, governments across the globe enacted laws to address a host of social problems: corrupt financial practices, pollution of the natural environment, and workplace health and safety hazards, to name just a few pressing concerns (Bardach and Kagan 2002). Although in many jurisdictions the pace of such lawmaking has slowed more recently, it has by no means stopped altogether. The more than 2,000-page-long Dodd-Frank Wall Street Reform and Consumer Protection Act of 2010, for example, attempted to restructure all aspects of the financial services industry in the United States (Labonte 2017). The U.S. Environmental Protection Agency (EPA), to pick another example, promulgated forty-six major regulatory actions during the Obama Administration, addressing environmental threats from greenhouse gases to toxic substances (McCarthy and Copeland 2016).

Despite the continued adoption of regulations by lawmakers and regulators, many of the problems that have spurred governments to issue new laws nevertheless have continued to persist. Financial services misconduct still exists, as witnessed by actions taken by employees of the bank Wells Fargo to create thousands of fraudulent consumer accounts in 2016 (Corkery 2016). During a recent seven-year period, US financial regulators assessed approximately $12 billion in fines and penalties for violations of a variety of financial rules (U.S. Government Accountability Office 2016) – presumably just the tip of the iceberg in terms of undetected or unsanctioned noncompliance (Lund and Sarin 2020). Noncompliance undoubtedly pervades other areas of regulation as well. In each of the past ten years, for example, the U.S. EPA initiated an average of about 2,500 civil actions for noncompliance – and in one year alone more than 1,500 additional facilities voluntarily reported instances of noncompliance to the agency (U.S. EPA 2018). Furthermore, despite many laws on the books to prevent employment discrimination, the #MeToo movement has revealed in recent years the pervasiveness of sexual harassment across nearly every sector of the US economy – with 38 percent of women reporting that they have experienced sexual harassment or assault in the workplace (Kearl 2018).

Clearly, the effectiveness of regulation depends not merely on what governments prohibit or require; it also vitally depends on the responses that these government regulations elicit from private sector managers and employees with the frontline responsibilities for compliance (Heimer 2013; Huising and Silbey 2011). After all, responsibility for compliance assurance does not fall exclusively on government, as government inherently lacks both the resources and the information required to guarantee compliance. Of course, government enforcement efforts do seek to *motivate* compliance, but in many domains regulators' oversight resources are small or even shrinking (Armour et al. 2016). For example, expenditures at the U.S. EPA for environmental monitoring and enforcement have remained at about $600 million to $620 million annually since the mid-1990s, despite the growing number and complexity of environmental rules (Shimshack 2014; Bardach and Kagan 2002). It is inevitable that, to address social problems more effectively, governments must draw on the expertise and authority of the people who are arguably best positioned to identify and root out noncompliance: private sector managers.

This chapter explains how organizations' compliance programs – or what we refer to as compliance management systems (CMSs) – can work to leverage the capacity of firms' managers to create internal plans, procedures, and information systems designed to help their organizations meet regulatory compliance obligations. After explaining what these systems are and how their proponents intend for them to work, we review the available empirical evidence that speaks to the extent to which CMSs can in fact help firms fulfill the letter as well as the spirit of regulatory obligations. We find that, despite some obvious theoretical advantages, CMSs do not guarantee full compliance on their own, nor is it exactly clear how much any formal system, qua system, matters, as opposed to other organizational factors, such as an organization's top managers' attitudes toward compliance or a less tangible compliance-supportive "culture." Of course, the best possible circumstance to support compliance would seem to consist of a well-designed CMS combined with strong leadership commitment to, and an organizational culture supportive of, faithful compliance. We end this chapter with a brief discussion of implications for future research and for public policy decision-making.

39.2 THE RISE OF COMPLIANCE MANAGEMENT SYSTEMS

Regulatory compliance has been a management challenge for as long as governments have imposed regulations on businesses and other organizations. As a result, some type of compliance management "system" has always existed to whatever extent that businesses and other organizations have created deliberate internal processes to ensure that they comply with applicable rules. In more recent decades, however, the management of compliance responsibilities has tended to grow more formal as the complexity of regulations has increased along with the complexity of business operations and transactions. Moreover, rather than merely relying on outside lawyers or tax accountants for advice, as organizations have long done, businesses have increasingly assigned particular staff members – such as in-house lawyers, accountants, and human resource professionals – to play key roles in ensuring compliance with legal requirements (Edelman 2016; Edelman and Suchman 1997). Today, many large businesses and nonprofit organizations have even created entirely separate compliance departments staffed by a set of professionals known as "compliance officers" (Miller 2017; Sokol 2016; Martin 2015).

Together, the establishment of professional staffs to manage compliance, combined with the implementation of a set of formal internal procedures and management structures to promote compliance, constitutes what we refer to as CMSs. These management systems are tools that allow "every business to be its own enforcement agency – identifying, correcting, and preventing its own noncompliance" (Parker and Nielsen 2006). Some of the common elements of CMSs include:

- establishment of internal compliance policies;
- design of business processes and procedures to carry out policies;
- accessibility of policies and procedures;
- training in policies and procedures;
- record-keeping and auditing to assess regulatory compliance and adherence to internal procedures;
- a confidential reporting hotline and a commitment to non-retaliation against whistleblowers; and

- procedures for corrective action of noncompliance.

Increasingly, an organization's compliance-related policies and procedures not only can be committed to operational manuals and training programs but can be incorporated into the design of the organization's information technology (IT) and digital systems as well. Not only can tasks be automated so that they are hard-wired to be consistent with legal requirements, but IT can also be designed to restrict access to certain information, ensure that only designated personnel give approvals to decisions (including exceptions to normal routines), and provide a digital basis for record-keeping and auditing.

CMSs are structured around the specific legal obligations that apply to the organizations within which they have been established – that is, around a host of substantive requirements that relate to financial accounting, tax reporting, employment practices, health care billing, interactions with government officials, workplace health and safety, environmental protection, and more. Although the specific rules that animate different organizations' CMSs vary, the general structure of a CMS often follows what is known as a "plan-do-check-act" model. That is, a CMS calls upon a firm's managers to develop a plan for how their organization will meet its applicable compliance obligations, and then to implement the plan, to check to be sure that the plan is working, and to act to correct problems as they occur. A firm's plan will typically start with assignment of distinct responsibilities for compliance to different members of the organization: its leaders and overseers (such as its boards of directors), its employees, and especially any staff dedicated to managing the overall compliance system. Overall, CMSs function as a type of organizational "checklist" that helps employees and managers to be informed of legal obligations and to overcome lapses in attentiveness that are common when personnel face competing demands (Gawande 2009: 36).

As regulatory noncompliance represents only one of the risks confronting an organization, it is not surprising that some CMSs are nested within larger risk management systems – or at least are related to such systems. In this way, CMSs belong to a larger family of management systems that has proliferated in business organizations over recent decades. CMSs' characteristic plan-do-check act model, for example, also characterizes a much more general management approach originally developed for promoting quality manufacturing.[1] This model's origin is often attributed to Japanese engineers of the 1950s, who themselves were inspired by the work of US engineer Edward Deming (Moen and Norman 2010). In 1987, the International Organization for Standardization (ISO) developed a set of standards, known as ISO 9000 and based on the plan-do-check-act model, to guide companies in improving the quality of their products and services (Stamatis 1995). These ISO 9000 standards then served as a model for the subsequent development in 1996 of additional international standards on environmental management systems (EMSs), known as the ISO 14000 series of standards (ISO 2015). CMSs bear a close affinity with all of these other management systems, including additional organizational practices that would fall under the rubric of enterprise risk management and the implementation of corporate codes of ethics.

Standards for CMSs have tended to grow more elaborate over time (Miller 2018), especially as CMSs in many countries have evolved from broad management principles to more detailed requirements calling for specific documentation and, in many cases, third-party verification. Recent guidance on CMSs issued by the U.S. Department of Justice (DOJ), for example, spells out regulators' current high level of expectations for the rigor, detail, and

[1] CMSs also have parallels to certain conformity assessment processes used by organizations to determine whether their products meet industry technical standards (Hunter 2009).

thoroughness of CMSs. Under DOJ's guidance, a CMS should be "comprehensive" and "well-integrated into the company's operations and workforce," taking into account the firm's specific risks, location, sector, competitive position, and customers, among other factors (U.S. Department of Justice Criminal Division 2019: 2–3).

As suggested by the existence of the DOJ guidance, governmental entities increasingly encourage companies to adopt CMSs. Governments even sometimes require firms to adopt them. A notable example of a CMS mandate in the United States can be found in section 404 of the Sarbanes-Oxley Act of 2002, enacted in the aftermath of the Enron and WorldCom financial scandals. Section 404 requires firms to adopt certain new components of "internal financial control" and to audit their processes for ensuring the validity of their financial reports (Moeller 2004). Other examples of US mandates for the adoption of CMSs or other comparable compliance-oriented processes include (Miller 2018; CFPB 2012):

- anti-money-laundering programs required under the Bank Secrecy Act;
- internal compliance programs on banks' proprietary trading required under the Dodd-Frank Financial Reform Act;
- overall CMSs expected under the Consumer Financial Protection Bureau's (CFPB's) supervisory authority;
- establishment of compliance officer positions in swap dealers and futures commission merchants as required under the Dodd-Frank Act; and
- "policies and procedures reasonably designed to prevent violation" of the law mandated under Securities and Exchange Commission (SEC) regulations imposed on investment advisors and investment companies.

Because these and other CMS requirements impose rules on organizations to develop systems designed to promote their compliance with yet other, subsidiary rules, they are sometimes considered a form of "meta-regulation" or "management-based regulation" (Parker 2002; Coglianese and Lazer 2003; Coglianese and Mendelson 2010; Coglianese 2019).[2]

In addition to embedding CMS requirements within statutes and regulations, governments sometimes require that firms accused of violating regulations adopt a CMS as part of an agreement settling a civil or criminal action (Miller 2018). For example, faced with a U.S. Federal Trade Commission (FTC) action over allegations that it violated federal privacy rules, the social media company Facebook agreed to establish a privacy-oriented CMS as part of its settlement agreement with the FTC. The settlement agreement specifically calls on Facebook to establish compliance officers and conduct privacy reviews on a quarterly basis, sharing these results with the company's CEO, an independent auditor, and the FTC. Under the agreement, Facebook must also document any violations of its privacy policies and the steps it takes to correct these violations (Federal Trade Commission 2019).

Government regulators have also taken other steps to encourage companies to adopt CMSs, even when firms are not officially required to do so. For example, implementation of a credible CMS is one of the factors that DOJ takes into account when determining the size of penalties against an organization and even whether to prosecute an organization or its managers at all (U.S. Department of Justice 2018: 928.300, 928.800, 928.1000; U.S.

[2] CMS requirements are a form of meta-regulation with respect to the goal of compliance with other regulations established to serve separate outcomes of solving problems or reducing risks. But meta-regulation can also be designed to mandate the adoption of management systems with respect to those separate outcomes themselves. For further discussion, see National Academies of Sciences, Engineering, and Medicine (2018).

Sentencing Commission 2018: §§ 8B2.1, 8C2.5(f)). The U.S. Occupational Safety and Health Administration's Voluntary Protection Program exempts certain firms with health and safety management systems from routine inspections, and the U.S. Department of Agriculture reduces inspections for food-processing facilities that institute systems for routine safety reviews (Short and Toffel 2010: 365–6). The U.S. EPA's Audit Policy reduces or waives penalties for violations that are discovered through a CMS and voluntarily disclosed to the agency (Pfaff and Sanchirico 2004; Short and Toffel 2010). From 2000 to 2006, the U.S. EPA ran the National Environment Performance Track program that exempted facilities from routine inspections if they implemented environmental management systems that, among other things, included procedures for third-party auditing of regulatory compliance (Coglianese and Nash 2014). The U.S. Department of Health and Human Services (HHS) has issued a variety of guidance materials designed to assist health care providers in establishing systems to track their compliance with federal billing and reimbursement requirements (HHS 2019).

Such enthusiasm for CMSs is not limited to governmental entities. Even without special mandates or incentives, many companies are individually seeing value in adopting and implementing CMSs. Not only do firms prefer to avoid the financial penalties that can arise from compliance failures, they also have reason to avoid adverse reputational consequences and shocks to their share prices that can stem from noncompliance. In addition, by managing compliance better, some firms have even said they find that they manage their overall operations better and achieve improvements in their financial performance (Biegelman 2008).

The purported benefits of CMSs have also led various industry organizations and other nongovernmental standard-setting bodies to establish expectations for sound compliance management. The New York Stock Exchange (NYSE), for example, requires all companies listed on the exchange to adopt a corporate code of "business conduct and ethics" that, among other things, "proactively promote[s] compliance with laws, rules and regulations, including insider trading laws" (NYSE 2019a). In addition, Exchange Rule 3130 requires each listed company to put "in place processes to establish, maintain, review, test and modify written compliance policies and written supervisory procedures reasonably designed to achieve compliance with applicable Exchange rules and federal securities laws and regulations" (NYSE 2019b).

Trade associations and other industry organizations see value for their members in responsible compliance management. The American Chemistry Council (ACC) – a trade association for the chemical manufacturing industry – requires its members to adopt "Responsible Care" management systems as a condition of membership. Through these systems, chemical companies identify a variety of risks to their operations, including noncompliance, and then implement processes to manage these risks and correct deficiencies promptly when they are discovered (ACC 2019).

Under the nongovernmental standards for environmental management systems known as ISO 14000, a facility must understand its regulatory obligations, develop a plan for meeting them, track progress, identify shortcomings, and take corrective action. As of 2018, nearly 450,000 facilities worldwide were operating such an EMS (ISO 2018). Many large manufacturers now require their suppliers, as a condition of doing business, to adopt EMSs that meet the nongovernmental ISO standard on EMSs.

In 2014, the ISO issued a new standard, ISO 19600, specifically on compliance management systems. Following the plan-do-check-act model, ISO 19600 calls on organizations to develop policies and plans designed to promote compliance with applicable legal obligations as well as other industry or internal standards (Figure 39.1). Although ISO 19600 is flexible as to how it is implemented – indeed, the ISO currently considers it a set of "guidelines" – it does

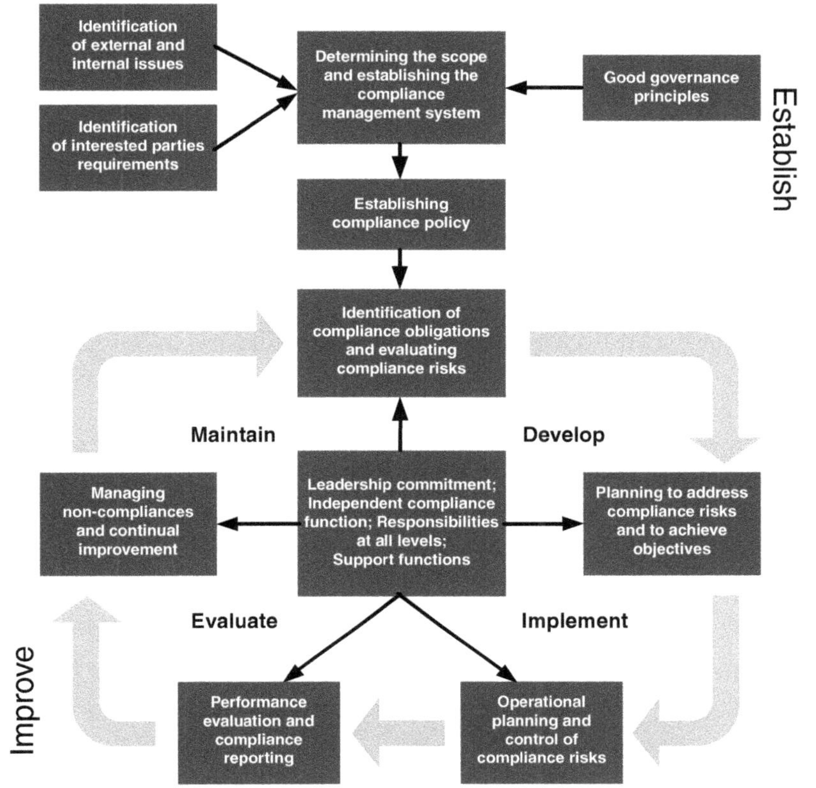

FIGURE 39.1 ISO flowchart of a model compliance management system[3]
Source: ISO (2014).

offer a detailed checklist of the organizational personnel, responsibilities, and activities needed for an organization to establish a comprehensive CMS. It specifically directs businesses to implement procedures and adopt measures for communication, employee training, internal controls, monitoring, reporting, auditing, and management review – all designed to carry out compliance policies and plans (ISO 2014). ISO 19600 also emphasizes the importance of an organization's leadership taking steps to ensure "the integration of the compliance management requirements into the organization's business processes" and "to continually improve the suitability, adequacy and effectiveness of the compliance management system" (ISO 2014). To ensure that problems of noncompliance can be identified, the standard calls on organizations to establish avenues for employees and customers to provide feedback, such as by providing helplines or other methods for reporting employee complaints and by establishing protections for whistleblowers.[4]

[3] Figure 39.1 is adapted from ISO 19600:2014, with permission of the American National Standards Institute (ANSI) on behalf of the International Organization for Standardization. ©ISO All rights reserved.

[4] Soltes (2019: 52) helpfully suggests that firms conduct random, anonymous surveys of employees asking about integrity problems, rather than exclusively seeking information on specific instances of noncompliance. When managers identify parts of their organizations where integrity problems are festering, they can better target interventions, such as by "redesigning incentives, creating new controls, or conducting training" (Soltes 2019: 53). Chen and Soltes (2018) further emphasize the need to evaluate CMS efforts using multivariate analysis and not individual metrics alone.

ISO 19600 is but one of a variety of nongovernmental efforts to promote and standardize the use of CMSs. As early as 1998, the leading Australian standard-setting organization adopted a standard on compliance programs, which it then revised in 2006 (Standards Australia 2006).[5] In 2011, Germany's accounting and auditing association, the Institut der Wirtschaftsprüfer in Deutschland eV (IDW), issued PS 980, a standard on how to audit compliance programs (IDW 2011). Austria's standard-setting organization established a standard on CMSs, ONR 192050, in 2013.

In addition to these various standards for general compliance systems, a number of other nongovernmental standards exist for systems intended to address specific regulatory issues, such as bribery (OECD 2010; ICC 2011) and antitrust (ICC 2013). Indeed, a year after issuing ISO 19600 on general CMSs, the ISO also adopted a similar standard, ISO 37001, on anti-bribery management systems. The ISO is currently at work on a still broader standard on organizational governance which will, among other things, aim to encourage the adoption of a governance system "supporting existing national legislation, policy, regulation, or guidance" (ISO 2019a). The ISO is also undertaking a process for updating ISO 19600 and making it more formal; once revised, ISO 19600 is expected to be renumbered as ISO 37301 (ISO 2019b).

39.3 DO COMPLIANCE MANAGEMENT SYSTEMS WORK?

The proliferation of governmental and nongovernmental standards, incentives, and mandates promoting the use of CMSs indicates that these systems have received widespread and rather enthusiastic support – most especially in the years following the financial crisis and Great Recession of 2007–8. Such support suggests that many people presumably believe that CMSs will work as intended to increase compliance with regulations. That belief accords with common sense. After all, any organization with leaders who deliberately and systematically manage operations with compliance in mind would seem more likely to produce behaviors, products, and outcomes that comport with the law, at least compared to an organization whose leaders pay no attention to regulatory compliance whatsoever and leave compliance entirely to chance or to the whims or consciences of individual managers and employees.

But, despite this common-sense expectation, the efficacy of CMSs remains an empirical question. If nothing else, persistent revelations of major cases of organizational illegalities offer reason to wonder whether the formalities associated with these systems really add all that much assurance of compliance.[6] After all, Volkswagen, Wells Fargo, and other companies at the heart of recent compliance scandals all had some kind of established compliance program staffed with compliance professionals (Grüninger and Schöttl 2017; Martinez 2020). Moreover, notwithstanding their own professional commitments, chief compliance officers are still human and might themselves be prone to negligence or mismanagement, if not perhaps, at times, corruption.

5 Standards Australia now considers its CMS standard to have been superseded by ISO 19600.

6 Martinez (2020) notes that "when one considers the significant compliance failures that continue to occur despite the adoption of increasingly sophisticated internal compliance programs, it suggests that it may be time to affirmatively question certain understandings and assumptions that serve as the foundation of modern-day compliance programs."

All this said, the mere existence of violations in organizations with CMSs does not mean that CMSs fail in general to promote compliance. The proper question is not whether a formal CMS prevents *all* instances of noncompliance. Nor is it whether an organization with a formal CMS simply fares better than an organization with a totally devil-may-care approach. The proper question is a counterfactual one, but it also needs to be a realistic one. It is realistic to ask whether the kinds of CMSs that have emerged in recent years – specifically those built around quality engineering concepts such as the plan-do-check-act model – tend to fare better on average than the more traditional, if less systematic, ways that companies have managed compliance for years. A still more important, but also more difficult, empirical question may be to understand when and how CMSs work – that is, to identify which ways of designing or operating a CMS prove most effective and under which kinds of conditions different designs work better than others.

Existing empirical studies on CMSs and related management systems have been motivated by questions like these. This research has not yet investigated relatively recent CMS standards such as ISO 19600, but considerable research exists on various older cousins of CMSs, such as corporate codes of ethics and EMSs adopted under ISO 14000. From that research, some possible lessons can be gleaned about the performance of CMSs.

39.3.1 *The Theory behind CMSs*

Before turning to the available empirical evidence, it is helpful to consider further the theoretical reasons why CMSs might be expected to generate improvements in compliance – that is, reasons beyond just a common-sense intuition that having a CMS is likely to be better than not having one. Any theoretical rationale for CMSs must stem ultimately from what it is that leads managers and employees within businesses and other organizations to violate the law. Although these drivers of disobedience are taken up in greater depth elsewhere in this volume, it suffices to focus here on three main factors: ignorance, incentives, and illegitimacy.[7]

With respect to ignorance, sometimes people working in organizations simply do not know how their own actions or the organizational activities in which they take part are regulated or what the rules require, a problem that grows more profound both as regulations increase in complexity (Fairman and Yapp 2005: 504–5) and as business operations increasingly depend on globally dispersed suppliers and customers. The internal procedures and routines that constitute a CMS should in principle ensure that employees know about applicable legal requirements (such as through regular training sessions) or, even when they do not know the rules, are steered in the direction of complying with them (such as through IT).

But even when they do know what the rules require, employees will not infrequently face incentives to cut corners or even outright cheat. These incentives can be substantial even if subtle. Whenever compliance makes it take longer or cost more for employees to accomplish a task, the overarching imperatives of nearly any organization will run in tension with the dictates of the law. This tension may be most pronounced in organizations facing significant employee turnover or low morale, or when managers or workers are chronically overworked (Bardach and Kagan 2002: 219). CMSs purport to shape the incentives that employees face, as

7 We do not mean to suggest that all noncompliance stems from one of these factors. After all, sometimes noncompliance occurs simply by accident – that is, even individuals who know the rules might forget to follow them or otherwise act inadvertently.

they seek to establish expectations for compliance that, at least to some degree, counteract other organizational pressures.

In addition, the documentation and auditing routines that constitute a CMS also aim to change the incentive calculus for managers and employees by making noncompliance more detectable, thereby enhancing deterrence. Although regulators themselves offer deterrence through the threat of fines and penalties, these consequences seldom directly affect the managers or workers who have the greatest impact on compliance. Ultimately, the managers of the firms themselves have authority to motivate their workforces on many dimensions – through recognition, promotion, or financial rewards. By helping managers identify and understand the rules they need to follow, CMSs may help "instill a kind of discipline of higher performance" (Gawande 2009: 35–6).

Finally, compliance behavior can be shaped by the law's perceived legitimacy (Tyler 1990). Research indicates that, when business managers and employees believe that regulatory requirements are legitimate, they are more like to follow them (Malesky and Taussig 2019). CMSs might help promote this pathway to compliance by ensuring that employees not only understand the rules but also understand why they are important. Furthermore, a CMS may signal to employees that the organization's top leadership views regulations as legitimate. By developing and implementing compliance management systems, managers may even help construct a "corporate conscience" (Selznick 1992: 352), elevating compliance to a place alongside other values such as earning profits.

Despite these theoretical reasons for expecting CMSs to promote compliance, there also exist reasons to be skeptical about whether CMSs will in fact reduce overall noncompliance – or at least to question how substantial their effects might be. Even CMSs intended to enhance compliance by promoting information, changing incentives, and promoting the law's legitimacy still might not be sufficient to address the major sources of noncompliance. Even if such systems are well designed, they might not be conscientiously or effectively implemented – or, even if well designed and sincerely implemented, they may still be too weak to make much of a difference. They might still be overwhelmed or counteracted by the pervasive corporate norms that drive individual and collective decision-making in ways incompatible with compliance.

In the end, cultural change within an organization truly might be what it takes to improve compliance (Huising and Silbey 2018). A CMS might be one indicator of an organizational culture of compliance, but by itself it may be too weak to change an organization's values, beliefs, and culture (Parker and Nielsen 2009). Scholars who study organizational change underscore how difficult it can be to effectuate deliberate and dramatic changes in existing values and patterns of behavior (Schein 2010; Howard-Grenville, Bertels and Boren 2015). Implementing a checklist probably does not hold much sway over the behavior of employees or managers compared to the pressures that stem from short-term shareholder expectations and the "tyranny" of quarterly earnings reports. In the face of financial pressures, employees and their managers might simply go through the motions in implementing CMSs without undertaking the real behavioral changes needed to avoid certain kinds of legal compliance problems – that is, they may engage in what is variously called "pencil whipping" (National Academies of Sciences, Engineering, and Medicine 2018), "window dressing" (Parker and Nielsen 2009: 9), or the creation of Potemkin villages (Gray 2006; Gray and Silbey 2014).[8] Such rote and meaningless execution of a CMS might especially be

[8] A similar type of mindlessness can pervade the process of auditing CMSs too. Audits may simply check that various procedures exist, rather than inquiring whether they are optimal, or even appropriate, for their intended purpose.

expected when CMSs are mandated by regulation or imposed on an organization as the result of an enforcement action, rather than voluntarily and enthusiastically embraced by an organization's top managers. If managers see their CMS simply as a means to negotiate reduced penalties or obtain official forbearance from regulators, the systems they put in place might even promote cynicism and weaken values that motivate compliance (Parker and Nielsen 2009: 9).

Furthermore, CMSs could well suffer, perhaps ironically, from their inherent focus on rules and on compliance with the *letter* of the law, dampening necessary attention to the adherence to the *spirit* of the law and to upholding other ethical values. Conceivably, a rule-oriented system might unintentionally undermine ethical decision-making by narrowing the scope of what managers and employees feel they need to address, leading them to "gloss over" the broader ethical dimensions of behavior (Michael 2006: 482–3). Although Volkswagen admitted to corporate wrongdoing, its engineers had, in fact, still designed diesel engines that met the letter of the required laboratory emissions test, fulfilling the technical parameters of the regulation. The problem was that the engineers designed the engines to recalibrate automatically after the testing time period once the engines were operating on the road, thus undermining the regulation's ultimate purpose (Coglianese and Nash 2017). When CMSs are oriented solely around avoiding the imposition of regulatory sanctions, they might even crowd out the intrinsic motivations needed to ensure that individuals act ethically and in full compliance with the law (Gneezy and Rustichini 2000; Gneezy, Meier, and Rey-Biel 2011; Stucke 2014). Such an effect could be significant in large organizations facing complex or changing regulatory demands, as their legal obligations probably cannot be fully anticipated by any simple compliance *system* per se; they must rely on the exercise of good judgment by their managers and employees.

39.3.2 *Empirical Evidence of Efficacy*

We know of no systematic empirical research comparing firms that have implemented systems meeting the ISO 19600 standard with firms that have not. Some empirical studies do exist on related organizational interventions, such as internal financial control systems, corporate codes of ethics, and ISO-certified environmental management systems. Furthermore, at least two studies have focused on consumer-oriented CMSs in Australia. We briefly survey these various studies and distill what they suggest about the efficacy of CMSs more generally. The evidence overall is limited and mixed. Some existing empirical research supports the theoretical expectation that CMSs can improve compliance, but other research also tends to reinforce a degree of skepticism about whether formal compliance systems lead to substantial improvements. Of particular concern is research indicating that an excessive emphasis on rules, to the exclusion of values, may undermine employees' motivation to act responsibly.

We begin with research on corporate codes of ethics, and the internal programs to support these codes, because they provide an analogue to a formal CMS. Paine (1994) has distinguished between ethics programs that emphasize compliance – perhaps the closest stand-in to a CMS – and those that emphasize integrity and values. Researchers have investigated empirically whether this distinction between compliance-based and values-based corporate ethics programs makes a difference, generally finding that values-based programs motivate ethical behavior more effectively than compliance-based ones (Trevino et al. 1999; Hofeditz et al. 2017, Goebel and Weissenberger 2017). As Weaver (2014) explains in a review of the literature, compliance-based programs appear to change behavior through "contractual, exchange-oriented relationship[s] involving doing (or not doing) one thing in order to achieve (or avoid) something else (namely, formal or informal reward or punishment)" (Weaver 2014: 298). As such, they are limited to shaping conduct "in a calculative way" (Weaver 2014: 298). But programs that instead appeal to deeply shared beliefs, such as fairness and altruism, are thought to have greater potential to impact employees' behavior on a deeper level (Weaver 2014: 298).

Survey research reinforces some caution about placing a heavy emphasis on compliance, as doing so may crowd out employees' intrinsic motivations to be ethical (Hofeditz et al. 2017: 40). Programs that emphasize "unquestioning obedience to authority" may backfire and actually promote misconduct (Trevino et al. 1999: 132; see also Gorsira et al. 2018). Indeed, "[w]hat hurts the most is . . . the perception that the ethics or compliance program exists only to protect top management from blame" (Trevino et al. 1999: 132). Based on a survey of about 10,000 employees across 6 major American companies, Trevino et al. (1999: 131) suggest "that specific characteristics of the formal ethics or compliance program matter less than broader perceptions of the program's orientation towards values and ethical aspirations." The more effective way to motivate compliance appears to be to provide workers with "a greater degree of involvement and a greater voice" in compliance-related decisions, thereby demonstrating "that compliance behavior is built on their own responsibility instead of control and external regulations" (Hofeditz et al. 2017: 40).

Of course, compliance and respect for the rule of law themselves represent important ethical values. Research on corporate ethics programs suggests that the best approach may be to combine a compliance-based emphasis with broader values-based efforts (Kaptein 2015; Ruiz et al. 2015; Bussmann, Niemeczek, and Vockrodt 2018). The most effective programs appear to be those that situate compliance management in a larger ethical context and that seek to demonstrate consistency between espoused values and actual behaviors, identifying and correcting behavior that managers define as deviating from those values. That alignment between values and policies appears crucial. If employees observe that managers do not themselves fully embrace compliance and other espoused values, cynicism may ensue, undermining compliance goals. An ethical organization depends on managers who respond with "direction, detection, and discipline" in the face of allegations of unethical behavior or legal violations – that is, respond with efforts to promote compliance (Weaver 2014: 298).

In addition to studies of corporate ethics programs, research exists on other initiatives related to compliance management. For example, one recent study modeled the impact on managers' compliance decisions of regulatory policies that promote self-policing and the disclosure of regulatory violations, deducing that financial incentives such as stock-based executive compensation packages are far more important in shaping the behavior of individual managers (Armour, Gordon, and Min 2020).

Other studies have examined empirically the impact of the compliance management requirement in section 404 of the Sarbanes–Oxley Act. This law requires certain companies to implement enhancements to their financial internal controls, specifically third-party auditing of internal financial control systems and senior officer reports on the effectiveness of these systems. A few studies comparing similar firms subject to and not subject to section 404 have found seemingly modest improvements (around a 3.5 percent change) in certain indicators of the effectiveness of these systems, such as the disclosure to the regulator of internal control breakdowns (Iliev 2010; Ge, Koester, and McVay 2017). Although these findings do not measure the overall impact of internal financial control systems on compliance per se, they suggest that companies tend to do a somewhat better job of managing their financial reporting once they implement the additional compliance management features called for by section 404. That said, it should be noted that several other empirical studies in recent years have failed to find any evidence at all consistent with improvements from section 404 enhancements (Fan, Li, and Raghunandan 2017; Bhaskar, Schroeder, and Shepardson 2019; McCallen et al. 2019).

Research on an entirely different type of compliance-oriented system – ISO 14000 environmental management systems – suggests that these systems might promote a modest increase in compliance with environmental regulations. ISO 14000-compliant systems aim not only toward improving a facility's environmental performance but also toward helping companies "fulfill ... compliance obligations" (ISO 2015). Potoski and Prakash (2006: 146–70) found that facilities that became certified to the ISO 14000 standard did spend less time out of compliance than comparable facilities. Although these improvements were statistically significant, the effects were substantively slight: the ISO-certified facilities were on average out of compliance only *one week* less than other facilities (Potoski and Prakash 2006).[9]

Toffel and Short (2011) studied firms that voluntarily reported information about their environmental regulatory compliance under a special federal policy that offers penalty relief to encourage self-auditing. They found that firms that voluntarily reported violations under this policy, which required having discovered them through self-policing, tended to be "subsequently cited for fewer regulatory violations by agency inspectors" (Toffel and Short 2011: 611). Based on careful analysis and the use of multiple dependent variables, Toffel and Short's (2011) results are quite robust; however, they cannot fully discern whether the firms that self-reported violations were in fact more compliant or whether these firms instead were just the recipients of greater regulatory forbearance when agency inspectors arrived.[10]

Parker and Nielsen (2006, 2009) come perhaps closest to the study of systems similar to those that conform to ISO 19600. In an initial study, Parker and Nielsen (2006) focused on the extent to which Australian companies adopted different types of CMS elements. Drawing on a sample of nearly a thousand large firms subject to antitrust and consumer protection regulations, Parker and Nielsen (2006: 471) found that most firms adopted only rather low-cost CMS elements, such as consumer complaint systems. Firms tended to avoid implementing CMS elements that "involve[d] more proactive internal management to identify and prevent misconduct in ways that are embedded in the organizational habits of management" (Parker and Nielsen 2006: 472). For example, relatively few firms established CMS elements such as compliance-oriented training programs, management accountability systems, and

9 Other data raise questions about the effectiveness of ISO 14000 in ensuring compliance. A 2007 investigation by the U.S. EPA's Inspector General investigated compliance performance among facilities that participated in the EPA's National Performance Track Program – a program that required facilities to have in place a formal environmental management system such as ISO 14000 that included third-party auditing of regulatory compliance. The Inspector General found that 37 percent of the Performance Track facilities it studied had greater compliance problems compared with the average firm in the same sector (U.S. EPA 2007).

10 In any study, such a possibility would be difficult to rule out based on data from regulatory inspections. In their analysis of the frequency of inspections, Toffel and Short (2011) did find possible evidence of another kind of regulatory forbearance, as the firms that in the past stepped forward to disclose their violations were inspected less frequently in the future. In another study, Short and Toffel (2010: 366) found that facilities under some pressure from regulators to self-audit and disclose regulatory violations failed to improve their compliance performance over time, possibly suggesting that facilities that implement self-policing in response to sanctions, or perhaps as part of the settlement of an enforcement action, might tend to be less committed to compliance in the first place and thus less effective at improving their self-policing.

whistleblowing protections. Only the smallest number of firms implemented programs for performance measurement and discipline based on compliance. Parker and Nielsen (2006: 472) attributed the varied and seemingly weak implementation of compliance system elements to the fact that the managers in their study did not necessarily see "any immediate financial or reputational gain" from adoption of the more substantial elements, whereas the adoption of simple complaint-processing elements provided for reporting of both compliance issues and the identification of customer concerns that could help firms improve their services and overall enhance their market competitiveness.

In subsequent analysis, Parker and Nielsen (2009) examined the relationship between CMS adoption and improved organizational compliance. Drawing on surveys of the same thousand large Australian firms, Parker and Nielsen (2009: 25) found that compliance was associated with firm size, resources, and management oversight. That is, the firms reporting fewer compliance problems tended to be larger, to have one or more staff members dedicated to promoting regulatory compliance, and to have clearly defined procedures for handling compliance failures. Parker and Nielsen (2009) distinguished between the formalities of CMSs on the books and what they called "compliance management in practice" – the resources, management attention, and values that make CMSs effective (Parker and Nielsen 2009: 29). They suggested that, without suitable staff resources, sufficient management attention, and reinforcing organizational values, CMSs fail to achieve meaningful results.

Overall, the empirical research on programs similar to CMSs reveals their potential for improving compliance, yet it also reinforces a degree of caution about expecting too much from the mere formalization of a compliance "system." In virtually any ongoing business or other organizational setting, individuals are undertaking activities each day that could potentially result in a violation of a regulation, a fact that suggests that, more than needing a mere *system*, what organizations need most may be clear *values* and ongoing *vigilance* focused on compliance (cf. Huising and Silbey 2011: 18). A certified CMS or other formal program may help, but such systems appear to be neither necessary nor sufficient for the attainment of compliance. As Parker and Gilad (2011: 175) have noted, even when companies have adopted compliance systems, a CMS "does not stand alone" but is instead "only one small aspect of the structure internal to the organization, which is itself a part of broader social structures." Understanding the precise contribution of a CMS is a difficult matter for empirical inquiry because compliance-oriented behavior within any organization will be a function of a variety of factors, both internal and external to that organization (Gunningham, Kagan, and Thornton 2003; Howard-Grenville, Nash, and Coglianese 2008), making it hard to isolate the precise effect of the CMS itself.[11] Researchers still have a long way to go toward understanding exactly what contributions CMSs can make and which types of, or elements within, CMSs are most effective in improving compliance and under exactly what conditions.

39.4 SYSTEMS VERSUS CULTURES

One perennial worry about CMSs – or any formalized management system – is that they might comprise merely "paper programs" that lack any meaningful impact on how an

[11] We should presumably expect, for example, that compliance will be a function of the nature and demands of the regulations themselves and the behavior of public regulators (Fairman and Yapp 2005; Black 2012; Coglianese 2019), factors which certainly need to be taken into account in any empirical inquiry into the efficacy of CMSs in promoting compliance.

organization operates (U.S. Department of Justice Criminal Division 2019: 9). This worry is often expressed in terms of the possibility of a disconnect between organizational *systems* and organizational *cultures*. Not infrequently, managers and executives find compliance systems to be an annoyance and a burden, "seeing them as a series of box-checking routines and mindless training exercises" entirely separate from their organization's real goals and values (Chen and Soltes 2018). Unless a compliance system aligns with, and is paired with, an overall culture within an organization that supports compliance, it is hard to see the system proving very effective. As Gunningham and Sinclair (2014: 516) argue, "culture can indeed 'eat systems for breakfast.'" Experienced compliance professionals recognize that, "[t]o be truly effective, the compliance program must be grounded in a culture based on integrity and strong ethical values" and that, "[w]ithout integrity, a compliance program will have form but not substance, and over time [it] will fail to do what it's designed to do" (Steinberg 2011: 33).

The relationship between compliance systems and cultures needs further research. The establishment of a CMS, after all, could well be one effective means for an organization to promote a culture of compliance. But the system and its operation might also just as easily assume a life of its own, divorced from the real values and beliefs held by those within an organization. It might even be viewed as "just a project or one-time idea" rather than an ongoing set of values baked into "the 'cultural mind-set' of all employees" and part of an ongoing effort toward continuous improvement (Biegelman and Bartow 2006).

A particular worry is that CMSs predicated on standards such as ISO 19600 will adhere to a systems-engineering mindset, when what it fundamentally takes to inspire people to follow the law, especially in the face of competing pressures to cut compliance corners, is a more psychological or humanistic mindset. The systems-engineering mindset upon which many contemporary CMSs are based might seem comprehensively rational, but that approach might also be more susceptible to the kinds of crowding-out and pencil-whipping effects about which researchers have expressed concern (Michael 2006; Ford 2008).

Important research findings by behavioral scientists Robin Ely and Debra Meyerson point toward what might prove a more promising alternative. Ely and Meyerson (2010) studied an offshore oil and gas company that adopted a novel approach to instilling respect for proper safety practices by rig workers. The company adopted intensive training programs in communication skills and personal growth designed to counteract traditional masculine traits exhibited by a nearly all-male workforce. Such traits – especially displays of fearlessness and risk-taking – are often antithetical to compliance, as workers look out for their own individual egos and well-being but not necessarily the needs of the entire operation. In particular, workers at the company studied by Ely and Meyerson had previously been reluctant to admit ignorance or mistakes, rarely asking for help and at times even willing to cover up the mistakes of others (Ely and Meyerson 2010: 6–8).

But the company found that safety practices improved dramatically – with a reported 84 percent decrease in accidents at the company – after its intensive initiative that focused largely on educational efforts designed to foster "collectivistic" goals of common purpose and acceptance (Ely and Meyerson 2010: 15). Workers were explicitly encouraged to find ways to contribute to the well-being of the group, rather than personal advancement. The company undertook numerous ongoing efforts to help employees link performance with a larger social good, imbuing their work with deeper meaning and promoting a willingness to learn and improve. As a result,

> [r]ather than hiding limitations or mistakes stemming from a lack of knowledge, as was common in other dangerous workplaces, workers ... brought them to the fore, thus further revealing vulnerability in behaviors anathema to conventional masculinity. When they were new, they welcomed guidance; when they didn't know how to solve a problem, they sought input from others; and when they made mistakes, they analyzed them. Rather than interpreting lack of knowledge, mistakes, and failures as self-image threats to be defended against, these workers saw them as opportunities to learn (Ely and Meyerson 2010: 17).

Importantly, after the company had implemented the intensive initiative, rig workers who failed to follow "safety rules" started to see that their "coworkers intervened" to help reinforce compliance (Ely and Meyerson 2010: 16). Overall, the initiative promoted an organizational culture that "gave priority to workers' safety and emphasized the importance of community, making clear management's concern for workers and reinforcing for workers their responsibilities to each other" (Ely and Meyerson 2010: 21–2).

The company in Ely and Meyerson's (2010) study focused its initiative on the larger purposes of safety and worker well-being – not on simply ensuring compliance with rules for their own sake. Also instrumental were the genuine ways that top managers signaled their commitment to their employees and led by example. In this respect, Ely and Meyerson's (2010) findings are consistent with those of many compliance professionals who emphasize the need for CMSs to enjoy the full support of senior leaders (U.S. Department of Justice Criminal Division 2019: 9–10). Walberg (2018: 246) notes that "[t]he oft-quoted mantra about the 'tone at the top' is more than just rhetoric; it makes a huge difference, especially for compliance officers" who must carry out an organization's CMS on a regular basis. As Biegelman (2008: 174) observes, employees pay attention to top leadership and to "every word they say and every action they take." Top managers' "commitment to all elements of compliance sets an example for everyone else. If an executive does not follow company policies and procedures, it is reasonable to assume that those below will not follow them either" (Biegelman 2008: 174). That kind of commitment by an organization's top leaders – combined with a supportive organizational culture – cannot be easily captured within a formal "system" per se, even though these less tangible factors may be, in the end, the most important ones for ensuring that an organization consistently complies with the law (cf. Coglianese and Nash 2001; Huising and Silbey 2018).

39.5 IMPLICATIONS FOR FUTURE RESEARCH AND POLICY DECISION-MAKING

As noted at the outset of this chapter, governmental authorities appear increasingly eager to require firms to adopt CMSs. Yet the available empirical evidence supporting such requirements is hardly extensive, nor does it provide great confidence that CMS mandates will yield substantial benefits in terms of improved compliance. Additional research would prove beneficial. Future research should both explore new questions and continue to address measurement and causal inference challenges of the kind to which we have alluded up to this point in this chapter.

Different measures of compliance – the key outcome for evaluating CMSs – will continue to present different strengths and limitations. Self-reported survey responses may be relatively easy to collect but they can be subject to obvious biases. Voluntary disclosures to regulators may prove similarly feasible to obtain but could be problematic for other reasons. Firms with greater compliance may ironically tend to be the same firms that report more violations, simply because they monitor more carefully or care more earnestly about being forthright with regulators. Relying alternatively on inspectors' reports or levied penalties may present its own source of bias if regulators systematically cut firms with CMSs some slack.

Adding to these measurement challenges is the perennial search for causal inference. Causation becomes harder to assess when firms voluntarily adopt CMSs, as these volunteers are presumably different from other firms in relevant ways. The same organizational factors that lead companies to choose to adopt a CMS – such as perhaps a managerial commitment to compliance – can also affect compliance. Even when CMSs are mandatory, other organizational factors will still be present and may need to be accounted for to determine the precise effects of CMSs (Gray and Silbey 2014; Huising and Silbey 2018).

These research challenges are hardly unique to the study of CMSs, but improving measurement and causal inference will remain a continued aspiration for research on CMSs. Beyond these perennial challenges, future research would benefit from the pursuit of answers on a range of new or relatively unexplored issues, including:

(1) *The relative efficacy of different types of CMSs.* With the proliferation of different CMS standards around the world, researchers should be open to the possibility that some types of CMSs might work better than others. Additional research should compare systems implemented in more holistic or values-based terms versus those more narrowly oriented toward compliance checklists.

(2) *The relative value of different elements within CMSs.* Are training programs more important than complaint hotlines? Are third-party audits more effective than internal audits? We currently know surprisingly little about which of the various elements common to CMSs are more important than others. We have also only scratched the surface when it comes to studying the use of digital tools in compliance management – tools which may be useful but cannot be presumed to be a panacea (Silbey and Agrawal 2011).

(3) *The conditions under which different types of CMSs or different elements tend to perform better.* Do CMSs (or certain CMS types or elements) work better in large companies versus small companies? Or in regulatory regimes characterized by principles-based requirements versus highly detailed prescriptions?

(4) *The ways that CMSs combine with other business programs and practices to promote ethical behavior.* When a company combines a CMS with a corporate code of ethics program, or with an environmental risk management system, how do these different systems or programs mesh with each other? Does their interaction synergistically improve the efficacy of each?

(5) *The role of organizational factors in the efficacy of CMSs.* Practitioners and researchers already recognize that other organizational factors such as leadership and culture matter. Researchers should do more to take such internal factors into account when studying CMSs (cf. Howard-Grenville, Nash, and Coglianese 2008; Huising and Silbey 2018).

(5) *The impact and interaction of outside factors, such as industry competitiveness or community demands.* Researchers who study the effect of government regulation on business behavior recognize the importance of businesses' social and economic "licenses" to operate (Gunningham, Kagan, and Thornton 2003). Further research is needed to investigate how these external factors affect CMS performance.

(7) *The role of government regulators, standards organizations, or public prosecutors in shaping CMS adoption and performance.* What steps can governments take to promote the effective use of CMSs? Do government mandates reinforce or undermine the motivation of business leaders to adopt CMSs?

Additional research on these kinds of questions would help improve both public- and private-sector decision-making related to CMSs.

When it comes to public policy, it is already apparent that CMS mandates, however intuitively appealing, raise a series of additional questions. If an effective CMS depends in substantial part on sincere top management support and a conducive organizational culture, a mandate could well prove counterproductive. The compulsory nature of a CMS might itself generate resistance or a begrudging, rote manner of implementation that crowds out more intrinsic motivations. Moreover, because it will be difficult to define in an enforceable rule what counts as *sufficient* management commitment or a *supportive* organizational culture, many CMS mandates will likely continue to take the form of a checklist of required actions or elements. When mandates take this form, they may lead organizations to approach compliance management in a rote, box-checking fashion.

Many regulatory agencies lack the capacity to identify insufficiently serious CMS implementation. This is a challenge that more generally plagues all types of management-based regulation: "Can government even know what truly constitutes 'good' management?" (Coglianese 2008a). Motivating businesses to do better at managing their own compliance calls for, at a minimum, a different skillset from that which most inspectors or auditors at regulatory agencies typically possess. Compliance management is all about human behavior and how to shape it, not just an exercise in legal analysis or systems engineering (Chen and Soltes 2018).

Ultimately, public policy decision-making should take into account both the benefits and the costs of mandating CMSs (Coglianese 2008b:19–22). These systems – even when implemented in a rote fashion – might well still produce paper trails that provide benefits in terms of helping government regulators detect underlying regulatory violations. Yet in terms of preventing such violations in the first place, the research evidence to date suggests some skepticism that these systems offer anything more than relatively modest benefits. Against modest benefits must be weighed the costs of mandating CMSs, which in some cases might be considerable. It should not be assumed that it simply "cannot hurt" to require firms to implement a CMS. The costs of mandating CMSs include the direct costs of complying with required planning, auditing, and other compliance management activities, which themselves can be substantial. The internal financial control requirements of the Sarbanes–Oxley Act, for example, apparently increased auditing fees as much as 36 percent (Ge, Koester, and McVay 2017) to 64 percent (McCallen et al. 2019). To these direct costs of complying with CMS mandates must be added any management time diverted from other productive activities, including potentially other activities that would be more effective in promoting compliance. Any perverse incentives that CMS mandates might produce, such as fostering more rote, checklist-oriented CMSs and crowding out other more productive behavior, should also be considered a cost. In the end, in many instances it may well be better for government agencies simply to encourage CMS adoption through the provision of resources or positive incentives, rather than imposing mandates that compel firms to go through the motions of systematic compliance management.

39.6 CONCLUSION

As reflected in an increasing array of government mandates and private standards, interest in CMSs appears to be growing. At least in theory, CMSs can help managers identify and address deficiencies in their operations that undermine regulatory compliance. They can provide a source of systematic discipline for how managers oversee the inner workings of their organizations, allowing managers essentially to take on the roles of inspectors and enforcers of legal rules established by regulatory authorities. Research suggests that CMSs may in some cases live up to their promise, at least to some degree, but, so far, the available studies also suggest that the impacts of CMSs in reducing regulatory violations may be rather modest.

Such seemingly modest results raise questions about whether most conventional CMSs can sufficiently overcome the significant organizational pressures that often lead many employees and managers to see compliance as being of at best secondary importance to their jobs. When it comes to changing what managers value and prioritize, CMSs may prove to be relatively weak instruments. Part of the reason that they seem to result in comparatively modest impacts may be that organizations have long engaged in other practices to promote compliance, even if these alternatives are less systematic and would not meet prevailing CMS standards. Furthermore, what may ultimately matter most for promoting compliance is the overall compliance commitment of an organization's top managers and the degree to which the organization's culture supports ongoing compliance vigilance. Additional research is needed on the relationship between compliance systems and these other factors affecting compliance, as well as on how government regulators can better encourage private organizations to engage in serious efforts to ensure that their employees and managers follow the rules.

REFERENCES

American Chemistry Council (ACC). 2019. *Responsible Care Management System Technical Specification*. Document No. RC101.06. https://responsiblecare.americanchemistry.com/Responsible-Care-Program-Elements/Management-System-and-Certification/RCMS-Technical-Specifications.pdf.

Armour, John, Dan Awrey, Paul Davies, Luca Enriques, Jeffrey N. Gordon, Colin Mayer, and Jennifer Payne. 2016. *Principles of Financial Regulation*. Oxford: Oxford University Press.

Armour, John, Jeffrey Gordon, and Geeyoung Min. 2020. "Taking Compliance Seriously." *Yale Journal on Regulation* 37: 1–66.

Bardach, Eugene, and Robert A. Kagan. 2002. *Going by the Book: The Problem of Regulatory Unreasonableness*. New Brunswick, NJ: Transaction.

Bhaskar, Lori Shefchik, Joseph H. Schroeder, and Marcy L. Shepardson. 2019. "Integration of Internal Controls and Financial Statement Audits: Are Two Audits Better than One?" *Accounting Review* 94: 53–81.

Biegelman, Martin T. 2008. *Building a World-Class Compliance Program: Best Practices and Strategies for Success*. Hoboken, NJ: John Wiley & Sons.

Biegelman, Martin T., and Joel T. Bartow. 2006. *Executive Roadmap to Fraud Prevention and Internal Control*. Hoboken, NJ: John Wiley & Sons.

Black, Julia. 2012. "Paradoxes and Failures: 'New Governance' Techniques and the Financial Crisis." *Modern Law Review* 75: 1037–63.

Bussmann, Kai D., Anja Niemeczek, and Marcel Vockrodt. 2018. "Company Culture and Prevention of Corruption in Germany, China and Russia." *European Journal of Criminology* 15: 255–77.

Chen, Hui, and Eugene Soltes. 2018. "Why Compliance Programs Fail – and How to Fix Them." *Harvard Business Review* 96: 116–25.

Coglianese, Cary. 2019. "Review of Meta-regulation in Practice." *Public Administration Review* 79: 794–8.

2008a. "The Managerial Turn in Environmental Protection." *New York University Environmental Law Journal* 17: 54–74.

2008b. *Management-Based Regulation: Implications for Public Policy*. OECD Paper No. GOV/PGC/REG. OECD. www.oecd.org/gov/regulatory-policy/41628947.pdf.

Coglianese, Cary, and David Lazer. 2003. "Management-Based Regulation: Prescribing Private Management to Achieve Public Goals," *Law & Society Review* 37: 691–730.

Coglianese, Cary, and Evan Mendelson. 2010. "Meta-regulation and Self-Regulation." In *Oxford Handbook of Regulation*, edited by Martin Cave, Robert Baldwin, and Martin Lodge, 146–68. Oxford: Oxford University Press.

Coglianese, Cary, and Jennifer Nash. 2017. "The Law of the Test: Performance-Based Regulation and Diesel Emissions Control." *Yale Journal on Regulation* 34: 33–90.

2014. "Performance Track's Postmortem: Lessons from the Rise and Fall of EPA's 'Flagship' Voluntary Program." *Harvard Environmental Law Review* 38: 1–86.

2001. "Environmental Management Systems and the New Policy Agenda." In *Regulating from the Inside: Can Environmental Management Systems Achieve Policy Goals?*, edited by Cary Coglianese and Jennifer Nash, 1–25. Washington, DC: Resources for the Future Press.

Consumer Financial Protection Bureau (CFPB). 2012. "CFPB Supervision and Examination Manual." https://files.consumerfinance.gov/f/201210_cfpb_supervision-and-examination-manual-v2.pdf.

Corkery, Michael. 2016. "Wells Fargo $185 Million for Fraudulently Opening Accounts." *New York Times*, September 8. www.nytimes.com/2016/09/09/business/dealbook/wells-fargo-fined-for-years-of-harm-to-customers.html.

Edelman, Lauren B. 2016. *Working Law: Courts, Corporations, and Symbolic Civil Rights*. Chicago, IL: University of Chicago Press.

Edelman, Lauren B., and Mark C. Suchman. 1997. "The Legal Environments of Organizations." *Annual Review of Sociology* 23: 479–515.

Ely, Robin J., and Debra E. Meyerson. 2010. "An Organizational Approach to Undoing Gender: The Unlikely Case of Offshore Oil Platforms." *Research in Organizational Behavior* 30: 3–34.

Fairman, Robyn, and Charlotte Yapp. 2005. "Enforced Self-Regulation, Prescription, and Conceptions of Compliance with Small Businesses: The Impact of Enforcement." *Law & Policy* 27: 491–519.

Fan, Yangyang, Chan Li, and Kannan Raghunandan. 2017. "Is SOX 404(a) Management Internal Control Reporting an Effective Alternative to SOX 404(b) Internal Control Audits?" *Auditing: A Journal of Practice and Theory* 36: 71–89.

Federal Trade Commission. 2019. "FTC Imposes $5 Billion Penalty and Sweeping New Privacy Restrictions on Facebook." www.ftc.gov/news-events/press-releases/2019/07/ftc-imposes-5-billion-penalty-sweeping-new-privacy-restrictions.

Ford, Cristie L. 2008. "New Governance, Compliance, and Principles-Based Securities Regulation." *American Business Law Journal* 45:1–60.

Gawande, Atul. 2009. *The Checklist Manifesto: How to Get Things Right*. New York: Metropolitan.

Ge, Weili, Allison Koester, and Sarah McVay. 2017. "Benefits and Costs of Sarbanes-Oxley Section 404 (b) Exception: Evidence from Small Firms' Internal Control Disclosures." *Journal of Accounting and Economics* 63: 358–84.

Gneezy, Uri, Stephan Meier, and Pedro Rey-Biel. 2011. "When and Why Incentives (Don't) Work to Modify Behavior." *Journal of Economic Perspectives* 25: 191–210.

Gneezy, Uri, and Aldo Rustichini. 2000. "A Fine Is a Price." *Journal of Legal Studies* 29: 1–18.

Goebel, Sebastian, and Barbara E. Weissenberger. 2017. "The Relationship between Informal Controls, Ethical Work Climates, and Organizational Performance." *Journal of Business Ethics* 141: 505–28.

Gorsira, Madelijne, Linda Steg, Adriaan Denkers, and Wim Huisman. 2018. "Corruption in Organizations: Ethical Climate and Individual Motives." *Administrative Sciences* 8: 1–19.

Gray, Garry C. 2006. "The Regulation of Corporate Violations: Punishment, Compliance, and the Blurring of Responsibility." British Journal of Criminology, 46: 875–92.

Gray, Garry C. and Susan S. Silbey. 2014. "Governing Inside the Organization: Interpreting Regulation and Compliance." *American Journal of Sociology* 120: 96-145.

Grüninger, Stephan and Lisa Schöttl. 2017. "Rethinking Compliance: Essential Cornerstones for More Effectiveness in Compliance Management." *Compliance Elliance Journal* 3: 3–17.

Gunningham, Neil, Robert A. Kagan, and Dorothy Thornton. 2003. *Shades of Green: Business, Regulation, and Environment*. Palo Alto, CA: Stanford University Press.

Gunningham, Neil, and Darren Sinclair. 2014. "The Impact of Safety Culture on Systemic Risk Management." *European Journal of Risk Regulation* 5: 505–16.

Heimer, Carol A. 2013. "Resilience in the Middle: Contributions of Regulated Organizations to Regulatory Success." *Annals of the American Academy of Political and Social Science* 639 (September): 139–56.

Hofeditz, Marcel, Ann-Marie Nienaber, Anders Dysvik, and Gerhard Schewe. 2017. "'Want To' versus 'Have To': Intrinsic and Extrinsic Motivators as Predictors of Compliance Behavior Intention." *Human Resource Management* 56(January–February): 25–49.

Howard-Grenville, Jennifer, Stephanie Bertels, and Brooke Boren. 2015. *What Regulators Need to Know about Organizational Culture*. Penn Program on Regulation Research Paper. www.law.upenn.edu /live/files/4708-howard-grenvillebertelsboren-ppr-researchpaper0620.

Howard-Grenville, Jennifer, Jennifer Nash, and Cary Coglianese. 2008. "Constructing the License to Operate: Internal Factors and Their Influence on Corporate Environmental Decisions." *Law & Policy* 30: 73–107.

Huising, Ruthanne, and Susan S. Silbey. 2018. "From Nudge to Culture and Back Again: Coalface Governance in the Regulated Organization." *Annual Review of Law and Social Science* 14: 91–114.

2011. "Governing the Gap: Forging Safe Science through Relational Regulation." *Regulation & Governance* 5: 14–42.

Hunter, Robert D. 2009. *Standards, Conformity Assessment, and Accreditation for Engineers*. Boca Raton, FL: CRC Press.

Iliev, Peter. 2010. "The Effect of SOX Section 404: Costs, Earnings Quality, and Stock Prices." *Journal of Finance* 65: 1163–96.

Institut der Wirtschaftsprüfer (IDW). 2011. *IDW AsS 980: Principles for the Proper Performance of Reasonable Assurance Engagements Relating to Compliance Management Systems*. Düsseldorf: IDW.

International Chamber of Commerce (ICC). 2013. "The ICC Antitrust Compliance Toolkit." https://iccwbo.org/content/uploads/sites/3/2013/04/ICC-Antitrust-Compliance-Toolkit-ENGLISH.pdf.

2011. "ICC Rules on Combating Corruption." https://iccwbo.org/content/uploads/sites/3/2011/10/ICC-Rules-on-Combating-Corruption-2011.pdf.

International Organization for Standardization (ISO). 2019a. "Projects Ongoing: ISO 37000 Guidance for the Governance of Organizations." https://committee.iso.org/sites/tc309/home/projects/ongoing/ongoing-1.html.

2019b. "Projects Ongoing: ISO 37301 Compliance Management Systems – Requirements with Guidance for Use." https://committee.iso.org/sites/tc309/home/projects/ongoing/ongoing-3.html.

2018. "The ISO Survey of Management System Certifications 2018." https://isotc.iso.org/livelink/livelink?func=ll&objId=18808772&objAction=browse&viewType=1.

2015. *ISO 14001: 2015 Environmental Management System – Requirement with Guidance for Use*. Geneva: ISO.

2014. *ISO 19600: 2014 Compliance Management Systems – Guidelines*. Geneva: ISO.

Kaptein, Muel. 2015. "The Effectiveness of Ethics Programs: The Role of Scope, Composition, and Sequence." *Journal of Business Ethics* 132: 415–31.

Kearl, Holly. 2018. *The Facts Behind the #MeToo Movement: A National Study on Sexual Harassment and Assault*. Reston, VA: Stop Street Harassment. www.stopstreetharassment.org/wp-content /uploads/2018/01/2018-National-Sexual-Harassment-and-Assault-Report.pdf.

Labonte, Marc. 2017. "Who Regulates Whom? An Overview of the U.S. Financial Regulatory Framework." Congressional Research Service 7–5700. https://fas.org/sgp/crs/misc/R44918.pdf.

Lund, Dorothy S., and Natasha Sarin. 2020. "The Cost of Doing Business: Corporate Crime and Punishment Post-Crisis." University of Pennsylvania Institute for Law and Economics Research Paper No. 20–13. https://papers.ssrn.com/sol3/papers.cfm?abstract_id=3537245.

Malesky, Edmund, and Markus Taussig. 2019. "Participation, Government Legitimacy, and Regulatory Compliance in Emerging Economies: A Firm-Level Field Experiment in Vietnam." *American Political Science Review* 113: 530–51.

Martin, Susan Lorde. 2015. "Compliance Officers: More Jobs, More Responsibility, More Liability." *Notre Dame Journal of Law, Ethics & Public Policy* 29: 169–98.

Martinez, Veronica Root. 2020. "Complex Compliance Investigations." *Columbia Law Review* 120(2): 249–308.

McCallen, Jennifer, Roy Schmardebeck, Jonathan Shipman, and Robert Whited. 2019. "Have the Costs and Benefits of SOX Section 404(b) Compliance Changed Over Time?" Working Paper. https://papers.ssrn.com/sol3/papers.cfm?abstract_id=3420787.

McCarthy, James E., and Claudia Copeland. 2016. "EPA Regulations: Too Much, Too Little, or On Track?" Congressional Research Service 7–5700. https://fas.org/sgp/crs/misc/R41561.pdf.

Michael, Michael L. 2006. "Business Ethics: The Law of Rules." *Business Ethics Quarterly* 16: 475–504.

Miller, Geoffrey P. 2018. "An Economic Analysis of Effective Compliance Programs." In *Research Handbook on Corporate Crime and Financial Misdealing*, edited by Jennifer Arlen, 247–62. Cheltenham, UK: Edward Elgar.

2017. "Compliance: Past, Present and Future." *University of Toledo Law Review* 48: 437–51.

Moeller, Robert R. 2004. *Sarbanes-Oxley and the New Internal Auditing Rules*. Hoboken, NJ: John Wiley & Sons.

Moen, Ronald D. and Clifford L. Norman. 2010. "Circling Back: Clearing Up Myths about the Deming Cycle and Seeing How It Keeps Evolving." *Quality Progress* 43: 22–8.

National Academies of Sciences, Engineering, and Medicine. 2018. *Designing Safety Regulations for High-Hazard Industries*. Washington, DC: The National Academies Press.

New York Stock Exchange (NYSE). 2019a. "Listed Company Manual – Section 303A.10 Code of Business Conduct and Ethics." https://nyse.wolterskluwer.cloud/listed-company-manual/document?treeNodeId=csh-da-filter!WKUS-TAL-DOCS-PHC-%7B0588BF4A-D3B5-4B91-94EA-BE9F17057DF0%7D–WKUS_TAL_5667%23teid–78.

2019b. "Rule 3130: Annual Certification of Compliance and Supervisory Processes." https://nyse.wolterskluwer.cloud/rules/document?treeNodeId=csh-da-filter!WKUS-TAL-DOCS-PHC-%7B4A07B716-0F73-46CC-BAC2-43EB20902159%7D–WKUS_TAL_5665%23teid–598.

Organisation for Economic Co-operation and Development (OECD). 2010. "Good Practice Guidance on Internal Controls, Ethics, and Compliance." www.oecd.org/daf/anti-bribery/44884389.pdf.

Paine, Lynn. 1994. "Managing for Corporate Integrity." *Harvard Business Review* 72(2): 106–17.

Parker, Christine. 2002. *The Open Corporation: Effective Self-Regulation and Democracy*. Cambridge: Cambridge University Press.

Parker, Christine, and Sharon Gilad. 2011. "Internal Corporate Compliance Management Systems: Structure, Culture, and Agency." In *Explaining Compliance: Business Responses to Regulation*, edited by Christine Parker and Vibeke Lehmann Nielsen, 170–95. Cheltenham, UK: Edward Elgar.

Parker, Christine, and Vibeke Lehmann Nielsen. 2009. "Corporate Compliance Systems: Could They Make Any Difference?" *Administration & Society* 41: 3–37.

2006. "Do Businesses Take Compliance Systems Seriously? An Empirical Study of the Implementation of Trade Practices Compliance Systems in Australia." *Melbourne University Law Review* 30: 441–94.

Pfaff, Alexander, and Christopher William Sanchirico. 2004. "Big Field, Small Potatoes: An Empirical Assessment of EPA's Self-Audit Policy." *Journal of Policy Analysis and Management* 23: 415–32.

Potoski, Matthew, and Aseem Prakash. 2006. *The Voluntary Environmentalists: Green Clubs, ISO 14001, and Voluntary Environmental Regulations*. Cambridge: Cambridge University Press.

Ruiz, Pablo, Ricardo Martinez, Job Rodrigo, and Cristina Diaz. 2015. "Level of Coherence among Ethics Program Components and Its Impact on Ethical Intent." *Journal of Business Ethics* 128: 725–42.

Schein, Edgar H. 2010. *Organizational Culture and Leadership*, 4th ed. San Francisco, CA: Jossey-Bass.

Selznick, Philip. 1992. *The Moral Commonwealth: Social Theory and the Promise of Community*. Berkeley: University of California Press.
Shimshack, Jay P. 2014. "The Economics of Environmental Monitoring and Enforcement: A Review." *Annual Review of Resource Economics (ARRE)* 6: 339–60.
Short, Jodi L., and Michael W. Toffel. 2010."Making Self-Regulation More than Merely Symbolic: The Critical Role of the Legal Environment." *Administrative Science Quarterly* 55: 361–96.
Silbey, Susan S., and Tanu Agrawal. 2011. "The Illusion of Accountability: Information Management and Organizational Culture." *Droit et société* 77: 69–86.
Sokol, Daniel D. 2016. "Teaching Compliance." *University of Cincinnati Law Review* 84: 1–21.
Soltes, Eugene. 2019. "Where Is Your Company Most Prone to Lapses in Integrity? A Simple Survey to Identify the Danger Zones." *Harvard Business Review* July-August: 51–4.
Stamatis, D. H. 1995. *Understanding ISO 9000 and Implementing the Basics to Quality*. New York: Marcel Dekker.
Standards Australia. 2006. "Australian Standard: Compliance Programs." http://aeaecompliance.com/images/documentos/AS-3806–2006-Compliance-Standard.pdf.
Steinberg, Richard M. 2011. *Governance, Risk Management, and Compliance*. Hoboken, NJ: John Wiley & Sons.
Stucke, Maurice E. 2014. "In Search of Effective Ethics and Compliance." *Journal of Corporate Law* 39: 770–832.
Toffel, Michael W., and Jodi L. Short. 2011. "Coming Clean and Cleaning Up: Does Voluntary Self-Reporting Indicate Effective Self-Policy?" *Journal of Law and Economics* 54: 609–49.
Treviño, Linda Klebe, Gary R. Weaver, David G. Gibson, and Barbara Ley Toffler. 1999. "Managing Ethics and Legal Compliance: What Works and What Hurt." *California Management Review* 4: 131–51.
Tyler, Tom R. 1990. *Why People Obey the Law*. Princeton, NJ: Princeton University Press.
U.S. Department of Health and Human Services (HHS). 2019. "Office of Inspector General – Compliance." https://oig.hhs.gov/compliance/.
U.S. Department of Justice. 2018. "Justice Manual." www.justice.gov/jm/justice-manual.
U.S. Department of Justice Criminal Division. 2019. "Evaluation of Corporate Compliance Programs, Guidance Document." www.justice.gov/criminal-fraud/page/file/937501/download.
U.S. Environmental Protection Agency (EPA). 2018. "EPA Enforcement and Compliance Annual Results." www.epa.gov/sites/production/files/2019–02/documents/fy18-enforcement-annual-results-data-graphs.pdf.
2007. "Performance Track Could Improve Program Design and Management to Ensure Value" Rep. No. 2007-P-00013. www.epa.gov/sites/production/files/2015–11/documents/20070329–2007-p-00013.pdf.
U.S. Government Accountability Office. 2016. "Fines, Penalties, and Forfeitures for Violations of Financial Crimes and Sanctions Requirements." www.gao.gov/assets/680/675987.pdf.
U.S. Sentencing Commission. 2018. "Guidelines Manual 2018." www.ussc.gov/sites/default/files/pdf/guidelines-manual/2018/GLMFull.pdf.
Walberg, Susan Lee. 2018. *Insider's Guide to Compliance: Real World Advice for Building a Successful Compliance Program*. Compliance Ala Carte.
Weaver, Gary R. 2014. "Encouraging Ethics in Organizations: Review of Some Key Research Findings." *American Criminal Law Review* 51: 293–316.

40

Business Codes: A Review of the Literature

Muel Kaptein

Abstract: The widespread use of business codes raises the questions of what we know about codes and what they do. This chapter presents an overview of what we currently know about the definitions, functions, and effectiveness of business codes. The chapter shows that business codes are an important method of self-regulation, that the many studies into the effectiveness of codes present a mixed picture, and that there are promising directions for future research on business codes. The chapter also provides suggestions for the development, implementation, and assessment of business codes in practice.

40.1 INTRODUCTION

There are many and different kinds of codes: codes for how students should behave at school, how visitors should behave at certain venues, how consumers should handle their products, how sportspeople should behave when exercising their sport, or for how members of religious communities should behave during and outside services. Work is also teeming with codes. Professionals and professional associations, like nurses and physicians, purchasers, politicians, preachers, stockbrokers, lawyers, marketers, and auditors, have their own codes. The same is true for various business and industrial sectors – such as banks, pension funds, private equity firms, textile and apparel companies, and pharmaceutical companies – and for the education sector, like universities. There are also corporate governance codes, for example, for companies listed at a stock exchange, which prescribe what such companies and their executive and nonexecutive directors should do.

Many business organizations have their own code. In 2014, 76 percent of the Fortune Global 200 companies have their own code (KPMG and EUR, 2014) compared to only 52.5 percent ten years earlier (Kaptein, 2004). At a national level, 77 percent of the largest companies in the UK (Dondé, 2016), 96 percent in Israel (Schwartz, 2012), and 90 percent in The Netherlands (VNO-NCW, 2016) have a code. In the following countries, the percentage of the working population that indicates their organization has a code are: Australia 73 percent (Dondé and Somasundaram, 2018), Ireland 74 percent, England 69 percent, Switzerland 61 percent, Portugal 60 percent, Spain 59 percent, Germany 52 percent, Italy 50 percent, and France 47 percent (Dondé, 2018). In the USA, 80 percent of those who work in an organization with more than 200 people indicate that their organization has its own code (KPMG, 2013).

The widespread use of business codes raises the questions of what we know about codes and what they do. This chapter presents an overview of what we currently know about the definitions, functions, and effectiveness of business codes. We will see from a compliance management perspective that business codes are an important method of self-regulation, that the many studies into the effectiveness of codes present a mixed picture, and that there are promising directions for future research on business codes.

40.2 Definition of a Business Code

Much has been written about what a business code is. Apart from "business code," other related terms used are business code of ethics, code of ethics, code of conduct, business principles, corporate credo, corporate philosophy, corporate ethics statement, and code of practice. Kaptein (2008) gives an overview of how companies refer to their code: code of integrity, declaration, deontological code, philosophy, policy principles, standards, and values statement. In their research among Canadian organizations, Bodolica and Spraggon (2015) came across other names: code of business practice, code of ethical conduct, and ethical behavior policy. Although the terms may indicate different views on what a code is in the context of business, Kaptein and Schwartz (2008) consider the term "business code" a concept that covers all types of code at the corporate level.

A widely used definition of a business code (BC) comes from Kaptein and Schwartz (2008: 113): "A distinct and formal document containing a set of prescriptions developed by and for a company to guide present and future behavior on multiple issues of its managers and employees toward one another, the company, external stakeholders and/or society in general." This definition is based on an analysis of existing definitions and it shows that (the concept of) a BC has at least four distinctive elements.

First, a BC is developed *for* and *by* a company. That a BC is developed *for* a company implies that the BC applies to those who represent the company and, thus, to all its managers and employees. A BC is therefore not meant only for a selection of those who work at a company (such as a specific department or function). That a BC is developed *by* a company means that a code is a method of self-regulation (Weller, 1988) and is soft law (Sobczak, 2006). Therefore, a BC is a specific and unique document that belongs and applies to one company and not to all companies within an industry or region. That BCs are a method of self-regulation does not necessarily imply that they are voluntary; companies may also be required by law or their stakeholders to develop one (cf. Sobczak, 2006).

A second element of a BC is a formal document. While codes in general can be informal and implicit (Weaver, 1993), a BC in particular is formal in the sense that for it to apply to all managers and employees, it should have the approval of the company's board, the highest corporate decision-making authority. If a BC could also be informal, then this would "both broaden and dilute the concept to such an extent that it would become synonymous with the ethical culture and climate of the organization" (Kaptein and Schwartz, 2008: 113).

A third element of a BC is its prescriptive character. A BC aims to guide the behavior of those who represent the company. This means that a BC does not necessarily describe current behavior but rather desirable behavior. In general, two important sources of behavioral prescriptions are laws and regulations and morality and ethics. There are two reasons why Kaptein and Schwartz (2008) do not include the adjective "ethics" in their definition of BC even though many scholars do. On the one hand, they consider a business code as already reflecting, in itself, what ethics entails: fundamental interests. On the other hand, this avoids the impossible task of judging whether codes are ethical, that is, whether a company is intrinsically driven to do the good thing by means of their code.

A fourth element of a BC is that it prescribes behavior on many issues. The adjective "business" implies that a BC prescribes on numerous behavioral issues because a company can only have one BC; a BC is the code of a company, so it should address all topics that (the board of) a company deems relevant. Hence, a code regarding one topic or issue, such as the use of the company's internet facilities, cannot be regarded as a BC; rather it is a subcode or what Gaumnitz and Lere (2004) call a vertical code. At the same time, together with a BC, companies can also have subcodes that describe in more detail what is expected of managers and employees regarding a particular issue (cf. Preuss, 2010; Weber and Wasieleski, 2013).

40.2.1 *Differences in Business Codes*

Because BCs are developed by and for a company, their contents can differ from one company to another. A BC addresses the topics that a company considers relevant, and it is a description in the company's own words of how its managers and employees should deal with these topics. Babri et al. (2019) give a good overview of the many studies on the content of BCs. There are two important dimensions of such studies, which are also related to the third and fourth elements of the above-given definition of a BC: the level of prescription and the type of topics. The level of prescription can range from general to specific. Kaptein (2008) proposes a four-layered pyramid of the possible behavioral prescriptions of a BC. The layers are, from the top (being generic and brief): (1) mission, purpose, and vision; (2) core values; (3) responsibilities, principles, and guidelines; and at the bottom (being specific and extensive): (4) norms, standards, and rules. Codes that cover only one layer can be called, from top to bottom, mission statement; values statement; business principles or stakeholder statute; and code of conduct. Next to how generic or specific a code is, a code can be classified according to how narrow or broad it is. BCs can range from addressing a few issues to more than a hundred issues (Webley and Dondé, 2016). As a result, the length of BCs can range from a single page up to around eighty pages (Kaptein, 2008).

Studies on the content of BCs show that there is indeed a big variety of BCs. For example, research on the Fortune Global 200 companies shows that 20 percent of the BCs describe the organization's mission and/or vision, 43 percent describe the organization's core values (with integrity being the most cited value in 50 percent of the BCs), and 95 percent describe the responsibilities of the company toward its employees. However, the responsibilities toward customers and shareholders are described in only 52 percent and 30 percent of the BCs, respectively. More than 80 percent of the BCs contain standards and rules regarding confidential or secret information, corruption and bribery, accuracy of reporting, protecting the organization's assets, accepting gifts, and performing sideline activities, while only 31 percent include standards regarding contact with the media, and 11 percent address the use of company time (KPMG and EUR, 2014).

40.2.2 *Functions of Business Codes*

Ruiz et al. (2015) suggest that a BC is the most common and concrete organizational instrument for promoting ethical decision-making. It is also the most frequently cited instrument for managing the ethics and compliance of business organizations (Kaptein and Schwartz, 2008). Codes are seen as cornerstones (Kaptein, 2011) and not having a BC is viewed as dangerous (Cohen, 2013). What then are the functions of a BC that make it so important?

The functions of BCs also differ, just like their contents. Frankel (1989), Wotruba et al. (2001), and Kaptein (2008) present an overview of the functions that a BC may have. From a compliance management perspective, the following important functions of a BC can be identified and categorized into internal and external functions.

Many internal functions are attributed to a BC when it concerns managers and employees. A BC may have a *signaling function* because it demonstrates that the company is concerned about ethics and compliance (Wotruba et al., 2001). A BC may have a *clarifying function* because it makes explicit what legal and moral behavior is expected of managers and employees (Kaptein, 2008). A BC may also have a *guiding function* because it gives direction to managers and employees, transmits what is expected of them, and enables their behavior (Frankel, 1989; Wotruba et al., 2001). A BC may also have a *motivating, supporting*, or *stimulating function* because it conveys the importance of ethics and appeals to the responsibility of managers and employees to act in an ethical and compliant way. A BC has a significantly intrinsic value (Somers, 2001; Stevens, 2004), and it sets the tone (Stohs and Brannick, 1999). A BC has also been ascribed a *correcting function* because it provides a ground for calling managers and employees to account and for sanctioning them when they misbehave (Kaptein, 2008). As Frankel (1989) suggests, a BC functions as a deterrent to unethical behavior. A BC can also have an *aligning function*, in the sense that it aims to ensure the compliance of all managers and employees with the same set of behavioral expectations (Ferrell et al., 2017).

Different external functions that partly overlap with the internal functions have also been attributed to BCs. A BC is said to have a *distinguishing function* in the sense that it makes known what the company stands for, its identity, and, as such, it makes the company discernible to other organizations. A frequently mentioned function of a BC is its *legitimating function*: it motivates, explains, and demonstrates to external stakeholders the company's practices (Wotruba et al., 2001) and its ethical, social, and legal awareness (cf. Erwin, 2011). A BC also works the other way around: a company can publicly distance itself from managers and employees who violate its BC (Kaptein, 2008). Another function mentioned in the literature is a *committing function:* a BC is a tangible endorsement of the legal and moral norms the company wants to comply with (Erwin, 2011; Singh, 2011). A BC can also have a *correcting function* not just for internal stakeholders but also for external stakeholders by giving them the ground to evaluate the company and call it to account (Frankel, 1989).

Due to these functions, many positive objectives and effects are ascribed to companies that have a BC. Based on the assumption or belief that a code leads to more ethical and legal behavior of managers and employees (Wotruba et al., 2001; Erwin, 2011), a BC can enhance stakeholders' trust in a company and preserve the company's reputation (Frankel, 1989; Singh, 2011; Winkler, 2011), strengthen employees' identity (Frostenson et al., 2012), encourage the authorities to relax onerous regulations and controls (Clark, 1980), decrease the amount of legal fines in case of transgressions (Pitt and Groskaufmanis, 1990), and retain the corporate license to operate (Preuss, 2010). It seems that many, if not all, objectives of a company are also seen as objectives of BCs.

Despite the many functions attributed to them, BCs are not exempt from criticisms. For example, BCs are seen to undermine the responsibilities of employees and to be accusatory, threatening, and demeaning (see Raiborn and Payne's (1990) overview). There is also the question of whether a BC can influence behavior at all because the employees who most need a BC will not adhere to it anyway, and the good employees do not need a BC in the first place because they already know what they ought to do (Ladd, 1985). Others suggest that a BC makes stakeholders more suspicious, cynical, and distrustful (Dobel, 1993). For Kaptein and Wempe (1998), a code by itself is nothing; it is not about the text but all about codifying, that is, the process of coming up with a code and implementing it. As they put it, "A code is nothing, coding is everything" (1998: 853). This expression relates to Petersen and Krings' (2009: 513) claim that BCs are "toothless tigers" unless they are implemented well and to Wood and Rimmer's (2003: 192) view that a code is not "self-sufficient" or a "stand-alone document." Mercier and Deslandes (2017) also argue that there are no codes, only interpretations; that codes receive meaning when interpreted and appropriated with practical wisdom by managers and employees.

40.3 THE EFFECTIVENESS OF BUSINESS CODES OF ETHICS

Given the many functions of a BC and its potential but disputed effectiveness, the question is whether BCs are indeed effective. There are several studies on this question. Using a questionnaire with 189 sales professionals working at smaller organizations in the USA, Valentine et al. (2019) find that the presence of a BC was associated with a more internal locus of control and stronger ethical judgment about workplace incivility. Tjosvold et al. (2009) interviewed 101 Chinese employees and asked them to describe a specific occasion when their ethical values were at issue. They found that BCs facilitated the open-minded discussion of opposing views. Stöber et al. (2019) asked 143 students and academic staff of a German university to put themselves in the role of an employee of a fictitious company. The results of their survey experiment indicate that the positive tone in which the code is written increases code familiarity and that a code signed by top managers sends a strong signal of their commitment to the code.

There are also a few meta-studies on the effectiveness of BCs. Kaptein and Schwartz (2008) show that 35 percent of the seventy-nine empirical studies published until 2006 found BCs to be effective, 16 percent found BCs to be slightly effective, 33 percent found no effectiveness, and 14 percent yielded mixed results. One study even found that BCs could be counterproductive. Babri et al. (2019) present a detailed overview of 100 empirical studies on BCs published from mid-2005 until mid-2016. They find that 50 percent of the publications can be classified as content-oriented studies, 15 percent as transformation studies (how BCs come into practice), and 35 percent as output studies (what effects BCs have). They also find that BCs lead to both positive and negative outcomes.

Kaptein and Schwartz (2008) and Babri et al. (2019) offer explanations for the mixed findings regarding the effectiveness of BCs. They claim that the wide variety of definitions, empirical bases, and research methods leads to a large variation in empirical findings. The findings depend on how the concept of BC is defined. For example, when a BC is defined as a description of core values, researchers tend to look for other results than when a BC is defined as a set of specific rules. It also makes a difference for the findings how a BC's effectiveness is defined: whether the objective of a BC is defined as making employees more familiar with the law or improving the corporate reputation. As Kaptein and Schwartz (2008) argue, the more difficult it is to realize the objectives of a BC, the greater the likelihood that it will be ineffective. Existing studies on the effectiveness of BCs also differ widely in their empirical basis: for example, the types of response group (students, managers, employees, organizations, and external stakeholders from different sectors and countries); sample size (ranging from one company to more than a thousand companies, and from fewer than twenty questionnaires to more than ten thousand questionnaires); and the response rate (from less than 10 percent to more than 50 percent). Much of the variance in the findings could also be explained by the use of different research methods: for example, desk research, laboratory experiments, vignettes (usually respondents are requested to select their preferred response to a set of hypothetical ethical dilemmas), perceptions about practice (often employees are asked about their perceptions of their organization), and objective data on practice (such as the frequency of civil actions and the price of shares). Only four of the seventy-nine studies that Kaptein and Schwartz (2008) reviewed used multiple methods. Kaptein and Schwartz (2008) also point out that there is a difference between examining whether BCs are actually effective and examining whether they are potentially effective. In the latter case, finding even one example where a BC is effective is sufficient, whereas the former case is much more complicated because for any BC to be found effective, it needs to be proven to be effective every time for the population being studied.

The complexity involved in examining the effectiveness of BCs can also explain the mixed findings about it. There are many explanatory, moderating, and mediating factors involved. Weller (1988) proposes twenty-five hypotheses on BC effectiveness. Kaptein and Schwartz (2008) propose an integrated research model with different levels of codes and different types of effects, antecedents, and relevant contextual characteristics. There being different types of BC with contents differing widely in practice makes the examination of the effectiveness of BCs complex. Furthermore, BCs can even have only indirect effects. This is what Frostenson et al. (2012: 271) found when they examined organizations whose BCs did not directly influence their employees' behavior but were instead "embedded in a wider normative self-understanding where the employees consider the organization to be fair and morally respectable." Furthermore, it is also difficult to prove causality, as Kaptein and Schwartz (2008) note. BCs may be adopted and implemented in circumstances where companies are confronted with unethical behavior, thereby reversing the causal relationship. It is also likely that having a BC leads to higher expectations by stakeholders and makes the company an easier target of criticisms. There are also time effects. BCs may be effective only during the introduction phase or only after a long time. Kaptein (2008) distinguishes different kinds of paths of BC effectiveness: the code as a rocket (only effective shortly after its introduction), as a boomerang (only effective shortly after the introduction and then becoming counterproductive), as a comet (becoming increasingly effective after its introduction and then staying effective), or as stairs (gradually and stepwise becoming more effective). So, assessing the effectiveness of BCs only shortly after their introduction does not say anything about their long-term effectiveness.

40.4 Future Research Directions

Despite the many studies that have been conducted on the effectiveness of BCs, there is still much to be studied about the matter. Given the complexity of studying BCs, there is as yet no conclusive evidence on whether and to what extent BCs can be effective at all, whether and to what extent BCs are effective in practice, and, if BCs can be effective, what are the (combination of) factors of this effectiveness. Many studies on the effectiveness of BCs have suggestions for future research (e.g., Babri et al., 2019; Kaptein and Schwartz, 2008; Kaptein, 2011; Singh, 2011; Valentine et al., 2019). Below are four future research directions that have not or hardly been mentioned.

Research into the development process of BCs is a promising research direction. As mentioned, scholars have emphasized that the process of how a code is developed is important or is even a prerequisite for understanding its effectiveness. In this regard, Hill and Rapp (2014) advocate that the cooperation of employees at all levels is necessary for the development of an effective BC. Murphy (1988) also suggests that BCs should be revised periodically, and Weller (1988) thinks that there is a relationship between the frequency of revisions and the effectiveness of BCs. To date, we know relatively little about how companies develop and update their BCs. Some exceptions are case descriptions by Kaptein and Wempe (1998) of how an airport developed its BC and by Messikomer and Cirka (2010) of how a national association of move managers developed its BC, and a survey research by Weber and Wasieleski (2013) on who is involved in the drafting or redrafting of BCs in large US companies. Hence, future research can look into identifying the types, factors, determinants, and issues involved in the development processes of BCs, and the current effectiveness of these processes.

The normative content of BCs is another promising research direction. There have been numerous studies on the content of BCs, and many frameworks have been developed for assessing the quality of BCs. Examples of the latter are Cressey and Moore (1983), Gaumnitz and Lere (2002), Kolk and Tulder (2002), Schwartz (2007), Donker et al. (2008), and Singh et al. (2011). Garegnani et al. (2015) developed an extensive framework that resulted in a scoring model for the quality of a code. The model contains six categories and a total of forty individual quality indicators that include, among other things, “introductory letter from top management,” “presence of examples and FAQs,” “existence of a reporting policy,” and “compliance procedures.” However, these frameworks hardly address the ethical content of BCs. Many frameworks are based on counting the issues and elements contained in a BC. Only a few studies analyze BCs in a substantial manner, for instance in terms of the language (Stöber et al., 2019) and ethical theory used (Hoover and Pepper, 2015; De Waegeneer et al., 2016). Because a BC is a rich manifestation of the desired ethics of a company, there are many things that call for examination, for example, the extent to which a company ascribes to itself a moral responsibility for every issue; the intensity, depth, and comprehensiveness of a company’s description of its responsibilities; the foundations and motivations for these responsibilities; and the progressiveness of a BC (whether it incorporates new ethical norms or what is called “leadership in ethics” or “moral entrepreneurship” (Kaptein, 2019)). A framework that addresses these elements can be used to better understand the articulated ethics of companies and how these ethics differ among each other and develop over time. Some interesting studies have already been done in this area. For example, Singh et al. (2011) examined the development of the content of BCs in Australia, Canada, and Sweden, and Bodolica and Spraggon (2015) classified the content of Canadian BCs into compliers, updaters, and promotors.

Another interesting research direction is the development and application of a framework for assessing the quality of the implementation of BCs. As stated, good implementation is essential for creating an effective BC. Some scholars propose and use a list of elements of a good implementation, for instance, Weller (1988), Scholtens and Dam (2007), Svensson et al. (2010), and Singh (2011). Singh (2011) uses eighteen variables for assessing the effectiveness of a BC, including variables that assess its implementation: whether the BC is communicated to all employees, whether ethics training is offered to all staff, and whether the company has an ethics ombudsman. Other proposed factors for assessing implementation are the other elements of ethics programs, such as ethics audits, ethics committees, ethics reporting lines, incentive policies, and pre-employment screening. Together with these hard controls, soft controls are also essential in creating an effective BC. For example, Petersen and Krings (2009) and Kaptein (2011) find that the support of management is a necessary condition. Other examples of elements of corporate soft controls or culture are openness to discussing dilemmas, transparency of behavior, and room to speak up about unethical behavior (Kaptein, 2017). A good framework for assessing the quality of the implementation of a BC should therefore include both these hard and soft controls. Having such a framework will open avenues for assessing how well a BC is implemented and embedded, what types of implementation are possible, what factors (such as the type of BC) determine the right mix of hard and soft controls, and to what extent the implementation of BCs should change over time.

A final direction for future research is the development and use of theories in studying BCs. Some of the theories that have been applied for understanding and assessing BCs are institutional theory (Weaver, 1995), new institutional theory (Egels-Zandén, 2014), information economics (Lere and Gaumnitz, 2003), ethical normative theories (Hoover and Pepper, 2015), and critical discourse theory (Winkler, 2011). However, "the majority of papers are still either not explicitly grounded in theory or completely atheoretical" (Babri et al., 2019: 34). Kaptein (2011) also points out the necessity of developing strong and coherent theories to better explain and predict the effectiveness of BCs. One way forward is to develop a coding theory. As far as I am aware, there is no such theory yet in the field of BC. Such a theory would start from the idea of what a code is and then work out how the processes of coding, decoding, and recoding work. Such a theory would not apply theories from other fields but would develop a theory from within, making the theory stronger and more robust.

In the same way that the creation of an effective BC is never-ending (Kaptein and Wempe, 1998), doing research on BCs is also never-ending. This is not only because BC is a complex research subject and a dynamic field but also because it is and remains an important field for managing and supervising the ethics and compliance of companies. I hope that this chapter has provided some inspiration and ideas for this subject.

REFERENCES

Babri, M., Davidson, B., and Helin, S. (2019). "An Updated Inquiry into the Study of Corporate Codes of Ethics: 2005–2016." *Journal of Business Ethics*. 10.1007/s10551-019-04192-x.

Bodolica, V., and Spraggon, M. (2015). "An Examination into the Disclosure, Structure, and Contents of Ethical Codes in Publicly Listed Acquiring Firms." *Journal of Business Ethics*, 126, 459–72.

Clark, M. (1980). "Corporate Codes of Ethics: A Key to Economic Freedom." *Management Review*, 69 (9), 60–2.

Cohen, S. (2013). "Promoting Ethical Judgment in an Organisational Context." *Journal of Business Ethics*, 117, 513–23.

Cressey, D. R., and Moore, C. A. (1983). "Managerial Values and Corporate Codes of Ethics." *California Management Review*, 25(4), 53–77.

De Waegeneer, E., Van De Sompele, J., and Willem, A. (2016). "Ethical Codes in Sports Organizations: Classification Framework, Content Analysis, and the Influence of Content on Code Effectiveness." *Journal of Business Ethics*, 136, 587–98.

Dobel, J. (1993). "The Realpolitik of Ethics Codes: An Implementation Approach to Public Ethics." In H. Frederickson (ed.), *Ethics and Public Administration*, 158–71. New York: Sharpe.

Dondé, G. (2016). *Corporate Ethics Policies and Programs: 2016 UK and Continental Europe Survey*. London: Institute of Business Ethics.

(2018). *Ethics at Work: 2018 Survey of Employees: Europe*. London: Institute of Business Ethics.
Dondé, G., and Somasundaram, K. (2018). *Ethics at Work: 2018 Survey of Employees: Australia*. London: Institute of Business Ethics.
Donker, H., Poff, D., and Zahir, S. (2008). "Corporate Values, Codes of Ethics, and Firm Performance: A Look at the Canadian Context." *Journal of Business Ethics*, 82, 527–37.
Egels-Zandén, N. (2014). "Revisiting Supplier Compliance with MNC Codes of Conduct: Recoupling Policy and Practice at Chinese Toy Suppliers." *Journal of Business Ethics*, 119, 59–75.
Erwin, P. M. (2011). "Corporate Codes of Conduct: The Effects of Code Content and Quality on Ethical Performance." *Journal of Business Ethics*, 99, 535–48.
Ferrell, O. C., Fraedrich, J., and Ferrell, L. (2017). *Business Ethics: Ethical Decision Making and Cases*. 11th ed. Boston, MA: Cengage Learning.
Frankel, M. S. (1989). "Professional Codes: Why, How, and With What Impact?" *Journal of Business Ethics*, 8, 109–15.
Frostenson, M., Helin, S., and Sandström, J. (2012). "The Internal Significance of Codes of Conduct in Retail Companies." *Business Ethics: A European Review*, 21, 263–75.
Garegnani, G. M., Merlotti, E. P., and Russo, A. (2015). "Scoring Firms' Codes of Ethics: An Explorative Study of Quality Drivers." *Journal of Business Ethics*, 126, 541–57.
Gaumnitz, B., and Lere, J. (2002). "Contents of Codes of Ethics of Professional Business Organizations in the United States." *Journal of Business Ethics*, 35, 35–49.
(2004). "A Classification Scheme for Codes of Business Ethics." *Journal of Business Ethics*, 49, 329–35.
Hill, R. P., and Rapp, J. M. (2014). "Codes of Ethical Conduct: A Bottom-Up Approach." *Journal of Business Ethics*, 123, 621–30.
Hoover, K. F., and Pepper, M. B. (2015). "How Did They Say That? Ethics Statements and Normative Frameworks at Best Companies to Work For." *Journal of Business Ethics*, 131, 605–17.
Kaptein, M. (2004). "Business Codes of Multinational Firms: What Do They Say?" *Journal of Business Ethics*, 50, 13–31.
(2008). *The Living Code: Embedding Ethics into the Corporate DNA*. Sheffield, UK: Greenleaf.
(2011). "Toward Effective Codes: Testing the Relationship with Unethical Behavior." *Journal of Business Ethics*, 99, 233–51.
(2017). "When Organizations Are Too Good: Applying Aristotle's Doctrine of the Mean to the Corporate Ethical Virtues Model." *Business Ethics: A European Review*, 26, 300–11.
(2019). "The Moral Entrepreneur: A New Component of Ethical Leadership." *Journal of Business Ethics*, 156, 1135–50.
Kaptein, M., and Schwartz, M. S. (2008). "The Effectiveness of Business Codes: A Critical Examination of Existing Studies and the Development of an Integrated Research Model." *Journal of Business Ethics*, 77, 111–27.
Kaptein, M., and Wempe, J. (1998). "Twelve Gordian Knots When Developing an Organizational Code of Ethics." *Journal of Business Ethics*, 17, 853–69.
Kolk, A., and Tulder, R. (2002). "Child Labor and Multinational Conduct: A Comparison of International Business and Stakeholder Codes." *Journal of Business Ethics*, 36, 291–301.
KPMG (2013). *Integrity Survey 2013*. KPMG Forensic.
KPMG and Erasmus University Rotterdam (2014). *The Business Codes of the Fortune Global 200: What the Largest Companies in the World Say and Do*. Amsterdam: KPMG.
Ladd, J. (1985). "The Quest for a Code of Professional Ethics." In D. G. Johnson and J. W. Snapper (eds.), *Ethical Issues in the Use of Computers*, 37–8. Belmont, CA: Wadsworth.
Lere, J. C., and Gaumnitz, B. R. (2003). "The Impact of Codes of Ethics on Decision Making: Some Insights from Information Economics." *Journal of Business Ethics*, 48, 365–79.
Mercier, G., and Deslandes, G. (2017). "There Are No Codes, Only Interpretations: Practical Wisdom and Hermeneutics in Monastic Organizations." *Journal of Business Ethics*, 145, 781–94.
Messikomer, C. M., and Cirka, C. C. (2010). "Constructing a Code of Ethics: An Experiential Case of a National Professional Organization." *Journal of Business Ethics*, 95, 55–71.
Murphy, P. E. (1988). "Implementing Business Ethics." *Journal of Business Ethics*, 7, 907–15.

Petersen, L. E., and Krings, F. (2009). "Are Ethical Codes of Conduct Toothless Tigers for Dealing with Employment Discrimination?" *Journal of Business Ethics*, 85, 501–14.
Pitt, H., and Groskaufmanis, K. (1990). "Minimizing Corporate Civil and Criminal Liability: A Second Look at Corporate Codes of Conduct." *Georgetown Law Journal*, 78, 1559–64.
Preuss, L. (2010)." Codes of Conduct in Organisational Context: From Cascade to Lattice-Work of Codes". *Journal of Business Ethics*, 94, 471–87.
Schwartz, M. S. (2007). "Universal Moral Values for Corporate Code of Ethics." *Journal of Business Ethics*, 59, 27–44.
(2012). "The State of Business Ethics in Israel: A Light unto the Nations?" *Journal of Business Ethics*, 105, 429–46.
Raiborn, C., and Payne, D. (1990). "Corporate Codes of Conduct: A Collective Conscience and Continuum." *Journal of Business Ethics*, 9, 879–89.
Ruiz, P., Martinez, R., Rodrigo, J., and Diaz, C. (2015). "Level of Coherence among Ethics Program Components and Its Impact on Ethical Intent." *Journal of Business Ethics*, 128, 725–42.
Scholtens, B., and Dam, L. (2007). "Cultural Values and International Differences in Business Ethics." *Journal of Business ethics*, 75, 273–84.
Singh, J. B. (2011). "Determinants of the Effectiveness of Corporate Codes of Ethics: An Empirical Study." *Journal of Business Ethics*, 101, 385–95.
Singh, J., Svensson, G., Wood, G., and Callaghan, M. (2011). "A Longitudinal and Cross-Cultural Study of the Contents of Codes of Ethics of Australian, Canadian and Swedish Corporations." *Business Ethics: A European Review*, 20, 103–19.
Sobczak, A. (2006). "Are Codes of Conduct in Global Supply Chains Really Voluntary? From Soft Law Regulation of Labour Relations to Consumer Law." *Business Ethics Quarterly*, 16, 167–84.
Somers, M. J. (2001). "Ethical Codes of Conduct and Organizational Context: A Study of the Relationship between Codes of Conduct, Employee Behavior and Organizational Values." *Journal of Business Ethics*, 30, 185–95.
Stevens, B. (2004). "The Ethics of the US Business Executive: A Study of Perceptions." *Journal of Business Ethics*, 54, 163–71.
Stöber, T., Kotzian, P., and Weißenberger, B. E. (2019). "Culture Follows Design: Code Design as an Antecedent of the Ethical Culture." *Business Ethics: A European Review*, 28, 112–28.
Stohs, J. H., and Brannick, T. (1999). "Code and Conduct: Predictors of Irish Managers' Ethical Reasoning." *Journal of Business Ethics*, 22, 311–26.
Svensson, G., Wood, G., and Callaghan, M. (2010). "A Corporate Model of Sustainable Business Practices: An Ethical Perspective." *Journal of World Business*, 45, 336–45.
Tjosvold, D. W., Snell, R. S., and Fang, S. S. (2009). "Codes of Conduct for Open-Minded Discussion and Resolution of Ethical Issues in China." *Journal of International Business Ethics*, 2(2), 3–20.
VNO-NCW (2016). *Leiderschap in Ethiek* [Leadership in Ethics]. The Hague: VNO-NCW.
Valentine, S. R., Hanson, S. K., and Fleischman, G. M. (2019). "The Presence of Ethics Codes and Employees' Internal Locus of Control, Social Aversion/Malevolence, and Ethical Judgment of Incivility: A Study of Smaller Organizations." *Journal of Business Ethics*, 160, 657–74.
Weaver, G. (1993). "Corporate Codes of Ethics: Purpose, Process and Content Issues." *Business and Society*, 32, 44–58.
Weaver, G. R. (1995). "Does Ethics Code Design Matter? Effects of Ethics Code Rationales and Sanctions on Recipients' Justice Perceptions and Content Recall." *Journal of Business Ethics*, 14, 367–85.
Weber, J., and Wasieleski, D. M. (2013). "Corporate Ethics and Compliance Programs: A Report, Analysis and Critique." *Journal of Business Ethics*, 112, 609–26.
Webley, S., and Dondé, G. (2016) *Codes of Business Ethics: Examples of Good Practice*. London: Institute of Business Ethics.
Weller, S. (1988). "The Effectiveness of Corporate Codes of Ethics." *Journal of Business Ethics*, 7, 389–96.

Winkler, I. (2011). "The Representation of Social Actors in Corporate Codes of Ethics: How Code Language Positions Internal Actors." *Journal of Business Ethics*, *101*, 653–65.
Wood, G., and Rimmer, M. (2003). "Codes of Ethics: What Are They Really and What Should They Be?" *International Journal of Value-Based Management*, 16, 181–95.
Wotruba, T. R., Chonko, L. B., and Loe, T. W. (2001). "The Impact of Ethics Code Familiarity on Manager Behavior." *Journal of Business Ethics*, 33, 59–69.

41

Third Party and Appointed Monitorships

Veronica Root Martinez[*]

Abstract: This chapter outlines the history and use of monitors in various contexts, beginning with the original conception of a court-appointed monitor and ending with the more recent development of the public relations and modern-day court-ordered monitor. It next discusses how the specific type of monitorship alters the duties and confidentiality expectations of the parties to the monitorship in both formal and informal ways. Next, it analyzes the sparse regulation of monitorships, suggesting that reputation may currently be the most effective limit on monitor overreach and capture. Finally, it ends by proposing two areas for scholarly focus going forward: (1) mechanisms for formally regulating monitors, and (2) empirical study of the overall effectiveness of monitorships.

41.1 INTRODUCTION

Monitorships are ubiquitous in today's society. From use in resolutions of formal court adjudications to negotiated settlement agreements with the government, organizations have long been aware that when an organization encounters a significant compliance failure (or series of failures) the retention of a monitor may become a part of its remediation effort. While perhaps best known for their role in the structural reform litigation efforts that helped to transform schools and prisons, monitors and their use have evolved significantly over time (Garrett 2014: 177). The use of modern-day monitorships was revolutionized by the corporate prosecution policies enacted by the U.S. Department of Justice (DOJ) in the late 1990s and early 2000s (Holder 1999). For example, approximately one-third of all resolutions of Foreign Corrupt Practice Act (FCPA) matters brought by the DOJ from 2004 to the present have resulted in the imposition of a monitor.[1]

And yet, despite the widespread use of monitors by courts, governmental enforcement authorities and even at times by private firms on their own initiative, monitors have operated and continue to operate largely in the shadows. There are no formal requirements for how monitors should be used, regulated, and structured to meet the various interests, concerns, and requirements of the parties to the monitorship.[2] Indeed, the inherent flexibility of the

[*] This chapter is dedicated to the many practitioners who have taken the time to speak with me informally to ensure that my academic take on a tool within industry remains rooted in reality. Many thanks to Malaina Weldy for invaluable assistance in putting together this chapter and to the many research assistants who have contributed to my scholarly work addressing the monitor phenomenon over the past several years. Special thanks to Carol Li and Caitlin-Jean Juricic for exceptional assistance.

[1] Statistical analysis on file with author; data pulled from Stanford FCPA database.

[2] There is, however, new guidance from the American Bar Association (2020).

monitorship structure has meant that monitorships continue to develop variations and nuances in purpose and scope, as the understanding of what it means to enter into a monitorship – as well as the contexts in which monitorships are used – expands.

This chapter offers an introduction to, and overview of, monitorships, examining how the use of monitors has developed over time and explaining how we arrived at our present-day understanding of monitorships. It also discusses when and why monitors are used, what a monitor's role is to the various parties, and how monitors in different contexts may have differing responsibilities or functions. The chapter concludes with suggestions for future lines of inquiry and research.

41.2 DEFINING MONITORS

After a violation of applicable regulations or the law, organizations are often required to remediate the underlying misconduct. When, however, there is a concern about the firm's ability to do so on its own – whether that concern stems from a lack of underlying trust or expertise – an independent third party is often brought in to oversee the remediation effort. Today's monitors are independent, private outsiders, employed after an institution is found to have engaged in wrongdoing, who effectuate remediation of the organization's misconduct, and provide information to outside actors about the status of the firm's remediation efforts (Root 2016: 123). At their core, monitorships are about assisting an organization in successfully completing a remediation effort prompted by a compliance failure and ensuring long-term compliance with applicable law (Morford 2008), industry standards, and the organization's own internal norms and policies. Although monitors today are used in a variety of different contexts and can accordingly vary in role, structure, and purpose – which will be examined more closely in Section 41.4 – this is the most universal understanding of what a monitor is and what a monitor does.

The key difference between a monitor and, say, an auditor who might be the first to signal that there are compliance problems within an organization is that the monitor does not come into the picture until *after* a structural compliance failure at the company has come to light (Root 2014: 535). This means that the monitor's role is less about finding new compliance issues (although that may be a small part of it) and more about working with the organization to address the compliance failure and assist the firm in its remediation efforts (Root 2014: 528). As such, monitors engage in activities that are distinct from traditional gatekeeping roles, which are often focused on preventing misconduct. Monitors, which are a type of external remediator, come in to help firms reform their policies after misconduct has already occurred (Root 2016: 156).

Monitors play an increasingly important role in our society, yet there is no universal definition of a monitor. The American Bar Association (ABA), for instance, defines a monitor as:

> [a] person or entity: [e]ngaged by a Host Organization pursuant to a Court Order or an Agreement and Engagement Letter; [w]ho is independent of both the Host Organization and the Government; [w]hose selection is approved by the Government or ordered by a court; and [w]hose responsibilities and authority are established by Court Order or by the Agreement and the Engagement Letter (American Bar Association n.d.).

Professors Vikramaditya Khanna and Timothy L. Dickinson, on the other hand, define corporate compliance monitors more simply as "people appointed to supervise a firm for a certain period of time as part of a Deferred Prosecution Agreement ('DPA') or NonProsecution Agreement ('NPA')" (Khanna and Dickinson 2007: 1714). The International Association of Independent Corporate Monitors (IAICM) explains that "[m]onitors may be given different titles or roles, but their essential function is to report to governmental agencies and other oversight organizations (the 'Reporting Agency') on the compliance of organizations (the 'Host Organization') with the terms and conditions of legal agreements between the Reporting Agency and Host Organization" (International Association of Independent Corporate Monitors 2016).

The variation in definitions of a monitor mirrors the variation in the roles that the monitor might play depending upon the type of remediation effort being overseen. Monitors are retained as a result of formal court adjudications but are also utilized as part of negotiated settlement agreements between the government and a firm to resolve allegations of misconduct (Root 2014: 524). Depending upon the scope of the engagement, a monitor may act as a quasi-probation officer, an investigator, a recommender, a legal advisor (outside an attorney–client relationship), or a consultant of sorts for the firm to which he or she has been assigned (Root 2014: 531). And, depending upon the agreement, the monitor may be referred to as a monitor, an independent consultant, an independent compliance consultant, or by another term. My own study of the phenomenon has led me to the definition outlined at the outset of this section: a monitor is an independent, private outsider, employed after an organization is found to have engaged in wrongdoing, who effectuates remediation of the firm's misconduct, and provides information to outside actors (e.g., the court, the government, prosecutors, or the public) about the status of the firm's remediation efforts.

Depending on the monitor's particular background, they may bring in a team of individuals to work with them to assess a firm's compliance with the remediation effort being overseen and may even assist in designing processes and programs to analyze the organization's culture (Root 2014: 532). Yet it is important to remember that, despite the many and varying roles of a monitor, the monitor's role is not to provide legal counsel for an organization per se, regardless of the monitor's background. Even if a monitor is an attorney, the monitorship does not purport to create an attorney–client relationship. The monitor is more akin to a third-party neutral as articulated in the Model Rules of Professional Conduct (American Bar Association 2019). The monitor is to provide advice beyond the bounds of the traditional legal relationship, due in large part to the monitor's role as an agent of interested parties beyond the monitored firm (e.g., the court or government) (Root 2014: 538).

The ultimate function a monitor is meant to undertake on behalf of a particular institution is determined by the scope of the monitorship as outlined in the agreement that prompted the retention of the monitor by the monitored firm. The scope of a monitorship can vary significantly from one organization to the next and will be tied both to the actors the monitor is required to report to and to the nature of the activity at the firm that the monitor is meant to oversee. Importantly, the scope of the monitorship is often dependent on the seriousness and pervasiveness of the underlying compliance failure. In an ideal scenario, the monitor's role is precisely delineated in the agreement between the corporation and the entity prompting the retention of the monitor, typically a court or government enforcement authority. However, being able to effectively anticipate and document every issue the monitor needs to address or every decision that must be made is fairly daunting and unrealistic, since, at the point of the agreement between the parties, the investigation into the underlying behavior that caused the compliance failure is sometimes not complete. Accordingly, the agreement often lays out the broad strokes of the monitorship and as many details as possible, trying to offer the monitor and the organization at least a shared understanding of the respective roles and power of each party. This ad hoc structure offers a springboard for the company and the monitor to work together. To the extent that there are disagreements regarding the scope of the monitor's role, the agreement resulting in the retention of the monitor should make clear who the arbiter of any disputes will be (Larence 2009).[3]

Ultimately, the monitor works pursuant to the monitorship agreement until the term of the agreement concludes. Occasionally, however, if the monitor believes that his or her job is complete, the monitor will petition the court for an early dismissal (Khanna and Dickinson 2007: 1716–17). Additionally, monitorships have sometimes been extended if sufficient progress toward the ultimate remediation goal has not been obtained (Root 2014: 524–5). When the monitorship is complete, the hope is that the monitor has assisted the company in a remediation effort that will ensure that corporate compliance failures (at least of this sort) do not occur in the future. There is, of course, never any guarantee that the corporation will take the reforms to heart or be able to successfully maintain legal and regulatory compliance once the monitorship concludes.

41.3 THE HISTORY AND USE OF MONITORS

Unlike traditional monitorships, which were court-imposed as part of a post-judgment action, modern-day corporate compliance monitorships are typically entered into voluntarily[4] as part of negotiated settlement agreements without a formal adjudicative decision from a court (Khanna and Dickinson 2007: 1716–17). Once the corporation agrees to the monitorship, the details and scope of the monitorship are set out in the agreement, as discussed in Section 41.2, and a monitor, typically of a legal background (but not necessarily), is selected to serve as the monitor for the firm (Root 2014: 524–5). The monitor, according to U.S. Attorney General Guidance, should be chosen on their merits, selected to prevent the existence or appearance of conflicts, and should generally impart confidence to the general public as someone who can effectively implement the goals of the monitorship (Morford 2008).

The government maintains that a monitorship should not be thought of as a penalty or as a probationary period but rather as a way for the government to more effectively shift the cost of the enforcement to the firm itself, while hopefully more effectively and efficiently bringing about the necessary change to the organization (Ford and Hess 2009: 703; Root 2016: 121; Root 2014: 533). The agreement to a monitorship does not occur instead of other punishments such as fines or restitution but oftentimes in conjunction with such measures. Nevertheless, voluntarily agreeing to a monitorship may help lower some of these government-imposed fines (Root 2016: 139): it shows that the corporation is focused on improving itself and genuinely (whether for purely financial reasons or not) wants to reform its systems and processes to prevent a compliance failure of a similar sort in the future.

3 The Government Accountability Office issued a report in 2009 regarding the need for additional guidance related to disputes between a monitor and the monitored-firm. Since this report, all deferred and nonprosecution agreements entered into between the DOJ and corporations have included language such that any disputes should be elevated to the DOJ for resolution.

4 There are many who would debate whether a monitorship that results from a negotiated settlement agreement is truly voluntary. Negotiated settlement agreements, however, are civil agreements that firms are not legally forced to enter into, making the terms contained in them technically voluntary. Larger discussions about the power of the government to effectively force organizations to enter into negotiated settlement agreements are beyond the scope of this chapter.

Modern-day monitorships have their roots in "[t]he power of a federal court to appoint an agent to supervise the implementation of its decrees," which has "been long established" (Root 2014: 529). Although these agents of the court were not exclusively called monitors, but rather referred to by an array of titles such as "receiver, Master, Special Master, master hearing officer, monitor, human rights committee, Ombudsman, and others" (Root 2014: 529), the courts have used monitors (in form, if not in name) to aid in pre- and post-judgment matters for decades. These "monitors" assisted the court in everything from calculating damages to helping with the discovery process (Khanna and Dickinson 2007: 1715).

The rise in popularity of the modern-day monitorship, however, is traced beyond the use of special masters to the expanded use of monitors in the Racketeer Influenced and Corrupt Organizations Act (RICO) and DOJ cases (Khanna and Dickinson 2007: 1716–17). This evolution of the monitorship has largely been an organic one, and is "an outgrowth of three related phenomena: the evolution of the use of traditional, court-appointed agents, an increase in the complexity of regulatory and legal requirements facing organizations, and the use of external gatekeepers to assist organizations in their efforts to comply with a more challenging and demanding regulatory environment" (Root 2016: 115). Yet the relatively fluid nature of the monitorship's transformation has occurred despite attempts to pass legislation to define and delineate both the use and the selection of monitors. For example, after Chris Christie, in his role as a New Jersey federal prosecutor, appointed his former boss, John Ashcroft, to serve as a monitor to Zimmer Holdings (a monitorship worth between $28 million USD and $52 million USD) without any public notice or bidding, the DOJ conducted an internal review (Root 2017: 2233). This review resulted in guidance referred to as the Morford Memo, which provides suggested standards for monitor independence, selection, communication, reporting obligations, and more. Yet the guidance is informal in nature, and legislation proposed by the House of Representatives, which was at least in part in response to the Chris Christie scandal – the Accountability in Deferred Prosecution Act – died in committee (Root 2017: 2233).

The proposed legislation would have changed how monitors are selected, which continues to be a topic of scholarly and practical consideration, as the appearance of independence remains an important component of public confidence in monitorships' ability to effect change within organizations. The legislation would have

> (i) required monitors to be selected from a public national pool of prequalified candidates, (ii) granted final monitor selection approval to a judge, (iii) dictated that the monitor selection process be 'an open and competitive one where the monitor's powers should extend no further than the compliance concerns at the [monitored] firm,' and (iv) required monitors to receive payments based on a flat- and fixed-fee structure (Root 2017: 2233).

However, the lack of legislation has never prevented the promulgation of informal guidance such as the Holder Memorandum in 1999 (Holder 1999), the Morford Memorandum in 2008 (Morford 2008), or the American Bar Association "Monitors Standards," with the ABA Standards in particular addressing this issue of monitor selection (American Bar Association n.d.). The Holder Memorandum sets out a number of practical factors for government prosecutors to consider before either appointing a monitor or charging a corporation criminally (Khanna and Dickinson 2007: 1719), while the ABA Standards provide a high-level view of monitorships and discuss issues such as selection, compensation, and the scope of the engagement (Root 2017: 2239).

Yet as we can see from the ad hoc guidance from various organizations and the dearth of regulation itself, modern-day monitorships are not well defined and are largely unregulated. Indeed, attempts by courts to oversee monitorships arising out of negotiated settlement agreements, as opposed to court order, have been rejected as beyond the power of the judiciary.[5] Accordingly, the structure and the principles guiding monitorships are susceptible to change and distortion over time – perhaps in undesirable ways – and are prone to inconsistent application (Diamantis 2019: 76). This ambiguity in the structure of the relationship in particular has important implications for duties and confidentiality in the monitorship context, which will be addressed in the next section.

41.4 TYPES OF MONITORSHIPS: IMPLICATIONS FOR DUTIES AND CONFIDENTIALITY

Although traditionally scholars have considered monitorships as one and the same, and accordingly proposed regulation that is consistent across the board, my own research suggests that there are actually several different types of monitor. Understanding the differences between these monitor types has importance in terms of the methods of regulation my fellow scholars and I have proposed, and also has particular import for assessing both duties and confidentiality in the monitorship setting.

The five different types of monitorships that I have identified to date are (1) traditional court-ordered monitorships, (2) enforcement monitorships, (3) corporate compliance monitorships, (4) modern-day court-ordered monitorships, and (5) public relations monitorships, each of which will be discussed in turn.

(1) Traditional court-ordered monitorships, as discussed earlier, are the root of the more modern monitorships we have today. The purpose of a traditional court-ordered monitorship is to ensure specific performance in line with the court's order (e.g., a desegregation order directed toward public schools). This means that the monitor acts as an agent of the court pursuant to a particular pre- or post-judgment order (Root 2016: 143–4).

(2) Enforcement monitorships are similar to traditional court-ordered monitorships but, instead of a court requiring their imposition, a government enforcement authority requires that the organization enter into the monitorship as one of several terms contained within a negotiated settlement agreement. Like traditional court-ordered monitorships, enforcement monitorships require the monitor to ensure that the monitored organization complies with the specific terms of the negotiated settlement agreement (Root 2016: 144–5). This is a "check-the-box" type monitorship. Practitioners and scholars debate how much power organizations have in rejecting or accepting enforcement monitorships, but they are typically entered into after the compliance failure within the organization becomes publicly known.

(3) Corporate compliance monitorships, although similar to enforcement monitorships, are more amorphous. This is because it is often more difficult to identify when the agreement between the parties is entered into, and exactly what aspects of the corporation's policies and procedures must be overhauled in order to achieve long-term compliance with the agreement as well as with the applicable regulatory and legal requirements. This means that the monitor's first task is to do a root cause analysis to identify the causes of the underlying compliance failure. This broader mandate means

[5] *United States* v. *HSBC Bank USA, N.A.*, 863 F. 3d 125 (2d Cir. 2017).

that the typical corporate compliance monitorship may be longer and more involved than the other types. It also means that the monitor will need to oversee more than whether the organization has specifically performed in line with a court or enforcement authority's mandate and will go beyond that to work with the organization to determine a set of novel, independent recommendations for the organization to implement in an effort to improve its compliance processes and procedures (Root 2016: 145–6).

(4) Modern-day court-ordered monitorships are entered into per an order by the court but (perhaps improperly) take on some of the characteristics of corporate compliance monitorships. This construct, if not fully consented to by the organization, may lead to significant problems and conflict. A key component of an effective corporate compliance monitorship is cooperation between the monitor and the firm, but court-ordered monitorships may arise despite significant objections from the firm to be monitored. This means that the monitor and the organization may have differing goals, as the monitor may be providing a largely unwanted service to the organization, which goes beyond simply monitoring specific compliance with a court's mandates. The court, by ordering the monitor to assist with the remediation effort rather than allowing the institution to "agree" to the remediation voluntarily, as in the corporate compliance monitorship context, may simply be utilizing the wrong form to achieve its stated goals. However, the use of this form appears to be less common, and the legality of it remains an open consideration (Root 2016: 146–7).

(5) Public relations monitorships, different from any of the other forms of monitorship and a relatively new phenomenon, are entered into by the institution without any involvement from the court or a governmental agency. Such monitorships are often entered into after the institution experiences some sort of pressure, real or perceived, from the public to initiate reforms after a scandal is discovered. The public relations monitor is retained by the institution as a service to the public, and accordingly – distinct from the other forms of monitorship – the institution typically distances itself from the monitor once he or she has been selected (e.g., by waiving any possible privilege at the outset of the engagement). This allows the monitor to assist with remediating the misconduct within the organization without the institution seemingly tainting the process. Although this form of monitorship is clearly about remediation, it is also in large part about rebuilding public trust that has been lost through the compliance failure or scandal (Root 2016: 147–8).

41.4.1 *Duties*

The differences in each of these five types of monitorships are significant when considering what duties the monitor might owe in each situation. It is not currently clear that duties necessarily flow from monitorship relationships, but walking through the different ways in which duties would align based on different monitorship structures helps reveal the differences among monitorship types (Root 2016: 151–2). For example, court-imposed monitors, both traditional and modern-day, owe duties principally to the court. Enforcement monitors, on the other hand, appear to primarily have a duty to the government enforcement authority that required their retention, although the agreements tend to state that enforcement monitors are not technically agents of the government. Additionally, enforcement monitors may also have duties to the public depending upon the underlying compliance failure (Root 2016: 151–2).

Corporate compliance monitors, on the other hand, have a more complicated structure and potential set of duties, both to the government pursuant to the voluntary agreement and to the monitored institution itself. A corporate compliance monitor acts as a dual agent of sorts, and may, similar to the enforcement monitor, owe additional duties to the public at large. Modern-day court-ordered monitors may owe duties to another entity besides the court. For example, it is an open question whether the monitor may owe duties to the shareholders of the monitored firm (Root 2016: 151–2).

Finally, public relations monitors present a difficult analysis: they are undertaken by the institution, yet are seemingly entered into for the benefit of the public, and the independence of a typical public relations monitor echoes this. Therefore, it may be challenging to determine to whom the duty should be owed in this situation, and it might need to be determined on a case-by-case basis (Root 2016: 152).

41.4.2 *Confidentiality and Transparency*

The analysis of when there should be confidentiality versus transparency in each of these various monitorship types is equally complex and consequential. Court-ordered (both traditional and modern-day), enforcement, and public relations monitorships can all be considered monitorships with high transparency and low confidentiality (Root 2016: 148). Because of the nature of each of these monitorships, the public benefits the most from gaining a full and accurate picture of the monitor's goals and activities, and the parties' expectations relative to this transparency are either set by the court or voluntarily elected in the case of the public relations monitor. The transparency of the information also allows victims of the organization's misconduct to receive information regarding the extent of the organization's remediation.

Corporate compliance monitors, on the other hand, benefit from a lower degree of transparency and a higher degree of confidentiality than the other monitorship types. This is because the agreement requires more than monitoring rote compliance with a court order or enforcement authority demands; it requires that the monitor work in a collaborative manner with the organization so that the monitor is able to determine the steps that the organization should take to ensure that similar misconduct does not reoccur. If the institution is assured a higher degree of confidentiality, this incentivizes the institution to be more forthcoming with the monitor. This in turn allows the monitor to work more effectively and develop a set of recommendations most likely to reform the organization (Root 2014).

* * * *

While the particular duties owed and the level of confidentiality to be expected in each type of monitorship have yet to be formally regulated, the understanding of the nuances among the different types is important when considering potential future legislation, which appears inevitable. Additionally, these nuances matter because in structuring the relationship and labeling it as a monitorship (or not), there are serious consequences for the parties involved.

41.5 FUTURE SCHOLARSHIP ON MONITORSHIPS

The use of monitorships is well known, but much of the work done by monitors is shrouded in secrecy. As such, monitors and monitorships are ripe for future scholarly work on both a theoretical and an empirical level.[6]

41.5.1 *Regulation of Monitors*

Monitors have been utilized to ensure that homeowners who were improperly foreclosed upon received financial remediation, to oversee reforms to compliance policies and procedures at firms engaged in widespread bribery of foreign officials, and to supervise efforts by universities that failed to protect children from predatory behavior (Root 2016). In other words, monitorships are as diverse as the misconduct that can be identified in firms of every type and size all over the country. This diversity has made regulating monitorships an exceedingly daunting task, as it seems unlikely that typical avenues will successfully capture the breadth and depth of the situations where monitors are retained.

As a result, I have come to the conclusion that instead of attempting to regulate monitorships, policymakers and academics should focus on ways to regulate the monitors themselves. Because monitors are not engaged in an attorney–client relationship and are often not lawyers, the ABA is limited in what it can do to regulate the conduct of monitors. It has certainly done its part by issuing Monitor Standards, but those standards are necessarily nonbinding. Additionally, because attempts by courts to regulate monitorships have been deemed improper, monitorships often operate in a space without formal and traditional oversight mechanisms.[7]

As a result, it appears that the only true and constant restraint on a monitor's behavior today is the monitor's own concerns about his or her reputation (Root 2017). Yet even that tool has been limited by the government's continued insistence that all information regarding monitorships should remain confidential. Indeed, it continues to litigate cases where relatively innocuous information regarding monitors is requested by members of the public, which makes reputation a particularly inept tool to regulate their role.[8] One by-product of this reality is that we have very little information about potential failed monitorships or conflicts that might arise between monitors and monitored firms. In other words, we have no way of knowing whether we should be concerned or not regarding the work that monitors are completing on behalf of organizations and the public.

It would be beneficial, then, if more scholars were to engage in theoretical inquiries into how monitors – important actors within compliance efforts – might be regulated. Would the creation of a self-regulatory organization be helpful? Might it be worth exploring new Securities and Exchange Commission (SEC) disclosures surrounding monitorships for public companies? Should the ABA adopt formal guidance to restrain lawyer-monitors and the Public Company Accounting Oversight Board (PCAOB) adopt standards to rein in accountant-monitors? Should Congress require standardization of the use of the term monitor by all administrative agencies to make it easier to (i) track the use of monitors and

6 For example, Global Investigations Review published *The Guide to Monitorships* in 2019 aiming to fill a gap in the literature, covering commonly raised issues (Barkow, Barofsky, and Perrelli 2019).

7 See *United States* v. *Fokker Services B.V.*, 818 F.3d 733 (D.C. Cir. 2016); *United States* v. *HSBC Bank USA, N.A.*, 863 F.3d 125 (2d Cir. 2017).

8 *Tokar* v. *U.S. Department of Justice*, 304 F. Supp. 3d 81 (D.D.C. 2018).

(ii) enact legislation to regulate monitors? These are just a few of many questions that could benefit from scholarly engagement from academics in a variety of disciplines.

41.5.2 *Ripe for Empirical Study*

In addition to theoretical scholarship, the study of monitors and monitorships would benefit from both qualitative and quantitative research studies. The most important question surrounding monitorships – are they effective? – remains unanswered. In part, this question is difficult to answer because the government, and more specifically the DOJ, has worked very hard to keep monitorships outside the public eye.[9] But it is also difficult because monitored firms have a very real interest in keeping information related to monitorships private in an effort to prevent both third-party litigation and good old-fashioned bad press.

Thus, the use of modern-day monitorships could benefit from qualitative and quantitative empirical research. It would be helpful to conduct robust qualitative studies focused on the perspectives of those at monitored firms who work with monitors, monitors themselves, and even government officials who have received information from monitors. Additionally, it would be helpful for empirically trained scholars to construct studies that might aid in determining whether monitored firms' outcomes post-monitorship are better or worse than those of their nonmonitored peers. In particular, it may be fruitful for scholars with accounting, finance, or economics expertise to engage in event studies that look at the effect of the imposition of monitorships for both short- and long-term stock returns.[10]

41.6 CONCLUSION

Modern-day monitorships come in many different forms, yet the various types of monitorships are advantageous in our increasingly complex regulatory environment. Each type of monitorship serves a unique purpose and plays a valuable role in helping to reform and transform organizations found to have engaged in misconduct. The diversity of monitorships, however, can make recognizing when a monitorship exists challenging. As monitorship structures continue to morph and develop, it will be increasingly important to focus on regulating monitors themselves. And, as the use of monitorships increases, scholars should strongly consider engaging in both qualitative and quantitative research surrounding such use and its effectiveness.

REFERENCES

American Bar Association. 2019. "Model Rules of Professional Conduct." www.americanbar.org/groups/professional_responsibility/publications/model_rules_of_professional_conduct/model_rules_of_professional_conduct_table_of_contents/.

2020. "ABA Standards for Criminal Justice Monitors and Monitoring." February 20. www.americanbar.org/products/inv/book/395343871/.

n.d. "Monitor Standards." www.americanbar.org/groups/criminal_justice/standards/MonitorsStandards.html.

[9] *Tokar* v. *U.S. Department of Justice*, 304 F. Supp. 3d 81 (D.D.C. 2018).

[10] My own initial inquiries into the feasibility of empirical studies suggests that they might be difficult to complete at the present moment, but within three to five years there should be a sufficient sample of monitorship cases to enable empirical studies worth completing.

Barkow, Anthony S., Neil M. Barofsky, and Thomas J. Perrelli. 2019. *The Guide to Monitorships*. London: Law Business Research Ltd. https://jenner.com/system/assets/publications/19193/original/GIR%20The%20Guide%20to%20Monitorships%20full%20book.pdf?1565117673.

Diamantis, Mihailis E. 2019. "An Academic Perspective." In *The Guide to Monitorships*, edited by Anthony S. Barkow, Neil M. Barofsky, and Thomas J. Perrelli, 75–84. London: Law Business Research Ltd.

Ford, Cristie, and David Hess. 2009. "Can Corporate Monitorships Improve Corporate Compliance?" *Journal of Corporation Law* 34: 679–737.

Garrett, Brandon. 2014. *Too Big to Jail*. Cambridge, MA: Belknap Press.

Holder, Jr., Eric. 1999. "Memorandum to All Component Heads and U.S. Attorneys." U.S. Department of Justice. June 16. www.justice.gov/sites/default/files/criminal-fraud/legacy/2010/04/11/charging-corps.PDF.

International Association of Independent Corporate Monitors (IAICM). 2016. "Preamble." Code of Professional Conduct. Last modified December 16, 2016. http://iaicm.org/about-independent-corporate-monitors/code-of-conduct/.

Khanna, Vikramaditya, and Timothy L. Dickinson. 2007. "The Corporate Monitor: The New Corporate Czar?" *Michigan Law Review* 105: 1713–55.

Larence, Eileen R. 2009. "Prosecutors Adhered to Guidance in Selecting Monitors for Deferred Prosecution and Non-prosecution Agreements, but DOJ Could Better Communicate Its Role in Resolving Conflicts." U.S. Government Accountability Office, November 19. www.gao.gov/products/GAO-10-260T.

Morford, Craig S. 2008. "Memorandum for Heads of Department Components and United States Attorneys." *U.S. Department of Justice*, March 7. www.justice.gov/sites/default/files/dag/legacy/2008/03/20/morford-useofmonitorsmemo-03072008.pdf.

Root, Veronica. 2014. "The Monitor-Client Relationship." *Virginia Law Review* 100: 523–85.

2016. "Modern-Day Monitorships." *Yale Journal on Regulation* 33: 109–63.

2017. "Constraining Monitors." *Fordham Law Review* 85: 2227–47.

42

Ethics and Compliance Training

David Hess

Abstract: An essential component of ethics and compliance programs is the training of organizational members. Training helps ensure that all employees understand their legal and regulatory obligations, and company policies. There are significant legal incentives for organizations to adopt training, but understanding when training is effective is challenging. After discussing the legal incentives, this chapter explores how effectiveness can be measured, and reviews those factors that the academic literature has identified as potentially having a positive impact on training effectiveness.

42.1 INTRODUCTION

Ethics and compliance training is a widespread practice in organizations and is commonly viewed as an essential part of ethics and compliance programs. In general, this type of training is used to help ensure that all employees understand, and comply with, their legal and regulatory obligations. In some cases, such as with sexual harassment, the law has made certain types of training mandatory. In other cases, organizations are motivated to adopt training practices to help prevent the organization from facing legal liability, or to help mitigate the organization's sanctions if one of its employees is found to have violated the law. Finally, organizations may use ethics training to help set the foundation for an ethical organizational culture by defining, and calling attention to, the values the organization seeks to promote and adhere to (Warren et al., 2014).

Just as organizations have different motivations to adopt training, their training practices can have different orientations and goals. Compliance programs are often loosely categorized as being compliance-oriented or values-oriented (Paine, 1994). Likewise, ethics and compliance training can have a compliance-orientation, which is focused on ensuring adherence to specific laws, regulations, or codes of conduct. Or, training can have a values orientation, and focus on training employees to engage in ethical decision-making consistent with the values of the organization. This latter type of training focuses on employees' discretionary decision-making skills and improving their ability to handle ethical challenges in the workplace (Weber, 2015). From a social psychology perspective, training should raise awareness of ethical issues, model appropriate behavior, and promote the modeled behavior (e.g., understanding the positive or negative consequences from certain behaviors) (Warren et al., 2014). Companies can, of course, use a combination of both approaches. Thus, in general, training should teach necessary standards, but it should also "help employees learn how to effectively recognize and respond to common ethical problems experienced in the workplace" (Sekerka, 2009: 78).

Due to organizations' multiple possible motivations for adopting training practices, training can have many possible goals, including but not limited to the following:

- to orient new employees to the organization's policies and legal requirements that they are required to follow;
- to remind, and update, all employees, and in some cases the agents of the organization, on the company policies and legal requirements that they are required to follow;
- to support the organization's efforts to build and maintain an ethical corporate culture;
- to raise awareness of the types of ethical issues that employees may face, and provide a framework for resolving those problems;
- to raise awareness of when and how employees should report any wrongdoing they observe;
- to comply with legal requirements and incentives on training, including demonstrating that the company has attempted to adopt an effective compliance and ethics program.

In structuring a training program, organizations must consider a wide variety of factors. Examples of such considerations include:

- What topics must training cover?
- For the various possible topics, do we need to train all employees of the organization on this topic, or just certain types or levels of employee?
- What resources do we have available to conduct training?
- Are we attempting to train employees on ethical decision-making, legal compliance, or both?
- Do we expect training to change employee attitudes toward the topic?
- Should the training be conducted in a live, face-to-face setting, or can it be computer-based?
- Should the training involve role-plays, simulations, case studies, and other forms of active engagement?
- How often should the training occur?
- How do we know if the training is effective?

This chapter will provide an overview of how the academic literature has studied some of these issues. In Section 42.2, the chapter provides a brief overview of some of the legal incentives that organizations have for adopting compliance and ethics training. In Section 42.3, the chapter discusses the general issue of whether compliance training is effective and how effectiveness can be measured. The remainder of the chapter, Section 42.4, explores those factors that the academic literature has identified as potentially having an impact on training effectiveness.

42.2 LEGAL INCENTIVES

In the United States, the greatest influence on corporations' adoption of compliance programs came from the 1991 Organizational Sentencing Guidelines (OSG). Under the OSG, a corporation convicted of violating a criminal law could receive a significantly reduced punishment if it had implemented an effective compliance program. The OSG listed seven basic requirements of such a program. The initial list of these minimum requirements did not include ethics or compliance training, but the 2004 amendments to the OSG added "effective training programs" for individuals at all levels of the organization (Hess, 2016).

Also, for criminal matters, the Department of Justice (DOJ) issued guidelines on the evaluation of corporate compliance programs (DOJ Criminal Division, 2019). The guidelines are intended to help prosecutors determine whether a corporation accused of wrongdoing had an effective compliance program in place and therefore may be deserving of a settlement agreement or declination instead of prosecution. For example, in 2012, the DOJ declined to prosecute Morgan Stanley for bribes paid by one of its employees because the company had exercised appropriate due diligence in attempting to prevent such payments. The DOJ's announcement of the declination emphasized the number of times the company had trained the offending employee on anti-bribery laws (DOJ, 2012). With respect to training and communications, the DOJ's guidelines seek to ensure that corporations are designing training programs specifically for the trainees' positions, roles, and areas of risk, as opposed to a one-size-fits-all training. In addition, the guidelines ask corporations to be able to articulate why they selected their particular training content and delivery method, and how they determine the effectiveness of their training (DOJ Criminal Division, 2019).

Sexual harassment is an example of an area of law where organizations have a strong incentive to provide ethics and compliance training. Due to the 1998 US Supreme Court rulings of *Faragher* v. *City of Boca Raton* and *Burlington Industries, Inc.* v. *Ellerth*, a key part of an organization's affirmative defense for a supervisor creating a hostile work environment is showing that the organization had exercised reasonable care to prevent harassment, which has been interpreted to include training employees on the organization's harassment policies and procedures. Some states have adopted laws requiring companies to provide sexual harassment training, either to all employees or to specified supervisors. The statute will often specify minimum requirements for the training; for example, the Delaware Code states the topics to be covered, requires some level of interactivity, and requires training of supervisors on the topics of prevention and correction of harassment.[1]

42.3 IS ETHICS TRAINING EFFECTIVE?

Due to the importance given to ethics and compliance training in various areas of the law, it is important to know when training is effective. Measuring effectiveness is a challenge faced by practitioners and academics alike. Based on the ideas of Kirkpatrick (1996), Steele et al. (2016) identify four categories of training evaluation methods:

- *Reaction.* This widely used method is a measure of the trainee's subjective evaluation of the training.
- *Learning.* This is a measure of the knowledge or skill gained in the training. For example, it could be knowledge of a code of conduct's provision, or demonstrated skill, such as competence in utilizing an ethical decision-making process. Learning could also measure attitudes, such as the "trainees' attitudes about the importance or relevance of ethics in business contexts" (Steele et al., 2016: 323).
- *Behavior.* This is a measure of behavioral outcomes in practice (that is, outside of the training context). For example, the organization could measure the levels of misconduct observed by employees both before and after training (though, being careful that employees are not observing more misconduct after training simply because they are now more aware of the misconduct).

[1] 19 Delaware Code § 711A: Unlawful employment practices; sexual harassment.

- *Results.* Results refers to organizational-level outcomes, including perceptions of the organization's ethical climate.

Practitioners have used a variety of metrics from the above categories. One study found that compliance officers relied on the following metrics (listed in order of reported value) (Weber, 2015 33):

1. Incidences of illegal activity by employees.
2. Employee feedback and evaluation of the program.
3. Willingness by employees to report bad news.
4. Employee completion rate of training.
5. Employee awareness of organization's code or reporting mechanism.

Measuring the effectiveness of training is complicated by the fact that a variety of factors will influence the overall impact of the training. In the context of sexual harassment training, Roehling and Huang (2018) classify these factors into three categories: "training design and delivery," "trainee characteristics," and "organizational context." Training design and delivery involves such factors as the frequency and length of time of training and how the organization delivers the content to the trainees. Relevant trainee characteristics include such factors as demographics, prior experience, personality traits, and preexisting attitudes toward the topic. The organizational context refers to the ethical culture of the company and leadership support.

These factors will influence proximal, intermediate, and distal outcomes, with reciprocal influences among these outcomes (Roehling and Huang, 2018). Proximal outcomes include changes in employees' knowledge, skills, attitudes, awareness, and perceived organizational tolerance. These will influence the intermediate outcomes, which are the number and seriousness of incidents of the wrongful conduct, such as sexual harassment, and the reporting of misconduct. Distal outcomes relate to impacts beyond changes in trainees' behaviors, knowledge, or attitudes, and include employee morale, employee safety, and reduction in the organization's legal liability (Roehling and Huang, 2018).

The following discussion provides an overview of the research on the effectiveness of ethics and compliance training by looking at factors in each of three categories identified by Roehling and Huang (2018). To aid in this review, this chapter relies on several meta-analyses of the empirical studies on the effectiveness of ethics training. Those meta-analytic studies include some focused on the ethics training in the sciences (e.g., Watts et al., 2017; Antes et al., 2009), and some focused on business ethics (e.g., Medeiros et al., 2017). It is important to note that the meta-analyses combine studies on professional training and academic training. In general, though, professional development programs have had a greater impact than academic programs (Medeiros et al., 2017).

There are several challenges in conducting meta-analyses in this area. First, the empirical studies used a variety of criteria to measure the effectiveness of the training. The dependent variable can make a significant difference in determining whether the training was effective. For example, some studies have shown that training on sexual harassment increases employees' understanding of what actions are unacceptable harassment (Feldblum and Lipnic, 2016). When the dependent variable is the trainees' change in attitudes toward sexual harassment, however, the results are mixed (Feldblum and Lipnic, 2016).

The various dependent variables include improved moral reasoning, knowledge, awareness of ethical issues, ethical decision-making strategies, and others. Watts and colleagues combined these measures into one variable to measure effectiveness and found that, overall, ethics training had positive "medium-sized effects" on outcomes (Watts et al., 2017: 364). Medeiros et al. (2017) found an overall small, positive effect on outcomes. They noticed a clear distinction between two categories of outcomes, behavioral and attitudinal, and conducted their analysis on those outcomes separately. The first category included measures on ethical decision-making and ethical behavior, and the second, an attitudinal category, included measures on attitudes, moral judgment, perceptions of self, and ethical awareness. Overall, the greatest positive impacts were on ethical decision-making and behavior, and the smallest were in the attitudinal category (Medeiros et al., 2017).

Another challenge is that the various studies used different methodologies to test effectiveness. Steele et al. (2016) provide a review of possible ethics training evaluation practices. They identify the following possibilities:

- Post-test only. The authors identify this as a relatively weak measure. Under this method, trainees are evaluated on the outcome of interest at the end of the training session. This evaluation is the easiest to implement but may be suited only to situations where the outcome of interest is some minimum level of competence.
- Control group. Under this design, the organization can compare the post-test performance of the group of employees that received training to a group that did not receive training.
- Pre-test. The above designs can be modified to include a test on the outcome of interest for all employees before they receive training (and also for the control group, if one is used). This allows the evaluator to control for any differences between the control group and the trainees, and helps show causality.

Another limitation is that few of the studies were longitudinal, and instead measured outcomes at just one point in time. For the studies that were longitudinal, the results are encouraging. For studies that used a follow-up test in addition to a post-test, the results showed no loss of skills or knowledge gained, which suggests that ethics training does have a long-term impact (Watts et al., 2017). Likewise, in a study of face-to-face ethics training at a multinational bank, Warren et al. (2014) found not only that the training had a positive relationship to various attributes of an ethical organizational culture but also that the positive relationship with ethical behaviors persisted over a period of years.

Finally, with a few exceptions, such as the Warren et al. (2014) study, there are a lack of studies conducted in the workplace. Feldblum and Lipnic (2016) identified this as a serious limitation in their review of sexual harassment training studies. One study they reviewed that did occur in the workplace found that training increased the reporting of sexual harassment but did not impact the frequency of sexual harassment behavior (Feldblum and Lipnic, 2016). In addition, and demonstrating the challenges of workplace studies, the authors noted that the increase in reporting may have been due to other factors implemented by the organization. The following reviews the literature on ethics and compliance training by utilizing the three categories identified by Roehling and Huang (2018): "training design and delivery," "trainee characteristics," and "organizational context."

42.3.1 *Training Design and Delivery*

Training can be conducted in a variety of ways, such as through lectures, group discussions of general issues, case studies, role-plays, and others (Weber, 2015). In addition, the organization can conduct some, or all, of its training online (computer-based). In general, researchers believed that face-to-face ethics training should be more effective than online training due to the importance of the social interaction aspects (Warren et al., 2014; Sekerka, 2009; Burke et al., 2006). Moreover, face-to-face training sessions conducted in smaller groups are expected to be especially beneficial, as such programs allow, for example, greater opportunities for trainees to practice desired behaviors in role-plays or simulations (Warren et al., 2014). These methods also allow for group discussion of complex issues, including possible resolutions of the ethical dilemmas (Weber, 2015). In addition, face-to-face training will typically have a higher level of employee engagement than computer-based training, where, for example, a trainee may be able to quickly click through the program (Weber, 2015).

Online training does have certain benefits. Online training allows the organization to quickly and easily reach all employees, it provides the employees with the flexibility to take the training when most convenient, and, perhaps most importantly, it requires significantly less organizational resources than live training. A face-to-face approach, by contrast, may be cost-prohibitive for many companies to offer for all employees (Sekerka, 2009). Thus, if the company offers face-to-face training, it may be only for a select group of managers, or, for example, the company may choose to conduct compliance-oriented training online and values-oriented training face-to-face (Sekerka, 2009).

From the studies, face-to-face, or a combination of face-to-face and online, performed better than online only programs (Medeiros et al., 2017). Online only courses had no impact on attitude criteria, and only a small positive effect on behavioral criteria (Medeiros et al., 2017). In addition, programs with at least some individual component, as opposed to entirely group or team-based, had higher outcomes (Watts et al., 2017; Medeiros et al., 2017).

For the instruction method, case-based instruction with a limited use of lectures had the most positive outcomes (Watts et al., 2017; Medeiros et al., 2017). In general, more active trainee participation opportunities, including practice opportunities, debates, and problem-solving activities, had more positive outcomes (Watts et al., 2017; Medeiros et al., 2017; Waples et al., 2009; Burke et al., 2006). Using a variety of these teaching methods in one training also created positive benefits (Antes et al., 2009). In a review of studies on safety trainings, Burke and Sockbeson (2016) found that more engaging training methods, as compared to more passive approaches, were more effective in improving knowledge and safety performance. In summing up their review of sexual harassment training, Feldblum and Lipnic (2016: 52) state: "[I]n general, repetition is a good thing, we caution against simply repeating the same training over and over, which risks becoming a rote exercise. Rather, we urge employers to consider training that is varied and dynamic in style, form, and content."

The length of time of the training can also make a difference. In most organizations, ethics training does not seem be a significant time involvement. One study found that over 90 percent of respondents had ethics training that lasted less than two hours, and training was typically given only annually (37 percent) or biannually (19 percent) (Weber, 2015). Full- or half-day workshops had a greater impact than longer-term courses (Medeiros et al., 2017;

Antes et al., 2009). Voluntary ethics training programs had larger effects than mandatory trainings (Watts et al., 2017; see also Waples et al., 2009).

Although the DOJ guidelines mentioned in Section 42.2 want organizations to be able to show why they believe their training program to be effective, a one-size-fits-all approach is still common. For example, Tippett (2018: 486) studied a variety of harassment training materials conducted between 1980 and 2016 and found that the trainings generally followed the same format of "authority figure summarizing legal rules, providing examples of prohibited conduct, and offering conduct advice." The likely explanation for this similarity across organizations and time is that managers demanded training approaches that allowed them to easily demonstrate to external observers that they had conducted training (Tippett, 2018). The managers were less focused on effectiveness and innovation, and more on conforming to industry practices.

Unfortunately, a minimalist approach may not just be ineffective; it may also be counter-productive. Others agree with Tippett (2018) that sexual harassment training often focuses on legal standards, identification of inappropriate behavior, and reviews of the company disciplinary process (Dobbin and Kalev, 2019). This approach to training sends the message to employees that they are potential harassers and can create a backlash (Dobbin and Kalev, 2019). For example, some studies found that those employees that are most likely to offend, as measured on a likelihood to harass scale, end up scoring even higher on the scale after training (even though the training improved their knowledge and awareness of the issue) (Dobbin and Kalev, 2019). By contrast, training that focused on bystander intervention and treated the trainees as allies of victims did not have these negative effects (Dobbin and Kalev, 2019).

The latter finding on bystander intervention training is consistent with other findings on trainings focused on problem-solving and decision-making. For example, one meta-analysis found benefits from including coverage of "possible reasoning errors in ethical decision making" and strategies for reasoning through an ethical problem (Antes et al., 2009: 393). Likewise, another study found benefits from teaching problem-solving skills (Waples et al., 2009).

In the context of sexual harassment training, Feldblum and Lipnic (2016) advocate for workplace civility training and bystander intervention training. Workplace civility training focuses on respect, interpersonal skills, conflict resolutions, and other factors that can help create an environment where harassment is less likely (Feldblum and Lipnic, 2016). Bystander intervention training focuses on giving trainees the skills and confidence to intervene when they observe wrongful behavior (Feldblum and Lipnic, 2016). Finally, Gentile (2010) has developed a "Giving Voice to Values" approach to ethics training, which has been adopted by some corporations. Consistent with the above, the focus is not just on knowledge and awareness of ethical issues but also on learning how to develop an action plan and the skills necessary to act effectively on your values.

42.3.2 *Trainee Characteristics*

Studies on ethics and compliance training have considered a variety of trainee characteristics, including gender, age, stage in career, work experience, prior exposure to ethics training, and education. In general, the studies indicate that those that benefited the most from ethics training were older professionals (thus with more work experience as compared to students) and/or who had no prior exposure to ethics training (Watts et al., 2017; Medeiros et al., 2017; Antes et al., 2009; Waples et al., 2009). One study, however, found no differences based on whether the trainees were students or professionals (Watts et al , 2017). In addition, there is some evidence that men benefit more than women from ethics instruction (Watts et al., 2017). This may be due to the fact that women generally score higher on ethical decision-making measures than men, and therefore men may show a larger gain from training.

42.3.3 *Organizational Context*

The organizational context may also influence ethics and compliance training. In some cases, a positive culture may improve training effectiveness. For example, for safety training, some studies have found a stronger relationship between safety training and safety performance in organizational departments with more positive safety climates (Burke and Sockbeson, 2016). In other cases, training is most needed, and has the greatest impact, when the organizational context is not supportive of ethical behavior. Smith-Crowe et al. (2014) studied the interaction between the organization's formal compliance system (which they measured by the presence of ethics training and a whistleblower hotline) and its informal system (which was measured by whether employees reported that they felt pressures to violate company policies). They found that the formal system reduced wrongdoing when employees faced pressure in the informal system to violate the rules. However, when employees did not face such pressures, the formal system did not have any impact on the level of wrongdoing. This suggests that any attempt to study the broader impact of ethics training must take into account the organizational context. As Smith-Crowe et al. (2014: 799) state: "Organizations that find that their formal systems do not impact behavior may erroneously conclude that formal systems are never useful and may be unlikely to rely on them in situations in which they would be most effective, namely when they are in the presence of informal pressures to do wrong." The organizational context can also matter for sexual harassment training. As discussed, there are some situations where sexual harassment training may be counterproductive due to creating a backlash. Research has found, however, that the presence of more women managers in the workplace can prevent the counterproductive effects in some situations (Dobbin and Kalev, 2019).

42.4 CONCLUSION

This chapter started by listing some of the potential goals of ethics and compliance training. These are questions of who, when, what, and how. There is evidence that training can be effective, but the picture is complicated. Some studies focus on the impact at the individual level. The outcome of interest may not be a measure of changed behavior but one of knowledge or attitude changes. For example, one study found that business professionals that underwent anti-corruption training were less likely to accept the common justifications for engaging in corrupt behavior compared to those without such training (Hauser, 2019). Other studies focus on the impact at the organizational level. For example, Parker and Nielsen's (2009) study of 999 large Australian businesses found that training new employees during an orientation phase was a significant part of an effective compliance program. Their study also found, however, that trainings at other times and for other types of employee were not significant. This raises the question of how ethics and compliance training and the organization's informal control system (or corporate culture) impact each other. When is training needed to improve the corporate culture (as well as the other aspects of the formal system)? And when does a positive corporate culture improve the effectiveness of training?

REFERENCES

Antes, Alison L., Stephen T. Murphy, Ethan P. Waples, Michael D. Mumford, Ryan P. Brown, Shane Connelly, and Lynn D. Devenport. 2009. "Meta-analysis of Ethics Instruction Effectiveness in the Sciences." *Ethics & Behavior* 19: 379–402.

Burke, M. J., and C. E. S. Sockbeson. 2016. "Safety Training." In S. Clarke, T. M. Probst, F. Guldenmund, and J. Passmore (eds.), *The Wiley Blackwell Handbook of the Psychology of Occupational Safety and Workplace Health*, 327–56. Chichester, UK: Wiley-Blackwell.

Burke, M. J., S. A. Sarpy, K. Smith-Crowe, S. Chan-Serafin, R. O. Salvador, and G. Islam. 2006. "Relative Effectiveness of Worker Safety and Health Training Methods." *American Journal of Public Health* 96: 315–24.

Dobbin, Frank, and Alexandra Kalev. 2019. "The Promise and Peril of Sexual Harassment Programs." *PNAS* 116(25): 12255–60. www.pnas.org/content/pnas/early/2019/05/29/1818477116.full.pdf.

Feldblum, Chai R., and Victoria A. Lipnic. 2016. *US Equal Employment Opportunity Commission, Select Task Force on the Study of Harassment in the Workplace*. Washington, DC: US Equal Employment Opportunity Commission.

Gentile, Mary C. 2010. *Giving Voice to Values: How to Speak Your Mind When You Know What's Right*. New Haven, CT: Yale University Press.

Hauser, C. 2019. "Fighting Against Corruption: Does Anti-corruption Training Make Any Difference?" *Journal of Business Ethics* 159(1): 281–99.

Hess, David. 2016. "Ethical Infrastructures and Evidence-Based Corporate Compliance and Ethics Programs: Policy Implications from the Empirical Evidence." *New York University Journal of Law and Business* 12(2): 317–68.

Kirkpatrick, D. L. 1996. "Great Ideas Revisited." *Training and Development* 50: 54–9.

Medeiros, K. E., L. L. Watts, T. J. Mulhearn, L. M. Steele, M. D. Mumford, and S. Connelly. 2017. "What Is Working, What Is Not, and What We Need to Know: A Meta-analytic Review of Business Ethics Instruction." *Journal of Academic Ethics* 15(3): 245–75.

Paine, L. S. 1994. "Managing for Organizational Integrity." *Harvard Business Review* 72(2): 106–17.

Parker, C., and V. L. Nielsen. 2009. "Corporate Compliance Systems: Could They Make Any Difference?" *Administration and Society*, 41(1): 3–37.

Roehling, Mark V., and Jason Huang. 2018. "Sexual Harassment Training Effectiveness: An Interdisciplinary Review and Call for Research." *Journal of Organizational Behavior* 39: 134–50.

Sekerka, Leslie E. 2009. "Organizational Ethics Education and Training: A Review of Best Practices and Their Application." *International Journal of Training and Development* 13(2): 77–95.

Smith-Crowe, K., A. E. Tenbrunsel, S. Chan-Serafin, A. P. Brief, E. E. Umphress, and J. Joseph. 2014. "The Ethics "Fix": When Formal Systems Make a Difference." *Journal of Business Ethics* 1: 10.1007/s10551-013-2022-6.

Steele, Logan M., Tyler J. Mulhearn, Kelsey E. Medeiros, Logan L. Watts, Shane Connelly and Michael D. Mumford. 2016. "How Do We Know What Works? A Review and Critique of Current Practices in Ethics Training Evaluation." *Accountability in Research* 23(6): 319–50.

Tippett, Elizabeth C. 2018. "Harassment Trainings: A Content Analysis." *Berkeley Journal of Employment and Labor Law* 39: 481–526.

U.S. Department of Justice (DOJ). 2012. "Former Morgan Stanley Managing Director Pleads Guilty for Role in Evading Internal Controls Required by FCPA." April 25, www.justice.gov/opa/pr/former-morgan-stanley-managing-director-pleads-guilty-role-evading-internal-controls-required.

U.S. Department of Justice (DOJ) Criminal Division. 2019. Evaluation of Corporate Compliance Programs (updated April 2019).

Waples, Ethan P., Alison L. Antes, Stephan T. Murphy, Shane Connelly, and Michael D. Mumford. 2009. "A Meta-analytic Investigation of Business Ethics Instruction." *Journal of Business Ethics* 87: 133–51.

Warren, Danielle E., Joseph P. Gaspar, and William S. Laufer. 2014. "Is Formal Ethics Training Merely Cosmetic? A Study of Ethics Training and Ethical Organizational Culture." *Business Ethics Quarterly* 24(1): 85–117.

Watts, Logan L., Kelsey E. Medeiros, Tyler J. Mulhearn, Logan M. Steele, Shane Connelly, and Michael D. Mumford. 2017. "Are Ethics Training Programs Improving? A Meta-analytic Review of Past and Present Ethics Instruction in the Sciences." *Ethics & Behavior* 27(5): 351–84.

Weber, James. 2015. "Investigating and Assessing the Quality of Employee Ethics Training Programs among US-Based Global Organizations." *Journal of Business Ethics* 129: 27–42.

43

The Social and Organizational Psychology of Compliance: How Organizational Culture Impacts on (Un)ethical Behavior

Elianne F. van Steenbergen and Naomi Ellemers

Abstract: In psychological theory and research, compliance is generally seen as the most superficial and weakest form of behavioral adaptation. The current contribution examines how the social context of work – the organizational culture – can be organized to stimulate ethical business conduct. By reviewing social psychological theory and research, we illustrate how an ethical culture can be developed and maintained through ethical leadership and by mainstreaming ethics into existing business models. This is markedly different from more common legal approaches. It requires that a commitment to ethical business conduct is visible from the tone at the top, that organizational leaders "walk the talk" on the work floor, and that this matches the implicit messages that organizational members receive on a day-to-day basis about what really matters and what should be prioritized. Attempts to increase rule compliance are bound to fail when organizational incentives and rewards focus on individual bottom-line achievement regardless of how this is done. Empirical evidence supports the claim that organizational culture is an important factor in stimulating ethical conduct. By creating an ethical culture, organizations develop an "ethical mindset" in organizational members, which helps them not only to understand and internalize existing guidelines in their current work but also to apply the "spirit" of these guidelines to new dilemmas and emerging situations. This makes investing in an ethical culture a sustainable business solution.

43.1 COMPLIANCE IN SOCIAL AND ORGANIZATIONAL PSYCHOLOGY

In psychological theory and research, the notion of "compliance" features as a potential outcome of attempts to influence people's behaviors (Cialdini and Goldstein, 2004). However, in the range of possibilities, "compliance" emerges as the *weakest form of behavioral adaptation*, instead of being considered a desired end-state. In psychology, the term compliance is used to indicate people acting in line with requirements, even when they don't agree or don't understand why this is important. Such behavioral adaptation can be elicited by social pressure (from leadership or peers), threat of sanctions, or by decreasing the opportunity to deviate from an established course of action (e.g., due to external restrictions or nudges). While at first sight this may seem a perfectly acceptable outcome ("never mind why, just do it"), in psychological theory and research, compliance is generally seen as the most superficial and weakest form of behavioral control, as it relies on continued monitoring and consistent implementation of sanctions and rewards (Raven, 1992; Tyler and Blader, 2005).

The chances of people "truly" adapting their behavior – even when nobody is watching, or in situations that are unforeseen – are much larger when they are *convinced* of the relevance and importance of behavioral guidelines ("conversion"), and is strongest when they incorporate these guidelines into their sense of *identity*, as indicating a key aspect of who they are and where they belong ("internalization"). This is also acknowledged in modern theories of effective leadership in organizations (Haslam, Reicher, and Platow, 2011). Thus, compliance with important guidelines will be most robust when these guidelines also engage with and define people's sense of self and social identity, while compliance is most fragile or even unlikely when the intended guidelines go against (locally) shared values and important self-views (Ellemers, 2017; Ellemers and Van der Toorn, 2015).

The pervasive influence of the social context is often ignored when inferring that those who fail to comply with explicit regulations must have a "deviant personality" or "lack a moral compass." Individual behavior is much more influenced by our social context (e.g., social norms) and the broader system in which we operate (e.g., implicit incentives) than many people think (Haslam and Ellemers, 2011; Kish-Gephart, Harrison, and Treviño, 2010; Treviño and Nelson, 2011; Van Steenbergen et al., 2019). An egoistic organizational culture, for example, was found to overrule personal norms of public and private sector employees regarding corruption, and enhanced the likelihood that those employees would accept bribes in exchange for preferential treatment (Gorsira et al., 2018).

Social and organizational psychology explicitly considers such social factors and studies how these influence human behavior in an organizational context. Research in this area examines how individuals are directly or indirectly, consciously or subconsciously, influenced by others in the organization, such as fellow team members, their manager, the CEO, or the broader organizational culture. This approach offers a valuable perspective from which to study corporate compliance. It can provide insight into the conditions under which individuals in organizations are inclined to obey, bend, or break the rules that apply to them – regardless of their character or personal values. The current contribution aims to examine how the social context of work – the organizational culture in particular – can be organized to stimulate ethical business conduct.

43.2 PREVENTING UNETHICAL BEHAVIOR AT WORK

Unethical behavior in a work context is defined as "any organizational member action that violates widely accepted (societal) moral norms" (Kish-Gephart et al., 2010: 2). Importantly, this definition does not rely on what is specified by the law or corporate conduct codes but refers to the violation of widely accepted (societal) moral norms. As such, it excludes mildly negative workplace behaviors such as gossiping or tardiness; even if these may deviate from organizational rules or codes of conduct, such behaviors do not violate widely accepted moral norms in society. This definition does include behaviors such as theft, sabotage, fraud, sexual harassment, lying to customers, and misrepresentation of information, *regardless of whether* these behaviors were specified in the organizational code of conduct or the law. This means that certain behaviors can be considered unethical even when not formally forbidden in organizational policy or by law.

The distinction and overlap between illegal and unethical behavior is illustrated in the Venn diagram in Figure 43.1 (drafted after Treviño and Nelson, 2011). The overlapping area in the middle concerns behavior that is both illegal and unethical, such as stealing money from the organization. The left category indicates illegal behavior, which is not

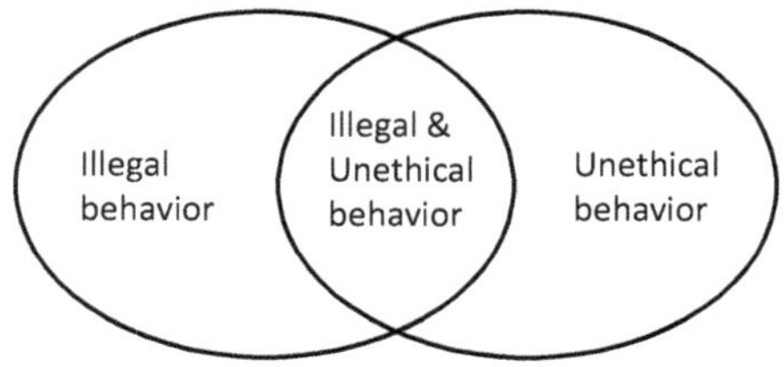

FIGURE 43.1 The partly overlapping categories of illegal and unethical behavior
Source: Adapted from Treviño and Nelson, 2011.

generally considered unethical, such as breaking the legal speed limit by 10 miles per hour in a company car. On the right are cases that are not illegal but generally considered unethical. Examples are the selling of financial products that are not appropriate to the customer's situation, giving or receiving large gifts to influence business relationships, or having sexual relationships with lower-ranked employees in the organization. These types of behavior are in many cases not illegal and, depending on the company, often not specifically prohibited in the corporate code. Nevertheless, there is widespread agreement in society that these types of behavior are "wrong" and morally objectionable (i.e., unethical; Kish-Gephart et al., 2010). Public scandals about corporate misconduct frequently concern the latter category.

In response to publicized incidents of misconduct, the standard response seems to be to extend or adjust legal rules and company regulations, and to monitor that everyone complies with these guidelines. In theory, such efforts to increase the overlap between what is considered unethical and what is defined as illegal reduces the ambiguity in what is considered acceptable behavior. It can also empower supervisors and regulators to enforce this by punishing those individuals who violate these guidelines. In practice, however, this raises concerns about "overregulation" and can have unintended side effects. As a result, some sectors now suffer from disproportionate costs and efforts invested in the process of monitoring rule adherence, enforcing, and sanctioning compliance, to the extent that this can undermine the time and resources available for core activities. Further, such regulatory efforts always run behind changing realities. Moreover, even if people can be forced to adhere to the *letter* of the law, this will not necessarily make them more mindful of the *spirit* of the law when new ethical dilemmas emerge (Tyler and Blader, 2005).

To complement existing perspectives, we propose to incorporate insights from social and organizational psychology, and to identify factors that contribute to an *ethical culture* within organizations. There are three reasons why this is important. First, rules and legal requirements alone are typically ineffective in steering human behavior in organizations as is the threat of fines or sanctions when breaking them (Feldman, 2018; Fehr and Rockenbach, 2003; FSB, 2018; Tenbrunsel and Messick, 1999). In fact, such attempts can even have counterproductive effects. Apart from anything else, this is because when sanctions are communicated as a means of deterring people from undesired behaviors, recipients of such communication feel distrusted, which undermines their willingness to follow these rules and actually reduces compliance (Mooijman et al., 2017). Second, the world is constantly evolving (e.g., as a result of new technologies, new ways of working, etc.), and we can never fully foresee which rules will steer humans in "the right" direction. Even societal norms about what is "wrong" and what is "the right thing to do" evolve. As a result, rule- and policymakers will oftentimes be too late, that is, act after unethical behavior has already taken place. Third, we argue that a legal response triggers a "legal mindset" in organizational members. This is known to invite moral disengagement, which undermines ethical reasoning in the organization (Moore, 2015). This can be the result of any measure that stimulates employees and managers to evaluate their behavior against regulations (Is it prohibited?), rather than against their individual or the group's morals and norms (Is it the right thing to do under these circumstances? And is it right for all stakeholders?).

This is why there is added value in examining factors that enhance or undermine ethical behavior, in addition to the question of whether adherence to relevant guidelines and regulations can be legally enforced. Theory in social and organizational psychology can help define characteristics of an "ethical culture" at work, and research evidence reveals how such a culture can be achieved and whether this helps prevent the emergence of unethical behavior.

43.3 THE SOCIAL NATURE OF ETHICAL GUIDELINES

Our analysis focuses on the internalization of shared norms and values, and is based on insights from Social Identity Theory (Tajfel and Turner, 1979; see also Ellemers and Haslam, 2011). This is one of the most influential theories in social and organizational psychology and explicitly considers people as "group animals" who define themselves in terms of relevant group characteristics, such as the political party they support, their profession, or the organization for which they work. Social Identity Theory examines the situational variations in identity aspects that come to the fore in different social contexts, and that guide individual behavioral choices. To decide what are acceptable behaviors in everyday work practice, people rely on the formal and informal guidelines they receive. These are derived from behaviors they observe in others as well as from implicit signals about relevant priorities and choices that tend to be rewarded. Such implicit observations define shared guidelines about "right" versus "wrong" behavior in the workplace. Understanding and acting in accordance with such guidelines helps workers communicate their awareness of what it takes to be a "good" professional and a "proper" member of the organization. Endorsing these norms secures inclusion and respect from others at work, and over time this can become internalized as defining people's work-related identity. In this way, social contexts and shared norms influence what we think is acceptable behavior in the workplace – beyond mere compliance. Importantly, these norms also prescribe which situations require moral reasoning (rather than being guided by business or legal considerations), and which stakeholders' outcomes should be taken into account (shareholders, employees, customers, the planet), to define priorities or weigh the implications of relevant decisions.

These social guidelines that indicate what is considered (un)acceptable behavior define the ethical *culture* in the workplace. This follows definitions of organizational culture as capturing "the set of shared, taken-for-granted implicit assumptions that a group holds and that determines how it perceives, thinks about, and reacts to its various environments" (Schein, 1996: 236). In short, we use the term culture to indicate people's shared views of "the way things are done around here" (Deal and Kennedy, 1982). This includes relatively local and concrete prescriptions of specific behaviors in relation to particular tasks or responsibilities at work, which some scholars refer to as the organizational or team "climate" (Victor and Cullen, 1988).

Acknowledging the influence of social contextual factors in this way has important implications for how we approach and sanction instances of (un)ethical behavior at work as well as the steps we might take to prevent this. Instead of focusing us on individuals and their deficiencies as "rotten apples" to be removed from the organization, this prompts us to examine which organizational structures, practices, and incentives may contribute to the emergence of "corrupting barrels" (Kish-Gephart, Harrison, and Treviño, 2010). Yet, investigations of misconduct (e.g., in the financial sector) often overlook the influence of these "corrupting barrels," while they keep on identifying and removing "rotten apples" (Scholten and Ellemers, 2016). This matches legal conceptions which aim to assign responsibility for misconduct to specific individuals but deprive organizations of the opportunity to examine and learn from broader circumstances that invited or condoned behaviors that were bound to cause problems, and allows for the development of "toxic cultures" (Van Rooij and Fine, 2018).

This happened at Wells Fargo, an American bank where employees were expected to achieve impossible sales targets, upon threat of losing their job (Reckard, 2013). This prompted them to do whatever was necessary to meet performance goals, including the opening of bank accounts without customer consent, and assigning unwanted credit cards to people who couldn't afford the fees. Another famous case is that of Kweku Adoboli, a "rogue trader" at Swiss investment bank UBS, who served a prison sentence for financial bookkeeping fraud. For many years Adoboli was a valued employee, who was rewarded with promotions and bonuses for the millions of earnings he realized for his bank. He was portrayed as "a rotten apple in an otherwise clean industry," but one of his colleagues said that everyone knew he was the man to turn to when you had screwed up: "We didn't know how he did it, but we didn't want to know" (Fortado, 2015). This case and many similar events illustrate that finding root causes of misconduct and preventing unethical behavior require a broader consideration of possible problems, including the behavior of colleagues and leaders that shapes the ethical culture characterizing the organization.

43.4 MONITORING ORGANIZATIONAL CULTURES TO PREVENT UNETHICAL BEHAVIOR

Culture in financial services is widely accepted as a key root cause of the major conduct failings that have occurred within the industry in recent history, causing harm to both consumers and markets.

— Jonathan Davidson, Financial Conduct Authority (FCA, 2018: 3).

The "culture" is often regarded as a root cause of unethical behavior in an organization or an entire sector. This was the case, for instance, in the Netherlands, where ING banking was sanctioned with the largest fine in Dutch history, €775,000,000, for doing too little to prevent money laundering. Afterwards ING, embodied by CEO Ralph Hamers, was accused of lacking "morals" and having a "commercial culture" in which the achievement of financial targets prevailed over the performance of background checks on clients (Arnold, 2018).

From a research perspective, there seems to be truth to the claim that organizational culture is an important factor in stimulating or preventing unethical behavior (for an overview, see Mayer, Kuenzi, and Greenbaum, 2010). A comparative analysis of high-profile corporate scandals in the United States (Enron, WorldCom, and HealthSouth) and Europe (Parmalat, Royal Ahold, and Vivendi Universal) emphasizes the influence of a "poor ethical climate" in these organizations, alongside external factors such as market developments, as well as political, legal, and regulatory laxness (Soltani, 2014). Other case studies of fraud also point to the role of corporate culture in creating the incentives, opportunities, and rationalizations that together constitute the three elements of the classic "fraud triangle" (Schuchter and Levi, 2016). For example, the results of a recent study show that the corporate culture of banks could account for risk-taking behavior of employees within those banks. Banks in which the culture was characterized by aggressive competition engaged in riskier lending practices (higher approval rate, lower borrower quality, fewer covenant requirements). These short-term performance goals and the behaviors they elicit ultimately harmed the organization as well as society, as such banks were found to have larger loan losses and contributed to systemic risk. The opposite pattern was found for banks whose culture was characterized by control and safety (Nguyen, Nguyen, and Sila, 2019).

In recent years, researchers have increasingly focused on the culture in the workplace as an explanatory characteristic that accounts for individual and organizational outcomes. Different scholars have used different labels and measures, such as culture of compliance, (Oded, 2017), or ethical culture (Kaptein, 2008a). However, the most well-known and widely used tool is the Ethical Climate Questionnaire (Cullen, Victor, and Bronson, 1993). This refers to the set of shared perceptions of procedures and policies, both formal and informal, which shape expectations for ethical behavior in the organization (Cullen et al., 1993). Three important dimensions can be distinguished in this measure that capture how ethical issues are dealt with (Ellemers, 2017; Martin and Cullen, 2006; Simha and Cullen, 2012). Scoring high on the *instrumental* dimension means that employees perceive that people in their company are primarily guided by personal self-interest (i.e., "What's in it for me?"). They have an individualistic and independent way of dealing with ethical issues in the organization and feel that decisions should be made solely in order to serve the economic interests of the organization (profitability, efficiency) or to provide personal benefits (Martin and Cullen, 2006; Pagliaro et al., 2018). This type of culture is indicated when employees express agreement with statements such as "People around here protect their own interest above other considerations." The *caring* dimension indicates that individuals perceive that decisions are and should be based on an overarching concern for the well-being of others within and outside the organization, such as coworkers, customers, or the public (e.g., as indicated by high agreement with statements such as "People are actively concerned about each other's interests."). The *principles* dimension refers to the value that is attached to working in accordance with company rules and codes and legal guidelines and professional standards (e.g., "Successful people in this company go by the book."; see also Ellemers, 2017). The vast majority of empirical research shows that high scores on the instrumental dimension go hand in hand with behavior such as lying, stealing, cheating, falsifying reports, harmful behavior toward customers, misreporting outcomes, acceptance of bribes, and other forms of corruption and fraud, whereas the caring and the principles dimensions tend to be negatively associated with these outcomes (Gorsira et al., 2018; Kaptein, 2011; Mayer et al., 2010; Pagliaro et al., 2018; Peterson, 2002; Simha and Cullen, 2012).[1]

Rather than examining the independent effects of these separate dimensions of culture, we propose that ethical culture can be best diagnosed by examining these three dimensions in coherence (see also Ellemers, 2017). When employees score low on the instrumental dimension and high on the caring and the principles dimensions, we consider this as indicating an "ethical" culture. In such an organization, concerns with employee self-interests and

[1] See also Van Steenbergen, Elianne F., and Naomi Ellemers, "On the Rightness of Rewarding B While Hoping for B: Promoting an Ethical Culture in the Financial Sector," unpublished data.

company outcomes are balanced by concerns for employee and customer relations, as well as professional rules and behavioral codes. Such an ethical culture stimulates employees and managers to evaluate whether decisions that seem right from an individualistic and economic point of view are also right in terms of compliance with rules and right for internal and external stakeholders such as the employees, customers, the general public, and even the planet.

43.5 THE IMPORTANCE OF ETHICAL LEADERSHIP

The insights and study results summarized so far speak to the dangers of "standard business practices" in many businesses as well as public organizations. The broad use of performance incentives that fuels the competition between individual workers to achieve set targets and ongoing efforts to increase the efficiency of work procedures implicitly communicates that it is less important to care for the interests of others or to invest time in following relevant prescriptions and guidelines. In such an organizational climate, simply emphasizing the importance of rule adherence is not enough. To stimulate an ethical culture in which workers become convinced of the importance of rule compliance and internalize this into their self-views as good organizational members, it is essential that top management, senior management, and line management demonstrate ethical leadership (Brown, Treviño, and Harrison, 2005; Garratt, 2010; Treviño and Nelson, 2011). Social Learning Theory (Bandura, 1977, 1986) helps us understand why.

Through the process of role modeling, individuals implicitly learn what is "really" important and appropriate (vs. less important or inappropriate) by observing the behavior of others. In an organizational context, individuals pay most attention to higher-ranked individuals because they embody important organizational goals and reveal how to be successful in the organization (Haslam et al., 2011). Leaders at all levels in the organization are generally regarded in this way by their subordinates, and hence function as legitimate models for normative behavior. When leaders emphasize performance achievement above all else, only express concern for the achievement of outcomes that serve their own self-interest, or are known to bend the rules they have set for those placed below them, this erodes the perceived importance of ethical concerns in the organization. Ethical leadership is displayed by leaders who clearly signal the priority of adhering to shared moral values – even when this is costly. They can do this for, instance, by indicating when and why they prioritize ethical concerns in their own decision-making (e.g., by taking responsibility for a product that did not meet quality standards, or investing in the improvement of production standards). Demonstrating such exemplary behavior instead of just paying lip service to ethical guidelines signals the true importance of rule compliance and makes it more likely that employees will do this too (Mayer et al., 2010).

Besides functioning as role-models in making their own strategic choices, there is a second process by which leaders communicate the ethical climate to lower-ranked employees. By choosing whom to punish and whom to reward, leaders also signal what is truly important to be valued as an organizational member and to get ahead at work. Take the employee who realizes high revenues by using a rather aggressive sales technique, or outperforms her co-workers by "stealing" their customers from them. Is she receiving compliments for her performance, or maybe even a promotion? Or is she reprimanded for acting irresponsibly toward clients and being disloyal to others in her team? Observing how people in the organization are generally treated is a much more powerful source of information than consulting formal policies. Such observations of different behaviors and their consequences communicate and maintain the organizational culture, as this reveals the extent to which leadership cares for the achievement of results and financial outcomes, and whether this happens irrespectively of how these were obtained (Van Yperen, Hamstra, and Van der Klauw, 2011). Importantly, individuals learn not only from their own experiences but also by observing their colleagues and what happens to them (vicarious learning, Bandura, 1977, 1986; Mayer et al., 2010). This means that an employee learns that the use of aggressive sales techniques is okay – and maybe even the way to go – from seeing that a colleague gets promoted after using them.

Building on these insights from Social Learning Theory, Brown et al. (2005) conceptualize ethical leadership as consisting of two main components. The first is the moral person of the leader him/herself, whether they display integrity, concern for others, justice, and trustworthiness. The second is the moral manager component. This refers to the extent to which the leader communicates and emphasizes ethical standards; for instance, the way he or she rewards or punishes ethical and unethical behavior. Ethical leadership is defined as "the demonstration of normatively appropriate conduct through personal actions and interpersonal relationships, and the promotion of such conduct to followers through two-way communication, reinforcement, and decision making" (Brown et al., 2005: 120). In other words, an ethical leader must *be* an ethical person and also *act* ethically in the leadership that he or she displays.

Brown et al. (2005) developed a measure to assess how employees rate their leaders, with statements such as "he/she can be trusted" and "he/she sets an example of how to do things the right way in terms of ethics." When employees rated their leader as more ethical on this measure, they were more willing to report problems to management, contributing to the resolution of these problems resulting in rule compliance (Brown et al., 2005). Ethical leadership – leaders' day-to-day behavior – thus plays a major role in creating an ethical culture (Stringer, 2002). Mayer et al. (2010) showed that ethical leadership relates to a more ethical culture and hence to less employee misconduct in a sample of 1,525 employees and their managers, working in 300 units in different organizations. Recently, we examined similar issues in a sample of more than 4,000 employees working in 18 organizations in the financial sector. Here, we examined how employees perceived the leadership they received from their board and their line management.[2] Specifically, we zeroed in on leaders' ethical behavior in regard to the tension between acting in the clients' interest (treating customers fairly) or in commercial interests, an area of tension in business in general and in finance especially (Ring et al., 2016). When employees felt that the board, line management, and the organization's reward system valued commercial interests over treating customers fairly, they perceived the organizational culture as less ethical and reported more instances of unethical behavior.[3] This research attesting to the central role of leadership and social learning at all levels in establishing and maintaining an ethical culture in the organization is relevant to understanding why so many attempts to enhance ethical behavior and rule compliance have failed.

43.6 ESTABLISHING AN ETHICAL CULTURE

Codes of conduct have become ubiquitous in organizations, yet day-to-day practices often deviate from what these codes prescribe and they are often little more than a façade. In line

[2] Ibid.

[3] Ibid. See also Mayer et al., 2010.

with this point, the well-known meta-analytic study by Kish-Gephart et al. (2010), covering more than thirty years of research, showed that merely having a code of conduct in place does not help to reduce unethical behavior. Only when employees are made to feel that they and others in the organization are held responsible for code compliance does the presence of such a code engender less unethical behavior. Based on this research, it makes sense to move beyond the question of whether or not a code of conduct exists. Instead, there is added value in considering how such codes can be effectively enforced and internalized to shape behavior in the workplace.

In this context, interesting questions are whether and how the introduction of a code of conduct can help to create an ethical culture. A recent experiment among students and academic staff of a university revealed that the use of a positive tone made the code easier to learn for participants, and hence increased familiarity with the code. In addition, participants rated top management's commitment to the code as higher when it was made clear that they had signed the code themselves (Stöber, Kotzian, and Weißenberger, 2019). This again points to the central role of leadership and role modeling in implementing ethical behavior. In sum, although this is an ongoing area of research, available findings suggest that a code of conduct is more effective as a tool to reduce unethical behavior when it is clearly "alive" in the organization and seems sincere in communicating values that are endorsed by the leadership and that are enforced in terms of the consequences of (non)adherence. In sum, the effectiveness of a code depends not only on its content but also on how it is embedded in the culture of the organization. This can be achieved through its explicit introduction, its integration in the core organizational goals and processes of the organization, its visible internalization into the hearts and minds of management and employees, and the institutionalization of its maintenance and monitoring of effectiveness (Kaptein, 2008b).

Accordingly, to establish and maintain an ethical culture, stimulate rule compliance, and prevent misbehavior in organizations, it is not enough to have in place formal descriptions of (un)acceptable conduct. In addition, key individuals in the organization need to embody and visibly enact the importance of these norms. This happens also by identifying, correcting, and communicating about small transgressions, even before "evidence" builds up that would have legal implications. Attending to relatively low-key issues, doing this immediately and visibly, also prevents these from being seen as isolated incidents that are attributed to the flawed character of specific individuals. Instead, inviting the conversation about what is acceptable and unacceptable behavior in the workplace allows for the examination of recurring patterns and helps prevent the development of a sequence of increasingly problematic behaviors.

This focus on specifying and communicating the behaviors that characterize a "good organizational member" is markedly different from more common legal approaches. It requires that a commitment to ethical business conduct is visible from the tone at the top, that organizational leaders also "walk the talk" on the work floor, and that this matches the implicit messages that organizational members receive on a day-to-day basis about what really matters and what should be prioritized. This requires leaders who have the courage to visibly impose sanctions on those who breach ethics guidelines – regardless of how successful or important they are (Oded, 2017). It also requires ongoing and explicit debate about priorities and their implications, as well as joint decision-making about emerging dilemmas due to new business or product developments. This in turn can foster employees' trust in leaders and more open communication between leaders and employees. In this context, talking about difficult decisions and personal failures is a sign not of weakness but of strength, and leaders only fortify their position and are awarded respect when they do this first. Adopting such an approach is the only way to avoid the slippery slope in which innocent bystanders start rationalizing fraudulent behavior and over time become guilty perpetrators themselves (Zyglipodopoulos and Fleming, 2008).

In this way, having an ethical culture functions as a *social correction mechanism* in an organization. There will always be individuals who misbehave or come up with ways to bend the rules, be it the colleague who makes sexual jokes at an office party, or the one who proposes a "quick fix" to a serious problem. What matters, however, is that *others* will feel safe to confront and correct that individual when small transgressions occur. Speaking up and holding such behavior against agreed-upon behavioral standards, instead of remaining silent or relegating such experiences to gossip, helps to prevent small transgressions from growing bigger over time (Welsh et al., 2015). When disapproval of small transgressions is voiced by others – that is, when an ethical culture is in place – social norms are upheld and reinforced, making future transgressions less likely. This way of "mainstreaming" ethics, rather than relegating them to a specific quality assurance or compliance department, makes ethical conduct the responsibility of all organizational members, and allows them to embrace, internalize, and even own and take pride in upholding important guidelines, instead of merely "complying" with them because they are forced to do so.

Of course, this is only possible when systems, practices, and reward systems allow organizational members to consider ethical concerns, instead of forcing them to focus on (financial) performance alone (Kish-Gephart et al., 2010; Mayer et al., 2010). Attempts to increase rule compliance are bound to fail when all organizational incentives and rewards focus on individual bottom-line achievement regardless of how this is done. Those who aim to implement a more ethical culture are only able to do so when they are willing to reconsider and modify "standard business practices" that undermine this ambition.

43.7 CONCLUSION

When unethical behavior occurs in business, there is often a call to punish those who misbehaved and to adapt or augment existing legal requirements and company policies. This contribution does not suggest that legal measures to steer humans in "the right direction" are unimportant. We do, however, emphasize the pervasive influence of social contextual factors – and the organizational culture in particular – that can invite unethical behavior (when the culture prioritizes instrumental outcomes above all else) or support ethical behavior and rule compliance (when the culture rewards care for others and adherence to important guidelines). The psychological theory and research we reviewed further illustrate how an ethical culture can be developed and maintained through ethical leadership and by mainstreaming ethics into existing business models.

By focusing on creating an ethical culture, the organization can develop an "ethical mindset" in organizational members, which helps them to understand and internalize existing guidelines as well as to apply the "spirit" of these guidelines to new dilemmas and emerging situations. This offers a powerful source of intrinsic motivation. Whereas procedures that aim for "mere compliance" with the rules only induce employees to ask themselves "Is this allowed?", an ethical culture will stimulate employees to also consider whether *it is the right thing to do*. Asking such questions stimulates employees to think for themselves, to discuss with others, to voice the dilemmas they encounter to their superiors, and to speak up when they observe transgressions in others.

Achieving such a state of "meaningful compliance" requires a different compliance strategy. Rather than merely stating *what* the rules are, and communicating that specific behavior is expected of employees, there is added value in explaining to employees *why* the rules are important and how they relate to key organizational values (Oded, 2017). Such a demonstration of ethical leadership is possible when behavioral guidelines connect to corporate purpose. In a context of aggressive and global competition, this raises the important question of whether "doing good" in the ethical domain is compatible with "doing well" in terms of commercial success. Here we note that traditional conceptions of an inherent tension between business ethics and a firm's economic performance are being reconsidered (Eisenbeiss, Van Knippenberg, and Fahrbach, 2015). In fact, some argue that paying attention to ethics and responsible business conduct nowadays is necessary to attract and retain investors, employees, and customers. This is illustrated by the results from an examination of thirty-two German companies from various industries, which revealed that ethical CEO leadership related to a more ethical culture and, through this, to higher firm performance, *provided that* there also was a strong corporate ethics program in place (Eisenbeiss et al., 2015). Indeed, managers increasingly recognize the positive long-term benefit that a reputation for ethics can bring to doing business (Treviño and Nelson, 2011). That is a hopeful note to conclude on, both for ethics *and* for business.

REFERENCES

Arnold, Martin. 2018. "ING to Pay €775 m in Money Laundering Case." *Financial Times* (September). www.ft.com/content/f3e64e3e-b02b-11e8-99ca-68cf89602132.

Bandura, Albert. 1977. "Self-Efficacy: Toward a Unifying Theory of Behavioral Change." *Psychological Review* 84:191–215.

1986. *Social Foundations of Thought and Action*. Englewood Cliffs, NJ: Prentice-Hall.

Brown, Michael E., Linda K. Treviño, and David A. Harrison. 2005. "Ethical Leadership: A Social Learning Perspective for Construct Development and Testing." *Organizational Behavior and Human Decision Processes* 97, no. 2 (July): 117–134. doi:10.1016/j.obhdp.2005.03.002.

Cialdini, Robert B., and Noah J. Goldstein. 2004. "Social Influence: Compliance and Conformity." *Annual Review of Psychology* 55: 591–621.

Cullen, John B., Bart Victor, and James W. Bronson. 1993. "The Ethical Climate Questionnaire: An Assessment of Its Development and Validity." *Psychological Reports* 73, no. 2 (October): 667–74. doi:10.2466/pr0.1993.73.2.667.

Deal, Terrence E., and Allan A. Kennedy. 1982. *Corporate Cultures: The Rites and Rituals of Corporate Life*. Reading, MA: Addison Wesley.

Eisenbeiss, Silke A., Daan Van Knippenberg, and Clemens M. Fahrbach. 2015. "Doing Well by Doing Good? Analyzing the Relationship between CEO Ethical Leadership and Firm Performance." *Journal of Business Ethics* 128, no. 3 (March): 635–51.

Ellemers, Naomi. 2017. *Morality and the Regulation of Social Behavior: Groups as Moral Anchors*. London/New York: Routledge.

Ellemers, Naomi, and Alexander S. Haslam. 2011. "Social Identity Theory." In *Handbook of Theories of Social Psychology*, edited by Paul A. M. Van Lange, Arie W. Kruglanski, and Tory Higgins, 379–98. London: Sage.

Ellemers, Naomi, and Jojanneke Van der Toorn. 2015. "Groups as Moral Anchors." *Current Opinion in Behavioral Sciences* 6: 189–94.

FCA. 2018. Transforming Culture in Financial Services. Discussion Paper 18/2, March 12. London: Financial Conduct Authority.

Fehr, Ernst, and Bettina Rockenbach. 2003. "Detrimental Effects of Sanctions on Human Altruism." *Nature* 422, no. 6928 (March): 137–40. doi:10.1038/nature01474.

Feldman, Yuval. 2018. *The Law of Good People: Challenging States' Ability to Regulate Human Behavior*. Cambridge: Cambridge University Press.

Fortado, Lindsay. 2015. "Kweku Adoboli: A Rogue Trader's Tale." *Financial Times* (October). www.ft.com/content/0fa0b42a-783a-11e5-a95a-27d368e1ddf7.

FSB. 2018. "Strengthening Governance Frameworks to Mitigate Misconduct Risk: A Toolkit for Firms and Supervisors." Report, Financial Stability Board, Basel, April 20.

Garratt, Bob. 2010. *The Fish Rots from the Head: The Crisis in Our Boardrooms: Developing the Crucial Skills of the Competent Director*. London: Profile Books.

Gorsira, Madelijne, Linda Steg, Adriaan Denkers, and Wim Huisman. 2018. "Corruption in Organizations: Ethical Climate and Individual Motives." *Administrative Sciences* 8, no. 1: 4.

Haslam, Alexander S., and Naomi Ellemers. 2011. "Identity Processes in Organizations." In *Handbook of Identity Theory and Research*, edited by Seth J. Schwartz, Koen Luyckx, and Vivian L. Vignoles, 715–44. New York: Springer.

Haslam, Alexander S., Stephen D. Reicher, and Michael J. Platow. 2011. *The New Psychology of Leadership: Identity, Influence, and Power*. Hove, UK: Psychology Press.

Kaptein, Muel. 2008a. "Developing and Testing a Measure for the Ethical Culture of Organizations: The Corporate Ethical Virtues Model." *Journal of Organizational Behavior* 29, no. 7 (October): 923–47.

2008b. *The Living Code: Embedding Ethics into the Corporate DNA*. Abingdon, UK/New York: Routledge.

2011. "Understanding Unethical Behavior by Unraveling Ethical Culture." *Human Relations* 64, no. 5 (June): 843–69. doi: 10.1177/0018726710390536.

Kish-Gephart, Jennifer J., David A. Harrison, and Linda K. Treviño. 2010. "Bad Apples, Bad Cases, and Bad Barrels: Meta-analytic Evidence about Sources of Unethical Decisions at Work." *Journal of Applied Psychology* 95, no. 4 (July): 791. doi:10.1037/a0020073.

Martin, Kelly D., and John B. Cullen. 2006. "Continuities and Extensions of Ethical Climate Theory: A Meta-analytic Review." *Journal of Business Ethics* 69: 175–94. doi:10.1007/s10551-006-9084-7.

Mayer, David M., Maribeth Kuenzi, and Rebecca L. Greenbaum. 2010. "Examining the Link between Ethical Leadership and Employee Misconduct: The Mediating Role of Ethical Climate." *Journal of Business Ethics* 95: 7–16. doi:10.1007/s10551-011-0794-0.

Mooijman, Marlon, Wilco W. van Dijk, Eric Van Dijk, and Naomi Ellemers. 2017. "On Sanction-Goal Justifications: How and Why Deterrence Justifications Undermine Rule Compliance." *Journal of Personality and Social Psychology* 112, no. 4 (April): 577–89. doi:10.1037/pspi0000084.

Moore, Celia. 2015. "Moral Disengagement." *Current Opinion in Psychology* 6: 199–204. doi:10.1016/j.copsyc.2015.07.018.

Nguyen, Duc Duy, Linh Nguyen, and Vathunyoo Sila. 2019. "Does Corporate Culture Affect Bank Risk-Taking? Evidence from Loan-Level Data." *British Journal of Management* 30, no. 1 (January): 106–33. doi:10.1111/1467-8551.12300.

Oded, Sharon. 2017. "The Intoxication of Force: When Enforcement Undermines Compliance." Inaugural Lecture. Erasmus Law Lectures 42.

Pagliaro, Stefano, Alessandro Lo Presti, Massimiliano Barattucci, Valeria A. Giannella, and Manuela Barreto. 2018. "On the Effects of Ethical Climate(s) on Employees' Behavior: A Social Identity Approach." *Frontiers in Psychology* 9: 1–10. doi:10.3389/fpsyg.2018.00960.

Peterson, Dane K. 2002. "The Relationship between Unethical Behavior and the Dimensions of the Ethical Climate Questionnaire." *Journal of Business Ethics* 41, no.4 (December): 313–26. doi:10.1023/A:1021243117958.

Raven, Bertram H. 1992. "A Power/Interaction Model of Interpersonal Influence: French and Raven Thirty Years Later." *Journal of Social Behavior and Personality* 7: 217–44.

Reckard, E. Scott. 2013. "Wells Fargo's Pressure-Cooker Sales Culture Comes at a Cost." *Los Angeles Times* (December). www.latimes.com/business/la-fi-wells-fargo-sale-pressure-20131222-story.html.

Ring, Patrick John, Cormac Bryce, Ricky McKinney, and Rob Webb. 2016. "Taking Notice of Risk Culture – the Regulator's Approach." *Journal of Risk Research* 19: 364–87. doi:10.1080/13669877.2014.983944.

Schein, Edgar H. 1996. "Culture: The Missing Concept in Organization Studies." *Administrative Science Quarterly* 41, no. 2 (June): 229–40. doi:10.2307/2393715.

Scholten, Wieke, and Naomi Ellemers. 2016. "Bad Apples or Corrupting Barrels? Preventing Traders' Misconduct." *Journal of Financial Regulation and Compliance* 24: 366–82.

Schuchter, Alexander, and Michael Levi. 2016. "The Fraud Triangle Revisited." *Security Journal* 29: 107–21. doi:10.1057/sj.2013.1.

Simha, Aditya, and John B. Cullen. 2012. "Climates and Their Effects on Organizational Outcomes: Implications from the Past and Prophecies for the Future." *Academy of Management Perspectives* 26, no. 4 (November): 20–34. doi:10.5465/amp.2011.0156.

Soltani, Bahram. 2014. "The Anatomy of Corporate Fraud: A Comparative Analysis of High Profile American and European Corporate Scandals." *Journal of Business Ethics* 120, no. 2 (March): 251–74. doi:10.1007/s10551-013-1660-z.

Stöber, Thomas, Peter Kotzian, and Barbara E. Weißenberger. 2019. "Culture Follows Design: Code Design as an Antecedent of the Ethical Culture." *Business Ethics: A European Review* 28, no 1. (January): 112–28. doi:10.1111/beer.12201.

Stringer, Robert. 2002. *Leadership and Organizational Climate*. Upper Saddle River, NJ: Pearson Education.

Tajfel, Henri, and John C. Turner. 1979. "An Integrative Theory of Intergroup Conflict." In *The Social Psychology of Intergroup Relations*, edited by William G. Austin and Stephen Worchel, 33–47. Monterey, CA: Brooks Cole.

Tenbrunsel, Ann E., and David M. Messick. 1999. "Sanctioning Systems, Decision Frames, and Cooperation." *Administrative Science Quarterly* 44, no. 4 (December): 684–707. doi: 10.2307/2667052.

Treviño, Linda B., and Katherine A. Nelson. 2011. *Managing Business Ethics: Straight Talk About How to Do It Right*. New York: Wiley.

Tyler, Tom R. and Steven L. Blader. 2005. "Can Businesses Effectively Regulate Employee Conduct? The Antecedents of Rule Following in Work Settings." *Academy of Management Journal* 40, no. 6 (December): 1143–58. https://doi.org/10.5465/amj.2005.19573114.

Van Rooij, Benjamin, and Adam Fine. 2018. "Toxic Corporate Culture: Assessing Organizational Processes of Deviancy." *Administrative Sciences* 8, no. 23. doi:10.3390/admsci8030023.

Van Steenbergen, Elianne F., Danny Van Dijk, Celine Christensen, Tessa Coffeng, and Naomi Ellemers. 2019. "Learn to Build an Error Management Culture." *Journal of Financial Regulation and Compliance* 28, no. 1 (February): 57–73. doi:10.1108/JFRC-12-2018-0156.

Van Yperen, Nico W., Melvyn R. W. Hamstra, and Marloes van der Klauw. 2011. "To Win, or Not to Lose, at Any Cost: The Impact of Achievement Goals on Cheating." *British Journal of Management* 22: S5–S15. doi:10.1111/j.1467-8551.2010.00702.x.

Victor, Bart, and John B. Cullen. 1988. "The Organizational Bases of Ethical Work Climates." *Administrative Science Quarterly* 33:101–25.

Welsh, David T., Lisa D. Ordóñez, Deirdre G. Snyder, and Michael S. Christian. 2015. "The Slippery Slope: How Small Ethical Transgressions Pave the Way for Larger Future Transgressions." *Journal of Applied Psychology* 100, no. 1 (January): 114–27. doi:10.1037/a0036950.

Zyglipodopoulos, Stelios C., and Peter J. Fleming. 2008. "Ethical Distance in Corrupt Firms: How Do Innocent Bystanders Become Guilty Perpetrators?" *Journal of Business Ethics* 78, no. 1–2 (March): 265–74. doi:10.1007/s10551-007-9378-4.

44

Organizational Factors and Workplace Deviance: Influences of Abusive Supervision, Dysfunctional Employees, and Toxic Work Environments

Anne Leonore de Bruijn

Abstract: As big corporate misconduct scandals continue to dominate newspaper headlines, it has never been more important to understand corporate deviance. The present chapter explains the reasons why organizations break rules and employees engage in deviant behavior. This chapter reviews existing literature on workplace deviance and examines the role of different organizational factors that stimulate and sustain it: abusive supervision, dysfunctional employees, and toxic work environments. It finds that the characteristics of leaders and how they treat employees, as well as the characteristics of employees and how they respond to the organization, are determinants of organizational deviancy. It also finds that there is more at play than individual leaders and employees or the interaction between them. The organizational culture or climate as a whole can become negative and come to sustain and stimulate deviancy. However, there is not yet a clear, validated understanding of what is a negative culture or climate and the individual elements that spur deviance. In all of this, the organizational psychology of deviant organizations does not yet clearly show exactly how deviance relates to legal compliance.

44.1 INTRODUCTION

Google has recently come under both internal and external pressure over its culture and business practices. It currently faces a multistate antitrust investigation that began after various employees spoke out about Google's unethical working processes that had created a toxic workplace (Chung 2018; Kelly 2019). Examples of Google's malpractices include tax avoidance, discrimination, misuse and manipulation of search results, and violations of people's privacy. Google is not alone; other recent examples of big corporate misconduct cases include Volkswagen and its long-term emission cheating scandal, Wells Fargo and its account fraud scandal, in which over a million unauthorized accounts were created, and Boeing and its failure to respond to safety problems that resulted in crashes involving the 737 Max. In news reporting, people respond with outrage each time another corporate scandal breaks. Often their immediate response is to ask for punishment for the highest-level executives. Yet the more important question to ask is exactly what is making these corporations engage in deviant behaviors.

This research was made possible through a generous grant from the European Research Council (ERC-2018-CoG - HomoJuridicus - 817680)

A core question in the study of compliance is: Why do organizations come to break rules and employees engage in deviant behavior? Structural misconduct in the workplace can be referred to as workplace deviance. Workplace deviance refers to behaviors that are intentional, violate organizational norms, and try to harm the organization, its employees, or both (Bennett and Robinson 2003; Puffer 1987). Workplace deviance can also have negative impacts outside the organization, such as huge economic losses or diminished economic growth of the country (Baharom, Bin Sharfuddin, and Iqbal 2017).

It is often thought that workplace deviance is a response by employees to *abusive supervision*. This suggests that workplace deviance stems from bad management/leadership. From another perspective, workplace deviance is thought to originate from *dysfunctional employees* themselves. In particular, employees with certain personality traits seem more likely to act out and engage in deviant behavior. Deviance in modern organizations is, however, more than the sum of negative leadership and bad employees. Recently, more and more companies have turned to the *organizational environment* to investigate and understand corporate crime and wrongdoing (van Rooij and Fine 2018). Companies have started hiring culture experts or forming a board of directors to evaluate toxic organizational factors in their company culture. This remains a challenge as organizational systems and processes are complex and difficult to investigate. Major corporate scandals illustrate how rules are broken and what external effects follow; yet it remains unclear exactly what happened within the organization itself that eventually led to workplace deviance.

This chapter provides a review of existing literature on workplace deviance and examines the influences of abusive leadership, dysfunctional employees, and toxic work environments.

By discussing these factors in detail, this chapter tries to understand exactly what causes people within an organization to act deviantly. Its conceptual framework can be viewed in Figure 44.1. Studies that are reviewed largely stem from work and organizational psychology and from business ethics. Importantly, this chapter is not meant to be a full review of all existing literature; rather, it tries to highlight the most important findings.

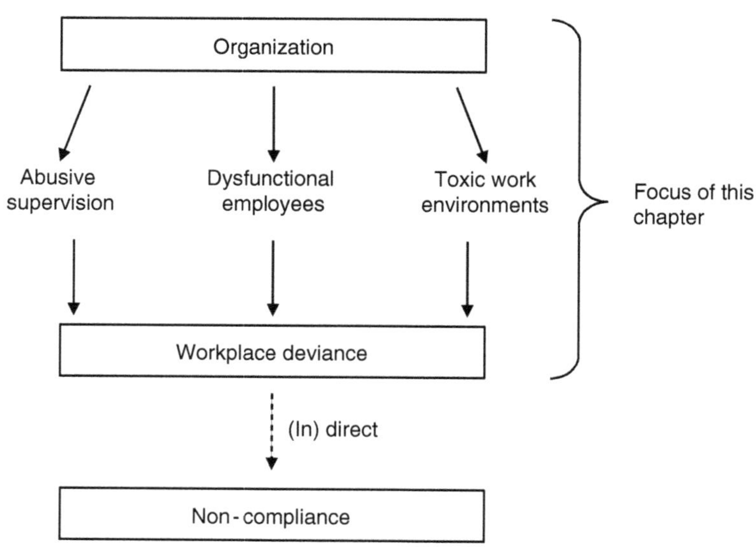

FIGURE 44.1 This chapter's conceptual framework

Before discussing the three factors that influence workplace deviance, the chapter will explain in more detail the concept of *workplace deviance*. In the workplace, employees can engage in deviant behavior within, against, or for the organization itself. Within the organization, employees can direct their deviant behavior toward their supervisors (*supervisor-directed deviance*) or their coworkers (*interpersonal deviance*). Employees can also direct their deviant behavior against the organization itself (*organizational deviance*) (Mitchell and Ambrose 2007; Robinson and Bennett 1995). Behavioral examples for each type of deviance, respectively, are retaliation against a supervisor (Mitchell and Ambrose 2007), playing a prank and acting rude toward a coworker (Henle, Giacalone, and Jurkiewicz 2005), or shirking duties and misrepresenting one's performance (Harvey et al. 2014). In addition, employees can also engage in deviant behaviors *for* (i.e., not against) the organization itself. This is known as *unethical pro-organizational behavior* and includes actions that are intended to benefit the organization or its members but that exceed ethical norms and limitations (Umphress and Bingham 2011). For example, giving false numbers to increase stock value or damaging documents to protect the organization (Liu and Qui 2015).

The typology of workplace deviance (Robinson and Bennett 1995) is another approach that is often used to break down the concept of workplace deviance. According to the typology, deviant workplace behavior can be divided along two dimensions. One axis represents the target of the deviance, varying from interpersonal (members of the organization) to organizational (the organization itself). The other axis represents the severity of the workplace deviance, varying from minor to serious. This creates four categories of workplace deviance: production deviance, property deviance, political deviance, and personal aggression. Examples for each type of deviance are leaving early, sabotaging equipment, showing favoritism, and verbal abuse, respectively (see Muafi 2011).

Finally, it is important to realize that individual deviant workplace behaviors can lead to workplace deviance throughout the entire organization. In particular, employees who engage in deviant behaviors influence coworkers. This can cause deviance contagion throughout the entire organization. Different explanations have been proposed (see Gutworth, Morton, and Dahling 2013). One of them is that employees who hear and witness deviance in the workplace can come to accept these behaviors. They can also experience social pressure from their "bad" coworkers to conform to the deviant norm. As more and more employees become accustomed to these behaviors, they are no longer considered deviant. Deviance becomes the social norm for the organization. This process has been described as the normalization of deviance (Vaughan 1996).

Workplace deviance is related to compliance; sometimes deviance not only violates organizational norms but also violates the law. In such cases, workplace deviance is equivalent to noncompliance. However, there can also be cases of workplace deviance, such as when employees shirk their duties or gossip, that are not in violation of the law and thus not directly related to compliance. These legally compliant forms of deviance may give rise to a negative culture or climate that, in and of itself, can cause organizations to eventually break the law. Thus, compliant deviance can stimulate noncompliance either directly or indirectly.

The present chapter does not directly assess the relationship between deviance and legal compliance because most of the studies in this field have not included measures of legal compliance. The chapter's main contribution to the field of compliance is that it allows a thorough understanding of three core organizational factors that stimulate deviance. In the end, such deviance in and of itself may directly or indirectly cause or sustain organizational noncompliance.

44.2 NEGATIVE LEADERSHIP: ABUSIVE SUPERVISION

Leadership plays a significant role within the organizational context and in workplace deviance. Leaders set the tone of the work environment, and their actions and decisions influence employee behavior. Research has shown that good and effective leadership produces an ethical work culture, greater employee satisfaction, increased organizational productivity and performance, and long-term business success (for an elaborate review see Chapter 43; see also Eisenbeiss, van Knippenberg, and Fahrbach 2015; Gibson and Mason 2011; Podsakoff, MacKenzie, and Bommer 1996; Shafiu, Manaf, and Muslim 2019). Bad leadership, on the other hand, leads to lower employee job satisfaction, weak organizational commitment, and poor psychological well-being (Mathieu et al. 2014; Schmidt 2014). It causes dysfunctional performance within the organization as it triggers unethical and counterproductive work behaviors from employees (Boddy 2014; Mitchell and Ambrose 2007; Tepper et al. 2008). More generally, bad leadership is associated with deviant workplace behaviors that can lead to serious organizational problems. Bad leadership has been conceptualized in many different ways. It has been described by a range of terms, such as petty tyranny (Ashforth 1994), supervisor undermining (Duffy, Ganster, and Pagon 2002), bad leadership (Kellerman 2004), narcissistic leadership (Burton and Hoobler 2011; Rosenthal and Pittinsky 2006), toxic leadership (Lipman-Blumen 2005; Reed 2004; Schmidt 2008), destructive leadership (Einarsen, Aasland, and Skogstad 2007; Schyns and Schilling 2013), and abusive supervision (Tepper 2000). In essence, these different concepts all explore and identify different antecedents and consequences of negative leadership.

The trait approach to leadership focuses solely on the leader itself. It tries to identify personal traits of leaders, such as personality characteristics, and assumes that these traits produce patterns of behavior that are consistent across situations (Fleenor 2011). It is believed that leaders are born with these traits and that they remain stable over time. Various personality studies have taken this approach and have tried to identify negative personality traits of leaders as determinants of bad leadership. Most research has focused on the "dark triad of personality," which refers to a constellation of three undesirable personality traits: narcissism, Machiavellianism, and psychopathy (Paulhus and Williams 2002). The three traits appear to be partially heritable (Petrides et al. 2011; Vernon et al. 2008), indicating that both genetic and environmental factors influence personality. Leaders with dark-side traits exhibit destructive leadership behaviors. Such toxic leaders negatively impact the career success or well-being of their subordinates (Prusik and Szulawski 2019; Volmer, Koch, and Göritz 2016). Yet the influence on employee deviant behavior of a leader with personality traits from the dark triad remains largely unstudied.

There is, however, a vast literature available on so-called *abusive supervision* and its effects on subordinates in work organizations. This chapter will, therefore, focus on negative leadership using the commonly studied concept of abusive supervision. Abusive supervision has been defined as "subordinates' perceptions of the extent to which their supervisors engage in the sustained display of hostile verbal and nonverbal behaviors, excluding physical contact" (Tepper 2007). This means that abusive supervision is viewed as a subordinate perception.

Research has argued that employees can differ in their opinions of whether or not a supervisor is abusive. Subordinates' perceptions of abuse seem to depend on their individual attribution styles (Martinko et al. 2011). In particular, subordinates with an external attribution style that favors stable attributions for failure (e.g., a supervisor's bad temper) are more likely to report abusive supervision. Perceptions of supervisory abuse are also affected by psychological entitlement. This is an individual trait that refers to the stable belief that preferential rewards and treatment are deserved irrespective of whether this is actually the case (Campbell et al. 2004; Harvey and Martinko 2009). Harvey et al. (2014) showed that entitled employees report higher levels of abusive supervision than other employees, even if they share the same supervisor. Importantly, such perceptions can motivate retaliatory behaviors like upward undermining (e.g., spreading rumors about a supervisor or failing to comply with requests) and organizational deviance. In general, however, subordinates seem to rate abusive supervision in a similar manner (see Taylor et al. 2019) and subordinate ratings are often used as valid indications of abusive supervisory behavior.

44.2.1 *Abusive Supervision and Workplace Deviance*

In the academic literature, abusive supervision has often been linked to workplace deviance (Alexander 2011; Avey, Wu, and Holley 2015; Harvey et al. 2014; Liu et al. 2010; Mawritz, Dust, and Resick 2014; Mitchell and Ambrose 2007; Park et al. 2017; Tepper et al. 2009; Tepper et al. 2008; Thau et al. 2009; Vogel, Homberg, and Gericke 2016; Zhang and Liao 2015). Most literature sees abusive supervision as a predictor of workplace deviance. Supervisors are viewed as causal actors that exhibit abusive behaviors that affect subordinates who react defiantly in return. However, it has been argued that the relationship between abusive supervision and employee deviance runs both ways, and both directions of the relationship have been theorized (Lian et al. 2014; Tepper et al. 2008; Thau et al. 2009). These studies propose that it is plausible to argue that subordinate deviance may lead to abusive supervision instead of vice versa.

For instance, research by Lian et al. (2014) used a cross-lagged panel design (i.e., variables are measured at multiple occasions) to examine twenty-month lagged effects of both abusive supervision and subordinate deviance. Interestingly, results from their first study showed that subordinate organizational deviance predicted abusive supervision, but not vice versa. In a second study, they included employees' self-control capacity and quit intentions as additional factors to investigate whether these affected the relationship between abusive supervision and subordinate organizational deviance. This time results showed that abusive supervision did predict subordinate organizational deviance, but only when subordinates had low self-control capacity and high intentions to quit their jobs.

This chapter will focus on the influence of abusive supervision on subordinate deviance in the workplace. There are multiple theories that help to recognize how abusive supervision directly influences subordinates' deviance. Section 44.2.2 will discuss six of these theories, namely the social exchange theory, the social information processing theory, the social learning theory, organizational injustice, the frustration-aggression theory, and the reactance theory. Section 44.2.3 will present various studies that illustrate the relationship between abusive supervision and workplace deviance. Section 44.2.4 will review different causes of abusive supervision.

44.2.2 *Abusive Supervision and Workplace Deviance: Theories*

One commonly discussed perspective is the *social exchange theory* (Blau 1964). This theory views the supervisor–employee relationship as a social exchange in which both parties seek to reciprocate the costs and benefits that they receive in order to maintain balanced contributions (Thau and Mitchell 2010). Employees who are treated poorly by their abusive supervisor will experience an aversive social cost, which leads to an exchange imbalance. As a result, they might feel the urge to restore balance. When they hold the supervisor accountable for the cost, they express their hostility by engaging in deviant behaviors toward him/her. Furthermore, the displaced aggression theory (Mitchell and Ambrose 2007) argues that when supervisors are not available to retaliate against, or when employees fear counter-retaliation from supervisors, employees might engage in deviance toward more readily available targets, such as coworkers or the organization.

The second perspective is the *social information processing theory* (Salancik and Pfeffer 1978). This theory explains that individuals who operate in a social environment adopt attitudes, beliefs, and behaviors in order to make sense of complex social settings. Within organizations, employees look for social cues regarding behavioral norms, such as leader behaviors and exchanges with peers, to develop expectations about acceptable social behavior and adapt their own behavior to these expectations. Employees who experience supervisors' abusive behaviors can view such behaviors as acceptable and supported in the organization. Consequently, employees can become more inclined to engage in similar behaviors. The work environment is important here as employees turn to this social context for information regarding perceived organizational norms. An environment with norms of hostility in which organizational deviance is seen as an appropriate means of anger will exacerbate employee deviance.

Similar to the social information processing theory is the *social learning theory*. This theory stresses the importance of observing and modeling the behaviors, attitudes, and emotions of others (Bandura 1977). In general, people can be exposed to abusive behaviors through role models at work, family upbringing, organizational norms, and country culture. They come to believe that these behaviors are acceptable and rewarding. Within organizations, this means that employees turn to credible role models in their close work environment (i.e., someone higher up in the hierarchy). Next, they emulate the behavior of these role models since they are seen as acceptable/normal. The two theories are related as employees first use the social context for information regarding behavioral norms (social information processing), then use this information to decide whose behaviors to imitate (social learning). As supervisors are highly visible and most employees are in direct contact with them, employees likely observe and mimic their supervisors' behaviors. Mawritz et al. (2012) lent support to the social learning theory as they showed that supervisors model the aggressive acts of their managers, acting in a similar manner toward their own subordinates, which can eventually prompt work group interpersonal deviance. In other words, negative behaviors trickle down through organizational hierarchies from managers to subordinates and ultimately result in employee deviant behaviors.

Organizational justice offers another explanation in which injustice caused by abusive supervision is seen as the primary cause of deviant workplace behavior. This perspective stems from equity theory (Adams 1963, 1965), which explains that employees value fair treatment and this motivates them to maintain the fairness within relationships in the organization. In particular, organizational justice refers to the degree to which employees view workplace procedures, interactions, and outcomes as fair (Baldwin 2006). Research shows that abusive supervision negatively impacts subordinate justice perceptions (Liang and Brown 2019). Subordinates who perceive injustice and feel mistreated may react with a range of negative behavioral responses. For example, Rizvi, Friedman, and Azam (2017) found that the perception of overall organizational injustice was positively correlated to workplace deviance and turnover intention. In conclusion, employees who experience situations of injustice at work due to abusive supervision can retaliate by acting in a deviant manner.

A fifth explanatory perspective is the *frustration-aggression theory* (Dollard et al. 1939; Fox and Spector 1999), which considers frustration to be the cause of workplace deviance. When workplace stressors (i.e., an abusive supervisor) interfere with individual goals, such as achieving valued work goals or attaining effective performance, employees become frustrated. This frustration leads to a stress reaction. Individuals can release this stress by engaging in destructive or counterproductive behaviors. Research supports this view, as the psychological state of frustration has been found to be associated with both interpersonal and organizational deviance (Bennett and Robinson 2000). Furthermore, results from a study by Ménard, Brunet, and Savoie (2011) showed that frustration was positively related to physical violence, which is a type of interpersonal deviant behavior in the workplace.

The last perspective that will be discussed is the *reactance theory* (Brehm 1966). According to this theory, individuals possess the freedom to engage in a number of "free behaviors." This is a set of realistically possible behaviors in which an individual can engage either physically or psychologically at the moment or at some time in the future (Brehm 1966). When the freedom to choose a course of action is threatened or eliminated, people become motivated to restore their freedom. The unpleasant motivational arousal that drives freedom restoration is called reactance (Steindl et al. 2015). In the workplace, abusive supervision can create a feeling of reduced autonomy for employees. They feel little or no control and experience psychological distress (Park et al. 2017; Restubog, Scott, and Zagenczyk 2011). As a means of restoring their personal freedom, they can become motivated to engage in deviant behaviors directed toward the supervisor, other employees, or the organization.

44.2.3 *Abusive Supervision and Workplace Deviance: Evidence*

Zhang and Liao (2015) conducted a meta-analysis in which they identified various consequences of abusive supervision. Results showed that abusive supervision was associated with subordinates' workplace behaviors. In particular, abusive supervision was positively related to all three types of workplace deviance (i.e., supervisor-directed, interpersonal-directed, and organization-directed). Abusive supervision explained 26 percent, 14 percent, and 14 percent, respectively, of the variance in the different types of workplace deviance. This suggests that subordinates who reported experiencing abusive supervision were also more likely to engage in deviant behaviors in the workplace. These deviant behaviors could be directed toward their supervisor, other coworkers, or the entire organization.

Tepper et al. (2009) investigated whether individual intentions to quit affected the strength of the relationship between abusive supervision and supervisor-directed or organization-directed deviance. First, the main effects of abusive supervision showed that it explained 8 percent of the variance in supervisor-directed deviance and 14 percent of the variance in organization-directed deviance. Results further showed that when intentions to quit were high, abusive supervision was more strongly related to both supervisor-directed and organization-directed deviance. More specifically, intention to quit refers to someone's intention that they will soon permanently leave their current employer (Cho, Johanson, and Guchait 2009). Employees who have high intentions to quit are less dependent on their supervisor and employment situation; they have less to lose by engaging in deviant behaviors and should thus perform these behaviors to a greater extent compared to coworkers with low intentions to quit.

Park et al. (2017) studied the indirect effect of subordinates' justice perceptions on the relationship between abusive supervision and employee deviance. In a meta-analytic research study, they adopted a multifoci approach to justice (Cropanzano et al. 2001). This approach highlighted the importance of assessing who is responsible for mistreatment within an organization (the source of injustice). The authors explained that employees who experience abusive supervision first identify the responsible party for the injustice, which can either be the supervisor or the organization. As they feel mistreated, this can prompt them to retaliate toward the wrongdoer. They might respond toward the responsible party with negative attitudes and behaviors. In this way, employees' justice perceptions are seen as an explanatory mechanism through which abusive leadership influences subordinates' deviant behaviors. This view is consistent with the explanatory perspective of organizational justice discussed just now. Results of the study showed that abusive supervision influenced subordinates' perceptions of justice, which eventually resulted in subordinate deviance. In particular, subordinates who identified their supervisor as the source of injustice were more likely to engage in deviance toward their supervisor; those who identified the organization as the source of injustice were more likely to engage in deviance toward the organization.

44.2.4 *Causes of Abusive Leadership*

As abusive supervision has numerous negative consequences for organizations, it is important to realize why leaders treat subordinates with hostility. A review of abusive supervision research by Martinko et al. (2013) identified various supervisor-level antecedents to abusive supervision. These antecedents included stress, histories of family violence, injustice perceptions, conflict levels, perceived abuse from their own supervisors, and leadership style.

Additionally, Tepper, Simon, and Park (2017) published a review in which they integrated all evidence that explored the causes and consequences of abusive supervision in work organizations. They described three processes that explain why supervisors engage in abusive behaviors: social learning, identity threat, and self-regulation impairment.

The first process refers to the social learning theory (Bandura 1977). As explained in Section 44.2.3, mid-level managers might observe and mimic the behaviors of their role models: the upper-level managers. More specifically, supervisors start to emulate their manager's abusive behaviors (see Mawritz et al. 2012) and, slowly, aggressive behaviors start spreading throughout the company. These behaviors will eventually become accepted organizational norms.

The second process draws on the social identity theory (Tajfel and Turner 1979), which explains that people make sense of who they are based on their group membership. People strive to maintain positive perceptions of the groups to which they belong because this confers self-esteem. However, when these perceptions get challenged, they experience a psychological threat that can manifest as negative emotions and behaviors. Organizational managers can experience threats to their identity as a leader from subordinate provocation, mistreatment of higher authorities, or their personal sensitivity to threat. In return, they might use hostile behaviors as a reparative strategy to restore their identity. As examples, Johnson et al. (2012) found that leaders with strong individual identities (i.e., those who hold overly favorable self-views and are highly critical toward subordinates) showed more daily abusive behaviors (Johnson et al. 2012) and Yu, Duffy, and Tepper (2018) found that downward envy of subordinates threatens supervisors' self-esteem, which can trigger them to use abusive behaviors in order to restore their identity.

The third and final process, self-regulation impairment, refers to a deficiency in self-regulatory and self-control abilities that can occur after the experience of abuse (Thau and Mitchell 2010). These self-regulatory abilities are necessary for someone to maintain normative behavior. As managers' psychological resources can become depleted, they struggle with self-regulation. It becomes harder for them to suppress impulses to act counternormatively to employees, and they are less likely to consider the potential costs of their actions, making destructive behaviors, such as abuse, more likely. In accordance, studies have suggested that supervisors are more abusive when they experience psychological distress (Li et al. 2016) or when they have previously shown behaviors (i.e., ethical behaviors) that drain self-regulatory resources (Lin, Ma, and Johnson 2016).

In conclusion, abusive supervision is a type of negative leadership that can have severe disadvantages for both the subordinates and the organization. In particular, abusive supervision has been linked to workplace deviance as it can spur employees to engage in deviant workplace behaviors. Six theories that help to understand how abusive supervision fosters workplace deviance have been discussed. In short, employees that experience abusive supervision might engage in deviant behaviors to try to restore the exchange imbalance in the employee–supervisor relationship (social exchange theory), to use the social context to understand what behaviors are acceptable and supported in the organization (social information processing theory), to emulate the behaviors of their role models (social learning theory), to try to restore justice because they feel mistreated (organizational injustice), to release stress because they feel frustrated (frustration–aggression theory), or to try to restore their freedom as they perceive reduced autonomy (reactance theory). In addition, meta-analytic and experimental research evidence that illustrates the link between abusive supervision and workplace deviance in a relationship was summarized. Finally, to answer the question of why leaders act abusively, three processes – the social learning theory, the social identity theory, and self-regulation impairment – were reviewed. In summary, leaders might copy destructive behaviors from those higher up in the organizational hierarchy, such as their managers (social learning theory); they can experience a threat to their identity as a leader and use hostile behaviors to restore this identity (social identity theory); or they might have a deficiency in self-regulatory and self-control abilities, which makes it harder for them to suppress abusive behaviors (self-regulatory impairment).

44.3 DYSFUNCTIONAL EMPLOYEES

Organizational deviance does not solely originate in leadership or relationships between supervisors and subordinates; it may also arise from employees themselves. Another line of research takes this approach and focuses on the individual employee as the source of workplace deviance. This perspective proposes that some employees are more likely to be deviant than others due to individual differences in personality traits. In particular, personality traits appear to be important in defining individual behaviors and can be seen as strong predictors of various forms of deviant workplace behavior. In this section, three personality components and their relation to workplace deviance will be discussed; these are the Big Five personality model, narcissism, and emotional intelligence.

44.3.1 *Big Five Personality Model*

Multiple studies have analyzed deviant workplace behaviors in relation to the Big Five personality model, a popular method for assessing personality traits. In particular, the Five-Factor Model (FFM) is a taxonomy for personality traits. The model proposes that individual personality is described in terms of five higher-order factors, namely extraversion, agreeableness, openness, conscientiousness, and neuroticism. *Extraversion* refers to an individual's comfort with relationships; *agreeableness* concerns individual inclination to defer to others; *openness* refers to an individual's range of interests and fascination for novelty; *conscientiousness* is a measure of reliability; and *neuroticism* refers to how someone copes with stress (Robbins and Judge 2009).

Colbert et al. (2004) investigated whether conscientiousness and emotional stability were related to the withholding of effort in the workplace, which is a form of organizational deviance. They also examined whether agreeableness was related to interpersonal workplace deviance. Results showed that emotional stability was not related to withholding effort but conscientiousness was; individuals who scored low on conscientiousness were more likely to withhold effort. A small effect size was reported, as conscientiousness explained 4 percent to 5 percent of the variance in withholding effort. Furthermore, agreeableness was related to interpersonal workplace deviance; individuals who scored low on agreeableness were more likely to show interpersonal workplace deviance. This effect was much larger, as agreeableness explained 25 percent to 30 percent of the variance in interpersonal workplace deviance. This suggests that, overall, the influence of agreeableness on interpersonal workplace deviance appeared to be stronger than the influence of conscientiousness on withholding effort. The effect of employees' perceptions of the work environment on deviance was also investigated. It appeared that employees with negative perceptions of the developmental environment who perceived no organizational support were also more likely to withhold effort. The effect of perceptions of the developmental environment on withholding effort appeared to be somewhat smaller than the effect of organizational support on withholding effort. The former explained between 2 percent and 5 percent of the variance in withholding effort, whereas these percentages varied between 8 percent and 14 percent for the latter. Next, the authors examined the joint effect of both situational perceptions and personality traits on workplace deviance. Results demonstrated that negative perceptions of the work situation did not cause people who were highly conscientious, emotionally stable, or agreeable to engage in deviant behaviors. These individuals appeared to be reluctant to withhold effort or engage in interpersonal deviance as such deviant behaviors were inconsistent with the individual's personality tendencies.

Agreeableness and conscientiousness also seem to play a role in individual deviance. A recent study by Aleksić and Vuković (2018) investigated the effect of personality traits on organizational deviance (OD) and interpersonal deviance (ID), depending on whether the deviant behavior was targeted at the organization or individuals, and overall deviant workplace behavior (DWB). Results showed that both agreeableness and conscientiousness were negatively connected with all forms of deviant behavior. Agreeableness explained 5 percent of the variance in OD, 16 percent of the variance in ID, and 11 percent of the variance in DWB. Conscientiousness explained 15 percent of the variance in OD, 6 percent of the variance in ID, and 13 percent of the variance in DWB.

Neuroticism also seems to be an important predictor of interpersonal deviance, organizational deviance, and overall workplace deviance (Kozako, Safin, and Abdul Rahim 2013; Lim, Teh, and Benjamin 2016). Garcia et al. (2015) examined the role of subordinates' neuroticism in the relationship between abusive supervision and workplace deviance. They found a stronger relationship between abusive supervision and workplace deviance for employees with high as opposed to low levels of neuroticism. This means that neurotic employees are more likely than non-neurotic employees to engage in deviant behaviors in response to perceived abusive supervision.

A different research approach by Raman, Sambasivan, and Kumar (2016) argued that individual personality traits indirectly affect counterproductive work behavior (CWB).

CWB includes employee behaviors that go against the goals of an organization, such as sabotage of equipment, gossiping, blaming others, or corruptness. In their study, the authors reported that personality factors drove emotional intelligence (EI), affectivity, emotional labor, and emotional exhaustion, which, in turn, affected CWB. In particular, employees with the following characteristics will be better at managing emotional labor and emotional exhaustion, and thus engage less in CWB: (1) high on personality traits, such as extraversion, agreeableness, openness, and conscientiousness, and low on neuroticism; (2) high levels of EI; and (3) low levels of negative affectivity.

44.3.2 *Narcissism*

Another important personality trait that influences workplace deviance is narcissism. Narcissism is a personality factor that is characterized by grandiosity, vanity, entitlement, and exploitativeness (Hyatt et al. 2018). Subordinates high in narcissism believe that they are special and unique, expect special treatment and exception, lack empathy, and often take advantage of other people. Others often view narcissists as arrogant, aggressive, self-promotional, and less likable (Buffardi and Campbell 2008). Furthermore, narcissists seem to be hypersensitive to threats to their self-esteem and to act out in aggressive ways when threats occur (Bushman and Baumeister 1998). In particular, ego-threatening information elicits negative emotions such as anger or frustration. These negative emotions may, in turn, lead to destructive outbursts such as workplace deviance. In support of this theory, Penney and Spector (2002) found that the relationship between narcissism and CWB was mediated by trait anger.

Grijalva and Newman (2015) published a meta-analytic review of the relationship between employees' narcissism and CWB. They showed that, after controlling for the Big Five personality traits, narcissism was the largest unique predictor of CWB. Together, these predictors explained a total of 36 percent of the variance in CWB. Thus, narcissism also appears to be an important predictor of workplace deviance.

As narcissism dictates the manner in which individuals cope with situational constraints at work (Penney and Spector 2002), it is important to look at the joint effect of narcissism and workplace stressors. Meurs et al. (2013) examined the interactive effect of narcissism and two work stressors (i.e., interpersonal conflict and organizational constraints) on workplace deviance. Results showed that individuals high on narcissism who experienced high levels of work stressors were more likely to engage in CWB directed at others or the organization. Although the interaction effect sizes were small, these findings suggest that narcissists are more likely than non-narcissists to respond to workplace stressors by engaging in deviant workplace behaviors. Overall, this shows that both personality and the work environment play an important role in workplace deviance.

44.3.3 *Emotional Intelligence*

Studies have shown that EI is also an important precursor of deviant workplace behaviors. EI can be defined as "the subset of social intelligence that involves the ability to monitor one's own and others' feelings and emotions, to discriminate among them and to use this information to guide one's thinking and actions" (Salovey and Mayer 1990). EI has often been associated with prosocial behaviors, which are behaviors that benefit other people and enhance their welfare. For example, higher EI has been linked to better social skills, closer and more affectionate social relationships, and higher marital satisfaction (Lopes, Salovey, and Straus 2003; Schutte et al. 2001).

However, EI has also been linked to various antisocial behaviors. For instance, Yunus, Khalid, and Nordin (2012) reported that EI was negatively related to deviant workplace behavior, which means that low-EI individuals have a greater tendency than do high-EI individuals to take part in such behavior. More specifically, a total of 11 percent of the variance in CWB was explained by EI. The authors considered that EI provides the necessary emotional competencies (i.e., high socialization and low impulsiveness) that enables employees to avoid committing deviant acts in the workplace.

Bibi, Karim, and Siraj ud Din (2013) also found that EI was negatively related to CWB, which implies that low-EI people tend to engage in CWB more frequently than high-EI people. EI explained roughly 11 percent to 14 percent of the variance in CWB. EI also affected the strength of the relationship between workplace incivility and CWB. Workplace incivility refers to low-intensity deviant workplace behavior with an ambiguous intent to harm (Andersson and Pearson 1999). Depending on EI, workplace incivility can cause an escalating spiral of wrongdoing in which one act of incivility can eventually lead to extreme forms of CWB. In particular, compared to high-EI people, low-EI people are less able to control themselves and will, therefore, cope less effectively with an uncivil environment, which leads them to act defiantly and to cause damage to the organization.

To conclude, in addition to the literature on negative leadership and organizational misconduct, another line of research has focused on the individual employee in order to understand why people engage in deviant workplace behaviors. This view suggests that workplace deviance is driven by various personality traits. Here, the influences of the Big Five personality model, narcissism, and EI were discussed.

44.4 TOXIC WORK ENVIRONMENTS

Workplace deviance is more than the sum of bad individual leaders and dysfunctional employees, however. A core idea that underlies another area of research is that the environment within an organization also plays a role in employee deviance (Appelbaum, Deguire, and Lay 2005; Peterson 2002). When the work climate is negative or hostile, employees feel envious, less trusting, and aggressive toward other organizational members (Mawritz et al. 2012), which can lead to deviant behaviors. In this section, the definition of the environment within an organization will first be discussed. Various studies will then be presented to illustrate how a toxic work environment affects employee misconduct. In particular, at what point does a work environment start to support or promote deviant workplace behaviors?

The environment at the workplace has been conceptualized in many ways. One commonly used operationalization is Schein's (1985, 2010) concept of organizational culture. Schein proposed a model of organizational culture in which he identified three distinct levels: *artifacts*, *espoused beliefs and values*, and *basic underlying assumptions*. In particular, artifacts refer to tangible or verbally identifiable elements of the organization, such as the organization's physical surroundings, dress code, languages, or office jokes. These are the visible elements that make the first impression on outsiders. For example, employees in toxic environments might gossip, make derogatory remarks to coworkers, and pull each other into controversies. Next, espoused beliefs and values encompass the ideals, goals, values, and aspirations shared among individuals within the organization. These are actively pursued in the company and communicated by upper management. Last, basic underlying assumptions are the hidden and deeply embedded, taken-for-granted beliefs, perceptions, thoughts, and feelings that drive values and action in an organization. They are integrated in office dynamics and unconsciously enacted by organization members. When there is misalignment among these layers, a company culture can fail or become toxic.

To give an example, Burke (2017) applied Schein's model to NASA's company culture at the time of the Challenger accident in 1986. An important value of NASA's culture at the time was openness. Employees could be blunt and confrontational with one another. This openness, however, was only demonstrated in peer interactions and top-down relationships. Prior to the accident, engineers spoke out about their technical concerns related to the O-rings that would ultimately cause the accident. Yet their managers were reluctant to deliver bad news to superiors. Incomplete and misleading information was communicated upward. Thus, although NASA's culture valued openness, the underlying assumption that was embedded in their culture appeared to be openness except with your boss.

Apart from Schein's influential approach of organizational culture, other research has focused on the term "working environment." Opperman (2002) defined the working environment as a composite of three sub-environments: the *technical* environment, the *human* environment, and the *organizational* environment. The first sub-environment refers to all technical elements of the workplace, such as tools, equipment, and infrastructure. The second sub-environment refers to the network of formal and informal interaction among colleagues, including peers, team and work groups, management, and leaders. The final sub-environment refers to all systems, procedures, practices, values, and philosophies that are controlled by management. A third line of research posits that there are two types of work environment: a conducive one and a toxic one (Kyko 2005). The former gives pleasurable experiences to subordinates and enables them to actualize their abilities and behavior, whereas the latter gives unpleasant experiences to subordinates and de-actualizes their behavior.

Overall, these different approaches have in common that they assume that there is a larger "organizational whole" (i.e., environment) at play rather than only individual components. Most studies have focused on work environments that are positive or healthy and are characterized by values such as openness, friendship, collaboration, encouragement, personal freedom, and trust (see Härtel and Ashkanasy 2010). In turn, positive work environments can have beneficial outcomes for companies, such as greater organizational commitment and increased worker productivity and performance (Bindu and Gunaseelan 2012; Hanaysha 2016; Jaskiewicz and Tulenko 2012). Yet recently, there seems to be a research shift in focus away from positive work environments toward negative or toxic work environments (Anjum and Ming 2018; Anjum et al. 2018; Tastan 2017; van Rooij and Fine 2018; van Rooij, Fine, and van der Graaf 2019).

There is, however, an apparent lack of academic definitions of exactly what is meant by a *toxic* work environment. A work environment can be conceptualized as the settings, situations, conditions, and circumstances under which people work (Oludeyi 2015), and toxicity refers to the quality of being toxic or poisonous (Merriam-Webster 2019). Researchers have used several terms to describe a company culture that is toxic, including hostile climate (Mawritz et al. 2014), hostile work environment (Abbas, Abd Hussein, and Khali 2017), unethical work environment (Appelbaum, Soltero, and Neville 2005), negative work culture (Baker et al. 2000), corrupt organizational culture (Campbell 2015), dysfunctional organizational culture (van Fleet and Griffin 2006), and dysfunctional organization (Balthazard, Cooke, and Potter 2006). Often researchers have tried to identify factors that constitute a toxic culture or environment at the workplace. The current state of the literature is still very fragmented; studies use different definitions, methods, and data, and researchers come to separate conclusions. Section 44.5 attempts to summarize the most important findings to date from the literature on toxic work environments and workplace deviance.

44.5 TOXIC WORK ENVIRONMENTS AND WORKPLACE DEVIANCE

As previously mentioned, toxic work environment is a relatively new construct. Research conducted so far has mainly focused on the identification of factors that constitute such an environment. These studies have linked varied toxic organizational factors to workplace deviance, such as job stressors, organizational frustration, or lack of organizational support (Chen, Fah, and Jin 2016; Lawrence and Robinson 2007; Silva and Ranasinghe 2017). Various studies will be discussed, with the first two studies primarily focused on the identification of factors of a toxic work environment and the final two studies additionally examining the effect of a toxic environment on workplace deviance.

To begin with, Chamberlain and Hodson (2010) used data coded from the full population of published book-length organizational ethnographies to find various toxic working conditions. Three types of toxic working conditions were distinguished: interpersonal conditions, occupational conditions, and organizational conditions. In particular, two toxic interpersonal conditions that were identified were conflict with supervisors, and customer interaction (i.e., this involves high emotional labor that can lead to the suppression of genuine feelings). Toxic occupational conditions included a lack of autonomy and a lack of job-specific skills. Finally, organizational chaos and unstable product market were recognized as toxic working conditions.

Campbell and Göritz (2014) studied similarities in organizational culture across different corrupt organizations to identify systematic characteristics. In their study, they interviewed experts about their experiences with corrupt organizations and addressed the three layers of organizational culture broken down by manager levels and employee levels: underlying assumptions, values, and norms of behavior (Schein 1992). Various characteristics of a corrupt organizational culture were identified. Important underlying assumptions shared by managers and employees in corrupt organizations were that company results were more important than the path to attaining these results (e.g., the end justified the means); both parties perceived themselves as fighting a war rather than facing ordinary competition within the market; and managers valued results and performance, concepts that were disconnected from ethical values. Furthermore, managers put pressure on their employees through three norms of behavior: goal setting, rewards, and punishment. To give an example, they punished employees who did not facilitate corruption (punishment) and rewarded employees that acted corruptly (rewards). The main values that employees shared were job security and team spirit. They started to separate themselves from non-corrupt coworkers and openly shared their secrets of corruption. However, no one talked about corruption-related issues; there was an organizational atmosphere of silence. Employees perceived group coercion within their work groups and felt pressure to follow (corrupt) group norms, which could eventually lead to even more deviant behaviors.

Nonetheless, research that explores the relationship between toxic work environments and workplace deviance remains scarce. Appelbaum and Roy-Girard (2007) published a comprehensive literature review on toxic organizations. They argued that toxicity in the workplace comes from multiple toxins (toxic leader, toxic manager, and toxic culture) within the organization. They explained that these toxins create a toxic work environment that negatively affects employees. In such an environment, employees engage in destructive deviant behaviors. This can have an adverse impact on the overall performance of work groups. Furthermore, these behaviors appear to be enormously costly to the organization. The costliest deviant behaviors identified by the authors were theft, sabotage, absenteeism, and the withholding of effort. Less costly deviant behaviors were verbal abuse, taking long breaks, gossiping, and substance abuse.

Mawritz et al. (2012) looked at the joint effect of abusive supervision and hostile work climate on workplace deviance. Results showed that a hostile climate strengthened the positive relationship between abusive supervisor behavior and work group interpersonal deviance. Although the effect size was small, this suggests that abusive supervision leads to even more workplace deviance in a hostile climate than in a non-hostile climate. The authors explained that a hostile climate at work creates a social context in which deviant behavior is promoted and encouraged. This creates expectations for hostile behaviors as well as pressure to conform to norms of hostility. In such a context, employees are more likely to accept and emulate their supervisors' abusive behaviors, which results in greater employee deviancy.

Although some studies have linked toxic work environments to employee deviance, there remains little empirical evidence for this connection. It continues to be a challenge for experimental research to identify toxic work environments and their effects on employee behavior. First, the exact definition of toxic work environment is still unclear and inconsistently used. Second, employees in a toxic work environment don't always speak up about toxicity in their organization. They have learned that speaking up is bad; it has potential costs for them, such as negative performance evaluations, undesirable job assignments, or termination from employment. As a consequence, they might respond inaccurately or falsely to survey questions about their organization. Last, researchers often have to convince companies to take part in research in order to access company structures. Companies sometimes refuse to participate as they think that closer examination will expose weakness or toxic elements within their company culture. Altogether, this makes it difficult to capture and investigate toxic work environments and their consequences.

In contrast, employee deviance has been studied extensively in relation to positive work environments (Di Stefano, Scrima, and Parry 2019; Lewicki et al. 1997; Peterson 2002; Vardi 2001). The effects of an absent positive work environment can help us to better understand the effects of a toxic work environment. Colbert et al. (2004) reported that positive perceptions of the developmental environment were negatively related to withholding effort, while perceived organizational support was negatively related to interpersonal deviance. In other words, employees who receive organizational support and have positive perceptions of the work environment are less likely to engage in workplace deviance. This suggests that employees who perceive their environment as negative might exhibit these deviant behaviors. Other research supports these findings, as it shows an inverse relationship between a positive ethical climate and employee deviant behaviors or unethical choices in the workplace (Appelbaum, Soltero, and Neville 2005; Kish-Gephart, Harrison, and Treviño 2010). In addition, Kanten and Ülker (2013) examined the effect of organizational climate on counterproductive behaviors. They focused on two types of counterproductive behavior: interpersonal counterproductive behaviors and organizational counterproductive behaviors. Five organizational factors showed a negative relationship with counterproductive behaviors. In particular, organizational climates with positive reward policies, a warm working environment, support and commitment, structure, and high standards influenced employees to behave positively. This implies that employees are more likely to exhibit deviant behaviors in work environments that lack these dimensions.

In conclusion, a toxic work environment also plays an important role in affecting workplace deviance. Exactly what constitutes a toxic work environment remains vague, and different approaches have tried to grasp the concept in their own way. Yet empirical evidence remains scarce regarding the effect of a toxic work environment on employee misconduct or deviance in the workplace. Thus, further research is required to develop a deeper understanding of the toxic work environment–workplace deviance relationship.

44.6 CONCLUSION

Compliance in organizational settings requires more than an understanding of what makes organizations act ethically and comply with the rules. It also requires an examination of factors that stimulate rule-breaking and deviant behavior. There is far less research on this negative side of organizational behavior than there is on the positive aspects. The available research shows that several factors play a role, some related to the leaders, some to the employees, and some to the overall work environment. This chapter has discussed the different literature and, as a general structure, has shown how these factors are related (see Figure 44.1 for the chapter's conceptual model).

Overall, the chapter shows several key insights about organizational deviance, as well as areas of focus for future research. It shows, for instance, that there is a link between organizational deviance and noncompliance. Yet, how minor deviant behaviors develop into behaviors that violate prevailing laws and regulations remains largely unstudied and unclear. Most studies have focused on less serious deviant acts within the organization. The chapter also concludes that leadership matters, as *abusive supervision* has repeatedly been linked to workplace deviance. However, the exact link between abusive supervisors and noncompliance remains understudied. Another finding is that *dysfunctional employees* are sources of workplace deviance. Research shows that personality traits can play a large role here. Yet again, there is limited work that explores how such employees spur noncompliance. Finally, a body of work has explored how a *toxic work environment* can cause deviance and rule-breaking behavior. Research findings here do link the work environment to rule-breaking and noncompliance to some extent. The problem is that the studies are conceptually fragmented, and there is limited cohesion in how they define and study toxic environments.

What becomes clear is how important these different organizational factors are for organizational compliance. Much human activity takes place in public or private organizations, and some of the worst, most damaging cases of noncompliance occur in organizations. As such, it is vital that the various organizational disciplines focus more on the joint effects of different toxic organizational factors on noncompliance. It is important that they come to integrate ideas about how leadership, employees, and work environments interact to shape deviancy and how such deviancy leads to noncompliance.

REFERENCES

Abbas, Ali Abdulhasan, Adel Abbas Abd Hussein, and Hussein Huraija Khali. 2017. "The Effect of Hostile Work Environment on Organizational Alienation: The Mediation Role of the Relationship

between the Leader and Followers." *Asian Social Science* 13(2): 140–58. https://doi.org/10.5539/ass.v13n2p140.
Adams, J. S. 1963. "Towards an Understanding of Inequity." *Journal of Abnormal and Social Psychology* 67(5): 422–36.
1965. "Inequity in Social Exchange." In *Advances in Experimental Social Psychology*, ed. L. Berkowitz, Vol. 2, 267–99. New York: Academic Press.
Aleksić, Ana, and Matea Vuković. 2018. "Connecting Personality Traits with Deviant Workplace Behaviour." *Journal of Media Critiques* 4(14): 119–29. https://doi.org/10.17349/jmc118209.
Alexander, Katherine. 2011. "Abusive Supervision as a Predictor of Deviance and Health Outcomes: The Exacerbating Role of Narcissism and Social Support." PhD dissertation, Bowling Green State University. https://doi.org/10.16194/j.cnki.31–1059/g4.2011.07.016.
Andersson, Lynne M., and Christine M. Pearson. 1999. "Tit for Tat? The Spiraling Effect of Incivility in the Workplace." *Academy of Management Review* 24(3): 452–71. https://doi.org/10.2307/259136.
Anjum, Amna, and Xu Ming. 2018. "Combating Toxic Workplace Environment: An Empirical Study in the Context of Pakistan." *Journal of Modelling in Management* 13(3): 675–97. https://doi.org/10.1108/JM2-02–2017-0023.
Anjum, Amna, Xu Ming, Ahmed Faisal Siddiqi, and Samma Faiz Rasool. 2018. "An Empirical Study Analyzing Job Productivity in Toxic Workplace Environments." *International Journal of Environmental Research and Public Health* 15(5): 1035. https://doi.org/10.3390/ijerph15051035.
Appelbaum, Steven H., Kyle J. Deguire, and Mathieu Lay. 2005. "The Relationship of Ethical Climate to Deviant Workplace Behaviour." *Corporate Governance* 5(4): 43–55. https://doi.org/10.1108/14720700510616587.
Appelbaum, Steven H., and David Roy-Girard. 2007. "Toxins in the Workplace: Affect on Organizations and Employees." *Corporate Governance* 7(1): 17–28. https://doi.org/10.1108/14720700710727087.
Appelbaum, Steven H., Ivan Ulises Soltero, and Keith Neville. 2005. "The Creation of an Unethical Work Environment: Organisational Outcome-Based Control Systems." *Equal Opportunities International* 24(2): 67–83. https://doi.org/10.1108/02610150510788024.
Ashforth, B. E. 1994. "Petty Tyranny in Organizations." *Human Relations* 47(7): 755–78. https://doi.org/10.1177/001872679404700701.
Avey, James B., Keke Wu, and Erica Holley. 2015. "The Influence of Abusive Supervision and Job Embeddedness on Citizenship and Deviance." *Journal of Business Ethics* 129(3): 721–31. https://doi.org/10.1007/s10551-014–2192-x.
Baharom, Mohd Nazri, Mohd Dino Khairi Bin Sharfuddin, and Javed Iqbal. 2017. "A Systematic Review on the Deviant Workplace Behavior." *Review of Public Administration and Management* 5(3): 1–8. https://doi.org/10.4172/2315–7844.1000231.
Baker, C., J. Beglinger, S. King, M. Salyards, and A. Thompson. 2000. "Transforming Negative Work Culture: A Practical Strategy." *Journal of Nursing Administration* 30(7–8): 357–63. https://doi.org/10.1097/00005110–200007000-00010.
Baldwin, Susanna. 2006. *Organisational Justice*. Brighton, UK: Institute for Employment Studies.
Balthazard, Pierre A., Robert A. Cooke, and Richard E. Potter. 2006. "Dysfunctional Culture, Dysfunctional Organization: Capturing the Behavioral Norms that Form Organizational Culture and Drive Performance." *Journal of Managerial Psychology* 21(8): 709–32. https://doi.org/10.1108/02683940610713253.
Bandura, A. 1977. *Social Learning Theory*. Englewood Cliffs, NJ: Prentice Hall.
Bennett, Rebecca J., and Sandra L. Robinson. 2000. "Development of a Measure of Workplace Deviance." *Journal of Applied Psychology* 85(3): 349–60. https://doi.org/10.1037/0021–9010.85.3.349.
2003. "The Past, Present, and Future of Workplace Deviance Research." In *Organizational Behavior: The State of the Science*, ed. J. Greenberg, 2nd ed., 247–81. Mahwah, NJ: Earlbaum.
Bibi, Zainab, Jahanvash Karim, and Siraj ud Din. 2013. "Workplace Incivility and Counterproductive Work Behavior: Moderating Role of Emotional Intelligence." *Pakistan Journal of Psychological Research* 28(2): 317–34.
Bindu, Anto Ollukkaran, and Rupa Gunaseelan. 2012. "A Study on the Impact of Work Environment on Employee Performance." *Namex International Journal of Management Research* 2(2): 71–85.

Blau, P. M. 1964. *Exchange and Power in Social Life*. New York: Wiley.
Boddy, Clive R. 2014. "Corporate Psychopaths, Conflict, Employee Affective Well-Being and Counterproductive Work Behaviour." *Journal of Business Ethics* 121(1): 107–21. https://doi.org/10.1007/s10551-013–1688-0.
Brehm, J. W. 1966. *A Theory of Psychological Reactance*. Oxford, UK: Academic Press.
Buffardi, L. E., and W. Keith Campbell. 2008. "Narcissism and Social Networking Web Sites." *Personality and Social Psychology Bulletin* 34(10): 1303–14. https://doi.org/10.1177/0146167208320061.
Burke, W. Warner. 2017. *Organization Change: Theory and Practice*. 5th ed. Thousand Oaks, CA: Sage.
Burton, James P., and Jenny M. Hoobler. 2011. "Aggressive Reactions to Abusive Supervision: The Role of Interactional Justice and Narcissism." *Scandinavian Journal of Psychology* 52(4): 389–98. https://doi.org/10.1111/j.1467–9450.2011.00886.x.
Bushman, Brad J., and Roy F. Baumeister. 1998. "Threatened Egotism, Narcissism, Self-Esteem, and Direct and Displaced Aggression: Does Self-Love or Self-Hate Lead to Violence?" *Journal of Personality and Social Psychology* 75(1): 81–105. https://doi.org/10.1037/0022–3514.75.1.219.
Campbell, Jamie-Lee, and Anja S. Göritz. 2014. "Culture Corrupts! A Qualitative Study of Organizational Culture in Corrupt Organizations." *Journal of Business Ethics* 120(3): 291–311. https://doi.org/10.1007/s10551-013–1665-7.
Campbell, Marlen Jamie-Lee. 2015. "Organizational Cultures' Impact on Employees' Corruption." PhD dissertation, Julius-Maximilians-Universität Würzburg. https://opus.bibliothek.uni-wuerzburg.de/opus4-wuerzburg/frontdoor/deliver/index/docId/12325/file/Campbell_Organizational_Cultures_Corruption.pdf.
Campbell, W. Keith, Angelica M. Bonnacci, Jeremy Shelton, Julie J. Exline, and Brad J. Bushman. 2004. "Psychological Entitlement: Interpersonal Consequences and Validation of a Self-Report Measure." *Journal of Personality Assessment* 83(1): 29–45. https://doi.org/10.1207/s15327752jpa8301_04.
Chamberlain, Lindsey Joyce, and Randy Hodson. 2010. "Toxic Work Environments: What Helps and What Hurts." *Sociological Perspectives* 53(4): 455–77. https://doi.org/10.1525/sop.2010.53.4.455.
Chen, Lim Li, Benjamin Chan Yin Fah, and Teh Choon Jin. 2016. "Perceived Organizational Support and Workplace Deviance in the Voluntary Sector." *Procedia Economics and Finance* 35: 468–75. https://doi.org/10.1016/s2212-5671(16)00058–7.
Cho, Seonghee, Misty M. Johanson, and Priyanko Guchait. 2009. "Employees Intent to Leave: A Comparison of Determinants of Intent to Leave versus Intent to Stay." *International Journal of Hospitality Management* 28(3): 374–81. https://doi.org/10.1016/j.ijhm.2008.10.007.
Chung, Frank. 2018. "Emails Reveal Extent of Google's Toxic Work Culture." *New Zealand Herald*, January 10. www.nzherald.co.nz/business/news/article.cfm?c_id=3&objectid=11972830.
Colbert, Amy E., Michael K. Mount, James K. Harter, and Murray R. Barrick. 2004. "Interactive Effects of Personality and Perceptions of the Work Situation on Workplace Deviance." *Journal of Applied Psychology* 89(4): 599–609. https://doi.org/10.1037/0021–9010.89.4.599.
Cropanzano, Russell, Zinta S. Byrne, D. Ramona Bobocel, and Deborah E. Rupp. 2001. "Moral Virtues, Fairness Heuristics, Social Entities, and Other Denizens of Organizational Justice." *Journal of Vocational Behavior* 58: 164–209. https://doi.org/10.1006/jvbe.2001.1791.
Di Stefano, Giovanni, Fabrizio Scrima, and Emma Parry. 2019. "The Effect of Organizational Culture on Deviant Behaviors in the Workplace." *International Journal of Human Resource Management* 30(17): 2482–2503. https://doi.org/10.1080/09585192.2017.1326393.
Dollard, J., L. W. Doob, N. E. Miller, O. H. Mowrer, and R. R. Sears. 1939. *Frustration and Aggression*. New Haven, CT: Yale University Press.
Duffy, Michelle K., Daniel C. Ganster, and Milan Pagon. 2002. "Social Undermining in the Workplace." *Academy of Management Journal* 45(2): 331–51. https://doi.org/10.5465/3069350.
Einarsen, Ståle, Merethe Schanke Aasland, and Anders Skogstad. 2007. "Destructive Leadership Behaviour: A Definition and Conceptual Model." *Leadership Quarterly* 18(3): 207–16. https://doi.org/10.1016/j.leaqua.2007.03.002.
Eisenbeiss, Silke Astrid, Daan van Knippenberg, and Clemens Maximilian Fahrbach. 2015. "Doing Well by Doing Good? Analyzing the Relationship between CEO Ethical Leadership and Firm Performance." *Journal of Business Ethics* 128(3): 635–51. https://doi.org/10.1007/s10551-014–2124-9.
Fleenor, John W. 2011. "Trait Approach to Leadership." *Encylopedia of Industrial and Organisational Psycology* 3(80): 103–41. https://doi.org/10.13140/2.1.3091.2804.

Fox, Suzy, and Paul E. Spector. 1999. "A Model of Work Frustration-Aggression." *Journal of Organizational Behavior* 20(6): 915–31. https://doi.org/10.1002/(SICI)1099-1379(199911)20:6<915::aid-job918>3.0.CO;2-6.

Garcia, Patrick Raymund James M., Lu Wang, Vinh Lu, Kohyar Kiazad, and Simon Lloyd D. Restubog. 2015. "When Victims Become Culprits: The Role of Subordinates' Neuroticism in the Relationship between Abusive Supervision and Workplace Deviance." *Personality and Individual Differences* 72: 225–9. https://doi.org/10.1016/j.paid.2014.08.017.

Gibson, Jane Whitney, and Jerry L. Mason. 2011. "Executive Leadership Development as a Strategy for Long Term Business Success." *Journal of Business & Economics Research (JBER)* 5(9): 19–26. https://doi.org/10.19030/jber.v5i9.2579.

Grijalva, Emily, and Daniel A. Newman. 2015. "Narcissism and Counterproductive Work Behavior (CWB): Meta-analysis and Consideration of Collectivist Culture, Big Five Personality, and Narcissism's Facet Structure." *Applied Psychology* 64(1): 93–126. https://doi.org/10.1111/apps.12025.

Gutworth, Melissa B., Dana M. Morton, and Jason J. Dahling. 2013. "Managing Organizational Deviance." In *Wisdom, Kernals of Truth, and Boundary Conditions in Organizational Studies*, edited by D. J. Svyantek and K. T. Mahoney, 153–80. Charlotte, NC: Information Age Publishing, Inc.

Hanaysha, Jalal. 2016. "Testing the Effects of Employee Engagement, Work Environment, and Organizational Learning on Organizational Commitment." *Procedia – Social and Behavioral Sciences* 229: 289–97. https://doi.org/10.1016/j.sbspro.2016.07.139.

Härtel, Charmine E. J., and Neal M. Ashkanasy. 2010. "Healthy Human Cultures as Positive Work Environments." In *The Handbook of Organizational Culture and Climate*, edited by N. M. Ashkanasy, C. P. M. Wilderom, and M. F. Peterson, 85–100. Thousand Oaks, CA: Sage. https://doi.org/10.4135/9781483307961.n6.

Harvey, Paul, Kenneth J. Harris, William E. Gillis, and Mark J. Martinko. 2014. "Abusive Supervision and the Entitled Employee." *Leadership Quarterly* 25(2): 204–17. https://doi.org/10.1016/j.leaqua.2013.08.001.

Harvey, Paul, and Mark J. Martinko. 2009. "An Empirical Examination of the Role of Attributions in Psychological Entitlement and Its Outcomes." *Journal of Organizational Behavior* 30(4): 459–76. https://doi.org/10.1002/job.549.

Henle, Christine A., Robert A. Giacalone, and Carole L. Jurkiewicz. 2005. "The Role of Ethical Ideology in Workplace Deviance." *Journal of Business Ethics* 56(3): 219–30. https://doi.org/10.1007/s10551-004–2779-8.

Hyatt, Courtland S., Chelsea E. Sleep, Joanna Lamkin, Jessica L. Maples-Keller, Constantine Sedikides, W. Keith Campbell, and Joshua D. Miller. 2018. "Narcissism and Self-Esteem: A Nomological Network Analysis." *PLoS ONE* 13(8): e0201088. https://doi.org/10.1371/journal.pone.0201088.

Jaskiewicz, Wanda, and Kate Tulenko. 2012. "Increasing Community Health Worker Productivity and Effectiveness: A Review of the Influence of the Work Environment." *Human Resources for Health* 10: 1–9. https://doi.org/10.1186/1478–4491-10–38.

Johnson, Russell E., Merlijn Venus, Klodiana Lanaj, Changguo Mao, and Chu-Hsiang Chang. 2012. "Leader Identity as an Antecedent of the Frequency and Consistency of Transformational, Consideration, and Abusive Leadership Behaviors." *Journal of Applied Psychology* 97(6): 1262–72. https://doi.org/10.1037/a0029043.

Kanten, Pelin, and Funda Er Ülker. 2013. "The Effect of Organizational Climate on Counterproductive Behaviors: An Empirical Study on the Employees of Manufacturing Enterprises." *Macrotheme Review* 2(4): 144–60.

Kellerman, Barbara. 2004. *Bad Leadership*. Boston, MA: Harvard Business Review Press.

Kelly, Jack. 2019. "Google under Investigation for Alleged Unfair Labor Practices." *Forbes*. www.forbes.com/sites/jackkelly/2019/12/11/google-under-investigation-for-alleged-unfair-labor-practices/#355c51266e77.

Kish-Gephart, Jennifer J., David A. Harrison, and Linda Klebe Treviño. 2010. "Bad Apples, Bad Cases, and Bad Barrels: Meta-analytic Evidence about Sources of Unethical Decisions at Work." *Journal of Applied Psychology* 95(1): 1–31. https://doi.org/10.1037/a0017103.

Kozako, Intan Nurul 'Ain Mohd Firdaus, Siti Zaharah Safin, and Abdul Rahman Abdul Rahim. 2013. "The Relationship of Big Five Personality Traits on Counterproductive Work Behaviour among Hotel Employees." *Procedia Economics and Finance* 7: 181–7. https://doi.org/10.1016/S2212-5671(13)00233-5.

Kyko, O. C. 2005. *Instrumentation: Know Yourself and Others*. New York: Longman.

Lawrence, Thomas B., and Sandra L. Robinson. 2007. "Ain't Misbehavin: Workplace Deviance as Organizational Resistance." *Journal of Management* 33(3): 378–94. https://doi.org/10.1177/0149206307300816.

Lewicki, Roy J., Tim Poland, John W. Minton, and Blair H. Sheppard. 1997. "Dishonesty as Deviance: A Typology of Workplace Dishonesty and Contributing Factors." In *Research on Negotiations in Organizations*, edited by Robert J. Bies, Roy J. Lewicki, and Blair H. Sheppard, Vol. 6, 53–86. Greenwich, CT: JAI Press.

Li, Yuhui, Zhen Wang, Liu Qin Yang, and Songbo Liu. 2016. "The Crossover of Psychological Distress from Leaders to Subordinates in Teams: The Role of Abusive Supervision, Psychological Capital, and Team Performance." *Journal of Occupational Health Psychology* 21(2): 142–53. https://doi.org/10.1037/a0039960.

Lian, Huiwen, D. Lance Ferris, Rachel Morrison, and Douglas J. Brown. 2014. "Blame It on the Supervisor or the Subordinate? Reciprocal Relations between Abusive Supervision and Organizational Deviance." *Journal of Applied Psychology* 99(4): 651–64. https://doi.org/10.1037/a0035498.

Liang, Lindie H., and Douglas J. Brown. 2019. "Abusive Leadership." In *Global Encyclopedia of Public Administration, Public Policy, and Governance*, edited by Ali Farazmand, 1–7. New York: Springer. https://doi.org/10.1007/978–3-319–31816-5.

Lim, Li-Chen, Choon-Jin Teh, and Chan-Yin-Fah Benjamin. 2016. "A Preliminary Study of the Effects of Personality Traits on Workplace Deviance in the Voluntary Sector." *International Review of Management and Marketing* 6(7S): 6–10.

Lin, Szu Han (Joanna), Jingjing Ma, and Russell E. Johnson. 2016. "When Ethical Leader Behavior Breaks Bad: How Ethical Leader Behavior Can Turn Abusive via Ego Depletion and Moral Licensing." *Journal of Applied Psychology* 101(6): 815–30. https://doi.org/10.1037/apl0000098.

Lipman-Blumen, Jean. 2005. *The Allure of Toxic Leaders: Why We Follow Destructive Bosses and Corrupt Politicians – and How We Can Survive Them*. New York: Oxford University Press.

Liu, Jun, Ho Kwong Kwan, Long-zeng Wu, and Weiku Wu. 2010. "Abusive Supervision and Subordinate Supervisor-Directed Deviance: The Moderating Role of Traditional Values and the Mediating Role of Revenge Cognitions." *Journal of Occupational and Organizational Psychology* 83(4): 835–56. https://doi.org/10.1348/096317909X485216.

Liu, Yaozhong, and Caibao Qui. 2015. "Unethical Pro-Organizational Behavior: Concept, Measurement and Empirical Research." *Journal of Human Resource and Sustainability Studies* 3 (3): 150–5. https://doi.org/10.4236/jhrss.2015.33020.

Lopes, Paulo N., Peter Salovey, and Rebecca Straus. 2003. "Emotional Intelligence, Personality, and the Perceived Quality of Social Relationships." *Personality and Individual Differences* 35(3): 641–58. https://doi.org/10.1016/S0191-8869(02)00242-8.

Martinko, Mark J., Paul Harvey, Jeremy R. Brees, and Jeremy Mackey. 2013. "A Review of Abusive Supervision Research." *Journal of Organizational Behavior* 34(SUPPL 1). https://doi.org/10.1002/job.1888.

Martinko, Mark J., Paul Harvey, David Sikora, and Scott C. Douglas. 2011. "Perceptions of Abusive Supervision: The Role of Subordinates' Attribution Styles." *Leadership Quarterly* 22(4): 751–64. https://doi.org/10.1016/j.leaqua.2011.05.013.

Mathieu, Cynthia, Craig S. Neumann, Robert D. Hare, and Paul Babiak. 2014. "A Dark Side of Leadership: Corporate Psychopathy and Its Influence on Employee Well-Being and Job Satisfaction." *Personality and Individual Differences* 59: 83–8. https://doi.org/10.1016/j.paid.2013.11.010.

Mawritz, Mary B., Scott B. Dust, and Christian J. Resick. 2014. "Hostile Climate, Abusive Supervision, and Employee Coping: Does Conscientiousness Matter?" *Journal of Applied Psychology* 99(4): 737–47. https://doi.org/10.1037/a0035863.

Mawritz, Mary Bardes, David M. Mayer, Jenny M. Hoobler, Sandy J. Wayne, and Sophia V. Marinova. 2012. "A Trickle-Down Model of Abusive Supervision." *Personnel Psychology* 65(2): 325–57. https://doi.org/10.1111/j.1744–6570.2012.01246.x.

Ménard, Julie, Luc Brunet, and André Savoie. 2011. "Interpersonal Workplace Deviance: Why Do Offenders Act Out? A Comparative Look on Personality and Organisational Variables." *Canadian Journal of Behavioural Science* 43(4): 309–17. https://doi.org/10.1037/a0024741.

Merriam-Webster.com Dictionary, s.v. "toxicity." www.merriam-webster.com/dictionary/toxicity.

Meurs, James A., Suzy Fox, Stacey R. Kessler, and Paul E. Spector. 2013. "It's All about Me: The Role of Narcissism in Exacerbating the Relationship between Stressors and Counterproductive Work Behaviour." *Work and Stress* 27(4): 368–82. https://doi.org/10.1080/02678373.2013.849776.

Mitchell, Marie S., and Maureen L. Ambrose. 2007. "Abusive Supervision and Workplace Deviance and the Moderating Effects of Negative Reciprocity Beliefs." *Journal of Applied Psychology* 92(4): 1159–68. https://doi.org/10.1037/0021–9010.92.4.1159.

Muafi. 2011. "Causes and Consequence Deviant Workplace Behavior." *International Journal of Innovation, Management and Technology* 2(2): 123–6. https://doi.org/10.7763/IJIMT.2011.V2.117.

Oludeyi, Olukunle S. 2015. "A Review of Literature on Work Environment and Work Commitment: Implication for Future Research in Citadels of Learning." *Human Resource Management* 18(2): 32–46. www.jhrm.eu/wp-content/uploads/2015/03/JournalOfHumanResourceMng2015vol18issue2-pages-32–46.pdf.

Opperman, C. S. 2002. *Tropical Business Issues*. In partnership with PriceWaterhouseCoopers. www.pricewaterhousecoopers//zambiaeconomists.com.

Park, Haesang, Jenny M. Hoobler, Junfeng Wu, Robert C. Liden, Jia Hu, and Morgan S. Wilson. 2017. "Abusive Supervision and Employee Deviance: A Multifoci Justice Perspective." *Journal of Business Ethics* 158(4): 1–19. https://doi.org/10.1007/s10551-017–3749-2.

Paulhus, Delroy L., and Kevin M. Williams. 2002. "The Dark Triad of Personality: Narcissism, Machiavellianism, and Psychopathy." *Journal of Research in Personality* 36(6): 556–63. https://doi.org/10.1016/S0092-6566(02)00505–6.

Penney, Lisa M., and Paul E. Spector. 2002. "Narcissism and Counterproductive Work Behavior: Do Bigger Egos Mean Bigger Problems?" *International Journal of Selection and Assessment* 10(1&2): 126–34. https://doi.org/10.1111/1468–2389.00199.

Peterson, Dane K. 2002. "Deviant Workplace Behavior and the Organization's Ethical Climate." *Journal of Business and Psychology* 17(1): 47–61. https://doi.org/10.1023/A:1016296116093.

Petrides, K. V., Philip A. Vernon, Julie Aitken Schermer, and Livia Veselka. 2011. "Trait Emotional Intelligence and the Dark Triad Traits of Personality." *Twin Research and Human Genetics* 14(1): 35–41. https://doi.org/10.1375/twin.14.1.35.

Podsakoff, Philip M., Scott B. MacKenzie, and William H. Bommer. 1996. "Transformational Leader Behaviors and Substitutes for Leadership as Determinants of Employee Satisfaction, Commitment, Trust, and Organizational Citizenship." *Journal of Management* 22(2): 259–98. https://doi.org/10.1016/S0149-2063(96)90049–5.

Prusik, Monika, and Michal Szulawski. 2019. "The Relationship between the Dark Triad Personality Traits, Motivation at Work, and Burnout among HR Recruitment Workers." *Frontiers in Psychology* 10: 1290. https://doi.org/10.3389/fpsyg.2019.01290.

Puffer, Sheila M. 1987. "Prosocial Behavior, Noncompliant Behavior, and Work Performance among Commission Sales People." *Journal of Applied Psychology* 72(4): 615–21. https://doi.org/10.1037//0021–9010.72.4.615.

Raman, Ponniah, Murali Sambasivan, and Naresh Kumar. 2016. "Counterproductive Work Behavior among Frontline Government Employees: Role of Personality, Emotional Intelligence, Affectivity, Emotional Labor, and Emotional Exhaustion." *Revista de Psicologia Del Trabajo y de Las Organizaciones* 32(1): 25–37. https://doi.org/10.1016/j.rpto.2015.11.002.

Reed, George E. 2004. "Toxic Leadership." *Military Review* 84(4): 67–71.

Restubog, Simon Lloyd D., Kristin L. Scott, and Thomas J. Zagenczyk. 2011. "When Distress Hits Home: The Role of Contextual Factors and Psychological Distress in Predicting Employees' Responses to Abusive Supervision." *Journal of Applied Psychology* 96(4): 713–29. https://doi.org/10.1037/a0021593.

Rizvi, Syed Tahir, Barry A. Friedman, and Rauf I. Azam. 2017. "Overall Injustice, Workplace Deviance and Turnover Intention among Educators and Supporters." *BRC Academy Journal of Business* 7(1): 45–71. https://doi.org/10.15239/j.brcacadjb.2017.07.01.ja03.
Robbins, Stephen P., and Timothy A. Judge. 2009. *Organisational Behaviour*. Upper Saddle River, NJ: Pearson Prentice Hall.
Robinson, Sandra L., and Rebecca J. Bennett. 1995. "A Typology of Workplace Behaviors: A Multidimensional Scaling Study." *Academy of Management Journal* 38(2): 555–72.
Rosenthal, Seth A., and Todd L. Pittinsky. 2006. "Narcissistic Leadership." *Leadership Quarterly* 17(6): 617–33. https://doi.org/10.1016/j.leaqua.2006.10.005.
Salancik, Gerald R., and Jeffrey Pfeffer. 1978. "A Social Information Processing Approach to Job Attitudes and Task Design." *Administrative Science Quarterly* 23(2): 224–53.
Salovey, Peter, and John D. Mayer. 1990. "Emotional Intelligence." *Imagination, Cognition, and Personality* 9(3): 185–211. https://doi.org/10.2190/DUGG-P24E-52WK-6CDG.
Schein, Edgar H. 1985. *Organizational Culture and Leadership*. San Francisco, CA: Jossey-Bass.
1992. *Organizational Culture and Leadership*. 2nd ed. San Francisco, CA: Jossey-Bass.
2010. *Organizational Culture and Leadership*. 4th ed. San Francisco, CA: Jossey-Bass.
Schmidt, Andrew A. 2008. "Development and Validation of the Toxic Leadership Scale." Master's thesis, University of Maryland. https://drum.lib.umd.edu/bitstream/handle/1903/8176/umi?sequence=1.
2014. "An Examination of Toxic Leadership, Job Outcomes, and the Impact of Military Development." PhD dissertation, University of Maryland. https://drum.lib.umd.edu/bitstream/handle/1903/15250/Schmidt_umd_0117E_15049.pdf?sequence=1&isAllowed=y.
Schutte, Nicola S., John M. Malouff, Chad Bobik, Tracie D. Coston, Cyndy Greeson, Christina Jedlicka, Emily Rhodes, and Greta Wendorf. 2001. "Emotional Intelligence and Interpersonal Relations." *Journal of Social Psychology* 141(4): 523–36. https://doi.org/10.1080/00224540109600569.
Schyns, Birgit, and Jan Schilling. 2013. "How Bad Are the Effects of Bad Leaders? A Meta-analysis of Destructive Leadership and Its Outcomes." *Leadership Quarterly* 24(1): 138–58. https://doi.org/10.1016/j.leaqua.2012.09.001.
Shafiu, Awwal Muhhammad, Halimah Abdul Manaf, and Sakinah Muslim. 2019. "The Impact of Leadership on Organizational Performance." *International Journal of Recent Technology and Engineering* 8(3): 7573–6. https://doi.org/10.35940/ijrte.C6158.098319.
Silva, H. Michelle S. V., and R. M. I. D. Ranasinghe. 2017. "The Impact of Job Stress on Deviant Workplace Behaviour: A Study of Operational Level Employees of Comfort Apparel Solutions Company in Sri Lanka." *International Journal of Human Resource Studies* 7(1): 74–85. https://doi.org/10.5296/ijhrs.v7i1.10901.
Steindl, Christina, Eva Jonas, Sandra Sittenthaler, Eva Traut-Mattausch, and Jeff Greenberg. 2015. "Understanding Psychological Reactance: New Development and Findings." *Zeitschrift Fur Psychologie* 223(4): 205–14. https://doi.org/10.1027/2151–2604/a000222.
Tajfel, Henri, and John Turner. 1979. "An Integrative Theory of Intergroup Conflict." In *The Social Psychology of Intergroup Relations*, eds. William G. Austin and Stephen Worchel, 33–7. Monterey, CA: Brooks/Cole.
Tastan, Seçil Bal. 2017. "Toxic Workplace Environment in Search for the Toxic Behaviours in Organizations with a Research in Healthcare Sector." *Postmodern Openings* 8(1): 83–109. https://doi.org/10.18662/po/2017.0801.07.
Taylor, Shannon G., Matthew D. Griffith, Abhijeet K. Vadera, Robert Folger, and Chaim R. Letwin. 2019. "Breaking the Cycle of Abusive Supervision: How Disidentification and Moral Identity Help the Trickle-Down Change Course." *Journal of Applied Psychology* 104(1): 164–82. https://doi.org/10.1037/apl0000360.
Tepper, Bennett J. 2000. "Consequences of Abusive Supervision." *Academy of Management Journal* 43 (2): 178–90. https://doi.org/10.2307/1556375.
2007. "Abusive Supervision in Work Organizations: Review, Synthesis, and Research Agenda." *Journal of Management* 33(3): 261–89. https://doi.org/10.1177/0149206307300812.
Tepper, Bennett J., Jon C. Carr, Denise M. Breaux, Sharon Geider, Changya Hu, and Wei Hua. 2009. "Abusive Supervision, Intentions to Quit, and Employees' Workplace Deviance: A Power/

Dependence Analysis." *Organizational Behavior and Human Decision Processes* 109(2): 156–67. https://doi.org/10.1016/j.obhdp.2009.03.004.

Tepper, Bennett J., Christine A. Henle, Lisa S. Lambert, Robert A. Giacalone, and Michelle K. Duffy. 2008. "Abusive Supervision and Subordinates' Organization Deviance." *Journal of Applied Psychology* 93(4): 721–32. https://doi.org/10.1037/0021–9010.93.4.721.

Tepper, Bennett J., Lauren Simon, and Hee Man Park. 2017. "Abusive Supervision." *Annual Review of Organizational Psychology and Organizational Behavior* 4(1): 123–52. https://doi.org/10.1146/annurev-orgpsych-041015–062539.

Thau, Stefan, Rebecca J. Bennett, Marie S. Mitchell, and Mary Beth Marrs. 2009. "How Management Style Moderates the Relationship between Abusive Supervision and Workplace Deviance: An Uncertainty Management Theory Perspective." *Organizational Behavior and Human Decision Processes* 108(1): 79–92. https://doi.org/10.1016/j.obhdp.2008.06.003.

Thau, Stefan, and Marie S. Mitchell. 2010. "Self-Gain or Self-Regulation Impairment? Tests of Competing Explanations of the Supervisor Abuse and Employee Deviance Relationship through Perceptions of Distributive Justice." *Journal of Applied Psychology* 95(6): 1009–31. https://doi.org/10.1037/a0020540.

Umphress, Elizabeth E., and John B. Bingham. 2011. "When Employees Do Bad Things for Good Reasons: Examining Unethical Pro-Organizational Behaviors." *Organization Science* 22(3): 621–40. https://doi.org/10.1287/orsc.1100.0559.

van Fleet, David D., and Ricky W. Griffin. 2006. "Dysfunctional Organization Culture: The Role of Leadership in Motivating Dysfunctional Work Behaviors." *Journal of Managerial Psychology* 21(8): 698–708. https://doi.org/10.1108/02683940610713244.

van Rooij, Benjamin, and Adam Fine. 2018. "Toxic Corporate Culture: Assessing Organizational Processes of Deviancy." *Administrative Sciences* 8(3): 1–38. https://doi.org/10.3390/admsci8030023.

van Rooij, Benjamin, Adam Fine, and J. van der Graaf. 2019. "Detoxing Corporate Culture: How to Assess Toxic Cultural Elements." Corporate Compliance and Enforcement at NYU School of Law (blog). https://wp.nyu.edu/compliance_enforcement/2019/02/04/detoxing-corporate-culture-how-to-assess-toxic-cultural-elements/.

Vardi, Yoav. 2001. "The Effects of Organizational and Ethical Climates on Misconduct at Work." *Journal of Business Ethics* 29(4): 325–37. https://doi.org/10.1023/A:1010710022834.

Vaughan, Diane. 1996. *The Challenger Launch Decision: Risky Technology, Culture, and Deviance at NASA*. Chicago, IL: University of Chicago Press.

Vernon, Philip A., Vanessa C. Villani, Leanne C. Vickers, and Julie Aitken Harris. 2008. "A Behavioral Genetic Investigation of the Dark Triad and the Big 5." *Personality and Individual Differences* 44 (2): 445–52. https://doi.org/10.1016/j.paid.2007.09.007.

Vogel, Rick, Fabian Homberg, and Alena Gericke. 2016. "Abusive Supervision, Public Service Motivation, and Employee Deviance: The Moderating Role of Employment Sector." *Evidence-Based HRM* 4(3): 214–31. https://doi.org/10.1108/EBHRM-08–2015-0034.

Volmer, Judith, and Iris K. Koch, and Anja S. Göritz. 2016. "The Bright and Dark Sides of Leaders' Dark Triad Traits on Subordinates' Career Success and Well-Being." *Personality and Individual Differences* 101: 413–18. https://doi.org/10.1016/j.paid.2016.06.046.

Yu, Lingtao, Michelle K. Duffy, and Bennett J. Tepper. 2018. "Consequences of Downward Envy: A Model of Self-Esteem Threat, Abusive Supervision, and Supervisory Leader Self-Improvement." *Academy of Management Journal* 61(6): 2296–318. https://doi.org/10.5465/amj.2015.0183.

Yunus, Othman Mohd, Khalizani Khalid, and Shahrina Nordin. 2012. "A Personality Trait and Workplace Deviant Behaviors." *Elixir Human Resource Management* 47(1): 8678–83.

Zhang, Yucheng, and Zhenyu Liao. 2015. "Consequences of Abusive Supervision: A Meta-analytic Review." *Asia Pacific Journal of Management* 32(4): 959–87. https://doi.org/10.1007/s10490-015–9425-0.

45

Corporate Social Responsibility, ESG, and Compliance

Elizabeth Pollman

Abstract: Notable business leaders and institutional investors have begun to support the idea that companies should be run for the benefit of all stakeholders – customers, employees, suppliers, communities, and shareholders. After decades of focus on maximizing shareholder value, corporate social responsibility ("CSR") and initiatives relating to environmental, social, and governance matters ("ESG") are gaining ground in the debate about corporate purpose. Despite their rising prominence, CSR and ESG are still highly contested and no consensus exists about their precise meaning. Diverging views about what constitutes socially responsible activity and the rationale for its pursuit have driven wide-ranging approaches to researching and implementing CSR and ESG practices. This chapter examines the shifting debate and landscape of CSR, ESG, and their connection to compliance. Although CSR and ESG are often connected conceptually to legal compliance, or taking actions that exceed such an aim, usage of the terms vary. Further, although many studies find a positive relationship between CSR or ESG and financial performance, the empirical evidence is mixed and does not conclusively establish whether CSR or ESG activity mitigates compliance, regulatory, litigation, or other business risks. Finally, the chapter observes that social responsibility initiatives are on the rise in the form of internal governance mechanisms, private principles, and third-party ratings and rankings, but the dizzying array of approaches and frameworks impedes a clear understanding of what it means for a company to "comply" with aims for CSR or ESG. The lack of a singular, universal system enables customization, but evolving norms and laws on corporate practices and disclosures could lead to new insights.

45.1 INTRODUCTION

In 2019, the CEO and chairperson of BlackRock, the world's largest asset manager, called for corporate leaders to embrace corporate purpose and create value for stakeholders, and 181 CEOs of the Business Roundtable committed to lead their companies for the benefit of all stakeholders – customers, employees, suppliers, communities, and shareholders. The idea that corporations should engage in socially responsible business practices ("CSR") or initiatives relating to environmental, social, and governance matters ("ESG") is gaining prominence but remains highly contested. Deeper examination reveals that each of these terms – CSR and ESG – lacks a singular meaning. From aligning shareholder and stakeholder interests for shared value and risk management, to going beyond compliance and profit-maximizing strategies, there is no consensus on what socially responsible activity entails and the rationale for its pursuit.

This chapter aims to illuminate the landscape of CSR, ESG, and their connection to compliance. Varying usage and mixed empirical research reveal that CSR and ESG lack a clearly defined connection to compliance. This indeterminacy extends to (1) whether CSR and ESG are correlated with or refer to greater levels of legal compliance, as well as (2) what it means for a corporation to "comply" with CSR or ESG goals in light of the proliferation of standards and metrics pertaining to sustainability and social impact. This examination reflects that the business world is in a state of flux regarding how companies take account of their impact on stakeholders and the environment, and, around the world, laws are evolving on issues such as sustainability disclosures that could help us better understand existing practices.

45.2 INTRODUCTION TO CSR AND ESG

The scope and contours of CSR are disputed and have shifted over time. Discussion of whether corporations primarily serve an economic role for shareholders or whether they more broadly serve society dates back to the famous Berle-Dodd debate of the 1930s (Bratton and Wachter 2008). The rise of large public corporations with separation of ownership and control raised concerns about corporate accountability and the question of whether corporate managers were trustees for shareholders or stewards with broader social obligations. The debate has never been fully resolved to a consensus view, nor have commentators agreed upon what constitutes socially responsible business practice.

The use of the term "social responsibility" – referring to the concept of incorporating stakeholders and their interests in how companies are run – emerged in the 1950s (Carroll 1999; Jackson 2010; Ostas 2004). Economist Howard Bowen's landmark book *The Social Responsibilities of the Businessman* launched discussion of "the obligations of businessmen to pursue those policies, to make those decisions, or to follow those lines of action which are desirable in terms of the objectives and values of our society" (Bowen 1953:6). Bowen's framing identified social duties that stemmed from the consequences of business activity and encompassed ethics to protect the well-being of workers and the general public (Carroll 1999; Ostas 2004).

Other mid-twentieth-century thinkers built on this idea, such as Keith Davis who espoused the "Iron Law of Responsibility" that "social responsibilities of businessmen need to be commensurate with their social power" (Davis 1960:71). According to Davis (1960:70), social responsibility refers to "business[persons'] decisions and actions taken for reasons at least partially beyond the firm's direct economic or technical interest." Such responsibility has two aspects: "a broad obligation to the community with regard to economic developments affecting the public welfare" and an obligation "to nurture and develop human values" (Davis 1960:70). Some socially responsible business decisions would be justified by aligning with long-term economic value for the corporation (Davis 1960:70). But, together with other scholars in this period such as Adolf Berle and Peter Drucker, Davis further recognized that society had certain expectations of business and that government regulation would need to step in to the extent that business leaders did not use their power responsibly (Ostas 2004; Pollman 2019). This view appreciated that social expectations could be addressed by the business community or through regulation, and if the former failed to live up to the task, the law would step in.

By the 1970s, the modern regulatory state indeed began to take shape with the rise of regulation concerning the environment, worker safety, and consumer protection. Expansive conceptions of CSR were met with criticism from economists and legal academics such as Milton Friedman and Henry Manne who presented a different view of how corporations should be run (Carroll 1999). Friedman famously argued that "there is one and only one social responsibility of business – to use its resources and engage in activities designed to increase its profits so long as it stays within the rules of the game, which is to say, engages in open and free competition without deception or fraud" (Friedman 1962:133). In Friedman's view, corporate managers are agents working on behalf of the shareholder-owners, and it is "pure and unadulterated socialism" to encourage such corporate managers to spend "other's people money" in pursuit of stakeholder interests that do not align with the profit motive (Friedman 1970). Along similar lines, Henry Manne expressed skepticism that "socially responsible" corporate expenditures were truly voluntary and independent acts of altruism, and argued that they were instead examples of corporate public relations or agency costs in the form of self-interested executives pursuing their own prestige to appear as "corporate statesmen" – both representing an abandonment of the free market in favor of ineffective programs that by his account were unlikely to increase social welfare (Manne and Wallich 1972).

This narrow view of corporate responsibility to maximize profits for shareholders "within the rules of the game" became known as the "shareholder primacy" view, and as it gained dominance in the United States through the late twentieth century, it came to stand in contrast to the preceding broader vision of CSR (Hansmann and Kraakman 2001). While the shareholder primacy view gained adherents, the literature on CSR nonetheless continued to flourish in the late twentieth century and writings multiplied on alternative concepts, theories, and models (Carroll 1999).

Approaches to the topic of CSR also became more diverse. Researchers studied relevant disclosures in annual reports, executive perceptions of CSR, and the relation between CSR and financial performance (Carroll 1999). Business practice expanded to include mechanisms of self-reporting, such as corporate codes of conduct and sustainability reports, and the adoption of nonbinding standards from nongovernmental organizations (NGOs) and international organizations. Assets in socially screened portfolios and investment funds for "socially responsible investing" increased substantially. Several legal scholars in the 1990s and 2000s developed a body of scholarship known as "progressive corporate law," which argues for more comprehensive, mandatory changes in corporate law in order to serve the public interest (Greenfield 2007).

In the twenty-first century, greater interest in whether there is a "business case" for CSR apart from altruistic and ethical justifications has shifted the debate to concepts of "sustainability" and environmental, social, and governance ("ESG") practices and risks. ESG is used "to refer not only to sustainability measures or to environmental, social, or governance practices specifically, but to all nonfinancial fundamentals that can impact firms' financial performance, such as corporate governance, labor and employment standards, human resource management, and environmental practices" (Harper Ho 2016:651). Underlying ESG initiatives is "evidence that accounting for both financial and nonfinancial risk can drive firm and portfolio performance" (Harper Ho 2016:647) – and an understanding that ESG is an important tool for mitigating risk, which is particularly valuable for large asset managers (Gadinis and Miazad 2020).

45.3 LEGAL COMPLIANCE AND CSR/ESG

With groundwork set out on CSR and ESG, this section now turns to examining how each concept is connected to legal compliance. First, this section parses how various definitions of

CSR and ESG relate to the law, demonstrating that each term has been used in reference to obedience or compliance, rooted in discourse on ethics or risk management. Second, this section reviews the related empirical literature and concludes that there is mixed support for a positive relationship between CSR or ESG and financial performance, and that some explanations for this linkage include compliance, regulatory, and litigation risk, but empirical support exists for alternative explanations as well.

45.3.1 *Conceptual Connections*

Although the debate on CSR has been wide ranging, as the discussion in the previous sections illustrates, usage of the term CSR could be understood in terms of three categories – references that "reduc[e] CSR to mere compliance with existing laws and market demands" (Kerr 2008:854); references that equate CSR with going "beyond compliance" (Rosen-Zvi 2011:532); and references that are broadly stated without relation to law, that "CSR merely implies that businesses share responsibility for societal conditions" (Jackson 2010:52).

The first usage, equating CSR with compliance and market demands, does not claim to take a capacious approach but instead typically references Delaware corporate law dictates for fiduciaries to maximize shareholder value and emphasizes the importance of government regulation to ensure that corporations do not generate excessive externalities (Strine 2012; Strine 2015). In this account, corporate fiduciaries are subject to a legal duty to aim to increase the value of the corporation for the benefit of the shareholders, and stakeholder interests should be pursued only insofar as they coincide with this goal or are required by law. Notably, the notion that the law requires shareholder primacy is contested (Stout 2012), and corporate law varies around the world (Berger-Walliser and Scott 2018). Furthermore, some jurisdictions have evolved to mandate conduct that was formerly understood as voluntary CSR engagement, such as India's mandatory corporate charity policy and California's supply chain transparency law – a trend some scholars have called the "legalization of CSR" (Berger-Walliser and Scott 2018:169). One concern expressed about this trend of hardening socially responsible practices into law is that it may ultimately reinforce a paradigm of shareholder primacy and undermine the understanding of CSR as a moral or ethical responsibility (Berger-Walliser and Scott 2018:170).

The second usage of CSR envisions it as voluntary, self-regulatory action requiring more than compliance (Afsharipour and Rana 2014). Myriad definitions, pledges, and programs use this framing of CSR as encouraging "companies to conduct business beyond compliance with the law and beyond shareholder wealth maximization" (Lin 2010:64; see also Bénabou and Tirole 2009). This usage "suggests that companies should do more than they are obligated under applicable laws governing product safety, environmental protection, labor rights, human rights, community development, corruption, and so on; it also suggests that companies should consider not only the interests of shareholders but also those of other stakeholders" (Lin 2010:64). One criticism of this definitional approach is that as certain areas that were once in the realm of voluntary CSR activity have become regulated, the notion of CSR as "an extralegal, voluntary activity" is called into question (Berger-Walliser and Scott 2018). Further, notions of CSR and what is required by law vary widely around the world so that activity that would be considered CSR in some countries is mere compliance in others (Berger-Walliser and Scott 2018).

The third usage similarly presents a pro-stakeholder perspective, but it does not reference a concept of acting "beyond compliance" or state a particular position with respect to the law.

For example, some scholars have proposed a definition of CSR as "activities that internalize costs for externalities resulting directly or indirectly from corporate actions, or processes and actions to consider and address the impact of corporation actions on affected stakeholders" (Berger-Walliser and Scott 2018:214–15). Many variations on these themes exist, such as the concept of "shared value" and "responsive CSR" which includes "acting as a good corporate citizen, attuned to the evolving social concerns of stakeholders, and mitigating existing or anticipated adverse effects from business activities" (Porter and Kramer 2006:85).

The newer term of ESG typically coincides with the second usage of CSR insofar as it envisions a scope that includes legal compliance as well as additional concerns. The difference is that whereas CSR is often framed in terms of social obligations, rooted in ethical or moral concerns, ESG is generally discussed in terms of risk management for firms and investors, individually or systemically. For example, a majority of US public companies have adopted enterprise risk management systems that "take account of nonfinancial or ESG risks, including compliance, regulatory, environmental and other operational risks, as well as strategic risks" (Harper Ho 2016:663). Risk management can contribute to financial performance "by reducing the cost of future liabilities due to enforcement actions, legal claims, and other negative risk events, as well as losses to investors when these events become known to the market" (Harper Ho 2016:664).

Framed in terms of risk management and the business case, "ESG investing, once a sideline practice, has gone decisively mainstream" (Goldman Sachs 2016). An ESG investment strategy "emphasizes a firm's governance structure or the environmental or social impacts of the firm's products or practices" (Schanzenbach and Sitkoff 2020:388). For example, as framing has shifted from socially responsible investing to ESG, "instead of avoiding the fossil fuel industry to achieve collateral benefits from reduced pollution, ESG proponents argued that the fossil fuel industry should be avoided because financial markets underestimate its litigation and regulatory risks, and therefore divestment would improve risk-adjusted return" (Schanzenbach and Sitkoff 2020:389). Further, ESG has a broader focus than compliance as it targets not only legal risk but also business risk from a wide variety of sources, and it can flexibly take account of a range of stakeholders (Gadinis and Miazad 2020).

The boundaries of these terms, however, are not precise – sometimes CSR and ESG are used interchangeably, and although ESG is frequently used in the context of risk management and risk-adjusted returns, it is also used sometimes to refer to social benefits.

45.3.2 *Empirical Literature*

The variation and evolution of definitions of CSR and ESG, and the lack of a standardized set of metrics, have posed challenges for empirical study (Clarkson 1995; Aguinis and Glavas 2012). The voluntary nature of much of this activity presents significant selection problems (Christensen et al. 2019). Notwithstanding these challenges, an enormous amount of research has focused on the key empirical question – whether there is a connection between CSR or ESG and financial performance – and the literature is mixed.

A minority of studies finds a negative relationship between various ESG or social performance indicators and financial performance. For example, one study of UK firms used a set of disaggregated indicators for environment, employment, and community activities and found a negative relationship between stock returns and environmental performance and, to a lesser extent, community activities, over a one- to three-year period (Brammer et al. 2006). Another study examined a panel of socially responsible investing funds over multiple decades and found that community relations screening increased financial performance but environmental and labor relations screening decreased financial performance (Barnett and Salomon 2006).

A majority of empirical studies, however, find "that although not all firm sustainability efforts translate into higher returns for investors, positive social performance has a positive or neutral effect on risk-adjusted returns, profitability, and other standard measures of financial performance at the firm and portfolio level" (Harper Ho 2016:665; see also Friede et al. 2015; Mahon and Griffin 1999; Margolis et al. 2009; Orlitzky et al. 2003). One survey of 159 articles found that "[t]he majority of studies show a positive relationship between [corporate social performance] and financial performance (63%); 15% of studies report a negative relationship, and 22% report a neutral or mixed relationship" (Peloza 2009:1521).

It is not clear whether a positive relationship between CSR or ESG and financial performance evidences the business case, and, if so, by what mechanism. The generation of financial performance might occur through improving relationships with stakeholders such as customers (Brown and Dacin 1997) or employees (Turban and Greening 1997). Several other explanations exist and some connect to compliance, regulatory, and litigation risk.

One alternative finding or interpretation of the empirical evidence is that CSR or ESG activity is a proxy for compliance or it creates goodwill that functions like insurance to protect the company if negative events occur such as an investigation or enforcement action (Armour et al. 2018; Godfrey et al. 2009; Husted 2005). One study found that participation in CSR activities aimed at a company's stakeholders or society can create value by tempering negative judgments and reducing sanctions (Godfrey et al. 2009). Companies with better CSR and ESG practices might better mitigate downside risks from environmental disasters, employee strikes or health and safety issues, product recalls and boycotts, or corporate criminal or civil liability (Koehler and Hespenheide 2013). A broader framing of this explanation is that CSR or ESG activity might help to quantify or mitigate compliance, regulatory, litigation, and other business risks (CFA Institute 2017). Monitoring and managing nonfinancial risk might also lower the cost of capital (Goss and Roberts 2011; Sharfman and Fernando 2008).

Another possibility is that CSR or ESG indicators might instead be a proxy for management quality. A recent survey of portfolio managers and research analysts found that 41 percent reported using ESG issues in investment analysis and decisions for this reason (CFA Institute 2017). One way in which the quality of management might be linked is that CSR might prevent short-sighted managerial decision-making or it could be a strategic move to strengthen market position, to "placat[e] regulators and public opinion to avoid strict supervision in the future, or to attempt to raise rivals' costs by encouraging environmental, labour or safety regulations that will particularly handicap competitors" (Bénabou and Tirole 2009:9–10). For example, "[a] firm that is better at regulatory compliance and managing environmental and social risks may be better managed and governed in general, making environmental and social factors a useful proxy for better management" (Schanzenbach and Sitkoff 2020:435). Another linkage might be that high-quality managers choose to work for companies with pro-social and environmental policies for their own reputational capital, self-image, or personal values (Schanzenbach and Sitkoff 2020:435).

45.4 CORPORATE GOVERNANCE AND CSR AND ESG INITIATIVES

Finally, CSR and ESG intersect with "compliance" in another meaning of the term – rather than focusing on legal obedience and related risks, a separate inquiry looks into what standards or metrics companies that claim to have CSR and ESG aims are trying to comply with or meet. The big picture is an evolving mix of internal governance mechanisms, private principles, and third-party ratings and rankings – without a clear set of content or standardized disclosure. Thus, companies may independently determine their own particularized CSR or ESG aims, and there is a high degree of variability and lack of a reliable mechanism to determine compliance with the stated aims.

In broad terms, the approaches can be categorized as "self-regulation," referring to internal corporate governance mechanisms that are adopted on a voluntary basis, and "meta-regulation," referring to external measurements (Gill 2008). Both are complements to formal governmental regulation and companies may engage in these "voluntary" activities in response to a range of internal factors or external social pressures (Aguinis and Glavas 2012; Howard-Grenville et al. 2008; Kagan et al. 2003). Recent years have witnessed a growing number of approaches in both of these categories and increasingly vociferous calls for improved disclosure and standardization.

Corporate governance mechanisms of "self-regulation" include corporate codes of conduct, CSR board committees, business ethics units, and supply chain assurance (Gill 2008). Corporate codes of conduct vary widely in addressing corporate ethics and articulating the norms and standards that a corporation voluntarily adopts on a range of key issues such as human rights, labor, and the environment. Such codes gained prominence in the 1990s particularly with multinational corporations operating in developing countries, but they have come under criticism as ineffective window dressing that may not actually improve corporate behavior unless accompanied by more significant organizational change (Gill 2008; Kaptein and Wempe 1998). This criticism is reflected in the variety of reasons that motivate corporations to adopt codes of conduct, including: "to prevent governmental intervention in the form of mandatory regulation . . .; to limit political opposition to the growing globalization of markets; as a response to pressures from consumer groups; and as a means to protect their reputation" (Rosen-Zvi 2011:537). Although corporate codes of conduct are among the "softest" form of voluntary self-regulation and are typically expressed in abstract and non-binding language, in some instances NGOs and advocacy groups have attempted to hold corporations to their stated commitments (Rosen-Zvi 2011:536, 538–40). Other internal governance mechanisms such as CSR board committees and business ethics units are means of carrying out and monitoring the principles adopted in the corporate code of conduct throughout the organizational hierarchy. These complement compliance departments within corporations, which also function to bring broader social interests into the firm (Griffith 2016). Supply chain assurance extends the corporation's voluntarily adopted principles into its external contracts through private ordering, requiring suppliers to use international business norms and standards of human rights, labor protection, and social responsibility (Blair et al. 2008; Park and Berger-Walliser 2015).

External forms of "meta-regulation" arise from institutional investors, regulators, NGOs, and other groups that develop schemes that guide, measure, and monitor corporate conduct. This area of "soft law" and "private regulation" has become a veritable alphabet soup of acronyms as third-party standards, ratings, and rankings have multiplied (Hall and Huber 2019; Park and Berger-Walliser 2015). Some provide substantive principles for incorporating CSR or ESG into corporate operations or investment practice, whereas others provide standards and metrics for disclosures. Prominent examples of frameworks with substantive standards on topics such as social impact, human capital, and the environment include the UN Global Compact (UNGC), the Global Reporting Initiative (GRI) Standards, and the

Organisation for Economic Co-Operation and Development's (OECD) Guidelines for Multinational Enterprises.

In the United States, federal securities regulation requires public companies to disclose "material" risk-related information, and the SEC has recognized that material ESG risks such as related to climate change must be disclosed under standard reporting requirements (SEC 2010). To date, the SEC has not required general sustainability disclosure, however, and a significant amount of the data available comes from voluntary reports that a majority of US public companies issue to describe their commitment to stakeholders and the environment (Fisch 2019; Harper Ho 2010). Uniform reporting and audit standards for this kind of "nonfinancial" reporting have not yet been widely adopted, and most disclosure regimes do not use standardized quantitative metrics (Harper Ho 2016). The Sustainability Accounting Standards Board (SASB) has made significant progress in providing a baseline for reporting CSR and ESG data, but researchers find that companies report data in more than twenty different ways with considerable inconsistencies (Kotsantonis and Serafeim 2019). Scholars have called for mandatory disclosure and reform in the United States (Fisch 2019; Lipton 2020), and several jurisdictions around the world have imposed or are considering mandatory "nonfinancial" or "sustainability" disclosures such as the 2014 European Union Directive on the Disclosure of Non-Financial and Diversity Information and the stakeholder disclosure provision of the UK Companies Act (Fisch 2019; Grewal et al. 2019; Harper Ho 2010).

On the investing front, a group of twenty leading institutional investors developed the United Nations' Principles for Responsible Investment (PRI), which promote institutional investor engagement with portfolio firms around ESG performance (Harper Ho 2010). Hundreds of institutional investors, representing trillions of dollars in assets under management, have signed on to the PRI (Harper Ho 2010). In addition, a number of international corporate governance codes direct institutional investors to promote better governance and risk management through their influence over asset managers, such as the International Corporate Governance Network (ICGN) Global Governance Principles, the OECD Principles of Corporate Governance, and stewardship codes in the United Kingdom, Canada, Australia, Japan, and the European Union (Harper Ho 2016).

Institutional investors, asset managers, and financial institutions increasingly use ESG third-party raters in assessing risk and managing their investments (Hall and Huber 2019). ESG rating agencies such as MSCI, Sustainalytics, RepRisk, and ISS are hobbled, however, in their efforts by nonstandardized disclosures, and their varying methodologies produce conflicting ratings subject to biases (Doyle 2018). Scholars and commentators have therefore observed that "[w]hile rigorous and reliable ratings might constructively influence corporate behavior, the existing cacophony of self-appointed scorekeepers does little more than add to the confusion" (Porter and Kramer 2006:81). In turn, researchers have found that ESG investing is an "essentially unregulated market" and the use of factors relating to the environment, social issues, and governance is generally opaque (Brakman Reiser and Tucker 2020).

In sum, social responsibility initiatives are on the rise in the form of both internal governance mechanisms and "meta-regulation," but the dizzying array of approaches and frameworks impedes a clear understanding of what it means for a company to comply with aims for CSR or ESG. Companies have flexibility to create their own structures for internal governance, their own channels for stakeholder engagement, their own selection of third-party guidelines or standards, and, in many jurisdictions, their own level of disclosure. The lack of a singular, universal system is beneficial insofar as it allows for customized approaches to CSR and ESG rather than one-size-fits-all governance and regulation. As corporate leaders and investors increasingly appreciate the importance of social responsibility and sustainability, however, the need for standardized, accurate, and audited information that provides transparency and allows for comparability becomes more pressing. Better information would in turn aid efforts to understand the relationship between CSR, ESG, and financial performance, as well as related topics such as compliance. New insights could further inform evolving norms and laws on issues of particular significance for workers, customers, communities, and the environment.

REFERENCES

Afsharipour, Afra, and Shruti Rana. 2014. "The Emergence of New Corporate Social Responsibility in China and India." *UC Davis Business Law Journal* 14:175–230.

Aguinis, Herman, and Ante Glavas. 2012. "What We Know and Don't Know about Corporate Social Responsibility: A Review and Research Agenda." *Journal of Management* 38(4):932–68.

Armour, John, Luca Enriques, Ariel Ezrachi, and John Vella. 2018. "Putting Technology to Good Use for Society: The Role of Corporate, Competition and Tax Law." *Journal of the British Academy* 6 (s1):285–321.

Barnett, Michael L., and Robert M. Salomon. 2006. "Beyond Dichotomy: The Curvilinear Relationship between Social Responsibility and Financial Performance." *Strategic Management Journal* 27:1101–22.

Bénabou, Roland, and Jean Tirole. 2009. "Individual and Corporate Social Responsibility." *Economica* 77:1–19.

Berger-Walliser, Gerlinde, and Inara Scott. 2018. "Redefining Corporate Social Responsibility in an Era of Globalization and Regulatory Hardening." *American Business Law Journal* 55:167–218.

Blair, Margaret M., Cynthia A. Williams, and Li-Wen Lin. 2008. "The New Role for Assurance Services in Global Commerce." *Journal of Corporation Law* 33:325–60.

Bowen, Howard E. 1953. *Social Responsibilities of the Businessman*. New York: Harper & Row.

Brakman Reiser, Dana, and Anne Tucker. 2020. "Buyer Beware: The Paradox of ESG & Passive ESG Funds." *Cardozo Law Review* 41:1921–2018.

Brammer, Stephen, Chris Brooks, and Stephen Pavelin. 2006. "Corporate Social Performance and Stock Returns: UK Evidence from Disaggregate Measures." *Financial Management* 35:97–116.

Bratton, William W., and Michael L. Wachter. 2008. "Shareholder Primacy's Corporatist Origins: Adolf Berle and the Modern Corporation." *Journal of Corporation Law* 34:99–152.

Brown, Tom J., and Peter A. Dacin. 1997. "The Company and the Product: Corporate Associations and Consumer Product Responses." *Journal of Marketing* 61(1): 68–84.

Carroll, Archie B. 1999. "Corporate Social Responsibility: Evolution of a Definitional Construct." *Business & Society* 38(3):268–95.

CFA Institute, Environmental, Social, and Governance (ESG). 2017. "Survey 2017," www.cfainstitute.org/-/media/documents/survey/esg-survey-report-2017.ashx.

Christensen, Hans B., Luzi Hail, and Christian Leuz. 2019. "Adoption of CSR and Sustainability Reporting Standards: Economic Analysis and Review." https://papers.ssrn.com/sol3/papers.cfm?abstract_id=3427748.

Clarkson, Max B. E. 1995. "A Stakeholder Framework for Analyzing and Evaluating Corporate Social Performance." *Academy of Management Review* 20:92–117.

Davis, Keith. 1960. "Can Business Afford to Ignore Social Responsibilities?" *California Management Review* 2:70–6.

Doyle, Timothy M. 2018. "Ratings That Don't Rate: The Subjective World of ESG Ratings Agencies." American Council for Capital Formation, http://accfcorpgov.org/wp-content/uploads/2018/07/ACCF_RatingsESGReport.pdf.

Fisch, Jill E. 2019. "Making Sustainability Disclosure Sustainable." *Georgetown Law Journal* 107:923–66.

Friede, Gunnar, Timo Busch, and Alexander Bassen. 2015. "ESG and Financial Performance: Aggregated Evidence from More than 2000 Empirical Studies." *Journal of Sustainable Finance & Investment* 5:210–33.

Friedman, Milton. 1962. *Capitalism and Freedom*. Chicago: University of Chicago Press.

1970. "The Social Responsibility of Business Is to Increase Its Profits." *NY Times Magazine*, September 13.

Gadinis, Stavros, and Amelia Miazad. 2020. "Sustainability in Corporate Law." *Vanderbilt Law Review* 73:1401–77.

Gill, Amiram. 2008. "Corporate Governance as Social Responsibility: A Research Agenda." *Berkeley Journal of International Law* 26: 452–78.

Godfrey, Paul C., Craig B. Merrill, and Jared M. Hansen. 2009. "The Relationship between Corporate Social Responsibility and Shareholder Value: An Empirical Test of the Risk Management Hypothesis." *Strategic Management Journal* 30:425–55.

Goldman Sachs. 2016. ESG Report, "What Is Powering the ESG Investing Surge?" www.goldmansachs.com/citizenship/sustainability-reporting/esg-content/esg-report-2016-highlights.pdf.

Goss, Allen, and Gordon S. Roberts. 2011. "The Impact of Corporate Social Responsibility on the Cost of Bank Loans." *Journal of Banking & Finance* 35(7):1794–810.

Greenfield, Kent. 2007. *The Failure of Corporate Law: Fundamental Flaws and Progressive Possibilities*. Chicago: University of Chicago Press.

Grewal, Jody, Edward J. Riedl, and George Serafeim. 2019. "Market Reaction to Mandatory Nonfinancial Disclosure." *Management Science* 65(7):3061–84.

Griffith, Sean J. 2016. "Corporate Governance in an Era of Compliance." *William & Mary Law Review* 57:2075–140.

Hall, Joseph A., and Betty M. Huber. 2019. "ESG in the US: Current State of Play and Key Considerations for Issuers." In *The International Comparative Legal Guide to: Corporate Governance 2019*, 12th ed., edited by Sabastian Niles and Adam Emmerich, 23–30. London: Global Legal Group.

Hansmann, Henry, and Reinier Kraakman. 2001. "The End of History for Corporate Law." *Georgetown Law Journal* 89:439–68.

Harper Ho, Virginia. 2010. "'Enlightened Shareholder Value': Corporate Governance Beyond the Shareholder-Stakeholder Divide." *Journal of Corporation Law* 36:59–112.

2016. "Risk-Related Activism: The Business Case for Monitoring Nonfinancial Risk." *Journal of Corporation Law* 41:647–704.

Howard-Grenville, Jennifer, Jennifer Nash, and Cary Coglianese. 2008. "Constructing the License to Operate: Internal Factors and Their Influence on Corporate Environmental Decisions." *Law & Policy* 30(1):73–107.

Husted, Brian W. 2005. "Risk Management, Real Options, and Corporate Social Responsibility." *Journal of Business Ethics* 60(2):175–83.

Jackson, Kevin T. 2010. "Global Corporate Governance: Soft Law and Reputational Accountability." *Brooklyn Journal of International Law* 35:41–106.

Kagan, Robert A., Dorothy Thornton, and Neil Gunningham. 2003. "Explaining Corporate Environmental Performance: How Does Regulation Matter?" *Law & Society Review* 37 (1):51–90.

Kaptein, Muel, and Johan Wempe. 1998. "Twelve Gordian Knots When Developing an Organizational Code of Ethics." *Journal of Business Ethics* 17: 853–69.

Kerr, Janet E. 2008. "The Creative Capitalism Spectrum: Evaluating Corporate Social Responsibility through a Legal Lens." *Temple Law Review* 81:831–70.

Koehler, Dinah A., and Eric J. Hespenheide. 2013. "Finding the Value in Environmental, Social, and Governance Performance." *Deloitte Review* 12:98–111.

Kotsantonis, Sakis, and George Serafeim. 2019. "Four Things No One Will Tell You about ESG Data." *Journal of Applied Corporate Finance* 31(2):50–8.

Lin, Li-Wen. 2010. "Corporate Social Responsibility in China: Window Dressing or Social Change?" *Berkeley Journal of International Law* 28:64–100.

Lipton, Ann. 2020. "Not Everything Is about Investors: The Case for Mandatory Stakeholder Disclosure." *Yale Journal on Regulation* 37:499–572.

Mahon, John F., and Jennifer J. Griffin. 1999. "Painting a Portrait: A Reply." *Business and Society* 38:126–33.
Manne, Henry G., and Henry C. Wallich. 1972. *The Modern Corporation and Social Responsibility*. Washington, DC: American Enterprise Institute for Public Policy Research.
Margolis, Joshua D., Hillary Anger Elfenbein, and James P. Walsh. 2009. "Does It Pay to Be Good . . . and Does It Matter? A Meta-analysis of the Relationship between Corporate Social and Financial Performance." https://papers.ssrn.com/sol3/papers.cfm?abstract_id=1866371.
Orlitzky, Marc, Frank L. Schmidt, and Sara L. Rynes. 2003. "Corporate Social and Financial Performance: A Meta-analysis." *Organization Studies* 24:403–41.
Ostas, Daniel T. 2004. "Cooperate, Comply, or Evade? A Corporate Executive's Social Responsibilities with Regard to Law." *American Business Journal* 41:559–94.
Park, Stephen Kim, and Gerlinde Berger-Walliser. 2015. "A Firm-Driven Approach to Global Governance and Sustainability." *American Business Law Journal* 52: 255–314.
Peloza, John. 2009. "The Challenge of Measuring Financial Impacts from Investments in Corporate Social Performance." *Journal of Management* 35(6):1518–41.
Pollman, Elizabeth. 2019. "Quasi Governments and Inchoate Law: Berle's Vision of Limits on Corporate Power." *Seattle University Law Review* 42:617–39.
Porter, Michael E., and Mark R. Kramer. 2006. "Strategy and Society: The Link Between Competitive Advantage and Corporate Social Responsibility." *Harvard Business Review* 84(12):76–92.
Rosen-Zvi, Issachar. 2011. "You Are Too Soft!: What Can Corporate Social Responsibility Do for Climate Change?" *Minnesota Journal of Law, Science & Technology*. 12:527–66.
Schanzenbach, Max M., and Robert H. Sitkoff. 2020. "The Law and Economics of Environmental, Social, and Governance Investing by a Fiduciary." *Stanford Law Review* 72:381–454.
Securities and Exchange Commission (SEC). 2010. "Commission Guidance Regarding Disclosure Related to Climate Change." www.sec.gov/rules/interp/2010/33–9106.pdf.
Sharfman, Mark P., and Chitru S. Fernando. 2008. "Environmental Risk Management and the Cost of Capital." *Strategic Management Journal* 29(6):569–92.
Stout, Lynn. 2012. *The Shareholder Value Myth: How Putting Shareholders First Harms Investors, Corporations, and the Public*. San Francisco: Berrett-Koehler Publishers.
Strine, Jr., Leo E. 2012. "Our Continuing Struggle with the Idea that For-Profit Corporations Seek Profit." *Wake Forest Law Review* 47:135–72.
2015. "The Dangers of Denial: The Need for a Clear-Eyed Understanding of the Power and Accountability Structure Established by the Delaware General Corporation Law." *Wake Forest Law Review* 40:761–93.
Turban, Daniel B., and Daniel W. Greening. 1997. "Corporate Social Performance and Organizational Attractiveness to Prospective Employees." *Academy of Management Journal* 40(3): 658–72.

46

Agency, Authority, and Compliance

Sean J. Griffith

Abstract: Compliance can and often does serve as a conduit through which regulators and enforcement authorities enlarge their authority beyond statutory bounds. The potential to do so is a function of the symbiotic relationship between compliance officers and regulatory authorities. Compliance officers owe their professional existence and their organizational authority to the interventions of regulators and enforcement agents. This creates a unique incentive structure and renders compliance officers especially receptive to regulators' extralegal pronouncements. As a result, the separation of compliance from legal and the elevation of the compliance function as the coequal of the legal department, a structure often insisted upon by regulators and enforcement authorities, effectively enlarges the compliance conduit through which the government may abuse the rule of law. Rather than separating compliance from legal, compliance should be subordinated to legal so that an officer accountable exclusively to the best interests of the firm is charged with interpreting the law and advising the firm on what the law requires. Only after this determination has been made should compliance officers be charged with the task of executing these decisions. A necessary condition to realigning organizational responsibilities in this way, however, is for the government to stop insisting on the alternative. More broadly, the government should not involve itself in the organizational details of compliance but, rather, should limit itself to making and enforcing the law.

46.1 INTRODUCTION

Law, ethics, and compliance are conceptually distinct. Law is what you must do – the rules and regulations originating from the sovereign, transgression of which may lead to deprivation of property or, in some cases, liberty. Ethics is what you should do. Ethical norms originate from somewhere other than the sovereign, and, when transgressed, may generate negative publicity and lead to adverse consequences in capital, product, or labor markets. Finally, compliance is what a person does in order to ensure that he or she is doing what they must or should. Or, more concisely: law and ethics are different ways of answering *what* to do, while compliance answers *how* to do it.

Legal and ethical requirements may be vague or ambiguous. This is true both internally – what law or ethics requires may not be clear – and in relation to each other – an action may be legal but not ethical, or vice versa. The question thus becomes one of authority. Who decides what law or ethics requires of the organization? And who decides what the organization ought to do in cases of conflict?

The answer, in many business organizations, is compliance. In addition to deciding *how* to execute the dictates of law or ethics, the compliance function increasingly also decides *what* law or ethics requires of the organization. This result is a natural consequence of the organization of compliance within firms. In the last two decades and especially since the global financial crisis of 2008, the importance of compliance departments has expanded vastly, largely due to the pressure of prosecutors and regulators. Compliance has largely subsumed ethics and, thanks again to regulatory pressure, established itself as independent from and equal in authority to the legal department in many firms. At such firms, the chief compliance officer (CCO) need not subordinate his or her judgment to the source of legal authority within the firm, the general counsel (GC), but rather can decide for him- or herself whether conduct is legal or ethical. The CCO makes policy determinations relating to law and ethics, then designs procedures to bring those policies into effect.

This reallocation of authority would not be worth serious scholarly attention were it purely internal to the firm. Management is ordinarily trusted to organize the internal departments of the firm in the same way that it is entrusted with deciding what to make and sell, whether to expand or contract, and whom to hire or fire. But, in fact, the organization of compliance does not come entirely from management. Compliance owes its existence and much of its authority to exogenous sources – prosecutors and regulators. As a result of its exogenous origins, compliance is not wholly accountable to intra-firm authority structures. This creates incentives for compliance officers to consider regulatory interests as coequal to the interests of the firm, making them receptive to regulatory pronouncements regardless of whether of those pronouncements meet the formal requirements of law. This in turn creates an opportunity for regulators to extend their *de jure* authority by exercising it through their *de facto* agents inside the firm. This result is inconsistent with fundamental rule of law values. No statute confers upon regulators the authority to pronounce law in this way. Yet regulators and enforcers have imposed an organizational structure upon firms that creates this authority for themselves.

This chapter analyzes agency and authority in the internal organization of compliance, ethics, and law departments. It describes how the allocation of authority to each of those roles has shifted in recent decades, due in large part to regulatory interventions. It also describes the effect of that shift. Far from the trivia of who reports to whom, the result is an organizational structure that facilitates governmental interventions in private firms and the taking of greater regulatory authority than has in fact been legally conferred upon regulators.

Compliance should be subordinated to legal rather than separated from it. Making compliance report to legal means putting the question of how after the question of whether or why. Furthermore, because the GC's authority flows from shareholders, not exogenous enforcement authorities, the GC is less likely than the CCO to confound the distinction between law – what the firm must do – and guidance – what regulators might prefer the firm to do. As long as this distinction is clear and clearly presented to agents capable of deciding what is best for the firm, larger rule of law concerns are mitigated. Nevertheless, in order for these authority and accountability structures to function as they should, the government, as the source of law, must limit itself to telling firms what they must do rather than also telling them how they must do it. Government, in other words, should make the rules and sanction firms for falling short. But it should not impose compliance structures on firms or deputize intra-firm agents to carry out its enforcement agenda.

From this introduction, this chapter proceeds as follows: In Section 46.2, it describes the rise of corporate ethics and documents how ethics functions have been effectively subsumed by compliance. In Section 46.3, it probes the origins of the modern compliance function, demonstrating the ways in which compliance has evolved in direct response to governmental interventions, typically through prosecutions or regulatory enforcement actions. In Section 46.4, it shows how the exogenous origins of compliance and continued governmental interventions into the structure of compliance corrupt intra-firm lines of accountability and transform compliance officers into quasi-governmental agents with incentives to align firm conduct with regulatory pronouncements. In Section 46.5, it demonstrates how this structure leads to regulatory rule-making that exceeds the limits of the law and brings the modern compliance function squarely into conflict with rule of law values. Finally, in Section 46.6, it attempts to show the way out, by subordinating compliance to legal and limiting government to making and enforcing the law, not to meddling with the internal organization of compliance.

46.2 COMPLIANCE SUBSUMES ETHICS

The idea of ethical business conduct is an old one, but corporate codes of ethics are more recent. Companies began adopting codes of ethics in the 1970s to commit themselves publicly to fair business practices and evolving norms against commercial bribery (de George 2015). These codes received a significant boost following the Enron and WorldCom scandals in 2001, after which the Sarbanes-Oxley Act required public companies to either adopt an ethics code or explain why they had not.[1] The New York Stock Exchange now also requires listed companies to adopt a code of ethics.[2] As a result, codes of ethics have become common among large corporations.

The results of research into the effect of ethics codes on corporate behavior, however, are not encouraging. Studies comparing firms that have adopted codes of ethics to firms that have not are mixed (Kaptein and Schwartz 2008). Some find that the adoption of a code of ethics has a significant positive effect; others find no significant effect; others find results somewhere in the middle. Other work challenges the methodology of these studies, which often rely on survey data, arguing that methodological weaknesses preclude serious reliance on their findings (Kraweic 2003). As a result, the effect of ethics codes on corporate conduct remains unclear.

Nevertheless, studies do find that when an ethical code is combined with additional monitoring or enforcement mechanisms, the effect on firm behavior is more pronounced (Nitsch et al. 2005; Rottig et al. 2001). The difference, it seems, is not the code itself but rather the systems the corporation has adopted for implementing it. This should come as no surprise. Codes are inert. They are brought to life only by mechanisms for implementing them. But the animating principle is what we have defined as compliance. Compliance is "the *processes* by which an organization seeks to ensure that employees and other constituents conform to applicable norms" (Miller 2014: 3).

Compliance has largely subsumed ethics. Many organizations combine ethics and compliance into a single department with a single head. Sometimes this person is given the title of Chief Ethics and Compliance Officer, but frequently it is just the CCO (PricewaterhouseCoopers 2014). On the one hand, this is natural. Once the conversation moves from principles to implementation, the subject has changed from ethics to compliance. And insofar as compliance

[1] Sarbanes-Oxley Act of 2002, 15 U.S.C. § 7264.

[2] New York Stock Exchange, "§ 303A.10 Code of Business Conduct and Ethics," *NYSE Listed Companies Manual* (last amended November 25, 2009), http://nysemanual.nyse.com/LCMTools/PlatformViewer.asp?selectednode=chp_1_1&manual=%2Flcm%2Fsections%2Flcm%2Dsections%2 F.

designs and implements policies and procedures, it is natural to allocate implementation of the corporate ethics code – a kind of policy – to compliance. So putting compliance together with ethics does not necessarily imply that compliance has swallowed ethics. It could be the other way around: perhaps ethics has swallowed or expanded into compliance.

The development of compliance, however, suggests that this is not the case. Instead, the explosive growth of compliance at American corporations, driven principally by prosecutions and regulatory interventions, has made ethics the junior partner in the relationship. This can be seen most clearly through a consideration of the origins of the compliance function, the subject of the next section.

46.3 THE EXOGENOUS ORIGINS OF COMPLIANCE

On June 7, 2018, the US Department of Commerce announced the terms of a settlement with the Chinese telecommunications firm ZTE, under which the firm agreed, in order to rectify past misconduct and ensure compliance going forward, to hire a team of "compliance coordinators selected by and answerable to [the Department of Commerce] for a period of 10 years" (Department of Commerce Press Release 2018). In other words, the settlement required the company to hire compliance officers to implement an enforcement agenda and, in doing so, report directly to the government. Although the example is a striking one – most compliance officers are not selected by or made to report directly to the government – something like it happens all the time.

The modern compliance function is a direct outgrowth of governmental interventions. Corporate compliance programs are expressly designed to meet governmental standards, and the authority of corporate compliance officers derives in large part from the government – as a kind of outsourced enforcement agent. As with ZTE's settlement with the Commerce Department, compliance reforms are often extracted as settlement conditions by the Justice Department. As a result, although ZTE presents an extreme case, it is a difference of degree, not kind. Compliance officers owe their positions and their authority to governmental interventions in the firm.

The government's first major foray into corporate compliance came during the drafting of the Organizational Sentencing Guidelines (Arlen 1994). In response to early drafts of the Guidelines that promised to vastly increase penalties for corporate criminal conduct, a number of leading corporations lobbied the Sentencing Commission to include compliance as a mitigating factor (Clark 1994). For example, the Martin Marietta Corporation implored the commission to "find a balance between imposing sentences on corporations for their wrongdoing and at the same time trying to incentivize corporations to develop meaningful compliance programs" (Clark 1994: section 2.7). Likewise, General Electric encouraged the Commission to adopt a system where there would be "no penalty fine for a corporation that has developed and implemented stringent policies and training, and yet has a low-level employee go astray" (Clark 1994: section 2.7). The Business Roundtable joined the lobbying effort, arguing that "compliance programs are the best way to encourage compliance with the law" and that corporate crime would best be reduced "by trying to encourage, enhance, build, expand not only the presence of compliance programs in corporations but also the effectiveness and vigor with which they are administered and enforced inside the corporation" (Clark 1994: section 2.7). The result was the inclusion of an "effective compliance program" as a factor mitigating the punishment of corporate crime.

Ultimately, the Guidelines articulated the features of an effective compliance program, including the now famous "seven factors."[3]

Of course, the Guidelines alone force compliance on no firm. They merely specify the sentences that judges may impose when corporations are convicted. Such convictions are rare (Henning 2007). But bargains are struck in the shadow of the law (Cooter et al. 1982). The real impact of the Guidelines and the compliance structures they encourage thus lies in the way they guide the parties toward settlement.

Compliance has become part of the settlement process in two ways. First, the existence and adequacy of a corporation's compliance program factor into the prosecutor's charging discretion according to a set of factors enshrined in the U.S. Attorney's Manual.[4] Second, prosecutors frequently make compliance enhancements a condition of settlement (Garrett 2014; Kaal and Lacine 2014). Compliance reforms extracted at settlement frequently focus on improvements to policies and procedures, training, and employee monitoring. These may include the adoption of a formal compliance charter or code, revisions to existing compliance policies, and improvements in communications or training. Settlements often call for the hiring of additional employees in compliance, and occasionally also provide for a new CCO or the establishment of a board-level committee or reporting structure. These are extensive internal reforms, far beyond simple commands to stop disobeying the law or fines for past violations (Barkow 2011). Moreover, the ability to extract these reforms enables regulators to "advance the agency's policy goals even if the original behavior was not clearly illegal – such as when a monitor believes a company's internal process for reviewing legal complaints is likely to miss future violations" (Van Loo 2019: 375).

Compliance reforms extracted by prosecutors and regulators have an impact not only on the counterparty to the settlement but often across an entire industry. In an accretive process not unlike the common law, the actions brought by prosecutors and the reforms agreed to in settlements have a precedential impact on similarly situated firms. However, unlike the common law, there is no adjudication and no meaningful judicial review. Companies and consulting firms track enforcement activity and heed the elements of compliance emphasized by enforcement authorities (PricewaterhouseCoopers 2014). Settlements thus have a strong signaling effect on the market as a whole as companies are pushed to adopt compliance functions similar to peer firms. Trade associations and industry-wide working groups, such as the Wolfsburg Group in the banking sector, can accelerate this process. The result is "compliance creep," a process by which compliance enhancements at one firm are soon mimicked across an entire industry.

In spite of recent efforts to subject compliance to empirical testing (Armour et al. in press (a); Armour et al. in press(b)), the effect of compliance enhancements on corporations remains unknown and largely untested (Griffith 2016). Still, one effect is clear. By creating strong incentives for firms to adopt compliance programs and taking the additional step of defining what specific features make a compliance program effective, government enforcement authorities have embedded within firms an agent to carry out their enforcement agenda. Corporate compliance departments owe their existence and their design in large part to an

3 The seven basic factors are: (1) rules, (2) high-level engagement and appropriate delegation, (3) diligence in hiring, (4) communication and training, (5) monitoring and testing, (6) alignment of incentives, and (7) appropriate remediation (Sentencing Guidelines, §8B2.1(b), www.ussc.gov/guidelines/2018-guidelines-manual/2018-chapter-8).

4 U.S. Department of Justice (DOJ), "Principles of Federal Prosecution of Business Organizations §9–28.700–900," U.S. Attorneys' Manual, www.justice.gov/jm/jm-9–28000-principles-federal-prosecution-business-organizations.

exogenous authority. This creates unique incentives for the agents operating within them, as described in the next section.

46.4 COMPLIANCE AGENTS

Given that compliance officers owe their professional existence, in large part, to the government, it is worth asking to whom these agents are accountable. The government? Or the firm? As we shall see, these questions cannot be answered unambiguously. As a result, it is perhaps most accurate to see compliance officers as accountable both to the firm and to the government. This dual accountability has predictable effects on the incentives of compliance officers, rendering them especially receptive to the policy agenda of prosecutors and regulators.

The compliance department, like any other corporate function, is administered by agents: the CCO and his or her staff. However, unlike other corporate officers who serve shareholder interests, compliance officers are not simply accountable to the interests of shareholders. As we have seen, prosecutors and regulatory authorities insist that compliance departments carry out a monitoring and enforcement agenda inside the firm. Failure to do so may lead to consequences not only from the firm but also from the government or regulator. In perhaps the most famous example, the Financial Crimes Enforcement Network (part of the Treasury Department) sought a $1 million penalty and a bar from future financial industry employment against a compliance officer for "failing to ensure that his company abided [by]" anti-money laundering law.[5] Likewise, FINRA fined and suspended a compliance officer at Brown Brothers Harriman & Co. for failing to detect and deter transactions potentially linked to money laundering.[6] Although personal liability remains rare, the replacement of compliance personnel in the wake of a governmental investigation is not.[7] Compliance officers are therefore likely to feel accountable to governmental regulators and enforcers as much as to the company employing them. As a result, they have their own incentives promptly to report any wrongdoing within the firm, lest they face personal penalties when it is later uncovered.

In this way, unlike other agents of the firm, compliance officers' first responsibility is not to maximize shareholder wealth but rather to maximize compliance. Doing so efficiently and effectively, of course, may have salutary effects on shareholder wealth. But at least so far as the government is concerned, compliance officers are there to ensure compliance full stop, without regard to efficiency. As a result, compliance officers maximize compliance first, shareholder wealth second, if at all.

Compliance officers also have their own incentives, including growth and advancement within their profession, to promote compliance beyond what shareholders might prefer. One

[5] FinCEN press release, "FinCEN Assesses $1 Million Penalty and Seeks to Bar Former MoneyGram Executive from Financial Industry," December 18, 2014, www.fincen.gov/sites/default/files/news_release/20141218.pdf.

[6] FINRA press release, "FINRA Fines Brown Brothers Harriman a Record $8 Million for Substantial Anti-money Laundering Compliance Failures," February 5, 2014, www.finra.org/newsroom/2014/finra-fines-brown-brothers-harriman-record-8-million-substantial-anti-money-laundering.

[7] See, e.g., DOJ press release, "BNP Paribas Agrees to Plead Guilty and to Pay $8.9 Billion for Illegally Processing Financial Transactions for Countries Subject to U.S. Economic Sanctions," June 30, 2014, www.justice.gov/opa/pr/bnp-paribas-agrees-plead-guilty-and-pay-89-billion-illegally-processing-financial (noting the replacement of employees in the compliance department); DOJ press release, "HSBC Holdings Plc. and HSBC Bank USA N. A. Admit to Anti-money Laundering and Sanctions Violations, Forfeit $1.256 Billion in Deferred Prosecution Agreement," December 11, 2012, www.justice.gov/opa/pr/hsbc-holdings-plc-and-hsbc-bank-usa-na-admit-anti-money-laundering-and-sanctions-violations (noting the clawback of compensation paid to compliance officers in the wake of corporate misconduct).

does not advance in any field by downplaying its importance. A better strategy would be to regularly promote the importance of the field, emphasize its complexity, and claim special knowledge of what works and what does not. Compliance officers do all of this.[8] Moreover, their dual accountability – to the government on the one hand, to the firm on the other – may assist them in this regard. Just as a servant of two masters is accountable to none, compliance agents can cite their government mandate when called to account by the firm and the interests of the firm when called to account by the government (Easterbrook and Fischel 1991).

One way that compliance officers have increased their own stature within the firm is by taking on the role of interpreting the rules with which the firm must comply. To use the dichotomy with which we began, compliance has taken on answering *what* as well as *how*. This authority is formalized in firms that separate compliance from legal, often at the behest of a regulator (DeStefano 2013). But even where compliance is not formally separated from legal, compliance may be able to expand its authority by interpreting regulatory guidance and embedding the interpretation as part of the firm's compliance program.

Consistent with this account, a recent study finds that compliance officers often fail to distinguish between regulatory guidance, which is formally nonbinding, and regulatory rules, which have the force of law (Parrillo 2019). Instead, compliance officers often follow guidance as though it were the law, using regulatory pronouncements as sources of authority to guide internal compliance policies and procedures. In doing so, however, they are complying not with law but with a regulator's view of what the law is or ought to be. For example, the bribery of foreign officials is made illegal by a statute, the Foreign Corrupt Practices Act (FCPA). That statute is enforced by the Department of Justice (DOJ) and the Securities and Exchange Commission (SEC) (the "enforcers"). That much is law. The enforcers have also promulgated guidance on how they intend to implement the law (FCPA Resource Guide 2012).[9] This guidance contains legal interpretations as well as specific recommendations, with examples, on how to design and conduct compliance programs consistent with the enforcers' objectives. The guidance is not law. In fact, it contains several highly contestable legal claims (Koehler 2012). Moreover, the enforcers often go further in making pronouncements, often in speeches, about specific features that may render a compliance program effective or ineffective (e.g., Caldwell 2014). Such pronouncements are another form of guidance, not law.

Whether a business organization ought to comply with guidance as well as law is a complex business decision. It requires distinguishing between the two, weighing the costs and benefits of the alternatives, factoring in probabilities, and determining whether the benefits exceed the costs. Compliance officers who view their role as maximizing compliance, not firm value, and who are at least partially accountable to an outside government enforcer may have a tendency to decide these issues in one way – that is, in favor of greater compliance. Indeed, compliance officers may simply incorporate guidance into compliance policies and training modules. This harms the firm insofar as the costs of complying with guidance exceed the benefits. But more important than the imposition of inefficiencies on the firm is that the

8 For example, compliance officers often write and speak to emphasize the complexities of compliance design and lessons learned from major enforcement actions. See, e.g., the FCPA Blog: News and Commentary about White-Collar Crime, Enforcement, and Compliance, www.fcpablog.com/ (featuring posts from compliance officers and experts in compliance).

9 See U.S. Department of Justice and Securities and Exchange Commission, 2012, "A Resource Guide to the U.S. Foreign Corrupt Practices Act," 57–62 (www.justice.gov/criminal-fraud/fcpa-resource-guide).

structure of compliance and the incentives of compliance officers create significant rule of law concerns, explored in the next section.

46.5 COMPLIANCE AND THE RULE OF LAW

The rule of law means that rulers must also follow rules. Under US law, the Administrative Procedure Act (APA) sets forth procedures that regulators must follow in passing rules affecting regulated entities. Among other things, the APA requires regulatory agencies to subject proposed rules to a set of constraints before they can be formally enacted. These include a cost–benefit analysis designed to ensure the efficacy of the rule as well as a period of notice and comment, designed to expose the proposed rule to the democratic process. Each of these is an important constraint on administrative rule-making, and rules have been overturned for failing under either or both requirements.[10] Guidance – regulatory pronouncements issued in the form of advisory manuals, policy statements, interpretative letters, FAQs, and so on – is formally exempted from these processes.

Rule of law concerns arise because guidance, although technically nonbinding, often has the same effect as administrative rule-making (Crews 2017).[11] This may be for several reasons, centrally including the development of compliance (Parrillo 2019). As discussed in Section 46.4, compliance officers not only treat guidance as binding, they owe their existence to and interpret their mandate as derived from the regulators themselves. The compliance department, in other words, operates as a conduit through which administrative agencies can influence firm conduct. The problem is that when agencies do so through guidance rather than through rule-making, they exceed the authority conferred upon them by statute.

The pronouncements of prosecutors and regulators, whether they interpret the law or suggest "effective" compliance structures, are checked neither by expert cost–benefit analysis nor by the democratic process of notice and comment. Instead, regulatory pronouncements are silently operationalized, through the intermediation of compliance, without public process or demonstration of efficacy. This is an enlargement of regulatory authority beyond the bounds of the law. Moreover, when the imposition comes from a prosecutor rather than a regulator, separation of powers concerns are raised as well. Prosecutors acting as rule-makers amounts to the executive usurpation of a legislative role. "The model of 'prosecutor-slash-regulator' is in tension with a government based on strict separation of powers" (Barkow 2011: 185).

This enlargement of regulatory and prosecutorial authority may not be wholly intentional. Regulatory and enforcement agents may not set out to enlarge their powers by acting strategically through the use of guidance (Parrillo 2019). But whether it is intentional or

[10] For decisions overturning rules for failure to conduct a persuasive cost–benefit analysis, see *Bus. Roundtable* v. *SEC*, 647 F.3d 1144, 1151 (D.C. Cir. 2011) (vacating the proxy access proposal on the basis of flawed cost—benefit analysis because the SEC "discounted the costs of [the proposed rule] – but not the benefits"); *Am. Equity Inv. Life Ins. Co.* v. *SEC*, 613 F.3d 166, 179 (D.C. Cir. 2010) (vacating the proposed rule for failure to conduct adequate cost–benefit analysis, specifically failure "to determine whether, under the existing regime, sufficient protections existed to enable investors to make informed investment decisions and sellers to make suitable recommendations to investors"); *Chamber of Commerce* v. *SEC*, 412 F.3d 133, 136 (D.C. Cir. 2005) (holding that the SEC violated the APA "by failing adequately to consider the costs mutual funds would incur in order to comply with the conditions"). For a canonical case overturning a rule for insufficient notice and comment, see *United States* v. *Nova Scotia Food Products Corp.*, 568 F.2d 240 (2d Cir. 1977).

[11] This concern forms the basis of two recent executive orders: Exec. Order, "Promoting the Rule of Law through Improved Agency Guidance Documents" (October 9, 2019); Exec. Order, "Promoting the Rule of Law through Transparency and Fairness in Civil Administrative Enforcement and Adjudication" (October 9, 2019).

not, the compliance conduit for regulatory rule-making is in tension with the rule of law and constitutional values.

46.6 A STRUCTURAL SOLUTION TO A STRUCTURAL PROBLEM

A simple way of ameliorating the situation would be to strip compliance departments of the authority to say *what* is lawful, leaving them with only the power to say *how* to comply. The best way of doing this would be to make compliance subservient to an organ of the firm that has both the informational resources to interpret the requirements of law and the incentive to do so from the perspective of the firm's shareholders, rather than an outside authority. The relevant organ of the firm, of course, is the legal department. The simplest way to address the problems raised so far is thus to make the CCO report to the GC.

Subordinating compliance to legal would make the officer charged with determining how to comply report separately to an officer charged with interpreting and applying the law. The GC has adequate training and information to understand the distinction between rules and guidance. Moreover, as a legal advisor, the GC is accustomed to complex risk–reward calculations. Most importantly, because his or her authority flows from shareholders, not prosecutors or other external enforcement agents, the GC is more likely to perform the cost–benefit calculation from the shareholders' perspective, ignoring guidance or seeking exemptive relief when compliance is not cost-justified to the firm.

This is not to suggest that GCs are perfect. Indeed, GCs may also use regulatory guidance as an interpretive tool. But because GC accountability is not ambiguous in the same way as CCO accountability, GCs have less incentive to overcomply or overrepresent the authority of guidance. The GC's role, as a legal advisor, is to counsel management on the risks associated with various alternatives, not to ensure a particular course for the organization.

Unfortunately, the recent momentum in compliance has been toward the separation of compliance from legal and the further insulation of compliance from other departments of the firm (DeStefano 2013). This is a regrettable development that should be reversed in order to prevent the compliance function from becoming a conduit through which the administrative state unaccountably enlarges its authority. In order to reverse this trend, however, the government must stop insisting upon the separation of compliance from legal. More broadly, the government should stop telling firms how to do compliance. The government should no longer seek to define "effective" compliance in the Sentencing Guidelines, the U.S. Attorneys' Manual, or various other guidance documents. And prosecutors and enforcement agents should stop seeking to extract compliance reforms in settlement.

Restricting the government's authority to say what effective compliance is and is not would eliminate much of its ability to operate beyond the confines of law. Without the threat that failure to implement a proposal will render a compliance program "ineffective," pronouncements made as guidance will lose much of their de facto mandatory nature. But government exit from compliance does not mean exit from enforcement. If the government got out of the business of corporate reform, it would still have the power to enforce the law to its fullest extent. It would still be able to impose massive penalties. And it would still have the power to settle and to give credit for cooperation. It simply could not insist upon compliance reforms. In sum, setting such limits does not mean allowing firms to break the law but rather ensuring that the government also follows it.

REFERENCES

Arlen, Jennifer. 1994. "The Potentially Perverse Effects of Corporate Criminal Liability." *Journal of Legal Studies* 23:839.

Armour, John, Brandon L. Garrett, Jeffrey N. Gordon, and Geeyoung Min. in press(a). "Board Compliance." *Minnesota Law Review*, ssrn.com/abstract=3205600.

Armour, John, Jeffrey N. Gordon, and Geeyoung Min. in press(b). "Taking Compliance Seriously." *Yale Journal on Regulation*, ssrn.com/abstract=3244167.

Barkow, Rachel E. 2011. "The Prosecutor as Regulatory Agency." In *Prosecutors in the Boardroom: Using Criminal Law to Regulate Corporate Conduct*, edited by Anthony S. Barkow and Rachel E. Barkow, 177. New York: NYU Press.

Caldwell, Leslie R. 2014. "Remarks," 22nd Annual Ethics and Compliance Conference. Atlanta, GA. October 1.

Clark, Nolan Ezra. 1994. "Corporate Sentencing Guidelines: Drafting History." In *Compliance Programs and the Corporate Sentencing Guidelines: Preventing Criminal and Civil Liability*, edited by Jeffrey M. Kaplan, § 2.16. Deerfield, IL: Clark Boardman Callaghan.

Cooter, Robert, Stephen Marks, and Robert Mnookin. 1982. "Bargaining in the Shadow of the Law: A Testable Model of Strategic Behavior." *Journal of Legal Studies* 11:225.

Crews, Clyde Wayne, Jr. 2017. "Mapping Washington's Lawlessness: An Inventory of 'Regulatory Dark Matter' 2017 Edition." *Competitive Enterprise Institute*. https://cei.org/sites/default/files/Wayne%20Crews%20-%20Mapping%20Washington%27s%20Lawlessness%202017.pdf.

De George, Richard T. 2015. "A History of Business Ethics." *Markkula Center for Applied Ethics*. www.scu.edu/ethics/focus-areas/business-ethics/resources/a-history-of-business-ethics/.

Department of Commerce. 2018. Press release: "Secretary Ross Announces $1.4 Billion ZTE Settlement; ZTE Board, Management Changes and Strictest BIS Compliance Requirements Ever." June 7. Office of Public Affairs (202) 482–4883.

DeStefano, Michele. 2013. "Creating a Culture of Compliance: Why Departmentalization May Not Be the Answer." *Hastings Business Law Journal* 10:71.

Easterbrook, Frank H., and Daniel R. Fischel. 1991. *The Economic Structure of Corporate Law*. Cambridge, MA: Harvard University Press.

Garrett, Brandon. 2014. *Too Big to Jail: How Prosecutors Compromise with Corporations*. Cambridge, MA: Belknap Press.

Griffith, Sean J. 2016. "Corporate Governance in an Era of Compliance." *William and Mary Law Review* 57:2075.

Henning, Peter J. 2007. "The Organizational Guidelines: R.I.P.?" *Yale Law Journal Pocket Part* 116:312. www.yalelawjournal.org/forum/the-organizational-guidelines-rip.

Kaal, Wulf A., and Timothy Lacine. 2014. "The Effect of Deferred and Non-prosecution Agreements on Corporate Governance: Evidence from 1993–2013." *Business Lawyer* 70:61.

Kaptein, Muel, and Mark S. Schwartz. 2008. "The Effectiveness of Business Codes: A Critical Examination of Existing Studies and the Development of an Integrated Research Model." *Journal of Business Ethics* 77:113–17.

Koehler, Mike. 2012. "Grading the Foreign Corrupt Practices Act Guidance." *Bloomberg BNA: White Collar Crime Report* 07 WCR 961:4–6.

Kraweic, Kimberly D. 2003. "Cosmetic Compliance and the Failure of Negotiated Governance." *Washington University Law Quarterly* 81:511 (leveling this criticism).

Miller, Geoffrey P. 2014. *The Law of Governance, Risk Management, and Compliance*. New York: Wolters Kluwer.

Nitsch, Detlev, Mark Baetz, and Christensen Hughes. 2005. "Why Code of Conduct Violations Go Unreported: A Conceptual Framework to Guide Intervention and Future Research." *Journal of Business Ethics* 57:327.

Parrillo, Nicholas R. 2019. "Federal Agency Guidance and the Power to Bind: An Empirical Study of Agencies and Industries." *Yale Journal on Regulation* 36:165.

PricewaterhouseCoopers. 2014. "What It Means to Be a 'Chief' Compliance Officer: Today's Challenges, Tomorrow's Opportunities." *State of Compliance 2014 Survey*:17–18. www.pwc.com/

us/en/risk-management/state-of-compliance-survey/assets/pwc-state-of-compliance-2014-survey.pdf [http://perma.cc/A9QU-BLTK].

Rottig, Daniel, Xenophon Koufteros, and Elizabeth Umphress. 2001. "Formal Infrastructure and Ethical Decision Making: An Empirical Investigation and Implications for Supply Management." *Decision Sciences* 42:163.

Van Loo, Rory. 2019. "Regulatory Monitors: Policing Firms in the Compliance Era." *Columbia Law Review* 119:369.

47

Life-Course Criminology and Corporate Offending

Arjan Blokland, Marieke Kluin and Wim Huisman

Abstract: Developmental and life-course criminology has evolved into a key perspective from which to understand individual offending. In this chapter we explore the benefits and pitfalls of applying a life-course perspective to corporate crime. We do so by systematically reviewing the cornerstones of current developmental and life-course criminology, consecutively addressing the criminal career paradigm, developmental criminology, life-course sociology and life history narratives. For each of these subfields of research we address both core theoretical assumptions and empirical findings, and explore how these would apply to corporate offending.

47.1 INTRODUCTION

After taking the criminological field by storm in the early 1990s, developmental and life-course criminology has stuck as one of the discipline's main explanatory frameworks (Blokland and Van der Geest, 2017; Farrington, Kazemian and Piquero, 2018; Gibson and Krohn, 2012). Taking a longitudinal perspective on criminal behavior, its causes and its consequences, developmental and life-course criminology has inspired a vast amount of theoretical and empirical work. Though at first gravitated toward the behavior of disadvantaged, urban young men, over the years life-course research has come to include both youths and adults (Sampson and Laub, 1993; Blokland, Nagin and Nieuwbeerta, 2005), men and women (Block et al., 2010; Loeber et al., 2017), and is beginning to be applied not only to street crime but to other types of crime (Blokland and Lussier, 2015; Campedelli et al., 2019; Van Koppen, De Poot and Blokland, 2010), including white-collar crime (Benson and Kerley, 2001; Morris and El Sayed, 2013; Piquero and Benson, 2004; Piquero and Weisburd, 2009; Van Onna et al., 2014; Van der Geest, Weisburd and Blokland, 2017; Weisburd and Waring, 2001). With white-collar crime, life-course criminology has entered the realm of corporate compliance.

The three cornerstones of developmental and life-course criminology are the criminal career paradigm, developmental criminology, and life-course sociology (Farrington, 2003), with ethnographic research constituting a possible fourth (Blokland and Nieuwbeerta, 2010a). Though different in their origins and specific focus, what links these fields of research is their focus on individual development over time. The criminal career paradigm provides researchers with the conceptual tools to meticulously describe the patterning of criminal behavior over the individual's life span, without committing itself to any particular theoretical explanation (Blumstein and Cohen, 1987). Developmental criminology focuses on the different developmental stages that individuals go through as they age, each with their own developmental challenges and milestones (LeBlanc and Loeber, 1998). Life-course sociology, on the other hand, seeks to understand how the social context, on both the micro and the macro level, influences the course of individuals' developmental pathways from birth to old age (Elder, 1995). Finally, narrative accounts focus on the lived experience of individuals as they grow and develop over time (Bertaux, 1981).

Here we seek to explore whether the developmental and life-course perspective has any merit in understanding law-breaking by corporations. Corporate law-breaking has been labeled in criminology as corporate crime, which we, following Clinard and Yeager (1980: 16), broadly define as "[a]ny act committed by corporations that is punished by the state, regardless of whether it is punished under administrative, civil, or criminal law." In the context of this handbook, corporate crime is a form of *non*compliance. It hardly needs a spoiler alert to note that we come to answer the question of developmental and life-course criminology's merit for understanding corporate crime and noncompliance affirmatively, both in terms of theory and in terms of empirical research. As not all students of corporate crime may be familiar with the life-course framework, rather than providing a comprehensive overview of corporate crime research through a life-course lens, here we concisely introduce the main themes of the developmental and life-course perspective, and illustrate how these could be applied to the study of corporate crime. Doing so, we explore the theoretical ramifications explicit or implicit to taking a life-course perspective, as well as its implications for designing future corporate crime research.

Applying a theoretical framework designed to explain the criminal development of individuals to that of corporations requires us to conceptualize the corporation as a demarcated entity with some level of durability.[1] In our daily speech we seem to have no problem accrediting corporations with individual-like properties. Corporations, for example, are said to have distinct identities, goals and reputations. Organizational sciences also view corporations as independent actors capable of goal-directed behavior (Morgan, 2006). Management and business theorists even speak of the corporate life cycle that is claimed to feature discernible life stages (Phelps, Adams and Bessant, 2007). In legal practice, in various jurisdictions, corporations are considered legal personalities, and are held liable for their actions in much the same way as are natural persons (Wells, 2001). Without losing sight of its limits, and cognizant of the philosophical complexities in defining what exactly constitutes a "corporation," here we take the functional corporation-individual analogy as a starting point and assume that corporations, like natural persons, can and do commit crimes (Sutherland, 1983; Clinard and Yeager, 1980; but see Cressey, 1989). We do so not because we argue that viewing corporations as individuals fully encompasses the essence of what a corporation is but rather because it opens new avenues of thought and research into which, when, how and why corporations transgress rules (Braithwaite and Fisse, 1990).

Another caveat best stated up front is that by applying the parlance of developmental and life-course criminology, we are not implying that all that is considered corporate crime is committed intentionally. In mainstream criminology, offenders may have different motivations for committing crimes, but intentionality of the behavior in question is usually implicitly or explicitly assumed. All citizens are expected to know the law and behave themselves accordingly. In the corporate crime literature, however, motivations to offend are considered different from the capacities to comply. A corporation might be willing to

[1] While this chapter was written with profit-driven corporations in mind, "corporate crime" could also be read to include noncompliance by other types of formal organization, e.g. governmental bodies or NGOs (Holtfreter, 2005).

comply but may not be aware of the applicable laws and obligations, or be aware of the rules but lack either the knowledge or the resources to comply (Huisman, 2016). Of course, the question then becomes to what extent the corporation has a responsibility to know or to have the means to adequately respond available. At this point, however, we happily leave this discussion on the table, and conclude that developmental and life-course models equally apply to both crimes of ill will and crimes of incompetence. This is relevant, because much corporate law-breaking takes the form of crimes of omission – not complying with legally prescribed action – contrary to most individual law-breaking being crimes of commission – legally prohibited action (Gross, 1978). Transitioning from one developmental stage to the next may affect corporations' motivations to offend, as well as their awareness and adaptability to relevant regulations. Changes in the corporations' micro- or macro-level environment may have similar effects (Vaughan, 2007). Corporate crime and corporate offending as used here thus refer solely to the nature of the behavior (Clinard and Yeager, 1980), not the motivations for that behavior.

The remainder of this chapter describes in more detail what are the cornerstones of developmental and life-course criminology, and explicates how these would translate to the study of corporate crime.

47.2 THE CRIMINAL CAREER PARADIGM

The criminal career paradigm defines the criminal career simply as the longitudinal sequence of crimes committed by an individual offender (Blumstein et al., 1986). Having a criminal career thus does not imply that the individual is earning a livelihood from committing crime, or is otherwise to be considered a professional criminal, for example by the term implying a certain level of criminal sophistication. In fact, everyone that commits a crime once is argued to have a criminal career, be it one of minimum volume and duration.

The criminal career paradigm distinguishes several different dimensions in which criminal careers can differ between individuals and within individuals over time (Piquero, Farrington and Blumstein, 2003). Participation distinguishes those that at one point engage in crime from those who do not, or offenders from abstainers. Frequency refers to the number of crimes per some unit of time. Duration is defined as the time between the first offense – also referred to as onset – and the last offense – also referred to as termination. Finally, crimes committed may vary in nature – crime mix – or seriousness. During the course of an individual's criminal career, offending frequency may go up or down, that is, accelerate or decelerate, become more or less diverse, that is, diversify or specialize, or become more or less serious, that is, aggravate or de-aggravate (LeBlanc and Loeber, 1998; Loeber and Leblanc, 1990).

Criminal career research has yielded important insights into the ways in which offending develops over the individual's life span. For instance, while participation in crime is rather common, the frequency distribution of offending is often found to be very skewed, with a minority of offenders responsible for a disproportionate share of all offenses (Martinez et al., 2017). On the aggregate level, both participation and frequency of offending steeply rise to a peak during adolescence, followed by a more general decline, yet on the individual level, offending patterns are much more diverse (Britt, 2019). For most offenders, criminal careers are of rather short duration (Francis, Soothill and Piquero, 2007). Finally, offending is usually found to be highly diverse – with offenders committing many different types of crime – though there are signs of specialization as offenders get older (Nieuwbeerta et al., 2011).

The criminal career paradigm is atheoretical in the sense that it is not committed to certain theories or lines of theoretical reasoning. It has, however, made researchers conscious of the fact that different career dimensions may be influenced by different causal processes (Blumstein and Cohen, 1987; Paternoster and Triplett, 1988). More specifically, asymmetrical causation refers to the fact that the factors that cause offenders to start, accelerate, diversify or aggravate their criminal career are likely to differ from those that make offenders stop, decelerate, specialize or de-aggravate their offending behavior (Paternoster, 1989). Distinguishing different career dimensions and exploring their possible causes requires longitudinal research following the same individual over time (Blumstein, Cohen and Farrington, 1988).

Developmental and life-course criminological theories designed to explain the findings from criminal career research include Moffitt's (1993) theory of life-course persistent offending, in which she argues that, unlike adolescence-limited offenders whose offending is temporal, less serious and argued to be contextually induced, persistent offenders showing criminal careers of high frequency, long duration and serious offending suffer from individual characteristics that continuously elevate their risk of offending regardless of changes in their environment. Gottfredson and Hirschi's (1990) general theory of crime similarly ascribes the diversity of offending to a set of underlying individual characteristics – which they refer to as low self-control – that makes individuals seek immediate gratification in an ill-thought-out manner, whether it be stealing or embezzling something of want, or physically attacking a perceived opponent. This is in sharp contrast to, for instance, Sutherland's (1947) theory of differential association, which assumes that the likelihood of different types of offending is conditional on the definitions of those behaviors that one is confronted with. These theories in turn have instigated methodological innovation as life-course researchers sought ways to operationalize career concepts, like the forward specialization coefficient (Stander et al., 1989) and the diversity index (Paternoster et al., 1998; Piquero et al., 1999), to contrast opposing theories. Perhaps most strongly linked to developmental and life-course criminology is Nagin's group-based trajectory model, which allows researchers to identify and describe groups of individuals following similar developmental pathways (Nagin, 1999, 2005).

The scant longitudinal research into corporate offending finds that participation in rule violation is widespread. In his seminal book *White-Collar Crime* (1949, 1983), Edwin Sutherland examined the records of the seventy largest nonfinancial US corporations at the time. He took into account all decisions of administrative commissions, stipulations, settlements, violations of food law, and opinions of the court that the defendant had violated the law (even though the court at a later stage dismissed the law suit) over a period of up to forty-five years. Sutherland found that all of these seventy corporations had violated the rules at least once during this time. In total, they had 980 decisions recorded against them, averaging a total of 14 violations each. Furthermore, his research showed that nearly all (97.1 percent) of the corporations were repeat offenders. A more recent study by Alalehto (2010) examining criminal, civil and administrative law violations among the seventy highest-ranking corporations in Swedish business over a ten-year period found that 85 percent of these corporations violated the legal rules at least once. Like in mainstream criminological research, the offense distribution found in corporate crime research is often skewed. In their study of 582 large US corporations, Clinard and Yeager (1980: 116) found that 13 percent of the firms accounted for 52 percent of the violations over a two-year period. In the aforementioned Swedish study, 7 percent of the Swedish corporations committed over thirty violations each and were responsible for a disproportionate share of all registered offending during the ten-year follow-up of the study

(Alalehto, 2010). In the largest longitudinal study on corporate crime to date, Kedia, Luo and Rajgopal (2017) collected data of enforcement actions by US federal government agencies from 1994 to 2011 on firms' violations against rules and laws on product-, market-, labor- and environment-related issues. Over 36 percent of these corporations were found to have broken the rules at least once. These researchers identified a group that they labeled "notoriously rule-breaking corporations," which they defined as each having committed at least one violation in eight of the ten years under scrutiny.

Theoretically interpreting these findings is a challenge. For one, whereas criminal career studies strive to cover at least the period of onset, for example by starting to observe individuals from the minimum age of criminal responsibility onward, longitudinal studies on corporate crime usually cover a more or less random period in the corporations' existence. This makes it impossible to reflect on career dimensions like onset, termination and duration. Another complicating factor is that, unlike in studies on individual criminal careers that order observations based on biological age, research into corporate criminal careers largely lacks such an intuitive timescale due to the much larger variation in corporate compared to individual life spans; some corporations have been around for centuries. Furthermore, the finding that corporate crime, like individual offending, is both varied and heavily skewed seems to point at the influence of some set of relatively stable corporate characteristics that for some (notoriously rule-breaking) corporations constantly elevate the offending risk. Common life-course criminological theories typically frame the stable risk factors underlying persistent offending as some psychological or personality characteristic (Lynam, 1996; Moffitt, 2015; Vaughn and Howard, 2005), while empirically it seems to be the number of risk factors to which youths are exposed that counts (Jolliffe et al., 2017). Much corporate crime research has been aimed at identifying such criminogenic dispositions for corporations, distinguishing structural, cultural and procedural characteristics that increase the odds of corporate offending (Gross, 1978; Shover and Hochstetler, 2006). Yet, what would be the functional corporate equivalent of something like impulsivity, low self-control or psychopathy, or whether risk factors for persistent corporate crime show a similar additive effect, is still far from clear.

A first important contribution of the criminal career paradigm to the study of corporate crime lies in the fine-grained distinction of different criminal career dimensions. This allows differentiation between corporations going far beyond the presently common dichotomy of compliant versus noncompliant (Jennings and Reingle, 2012). It also allows discerning of important changes within a single corporation in the level, diversity and seriousness of rule violations over time, painting a more complete picture of corporate crime development. Innovative life-course methodologies, like group-based trajectory modeling (Nagin, 2005), could be applied to corporate crime data to replace present ad hoc definitions of notoriousness. Furthermore, such fine-grained descriptions of corporate criminal development will provide the theoretical impetus for designing new and better explanations of corporate offending: theories that, for instance, encompass the notion of asymmetrical causation (Uggen and Piliavin, 1998). In terms of study design, adopting the criminal career paradigm would urge corporate crime researchers to try to create corporate equivalents of birth cohorts, which would allow tracking of corporate crime from onset till termination (Farrington, 2013), and which would provide a more intuitive timescale within which to interpret the results found.

47.3 DEVELOPMENTAL CRIMINOLOGY

Developmental psychology is the branch of psychology that is concerned with how individuals grow and change as they progress from childhood to adolescence into adult life. Developmental psychologists are interested in how individuals' physical, intellectual and emotional growth influences their thinking, feeling and behavior. Specifically applied to crime, developmental criminologists seek to understand how these life-span changes affect individuals' delinquency and crime.

Many influential developmental scientists have divided the human life span into a sequence of life stages (Erikson, 1950; Havighurst, 1948; Levinson, 1978). These stages arguably represent the different phases that all individuals go through in a normal life cycle. Each stage is characterized by a different set of developmental challenges, like reaching physical maturity, realizing the full potential of one's intellectual abilities, or becoming emotionally independent from one's primary caregivers. In general, not meeting the developmental challenges of one particular stage will echo through to the subsequent life stage and have a detrimental impact on the individual's overall developmental trajectory.

Developmental criminology has come up with different models explaining delinquent and criminal development in young people. Loeber et al. (1993), for instance, distinguish between the authority conflict pathway, the covert pathway and the overt pathway, each characterized by a certain order of events. This model is a typical escalation model in which less serious offenses precede more serious ones. For example, for the authority conflict pathway, stubborn behavior during childhood is argued to precede defiance and disobedience in the second stage, while leading to authority avoidance, like truancy and running away, in the third stage. Both the covert and the overt pathways, differing primarily in the use of violence, show similar escalations from innocuous to very serious nonviolent and violent behaviors, respectively (Loeber and Burke, 2011). Taking a different angle, Moffitt's (1993, 1997) theory of adolescence-limited offending ascribes the common onset of delinquency and crime during late adolescence to the typical challenges that young people face during this life stage. While physically fully mature, adolescents are not yet treated as adults by modern-day society, which bestows them with different kinds of obligation and limitation, like compulsory education and a legal minimum age for driving an automobile, buying tobacco products and consuming alcoholic beverages. This discrepancy between their physical and their social status leads adolescents to seek alternative ways to gain their desired adult status, including delinquency and crime (Piquero et al., 2013). Importantly, once, with increasing age, conventional adult opportunities do become available, offenders of the adolescence-limited type do not need any outside encouragement to grasp these opportunities, plus they have the skills to make these opportunities work (Moffitt, 1997).

Organizational life-cycle models have been around since the 1950s. Like developmental psychology, corporate life-cycle theory proposes that corporations tend to follow a predictable developmental pattern which is characterized by different phases of development which cannot easily be reversed (Quinn and Cameron, 1983). Though the stages of the corporate life cycle are less agreed on than the stages in the individual life cycle, most models distinguish between a "birth" stage, in which corporations are characterized by simple and informal structures and are dominated by their owners; a second or "growth" stage, in which the corporation increases in scale, procedures become formalized and middle management is introduced; and a "maturity" stage, during which bureaucracy reaches its peak. Once maturity is attained, corporate life-courses may diverge. Some corporations move into a "revival" stage, which is characterized by product diversification and the corporation venturing into different markets, adopting a more divisionalized structure along the way. Others may enter a stage of "decline" in which shrinking markets stagnate corporate growth. If decline is not countered by revival, this stage may prelude the "death" of the corporation (Miller and Friesen, 1984).

Like developmental stages in the individual's life span, the different stages of the corporate life cycle are characterized by particular challenges and risks, such as trial and error learning and the need for entrepreneurial risk taking during early stages, and consolidation and structuring business processes during the maturity stage (Phelps, Adams and Bessant, 2007). Overcoming these challenges and mitigating these risks are seen as conditional for a corporation developing into the next life phase. While recognized as a potentially fruitful avenue for future research (Simpson, 2019), these stages have yet to be convincingly linked to levels of noncompliance. On the one hand, small and growing firms may fail to reserve sufficient budget to ensure compliance, for example by investing in education and training of their personnel or by hiring designated compliance officers. On the other hand, despite available resources, the business processes of larger corporations might be more multifaceted and difficult to oversee, while their complex managerial structures may lead to internal competition and diffusion of responsibility, thus enhancing both motivation and opportunity for regulatory transgressions (Tombs, 1995). Finally, corporate life stage, and the size and legal structures that go with it, may also determine the way the corporation is regulated (Hanlon and Heitzman, 2010). Various studies have found a positive correlation between corporation size and the level of corporate crime (Dalton and Kesner, 1988; Simpson, 1986; Tillman and Pontell, 1995), leading Simpson and Rorie (2011) to conclude that this positive association is one of the most consistent findings in the corporate crime literature. Yet others have found rather the opposite (Borck and Coglianese, 2011).

Much of developmental criminology leads us to expect that, if not adequately addressed, problematic behavior tends to escalate from bad to worse. Developmental criminologists therefore conclude that it is "never too early" to intervene, even if this means that intervention precedes the actual behavior of interest (Farrington and Welsh, 2007). With regard to corporate crime, prevention might also be better than cure, and regulatory agencies would benefit from empirical studies identifying the major risk factors for participation and escalation in corporate crime. Developmental stage models offer ground for even more specified hypotheses, linking the types of crime committed to the goals, challenges and opportunities that characterize a certain life stage. Like escalation theories, though, stage models also assume behavior to worsen with each subsequent stage when stage-typical challenges are not sufficiently met in legal ways. In terms of methods, developmental criminology challenges researchers of corporate crime to reach consensus on the different stages in the corporate life cycle and on how these stages can be satisfactorily operationalized (Lichtenstein and Lyons, 2008), so that they can be linked to the frequency, nature and seriousness of corporate offending.

47.4 LIFE-COURSE SOCIOLOGY

Whereas the emphasis in developmental criminology is on the onset and subsequent development of individuals' criminal careers during childhood and adolescence, life-course sociology tends to consider adult outcomes. In life-course criminology, this translates into a focus on the processes underlying desistance and persistence in crime – the right-hand side of the age crime curve (Laub and Sampson, 2001). Another important distinction between developmental criminology and life-course criminology is that the former tends to focus on the "typical" developmental pathway, whereas life-course criminology is primarily interested in variation in individuals' lives, along with variation by generation and historical context (Blokland and Nieuwbeerta, 2010a; Sampson and Laub, 2004).

Life-course studies share four paradigmatic factors (Elder, 1998; Elder and Giele, 2009). The first is a focus on the timing of events and transitions in the individual's life. What the consequences are of a certain event or transition is deemed to depend on whether these events and transitions occur relatively early or late compared to other people or normative expectations, both in terms of calendar age as well as in terms of the sequencing of events. A closely tied second emphasis is that on geographical and historical context (Elder, 1995). The timing of lives, and hence what is considered "too early" or "too late" is governed by normative expectations which differ between communities and across historical time (Neugarten, 1979). Regardless of their societal evaluation, observed transitions may also signal different processes and consequences depending on the constellation of macro-level contextual factors. Third, the life-course paradigm stresses the notion of linked lives (Bengston, Elder and Putney, 2005). Just as lives do not evolve in the abstract, they do not do so in isolation. Individuals' lives are linked to those of many others in complicated chains of interdependence. Finally, it is recognized that, despite the constraints resulting from the timing of events, contextual factors and the ties to others, individuals can and do make deliberate choices that steer their life trajectory in divergent directions (Hitlin and Elder, 2007). This capacity of agency and personal control makes for a situation in which individuals' lives are not fully determined by their surroundings.

The life-course paradigm was convincingly introduced to the criminological literature by Sampson and Laub's (1993; Laub and Sampson, 2003) seminal studies on the lives of 500 formerly institutionalized youths, which they followed up to old age. These researchers were able to show that, even after controlling for preexisting individual differences, life-course events and transitions, like employment stability and marriage, had an impact on individuals' criminal development. These findings were first interpreted as evidencing the social control originating from investments in conventional institutions (Sampson and Laub, 1993), though later insights from other theoretical families, like routine activities and learning theories, were incorporated (Laub and Sampson, 2003). In the wake of these studies, a tidal wave of empirical research examining the effects of these and other transitions followed, all but flooding the criminological landscape (for reviews, see Craig, Diamond and Piquero, 2014; Laub, Rowan and Sampson, 2018, Nguyen and Loughran, 2018; Rocque, 2017, Siennick and Osgood, 2008; Uggen and Wakefield, 2008).

Adopting a life-course perspective also led criminologists to view crime itself as a potentially important event in individuals' lives (Hagan and Palloni, 1988). Building on insights from interactionist sociological theory, Sampson and Laub (1997) argued that being arrested, convicted or sentenced could set in motion a downward spiral in which offenders increasingly find conventional opportunities blocked as a result of them having been labeled "criminal" in the past. Rather than promoting desistance, this process of cumulative disadvantage following state intervention would perpetuate offending. Likewise, Moffitt (1997) stated that adolescence-limited-type offenders could become "ensnared" by the collateral effects of their rule-breaking behavior, prolonging the frequency and duration of their criminal career. Research suggests that crime, or the formal reactions to it, indeed influences development in other life-course trajectories (Kirk and Sampson, 2013; Verbruggen, 2016). Additionally, empirical studies contrasting the enduring effects of stable risk factors with those of dynamic, state-dependent processes have found evidence of both processes influencing criminal continuity (for a review, see Blokland and Nieuwbeerta, 2010b).

More recently, life-course criminological research has begun addressing other aspects of the life-course paradigm, including the differential effects of transitions by timing and historical context (Bersani, Laub and Nieuwbeerta, 2009; Martin et al., 2014). The life-course theme of linked lives echoes most audibly in research on the effects of partnering a criminal spouse and in studies on the intergenerational transmission of delinquency and crime (Eichelsheim and Van de Weijer, 2018; Van Schellen, Apel and Nieuwbeerta, 2012). Finally, a considerable qualitative literature now addresses the role of human agency in the desistance process, arguing that individuals may consciously choose between a range of possible future selves, both desired and feared, adapting their behavior accordingly (Giordano, Cernkovic and Rudolph, 2002; Paternoster and Bushway, 2009).

Rather than social control, transitions in the corporate life have been attributed to changes in business performance and patterns of profitability (such as asset turnover and profit margin) (Dickinson, 2011). Profitability, or rather lack thereof, is generally seen as a motivator for corporate offending (Shover and Hochstetler, 2006). Many empirical studies into the drivers of corporate crime have therefore taken criminological strain theory as a vantage point (Wang and Holtfreter, 2012). In strain theory, blockage of goals is thought to increase the risk of "innovation," where groups are trying to achieve the same goals but with illegitimate means. As one of the main goals of corporations is to make money, and as compliance generally is costly by itself, the actual or perceived inability to reach current or future financial goals as an explanation for regulatory transgressions has a clear intuitive ring to it. Empirically, however, the emerging picture is much murkier and the link between financial stress and corporate offending far from robust. In one of the few long-term longitudinal studies on corporate crime, for instance, Simpson (1986) finds that in the fifty-two American corporations in continuous business between 1927 and 1984, a general decline in the business cycle, rather than corporate profit, seems to affect antitrust offending, and that this applies to some types of antitrust crime but not others.

Another line of corporate crime research has considered the effects of managerial turnover. The "tone at the top" is deemed important when it comes to corporate compliance, as lower-level employees are expected to adopt the definitions and behaviors of top-level managers. A change in the corporation's CEOs, much like an individual's change to or from a criminal romantic partner, may thus create a micro-environment that is either more or less conducive to misbehavior. Management turnover is indeed found to be associated with lower levels of corporate offending, arguably because employees need some time to assure themselves of the extent to which their new CEO is committed to regulatory compliance (Simpson and Koper, 1997). Besides managerial turnover, gender diversity of board composition is associated with corporate compliance. Recent studies show a negative correlation between corporate offending and gender diversity in the board (Cumming, Leung and Rui, 2015; Wahid, 2019). Arguably the most important takeaway from life-course criminology is its focus on the variability of life-course trajectories and the ways in which these variabilities are linked to changes in the contexts in which these trajectories are played out. The major challenge offered by the life-course approach to the study of corporate crime is to identify contextual factors at different levels of aggregation that will help explain corporations' divergent rule-violating pathways and provide the theoretical underpinnings that would clarify why this would be the case. Framing formal reactions to noncompliance as a special type of life-course event also brings in the study of the effects of regulatory enforcement on the future development of compliance as central to a life-course approach to corporate crime. While corporations may not be labelled for their noncompliance to the same extent that individual offenders are (Brown, 2001), past rule-breaking could affect the ways in which market actors and regulatory agencies will subsequently approach a corporation (Macher, Mayo and Nickerson, 2011; Weil and Pyles, 2005). Looking at longitudinal variations in the likelihood of regulatory violations using data on occupational safety and health act transgressions of fifty-five US companies, Simpson and Schell (2009) found that once corporate differences were taken into account, corporations with prior violations actually had lower violation rates in subsequent years, suggesting an effect of regulatory enforcement on corporate criminal career development.

In terms of methodology, vivid past and current debates in extant life-course research remind us of the need for rich and longitudinal data on a broad range of corporate and contextual variables, so that research may differentiate mere correlation from actual causation. Despite researchers of corporate crime facing the same hurdles as those of individual offenders and then some, data on corporate transgressions may also have benefits that are unique to corporate crime data. Most importantly, while, in criminal career research, police attention for various types of crime is implicitly assumed to be indiscriminate, regulatory enforcement data may allow corporate crime researchers not only to track corporate violations but also to include the specific labors of regulatory agencies, in terms of the frequency, intensity and specific topics of their inspection efforts, in the equation. Research into the discretionary authority of regulatory agencies – and how this is subject to political influence – suggests that this is not an unnecessary luxury (Etienne, 2015; Schinkel, Toth and Tuinstra, 2020).

47.5 LIFE HISTORY NARRATIVES

Developmental and life-course criminology has adopted increasingly sophisticated statistical methods to allow for making stronger causal inferences. In the midst of this methodological nitpicking, some have warned that quantitative methods, regardless of their level of sophistication, will always provide a fragmented image of the developmental processes of interest. Following in the footsteps of their famous Chicago school predecessors, by focusing on a single life course these scholars present an insider's view of criminal development as experienced and narrated by those who actually went through it, or, in some cases, are still very much going through it (Goodman, Steffensmeier and Ulmer, 2005; Shover, 1996). The life stories of these former and current criminals add necessary detail to the complex processes that bring about persistence and desistance in offending. Especially the many qualitative studies on desistance from offending highlight the importance of internal processes of self-evaluation and reflection, as well as structural elements like the real or symbolic opportunity structure provided by individuals in the offender's micro-space (Veysey, Martinez and Christian, 2013). Giordano and colleagues, for example, speak of structural opportunities as "hooks for change" that may be used to scaffold the individual's agency toward a desired self (Giordano, Cernkovic and Rudolph, 2002). Likewise, Paternoster and Bushway (2009) suggest that negative events in the individual's life course may serve as vivid prompts of a future feared self, causing individuals to make conscious decisions that serve to avoid such an outcome. As such, these life history narratives provide valuable insight into the elements key to the life-course approach – geographical and historical context, social relationships, human agency, and adaptation to life events and transitions – and their often complex interdependencies in shaping individual criminal careers.

Most extant research into corporate crime consists of qualitative case studies (Dabney, 2016; Verhage, 2011). Recent examples include the Volkswagen scandal (van Rooij and Fine, 2018; Spapens, 2018), the corruption of Siemens (Klinkhammer, 2015) or the Trafigura case (van Wingerde, 2015). Importantly, not all available case studies into corporate crime were conducted by academics; there have also been studies by investigative journalists and nongovernmental organizations (NGOs), including that of Enron (McLean and Elkind, 2003), Greenpeace's (2018) report on twenty case studies of corporate wrongdoing, and the International Consortium of Investigative Journalism's (ICIJ) publication of the Panama Papers (2016)[2] and the Paradise Papers (2017)[3]. Perhaps more so than researchers of individual crime, corporate crime scholars are usually very much aware of the many different actors at different "levels of aggregation" that are involved in bringing about the situation in which corporate crime can and does occur, including corporations themselves, victims, lawyers, inspection authorities, governments, and NGOs (van Wingerde, 2015).

Most corporate crime cases studied, however, are serious, and therefore relatively exceptional cases often occur in large and well-known corporations. High-profile cases or unusually harmful crimes and the organizations in which they occurred are singled out repeatedly, in the process becoming "landmark narratives" of scholarship on organizational crime (Shover and Hochstetler 2002: 9). While these studies are informative, the relevance of their findings for explaining more common instances of corporate noncompliance as yet remains unclear. Since these studies are mostly limited to the period directly before and after the scandal under scrutiny emerged, the majority of the available case studies cannot truly be considered to entail corporate life histories. Nevertheless, the detailed analysis of the chronology of the particular incident provided by these studies sometimes dates back multiple years. Furthermore, case study research of corporate crime usually has a strong emphasis on the circumstances both within corporations and within markets in which rule violations occur (van Wingerde, Verhage and Bisschop, 2018). Fully in line with the life-course approach, Van Baar (2019), for example, showed that detailed analysis of the historical, political and economic context in the life history narratives of her three case studies (Topf and Söhne; Shell; and AngloGold Ashanti) was crucial in understanding the corporations' involvement in international crimes.

47.6 CONCLUSION

Developmental and life-course criminology has proven an enlightening perspective that can help explain both the empirical regularities in the development of delinquency and crime over the life span, as well as the variety found in individual criminal career patterns both within and across historical time and geographical place. In this chapter, we have argued that our understanding of corporate crime could benefit from taking a life-course perspective as

[2] The Panama Papers is the name given to one of the biggest leaks of documents and largest collaborations of journalists in history. Published in 2016, the Panama Papers involved more than 350 reporters from 80 countries and was coordinated by the ICIJ. Since then, dozens more journalists have been added to the collaboration, and the investigation has continued.

[3] The Paradise Papers was the ICIJ's 2017 global investigation into the offshore activities of some of the world's most powerful people and companies.

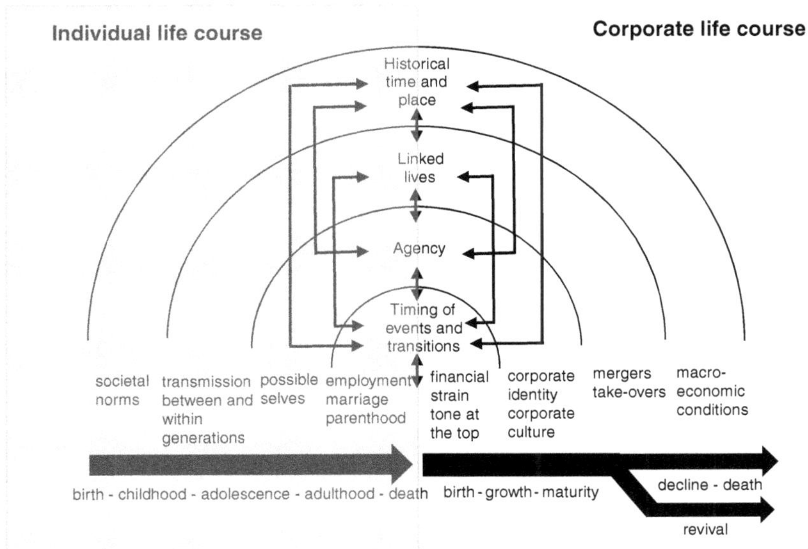

FIGURE 47.1 Schematic representation of the life course perspective as applied to individuals and corporations
Source: Based on Elder and Giele, 2009.

well. Doing so, we have highlighted the origins of present-day developmental and life-course criminology, and have explored how the theoretical and methodological approaches of developmental and life-course criminology would translate to the realm of corporate crime. For some aspects, this seems intuitively clear; for others, the conceptual leap of imagination needed is somewhat larger, demanding additional theorizing. Our main argument is summarized by Figure 47.1, which captures the essence of the life-course approach and directly compares its application to individual offenders with that to corporate crime. Figure 47.1 is also meant to illustrate the ways in which the different levels and processes of causal influence are linked.

As such, Figure 47.1 dares students of corporate crime to think of corporate counterparts of concepts central to the individual life span, like birth, continuity and death, and what these phases mean for corporate compliance and corporate offending. Whereas every year many start-ups enter the corporate population, other corporations may result from the merger of two or more existing others, or rather from splitting off of some larger business. Which of these events could be considered to involve the "birth" of a corporation? And can this be determined on legal grounds alone, or are substantive considerations, like the continuation of commercial activities in the same market, important too? Similar questions apply to the "death" of a corporation as well (Macey, 2013), as even bankruptcy may obscure some form of corporate continuation. Given that individual-level continuity is at the heart of the life-course approach, corporate crime researchers wishing to apply the life-course approach to corporations at least have to offer some working solution to the famous Theseus paradox.[4] Another

4 The Theseus paradox refers to the thought experiment of the sailing vessel of Greek hero king Theseus being kept in a harbor as a monument to the king's naval victories. Over the years, the ship's rotting boards are replaced, until all old boards have been substituted for new ones. Philosophers have been arguing for centuries over whether the refurbished ship can still be considered king Theseus's ship, or rather constitutes a new ship altogether.

complicating factor is the nonlinearity of the corporate life course. Whereas in natural persons the sequencing and duration of the different life stages closely parallel calendar age, the life of corporations is much more flexible and cyclical in nature, rendering corporate age a much less informative variable.

Figure 47.1 also highlights the different realms of causal influence which together shape individual-level development over the life span. Whereas some contextual factors, like the macro-economic climate of a particular era or region, can easily be imagined to influence both the trajectories of individuals and those of corporations, other factors may be less intuitive. What, for example, would constitute the corporate equivalents of social control enhancing transitions like marriage and employment – life-course transitions that figure prominently in life-course criminology? Extant theoretical and empirical work on corporate crime highlights some factors that seem to affect the level of corporate rule violation, like financial strain, but other factors are likely still to be discovered. Figure 47.1 also suggests these different realms to be linked, such that macro-level contextual factors may shape the individual's choice of behavioral opportunities, as well as the consequences of going through a particular transition.

Like individuals, corporations are not just playthings of fate. Corporations have the ability to choose between alternative courses of action that are available to them at a particular point in time. In individual life-course criminology, a narrative conceptualization of agency has given rise to theories in which past, present and future possible selves are linked in a perpetual motion of evaluation and reevaluation. In turn, this continuously "work-in-progress" self is seen as the driver of agentic choice. Depicted by the arrows in Figure 47.1, historical time and geographical place provide for the choice alternatives available as well as the storylines by which these alternatives can be perceived. In that sense, individual agency is not strictly a private but also a very public matter.

Corporate decision-making adds additional layers of complexity to the study of agentic choice as corporate agency typically involves the decision-making of multiple individuals, whether it be multiple members of the board or the individual choices of those linked through the corporate chain of command. Corporate culture and identity may likewise shape the perception of behavioral alternatives and provide the scripts to justify employer actions, yet, when not fully internalized, they also leave room for both employee misbehavior and whistleblowing originating from the individual's own self-perception.

Ideally, life-course studies, be it those on individual or corporate behavioral development, combine information on all different paradigmatic elements. Needless to say, few – if any – studies on individual development meet this demand. Obstacles for those attempting a life-course approach to corporate crime may be even more daunting. First and foremost, longitudinal data are needed on corporate transgressions. Whereas individual life-course criminological research can typically resort to police or court registers on a state or even national level, the monitoring of corporate compliance is often decentralized, resulting in various regulatory agencies keeping their own records. At best this requires only the extra effort of gaining access to these different data sources and of combining them to an overarching dataset. More often than not, however, these data sources differ not only in jurisdiction but also in the way these local registries are designed, filled and archived, rendering their combination much more effortful, if not on the brink of impossible.[5] Furthermore, whereas

[5] Some of the drawbacks of register data could be compensated by making use of prospective longitudinal surveys in which respondents are questioned on their behavior at regular intervals. In fact, such panel studies constitute an important part of life course criminology (Farrington, 2015). The use of longitudinal self-report data, however, has

police and court records cover a plethora of offenses, researchers of corporate noncompliance are confronted with a range of regulatory and law enforcement agencies each responsible for a very specific area of regulation, complicating the study of corporate crime mix and offending diversity.

Similar hurdles may be faced when collecting data on events and transitions in other corporate life-course domains. Whereas micro-level data on the life course of individuals is increasingly becoming available through the national bureau of statistics in many countries, information on important aspects of the corporate life course tends to be less well documented. Relevant data might be incomplete, available for only a short period of time, or both. Data may also have been collected on a level of aggregation inappropriate for studying the life course of a single corporation, for example only provide information on the parent company level instead of on that of the local businesses. Commercial parties offer access to data relevant to explain developmental trajectories in corporate crime, yet these data may come at a price that is beyond the budget typically available in scientific research projects. Finally, third parties may be reluctant to share the information they have access to. One reason might be that these data contain commercially sensitive information on the corporation's positioning in the market. Another might be that regulatory agencies fear that research outcomes might reflect badly on their daily practice. Establishing and maintaining good relationships with both the regulatory bodies and the corporations under their jurisdiction is therefore pivotal for researchers of corporate crime.

A number of recent initiatives, however, show that, while daunting, it is not impossible to compile longitudinal data on corporate noncompliance and corporate features that may explain the variation both within and between corporations. Simpson, Garner and Gibbs (2007), for instance, followed seventy-three US companies in the pulp, paper, steel and oil industries for a period of six years, collecting data on administrative, civil and criminal court cases, alongside information on the industrial classification of each corporation, the number of employees, the number of facilities, and several measures of profitability. Stockholder equity was found to be associated with lower environmental violation rates, with fewer violations being registered in more profitable years. Simpson et al. (2020) tracked 3,327 public US-based companies from 1996 through 2013 combining corporate data (i.e., size, economic performance, board composition) with data on financial/corruption (i.e., FCPA violations), environmental and anticompetitive offenses. Nearly one in four corporations was found to engage in illegal activities, the majority of which were environmental violations. The gender diversity of the board and the type of intervention (i.e., criminal, civil, regulatory) were found to be only weakly correlated with corporate (re)offending. Most recently, Kluin et al. (2020) have constructed a 10-year longitudinal database comprising the regulatory violation data of 494 Dutch corporations working with dangerous substances that need to adhere to the European Seveso Directive. These data also hold information on corporate characteristics, like industrial classification, and enforcement actions taken by the relevant inspection agencies. At present, these data are being augmented with information regarding these corporations' size and governance type, and corporate-, sector- and national-level information on financial performance.

its own disadvantages, including problems obtaining large and representative samples, minimizing sample attrition, and bias resulting from social desirable responses and testing effects. Obviously, the typical strategy of offering monetary incentives to respondents to limit the first two of these problems does not fit corporate crime research very well.

Developmental and life-course criminology has provided a fertile soil for both theory and empirical research on the development of delinquency and crime across the individual life course. It has both revived old theories and given rise to new ways of thinking. It has triggered new data collections and fueled the development of innovative methodologies for analyzing these data. While it would be foolish to expect it to provide us with all the answers, taking a life-course perspective has significantly increased our knowledge on the evolution of crime across the individual's life span. We see no reason to expect these benefits of taking a life-course perspective not also to apply to our efforts in understanding corporate crime.

REFERENCES

Alalehto, Tage. 2010. "The Wealthy White-Collar Criminals: Corporations as Offenders." *Journal of Financial Crime* 17, 3: 308–20. doi:10.1108/13590791011056273.

Bengston, Vern L., Glen H. Elder and Norella M. Putney. 2005. "The Lifecourse Perspective on Ageing: Linked Lives, Timing, and History." In *The Cambridge Handbook on Age and Ageing*, pp. 493–501, edited by Malcolm L. Johnson. Cambridge: Cambridge University Press.

Benson, Michael L., and Kent R. Kerley. 2001. "Life Course Theory and White Collar Crime." In *Contemporary Issues in Crime and Criminal Justice: Essays in Honor of Gil Geis*, pp. 121–36, edited by Henry N. Pontell and David Shichor. Upper Saddle River, NJ: Prentice Hall.

Bersani, Bianca E., John H. Laub and Paul Nieuwbeerta. 2009. "Marriage and Desistance from Crime in the Netherlands: Do Gender and Socio-historical Context Matter?" *Journal of Quantitative Criminology* 25: 3–24.

Bertaux, Daniel. 1981. *Biography and Society*. Thousand Oaks, CA: Sage.

Block Carolyn R., Arjan A. J. Blokland, Cornelia van der Werff, Rianne van Os and Paul Nieuwbeerta. 2010. "Long-Term Patterns of Offending in Women." *Feminist Criminology* 5, 1: 73–107.

Blokland, Arjan A. J. and Patrick Lussier. 2015. *Sex Offenders: A Criminal Career Approach*. Chichester: Wiley.

Blokland, Arjan A.J., Daniel Nagin and Paul Nieuwbeerta. 2005. "Life Span Offending Trajectories of a Dutch Conviction Cohort." *Criminology* 43, 4: 919–54.

Blokland, Arjan A. J. and Paul Nieuwbeerta. 2010a. "Life Course Criminology." In *International Handbook of Criminology*, pp. 77–120, edited by Shlomo Giora Shoham, Paul Knepper and Martin Kett. Boca Raton, FL: CRC Press.

2010b. "Considering Criminal Continuity: Testing for Heterogeneity and State Dependence in the Association of Past to Future Offending." *Australian and New Zealand Journal of Criminology* 43, 3: 526–56.

Blokland, Arjan A. J. and Victor R. van der Geest. 2017. *Routledge International Handbook of Life-Course Criminology*. New York: Routledge.

Blumstein, Alfred, and Jacqueline Cohen. 1987. "Characterizing Criminal Careers." *Science* 237: 985–91.

Blumstein, Alfred, Jacqueline Cohen, Jeffrey A. Roth and Christy A. Visher. 1986. *Criminal Careers and Career Criminals*. Washington, DC: National Academy Press.

Blumstein, Alfred, Jacqueline Cohen and David P. Farrington. 1988. "Criminal Career Research: Its Value for Criminology." *Criminology* 26, 1: 1–35.

Borck, Jonathan C. and Cary Coglianese. 2011. "Beyond Compliance: Explaining Business Participation in Voluntary Environmental Programs." In *Explaining Compliance: Business Response to Regulation*, pp. 139–69, edited by Christine Parker and Vibeke Lehmann Nielsen. Cheltenham, UK: Edward Elgar.

Braithwaite, John, and Brent Fisse. 1990. "On the Plausibility of Corporate Crime Theory." In *Advances in Criminological Theory*, Vol. 2, pp. 5–38, edited by William Laufer and Freda Adler. New Brunswick, NJ: Transaction.

Britt, Chester L. 2019. "Age and Crime." In *The Oxford Handbook of Developmental and Life-Course Criminology*, pp. 13–33, edited by David P. Farrington, Lila Kazemian and Alex R. Piquero. Oxford: Oxford University Press.

Brown, Darryl K. 2001. "Street Crime, Corporate Crime, and the Contingency of Criminal Liability." *University of Pennsylvania Law Review* 149, 5: 1295–360.

Campedelli, Gian Maria, Francesco Calderoni, Tommaso Comunale and Cecilia Meneghini. 2019. "Life-Course Criminal Trajectories of Mafia Members." *Crime and Delinquency*: 1–31. https://doi.org/10.1177/0011128719860834.

Clinard, Marshall B., and Peter C. Yeager. 1980. *Corporate Crime*. New York: Free Press.

Craig, Jessica M., Brie Diamond and Alex R. Piquero. 2014. "Marriage as an Intervention in the Lives of Criminal Offenders." In *Effective Interventions in the Lives of Criminal Offenders*, pp. 19–37, edited by John A. Humphrey and Peter Cordella. New York: Springer-Verlag.

Cressey, Donald. 1989. "The Poverty of Theory in Corporate Crime Research." In *Advances in Criminological Theory*, Vol 1, pp. 31–56, edited by William S. Laufer and Freda Adler. New Brunswick, NJ: Transaction.

Cumming, Douglas, T. Leung and Oliver Rui. 2015. "Gender Diversity and Securities Fraud." *Academy of Management Journal* 58, 5: 1572–93.

Dabney, Dean A. 2016. "White-Collar Criminals: Ethnographic Portraits of Their Identities and Decision Making." In *The Oxford Handbook of White-Collar Crime*, pp. 127–48, edited by Shanna R. Van Slyke, Michael L. Benson and Francis T. Cullen. New York: Oxford University Press.

Dalton, Dan R., and Idalene F. Kesner. 1988. "On the Dynamics of Corporate Size and Illegal Activity: An Empirical Assessment." *Journal of Business Ethics* 7: 861–70.

Dickinson, Victoria. 2011. "Cash Flow Patterns as a Proxy for Firm Life Cycle." *Accounting Review* 86, 6: 1969–94.

Eichelsheim, Veroni I., and Steve G. A. van de Weijer. 2018. *Intergenerational Continuity of Criminal and Antisocial Behavior: An International Overview of Studies*. New York: Routledge.

Elder, Glen H. Jr. 1995. "Time, Human Agency, and Social Change: Perspectives on the Life Course." *Social Psychology Quarterly* 57: 4–15.

1998. "The Life Course as Developmental Theory." *Child Development* 69, 1: 1–12.

Elder, Glen H., Jr., and Jant Z. Giele. 2009. "Life Course Studies. An Evolving Field." In *The Craft of Life Course Research*, pp. 1–24, edited by Glen H. Elder, Jr. and Janet Z. Giele. New York: Guilford Press.

Erikson, E. 1950. *Childhood and Society*. New York: W.W. Norton & Company.

Etienne, J. 2015. "The Politics of Detection in Business Regulation." *Journal of Public Administration Research and Theory* 25, 1: 257–84.

Farrington, David P. 2003. "Developmental and Life-Course Criminology: Key Theoretical and Empirical Issues – The 2002 Sutherland Award Address." *Criminology* 41, 2: 221–5.

2013. "Longitudinal and Experimental Research in Criminology." *Crime and Justice* 42: 453–528.

2015. "Prospective Longitudinal Research on the Development of Offending." *Australian and New Zealand Journal of Criminology* 48, 3: 314–35.

Farrington, David P., and Brandon C. Welsh. 2007. *Saving Children from a Life of Crime. Early Risk Factors and Effective Interventions*. New York: Oxford University Press.

Farrington, David P., Lila Kazemian and Alex R. Piquero. 2018. *The Oxford Handbook of Developmental and Life-Course Criminology*. Oxford: Oxford University Press.

Francis, Brian, Keith Soothill and Alex R. Piquero. 2007. "Estimation Issues and Generational Changes in Modeling Criminal Career Length." *Crime and Delinquency* 53, 1: 84–105.

Gibson, Chris L. and Marvin D. Krohn. 2012. *Handbook of Life-Course Criminology. Emerging Trends and Directions for Future Research*. New York: Springer.

Giordano, Peggy C., S. A. Cernkovich and J. L. Rudolph. 2002. "Gender, Crime and Desistance: Toward a Theory of Cognitive Transformation." *American Journal of Sociology* 107, 4: 990–1164.

Gottfredson, Michael R. and Travis Hirschi. 1990. *A General Theory of Crime*. Stanford: Stanford University Press.

Goodman, Sam, Darrell J. Steffensmeier and Jeffery T. Ulmer. 2005. *Confessions of a Dying Thief: Understanding Criminal Careers and Illegal Enterprise*. New Brunswick, NJ: AldineTransaction.

Greenpeace. 2018." Justice for People and Planet. Ending the Age of Corporate Capture, Collusion and Impunity." www.greenpeace.de/sites/www.greenpeace.de/files/publications/justice_report_0.pdf.

Gross, Edward. 1978. "Organizations as Criminal Actors." In *Two Faces of Deviance: Crimes of the Powerless and Powerful*, pp. 198–213, edited by Paul R. Wilson and John Braithwaite. Brisbane: University of Queensland Press.

Hagan, John, and Alberto Palloni. 1988. "Crimes as Social Events in the Life Course: Reconceiving a Criminological Controversy." *Criminology* 26: 87–100.

Hanlon, Michelle, and Shane Heitzman. 2010. "A Review of Tax Research." *Journal of Accounting and Economics* 50, 2–3: 127–78.

Havighurst, Robert J. 1948. *Developmental Tasks and Education*. New York: McKay.

Hitlin, Steven, and Glenn H. Elder, Jr. 2007. "Agency: An Empirical Model of an Abstract Concept." *Advances in Life Course Research* 11: 33–67.

Holtfreter, Kristy. 2005. "Is Occupational Fraud 'Typical' White-Collar Crime? A Comparison of Individual and Organizational Characteristics." *Journal of Criminal Justice* 33: 353–65.

Huisman, Wim. 2016. "Criminogenic Organizational Properties and Dynamics." In *The Oxford Handbook of White-Collar Crime*, pp. 435–62, edited by Shanna R. van Slyke, Michael L. Benson and Francis T. Cullen. Oxford: Oxford University Press.

Jennings, Wesley G., and Jennifer M. Reingle. 2012. "On the Number and Shape of Developmental/Life-Course Violence, Aggression, and Delinquency Trajectories: A State-of-the-Art Review." *Journal of Criminal Justice* 40, 6: 472–89.

Jolliffe, Darrick, David P. Farrington, Alex R. Piquero, Rolf Loeber and Karl G. Hill. 2017. "Systematic Review of Early Risk Factors for Life-Course-Persistent, Adolescence-Limited, and Late-Onset Offenders in Prospective Longitudinal Studies." *Aggression and Violent Behavior* 33: 15–23.

Kedia, Simi, Shuqing Luo and Shivaram Rajgopal. 2017. *Profiling: Does Past Compliance Record Predict Financial Reporting Risk?* Columbia Business School.

Kirk, David S., and Robert J. Sampson. 2013. "Juvenile Arrest and Collateral Educational Damage in the Transition to Adulthood." *Sociology of Education* 86, 1: 36–62.

Klinkhammer, Julian. 2015. "Varieties of Corruption in the Shadow of Siemens: A Modus Operandi Study of Corporate Crime on the Supply Side of Corrupt Transactions." In *The Routledge Handbook of White-Collar and Corporate Crime in Europe*, pp. 318–35, edited by Judith van Erp, Wim Huisman and Gudrun Vande Walle, London: Routledge.

Kluin, Marieke H. A, Ellen Wiering, Marlijn P. Peeters, Arjan A. J. Blokland and Wim Huisman. 2020. *Regelovertreding en incidenten bij Brzo-bedrijven: Een longitudinale benadering*. Den Haag: Boom Criminologie.

Laub, John H., Zachari R. Rowan and Robert J. Sampson. 2018. "The Status of the Age-Graded Theory of Informal Social Control." In *The Oxford Handbook on Developmental and Life-Course Criminology*, pp. 295–324, edited by David P. Farrington, Lila Kazemian and Alex R. Piquero. Oxford: Oxford University Press.

Laub, John H., and Robert J. Sampson. 2001. "Understanding Desistance from Crime." *Crime and Justice* 28: 1–69.

2003. *Shared Beginnings, Divergent Lives: Delinquent Boys to Age 70*. Cambridge, MA: Harvard University Press.

LeBlanc, Marc, and Rolf Loeber. 1998. "Developmental Criminology Updated." *Crime and Justice* 23: 115–97.

Levinson, Daniel J. 1978. *The Seasons of a Man's Life*. New York: Knopf.

Lichtenstein, Gregg A., and Thomas S. Lyons. 2008. "Revisiting the Business Life-Cycle Proposing an Actionable Model for Assessing and Fostering Entrepreneurship." *Entrepreneurship and Innovation* 9, 4: 241–50.

Loeber, Rolf, and Jeffrey D. Burke. 2011. "Developmental Pathways in Juvenile Externalizing and Internalizing Problems." *Journal of Research on Adolescence* 21, 1: 34–46.

Loeber, Rolf, and Marc Le Blanc. 1990. "Toward a Developmental Criminology." *Crime and Justice* 12: 375–473.

Loeber, Rolf, Wesley G. Jennings, Lia Ahonen, Alex R. Piquero and David P. Farrington. 2017. *Female Delinquency from Childhood to Young Adulthood: Recent Results from the Pittsburgh Girls Study*. New York: Springer.

Loeber, Rolf, Phen Wung, Kate Keenan, Bruce Giroux, Magda Stouthamer-Loeber, Welmoet B. Van Kammen and Barbara Maugham. 1993. "Developmental Pathways in Disruptive Child Behavior." *Development and Psychopathology* 5, 1–2: 103–33.

Lynam, Donald R. 1996. "Early Identification of Chronic Offenders: Who Is the Fledgling Psychopath?" *Psychological Bulletin* 120, 2: 209–34.

Macey, Jonathan. 2013. *The Death of Corporate Reputation: How Integrity Has Been Destroyed on Wall Street*. Upper Saddle River, NJ: FT Press.

Macher, Jeffrey T., John W. Mayo, and Jack A. Nickerson. 2011. "Regulator Heterogeneity and Endogenous Efforts to Close the Information Asymmetry Gap." *Journal of Law and Economics* 54, 1: 25–54.

Martin, Monica J., Shelley A. Blozis, Daria K. Boeninger, April S. Masarik and Rand D. Conger. 2014. "The Timing of Entry into Adult Roles and Changes in Trajectories of Problem Behaviors during the Transition to Adulthood." *Developmental Psychology* 50, 11: 2473–84.

Martinez, Natalie N., YongJei Lee, John E. Eck and SooHyun O. 2017. "Ravenous Wolves Revisited: A Systematic Review of Offending Concentration." *Crime Science* 6, 10. https://doi.org/10.1186/s40163-017-0072-2.

McLean, Bethany, and Peter Elkind. 2013. *The Smartest Guys in the Room: The Amazing Rise and Scandalous Fall of Enron*. New York: Penguin.

Miller, Danny, and Peter H. Friesen. 1984. "A Longitudinal Study of the Corporate Life Cycle." *Management Science* 30, 10: 1161–83.

Moffitt, Terrie E. 1993. "Adolescence-Limited and Life-Course-Persistent Antisocial Behavior: A Developmental Taxonomy." *Psychological Review* 100: 674–701.

1997. "Adolescence-Limited and Life-Course-Persistent Offending: A Complementary Set of Theories." In *Developmental Theories of Crime and Delinquency*, pp. 11–54, edited by Terence P. Thornberry. New Brunswick, NJ: Transaction.

2015. "Life-Course-Persistent versus Adolescence-Limited Anti-Social Behavior." In *Developmental Psychopathology, Vol. 3*, edited by Dante Cicchetti and Donald J. Cohen. Chichester, UK: Wiley.

Morgan, Gareth. 2006. *Images of Organization*. Beverly Hills, CA: Sage.

Morris, Robert G., and Sarah El Sayed. 2013. "The Development of Self-Reported White-Collar Offending." *Journal of Contemporary Criminal Justice* 29, 3: 369–84.

Nagin, Daniel S. 1999. "Analyzing Developmental Trajectories: A Semiparametric, Group-Based Approach." *Psychological Methods* 4, 2: 139–57.

2005. *Group-Based Modeling of Development over the Life Course*. Cambridge, MA: Harvard University Press.

Neugarten, Bernice L. 1979. "Time, Age, and the Life Cycle." *American Journal of Psychiatry* 136, 7: 887–94.

Nguyen, Holly, and Thomas A. Loughran. 2018. "On the Measurement and Identification of Turning Points in Criminology." *Annual Review of Criminology* 1: 335–58.

Nieuwbeerta, Paul, Arjan Blokland, Alex Piquero and Gary Sweeten. 2011. "A Life-Course Analysis of Offence Specialization: Introducing a New Method for Studying Individual Specialization over the Life Course." *Crime and Delinquency* 57, 1: 3–28.

Paternoster, Raymond. 1989. "Decisions to Participate in and Desist from Four Types of Common Delinquency: Deterrence and the Rational Choice Perspective." *Law and Society Review*: 7–40.

Paternoster, Raymond, Robert Brame, Alex Piquero, Paul Mazerolle and Charles W. Dean. 1998. "The Forward Specialization Coefficient: Distributional Properties and Subgroup Differences." *Journal of Quantitative Criminology* 14, 2: 133–54.

Paternoster, Raymond, and Shawn Bushway. 2009. "Desistance and the Feared Self: Toward an Identity Theory of Desistance." *Journal of Criminal Law and Criminology* 99, 4: 1103–56.

Paternoster, Raymond, and Ruth Triplett. 1988. "Disaggregating Self-Reported Delinquency and Its Implications for Theory." *Criminology* 26: 591–626.

Phelps, Robert, Richard Adams and John Bessant. 2007. "Life Cycles of Growing Organizations: A Review with Implications for Knowledge and Learning." *International Journal of Management Reviews* 9, 1: 1–30.

Piquero, Nicole L., and Michael L. Benson. 2004. "White-Collar Crime and Criminal Careers: Specifying a Trajectory of Punctuated Situational Offending." *Journal of Contemporary Criminal Justice* 20, 2: 148–65.
Piquero, Nicole L., and David Weisburd. 2009. "Development Trajectories of White-Collar Crime." In *Criminology of White-Collar Crime*, pp. 153–71, edited by Sally S. Simpson and David Weisburd. New York: Springer.
Piquero, Alex R., Brie Diamond, Wesley G. Jennings, and Jennifer M. Reingle. 2013. "Adolescence-Limited Offending." In *Handbook of Life-Course Criminology*, pp. 129–42. New York: Springer.
Piquero, Alex R., David P. Farrington and Alfred Blumstein. 2003. "The Criminal Career Paradigm: Background and Recent Developments." In *Crime and Justice: A Review of Research*, Vol. 30, edited by Michael Tonry. Chicago: University of Chicago Press.
Piquero, Alex, Raymond Paternoster, Robert Brame, Paul Mazerolle and Charles Dean. 1999. "Onset Age and Offense Specialization." *Journal of Research in Crime and Delinquency* 36: 275–99.
Quinn, Robert E., and Kim Cameron. 1983. "Organizational Life Cycles and Shifting Criteria of Effectiveness: Some Preliminary Evidence." *Management Science* 29, 1: 33–51.
Rocque, Michael. 2017. *Desistance from Crime: New Advances in Theory and Research*. New York: Palgrave Macmillan.
Sampson, Robert J. and John H. Laub. 1993. *Crime in the Making*. Cambridge, MA: Harvard University Press.
1997. "A Life-Course Theory of Cumulative Disadvantage." In *Developmental Theories of Crime and Delinquency*, pp. 133–61, edited by Terence P. Thornberry. New Brunswick, NJ: Transaction.
2004. "A General Age-Graded Theory of Crime: Lessons Learned and the Future of Life-Course Criminology." In *Advances in Criminological Theory Vol. 13: Testing Integrated Developmental/Life Course Theories of Offending*, edited by David P. Farrington. New Brunswick, NJ: Transaction.
Schinkel, Maarten P., Lukáš Tóth and Jan Tuinstra. 2020. "Discretionary Authority and Prioritizing in Government Agencies." *Journal of Public Administration Research and Theory* 30, 2: 240–56.
Shover, Neal. 1996. *Great Pretenders: Pursuits and Careers of Persistent Thieves*. Boulder, CO: Westview Press.
Shover, Neal, and Andy Hochstetler. 2002. "Cultural Explanation and Organizational Crime." *Crime, Law, and Social Change* 37: 1–18.
2006. *Choosing White-Collar Crime*. New York: Cambridge University Press.
Siennick Sonja E. and D. Wayne Osgood. 2008. "A Review of Research on the Impact on Crime of Transitions to Adult Roles." In *The Long View of Crime: A Synthesis of Longitudinal Research*, pp. 161–87, edited by Akavi M. Liberman. New York: Springer-Verlag.
Simpson, Sally S. 1986. "The Decomposition of Antitrust: Testing a Multi-level, Longitudinal Model of Profit-Squeeze." *American Sociological Review* 51: 859–75.
2019. "Reimagining Sutherland 80 Years after White-Collar Crime." *Criminology* 57, 2: 189–207.
Simpson, Sally S., and Christopher S. Koper. 1997. "The Changing of the Guard: Top Management Characteristics, Organizational Strain, and Antitrust Offending." *Journal of Quantitative Criminology* 13: 373–404.
Simpson, Sally S., and Melissa Rorie. 2011. "Motivating Compliance: Economic and Material Motives for Compliance." In *Explaining Compliance: Business Response to Regulation*, edited by Christine Parker and Vibeke Lehmann Nielsen. Cheltenham, UK: Edward Elgar.
Simpson, Sally S., and Natalie Schell. 2009. "Persistent Heterogeneity or State Dependence? An Analysis of Occupational Safety and Health Act Violations." In *The Criminology of White-Collar Crime*, pp. 63–78, edited by Sally S. Simpson and David Weisburd. New York: Springer.
Simpson, Sally S., Joel Garner and Carole Gibbs. 2007. "Why Do Corporations Obey Environmental Law? Assessing Punitive and Cooperative Strategies of Corporate Crime Control." A report by the US Department of Justice, Document 220693.
Simpson, Sally S., Debra L. Shapiro, Christine M. Beckman and Gerald S. Martin. 2020. "Preventing and Controlling Corporate Crime: The Dual Role of Corporate Boards and Legal Sanctions." Final report, National Institute of Justice Grant 2015-IJ-CX-0008. Washington, DC: Office of Justice Programs, U.S. Department of Justice. www.ncjrs.gov/pdffiles1/nij/grants/254622.pdf.

Spapens, Toine. 2018. "The 'Dieselgate' Scandal: A Criminological Perspective." In *Green Crimes and Dirty Money*, pp. 91–112, edited by Toine Spapens, Rob White, Daan van Uhm and Wim Huisman. London/New York: Routledge.

Stander, J., D. Farrington, G. Hill and P. Altham. 1989. "Markov Chain Analysis and Specialization in Criminal Careers." *British Journal of Criminology* 29: 317–35.

Sutherland, Edwin H. 1947. *Principles of Criminology*. 4th edition. Philadelphia: Lippincott.

1949. *White Collar Crime*. New York: Dryden.

1983. *White Collar Crime: The Uncut Version*. New Haven, CT: Yale University Press.

Tillman, Robert, and Henry Pontell. 1995. "Organizations and Fraud in the Savings and Loan Industry." *Social Forces* 73: 1439–63.

Tombs, Steve. 1995. "Corporate Crime and New Organizational Forms." In *Corporate Crime: Contemporary Debates*, edited by Frank Pearce and Laureen Snider. Toronto: University of Toronto Press.

Uggen, Christopher, and Irvin Piliavin. 1998. "Asymmetrical Causation and Criminal Desistance." *Journal of Criminal Law and Criminology* 88, 4: 1399–1422.

Uggen, Christopher, and Sarah Wakefield. 2008. "What Have We Learned from Longitudinal Studies of Work and Crime?" In *The Long View of Crime: A Synthesis of Longitudinal Research*, pp. 191–219, edited by Akavi M. Liberman. New York: Springer-Verlag.

van Baar, Annika. 2019. *Corporate Involvement in International Crimes: In Nazi Germany, Apartheid South Africa and the Democratic Republic of the Congo*. PhD dissertation, VU Amsterdam.

van der Geest, Victor R., David Weisburd and Arjan A. J. Blokland. 2017. "Developmental Trajectories of Offenders Convicted of Fraud: A Follow-Up to Age 50 in a Dutch Conviction Cohort." *European Journal of Criminology* 14, 5: 543–65.

van Koppen, M. Vere, Christianne J. de Poot and Arjan A. J. Blokland 2010. "Comparing Criminal Careers of Organized Crime Offenders and General Offenders." *European Journal of Criminology* 7: 356–74.

van Onna, Joost, Victor R. van der Geest, Wim Huisman and Adriaan Denkers. 2014. "Criminal Trajectories of White-Collar Offenders." *Journal of Research in Crime and Delinquency* 51, 6: 759–84.

Van Rooij, Benjamin, and Adam Fine. 2018. "Toxic Corporate Culture: Assessing Organizational Processes of Deviancy." *Administrative Sciences* 8, 23. doi:10.3390/admsci8030023.

van Schellen, Marieke, Robert Apel and Paul Nieuwbeerta. 2012. "Because You're Mine, I Walk the Line? Marriage, Spousal Criminality, and Criminal Offending Over the Life Course." *Journal of Quantitative Criminology* 28: 701–23.

van Wingerde, Karin G. 2015. "The Limits of Environmental Regulation in a Globalized Economy: Lessons from the Probo Koala Case." In *The Routledge Handbook of White-Collar and Corporate Crime in Europe*, pp. 260–75, edited by Judith van Erp, Wim Huisman and Gudrun Vande Walle. London: Routledge.

van Wingerde, Karin G., Antoinette Verhage and Lieselot Bisschop. 2018. "Organisatiecriminaliteit en de aanpak ervan in de Lage Landen." *Tijdschift voor Criminologie* 60, 4: 404–20.

Vaughan, Diane. 2007. "Beyond Macro- and Micro-Levels of Analysis, Organizations, and the Cultural Fix." In *International Handbook of White-Collar and Corporate Crime*, pp. 3–24, edited by Gilbert Geis and Henry Pontell, New York: Springer.

Vaughn, Michael G., and Matthew O. Howard. 2005. "The Construct of Psychopathy and Its Potential Contribution to the Study of Serious, Violent, and Chronic Youth Offending." *Youth Violence and Juvenile Justice* 3, 3: 235–52.

Verbruggen, Janna. 2016. "Effects of Unemployment, Conviction and Incarceration on Employment: A Longitudinal Study on the Employment Prospects of Disadvantaged Youths." *British Journal of Criminology* 56, 4: 729–49.

Verhage, Antoinette. 2011. *The Anti-Money Laundering Complex and the Compliance Industry*. Abingdon, UK: Routledge.

Veysey, Bonita M., Damian J. Martinez and Johnna Christian. 2013. "Getting Out: A Summary of Qualitative Research on Desistance across the Life Course." In *Handbook of Life-Course Criminology: Emerging Trends and Directions for Future Research*, pp. 233–60, edited by Chris L. Gibson and Marvin D. Krohn. New York: Springer.

Wahid, Aida S. 2019. "The Effects and the Mechanisms of Board Gender Diversity: Evidence from Financial Manipulation." *Journal of Business Ethics* 159: 705–25.

Wang, Xia, and Kristy Holtfreter. 2012. "The Effects of Corporation- and Industry-Level Strain and Opportunity on Corporate Crime." *Journal of Research in Crime and Delinquency* 49: 151–85.

Weil, David, and Amanda Pyles. 2005. "Why Complain – Complaints, Compliance, and the Problem of Enforcement in the US Workplace." *Comparative Labor Law and Policy Journal* 27: 59.

Weisburd, David, and Elin E. Waring. 2001. *White-Collar Crime and Criminal Careers*. New York: Cambridge University Press.

Wells, Celia. 2001. *Corporations and Criminal Responsibility*. New York: Oxford University Press.

PART VIII

Measuring and Evaluating Compliance

48

Laboratory Experiments

James Alm and Matthias Kasper

Abstract: In this chapter, we assess the use of laboratory experiments in tax compliance research. We first discuss the reasons for using laboratory experiments, and we then describe the basic design of most experiments, including their main limitations. We also summarize some of the main results of these studies, and we discuss how the insights obtained from experimental research can help shape better tax policies. We conclude with some suggestions on new areas of research on tax compliance in which laboratory experiments may be usefully applied in the future.

48.1 INTRODUCTION

Compliance is a multifaceted phenomenon that has been investigated in disciplines as diverse as economics, law, psychology, accounting, and sociology. To better understand compliance behavior, researchers from these disciplines have applied a variety of methods to examine incentives, administrative processes, attitudes, motivation, and behavior (Parker and Nielsen, 2009).

However, studying compliance is difficult. A major challenge in compliance research is simply the measurement of noncompliance. Direct measures of noncompliant behavior are seldom possible, at least without detailed and expensive observation of individual behavior through (say) audits. Indirect measures of compliance are problematic because of the likelihood of significant measurement errors. In either case, measurement raises ethical concerns if people are not aware that their behavior is being studied. Even if measurement is possible, an additional challenge of compliance research is establishing causal relationships between the many factors that are thought to affect compliance behavior, known as "identification." Both factors contribute to the challenge of studying compliance behavior.

The difficulties of empirically assessing compliance are especially daunting for tax compliance.[1] Reliable and useful evidence on tax compliance is very hard to find, for obvious reasons, and indeed the fundamental difficulty in analyzing empirically tax compliance behavior is the lack of such information on taxpayer compliance. After all, tax evasion is illegal, and individuals have strong incentives to conceal their cheating, given financial and other penalties that are imposed on individuals who are found cheating on their taxes.

[1] There are several comprehensive surveys of the tax compliance literature. See especially Cowell (1990); Pyle (1991); Andreoni, Erard, and Feinstein (1998); Slemrod and Yitzhaki (2002); Kirchler (2007); Slemrod (2007); Torgler (2007); Alm (2012, 2019); Sandmo (2012); Slemrod and Weber (2012); and Hashimzade, Myles, and Tran-Nam (2013). Also, see Torgler (2002) and Mascagni (2018) for reviews that focus upon the use of experiments on tax compliance, including laboratory and field experiments.

Laboratory experiments represent a methodological approach that has become a popular and powerful tool for examining compliance behavior, and tax compliance in particular, because it generates direct measures of compliance choices and allows testing of causal relationships between factors that are otherwise unobservable. As a consequence, laboratory experiments are increasingly applied both to a wide range of different behaviors and also to a wide range of different disciplines.

In this chapter, we assess the use of laboratory experiments in tax compliance research. We first discuss the reasons for using laboratory experiments, and we then describe the basic design of most experiments, including their main limitations. We also summarize some of the main results of these studies, and we discuss how the insights obtained from experimental research can help shape better tax policies. We conclude with some suggestions on new areas of research on tax compliance, and compliance more broadly, in which laboratory experiments may be usefully applied in the future.

48.2 WHY USE LABORATORY EXPERIMENTS IN TAX COMPLIANCE RESEARCH?

As emphasized earlier, a fundamental difficulty in analyzing tax compliance behavior is the lack of reliable and useful information on taxpayer compliance. There have been many approaches to measurement, including direct and indirect methods of measurement using naturally occurring field data, survey data, and administrative data, as well as controlled field experiments (or randomized controlled trials), simulation studies, and qualitative methods. All of these approaches can contribute to our understanding of the drivers of tax compliance. However, all of these approaches also have limitations, some more severe than others. The quality and accuracy of many forms of these data are particularly worrisome (Slemrod and Weber, 2012; Torgler, 2016). After all, research requires measuring something that people by their very nature are trying to conceal. Even aside from these concerns about the quality and accuracy of the data, researchers have become increasingly skeptical about the ability of naturally occurring field data to achieve identification of the causal effects of policies (Angrist and Pischke, 2010). Controlled field experiments avoid some of these issues by their ability to identify causal factors in the compliance decision, but they have problems of their own: they seldom generate direct measures of evasion; they are expensive; they are typically one-time interventions; and they cannot examine many relevant factors in the compliance decision.[2] Also, the inability to replicate remains widespread in economics research (Christensen and Miguel, 2018).

Given these difficulties, laboratory experiments have become an increasingly common approach in economic research. What can laboratory experiments do? They can generate direct measures of tax compliance under different settings in which there is control over extraneous influences. In particular, they can provide a controlled environment that allows one to examine the mechanisms of interest, as well as the changes in these environments and institutions, in isolation from each other; they are relatively inexpensive; they can be easily replicated; and they have a high degree of internal validity. In short, laboratory experiments give a researcher the twin advantages of *control* (including *identification, data generation*, and *replicability* from this control) and *flexibility*.

First, laboratory methods allow the investigator to *control* the institutions and incentives facing subjects in order to allow *identification* of the causal mechanisms of main interest.

[2] See Hallsworth (2014) for a critical discussion of controlled field experiments.

Relatedly and importantly, laboratory methods allow the investigator to *generate data* on individual and group choices in settings where these institutions and incentives can be varied singly and independently in order to examine responses to separate changes in these factors. In the naturally occurring world, such control is seldom if ever available. Further, data on the responses of individuals to the myriad factors thought to influence the compliance decision may confound these many influences, making it difficult to disentangle their effects on compliance. Finally, it is likely that independent variation in many of these influences is simply not possible in the naturally occurring world, making it impossible to measure their effects on individual and group behavior. Laboratory experiments allow such data to be generated in a setting in which each relevant factor can be separately manipulated and outcomes of subject choices reliably observed. They also allow other investigators to *replicate* more-or-less identical laboratory settings in order to determine whether the results are robust, an essential attribute of any science.

Second, laboratory methods give the investigator substantial *flexibility* in examining the effects of supposedly relevant considerations on individual and group decisions. It is difficult to imagine real-world settings in which, say, notions of fairness, altruism, and trust can be manipulated in a reliable manner. Carefully designed experiments give the investigator precisely this flexibility, thereby allowing theories based on these notions (and the assumptions of these theories) to be tested in a controlled environment.

However, despite the demonstrated usefulness of experimental methods, there are sound reasons for caution in interpreting and generalizing experimental results. Some early experiments did not follow some now widely accepted procedures of the experimental paradigm, such as the use of repeated decisions and of neutral instructions. Much early work also lacked realism because values of the various policy parameters did not approximate real-world values.

Although more recent experimental research has generally addressed these problems, some concerns remain, some of which are more legitimate than others. The most common criticism of laboratory experiments – not simply in compliance behavior but more broadly – is that the student subjects typically used may not be representative of taxpayers. For example, students have typically little experience in filing and paying taxes, and so their behavior in an experimental setting might be different from the behavior of, say, self-employed individuals who have stronger incentives to minimize their tax payments and also more to lose if their noncompliance is detected. As a result, there is a concern that experimental results on policy innovations that rely upon student subjects cannot generalize to the population. However, there is now much evidence that the experimental responses of students are seldom different from the responses of other subject pools (Plott, 1987), including in the specific context of tax compliance (Alm, Bloomquist, and McKee, 2015). In a more fundamental sense, there is no reason to believe that the cognitive processes of students are different from those of "real" people, which suggests that the burden must be on skeptics to prove that these processes actually do differ.

Another common criticism is that it is not possible to control for many relevant factors in the laboratory. However, if one cannot control for such factors in the laboratory where the experimenter establishes the institutions, the rules, and the reward structure, then one cannot hope to control for these factors in the naturally occurring world.

Of more legitimate concern, the results may well be sensitive to the specific experimental design. Indeed, a laboratory experiment is only as good as its design: if the institutions and environments imposed in the lab do not parallel systems of interest in the world, the resulting experimental data can be useless or misleading. Replication is therefore crucial (Olsen et al., 2019b).

It is also possible that subjects may modify their behavior simply because they know that they are participating in an experiment, exhibiting more "obedience to authority" and more "prosocial behavior" in the laboratory than in the naturally occurring world. Most critically, there is a certain artificiality in any laboratory setting since laboratory experiments cannot fully reflect the incentive structure of a real-world tax compliance decision. A decision to report, say, three tokens of income in a tax compliance experiment is clearly different from a decision to report actual income on an annual tax return, even if the laboratory incentives are salient. In particular, the laboratory setting cannot capture certain types of incentives (e.g., a catastrophic loss such as jail), and it cannot capture the social stigma that some surveys suggest is an important factor in taxpayer reporting.

The crucial issue in experimental methods is therefore the "external validity" of laboratory methods; that is, do the results in the laboratory apply more broadly to the "naturally occurring world"?[3] This is an issue that cannot be answered in general for all experimental studies but must be addressed in each specific case. (It is often forgotten that this is also an issue that any empirical analysis must address.[4]) In the specific case of tax compliance experiments, there is now emerging evidence that the results found in the laboratory do in fact achieve such external validity.[5] These results are consistent with many other experimental studies that demonstrate that student and nonstudent subjects behave and respond similarly (Amberger, Eberhartinger, and Kasper, 2019).

In short, one must use the results from laboratory experiments with some care. However, such use depends largely upon the purpose of the experiment. According to Roth (1987), experiments can be classified into three broad categories that depend upon the dialogue in which they are meant to participate. "Speaking to Theorists" includes those experiments designed to test well-articulated theories. "Searching for Facts" involves experiments that examine the effects of variables about which existing theory has little to say. "Whispering in the Ears of Princes" identifies those experiments motivated by specific policy issues. To date, most experiments in behavioral public economics have fallen into the first two categories. However, this is now changing, and experiments are increasingly being used to illuminate numerous areas of public policy, especially tax compliance. This reflects a broader shift toward a "multi-method" approach where research questions are investigated from different perspectives to overcome the shortcomings of a single method. For example, laboratory experiments can complement field studies to better understand why, and under which circumstances, individuals exhibit certain behaviors.

48.3 The Design of Laboratory Experiments

The use of laboratory experiments in economics began in earnest in the early 1960s with work on resource allocation under alternative forms of market organization. Growth in its applications came with the establishment of a well-defined framework for experimental work

[3] See Levitt and List (2007) for a general critique of laboratory experiments. For robust responses to this critique, see Falk and Heckman (2009); Camerer (2015); Frechette (2015); Harrison, Lau, and Rutström (2015); Kagel (2015); and Kessler and Vesterlund (2015).

[4] For example, field experiments do not fully control subject valuations of commodities used in the field; they cannot generalize beyond the specific subject pool that is investigated; and they face significant difficulties in conducting replications.

[5] Again, see Alm, Bloomquist, and McKee (2015) for specific evidence on the external validity of tax compliance experiments, who find that student and nonstudent behaviors are similar. See Choo, Fonseca, and Myles (2016) for an alternative view on student versus nonstudent behaviors.

by Smith (1976, 1982), and laboratory methods are now widely accepted as a methodological approach in the analysis of theory and policy.[6]

Experimental economics involves the creation of a real microeconomic system in the laboratory, one that parallels the naturally occurring world that is the subject of investigation and one in which subjects (usually students) make decisions that yield individual financial payoffs whose magnitude depends on their decisions. The essence of such a system is control over the environment, the institutions, the incentives, and the preferences that subjects face. Of these, control over preferences is particularly crucial. As emphasized by Smith (1976), "[s]uch control can be achieved by using a reward structure to induce prescribed monetary value on actions."[7]

Smith (1982) identifies a set of sufficient conditions for control over preferences to be established:

- *Nonsatiation*: Subjects prefer more to less of the reward medium.
- *Saliency*: The rewards received by subjects are related to their decisions, so that subjects recognize that their actions affect their outcomes.
- *Reward Dominance*: The rewards are large enough to offset any subjective costs or benefits that subjects place on participation in the experiment.
- *Privacy*: Each subject knows only his or her own payoffs, so that they do not receive any subjective value from the payoffs of other subjects.

Nearly all recent experimental studies invoke these conditions.[8]

Several other procedures should also be followed in experiment. The experiment should be administered in a uniform and consistent manner to allow replicability. The experiment should not be excessively long or complicated, since subjects may become bored or confused. Subjects must believe that the procedures described to them are the procedures actually followed. The instructions provided to subjects should be understandable, should avoid the use of examples that lead subjects to anchor on certain choices that are the focus of the experiment, and should be phrased in "neutral" rather than "loaded" terms, in order to mask the context of the experiment and to avoid direct reference to the real-world phenomena under investigation.[9]

48.4 The Basic Design of Laboratory Experiments in Tax Compliance

The standard economics-of-crime model of compliance is based upon the work of Allingham and Sandmo (1972) and Srinivasan (1973), and it is this theory that underlies most all laboratory

6 For comprehensive surveys of experimental methods, see Davis and Holt (1993) and Kagel and Roth (1995).

7 Smith (1976) goes on to write that a maintained assumption in experimental economics is the following: "Given a costless choice between two alternatives, identical except that the first yields more of the reward medium ... than the second, the first will always be chosen (preferred) over the second." It is in this sense that Smith (1976) refers to experimental economics as "induced value theory."

8 There are, however, some exceptions to these conditions. For example, one does not want to impose *Privacy* in an experiment on, say altruism because the payoffs to others are an essential part of the research issue.

9 Neutrality increases the experimenter's control over subject preferences, and avoids leading subjects to invoke different "mental scripts," which may enable them to fill in (potentially) missing information in the instructions but which also may unpredictably influence their choices. It is sometimes claimed that the use of neutral instructions limits the ability to generalize from the experimental to the naturally occurring setting. In fact, however, as argued by most experimental economists, it is not possible to generalize beyond the laboratory unless one uses neutral instructions, since the experimenter cannot control (or induce) the values that subjects associate with loaded terms.

experiments. In its simplest form, an individual is assumed to receive a fixed amount of income I, and must choose how much of this income to declare to the tax authorities and how much to underreport. The individual pays taxes at rate t on every dollar R of income that is reported, while no taxes are paid on underreported income. However, the individual may be audited with a fixed, predetermined probability p; if audited, then all underreported income is discovered, and the individual must pay a penalty at rate f on each dollar that he or she was supposed to pay in taxes but did not pay. The individual's income I_C if caught underreporting equals $I_C=I-tR-f[t(I-R)]$, while if underreporting is not caught income I_N is $I_N=I-tR$. The individual chooses declared income to maximize the expected utility $EU(I)$ of the evasion gamble, or $EU(I)=pU(I_C)+(1-p)U(I_N)$, where E is the expectation operator and utility $U(I)$ is a function only of income. Numerous extensions to this basic model have been made since the original Allingham and Sandmo (1972) paper, extensions that enrich but also complicate the analysis and that render clear-cut analytical results quite difficult.[10]

Applying this framework to the laboratory in the study of tax compliance is straightforward, and, beginning with the seminal experimental study of Friedland, Maital, and Rutenberg (1978), the basic design of most compliance experiments has been similar. Human subjects (generally students) in a controlled laboratory are told that they should feel free to make as much income as possible. At the beginning of each round of the experiment, each subject is given (or earns) income and must decide how much income to report. Taxes are paid at some rate on all reported, but not on underreported, income. However, underreporting is discovered with some fixed probability, and the subject must then pay a fine on unpaid taxes. This process is repeated for a given number of rounds. At the completion of the experiment, each subject is paid an amount that depends upon his or her performance during the experiment. Into this microeconomic system, various policy changes can be introduced one at a time, such as changes in audit probabilities or audit rules, in penalty rates, in tax rates, in public good provision, and in any other relevant institutions, and their separate and independent impacts on tax compliance are identified.

To date, laboratory experiments have examined virtually all factors that have been suggested as determinants of what motivates tax compliance, including:

- audit rates
- effectiveness of audits
- audit selection methods (e.g., targeted audit programs)
- tax rates and tax structures
- tax withholding systems
- matched versus nonmatched income
- fine rates
- public disclosure of compliance
- group rewards (e.g., public goods)
- individual rewards
- tax amnesties
- overweighting of low probabilities
- taxpayer communication ("cheap talk") and information dissemination

10 For discussions of the theoretical literature and its many extensions, see Andreoni, Erard, and Feinstein (1998); Slemrod and Yitzhaki (2002); and Alm (2012, 2019). Note that some recent work has incorporated aspects of "behavioral economics," in which insights from other social sciences (especially psychology) are incorporated. See, e.g., Yaniv (1999); Bernasconi and Zanardi (2004); and Dhami and al-Nowaihi (2007).

- collective decision processes (including voting)
- social norms
- perceptions of inequity (e.g., differences in tax burdens)
- complexity and uncertainty
- taxpayer services
- choice of tax preparers.

We discuss the results from these many laboratory experiments next.

48.5 SOME RESULTS FROM LABORATORY EXPERIMENTS

The many laboratory experiments on tax compliance have generated many insights, indicating clearly that individuals respond predictably, if not always significantly, to a wide array of policies. Here we summarize some of the main findings. Note that these issues have of course been examined via other empirical approaches, especially with naturally occurring field data and increasingly with controlled field experiments.[11] We emphasize here mainly the results from laboratory experiments.

48.5.1 *Audits – Both the Level and the Type of Audit – Matter, and Matter a Lot*

There is much evidence that suggests that more audits increase compliance, with an estimated reported income-audit rate elasticity that generally falls between 0.2 and 0.4.[12] Audits also typically have a "spillover" effect, or an increase in compliance independent of revenues generated directly from the audits themselves, whose magnitude varies from 4 to 12 (e.g., "general deterrence"). Audits also have a greater deterrent impact than fines, despite their theoretical equivalence, at least in an expected value sense. Even so, the reported income-audit rate elasticity is small and varies across studies. Also, telling individuals that they will be subject to "more scrutiny" via a message often has some impact on compliance, even if of small size and of unknown duration. Further, laboratory experiments have generally found that the impact of increased audits is nonlinear, so that the deterrent effect seems to diminish (and may even be reversed) with higher audit rates. Relative to a random audit selection rule, strategic audit selection (especially a "cutoff rule") is far more effective in increasing compliance than random audit selection, although some random selection seems necessary for audit schemes to work. Of some note, there is often some compliance even with no audits. As noted in Section 48.5.2, there is also some evidence that higher audit rates can sometimes backfire, leading to lower post-audit compliance.

48.5.2 *Perceptions of Audit Rates Affect Compliance; that is, Cognitive Considerations Matter*

In particular, individuals appear to substantially misperceive audit rates, typically overweighting a (low) probability of audit (Alm, McClelland, and Schulze, 1992; Kinsey, 1992). Also,

[11] See Alm (2019) for a summary of all of these empirical studies.

[12] The impact of audits on compliance has been examined perhaps more than most any other policy intervention in laboratory experiments. See Friedland, Maital, and Rutenberg (1978); Spicer and Hero (1985); Baldry (1987); Webley (1987); Beck, Davis, and Jung (1991); Alm, Jackson, and McKee (1992a, 1992b); Alm, McClelland, and Schulze (1992); and Alm, Cronshaw, and McKee (1993); Alm and McKee (2004, 2006); Alm et al. (2010, 2012); Andrighetto et al. (2016); Zhang et al. (2016); Alm, Bloomquist, and McKee (2017); and Alm et al. (2017); also, see Blackwell (2010) and Alm and Malézieux (in press) for meta-analyses of laboratory experiments.

post-audit behavior of audited taxpayers (e.g., "specific deterrence") is mixed and appears to depend on the audit effectiveness (i.e., the amount of noncompliance that an audit detects) as well as prior reporting levels (Kasper and Alm, 2020). There is some evidence that an audited individual may actually reduce his or her post-audit compliance, sometimes termed a "bomb-crater effect" (Guala and Mittone, 2005). This effect is found in several laboratory experiments in which tax compliance of audited taxpayers falls immediately after an audit (Mittone, 2006; Maciejovsky, Kirchler, and Schwarzenberger, 2007; Kastlunger et al., 2009), before recovering somewhat in succeeding rounds. One explanation for the bomb-crater effect is that individuals may update their subjective audit probabilities following an audit (Mittone, Panebianco, and Santoro, 2017). Another explanation is that deterrence may "crowd out" an individual's "intrinsic motivation" to pay taxes (Frey, 1997; Feld and Frey, 2002). Nevertheless, field data generally find little or no evidence of a bomb-crater effect (Erard, 1992; Advani, Elming, and Shaw, 2015), although there are exceptions (DeBacker et al. 2015). Indeed, some researchers question whether the bomb-crater effect generalizes beyond laboratory settings, largely because these researchers believe that laboratory experiments cannot adequately reflect the real-life consequences of noncompliance. However, some recent work using field data suggests that the specific deterrence effect of tax audits might depend on the audit outcome. These studies argue that one must distinguish between the effects of audits on taxpayers found to be compliant and those found to be noncompliant (Gemmell and Ratto, 2012; Beer et al., 2020): audited taxpayers who are found to have additional tax liabilities tend to increase their compliance following an audit, while audits tend to reduce compliance for audited taxpayers with no additional assessment following an audit. There is also some work that finds that delayed feedback on tax audits is more effective in improving compliance than immediate feedback, possibly because delay leads individuals to overweight audit probabilities (Kogler, Mittone, and Kirchler, 2016).

48.5.3 *Fines, whether Financial or Nonfinancial, Affect Compliance, but Their Deterrent Effects Are Small*

Fines are one policy intervention that have been almost exclusively examined using laboratory experiments, due largely to difficulties of generating independent variation in fine rates (Friedland, Maital, and Rutenberg, 1978; Beck, Davis, and Jung, 1991; Alm, Jackson, and McKee, 1992a, 1992b; Alm, McClelland, and Schulze, 1992).[13] Laboratory experiments typically find that a higher fine rate leads to marginally more compliance, with an estimated reported income-fine rate elasticity less than 0.1. Of some note, there is now much evidence (some from field studies) that nonfinancial penalties (e.g., public disclosure) may also act as a deterrent (Bosco and Mittone, 1997; Fortin, Lacroix, and Villeval, 2007; Coricelli et al., 2010; Hasegawa et al., 2013; Casagrande et al., 2015; Lefebvre et al., 2015; Perez-Truglia and Troiano, 2018; Casal and Mittone, 2016; Alm et al., 2017).

48.5.4 *Positive Inducements, whether to Individuals or to Groups, Improve Compliance*

Laboratory experiments consistently find that rewards to *individuals* increase compliance, including programs in which an individual who reports more income receives more

[13] However, see Alm, Bahl, and Murray (1990) for evidence on the deterrent effect of fines using naturally occurring field data for Jamaica.

government benefits (e.g., social insurance benefits) (Alm et al., 2012) or an individual who is found to be honest becomes eligible for rewards (e.g., a lottery) (Alm, Jackson, and McKee, 1992a; Feld, Frey, and Torgler, 2006; Bazart and Pickhardt, 2011). Laboratory experiments also find that an increase in payoffs to *groups*, such as public goods financed by tax payments, improves compliance (Becker, Buchner, and Sleeking, 1987: Alm, McClelland, and Schulze, 1992, 1999; Alm, Jackson, and McKee, 1992a, 1992b; Fochmann and Kroll, 2016).

48.5.5 *Tax Rates Affect Compliance, but the Effects Are Nuanced*

For example, the *level* of tax rates matters in an individual's compliance decision, with an increase in tax rates generally (though not always) reducing reported income (Alm, Jackson, and McKee, 1992b). However, Alm, Sanchez, and de Juan (1995) find that reporting actually increases with higher tax rates in their experimental study. In addition, one's tax rate *relative* to others' (e.g., "fiscal inequity") matters; that is, if an individual believes that his or her tax rate is "too high" relative to others, then the individual will tend to comply less (Spicer and Becker, 1980; Alm, McClelland, and Schulze, 1999).[14]

48.5.6 *The Social and Institutional Environment in which Individuals Live Affects Compliance*

The overall setting in which an individual lives, works, and functions has important effects on individual compliance, effects that go well beyond the ways by which the environment affects behavioral incentives. The importance of this overall social and institutional environment as one explanation for what motivates tax compliance has been consistently demonstrated by empirical findings of differences in compliance behavior in countries with similar fiscal systems (e.g., tax rates, audit rates, fine rates) but different social and institutional environments (Alm, Sanchez, and de Juan, 1995; Cummings et al., 2009; Andrighetto et al., 2016; Zhang et al., 2016). One compelling explanation for these differences in compliance behavior is that there seems to be a "social norm" of compliance, in which one's compliance depends upon various factors that reflect and capture the many aspects of one's environment (Alm, McClelland, and Schulze, 1992, 1999; Alm et al., 2019a). Further, these social norms seem to be affected by the institutions that face individuals and by individuals' attitudes toward these institutions (Alm, Jackson, and McKee, 1993a; Alm, McClelland, and Schulze, 1999). For example, individuals who have a negative attitude toward government tend to comply less (Webley et al., 1991).[15] Further, "trust" in institutions affects the viability of government policies by affecting these social norms: when individual trust in government is greater, enforcement tends to be more effective in deterring noncompliance (Kirchler,

14 Note that the level and the perception of tax rates can have behavioral effects beyond tax compliance. For example, tax rates may jointly affect labor supply and tax compliance decisions. See Collins and Plumlee (1991) and Doerrenberg and Duncan (2014) for somewhat conflicting experimental studies of the joint labor-evasion decision.

15 Similarly, justice and fairness perceptions have been identified as determinants of voluntary tax compliance by Tyler (1990). He finds that taxpayers comply with the law when they perceive political and legislative procedures as fair ("procedural justice"), when they find that the public goods they receive reflect their contribution to society ("distributive justice"), and when the tax burden is allocated in a fair way among taxpayers with equal ("horizontal equity") and unequal incomes ("vertical equity"). However, other compelling experimental evidence on the effect of fairness on compliance is scarce.

Hoelzl, and Wahl, 2008; Guala and Mittone, 2010; Kogler et al., 2013; Kasper, Kogler, and Kirchler, 2015; Karakostas and Zizzo, 2016).

48.5.7 *Individual Participation in the Choice of Institutions Affects Compliance; that is, Process (versus Outcome) Is an Essential Determinant of Compliance*

A related and important finding is that individual participation in the choice of institutions – the process as distinct from the outcome – has real effects, independent of the actual levels of tax, audit, and fine rates. For example, subjects in laboratory experiments pay more when they choose the use of their taxes by voting than when the identical use is imposed upon them; their compliance is greater when the vote indicates a clear group consensus; and their compliance is significantly and dramatically lowered by the imposition without taxpayer choice of an unpopular program, even an unpopular program with no financial benefits to individuals (Alm, Jackson, and McKee, 1993a; Alm, McClelland, and Schulze, 1999; Feld and Tyran, 2002; Wahl, Muehlbacher, and Kirchler, 2010; Casal et al., 2016). There is also some emerging work on how different forms of communication between the tax authorities and the taxpayers may sometimes increase the social norm of compliance (Onu and Oats, 2016).

48.5.8 *The Information that Tax Authorities Have on Income Sources Is an Essential Component of a Compliance Strategy*

Compliance is far greater on income subject to employer withholding and to third-party information sources than on income not subject to these features. In particular, withholding taxes at source via employer source withholding vastly improves compliance (at least on items subject to withholding) (Martinez-Vazquez, Harwood, and Larkins, 1992; Alm, Deskins, and McKee, 2009).[16]

48.5.9 *The Information that Individuals Are Provided about the Tax System and about Other Individuals Affects Compliance, but in Sometimes Surprising Ways*

For example, higher audit rates have no impact on compliance if this “official” information is not provided; if it is provided, higher audit rates increase compliance (Alm, Jackson, and McKee, 2009). However, the effects of information on compliance can also be counterintuitive. Telling individuals that they will be “closely examined” (via a message) generally increases the compliance rate of these individuals; however, the compliance rate of those individuals who infer that they will not be closely examined falls, and the net impact on overall compliance is often negative (Alm and McKee, 2006). Relatedly, knowing what your “neighbors” are doing affects your own decisions, and not always in a way that increases compliance: if you know that your neighbors are cheating, you will tend to cheat yourself, and vice versa (Alm, Bruner, and McKee, 2016; Alm, Bloomquist, and McKee, 2017). This result

16 There is also very strong empirical support for the compliance effects of employer withholding and third-party information sources (Internal Revenue Service, 2006, 2012, 2016; Kleven et al., 2011). However, these effects are not always clear-cut. For example, withholding that applies to only some sources of reporting has been found to improve compliance of these sources (Agostini and Martinez, 2014; Pomeranz, 2015; Fack and Landais, 2016). However, if there are other margins of behavior that are not subject to withholding, individuals have been found to reduce compliance along these other margins (Carillo, Pomeranz, and Singhal, 2017).

implies that telling people about audits can sometimes backfire because what your neighbors do affects what you do. Finally, as noted earlier, knowing how your tax dollars are spent often has a positive, if small, impact on compliance (Alm, Jackson, and McKee, 1993a; Alm, McClelland, and Schulze, 1999). Consequently, information that individuals have about the tax system and about other individuals does not always improve compliance.

48.5.10 *The Knowledge (or Understanding) that Taxpayers Have – or Do Not Have – about the Tax System Affects Compliance, but the Impacts Are Unresolved*

Taxpayers often do not know what they should pay in taxes, given a complex and uncertain tax system. As a result, they have increasingly come to rely upon paid tax practitioners (and also tax preparation software) in the preparation of their taxes. Indeed, field data suggest that an increase in complexity leads to greater use of a tax practitioner. Laboratory experiments suggest that a more complicated tax system often (if not always) tends to decrease compliance and that better administrative services that make it easier for an individual to pay taxes tend to improve compliance (Alm, Jackson, and McKee, 1993b; Alm et al., 2010; Alm et al., 2019b). Even so, these effects are weak and variable and other experimental work finds that increasing complexity increases reported income (Beer, Kasper, and Loeprick, 2019). It may well be that "mental accounting" may help explain the impacts of complexity (Muehlbacher, Hartl, and Kirchler, 2017; Olsen et al., 2019a).

48.5.11 *Demographics Matter*

There is consistent evidence that compliance may be motivated, or at least affected, by numerous demographic variables. For example, individuals in laboratory experiments are more likely to decrease their compliance if they are male, if they are younger, and if they do not prepare their own taxes (Friedland, Maital, and Rutenberg, 1978; Baldry, 1987; Alm, Jackson, and McKee, 1992a; Alm and McKee, 2004, 2006; Alm et al., 2010, 2012; Alm, Bloomquist, and McKee, 2017). The effects of most other demographic variables are uncertain. These results indicate clearly the great heterogeneity of individual behavior, a finding that has been consistently found in survey evidence going all the way back to Vogel (1974) and continuing more recently with Torgler (2003) and Hofmann et al. (2017): individuals who are otherwise identical but differ only in (say) age exhibit very different compliance behaviors.[17]

48.5.12 *Individuals Are Motivated by Many Factors beyond Narrow Financial Interest*

Individuals who are identified as having greater sympathy (e.g., "concern for another's well-being," measured by the frequency of prosocial behavior) are more compliant, and individuals who are "primed" to elicit empathy (e.g., "putting yourself in someone else's shoes") or to do the "moral" action are more compliant (Christian and Alm, 2014). Other motivations have also been found to affect compliance. For example, Konrad and Qari

[17] Some evidence for the role of demographics comes from the Taxpayer Compliance Measurement Program (TCMP) of the Internal Revenue Service (IRS). These data suggest that compliance tends to be lower for individuals who are younger, who are single, and who are self-employed (Clotfelter, 1983; Witte and Woodbury, 1985; Dubin and Wilde, 1988; Dubin, Graetz, and Wilde, 1990; Feinstein, 1991; Beron, Tauchen, and Witte, 1992; Erard, 1993; Erard and Ho, 2001; Alm, Clark, and Leibel, 2016).

(2012) and Gangl, Torgler, and Kirchler (2016) find empirical evidence that individuals who exhibit greater "patriotism" are more compliant, possibly because more patriotism generates more cooperation. In promising if still tentative work, there is emerging evidence that the compliance decision creates emotional (or psychic) distress, as measured by skin conductance responses (Coricelli et al., 2010) or heart rate variability (Dulleck et al., 2016). However, the role of emotions in tax compliance decisions remains largely unexamined (Olsen et al., 2018; Enachescu et al., 2020).

48.5.13 *Summary*

The evidence from most all laboratory experiments indicates that individuals are motivated by narrowly defined, and individually based, financial considerations (e.g., audits, penalties). However, the evidence also indicates that they are motivated by nonfinancial considerations (e.g., trust, sympathy, empathy, guilt, shame, morality). Further, there is some evidence that they are motivated by social considerations (e.g., social norms, public goods, voting, neighbor behavior). There is also evidence that individuals are motivated by information and by the ways in which they process this information. Finally, the evidence is clear that there is great heterogeneity across individuals; that is, individuals cannot be represented by a single representative agent but must be considered a collection of different segments.

This last conclusion – on individual heterogeneity – is especially important. Put differently, there is no "typical" individual who responds predictably and reliably to all policies. People are complicated, motivated by many different factors, and responsive (if at all) in different ways. In this regard, Gould (1996) emphasizes that it is grossly misleading to represent a complex system by a single, so-called representative agent, who behaves in some average or typical way. Instead, most systems have incredible variety – a "full house" of individual behaviors – and the proper understanding of any system requires recognition of this basic fact. Indeed, Gould (1996) argues that the ways in which a system changes over time are attributable largely to changes in the amount of variation within the system, rather than to changes in some largely meaningless "average" behavior across its individual members.

This lesson seems especially apt for tax compliance. People exhibit a remarkable diversity in their behavior. There are individuals who always cheat and those who always comply, some who behave as if they maximize the expected utility of the tax evasion gamble, others who seem to overweight low probabilities, individuals who respond in different ways to changes in their tax burden, some who are at times cooperative and at other times free-riders, and many who seem to be guided by such things as social norms, moral sentiments, and equity.

Indeed, recent research both by the Internal Revenue Service (2010) and by Her Majesty's Revenue and Customs Service (HMRC, 2009) suggests that understanding the "full house" of taxpayer heterogeneity is essential in determining a "full house" of policies to control evasion. Devising policies to improve compliance requires recognizing the existence of these many types of taxpayer and then targeting policies appropriately, as we discuss next.

48.6 DEVISING POLICIES TO IMPROVE COMPLIANCE

What does all of this work suggest about devising government policies to improve compliance?

We believe that there are three "paradigms" for tax administration that emerge from this experimental research. These paradigms start with a government compliance strategy based on detection and punishment. However, these paradigms also go well beyond one that emphasizes only enforcement to include a range of additional policies for which much theoretical and empirical support is now emerging.

Under a first paradigm – what we term the traditional *"Enforcement Paradigm"* – the emphasis is exclusively on repression of illegal behavior through frequent audits and stiff penalties. This has been the conventional paradigm of tax administrations throughout history, and it fits well the standard portfolio model of tax evasion based upon the economics-of-crime theory (Becker, 1968).

However, laboratory experiments also suggest a second paradigm, one that acknowledges the role of enforcement but also recognizes the role of tax administration as a facilitator and a provider of services to taxpayer-citizens, in order to assist taxpayers in every step of filing their returns and paying taxes. This new *"Service Paradigm"* for tax administration fits squarely with the perspective that emphasizes the role of government-provided services as a consideration in the individual tax compliance decision. Indeed, the most recent literature on tax administration reform has emphasized this new paradigm for tax administration, as a facilitator and a provider of services to taxpayer-citizens, and many recent administrative reforms around the world have embraced this new paradigm with great success.

A third paradigm is also suggested by recent laboratory experiments, especially the emerging work that sees the taxpayer as a member of a larger group, as a social creature whose behavior depends upon his or her own moral values (and those of others) and also upon his or her perception of the quality, credibility, and reliability of the tax administration. We term this a *"Trust Paradigm"*. It is consistent with the role of various behavioral economics factors like social norms broadly defined in the compliance decision. It is based on the notion that individuals are more likely to respond either to enforcement or to services if they believe that the government generally and the tax administration specifically are honest, and if they believe that other individuals are similarly motivated; that is, "trust" in the authorities – and in other individuals – can have a positive impact on compliance.

Given this discussion, designing strategies to control tax evasion falls into three main categories, each consistent with one of the three paradigms: increase the likelihood and the threat of punishment; improve the provision of tax services; and change the tax culture.

First, there is scope for improvement in policies to increase detection and punishment (e.g., the Enforcement Paradigm). Traditionally, there are three main aspects of tax administration: taxpayer registration, taxpayer audit, and collections. Improvements in each of these areas are feasible, all of which would enhance detection and punishment.

Second, there is scope for improvement in the services of the tax administration by becoming more "consumer-friendly," along the lines of the Service Paradigm. Such policies include promoting taxpayer education, providing taxpayer services to assist taxpayers in filing returns and paying taxes, improving phone advice service, improving the tax agency website, simplifying taxes and tax forms, and simplifying the payment of taxes. The basic thrust of these actions is to treat the taxpayer more as a client than as a potential criminal.

Third, there may be scope for a government-induced change in the culture of paying taxes, consistent with the Trust Paradigm, by using the mass media to reinforce tax compliance as the ethical form of behavior, publicizing cheaters, emphasizing the link between payment of taxes and the receipt of government services, targeting certain groups (e.g., new firms or employees) in order to introduce from the start the notion that paying taxes is "the right thing to do," enlisting other organizations to promote compliance, avoiding actions that lead individuals to think cheating is "okay" (e.g., a tax amnesty), addressing perceived inequities in the ways people feel that they are treated, and promoting a tax administrator – and a taxpayer – "code of ethics." It is this third paradigm that is, we believe, an essential but largely neglected strategy for improving compliance.

48.7 CONCLUSIONS: THE PAST, PRESENT, AND FUTURE OF LABORATORY EXPERIMENTS

What can laboratory experiments teach us about tax compliance and about compliance more broadly? Early experimental work investigated the traditional deterrence model of tax compliance, and analyzed the effects of audit probabilities, fines, and tax rates. These studies provided strong indication for a deterrence effect of audits, weaker evidence on the deterrence effects of fines, and somewhat nuanced effects of tax rates on compliance. More recent experimental research has added additional perspectives to the traditional deterrence model. For instance, individual rewards and public goods seem to increase compliance, particularly so when taxpayers can participate in the choice of institutions. Social norms, as reflected in part in a reliable and trusted institutional environment, also increase compliance. Compliance has been found to be affected by communication with the tax administration and with other taxpayers. Experimental research has shown that third party reporting reduces noncompliance substantially, and that younger people and men are less compliant than older people and women. Of some note, experiments have shown that factors that go well beyond financial interest affect compliance, factors such as tax morale, sympathy, and social norms, as reflected in part in a reliable and trusted institutional environment.

In short, there should be a "full house" of strategies to address the "full house" of motivations. Even so, the actual evidence supporting these paradigms is not always compelling. Clearly, additional research is required on the potential impacts of the three paradigms of enforcement, service, and trust.

Indeed, many of the experimental findings on tax compliance behavior are instructive for our understanding of compliance behavior more broadly. For instance, the effect of deterrence is often weaker than theoretically predicted, so it seems unlikely that regulatory approaches that rely on deterrence alone will be successful in achieving high levels of compliance. The social dilemma that many experiments on tax compliance investigate might be of even greater relevance in other domains, such as environmental protection, where the consequences of noncompliance can be more visible than they are for tax evasion. As a consequence, the effects of social norms and mutual trust might be more relevant here. The provision of services that make it easier for individuals and firms to comply with government enforcement and regulatory policies may also represent a potentially useful policy tool in achieving compliance in domains beyond tax compliance.[18]

Given these considerations, we believe that there are several areas where the use of laboratory experiments has the potential to provide important new evidence on compliance behavior, shedding light on issues that are not yet fully understood in tax compliance and beyond. For instance, what are the drivers of different responses to tax audits and to enforcement more broadly? How does legal complexity affect compliance? What is the role of advisors or consultants in compliance decisions? How do individuals respond if the

[18] See especially Alm and Shimshack (2014) for a discussion of how the lessons from research on tax compliance (and other fields) have lessons for environmental enforcement.

administration fails to detect and prosecute noncompliant behavior? How does the subjective appraisal of an audit affect the willingness to comply in the future? How will technological advancements (e.g., digitization of (taxpayer) services, filing improvements, advances in third-party information capabilities) change the dynamics between individuals and tax agencies? How does taxpayer "numeracy" affect taxpayer compliance and, more broadly, how does education affect the willingness and ability to comply? Finally, future studies might explore how long-lasting are the effects of policy interventions.

These – and many other questions – seem well-suited to the application of laboratory experiments, including those that investigate decision processes (rather than decision outcomes) and the dynamic and interactive aspects of compliance behavior. In this work, we anticipate that laboratory experiments will continue to play an important role. They provide important insights into aspects of compliance that are difficult to observe outside the laboratory, even though they cannot fully reflect the real-world complexity that individuals face in their actual compliance choices. We remain convinced that the insights obtained from laboratory experiments can, and should, inform the policy debate in ongoing efforts to improve compliance and the work of public administrations.

REFERENCES

Advani, Arun, William Elming, and Jonathan Shaw. 2015. "How Long-Lasting Are the Effects of Audits?" TARC Discussion Paper 011–15. Exeter, UK: Tax Administration Research Centre, University of Exeter.

Agostini, Claudio A., and Claudia Martínez. 2014. "Response of Tax Credit Claims to Tax Enforcement: Evidence from a Quasi-experiment in Chile." Fiscal Studies 35(1): 41–65.

Allingham, Michael G., and Agnar Sandmo. 1972. "Income Tax Evasion: A Theoretical Analysis." *Journal of Public Economics* 1(3–4): 323–38.

Alm, James. 2012. "Measuring, Explaining, and Controlling Tax Evasion: Lessons from Theory, Field Studies, and Experiments." *International Tax and Public Finance* 19(1): 54–77.

2019. "What Motivates Tax Compliance?" *Journal of Economic Surveys* 33(2): 353–88.

Alm, James, and Antoine Malézieux. in press. "40 Years of Tax Evasion Games: A Meta-analysis." *Experimental Economics*.

Alm, James, and Michael McKee. 2004. "Tax Compliance as a Coordination Game." *Journal of Economic Behavior & Organization* 54(3): 297–312.

2006. "Audit Certainty, Audit Productivity, and Taxpayer Compliance." *National Tax Journal* 59(4): 801–16.

Alm, James, and Jay Shimshack. 2014. "Environmental Enforcement and Compliance: Lessons from Pollution, Safety, and Tax Settings." *Foundations and Trends in Microeconomics* 10(4): 209–74.

Alm, James, Roy Bahl, and Matthew N. Murray. 1990. "Tax Structure and Tax Compliance." *Review of Economics and Statistics* 72(4): 603–13.

Alm, James, Betty R. Jackson, and Michael McKee. 1992a. "Deterrence and Beyond: Toward a Kinder, Gentler IRS." In *Why People Pay Taxes: Tax Compliance and Enforcement*, Joel Slemrod (ed.). Ann Arbor: University of Michigan Press, 311–29.

1992b. "Estimating the Determinants of Taxpayer Compliance with Experimental Data." *National Tax Journal* 45(1): 107–14.

1993a. "Fiscal Exchange, Collective Decision Institutions, and Tax Compliance." *Journal of Economic Behavior & Organization* 22(4): 285–303.

1993b. "Institutional Uncertainty and Taxpayer Compliance." *American Economic Review* 82(4): 1018–26.

2009. "Getting the Word Out: Increased Enforcement, Audit Information Dissemination, and Compliance Behavior." *Journal of Public Economics* 93(3–4): 60–84.

Alm, James, Gary H. McClelland, and William D. Schulze. 1992. "Why Do People Pay Taxes?" *Journal of Public Economics* 48(1): 21–38.

1999. "Changing the Social Norm of Tax Compliance by Voting." *Kyklos* 52(2): 141–71.
Alm, James, Mark B. Cronshaw, and Michael McKee. 1993. "Tax Compliance with Endogenous Audit Selection Rules." *Kyklos* 46(1): 27–45.
Alm, James, Isabel Sanchez, and Anna de Juan. 1995. "Economic and Noneconomic Factors in Tax Compliance." *Kyklos* 48(1): 3–18.
Alm, James, John Deskins, and Michael McKee. 2009. "Do Individuals Comply on Income Not Reported by Their Employer?" *Public Finance Review* 37(2): 120–41.
Alm, James, Todd L. Cherry, Michael Jones, and Michael McKee. 2010. "Taxpayer Information Assistance Services and Tax Reporting Behavior." *Journal of Economic Psychology* 31(4): 577–86.
2012. "Social Programs as Positive Inducements for Tax Participation." *Journal of Economic Behavior & Organization* 84(1): 85–96.
Alm, James, Kim M. Bloomquist, and Michael McKee. 2015. "On the External Validity of Laboratory Tax Compliance Experiments." *Economic Inquiry* 53(2): 1170–86.
2017. "When You Know Your Neighbor Pays Taxes: Information, Peer Effects, and Tax Compliance." *Fiscal Studies* 38(4): 587–613.
Alm, James, David Bruner, and Michael McKee. 2016. "Honesty and Dishonesty in Taxpayer Communications in an Enforcement Regime." *Journal of Economic Psychology* 56: 85–96.
Alm, James, Jeremy Clark, and Kara Leibel. 2016. "Enforcement, Socio-economic Diversity, and Tax Filing Compliance in the United States." *Southern Economic Journal* 82(3): 725–47.
Alm, James, Michele Bernasconi, Susan Laury, Daniel J. Lee, and Sally Wallace. 2017. "Culture, Compliance, and Confidentiality: Taxpayer Behavior in the United States and Italy." *Journal of Economic Behavior & Organization* 140: 176–96.
Alm, James, William D. Schulze, Carrie von Bose, and Jubo Yan. 2019a. "Appeals to Social Norms and Taxpayer Compliance." Department of Economics Working Paper. New Orleans, LA: Tulane University.
2019b. "A Taxpayer's Use of a Tax Preparer: Choice Considerations and Compliance Effects." Department of Economics Working Paper. New Orleans, LA: Tulane University.
Amberger, Harald, Eva Eberhartinger, and Matthias Kasper. 2019. "Tax-Rate Biases in Tax-Planning Decisions: Experimental Evidence." WU International Taxation Research Paper Series. Vienna.
Andreoni, James, Brian Erard, and Jonathan Feinstein. 1998. "Tax Compliance." *Journal of Economic Literature* 36(2): 818–60.
Andrighetto, Giulia, Nan Zhang, Stefania Ottone, Ferruccio Ponzano, John D'Attoma, and Sven Steinmo. 2016. "Are Some Countries More Honest than Others? Evidence from a Tax Compliance Experiment in Sweden and Italy." *Frontiers in Psychology* 7. www.frontiersin.org/articles/10.3389/fpsyg.2016.00472/full.
Angrist, Joshua D., and Jorn-Steffen Pischke. 2010. "The Credibility Revolution in Empirical Economics: How Better Research Design Is Taking the Con out of Econometrics." *Journal of Economic Perspectives* 24(2): 3–30.
Baldry, Jonathan C. 1987. "Income Tax Evasion and the Tax Schedule: Some Experimental Results." *Public Finance* 42(3): 357–83.
Bazart, Cecile, and Michael Pickhardt. 2011. "Fighting Income Tax Evasion with Positive Rewards." *Public Finance Review* 39(1): 124–49.
Beck, Paul J., Jon S. Davis, and Woon-Oh Jung. 1991. "Experimental Evidence on Taxpayer Reporting Behavior." *Accounting Review* 66(3): 535–58.
Becker, Gary S. 1968. "Crime and Punishment – An Economic Approach." *Journal of Political Economy* 76(2): 169–217.
Becker, Winfried, Heinz-Jurgen Buchner, and Simon Sleeking. 1987. "The Impact of Public Transfer Expenditures on Tax Evasion: An Experimental Approach." *Journal of Public Economics* 34(2): 243–52.
Beer, Sebastian, Mattias Kasper, and Jan Loeprick. 2019. "Puzzling Tax Law – Behavioral Responses to Complex Rules." Working Paper.
Beer, Sebastian, Matthias Kasper, Erich Kirchler, and Brian Erard. 2020. "Do Audits Deter or Provoke Future Tax Noncompliance? Evidence on Self-Employed Taxpayers." *CESifo Economic Studies* 66(3): 248–64.

Bernasconi, Michele, and Alberto Zanardi. 2004. "Tax Evasion, Tax Rates, and Reference Dependence." *FinanzArchiv* 60(3): 422–45.

Beron, Kurt J., Tauchen, Helen V., and Ann D. Witte. 1992. "The Effect of Audits and Socio-economic Variables on Compliance." In *Who Pays Their Taxes and Why?* Joel Slemrod (ed.), Ann Arbor: University of Michigan Press, 67–89.

Blackwell, Calvin. 2010. "A Meta-analysis of Incentive Effects in Tax Compliance Experiments." In *Developing Alternative Frameworks for Explaining Tax Compliance Behavior*, James Alm, Jorge Martinez-Vazquez, and Benno Torgler (eds.). New York: Routledge, 97–112.

Bosco, Luigi, and Luigi Mittone. 1997. "Tax Evasion and Moral Constraints: Some Experimental Evidence." *Kyklos* 50(3): 297–324.

Camerer, Colin F. 2015. "The Promise and Success of Lab-Field Generalizability in Experimental Economics: A Reply to Levitt and List." In *The Methods of Modern Experimental Economics*, Guillaume R. Frechette and Andrew Schotter (eds.). New York: Oxford University Press, ch. 14.

Carillo, Paul, Dina Pomeranz, and Monica Singhal. 2017. "Dodging the Taxman: Firm Misreporting and Limits to Tax Enforcement." *American Economic Journal: Applied Economics* 9(2): 144–64.

Casagrande, Alberto, Daniela Di Cagno, Alessandro Pandimiglio, and Marco Spallone. 2015. "The Effect of Competition on Tax Compliance: The Role of Audit Rules and Shame." *Journal of Behavioral and Experimental Economics* 59: 96–110.

Casal, Sandro, Christoph Kogler, Luigi Mittone, and Erich Kirchler. 2016. "Tax Compliance Depends on Voice of Taxpayers." *Journal of Economic Psychology* 56: 141–50.

Casal, Sandro, and Luigi Mittone. 2016. "Social Esteem versus Social Stigma: The Role of Anonymity in an Income Reporting Game." *Journal of Economic Behavior & Organization* 124: 55–66.

Choo, C. Y. Lawrence, Miguel A. Fonseca, and Gareth D. Myles. 2016. "Do Students Behave like Real Taxpayers in the Lab? Evidence from a Real Effort Tax Compliance Experiment." *Journal of Economic Behavior & Organization* 124: 102–14.

Christensen, Garret, and Edward Miguel. 2018. "Transparency, Reproducibility, and the Credibility of Economics Research." *Journal of Economic Literature* 56(3): 920–80.

Christian, Roberta Calvet, and James Alm. 2014. "Sympathy, Empathy, and Tax Compliance." *Journal of Economic Psychology* 40: 62–82.

Clotfelter, Charles T. 1983. "Tax Evasion and Tax Rates: An Analysis of Individual Returns." *Review of Economics and Statistics* 65(3): 363–73.

Collins, Julie H., and R. David Plumlee. 1991. "The Taxpayer's Labor and Reporting Decisions: The Effect of Audit Schemes." *Accounting Review* 66(3): 559–76.

Coricelli, Giorgio, Mateus Joffily, Claude Montmarquette, and Marie Claire Villeval. 2010. "Cheating, Emotions, and Rationality: An Experiment on Tax Evasion." *Experimental Economics* 13(2): 226–47.

Cowell, Frank A. 1990. *Cheating the Government: The Economics of Evasion*. Cambridge, MA: MIT Press.

Cummings, Ronald G., Jorge Martinez-Vazquez, Michael McKee, and Benno Torgler. 2009. "Tax Morale Affects Tax Compliance: Evidence from Surveys and an Artefactual Field Experiment." *Journal of Economic Behavior & Organization* 70(3): 447–57.

Davis, Douglas D., and Charles A. Holt. 1993. "Experimental Economics: Methods, Problems, and Promise." *Estudios Economicos*: 179–212.

DeBacker, Jason, Bradley T. Heim, Anh Tran, and Alexander Yuskavage. 2015. "Legal Enforcement and Corporate Behavior: An Analysis of Tax Aggressiveness after an Audit." *Journal of Law and Economics* 58(2): 291–324.

Dhami, Sanjit, and Ali al-Nowaihi. 2007. "Why Do People Pay Taxes? Prospect Theory versus Expected Utility Theory." *Journal of Economic Behavior & Organization* 64(1): 171–92.

Doerrenberg, Philipp, and Denvil Duncan. 2014. "Experimental Evidence on the Relationship between Tax Evasion Opportunities and Labor Supply." *European Economic Review* 68: 48–70.

Dubin, Jeffrey, Michael Graetz, and Louis L. Wilde. 1990. "The Effect of Audit Rates on the Federal Individual Income Tax, 1977–1986." *National Tax Journal* 43(4): 395–409.

Dubin, Jeffrey A., and Louis L. Wilde. 1988. "An Empirical Analysis of Federal Income Tax Auditing and Compliance." *National Tax Journal* 41(1): 61–74.

Dulleck, Uwe, Jonas Fooken, Cameron Newton, Andrea Ristl, Markus Schaffner, and Benno Torgler. 2016. "Tax Compliance and Psychic Costs: Behavioral Experimental Evidence Using a Physiological Marker." *Journal of Public Economics* 134: 9–18.

Enachescu, Janina, Žiga Puklavec, Christian Martin Bauer, Jerome Olsen, Erich Kirchler, and James Alm. 2020. "Incidental Emotions, Integral Emotions, and Decisions to Pay Taxes." In *Behavioral Public Finance: Individuals, Society, and the State*, Larissa Batrancea, Savas Cevik, and M. Mustafa Erdoğdu (eds.). New York: Routledge.

Erard, Brian. 1992. "The Influence of Tax Audits on Reporting Behavior." In *Why People Pay Taxes: Tax Compliance and Enforcement*, Joel Slemrod (ed.). Ann Arbor: University of Michigan Press, 95–114.

1993. "Taxation with Representation: An Analysis of the Role of Tax Practitioners in Tax Compliance." *Journal of Public Economics* 52(2): 163–97.

Erard, Brian, and Chih-Chin Ho. 2001. "Searching for Ghosts: Who Are the Nonfilers and How Much Tax Do They Owe?" *Journal of Public Economics* 81(1): 25–50.

Fack, Gabrielle and Camille Landais. 2016. "The Effect of Tax Enforcement on Tax Elasticities: Evidence from Charitable Contributions in France." *Journal of Public Economics* 133: 23–40.

Falk, Armin, and James J. Heckman. 2009. "Lab Experiments Are a Major Source of Knowledge in the Social Sciences." *Science* 326(5952): 535–8.

Feinstein, Jonathan S. 1991. "An Econometric Model of Income Tax Evasion and Its Detection." *RAND Journal of Economics* 22(1): 14–35.

Feld, Lars P., and Bruno S. Frey. 2002. "Trust Breeds Trust: How Taxpayers Are Treated." *Economics of Governance* 3(2): 87–99.

Feld, Lars P., Bruno S. Frey, and Benno Torgler. 2006. "Rewarding Honest Taxpayers." In *Managing and Maintaining Compliance*, Henk Elffers, Peter Verboon, and Wim Huisman (eds.). The Hague: Boom Legal Publishers, 45–61.

Feld, Lars P., and Jean-Robert Tyran. 2002. "Tax Evasion and Voting: An Experimental Analysis." *Kyklos* 55(2): 197–221.

Fochmann, Martin, and Eike B. Kroll. 2016. "The Effects of Rewards on Tax Compliance Decisions." *Journal of Economic Psychology* 52: 38–55.

Fortin, Bernard, Guy Lacroix, and Marie Claire Villeval. 2007. "Tax Evasion and Social Interactions." *Journal of Public Economics* 91(11–12): 2089–2112.

Frechette, Guillaume R. 2015. "Laboratory Experiments: Professionals versus Students." In *The Methods of Modern Experimental Economics*, Guillaume R. Frechette and Andrew Schotter (eds.). New York: Oxford University Press, ch. 17.

Frey, Bruno. 1997. *Not Just for the Money: An Economic Theory of Personal Motivation*. Cheltenham, UK: Edward Elgar.

Friedland, Nehemiah, Shlomo Maital, and Aryeh Rutenberg. 1978. "A Simulation Study of Income Tax Evasion." *Journal of Public Economics* 10(1): 107–16.

Gangl, Katharina, Benno Torgler, and Erich Kirchler. 2016. "Patriotism's Impact on Cooperation with the State: An Experimental Study on Tax Compliance." *Political Psychology* 37(6): 867–81.

Gemmell, Norman, and Marisa Ratto. 2012. "Behavioral Responses to Taxpayer Audits: Evidence from Random Taxpayer Inquiries." *National Tax Journal* 65(1): 33–58.

Gould, Stephen Jay. 1996. *Full House: The Spread of Excellence from Plato to Darwin*. New York: Harmony Books.

Guala, Francesco, and Luigi Mittone. 2005. "Experiments in Economics: External Validity and the Robustness of Phenomena." *Journal of Economic Methodology* 12: 495–515.

2010. "How History and Convention Create Norms: An Experimental Study." *Journal of Economic Psychology* 31(4): 749–56.

Hallsworth, Michael. 2014. "The Use of Field Experiments to Increase Tax Compliance." *Oxford Review of Economic Policy* 30(4): 658–79.

Harrison, Glenn W., Morten Lau, and E. Elisabet Rutström. 2015. "Theory, Experimental Design and Econometrics Are Complementary (and So Are Lab and Field Experiments)." In *The Methods of Modern Experimental Economics*, Guillaume R. Frechette and Andrew Schotter (eds.). New York: Oxford University Press, ch. 15.

Hasegawa, Makoto, Jefrey L. Hoopes, Ryo Ishida, and Joel Slemrod. 2013. "The Effect of Public Disclosure on Reported Taxable Income: Evidence from Individuals and Corporations in Japan." *National Tax Journal* 66(3): 571–608.

Hashimzade, Nigar, Gareth D. Myles, and Binh Tran-Nam. 2013. "Applications of Behavioural Economics to Tax Evasion." *Journal of Economic Surveys* 27(5): 941–77.

Her Majesty's Revenue and Customs (HMRC). 2009. *Individual's Prioritisation: An Investigation into Segmentation of the Individuals Customer Base*. London: HMRC.

Hofmann, Eva, Martin Voracek, Christine Bock, and Erich Kirchler. 2017. "Tax Compliance across Sociodemographic Categories: Meta-analyses of Survey Studies in 111 Countries." *Journal of Economic Psychology* 62: 63–71.

Internal Revenue Service (IRS). 2006. *Tax Year 2001 Federal Tax Gap* (Extended Version). Washington, DC: IRS Office of Research, Analysis, and Statistics. www.irs.gov/pub/irs-soi/01rastg07map.pdf.

2010. *Final Report for Planning Theoretical Research (T.O. 0002)*. Washington, DC: Internal Revenue Service.

2012. *Tax Gap Estimates for Tax Year 2006 – Overview*. Washington, DC: IRS Office of Research, Analysis, and Statistics. www.irs.gov/pub/newsroom/overview_tax_gap_2006.pdf.

2016. *Tax Gap Estimates for Tax Years 2008–2010*. Washington, DC: IRS Office of Research, Analysis, and Statistics. www.irs.gov/pub/newsroom/tax%20gap%20estimates%20for%202008%20through%202010.pdf.

Kagel, John H. 2015. "Laboratory Experiments: The Lab in Relationship to Field Experiments, Field Data, and Economic Theory." In *The Methods of Modern Experimental Economics*, Guillaume R. Frechette and Andrew Schotter (eds.). New York: Oxford University Press, ch. 16.

Kagel, John H., and Alvin E. Roth (eds.). 1995. *The Handbook of Experimental Economics*. Princeton, NJ: Princeton University Press.

Karakostas, Alexandrow, and Daniel John Zizzo. 2016. "Compliance and the Power of Authority." *Journal of Economic Behavior & Organization* 124: 67–80.

Kasper, Matthias, and James Alm. 2020. "Audits, Audit 'Effectiveness', and Post-audit Tax Compliance." WU International Taxation Research Paper Series 2020-12.

Kasper, Matthias, Christoph Kogler, and Erich Kirchler. 2015. "Tax Policy and the News: An Empirical Analysis of Taxpayers' Perceptions of Tax-Related Media Coverage and Its Impact on Tax Compliance." *Journal of Behavioral and Experimental Economics* 54: 58–63.

Kastlunger, Barbara, Erich Kirchler, Luigi Mittone, and Julia Pitters. 2009. "Sequences of Audits, Tax Compliance, and Taxpaying Strategies." *Journal of Economic Psychology* 30(3): 405–18.

Kessler, Judd B., and Lise Vesterlund. 2015. "The External Validity of Laboratory Experiments: The Misleading Emphasis on Quantitative Effects." In *The Methods of Modern Experimental Economics*, Guillaume R. Frechette and Andrew Schotter (eds.). New York: Oxford University Press, ch. 18.

Kinsey, Karyl A. 1992. "Deterrence and Alienation Effects of IRS Enforcement: An Analysis of Survey Data." In *Why People Pay Taxes: Tax Compliance and Enforcement*, Joel Slemrod (ed.). Ann Arbor: University of Michigan Press, 259–85.

Kirchler, Erich. 2007. *The Economic Psychology of Tax Behaviour*. Cambridge: Cambridge University Press.

Kirchler, Erich, Erik Hoelzl, and Ingrid Wahl. 2008. "Enforced versus Voluntary Tax Compliance: The 'Slippery Slope' Framework." *Journal of Economic Psychology* 29(2): 210–25.

Kleven, Henrik J., Martin B. Knudsen, Claus T. Kreiner, Søren Pedersen, and Emmanuel Saez. 2011. "Unwilling or Unable to Cheat? Evidence from a Randomized Tax Audit Experiment in Denmark." *Econometrica* 79(3): 651–92.

Kogler, Christoph, Larissa Batrancea, Anca Nichita, Jozsef Pantya, Alexis Belianin, and Erich Kirchler. 2013. "Trust and Power as Determinants of Tax Compliance: Testing the Assumptions of the Slippery Slope Framework in Austria, Hungary, Romania, and Russia." *Journal of Economic Psychology* 34(1): 169–80.

Kogler, Christoph, Luigi Mittone, and Erich Kirchler. 2016. "Delayed Feedback on Tax Audits Affects Compliance and Fairness Perceptions." *Journal of Economic Behavior & Organization* 124: 81–7.

Konrad, Kai A., and Salmai Qari. 2012. "The Last Refuge of a Scoundrel? Patriotism and Tax Compliance." *Economica* 79(315): 516–33.

Lefebvre, Mathieu, Pierre Pestieau, Arno Riedl, and Marie Claire Villeval. 2015. "Tax Evasion and Social Information: An Experiment in Belgium, France, and the Netherlands." *International Tax and Public Finance* 22(3): 401–25.
Levitt, Steven D., and John A. List. 2007. "What Do Laboratory Experiments Measuring Social Preferences Reveal about the Real World?" *Journal of Economic Perspectives* 21(2): 153–74.
Maciejovsky, Boris, Erich Kirchler, and Herbert Schwarzenberger. 2007. "Misperceptions of Chance and Loss Repair: On the Dynamics of Tax Compliance." *Journal of Economic Psychology* 28(6): 678–91.
Martinez-Vazquez, Jorge, Gordon B. Harwood, and Ernest R. Larkins. 1992. "Withholding Position and Income Tax Compliance: Some Experimental Evidence." *Public Finance Review* 20(2): 152–74.
Mascagni, Giulia. 2018. "From the Lab to the Field: A Review of Tax Experiments." *Journal of Economic Surveys* 32(2): 273–301.
Mittone, Luigi. 2006. "Dynamic Behaviour in Tax Evasion: An Experimental Approach." *Journal of Socio-Economics* 35(5): 813–35.
Mittone, Luigi, Fabrizio Panebianco, and Alessandro Santoro. 2017. "The Bomb-Crater Effect of Tax Audits: Beyond the Misperception of Chance." *Journal of Economic Psychology* 61: 225–43.
Muehlbacher, Stephan, Barbara Hartl, and Erich Kirchler. 2017. "Mental Accounting and Tax Compliance: Experimental Evidence for the Effect of Mental Segregation of Tax Due and Revenue on Compliance." *Public Finance Review* 45(1): 118–39.
Olsen, Jerome, Matthias Kasper, Janina Enachescu, Tamer Budak, Serkan Benk, and Erich Kirchler. 2018. "Emotions and Tax Compliance among Small Business Owners: An Experimental Survey." *International Review of Law and Economics* 56: 42–52.
Olsen, Jerome, Matthias Kasper, Christoph Kogler, Stephan Muehlbacher, and Erich Kirchler. 2019a. "Mental Accounting of Income Tax and Value Added Tax among Self-Employed Business Owners." *Journal of Economic Psychology* 70: 125–39.
Olsen, Jerome, Christoph Kogler, Mark J. Brandt, Linda Dezső, and Erich Kirchler. 2019b. "Are Consumption Taxes Really Disliked More than Equivalent Costs? Inconclusive Results in the USA and No Effect in the UK." *Journal of Economic Psychology* 75, 102145, DOI: 10.1016/j.joep.2019.02.001.
Onu, Diana, and Lynne Oats. 2016. "'Paying Tax Is Part of Life': Social Norms and Social Influence in Tax Communications." *Journal of Economic Behavior & Organization* 124: 29–42.
Parker, Christine, and Vibeke Nielsen. 2009. "The Challenge of Empirical Research on Business Compliance in Regulatory Capitalism." *Annual Review of Law and Social Science* 5: 45–70.
Perez-Truglia, Ricardo, and Ugo Troiano. 2018. "Shaming Tax Delinquents." *Journal of Public Economics* 167: 120–37.
Plott, Charles R. 1987. "Dimensions of Parallelism: Some Policy Applications of Experimental Methods." In *Laboratory Experimentation in Economics: Six Points of View*, Alvin E. Roth (ed.). New York: Cambridge University Press, 193–219.
Pomeranz, Dina. 2015. "No Taxation without Information: Deterrence and Self-Enforcement in the Value Added Tax." *American Economic Review* 105(8): 2539–69.
Pyle, D. J. 1991. "The Economics of Taxpayer Compliance." *Journal of Economic Surveys* 5(2): 163–98.
Roth, Alvin E. 1987. "Laboratory Experimentation in Economics." In *Advances in Economic Theory, Fifth World Congress*, Truman Bewley (ed.). Cambridge: Cambridge University Press, 269–99.
Sandmo, Agnar. 2012. "An Evasive Topic: Theorizing about the Hidden Economy." *International Tax and Public Finance* 19(1): 5–24.
Slemrod, Joel. 2007. "Cheating Ourselves: The Economics of Tax Evasion." *Journal of Economic Perspectives* 21(1): 25–48.
Slemrod, Joel, and Caroline Weber. 2012. "Evidence of the Invisible: Toward a Credibility Revolution in the Empirical Analysis of Tax Evasion and the Informal Economy." *International Tax and Public Finance* 19(1): 25–53.
Slemrod, Joel, and Shlomo Yitzhaki. 2002. "Tax Avoidance, Evasion, and Administration." In *Handbook of Public Economics, Volume 4* (ch. 22), Alan J. Auerbach and Martin Feldstein (eds.). Amsterdam, London, New York: Elsevier B.V. North Holland Publishers, 1423–70.
Smith, Vernon L. 1976. "Experimental Economics: Induced Value Theory." *American Economic Review* 66(2): 274–9.

1982. "Microeconomic Systems as an Experimental Science." *American Economic Review* 72(5): 923–55.
Spicer, Michael W., and Lee A. Becker. 1980. "Fiscal Inequity and Tax Compliance: An Experimental Approach." *National Tax Journal* 33(2): 171–5.
Spicer, Michael W., and Rodney E. Hero. 1985. "Tax Evasion and Heuristics: A Research Note." *Journal of Public Economics* 26(2): 263–7.
Srinivasan, T. N. 1973. "Tax Evasion: A Model." *Journal of Public Economics* 2(4): 339–46.
Torgler, Benno. 2002. "Speaking to Theorists and Searching for Facts: Tax Morale and Compliance in Experiments." *Journal of Economic Surveys* 16(5): 657–83.
2003. "Tax Morale, Rule-Governed Behaviour, and Trust." *Constitutional Political Economy* 14(2): 119–40.
2007. *Tax Compliance and Tax Morale: A Theoretical and Empirical Analysis*. Cheltenham, UK: Edward Elgar.
2016. "Tax Compliance and Data: What Is Available and What Is Needed." *Australian Economic Review* 49(3): 352–64.
Tyler, Tom R. 1990. *Why People Obey the Law*. New Haven, CT: Yale University Press.
Vogel, Joachim. 1974. "Taxation and Public Opinion in Sweden: An Interpretation of Recent Data." *National Tax Journal* 27(4): 499–514.
Wahl, Ingrid, Stephan Muehlbacher, and Erich Kirchler. 2010. "The Impact of Voting on Tax Payments." *Kyklos* 63(1): 144–58.
Webley, Paul. 1987. "Audit Probabilities and Tax Evasion in a Business Simulation." *Economics Letters* 25(3): 267–70.
Webley, Paul, Henry Robben, Henk Elffers, and Dick Hessing. 1991. *Tax Evasion: An Experimental Approach*. Cambridge: Cambridge University Press.
Witte, Ann D., and Diane F. Woodbury. 1985. "The Effect of Tax Laws and Tax Administration on Tax Compliance." *National Tax Journal* 38: 1–13.
Yaniv, Gideon. 1999. "Tax Compliance and Advanced Tax Payments: A Prospect Theory Analysis." *National Tax Journal* 52(4): 753–64.
Zhang, Nan, Giulia Andrighetto, Stefania Ottone, Ferruccio Ponzano, and Sven Steimo. 2016. "'Willing to Pay'? Tax Compliance in Britain and Italy: An Experimental Analysis." *PLoS ONE* 11(2). http://journals.plos.org/plosone/article?id=10.1371/journal.pone.0150277.

49

Compliance Experiments in the Field: Features, Limitations, and Examples

Dane Thorley

Abstract: Randomized experiments are broadly considered to be the gold standard for making empirically informed causal claims. Field experiments (often called randomized controlled trials or RCTs) are randomized studies that feature naturalistic context, participants, treatments, and outcomes in order to provide researchers and policy-makers with the most accurate vision of how laws and practices will play out in the real world. This methodology is particularly well-suited for evaluating if, how, and why individuals and organizations respond to rules and regulations and should be an essential piece in the puzzle of compliance studies. This chapter begins with a brief primer on field experiments, outlining why randomized experiments are so valuable as a methodological tool and how the unique attributes of field experiments provide a distinct set of benefits from similar causality-focused approaches such as laboratory experiments and natural experiments. The chapter then highlights the important assumptions and practical difficulties in conducting and analyzing field experiments, paying particular attention to how these factors can be limitations when studying compliance. The chapter concludes by considering what sorts of compliance-related field experiments are possible by focusing on two areas in which their use is well established – tax compliance and criminal deterrence – and then highlights individual experiments testing a diversity of substantive topics less commonly explored by field experimentalists such as international law, food safety inspections, and the behavior of political elites.

49.1 INTRODUCTION

As the chapters in this handbook have shown, the field of compliance covers an extensive range of substantive topics and involves scholars from numerous disciplines. While the specific theories, mechanisms, and arenas that these scholars focus on inevitably vary, the base questions that serve as the foundation for their inquiries are more or less the same: How are rules, laws, and policies selected, implemented, and enforced? How do people or groups of people respond to those policies? And *why* do people respond in the ways that they do?

The interaction between rules and behavior has an inherently causal element, and so empirically minded compliance scholars have long pursued approaches and methodologies that can reliably identify the existence and scope of causal effects (Schwartz 1961). However, due in large part to what Angrist and Pischke (2010) have termed the "credibility revolution," the way in which empirical scholars (both inside and outside compliance studies) have approached causal identification has experienced a palpable shift over recent decades.

While traditional causal research sought to achieve identification through systematically modeling the relationship between the variables of interest and other potentially confounding variables, social scientists have become increasingly skeptical of the ability of these approaches – often called "observational" research – to address the problems caused by omitted variable bias (Gerber, Green, and Kaplan 2004).

Randomized experimentation is an alternative to observational research that is particularly well-suited to causal identification because it can overcome omitted variable bias through the exogenous assignment of the dependent variable. Laboratory experiments are the most common form of experimentation in the field of compliance and a powerful tool in this enterprise, but they are characteristically limited by the controlled and artificial environment in which they are conducted (Levitt and List 2007, 2008). Many compliance scholars are, understandably, interested in how the field's theories and empirical observations translate to the practical realities of the real world. What is the most cost-effective way to get people to actually pay their taxes? What sort of impact, if any, does incarceration have on future criminality? Does international law have any effect on individual-level behavior? How well do our laws govern the government itself?

These sorts of question are particularly fertile grounds for field experiments, which blend the causal-identification power of random assignment with the naturalism of in-the-field studies (Gerber and Green 2012). As such, field experiments are an essential methodological tool for exploring the theoretical mechanisms that underpin compliance studies, understanding the practical interaction between actual laws and behavior, and developing effective real-world policies and laws. With a few exceptions, field experiments had been sparingly used to study compliance throughout the latter half of the twentieth century, and although they have been more fully adopted by compliance scholars within some subfields over the last two decades, they are still uncommon, particularly among legal scholars (Green and Thorley 2014).

This chapter discusses why field experiments are valuable to compliance scholars and highlights how they have already been used to study compliance. It begins with a brief primer on field experiments, emphasizing why random assignment is so valuable as a methodological tool and how the unique attributes of field experiments provide a set of benefits that is distinct from those of similar approaches such as laboratory experiments. The chapter then outlines the important assumptions and practical difficulties required to conduct and analyze field experiments, paying particular attention to how these issues can be important limiting factors when studying compliance. The chapter also illustrates what sorts of compliance-related field experiments are possible, first by focusing on two areas in which their use is well established – tax compliance and criminal deterrence – and then by highlighting individual experiments conducted on a diversity of substantive topics less commonly explored by field experimentalists such as international law, food safety inspections, and the behavior of political elites. The chapter concludes with a summary.

49.2 FIELD EXPERIMENTS

49.2.1 *Randomized Experiments as a Solution to Omitted Variable Bias*

Suppose that you are a tax administrator for a country that struggles with tax evasion and are seeking the most efficacious policy for increasing individual-level tax compliance. In particular, you would like to know if and how much tax audits influence the likelihood of individuals underreporting their income in future years.

You have the administrative data on all tax returns over a ten-year period and also know whether and in what year a given individual was audited. An intuitive approach to determining the effect that audits have on tax compliance would be to simply measure the reported income of those individuals who were audited in the year prior against those who were not audited. If audits reduce the likelihood of underreporting income, we would expect to see a greater increase in reported income among those who were audited than among those who were not audited.

However, as an administrator, you know that individuals are, in accordance with department policy, selected for audits based on a risk-assessment score that accounts for several factors, including reported incomes in previous years, the complexity of a tax return, and whether the individual had been caught for reporting discrepancies in the past. This audit policy is an empirical problem because each of these factors is also likely to affect the outcome of interest in your study (the change in reported income), and so the treatment effect you identify from simply comparing the two subject groups is likely not exclusively reflective of the effect of audits.

Using various statistical techniques, you attempt to model and control for these various "confounding" variables. Yet, upon conducting this updated comparison, you also remember that the number of audits that your department is able to conduct over a given time period hinges on available funds, which vary from year to year. Additionally, you are concerned that some government employees may be selecting individuals to audit based on race. So, you consequently control for year and race. Have you properly modeled for these confounding variables, and have you missed any other important factors that could influence your outcome of interest? This problem – the possibility that an unknown or unmeasurable variable is driving the causal estimate in your analysis – is called omitted variable bias and has long been a serious limitation in empirical studies designed to identify causal effects. And while the methodological problems in the above example are undoubtably simplistic (and there are much more sophisticated empirical techniques than simply "controlling" for variables), they reflect the difficulty in overcoming omitted variable bias and identifying causal effects using datasets in which the way the treatment allocated is either unknown or systematically endogenous to the outcome of interest.

Randomized experiments solve the problem of omitted variable bias by randomly and independently assigning the dependent variable across the subject pool. When properly administered, random assignment ensures that the comparison groups in a study are equal in expectation across all possible criteria, except for the fact that only one of the groups has been exposed to the "treatment." As a result, any difference in the measured outcomes between the two groups reflects *only* the causal effect that the researcher is interested in. Consequently, randomized experiments are seen as the gold standard for identifying causal estimates and have been widely adopted by causality-oriented scholars, including those in compliance studies.

49.2.2 *Field Experiments and the Benefits of Naturalism*

Field experiments, commonly referred to as randomized controlled trials (RCTs), are part of the broader family of randomized experiments and therefore produce – under the proper assumptions – an unbiased estimate of the effect of whatever treatment is administered by the researcher. The key distinguishing feature of a field experiment is the emphasis on naturalism or the attempt at designing the experiment so that "[s]ubjects are studied in a natural context where they would have been even if no study had been conducted" (Schwartz and Orleans 1967: 285). As Gerber and Green (2012) identify in their foundational text on field experiments, naturalism can be measured in four ways: (1) how similar the randomized treatment is to the actual law, policy, or intervention; (2) how similar the subjects in the study are to the actual individuals or organizations that will interact with the law, policy, or intervention; (3) how similar the outcome measured in the study is to the actual outcomes; and (4) how similar the context in which the previous three elements interact with each other is to the circumstances that the researchers want to extrapolate to. While not all field experiments feature all four of these criteria, they generally attempt to maximize naturalism to the extent possible.

This emphasis on naturalism yields important benefits for compliance scholars. First, it often (although not always) means that the design and results of an experiment will be more practically intuitive and understandable for individuals without a background in statistics or compliance theory – including policy-makers and government officials – to turn research findings into legal reality. Second, a naturalistic field experiment will produce outcomes that more accurately reflect the true behavior of individuals, both because the subjects are responding to everyday incentives and substantial consequences for noncompliance and because the subjects are not consistently aware that they are being studied. This allows researchers and policy-makers to extrapolate the results to a real-world setting while having to rely on fewer assumptions (Gerber and Green 2012; Duflo and Banerjee 2017).

To make these features more salient, let us return to the tax compliance example from earlier. Under the criteria outlined above, a model field experiment that tests the effect of audits on future tax reporting would randomly assign real audits to evaluate the tax returns of actual taxpayers and then use those individuals' subsequent tax returns to measure changes in reporting behavior, all done through the administrative office that normally presides over such functions. While a study matching this description may seem improbable, this exact field experiment has already been conducted in cooperation with the Denmark tax collection agency (Kleven et al. 2011). The experiment involved more than 40,000 individual taxpayers, and the results showed that audits cause a positive and statistically significant 1 percent increase in reported income, while the threat of future audits (another randomly assigned treatment arm in the experiment) also led to higher reporting.

A close relative of the field experiment is the naturally occurring randomization. Whereas the random assignment process in a field experiment is conducted and/or designed by the researcher herself, researchers relying on naturally occurring randomization identify and utilize a random assignment scheme that was implemented by an outside party. Common examples include the random assignment of judges to court cases or the lottery distribution of a program or benefit that is too costly to provide to all potential recipients. Although this sort of randomization is often implemented without a consideration for the empirical benefits of random assignment, with the proper assumptions, it yields the same causal benefits as a researcher-driven field experiment. For this reason, this chapter treats field experiments and naturally occurring randomizations in the same light and includes reviews of studies utilizing both approaches in Section 49.4.

49.2.3 *How Field Experiments Differ from Lab Experiments*

As James Alm and Matthias Kasper demonstrated in Chapter 48 of this volume, laboratory experiments also provide an escape from the empirical dilemma of omitted variable bias and are a powerful tool for identifying causal effects. Indeed, particularly within compliance studies, lab experiments are nearly ubiquitous: "[v]irtually all aspects of compliance have been examined in some way in experimental work" (Alm 2012: 66). While field experiments are technically included in that observation, lab experiments have long been the method of choice for behavioral economists and psychologists who are interested in testing the theories and predictions regarding the interaction of laws and human behavior.

As their moniker suggests, lab experiments differ from field experiments in that they generally take place in an artificial, tightly controlled environment (a "lab"), often a plainly decorated room at a university.[1] In addition to the physical setting, lab experiments often also feature abstract treatments and restrict the interaction between subjects and the intervention to computers or stylized games. This lack of naturalism is an intentional feature of lab experiments, as it avoids much of the methodological "messiness" of field experiments and grants researchers greater precision and control in order to more tightly test specific theoretical mechanisms and nuances of human behavior (Falk and Heckman 2009).

However, the increased control in lab experiments comes at the cost of external validity. Experimental subjects know that they are part of a study and are sometimes even aware of what the inquiry of interest is. Additionally, lab experiments are unable to replicate the high stakes and long-term behavioral timelines inherent in many of the arenas that compliance scholars are interested in. For these and other reasons, scholars and policy-makers are often wary about how well the findings of lab experiments will translate to real-world policy and behavior (Levitt and List 2007, 2008).

49.3 SOME IMPORTANT ASSUMPTIONS AND LIMITATIONS

While field experimentation is a powerful tool in studying compliance, it is constrained by several factors. This section focuses specifically on two key methodological assumptions – true random assignment and noninterference (spillover) – and three practical limitations – cost, ethics, and external validity.[2] While none of these limitations are unique to field experiments in compliance studies (or field experiments more generally), the necessity of grounding field experiments in naturalism means that they will be more prevalent for scholars looking to identify the relationship between law and behavior. Good planning and clean execution can remedy most of these difficulties, but in some cases, a particular question or arena within compliance may be (currently) out of reach for field experimentalists.

[1] Note that compliance experimentalists have also begun to implement "lab-in-the-field" experiments, where the setting for the study is designed to be more naturalistic (e.g. Cummings et al. 2009). While these studies generally do yield some of the benefits of naturalism, they are still subject to most of the limitations and benefits related to standard lab experiments. Gneezy and Imas (2017) provide a broader view on lab-in-the-field experimentalists in the social sciences.

[2] This is by no means a comprehensive discussion of such limitations. Potential producers and consumers of field experimental research should look to the growing number of empirical treatises that specifically and comprehensively address these assumptions and limitations along with other issues not covered in this chapter, such as excludability and attrition. Gerber and Green (2012) and Duflo and Banerjee (2017) constitute two particularly helpful and approachable references.

49.3.1 *Truly Random Assignment*

Beginning with the methodological assumptions required for a field experiment, we look first to the necessity of *truly* random assignment of treatment conditions. While random assignment may seem like a given in a field experiment, the increased reliance on naturally occurring randomization and on nonresearcher field partners (such as government institutions, nongovernmental organizations (NGOs), and private business) means that the randomization and/or assignment process is not always squarely in the hands of the researcher. For example, scholars studying criminal deterrence have long used the random assignment of judges as a source of naturally occurring random assignment, understandably keen on harnessing experimental analysis in an arena that is not traditionally seen as amenable to experimental design. As simple as judicial assignment may seem, however, legal empiricists have recently begun to question the assumption of random assignment, noting that aggregated data suggest some degree of nonrandom assignment in certain courts (Hall 2010; Chilton and Levy 2015) and that the complicated procedural life of a case can often introduce nonrandom elements into an otherwise "usable" random mechanism (Thorley 2020).

Additionally, as researcher-driven field experiments become larger and more ambitious, the potential for nonrandomness to creep into experimental designs also increases. While the researchers implementing lab experiments can almost assuredly prevent subjects from either rejecting their treatment assignment or adopting someone else's treatment assignment, field experimentalists must often deal with the self-selective behavior of research participants. The field has developed some methodologies that account for this sort of "noncompliance,"[3] such as redefining the assignment of treatment categories as the experimental treatment as opposed to the actual reception of the treatment itself (often called the ITT, or intent-to-treat effect), but all of them require methodological sacrifices of some degree or another (Gerber and Green 2012: chapters 5 and 6).

49.3.2 *The Problem of Noninterference*

In order to identify an unbiased causal effect, a field experimenter must be certain (or at least have good reason to assume) that a subject's potential outcomes are not impacted by the assignment conditions of the other subjects in the study. Whereas the highly controlled and sterilized environment of lab studies allow researchers to credibly isolate each of the subjects from each other, field experiments will often take place under circumstances in which the subjects will interact with each other. While this interaction may be reflective of how individuals actually interact, it is nonetheless an empirical problem because the resulting causal estimate provided by the experimental data will no longer be a clean comparison of the subjects who received the treatment against those who didn't (Gerber and Green 2012).

The analysis by Drago, Mengel, and Traxler (2020) provides a real example of the threat that interference poses for compliance scholars hoping to use field experiments.[4] The authors examine a previous study in which researchers (Fellner, Sausgruber, and Traxler 2013) had partnered with the Austrian government to measure the effect that various mailings had on TV license fee evasion. Subjects – individuals who were delinquent in their payments – were

3 Confusingly, experimental noncompliance is completely unrelated to the substantive study of compliance that is the focus of this book.

4 Ariel, Sutherland, and Sherman (2018) conduct a similar analysis in the context of field experiments relating to police body cameras.

randomly divided into three groups: one group did not receive any mailing, one group received a mailing from the Austrian broadcasting company asking why they had not paid the fee, and one group received a mailing that highlighted the likelihood of financial and legal consequences for continued delinquency. Under an assumption of noninterference, the letters sent to the treatment groups should have had no effect on the likelihood that individuals who did not receive the letter would pay their fines. However, using a sophisticated networking model based on geographic proximity, Drago, Mengel, and Traxler (2020) found that households who were not part of the field experiment but lived within 50 meters of subjects who received letters were as much as 5 percentage points more likely to pay their fines than those who lived further than 50 meters from subjects – a finding that is simultaneously valuable as a measure for how compliance strategies work in the real world and a reminder of the added complexity that the naturalism of field experiments produces.

Although the field experiment literature has continually produced new methodologies that allow researchers to map out and, to some degree, control for this sort of spillover (e.g. Aronow and Samii 2017), subject-to-subject interference is still a common concern. And field experiments exploring the interactions between laws and human behavior may, by the nature of the treatment they employ, be even more susceptible to a violation of the noninterference assumption.

49.3.3 *Cost*

Although not a methodological limitation, the difficulty in and cost of implementing field experiments can be a substantial practical barrier for many scholars (Bothwell et al. 2016), including those who study law and policy (Abramowitz, Ayres, and Listokin 2011). Because field experiments emphasize naturalism, the implementation of field experiments in compliance often involves the random allocation of resource-heavy audits (e.g. Kleven et al. 2011) or complex and novel policing strategies (e.g. Braga and Bond 2008). And, of course, the cost of a field experiment is not limited only to the assignment and distribution of the treatments: collecting the necessary outcome data can be equally, if not more, difficult.[5]

Nonetheless, large and complicated field experiments do not necessarily have to break the bank, particularly given the questions and issues that compliance scholars are commonly interested in exploring. Many field experiments will inherently require the close participation of government agencies or large institutions, which are already implementing costly rules or policies that can simply be replaced with the intervention of choice. Alternatively, the institution may have already been interested in creating a new policy and can work with researchers to design roll-out strategies that are conservative while still yielding valuable experimental data (Handan-Nader, Ho, and Elias 2020).

49.3.4 *Ethical Considerations*

Compliance-based field experiments involve actively intervening with and observing the behavior of human beings, either on an individual level or within the context of communities or institutions. While this interaction is true of all experimental techniques, the emphasis that field experiments put on naturalism brings with it a number of ethical concerns that are

[5] Researchers – particularly those fighting the tenure clock – will also have to be aware of the relatively higher risk of pursuing field experiments, which requires a substantial amount of upfront work in the design and coordination of a study that may (for various reasons) not even end up being implemented.

particularly salient. For example, the scope of many field experiments makes it extremely difficult or even unfeasible to receive informed consent from each of the individuals impacted by the study. Indeed, seeking informed consent is likely to negate the benefits that come from naturalism, as many studies have shown that those who know they are being observed will act differently. It is therefore incumbent upon the field experimentalist to grapple with the balance between the production of knowledge and the autonomy of the subjects.

Traditional sources of ethical standards in human subject research such as *The Belmont Report* (National Commission 1979) and the Institutional Review Board (IRB) process are helpful in this regard, but, as scholars have noted, most existing ethical standards were created to address the challenges most commonly encountered in the "hard" and medical sciences and are therefore poorly applied to field experiments in the social sciences (Humphreys 2015). This can also mean that IRB review is frustratingly inconsistent across different institutions (Yanow and Schwartz-Shea 2008). To make matters more complicated, the ethical norms in regard to issues such as informed consent and deception also vary across the spectrum of disciplinary fields that study compliance (Hertwig and Ortmann 2008; Desposato 2015; Rousu et al. 2015). Recently, field experimentalists have begun to build up a corpus of resources that address this lacuna of ethical standards (e.g. Teele 2014), but compliance scholars seeking to design and implement field experiments are likely to come across novel ethical considerations that necessitate careful consideration, in addition to the required institutional approval.

49.3.5 *External Validity*

When properly designed, conducted, and analyzed, a field experiment will allow compliance scholars to identify an unbiased estimate of the average treatment effect of the law, rule, or compliance strategy that they are evaluating. Indeed, because of the naturalism that is the hallmark of field experimentation, compliance scholars can be confident that the estimate is an accurate reflection of how people will actually behave in relation to that law or strategy. However, without additional assumptions, that estimate is only justifiably reflective of the specific context in which the experiment is conducted. The particular outcomes observed, while well identified, may have been different (possibly even substantially different) were the experiment conducted at a different time, in a different venue, or with a different set of subjects. Similarly, the particular outcomes of interests that were assessed in an individual field experiment may be imperfect measures of the sometimes-latent constructs that are the most theoretically or practically important (Harrison 2013).[6]

Scholars and policy-makers should therefore not assume that research will provide absolutely generalizable results simply because they are the product of a field experiment. This limitation is, of course, hardly unique to field experiments or experimental research more broadly (Guala 2005:chapter 7; Guala 2009). All empirical evidence, both quantitative and qualitative, must be understood within the context from which it is produced. Due, however,

6 External validity concerns, combined with the relatively high cost of field experiments, are often used to argue that field experimentation is simply a sophisticated form of program evaluation, as opposed to a tool for studying and advancing theory. While it is indeed true that the challenges involved in running field experiments in the field of compliance can make theory-driven research more difficult, thoughtfully designed field experiments are well-suited to identifying intermediate causal mechanisms, moderating conditions, and mediating processes (Wenzel and Taylor 2003).

to the relative difficulty in conducting field experiments, the temptation to simply extrapolate findings instead of performing the replications necessary to confirm findings across a wide variety of settings may be particularly enticing.

49.4 EXAMPLES OF FIELD EXPERIMENTS IN COMPLIANCE

Aside from the limitations highlighted in Section 49.3, likely the primary hurdle that has prevented field experiments from becoming more common in compliance studies is the perceived impracticality or even impossibility of implementing them. As the following studies demonstrate, however, scholars have found ways to implement field experiments to study compliance theories in a wide diversity of venues. To emphasize the potential for additional experiments, the review in this section focuses more on the design and creativity of these field experiments than it does on synthesizing the empirical results that they produce – the latter of which has already been comprehensively addressed by the various reviews and meta-analyses that exist for the more "mature" field experimental literatures reviewed in Sections 49.4.1 and 49.4.2.

49.4.1 *Tax Compliance*

Compliance scholars had been musing about the possibility of running field experiments on federal tax policy long before such an approach was widely thought to be feasible. In the early 1960s, Schwartz and Skolnick (Schwartz 1961; Schwartz and Skolnick 1963) proposed an experiment that would vary the distribution of television publicity campaigns and then measure the impact that those communications had on individual-level income tax compliance. While this study was never conducted, it was a forerunner for the first truly randomized field experiment on tax compliance (and among the first field experiments on the social sciences more generally), in which Schwartz and Orleans (1967) tested the contrasting effects of the threat of sanctions and appeals to conscience on federal tax compliance. Subjects in the study (there were only 273) were interviewed in the months prior to tax season, and the researchers randomly assigned them to one of three interview scripts: one that contained questions that highlighted that "a jail sentence ... could be imposed for willful failure to pay tax on interest" (p. 286); one that suggested that "a citizen's willful failure to pay tax on interest [is] an indication that he is unwilling to do something for the country as a whole" (p. 287); and a placebo script that did not include any accentuation language. The researchers then measured the behavioral effect of these questions on the reported income in the subjects' personal tax returns. They found that subjects who received the appeals to conscience reported substantial higher increases in income (+$804) than those who received the threat of sanction (+$181) and those who were in the placebo group (-$87).

Although only one other field experiment on tax compliance was published in the twentieth century (Coleman 1996), the last two decades have brought about an explosion in the number of such investigations. Recent reviews of the empirical literature have chronicled nearly thirty tax compliance field experiments (Hallsworth 2014; Mascagni 2018), and half a dozen additional field experiments that were not included in these reviews or have been released in just the last year were identified over the course of researching for this chapter. These studies test a wide variety of compliance theories on hundreds of thousands of individual and corporate taxpayers in tax regimes from across the globe.

When measured against the much more established field of lab experiments dealing with tax compliance (Alm and McKee 1998), the number of these field experiments may appear trivial, but this corpus of studies provides invaluable insights into real-world tax administration and serves as a prime example of the potential that this approach has for impacting the field of compliance as a whole.

Looking first to the mechanism through which the treatments were administered, the vast majority of these field experiments utilized mailed letters or surveys. For example, Hallsworth et al. (2017) sent reminder letters to over 100,000 individuals in the United Kingdom who had filed a tax return but had not yet paid the appropriate amount (a preexisting practice by the UK tax administration). The randomized treatments – various appeals to norms and gain- and loss-framed public goods messages – were then embedded into the letters, and the likelihood of tax-debt payments was compared across groups. The experiments analyzed by Wenzel (2005, 2006), Iyer, Reckers, and Sanders (2010), and Dwenger et al. (2016) employed a similar informational-letter strategy in Australia, the United States, and Germany, respectively. Other experiments have featured message-based treatments conveyed via email and SMS (Ortega and Scartascini 2020; Mascagni, Nell, and Monkam 2017).

A few experiments attempted to increase compliance through direct government contact. In the field experiment that inspired the working example we explored in Section 49.2, Kleven et al. (2011) reported the results of randomizing actual tax audits, comparing the post-audit behavior of Danes who were audited against those who were not. Similarly, Gangl et al. (2014) randomly assigned a treatment that included supervision and tax counseling by the Austrian tax auditors, and Doerrenberg and Schmitz (2015) compared the effects of delivering a compliance-inducing message through mail and through an in-person visit by Slovenian tax officials. Ortega and Scartascini (2020) directly test personal contact against letter- and email-based methods, finding that – conditional on successful deployment – in-person interventions are most effective in inducing compliance.

Due to the centrality of deterrence theory to compliance studies and the wide use of letter-based informational treatments, many of the existing tax compliance experiments were designed to test the behavioral effect of varying probabilities of audit and enforcement (e.g. Hasseldine et al. 2007; Appelgren 2008; Iyer, Reckers, and Sanders 2010; OECD 2010; Kleven et al. 2011; Pomeranz 2015; Harju, Kosonen, and Ropponen 2014; Del Carpio 2013). Alternatively, some allocated social or financial awards (Dwenger et al. 2016) or appeals to social norms, morality, fairness, and civic duty (Wenzel 2006; Ariel 2012; Torgler 2013; Castro and Scartascini 2015). Other experiments simply measured the effect of providing citizens with tax-related information such as the address of the tax office (Ortega and Sanguinetti 2013), rental property schedules (Wenzel and Taylor 2004), or a basic reminder of tax obligations (Del Carpio 2013; Moulton et al. 2019).

Importantly, these field experiments also varied in venue and subject pool. A majority of these studies involved individual income taxpayers, but some distributed treatments to firms (Iyer, Reckers, and Sanders 2010; Ariel 2012; Harju, Kosonen, and Ropponen 2014; Ortega and Sanguinetti 2013; Pomeranz 2015; Gangl et al. 2014; Bergolo et al. 2019), property or business owners (Wenzel and Taylor 2004; Hasseldine et al. 2007; Castro and Scartascini 2015; Del Carpio 2013; Chirico et al. 2016; Moulton et al. 2019), and individuals liable for a church tax (Dwenger et al. 2016). And while most of the studies took place in first-world countries such as Australia (Wenzel 2005, 2006), Denmark (Kleven et al. 2011), Switzerland (Torgler 2013), and the United States (Iyer, Reckers, and Sanders 2010; Chirico et al. 2016), a number of more recent studies have featured experiments in middle- and low-income countries such as Argentina (Castro and Scartascini 2015), Mexico (OECD 2010), Rwanda (Mascagni, Nell, and Monkam 2017), Slovenia (Doerrenberg and Schmitz 2015), and Uruguay (Bergolo et al. 2019). As Mascagni (2018) notes in her review of the literature, the diversity provided by these later studies is particularly important because of how "deeply intertwined" tax compliance is "with the political environment that shapes the social contract between citizens and state" (p. 273).

It is also worth noting that these experimental designs have been applied to test enforcement strategies in non-tax regimes that are nonetheless similarly interested in decreasing evasion and can therefore speak to the theoretical underpinnings of compliance more broadly. Fellner, Sausgruber, and Traxler (2013) worked with the Austrian public broadcasting company to identify the most efficacious means for decreasing evasion of the individual-level fee charged to Austrians who own a TV or radio. Much like those studied in the tax experiments, the 50,000 subjects in this experiment were sent mailings that included a threat, a moral appeal, a social appeal, or no compliance-inducing language at all (some received no mailings and some received mixes of various treatment arms). The authors found that all the treatments significantly increased compliance rates (by nearly 7 percentage points), with the threat having the largest positive effect. In Bursztyn et al. (2019), a random selection of delinquent credit card clients of an Islamic bank in Indonesia were sent a variety of text messages meant to induce payment, including the promise of a partial rebate, social and moral appeals, reminders, and quotes from the Prophet Muhammad that highlighted the "injustice" of not paying one's debts. Haynes et al. (2013) also used text messages to induce the payment of fines, which they varied in whether they included the name of the individual and the amount of the fine.

Given the scope and logistical difficulty of administering the experiments highlighted above, it is worth briefly considering why tax compliance has been such a fruitful arena for running field experiments relative to other subfields within compliance studies. Schwartz and Orleans (1967) suggest a number of factors, including the inherently vast potential-subject pool, the highly consistent and centralized outcome data, the varying degrees of compliance possible, and the potential for replication due to the ubiquity of taxation regimes across the world. Hallsworth (2014) also highlights that, due to the importance of capturing lost revenue, governments agencies are highly motivated to identify the cheapest and easiest methods for increasing tax compliance, which makes it easier for researchers to find cooperative administrative partners willing to help shoulder the burden of such expansive studies. Additionally, the early calls for and adoption of field experimentation on tax compliance likely served as self-fulfilling prophecies, working against or even preempting the common assumption that experiments of such scope and complexity are simply not feasible.

49.4.2 *Policing and Criminal Deterrence*

Criminal justice is another subfield which has fully embraced field experimentalism[7] as a viable approach to understanding the interaction between law and behavior, with methodological reviews that included field experiments appearing as early as 1980 (Empey 1980;

[7] For clarity, it should be noted that use of the term randomized controlled trial (RCT) in place of field experiment is particularly prevalent in these studies.

Farrington 1983). As with the previous discussion of tax compliance experiments, the below review is by no means comprehensive, and a number of existing works already provide extensive reviews of the results of these studies for specific areas.[8] However, an overview of some examples of how scholars have designed their experiments and found willing institutional partners – often law enforcement and courts – to either randomize policies or provide data should inspire confidence in compliance scholars interested in field experiments more broadly. This subsection focuses specifically on experiments that vary law enforcement policies and approaches and naturally occurring randomization studies evaluating the effect that incarceration has on recidivism.

For better or for worse, the behavior of law enforcement officials, particularly those patrolling American cities, has come under increased scrutiny over the last decade. Many believe that increased utilization of officer-worn body cameras stands as a direct strategy for both increasing police compliance and accountability while also inducing increased compliance and cooperation by the citizens that come into contact with the criminal justice system through police encounters (Miller et al. 2014). In response, scholars have conducted upwards of twenty field experiments that utilized treatments relating to the use and effect of officer-worn body cameras, nearly all of which were published within the last five years. The experimental designs of the vast majority of these studies involve randomly distributing body cameras at the officer or shift level and measuring the resulting differences in the frequency of police force (e.g. Ariel, Farrer, and Sutherland 2015; Henstock and Ariel 2017), citizen complaints (e.g. Jennings, Lynch, and Fridell 2015; Ariel et al. 2017), stops (e.g. Peterson, Yu, and La Vigne 2018), arrests (e.g. Braga et al. 2018; Yokum, Ravishankar, and Coppock 2019), and long-term outcomes such as whether criminal charges were prosecuted and how the criminal adjudication concluded (e.g. Yokum, Ravishankar, and Coppock 2019).

Although body-cam experiments are rather new (due mostly to the novelty of the underlying technology), criminal compliance scholars have been using field experiments for nearly thirty years to study the effects of other law enforcement strategies such as focusing the intensity of police patrols in certain areas – an approach often called "hot spot" policing. The "subjects" in these experiments were generally geographical areas such as city blocks or patrol beats, most often those with the highest crime rates. The treatments were mostly of two types: either increased saturation of police presence or supervision (e.g. Sherman and Weisburd 1995; Ratcliffe et al. 2011; Taylor, Koper, and Woods 2011; Piza et al. 2015) or the use of problem-oriented policing, an alternative approach where police focus on underlying causes of crime as opposed to responding to individual incidents (e.g. Weisburd and Green 1995; Braga et al. 1999; Mazerolle, Price, and Roehl 2000; Braga and Bond 2008; Taylor, Koper, and Woods 2011). Other field experiments have varied the way in which the citizen-offender is treated, such as the well-known and influential Minneapolis Experiment, where the Minneapolis Police Department randomly assigned domestic violence suspects to be arrested, temporarily sent away from the location where the violence occurred, or advised (along with the victim) (Sherman and Cohn 1989).

Moving beyond policing strategies, deterrence scholars have also long been interested in identifying the causal impact that incarceration has on future behavior (Blumstein, Cohen, and Nagin 1978). However, even the most ardent proponents of field experiments appreciate the ethical and political complexity of randomizing the existence and length of confinement

[8] For example, Lum et al. (2019) review police-worn body camera studies, including field experiments; Braga, Papachristos, and Hureau (2014) review hot spot policing studies, including field experiments; and Neyroud (2017) conducts a fantastically comprehensive review of field experiments in policing more generally.

(e.g. Abramowitz, Ayres, and Listokin 2011). Taking advantage of the prevalence of the random assignment of judges to criminal proceedings, scholars have found creative ways to measure the impact of short- and long-term incarceration on future criminality. By using the initial randomization of judges paired with the reality that judges vary in how punitively they treat defendants (Anderson, Kling, and Stith 1999), researchers can instrument for imprisonment. In two such evaluations, Green and Winik (2010) and Loeffler (2013) assessed the effect of incarceration on post-trial recidivism among Washington, DC drug cases and general criminal cases in Chicago (Cook County), yielding mixed results. Aizer and Doyle (2015) utilized random judicial assignment to over 35,000 juvenile cases in Illinois and found that, under their most sophisticated model, juvenile incarceration increased adult recidivism by a massive 22 percentage points (it also decreased high school graduation rates by 13 percentage points). This same methodological approach has also recently been applied to the long-term behavioral impacts of short-term incarceration by instrumenting on variations in pre-trial judges' allocation of bail and pre-trial detainment (Gupta, Hansman, and Frenchman 2016; Leslie and Pope 2017; Dobbie, Goldin, and Yang 2018).[9]

49.4.3 *Additional Examples*

The previous subsections reviewed two of the most mature arenas of field experiments in compliance studies. However, government administrators and scholars in many other subfields have conducted a variety of informative and creative studies that are worth consideration. What follows is a "grab-bag" of field experiments that address (sometimes implicitly) important questions within compliance studies. While not comprehensive of all such field experiments, the studies described here are either particularly influential or particularly novel and should engage the imagination of compliance scholars looking to employ this methodology in their work.

Beginning with one of the more audacious examples of the potential for field experiments to provide insights for compliance scholars, Baradaran et al. (2013, 2014) conducted a series of expansive experiments on the effect of international laws and norms on the compliance behaviors of international incorporation firms from across the globe (see also Findley, Nielson, and Sharman 2013, 2014, 2015). In order to both measure the rates of compliance with international standards and identify the causes of noncompliance, the researchers posed as international business consultants who were looking to anonymously incorporate their companies. Using email as the means of communication, the researchers reached out to nearly 3,500 incorporation firms in over 175 countries and randomly varied the content of their messages, including the country of origin, references to various international and national regulations relating to incorporation, references to the punishment for violating those regulations, monetary incentives for noncompliance, and allusions to various terrorism-financing risks that had been flagged by international organizations (among other treatments). The results demonstrated how easy it is to set up illegal shell corporations – particularly in OECD countries and despite increased international efforts to prevent such behavior – and provided tests of traditional compliance theories in a context in which experimental work was thought to be out of reach.

9 Also notable is the 1981 Philadelphia Bail Experiment, where bail judges were randomly assigned to either use a newly formed set of bail guidelines or determine bail amounts independently. While a recent analysis of the data does not include post-trial recidivism outcomes, the authors nonetheless provide valuable insights into how defendants value freedom and behave before trial (Abrams and Rohlfs 2011).

Many compliance scholars are naturally interested in whether enforcement strategies impact behavior beyond behavior targeted by the strategy. Does direct exposure to a deterrence institution increase an individual's perception of enforcement, thereby decreasing future noncompliance, or does exposure indicate that noncompliance is the norm, thereby increasing noncompliance (Dickinson, Dutcher, and Rodet 2015)? Galeotti, Maggian, and Villeval (2019) designed a particularly creative field experiment to test these downstream effects, and while their treatment and outcome measurements are a bit more complex than most of the experiments we have reviewed so far, it is worth detailing their approach. The authors employed research assistants to board public transportation (a bus or tram) in Lyon, France and passively identify passengers who boarded without validating their boarding pass (i.e. not paying for the ride). When a noncomplier departed the vehicle, either they were approached by ticket inspectors – and made to pay a fine – or they were not inspected (note, this did not appear to be random). The actors then followed the individuals down the street, where one of the research assistants, while appearing to talk on a cellular phone, bent down to pick up a 5 euro note and asked the noncomplier if they had dropped the money. The researchers recorded whether the individual took the money as a measure of honesty and compared the behavior of those who were investigated against those who were not. They found that those who were investigated were 14 percentage points more likely to take the money. Interestingly, they also ran this experiment on individuals who did initially pay for their ride and found that investigation resulted in an even larger increase in dishonesty (18 percentage points).

Whereas the vast majority of field experiments reviewed in this chapter study the effect of government rules and compliance strategies on the behavior of citizens, a growing number of experiments look at whether government officials and employees are properly administering goods and services. Ho (2017) partnered with public health departments in the state of Washington to randomly implement a peer-review system among their restaurant food-safety inspectors. The inspectors assigned to the "peer-review" treatment – who knew that a coworker would conduct an independent review of the same restaurant and also participated in group meetings regarding any variations – were 2 percentage points more likely to find a health violation and were less likely to produce reports that varied from their coworkers'.

In a similar vein, the experiments featured in Dustan, Maldonado, and Hernandez-Agramonte (2018) used targeted text messaging to induce compliance of civil servants in Peru who were tasked with using federal funds to improve their local education infrastructure. Like many of the treatments discussed to this point, the treatment arms were designed to test the impact of various strategies derived from compliance theory, including simple reminders, increased monitoring, social norms, shaming, and threat of audit. The authors found that all these messages had significant, positive effects on bureaucrat compliance (measured through expense reports and bank account activity), particularly the treatment arms focused on social norms and monitoring. Daniels, Buntaine, and Bangerter (2020) conducted a similar field experiment in Uganda's Bwindi Impenetrable Forest National Park. Working with park officials, the researchers randomly assigned a two-prong transparency treatment: certain rural communities within the park received information whenever the park transferred money for local development projects to the local district's chief administrative office and were also provided with a platform for reporting about the implementation of the projects. Communication networks in the park are so poor that both prongs were nonexistent in the villages assigned to the control group. Interestingly, audits and interviews on both sets of villages showed no significant difference in how the park funds were allocated at the village level.

Other such studies have found creative ways to study the behavior of political "elites" such as judges and congresspeople. Krasno et al. (in press) implemented a field experiment to test the effect of third-party watchdog observation on whether elected judges in the United States recused themselves from cases in which one of the attorneys had donated to the judge's previous political campaigns. A random selection of judges presiding over such cases were sent a letter that identified the potential conflict (including the name of the attorney and the amount they had donated) and asked the judge to recuse themselves. The treatment letter had no significant effect on recusal behavior but did substantially increase on-the-record judicial disclosures of the potential conflicts. Ho et al. (2019) utilized a naturally occurring randomization where a portion of draft opinions by administrative judges in the US Board of Veterans' Appeals were assigned to staff attorneys for review. The authors collected almost 600,000 cases decided over a 13-year period and compared the appeal and reversal rates for those decision drafts that received attorney review against those that did not, finding that "peer" review had no effect on either outcome. Looking to the legislature, Kalla and Broockman (2015) worked with a political organization to reach out to US congresspeople to attempt to schedule meetings with them. The authors randomly varied whether the congresspeople were informed that the individuals who were seeking a meeting had donated to their political campaign. Politicians were three times as likely to agree to meet with donors as they were with nondonors.

49.5 CONCLUSION

Although this chapter featured many examples of how field experiments can be used to study compliance, such studies are still uncommon in the field. This is due in large part to the relative novelty of the methodology combined with the practical difficulties in running randomized field studies testing the theories and issues that compliance scholars are interested in. However, field experiments can and should become wholly incorporated into the methodological ecosystem of compliance studies, both as an additional tool for exploring theory and as a reliable approach for researchers and policy-makers who wish to translate the field's findings into practical real-world law and policy.

REFERENCES

Abramowitz, Michael, Ian Ayres, and Yair Listokin. 2011. "Randomizing Law." *University of Pennsylvania Law Review* 159(4): 929.

Abrams, David S., and Chris Rohlfs. 2011. "Optimal Bail and the Value of Freedom: Evidence from the Philadelphia Bail Experiment." *Economic Inquiry* 49(3): 750–70.

Aizer, Anna, and Joseph J. Doyle, Jr. 2015. "Juvenile Incarceration, Human Capital, and Future Crime: Evidence from Randomly Assigned Judges." *Quarterly Journal of Economics* 130(2): 759–803.

Alm, James. 2012. "Measuring, Explaining, and Controlling Tax Evasion: Lessons from Theory, Experiments, and Field Studies." *International Tax and Public Finance* 19(1): 54–77.

Alm, James, and Michael McKee. 1998. "Extending the Lessons of Laboratory Experiments on Tax Compliance to Managerial and Decision Economics." *Managerial and Decision Economics* 19(4/5): 259–75.

Anderson, James M., Jeffrey R. Kling, and Kate Stith. 1999. "Measuring Inter-judge Sentencing Disparity before and after the Federal Sentencing Guidelines." *Journal of Law and Economics* 42: 271.

Angrist, Joshua D., and Jörn-Steffen Pischke. 2010. "The Credibility Revolution in Empirical Economics: How Better Research Design Is Taking the Con out of Econometrics." *Journal of Economic Perspectives* 24(2): 3–30.

Appelgren, Leif. 2008. "The Effect of Audit Strategy Information on Tax Compliance – An Empirical Study." *eJournal of Tax Research* 6(1): 67–81.

Ariel, Barak. 2012. "Deterrence and Moral Persuasion Effects on Corporate Tax Compliance: Findings from a Randomized Controlled Trial." *Criminology* 50(1): 27–69.

Ariel, Barak, Alex Sutherland, Darren Henstock, Josh Young, Paul Drover, Jayne Sykes, Simon Megicks, and Ryan Henderson. 2017. "Contagious Accountability: A Global Multistate Randomized Controlled Trial on the Effect of Police Body-Worn Cameras on Citizens' Complaints against the Police." *Criminal Justice and Behavior* 44(2): 293–316.

Ariel, Barak, Alex Sutherland, and Lawrence W. Sherman. 2018. "Preventing Treatment Spillover Contamination in Criminological Field Experiments: The Case of Body-Worn Police Cameras." *Journal of Experimental Criminology*: 1–23.

Ariel, Barak, William A. Farrer, and Alex Sutherland. 2015. "The Effect of Police Body-Worn Cameras on Use of Force and Citizens' Complaints against the Police: A Randomized Controlled Trial." *Journal of Quantitative Criminology* 31(3): 509–35.

Aronow, Peter M., and Cyrus Samii. 2017. "Estimating Average Causal Effects under General Interference, with Application to a Social Network Experiment." *Annals of Applied Statistics* 11(4): 1912–47.

Baradaran, Shima, Michael Findley, Daniel Nielson, and Jason C. Sharman. 2013. "Does International Law Matter?" *Minnesota Law Review* 97(3): 743–837.

2014. "Funding Terror." *University of Pennsylvania Law Review* 162(3): 477–536.

Bergolo, Marcelo, Rodrigo Ceni, Guillermo Cruces, Matias Giaccobasso, and Ricardo Perez-Truglia. 2019. "Tax Audits as Scarecrows. Evidence from a Large-Scale Field Experiment." IZA Institute of Labor Economics Discussion Paper No. 12335.

Blumstein, Alfred, Jacqueline Cohen, and Daniel S. Nagin, eds. 1978. *Deterrence and Incapacitation: Estimating the Effects of Criminal Sanctions on Crime Rates*. National Academy Press.

Bothwell, Laura E., Jeremy A. Greene, Scott H. Podolsky, and David S. Jones. 2016. "Assessing the Gold Standard – Lessons from the History of RCTs." *New England Journal of Medicine* 374(22): 2175–81.

Braga, Anthony A., and Brenda J. Bond. 2008. "Policing Crime and Disorder Hot Spots: A Randomized Controlled Trial." *Criminology* 46(3): 577–608.

Braga, Anthony A., Andrew V. Papachristos, and David M. Hureau. 2014. "The Effects of Hot Spots Policing on Crime: An Updated Systematic Review and Meta-analysis." *Justice Quarterly* 31(4): 633–63.

Braga, Anthony A., David L. Weisburd, Elin J. Waring, Lorraine G. Mazerolle, William Spelman, and Francis Gajewski. 1999. "Problem-Oriented Policing in Violent Crime Places: A Randomized Controlled Experiment." *Criminology*, 37(3): 541–80.

Braga, Anthony A., William H. Sousa, James R. Coldren, Jr., and Denise Rodriquez. 2018. "The Effects of Body-Worn Cameras on Police Activity and Police-Citizen Encounters: A Randomized Controlled Trial." *Journal of Criminal Law and Criminology* 108(3): 511–38.

Bursztyn, Leonardo, Stefano Fiorin, Daniel Gottlieb, and Marin Kanz. 2019. "Moral Incentives in Credit Card Debt Repayment: Evidence from a Field Experiment." *Journal of Political Economy* 127(4): 1641–83.

Castro, Lucio, and Carlos Scartascini. 2015. "Tax Compliance and Enforcement in the Pampas: Evidence from a Field Experiment." *Journal of Economic Behavior and Organization* 116: 65–82.

Chilton, Adam S., and Marin K. Levy. 2015. "Challenging the Randomness of Panel Assignment in the Federal Courts of Appeal." *Cornell Law Review* 101: 1.

Chirico, Michael, Robert P. Inman, Charles Loeffler, John MacDonald, and Holger Sieg. 2016. "An Experimental Evaluation of Notification Strategies to Increase Property Tax Compliance: Free-Riding in the City of Brotherly Love." *Tax Policy and the Economy* 30(1): 129–61.

Coleman, Stephen. 1996. "The Minnesota Income Tax Compliance Experiment: State Tax Results." MPRA Paper No. 4827. University of Munich.

Cummings, Ronald G., Jorge Martinez-Vazquez, Michael McKee, and Benno Torgler. 2009. "Tax Morale Affects Tax Compliance: Evidence from Surveys and an Artefactual Field Experiment." *Journal of Economic Behavior and Organization* 70(3): 447–57.

Daniels, Brigham, Mark Buntaine, and Tanner Bangerter. 2020. "Testing Transparency." *Northwestern University Law Review* 114(5): 1263–1333.
Del Carpio, Lucia. 2013. "Are the Neighbors Cheating? Evidence from a Social Norm Experiment on Property Taxes in Peru." Princeton University Working Paper.
Desposato, Scott, ed. 2015. *Ethics and Experiments: Problems and Solutions for Social Scientists and Policy Professionals*. Routledge.
Dickinson, David L., E. Glenn Dutcher, and Cortney S. Rodet. 2015. "Observed Punishment Spillover Effects: A Laboratory Investigation of Behavior in a Social Dilemma." *Experimental Economics* 18: 136–53.
Dobbie, Will, Jacob Goldin, and Crystal Yang. 2018. "The Effects of Pre-trial Detention on Conviction, Future Crime, and Employment: Evidence from Randomly Assigned Judges." *American Economic Review* 108(2): 201–40.
Doerrenberg, Phillip, and Jan Schmitz. 2015. "Tax Compliance and Information Provision – A Field Experiment with Small Firms." *Journal of Behavioral Economics for Policy* 1(1): 47–54.
Drago, Francesco, Friederike Mengel, and Christian Traxler. 2020. "Compliance Behavior in Networks: Evidence from a Field Experiment." *American Economic Journal: Applied Economics* 12(2): 96–133.
Duflo, Esther, and Abhijit Banerjee, eds. 2017. *Handbook of Field Experiments*, Volume 1. North Holland.
Dustan, Andrew, Stanislao Maldonado, and Juan Manuel Hernandez-Agramonte. 2018. "Motivating Bureaucrats with Non-monetary Incentives when State Capacity Is Weak: Evidence from Large-Scale Field Experiments in Peru." MPRA Working Paper No. 90952.
Dwenger, Nadja, Henrik Kleven, Imran Rasul, and Johannes Rinke. 2016. "Extrinsic and Intrinsic Motivations for Tax Compliance: Evidence from a Field Experiment in Germany." *American Economic Journal: Economic Policy* 8(3): 203–32.
Empey, LaMar T. 1980. "Field Experimentation in Criminal Justice: Rationale and Design." In *Handbook of Criminal Justice Evaluation*, eds. Malcolm Klein and Katherine Teilman, 143–76. Sage.
Falk, Armin, and James J. Heckman. 2009. "Lab Experiments Are a Major Source of Knowledge in the Social Sciences." *Science* 326(5952): 535–8.
Farrington, David P. 1983. "Randomized Experiments on Crime and Justice." *Crime and Justice* 4: 257–308.
Fellner, Gerlinde, Rupert Sausgruber, and Christian Traxler. 2013. "Testing Enforcement Strategies in the Field: Threat, Moral Appeal and Social Information." *Journal of the European Economic Association* 11(3): 634–60.
Findley, Michael, Daniel L. Nielson, and Jason C. Sharman. 2013. "Using Field Experiments in International Relations: A Randomized Study of Anonymous Incorporation." *International Organization* 67(4): 657–3.
2014. *Global Shell Games: Experiments in Transnational Relations, Crime, and Terrorism*. Cambridge University Press.
2015. "Causes of Noncompliance with International Law: A Field Experiment on Anonymous Incorporation." *American Journal of Political Science* 59(1): 146–61.
Galeotti, Fabio, Valeria Maggian, and Marie Claire Villeval. 2019. "Fraud Detterrence Institutions Reduce Intrinsic Honesty." Groupe d'Analyse et de Théorie Economique Working Paper.
Gangl, Katharina, Benno Torgler, Erich Kirchler, and Eva Hofmann. 2014. "Effects of Supervision on Tax Compliance: Evidence from a Field Experiment in Austria." *Economics Letters* 123(3): 378–82.
Gerber, Alan S., Donald P. Green, and Edward H. Kaplan. 2004. "The Illusion of Learning from Observational Research." In *Problems and Methods in the Study of Politics*, eds. Ian Shapiro, Rogers M. Smith, and Tarek E. Masoud, 251–73. Cambridge University Press.
Gerber, Alan S., and Donald P. Green. 2012. *Field Experiments: Design, Analysis, and Interpretation*. W. W. Norton.
Gneezy, Uri, and Alex Imas. 2018. "Lab in the Field: Measuring Preferences in the Wild." In *Handbook of Economic Field Experiments*, Volume 1, eds. Abhijit Vinayak Banerjee and Esther Duflo. North-Holland.

Green, Donald P., and Dane R. Thorley. 2014. "Field Experimentation and the Study of Law and Policy." *Annual Review of Law and Social Science* 10: 53–72.
Green, Donald P., and Daniel Winik. 2010. "Using Random Judge Assignments to Estimate the Effects of Incarceration and Probation on Recidivism among Drug Offenders." *Criminology* 48 (2): 357–87.
Guala, Francesco. 2005. *The Methodology of Experimental Economics*. Cambridge University Press.
2009. "Methodological Issues in Experimental Design and Interpretation." In *The Oxford Handbook of the Philosophy of Economics*, eds. Don Ross and Harold Kincaid, 280–305. Oxford University Press.
Gupta, Arpit, Christopher Hansman, and Ethan Frenchman. 2016. "The Heavy Costs of High Bail: Evidence from Judge Randomization." *Journal of Legal Studies* 45(2): 471–505.
Hall, Matthew. 2010. "Randomness Reconsidered: Modeling Random Judicial Assignment in the U.S. Courts of Appeals." *Journal of Empirical Legal Studies* 7: 574.
Hallsworth, Michael. 2014. "The Use of Field Experiments to Increase Tax Compliance." *Oxford Review of Economic Policy* 30(4): 658–79.
Hallsworth, Michael, John A. List, Robert D. Metcalfe, and Ivo Vlaev. 2017. "The Behavioralist as Tax Collector: Using Natural Field Experiments to Enhance Tax Compliance." *Journal of Public Economics* 148: 14–31.
Handan-Nader, Cassandra, Daniel E. Ho, and Becky Elias. 2020. "Feasibly Policy Evaluation by Design: A Randomized Synthetic-Wedge Trial of Mandated Disclosure in King County." *Evaluation Review* 44(1): 3–50.
Harju, Jarkko, Tuomas Kosonen, and Olli Ropponen. 2014. "Do Honest Hairdressers Get a Haircut?" Government Institute for Economic Research (VATT) Working Paper.
Harrison, Glenn W. 2013. "Field Experiments and Methodological Intolerance." *Journal of Economic Methodology* 20(2): 110–11.
Hasseldine, John, Peggy Hite, Simon James, and Marika Toumi. 2007. "Persuasive Communications: Tax Compliance Enforcement Strategies for Sole Proprietors." *Contemporary Accounting Research* 24(1): 171–94.
Haynes, Laura C., Donald P. Green, Rory Gallagher, Peter John, and David J. Torgerson. 2013. "Collection of Delinquent Fines: An Adaptive Randomized Trial to Assess the Effectiveness of Alternative Text Messages." *Journal of Policy Analysis and Management* 32(4): 718–30.
Henstock, Darren, and Barak Ariel. 2017. "Testing the Effects of Police Body-Worn Cameras on Use of Force during Arrests: A Randomised Controlled Trial in a Large British Police Force." *European Journal of Criminology* 14(6): 720–50.
Hertwig, Ralph, and Andreas Ortmann. 2008. "Deception in Experiments: Revisiting the Arguments in Its Defense." *Ethics and Behavior* 18(1): 59–92.
Ho, Daniel E. 2017. "Does Peer Review Work? An Experiment of Experimentalism." *Stanford Law Review* 69: 1–119.
Ho, Daniel E., Cassandra Handan-Nader, David Armes, and David Marcus. 2019. "Quality Review of Mass Adjudication: A Randomized Natural Experiment at the Board of Veterans Appeals, 2013–16." *Journal of Law, Economics, and Organization* 25: 239–88.
Humphreys, Macartan. 2015. "Reflections on the Ethics of Social Experimentation." *Journal De Gruyter* 6: 87.
Iyer, Govind S., Phillip M. J. Reckers, and Debra L. Sanders. 2010. "Increasing Tax Compliance in Washington State: A Field Experiment." *National Tax Journal* 63(1): 7–32.
Jennings, Wesley G., Matthew D. Lynch, and Lorie A. Fridell. 2015. "Evaluating the Impact of Police Officer Body-Worn Cameras (BWCs) on Response-to-Resistance and Serious External Complaints: Evidence from the Orlando Police Department (OPD) Experience Utilizing a Randomized Controlled Experiment." *Journal of Criminal Justice* 43(6): 480–6.
Kalla, Joshua L., and David E. Broockman. 2015. "Campaign Contributions Facilitate Access to Congressional Officials: A Randomized Field Experiment." *American Journal of Political Science* 60(3): 545–58.
Kleven, Henrik J., Martin B. Knudsen, Claus Thustrup Kreiner, Soren Pederson, and Emmanuel Saez. 2011. "Unwilling or Unable to Cheat? Evidence from a Tax Audit Experiment in Denmark." *Econometrica* 79(3): 651–92.

Krasno, Jonathan S., Donald P. Green, Costas Panagolpoulos, Dane Thorley, and Michael Schwam-Baird. in press. "Campaign Donations, Judicial Recusal, and Disclosure: A Field Experiment." *Journal of Politics*.

Leslie, Emily, and Nolan G. Pope. 2017. "The Unintended Impact of Pretrial Detention on Case Outcomes: Evidence from New York City Arraignments." *Journal of Law and Economics* 60: 529–57.

Levitt, Steven D., and John A. List. 2007. "What Do Laboratory Experiments Measuring Social Preferences Reveal About the Real World?" *Journal of Economic Perspectives* 21(2): 153–74.

2008. "*Homo Economicus* Evolves." *Science* 319(5856): 909–10.

Loeffler, Charles E. 2013."Does Imprisonment Alter the Life Course? Evidence on Crime and Unemployment from a Natural Experiment." *Criminology* 51: 137.

Lum, Cynthia, Megan Stoltz, Christopher Koper, and J. Amber Scherer. 2019. "Research on Body-Worn Cameras." *Criminology and Public Policy* 18(1): 93–118.

Mascagni, Giulia. 2018. "From the Lab to the Field: A Review of Tax Experiments." *Journal of Economic Surveys* 32(2): 273–301.

Mascagni, Giulia, Christopher Nell, and Nara Monkam. 2017. "One Size Does Not Fit All: A Field Experiment on the Drivers of Tax Compliance and Delivery Methods in Rwanda." ICTD Working Paper 58.

Mazerolle, Lorraine G., James F. Price, and Jan Roehl. 2000. "Civil Remedies and Drug Control: A Randomized Field Trial in Oakland, California." *Evaluation Review* 24(2): 212–41.

Miller, Lindsay, Jessica Toliver, and Police Executive Research Forum. 2014. "Implementing a Body-Worn Camera Program: Recommendations and Lessons Learned." Washington, DC: Office of Community Oriented Policing Services Report.

Moulton, Stephanie, J. Michael Collins, Cäzilia Loibl, Donald Haurin, and Julia Brown. 2019. "Reminder to Pay Property Tax Payments: A Field Experiment of Older Adults with Reverse Mortgages." Working Paper.

National Commission for the Protection of Human Subjects of Biomedical and Behavioral Research. April 18, 1979. "The Belmont Report: Ethical Principles and Guidelines for the Protection of Human Subjects of Research."

Neyroud, Peter W. 2017. "Learning to Field Test in Policing: Using an Analysis of Completed Randomised Controlled Trials Involving the Police to Develop a Grounded Theory on the Factors Contributing to High Levels of Treatment Integrity in Police Experiments." University of Cambridge Doctoral Dissertation.

OECD. 2010. "Understanding and Influencing Taxpayers' Compliance Behavior."

Ortega, Daniel E., and Carlos Scartascini. 2020. "Don't Blame the Messenger: The Delivery Method of a Message Matters." *Journal of Economic Behavior & Organization* 170: 286–300.

Ortega, Daniel E., and Pablo Sanguinetti. 2013. "Deterrence and Reciprocity Effects on Tax Compliance: Experimental Evidence from Venezuela." CAF Working Paper, 2013/08.

Peterson, Bryce E., Lilly Yu, and Nancy La Vigne. 2018. "The Milwaukee Police Department's Body-Worn Camera Program: Evaluation Findings and Key Takeaways." Urban Institute Report.

Piza, Eric L., Joel M. Caplan, Leslie W. Kennedy, and Andrew M. Gilchrist. 2015. "The Effects of Merging Proactive CCTV Monitoring with Directed Policy Patrol: A Randomized Controlled Trial." *Journal of Experimental Criminology* 11(1): 43–69.

Pomeranz, Dina. 2015. "No Taxation without Information: Deterrence and Self-Enforcement in the Value Added Tax." *American Economic Review* 105(8): 2538–69.

Ratcliffe, Jerry H., Travis Taniguchi, Elizabeth R. Groff, and Jennifer D. Wood. 2011. "The Philadelphia Foot Patrol Experiment: A Randomized Controlled Trial of Police Patrol Effectiveness in Violent Crime Hot Spots." *Criminology* 49(3): 795–831.

Rousu, Matthew C., Gregory Colson, Jay R. Corrigan, Carola Grebitus, and Maria L. Loureiro. 2015. "Deception in Experiments: Towards Guidelines on Use in Applied Economics Research." *Applied Economic Perspectives and Policy* 37(3): 524–36.

Schwartz, Richard D. 1961. "Field Experimentation in Sociolegal Research." *Journal of Legal Education* 13: 401.

Schwartz, Richard D., and Sonya Orleans. 1967. "On Legal Sanctions." *University of Chicago Law Review* 34: 274–300.

Schwartz, Richard D., and Jerome H. Skolnick. 1963. "Televised Communication and Income Tax Compliance." In *Television and Human Behavior: Tomorrow's Research in Mass Communication*, eds. Mark A. May and Leon Arons, 155. Appleton-Century-Crofts.

Sherman, Lawrence W., and Ellen G. Cohn. 1989. "The Impact of Research on Legal Policy: The Minneapolis Domestic Violence Experiment." *Law and Society Review* 23(1): 117–44.

Sherman, Lawrence W., and David Weisburd. 1995. "General Deterrent Effects of Police Patrol in Crime Hot Spots: A Randomized Controlled Trial. *Justice Quarterly* 12:x625–48.

Taylor, Bruce, Christopher S. Koper, and Daniel J. Woods. 2011. "A Randomized Controlled Trial of Different Policing Strategies at Hot Spots of Violent Crime. *Journal of Experimental Criminology* 7(2): 149–81.

Teele, Dawn L. 2014. "Reflections on the Ethics of Field Experiments." In *Field Experiments and Their Critics*, ed. Dawn L. Teele, 115–40. Yale University Press.

Thorley, Dane R. 2020. "Randomness Pre-Considered: Recognizing and Accounting for 'De-Randomizing' Events When Utilizing Random Judicial Assignment." *Journal of Empirical Legal Studies* 17(2): 342–82.

Torgler, Benno. 2013. "A Field Experiment in Moral Suasion and Tax Compliance Focusing on Underdeclaration and Overeducation." *FinanzArchiv: Public Finance Analysis* 69(4): 393–411.

Weisburd, David, and Lorraine Green. 1995. "Policing Drug Hot Spots: The Jersey City DMA Experiment." *Justice Quarterly* 12(4): 711–36.

Wenzel, Michael. 2005. "Misperceptions of Social Norms about Tax Compliance: From Theory to Intervention." *Journal of Economic Psychology* 26(6): 862–83.

2006. "A Letter from the Tax Office: Compliance Effects of Informational and Interpersonal Justice." *Social Justice Research* 19: 345–64.

Wenzel, Michael, and Natalie Taylor. 2003. "Toward Evidence-Based Tax Administration." *Australian Journal of Social Issues* 38(3): 413–32.

2004. "An Experimental Evaluation of Tax-Reporting Schedules: A Case of Evidence-Based Tax Administration." *Journal of Public Economics* 88(12): 2785–99.

Yanow, Dvora, and Peregrine Schwartz-Shea. 2008. "Reforming Institutional Review Board Policy: Issues in Implementation and Field Research." *PS, Political Science and Politics* 41: 483–94.

Yokum, David, Anita Ravishankar, and Alexander Coppock. 2019. "A Randomized Control Trial Evaluating the Effects of Police Body-Worn Cameras." *PNAS* 116(21): 10329–32.

50

Naming and Shaming: Evidence from Event Studies

John Armour, Colin Mayer and Andrea Polo

Abstract: A firm's 'reputation' reflects the expectations of its partners of the benefits of trading with it in the future. An announcement by a regulator that a firm has engaged in misconduct may be expected to impact negatively on trading parties' (i.e. consumers or investors) expectations for a firm's future performance, and hence on its market value. How can we identify reputational losses from share price reactions? How large are these losses for different types of misconduct? The chapter seeks to answer the above questions in the light of recent empirical evidence and draws implications for regulatory enforcement policy.

50.1 INTRODUCTION

An important function of financial regulators is to uncover and discipline misconduct. In the absence of effective monitoring and enforcement of rules of conduct, financial markets are particularly prone to abuse. Indeed, Dyck, Morse and Zingales (2014) estimate the probability of a company engaging in fraud in any given year to be as high as 14.5 per cent. The imposition of penalties for misconduct is an important weapon in the armoury available to regulators, which, following the financial crisis, they have shown a greater willingness to deploy. However, this chapter suggests that such penalties are only one, and actually a surprisingly small, component of the overall sanctions following regulatory enforcement. There is another, far more potent consequence.

A firm's reputation reflects the expectations that its partners have of the benefits of trading with it in the future. In general, this is difficult to measure, but the release of new information provides an opportunity to do so. Following a firm's 'naming' as a wrongdoer by a regulator, it may suffer 'shaming' in terms of lost reputation.

It is important to understand the role of 'reputational sanctions' in regulating corporate enterprise and the degree to which they add meaningfully to deterrence. Understanding enforcement is crucial to making sense of the links between legal institutions and financial development, much emphasized in the 'law and finance' literature (La Porta et al. 1997, 1998, 2008). Whilst there is agreement that accurate indexing of the efficacy of legal institutions requires account to be taken of enforcement, no consensus has emerged as to the best way to measure its intensity or effect. Looking at regulators' legal powers (La Porta et al. 2006) or budgets (Jackson and Roe 2009) fails to account for differing institutional efficiency amongst enforcers and looking at the size of financial penalties (Coffee 2007) omits deterrent effects of reputational penalties.

Karpoff (2012) surveys a growing empirical literature on reputational sanctions which shows that such sanctions are large when a regulator reveals misconduct against customers or investors – types of trading partner – but are negligible when the misconduct is against a third party, with whom the firm does not trade. This literature, based on event studies, suffers from some methodological weaknesses. As Karpoff, Lee and Martin (2017) note, the precision of existing tests is seriously compromised by problems of identifying an 'event'. They are based on data from the United States, where financial misconduct investigations typically involve a sequence of public announcements that stretches over several years. This means that these data suffer from confounding multiple events, which make it hard to distinguish reputational from other losses.

This chapter describes the results of previous studies, discusses the event study methodology and underlines the empirical challenges. We then present the evidence from one unique study that meets all necessary conditions for identification of reputational sanctions from event studies (Armour, Mayer and Polo 2017). This paper focuses on the UK, where, in contrast to the USA during the period of this study, regulators made public announcements only at the successful *completion* of an enforcement process. The Financial Services Authority (FSA) and the London Stock Exchange (LSE) investigated firms for possible violations of financial regulation and listing rules but only made their investigations public once misconduct had been established and a fine and/or order to pay compensation had been imposed. This made the announcement of misconduct in the UK context a well-specified event, for which the reputational consequences can be established with far greater precision than in the USA. The study confirms that reputational sanctions are very real: their stock price impact is on average nine times larger than the financial penalties imposed by the FSA/LSE. However, the reputational damage is unrelated to the scale of fines imposed by regulators or the compensation paid by firms. Moreover, also in this study, reputational losses are confined to misconduct that directly affects those who trade with the firm, such as customers and investors. The announcement of a fine for wrongdoing that harms third parties who do not trade with the firm has, if anything, a weakly positive effect on stock price.

Dyck, Morse and Zingales (2014) offer an estimate of the social cost of fraud, calculated as the difference between the value of an enterprise after a fraud is revealed and what (based on various assumptions) the enterprise value would have been in the absence of the fraud. In their analysis, corporate fraud costs investors an average of 3 per cent of enterprise value across all firms. The results from the empirical literature on reputational sanctions reveal that this is only a portion of the true social cost of corporate wrongdoing. When the misconduct harms third parties, the share price of the wrongdoer firm is unaffected even when the wrongdoing is publicly revealed, but the misconduct nevertheless has a cost to society.

If we generalize, these findings – that firms suffer large reputational sanctions where harms against a firm's trading partners are revealed, but no corresponding reputational consequences where harms are revealed against third parties – have important implications for the design and effects of corporate and financial regulation. They suggest that, in some areas, the primary weapon that regulators have in their armoury is not fines but reputational sanctions. In relation to wrongs to trading partners, fines appear largely irrelevant to, and uncorrelated with, the overall loss inflicted on the firm by the announcement of its wrongdoing. In contrast, reputational incentives are either non-existent or perverse where the misconduct afflicts third parties. In these cases, fines are the only effective sanction, and need to be substantially greater than they are at present if they are to have the same overall level of deterrence associated with wrongs harming trading partners.

The rest of this chapter is structured as follows. Section 50.2 reviews theory and prior literature on how reputational sanctions may penalize wrongdoings. Section 50.3 describes the role of law enforcement in financial regulation. Section 50.4 analyzes the interaction between regulatory sanctions and reputational losses in the deterrence of wrongdoings. In Section 50.5, we describe the event study methodology used to calculate reputational sanctions. Section 50.6 describes the methodological challenges and presents the results from one study which meets all the necessary identification conditions. Section 50.7 concludes and summarizes the implications for the design of regulatory enforcement.

50.2 CORPORATE REPUTATION

A firm's 'reputation' reflects the expectations of partners of the benefits of trading with it in the future. With asymmetries of information in product and capital markets, firms commit resources to activities, which, independently of the quality of past performance, might raise these expectations. For product markets, this includes investment in advertising and brand development. Such investments, which are lost if performance subsequently turns out to be poor, are thought to act as a credible commitment by the firm not to renege opportunistically (Klein and Laffler 1981; Shapiro 1983). For capital markets, firms invest in the production of reports for investors, and pay out free cash flows as dividends in order to signal the quality of their future projects (Bhattacharya 1979; Easterbrook 1984).

Certain types of revelation may be expected to impact negatively on trading parties' expectations of a firm's future performance. For example, if a firm is found to have produced goods which do not meet mandated standards of quality or to have been at fault in accidents in which it was involved then it may be deemed to have taken inadequate prior precautions (Jarrell and Peltzman 1985; Mitchell and Maloney 1989). Or if information conveyed to trading partners through advertising or financial statements is found to be false then trading partners will be sceptical about relying on them in the future (Peltzmann 1981; Karpoff and Lott 1993; Alexander 1999; Karpoff, Lee and Martin 2008). Similarly, providers of finance offer less generous terms to firms that are revealed to have made accounting mis-statements (Hribar and Jenkins 2004; Graham, Li and Qiu 2008; Kravet and Shevlin 2010). An announcement by a regulator that a firm has engaged in misconduct may constitute precisely this type of revelation.

Adverse revisions of trading partners' expectations should negatively affect a firm's future terms of trade and consequently its market value. The firm may also need to commit additional resources to bonding or monitoring mechanisms, such as advertising and brand investment. Murphy, Shrieves and Tibbs (2009) show that share price reactions to the announcement of corporate misconduct are associated with subsequent changes in the level or certainty of earnings. We define the present value of such losses as a reputational cost.

Conversely, since reputation is associated with the value of future trading opportunities, revelations of misconduct that do not have implications for parties who contract with the firm should not devalue its reputation. For example, the firm's degree of compliance with laws designed to internalize social costs – tort laws and environmental regulations – will not affect its consumers and investors, other than through the direct costs of compliance (and penalties for non-compliance). Consequently, an adjudication that a firm is in breach of such laws should result in a decline in market value equivalent to no more than the expected cost of legally imposed penalties, compensation awards and remedial measures. This prediction receives support from US studies considering breaches of environmental law (Jones and Rubin 2001; Karpoff, Lott and Wehrly 2005), tort law (Karpoff and Lott 1999) and other regulatory crimes that do not affect parties in contractual arrangements with the defendant (Karpoff and Lott 1993). Particularly revealing is the more recent evidence on anti-bribery regulation (Karpoff, Lee and Martin 2017). Using data from enforcement actions initiated under the U.S. Foreign Corrupt Practices Act (FCPA), the authors find that for firms that are caught, the reputational loss is negligible (the average *ex post* net present value (NPV) net of penalties of paying a bribe is still non-negative). Only for a subset of firms that simultaneously face charges for financial fraud are the reputational losses large (in each of these cases also the direct cost is larger and so the *ex post* NPV is negative). Bribery charges by themselves do not lead to reputational damage. At times, firms that are targets of bribery enforcement actions experience large fines and regulatory penalties but the announcement of the fines does not seem to harm the firm's business relationships with its customers, suppliers or investors.

A different perspective is offered by studies focusing on corporate social responsibility (CSR). Godfrey, Merrill and Hansen (2009) report that firms that participate in 'social initiatives' likely to benefit third parties tend to suffer less adverse stock price reaction following the announcement of a lawsuit or regulatory enforcement action against the firm than firms that do not participate in such initiatives. In contrast, firms undertaking initiatives calculated to benefit their trading partners experience no such reduction in the intensity of adverse stock price reaction. The authors interpret this as consistent with the theory that CSR investments tend to provide a kind of reputational insurance when negative events such as litigation occur. However, the study does not control for the amounts of the penalties actually imposed on firms, or the nature of the wrongs for which enforcement occurred.

50.3 FINANCIAL REGULATION AND ENFORCEMENT

The 'law and finance' literature emphasizes the significance of legal institutions for the successful functioning of capital markets (La Porta et al. 1997, 1998, 2008). Effective investor protection rules, it is argued, mitigate agency problems between outside investors and management or controlling shareholders, thereby stimulating investment (Shleifer and Vishny 1997). A recurring criticism of this literature, however, has been its reductionist conception of 'legal institutions' (Armour et al. 2009a; Spamann 2009). In particular, it is said to underplay the potential role of enforcement in measuring the efficacy of laws (Coffee 2007; Jackson and Roe 2009).

If legal rules are understood as shaping the incentives of market actors, their practical impact will be a function of *both* the substantive rule and the enforcement technology. It is probably much more difficult to create effective enforcement institutions than it is to transplant substantive rules. Consequently, to focus simply on the 'law on the books' is to omit potentially the most important variables relating to legal institutions.

Whilst the potential significance of enforcement is now widely understood, no consensus has yet emerged on how best to measure its efficacy. An early attempt looks simply at the extent of the statutory powers available to regulators as regards penalties and compensation orders (La Porta et al. 2006). The authors conclude that private enforcement (class action lawsuits) is more strongly associated with deep and liquid securities markets than is public enforcement. However, their measure of enforcement fails to take into account differences in the *use* of enforcement powers.

Jackson and Roe (2009) proxy for enforcement intensity by focusing on the resources available to securities regulators: that is, their annual staffing and budget. They report that this measure of public enforcement explains variations in stock market liquidity better than measures of private enforcement used in La Porta et al. (2006). However, this measure itself fails to take into account differences in deployment of resources allocated to enforcers. Coffee (2007) argues that the most meaningful measure of enforcement intensity is one that focuses on outputs rather than inputs: that is, how many dollars of fines are paid, or years of jail time served, by wrongdoers. These measures, divided by the population of those regulated, give a clearer indication of the incentive effects of legal rules on rational parties' behaviour. Even measuring such penalties, however, will be misleading if announcements of enforcement activity carry with them additional reputational losses for malefactors.

In particular, if enforcement intensity is measured by financial penalties, the United States looks to be an outlier in world enforcement activity (Coffee 2007; Armour et al. 2009b). The gap in aggregate fines, even adjusted for differences in market capitalization, is so large (an order of four or five times anywhere else) as to pose the question whether misconduct outside the USA in fact goes unpunished. However, it may be that regulators elsewhere – whose budgets are no less, in per capita terms, than those of the USA – rely more heavily on reputational than financial penalties (Jackson 2008; Armour 2009). The difference may be more one of enforcement style than intensity.

50.4 DETERRENCE, COMPENSATION AND REPUTATION

For a legal penalty to deter a wrong from which the defendant can gain a benefit w, the inequality

$$w < pD \tag{1}$$

must be satisfied (Becker 1968), where D is size of financial penalty and p ($0 < p < 1$) is the probability of enforcement. Further, w can be earned at the expense of the firm's own customers and investors (causing loss to such 'second parties', s, who trade with the firm) or third parties (such as other firms, market participants and the general public, which we denote t).[1] Put in legal terms, this distinction captures the essence of the difference between breaches of contract (harming second parties) and torts (harming third parties).[2] The theory of optimal deterrence implies that policymakers should calibrate the right-hand side of inequality (1) according to the social cost of the wrong in question (s or t), through either the amount spent on detection and enforcement (p) or the size of the penalty (D). In reality, budget constraints for regulators mean that p is often quite small. Moreover, there may be constitutional law restrictions on the maximum size of D ($D_{\max}$) that can be levied, such that for serious offences, $w > pD_{\max}$. However, if the announcement of a penalty D triggers an additional reputational sanction R for the defendant, deterrence is now achieved where

$$w < p(D + R) \tag{2}$$

This implies that reputational sanctions may help regulators to increase the upper bound of sanction efficacy in the presence of limitations on the size of feasible p and D.

When a corporate penalty for wrongdoing is announced, any associated reputational damage, R, comes from a worsening of the terms of trade of the firm with its second parties.

[1] The terminology is derived from the legal literature on enforcement (e.g. Ellickson 1991), which distinguishes between the 'first party' (the actor itself), 'second parties' (private persons contracting with the actor) and 'third parties' (persons who have no prior relationship with the actor).

[2] Of course, in the context we examine, enforcement is by a public agency, rather than private actors as in the case of contracts and torts.

We would therefore expect R to be related to the magnitude of s but not t, with customers and investors trading on less favourable terms than previously with a firm that has inflicted a sizeable loss, s, on them but not on third parties, t. In contrast, regulators will be concerned with the total social losses, $s + t$. If markets sanction s but not t, it is optimal for D to be smaller in 'contract pattern' wrongs, where R is larger, but for D to be larger in 'tort pattern' wrongs, where R is smaller. This would imply a negative correlation between D and R; that is, regulatory sanctions would substitute for reputational ones across but not within the two classes of wrongs.[3]

We would anticipate the worsening in the terms of trade of the firm to be reflected in a decline in its market value, V. The total fall in value on revelation of a wrong will reflect R, the loss in value of the profitable activities (W – the present value of forgone future values of w) and D. To the extent that the market anticipates that firms engage in wrongs then the market reaction will reflect new information that is not available from private sources such as market analysts and credit ratings about the size and composition of wrongs. To the extent that D is informative about this, then it will be correlated with V and R so making regulatory sanctions and reputational damage complementary within types of wrong.[4]

The presence of reputational sanctions may also have implications for the design of prudential regulation for financial firms. Whilst capital adequacy regulation is primarily aimed at the mitigation of systemic risk, it is also applied to non-systemically important financial institutions with the goal of ensuring that financial firms have sufficient assets to pay regulatory penalties, thereby avoiding the problem of 'judgment-proofing' (Clark 1976; Correia, Franks and Mayer 2002). Capital is conventionally measured in accounting terms and, indeed, if it is held in part to ensure that sufficient resources are available to pay for regulatory penalties (D), then there will be a need for adequate assets on the books. However, to the extent that the 'true' sanction, including a reputational component ($D + R$), differs from the financial payment (D), then capital requirements calibrated on D alone will not be effective.

A further difficulty with reputational sanctions is that, unlike a financial payment, but like incarceration (Becker 1968), they represent not a transfer of resources but a destruction of value. For the firm to remain solvent after the regulatory intervention (that is, $V_a > 0$, where V_a is the post-event equity market value of the firm), the compensation payable (C) together with the combined regulatory and reputational penalties ($D + R$) cannot exceed the pre-event equity market value of the firm (V_b), that is, $V_b > C + D + R$ and $C < V_b - D - R$.[5] Conventional measures of capital, which do not take into account the expected destruction in

[3] However, this posited correlation may not hold if regulators hold firms liable not as primary wrongdoers but as gatekeepers. Wrongs perpetrated by a corporate actor are in fact committed by individuals working for the firm. Where the social harm is large, then large financial penalties will likely exceed the budget constraints of individual wrongdoers. Greater marginal deterrence is consequently achieved by increasing the associated probability of enforcement. In the context of wrongdoing associated with corporate activity, it is possible to recruit the firm as an additional monitor of its employees, in what may be termed a 'gatekeeper' view of corporate liability (Arlen and Kraakman 1997). If corporate penalties for such wrongs are conditioned not directly on the social cost of the harm but on the level of monitoring and policing in which the firm has engaged to prevent employees taking proscribed actions, then firms will have incentives to engage in monitoring of employees *ex ante*. This in turn increases the effective size of p faced by individual would-be wrongdoers.

[4] Whereas there is no direction of causation implied in the substitutability relation across types, there is a suggestion here that the complementarity causation runs from the disclosure of information by regulators to the reputational response by markets. We examine this empirically later in the chapter.

[5] Note that this assumes that it is solvency, not liquidity, that determines the amount of compensation that can be paid. That is, if necessary, firms can raise external finance to pay compensation.

value of R, may therefore be insufficient to ensure that compensation can be paid.[6] This negative-sum feature of reputational sanctions introduces a tension between *ex ante* deterrence and *ex post* compensation: the greater the reputational damage imposed by the revelation of wrongdoing, the smaller is the capacity of the firm to pay compensation to its victims.

This poses a potential dilemma for regulators concerned about the ability of firms to pay compensation to customers and investors as well as the incentive effects of markets: the more adverse the likely market reaction to the revelation of failure, the less will remain to pay compensation. The dilemma is particularly acute if the reputational effects are not restricted to the firm in question but spill over to others and thereby have wider systemic consequences. Arguably, some of the past inadequacies of regulation reflect a failure to resolve this dilemma.[7]

The above raises several empirical questions:

1 How large is R relative to D?
2 How predictable is the relation between R and D and what are the factors that influence the relation?
3 Are R and D sufficiently large relative to the value of the firm to threaten the solvency of the firm and its ability to pay compensation?

Reputational losses will enhance regulatory enforcement if they are large and predictable relative to D, but not so large as to threaten solvency. On the other hand, regulators may be reluctant to disclose failures if the reputational consequences are unpredictable and potentially so large as to threaten the solvency of firms.

50.5 MEASURING REPUTATIONAL LOSSES FROM REGULATORY ANNOUNCEMENTS

How can a researcher measure the reputational loss (R)? Several studies have estimated reputational losses by measuring stock price reactions around announcements by regulators of misconduct. The standard event study methodology pioneered by Fama et al. (1969) is usually adopted to evaluate the stock price reaction around the public announcement. We calculate the abnormal share price reaction around the event. We use the market model as a benchmark of normal returns. The abnormal return for firm i at time t is defined as

$$AR_{i,t} = R_{i,t} - \alpha_i - \beta_i R_{m,t} \quad (1)$$

where $R_{i,t}$ and $R_{m,t}$ are the returns on firm i's common stock on day t and the index of market returns on day t, respectively. The coefficients α_i and β_i are estimated from an ordinary least squares regression of $R_{i,t}$ on $R_{m,t}$ using a 260-day period consisting of days -261 to -2 relative to the announcement day.[8] The average abnormal return for each day t in the event window is computed as

6 Conversely, if the inequality holds, conventional capital requirements are unnecessary.

7 For example, there have been concerns about revelation of the results of stress tests on banks since revelation of the true degree of their fragility may provoke precisely the runs and systemic crises that the tests are designed to avoid.

8 In this case, we describe the event study methodology, using the market model as a benchmark of normal returns. Alternative models for normal returns may be used, that is, the Capital Asset Pricing Model (CAPM). However, in short-horizon event studies, the test statistic specification is not highly sensitive to the benchmark model of normal returns (Kothari and Warner 2007).

$$AR_t = \frac{\sum_{i=1}^{N} AR_{i,t}}{N} \quad (2)$$

where N is the number of firms over which abnormal returns are averaged on day t. The cumulative average abnormal return for small windows of t days (usually one, three or five days) is defined as

$$CAR(t_1, t_2) = \sum_{t=t_1}^{t_2} AR_t \quad (3)$$

Parametric t-statistics for the mean abnormal returns are calculated from the cross-section standard error of abnormal returns.

Once this measure of abnormal share price reaction in the event window around the announcement of misconduct by the regulator is built ($\Delta Vt=Vt\text{-}Vt\text{-}1$), researchers subtract any financial payments the firm is required to make (fines, compensation orders, etc.) from the total stock price effect, and measure the reputational loss as the residual component of the firm's stock price decline:

$$\text{Reputational loss} = \Delta Vt - \text{Fine} - \text{Compensation} \quad (4)$$

This approach to disentangle reputational losses from share price reaction is valid only if the following three conditions are verified: a) there should be a clearly defined revelation of information relating to a firm's conduct, b) all information relevant to the firm's conduct should be released simultaneously, and c) the direct costs associated with the revelation of information (for example, in this case, the size of both publicly imposed fines/compensation and private litigation) should be measurable when it is disclosed and distinguishable from the additional reputational loss. Finally, also if the three conditions are satisfied, the researcher needs to further consider whether some or all of these residual losses may be explicable as profits that will be forgone from loss of future earnings on the proscribed activity in question.

50.6 THE EVIDENCE

Data limitations owing in particular to the structure of US enforcement institutions have meant that these three conditions have not been satisfied in the prior literature discussed in Section 50.1.[9]

As Karpoff, Lee and Martin (2017) have noted, a problem with this methodology is that there are frequently multiple announcements associated with a particular enforcement action. The first announcement is often that the regulator has commenced an investigation (though even this may be preceded by speculation in the press of a potential investigation). The second announcement concerns the conclusion of the investigation and whether the defendant has been found guilty or innocent, along with the size of any fine. Finally, consequent on the regulatory ruling, there may be subsequent private litigation by investors.[10] Indeed, firms more often make payments in response to follow-on class actions

9 For a more complete survey, see Karpoff (2012).

10 Bhagat, Bizjak and Coles (1998) and Prince and Rubin (2002) measure stock price reactions to announcements that lawsuits have been filed in respect of damages for product liability. They report small negative stock price reactions.

by investors than fines imposed by regulators; for example, Karpoff, Lee and Martin (2008) report 231 cases in their data set of financial settlements as part of class actions but only 47 cases of regulatory fines. According to Karpoff, Lee and Martin (2017), in the USA, financial misconduct typically prompts a sequence of public announcements that can stretch over several years.

The response by previous researchers to such multiple events is simply to sum the total abnormal returns across all the events. However, with multi-stage events, it is difficult to be sure that the later stages really relate to the original announcement and not to further information that was released during subsequent stages, or conversely that relevant information was not released between the reported stages. In particular, share price movements around observed events may merely reflect the degree to which regulatory interventions were more or less onerous than previously anticipated, not the overall reputational damage that they inflict. Summing share price reactions therefore risks both over- and under-inclusion of information. This makes the challenge of distinguishing reputational from other losses even harder.

We have been able to address these concerns by looking at the UK (Armour, Mayer and Polo 2017), where the entire enforcement process involves only *one* public announcement, which includes information about associated legal penalties. During the period of the study (2001–11), UK regulators made public announcements only on completion of the enforcement process. The FSA and the LSE investigated firms but only made their investigations public once misconduct had been established and a fine and/or order to pay compensation had been determined.[11] Moreover and again in contrast to the USA, the announcement of an FSA/LSE enforcement action was unlikely to trigger any private litigation. Securities litigation, for example, is practically non-existent in the UK (Armour et al. 2009b), owing to differences in substantive law and litigation funding rules (Davies 2007). The foregoing features mean that the FSA/LSE's announcement of a final notice was a unique event associated with each enforcement action, conveying information that in a typical SEC case would encompass three or four separate announcements – investigation, conclusion, penalty and civil actions. This is highly significant for our purposes, because it gives a much more precise and complete announcement to the market. It makes the event study less prone to distortion from multiple announcements. Moreover, the immediate inclusion of information about the size of financial payments and the lack of class action claims means that no assumptions need be made about the accuracy of the market's estimates of future financial penalties.

We conducted an event study of the impact of announcements of regulatory sanctions on disciplined firms in the UK. We split the sample into sanctions where the prohibited conduct imposes losses on customers and/or investors (for example, mis-selling financial products or mis-statements in financial reports) and sanctions where the injured parties do not trade with the firm (for example, failure to comply with rules about money laundering or reporting of trades in other firms' stocks). The three-day average cumulative abnormal return is -1.68 per cent and statistically significant (the t-statistic is -1.97). However, this number is an average of the effect of all press statements in our sample. By decomposing the sample into cases involving second- and third-party wrongs, we show that misconducts against customers and investors are associated with a -2.62 per cent share price reaction that is strongly

11 After our sample period, the UK regulatory practices changed. It is now common for the UK authorities to announce the start of the investigation.

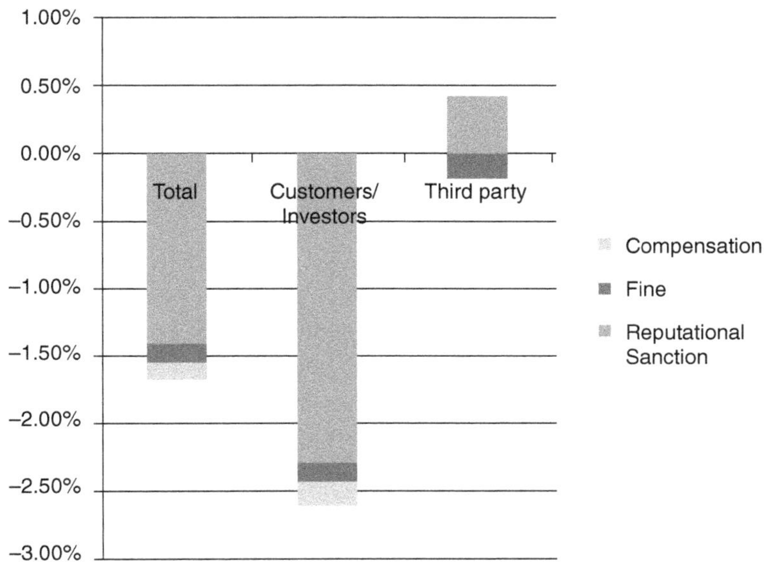

FIGURE 50.1 Reputational losses
This figure shows the reputational losses calculated by subtracting the financial penalty (fine and compensation as a percentage of the market capitalization) from the market reaction (cumulative abnormal reaction (CAR) in the three days around the announcement). In the first vertical bar, we report the results for the all sample; in the other two bars we split the sample between wrongdoings against second (customers/investors) and third parties.
Source: Armour, Mayer and Polo (2017).

statistically significant while third-party wrongs are in fact characterized by a positive stock price reaction of 0.24 per cent, although this is not statistically significant.[12]

When we subtract the total financial payment from the market reaction to measure the reputational loss as the residual, we confirm that the differences in overall market reaction are driven by differences in reputational losses rather than financial payments.[13] The reputational loss for the customers/investors subgroup is -2.31 per cent of market value, while for wrongs to third parties, the reputational effect is in fact positive (0.43 per cent). Figure 50.1 shows these results graphically. In cross-sectional regressions, we find that the reputational sanction is unrelated to the size of financial penalties levied, is smaller for larger firms, and increases in intensity since the financial crisis of mid-2007. In robustness tests, we are also able to discount the possibility that the reputational losses we observe are explicable as profits forgone from loss of future earnings through the proscribed activity in question.

The results in Armour, Mayer and Polo (2017) are consistent with those of previous studies (Section 50.1). The more precise identification of announcement dates in this paper therefore supports and significantly reinforces inferences about reputational losses that have been drawn from previous ones.

12 Crucially for identification, both types of misconduct are sanctioned by the same regulatory institution, allowing us to rule out effects due to the reputation of the authority itself.

13 The fine, as a percentage of market capitalization, is 0.19 per cent for wrongs against third parties and 0.13 per cent for wrongs against the customers and/or investors subgroup. The amount of compensation is zero for the former subgroup and 0.18 per cent for the latter.

50.7 CONCLUSIONS AND IMPLICATIONS

A large literature surveyed by Karpoff (2012) shows that announcements by regulators about corporate misconducts attract large reputational losses for the 'named' firm'; however, these losses are confined to misconducts related to customers or investors and are negligible for misconducts against third parties. This literature calculates reputational losses by calculating the abnormal share price reactions around the regulatory announcements and then subtracting the cost of fines and compensation.

We described in this chapter the several methodological challenges in obtaining credible estimates of reputational sanctions from event studies and we report the results of a unique study which is able to meet all these challenges, producing very precise estimates of reputational losses. Reassuringly, this study confirms and reinforces previous findings.

Reputational sanctions are very real: their stock price impact is on average nine times larger than the imposed financial penalties. However, the announcement of a fine for wrongdoing that harms 'third parties' who do not trade with the firm has, if anything, a weakly positive effect on stock price.

These results have significant implications for debates about regulatory policy. In terms of the criteria described in Section 50.4, reputational losses are important forms of regulatory enforcement. They dwarf regulatory penalties such that, intended or not, they are the primary consequence for a firm of a revelation of its misconduct. At approximately 2.3 per cent of market value, they are, however, a long way from threatening the solvency of firms and preventing full compensation being paid to customers and investors.

What is more questionable is the calibration of the penalties imposed. The absence of reputational damage in the event of revelation of third-party wrongs suggests that market processes are wholly inadequate for restraining such activity. Penalties should therefore be much greater in third-party than second-party wrongs, but, in the UK, there is no evidence that they are and penalties would seem to be too modest to restrain third-party wrongs. US enforcement appears more appropriate in this regard: penalties are larger and, according to Murphy, Shrieves and Tibbs (2009), the mean legal fine for violations that affect third parties is almost double the size of frauds committed against related parties.

Finally, a transmission mechanism that emerged in the last few years and deserves further research in the future is political punishment of third-party wrongs. While the direct economic consequences, in terms of reputational sanctions, of third-party wrongs are very small, the political ramifications resulting from negative public reactions can be substantial. The large drops in share prices after revelations of third-party wrongs in the case of BP's oil spill in the Gulf of Mexico in 2010 or Barclays' Libor-fixing scandal in 2012 illustrate the case. Initially, the share prices of these companies reflected only the potential fines and class action settlements but they collapsed after a few hours when damaging political interventions were disclosed by the governments.

REFERENCES

Alexander, Cindy R. 1999. 'On the Nature of the Reputational Penalty for Corporate Crime: Evidence'. *Journal of Law & Economics*. 42: 489–526.

Arlen, Jennifer, and Reinier Kraakman. 1997. 'Controlling Corporate Misconduct: An Analysis of Corporate Liability Regimes'. *New York University Law Review*, 72(4): 687–779.

Armour, John. 2009. 'Enforcement Strategies in UK Corporate Governance'. In John Armour and Jennifer Payne (eds.), *Rationality in Company Law*, 71–119. Oxford: Hart.
Armour, John, Simon Deakin, Mathias Siems and Ajit Singh. 2009a. 'Shareholder Protection and Stock Market Development: An Empirical Test of the Legal Origins Hypothesis'. *Journal of Empirical Legal Studies*, 6(2): 343–80.
Armour, John, Bernard S. Black, Brian R. Cheffins and Richard Nolan. 2009b. 'Private Enforcement of Corporate Law: An Empirical Comparison of the United Kingdom and the United States'. *Journal of Empirical Legal Studies*, 6(4): 701–45.
Armour, John, Colin Mayer and Andrea Polo. 2017. 'Regulatory Sanctions and Reputational Damage in Financial Markets'. *Journal of Financial and Quantitative Analysis* 52(4): 1429–48.
Becker, Gary. 1968. 'Crime and Punishment: An Economic Approach'. *Journal of Political Economy*, 76(2): 169–217.
Bhagat, Sanjai, John Bizjak and Jeffrey L. Coles. 1998. 'The Shareholder Wealth Implications of Corporate Lawsuits'. *Financial Management*, 5–27.
Bhattacharya, Sudipto. 1979. 'Imperfect Information, Dividend Policy, and the "Bird in the Hand" Fallacy'. *Bell Journal of Economics*, 10(1): 259–70.
Clark, Robert C. 1976. 'The Soundness of Financial Intermediaries'. *Yale Law Journal*, 86(1): 1–102.
Coffee, John C. Jr. 2007. 'Law and the Market: The Impact of Enforcement'. *University of Pennsylvania Law Review*, 156(2): 229–311.
Correia, Luis, Julian Franks and Colin Mayer. 2002. *Asset Management and Investor Protection*. Oxford: Oxford University Press.
Davies, Paul. 2007. *Davies Review of Issuer Liability: Final Report*. London: HM Treasury.
Dyck, Alexander, Adair Morse and Luigi Zingales. 2014. 'How Pervasive Is Corporate Fraud?' Working Paper No. 2222608, Rotman School of Management.
Easterbrook, Frank H. 1984. 'Two Agency-Cost Explanations of Dividends'. *American Economic Review*, 74(4): 650–9.
Ellickson, Robert C. 1991. *Order Without Law: How Neighbors Settle Disputes*. Cambridge, MA: Harvard University Press.
Fama, Eugene F., Lawrence Fisher, Michael C. Jensen and Richard Roll. 1969. 'The Adjustment of Stock Prices to New Information'. *International Economic Review*, 10(1): 1–21.
Godfrey, Paul C., Craig B. Merrill and Jared M. Hansen, 2009. 'The Relationship Between Corporate Social Responsibility and Shareholder Value: An Empirical Test of the Risk Management Hypothesis'. *Strategic Management Journal*, 30: 425–45.
Graham, John R., Si Li and Jiaping Qiu. 2008. 'Corporate Misreporting and Bank Loan Contracting'. *Journal of Financial Economics*, 89(1): 44–61.
Hribar, Paul, and Nicole Thorne Jenkins. 2004. 'The Effect of Accounting Restatements on Earnings Revisions and the Estimated Cost of Capital'. *Review of Accounting Studies*, 9(2–3), 337–56.
Jackson, Howell E. 2008. 'Response. The Impact of Enforcement: A Reflection'. *University of Pennsylvania Law Review*, 156(2): 400–11.
Jackson, Howell E., and Mark J. Roe. 2009. 'Public Enforcement of Securities Laws: Preliminary Evidence'. *Journal of Financial Economics*, 93(2): 207–38.
Jarrell, Gregg, and Sam Peltzman. 1985. 'The Impact of Product Recalls on the Wealth of Sellers'. *Journal of Political Economy*, 93(3): 512–36.
Jones, Kari, and Paul H. Rubin. 2001. 'Effects of Harmful Environmental Events on Reputations of Firms'. In Mark Hirschey, Kose John and Anil Makhija (eds.), *Advances in Financial Economics*, Vol. VI, 161–82. Amsterdam: JAI Press.
Karpoff, Jonathan M. 2012. 'Does Reputation Work to Discipline Corporate Misconduct?' In *Oxford Handbook of Corporate Reputation*. 361–83. Oxford: Oxford University Press.
Karpoff, Jonathan M., and John R. Lott, Jr. 1993. 'The Reputational Penalty Firms Bear from Committing Criminal Fraud'. *Journal of Law & Economics*, 36(2): 757–802.
1999. 'On the Determinants and Importance of Punitive Damage Awards'. *Journal of Law & Economics*, 42(S1): 527–73.
Karpoff, Jonathan M., John R. Lott, Jr. and Eric W. Wehrly. 2005. 'The Reputational Penalties for Environmental Violations: Empirical Evidence'. *Journal of Law & Economics*, 48(2): 653–75.

Karpoff, Jonathan M., D. Scott Lee and Gerald S. Martin. 2008. 'The Cost to Firms of Cooking the Books'. *Journal of Financial and Quantitative Analysis*, 43(3): 581–611.

2017. 'Foreign Bribery: Incentives and Enforcement'. Working paper. University of Washington.

Klein, Benjamin, and Keith B. Laffler. 1981. 'The Role of Market Forces in Assuring Contractual Performance'. *Journal of Political Economy*, 89(4): 615–41.

Kothari, S. P., and Jerrold B. Warner 2007. 'Econometrics of Event Studies'. In B. Espen Eckbo (ed.), *Handbook of Corporate Finance: Empirical Corporate Finance, Vol 1*. Amsterdam: Elsevier: 3–36.

Kravet, Todd, and Terry Shevlin. 2010. 'Accounting Restatements and Information Risk'. *Review of Accounting Studies*, 15(2): 264–94.

La Porta, Rafael, Florencio Lopez-de-Silanes, Andrei Shleifer and Robert Vishny. 1997. 'Legal Determinants of External Finance'. *Journal of Finance*, 52(3): 1131–50.

1998. 'Law and Finance'. *Journal of Political Economy*, 106(6): 1113–55.

La Porta, Rafael, Florencio Lopez-de-Silanes and Andrei Shleifer. 2006. 'What Works in Securities Laws?' *Journal of Finance*, 61(1): 1–32.

2008. 'The Economic Consequences of Legal Origins'. *Journal of Economic Literature*, 46(2): 285–332.

Mitchell, Mark L., and Michael T. Maloney. 1989. 'Crisis in the Cockpit? The Role of Market Forces in Promoting Air Travel Safety'. *Journal of Law & Economics*, 32(2): 329–55.

Murphy, Deborah L., Ronald E. Shrieves and Samuel L. Tibbs. 2009. 'Understanding the Penalties Associated with Corporate Misconduct: An Empirical Examination of Earnings and Risk'. *Journal of Financial and Quantitative Analysis*, 44(1): 55–83.

Peltzman, Sam. 1981. 'The Effects of FTC Advertising Regulation'. *Journal of Law & Economics*, 24(3): 405–48.

Prince, David W., and Paul H. Rubin. 2002. 'The Effects of Product Liability Litigation on the Value of Firms'. *American Law and Economics Review*, 4(1): 44–87.

Shapiro, Carl. 1983. 'Premiums for High Quality Products as Returns to Reputations'. *Quarterly Journal of Economics*, 98(4): 659–80.

Shleifer, Andrei, and Robert W. Vishny. 1997. 'A Survey of Corporate Governance'. *Journal of Finance*, 52(2): 737–83.

Spamann, Holger. 2009. 'The "Antidirector Rights Index" Revisited'. *Review of Financial Studies*, 23(2): 467–86.

51

Validity Concerns about Self-Reported Surveys on Rule Compliance

Henk Elffers

Abstract: Many studies into rule compliance use the method of self-reports about compliance or non-compliance among people or organizations that have to comply with given rules. This chapter discusses a number of validity threats associated with this method. Three major sources of distortion are discussed: misinformation, misunderstanding, and misleading. In a number of examples, it is shown that self-reports may indeed fail to mirror the behaviour of a rule addressee. Some notes on the use of multiple questions and on randomized response methods are added.

51.1 INTRODUCTION

How to establish whether a given rule that intends to govern behaviour has been obeyed by those under the scope of that rule? Investigation by law enforcement officers on what has happened or is happening may be a powerful method, but, for practical and cost reasons, law enforcement personnel can't but look into the behaviour of just a rather small subset of all cases, and they have to focus on supposedly non-compliant cases. Results of law enforcement investigation are often not made public.[1]

It is no wonder then that the method of *self-report surveys on past compliance with rules* (SRSC) is one of the most frequently used approaches.[2] In this contribution I will discuss a few validity problems of SRSC methods.

This chapter concentrates on methodological issues. Hence, it is, except in some examples, abstracting from the content of the rules the circumstances in which they apply, the type of rule transgressions that are possible and which people or organizations must comply.

For simplicity's sake, I use the terminology as introduced in Table 51.1: I speak of a rule **R**, a behaviour[3] prescribed by that rule **BP**, a person or organization[4] under

[1] But sometimes outsiders do get access to law enforcement documentation, for example Elffers (1991) on tax evasion. Also, sometimes insiders do studies that are made public, for example, Van Onna et al. (2014) on prosecution files about organizational crime.

[2] There are of course, at least in principle, other methods: observation, experiment. An example of observational work in the real world is, for example, Van Giels et al. (1991a) on red light jumping. Experimental work is often not possible due to ethical restrictions.

[3] I have written this contribution as if a case of rule compliance is an instantaneous event: for example, an export firm has to declare to customs what is in the lorry it sends from Rotterdam to Glasgow. However, many cases of rule non-compliance have a character of being done over a period of time, for example, if an abattoir is not complying with hygiene rules, it does so for a continuous stretch of time.

[4] While it is clear that compliance by organizations is more complex than that of individuals, I abstract from that difference here.

TABLE 51.1 *Notation*

Symbol	Explanation
R	Rule that governs behaviour
BP	Behaviour as Prescribed by rule R
RA	Rule Addressee, i.e., person or organization that should comply to rule R
AB	Behaviour that is Actually displayed by RA
C	AB is Compliant, i.e., AB equals BP; i.e., RA does not commit an offence
NC	AB is Non-compliant, i.e., AB does not equal BP; i.e., RA commits an *offence*
RB	By RA Reported Behaviour, which may be congruent with AB or not

the prescription of that rule, that is, the Rule Addressee **RA**, the RA's actual behaviour **AB**, which then can be either compliant **C**, or non-compliant **NC**, and finally **RB** is what RA reports about their behaviour AB, a report that can be congruent with AB or not.

The chapter discusses only survey studies addressing past behaviour, and will not treat self-reports on intended behaviour in hypothetical situations, by various methods such as simple questioning, presenting of vignettes, videos, behavioural lab stimuli, computer-simulated environments, or virtual reality (see, e.g., Van Gelder et al., 2017), though much of the considerations here will have relevance for such situations as well.

51.2 SRSC ON PAST BEHAVIOUR

The standard example of an SRSC for rule R recognizes two steps:

(1) Identify the population of people that, in the context of the research, should behave according to a given rule R, that is {RA|*RA is a person or organization whose behaviour falls under the scope of the rule R*} and approach a sample from this population.
(2) Ask the members of the sample to complete a questionnaire that contains questions about their behaviour in cases governed by R in a certain time frame.[5]

Discussion on the first issue is of course relevant for research, but it is not or not necessarily a validity issue. I just mention how important it is to delimit the population of interest to those people who have been in the relevant situation and not contaminate the research sample with people who have not.

Let us therefore look into the second issue, the use of questionnaires. A typical example of such a question, meant for naval officers, is: '*As an employee of your shipping company, have you in the past year been instrumental in dumping waste when on the high seas?*" We will use this question throughout as an example. Coming back to the issue of who to approach for questioning, it is of no use interrogating sea officers who serve on ships that cannot transport waste at all.

It is immediately clear that we may wonder whether answers given to such questions could form a sound basis for reconstructing whether the RAs have complied or not, that is, whether the measure is valid.

[5] Notice that when the Rule Addressee is an organization, we need a further description of which person or persons in that organization should complete the questionnaire.

51.2.1 *Validity Concerns*[6]

When we contemplate the use of statements of RAs about the way they have committed an offence, we find ourselves right in the middle of the long-standing and ongoing debate on validity problems of self-reports on behaviour in general. When we intend to use RAs' statements as source of information about their past behaviour, the validity question takes centre stage: to what degree can we interpret RAs' statements on their behaviour as a true representation of what has happened in the past, when they were considering, making decisions about, and executing an offence, i.e. of AB, their actual behaviour? Often, though not always, we are not interested in the RA as such, but we use him or her as an instrument that makes available information about that offence and its associated decision-making.

The aim of the present chapter is to provide a short and systematic list of validity threats in the context of self-reports, with the explicit goal of taking validity problems as seriously as we can. I want to go a step further than a ritual writing down that the problem exists:

> [M]ost investigators using such measures have simply acknowledged an awareness of the scepticism surrounding the reliability and validity of self-reported data. Sobell (1976:2)

Many researchers then go on with their research, as if just stating awareness of validity issues is equal to having solved them. If we are aware of validity problems, we should counter them as well as we can.

The basic structure of the problem recognizes three entities: the *researcher*, the *RA*, and the *actual behaviour AB*, which may be either compliant (C) or non-compliant (NC). The researcher asks the RA to inform him or her about certain characteristics of the BA, and especially whether it was an offence, a case of non-compliance, NC, or a case of compliance, C. The term 'offence' is used here in a rather broad sense: e.g., I consider also RA's decisions about the offence as offence characteristics.

This chapter concentrates on validity problems, which certainly does not deny the importance of many other problems we may meet when trying to use RAs' statements. I just mention a few here: the RA outright refuses to give an answer to the question; the person interviewed is not the real RA but mistakenly assumed to be so; the RA is physically or mentally not fit to answer questions; authorities prohibit questioning the RA; the RA is no longer available for interviewing, ... Such problems may well be very relevant and very unpleasant, but I will not treat them here; they do not concern validity problems.

If indeed an RA has been correctly localized, and has been interrogated (by whatever means: face-to-face interview, questions on paper, internet survey) about their behaviour AB, we may wonder whether this respondent has given us correct information. For what reasons could information provided by the responding RA misrepresent the offence characteristics?

Three types of problem may be identified:

- misinformation: the responding RA does not have access to the sought-after information;
- misunderstanding: mutual misunderstanding between the RA and the researcher about what is being communicated, leading to the respondent answering a different question from that which was intended by the researcher;

[6] I closely follow here my earlier treatment of validity issues in Elffers (2010), adding some new insights where appropriate.

- misleading: the RA is unwilling to tell the truth to an outsider, so is actually trying to mislead the researcher by knowingly returning an incorrect answer.[7]

In terms of the example question on waste dumping, it may be the case that the RA simply does not know whether dumping has occurred, because he or she is only a subaltern officer and has not been taken into the confidence of the captain (*misinformation*). Or the RA (*miscommunication*) has served every now and then on ships chartered for the company that indeed have dumped waste, but he or she considers only ships owned by the company, and not chartered ships, as 'belonging to your shipping company'. If the researcher rejects this interpretation of what ships belong to the company, but is unaware of this definitional difference between him- or herself and the RA, the researcher will misinterpret the answer: underreporting. Or, when an RA reports waste dumping that actually occurred eighteen months ago, or not on the high seas but in coastal waters (not hearing or pretending not to hear the geographic and temporal limits, or not sure about times or places in the past), the researcher may overreport. The case of *misleading* is simple: the RA has actively taken part in dumping from a ship on which he or she served, but prefers not to disclose that to the researcher, and therefore denies any dumping.

Let us look in a bit more detail at the three types of misrepresentation.

51.2.2 *Misinformation*

Even if it is beyond all doubt that a person has been participating in an event of non-compliance, it by no means follows that they can inform us about each and every detail of what has happened: after all, they may *not be well informed* themselves. There may be two reasons for that: either the respondent has never had access to the sought-after information, or indeed they may have possessed the relevant information but have meanwhile *forgotten* it.

51.2.2.1 Misinformation: Uninformedness

The first of those, never having possessed the information, may be on a trivial level, such as when the informant simply did not get information that in principle was available but, somehow, they did not pick up on it. People cannot inform about whether their boss was present at the scene of a non-compliance if they did not observe it, affirmatively or negatively, during the act itself. In such a case, follow-up questions on what the RA did or did not do or thought after having noticed an event become irrelevant. In SRSC we should pay ample attention to what follow-up questions are still relevant. In ordinary conversation we easily mix up questions of what the case actually was and what we think or would have thought about it, had we been aware of it. If a friend has bought a red sweater in a shop where you know they also sell purple ones, you may remark '*So you did not like the purple sweaters?*' and get as an answer '*I really prefer red*', which may mean '*Indeed, I compared the red and purple sweaters, and I happened to prefer the red one*', but also '*I did not see a purple one, but anyway, in general I like red more than purple*', or perhaps '*I was immediately so much charmed by this red one that I did not care for any other, purple or not*'. So, it remains wholly unclear whether the friend actually observed that purple sweaters were on sale or not, or whether their stated preference was formed based on the actual purple sweaters on sale. In everyday conversation, we usually

[7] Following Cronbach (1959) and Nunnally (1978), many authors discuss validity issues by distinguishing between content, criterion, predictive, and construct validity. I do prefer the distinction proposed here.

do not sort out such ambiguous statements, but when gathering information on non-compliance, it pays to be more alert. The lesson to learn from this is that we should meticulously work out the formulation of our questions, in order to be able to take the respondent by hand and guide them through the questionnaire such that we get exactly the detailed information we need.

Sometimes we see questionnaires that ask an RA about what they would have done or thought, had they been aware of what the case was, or even when something would have happened that actually has not happened now. In many a case, indeed, it may be argued that it is useless to ask people certain questions because they simply cannot have access to the relevant process. Champions of this argument when it considers motivations (‘*Why did you did this or that?*’) are Nisbett and Wilson (1977) in their famous article ‘Telling More than We Can Know’. They hold that it is useless to ask people about their motivations, arguing that they are generally unaware of *why* they did something. The argument largely hinges on the idea that many choices are made subconsciously, and that asking people to explain the whys of a choice only leads to the construction of a rationalization tale that is made up after the fact. In fact, following Calahan (1968), Nisbett and Wilson (1977) point out that people sometimes even do not know that they have made a choice or even that they have displayed a certain behaviour. The lesson here is that forcing people to give answers to motivation questions may well force them to return answers that have only a feeble relation to reality.

51.2.2.2 Misinformation: Memory Problems

The second problem about not being able to give an informative answer to questions about offences is the memory problem. It is well documented that memory about offences lacks precision. Already Medanik (1982) showed that accuracy of verbal statements about problem behaviour deteriorates with time, and the feared telescoping effect (people remembering events either much too early or much too late in time) is usually formidable in size (e.g., Averdijk and Elffers, 2012). Suffice it to say that reports about offences seem to be rather dependent on the time elapsed between behaviour and questioning (e.g., Farrington, 1973; Elffers, 1991:28).

Psychology has produced an impressive literature about memory and memory lapses (e.g., Cohen, 1996; Stein et al., 1997; Wolters, 2002). One of the phenomena that is of interest for RA interviewing is *consistency bias*: memories about former feelings and attitudes tend to be biased towards present-day feelings and attitudes. This is of course especially problematic when we interview offenders during detention about events that led to their conviction; for example, looking back, they may well remember that they had already evaluated the crime as a rather risky one (and rightly so, as it finished in arrest), even when that had not been true in the moment itself. They will tend to report what happened with the hindsight that it went wrong. Moreover, people often tend to remember events and behaviours by adapting them to so-called schemata: events will be remembered according to what people perceive as a normal or model *schema* of such an event. So people having bribed a customs officer in order to let it go when he discovers clearly faked import documents may report that the officer looked like their schematized image of a customs officer (broad-shouldered, moustache, sticking to the rules), even when the guy was clean-shaven and of slim build and with a flexible attitude on rules. Such adaptive recollection is most likely to occur in peripheral details that do not take centre stage in the event being questioned and recollected.

In this context, a great problem with memory is that people usually suffer from inadequate *source monitoring*, that is, not knowing where a remembered detail comes from. In the literature about police interrogation and false memories, it has been shown that repeatedly talking about an event, such as occurs in often repeated interrogations, may bring details into somebody's memory, not because they remember them from the event itself but because they remember them from a previous session in which that element was mentioned or discussed between them and the investigators. For example, a suspect might say that they do not know in what type of car they helped to transport illegally dumped chemicals, but then the interrogation officer says '*Come on, man, your mate has told us it was a grey Toyota pick-up*'. The suspect may then, in the next session, honestly but erroneously remember the car being grey out of their own knowledge. Actually, they do remember that detail, but they are not able to recognize that it comes from a different source than their own observation.

These points must be taken into consideration when we approach RAs on past behaviour. We ought to be very conscious about not planting cues into the RA's memory by talking (or writing) about various aspects of the actual behaviour that we may know already from other sources, and we must be aware of consistency bias. In my opinion, these problems point to a requirement for a rather strict protocol on what to ask and what to say, in order to be able to control for these types of bias. A less formal interview style (open interviewing) may be much more vulnerable. On the other hand, using closed answer formats will certainly be instrumental to getting distorted or imagined versions of the report of events. So, it is my impression that a rather strict protocol on the interviewer's side, and an open answer format for the RA, in one session only, should be seen as the least problematic with respect to memory problems. If we are talking about written or internet questionnaires, strictness about the wording on the side of the researcher is given by the format: we have to write out the complete questions. The advice here is then to consider whether open answer formats should be used.

51.2.3 *Misunderstanding*

Under the misunderstanding heading, we can classify the problem of mismatching reference frames, for example, '*money laundering*' meaning something different to the respondent than to the interviewer. A good example is from my own interviewing of people about tax fraud (Elffers, 1991; cf Webley et al., 2006). One of my respondents was a successful plumber who was adamant about always paying every cent of his taxes, otherwise he would lose his self-respect, he said. Later on in the interview, it turned out that he had an active moonlighting business on the side, for which he paid no tax, of course. Confronted with that, he was seriously surprised at my questioning that practice. '*That's not tax dodging. Tax fraud is if you don't pay over your regular daylight business.*' No tax inspector will agree, I'm afraid. Such mismatching definition problems will occur pretty often in RA interviewing, as long as the interviewer has not, or not yet, the insider's perspective. This seems to call for a rather open interview style, in which it is first left to the respondent to tell their story in their own words, after which the researcher can probe into what exactly is meant by terms and so on. Notice that this advice is contrary to that given in Section 51.2.2.2 on memory problems!

Under the misunderstanding heading, we should of course also attend to common 'good questioning practice' as taught in any standard methods book on interviewing or survey design, in order to safeguard ourselves against common errors like not listening, taking undeserved shortcuts, misunderstanding of questions or answers. A special problem is when the interviewer and the RA don't share the same mother tongue.

51.2.4 *Misleading*

People may actively or passively try to give a wrong picture to the interviewer. In the case of reporting about non-compliance, this may go both ways: either denying that any offence has taken place or at least underplaying the role of the respondent in it, or, at the other end of the scale, bragging about their criminal adventures, reporting non-existing or overstated cases of non-compliance. Underreporting is often driven by the fact that admitting to non-compliance may make the RA vulnerable to law enforcement prosecution, and the first thing to do, as a researcher, is of course to try to convince them that you will not inform the authorities.[8] Both under- and overreporting fall under the denominator of *social desirability* (Crowne and Marlowe, 1960; Edwards, 1990), that is, the tendency of the RA is to adapt their answer to what they think is expected of them in a social context, such as family, friends, workmates, irrespective of the true AB.[9] Notice that the first and foremost social context is that of the interaction between the RA and the researcher, in which case an RA may report what they think the researcher (interviewer) would perceive as correct behaviour. Paulhus (1984) showed that social desirability may come in two varieties: either the wish to deceive the interviewer, or, more fundamentally, the wish to present a picture to one's self, and therefore also to the outside world, that is more in accordance with what the reporter would wish it to be; that is, the RA is unwilling to tell the truth to themselves. In such a case, the RA may prefer to re-interpret events within the coveted frame of their self-image (self-presentational concern, Baumeister, 1982; dissonance reduction, Bem and McConnell, 1970; Goffman, 1959), which, as said, may go both ways: understating or overstating. Calahan summed this problem up nicely:

> [I]t may well be that certain questions on past behaviour do not lend themselves to accurate measurement through survey research approaches, not because people do not want to tell the truth to others, but because they cannot tell the truth to themselves. Calahan (1968:609)

A special case may take the form of *momentary consistency bias*, that is, people in an interview do not like to give an inconsistent picture of themselves and therefore bring their later answers in line with previous ones. People like to be, in fact need to be, consistent in the way they see themselves. They cannot imagine themselves doing things that are not in accordance with their self-image; therefore, they will bring their answers in line with their self-image. Deviating from this course would imply a major restructuring of the way they see themselves. It is unlikely that a simple interview could trigger such a profound exercise (Hessing et al., 1988). Goffman (1959) argued that people perceive their lives as stories, in which they may be motivated to increase the shapeliness of their personal stories to protect their self-image. Momentary consistency bias will appear when, in one and the same session, we first ask an RA about whether they committed a certain offence, and later on ask about their attitudes with

8 This may not always be possible: in many jurisdictions, citizens are legally bound to report if they have knowledge about the past or future occurrence of certain types of serious crime, such as murder or terrorism.

9 A special case, not discussed here, is *acquiescence*, the 'disposition of a respondent to respond systematically to questions in another way than he would if the questions were offered in another form' (Billiet and McClendon, 2000).

respect to that offence. It is hardly possible to report in a single time frame being a street robber but having a very negative attitude with respect to street robbery. The same holds when we offer questions in the opposite direction, first asking about attitudes, then asking for self-report: it is difficult to admit to non-compliance after having sketched a very negative picture of it. People go on in the mood they adopted at the beginning of the interview.

The misleading problem is perhaps the hardest to tackle. Of course, obvious prerequisites like convincing assurance of anonymity are important, and some researchers hope that interviewing detained prisoners provides them with such a welcome break from dull prison life that they will be more open. However, it is hard to believe that the self-presentation problem will be overcome this way. Psychological literature is pretty equivocal about the impossibility of classifying statements as lies in a reliable way (Vrij, 2008) without outside corroboration, and, though various instruments for measuring social desirability tendencies have been proposed (Paulhus, 1991; Tourangeau and Smith, 1996; cf also Wentland and Smith, 1993), an operational strategy to 'correct' answers has not emerged from this literature.

Now, many of the concerns voiced in this section address the direct admitting or denying of an offence. In some SRSC research we may hope that the fact that an offence has taken place is granted by the offender, especially if they are going to be interviewed when in custody after being convicted of it; in that case, they know very well that the interview is because of their offence. The focus of such an interview is on the ways and means, the choices and deliberations, and may, hopefully, be understood by the offender as addressing him or her in their professional capacity as offender. Will this improve the situation? Maybe it is helpful against underreporting, but, on the flip side, it may enhance bragging?

51.3 IT MAY BE A PROBLEM, BUT IS IT A PROBLEM?

In the previous sections we raised awareness of validity concerns on self-reported rule compliance. However, the fact that problems *may* occur does not imply that they *will* occur. We may be afraid that reported behaviour, RB, is not exactly equal to actual behaviour, AB, but what is the problem, if an eventual difference between the two is after all rather small? Maybe the hope that only small differences may be expected is why so many investigators are content, as Sobell is quoted as observing in Section 51.2.1, to just state their awareness and go on as if no problem exists. But how do we know whether only small differences will occur?

The standard way of approaching this question is by doing an instrument development study on the quality (in terms of both validity, our topic here, and reliability) of eliciting an answer RB from an RA. This is usually done by taking a concurring way of measuring, say RB', and studying the correlation between RB and RB' (concurrent validity approach). The optimal study, of course, is when we are able to actually observe the real behaviour AB, that is, RB'= AB (gold standard approach). We may be optimistic about how well RB approximates to the true behaviour as displayed, AB, if the correlation ρ(RB, RB') between RB and RB' is very high. We should have pretty severe standards for what we call high; elsewhere I have argued that values of ρ must be at the very least 0.70 (Elffers, 1980). In social sciences, however, such high values are rather exceptional.

Starting with an instrument development study is an excellent idea, but in most research efforts this is not done: no time, no money, no awareness. It is not very consoling then that, indeed, in many cases SRSC has been very misleading or at least suspicious, as can be derived from the disappointing low correlations that were observed in a number of studies listed in

TABLE 51.2 *Correlation between self-reports and alternative operationalizations of non-compliance**,**

Study	Topic	RB	RB'	ρ(RB, RB')
Hessing et al. (1988:409)[10]	Income tax fraud	Self-report	Tax inspector's judgement	.02
Van Giels et al. (1991a)	Red light jumping	Self-report	Observation***	.22
Van Giels et al. (1991b)	Parking violations	Self-report	Observation***	.39
Hessing et al. (1993:235)	Social security fraud	Self-report	Social security inspector's report	.51
Fetchenhauer (1998:236)	Insurance fraud	Self-report	Behaviour in public good game	.40
Webley & Siviter (2000)	Dog fouling	Self-report	Observation***	.47

* For operationalizations of all measures, see the original publications.

** Correlation type according to original publications; most publications report several measures, but I selected one here.

*** Notice that 'observation' of the behaviour concerned results in the actual behaviour AB.

Table 51.2. Even those who think my proposed threshold value of 0.70 is too severe will agree that these values are often too low to speak of concurrent validity.

The lesson to be learned here is twofold:

(1) In some circumstances, reported behaviour, RB, is not only a bad approximation of the actual behaviour, BA, it may even be totally uncorrelated with it.
(2) In other circumstances, there may be a modest correlation between RB and an alternative measure.

The inevitable conclusion seems to me to be that SRSC is to be advised only after an instrument development study has shown that concurrent validity is high enough, or when earlier studies show that such a conclusion is supported.

Listing possibly threatening factors is by no means demonstrating that self-reports are useless. In any given case, a threat may not materialize itself, or it will affect responses only marginally, or no other method will do better. Only by doing special studies into validity will we gather enough knowledge to either trust or distrust a given self-reported measure.

Whoever has to admit that interviewing RAs on past offending behaviour, in their case, may be too vulnerable to serious validity threatening factors should then consider whether it is possible to try to extract information from RAs on offending by different methods: observations, interrogating offenders on different hypothetical scenarios, discussing with offenders in the real world how they would operate if contemplating an offence and so on.

51.4 WHAT ELSE CAN WE DO?

51.4.1 *Multiple Questions?*

Is it helpful to try the age-old trick of using multiple questions on the same issue, in the hope that errors (in the sense of the difference between truth (AB) and self-report (RB)) will tend to

[10] These authors did also show an interesting structure in self-reported compliance measures as compared to outsiders' rating of that behaviour: the former are correlated with attitudes of RA, the latter with personality indicators of RA, cf Weigel et al. (1987).

cancel out? Multiple questions are first and foremost useful to enhance *reliability* of results, ie to make outcomes of the measurement procedure less sensitive or even insensitive to unrelated influence, and for that goal they are very useful. However, there is no reason to suppose that they also help validity. Notice that the concept of 'errors cancelling each other out' is based on the idea that such errors will be random errors, unrelated to the phenomenon being measured. The type of misrepresentations we have discussed here – misinformation, misunderstanding, and misleading – are of a different kind, and there is every reason to believe that such errors will not cancel each other out; on the contrary, they will all be in the same direction: if an RA does not want to confess their non-compliance, they will tend to stick to that in whatever question format. The same holds true when the source of error is lying in misinformation or misunderstanding.

51.4.2 *Randomized Response*

Randomized response is sometimes proposed as a method to counter validity problems born of social desirability. Indeed, this method has produced a number of impressive results (Van den Hout et al. 2007). A short refresher on randomized response: it does not ask the RA straight out to report on their actual behaviour, AB; rather, it first lets them throw a die, the outcome of which only the RA knows. If they threw a three, four, five or six, they must answer a question on the AB ("Did you transgress the rule?"), but if they threw a one or a two, they must answer a question with a known distribution of answers ("Was your mother's birthday in January?"). The idea is that the RA will become aware that if they say 'Yes' to this layered question, the researcher has no way to sort out whether the RA was non-compliant or whether their mother was born in January. Nevertheless, the researcher can compute from the distribution of the answers, through taking into account the known distribution of the eyes of a die, and the distribution of birthdays over a year, the distribution of non-compliance over the whole sample.[11] Notice that randomized response techniques do not make it possible to establish the outcomes for individual RAs; they produce aggregated results only. Also, they do not solve other issues we treated earlier in this chapter, only those generated by social desirability, and even on social desirability the method may perhaps deal with what Paulhus (1991) calls the wish to deceive the researcher, rather than those problems that come from self-presentational concern. Even if the complex construction of randomized response questions is convincing the RA that they may safely report non-compliance to the researcher, it is not helpful in seducing them to admit it to themselves (for a different point of view, see Cruyff et al. 2007). If I am right in this respect, randomized response reassurance will remove the RA's wish to maintain an earlier constructed self-image. Regardless, an instrument development study remains necessary.

REFERENCES

Averdijk, M., and H. Elffers. 2012. 'The Discrepancy between Survey-Based Victim Accounts and Police Reports Data Revisited'. *International Review of Victimology*, 18(2), 91–107.

Baumeister, R. F. 1982. 'A Self-Presentational View of Social Phenomena'. *Psychological Bulletin*, 91, 3–26.

Bem, C. G., and H. K. McConnell. 1970. 'Testing the Self-Perception Explanation of Dissonance Phenomena: On the Salience of Premanipulation Attitudes'. *Journal of Personality and Social Psychology*, 14, 23–31.

[11] There are many varieties of executing randomized response techniques; see Van den Hout et al. (2007).

Billiet, J., and J. McClendon. 2000. 'Modelling Acquiescence in Measurement Models for Two Balanced Sets of Items'. *Structural Equation Modeling*, 7(4), 608–28.

Calahan, D. 1968. 'Correlates of Respondent Accuracy in the Denver Reliability Survey'. *Public Opinion Quarterly*, 32, 608–21.

Cohen, G. 1996. *Memory in the Real World*, 2nd ed. Hove: Psychology Press.

Cronbach, L. J. 1959. *Essentials of Psychological Testing*, 2nd ed. London: Harper and Row.

Crowne, D. P., and D. Marlowe. 1960. 'A New Scale of Social Desirability Independent of Psychopathology'. *Journal of Consulting Psychology*, 24, 349–54.

Cruyff, M. J., A. van den Hout, P. G. van der Heijden, and U. Böckenholt. 2007. 'Log-Linear Randomized-Response Models Taking Self-Protective Response Behavior into Account'. *Sociological Methods and Research*, 36(2), 266–82.

Edwards, A. L. 1990. 'Construct Validity and Social Desirability'. *American Psychologist*, 45, 287–9.

Elffers, H. 1980. 'On Interpreting the Product Moment Correlation Coefficient'. *Statistica Neerlandica*, 34, 3–11.

Elffers, H. 1991. *Income Tax Evasion: Theory and Measurement*. Deventer: Kluwer.

Elffers, H. 2010. 'Misinformation, Misunderstanding and Misleading S Validity Threats to Offenders' Accounts of Offending'. In W. Bernasco (ed.), *Offenders on Offending. Learning about Crime from Criminals*, 13–22. Cullompton: Willan Publishing.

Farrington, D. P. 1973. 'Self-Reports of Deviant Behaviour: Predictive and Stable?' *Journal of Criminal Law and Criminology*, 64, 99–110.

Fetchenhauer, D. 1998. *Versicherungsbetrug: Eine theoretische und empirische Analyse betrügerischen Verhaltens gegenüber einem anonymen Geschädigten*. Nomos-Verlag-Ges.

Goffman, E. 1959. *The Presentation of Self in Everyday Life*. New York: Doubleday.

Hessing, D. J., H. Elffers, and R. H. Weigel. 1988. 'Exploring the Limits of Self-Reports and Reasoned Action: An Investigation of the Psychology of Tax Evasion Behavior'. *Journal of Personality and Social Psychology*, 54, 405–13.

Hessing, D. J., H. Elffers, H. S. J. Robben, and P. Webley. 1993. 'Needy or Greedy? The Social Psychology of Individuals Who Fraudulently Claim Unemployment Benefits'. *Journal of Applied Social Psychology*, 23(3), 226–43.

Medanik, L. 1982. 'The Validity of Self-Reported Alcohol Consumption and Alcohol Problems: A Literature Review'. *British Journal of Addiction* 77, 357–82.

Nisbett, R. E., and T. D. Wilson. 1977. 'Telling More than We Can Know: Verbal Reports of Mental Processes'. *Psychological Bulletin* 84, 231–57.

Nunnally, J. C. 1978. *Psychometric Theory*. New York: McGraw-Hill.

Paulhus, D. L. 1984. 'Two-Component Models of Socially Desirable Responding'. *Journal of Personality and Social Psychology*, 46(3), 598–609.

Paulhus, D. L. 1991. 'Measurement and Control of Response Bias'. In J. Robinson, P. Shaver, and L. Wrightman (eds.), *Measures of Personality and Social Psychological Attitudes*, 17–60. San Diego, CA: Academic Press.

Sobell, L. C. 1976. 'The Validity of Self-Reports. Towards a Predictive Model'. Unpublished dissertation, University of California, Irvine.

Stein, N. L., P. A. Ornstein, B. Tversky, and C. Brainerd. (eds.) 1997. *Memory for Everyday and Emotional Events*. Mahwah, NJ: Laurence Erlbaum Associates.

Tourangeau, R., and T. W. Smith. 1996. 'Asking Sensitive Questions: The Impact of Data Collection Mode, Question Format, and Question Context'. *Public Opinion Quarterly*, 60, 275–304.

Van den Hout, A., P. G. van der Heijden, and R. Gilchrist. 2007. 'The Logistic Regression Model with Response Variables Subject to Randomized Response'. *Computational Statistics and Data Analysis*, 51(12), 6060–9.

Van Gelder, J. L., C. Nee, M. Otte, A. Demetriou, I. Van Sintemaartensdijk, and J. W. Van Prooijen. 2017. 'Virtual Burglary: Exploring the Potential of Virtual Reality to Study Burglary in Action'. *Journal of Research in Crime and Delinquency*, 54(1), 29–62.

Van Giels, B., D. J. Hessing, and H. Elffers. 1991a. *Rood Rijden: Determinanten van het Rijden door Rood onder Automobilisten [Determinants of Red Light Jumping]*. Rotterdam: ECSTR.

Van Giels, B., D. J. Hessing, and H. Elffers. 1991b. *Dubbel Parkeren: Determinanten van het Dubbel Parkeren onder Automobilisten [Determinants of Illegal Parking]*. Rotterdam: ECSTR.

Van Onna, J. H., V. R. Van Der Geest, W. Huisman, and A. J. Denkers. 2014. 'Criminal Trajectories of White-Collar Offenders'. *Journal of Research in Crime and Delinquency*, 51(6), 759–84.
Vrij, A. 2008. *Detecting Lies and Deceit: Pitfalls and Opportunities*. 2nd ed. Chichester: John Wiley and Sons.
Webley, P., C. Adams, and H. Elffers. 2006. 'Value Added Tax Compliance'. In E. J. McCaffery and J. Slemrod (eds.), *Behavioral Public Finance*. New York: Russell Sage Foundation, 175–205.
Webley, P., and C. Siviter. 2000. 'Why Do Some Dog Owners Allow Their Dogs to Foul the Pavement? The Social Psychology of Minor Rule Transgression'. *Journal of Applied Social Psychology* 30, 1371–80.
Weigel, R. H., D. J. Hessing, and H. Elffers. 1987. 'Tax Evasion Research: A Critical Appraisal and Theoretical Model'. *Journal of Economic Psychology*, 8, 215–35.
Wentland, E. J., and K. W. Smith (1993. *Survey Responses: An Evaluation of Their Validity*. San Diego: Academic Press.
Wolters, G. 2002. 'Herinneren door getuigen [Eyewitness Memory]'. In P. J. van Koppen, D. J. Hessing, H. L. G. J. Merckelbach and H. F. M. Crombag (eds.), *Het Recht van Binnen. Psychologie van het Recht* [Handbook of Psychology of Law]. Deventer: Kluwer.

52

Factorial Surveys and Crime Vignettes

Nicole Leeper Piquero, Vrishali Kanvinde, and Whitney Sanders

Abstract: Factorial surveys or vignettes have become a popular research methodology for social scientists to use when studying issues surrounding compliance, crime, and justice. This chapter provides an overview of this specially designed self-report survey methodology, highlighting its strengths and weaknesses while also providing current examples within the field of criminology.

52.1 INTRODUCTION

Understanding decision-making is key to studying many issues surrounding compliance, crime, and justice. Theorists seek to explain why crimes or rule violations occur while others set out to understand the operations of the various systems of justice including criminal, regulatory, and civil. Both lines of inquiry require understanding of the complex circumstances surrounding the situations that individuals find themselves in and then measuring the social judgments or decisions that individuals have to make when in those circumstances. The question then becomes how best to measure and capture these social judgments in the dynamic situations that individuals find themselves in. Since having people stop at the moment of every decision and fill out a survey is not very feasible – and may in fact alter decision-making, Rossi and Nock (1982) proposed that one way to capture decision-making in a situational context is through a factorial survey approach.

Scholars have used a variety of terms, such as factorial surveys, vignette surveys, or even scenario methodology, to refer to this methodological approach. Regardless of the moniker given to the methodology, its administration is rather quite simple as it is essentially a specially designed self-report survey most often administered in a controlled setting (a point we return to later).

52.2 THE VIGNETTE APPROACH

In the vignette approach, respondents are asked to complete a survey that includes hypothetical vignettes or scenarios depicting real-life situations in which decisions need to be made. In each scenario, the actor takes a decisive action (e.g., engages in price-fixing or drunk driving). After reading each scenario, respondents are told to imagine that they are the actor depicted in the story and then asked to estimate how likely (or unlikely) it is that they would do what the character did; typically, on a Likert scale (0 = no chance to 10 = 100 percent likely).

For example, Schoepfer, Piquero, and Langton (2014) sampled undergraduate students and used the following scenario to examine intentions to embezzle from their place of work:

> Jamie is a college student at a local university who has to work to earn money for tuition and fees. Jamie has been working evenings and weekends at a local grocery store stocking shelves and serving as a cashier. Just before classes are to begin, Jamie is short on registration fees by about $250. Jamie's parents cannot afford to pay the fee so, when another employee forgets to lock the cash register before leaving one night, Jamie takes $250 from that employee's cash register.

Scenarios are constructed with at least one factor or dimension of a complex situation that can be manipulated across survey administrations such that different subjects respond to a slightly different vignette but all ultimately have to decide the extent to which they would do what the character in the scenario did. The factors selected are pulled from findings and are designed to recreate the real-world circumstances an individual might find him or herself in when making the choice depicted in the scenario. These elements or factors are then randomly assigned across respondents. For example, Simpson and Piquero (2002) were interested in understanding firm-level influences on decisions to engage in various forms of corporate offending so they randomly assigned three different levels of firm size (i.e., small, medium, or large) in their scenario. Other scholars working on testing aspects of deterrence and rational choice theory varied the likelihood/risk of detection (e.g., 20 percent or 75 percent) and/or how long a character had to drive home while drunk (e.g., 1 mile or 5 miles) (see Nagin and Paternoster, 1993; Piquero and Tibbetts, 1996). Like all surveys, factorial surveys also include a battery of other questions asking respondents about their attitudes and perceptions, their demographic characteristics, and other theoretical constructs (e.g., elements of low self-control or rational choice theory) of interest to the research question(s), which are also used as independent variables for predicting the penultimate response question given by the scenario.

This methodological approach can be described as a hybrid quasi-experimental research design as it integrates a randomized experimental design with the social survey approach (Aviram, 2012; Wallander, 2009) and as such pulls from the strengths of both approaches, mainly improving internal validity and increasing generalizability from the findings. As such, there are a number of advantages to using such a research approach to assess decision-making in a situational context.

First, as with experimental designs, researchers utilizing a factorial survey approach have a high degree of control and manipulation of the independent variables(s) they believe are causally linked to the variable(s) of interest. As noted by Aviram (2012: 463), "all control over the text of the scenario lies with the researcher," therefore a well-constructed vignette will present respondents with concrete and detailed descriptions of situations where researchers are manipulating and isolating the specific factors of interest while at the same time controlling for potentially confounding influences in the decision-making process. Nagin and Paternoster (1993) contend that if respondents are not provided with specific details in the scenario (i.e., the name of a local bar, etc.), they are likely to impute their own circumstances or definitions, which, of course, will vary across persons and affect response outcomes.

The randomization of vignette dimensions across respondents allows for causal inferences to be more readily assessed. As noted, if the researcher believes that the likelihood of detection and/or the distance to be traveled are variables that could be intimately related to the decision to drive home drunk, then manipulation of those variables in a scenario allows the researcher the direct ability to test for such effects. Of course, there are only so many variables that can be manipulated within a scenario. Accordingly, the researcher must take care to ensure that s/he has enough subjects to cover the number of manipulations in the scenario.

Second, as Wallander (2009) argues, the factorial survey approach may also reduce social desirability bias, or the tendency to provide answers that the researcher is looking for or to answer in such a way as to come across as a good person, compared to results from a conventional survey approach (see also Alexander and Becker, 1978). This lessening of social desirability bias within the vignette methodology is enhanced because respondents are not fully aware of the manipulation of the variables of interest across the vignette. Since the underlying purpose of the factorial survey approach is to manipulate variables of interest in the vignette and respondents are not privy to the construction of vignettes, they do not know or are not aware of which variable(s) were varied in other versions of the scenario.

Third, while typical self-report surveys are often plagued with temporal ordering problems, this is not the case with factorial surveys. In both cross-sectional and panel survey research designs, researchers must contend with the issue of lag time between independent and dependent variables (Nagin and Paternoster, 1993). For example, researchers utilizing self-report surveys have to contend with the issue of how long is too long for a recall period for respondents to report events? Or how long should the interval be between time one and time two data collection? Thus, the factorial survey approach gives researchers the advantage that they are examining the instantaneous relationship between the independent variables and the self-reported intentions to offend.

In particular, not only do the majority of vignette-style studies tend to include demographic and other variables that are theoretically related to the key outcome variable (e.g., elements of low self-control or desire for control) but the manipulated conditions within the scenario are also collected in "real time." Thus, because the main outcome variable in a scenario design asks respondents to indicate the probability or likelihood that they would do what the character in the scenario did (i.e., the character always does the action), that response is a future behavior and the other variables precede it (i.e., they are measured in the present instance) such that temporal order has been better established. Finally, it is also worth pointing out that there is good evidence to suggest that what people say they are likely to do in a vignette format correlates well with what they actually end up doing, say, six months later in follow-up studies (see Fishbein and Ajzen, 1975; Green, 1989; Kim and Hunter, 1993; Pogarsky, 2004).

Fourth, the factorial survey design approach allows researchers to study behaviors that are difficult to gather information on or for which data are not routinely available (e.g., white-collar and corporate offenses). Therefore, they allow researchers to study hard-to-reach populations and sensitive topics (Aviram, 2012).

In particular, corporate crime scholars cannot easily rely on official records to examine corporate offending because few existing data collection efforts include such offenses. Likewise, populations of corporate executives and high-level business managers are not easily attainable or accessible. Therefore, many white-collar and corporate crime scholars have utilized this approach by surveying student populations, particularly those enrolled in Masters of Business Administration (MBA) and Executive MBA programs (Elis and Simpson, 1995; Paternoster and Simpson, 1996; Piquero, Exum, and Simpson, 2005; Piquero, Tibbetts, and Blankenship, 2005; Piquero, Schoepfer, and Langton, 2010; Simpson, 2002; Simpson and Piquero, 2002; Vieraitis et al., 2012). Vignette designs are particularly useful when trying to understand the causes of corporate crime because of the complexity of the decision-making process. As noted by many organizational theories, the challenges to understanding motivations to offend are at both the macro- and the micro-level and include elements such as normative organizational considerations, organizational costs and benefits, authority and group influences, as well as individual self-interests (see Simpson and Piquero, 2002). Piquero, Exum, and Simpson (2005) set out to examine the extent to which individuals with high levels of desire for control, or the general wish to be in control of everyday life events, were more likely to engage in corporate crime. In order to do this, they created the following vignette that included ten variable dimensions (nine of which are in italics below) that may be present in a corporate decision-making context and administered it to a sample of MBA and Executive MBA students:

> Lee, a manager at Steelcorp, considers whether to order an employee to meet with competitors to discuss product pricing for the next year. Lee thinks that *the law governing this act is unreasonably applied to companies* like Steelcorp. Steelcorp is *a diversified company*, currently *experiencing growing sales and revenues* in an industry that is *losing ground to foreign competitors*. If successful, the act may *result in a positive impression of Lee by top management*. Lee also believes that the act will *greatly increase firm revenues*. The firm *has mandatory ethics training*, and *an employee was severely reprimanded after being discovered* by the firm engaging in a similar act. Lee decides *to order an employee* to meet with competitors to discuss product pricing for next year.

The ten dimensions built into the scenario were (Piquero, Exum, and Simpson, 2005: 264):

1. Information regarding the depicted manager's perceptions of legal fairness; whether the manager thinks the law governing the act is unreasonably applied versus no information regarding the law
2. Whether the company was diversified versus no information about diversification
3. Economic pressures on the firm to include experiencing either growing sales and revenues versus experiencing declining sales and revenues
4. Environmental constraints such that the industry was losing ground to foreign competitors, was economically healthy or economically deteriorating
5. The benefits of noncompliance to the manager that could result in a positive impression by top management, a promotion and salary bonus, or an increase in co-worker admiration
6. The benefits of noncompliance to the firm such greatly increasing firm revenues versus modestly increasing revenues
7. Internal compliance indicators such as whether the company had mandatory ethics training, versus a code of ethics, a hotline, or ethic audits
8. The nature of vicarious punishment experienced assuming the act was discovered and an employee was severely reprimanded, versus the firing of an employee, or no action taken
9. The locus of control of the decision represented by whether the manager orders an employee to engage in the act or is ordered by a supervisor to do so
10. Corporate culture regarding similar behaviors measured as the act is common within the firm, common within the industry, or no information about culture (note: the last option is used in the vignette above).

In addition to hard-to-reach populations and crime types, vignette designs are useful when dealing with sensitive topics, particularly those dealing with moral or ethical dilemmas (Aviram, 2012). For example, Piquero and Hickman (1999) used a vignette design to better understand deviant sexual practices among college students; Hickman et al. (2001) applied the scenario methodology to police officers in order to gauge their intentions to physically abuse a suspect in custody and Klepper and Nagin (1989) have used the approach to study tax evasion.

52.3 CRITICISMS OF THE VIGNETTE APPROACH

Although the scenario methodology entails many advantages and offers "theory testers" and researchers interested in decision-making a relatively straightforward and low-cost approach to examining individual decision-making in situational context, especially when compared to randomly controlled experiments, as is the case with any research methodology, researchers have raised some concerns.

First, because the vignette approach is hypothetical, some have claimed that it does not address "real" behavior or the actions that an individual "would actually" do. There is, of course, no denying that this is true. However, as noted earlier, there is research examining the concordance between behavioral intentions and actual behaviors (Fishbein and Ajzen, 1975; Green, 1989; Kim and Hunter, 1993; Pogarsky, 2004). Green (1989) conducted a two-wave panel study to examine the effects of deterrence theory on driving under the influence among a random sample of adults. At wave one, respondents were asked whether or not they thought they would drive under the influence in the next year while at wave 2, approximately one year later, they were asked to self-report whether they had or had not driven under the influence in the past twelve months. He found a strong and significant correlation (r=.83) between the two measures of drinking and driving. Kim and Hunter (1993) conducted a meta-analysis to examine whether or not attitudinal relevance affected the correlation between attitudes and behavior. They found a strong relationship (r=.79) between attitudes and behaviors and noted that the higher the attitudinal relevance, the stronger the relationship between attitudes and behaviors.

To further examine the connection between intentions to offend and actual offending behavior, Pogarsky (2004) integrated a vignette-based survey with a randomized laboratory experiment. The first part of the study asked respondents to complete a survey including a scenario about drinking and driving while the second part, the experiment, offered the respondents an opportunity to cheat on the final part of a survey that would allow them to earn additional money. He found that those who cheated on the experiment part of the study were significantly more likely to project that they would drink and drive. As he summarized, "the results reflect a strong correlation between projected offending and contemporaneous rule violation" (Pogarsky, 2004: 124).

Second, even if intentions to offend are likely to predict actual behavior, we still must contend with the issue of whether or not the scenario simulates the real world. While vignettes are designed to manipulate known conditions that may affect an individual's decision-making, the respondent must also believe in the realism of the scenario. Aviram (2012) notes that respondents must not only be engaged with the story but also have the ability to place themselves in it. He further argues that if they are not imagining themselves experiencing the situation, they may be more emotionally removed from it, and that emotional distance may influence the social desirability of their responses. One way to account for this concern is to simply include a question asking respondents to assess the realism of each scenario and to drop the cases that were deemed to be unrealistic. Importantly, the majority of scenario-based studies yielded very high (> 90 percent) realism estimates.

Third, since many scenario studies are interested in manipulating a number of characteristics within the vignette that are believed to be related to an individual's penultimate decision, a researcher must take care to ensure that she or he has enough subjects in order to have sufficient statistical power to generate adequate model estimations. Relatedly, researchers will often provide subjects with more than one scenario per survey. For example, Schoepfer, Piquero, and Langton (2014) surveyed a large sample of university students and included three separate hypothetical scenarios related to occupational crime (embezzlement), corporate crime (shredding documents), and traditional crime (shoplifting) to examine the effects of low self-control and the desire for control on different types of offending intention. While each of the different scenarios has its own manipulations factored into it, there is still a built-in tendency, or unobserved individual differences, that may be operating in the overall survey responses. Because the scenarios are often used as the unit of analysis and individuals are responding to multiple scenarios, there will be bias or correlation in the way an individual responds to each scenario. While there are statistical techniques, particularly the fixed-effects model, that researchers can use to deal with this unobserved individual difference, they too have some disadvantages that researchers must weigh in their overall research.

In the end, the vignette approach has very desirable features and, because of that, it has been used to study a wide variety of behaviors, including many of the antisocial ones discussed here; however, it is important to note that it has also been used to understand prosocial decisions. For example, Piquero, Cohen, and Piquero (2011) used such an approach to ask people about their willingness to pay for identity theft prevention programs and Nagin et al. (2006) queried respondents about whether they would prefer to spend money on juvenile offender rehabilitation or punishment. Because of the flexibility of the factorial survey approach, we believe that it will continue to serve as a popular research methodology for social scientists who want to understand causal factors in understanding decision-making patterns in specifically defined social contexts. That said, it is incumbent on each researcher using this strategy to ensure the integrity of the scenario by making sure that it is grounded in the extant literature such that it truly depicts a real-world situation that the decision-maker could find her or himself in with as much real-world specificity built into the scenario as possible.

REFERENCES

Alexander, C. S., and Becker, H. J. (1978). "The Use of Vignettes in Survey Research." *Public Opinion Quarterly*, 42: 93–104.

Aviram, H. (2012). "What Would You Do? Conducting Web-Based Factorial Vignette Surveys." In L. Gideon (ed.), *Handbook of Survey Methodology for the Social Sciences*, 463–73. New York: Springer.

Elis, L. A., and Simpson, S. S. (1995). "Informal Sanction Threats and Corporate Crime: Additive versus Multiplicative Models." *Journal of Research in Crime and Delinquency*, 32: 399–425.

Fishbein, M., and Ajzen, I. (1975). *Belief, Attitude, Intention, and Behavior*. Reading, MA: Addison-Wesley.

Green, D. E. (1989). "Measures of Illegal Behavior in Individual-Level Deterrence Research." *Journal of Research in Crime and Delinquency*, 26(3): 253–75.

Hickman, M., Piquero, A., Lawton, B., and Greene, J. (2001). "Applying Tittle's Control-Balance Theory to Police Deviance." *Policing*, 24: 497–520.

Kim, M., and Hunter, J. E. (1993). "Attitude-Behavior Relations: A Meta-analysis of Attitudinal Relevance and Topic." *Journal of Communications*, 43(1): 101–42.

Klepper, S., and Nagin, D. S. (1989). "Tax Compliance and Perceptions of the Risks of Detection and Criminal Prosecution." *Law & Society Review*, 23: 209–40.

Nagin, D. S., and Paternoster, R. (1993). "Enduring Individual Differences and Rational Choice Theories of Crime." *Law & Society Review*, 27(3): 467–96.

Nagin, D. S., Piquero, A. R., Scott, E. S., and Steinberg, L. (2006). "Public Preferences for Rehabilitation versus Incarceration of Juvenile Offenders: Evidence from a Contingent Valuation Survey." *Criminology & Public Policy*, 5: 627–52.

Paternoster, R., and Simpson, S. (1996). "Sanction Threats and Appeals to Morality: Testing a Rational Choice Model of Corporate Crime." *Law & Society Review*, 30: 549–83.

Piquero, A. R., and Hickman, M. (1999). "An Empirical Test of Tittle's Control Balance Theory." *Criminology*, 37: 319–42.

Piquero, A., and Tibbetts, S. (1996). "Specifying the Direct and Indirect Effects of Low Self-Control and Situational Factors in Offending Decision Making: Toward a More Complete Model of Rational Offending." *Justice Quarterly*, 13: 481–510.

Piquero, N. L., Exum, M. L., and Simpson, S. S. (2005). "Integrating the Desire for Control and Rational Choice in a Corporate Crime Context." *Justice Quarterly*, 22(2): 253–80.

Piquero, N. L., Tibbetts, S. G., and Blankenship, M. (2005). "Examining the Role of Differential Association and Techniques of Neutralization in Explaining Corporate Crime." *Deviant Behavior*, 26(2): 159–88.

Piquero, N. L., Schoepfer, A., and Langton, L. (2010). "Completely Out of Control or the Desire to Be in Complete Control? An Examination of How Low Self-Control and the Desire for Control Relate to Corporate Offending." *Crime & Delinquency*, 56(4): 627–47.

Piquero, N. L., Cohen, M., and Piquero, A. R. (2011). "How Much Is the Public Willing to Pay to Be Protected from Identity Theft?" *Justice Quarterly*, 28(3): 437–59.

Pogarsky, G. (2004). "Projected Offending and Contemporaneous Rule-Violation: Implications for Heterotypic Continuity." *Criminology*, 42: 111–35.

Rossi, P. H., and Nock, S. L. (eds.) (1982) *Measuring Social Judgments: The Factorial Survey Approach*. Beverly Hills, CA: Sage Publications.

Schoepfer, A., Piquero, N. L., Langton, L. (2014). "Low Self-Control versus the Desire-for-Control: An Empirical Test of White-Collar Crime and Conventional Offending." *Deviant Behavior*, 35: 197–214.

Simpson, S. (2002). *Corporate Crime, Law, and Social Control*. New York: Cambridge University Press.

Simpson, S. S., and Piquero, N. L. (2002). "Low Self-Control, Organizational Theory, and Corporate Crime." *Law & Society Review*, 36(3): 509–47.

Vieraitis, L. M., Piquero, N. L., Piquero, A. R., Tibbetts, S. G., and Blankenship, M. (2012). "Do Women and Men Differ in Their Neutralizations of Corporate Crime?" *Criminal Justice Review*, 37(4): 480–94.

Wallander, L. (2009). "25 Years of Factorial Surveys in Sociology: A Review." *Social Science Research*, 38: 505–20.

53

Qualitative Methods and the Compliance Imagination

Garry Gray

Abstract: Qualitative research is valuable because it allows us to gain a deeper appreciation for the everyday lived experiences of individuals and groups across a wide spectrum of compliance settings. The insights gained from qualitative research may also provide an opportunity to challenge traditional assumptions held in the literature by revealing what we miss when we fail to account for the social context of compliance. In this chapter, qualitative researchers are encouraged to draw on their compliance imaginations in order to develop innovative and creative research projects that explore everyday practices of (non-)compliance.

53.1 INTRODUCTION

Qualitative research provides audiences a different view into the routine experiences of regulatory compliance by revealing how legal rules interact with individual and organizational behaviour in everyday practice. In contrast to quantitative research, which focuses primarily on the statistical analysis of numerical data, the goal of most qualitative researchers is to provide an in-depth understanding of the social context of legality. In the compliance field, qualitative approaches help researchers provide insights into the lived experiences of regulatory settings by revealing the social meanings that individuals and groups attach to their (non-)compliance behaviours. Qualitative research highlights what we miss when we fail to take account of what occurs at the frontline of regulatory fields (cf. Gray and Lindsay 2019; van Rooij et al. 2012; Abrego 2011; Gray 2002; Heimer 1999; Ewick and Silbey 1998; Vaughan 1996).

There are a wide range of qualitative methodologies and data collection techniques that researchers can draw on when conducting compliance-related research. While popular qualitative research methods tend to involve interviews, fieldwork, and ethnography, qualitative research also routinely draws on focus groups, content analysis, narrative analysis, and historical research.[1] Furthermore, as Denzin and Lincoln (2005: 2) note, qualitative research also involves 'the studied use and collection of a variety of empirical materials – case study, personal experience, introspective, life story, interview, observational, historical, interactional, and visual texts – that describe routine and problematic moments and meanings in individuals' lives'. In other words, as one of the founders of the seminal work on the discovery of grounded theory (Glaser 2001) notes – 'all is data'.[2] In this chapter, I combine the

[1] For more information on different qualitative methodologies and data collection techniques, see Morgan 2019; Coffey 2018; Leavy 2014; Bourgeault et al. 2010.

[2] According to Glaser (2001), the dictum *all is data* 'means exactly what is going on in the research scene is the data, whatever the source, whether interview, observations, documents, in whatever combination. It is not only what is

grounded theory dictum that 'all is data' with C. Wright Mills's (1959) classic concept of the 'sociological imagination' to advocate for future qualitative research that is inspired by a *compliance imagination* towards the examination of governance in everyday life.[3]

53.2 THE COMPLIANCE IMAGINATION

Qualitative research holds great promise for innovative researchers willing to engage their compliance imaginations and the idea that 'all is data'. For example, while voluntary and self-regulation, as well as consumer choice models of regulation, involve less regulatory oversight and, as a result, less official data, a researcher who uses their compliance imagination and the idea that all is data can still observe compliance in practice. The following two studies, one involving free-range eggs and a second one on video games, illustrate how compliance fieldwork can be enacted when researchers adopt an openness to what counts as data.

The first study, on the regulation of free-range eggs, used a recursive data collection approach 'beginning and ending with the researcher[s] [putting themselves] in the place of the retail consumer seeking to buy free-range eggs' (Parker 2013: 54). After purchasing a variety of differently labelled non-cage eggs (free-range, organic, and barn-laid) from twenty-two different stores covering a variety of socio-demographic locations in Australia, the authors described their methodological approach:

> We took written notes (using a standard form) and photographs of how eggs were displayed for sale in their retail context at the time of purchasing the eggs. Later we also performed a content analysis of the branding and labelling on the cartons themselves and on any associated websites. We focused on what claims were made – explicitly (in words) and implicitly (in pictures, signs, and symbols and by context) in any material on the shelves or surrounding the retail display and on the egg cartons – about being 'free-range' and what images, logos, and graphic elements were used to support or add to the claims made in words on the cartons. Finally, we also looked for what evidence (if any) was available to the consumer about how the eggs were in fact produced and how the production systems addressed the animal welfare, agro-ecological, and health aspects of egg production differently (and better) than intense cage production. (Parker, Brunswick, and Kotey 2013: 172)

By situating themselves as consumers, these researchers creatively sought to engage how customers experience the self-regulatory and voluntary compliance practices of major retailers selling free-range eggs. In addition, the authors continued to inductively develop their methodological approach by drawing on grounded theory (Glaser and Strauss 1967).[4] After their study was completed, the authors concluded that

being told, how it is being told and the conditions of its being told, but also all the data surrounding what is being told ...' (145; see also Glaser and Strauss 1967).

3 Mills (1959: 7) notes that 'the sociological imagination is the most fruitful form of self-consciousness' as it allows us to observe how things interact and hold influence in our everyday lives. Drawing influence from Mills, Young (2011: 2–3) notes that the role of the sociological imagination is 'to bridge the gap between the inner life of human actors and the historical and social setting in which they find themselves. It is this fundamental triangle of the individual placed in a social structure at a particular place and time that is the centre of Mills' work.' The upside of adopting a sociological imagination, Young states 'is an increased reflexivity, dereification of the social world, and an awareness of the ever-present possibility of change' (ibid.). In the field of regulation, the sociological imagination helps us to become, or at least better understand, Susan Silbey's (2011) construct of a 'sociological citizen' in everyday forms of relational regulation.

4 For a full methodological description of their project as well as additional details surrounding their findings, see Parker and De Costa 2016; Parker 2013; Parker, Brunswick, and Kotey 2013.

> the consumer choice approach to free-range egg regulation and labeling in Australia 'responsibilizes'[5] consumers more than it empowers them. It appears to give consumers the power to 'regulate' the food chain by choosing the production method that they want to valorize, but in reality it creates a distinction between those who are 'ethically competent'[6] – consumers who are willing, able, and informed enough to invest time, money, and social and emotional intelligence into seeking out information and retail spaces where they can find alternatives – and those who allow the dominant retailers to construct their choices for them. (Parker 2013: 66–7)

This downloading of responsibility onto consumers is part of a broader reconfiguration of individual responsibility for risk under neo-liberalism. In other words, rather than governments officially enforcing regulation to ensure compliance, we often observe in everyday practice regulation through the individual responsibility of consumers, workers, and ordinary citizens. Qualitative and mixed method approaches, as illustrated in the socio-legal work done by Christine Parker and her colleagues on free-range egg regulation, illustrate the value of thinking creatively about everyday forms of regulation and compliance.[7]

The second case on video games provides another example of the compliance imagination and the notion that all is data. This particular study began when Tomas, a student in my research methods class, informed me that he would like to conduct research on one of his two passions – football and video games. So, taking one of his passions – video games – we worked together to develop a research design that involved participant observation through a unique interactive content analysis. The purpose of the research was to examine the amount and forms of violence, racial discrimination, and ethnic and gender stereotyping in the top ten most popular and played video games at the time.

> We drew on the roles of both observer *and* interactive-participant whereby each game was initially played for 60 full minutes, recording any notable actions on coding sheets. We then reviewed the coding sheets and entered the data into a database. When the hour had passed, game-play would stop and the recorded data was then immediately analyzed. Upon completing an extensive review of our findings, we made notes of any voids and findings that required further clarification. The game would be played again for an additional 30 minutes in an attempt to clarify and confirm earlier observations. The interactive participant method in content analysis that we used here is reminiscent of the principles of Grounded Theory where the researcher continually reviews field notes and returns to the site (in this study, back to the interactive video game) for the theoretical saturation of ideas and concepts. (Gray and Nikolakakos 2007: 99)

Using these findings, we then examined the accuracy of video game company disclosures to the Entertainment Software Rating Board (ESRB), the self-regulatory body responsible for video game ratings. The findings revealed not only non-compliance but also that certain companies did not accurately disclose the content of their video games to the ratings board. The discrepancies between the findings from our interactive content analysis and the ESRB descriptors were significant.

Similar to the research on free-range eggs, our qualitative study on video games also showed that compliance with voluntary and self-regulation eventually resulted in a downloading of individual responsibility for risk onto consumers. These studies both illustrate the

5 See Clarke 2005; Gray 2009; see also Roff 2007.

6 See Miele and Evans 2010.

7 For a qualitative study of compliance in the food industry that draws on traditional qualitative methods, in particular interviews and focus groups, see Yapp and Fairman 2005.

value of drawing on qualitative methods to examine behavioural compliance under responsibilization strategies of regulation (Gray 2009). For examples of other studies that qualitatively examine the downloading of individual responsibility for risk onto individuals on the frontline, see van Wijk and Mascini 2019; McDermott et al. 2018; Rasmussen 2011; and Gray 2006.

53.3 THE VALUE OF QUALITATIVE RESEARCH

Qualitative methods are an incredibly useful resource for examining compliance. By examining the everyday lived experiences of individuals and groups, these approaches can challenge traditional assumptions held in the literature by revealing what we miss when we fail to account for the social context of compliance. For example, in both the regulation and the compliance literature, the organization is often portrayed in terms consistent with the doctrinal fiction of the corporate person: a unitary actor subject to rules and legal regulations rather than a network of human transactions (Gray and Silbey 2011). Researchers drawing on qualitative methods are well positioned to challenge this implicit assumption of the firm/organization in regulatory compliance by examining how individuals and groups inside organizations and across professional fields experience and negotiate compliance in everyday practice. Observing and talking to individuals via ethnographies, fieldwork, and interviews create opportunities for us to see individuals as compliance agents in a broader network of organizational and institutional compliance (cf. van Wijk and Mascini 2019; Gray and Pélisse 2019; van Rooij et al. 2012; Mascini and van Wijk 2009; Hutter 2001; Heimer 1999).

Further, qualitative approaches allow us to describe and highlight how differential capacity to meaningfully engage in compliance is influenced by organizational role across social settings. In a multi-sited ethnographic collaboration I participated in with Susan Silbey, we used qualitative approaches to examine how individuals inside university labs, factories, and the trucking industry interpret and experience rules, regulations, and regulators. We found that in the everyday lived experiences of regulatory compliance, individuals would often conceptualize regulators in the following three ways: (i) *regulator as threat*, (ii) *regulator as ally*, and (iii) *regulator as obstacle*. These constructions of the regulator varied with an individual's level of workplace expertise, authority, and continuity of relationship with a regulator and/or middle-manager who occupied a legal intermediary role (Gray and Silbey 2014).

In addition to challenging traditional assumptions in the literature, qualitative methods can also be used to shape entire fields of research, as exemplified by the growth in legal consciousness research after Patricia Ewick and Susan Silbey (1998) published their influential book *The Common Place of Law: Stories from Everyday Life*. Drawing on qualitative data analysis of 141 interviews (from a larger sample of 430 interviews), these authors demonstrated that 'legality is an emergent feature of social relations rather than an external apparatus acting upon social life' (Ewick and Silbey 1998: 17; see also Merry 1990). By examining narratives of how people interpret and experience law, they were able to map three general modes of legal consciousness in everyday practice – (i) conformity *before* the law, (ii) engagement *with* the law, and (iii) resistance *against* the law (Ewick and Silbey 1998: 45). Researchers across many different studies of everyday legality have been inspired by the qualitative research of Ewick and Silbey (including myself with the above typology on how individuals socially construct regulators as threat, ally, or obstacle). For instance, several scholars who have drawn on their legal consciousness approach have qualitatively shown that how people think about and act (or do not act) towards everyday injustices and legal right violations influences the overall social context of compliance with legal rights (cf. Pélisse 2006; Marshall 2005; Gray 2002; Nielsen 2000).

Another influential body of qualitative work that has challenged traditional literatures and shaped new directions in research is that by Diane Vaughan on the 1986 Space Shuttle Challenger disaster (2004, 1996). Vaughan's research consisted of a historical ethnography of the individual decision-making processes that produced the accident. This involved the following methods: (i) qualitative interviews she conducted; (ii) detailed analysis of the official investigation interview transcripts; and (iii) examination of archival data on the case. Her qualitative methodology involved analogical theorizing (Vaughan 2004), which consists of theoretically comparing similar activities and/or events across various social settings. This approach was instrumental in challenging rational choice models of individual decision-making inside organizations that she argues decontextualize decision-making. Vaughan's innovative approaches to using qualitative methods showed that risk is often adopted incrementally and can contribute to the normalization of deviance in everyday (non-)compliance. Her study found that 'in the years preceding the Challenger launch, engineers and managers together developed a definition of the situation that allowed them to carry on as if nothing were wrong when they continually faced evidence that something was wrong'. This, Vaughan states, 'is the problem of the normalization of deviance' (Vaughan 1998: 36).

A new generation of compliance scholars is also drawing on qualitative methods to ask important questions about compliance in developing regulatory compliance contexts. For instance, Na Li (2016) has produced an insightful ethnographic account of workplace safety in the Chinese construction industry. In her research, she argues that compliance is a process and demonstrates this idea by examining compliance in everyday practice through participant observation and in-depth qualitative interviews with construction regulators (external regulatory process), managers (organizational process), and frontline workers (individual process). In another study involving China, Yunmei Wu (2017) explored compliance behaviours in the restaurant industry by conducting a participant observation study of two different restaurants. In this study, she was a full participant (she worked as a waitress/server) and also interviewed employees, managers, and owners on their experiences with compliance and interactions with regulators (see also Wu and van Rooij 2019). Both of these qualitative studies of compliance in China adopted a frontline approach (Almond and Gray 2017) and illustrate the importance of examining the social context of observable compliance behaviours. The above studies are also reminiscent of earlier ethnographies and qualitative fieldwork conducted in the United States on the construction industry (Hass 1977), underground mines (Fitzpatrick 1980), industrial factories (Jurovich 1985), restaurant service workers (Loe 1996; Mars and Nicod 1984), door-to-door salespersons (Biggart 1989), and corporate managers (Jackall 1998).

53.4 CONCLUDING NOTE

This chapter introduced several themes to consider when engaging qualitative research. First, researchers should draw on their compliance imaginations in order to develop innovative and creative research projects that explore everyday practices of (non-)compliance. Second, compliance researchers should also remain open to what counts as data and take seriously the grounded theory notion that 'all is data'. Third, qualitative research is valuable because it allows us to gain a deeper appreciation for the everyday lived experiences of individuals and groups across a wide spectrum of compliance settings. And, finally, the insights gained from qualitative research may provide an opportunity to challenge traditional assumptions held in the literature by revealing what we miss when we fail to account for the social context of compliance.

REFERENCES

Abrego, Leisy. 2011. 'Legal Consciousness of Undocumented Latinos: Fear and Stigma as Barriers to Claims-Making for First- and 1.5-Generation Immigrants'. *Law & Society Review* 45(2): 337–69.

Almond, Paul, and Garry Gray. 2017. 'Frontline Safety: Understanding the Workplace as a Site of Regulatory Engagement'. *Law & Policy* 39(1): 5–26.

Biggart, Nicole. 1989. *Charismatic Capitalism: Direct Selling Organizations in America*. Chicago: University of Chicago Press.

Bourgeault, Ivy, Robert Dingwall, and Raymond de Vries (eds.). 2010. *The Sage Handbook of Qualitative Methods in Health Research*. London: Sage.

Clarke, John. 2005. 'New Labour's Citizens: Activated, Empowered, Responsibilized, Abandoned?'. *Critical Social Policy* 25(4): 447–63.

Coffey, Amanda. 2018. *Doing Ethnography*, 2nd ed. London: Sage.

Denzin, Norman, and Yvonna Lincoln. 2005. 'Introduction: The Discipline and Practice of Qualitative Research'. In *The Sage Handbook of Qualitative Research*, edited by Normal Denzin and Yvonna Lincoln, 1–32. Thousand Oaks, CA: Sage.

Ewick, Patricia, and Susan Silbey. 1998. *The Common Place of Law: Stories from Everyday Life*. Chicago: University of Chicago Press.

Fitzpatrick, J. S. 1980. 'Adapting to Danger: A Participant Observation Study of an Underground Mine'. *Sociology of Work and Occupations* 7(2): 131–58.

Glaser, Barney. 2001. *The Grounded Theory Perspective: Conceptualization Contrasted with Description*. Mill Valley, CA: Sociology Press.

Glaser, Barney, and Anselm Strauss. 1967. *The Discovery of Grounded Theory: Strategies for Qualitative Research*. Chicago: Aldine.

Gray, Garry. 2009. 'The Responsibilization Strategy of Health and Safety: Neo-liberalism and the Reconfiguration of Individual Responsibility for Risk'. *British Journal of Criminology* 49: 326–42.

2006. 'The Regulation of Corporate Violations: Punishment, Compliance, and the Blurring of Responsibility'. *British Journal of Criminology* 46: 875–92.

2002. 'A Socio-legal Ethnography of the Right to Refuse Dangerous Work'. *Studies in Law, Politics & Society* 24: 133–69.

Gray, Garry, and Katie Lindsay. 2019. 'Workplace Violence: Examining Interpersonal and Impersonal Violence among Truck Drivers'. *Law & Policy* 41(3): 271–85.

Gray, Garry, and Tomas Nikolakakos. 2007. 'The Self-Regulation of Virtual Reality: Issues of Voluntary Compliance and Enforcement in the Video Game Industry'. *Canadian Journal of Law and Society* 22(1): 93–108.

Gray, Garry, and Jérôme Pélisse. 2019. 'Frontline Workers and the Role of Legal and Regulatory Intermediaries'. Sciences Po LIEPP Working Paper No. 94, 2019–10-12.

Gray, Garry, and Susan Silbey. 2014. 'Governing Inside the Organization: Interpreting Regulation and Compliance'. *American Journal of Sociology* 120: 96–145.

2011. 'The Other Side of the Compliance Relationship'. In *Explaining Compliance: Business Responses to Regulation*, edited by Christine Parker and Vibeke Lehmann Nielsen, 123–38. Cheltenham, UK: Edward Elgar.

Haas, Jack. 1977. 'Learning Real Feelings: A Study of High Steel Ironworkers' Reactions to Fear and Danger'. *Sociology of Work and Occupations* 4(2): 147–70.

Heimer, Carol 1999. 'Competing Institutions: Law, Medicine, and Family in Neonatal Intensive Care'. *Law & Society Review* 33(1): 17–66.
Hutter, Bridget. 2001. *Regulation and Risk: Occupational Health and Safety on the Railways*. Oxford: Oxford University Press.
Jackall, Robert. 1998. *Moral Mazes: The World of Corporate Managers*. New York: Oxford University Press.
Jurovich, Tom. 1985. *Chaos on the Shop Floor: A Worker's View of Quality, Productivity, and Management*. Philadelphia: Temple University Press.
Leavy, Patricia (ed.). 2014. *The Oxford Handbook of Qualitative Research*. New York: Oxford University Press.
Li, Na. 2016. 'Compliance as Process: Work Safety in the Chinese Construction Industry'. PhD Dissertation. Faculty of Law, University of Amsterdam.
Loe, Meika. 1996. 'Working for Men at the Intersection of Power, Gender, and Sexuality'. *Sociological Inquiry* 66(4): 399–422.
Mars, Gerald, and Michael Nicod. 1984. *The World of Waiters*. London: George Allen and Unwin.
Marshall, Anna-Maria. (2005). 'Idle Rights: Employees' Rights Consciousness and the Construction of Sexual Harassment Policies'. *Law & Society Review* 39(1): 83–124.
Mascini, Peter, and Eelco van Wijk. 2009. 'Responsive Regulation at the Dutch Food and Consumer Product Safety Authority: An Empirical Assessment of Assumptions Underlying the Theory'. *Regulation & Governance* 3(1): 27–47.
McDermott, Vanessa, Kathryn Henne, and Jan Hayes. 2018. 'Shifting Risk to the Frontline: Case Studies in Different Contract Working Environments'. *Journal of Risk Research* 21(12): 1502–16.
Merry, Sally Engle. 1990. *Getting Justice and Getting Even: Legal Consciousness among Working-Class Americans*. Chicago: University of Chicago Press.
Miele, Mara, and Adrian Evans. 2010. 'When Foods Become Animals: Ruminations on Ethics and Responsibility in Care-Full Practices of Consumption'. *Ethics, Place and Environment* 13: 171–90.
Mills, C. Wright. 1959. *The Sociological Imagination*. New York: Oxford University Press.
Morgan, David. 2019. *Basic and Advanced Focus Groups*. Singapore: Sage.
Nielsen, Laura Beth. 2000. 'Situating Legal Consciousness: Experiences and Attitudes of Ordinary Citizens about Law and Street Harassment'. *Law & Society Review* 34(4): 1055–90.
Parker, Christine. 2013. 'Voting with Your Fork? Industrial Free-Range Eggs and the Regulatory Construction of Consumer Choice'. *Annals of the American Academy of Social and Political Science* 649: 52–73.
Parker, Christine, and Josephine De Costa. 2016. 'Misleading the Ethical Consumer: The Regulation of Free-Range Egg Labelling'. *Melbourne University Law Review* 39: 895–949.
Parker, Christine, Carly Brunswick, and Jane Kotey. 2013. 'The Happy Hen on Your Supermarket Shelf: What Choice Does Industrial Strength Free-Range Represent for Consumers?'. *Bioethical Inquiry* 10(2): 165–86.
Pélisse, Jérôme. 2006. 'Time, Legal Consciousness and Power: The Case of France's 35-Hour Workweek Laws'. In *The New Civil Rights Research: A Constitutive Approach*, edited by Benjamin Fleury-Steiner and Laura Beth Nielson, 201–15. Burlington, VT: Ashgate Publishing.
Rasmussen, Joel. 2011. 'Enabling Selves to Conduct Themselves Safely: Safety Committee Discourse as Governmentality in Practice'. *Human Relations* 64(3): 459–78.
Roff, Robin Jane. 2007. 'Shopping for Change? Neoliberalizing Activism and the Limits to Eating Non-GMO'. *Agriculture and Human Values* 24: 511–22.
Silbey, Susan. 2011. 'The Sociological Citizen: Pragmatic and Relational Regulation in Law and Organizations'. *Regulation & Governance* 5: 1–13.
Van Rooij, Benjamin, Anna Lora Wainwright, Yunmei Wu, and Yiyun Zhang. 2012. 'The Compensation Trap: The Limits of Community-Based Pollution Regulation in China'. *Pace Environmental Law Review* 29(3): 701–45.
Van Wijk, Eelco, and Peter Mascini. 2019. 'The Responsibilization of Entrepreneurs in Legalized Local Prostitution in the Netherlands'. *Regulation & Governance*. DOI:10.1111/rego.12273.
Vaughan, Diane. 2004. 'Theorizing Disaster: Analogy, Historical Ethnography, and the Challenger Accident'. *Ethnography* 5(3): 315–47.

1998. 'Rational Choice, Situated Action, and the Social Control of Organizations'. *Law & Society Review* 32(1): 23–62.
1996. *The Challenger Launch Decision: Risky Technology, Culture, and Deviance at* NASA. Chicago: University of Chicago Press.
Wu, Yunmei. 2017. 'Compliance Pluralism and Processes: Understanding Compliance Behavior in Restaurants in China'. PhD Dissertation. Faculty of Law, University of Amsterdam.
Wu, Yunmei, and Benjamin van Rooij. 2019. 'Compliance Dynamism: Capturing the Polynormative and Situational Nature of Business Responses to Law'. *Journal of Business Ethics*. DOI:.org/10.1007/s10551-019-04234-4.
Yapp, Charlotte, and Robyn Fairman. 2005. 'Assessing Compliance with Food Safety Legislation in Small Businesses'. *British Food Journal* 107(3): 150–61.
Young, Jock. 2011. *The Criminological Imagination*. Cambridge: Polity Press.

54

Policy Evaluation

Saba Siddiki

Abstract: A key objective of policy evaluation is assessing the efficacy of public policies. When evaluating public policy, compliance is treated both as an indicator of policy effectiveness and as a necessary intermediary outcome for achieving policy goals. Given the importance of compliance within broader assessments of policy efficacy, scholars have dedicated substantial attention to identifying policy, individual, and organizational factors linked to policy compliance. This chapter discusses what is meant by compliance in the context of policy evaluation and ways that it can be measured therein. It also provides an overview of recent scholarship that addresses determinants of compliance as relevant for policy evaluation.

54.1 INTRODUCTION

This chapter covers the topic of policy evaluation as it relates to the overarching theme of this *Handbook* – how legal rules interact with individual and organizational behavior, and related implications for compliance. To effectively engage on the topic of policy evaluation around this theme, it is necessary to (i) define policy evaluation; (ii) posit the relevance of compliance in relation to policy efficacy; and (iii) identify various factors that influence compliance. This chapter addresses generally these three points, drawing on theoretical and empirical scholarship from various fields such as public administration, political science, economics, and social psychology.

54.2 POLICY EVALUATION: DEFINING

Fundamentally, policy evaluation is concerned with determining whether policies work. It involves ascertaining the outputs, outcomes, and impacts that result from the application of public policies, assessing the qualities of these outputs, outcomes, and impacts (e.g., evaluating their magnitude, or scale), and evaluating whether generated products actually improve the well-being of constituents (Heinrich 2002; Siddiki and Goel 2017). Vedung (1997: 3) offers the following informative and concise definition of policy evaluation: "Evaluation [is the] careful retrospective assessment of the merit, worth, and value of administration, output, and outcome of government interventions, which is intended to play a role in future, practical action situations."

Attainment of policy goals, which are typically cast in terms of outputs, outcomes, and/or impacts, is in most cases contingent on behavior change on the part of policy targets. As noted by Schneider and Ingram (1990), a key function of public policies is to compel particular types of behavioral change that are deemed to logically link to policy goals. What becomes critical, thus, is not just that policy targets alter their behavior in response to public policy directives but, rather, that they change their behavior in the specific ways directed through policy design. In essence, what matters is that they *comply* with the specific directives embodied within public policies that specify what individuals are required, permitted, and forbidden to do within certain temporal, spatial, and/or procedural parameters (Crawford and Ostrom 1995). Compliance thus can be conceived of both as an indicator of policy effectiveness (i.e., an outcome measure) and as a necessary intermediary outcome for achieving policy goals. In Section 54.3, policy compliance is defined more fully. Additionally, a range of considerations regarding the measurement of compliance within policy evaluation are presented.

54.3 POLICY COMPLIANCE: DEFINING AND MEASURING

Compliance in the policy realm is generally defined as conformance with policy directives. Others add nuance to this general definition by casting it as the extent of adherence with policy directives (May and Wood 2003). Extending this definition further, Siddiki et al. (2019: 17) define compliance as "a behavioral state in a specific time, situation, and place that conforms completely or partially to behavioral directives, such as those embodied in laws. . . ." Siddiki et al.'s (2019) definition of compliance is useful because, in addition to providing a clear operational definition of compliance, it also highlights key dimensions of compliance that those engaged in policy evaluation must account for in their measurement of such. One of these dimensions is that compliance can be situational – while a directive to behave in a certain way is mostly static (i.e., until it has been amended), how policy targets actually respond to a directive may not be. A policy target may sometimes comply with a policy directive, and, at other times, not. Another dimension of compliance highlighted in Siddiki et al.'s (2019) definition of compliance is that one can be partially or fully in compliance with the constellations of directives that comprise public policies. That is, policy targets may comply with some policy directives but not others, some or all of the time. Siddiki et al.'s (2019) definition implicitly suggests the value of treating policy directives constituting policies as the unit of analysis in compliance assessments, rather than whole policies.

The situationality and partiality dimensions of compliance highlighted so far pose questions of measurement for the policy evaluator. For example, the situationality dimension prompts the need for the policy evaluator to consider whether he or she is interested in situational or consistent compliance with a policy directive, or group of directives, when compliance itself is the outcome measure of interest. When policy compliance is assessed as an intermediary outcome – that is, when the evaluator is most concerned with the downstream effects of compliance/noncompliance – so too will the evaluator need to consider whether situational and consistent compliance is of interest.

Another dimension of compliance that must be taken into account in the context of measurement, which is not reflected in Siddiki et al.'s (2019) definition but is addressed at length in their compliance framework, is the level at which compliance is being measured: the micro-level, meso-level, or macro-level. At the micro-level, the focus is on individual-level compliance. At the meso-level, the focus is on compliance among groups, for example, organizations. At the macro-level, the focus is on aggregate compliance, for example, communities of individuals or organizations comprising a social system of some kind. Siddiki et al. (2019) also situate assessments of individual compliance decision-making occurring within group settings (so as to pick up on social influences thereon, for example) at the meso-level. Similarly, they place studies of individual decision-making in aggregate settings at the macro-level. Identifying at what level an analyst is evaluating compliance is essentially provoking attention to the unit of analysis that will serve as the basis for measurement. Most basically, it brings into focus whether the analyst is principally concerned with individual, group, or systemic compliance outcomes.

Having established the importance of compliance within policy evaluation, and articulated key considerations in the measurement of compliance, attention in this chapter now turns to factors that have been found to influence compliance in scholarship across a variety of disciplines. Understanding factors that contribute to compliance within specific domains is important as the policy evaluator, in addition to assessing policy efficacy, is also often in the position to advise on the design and implementation of policies leveraging this understanding. The academic study of compliance has largely focused on identifying individual, social, and policy-related determinants of compliance. Key findings from this scholarship are highlighted in the following section.

54.4 FACTORS INFLUENCING COMPLIANCE

Given the diversity of factors that have been studied and shown to influence compliance, some heuristic for organizing these factors is useful. For the general overview of compliance determinants presented here, this chapter again relies on Siddiki et al.'s (2019) compliance framework for studying compliance. Siddiki et al. (2019) identify four categories of factors that influence compliance, and then identify a nonexhaustive list of specific factors that fall within each category, drawing on theoretical and empirical scholarship. The four categories of factors are: (i) degree and type of monitoring and enforcement; (ii) policy design; (iii) compliance capacity; and (iv) individual psychological factors. Factors falling within the monitoring and enforcement category are frequency of monitoring and enforcement, and style of enforcement. Factors falling within the policy design category include the types and features of incentives (e.g., rewards and sanctions) embedded within policy as well as the compatibility among the designs of policies that are jointly applied within a given domain among common policy targets (May et al. 2006). Factors falling within the compliance capacity category include policy targets' resources, knowledge, and experience. Finally, factors falling under the individual psychological factors category include individuals' developmental psychological context, perceived costs of sanctions relative to benefits of noncompliance, attitudes about rules, attitudes about compliance, and perceptions of monitoring and enforcement. Provided in the rest of this section is an elaborated discussion of some of these factors within the context of extant compliance scholarship.

54.4.1 *Monitoring and Enforcement*

Regulatory scholars have consistently linked the monitoring and enforcement practices of regulatory personnel with compliance. Two stylistic factors in particular, are found to matter – frequency of monitoring and enforcement, and enforcement style. Unsurprisingly, more frequent monitoring is associated with higher rates of compliance (Gunningham et al. 2003; May and Wood 2003; Burby and Paterson 1993). Relating to enforcement style, scholars have given particular attention to examining the influence of more formalistic versus more facilitative enforcement (Carter and Siddiki in press; May and Burby 1998). Formalistic enforcement is evidenced by rigidity in the interpretation and application of policy directives by enforcement personnel (May and Wood 2003: 119). In contrast, facilitative enforcement is evidenced by more lenient interpretation and application of policy directives, as well as a tendency of enforcement personnel to assist regulatees in coming into compliance by providing compliance-supporting information or education (Carter and Siddiki in press). Scholz and Gray (1997) find that both formalistic and facilitative enforcement styles can promote compliance, but that one style may be more or less effective depending on the context. In contexts marked by greater levels of hostility between regulators and regulatees, formalistic enforcement styles may be more effective in promoting compliance. Conversely, where the relationship between regulators and regulatees is relatively harmonious, facilitative modes of enforcement may be more effective.

54.4.2 *Policy Design*

Siddiki et al.'s (2019) compliance framework points to two features of policy design that have implications for policy compliance: policy incentives and policy compatibility. Early research on compliance was steeped in the idea that a fear of civil or criminal penalty would in most cases be sufficient to thwart compliance, assuming penalties were set sufficiently high (Becker 1968). This idea, rooted in a rational actor model of decision-making, assumes individuals to be utility maximizers – incentivized by positive payoffs (i.e., monetary profit) and repelled by negative ones. Based on this conception of individual decision-making, tangible payoffs conveyed through positive and negative incentives embedded in policy design are often assumed to be largely sufficient to induce compliance (Schneider and Ingram 1990). The role of incentives in encouraging compliance has been consistently studied and validated.

Recently there has also been a growing interest in compliance research that draws insights from behavioral science, behavioral economics, social psychology, and cognate fields, to understand the role of human cognition and psychology in influencing how individuals interpret and respond to policy, including when and how they comply with it (Camerer et al. 2003; Chetty 2015; DeCaro 2018; Madrian 2014). This new wave of research is relevant for thinking about policy design in relation to compliance because the instruments presented as alternatives to incentives (and mandates) are also operationally reflected within policy design. Unlike incentives and mandates, these alternative instruments neither require nor forbid behavior, nor do they rely on material incentives to compel behavior (Loewenstein and Chater 2017; Siddiki 2020). Instead, they rely, for example, on the strategic framing of policy-relevant information, adjusting the scope of policy-relevant choice sets, and communicating personalized as well as more easily accessible information to decision-makers (Madrian 2014). As Siddiki (2020) notes, behaviorally rooted instruments are often designed to respond to various types of informational constraint that individuals face, which in turn can inhibit their compliance with policy.

Regarding policy compatibility, it is increasingly recognized that policy issues are often addressed with the simultaneous application of multiple policies (Howlett and Rayner 2007). It is also recognized that the joint application of policies is not always done as part of a coordinated exercise, with the implication that the various policies that policy targets are simultaneously exposed to may pose conflicting incentives (Siddiki et al. 2018). Siddiki (2020) refers to a lack of alignment among incentives – as well as among policy goals and instruments – between policies with common domains, foci, and targets as policy *incompatibility*.

54.4.3 *Compliance Capacity*

The ability of policy targets to comply with policy directives, relative to the behavioral change needed for compliance, has been found to shape compliance behavior (Winter and May 2001; Sabatier and Mazmanian 1980). This ability is tied to capacity, which can be conceived of in terms of various types of resources that policy targets need in order to follow directives. Examples of such resources include knowledge or information that a policy target possesses about policy directives, as well as experience with situations where directives apply. Compliance can also be costly in monetary terms, if, for example, policy targets have to invest in material resources, equipment, or personnel development to maintain or come into compliance (Winter and May 2001). As such, capacity to comply can also come in the form of financial resources. As Siddiki et al. (2019) note, however, capacity is relative. Some behavior change needed for compliance is much more extensive than others. Extensive behavioral change or highly complex changes are likely to require more capacity than behavior that is less complex. However, individual-level complexity can also emerge if compliance decisions or behaviors involve multiple steps. Capacity can also have an interactive effect on an individual's cognitive characteristics, whereby capacity may shape, for instance, perceptions of the cost of compliance.

54.4.4 *Individual Psychological Factors*

Within the context of their framework, Siddiki et al. (2019) highlight several individual-level factors that have been found to motivate compliance in policy and other rule-governed settings. Among them is perceptions of the costs and benefits or payoffs of following a given rule. The perceptions of costs could be contingent upon external sanctions or the likelihood of getting caught with specified negative consequences. Perceptions of sanctions as an individual-level factor is distinct from the actual presence and design of sanctions identified as a policy design factor in Section 54.4.2, as the former relates to how one interprets the sanction, not whether and how it embeds within public policies. Other individual factors found to influence compliance include judgments about whether following or breaking policy directives is compatible or not with individual values or norms around rule-following behavior (i.e., whether compliance is perceived as the "right thing to do"), the perceived appropriateness of enforcement, or the perceived legitimacy of the policy itself (Siddiki 2014).

DeCaro (2018) situates several of the above, and other, factors within a broader discussion of determinants of cooperation and compliance in rule-governed environments. DeCaro (2018) is fundamentally interested in evaluations of when and why individuals undercomply with mandates, and, conversely, when and why they overcomply with voluntary standards. According to DeCaro (2018), decision-making in rule-governed contexts is grounded in perceptions of fundamental needs, such as procedural justice, self-determination, competence, belonging, and security. He also posits the relevance of intrinsic motivations. Examples of intrinsic motivations are acceptance (i.e., perceived appropriateness of rule-directed behaviors within the context of broader norms) and internalization (i.e., perceived accordance of rule-directed behaviors with one's beliefs). As noted by Siddiki (2020), the concept of acceptance has also been addressed by others, for example, by March and Olsen (1995), who refer to it in terms of a logic of appropriateness, and by Young (2002), who refers to it as institutional fit. The concept of internalization has also been addressed by others such as Ryan and Deci (2000).

Finally, there are also various externally oriented individual-level factors that scholars have found to influence compliance. These are sometimes referred to as relational, or group, cognitions. Among them are perceptions of interpersonal trust, shared understanding, and self–other merging (DeCaro 2018; Beratan 2007). DeCaro (2018) defines self–other merging in terms of perceived belonging to a group. The concept of group cognitions can even be extended further to encapsulate, generally, the roles of culture, context, and history in shaping human cognition and the influence of such on responses to governing rules (Hutchins 1995; Siddiki 2020).

Within the context of this discussion, it is also important to note, as Siddiki et al. (2019) do, that individuals may not always base their decision calculus on a conscious assessment of costs or normative values. Some behavioral decisions might result from unconscious decisions - such as habits. Alternatively, biological predispositions to act impulsively, without rational calculation (i.e., as a result of fight or flight response mechanisms), can lead to actions not based on conventional rational choice.

Finally, Siddiki et al. (2019: 13) highlight various factors relating to individuals' developmental psychological context, or their individual biographies over the life-course, that influence compliance, noting:

> The extent to which decisions about compliance are affected by patterns of childhood development, or past experiences of rewards and/or pain and trauma, can trigger subsequent compliance decisions. Indeed, compliance may reflect this developmental context that can affect families and can be transmitted inter-generationally to the point where some people become non-compliant-persistent (meaning they fail to follow directives over the life course). They may also become non-compliant-limited, or exhibit non-compliant behavior during young adulthood but because of life course events triggers and changes, such as marriage, family, career, desist and begin to follow rules or norms of convention resulting in compliance. This is a familiar pattern with juvenile delinquents (Moffitt, 1993; Sampson and Laub, 1993). Yet others may fall between these positions and become compliant-limited in that they follow rules to a point but modify, reinterpret and otherwise fail to comply systematically over time.

The policy evaluator who can provide insight into the design and implementation of policy and supporting mechanisms based on his/her assessment of compliance and factors potentially contributing thereto within a particular domain might perceive recommendations regarding monitoring and enforcement, policy design, and capacity as being easier to make and enforce. However, care should also be given to unearthing individual psychological factors such as those highlighted in this section. Understanding and paying attention to such factors will help policy evaluators advise on policy design based on awareness of the underlying causes rather than just the symptoms of noncompliance where it is observed.

54.5 CONCLUSION

This chapter posits the importance of measuring compliance within policy evaluation. This position is grounded in the assumption that the efficacy of public policies ultimately depends on how individuals interpret the behavioral directives embedded within public policies (Siddiki 2014). More specifically, it depends on whether individuals, or policy targets, respond to policies in the ways intended – whether they *comply* with them. In concluding this chapter, a few key points are reiterated.

First, there are qualities of compliance that have a bearing on its measurement in policy evaluation. One quality of compliance highlighted in this chapter is that compliance is often situational; sometimes policy targets comply with specific policy directives, and sometimes they don't. Another quality of compliance highlighted in this chapter is that policy compliance can be partial; policy targets within a particular domain can be compliant with some parts of a policy but not others. The key implication of these qualities of compliance for measurement is that it begs clarity on the part of the policy evaluator regarding what specific types of compliance he or she is interested in evaluating as either a final or an intermediate outcome. This requires thinking about what types of compliance most significantly contribute to, or hinder, policy efficacy. A second point presented in this chapter is that, given the salience of compliance, it is also useful for the policy evaluator to be aware of factors that contribute to it. Ultimately, this understanding will enable policy evaluators to advise on designing policies and mechanisms that support the monitoring and enforcement of these policies, to encourage compliance within different domains. This second point links to a third offered in this chapter, which links to the core theme of this *Handbook* – how people respond to legal rules and other types of public policy (e.g., regulation) will depend on a constellation of factors relating to individuals' personal, social, policy, and other contexts.

REFERENCES

Becker, Gary. 1968. "Crime and Punishment: An Economic Approach." *Journal of Political Economy* 76, No. 2: 523–37.

Beratan, Kathi K. 2007. "A Cognition Based View of Decision Processes in Complex Social-Ecological Systems." *Ecology & Society* 12, No. 1: 27.

Burby, Raymond J., and Robert G. Paterson. 1993. "Improving Compliance with State Environmental Regulations." *Journal of Policy Analysis and Management* 12: 753–72.

Camerer, Colin, Samuel Issacharoff, George Loewenstein, Ted O'Donoghue, and Matthew Rabin. 2003. "Regulation for Conservatives: Behavioral Economics and the Case for Asymmetric Paternalism." *University of Pennsylvania Law Review* 151, No. 3: 1211–54.

Carter, David, and Saba Siddiki. in press. "Participation Rationales, Regulatory Enforcement, and Compliance Motivations in a Voluntary Program Context." *Regulation & Governance*.

Chetty, Raj. 2015. "Behavioral Economics and Public Policy: A Pragmatic Perspective." *American Economic Review* 105, No. 5: 1–33.

Crawford, Sue E. S., and Elinor Ostrom. 1995. "A Grammar of Institutions." *American Political Science Review* 89, No. 3: 582–600.

DeCaro, Daniel. 2018. "Humanistic Rational Choice and Compliance Motivation in Complex Societal Dilemmas." In *Contextualizing Compliance in the Public Sector: Individual Motivations, Social Processes, and Institutional Design*, edited by Saba Siddiki, Salvador Espinosa, and Tanya Heikkila. New York: Routledge.

Gunningham, Neil A., Robert A. Kagan, and Dorothy Thornton. 2003. *Shades of Green: Business, Regulation, and Environment*. Stanford, CA: Stanford University Press.

Heinrich, Carolyn J. 2002. "Outcomes-Based Performance Measurement in the Public Sector: Implications for Government Accountability and Effectiveness." *Public Administration Review* 62, No. 6: 712–25.

Howlett, Michael, and Jeremy Rayner. 2007. "Design Principles for Policy Mixes: Cohesion and Coherence in 'New Governance Arrangements.'" *Policy & Society* 26, No. 4: 1–18.

Hutchins, Edwin. 1995. *Cognition in the Wild*. Cambridge, MA: MIT Press.

Loewenstein, George, and Nick Chater. 2017. "Putting Nudges in Perspective." *Behavioural Public Policy* 1, No. 1: 26–53.

Madrian, Brigitte C. 2014. "Applying Insights from Behavioral Economics to Policy Design." *Annual Review of Economics* 6: 663–88.

March, James G., and Johan Olsen. 1995. *Democratic Governance*. New York: Free Press.

May, Peter J., and Raymond J. Burby. 1998. "Making Sense Out of Regulatory Enforcement." *Law & Policy* 20, No. 2: 157–82.

May, Peter J., and Robert S. Wood. 2003. "At the Regulatory Front Lines: Inspectors' Enforcement Styles and Regulatory Compliance." *Journal of Public Administration Research and Theory* 13, No. 2: 117–39.

May, Peter J., Joshua Sapotichne, and Samuel Workman. 2006. "Policy Coherence and Policy Domains." *Policy Studies Journal* 34, No. 2: 381–403.

Moffitt, T. E. 1993. "Adolescence-Limited and Life-Course Persistent Antisocial Behavior: A Developmental Taxonomy." *Psychological Review* 100, No. 4: 674–701.

Ryan, Richard M., and Edward L. Deci. 2000. "Self-Determination Theory and the Facilitation of Intrinsic Motivation, Social Development, and Well-Being." *American Psychologist* 55, No. 1: 68–75.

Sabatier, Paul, and Daniel Mazmanian. 1980. "The Implementation of Public Policy: A Framework for Analysis." *Policy Studies Journal* 8, No. 4: 538–60.

Sampson, Robert J., and John H. Laub. 1993. *Crime in the Making: Pathways and Turning Points through Life*. Cambridge: Cambridge University Press.

Schneider, Anne, and Helen Ingram. 1990. "Behavioral Assumptions of Policy Tools." *Journal of Politics* 52, No. 2: 510–29.

Scholz, John T., and Wayne B. Gray. 1997. "Can Government Facilitate Cooperation? An Informational Model of OSHA Enforcement." *American Journal of Political Science* 41, No. 3: 693–717.

Siddiki, Saba. 2014. "Assessing Policy Design and Interpretation: An Institutions-Based Analysis in the Context of Aquaculture in Florida and Virginia, United States."*Review of Policy Research* 31, No. 4: 281–303.

2020. *Understanding and Analyzing Public Policy Design*. Cambridge: Cambridge University Press.

Siddiki, Saba, and Shilpi Goel. 2017. "Assessing Collaborative Policymaking Outcomes: An Analysis of U.S. Marine Aquaculture Partnerships." *American Review of Public Administration* 47, No. 2: 253–71.

Siddiki, Saba, Sanya Carley, Nikolaos Zirogiannis, Denvil Duncan, and John Graham. 2018. "Does Dynamic Federalism Yield Compatible Policies? A Study of the Designs of Federal and State Vehicle Policies." *Policy Design and Practice* 1, No. 3: 215–32.

Siddiki, Saba, Salvador Espinosa, and Tanya Hekkila, eds. 2019. *Contextualizing Compliance in the Public Sector: Individual Motivations, Social Processes, and Institutional Design*. New York: Routledge.

Vedung, Evert. 1997. *Public Policy and Program Evaluation*. New York: Routledge.

Winter, Soren C., and Peter J. May. 2001. "Motivation for Compliance with Environmental Regulations." *Journal of Policy Analysis and Management* 20, No. 4: 675–98.

Young, Oran. 2002. *The Institutional Dimensions of Environmental Change: Fit, Interplay, and Scale*. Cambridge, MA: MIT Press.

PART IX

Analysis of Particular Fields

55

Strengthening Tax Compliance by Balancing Authorities' Power and Trustworthiness

Erich Kirchler

Abstract: The traditional economic approach to enforcing tax compliance rests on the assumption that taxpayers are reluctant to pay their share, are inclined to maximize their egoistic goals by rationally considering audit probability and fines in case of detected evasion, and comply only if forced to. Behavioral economic and psychological insights draw a more complex picture of determinants of compliance and point to differences between taxpayers and their inclination to be compliant, which calls for differential strategies to ensure compliance rather than a one-size-fits-all strategy. This chapter describes actors in the tax arena and interaction dynamics. Interaction is shaped by the power of the authorities and their trustworthiness, which, combined, are the underlying dimensions of the tax climate. As conceptualized in the slippery slope framework and its extension, it is argued that a distinction between coercive and legitimate power, and between reason-based trust and implicit trust, is necessary to understand the interaction dynamics. Subsequently, emotions elicited by the power of the authorities and their trustworthiness are described, followed by speculations about the impact on compliance of anger, fear or feelings of protection and security. Finally, strategies to shift from control to cooperation are summarized.

55.1 INTRODUCTION

Why do people pay taxes? Generally, there are two answers: on the one hand, people pay because they fear enforcement; on the other hand, they feel a moral obligation to contribute their share to the community. In this chapter, both views are presented and integrated. Moreover, emotions related to tax decisions and compliance behavior are discussed.

Levying taxes serves to provide public goods, incentivize desired behavior and discourage undesired behavior among citizens and businesses. These goals tend to enjoy broad acceptance. In particular, progressive taxation aimed at correcting excessive income and wealth differences in society appears to be perceived as just and has positive effects on people's happiness. For example, Oishi, Schimmack, and Diener (2012) found progressive taxation to be associated with nations' subjective well-being. On a global level, nations with higher progressive taxation and high satisfaction with the provision of public goods evaluate life more favorably.

We should be in favor of taxes. Noam Chomsky claimed that in a functioning democracy, people ought to celebrate on tax day:

> Here we've gotten together as a community, we've decided on certain policies and now we're moving to implement them by our own participation. That's not the way it's viewed in the United States. That's a day of mourning. There's this alien entity, sort of like a—as if it's from Mars somewhere, which is stealing our hard-earned money from us. (https://bigthink.com/videos/when-paying-taxes-became-un-american, July 1, 2019).

Conversely, already in the Middle Ages, Thomas Aquinas (1225–74) reportedly said that taxes are "legal theft," and in 2010 Peter Sloterdijk described the welfare state as a "kleptocracy." No doubt, paying taxes and levies is often felt as a burden. Webley et al. (1991) point out that the allocation of taxes was always perceived as unjust even when taxation was minimal relative to today's rates. Consequently, taxes are frequently viewed negatively. Accordingly, it is questionable whether tax morale is high.

If at best we consider paying taxes a moral obligation, and at worst we judge taxes to be legal theft, how do taxpayers decide whether or not to pay their share and how should tax authorities ensure that citizens comply with the law? What determines tax compliance and how can authorities shape the interaction climate to better foster taxpayer cooperation?

In this chapter, the traditional economic approach to enforcing tax compliance, economic determinants of compliance, and psychological forces to increase compliance are described. It is argued that taxpayers are not a uniform group of people; they differ with regard to their motivation to comply, and, consequently, a one-size-fits-all strategy to ensure compliance is less effective than a differential approach by the tax authorities. Moreover, the complex interplay between actors in the field of taxes is discussed, which requests focusing on the interaction dynamics between state authorities and citizens. Interaction processes are shaped by the power of the authorities and their trustworthiness, which, combined, are the underlying dimensions of the tax climate. As conceptualized in the slippery slope framework (Kirchler, 2007), power and trust lead to either enforced or voluntary compliance. It is argued that a distinction between coercive and legitimate power, and between reason-based trust and implicit trust, is necessary to understand the interaction dynamics. Subsequently, an attempt is made to integrate the emotions of taxpayers in the framework, by speculating about anger, fear and feelings of protection and security, which moderate the impact of coercive power on compliance. Finally, strategies to shift from control to cooperation are summarized.

55.2 DETERMINANTS OF TAX COMPLIANCE

55.2.1 *Economic and Psychological Determinants of Tax Compliance*

One conceptual approach to understanding tax compliance is individual cost–benefit analysis where the focus has been on the deterrent effect of audits and fines. According to the economic theory of criminal behavior (Becker, 1968) and its application to tax behavior by Allingham and Sandmo (1972) and Srinivasan (1973), taxpayers consider the costs and benefits of paying or not paying taxes and then make a calculated decision on how to maximize their profit. Since the 1970s, research in the field of tax behavior has focused on individual taxpayers and been dominated by the assumption that compliance depends on the probability of an audit and the level of fines in case of detected evasion. Although the effect of audits and negative sanctions on compliance has been empirically confirmed, it is rather weak (for a meta-analysis see Blackwell, 2007). Besides economic determinants, tax compliance is driven by psychological determinants. Already Allingham and Sandmo (1972, p. 326) state that their theory

> may perhaps be criticized for giving too little attention to nonpecuniary factors in the taxpayer's decision on whether or not to evade taxes. It need hardly be stressed that in addition to the income loss there may be other factors affecting utility if one's attempt at tax evasion is detected. These factors may perhaps be summarily characterized as affecting adversely one's reputation as a citizen of the community.

Recent studies provide convincing evidence that audits and fines explain only part of compliance and can have effects opposite to what was intended. For instance, audits can backfire when employed too often (Mendoza, Wielhouwer and Kirchler, 2015) or when the auditing climate and outcome evoke anger and fear (Erard et al., 2019). Frequent audits can impair voluntary compliance. Beer et al. (2015, 2017) found that audits have a positive long-term impact on compliance among self-employed taxpayers who filed incorrectly and experienced adjustments; however, taxpayers who were found to be compliant reported less income in subsequent years. Gemmell and Ratto (2012) report similar effects: random tax audits reduce subsequent reporting compliance among taxpayers who were found to be compliant. Possible explanations are that taxpayers misperceive the probability of future audits (Kastlunger et al., 2009; Mittone, Panebianco and Santoro, 2017); audited taxpayers might infer that the risk of a future audit is low given that the auditor was unable to detect additional taxable income during an audit (Lederman, 2019). Moreover, tax audits might undermine willingness to cooperate with the tax authorities if an audit was experienced as threat and the interaction as hostile. Mooijman et al. (2016) offer similar explanations in their study on the effects of justifications for sanctions. Audits may crowd out the motivation to comply among honest individuals because they signal distrust or the interaction with the auditor is perceived as negative.

Research in economic psychology and behavioral economics has shed doubt on the neoclassical economic assumption that taxpayers are generally driven by utility maximization and seek to avoid taxes by exploiting loopholes or evasion if the risk of audits is considered low and fines in the case of detected evasion are mild. Compliance is driven not only by economic factors but also by personal, societal and situational considerations, such as attitudes toward the state and taxation, complexity of the law and understanding of one's duties and rights, personal and social norms, and perceptions of distributive, procedural and retributive justice. Alm, Kirchler and Muehlbacher (2012; see also Kirchler, 2007 and Kirchler and Hoelzl, 2018) summarized the results of various studies and created a list of economic and psychological determinants (Table 55.1).

TABLE 55.1 *Determinants of tax compliance*

Economic determinants

- Audits: the probability of audits affects compliance; subjective probability appears to have a higher impact on compliance than objective probability.
- Fines: punishment in case of detected evasion has a deterrent effect.
- Marginal tax rate: tax rate effects are not unequivocally confirmed empirically.
- Income level: empirical results reveal an unclear pattern for the effects of income on compliance.

(continued)

TABLE 55.1 *(continued)*

- Opportunity to avoid or evade taxes: self-employed persons with ample opportunities to evade taxes are more likely to be noncompliant than taxpayers with limited opportunities to evade.

Psychological determinants

- Complexity of tax law: for the average individual, tax law is too complicated and thus compliance is difficult even when explicitly striven for.
- Attitudes/tax morale: opinions and assessments of the criminality of tax fraud, tax evasion and aggressive avoidance, the tax authorities, etc. shape compliance behavior. Attitudes are often treated as the source of tax morale.
- Norms that have an effect on compliance:
  - personal norms (internalized values or the personal tendency to obey the law)
  - social norms (norms and values in a social environment)
  - societal norms (norms and values in a society as a whole).
- Justice effects on compliance:
  - Distributive justice: distinctions are made between horizontal fairness (an individual's tax burden compared to others), vertical fairness (an individual's tax burden compared to those capable of contributing more or less) and exchange fairness (tax burden relative to the provision of public goods financed by tax revenues).
  - Procedural justice: the fairness of tax-related decision-making procedures (having a voice in policy-making, transparency, consistency, neutrality, etc., and fairness of interactions between authorities and taxpayers).
  - Retributive justice: fairness of the form and severity of punishment (e.g., monetary, imprisonment, damage to one's reputation).

Source: Adapted from Alm, Kirchler and Muehlbacher, 2012, p. 138; Kirchler and Hoelzl, 2018, p. 257.

Rather than rationally calculating how to maximize their profits, most taxpayers are committed to contributing. Onu and Oats (2018) conclude from their analyses of "tax talks" in social media that most people seem motivated to pay their fair share; they are less concerned with audits and fines, and "whether" to comply, and more concerned with "how" to comply. "[T]he gloomy picture of nobody paying a penny in taxes is a phantom picture, not to be observed in reality" (Elffers, 2000, p. 184). The motivation to comply or not to comply differs among taxpayers.

55.2.2 *Differential Motives*

Motivation to comply with tax law differs among citizens, as Braithwaite (2003, 2009) convincingly argues. The majority of taxpayers feel a moral commitment to defer to the authorities' rules and processes and to contribute to society. Committed taxpayers express a responsibility to behave in the interest of society. In contrast, the motivational posture of "capitulation" describes acquiescing to the law in order to avoid trouble. The motivational postures of commitment and capitulation prevail. A small share of taxpayers express negative motivational tendencies, exhibiting postures known as "resistance," "disengagement" and "game playing." They doubt the authorities' good intentions, are angry about how they operate, and are resistant. Disengaged citizens judge the tax authority as irrelevant and refrain from cooperation. Game players see the law as a game that can be cleverly used to one's own advantage.

The motivation to cooperate dominates in society and should not be put at risk through authorities' signals of mistrust (i.e., a view of taxpayers as criminals, frequent and random controls, and inappropriate fines). Most empirical research on this topic focuses on individual behavior and considers how individual characteristics affect the decision process. Braithwaite (2003), however, points to the relevance of the relationship between taxpayers and authorities and the quality of their interactions. Motivational postures develop and change in response to the authorities' actions. Consequently, authorities need to apply a differentiated approach to regulating citizens' behavior rather than a one-size-fits-all "command-and-control approach." Most of the time, the tax authorities must have a service orientation and take a sensitive approach; but a stick is needed for cases in which taxpayers repeatedly violate the law.

If most taxpayers are willing to pay their share, while a minority engages in exploiting the system, tax authorities need to apply different strategies to maintain willingness to cooperate and to prevent free-riders from bringing the system of cooperation to tilt. Henk Elffers (2000) developed a model – Willing-Being Able-Daring (WBAD) – illustrating which steps need to be undertaken by the authorities, depending on taxpayers' willingness to cooperate, their ability to cooperate and their inclination and opportunity to evade taxes. Measures to be taken to increase willingness and ability to cooperate are teaching and services, and investment into the reputation of the tax authorities. Opportunities to evade must be closed to reduce inclination to evade, and deterrence measures are appropriate if taxpayers repeatedly and intentionally evade their taxes.

So far, the focus has been on individual taxpayers and personal and situational characteristics determining the inclination to comply and to authorities' approaches to ensure compliance. Taking a systemic view, however, calls for consideration of all actors in the tax arena and their interaction dynamics. The following sections describe actors and their interaction dynamics.

55.3 THE TAX ARENA

The interaction between various actors in the tax arena is complex. In order to understand taxpayer behavior, it is necessary to consider the relationships among tax authorities and the government, tax accountants and intermediaries, and taxpayers. Alm, Kirchler and Muehlbacher (2012) illustrate the relationships among government, tax authorities, accountants and taxpayers that determine the interaction climate (Figure 55.1). Reiterating Alm, Kirchler and Muehlbacher (2012, p. 135), when government officials legislate, their assumptions about the effect of tax rates and acceptance by the paying class are relevant. Tax authorities' actions are shaped by their knowledge, beliefs and attitudes about the government, tax intermediaries and taxpayers. Accountants act according to their own conceptions of the authorities and their clients, the taxpayers. Recently, Wurth and Braithwaite (2018) and Frecknall-Hughes and Kirchler (2015) analyzed tax practitioners' multiple roles in the tax arena. Lozza and Castiglioni (2018) analyzed tax-talks in Italian and Swiss media using a lexicographical approach and were able to differentiate between an antagonistic and a synergistic climate in the countries, which affects actors' behavior. Taxpayers' intrinsic and extrinsic motivation to cooperate depend on conceptions of taxation among members of the public, taxpayers' personal values and judgments about the other actors in the field.

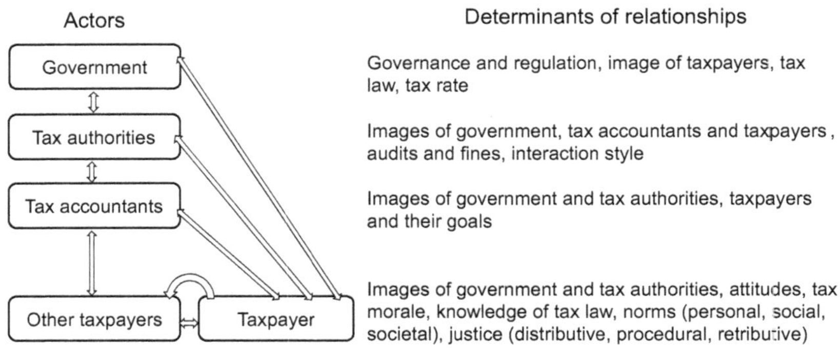

FIGURE 55.1 Actors in the tax behavior arena and determinants of relationships
Source: Adapted from Alm, Kirchler and Muehlbacher, 2012, p. 136.

Taxpayers react to the behavior of authorities, to controls and punishment, to the fairness of procedures and to violations of fairness. They also react to the behavior of other taxpayers and are shaped by established social norms. Frequent audits, the undifferentiated treatment of taxpayers, and harsh punishments when intended or unintended violations of the law are detected can undermine people's willingness to cooperate, which is motivated by a sense of responsibility and loyalty to society that Orviska and Hudson (2002) call "civic duty" and Braithwaite and Ahmed (2005) refer to as an "internalized obligation." Audits and fines can signal distrust and crowd out intrinsic motivation to comply with the law (Frey 1992, 1997). Consequently, Feld and Frey (2007, 2010) encourage the development of a cooperative relationship between authorities and taxpayers to promote and strengthen tax compliance. They highlight the norm of "reciprocity of commitments" between authorities and taxpayers and introduce the concept of the "psychological contract." In a psychological contract, citizens expect that authorities and politicians will be competent, behave transparently, act with integrity and benevolence, and will not violate the trust placed in them. When taxpayers trust the authorities, they will cooperate; when distrust prevails, cooperation can at best be enforced. The concept of a psychological contract among actors in the tax arena shifts attention away from the taxpayer as an individual toward the relationships among parties.

To ensure compliance, all actors in the tax arena and the relationships among them need to be taken into account, and interactions need to be structured in a way that promotes cooperation. Cooperation works as long as neither party disappoints the other, that is, as long as interacting partners trust each other. The quality of the relationship between authorities and citizens and the authorities' power and trustworthiness defines the overall interaction climate in a country. The interaction climate determines whether cooperation takes place voluntarily or needs to be enforced. In the following section, the power of authorities and trust in authorities are described, which in combination define the slippery slope framework.

55.4 POWER AND TRUST

55.4.1 *Power, Trust and the Slippery Slope of Compliance*

Traditionally, scholarship on tax compliance was fragmented into legal, economic and psychological camps. Kirchler (2007) reviewed empirical findings in economics and social psychology and attempted to integrate them in a coherent frame, which he termed the "slippery slope framework." This framework is based on two dimensions: the power of authorities to control taxpayers effectively and citizens' trust in the authorities.

Power refers to the authorities' capacity to detect and fine tax evasion. Audit probability and the effectiveness of fines are their core forms of power. Trust refers to taxpayers' belief that the authorities can be trusted to act in the interests of the collective. Trust refers to actors' competence, benevolence and integrity (Mayer, Davis and Schoorman, 1995) and is positively related to transparent and fair procedures. Uncertainty breeds distrust (Alm, 2014). Trust and perceptions of power also stem from communication about taxation, the appropriateness of fines, and the perceived behavior of other taxpayers (Alm, Jackson and McKee, 2009).

The slippery slope framework assumes that compliance depends on the power of the authorities and taxpayers' trust in them. Depending on the levels of citizens' trust and authorities' power, voluntary compliance, enforced compliance or no compliance is likely to result. When trust in authorities is high, voluntary compliance is also assumed to be high. If the authorities' power increases, enforced tax compliance increases. The term "slippery slope" stems from a three-dimensional concept including the dimensions of trust, power and compliance: when trust in the authorities and the authorities' power are at their maximum value, compliance is highest. As trust and power decrease, taxpayers act selfishly by maximizing their own gains through noncompliance (see Figure 55.2).

Survey studies and laboratory experiments have manipulated the power of authorities and trust in authorities by describing scenarios related to an imaginary country in which tax authorities either were or were not trustworthy and were either powerful or lacking strategies to deter noncompliance. In most studies, the participants were endowed with a basic income plus additional income that depended on their performance on a task. Over several rounds,

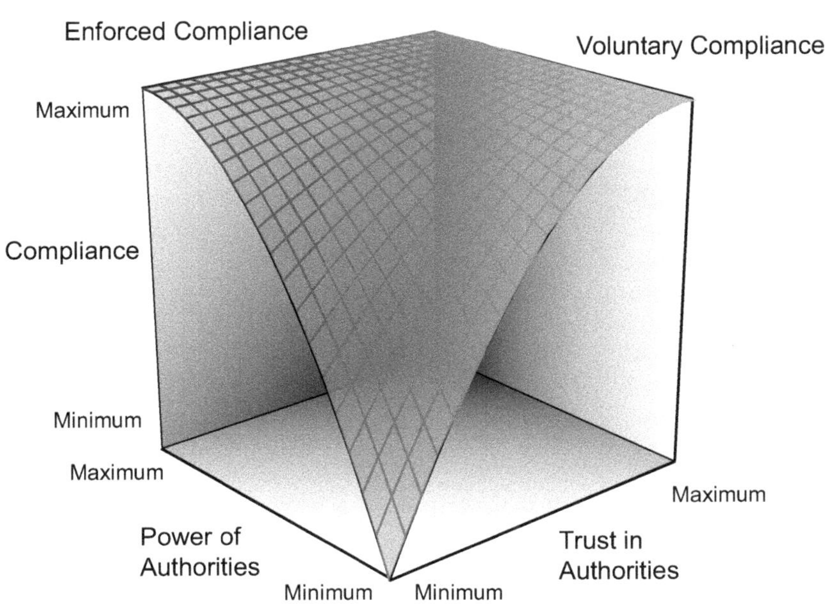

FIGURE 55.2 The slippery slope framework
Source: Adapted from Kirchler, 2007, p. 205.

they were informed about the audit probability and fines in the case of detected evasion and had to file taxes on their income.

For example, a survey with a representative sample of Austrian self-employed taxpayers was in line with expectations: participants imagined living in a country with authorities who were either trustworthy or not and powerful or not and indicated whether they would comply with the tax law. Figure 55.3 shows that the relationships among power, trust and compliance resemble the theoretical model. High power and high trust were associated with high compliance. Furthermore, high power was strongly related to enforced compliance, while high trust was associated with voluntary compliance (Figures 55.4a, 55.4b; Kirchler, Kogler and Muehlbacher, 2014; Muehlbacher and Kirchler, 2010).

The scenario technique was also used in two cross-national studies. Kogler et al. (2013) presented Austrian, Hungarian, Romanian and Russian taxpayers with a scenario in which the authorities were described as either trustworthy or not and powerful or not and then asked them about their willingness to comply with the tax law. The impact of power and trust on compliance was observed in all countries, independent of institutional, political and societal differences (Figure 55.5). The study was eventually repeated in forty-four countries in all, yielding similar effects (Batrancea et al., 2019).

In the earliest conceptualization of the slippery slope framework, trust and power were assumed to act as substitutes, with both dimensions independently leading to high compliance, either voluntary or enforced. However, empirical works shows that compliance rates are highest in situations with both high power and high trust. In other words, it is not

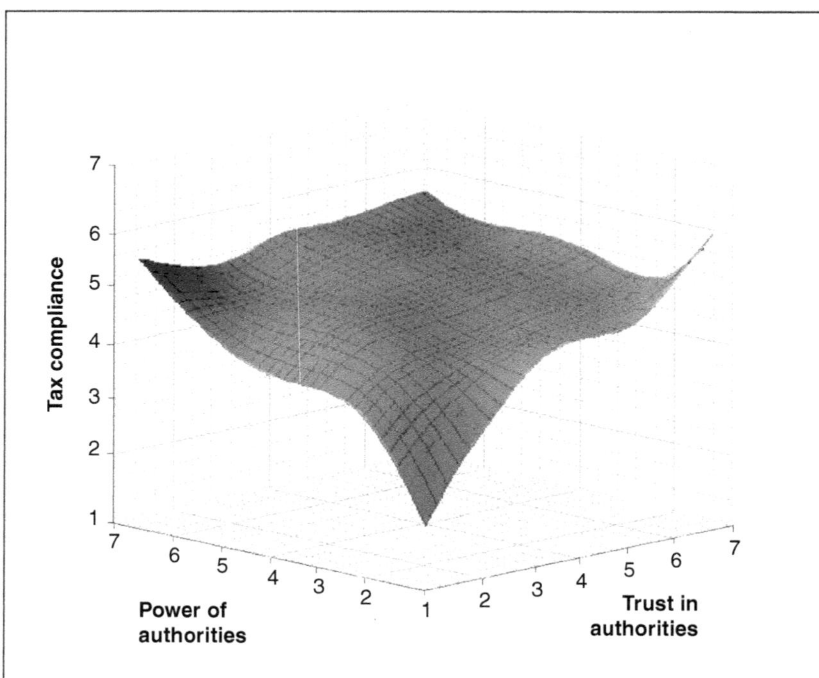

FIGURE 55.3 Relationships among power, trust and tax compliance
Source: Adapted from Kirchler, Kogler and Muehlbacher, 2014, p. 90.

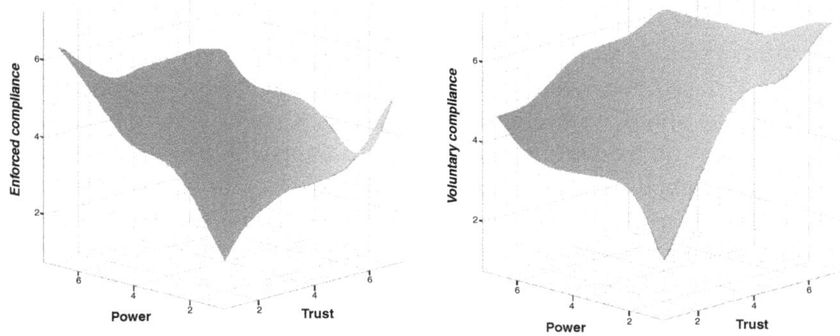

FIGURES 55.4A AND 55.4B Relationships among power, trust and enforced versus voluntary tax compliance

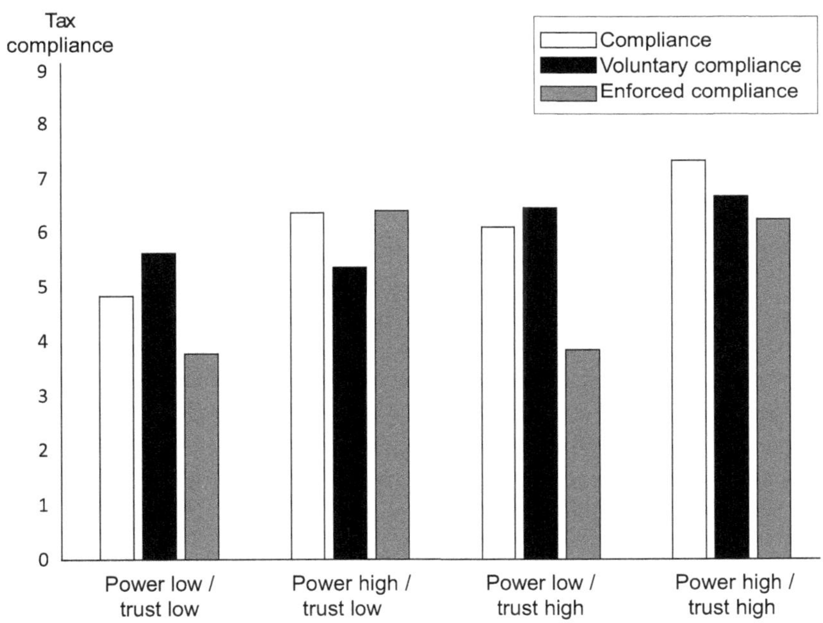

FIGURE 55.5 Tax compliance, voluntary compliance and enforced compliance by power of authorities and trust in authorities
Source: Kogler et al., 2013, p. 174, Table 2.

power or trust that leads to compliance but both dimensions together that yields the highest compliance rates. Power and trust appear to have an additive effect on compliance. With respect to the distinction between voluntary and enforced compliance, societies that trust their authorities exhibit greater levels of voluntary compliance than those that rely on power.

55.4.2 *Coercive versus Legitimate Power and Reason-Based Trust versus Implicit Trust*

The nature of the interplay between power and trust depends on the type of power and trust. Wielding power may evoke suspicion and mistrust, and signals of mistrust by authorities can provoke mistrust in taxpayers, which in turn can further strengthen the authorities' mistrust (e.g., Castelfranchi and Falcone, 2010, Farrell and Knight, 2003, Nooteboom, 2002). Wielding power can undermine trust if perceived as unfair or randomly applied to both compliant and noncompliant citizens. Manifestations of power can also positively affect trust. Seeing that free-riders are detected and fined by legitimate authorities might enhance trust in the authorities among compliant taxpayers. Bachmann (2001), for instance, holds that depersonalized forms of power such as the law can be a necessary precondition for trust, if the law and its enforcement are perceived as defining the norms of behavior. If power is perceived as a legitimate means by which to enforce societal norms, trust might increase with increasing power (Mulder et al., 2006; Mulder, Verboon and de Cremer, 2009).

This complex interplay between power and trust highlights the need to distinguish among different types of power and different types of trust. According to French and Raven (1959) and Raven (1965), power – the potential and perceived ability of one party to influence another party – is based on six sources of "legitimate power" and "coercive power," respectively. The authors distinguish among coercive power, reward power, legitimate power, expert power, referent power, and information power. Coercive power is defined as harsh pressure applied through either punishment or remuneration. It is wielded based on the expectation that the party being influenced will not voluntarily cooperate. Legitimate power originates from legitimization, expertise, information and identification, or referent power. Transferred to the tax context, legitimate power is based on positive evaluations of the authorities' power, whereas coercive power is based on the authorities' ability to enforce the law regardless of its societal acceptance.

Legitimate power and trust are highly related to one another. Legitimacy originates from two sources. The instrumental source consists of control and outcome favorability. The relational source concerns the quality of interactions among parties, and thus encompasses procedural justice and trustworthiness (Tyler, 1997). In theory, a political authority, government or organization management team may have the legitimacy to wield power and have professional capacities but need not be perceived as trustworthy. In empirical research, however, it is often very difficult to measure the two concepts independently. In particular, there is substantial conceptual overlap between trust and legitimate power originating from the quality of interactions among parties.

Coercive or harsh power is likely to have different effects on trust than legitimate or soft power (e.g., Freiberg, 2010; French and Raven, 1959). For instance, trust is likely to be undermined if coercive power is used inappropriately to enforce cooperation, whereas power exerted by an authority that is perceived as legitimate can increase trust (Korczynski, 2000). Wang and Murnighan (2017), for instance, found that punishment enhances trust if deserving perpetrators are punished by an authority that does not act out of self-interest and avoids overpunishing less-deserving perpetrators. In turn, trust can affect power and its effectiveness. Balliet and van Lange (2013) conclude in their meta-analysis that punishment promotes cooperation in societies with high trust. The double-edged nature of coercive power can be explained by the moderating influence of trust and the authority's perceived legitimacy (Balliet and van Lange, 2013). In high-trust societies, violating the law is perceived as a violation of social norms that should be punished in order to maintain the society's high

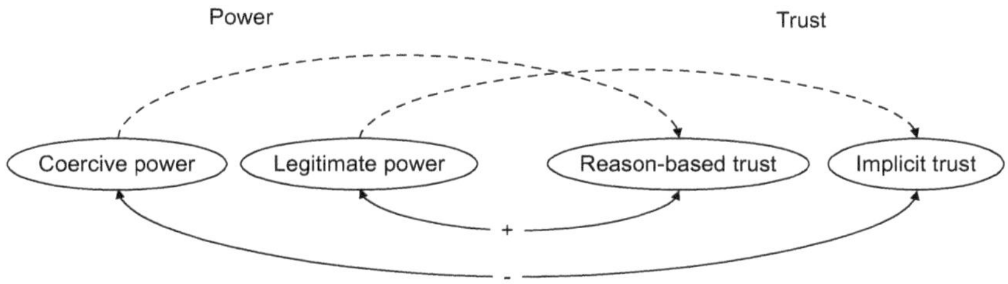

FIGURE 55.6 Dynamics between legitimate versus coercive power and reason-based trust versus implicit trust
Source: Adapted from Gangl, Hofmann and Kirchler, 2015, p. 17.

moral standards. If trust in the authorities is low, audits and fines may induce anger and fear and promote retaliation. Trust appears to make punishment effective when members of a society cooperate and when power serves to punish norm violations.

Castelfranchi and Falcone (2010; see also Tyler, 2003) distinguish between trust resulting from automatic and affective processes and trust resulting from a rational assessment of the predictability of others' behavior. Trust – defined as agreeing to make oneself vulnerable to the behavior of another party (Lewis and Weigert, 1985) – can stem from experiences and reasoning that the trusted person is competent and benevolent; in such cases, it is reason-based. On the other hand, trust can also refer to a general attitude by the trusting person toward others; in such cases, it is implicit. Dynamics among the types of power and the types of trust are shown in Figure 55.6.

Enachescu and Kirchler (2019) reviewed studies investigating the assumptions of the slippery slope framework and its extension. Survey studies and experiments generally lend support to the relevance of coercive and legitimate power and reason-based trust for understanding compliance (e.g., Ali and Ahmad, 2014; Benk, Çakmak and Budak, 2011; Fischer and Schneider, 2009; Gangl et al., 2013; Hofmann et al., 2014; Kasper, Kogler and Kirchler, 2015; Kastlunger et al., 2013; Kogler et al., 2013; Lemoine and Roland-Lévy, 2013; Lisi, 2012, 2019; Lozza et al., 2013; Muehlbacher, Kirchler and Schwarzenberger, 2011; Niesiobędzka, 2014; Pukelienė and Kažemekaitytė, 2016; Ruiu and Lisi, 2011; Tsikas, 2017; Wahl, Kastlunger and Kirchler, 2010; and Wilks and Pacheco, 2014. Further, Prinz, Muehlbacher and Kirchler, 2014, presented a simulation of the framework; while Mas'ud, Manaf and Saad, 2019, investigated the relationship between proxies of power and trust and compliance on the aggregated level of 158 countries.). High power and high trust are related to high compliance. Trust is often the main driver of compliance (e.g., Kaplanoglou and Rapanos, 2015; Kaplanoglou, Rapanos and Daskalakis, 2016). Voluntary compliance is related to trust in authorities, whereas the power of authorities is closely related to enforced compliance. However, some studies also yielded inconclusive or non-supporting results (e.g., Gobena and van Dijke, 2017; Hauptman, Gürarda and Korez-Vide, 2015; Mas'ud, Manaf and Saad, 2015).

55.5 INTERACTION CLIMATE

The slippery slope framework (Kirchler, 2007; Kirchler, Hoelzl and Wahl, 2008) considers not only the relationship between authorities and citizens but also the interaction climate. In the framework, the interaction climate varies on a continuum between antagonistic and synergistic. While an antagonistic climate is characterized by a cops-and-robbers mentality, the synergistic climate is defined by mutual trust and voluntary cooperation.

A tax administration relying on deterrence measures such as high audit density and severe fines creates and operates in an antagonistic climate. Taxpayer compliance with the tax regulations needs to be enforced. A synergistic climate prevails if procedures are transparent and authorities and citizens interact with integrity and mutual benevolence. In a synergistic climate, cooperation should take place voluntarily; in an antagonistic climate, authorities can enforce compliance only if they have the power to exert sufficient pressure on taxpayers. It is assumed that a synergistic climate stimulates spontaneous cooperation, whereas an antagonistic climate leads to calculated compliance or evasion when it pays to take the risk (see Rand, Greene and Nowak, 2012, on spontaneous giving and calculated greed).

Instead of relying predominantly on enforcement, tax administrations should invest in the creation of a synergistic climate. This is in line with the "trust paradigm," which Alm and Torgler (2011) describe as one of three major paradigms of tax administration. It emphasizes the relevance of building trust in order to promote compliance. The "trust paradigm" contrasts with the traditional "enforcement paradigm," which considers taxpayers as potential "robbers" who need to be monitored and fined in the case of evasion. The "service paradigm" stresses the need to facilitate tax compliance by offering services. The necessity of providing services to taxpayers is also constantly demanded by the US Taxpayer Advocate (Olson, 2015).

In the tax context, increased knowledge of the interplay between legitimate versus coercive power and reason-based versus implicit trust has led to an extension of the slippery slope framework (Gangl, Hofmann and Kirchler, 2015; Hofmann et al., 2014). The extended version distinguishes among antagonistic, service and confidence climates. Just as, in the original version of the framework, coercive measures are believed to lead to an antagonistic climate in which taxpayers exhibit enforced compliance, so legitimate power in combination with reason-based trust is argued to lead to a service climate in which taxpayers comply voluntarily, and implicit trust is assumed to lead to a confidence climate and to committed cooperation. Figure 55.7 shows the three tax climates and the forms of compliance associated with them.

In an antagonistic climate, authorities exert coercive power. Taxpayers are likely to feel persecuted and harassed by the authorities' actions. Mutual mistrust and resentment predominate, and voluntary cooperation is low. The classical economic model may best describe taxpayers' decision processes about whether to comply or not. In addition to costly audits, an antagonistic climate is likely to fuel opposition and reactance motives among taxpayers (Braithwaite, 2009; Hofmann et al., 2014).

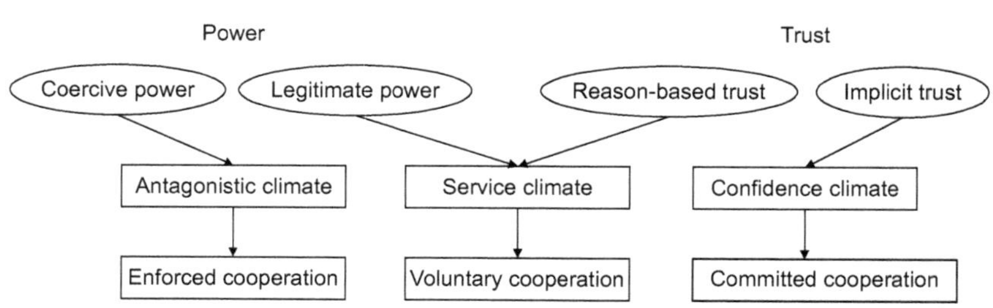

FIGURE 55.7 Coercive versus legitimate power, reason-based trust versus implicit trust and tax climates and compliance
Source: Adapted from Gangl, Hofmann and Kirchler, 2015, p. 19.

Cooperation between citizens and authorities requires a synergistic climate in the state. Authorities must administer the country in accordance with the people's mandate. They need to establish cooperative relationships (OECD, 2013), provide services that facilitate compliance, and also ensure that cooperative taxpayers are not exploited by free-riders.

55.6 INTEGRATING EMOTIONS IN COMPLIANCE DECISIONS

Emotions and their impact on decision-making and compliance behavior have received little attention in tax research (for exceptions, see Coricelli et al., 2010; Murphy and Tyler, 2008). This lack of attention to emotion cannot be traced back to the origins of the rational choice paradigm that long dominated the field of tax research. Elffers (2015, p. 53) points out that the founding fathers of the rational choice paradigm in the social sciences placed substantial emphasis on feelings and emotions:

> Dirck Coornhert, Adam Smith, and Jeremy Bentham – introduced in their original writings their perspectives in terms of norms, guilt, conscience, pity and other affects .... When considering Smith's work, even the title of his treatise, *The Theory of Moral Sentiments* (Smith 1759/1982), is an illustration of the point.

In psychology, emotions are most generally described as states of feeling accompanied by physical and psychological changes that affect behavior. Emotions are subjective, conscious experiences that are characterized by psychophysiological reactions and biological states as well as mental states and interpretations of the situation, experiences or objects. Emotions are closely related to motivation and behavior.

In his components processing model, Scherer (2005) distinguishes among cognitive appraisal, bodily symptoms, action tendencies, expressions and feelings. Cognitive appraisal refers to evaluations. Bodily symptoms reflect the physiological component of emotions. Action tendencies refer to the motivational aspects of emotions. Facial and vocal expressions indicate the subjective experience of an emotional state. In the "Geneva Emotions Wheel," he distinguishes among twenty specific emotion qualities varying from negative to positive valence and from low to high control. It is important to consider specific emotions in order to understand tax behavior. For instance, anger and fear are two emotions of similar negative valence (Lerner and Keltner, 2000); however, fear is often associated with flight, while anger evokes fight.

55.6.1 *Emotions and Decision-Making*

Loewenstein and Lerner (2003) and Lerner et al. (2015) developed a framework – the emotion-imbued choice model – describing different paths of influence of emotions on decisions. They distinguish between anticipated and immediate emotions, which are either integral or incidental.

Anticipated emotions originate from expected outcomes of a decision. In tax decisions, an individual may consider paying the full share or not, claim illegal deductions or conceal income. The decision to fully comply or not is likely affected by the anticipated feelings in case of detected evasion, for example, shame or regret.

Immediate emotions are experienced at the time of decision-making. They can be either incidental (i.e., not related to decision context, such as a weather effect or mood) or integral to the decision context (i.e., elicited directly by the decision situation). For instance, individuals filing their taxes might be in a good mood due to positive experiences before deciding to complete their tax forms and their decisions might be affected by their mood. Positive feelings might affect risk perception and risk evaluation and subjective weighting of probabilities of audits. Positively tuned persons might be overoptimistic and underestimate consequences of audits, and thus be inclined to be noncompliant. Negative mood, on the other hand, might lead to more pessimistic evaluations and prudence.

Emotions are also likely to originate from the activity at stake and to impact on people's decision-making and behavior. Filing one's taxes might be perceived as tedious bureaucratic work and evoke anger and frustration. Search for information about correct tax filing and avail of service by the tax office might be successful and correlate with correct filing. Direct experiences with the authorities might be perceived either as positive and stimulate willingness to cooperate on the taxpayers' side, or as negative and lead to anger and the inclination to evade, or to fear and resistance.

Decisions are assumed to vary, depending on the characteristics of the decision-maker, the characteristics of the decision situation, as well as the immediate-integral, incidental and anticipated emotions. The different paths of emotional influences on decision-making are illustrated in the emotion-imbued choice model by Lerner et al. (2015, p. 815; Figure 55.8).

55.6.2 *Emotions and Tax Compliance Decisions*

Studies on emotions and tax behavior are generally rare. Most research has focused on anticipated emotions: shame, guilt and regret. Taxpayers who consider evading taxes may refrain from doing so if they anticipate experiencing regret in the case of being detected and punished. Erard and Feinstein (1994) argue that shame and guilt are highly relevant anticipated "moral costs." Emotions as "moral costs" are of great relevance for tax filing decisions (e.g., Bosco and Mittone, 1997; Blaufus et al., 2017; Grasmick and Bursik, 1990).

Fochmann and colleagues (2019) conducted a study exploring the role of incidental emotions in the tax context. A survey of more than 22,000 German taxpayers yielded evidence that positive mood correlated with lower compliance than neutral or negative mood. If taxes were filed on days associated with positive mood (e.g., weekends), compliance was lower compared to days associated with less positive mood (e.g., working days). In a laboratory experiment, positive and negative emotions were induced by pictures depicting positive and funny versus negative, disgusting and fear-evoking scenes. The participants were less willing to comply after being primed with pictures evoking positive emotions compared to aversive emotions. Positive mood seems to correlate with dishonesty and the willingness to take risk.

While incidental emotions can arise from various circumstances unrelated to the actual activity, emotions integral to the taxation context can be related to thoughts and discussions about taxes and taxation in general, tax filing, audit experiences or the tax authorities. For instance, tax authorities can provide professional and useful services, which evokes positive feelings. In contrast, lack of professional advice can cause frustration and anger among taxpayers.

Coricelli and colleagues (2010) investigated integral emotions in the tax context by measuring arousal through skin conductance response in an income-reporting game. Intensity of emotions was positively related to tax evasion. A study employing an experimental survey design with self-employed taxpayers in Turkey (Olsen et al., 2018) suggests that taxpayers report different emotions in response to different enforcement strategies. Harsh enforcement, such as audits and fines, appears to evoke negative emotions and the intention

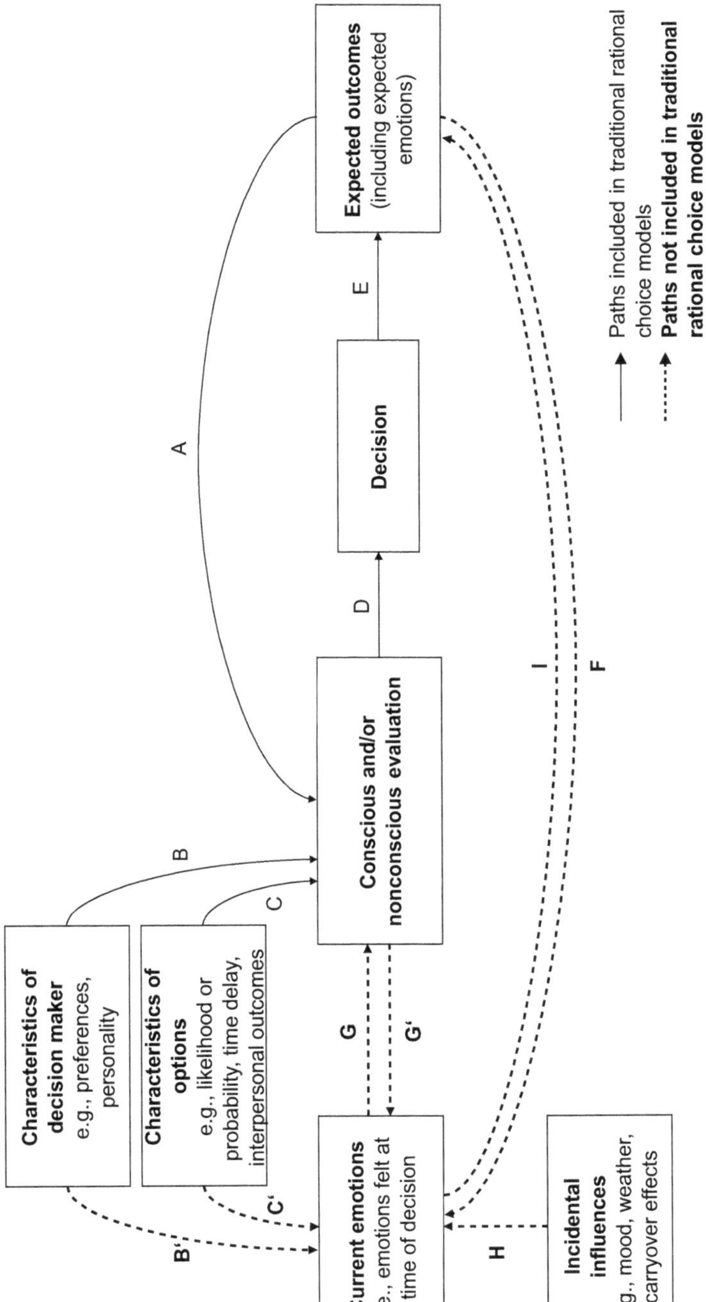

FIGURE 55.8 Emotion-imbued choice model
Source: Lerner et al., 2015, p. 815.

to evade. Trust reduces negative emotions and is related to the intention to comply with the tax law. Enachescu et al. (2019) investigated emotions related to preparatory accounting tasks, filing tasks, contacts with the authorities and feedback from them, receiving an audit announcement, experiencing an audit and the decision to evade taxes. The specific emotions identified were categorized into positive emotions, anger, fear and self-blame (shame and guilt). Positive emotions were high when tax documents were successfully prepared, when taxes were filed and when experiencing useful contact and feedback from the authorities. Audit announcements and audit experiences were not related to positive emotions but rather to fear, even when no adjustments were made. Anger was high when contacting the authorities for information and when experiencing a negative audit. Self-blame was highest when participants imagined evading taxes, even if evasion was not detected in an audit.

55.6.3 *Integrating Emotions in the Slippery Slope Framework*

In the remainder of this chapter, we attempt to integrate the insights from the studies considering emotions in the tax arena into the slippery slope framework. It can be assumed that taxpayers who perceive the authorities as legitimized and professional do not experience negative emotions but instead feel neutral or positive in general and are willing to spontaneously cooperate and pay their taxes. Coercive power, however, can be a double-edged sword. When taxpayers perceive that the tax authorities wield legitimate power, they develop trust. Specifically, when the tax authorities engage in coercive measures precisely targeted at free-riders who take advantage of cooperative citizens, feelings of satisfaction and being protected should be evoked. However, if coercive power is perceived as directed randomly at anyone and everyone, people might perceive the authorities as untrustworthy and their behavior as illegitimate, and react with either anger or fear. Feelings of anger are especially likely to be evoked when honest taxpayers are audited and thus perceive themselves as being treated as criminals. Anger has been shown to provoke retaliation behavior (e.g., Bougie, Pieters and Zeelenberg, 2003), and is likely to lead to tax avoidance or tax evasion. Moreover, rather than spontaneously cooperating, angry taxpayers are assumed to deliberately consider the pros and cons of cooperation and evasion and choose their most profitable option. When they feel fear, taxpayers are more likely to respond with enforced compliance. Figure 55.8 shows the trajectory from perceived power and trust to emotions and behavior. In summary, we assume that trust, legitimate power and well-targeted coercive power lead to spontaneous cooperation, whereas randomly wielded coercive power leads to either anger or fear. In both of the latter cases, taxpayers act strategically and deliberately decide which alternative to take (Figure 55.9). However, there is still a lack of empirical evidence on integral emotions in the context of the slippery slope framework.

55.7 CONTROL VERSUS COOPERATION

Research in economic psychology and behavioral economics has contributed to rethinking public administration paradigms. Concepts such as "good public governance" explicitly acknowledge the importance of cooperative relations and services. The importance of the quality of the relationships between authorities and taxpayers has also been recognized by the Organisation for Economic Co-operation and Development (OECD). In 2008, the OECD Forum on Tax Administration (OECD, 2008) developed the concept of "enhanced relationships," which was later renamed "cooperative compliance" (OECD, 2013). In

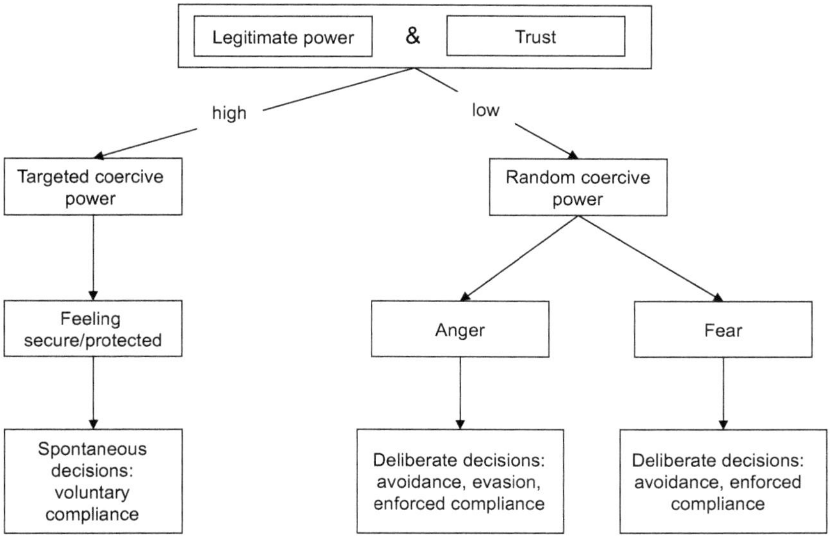

FIGURE 55.9 Emotions in the slippery slope framework

cooperative compliance programs such as Horizontal Monitoring in the Netherlands, the "vertical" relationship between authorities and taxpayers switches to cooperation on equal terms (Siglé, 2019; Stevens et al., 2012). The move to horizontal rather than vertical monitoring rests on seven pillars: "commercial awareness, impartiality, proportionality, openness through disclosure and transparency and responsiveness by revenue bodies and disclosure and transparency by taxpayers in their dealings with revenue bodies" (OECD, 2013).

Cooperative compliance programs have been developed in various countries. So far, in many countries, compliance programs address large firms and medium-sized businesses. Regarding individual taxpayers, Alm, Kirchler and Muehlbacher (2012) and Kirchler and Hoelzl (2018; see also Alm and Torgler, 2011; James et al., 2003) propose shifting from an exclusive command-and-control orientation to a service and cooperation paradigm by applying various strategies that are based on both economic and psychological insights. They stipulate a series of measures to promote mutual trust and cooperation that they summarized as follows (Kirchler and Hoelzl, 2018, p. 281):

- Tax law must be simplified so that taxpayers understand it.
- Instead of a plethora of rules with exceptions, principles of behaviour need to be fixed in the law to minimise the room for interpretation and negotiation.
- Tax authorities and above all tax auditors need to be efficiently trained so that they are experts in tax law and are able to treat taxpayers according to their motivations and abilities in order to apply regulation strategies effectively.
- Tax authorities need to cooperate intensively with legislators, judges, and international authorities.
- The use of tax money must be transparent; advertising campaigns should be used to inform the public of the services available so that the fair exchange of tax contributions for state services is clear.

- Social norms of correct behaviour need to be promoted and communicated, and measures need to be taken that strengthen citizens' and residents' identification with the community.
- Justice needs to be achieved on the distributive, procedural, and retributive levels.
- Taxpayers need to be segmented according to their needs so that appropriate services can be offered to facilitate tax honesty, tailored to meet individual needs at the 'point of sale'.
- Audits are necessary to protect honest taxpayers from free riders. Audits need to be directed at high-risk groups and to be effectively implemented.
- Negative sanctions are necessary at an adequate level and in the proper form, and should depend on the tax offender's ability to pay. Fines or prison sentences are two possible forms of retribution, while the publication of offenders' names or the requirement of compulsory community service represent alternative sanctions.

55.8 CONCLUSION

Research on tax compliance has generally addressed compliance as the result of a decision that considers tax authorities' enforcement strategies and the expected consequences of detected evasion, or as the result of people's sense of duty to contribute to the commons.

Traditionally, research has predominantly addressed enforcement measures such as audits and fines. However, audits and fines poorly explain high levels of tax compliance; moreover, they can have opposite than intended effects. Besides enforcement of compliance by power measures, trust in tax authorities is essential to ensure compliance. While trust and legitimate power are essential to ensure voluntary compliance, well-targeted coercive power is also necessary to enforce the law and to ensure that a trustworthy and legitimate authority is perceived as being capable of protecting cooperative citizens from exploitation by noncooperative ones. Insights from behavioral economics and psychology yield ample evidence that a shift from a command-and-control paradigm to a trust and service paradigm is necessary, and that, in practice, tax administrations should not continue to rely only on enforcement as the most powerful tool to ensure compliance. Enforcement is necessary. However, enforcement needs to be well targeted to protect cooperative citizens from being exploited by free-riders. Among cooperative citizens, enforcement should give rise to feelings of security and protection rather than anger, while citizens tempted to evade should fear unerring audits and appropriate punishment.

REFERENCES

Ali, A., and Ahmad, N. (2014). "Trust and Tax Compliance among Malaysian Working Youth." *International Journal of Public Administration* 37(7), 389–96. Doi:10.1080/01900692.2013.858353.

Allingham, M. G., and Sandmo, A. (1972). "Income Tax Evasion: A Theoretical Analysis." *Journal of Public Economics* 1, 323–38. Doi:10.1016/0047-2727(72)90010-2.

Alm, J. (2014). "Does an Uncertain Tax System Encourage 'Aggressive Tax Planning'?" *Economic Analysis and Policy* 44, 30–8. Doi:10.1016/j.eap.2014.01.004.

Alm, J., Jackson, B. R., and McKee, M. (2009). "Getting the Word Out: Enforcement Information Dissemination and Compliance Behavior." *Journal of Public Economics* 93(3/4), 392–402. Doi:10.1016/j.jpubeco.2008.10.007.

Alm, J., Kirchler, E., and Muehlbacher, S. (2012). “Combining Psychology and Economics in the Analysis of Compliance: From Enforcement to Cooperation.” *Economic Analysis and Policy* 42, 133–51.

Alm, J., and Torgler, B. (2011). “Do Ethics Matter? Tax Compliance and Morality.” *Journal of Business Ethics* 101, 635–51.

Bachmann, R. (2001). “Trust, Power and Control in Trans-organizational Relations.” *Organization Studies* 22, 337–65.

Balliet, D., and van Lange, P. A. M. (2013). “Trust Punishment and Cooperation across 18 Societies: A Meta-analysis.” *Perspectives on Psychological Science* 8, 363–79. Doi:10.1177/1745691613488533.

Batrancea, L., Nichita, A., Olsen, J., Kogler, C., Kirchler, E., Hoelzl, E., . . . Zukauskas, S. (2019). “Trust and Power as Determinants of Tax Compliance across 44 Nations.” *Journal of Economic Psychology* 74, 102191. Doi.org/10.1016/j.joep.2019.102191.

Becker, G. S. (1968). “Crime and Punishment: An Economic Approach.” *Journal of Political Economy* 76(2), 169–217.

Beer, S., Kasper, M., Kirchler, E., and Erard, B. (2015). “Audit Impact Study. Taxpayer Advocate Service Annual Report to Congress.” www.taxpayeradvocate.irs.gov/Media/Default/Documents/2015ARC/ARC15_Volume2_3-AuditImpact.pdf.

(2017). “Do Audits Deter Future Noncompliance? Evidence on Self-Employed Taxpayers.” IRS Research Bulletin, pp. 9–11. www.irs.gov/uac/soi-tax-stats-2016-irs-tpc-research-conference.

Berk, S., Çakmak, A. F., and Budak, T. (2011). “An Investigation of Tax Compliance Intention: A Theory of Planned Behavior Approach.” *European Journal of Economics, Finance and Administrative Sciences* 28(1), 180–8.

Blackwell, C. (2007). “A Meta-analysis of Tax Compliance Experiments.” International Studies Program Working Paper 07–24. Atlanta: Andrew Young School of Policy Studies, Georgia State University.

Blaufus, K., Bob, J., Otto, P. E., and Wolf, N. (2017). “The Effect of Tax Privacy on Tax Compliance: An Experimental Investigation.” *European Accounting Review* 26, 561–80.

Bosco, L., and Mittone, L. (1997). “Tax Evasion and Moral Constraints: Some Experimental Evidence.” *Kyklos* 50, 297–324.

Bougie, R., Pieters, R., and Zeelenberg, M. (2003). “Angry Customers Don’t Come Back, They Get Back: The Experience and Behavioral Implications of Anger and Dissatisfaction in Services.” *Journal of the Academy of Marketing Science* 31, 377–93. Doi: 10.1177/0092070303254412.

Braithwaite, V. (2003). *Taxing Democracy*. Aldershot, UK: Ashgate.

(2009). *Defiance in Taxation and Governance: Resisting and Dismissing Authority in a Democracy*. Cheltenham, UK: Edward Elgar.

Braithwaite, V., and Ahmed, E. (2005). “A Threat to Tax Morale: The Case of Australian Higher Education Policy.” *Journal of Economic Psychology* 26, 523–40.

Castelfranchi, C., and Falcone, R. (2010). *Trust Theory: A Socio-cognitive and Computational Model*. Chichester, UK: Wiley.

Coricelli, G., Joffily, M., Montmarquette, C., and Villeval, M. C. (2010). “Cheating, Emotions, and Rationality: An Experiment on Tax Evasion.” *Experimental Economics* 13, 226–47. Doi: 10.1007/s10683-010-9237-5.

Elffers, H. (2000). “But Taxpayers Do Cooperate!” In M. van Vugt, M. Snyder, T. R. Tyler and A. Biel (eds.), *Cooperation in Modern Society: Promoting the Welfare of Communities, States, and Organizations* (pp. 184–94). London: Routledge.

(2015). “Multiple Interpretations of Rationality in Offender Decision Making.” In W. Bernasco, J.-L. van Gelder and H. Elffers (eds.), *The Oxford Handbook of Offender Decision Making* (pp. 52–66). Oxford: Oxford University Press.

Enachescu, J., and Kirchler, E. (2019). “The Slippery Slope Framework of Tax Behaviour: Reviewed and Revised.” In S. Goslinga, L. van der Hel-van Dijk, P. Mascini and A. van Steenbergen (eds.), *Tax and Trust. Institutions, Interactions and Instruments* (pp. 87–120). The Hague: Eleven.

Enachescu, J., Olsen, J., Kogler, C., Zeelenberg, M., Breugelmans, S. M., and Kirchler, E. (2019). “The Role of Emotions in Tax Compliance Behavior: A Mixed-Methods Approach.” *Journal of Economic Psychology* 74. Doi.org/10.1016/j.joep.2019.102194.

Erard, B., and Feinstein, J. S. (1994). "The Role of Moral Sentiments and Audits Perceptions in Tax Compliance." *Public Finance* 49 Supplement, 70–89.

Erard, B., Kasper, M., Kirchler, E., and Olsen, J. (2019). "What Influence Do IRS Audits Have on Taxpayer Attitudes and Perceptions? Evidence from a National Survey." TAS Research and Related Studies. https://taxpayeradvocate.irs.gov/Media/Default/Documents/2018-ARC /ARC18_Volume2_04_InfluenceAudits.pdf.

Farrell, H., and Knight, J. (2003). "Trust, Institutions, and Institutional Change: Industrial Districts and the Social Capital Hypothesis." *Politics and Society* 31, 537–66.

Feld, L. P., and Frey, B. S. (2007). "Tax Compliance as the Result of a Psychological Tax Contract: The Role of Incentives and Responsive Regulation." *Law and Policy* 29, 102–20. Doi: 10.1111/j.1467-9930.2007.00248.x.

(2010). "Tax Evasion and the Psychological Tax Contract." In J. Alm, J. Martinez-Vazquez and B. Torgler (eds.), *Developing Alternative Frameworks for Explaining Tax Compliance* (pp. 74–94). London: Routledge.

Fischer, J. A. V., and Schneider, F. G. (2009). "The Puzzle of Tax Compliance Revisited: Testing the 'Slippery Slope' Hypothesis for Trust and Power against Field Data." Working Paper SGVS. Paris: OECD.

Fochmann, M., Hechtner, F., Kirchler, E., and Mohr, P. N. C. (2019). "When Happy People Make Society Unhappy: How Incidental Emotions Affect Compliance Behavior." https://papers .ssrn.com/sol3/papers.cfm?abstract_id=3259071.

Frecknall-Hughes, J., and Kirchler, E. (2015). "Towards a General Theory of Tax Practice." *Social and Legal Studies* 24(2) 289–312.

Freiberg, A. (2010). *The Tools of Regulation*. Leichhardt, Australia: Federation Press.

French, J. R. P., and Raven, B. (1959). "The Bases of Social Power." In D. Cartwright (ed.), *Studies in Social Power* (pp. 150–67). Ann Arbor: University of Michigan Press.

Frey, B. S. (1992). "Tertium Datum: Pricing, Regulating, and Intrinsic Motivation." *Kyklos* 45, 161–84.

(1997). "A Constitution for Knaves Crowds Out Civic Virtues." *Economic Journal* 107, 1043–53.

Gangl, K., Hofmann, E., and Kirchler, E. (2015). "Tax Authorities' Interaction with Taxpayers: A Conception of Compliance in Social Dilemmas by Power and Trust." *New Ideas in Psychology* 37, 13–23. Doi: 10.1016/j.newideapsych.2014.12.001.

Gangl, K., Muehlbacher, S., de Groot, M., Goslinga, S., Hofmann, E., Kogler, C., Antonides, G., and Kirchler, E. (2013). "'How Can I Help You?' Perceived Service Orientation of Tax Authorities and Tax Compliance." *FinanzArchiv: Public Finance Analysis* 69(4), 487–510. Doi: 10.1628/001522113X675683.

Gemmell, N., and Ratto, M. (2012). "Behavioral Responses to Taxpayer Audits: Evidence from Random Taxpayer Inquiries." *National Tax Journal* 65(1), 33–58.

Gobena, L. B., and van Dijke, M. (2017). "Fear and Caring: Procedural Justice, Trust, and Collective Identification as Antecedents of Voluntary Tax Compliance." *Journal of Economic Psychology* 62, 1–16. Doi: 10.1016/j.joep.2017.05.005.

Grasmick, H. G., and Bursik Jr., R. J. (1990). "Conscience, Significant Others, and Rational Choice: Extending the Deterrence Model." *Law and Society Review* 24(3), 837–61.

Hauptman, L., Gürarda, Ş. , and Korez-Vide, R. (2015). "Exploring Voluntary Tax Compliance Factors in Slovenia: Implications for Tax Administration and Policymakers." *Lex Localis* 13(3), 639–59. Doi: 10.4335/13.3.639-659(2015).

Hofmann, E., Gangl, K., Kirchler, E., and Stark, J. (2014). "Enhancing Tax Compliance through Coercive and Legitimate Power of Tax Authorities by Concurrently Diminishing or Facilitating Trust in Tax Authorities." *Law and Policy* 36(3), 290–313. Doi: 10.1111/lapo.12021.

James, S., Hasseldine, J. D., Hite, P. A., and Toumi, M. (2003, December). "Tax Compliance Policy: An International Comparison and New Evidence on Normative Appeals and Auditing." Paper presented at the ESRC Future Governance Workshop. Vienna, Austria: Institute for Advanced Studies.

Kaplanoglou, G., and Rapanos, V. T. (2015). "Why Do People Evade Taxes? New Experimental Evidence from Greece." *Journal of Behavioral and Experimental Economics* 56, 21–32. Doi: 10.1016/j.socec.2015.02.005.

Kaplanoglou, G., Rapanos, V. T., and Daskalakis, N. (2016). "Tax Compliance Behaviour during the Crisis: The Case of Greek SMEs." *European Journal of Law and Economics* 42(3), 405–44. Doi: 10.1007/s10657-016-9547-y.

Kasper, M., Kogler, C., and Kirchler, E. (2015). "Tax Policy and the News: An Empirical Analysis of Taxpayers' Perceptions of Tax-Related Media Coverage and Its Impact on Tax Compliance." *Journal of Behavioral and Experimental Economics* 54, 58–63. Doi: 10.1016/j.socec.2014.11.001.

Kastlunger, B., Lozza, E., Kirchler, E., and Schabmann, A. (2013). "Powerful Authorities and Trusting Citizens: The Slippery Slope Framework and Tax Compliance in Italy." *Journal of Economic Psychology* 34, 36–45. Doi: 10.1016/j.joep.2012.11.007.

Kastlunger, B., Kirchler, E., Mittone, L., and Pitters, J. (2009). "Sequences of Audits, Tax Compliance, and Taxpaying Strategies." *Journal of Economic Psychology* 30, 405–18.

Kirchler, E. (2007). *The Economic Psychology of Tax Behavior*. Cambridge: Cambridge University Press.

Kirchler, E., and Hoelzl, E. (2018). *Economic Psychology: An Introduction*. Cambridge: Cambridge University Press.

Kirchler, E., Hoelzl, E., and Wahl, I. (2008). "Enforced versus Voluntary Tax Compliance: The 'Slippery Slope' Framework." *Journal of Economic Psychology* 29, 210–25. Doi: 10.1016/j.joep.2007.05.004.

Kirchler, E., Kogler, C., and Muehlbacher, S. (2014). "Cooperative Tax Compliance: From Deterrence to Deference." *Current Directions in Psychological Science* 23(2), 87–92.

Kogler, C., Batrancea, L., Nichita, A., Pantya, J., Belianin, A., and Kirchler, E. (2013). "Trust and Power as Determinants of Tax Compliance: Testing the Assumptions of the Slippery Slope Framework in Austria, Hungary, Romania and Russia." *Journal of Economic Psychology* 34, 169–80. Doi: 10.1016/j.joep.2012.09.010.

Korczynski, M. (2000). "The Political Economy of Trust." *Journal of Management Studies* 37, 1–21.

Lederman, L. (2019). "Does Enforcement Reduce Voluntary Tax Compliance?" *Brigham Young University Law Review Collections* 2018(3), 623–93. https://digitalcommons.law.byu.edu/lawreview/vol2018/iss3/6.

Lemoine, J., and Roland-Lévy, C. (2013). "Are Taxpayers, Who Pay Their Taxes, All Cooperative Citizens?" *Citizenship Teaching and Learning* 8(2), 195–213. Doi: 10.1386/ctl.8.2.195_1.

Lerner, J. S., and Keltner, D. (2000). "Beyond Valence: Toward a Model of Emotion-Specific Influences on Judgement and Choice." *Cognition and Emotion* 14(4), 473–93. Doi: 10.1080/026999300402763.

Lerner, J. S., Li, Y., Valdesolo, P., and Kassam, K. S. (2015). "Emotion and Decision Making." *Annual Review of Psychology* 66, 799–823. https://doi.org/10.1146/annurev-psych-010213-115043.

Lewis, J. D., and Weigert, A. (1985). "Trust as a Social Reality." *Social Forces* 63(4), 967–85.

Lisi, G. (2012). "Unemployment, Tax Evasion and the Slippery Slope Framework." *International Review of Economics* 59, 297–302.

(2019). "Slippery Slope Framework, Tax Morale and Tax Compliance: A Theoretical Integration and an Empirical Assessment." Discussion Paper in Economic Behaviour, DPEP 02/19. Cassino, Italy: University of Cassino, Department of Economics and Law.

Loewenstein, G., and Lerner, J. S. (2003). "The Role of Affect in Decision Making." In R. J. Davidson, H. H. Goldsmith and K. R. Scherer (eds.), *Handbook of Affective Science* (pp. 619–42). Oxford: Oxford University Press.

Lozza, E., and Castiglioni, C. (2018). "Tax Climate in the National Press: A New Tool in Tax Behavior Research." *Journal of Social and Political Psychology* 6(2), 401–19.

Lozza, E., Kastlunger, B., Tagliabue, S., and Kirchler, E. (2013). "The Relationship between Political Ideology and Attitudes toward Tax Compliance: The Case of Italian Taxpayers." *Journal of Social and Political Psychology* 1(1), 51–73. Doi: 10.5964/jspp.v1i1.108.

Mas'ud, A., Manaf, N. A. A., and Saad, N. (2015). "Testing Assumptions of the 'Slippery Slope Framework' Using Cross-Country Data: Evidence from Sub-Saharan Africa." *International Journal of Business and Society* 16(3), 408–21.

(2019). "Trust and Power as Predictors of Tax Compliance: Global Evidence." *Economics and Sociology* 12(2), 192–204.

Mayer, R. C., Davis, J. H., and Schoorman, F. D. (1995). "An Integrative Model of Organizational Trust." *Academy of Management Review* 20(3), 709–34.

Mendoza, J. P., Wielhouwer, J. L., and Kirchler, E. (2015). "The Backfiring Effect of Auditing on Tax Compliance." SSRN Electronic Journal. Doi: 10.2139/ssrn.2597479.
Mittone, L., Panebianco, F., and Santoro, A. (2017). "The Bomb-Crater Effect of Tax Audits: Beyond the Misperception of Chance." *Journal of Economic Psychology* 61, 225–43.
Mooijman, M., van Dijk, W. W., van Dijk, E., and Ellemers, N. (2016). "On Sanction-Goal Justifications: How and Why Deterrence Justifications Undermine Rule Compliance." *Journal of Personality and Social Psychology* 111. Doi: 10.1037/pspi0000084.
Muehlbacher, S., and Kirchler, E. (2010). "Tax Compliance by Trust and Power of Authorities." *International Economic Journal* 24(4), 607–10. Doi: 10.1080/10168737.2010.526005.
Muehlbacher, S., Kirchler, E., and Schwarzenberger, H. (2011). "Voluntary versus Enforced Tax Compliance: Empirical Evidence for the 'Slippery Slope' Framework." *European Journal of Law and Economics* 32(1), 89–97. Doi: 10.1007/s10657-011-9236-9.
Mulder, L. B., Verboon, P., and de Cremer, D. (2009). "Sanctions and Moral Judgments: The Moderating Effect of Sanction Severity and Trust in Authorities." *European Journal of Social Psychology* 39, 255–69.
Mulder, L. B., van Dijk, E., de Cremer, D., and Wilke, H. A. M. (2006). "Undermining Trust and Cooperation: The Paradox of Sanctioning Systems in Social Dilemmas." *Journal of Experimental Social Psychology* 42, 147–62.
Murphy, K., and Tyler, T. R. (2008). "Procedural Justice and Compliance Behaviour: The Mediating Role of Emotions." *European Journal of Social Psychology* 38, 652–68. Doi: 10.1002/ejsp.
Niesiobędzka, M. (2014). "Relations between Procedural Fairness, Tax Morale, Institutional Trust and Tax Evasion." *Journal of Social Research and Policy* 5(1), 1–12.
Nooteboom, B. (2002). *Trust: Forms, Foundations, Functions, Failures and Figures*. Cheltenham, UK: Edward Elgar.
OECD. (2008). "Study into the Role of Tax Intermediaries." www.oecd.org/tax/administration/39882938.pdf.
(2013). "Co-operative Compliance: A Framework: From Enhanced Relationship to Co-operative Compliance." http://dx.doi.org/10.1787/9789264200852-en.
Oishi, S., Schimmack, U., and Diener, E. (2012). "Progressive Taxation and the Subjective Well-Being of Nations." *Psychological Science* 23, 86–92.
Olsen, J., Kasper, M., Enachescu, J., Benk, S., Budak, T., and Kirchler, E. (2018). "Emotions and Tax Compliance among Small Business Owners: An Experimental Survey." *International Review of Law and Economics* 56(May), 42–52. Doi: 10.1016/j.irle.2018.05.004.
Olson, N. E. (2015). "Procedural Justice for All: A Taxpayer Rights Analysis of IRS Earned Income Credit Compliance Strategy." *Advances in Taxation* 22, 1–35.
Onu, D., and Oats, L. (2018). "Tax Talks: An Exploration of Online Discussions among Taxpayers." *Journal of Business Ethics* 149, 931–44.
Orviska, M., and Hudson, J. (2002). "Tax Evasion, Civic Duty and the Law Abiding Citizen." *European Journal of Political Economy* 19, 83–102.
Prinz, A., Muehlbacher, S., and Kirchler, E. (2014). "The Slippery Slope Framework on Tax Compliance: An Attempt to Formalization." *Journal of Economic Psychology* 40, 20–34. Doi: 10.1016/j.joep.2013.04.004.
Pukelienė, V., and Kažemekaitytė, A. (2016). "Tax Behaviour: Assessment of Tax Compliance in European Union Countries." *Ekonomika* 95(2), 30–56. Doi: 10.15388/Ekon.2016.2.10123.
Rand, D. G., Greene, J. D., and Nowak, M. A. (2012). "Spontaneous Giving and Calculated Greed." *Nature* 489, 427–30.
Raven, B. H. (1965). "Social Influence and Power." In I. D. Steiner and M. Fishbein (eds.). *Current Studies in Social Psychology* (pp. 371–82). New York: Holt, Rinehart, Winston.
Ruiu, G., and Lisi, G. (2011). "Tax Morale, Slippery-Slope Framework and Tax Compliance: A Cross-Section Analysis." Dipartimento di Scienze Economiche. http://core.kmi.open.ac.uk/download/pdf/6279366.pdf.
Scherer, K. R. (2005). "What Are Emotions? And How Can They Be Measured?" *Social Science Information* 44, 695–729. Doi: 10.1177/0539018405058216.

Siglé, M. A. (2019). The Effects of Cooperative Compliance Programs. Thesis, Nyenrode Business University, NL.

Sloterdijk, P. (2010). *Die nehmende Hand und die gebende Seite [The Hand that Takes and the Side that Gives]*. Berlin: Suhrkamp.

Srinivasan, T. N. (1973). "Tax Evasion: A Model." *Journal of Public Economics* 2, 339–46. Doi: 10.1016/0047-2727(73)90024-8.

Stevens, L. G. M., Pheijffer, M., van den Broek, J. G. A., Keijzer, T. J., and van der Hel-van Dijk, E. C. J. M. (2012). "Tax Supervision – Made to Measure." https://download.belastingdienst.nl/belastingdienst/docs/tax_supervision_made_to_measure_tz0151z1fdeng.pdf.

Tsikas, S. A. (2017). "Enforce Tax Compliance, but Cautiously: The Role of Trust in Authorities and Power of Authorities." Hannover Economic Papers No. 589. http://diskussionspapiere.wiwi.uni-hannover.de/pdf_bib/dp-589.pdf.

Tyler, T. R. (1997). "The Psychology of Legitimacy: A Relational Perspective on Voluntary Deference to Authorities." *Personality and Social Psychology Review* 1(October), 323–45. Doi: 10.1207/s15327957pspr0104.

(2003). "Trust within Organisations." *Personnel Review* 32, 556–68.

Wahl, I., Kastlunger, B., and Kirchler, E. (2010). "Trust in Authorities and Power to Enforce Tax Compliance: An Empirical Analysis of the 'Slippery Slope Framework'." *Law and Policy* 32, 383–406. Doi: 10.1111/j.1467-9930.2010.00327.

Wang, L., and Murnighan, J. K. (2017). "The Dynamics of Punishment and Trust." *Journal of Applied Psychology* 102(10), 1385–402.

Webley, P., Robben, H. S. J., Elffers, H., and Hessing, D. J. (1991). *Tax Evasion: An Experimental Approach*. Cambridge: Cambridge University Press.

Wilks, D. C., and Pacheco, L. (2014). "Tax Compliance, Corruption and Deterrence: An Application of the Slippery Model." In A. Teixeira (ed.), *Interdisciplinary Insights on Fraud* (pp. 87–104). Newcastle upon Tyne: Cambridge Scholars Publishing.

Wurth, E., and Braithwaite, V. (2018). "Tax Practitioners and Tax Avoidance." In N. Hashimzade and Y. Epifantseva (eds.), *The Routledge Companion to Tax Avoidance Research* (pp. 320–39). London: Routledge.

56

Compliance in Occupational Safety and Health

John Mendeloff

Abstract: Quite apart from government regulations and enforcement, employers usually have many incentives to keep workers safe and these have led to major reductions in deaths and injuries. But safety can be costly and disagreements about the worth of some safety measures are inevitable. Leaders of small firms will often have limited information about the risks they face and survey data show that they are less likely to recognize the benefits of safety investments. Preventing long-term exposures that can cause chronic diseases is especially costly and less likely to offer benefits to employers. Governments differ in their approaches to workplace safety. Some, like the United States, essentially train inspectors to identify, cite and punish failures to comply with a detailed list of requirements. Others rely less on punishment and more on training inspectors to offer advice to firms about how to improve. The latter focus less on compliance with detailed standards and more on systematic procedures to give more weight to safety. Evidence from manufacturing that inspections with penalties are followed by reductions in injuries indicates that inspections can affect outcomes beyond compliance. These studies rarely find that the size of the penalty has an effect, although it seems likely that unusually large penalties would draw management's attention. Important reasons to comply with standards also include beliefs about the legitimacy of regulatory authorities and the fairness of the enforcement process as well as professional norms and empathy.

56.1 INTRODUCTION

In 1918, the workers' compensation agency in Pennsylvania recorded 3,403 fatal injuries (Commonwealth of Pennsylvania 2006). Compared to this, the US rate for acute fatal work injuries has fallen over 97 percent in the last century. Much of the drop resulted from shifts in employment away from dangerous trades, but it is also true that death rates have dropped sharply within those industries as employers have adopted safer practices. One contributor to this decline, although not the most important one, has been the development of government regulatory agencies devoted to enforcing rules and behaviors that reduce the hazards of work.

Enforcement required the development of some sort of standards for employers to meet. Along with public sector activity, businesses fostered the development of private standard-setting organizations that provided guidance to firms and could provide a substitute for government action; although, once developed, they could also be adopted by regulators.

We focus in this chapter on compliance in the United States, but we do include some comparisons with other systems. We follow this path: we ask what is it that employers (and occasionally workers) are required to comply with, how is compliance identified and measured, and what kinds of explanations of compliance have been offered that are relevant to workplace safety and health. We then look at survey evidence about employer actions and motivations, and research on violations, before offering some concluding thoughts.

56.2 COMPLIANCE WITH WHAT?

Before talking about why employers comply or don't comply with occupational safety and health standards, we should clarify what it is that they need to comply with (Hopkins 1994). When setting requirements, policymakers should consider whether they are understandable, effective, technically and economically feasible, economically worthwhile, legally enforceable, equitable in their effects across firms and responsive to and encouraging of innovation (Mendeloff 1988). Except for the last item, compliance should increase when standards meet these criteria. In short, when they are more "reasonable." Without these qualities, we can expect compliance to be worse.

There are two broad approaches to setting workplace safety and health standards. Almost all countries have standards regarding specific hazards, but some place a much heavier emphasis on assessing the quality of the employer's management system for health and safety. The choice of approach is linked with the country's enforcement style. The emphasis on individual standards tends to be linked to a more legalistic approach to enforcement. The inspector is not there to assess the overall program or to provide guidance but rather to identify violations, which usually carry fines (Kelman 1981; Lofgren 1989). In the United States, the federal Occupational Safety and Health Administration (OSHA) does have a recommended safety and health program, but it plays little role in the enforcement process. Some states have regulations requiring such programs and they are sometimes the most frequently cited standard; evidence from California indicates, however, that the firm is usually cited simply for failing to have a written document. How well a safety program is actually implemented by the firm and how it is using it are rarely the subject of scrutiny or citations (Mendeloff et al. 2012). A key shortcoming of the US approach is that only a minority of reported injuries are caused by violations of standards, a result stemming in part from the fact that about one-third of those injuries are sprains and strains, which are not addressed by any current OSHA standard (Mendeloff 1979). Bardach and Kagan (1982) focused on problems of "regulatory unreasonableness" in OSHA and other programs. Employers were often frustrated by the OSHA guidance of "cite what you see" that limited the ability of inspectors to exercise discretion and to distinguish important hazards from lesser ones.

I estimate that OSHA has well over 10,000 separate safety and health requirements for employers, although the number pertaining to a given employer may be closer to 1,000. Some apply only to certain industries; others apply to the control of specific hazards that may or may not be present in a workplace. To give a flavor, 86 requirements apply to walking surfaces, 70 to exits, 216 to powered platforms, 103 to ventilation, 88 to noise and so on.[1] About 80 percent of OSHA inspections assess penalties, which average about $4,000 per inspection.

It is noteworthy, however, that the federal and state OSHA programs together now conduct only about 70,000 inspections per year, an inspection rate per worker or establishment dwarfed by most other developed countries. The province of British Columbia in Canada

1 Calculations by the author.

conducted 34,000 inspections for 2.5 million workers in 2017, a ratio about 30 times higher that of the USA (McClure 2019).

In contrast to the US approach, inspectors of the Health and Safety Executive (HSE) in the United Kingdom issue fines in about 2 percent of inspections (2006/7 data). That 2 percent was taken to court and fined more than $25,000 on average (Mendeloff and Staetsky 2014). HSE inspectors issue notices to employers about conditions that need to be fixed; failure to fix them can lead to fines. HSE inspectors spend more time discussing safety and health program management (Hawkins 2002). In the last 20 years, HSE inspections have been reduced by half, although prosecutions leveled off at about 500 per year for the last decade. Even with the reduced numbers, the 30,000 or so HSE inspections represent an inspection rate about 3 times the rate in the USA and that doesn't count a larger effort by local health authorities (Walters et al. 2011; Blanc 2018).

In Sweden, which also rarely levies fines, deficiencies in the Systematic Work Environment Management (SWEM) provisions constituted about 40 percent of the notices to employers (Walters et al. 2011). A significant share of inspections there is devoted to SWEM's implementation, including the adequacy of risk assessments. However, some observers state that inspectors still usually fail to use SWEM to encourage a continuous quality improvement process.

56.3 HOW IS NONCOMPLIANCE IDENTIFIED AND MEASURED?

Ideally, we would first want to know how workplaces differ in the number of situations (conditions or activities) where standards require compliance. For example, a workplace with no machines will not have exposures related to machinery standards. In general, larger workplaces will have more exposures, but the relevance of standards varies substantially among industries. Second, we would want to know what percentage of all exposures are in a state of noncompliance and for how long. Thus, we would ask both the number and the percentage of noncompliant exposures at a point in time and the duration of the noncompliances.

What we can, in fact, observe is something different: the number of violations cited by the compliance officers during inspections which are, typically, widely spaced in time. Opportunities to observe exposures increase as inspections become more frequent and more comprehensive. In addition, some noncompliant exposures are more likely to be cited than others. Noncompliance with some standards may be relatively easy to detect (Mendeloff 1984); or inspectors may be looking more intently for some violations than for others.

A few opportunities exist to look at compliance outside of the inspection context. One comes from data on consultations provided by OSHA or state agencies, visits that did not carry any direct threat of penalties (Mendeloff and Gray 2001). These typically identified roughly twice as many violations as inspections did. An OSHA experiment in Maine in the early 1990s asked participating firms to conduct a self-audit of violations at their workplaces. In some cases, firms reported several thousand needed corrections (Mendeloff 1995). These cases suggest that OSHA "under-enforces" due to a number of organizational and policy constraints. Some violations will pose trivial hazards; finding and citing violations is time-consuming and enforcing all standards will antagonize many employers. To some degree, OSHA has responded to earlier criticism that its enforcement effort epitomized nit-picking.

Many more violations were cited during OSHA's first decade in the 1970s, although penalties then were considerably smaller (Siskind 2002).[2]

Regimes that focus on management systems also face measurement problems. OSHA discovered that when it considered developing a safety and health program rule. How would inspectors judge whether programs were good or bad? The proposal was to assess more than twenty different components of programs, but how should they be weighted? And assessments of inter-rater reliability indicated that the level of agreement among inspectors viewing the same facility was not high. In addition, evidence about the validity of these components as contributors to safety was often sketchy.

These facts posed serious problems for an agency that wanted to use a management measure within a legalistic framework. The problems are less severe in a more consultative program where inspectors have more discretion to emphasize elements that seem most germane to the worksite.

56.4 CONCEPTUAL PERSPECTIVES

One debate among scholars across many subjects of regulation has been the role of economic factors, especially of deterrence, compared to other factors affecting employer compliance.

If the fine and the probability of detection are really high, it seems clear that deterrence can achieve widespread compliance. The relevant question, however, is, given the existing (or other feasible) level of deterrence, what role does it play compared to other factors?

While deterrence has received considerable attention (Becker 1968), employers often have substantial economic incentives to improve safety apart from regulation. Injuries are generally costly to them as well as to employees. Economic incentives often include higher wages paid for riskier jobs, higher workers' compensation premiums, higher rates of turnover, fears of liability, reputational loss in the marketplace and lower worker morale (Viscusi 1983), although these are not found in every situation. As workers become wealthier, better educated and better organized, employers feel greater pressures to respond.

In response to their concerns, employers sponsored the development of private standard-setting organizations – for example, the International Standards Organization, the American National Standards Institute, the National Fire Protection Association. To some degree these were supported because they warded off government actions, but it is clear that they have provided useful guidance for many firms (Cheit 1990; Castleman and Ziem 1988).

Another signal of the importance of economic concerns is that employers have been less concerned to protect workers from long-latency diseases than from acute hazards. With these diseases, a larger share of the costs can be externalized to the workers, who often sicken as they near retirement, and to governments and charities.

Of course, economic incentives are only part of the story. Sociolegal scholars (e.g., Ayres and Braithwaite 1992; Hawkins 2002; Hutter 1988; Kagan, Gunningham and Thornton 2011; Kagan 1994; Simpson and Rorie 2011) have stressed the role of organizational, legal and ethical factors in shaping compliance behavior, as well as the role of limited information.

[2] OSHA does have some flexibility in enforcement: violations can be "serious," "other than serious" or "de minimus," with different levels of penalty. Employers can also get penalty reductions for evidence of "good faith" and a good previous inspection history. Also, in the twenty-one states where the OSHA program is run by the state government, rather than by federal OSHA, the penalties are usually substantially lower and the frequency of inspections is usually much higher. A noteworthy finding is that fatality rates in most of the state-run programs are lower than in the states where federal OSHA operates the program (Bradbury 2006; Mendeloff and Burns 2013).

Many studies have identified shortfalls in the predictive power of simple rational choice models. While the owners of small, struggling firms can find that cutting corners is tempting, Braithwaite and Makkai (1991) found that nurses in nursing homes emphasized their professional responsibility and moral standards rather than any economic incentive to provide good care.

Evidence for the limited role of deterrence comes from firms that have moved strongly to exceed the performance required by the law. These are disproportionately larger firms and their motives surely include other economic incentives as well as a desire to be good corporate citizens (Shapiro and Rabinowitz 1997, 2000; Borck and Coglianese 2011).

Blanc (2016) has proposed one useful way of categorizing the "different foundations of compliance" into four groups:

— enabling conditions: knowledge and understanding of rules, financial and technical ability to comply without putting the business viability in jeopardy;
— economic incentives: deterrence (probability of detection primarily, amount of potential sanctions as a secondary aspect – and also risk of reputation loss), potential economic benefits of compliance (improved reputation leading to improved market position, or compliance investments resulting in higher productivity, reduced losses etc.);
— social and cultural drivers: group conformity (other group members or models behave in a compliant way), group ethical values (ethical values aligned with the values of the regulation and/or posit legal compliance as an absolute good);
— legitimacy and interactions – individual psychological drivers: legitimacy of authorities (influenced by social and cultural drivers, but also directly by individual experience), procedural justice (or lack thereof) experienced in interactions with authorities, regulators.

These categories are an analytical device, and not absolute.[3]

In work on environmental protection, Gunningham, Thornton and Kagan (2005) have advanced the concept that firms require a "social license" to operate. To obtain this, firms must avoid the perception that the harms they cause are so great that they undermine the legitimacy they normally enjoy.

> Sustained inspection and enforcement activity seem to have inculcated a 'culture of compliance.' Consequently, *the regulations themselves*, not the fear of enforcement action, currently have the strongest impact on behavior. Rather than simply providing a threat, regulations and inspections acted as a reminder or guide to enterprises as to what was required of them (Gunningham et al. 2005: 312).

Even here we can wonder whether a "culture of compliance" emerges independently of the belief that resistance would be unproductive.

Systematic interview data is relatively scarce for OSHA. Not always representative given the small sample sizes, interviews nevertheless are often deeply informative. One interesting resource (Lofgren 1989) comes from an inspector's review of his interactions with employers. He judged that 80 percent of employers complied with no protest.

[3] Paternoster and Simpson (1993) provide a somewhat similar list which includes nine different factors.

56.5 SIMS'S STUDY OF COMPLIANCE ACTIVITIES IN THE UNITED STATES

One of the most useful studies of workplace safety compliance activities in the USA, especially among small firms, was conducted by Robert Sims (1988) in an unpublished PhD dissertation. Because it is little known, I will devote space to describing his findings. He obtained responses from 1,863 firms out of 8,000 contacted in July 1983. Seventy percent were in high-risk industries and 43 percent had fewer than 10 employees, 23 percent had 10–19 and 20 percent had 20–49; only 2 percent (N=37) had more than 250 workers.

The study's dependent variable was whether the firm had taken various actions to abate hazards, including safety training, self-inspections, having a safety committee, reducing worker exposures, using an OSHA or private consultant and others. Unsurprisingly, actions varied systematically with size and industry risk level. What seems especially interesting is the impact of these two factors on firms' perceptions of hazards and their beliefs about the efficacy of preventive measures.

Small firms and those in lower-risk industries were less likely to have taken preventive actions. In high-risk industries, the share of firms saying that their injury rate was below the industry average was 80 percent for those with 1–9 employees and 45–50 percent for those with more than 50. When the annual injury rate is often 0 percent, the perception of good performance is common. Smaller firms in high-risk industries were also less likely to say that they were "seriously concerned" about hazards. That percentage rose steadily from about 30 percent in group size 1–9 to over 80 percent in those with more than 250.

Those firms that had taken actions were asked if they received any of the following benefits: higher productivity, better morale, less turnover and absences, reduced losses to equipment and goods, lower premiums. Among high-risk firms, 50 percent of those with 1–9 workers said that they received none of these benefits versus less than 20 percent in the largest firms.

Among high-risk firms, only 19 percent of firms with 1–9 workers with an abatement action indicated that the actions reduced the number of accidents versus 48 percent among those with 100 or more. The percentages saying "no" were fairly similar, but 60 percent of the smaller firms said that they were "uncertain" versus about 20 percent in the largest firms. More than 70 percent in both small and large firms found personal observation very useful for making decisions about hazards. But safety records were judged very useful as well by 60 percent of those in firms above 250, but by less than 10 percent in firms with 1–9 workers.

Also, in addition to their own limited experience, small firms tended to have less information from other sources about risks. In high-risk industries, 30 percent of firms with 1–9 workers had a designated safety person versus 95 percent in firms with 250+. The figure was 47 percent in all high-risk industry firms versus 30 percent in all low-risk industry firms. Among all high-risk firms, the owner or general manager was responsible for safety in 85 percent. For high-risk firms with more than 250 workers, only 20 percent had this responsibility. Despite this burden on the owner, small firms were not more likely to hire consultants. But, except for high-risk firms above 250, no other category of firms reported more than 10 percent use of consultants.

Small firms did have one advantage. Eighty percent of firms with more than 100 employees reported that it was "very or somewhat difficult to get employees to observe safe work practices"; in contrast, 36 percent of firms with fewer than 10 reported the same difficulty. It is easier to keep tabs on a smaller workgroup, and it may be easier to instill a common standard.

Sims (1988) used a logistic regression with 965 firms in high-risk industries to explain whether a firm had a "serious concern" with occupational health and safety. The only significant variables were whether the firm had received loss control visits from its workers' compensation (WC) insurer and whether safety and health had been issues in collective bargaining. Firm size was not significant, but these two variables are strongly correlated with size.

WC loss control inspections increase monotonically with firm size with more than a 10-fold increase between firms with 1–9 versus those with more than 250. Unlike larger firms, firms with fewer than twenty employees usually (65 percent of the time) viewed the information provided in these visits as not useful. For bigger firms, the useful fraction was 70–80 percent. As Sims (1988: 82) noted: "Unfortunately, it is unclear if smaller firms are less able to take advantage of the information due to the less sophisticated hazard management capabilities of smaller firms, or if the information is less useful as a consequence of the lower hazard abatement benefits available to smaller firms."

The presence of unions increased with firm size. In high-risk industries, unions represented workers at only 5 percent of establishments with 1–9 employees; above 250 employees, the percentage was 55 percent. The percentage that was unionized was always below 30 percent, except for high-risk firms with more than 250 employees, when it hit 55 percent. Overall, respondents said that safety was important in collective bargaining for fewer than 30 percent of unionized firms. For those with more than 250 employees, the figure was 70 percent.

The picture that emerges reinforces the conclusion that small firms have less information about risks and hazards than larger firms do. Since they have more events, big firms will have a greater understanding of the hazards. Big firms will have better data to assess impacts than small ones will. Thus, it is hard for small firms to know, on the basis of their own experience, whether abatement actions work.

56.6 RESEARCH ON VIOLATIONS

This section focuses on quantitative studies of violations. Such studies are rarer in Europe (especially on the Continent) than in the United States.[4] US data indicate that small establishments have poorer compliance. Bigger establishments provide more opportunities for noncompliance, but in inspections labeled as "comprehensive" the number of serious violations cited is similar across size groups.[5] The most relevant evidence comes from complaint inspections, where the inspector is focusing on whether a particular standard is violated. The number of serious violations cited in safety complaint inspections decreases monotonically from 4.9 in establishments with 1–19 employees to 2.1 for those with over 100; for health inspections, the number drops from 4.9 to 1.7 (Mendeloff et al. 2014).[6] Although some data systems report lower non-fatal injury rates at smaller firms, the general finding that fatality rates decrease sharply with size indicates that the non-fatal injury data suffer greater underreporting at small firms (Mendeloff and Burns 2013; Mendeloff and Staetsky 2014; Oleinick, Gluck and Guire 1995; Nichols 1997).

4 Surveys by the European Agency for Safety Health at Work (2010) do quantify some firm practices, but they don't provide as much information about why firms don't comply.

5 For OSHA, the definition of a "serious" violation requires only that, if an injury occurred as a result of the violation, it would be a serious injury. The probability that an injury would occur is not part of that determination, although it does affect the size of the penalty.

6 This sample includes all complaint inspections in the manufacturing sector by federal OSHA from 2001 to 2007.

Several articles have examined OSHA enforcement in the USA to test hypotheses about the effects of political forces (Scholz and Wei 1986; Scholz, Twombly and Headrick 1991; Jung and Makofsky 2014). All claim to find various examples of political influence, although the last also find anomalous results. However, other studies provide contrary findings (Schell-Busey 2017) or provide different interpretations (Huber 2007). Huber (2007) argued that findings that others attributed to interventions by Congressmen usually reflected instead the variations in preferences among workers in more or less conservative or unionized constituencies. For example, where workers are more likely to request inspections, the inspection rate will be higher not because the Congressman is more liberal but because the workers are more active. The discussion here is not meant to deny that political forces can be important. The shift from President Carter to President Reagan in 1981 reduced regulatory resources across many programs (Wood and Waterman 1994).

A large number of studies of European occupational safety and health regimes include discussions of compliance policies (Hawkins 2002; Walters et al. 2011; Blanc 2018), but most lack inspection-level data on firms that allow examination of the relation between compliance and the characteristics of firms or individual standards.

56.7 FINDINGS ABOUT VIOLATIONS

Most quantitative studies of workplace safety and health enforcement have been carried out in the United States. Here we review what we have learned from these studies about noncompliance. Figure 56.1 shows the number of OSHA violations in the USA cited as "serious" or "other than serious" by year. The big swings that we see are the result of enforcement policy choices, not actual changes in compliance. As a result, it is often difficult to know whether the number of actual violations at inspected workplaces is declining. Exposures to noise and toxic substances are an exception because we have numerical measurements to refer to; these show substantial reductions for most of the hazards that have been the subject of OSHA standard-setting.

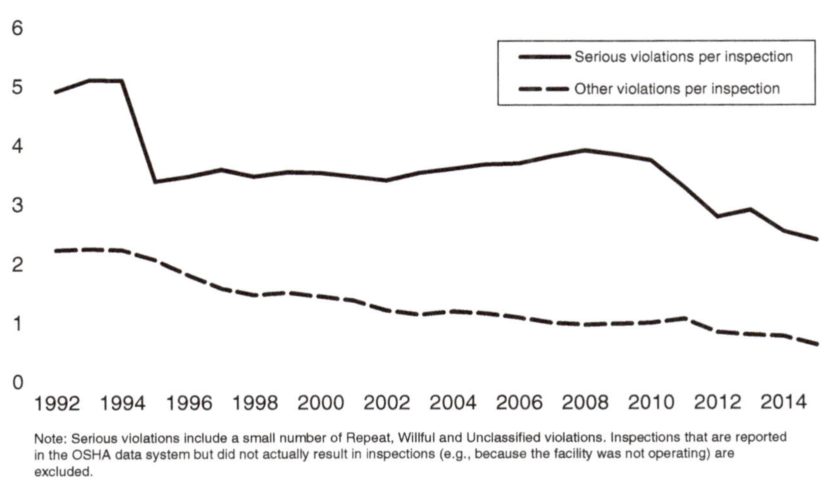

FIGURE 56.1 Trends in violations per inspection in federal OSHA manufacturing inspections, 1992–2015

Studies by Gray and Jones (1991a, 1991b) were the first to focus on the role of inspection sequence in a large data set, examining almost 300,000 individual plant inspection records from OSHA's IMIS system through 1983. They found that the number of violations cited by OSHA fell by approximately 30–40 percent from the first inspection to the second and then continued to drop, although much more slowly, in subsequent inspections. Ko, Mendeloff and Gray (2010) looked at federal OSHA inspections in manufacturing from 1972 through 2006 and found a very similar pattern of declines after the first inspection in each subperiod. These studies, along with those by Scholz and Gray (Scholz and Gray 1990; Gray and Scholz 1993), showed that inspections with penalties appeared to reduce injuries, while inspections without penalties did not. Scholz and Gray (1990) did not find that higher penalties led to bigger reductions. Weil (1996) demonstrated that, even in the absence of large initial penalties, the prospects of later penalties could be large enough to make compliance rational.

Viscusi (1986) reported moderate evidence that injury rates declined when inspection rates were higher, but found no effect of the size of the penalty. Bartels and Thomas (1985) found that more heavily inspected industries showed greater subsequent declines in violations, although they did not detect any effects of inspections on industry injury rates. Two studies (Mendeloff and Gray 2005; Haviland et al. 2010) explored the relations between violations of particular groups of standards and injuries, finding that inspections citing violations of personal protective equipment (PPE) standards appeared to be particularly effective. However, a more recent study, still unpublished, found stronger evidence of the effect of machine guarding standards.

It is difficult to study the distinct impacts of general deterrence and specific deterrence.[7] Events that may claim to focus on the former are the first-time inspections discussed above and inspections that take place after a new standard is promulgated. For standards regulating toxic exposures, we usually find that exposures have often decreased by the time that inspectors begin checking compliance with the new standard (Mendeloff 1988).

It seems clear that employers do abate the great majority of violations that OSHA cites Mendeloff et al. (2020). An important issue is whether violations that are abated stay abated. That study looked at all of the serious violations of ninety-one commonly cited standards identified during 1992–2004 in manufacturing inspections and followed the establishments where they had been cited to determine whether the exact same standard was cited there again during the next ten years. Mendeloff et al. (2020) argue that the proper analysis is to look at "re-violations" of safety standards only in subsequent safety inspections and to look at "re-violations" of health standards only in subsequent health inspections. When this is done, re-violations of the same standard exceeded 10 percent for about one-third of the ninety-one standards. When the authors looked at violations of health standards – toxic substances and noise – the percentages were 15 percent to 20 percent. Thus, re-violations are a source, but far from the major source, of violations that are cited in subsequent inspections.

A benefit–cost framework for the employer would lead us to expect that, prior to an inspection, several factors will lead to better compliance:

1. higher perceived probability of OSHA inspection;
2. greater expected penalties, if inspected;
3. lower costs to comply, especially if costs are one-time, instead of ongoing, and have limited impact on productivity;

[7] The former refers to the impact of the threat of punishment on all who are subject to the law; the latter, to the effect on the future behavior of those who are actually punished.

4. less difficulty in monitoring workers' behavior, especially if requirements are uncomfortable to workers or impede worker productivity when they are paid on piecework rate;
5. larger facilities because smaller establishments are less likely to have safety professionals and to be aware of hazards, safety requirements and methods of prevention. Also, smaller firms will generally have lower marginal benefits for preventing injuries because they are subject to a lower degree of experience rating under workers' compensation;
6. higher perceived safety benefits (injury prevention, cost savings). These estimates depend (as we saw in the Sims (1988) study) on the employer's perception that compliance will prevent injuries but will also vary depending on the skill level of workers; for lower-skilled workers, the costs of replacement will be lower when a worker is injured or quits;
7. union workplaces – unions may be an alternative source of information and a source of pressure for compliance. They make complaints to OSHA more likely and may lead to greater detection of noncompliance during an inspection.

In the study of re-violations, the evidence on these propositions was mixed. Violations that OSHA views as especially hazardous were more, not less, likely to be cited again, although this may reflect inspectors' greater vigilance rather than employers' lower compliance. The size of penalties for the particular standard was positively, not negatively, related to re-violations. The total penalty for the incident inspection did have a negative coefficient on re-violations, but it was mostly limited to penalties above $20,000. As noted already, the findings from complaint inspections showed that re-violations of a given standard were more likely at smaller workplaces.

As a measure of the difficulty and cost of abatement, the study used the length of time that OSHA allowed the firm for abatement. The hypothesis had been that high up-front costs would be associated with a lower probability of re-violation. The finding was the opposite, although it was significant only at a level of 0.10. Types of standards categorized as requiring continuous action were usually re-violated more often; for example, standards requiring housekeeping and maintenance rather than standards requiring that employers have written safety plans. Although re-violations were considerably more common than measures of repeat violations had indicated, this research does confirm that getting cited and penalized does substantially reduce later noncompliance (over a ten-year period).

Protecting a firm's reputation is one of the motivations that plays a role in compliance choices. Johnson (2020) used federal OSHA's policy of issuing press releases to local newspapers when an inspection resulted in more than $40,000 in penalties to assess the possible spillover effects on other employers. About 1 percent of inspections reached this threshold. He found that the number of violations cited declined significantly in inspections in the same sector and within 5 kilometers. On average, the effects lasted several years and were still significant up to 50 kilometers. "Furthermore, the evidence overwhelmingly suggests the observed responses are due to employers making defensive investments to avoid their own publicity, rather than using the information to update their beliefs about the probability and severity of regulatory enforcement." Interestingly, however, Johnson (2020) did not find that the number of violations at the penalized employers declined during their next inspection.

56.8 CRIMINAL ACTS?

Writers from the sociolegal perspective, starting from an interest in "white-collar crime," often discuss OSHA violations in terms of criminality. From other perspectives, this has an odd ring. Do the 500,000 or so violations cited each year constitute 500,000 crimes? Does it matter what we call them? Talking about "crimes" creates a moral onus that is considerably stronger than language about "violations." There may be normative reasons to prefer one term or another depending on the desire to stigmatize the actions. From a less normative position, we need to address the possible limits of treating morality as a causal factor. Does the existence of violations depend on whether the supervisor of the worker (at whatever level) is acting ethically? In some cases, yes, but, in the great majority, probably not.

OSHA does have a category of "willful" violations. According to the OSHA Field Operations Manual (2011), "[a] willful violation exists under the Act where an employer has demonstrated either an intentional disregard for the requirements of the Act or a plain indifference to employee safety and health."[8] It goes on to state: "It is not necessary that the violation be committed with a bad purpose or malicious intent to be deemed 'willful'. It is sufficient that the violation was deliberate, voluntary or intentional as distinguished from inadvertent, accidental or ordinarily negligent."[9] In recent years, federal OSHA has cited about 250 willful violations per year in manufacturing, a rate of about 2.5 per 1,000 inspections.

I am unclear about exactly how "ordinary negligence" is distinguished from the sort of negligence shown by someone who shows "a plain indifference to employee safety," but it seems evident that there is a difference. It seems important to distinguish between behavior of this type and behaviors generated by mistakes that the well-intentioned will make (Reason 1997; Cyert and March 1963).

56.9 Concluding Thoughts

Does our understanding of compliance help us to design better public policies? People will not, of course, all agree about what constitutes "better." Still, many scholars in this field have praised the 1992 Ayres and Braithwaite book *Responsive Regulation* for its advocacy of a mix of regulatory approaches that recognize the variety of motivations and capabilities among firms. Many regulatory agencies make attempts to act on this recognition; those that are more legalistic find it harder to achieve this flexibility. In the United States, the legalistic system reflects fears of both abuse of discretion and agency capture. Bureaucrats reasonably fear political criticism if evidence of either appears.

The US emphasis on compliance is especially unfortunate because of the limited scope of existing workplace safety standards. Good compliance with them does not preclude poor safety performance. (In contrast, health standards *are* designed to deal with the causes of most illnesses.) Bardach and Kagan (1982) have described the difficulties that stand in the way of more flexible approaches. A more flexible approach requires more trust by employers and employees in the competence and probity of inspectors, more freedom for administrators to design programs that may lack the uniformity that is sometimes demanded of enforcement. Perhaps most importantly, choices about compliance strategies should be guided by a better understanding of the consequences for workplace safety. Although outside evaluators can contribute to this understanding, the agencies themselves could do it best. However, most agencies are designed to serve an original mission, not to experiment to learn how to do better.

8 OSHA Field Operations Manual (2011), chapter 4, section 5, pp. 4–28.

9 OSHA Field Operations Manual (2011), chapter 4, section 5(B)(2), pp. 4–30.

REFERENCES

Ayres, Ian, and John Braithwaite. 1992. *Responsive Regulation: Transcending the Deregulation Debate*. New York: Oxford University Press.

Bardach, Eugene B., and Robert A. Kagan. 1982. *Going by the Book: The Problem of Regulatory Unreasonableness*, Philadelphia, PA: Temple University Press.

Bartels, Ann P., and Lacy Glenn Thomas. 1985. "Direct and Indirect Effects of Regulation: A New Look at OSHA's Impact." *Journal of Law and Economics* 28:1–25.

Becker, Gary S. 1968. "Crime and Punishment: An Economic Approach." *Journal of Political Economy* 76:169–217.

Blanc, Florentin. 2016. "From Chasing Violations to Managing Risks: Origins, Challenges and Evolutions in Regulatory Inspections." PhD dissertation, University of Leiden.

2018. "Tools for Effective Regulation: Is 'More' Always 'Better'?" *European Journal of Risk Regulation* 9:465–82.

Borck, Jonathan C., and Cary Coglianese. 2011. "Beyond Compliance: Explaining Business Participation in Voluntary Environmental Programs." Penn Law School Public Law and Legal Theory, Research Paper No. 12–06.

Bradbury, J. C. 2006. "Regulatory Federalism and Workplace Safety: Evidence from OSHA Enforcement, 1981–1995". *Journal of Regulatory Economics* 29:211–24.

Braithwaite J., and T. Makkai. 1991. "Testing an Expected Utility Model of Corporate Deterrence." *Law and Society Review* 25:7–39.

Castleman, Barry I., and G. E. Ziem. 1988. "Corporate Influence on Threshold Limit Values." *American Journal of Industrial Medicine* 13:531–59.

Cheit, Ross. 1990. *Setting Safety Standards*. Berkeley: University of California Press.

Commonwealth of Pennsylvania. 2006. "Pennsylvania Workers' Compensation and Safety Annual Report." Harrisburg, PA: Department of Labor and Industry.

Cyert, Richard, and James G. March. 1963. *A Behavioral Theory of the Firm*. Englewood Cliffs, NJ: Prentice-Hall.

European Agency for Safety Health at Work. 2010. European Survey of Enterprises on New Emerging Risks: Managing Safety Health at Work. Bilbao, Spain: European Agency for Safety Health at Work. European Risk Observatory Report TE-RO-10–002-EN-C, 2010. As of December 30, 2011. http://osha.europa.eu/en/publications/reports/esener1_osh_management.

Gray, Wayne B., and Carole A. Jones. 1991a. "Are OSHA Health Inspections Effective? A Longitudinal Study in the Manufacturing Sector." *Review of Economics and Statistics* 73:504–8.

1991b. "Longitudinal Patterns of Compliance with Occupational Safety and Health Administration Health and Safety Regulations in the Manufacturing Sector." *Journal of Human Resources* 26:623–53.

Gray, Wayne B., and John Scholz. 1993. "Does Regulatory Enforcement Work? A Panel Analysis of OSHA Enforcement." *Law & Society Review* 27:177–213.

Gunningham, Neil, Robert A. Kagan and Dorothy Thornton. 2003. *Shades of Green: Business, Regulation, and Environment*. Stanford, CA: Stanford University Press.

Haviland, Amelia, Rachel Burns, Wayne B. Gray, Teague Ruder and John Mendeloff. 2010. "What Kinds of Injuries Do OSHA Inspections Prevent?" *Journal of Safety Research* 41:339–45.

Hawkins, Keith. 2002. *Law as Last Resort: Prosecution Decision-Making in a Regulatory Agency*. New York: Oxford University Press.

Hopkins, Anthony. 1994. "Compliance with What?" *British Journal of Criminology* 34:431–443.

Huber, Gregory. 2007. *The Craft of Bureaucratic Neutrality: Interests and Influence in Governmental Regulation of Occupational Safety*. Cambridge: Cambridge University Press.

Hutter, Bridget M. 1988. *The Reasonable Arm of the Law? The Law Enforcement Procedures of Environmental Health Officers*. Oxford: Clarendon Press.

Johnson, Matthew S. 2020. "Regulation by Shaming: Deterrence Effects of Publicizing Violations of Workplace Safety and Health Laws." *American Economic Review* 110(6):1866–1904.

Jung, Juergen, and Michael D. Makowsky. 2014. "The Determinants of Federal and State Enforcement of Workplace Safety Regulations: OSHA Inspections 1990–2010." *Journal of Regulatory Economics* 45:1–33.

Kagan, Robert A. 1994. "Regulatory Enforcement." In *Handbook of Regulation and Administrative Law*, D. H. Rosenbloom and R. D. Schwartz, eds. New York: Marcel Dekker.

Kagan, Robert A., Neil Gunningham and Dorothy Thornton. 2011. "Fear, Duty, and Regulatory Compliance: Lessons from Three Research Projects." In *Explaining Compliance: Business Responses to Regulation*, Christina Parker and Vibeke Neilsen, eds. Cheltenham, UK: Edward Elgar.

Kelman, Steven. 1981. *Regulating America, Regulating Sweden: A Comparative Study of Occupational Safety and Health Policy*. Cambridge, MA: MIT Press.

Ko, Kilkon, John Mendeloff and Wayne Gray. 2010. "The Role of Inspection Sequence in Compliance with the US Occupational Safety and Health Administration's (OSHA) Standards: Interpretations and Implications." *Regulation and Governance* 4:48–70.

Lofgren, Don J. 1989. *Dangerous Premises: An Insider's View of OSHA Enforcement*. Ithaca, NY: Cornell University Press.

McClure, Kim V. 2019. "Understanding Regulatory Workplace Safety Inspections in British Columbia: Theory and Evidence." PhD dissertation, University of British Columbia.

Mendeloff, John. 1979. *Regulating Safety: A Political and Economic Analysis of OSHA*. Cambridge, MA: MIT Press.

1984. "The Role of OSHA Violations in Serious Workplace Accidents." *Journal of Occupational Medicine* May: 353–60.

1988. *The Dilemma of Toxic Substance Regulation*. Cambridge, MA: MIT Press.

1995. "An Evaluation of OSHA's 'Top 200' Program in Maine." A Report to the OSHA Office of Policy.

Mendeloff, John, and Rachel Burns. 2013. "States with Low Non-fatal Injury Rates Have High Fatality Rates and Vice-Versa." *American Journal of Industrial Medicine* 56:509–19.

Mendeloff, John, and Wayne B. Gray. 2001. "An Evaluation of OSHA's Consultation Program." Report to the OSHA Office of Policy.

2005. "Inside the Black Box: What Kinds of Injuries Do OSHA Inspections Prevent?" *Law and Policy* 27:219–37.

Mendeloff, John, and Laura Staetsky. 2014. "Occupational Fatality Risks in the United States and the United Kingdom." *American Journal of Industrial Medicine* 57:4–14.

Mendeloff, John, Amelia Haviland, Wayne B. Gray, Regan Main and Jing Xia. 2012. "An Evaluation of the California Injury and Illness Prevention Program." Santa Monica, CA: RAND Corporation, TR-1190, 2012.

Mendeloff, John, Michael Dworsky, Wayne B. Gray and Jose Castillo. 2014. "Options for Improving Complaint Inspections and Follow-Up Inspections in the Cal-OSHA Program." RAND Corporation, PR-1261, November 2014.

Mendeloff, John, Wayne B. Gray, Philip Armour and Frank Neuhauser. 2020. "The Re-Occurrence of Violations in Occupational Safety and Health Administration Inspections." Forthcoming in *Regulation and Governance*.

Nichols, Theo. 1997. *The Sociology of Industrial Injury: Employment and Work Relations in Context*. London: Mansell.

Occupational Safety and Health Administration Field Operations Manual. 2011.

Oleinick, A., J. V. Gluck and K. E. Guire. 1995. "Establishment Size and Risk of Occupational Injury." *American Journal of Industrial Medicine* 28:1–21.

Parker, Christina and Vibeke Neilsen. 2011. eds. *Explaining Compliance: Business Responses to Regulation*. Cheltenham UK: Edward Elgar.

Paternoster, Raymond, and Sally S. Simpson. 1993. "A Rational Choice Theory of Corporate Crime." In *Routine Activity and Rational Choice: Advances in Criminological Theory Vol. 5*, Ronald V. Clarke and Marcus Felson, eds. New Jersey: Transaction Publishers.

Reason, James. 1997. *Managing the Risks of Organizational Accidents*. Aldershot, UK: Ashgate.

Schell-Busey, Natalie. 2017. "Do Extralegal Variables Impact the Post-Inspection Process of the Occupational Safety and Health Administration?" *Crime, Law and Social Change* 68:187–216.

Scholz, John T., and Feng Heng Wei. 1986. "Regulatory Enforcement in a Federalist System." *American Political Science Review* 80:1249–70.

Scholz, John T., and Wayne B. Gray. 1990. "OSHA Enforcement and Workplace Injuries: A Behavioral Approach to Risk Assessment." *Journal of Risk and Uncertainty* 3:283–305.
Scholz, John T., Jim Twombly and Barbara Headrick. 1991. "Street-Level Political Controls over Federal Bureaucracy." *American Political Science Review* 85:829–50.
Shapiro, Sidney, and Randi Rabinowitz. 1997. "Punishment versus Cooperation in Regulatory Enforcement: A Case Study of OSHA." *Administrative Law Review* 49:713–62.
2000. "Voluntary Regulatory Compliance in Theory and Practice: The Case of OSHA." *Administrative Law Review* 52:97–155.
Simpson, Sally S., and Melissa Rorie. 2011. "Motivating Compliance: Economic and Material Motives for Compliance." in Parker, Christina and Vibeke Neilsen. eds. *Explaining Compliance: Business Responses to Regulation*. Cheltenham UK: Edward Elgar.
Sims, Robert H. 1988. "Hazard Abatement as a Function of Firm Size." PhD Dissertation, RAND Graduate School.
Siskind, Frederick B. 2002. "Twentieth Century OSHA Enforcement Data: A Review and Explanation of the Major Trends." Washington, DC: US Department of Labor, Office of the Assistant Secretary for Policy, Evaluation, and Research.
Viscusi, W. Kip. 1983. *Risk by Choice*. Cambridge, MA: Harvard University Press.
1986. "The Impact of Occupational Safety and Health Regulation, 1973–83." *RAND Journal of Economics* 17:567–80.
Walters, David, Richard Johnstone, Kaj Frick, Michael Quinlan, Genevieve Baril-Gingras and Annie Thebaud-Mony. 2011. *Regulating Workplace Risks: A Comparative Study of Inspection Regimes in Times of Change*. Cheltenham, UK: Edward Elgar.
Weil, David. 1996. "If OSHA Is So Bad, Why Is Compliance So Good?" *RAND Journal of Economics* 27:618–40.
Wood, Dan B., and Richard W. Waterman. 1994. *Bureaucratic Dynamics: The Role of Bureaucracy in a Democracy*. Boulder, CO: Westview Press.

57

Intellectual Property Compliance: Systematic Methods for Building and Using Intellectual Property

Richard S. Gruner and Jay P. Kesan

Abstract: Systematic methods for building and using intellectual property (IP) support companies in creative projects. These methods ensure compliance with IP laws to both establish IP interests and enforce those interests. More than just systematic means to advance legal interests, well-crafted and carefully operated IP compliance programs serve as reliable sources of new creative assets and IP-enhanced profits. At the same time, IP compliance programs are often preventative. IP owned by other parties can severely limit companies' freedom of action and produce unexpected liabilities that can scuttle major business enterprises. IP compliance programs can prevent commitments to business actions that will conflict with other parties' IP interests, allowing alternatives avoiding the conflicts to be considered or the requisite permissions obtained to allow use of the needed IP.

57.1 INTRODUCTION

This chapter considers four main topics. First, it examines the distinctive features of intellectual property (IP) compliance programs as asset builders and positive contributors to the opportunities and potential profits of business enterprises. Second, it considers the more traditional role of IP compliance programs as problem identifiers and liability preventers much like compliance programs in other fields of law. Third, it provides an overview of ways in which systematic compliance methods developed for other types of law compliance (such as compliance with criminal law standards) can serve IP compliance goals. Fourth, it summarizes prior research into the aims and features of IP compliance programs. Taken together, these discussions describe how IP compliance programs both differ from and conform to other types of law compliance program.

57.2 DEFINING INTELLECTUAL PROPERTY COMPLIANCE SUCCESS

IP compliance programs systematically manage organizational activities in light of IP opportunities and risks.[1] Success in these programs and the features that will produce it differ materially from other types of law compliance program.

[1] IP compliance programs are:

> systematic management programs for addressing IP production and use in business organizations. These sorts of IP management programs – built on the same management techniques that companies use to

More than compliance programs in most other legal fields, IP compliance programs can be both constructive (as when practices ensure that parties creating new IP protect it through legal means and use the resulting IP rights to promote organizational benefits) and harm-preventing (as when programs anticipate and avoid situations where IP interests of other parties are exerted in ways that harm or limit an enterprise).[2] Complete IP compliance programs have components addressing both IP construction and IP avoidance. Both components involve managing organizational activities within legal constraints – as defined by IP laws. But unlike most fields where compliance steps are primarily aimed at avoiding major liabilities (e.g., criminal law compliance) or adhering to regulatory requirements limiting organizational actions (e.g., environmental law compliance), IP compliance programs go beyond IP legal threats to extend to positive opportunities for creating and effectively handling IP value for organizational benefit.[3]

A short definition of success in IP compliance would be "management practices to maximize IP assets and minimize problems with IP of others."[4] This captures the twofold concerns of IP compliance with both outbound IP (that is, IP created by an organization that is primarily of value as it is exerted outward in markets or rights enforcement against other parties) and inbound IP (that is, IP held by other parties that serves as an inbound constraint on organizational activities that may produce unexpected liabilities and that must be dealt

> address other important aspects of business performance such as product safety or financial reporting – involve careful attention to such steps as standard setting, employee education, reporting on corporate performance, audits of key aspects of performance, and evaluations and business practice reforms following incidents of poor performance (Gruner, Ghosh and Kesan 2018: 17).

The best practices for managing IP compliance programs will vary substantially based on the industry and the IP characteristics of the organizations developing and maintaining such programs. *See generally* Frankel et al. 2018: §§ 3:1 to 3:156.

2 The dual goals of IP management – to maximize IP assets and to minimize IP liabilities – are captured in the following description of proper IP management for corporate organizations:

> A company's first step in developing a strategy for the management of intellectual property issues is understanding what assets are in its portfolio and how the intellectual property is connected with the company's products and key product features, as well as those of its competitors. A good intellectual property strategy should be able to address the company's needs from an offensive viewpoint (what intellectual property protection is needed for the company's own work) and from a defensive viewpoint (what risks exist for the portion of the company's business which is dependent on intellectual property) (Bochner and Krause 1989: 453).

See also Gruner and Brunell 2018: § 8:89 (Systematic legal audits of intellectual property practices in organizations "are aimed at identifying the procedures a business or other organization should undertake to best utilize its intellectual property and to minimize its risk of liability for the use of the intellectual property of others. In essence, intellectual property audits are the core of a managed approach to determining what operating procedures should be put in place with respect to intellectual property and when such procedures should be used.").

3 The need for compliance measures addressing both IP opportunities and risks derives directly from the multiple and often central roles played by IP in modern business enterprises. IP interests have key roles as 1) business products, 2) business inputs, 3) tools for constraining threatening actions by others and 4) sources of constraints on business actions under inbound enforcement of IP rights held by others. *See* Gruner, Ghosh and Kesan 2018: 9–11. IP compliance measures can further organizational interests by ensuring effective IP use and IP risk avoidance across all of these IP-related dimensions of business performance.

4 *Cf.* International Chamber of Commerce 2007 (noting that model business practices concerning IP include systematic measures to ensure that companies acquire and use IP of others with proper permissions and further "reasonable steps to identify and protect the company's own intellectual property"); Frankel et al. 2018: § 3:1 ("An intellectual property compliance program [should address] procedures needed to establish, maintain, exploit, and enforce the corporation's intellectual property rights as well as procedures needed to avoid violating the intellectual property rights of others.").

with in future activities through either IP licenses to gain use of the IP or altered practices that will not infringe the IP).

This short definition of successful IP compliance also addresses the forward-looking aims of IP compliance.[5] IP compliance programs are examples of preventive law practices targeting the future "IP health" of organizations.[6] Just as preventive medicine seeks to detect potential or developing health problems at early stages and to prevent further adverse impacts, IP compliance measures are aimed at detecting and addressing potential losses of valuable IP or potential conflicts of planned organizational activities with the IP rights of others.[7]

Early detection of potential IP problems gives firms the broadest possible means for dealing with them. On the positive side, identifying settings where IP is being or will be created can give organizations opportunities to determine how (or whether) they want to protect the IP and commercialize it, as well as to take steps to perfect their IP rights and to avoid forfeiture of valuable IP assets. On the negative side, early detection in planning stages of unauthorized use of other parties' IP gives firms the ability to seek advanced permission for such use (without the bargaining weakness of seeking permission while already being liable for past IP infringement). Early detection may also give firms the ability to take another tack altogether, as where a firm decides not to go forward with a project once it sees that the project is not profitable in light of its full IP costs or where a firm reformulates a project to use alternative IP without the need for dealing with a threatening IP rights holder. Expanding these types of advantageous decision choice to avoid (or at least minimize) future legal problems is a key objective of preventive law practices generally and of IP compliance programs in particular.

One further implication of the definition of IP compliance success above is that it suggests the boundaries for compliance activities. IP compliance serves to benefit organizational well-being. Particular compliance activities should adhere to this same benefit measure – that is, they should be cost-effective for the organization involved. Perfection in IP-related conduct is not the goal, only reasonable advancement of a party's IP-mediated interests as limited by the boundaries of cost-effective actions.[8] Hence, successful IP compliance involves forward-

[5] Preventing IP disputes is a primary goal of IP compliance programs. Analysts of IP risks have seen IP compliance programs as an affirmative form of "self-insurance" against IP claims, thereby providing an alternative to more traditional insurance policies covering IP-based claims. See Simensky and Osterberg 1999: 322: "It is axiomatic that the best way to limit one's potential liability is to take steps to insure that one does not become involved in a dispute in the first place. Thus, the first step a company should take to manage intellectual property risks is to initiate an effective intellectual property legal compliance program." Despite the clear potential for IP compliance programs to prevent future IP liabilities, many companies perceive only the benefits of such programs and adopt meaningful IP compliance programs once they have been stung by major IP liabilities. As noted by two specialists in IP litigation risks, "[t]hose who own intellectual property should initiate an effective intellectual property legal compliance program .... Unfortunately, many companies only create such compliance programs in response to litigation" (Magarick and Brownlee 2019: 3:§ 48:32 (quoting Fay and Frymark 2005)).

[6] See, e.g., Boyle 1998 ("One of the now popular methods for making preventive law real is the adoption of a compliance program.").

[7] Preventive law has always embraced the dual goals of cultivating legally mediated opportunities and avoiding legally dictated risks. As noted by Louis M. Brown (1995), the original advocate of preventive law as a framework for shaping future actions and related legal counseling, preventive law is "an effort to help people stay within the bounds of law (i.e. minimize the risk of legal trouble); and take advantage of legal opportunities (i.e. maximize the legal benefits)."

[8] In all areas of the law, successful compliance is recognized as the pursuit of reasonable law compliance, not perfect law compliance. This point is well understood in connection with compliance and ethics programs targeting criminal law compliance. Standards promulgated by the US Sentencing Commission (2018: §8B2.1) describe an effective program as including management practices "reasonably designed, implemented, and enforced so that the program is generally effective in preventing and detecting criminal conduct."

looking and cost-effective steps to gather information, evaluate its implications for both IP assets and liabilities, and make associated decisions about future organizational actions that will improve (or minimize harms to) the well-being of the organization at hand.

57.3 RELATION TO BROADER TYPES OF LAW COMPLIANCE SYSTEM

In serving the distinctive goals of IP compliance programs just described, organizations use many of the same compliance tools applied in other types of compliance program. Lessons learned from other compliance fields provide insights for parties operating IP compliance programs – particularly lessons from criminal law compliance where compliances measures have been under the longest development by managers and standards for such programs have been most thoroughly addressed by government officials.[9] However, these lessons (and the compliance practices they suggest) need always to be reshaped, both to bring them into the world of IP and to ensure that they serve the dual goals of building IP assets and avoiding IP liabilities.

In other fields like criminal law compliance, most compliance programs promote adherence to negative legal standards prohibiting certain actions.[10] The aim is to direct parties away from the prohibited actions, to help them understand how to do this, and to detect and react when they nonetheless undertake prohibited conduct. Many of the same techniques for directing organizational behaviors away from prohibited conduct can also be used to direct actions toward desired ends. In IP contexts, the types of compliance measure gaining acceptance in criminal law compliance can serve (with somewhat different content and focus) the dual objectives of directing organizational personnel toward IP asset creation and

[9] The development of law compliance programs in the criminal law sphere has a long history. In 1991, the US Sentencing Commission implemented standards that defined features of effective criminal law compliance programs and that provided significant criminal sentencing benefits to corporations and other organizations that maintained generally effective programs at the time of an organizational offense. *See* Desio 2003. Subsequently, other federal agencies developed standards based on the Sentencing Commission's criteria for effective compliance programs (Desio 2003). Private parties and industry groups also made significant efforts to develop and exchange information on best practices for complying with the Sentencing Commission's standards. *See* Desio 2003. Hence, the Sentencing Guidelines' standards for effective compliance programs have had broad and fundamentally important impacts on both government and private understanding of law compliance programs.
The Sentencing Commission itself assessed and revised its compliance program standards in 2004 through an extensive study conducted by a panel of government and private compliance specialists. The panel's report, in addition to containing recommended changes in compliance program standards that were largely adopted by the Sentencing Commission, contains extensive summaries of the evolving compliance program practices used by companies and other organizations to promote criminal law compliance. *See* Ad Hoc Advisory Group on the Organizational Sentencing Guidelines. 2003 (Richard S. Gruner served as a member of the Advisory Group that prepared this report).

[10] The avoidance of harmful organizational liability is seen by many parties as the main function of all types of compliance program. For example, this theme was adopted by the National Center for Preventive Law (NCPL) in the 1990s when it developed Corporate Compliance Principles to guide the creation and operation of compliance programs. The NCPL (1996) described compliance programs and their goals as follows:

> Carefully planned and implemented compliance programs can reduce [risks to companies from liability and reputational harm] by preventing illegal conduct and mitigating or eliminating punishments and liabilities for those offenses which still occur. Achieving and maintaining compliance can also produce other positive results. These include: increasing consumer and shareholder confidence, reducing the costs of doing business, improving relationships with investment bankers, commercial lenders and the stock and bond brokerage community, boosting management and employee morale, increasing profits, and cutting legal and administrative costs. The problem confronting most businesses now is not whether to adopt a compliance program, but rather how to establish and maintain such a program.

away from activities producing IP infringement liabilities. The teachings of techniques from experienced compliance fields like criminal law compliance inform effective practices in IP compliance.

Thus, in comparison to other compliance domains, IP compliance is both like other compliance fields (in sharing compliance techniques and the ability to prevent adverse organizational liabilities) and different from those fields (in using techniques derived from restrictive fields like criminal law compliance to serve positive ends by identifying and realizing IP asset-building and use opportunities).

57.4 IP COMPLIANCE METHODS

Compliance methods developed in other fields such as criminal law compliance can be used, with appropriate modifications, to (1) maximize IP asset-building and use opportunities and (2) prevent liability threats and conduct limitations based on IP rights of other parties. To simplify the discussion here, these dual aims of IP compliance programs will be discussed in terms of minimizing IP risks, with the relevant risks understood to include both risks of missing IP opportunities and further risks of organizational losses or constraints due to IP rights infringement.

IP compliance programs are specially focused quality control programs aimed at ensuring a very specific type of high-quality organizational performance – that is, performance that minimizes IP risks.[11] Techniques used in other quality control settings can be used with effect in the specific context of managing organizational IP performance. Experience with criminal law compliance programs has revealed the minimum features of effective quality control measures aimed at ensuring that organizational affairs generally comply with criminal laws. These minimum quality control measures constitute the minimum features of effective criminal law compliance programs given legal recognition in a number of corporate charging and sentencing contexts. Legal standards for effective compliance programs have been extended to a number of regulatory contexts as well. This chapter uses this framework drawn from standards for criminal law compliance programs to describe the minimum elements of parallel programs aimed at avoiding IP risks and maximizing organizational IP performance.

Overall, the elements of a successful compliance program – aimed at IP risks or any other type of legal threat – implement a learning process for managing organizational responses to legal risks. Compliance programs detect legal risks, direct organizational employees and other agents toward conduct minimizing those risks, monitor completion of the directed conduct, evaluate the sufficiency of the conduct to minimize the targeted risks, and revise the

[11] Compliance programs in all fields are examples of performance quality control programs. Appreciation of this allows organizational management principles and quality control experience from diverse fields to be brought to bear to guide the design and operation of law compliance programs. *See* Gruner 2018: § 15.01. In the specific setting of IP compliance, according to Simensky and Osterberg (1999: 324–5), the benefits of compliance programs include the following:

> Primarily, a company benefits when its [IP] compliance program highlights situations that are ripe for future legal troubles before they occur. Other significant benefits include: improved corporate image; reduced instances of findings of willful infringement by the business, its employees, contractors, agents, consultants, licensees, and franchisees; reduction in the cost of litigation as a result of a more streamlined process of gathering and producing evidence; reduction in the number of registration applications not timely filed; prevention of constructive abandonment of trademarks, and; reduction in the number of lost chances to augment the equity of the company's intellectual property portfolio.

compliance steps to achieve better results in future organizational activities. This type of "feedback" and learning cycle is actually a universal tool of organizational management, used in diverse settings to promote corporate aims from manufacturing quantity goals to marketing program successes.[12] Because they are based on long experience with well-tested management tools, IP compliance programs do not require creative management processes as much as extension of well-known organizational techniques to the specific ends of IP risks management.[13]

Existing legal standards for effective compliance programs – as well as guidance from management specialists on means to promote high-quality organizational performance in a wide variety of contexts – indicate that the following comprise the minimum features of generally effective IP compliance programs:[14]

1. An IP risk assessment (investigating the frequency and scope of organizational impacts from various IP risks and updated with corporate experience as unanticipated IP risks materialize); and
2. Systematic responses to the detected risks through IP compliance management programs involving seven key components:
   i) standards and procedures to minimize IP risks (including risks of missed opportunities to perfect, retain, or use IP interests);[15]
   ii) high-level oversight of IP-related organizational performance by senior organizational managers and a specific individual or individuals within senior organization management who is responsible for the entity's IP performance;
   iii) reasonable steps to exclude from top organizational management individuals who have ineffectively addressed IP risks;
   iv) reasonable efforts to communicate standards and methods for minimizing IP risks to organizational employees and agents (including training on IP standards and procedures);
   v) reasonable measures to audit, monitor, and evaluate whether IP risks are being successfully addressed (including efforts to periodically assess the adequacy of the organization's IP compliance program);
   vi) enforcement of IP standards and procedures through incentives and discipline; and
   vii) improvements in IP compliance measures following the detection of a mishandled IP risk or opportunity, including the completion of a reasonable evaluation of the

12 A wide variety of organizational quality control practices – and approaches to quality control management – can inform and guide IP compliance programs and similar programs in other legal fields. See, e.g., Gruner 2018: § 17.04 (describing how experience with product quality control measures can suggest parallel features of compliance management practices).

13 *See* Gruner 2018: § 15.02 (describing means to use organizational management principles to construct and evaluate organizational law compliance programs).

14 These essential components of IP compliance programs parallel, in the context of IP risk management, the features of minimally adequate criminal law compliance programs described in US Sentencing Commission 2018: §8B2.1. Other analysts have recognized that the compliance program standards in these Sentencing Guidelines provide valuable frameworks for designing IP compliance programs. *See* Carr, Morton and Furniss 2000: 200–9 (using federal Sentencing Guideline standards for compliance programs as a template for designing IP compliance programs addressing potential violations of the federal Economic Espionage Act). *See also* Gutterman 2018: § 1:3 (describing similar compliance activities to be undertaken as part of an IP management strategy for corporations and other organizations); Harris and Burgess 2003: 26–9 (describing features of IP compliance programs aimed at prevention of IP crimes).

15 Standards for IP handling and risk avoidance should address a number of dimensions of IP management, including procedures for obtaining, maintaining, exploiting and enforcing an organization's IP rights and for avoiding use and misappropriation of IP owned by other parties. *See* Frankel et al. 2018: §§ 3:1 to 3:141.

sources of the IP mishandling and means to prevent a repetition, steps to implement the identified improvements in IP compliance practices, and heightened monitoring to evaluate the sufficiency of the improved practices.

These practices are aimed at preventing both intentional disregard of IP risks and opportunities and inadvertent or unknowing losses of IP or failures to use IP interests to maximum organizational advantage. In the aggregate, they translate organizational interest in strong IP health and well-being into concrete organizational actions.

57.5 AN IP COMPLIANCE CASE STUDY: SOFTWARE LICENSE MANAGEMENT SYSTEMS

Some of the practical features of IP compliance programs are best illustrated by a case study of one example program. This section describes compliance program practices applied to the particular legal risks of software license management.

57.5.1 *Software Licensing Risk Assessment*

Proprietary software products produced by Microsoft and other vendors are licensed to users under copyright and trade secret licenses (Dawson, DeZabala and King 2017). One key goal of software IP compliance programs is to ensure that proper licenses are in place for software in use and that the duties under these licenses are met.[16]

In large organizations, the number and scope of such licenses are very complex. Assessments of needed licenses – including identifying both absent licenses that are needed and present licenses that are not needed – can be very difficult. Once the needed licenses at a given time are determined, further corporate administrative steps are required to obtain the licenses, ascertain conduct obligations under the licenses, complete payments and other actions required by the licenses, and periodically reassess the match between existing licenses and the software needs of the organization involved. All of these actions fall within the scope of IP compliance programs aimed at software license management.[17]

Preventing use of unlicensed software is another key objective of such compliance programs. Unlicensed software use represents potentially large financial and operational risks for organizations (Business Software Alliance 2019b). The use of unlicensed software (adopted with or without approval of company management) may be widespread in an organization, leading to hidden risks of widespread IP liability when past unlicensed use of the software surfaces and the company involved needs to pay damages for past IP misuse. In addition, uses of unlicensed software may lead to business interruptions where the use is discovered, a company is unable to come to licensing terms with the software's source (or cannot pay

[16] IP compliance programs concerning proprietary software are frequently focused on identifying and gaining the range of IP licenses needed to support a company's actual use of proprietary software along with payment of the full royalties due under these licenses. *See* Watts and Davis 2018; Microsoft Corporation 2004. A different form of IP compliance program (or component of a program) is sometimes focused on open source software and its use in organizations. These sorts of IP compliance programs are primarily concerned with tracking the use of software code and components covered by open source licenses and with ensuring that the use restrictions under open sources licenses are adhered to. *See* Copenhaver 2008; Haislmaier 2009.

[17] Processes for managing the initiation and administration of software licenses are sometimes part of broader software asset management (SAM) systems aimed at both identifying software needs and supplying corresponding resources (such as IP licenses). *See* Dawson, DeZabala and King 2017.

the amounts proposed to be charged for licensed use), and is no longer able to use software that is critical to a business function.

Finally, unlicensed software may raise further risks because it is either flawed or the bearer of affirmatively harmful malware (Business Software Alliance 2019b). Unlicensed software that has been pirated (that is, illegally copied or distributed) from a legitimate source may lack the types of software fixes and updates applied to properly licensed software, meaning that the unlicensed versions will contain dysfunctional components and incompatibilities with other software that have been fixed in licensed versions. In particular organizations, the flaws in unlicensed software may undercut the usefulness of the software and create corresponding organizational performance problems.

Even more damaging results may flow from malware carried forward into organizations with unlicensed software (Business Software Alliance 2019b). Empiric studies of unlicensed software have revealed that it is often contaminated with malware components added to the original proprietary software and distributed (often unknowingly) as the unlicensed software is copied and reused. The harms caused by malware located on organizational computers via unlicensed software can be very extensive. And, because they are not part of the product screening and update programs applied to licensed software, unlicensed programs are unlikely to be subject to the sorts of malware detection and screening that apply to licensed software.

These aspects of unlicensed software use define the legal (and operational) risks that are the targets of IP compliance programs aimed at software licensing. Software license management programs represent a specialized type of IP compliance program with narrowly focused IP risks and corresponding risk reduction methods.[18]

57.5.2 *Compliance Program Components for Managing Software Licensing in Media Replication*

The following discussion illustrates how software licensing risks can be matched with systematic practices to comprise an IP compliance program. The program is designed to prevent unlicensed software reproduction by parties engaging in recorded media production

[18] According to the Business Software Alliance (2019a), an effective compliance program for software licensing involves a "process of collecting, auditing, comparing, planning and executing" consisting of the following steps:

1. Find out what you have (number of PCs, servers, which software is installed, who is responsible for software purchases, etc.)
2. Conduct an audit/inventory (either using your own resources or using third party consultants) and prepare a detailed report
3. Compare information on existing licensing documentation to the audit report, revealing cases where you have a surplus or shortage of licenses
4. Address any surpluses or shortages of licenses to optimize costs and mitigate risks
5. Now that you have first addressed the immediate point-in-time issues, develop a plan for how you will standardize, use, control and purchase software. Specifically, your plan should focus on licensing management, which includes analysing your requirements, training your team on software use, planning technical support expenses cuts and regular software audits

. . .

[6.] [K]eep doing it. It's not a one-and-done action, but an ongoing cycle. This is critical as, not only is the first attempt never perfect, nothing is constant – everything, whether the industry you operate in, the technology you use or your own business, changes and evolves. The best way to keep it going and ensure that you continue to get the most value out of your software is to implement a continuous cycle of improvement.

Cf. Tomeny 2013 (describing similar features in a software license compliance system); Microsoft Corporation 2005 (same).

(Content Delivery & Security Association 2012). The practices described in this compliance program illustrate how one industry has operationalized the features of an effective IP compliance program, described in Section 57.4. The program described here includes compliance techniques that will be valuable not only in media reproduction settings but also, with appropriate refocusing to address other types of specific IP risk, as models for compliance programs aimed at other IP risks or even larger ranges of legal threats.

According to the Content Delivery & Security Association (CDSA), a model copyright and licensing verification program should include the following components.[19]

57.5.2.1 Personnel and Resources

The responsibility and authority of personnel involved with the compliance program should be defined in writing and should include at a minimum their authority to:

A. initiate any preventive actions to avoid nonconformities relating to program standards;
B. identify problems and recommend, initiate, provide and verify solutions;
C. identify, stop, segregate and dispose of nonconforming products or, in the event that the products have been manufactured, ensure that they are not shipped;
D. contact the relevant rights holder regarding nonconforming products.

Company management should appoint a program manager responsible for ensuring that operating systems, procedures, processes and documents are established and maintained in accordance with the compliance program. The program manager should report system performance for management review. Company managers should identify and provide resources for control, work performance and verification (including audits) in carrying out compliance program activities. Company managers should review compliance system performance at specified intervals to ensure continuing system effectiveness. Such performance reviews should be documented, with records kept in accordance with the compliance program standards. Company managers should establish and maintain a program manual to document the firm's compliance systems, procedures, processes, policies, responsibilities and authorities, and the firm's conformity to the CDSA Anti-Piracy & Compliance Program Standards.

57.5.2.2 Documents and Data Control

A company operating a copyright and licensing verification program should establish and maintain documented procedures to control all documents (paper or electronic) that relate to the program. The control procedures should address parties authorized to create or modify key documents, as well as means for recording changes to such documents and the reasons for the changes.

57.5.2.3 Product Inspections and Testing

The compliance program operator should establish and maintain procedures to ensure that copyright and licensing standards are being met, including proper licensing of any IP-protected materials being reproduced or used.

[19] The full model compliance program includes many detailed components; the account here describes key features of the program.

57.5.2.4 Identifying Conforming and Nonconforming Products

The compliance program operator should implement control procedures to ensure that unauthorized use of IP-protected materials does not occur. Once IP-protected materials without use authorizations are located, they should be identified as such and separated from authorized materials. Either the unauthorized materials should be destroyed or a specific plan should be put in place to ensure that they are not used until proper authorization is obtained.

57.5.2.5 Corrective and Preventive Actions

The compliance program operator should establish, maintain and implement documented procedures that ensure the documentation, implementation and effectiveness of corrective and preventive actions following incidents of detected misuse of IP-protected materials.

57.5.2.6 Records Retention

Records on IP licensing and the use of related materials should be kept for a period specified in the company's compliance program (generally, for a minimum of three years).

57.5.2.7 Internal Audit

The compliance program operator manufacturer should establish, maintain and implement internal auditing procedures to ensure that copyright observance and licensing activities comply with the CDSA Anti-Piracy & Compliance Program Standards. Results of audits should be recorded and reported to personnel having responsibility for the areas audited. Corrective activities following up on adverse audit findings should be recorded and evaluated for effectiveness. Results of internal audits, and a summary of the corrective and preventive actions planned and implemented, should be reviewed periodically by senior corporate management.

57.5.2.8 External Audits

Independent auditors, retained by CDSA, should audit a company's compliance procedures and documentation. If minor nonconformities with CDSA Anti-Piracy & Compliance Program Standards are found in an external audit, a company shall have thirty days to submit a corrective action report to the CDSA auditor. In the case of major or systemic nonconformities, the company, prior to the CDSA auditor returning for a required re-audit, must undertake a corrective action program. Successful completion of this audit shall result in the plant being certified for a six-month time period. At the end of the six-month period (six months after the initial certification), the company must undergo an external surveillance audit performed by a CDSA auditor. A successful six-month surveillance audit leads to certification for a period of one year. Thereafter, the company must undergo an annual external audit performed by a CDSA auditor. In addition, the manufacturer must conduct its own internal audits. CDSA reserves the right to conduct such external audits at intervals other than one year for specific reasons.

57.5.2.9 Anti-Piracy Training

A company operating a copyright and licensing compliance program should establish, maintain and implement procedures for anti-piracy training of personnel performing activities affecting the use of IP-protected materials. Records of all such training should be maintained for three years and should include the topic, date, place of training, the instructor's name(s) and the names of the individuals trained.

57.5.2.10 Anti-Piracy Guidelines

A company's copyright and licensing compliance program should require adherence to specific standards addressing procedures and approvals for transactions and activities with high risks of copyright infringement or other IP rights infringement. These procedures should be aimed at preventing infringement (particularly widespread infringement) through identification of IP-protected materials and either avoiding use and reproduction of such materials until appropriate authorizations have been secured or, if the materials have already been reproduced, sequestering the improperly copied materials until authorization is obtained (with destruction of the improperly copied materials to follow if permission to use them is not forthcoming).

57.6 SUMMARY OF PAST STUDIES OF IP COMPLIANCE

Past studies addressing IP compliance have approached the topic from several perspectives. Some treatments have examined the benefits of IP compliance programs and the major components needed to make such programs effective. Other works have described particular features of IP compliance programs without addressing the full range of practices needed to make these programs effective. Additional studies have considered specialized forms of IP compliance programs applicable to specific circumstances or industries. Yet additional studies have considered IP compliance as an adjunct to or component of anti-counterfeit goods programs. This section provides brief overviews of the past studies in this field.

57.6.1 *Guides to Constructing and Operating IP Compliance Programs*

Frankel et al. (2018) presents comprehensive discussions of procedures needed to establish, maintain, exploit and enforce a business's IP rights as well as procedures needed to avoid violating the IP rights of others.

Brownlee (2019) assesses systematic measures for retaining and expanding IP interests following corporate acquisitions of firms that include important IP rights.

Gutterman (2018) describes the key elements of an IP management strategy for corporations and other organizations. The discussion includes treatments of many specific IP-risk mitigation actions that should be included in IP compliance programs.

Simensky and Osterberg (1999) assesses the advantages of IP compliance programs and some of the key components of such programs. The authors consider IP compliance programs to be a form of affirmative "self-insurance" against IP-based legal claims.

Harris and Burgess (2003) describes recommended elements of compliance planning and compliance program designs for preventing IP crimes. Many of the compliance program features highlighted will apply equally well in broader compliance programs aimed at preventing and reducing civil liability claims based on IP misuse.

Carr, Morton and Furniss (2000) recommends elements of an IP compliance program aimed at preventing violations of the federal Economic Espionage Act (EEA). While the EEA primarily addresses trade secret misuse – and, hence, this article focuses primarily on compliance measures for preventing trade secret misuse – many of the compliance techniques described here will be valuable in all types of IP compliance program.

57.6.2 *Specific Components of IP Compliance Programs*

57.6.2.1 Conduct Codes Promoting IP Compliance

American Health Lawyers Association (2019) presents a model code of conduct to clarify practices and procedures concerning IP created and used by healthcare entities.

Hancock (2005) provides sample IP codes of conduct used by publicly traded companies. The codes were obtained through documents filed with the federal Securities and Exchange Commission (SEC) and recorded in the SEC's Electronic Data Gathering, Analysis, and Retrieval System (EDGAR).

57.6.2.2 IP-Focused Legal Audits

Gruner and Brunell (2018) describes systematic legal audits of IP practices aimed at identifying procedures that a business or other organization should adopt to best utilize its IP and to minimize its risk of liability for the use of the IP of others. These sorts of IP audits are at the core of management processes specifying (1) operating procedures with respect to IP, (2) when and where such procedures should be used and (3) means for improving such procedures in light of experience with their effectiveness (or lack of it).

Gutterman (2019) considers the importance of IP legal audits, particularly for high-technology companies that rely heavily on IP protections for business success. Discussions address the steps needed in regular audits to focus on the creation of IP assets and ownership rights therein, the procedures used to perfect and maintain all legal rights in the asset and the risk that the use of the assets might infringe upon the valid legal claims or the contractual rights of others.

Brownlee (2019) assesses the importance of IP audits in connection with corporate acquisitions. This work includes steps for systematic consideration of patent, trademark, domain name, copyright, database, semiconductor chip and trade secret assets.

57.6.3 *Specialized Forms of IP Compliance Programs*

57.6.3.1 Software Licensing Programs

Content Delivery & Security Association (2012) presents standards for copyright and licensing assurance compliance programs in firms reproducing IP-protected materials (such as software and movies) in DVDs and related products. The standards are modeled on the ISO 9000 Program concerning quality management and quality assurance.

57.6.3.2 Import Compliance Programs

Proctor (2019) describes the steps that companies should include in an import compliance program, including measures to ensure that imported items do not include infringing IP.

57.6.3.3 Anti-Counterfeit Programs

Programs to prevent acquisition or use of counterfeit goods (usually bearing fraudulently applied trademarks and potentially containing contents that infringe patents, copyrights and trade secrets) overlap in focus with programs aimed at preventing IP misuse. This subsection summarizes several works on anti-counterfeit goods programs.

57.6.3.3.1 PROGRAMS COMBATING COUNTERFEIT DRUGS Scheineson and Klinger (2005) describes the features of compliance programs for entities – including drug manufacturers and distributors – engaged in the marketing and supply of pharmaceutical drugs. The compliance programs addressed are aimed at ensuring compliance with applicable laws including prohibitions on the marketing of mislabeled or counterfeit drugs.

Freyer (1996: esp. 225–30, 234–40) evaluates the advantages and desirable features of compliance programs aimed at ensuring compliance with laws governing the sale and provision of pharmaceutical drugs and medical devices, including laws prohibiting sales of counterfeit drugs and medical devices.

57.6.3.3.2 PROGRAMS COMBATING OTHER COUNTERFEIT GOODS Kendall (2012) provides guidance to federal Department of Defense (DoD) suppliers on systematic steps for preventing delivery of counterfeit goods in performance of DoD supply contracts.

Livingston (2013) describes elements of compliance programs for preventing the delivery of counterfeit parts under supply contracts.

The National Defense Authorization Act for Fiscal Year 2012 is legislation requiring suppliers of electronic parts to the federal DoD to establish policies and procedures to eliminate counterfeit electronic parts from the defense supply chain.[20] Required systematic actions include provisions for (i) the training of personnel; (ii) the inspection and testing of electronic parts; (iii) processes to abolish counterfeit parts proliferation; (iv) mechanisms to enable traceability of parts; (v) use of trusted suppliers; (vi) the reporting and quarantining of counterfeit electronic parts and suspect counterfeit electronic parts; (vii) methodologies to identify suspect counterfeit parts and to rapidly determine if a suspect counterfeit part is, in fact, counterfeit; (viii) the design, operation and maintenance of systems to detect and avoid counterfeit electronic parts and suspect counterfeit electronic parts; and (ix) the flow down of counterfeit avoidance and detection requirements to subcontractors.

US Department of Defense (2014) specifies the required features of contractors' counterfeit electronic part detection and avoidance systems, indicating that such systems should include "risk-based policies and procedures" addressing, at a minimum, the following areas: (1) training of personnel; (2) inspection and testing of electronic parts, including criteria for acceptance and rejection; (3) processes to abolish counterfeit parts proliferation; (4) processes for maintaining electronic part traceability; (5) use of suppliers that are the original manufacturer, sources with the express written authority of the original manufacturer or current design activity, including an authorized aftermarket manufacturer or

[20] National Defense Authorization Act for Fiscal Year 2012 § 818(e) (Public Law 112–081).

suppliers that obtain parts exclusively from one or more of these sources; (6) reporting and quarantining of counterfeit electronic parts and suspect counterfeit electronic parts; (7) methodologies to identify suspect counterfeit electronic parts and to rapidly determine if a suspect counterfeit electronic part is, in fact, counterfeit; (8) design, operation and maintenance of systems to detect and avoid counterfeit electronic parts and suspect counterfeit electronic parts; (9) flow down of counterfeit detection and avoidance requirements; (10) a process for keeping continually informed of current counterfeiting information and trends; (11) a process for screening the Government-Industry Data Exchange Program (GIDEP) reports and other credible sources of counterfeiting information; and (12) control of obsolete electronic parts.

57.6.3.3.3 OTHER SPECIALIZED IP COMPLIANCE PROGRAMS Gollin (1991: esp. 229–33) describes the features of an environmental technology management program that includes features aimed at systematically maximizing IP opportunities and minimizing IP risks.

57.7 FUTURE IP COMPLIANCE DEVELOPMENT

Trends in other areas of law compliance management suggest some potentially valuable practices for future IP compliance development. This section briefly describes some of these developing compliance practices and their potential application to IP compliance.

57.7.1 *Monitoring and Auditing of Compliance Results*

Monitoring and evaluation of compliance program results (as opposed to just efforts to comply as part of those programs) are increasingly seen as core elements of compliance programs. The ultimate value of a compliance program lies in the legally beneficial behaviors that the program achieves. The proof of a high-quality compliance program accordingly requires the measurement and confirmation of high-quality results.

Many recently developed standards for evaluating compliance programs – both government and private criteria – emphasize the importance of continually improving compliance programs through assessment of results achieved and evaluation of program failures to learn how to make improvements. For example, the federal Department of Justice's standards for evaluating corporate programs for criminal law compliance emphasize that these programs should include reasonable steps to detect adverse program results such as criminal misconduct, evaluate the sources of misconduct and improve compliance programs in light of lessons learned (US Department of Justice 2019).

Limiting compliance program evaluations only to efforts made to comply with legal standards or to undertake legally desirable behavior raises several risks for organizations. First, this limited monitoring may just measure completion of compliance efforts mistakenly thought to be effective while leaving actual compliance problems unaddressed. Misconduct may slip by that was preventable (or at least containable in the early stages). Second, positive findings based on completed but ineffective efforts may lead to undue complacency and waste of compliance resources. Resources may be wasted on ineffective compliance efforts, while the need for different, more effective actions goes unaddressed. Directing compliance resources and actions to avoid these sorts of errors and waste requires that companies continuously monitor the relationships between compliance actions taken and results achieved.

Increased evaluation of IP management results in future IP compliance programs that have the potential to avoid these types of errors and waste. Evaluation of IP results can help companies gain the maximum benefits from IP management efforts and avoid waste on unproductive practices. Types of results monitoring practice already developed and implemented in criminal law compliance and other compliance settings may prove similarly desirable in IP compliance programs. Regular and detailed evaluation of IP problems (such as projects frustrated by unanticipated assertions of IP rights held by other parties) or audits of the handling of new and potentially valuable IP generated by operations producing creative products can ascertain whether present IP management practices are effective and avoid waste on ineffective actions. Such studies can also point to steps in company operations where better IP management was possible, thereby suggesting some of the features of improved IP program practices.

Because evaluation techniques for monitoring IP program impacts and results have the potential to benefit many IP producers and users, gaining improved understanding of these techniques is a highly significant future research target. Studies by management experts and IP specialists to develop and publicize techniques for critiquing and improving IP compliance results have the potential to increase both the effectiveness and the efficiency of IP compliance programs in advancing IP rights management.

57.7.2 *Computer-Enhanced Analytic Methods for Assessing IP Compliance*

Future techniques for evaluating IP management will benefit from ongoing changes and improvements in computer-based information gathering and analyses. Enhanced systems for information gathering, storage, analysis and reporting will enable many new methods for detecting illegal or otherwise harmful handling of IP, as well for monitoring the completion and results of activities mandated by IP compliance programs.

A significant range of computer-enhanced IP monitoring will benefit from data analytics applied to compliance management. Data analytics involves the detection of patterns of activities (or breaks in such patterns), where the aberrant or changed activities have operational significance (Chen 2019). In compliance contexts, aberrant activities may correspond to illegal conduct (or at least conduct raising sufficient risks of illegal actions to warrant further investigation). For example, as noted by Hui Chen, former Compliance Counsel to the federal Department of Justice, "When [companies] interpret [their] number and types of investigations over a certain time period to form inferences such as 'our cases involving breaches of financial control are on the rise,' [they] are already performing data analytics" (Chen 2019).

Growth in computer capabilities promises to strengthen data analytics as a future compliance tool. Compliance applications of data analytics will require companies to complete four underlying tasks: (1) selection of meaningful data metrics corresponding to compliance success or progress toward such success, (2) collection of data indicating whether or not the metrics are attained, (3) evaluations of collected data (often via computer-based systems) to assess results or progress against data metric standards and (4) reactions to negative evaluation results with appropriate follow-up investigations or changes in operating practices.

Potential future applications of data analytics in IP compliance settings include systems to detect both successes and failures in IP management. Systems measuring the completion of steps to perfect IP interests can confirm activities promoting IP rights perfection and strength.

Other systems can be aimed in the opposite direction – that is, at the detection of actions tending to promote or correlate with misuse of valuable IP rights.

Additional types of IP data analytics can monitor and evaluate IP compliance program activities, including the completion of required IP compliance program actions (such as completion of compliance-promoting employee training) or the failure to undertake required actions (such as the absence of regular compliance audits). Enhanced systems of this sort – enabled by increased computer resources and informed by the experience of organizations with data analytics in other operational and compliance settings – will aid organizations in both effective IP compliance program administration and the detection of potentially harmful IP-related practices.

57.7.3 *External Assessment and Certification of IP Compliance Program Effectiveness*

One additional trend seen in other compliance contexts that may affect future IP compliance programs involves the certification of program quality by independent certification agencies. Such certification processes are presently applicable to other types of compliance program. For example, the ISO 37001: Anti-Bribery Management System Standard (International Organization for Standardization 2016), in addition to specifying standards for companies to use internally in establishing, implementing, maintaining, reviewing and improving anti-bribery management systems, is structured to provide for certification of compliance with the Standard through reviews of company practices by accredited third-party certification agencies (Cottrell 2016).

Similar arrangements for certifying adherence of IP compliance programs with quality standards may have several desirable impacts on the development of such programs. First, certification processes (along with internal company audits and other self-evaluations preceding certification requests submitted to third-party agencies) may identify previously hidden weaknesses in IP management systems and expand opportunities for improvements. Second, companies may obtain marketing advantages from IP program certification by advertising their certification status to customers. Third, third-party certifications may aid companies in establishing the soundness of IP management processes and confirming the likely and continuing value of IP assets, thereby aiding in investment fundraising or other business transactions. Fourth, where companies have suffered from past IP management errors, certification of revised IP programs may help companies reestablish positive IP management reputations and regain the trust of both investors and potential business partners. In these ways, certification processes can have substantial impacts on both internal IP management and external business activities influenced by IP rights and assets.

57.8 SUMMARY

As the protectors of key assets in many companies, IP compliance programs are central management and legal features of diverse enterprises. In operating such programs, organizations can benefit greatly from the rapidly growing expertise of business and legal specialists concerning compliance programs in other fields. Future improvements of IP compliance programs can spring from two important sources: learning from compliance experience and developing new compliance methods tailored to the IP field.

Leaders of IP compliance programs should continue to look broadly at compliance program progress in other fields and to draw effective practices from those fields into the domain of IP rights management. Careful translation of methods from other compliance domains into IP compliance programs can gain firms the substantial benefits of rapid changes and improvements now surrounding compliance methods generally.

Program leaders should also be attentive to the distinctive features of IP compliance – particularly the potential of IP management to be constructive and to create important new business assets – and seek to develop additional compliance practices that are peculiar to IP. Through the development of distinctive methods for creating and using IP assets in positive ways, IP program leaders can ensure that IP management programs closely match the requirements and problems of specific IP standards and fields.

Through these two processes – looking to compliance developments generally and to IP needs specifically – IP program leaders can increase understanding and use of the full range of potentially beneficial methods for IP management and compliance program operation.

REFERENCES

Ad Hoc Advisory Group on the Organizational Sentencing Guidelines. 2003. *Advisory Group Report*. Washington, DC: US Sentencing Commission. www.ussc.gov/guidelines/organizational-guidelines/report-ad-hoc-advisory-group-organizational-sentencing-guidelines-october–7–2003.

American Health Lawyers Association. 2019. "Intellectual Property Policy." *In Health Law Practice Guide* 4:App. C–148.

Bochner, Steven E., and Susan P. Krause. 1989. "Intellectual Property Management and Board Liability." In *Securities Law Institute*. New York: Practising Law Institute.

Boyle, Gary W. 1998. "The Foundation of Preventive Law in Corporate America." *National Center for Preventive Law Essays*, www.preventivelawyer.org/main/default.asp?pid=essays/boyle.htm.

Brown, Louis M. 1995. "The Other Side of the Law." In *What Is Preventive Law?* Cyber Institute. www.cyberinstitute.com/preventivelaw/week1.htm.

Brownlee, L. M. 2019. "Post-Transaction Intellectual Property Management." In *IP Due Diligence in Corporate Transactions*, April 2019 Updates at §§ 13:55 to 13:117.

Business Software Alliance. 2019a. *Software Licensing Basics*, https://smeinfoportal.org/blog/software-licensing-basics/.

Business Software Alliance. 2019b. *The Software Asset Management Blueprint*, https://smeinfoportal.org/blog/the-software-asset-management-blueprint–2/.

Carr, Chris, Jack Morton and Jerry Furniss. 2000. "The Economic Espionage Act: Bear Trap or Mousetrap?" *Texas Intellectual Property Law Journal* 8: 159.

Chen, Hui. 2019. "Don't Let Your Compliance Program Fail Because You're Afraid of Data." *Bloomberg Law*, Feb. 12, https://huichenethics.files.wordpress.com/2019/02/afraidofdata.pdf.

Content Delivery & Security Association. 2012. *Copyright & Licensing Verification (CLV) Program Standards & Procedures*, www.mesalliance.org/wp-content/uploads/2016/04/CDSA-APCP-5-CLV-Standard-September-2012.pdf.

Copenhaver, Karen Faulds. 2008. "Managing Compliance with Open Source Software Licenses." *Practical Lawyer* 54: 21.

Cottrell, Eric. 2016. "ISO 37001 – The Potential Impact of the New International Anti-Bribery Management System Standard." *JD Supra*, Dec. 13, https://www.jdsupra.com/legalnews/iso-37001-the-potential-impact-of-the–69322/.

Dawson, Dave, Ted DeZabala and Joe King. 2017. "A Strategic Approach to Software Asset Management." CIO Insights and Analysis from Deloitte, https://deloitte.wsj.com/cio/2018/10/03/a-strategic-approach-to-software-asset-management/.

Desio, Paula. 2003. "An Overview of the Organizational Guidelines." In US Sentencing Commission. *Organizational Guidelines*. Washington, DC: US Sentencing Commission. www.ussc.gov/sites/default/files/pdf/training/organizational-guidelines/ORGOVERVIEW.pdf.

Fay, Erin, and Julie Frymark. 2005. "Businessowners Beware: You May Have Insurance, But Does It Cover Your Intellectual Property?" *Fire Casualty & Surety Bulletins* (April/May).

Frankel, William H., Christopher M. Dolan, Bradley G. Lane and Timothy K. Sendek. 2018. *Designing an Effective Intellectual Property Compliance Program*. Eagan, MN: Thompson Reuters.

Freyer, Dana H. 1996. "Corporate Compliance Programs for FDA-Regulated Companies." *Food & Drug Law Journal* 51: 225.

Gollin, Michael A. 1991. "Using Intellectual Property to Improve Environmental Protection." *Harvard Journal of Law & Technology* 4: 193.

Gruner, Richard S. 2018. *Corporate Criminal Liability and Prevention*. New York: Law Journal Press.

Gruner, Richard S., and Norman E. Brunell. 2018. "Goals of Intellectual Property Audits." In *The Legal Audit: Corporate Internal Investigation*, edited by Louis M. Brown, Anne O. Kandel and Richard S. Gruner. Eagan, MN: Thompson Reuters.

Gruner, Richard S., Shubha Ghosh and Jay Kesan. 2018. *Transactional Intellectual Property: From Startups to Public Companies*, 4th ed. Durham, NC: Carolina Academic Press.

Gutterman, Alan S. 2018. "Business Uses of Intellectual Property Rights – Value and Uses of Intellectual Property Rights." *Corporate Counsel's Guide to Technology Management & Transactions* 1 Dec. 2018 Updates at § 1:3.

Gutterman, Alan S. 2019. "Executive Summary for Clients Regarding Intellectual Property Audits." *Business Transactions Solutions*. April 2019 Updates at § 206:44.

Haislmaier, Jason. 2009. "Practical Strategies for Developing Open Source Compliance Programs: Why Compliance (Increasingly) Matters." *Practical Lawyer* 55: 45.

Hancock, William A. 2005. "Drafting Intellectual Property Provisions for Codes of Conduct." *Intellectual Property Counselor* (Nov.).

Harris, Ray K., and James D. Burgess. 2003. "Compliance Planning for Intellectual Property Crimes." *Buffalo Intellectual Property Law Journal* 2: 1.

International Chamber of Commerce. 2007. *Model Intellectual-Property Guidelines for Business*. Paris: International Chamber of Commerce. www.wipo.int/edocs/mdocs/sme/en/wipo_icc_smes_08/wipo_icc_smes_08_topic03-related2.pdf.

International Organization for Standardization. 2016. *ISO 37001:2016 Anti-Bribery Management Systems – Requirements with Guidance for Use*, www.iso.org/obp/ui/#iso:std:iso:37001:ed-1:v1:en.

Kendall, Frank (Acting Under Secretary of Defense). 2012. *Overarching DoD Counterfeit Prevention Guidance*, www.acq.osd.mil/log/SCI/.anti-counterfeit.html/Counterfeit-Prevention-Guidance.pdf.

Livingston, Henry. 2013. "Compliance Programs for Counterfeit Parts Avoidance and Detection." *Contract Management*, May: 46.

Magarick, Pat, and Ken Brownlee. 2019. "Intellectual Property." In *Casualty Insurance Claims*, 4th ed. May 2019 Update, 3:§ 48:32. Eagan, MN: Thompson Reuters.

Microsoft Corporation. 2004. *A Guide to Software Asset Management*, http://download.microsoft.com/documents/australia/piracy/MIC035_SAM_Guide_FINAL.pdf.

Microsoft Corporation. 2005. *Software Asset Management (SAM) Implementation Guide*, http://download.microsoft.com/download/f/8/5/f859245b-f740-4168-8dbb-a92d72a62f6d/samguide.pdf.

National Center for Preventive Law. 1996. *Corporate Compliance Principles*. San Diego, CA: National Center for Preventive Law. www.preventivelawyer.org/content/pdfs/corporate.pdf.

Proctor, Melissa. 2019. "Core Elements of an Import Compliance Program." *Westlaw Practice Notes*, www.westlaw.com/w-005-2872?transitionType=Default&contextData=(sc.Default)&VR=3.0&RS=cblt1.0.

Scheineson, Marc J., and Shannon Thyme Klinger. 2005. "Lessons from Expanded Government Enforcement Efforts Against Drug Crime." *Food & Drug Law Journal* 60: 11–14.

Simensky, Melvin, and Eric C. Osterberg. 1999. "The Insurance and Management of Intellectual Property Risks." *Cardozo Arts & Entertainment Law Journal* 17: 321.

Tomeny, John. 2013. "Software License Compliance: Five Essential Steps." *Sassafras Software News*, Nov. 22, https://web.archive.org/web/20180813041551/www.sassafras.com/software-license-compliance/.

United States Department of Defense. 2014. Defense Federal Acquisition Regulation Supplement: Detection and Avoidance of Counterfeit Electronic Parts. 79 FR 26092–01 (May 6).

United States Department of Justice. 2019. *Evaluation of Corporate Compliance Programs* (April 2019), www.justice.gov/criminal-fraud/page/file/937501/download.

United States Sentencing Commission. 2018. *Sentencing Guidelines Manual*. Washington, DC: United States Sentencing Commission.

Watts, Stephen, and Scott Davis. 2018. "Software License Management (SLM) Explained." *The Business of IT Blog*, Feb. 5, www.bmc.com/blogs/software-license-management/.

58

Insider Trading Compliance Programs

Stephen M. Bainbridge

Abstract: "A significant purpose of the Exchange Act was to eliminate the idea that use of inside information for personal advantage was a normal emolument of corporate office."[1] In pursuit of that goal, federal law creates significant incentives for corporations to adopt policies designed to prevent illegal trading by insiders. Such policies protect the insiders by providing guidance as to when trading is least likely to result in liability. Given the severe penalties for inside trading, and the inevitable temptation to profit from access to inside information, such policies are necessary to, in a sense, protect insiders from themselves. Even more important, however, such policies also protect the issuer itself from potential controlling person liability. Not surprisingly, perhaps, most public corporations have adopted such policies. This chapter provides an overview of corporate insider trading compliance programs. It sets out the basic legal framework of the federal insider trading prohibition. It then reviews the reasons why corporations adopt compliance programs. The chapter next reviews the basic elements of an insider trading compliance program. Finally, the chapter examines the special case of Rule 10b5-1 compliance programs.

58.1 INTRODUCTION

"A significant purpose of the Exchange Act was to eliminate the idea that use of inside information for personal advantage was a normal emolument of corporate office."[2] In pursuit of that goal, federal law creates significant incentives for corporations to adopt policies designed to prevent illegal trading by insiders. Such policies protect the insiders by providing guidance as to when trading is least likely to result in liability. Given the severe penalties for inside trading, and the inevitable temptation to profit from access to inside information, such policies are necessary to, in a sense, protect insiders from themselves. Even more important, however, such policies also protect the issuer itself from potential controlling person liability. Not surprisingly, perhaps, most public corporations have adopted such policies (Steinberg and Fletcher 1994:1828).

[1] *Dirks* v. *SEC*, 463 U.S. 646, 653 n.10 (1983).

[2] See note 1.

58.2 THE LEGAL FRAMEWORK

58.2.1 *The Federal Prohibition of Insider Trading*

Under current federal law, there are three basic theories under which trading on inside information becomes unlawful.[3] The disclose or abstain rule and the misappropriation theory were created by the courts under § 10(b) of the Securities Exchange Act of 1934 ("Exchange Act") and Rule 10b–5 thereunder. Pursuant to its rule-making authority under Exchange Act § 14(e), the SEC has also adopted Rule 14e–3 to specifically proscribe insider trading involving information relating to tender offers.

58.2.1.1 The Disclose or Abstain Rule

In a pair of cases in the early 1980s, *Chiarella* v. *United States* and *Dirks* v. *SEC*,[4] the US Supreme Court held that inside traders could not be held liable merely because they had more information than other investors in the marketplace. Instead, liability could be imposed only if the defendant was subject to a duty to disclose prior to trading and failed to do so. In turn, the requisite duty to disclose arises only where the potential inside trader owes a preexisting fiduciary duty or similar relationship of trust and confidence to the persons with whom they will trade. If an insider subject to such a duty possesses material nonpublic information, the insider must disclose that information before trading – which normally will be prohibited by agency law duties of confidentiality – or abstain from trading (Bainbridge 1999:1608–9).

Under *Chiarella* and *Dirks*, the prohibition of insider trading is not limited to true insiders, such as officers, directors, and controlling shareholders, but also picks up corporate outsiders in two important ways. First, the prohibition applies to a wide variety of nominal outsiders whose relationship with the issuer is sufficiently close to the issuer of the affected securities to justify treating them as "constructive insiders." The outsider must obtain material nonpublic information from the issuer. The issuer must expect the outsider to keep the disclosed information confidential. Finally, the relationship must at least imply such a duty. If these conditions are met, the putative outsider will be deemed a "constructive insider" and subject to the disclose or abstain rule in full measure.[5]

The rule also picks up so-called "tippees," who are outsiders who receive inside information from either true insiders or constructive insiders. There are a number of restrictions on tippee liability, however. Most important for present purposes, the tippee's liability is derivative of the tipper's, "arising from his role as a participant after the fact in the insider's breach of a fiduciary duty."[6] As a result, the mere fact of a tip is not sufficient to result in liability. What is proscribed is not merely a breach of confidentiality by the insider but, rather, a breach of the duty of loyalty imposed on all fiduciaries to avoid personally profiting from information entrusted to them. Thus, looking at objective criteria, the courts must determine whether the insider personally will benefit, directly or indirectly, from his or her

[3] Although insider trading originally was governed in the United States by state corporate law, and those state rules remain on the books, federal law has long since supplanted state law in this area (Bainbridge 2014:11–20). Insider trading may also violate other federal statutes, such as the mail and wire fraud laws, which are beyond the scope of this chapter (Wang 2015).

[4] *Chiarella* v. *United States*, 445 U.S. 222 (1980); *Dirks* v. *SEC*, 463 U.S. 646 (1983).

[5] *Dirks*, 463 U.S. at 655 n.14.

[6] Ibid., at 659.

disclosure. So once again, a breach of fiduciary duty is essential for liability to be imposed: a tippee can be held liable only when the tipper has breached a fiduciary duty by disclosing information to the tippee, and the tippee knows or has reason to know of the breach of duty.[7]

58.2.1.2 Rule 14e–3

Rule 14e–3 prohibits insiders of the bidder and target from divulging confidential information about a tender offer to persons who are likely to violate the rule by trading on the basis of that information: "A person violates Rule 14e–3(d) when he communicates to another person material nonpublic information acquired from an insider relating to a tender offer under circumstances where it is reasonably foreseeable that such communication is likely to result in unlawful trading."[8] The rule also, with certain narrow and well-defined exceptions, prohibits any person who possesses material information relating to a tender offer by another person from trading in target company securities if the bidder has commenced or has taken substantial steps toward commencement of the bid. Fisch (1991:251) explains that Rule 14e-3

> regulates trading whenever a bidder has either taken substantial steps to commence or has commenced a tender offer. Absent public disclosure, the rule prohibits trading by anyone who is in possession of material nonpublic information concerning the offer and who knows or has reason to know that the information came from the bidder or the target company, directly or indirectly. The bidder is exempted from this prohibition.

Rule 14e-3 differs importantly from the prohibition under Rule 10b-5. In particular, Rule 14e–3 prohibits insider trading "without requiring a showing that the trading at issue entailed a breach of fiduciary duty."[9] Some courts and commentators therefore argued that the SEC lacked authority to adopt the Rule. In *United States* v. *O'Hagan*, however, the Supreme Court rejected those arguments, holding that the SEC, pursuant to its authority under Exchange Act § 14 to "define ... such acts and practices as are fraudulent" in connection with a tender offer, may prohibit that acts are not themselves fraudulent under common law or § 10(b) of Securities Exchange Act, if prohibition is "reasonably designed to prevent acts and practices that are fraudulent."[10] According to the Court, Rule 14e-3 constituted "a 'means reasonably designed to prevent' fraudulent trading on material, nonpublic information in the tender offer context."[11]

Note that the Rule's scope is very limited. One prong of the Rule (the prohibition on trading while in possession of material nonpublic information) is not triggered until the offeror has taken substantial steps toward making the offer. More important, both prongs of the Rule are limited to information relating to a tender offer. As a result, most types of inside information remain subject to the duty-based analysis of *Chiarella* and its progeny.

58.2.1.3 Misappropriation

Like the traditional disclose or abstain rule, the misappropriation theory requires a breach of fiduciary duty before trading on inside information becomes unlawful. It is not unlawful, for

7 *Salman* v. *U.S.*, 137 S. Ct. 420, 423 (2016).
8 *SEC* v. *Falbo*, 14 F. Supp. 2d 508, 525 (S.D.N.Y. 1998).
9 *U.S.* v. *O'Hagan*, 521 U.S. 642, 666–7 (1997).
10 Ibid., at 673.
11 Ibid., at 672.

example, for an outsider to trade on the basis of inadvertently overheard information.[12] The fiduciary relationship in question, however, is a quite different one. Under the misappropriation theory, the defendant need not owe a fiduciary duty to the investor with whom he or she trades. Nor does he or she have to owe a fiduciary duty to the issuer of the securities that were traded. Instead, the misappropriation theory applies when the inside trader violates a fiduciary duty owed to the source of the information. The Supreme Court validated the misappropriation theory in *U.S.* v. *O'Hagan*.[13]

58.2.2 *Control Person Liability*

Exchange Act § 20(a) provides that any "person who, directly or indirectly, controls any person liable under any provision of this chapter or of any rule or regulation thereunder shall also be liable jointly and severally with and to the same extent as such controlled person to any person to whom such controlled person is liable . . ., unless the controlling person acted in good faith and did not directly or indirectly induce the act or acts constituting the violation or cause of action." Both liability of the controlled person to private persons and the SEC can trigger controlling person liability.

The Act does not define what constitutes control for this purpose. In *Brown* v. *Enstar Group*,[14] the court defined a controlling person as someone who has "the power to control the general affairs of the entity primarily liable at the time the entity violated the securities laws . . . [and] had the requisite power to directly or indirectly control or influence the specific corporate policy which resulted in the primary liability." The court noted an alternative test used by the Eighth Circuit, which requires a showing that the allegedly controlling person actually exercised the power to control the primarily liable defendant and further noted that other courts merely require the abstract ability to control.[15]

Because the purpose of controlling person liability is to encourage employers and the like to supervise their employees so as to prevent violations by the latter, there is no need to show that the controlling person was involved in the wrongful conduct. As the Eighth Circuit held in *Martin* v. *Shearson Lehman Hutton*,[16] for example, liability does "not depend on the controlling person's having exercised control over the particular transaction that gave rise to the violation .... Shearson had the ability to discipline O'Leary's conduct, and it was this conduct that gave rise to the loss." Similarly, in *In re Initial Public Offering Sec. Litig.*,[17] the Southern District of New York held that "culpable participation" is not required for the controlling person to be liable under § 20(a).

Good faith on the part of the controlling person is an affirmative defense under § 20(a) (*Frank* v. *Dana Corp.*).[18] In order to establish the good faith defense, the controlling person first must show that it did not induce the primary actor's violations. The controlling person then must show that it maintained and enforced a reasonable and proper system of supervision and internal control over the pertinent personnel (*SEC* v. *First Jersey Securities*).[19]

12 *SEC* v. *Switzer*, 590 F. Supp. 756, 766 (W.D. Okla. 1984).
13 *O'Hagan*, 521 U.S. 642 (1997).
14 *Brown* v. *Enstar Group, Inc.*, 84 F.3d 393, 396 (11th Cir. 1996), cert. denied, 519 U.S. 1112 (1997).
15 Ibid., at 396.
16 *Martin* v. *Shearson Lehman Hutton, Inc.*, 986 F.2d 242 (8th Cir. 1993), cert. denied, 510 U.S. 861 (1993).
17 *In re Initial Public Offering Sec. Litig.*, 241 F. Supp. 2d 281, 392–97 (S.D.N.Y. 2003).
18 *Frank* v. *Dana Corp.*, 646 F.3d 954 (6th Cir. 2011).
19 *SEC* v. *First Jersey Securities, Inc.*, 101 F.3d 1450, 1473 (2d Cir.1996).

In 1988, the Insider Trading and Securities Fraud Enforcement Act (ITSFEA) further revised controlling person liability in insider trading cases.[20] On the one hand, it extended the Insider Trading Sanctions Act of 1984 (ITSA) treble money penalty to controlling persons. On the other hand, before an ITSA penalty could be imposed on a controlling person, ITSFEA required the SEC to show that the controlling person "knew or recklessly disregarded the fact that such controlled person was likely to engage in the act or acts constituting the violation and failed to take appropriate steps to prevent such act or acts before they occurred" or, in the case of a broker or dealer, that the controlling person knowingly or recklessly failed to establish, maintain, or enforce "insider trading prevention compliance programs that such failure substantially contributed to or permitted the occurrence of the act or acts constituting the violation."

58.3 THE RATIONALE FOR COMPLIANCE PROGRAMS

As we have seen, the good faith defense available under § 20(a) "provides an incentive [for issuers] to implement procedures to preserve confidential information and to deter insider trading" (Steinberg and Fletcher 1994:1786). The incentive to adopt such compliance programs was enhanced following the 1988 adoption of ITSFEA, because adoption and effective implementation of a reasonable compliance program make it significantly more difficult for the SEC to show that the issuer acted recklessly and/or failed to take appropriate steps with respect to potential illegal trading by its insiders. Accordingly, good corporate practice mandates creation and rigorous enforcement of effective corporate compliance programs intended to prevent insider trading by officers and other employees of the issuer: "given the astronomical liability exposure and the emergence of organizational compliance programs directed against insider trading as an industry norm, the absence of a reasonably effective compliance program in this context makes little sense" (Steinberg and Fletcher 1994:1786).

A further incentive for such programs is provided by the U.S. Sentencing Guidelines, which provide for a penalty mitigation if an organization convicted of a crime had an effective compliance and ethics program. In order to get the benefit of that mitigation, the Sentencing Guidelines require that the organization "shall" meet various requirements, such as establishing "standards and procedures to prevent and detect criminal conduct" (U.S. Sentencing Commission 2016: § 8B2.1(b)(1)). To be sure, the Sentencing Guidelines are not mandatory and, moreover, come into play only if an organization faces criminal charges. The Guidelines, however, have been a highly influential motivator for corporate governance and compliance reform. In Chancellor Allen's well-known *Caremark* decision, which laid the legal foundation for the directors' duty to ensure that their corporation has adequate law compliance programs, for example, he emphasized the role of the Guidelines in providing "powerful incentives for corporations today to have in place compliance programs to detect violations of law, promptly to report violations to appropriate public officials when discovered, and to take prompt, voluntary remedial efforts."[21] The Guidelines thus served as one of the developments he cited as justifying recognizing the board of directors' "duty to attempt in good faith to assure that a corporate information and reporting system, which the board concludes is adequate, exists . . .."[22]

20 15 U.S.C. § 78 u–1(a)(3).
21 *In re Caremark Intern. Inc. Derivative Litig.*, 698 A.2d 959, 969 (Del. Ch. 1996).
22 Ibid., at 970.

As Barnard (1999:987) explained, Chancellor Allen pointed to the "powerful incentives" provided by the Sentencing Guidelines and argued "that 'any rational person attempting in good faith to meet an organizational governance responsibility' must take those incentives into account"). Professor Barnard further noted that Chancellor Allen could have cited other federal statutes in support of his decision, "including the Foreign Corrupt Practices Act of 1977 (FCPA), the Insider Trading and Securities Fraud Enforcement Act of 1988 (ITSFEA), and the Private Securities Litigation Reform Act of 1995 (PSLRA)," all of which "also impose obligations on companies to have in place data gathering and reporting programs aimed at specific forms of misconduct" (Barnard 1999:989). In addition, one might now add the mandatory compliance and governance provisions imposed by Sarbanes-Oxley and Dodd-Frank (Park 2017:160–1).

Another consideration is that evidence of insider transactions is highly relevant to private securities litigation. Public corporations, especially in technology sectors, have become highly vulnerable to such litigation. A technology corporation that fails to meet its quarterly earnings projection will experience a drop in its stock price when that news is announced, and often will be sued shortly thereafter for fraud under Rule 10b–5.

In 1995, Congress adopted the Private Securities Litigation Reform Act (PSLRA) to curtail what Congress believed was a widespread problem of merit-less strike suits.[23] Of particular relevance to insider trading compliance programs, one of the PSLRA's provisions established a new (and arguably higher) pleading standard with respect to the scienter element of Rule 10b–5, requiring that a complaint detail facts giving rise to a "strong inference" of scienter.[24]

Post-PSLRA, plaintiffs' securities lawyers began routinely seeking to satisfy the scienter pleading standard by alleging that insiders sold shares in suspicious amounts and/or at suspicious times. Insider sales supposedly provided inferential evidence that senior management knew that earnings forecasts would not be met and sold to avoid the price drop that follows from announcements of lower than expected earnings. Evidence that transactions took place during a trading window established by a corporate insider trading compliance program will help rebut claims that the insider transactions established the existence of scienter.

In addition, insider selling activity can be used as evidence that the nonpublic information in question was material. Finally, the board of directors may have a state law fiduciary duty under *Caremark* to ensure that the corporation has adopted an insider trading compliance program.

58.4 BASIC ELEMENTS OF AN ISSUER'S COMPLIANCE PROGRAM

Insider trading compliance programs commonly have two components. First, corporate policies commonly limit trading by insiders to specified time periods. Second, at least as to directors and Section 16 officers, corporate insider trading compliance programs commonly require preapproval of proposed transactions by a specified compliance officer. As a matter of good corporate practice, an issuer's insider trading compliance program commonly will apply to any and all transactions in any of the issuer's securities, including not just common stock but also preferred stock, convertible debentures, options, warrants, and any derivatives.[25]

23 Pub. L. 104–67, 109 Stat. 737 (1995).
24 15 U.S.C. § 78 u–4(b)(2).
25 Issuer compliance with Regulation FD's prohibition of selective disclosure is outside the scope of this chapter.

58.4.1 Timing

As a matter of good corporate practice, an insider trading compliance program should create prophylactic rules governing the timing of insider transactions. In *SEC* v. *Texas Gulf Sulphur Co.*,[26] the Second Circuit established a rule that an insider who possesses material nonpublic information may not trade until such information has been widely disseminated. At a minimum, the court opined, insiders therefore must wait until the news could reasonably be expected to appear over the Dow Jones broad tape – the news service that transmits investment news to brokers and investment professionals.

While the *Texas Gulf Sulphur* standard works well for the sort of dramatic, one-time event news at issue there, it works less well for the more mundane sorts of nonpublic information to which insiders routinely have access. An issuer always has undisclosed information about numerous different aspects of its business. By the time all of that information has been disseminated publicly, moreover, new undisclosed information doubtless will have been developed. In response to this concern, firms should develop policies limiting the periods within which insiders may trade.

Prophylactic trading restrictions of this sort typically are tied to the company's periodic disclosure process. Per SEC regulations, public corporations must send an annual report to the shareholders and also file with the SEC a Form 10–Q after each of the first three quarters of their fiscal year and a Form 10–K after year's end. Because of the substantial and wide-ranging disclosures required in these reports, which are publicly available, there is a relatively low probability that an insider who trades during the time immediately following their dissemination will be deemed to have traded on material nonpublic information. As *Texas Gulf Sulphur* suggests, however, the insider may not trade the moment the report is disseminated. Instead, the insider must wait until the market has had time to digest the report.

Corporate insider trading compliance policies typically create a "trading window" during which insiders are affirmatively permitted to trade. The window commonly opens a day or two after filing of the periodic report and closes a specified number of days later (commonly ten to thirty) (Dye 2000). The premise underlying the delay between the release of operating results and the opening of the trading window a day or two later is that it takes time for information to be absorbed by the marketplace. As we have seen, providing the market with such an opportunity is effectively mandated by *Texas Gulf Sulphur*.

A corporate compliance program establishing a trading window, of course, may not trump the federal securities laws. Because corporations generally do not have an affirmative duty to disclose information simply because it is material, there will be many instances where insiders have access to material information that is not yet ripe for disclosure. An insider who possesses material information that has not been disclosed must refrain from trading at all times – whether or not a trading window is open. As a matter of good corporate practice, public corporations should prohibit trading during an otherwise open trading window whenever insiders have access to undisclosed material nonpublic information even though the company has timely released its financial operating results in a periodic disclosure statement. This is referred to as "closing the window" or as a "blackout period." The window can be closed either through a general announcement that trading should not occur or by declining to preclear specific proposed transactions.

A trading window is appropriately closed during the period prior to the announcement of a proposed merger or acquisition or the announcement of a significant joint venture or other

[26] *SEC* v. *Texas Gulf Sulphur Co.*, 401 F.2d 833, 854 (2d Cir.), cert. denied, 394 U.S. 976 (1968).

strategic partnering relationship. Because the insider trading prohibition requires the insider to either disclose the information or abstain from trading, and because the insider has no right to disclose confidential corporate information, the insider is effectively obliged to comply with a company-imposed closure and refrain from trading during the period the issuer chooses to keep the information confidential.

A trading window approach contemplates a limited period in which insiders are permitted to trade, while prohibiting them from trading outside that period. In contrast, some corporations adopt so-called "blackout periods" during which insiders are prohibited from trading. A corporation might, for example, adopt a policy prohibiting insiders from trading during the period immediately prior to dissemination of a quarterly or annual report. Steinberg and Fletcher (1994:1832) suggest that issuers adopt a blackout period prohibiting trading by officers and directors "three weeks before and forty-eight hours after public announcement (and dissemination) of the company's earnings." Outside the blackout period, insiders are presumptively free to trade, although transactions by officers and directors should be precleared on a case-by-case basis as described in Section 58.4.2.

An effective blackout policy obviously must preclude insiders from trading stock they hold directly. In order to ensure compliance, however, it should also apply to stock held indirectly, such as stock held in a 401(k) plan or other employee benefit program.

Abuse of just such a blackout policy was one of the most unsavory features of the infamous Enron scandal. As Enron was going down the tubes, rank-and-file Enron employees were prevented from selling Enron stock held in their 401(k) plans during a lengthy blackout period imposed while the plan changed administrators. At the same time, however, top Enron executives were selling large amounts of stock they owned directly.

Section 306 of the Sarbanes-Oxley Act was adopted in direct response to this part of the Enron saga. Under it, directors and executive officers of a corporation are forbidden from trading any of their company's equity securities during any blackout period in which 50 percent or more of the issuer's employees are banned from trading stocks held in pension and benefit accounts.[27] If an executive officer or director violates the trading ban, the company can sue to recover any profit the executive earns from the trade. If the company fails to do so, § 306 expressly authorizes shareholders of the company to sue derivatively on the company's behalf to force the executive to disgorge profits.

58.4.2 *Preclearance*

Many commentators argue that, as a matter of good corporate practice, the issuer should require preclearance of trading by corporate directors and § 16 officers even during an otherwise open trading window (Dye 2000:1065; Steinberg and Fletcher 1994:1832). Nonofficer employees are typically exempted from the preclearance requirement. In my opinion, the greater access of corporate directors and § 16 officers to material nonpublic information mandates the adoption of such policies as a matter of good corporate practice.

Corporate compliance programs directed at insider trading by directors and officers in fact customarily include a requirement for preclearance of their transactions by a specified corporate official. Typically, the compliance officer will be a very senior corporate officer,

[27] As the Eastern District Court of Pennsylvania held in *Neer* v. *Pelino* (389 F. Supp. 2d 648 (E.D. Pa. 2005)), § 306 "makes it unlawful for directors or executive officers to buy or sell any of the issuer's equity securities during a pension fund blackout period if such securities were acquired in connection with the director or executive officer's employment." Ibid., at 654.

such as the general counsel, corporate secretary, or chief financial officer. As explained by Scott Killingsworth, a partner in the corporate and technology group at Powell Goldstein, "we'll give somebody a vice president's title and call him chief compliance officer or in most cases it's going to be the general counsel or the CFO or chief administrative officer taking on a second job" (Panel Discussion 2008: 558).

A director or officer wishing to trade in the company's securities should notify the compliance officer one or more business days before the proposed transaction is to be effected. In a trading window-based program, the compliance officer may disapprove the proposed transaction even though the trading window is open.

Clearly, the compliance officer should not approve a transaction when the insider seeking approval is known to possess material nonpublic information. If the compliance officer is not a lawyer trained in insider trading jurisprudence, it will be appropriate for the officer to consult knowledgeable counsel in close cases, because ambiguities in the law of insider trading can make resolving close cases difficult (Anderson 2016: 289).

As a matter of sound corporate practice, moreover, it would be appropriate for the compliance officer to disapprove a proposed transaction where there is material nonpublic information presently unknown to the insider requesting approval but to which that insider might have access. Indeed, because insider trading compliance programs have such a substantial prophylactic component, it would be appropriate for the compliance officer to disapprove a transaction even where the insider in question does not have authorized access to the material nonpublic information in question. Disapproval of a proposed transaction under such circumstances is appropriate because (1) it prevents subsequent litigation of the question "what did the insider know and when did he/she know it?" and (2) insiders without authorized access to nonpublic information nevertheless often come into possession of such information inadvertently or surreptitiously.

58.4.3 *Insulation Walls*

Sound compliance programs should include insulation walls so that only persons with need for material nonpublic information have access to such information. Such walls were formerly known in colloquial legal speech as "Chinese walls." As a California appellate judge aptly noted, however:

> "Chinese Wall" is [a] piece of legal flotsam that should be emphatically abandoned. The term has an ethnic focus that many would consider a subtle form of linguistic discrimination. Certainly, the continued use of the term would be insensitive to the ethnic identity of the many persons of Chinese descent. . . .
>
> Aside from this discriminatory flavor, the term "Chinese Wall" is being used to describe a barrier of silence and secrecy . . . . [But] "Chinese Wall" is not even an architecturally accurate metaphor for the barrier to communication created to preserve confidentiality. Such a barrier functions as a hermetic seal to prevent two-way communication between two groups. The Great Wall of China, on the other hand, was only a one-way barrier. It was built to keep outsiders out – not to keep insiders in (Peat, Marwick, Mitchell & Co. v. Superior Court, 245 Cal. Rptr. (App. 1988) (Low, P.J., concurring)).

In law firms, terms such as "ethical wall" or "ethical screen" are emerging as alternatives (St. John 2005). In the present context, however, the term "insulation wall" seems superior (Shapiro and Wyland 1993). First, it does not connote the professional responsibility aspects associated with the ethical wall terminology. Second, it provides a more exact "architecturally accurate metaphor" than does ethical wall.

Key features of such a wall would include organizational and physical separation of persons with access to information especially likely to be abused from persons who do not need such access. Prohibitions against and penalties for discussing confidential matters with unauthorized personnel or in locations where such discussions could be overheard are also an important part of the insulation wall. Likewise, the firm will need procedures for preventing unapproved personnel from accessing confidential information and files, delinking approved personnel compensation from trading profits, and regular training of personnel on their legal and commercial responsibilities.[28]

58.5 RULE 10B5-1 PLANS

The SEC has long argued that trading while in knowing possession of material nonpublic information satisfies Rule 10b–5's scienter requirement. During the 1990s, however, a split developed between the Second and Eleventh Circuits on that issue. The former adopted a knowing possession standard (*Teicher*),[29] while the latter held that "when an insider trades while in possession of material nonpublic information, a strong inference arises that such information was used by the insider in trading. The insider can attempt to rebut the inference by adducing evidence that there was no causal connection between the information and the trade – i.e., that the information was not used" (*Adler*).[30]

In 2000, the SEC resolved this split by adopting Rule 10b5–1, which states that Rule 10b–5's prohibition of insider trading is violated whenever someone trades "on the basis of" material nonpublic information. Because one is deemed, subject to certain affirmative defenses, to have traded "on the basis of" material nonpublic information if one was aware of such information at the time of the trade, Rule 10b5–1 formally rejects the *Adler* position.[31]

There are three affirmative defenses available under Rule 10b5–1, under each of which:

> [A] person's purchase or sale is not "on the basis of" material nonpublic information if the person making the purchase or sale demonstrates that:
> (A) Before becoming aware of the information, the person had:
> (1) Entered into a binding contract to purchase or sell the security,
> (2) Instructed another person to purchase or sell the security for the instructing person's account, or
> (3) Adopted a written plan for trading securities .... (Ibid., § 240.10b5–1(c)(1)(i).)

These affirmative defenses are available only if the contract, instruction, or plan meets the following conditions:

(1) Specified the amount of securities to be purchased or sold and the price at which and the date on which the securities were to be purchased or sold;

28 The court in *Henriksen* v. *Great Am. Sav. & Loan* (14 Cal. Rptr. 2d 184 (App. 1992)) discussed in detail these key elements of an insulation wall in a law firm. For discussion of the origin and development of insulation walls, see Dolgopolov (2008). To be sure, insulation walls often are imperfect, as illustrated by Seyhun's (2008) study of investment banks with representatives on client boards of directors, which concluded that the insulation walls at these banks were "porous." But this is an argument for improving such walls, rather than doing away with them.

29 *U.S.* v. *Teicher*, 987 F.2d 112 (2d Cir.1993).

30 *SEC* v. *Adler*, 137 F.3d 1325, 1337 (11th Cir. 1998).

31 17 C.F.R. § 240.10b5–1(a).

(2) Included a written formula or algorithm, or computer program, for determining the amount of securities to be purchased or sold and the price at which and the date on which the securities were to be purchased or sold; or
(3) Did not permit the person to exercise any subsequent influence over how, when, or whether to effect purchases or sales; provided, in addition, that any other person who, pursuant to the contract, instruction, or plan, did exercise such influence must not have been aware of the material nonpublic information when doing so . . ..[32]

The purchase or sale must be made pursuant to the plan, which includes a requirement that the plan not have been changed so as to permit the transaction. Finally, the plan must have been established "in good faith and not as part of a plan or scheme to evade the prohibitions of this section."[33] While the foregoing affirmative defenses are available to both individuals and entities, an additional affirmative defense is available solely to entities:

A person other than a natural person also may demonstrate that a purchase or sale of securities is not "on the basis of" material nonpublic information if the person demonstrates that:

(i) The individual making the investment decision on behalf of the person to purchase or sell the securities was not aware of the information; and
(ii) The person had implemented reasonable policies and procedures, taking into consideration the nature of the person's business, to ensure that individuals making investment decisions would not violate the laws prohibiting trading on the basis of material nonpublic information. These policies and procedures may include those that restrict any purchase, sale, and causing any purchase or sale of any security as to which the person has material nonpublic information, or those that prevent such individuals from becoming aware of such information.[34]

There is growing evidence that many executives are abusing Rule 10b5–1 by establishing or amending trading plans while in possession of material nonpublic information on the basis of which they proceeded to trade while using the plan for cover (Thomsen 2007). Because such abuse may give rise to controlling person liability for the issuer, it is essential that issuers ensure that employees with access to material nonpublic information trade through approved Rule 10b5-1 plans.

As Lamarre (2009:20) notes:

In one high-profile example, the SEC filed a civil complaint on June 4, 2009, against the former CEO of Countrywide Financial, Angelo Mozilo, and other former Countrywide executives, alleging that they used Rule 10b5–1 plans to trade illegally on inside information (to the tune of nearly $140 million, in Mr. Mozilo's case). Although all of these sales occurred through Rule 10b5–1 plans, the SEC alleges – citing internal correspondence such as an e-mail stating that the company was "flying blind" – that Mr. Mozilo had material nonpublic information about Countrywide's deteriorating mortgage business when he instituted his trading plans. The SEC also took particular note of the fact that he implemented no fewer than four separate plans during a three-month period, and that sales under the plans began soon after their adoption

[32] Ibid., § 240.10b5–1(c)(1)(i)(B).
[33] Ibid., § 240.10b5–1(c)(1)(ii).
[34] Ibid., § 240.10b5–1(c)(2).

There are a number of best practices to minimize the risk that a corporation's insiders will abuse their Rule 10b5–1 plan. First, the board of directors should assign responsibility for overseeing Rule 10b5–1 plans for senior corporate insiders to the nominating and corporate governance committee or compensation committee. The responsible board committee should preclear plan adoptions, amendments, and terminations by such insiders. As for less-senior managers, review and preclearance of Rule 10b5–1 plan adoptions, amendments, and terminations should be assigned to the firm's compliance officer.[35] In addition to preclearance, issuers should prohibit Rule 10b5–1 plans from being modified during trading blackout periods under the company's insider-trading policy.

Second, the issuer's chosen board committee should select a single broker to administer Rule 10b5–1 plans and require that all of the issuer's insiders establish and administer their plans exclusively through that broker. The insiders should not use the chosen broker for any security transactions outside of the plan.[36] The issuer's compliance office and the chosen board committee should work with the broker to develop a standard Rule 10b5–1 plan template that all insiders will adopt (Sawyer 2013). The template "may include features, such as waiting periods, restrictions on having multiple plans, requirements regarding plan duration and other alleged 'best practices' that are not technically required by Rule 10b5-1" (Sawyer 2013).

Although not required by Rule 10b5-1, a waiting period before the insider is allowed to make the initial trade under the plan is helpful to avoid the possibility that the insider set up the plan precisely so as to effect a trade on the basis of material nonpublic information then in the insider's possession. The influential proxy advisor service Institutional Shareholder Services (ISS) has adopted a policy of supporting shareholder proposals that require a ninety-day waiting period (Institutional Shareholder Services 2018:15).

Another common plan feature that is not required by the text of Rule 10b5-1, but which has emerged as a best practice, is voluntary disclosure of plan adoptions, modifications, and terminations. ISS's proxy voting guidelines call for disclosure on Form 8-K of a plan adoption, amendment, or termination within two business days (Institutional Shareholder Services 2018:51). In addition, if the insider is subject to reporting obligations under Exchange Act § 16(a), whether a transaction was effected within or outside the plan should be disclosed on the Form 4 reporting the transaction.

Corporate policies should discourage company insiders from adopting multiple Rule 10b5–1 plans with overlapping execution terms, since this can be viewed as an attempt to use timing to take advantage of material nonpublic information.

35 As James Ball (2003:15) observed, "companies should consider requiring insiders who wish to implement a trading plan under SEC Rule 10b5-1 to first clear the plan with the pre-clearance official." Similarly, Melissa Sawyer (2013) observed that because "compliance departments are often now asked to make subjective judgments about the permissibility of cancelling or modifying existing plans," "some companies expressly require that all plan modifications be pre-cleared through their compliance department."

36 Scheer (2013:3) argues that it is generally advisable to prohibit transactions outside of the plan:

> Rule 10b5-1 does not prohibit a person who establishes a trading plan under the rule from trading outside of the plan, though it does prohibit non-plan, corresponding, or hedging transactions or positions with respect to the company's stock. Non-plan trading will not be covered by the rule's affirmative defense, however, and must not occur at a time when the insider is aware of material nonpublic information. Once a trading plan is in place, non-plan trading should be kept to a minimum or avoided altogether, as parallel trading could be viewed with suspicion. For example, in the case of a Rule 10b5-1 trading plan to sell securities, the SEC or a federal prosecutor challenging non-plan sales by the insider might argue that because the insider already had a trading plan, presumably to diversify the insider's investment portfolio, the insider was seeking to take advantage of material nonpublic information in making the non-plan sales.

It is generally recommended that plans have a term of at least a year, because short-term plans are more likely to be set up so as to trade while in possession of nonpublic information. In addition, although the SEC permits a plan to "be modified so long as the modification is made in good faith and at a time when the insider is not aware of material nonpublic information" (Scheer 2013:2), ISS recommends that the issuer should permit amendment or early termination of a Rule 10b5-1 plan only in "extraordinary circumstances, as determined by the board" (Institutional Shareholder Services 2018:51). As noted earlier in this section, moreover, amendment or termination also should receive preclearance so as to ensure that the insider does not possess material nonpublic information at time of termination.

REFERENCES

Anderson, John P. 2016. "Solving the Paradox of Insider Trading Compliance." *Temple Law Review* 88: 273.

Bainbridge, Stephen M. 1999. "Insider Trading Regulation: The Path Dependent Choice between Property Rights and Securities Fraud." *SMU Law Review* 52: 1589.

Bainbridge, Stephen M. 2014. *Insider Trading Law and Policy*. St. Paul, MN: Foundation Press.

Ball, James H. 2003. "Suggestions for Implementing Sarbanes-Oxley Act Requirements." *Andrews Securities Regulation Litigation & Regulation Report* 8 (25): 15.

Barnard, Jayne W. 1999. "Reintegrative Shaming in Corporate Sentencing." *Southern California Law Review* 72: 959.

Dolgopolov, Stanislav. 2008. "Insider Trading, Chinese Walls, and Brokerage Commissions: The Origins of Modern Regulation of Information Flows in Securities Markets." *Journal of Law, Economics, and Policy* 4: 311.

Dye, Alan L. 2000. "Securities Law Compliance Programs." ALI-ABA (American Law Institute and American Bar Association) Postgraduate Course in Federal Securities Law. Chicago, IL: American Law Institute-American Bar Association Committee on Continuing Professional Education.

Fisch, Jill E. 1991. "Start Making Sense: An Analysis and Proposal for Insider Trading Regulation." *Georgia Law Review* 26: 179.

Institutional Shareholder Services. 2013. *U.S. Proxy Voting Guidelines*. Vol. 2013. Rockville, MD: ISS Governance.

Lamarre, David. 2009. "Keeping Current: Securities." *Business Law Today* 19 (December): 20.

Panel Discussion. 2008. "Corporate Compliance: The Role of Company Counsel." *Georgetown Journal of Legal Ethics* 21: 491.

Park, James J. 2017. "The Limits of the Right to Sell and the Rise of Federal Corporate Law." *Oklahoma Law Review* 70: 159.

Sawyer, Melissa. 2013. "Corporate Governance Feature: 10b5-1 Plans and M&A Transactions." *Mergers & Acquisitions Lawyer* 17 (7): 25.

Scheer, Craig M. 2013. "Rule 10b5–1 Trading Plans in the Current Environment: The Importance of Doing It Right." *Business Law Today* 2013 (February): 1.

Seyhun, H. Nejat. 2008. "Insider Trading and the Effectiveness of Chinese Walls in Securities Firms." *Journal of Law, Economics, and Policy* 4: 369.

Shapiro, Bernard, and Neil D. Wyland. 1993. "Ethical Quandaries of Professionals in Bankruptcy Cases." C836 ALI-ABA (American Law Institute and American Bar Association) 15.

St. John, Ronald R. 2005. "When an Ethical Screen Can Be Used to Avoid Vicarious Disqualification of a Law Firm Remains Unsettled." *L.A. Lawyer*, February, 29.

Thomsen, Linda Chatman. 2007. "Speech by SEC Staff: Opening Remarks before the 15th Annual NASPP Conference," Washington, DC, October 10. www.sec.gov/news/speech/2007/spch101007lct.htm.

U.S. Sentencing Commission. 2016. "Sentencing Guidelines Manual § 8B2.1." October 27. www.ussc.gov/guidelines/2016-guidelines-manual/2016-chapter-8#NaN.

Wang, William K. S. 2015. "Application of the Federal Mail and Wire Fraud Statutes to Criminal Liability for Stock Market Insider Trading and Tipping." *University of Miami Law Review* 70: 220.

59

Antitrust Compliance: Collusion

Johannes Paha and Florence Thépot

Abstract: Focusing on collusive behavior, this chapter outlines the complexity associated with both the *ex ante* design of antitrust compliance programs and the *ex post* assessment of their impact. Following an interdisciplinary review of relevant literature, the chapter provides a structured cost–benefit approach to compliance and challenges the idea that compliance cannot be rationalized. We recognize that measurement of compliance programs may be particularly difficult in light of the importance of less-tangible factors such as corporate culture. Yet, the chapter proposes that a principled approach to compliance would considerably support the work of practitioners. Future research should concentrate on studying the interaction effects of compliance mechanisms and corporate culture. Such large-scale empirical studies on individual and firm-specific factors of compliance might be promoted and coordinated by competition authorities.

59.1 INTRODUCTION

This chapter outlines the complex nature of antitrust compliance focusing on (illegal) collusive behavior such as price fixing, bid rigging, market or customer allocation.[1] The complexity of antitrust compliance raises challenges both to the *ex ante* design of compliance programs by firms that operate within budgetary constraints and to the *ex post* assessment of the programs' efficiency by competition authorities or external auditors. The aim of this chapter is to highlight gaps in the research literature on antitrust compliance specifically and to discuss practical implications.[2]

Among all types of antitrust offense, this chapter focuses on collusion. Risks of engaging in collusive behavior are widespread since collusion concerns all company types, while other antitrust offenses may be committed only by certain firms (e.g., those in a dominant position). Moreover, prohibitions of collusive agreements exist across all jurisdictions having a competition law regime; and the consequences of a breach may be substantial (penalties ranging from large monetary fines to criminal sanctions). Collusive behavior is also the best-documented area of compliance research, with the work by Schwalbe (2016) being one rare example of antitrust compliance research in areas other than collusion.

This chapter explains how antitrust compliance research builds on knowledge from different disciplines; and it demonstrates that causes of collusion are manifold, ranging

[1] The terms "compliance program" or "compliance management system" refer to measures taken by firms to ensure compliance with antitrust laws, including internal prevention and detection tools.

[2] Please see Part IX for insights into other areas of compliance.

from industry-, to firm- or employee-specific factors. It highlights the need for further research on the effectiveness, design, and assessment of compliance programs. We also argue that empirical research about the internal and external drivers of compliance should be promoted by competition authorities to enhance our understanding of the efficiency of compliance programs. This could be achieved by a large-scale statistical study, to complement existing small-scale studies. Taking stock of existing literature, we argue that we need, in particular, a better understanding of firm-specific and employee-specific factors contributing to the violation of competition rules.

Turning to practice, in their efforts to design compliance programs effectively, compliance officers face the challenge of assessing the risks being created by the factors causing antitrust infringements. The complex interactions of these factors render the assessment of compliance risks particularly difficult. A thorough risk assessment is equally important for deciding how to prioritize compliance efforts and for using the budget allocated to the compliance department efficiently. Assessing the risks by means of a formalized process may also help compliance officers in demonstrating the effectiveness and efficiency of their programs to third parties such as antitrust authorities. This may be particularly important in jurisdictions where effective compliance programs are rewarded by antitrust authorities. In this context, we also show that the measures implemented to ensure compliance with antitrust laws are diverse, ranging from training about antitrust laws to less-tangible factors such as corporate culture, which creates challenges when it comes to assessing the efficacy of antitrust law compliance programs.

Following an interdisciplinary overview of research literature on antitrust compliance, the chapter considers and presents the type of cost and benefit approach to compliance that is necessary when a firm envisages possible strategies for mitigating the noncompliance risk. In this context, the term *cost* needs to be understood not strictly as an accounting cost but in its broader sense of opportunity cost, embracing monetary and nonmonetary costs associated with a given action.[3] Besides suggesting avenues for future research, a further purpose of this chapter is to reflect on, and provide avenues for, a structured, yet flexible approach to compliance for professionals who need to design, implement, and evaluate compliance measures both efficiently and effectively. Ultimately, this chapter demonstrates the importance of cost-related considerations in antitrust enforcement against collusive behavior.

59.2 LITERATURE ON ANTITRUST COMPLIANCE

This section explains that – departing from its roots in law and economics – research on antitrust compliance needs to be truly interdisciplinary, additionally factoring in results from psychology and corporate governance.[4] Further research is required both to understand antitrust compliance as a complex multilayered phenomenon and to measure its determinants appropriately.

Economists have sought to explain the drivers of noncompliance, that is, collusive behavior, by analyzing market conditions that give rise to breaches of competition rules. In economics, collusion is typically modeled as firms behaving like a single firm, maximizing a joint rather than individual profits. Owing to the incentive of firms to deviate from the collusive agreement, economic research identifies specific market factors that help to sustain

[3] Also see Chapter 2 in this volume on the costs and benefits of compliance.

[4] The relevant literature in those fields is extensive so that the articles presented here must necessarily remain selective.

collusion from both a theoretical (Stigler 1964) and an empirical perspective (Levenstein and Suslow 2006, 2015). These factors of cartel stability may, however, differ from the factors contributing to cartel formation (Herold and Paha 2018). On top of market factors, organizational factors are important determinants of noncompliance. In the seminal contribution by Beckenstein and Gabel (1986) on this issue, antitrust offenses are explained or affected especially by "imperfect information and uncertainty, costly communication, perverse incentives, impacted information, and bounded rationality."[5]

Corporate governance researchers thus have analyzed how incentive systems may facilitate collusion. Indeed, firms may choose to delegate the pricing decision to managers within the firm to sustain a collusive agreement. This is because managers would set prices in such a way as to maximize their individual utility, which is determined by the structure of remuneration (Fershtman and Judd 1987; see Herold 2016 for a literature review). As a consequence, the literature on corporate governance and agency theory (Jensen and Meckling 1976) suggests that corporate compliance may be designed to reduce moral hazard problems characteristic to agency relationships. Indeed, white-collar crimes, including price-fixing, may be understood as a specification of the moral hazard problem, made possible by the potential divergence of interests and the asymmetry of information between the owners of the firm and those who conduct the firm's daily operations (Thépot 2019).

Several law and economics authors have therefore studied corporate governance factors as determinants of antitrust breaches, finding that behavioral aspects and bounded rationality also contribute to managerial wrongdoing. For example, Sonnenfeld (2002) stresses the importance of social elements such as trust, respect, and candor within the board of directors for preventing corporate misconduct, in addition to structural factors such as the presence of audit and compensation committees, or directors holding shares of the company or attending meetings regularly.[6] The empirical study by González and Schmid (2012) suggests that companies with a high proportion of busy directors, that is, members of more than one board, are more likely to engage in a cartel. In addition, González et al. (2017) empirically show that companies involved in cartels may favor passive directors, are less likely to replace directors who resign, and may change auditing companies less often than is the norm. Campello et al. (2017:244) also establish a link between the share of independent directors and the likelihood of applying for leniency and replacing "their scandal-laden CEOs following announcements of cartel prosecution."

Psychology researchers provide further insights into the determinants of corporate misconduct, which may well apply to collusive behavior. Such wrongdoing may be caused by characteristics of the individual (e.g., personality features), of the group or team (group dynamics and interpersonal interactions), or organizational features (e.g., perceptions of prevailing practices and corporate culture; Paruzel et al. 2016). Psychologists further enrich the study of compliance by deconstructing noncompliant behavior carried out either in favor of or against the company's interests. For example, Umphress et al. (2010) show that constructs thought to benefit the organization, such as a strong sense of employees' identification with their company, can drive breaches of the law committed by individuals who wish to act in a manner that benefits their companies. This is defined as "unethical pro-organizational behavior." Price-fixing could be such an example of individuals using unlawful means to

[5] Related questions have also been studied by researchers in sociology and criminology. For example, Simpson (1986) empirically studied the effects of business cycle fluctuations and corporate performance on antitrust offenses using a US data set spanning the years 1927–81.

[6] Also see Chapter 43 in this volume on the social and organizational psychology of compliance.

inflate the firm's profits. Other studies explore the determinants of noncompliance as counterproductive or deviant work-behavior, where the breach may be carried out directly or indirectly to harm the company (Bennett and Robinson 2000; Marcus et al. 2000), which fits antitrust particularly well in jurisdictions such as Europe where sanctions are mostly levied on the firms instead of the individuals who broke the law and, thus, harmed the firm directly.

Legal scholars typically study antitrust compliance from the perspective of enforcement of the law by authorities (see, e.g., Stephan 2010; Wagner-von Papp 2016; Rummel 2016). For example, in the scholarly debate between Wils (2013) and Geradin (2013), the core question is whether mechanisms of compliance ought to be encouraged and rewarded in the context of investigations for a breach. Opponents to such rewards (reflecting the approach of most competition authorities) usually warn against the negative consequences of rewarding compliance mechanisms. The deterrence function of fines may indeed be diminished if they are reduced to reward compliance efforts. Stephan (2010) also reflects on the effectiveness of compliance programs: such programs are deemed to be ineffective if managers do not face any consequences for engaging in collusive behavior, which still seems to be the case in most of Europe. Researchers advocating the need to complement classic approaches to enforcement with self-regulation or responsive regulation tools also emphasize the role of compliance mechanisms from a regulatory perspective (Fisse and Braithwaite 2010; Parker 2002; Simpson 2002). According to this stream, regulation should encompass a variety of tools, with more emphasis on education and prevention, moving away from a strict "command-and-control" approach. Providing insights into other areas of compliance (e.g., anti-corruption[7]), legal researchers also advocate the need for further interdisciplinary research and the need to supplement classic enforcement instruments with other regulation approaches with greater consideration of compliance mechanisms (Riley and Sokol 2015; Sokol 2012; Thépot 2015, 2016, 2019).

Advocating the need for greater understanding of the organizational dimension of compliance, compliance and ethics scholars highlight the essential role of authorities in steering compliance efforts by companies. They also develop an understanding of the compliance risk factors, with emphasis on the key role of senior management in promoting a culture of compliance; thereby providing practical tools for companies in the prevention and detection of corporate wrongdoing (see Murphy 2010).

This overview of the literature illustrates that antitrust violation constitutes a multifaceted risk, with potentially significant consequences (including fines, payment of damages, or loss of shareholder value). Risk factors may be external to the firm (e.g., industry factors) as well as organizational, that is, firm- or employee-specific. A risk-based approach to the implementation and design of compliance management systems thus requires an understanding and assessment of these factors in their complexity.

59.3 THE ASSESSMENT AND EFFECTIVENESS OF COMPLIANCE

This section presents a model that purports to define and delineate the risks and the associated costs of antitrust compliance for a given company. A structured assessment of risks and costs is necessary both to the *ex ante* design of competition law compliance programs

7 Authorities in the areas of anti-corruption may have a very different approach; in some jurisdictions, companies may be relieved from liability if they show they had adequate and effective compliance programs in place (Thépot 2015).

and to their *ex post* assessment as is required, for example, in the US Department of Justice's (DoJ) 2019 guidance document on the *Evaluation of Corporate Compliance Programs*. Based on the compliance risk model, we illustrate the complex nature of risk mitigation strategies. The model supports the idea that it is crucial to design antitrust compliance programs optimally because firms operate under tight budgetary constraints and cannot abstract from considerations of optimality and effectiveness in their compliance-related decisions. Presenting a model of compliance risks enables firms to deconstruct the different components of compliance (i.e., risk factors and mitigation strategies) and reflect on challenges in the assessment of each component. Highlighting that more research is needed on the factors driving antitrust risk, this chapter feeds into the delicate question of the evaluation of costs of compliance mechanisms adequate to mitigate the compliance risk faced by firms. Ultimately, this chapter demonstrates that cost-related considerations find their place in the policy debate on enforcement.

59.3.1 *The Compliance Risk Model*

The compliance risk model includes the monetary and nonmonetary costs incurred by a firm in consequence of a violation, which we call the costs of noncompliance *CN*.[8] None of the individual components of these costs may be evaluated with certainty, as will be explained; yet understanding the different cost components and attempting to approximate these is useful for risk mitigation purposes.

Following Paha and Götz (2015), the costs of noncompliance *CN* incurred by the firm as a whole may be decomposed into fines *F*, damages *D*, litigation costs *L*, and additional costs C_{ad} (see equation (1)). The last comprises, for example, the decrease in a company's value in response to the discovery of the anticompetitive conduct, or less-tangible costs that may be associated with reputation damages. To be specific, *CN* is defined using the concept of opportunity costs that exist beyond monetary costs.

$$CN = F + D + L + C_{ad} \tag{1}$$

The costs of noncompliance *CN* are incurred if employees violate antitrust law occurring with probability *RR*, that is, the residual risk of antitrust compliance. In other words, *RR* stands for the probability that a violation occurs despite the existence of a compliance program. This acknowledges that, depending on the effectiveness of a compliance program, the risk of noncompliance may not be eliminated entirely despite such a program being in place.

$$RR = IR1 \cdot \ IR2 \cdot \ CR \cdot \ DR \tag{2}$$

The probability *RR* depends on a number of factors. One of them is the inherent risk *IR*, that is, the "external risk" that is unrelated to the existence of a compliance program within the firm. The risk *IR* is deconstructed further into two types of risk. The factor *IR1* refers to the risk specific to a market, depending on characteristics such as the type of industry, the degree of product differentiation, or the number of competitors, which may all affect the occurrence of collusion. The factor *IR2* expresses the probability that recent events in a firm's external

[8] The compliance risk model phrases compliance in the context of risk management. A further discussion of the links between compliance and risk management may be found in Chapter 10 of this volume.

business environment trigger collusion. For example, external demand shocks may explain the formation of some cartels (Herold and Paha 2018).

The probability RR also depends on the ability of internal mechanisms of compliance to prevent and detect the wrongdoing internally; being further deconstructed into the control risk CR and the detection risk DR. The control risk refers to the ability of preventive measures, such as training sessions or incentives produced via remuneration, to reduce the residual risk of noncompliance. The detection risk refers to the ability of internal processes to detect the occurrence of a violation (e.g., whether internal audits are run, whether there is a reporting mechanism, etc.). The effectiveness of a compliance program depends on how the employees of the firm react to its elements. For example, individuals that are overconfident may sustain a collusive behavior in spite of effective internal detection mechanisms. Such effects have to be considered when assessing CR and DR as is explained in greater detail in Section 59.3.2 and 59.3.3.

Putting the costs and the residual risk of noncompliance together, and considering that the collusive agreement is detected by a competition authority with probability p, the expected costs of noncompliance EC can be written as in equation (3).

$$EC = p \cdot RR \cdot CN \tag{3}$$

While the inherent risks $IR1$ (susceptibility of the market to collusive conduct) and $IR2$ (occurrence of events initiating collusion) relate to external factors that cannot be mitigated by a company, CR and DR may well be reduced by implementing appropriate compliance procedures. A risk-management approach suggests that a company should choose to implement compliance measures such that the expected costs EC are outweighed by the amount of risk that the firm is willing to accept (i.e., its so-called risk appetite RA; Scheld et al. 2016).[9]

$$EC \leq RA \tag{4}$$

The compliance risk model also enables us to highlight the challenges that companies may face in the *ex ante* implementation of compliance management systems as well as in the *ex post* assessment of their effectiveness. Firstly, the *assessment* of the parameters described above, such as those contributing to the inherent risks $IR1$ and $IR2$, may be particularly difficult due to incomplete and imperfect information. Secondly, the *effectiveness* of compliance management systems, or, in other words, the extent to which compliance efforts contribute to reducing the risks CR and DR, is difficult to estimate.

59.3.2 *Assessment*

A first challenge is the assessment of the costs of noncompliance CN, which determine the appropriate level of compliance efforts to undertake. Measuring the expected fine F, the payment of damages D, and the litigation costs L is complicated by a range of factors including the discretion of competition authorities, the setting of sanctions, unpredictable

9 Risk appetite is a standard concept used in risk management to define the level of risk that a firm is willing to accept in pursuit of its goals, for example, the risk associated with certain investment opportunities. Compliance experts may argue that using this term puts noncompliant conduct on the same level as other risky but legal business opportunities, which may erode the effect of social norms that would otherwise have contributed to compliance by functioning as informal sanctions on illegal conduct. We acknowledge this risk when it comes to compliance in practice. In terms of this research-oriented chapter, we nonetheless stick to the term *risk appetite* to keep the terminology consistent with the related literature in risk management.

events related to leniency policy (who is going to be first applicant), or the quality of the data available to the plaintiffs in damages cases. An empirical study by Aguzzoni et al. (2013) suggests that only 10 percent of a firm's total decrease in stock market value is due to the imposition of fines in Europe. As a result, the additional costs of noncompliance C_{ad} potentially have considerable importance: such costs include, for example, the reduction of future cash flows when prices come back to competitive levels or reputational damages, which are even harder to assess than F, D, and L.

The probability p of the collusive conduct being detected by an antitrust authority is equally difficult to measure. For example, using US data, Bryant and Eckard (1991) estimate a 13–17 percent probability of a cartel being detected, which appears to be supported by the 17 percent estimate of Harrington and Wei (2017). However, using EU data for 1969–2007, Combe et al. (2008) estimate such probability to be in the range of only 12.9 to 13.2 percent, whereas Ivaldi et al. (2016) estimate a probability of 24 percent using a dataset for 249 cartels prosecuted in 20 developing countries between 1995 and 2013. While these are estimates of the *average* detection probability, estimating the actual probability p for a specific firm in a specific industry, operating within specific jurisdictions (and within the remit of their competition authorities), is more complicated because of idiosyncratic effects.

Factors contributing to the inherent risk $IR1$, that is, market-specific factors leading to collusion, were analyzed, among others, by Levenstein and Suslow (2006, 2015). Herold and Paha (2018) studied factors preceding cartel formation and, thus, the determinants of the inherent risk $IR2$. None of these studies can actually quantify the product $IR1 \cdot IR2$ because, firstly, the number of detected cartels is too small relative to the number of determinants of collusion, so that these probabilities can hardly be estimated by econometric methods. Secondly, one can only draw inferences about detected cartels so that quantification attempts may be biased if an industry is wrongly considered cartel-free although collusion may exist in absence of its detection. Thirdly, it is difficult determining the interactions of $IR1$ and $IR2$ because, for example, buyer power is often considered to lower the suitability of a market for collusion (causing a low value of $IR1$) while it may also be an event that triggers collusion (causing a high value of $IR2$).

59.3.3 *Effectiveness*

Evaluating the control risk CR and the detection risk DR, which closely relate to the effectiveness of compliance efforts, is another critical component of risk-mitigation strategies. The risk of anticompetitive conduct occurring in spite of prevention mechanisms (CR) or of such conduct remaining undetected internally despite the existence of internal detection mechanisms (DR) is maximal (CR_{max}, DR_{max}) in the absence of any formal compliance procedures. These maxima need not be 100 percent. They can, in fact, be lower because of the existence of less-tangible aspects impacting the level of compliance, such as corporate culture and ethical considerations, as is explained below.

Due to differences in less-tangible but important aspects of compliance, the maximum risk levels CR_{max} and DR_{max} may also differ across firms, business units within these firms, and individual employees within these business units. Because of these firm- and employee-specific effects, one and the same formal compliance mechanism may reduce CR and DR more (and thus be more effective) in one firm than in another. This is also considered in the guidance document issued by the US DoJ (2019), which recognizes "that each company's risk profile and solutions to reduce its risks warrant particularized evaluation." This is why the design of compliance programs needs to reflect the importance of these less-tangible components related to corporate culture and ethics.

Moral commitment to compliance and personal ethical values may explain why individuals abstain from breaking the law, even if the violation would be considered profitable absent these influences. Yet, even in the absence of such personal ethical values, individuals may still comply with the relevant laws if they perceive that wrongdoing may affect them negatively socially (ranging from a loss of reputation to social ostracism); and these influences would be effective even in the absence of formal punishment mechanisms (McAdams and Rasmusen 2007). A strong moral commitment to the adherence to antitrust laws is likely to be more effective and spread within the organization if adopted at the very top of the hierarchy and backed up by concrete actions (Murphy 2014, 2017), especially if they serve as credible signals in a game-theoretic sense about top managers' commitment to compliance.

These considerations illustrate why firms are likely to have differing levels of CR_{max} and DR_{max}, that is, depending on the strength of their compliance culture. As a consequence, two firms may have to take different efforts and incur different costs to attain the same level of residual risk of compliance. Moreover, the compliance culture may vary over time calling for a continuous reassessment of the risks and a firm's optimal responses to them. In other words, one size does not fit all: effectiveness of compliance systems across firms and over time means that a firm with a strong compliance culture is likely to reduce compliance risk at lower cost than one with a weak compliance and ethics culture. As an important implication, a strong culture of compliance leverages the effectiveness of compliance mechanisms and may enable cost savings.

Another implication is that although a strong culture of compliance adopted at the top may be evidenced concretely *ex post* (Murphy 2014, 2017), it may be difficult to design and to cost *ex ante* a compliance program that is adequate to the company's specific risk (in line with risk management principles). For example, how may a compliance officer budget for some training sessions or the implementation of an internal hotline, if less-tangible factors affect a firm's risk of noncompliance and, thus, the costs of promoting law-abiding behavior perceptibly? Indeed, antitrust compliance training may be quite effective in lowering CR if employees merely lack information about antitrust laws, but it will probably be less effective if some employees are driven by overconfidence or anti-ethical behavior.

It is also of utmost importance to reflect on how the various parameters may interact and take stock of possible crowding out effects between different compliance mechanisms. For example, the introduction of formal compliance mechanisms may undermine the positive impact of a strong ethics culture.[10] Other compliance mechanisms may be unrelated, substitutional (e.g., online training or face-to-face-training), or complementary (e.g., doing an automated screening of accounting information may enhance the effectiveness of other audits by guiding auditors' attention to suspect areas).

10 Deci et al. (1999) review evidence showing that rewards may crowd out intrinsic motivation, which in the compliance context may be taken to suggest "that formal controls can 'crowd out' psychological motivations that would lead to desired behavior even in the absence of controls" (Tayler and Bloomfield 2011: 754). Bénabou and Tirole (2003) show in a game-theoretic model that "forbidden fruits," i.e., actions sanctioned by a fine, may be particularly appealing because – speaking intuitively – the wrongdoer may have inferred from the sanction that the task is forbidden because it yields a gain at particularly low costs. Also see Chapter 9 and Part IV in this volume that are specifically concerned with the crowding out of social norms as well as the links between compliance and internal firm behavior.

Hence, the external assessment of a compliance system, by auditors or authorities, needs to take into account the full set of factors impacting compliance, including less-tangible factors such as those related to the corporate culture. External auditors or competition authorities assessing firms' compliance efforts thus need to be particularly conscious of understanding the adequacy of measures in place to meet the firm's specific risk. Two compliance programs may be equally effective while adopting different ranges of techniques. Yet, important factors such as the compliance culture may be more difficult to evaluate in a systematic way than formal compliance mechanisms that are somewhat easier to observe. Spelling out standards for the assessment of a strong commitment to the norm helps structure the evaluation of compliance programs in a manner that is useful for both the *ex ante* design and the *ex post* evaluation. Research on antitrust compliance should thus help identify tangible elements that reflect and enable the evaluation of these less-tangible aspects.

59.3.4 *Empirics*

The quantification of the risks listed in the previous section would be facilitated if there were large-scale empirical studies on the factors driving (non)compliance. The available studies, which are reviewed in this section, are characterized by a variety of designs and methods. This variety poses difficulties for comparing the studies and, especially, for pooling the raw data for further analyses. We suggest that competition authorities should play a role in coordinating research efforts, which would likely be to the benefit of the authorities themselves as well as the firms and the researchers.

Large-scale empirical studies would allow researchers to econometrically regress instances of observed wrongdoing both on factors that are deemed to be promoting lawbreaking and on the components of compliance management systems believed to promote compliance with the laws. The coefficients estimated by these regressions may help in determining whether both types of factors have the hypothesized effect on wrongdoing. Such studies would also allow identification of which compliance mechanisms are particularly effective.

The main obstacle to such research is the lack of a comprehensive panel-data set with a considerably large number of observations across a sufficiently large number of firms and a sufficiently long timespan. Recent empirical analyses have mostly relied on data with moderate sample sizes of less than 100 up to somewhat above 1,000 firms. Moreover, researchers have often collected cross-section data on multiple firms at just one point in time. This applies to studies conducted by researchers (Parker and Nielsen 2009; Sokol 2012; Götz et al. 2016), consultancies (KPMG 2016; Bussmann et al. 2018; EY 2018), or on behalf of competition authorities (Rodger 2015; van der Noll and Baarsma 2017) alike. As a further relevant characteristic of these data sets, they have typically relied on customized sets of questions and used different measures for quantifying (non)compliance.

Though this research allows for a quite targeted study of the questions posed, the data collected cannot be pooled in a larger data set. Yet, the availability of a larger data set would help to increase the statistical validity of the study results and allow for the application of more refined statistical techniques. A larger data set would also allow for controlling for the factors promoting noncompliance. This may be expected to reduce the variance of the error term sufficiently for achieving statistically significant results concerning the effect of the compliance measures on preventing collusion. One might also inquire whether data collected in some studies support the conclusions reached in others. Yet, such studies would need to follow a joint set of design rules and feature the same survey questions.

In this context, competition authorities may play a central role in harmonizing research efforts. Owing to different authorities' (presumably) common interest toward compliance research, they might coordinate efforts when it comes to developing a common and standardized approach for designing and commissioning studies. As a result of such a standardized approach, which could be developed within the European Competition Network, further research and analysis could build on a joint data set. Similar to commercial research agreements, cooperation among competition authorities would be capable of bringing together different research capabilities that allow the parties to streamline research efforts and enhance empirically grounded policymaking.

Ensuring compatibility of data sets would enable greater (statistical and economic) significance of studies for higher-quality research. The surveyed firms as providers of the data would also benefit from a "one-stop" questionnaire filing while receiving statistically more reliable answers in return.

Researchers might be granted access to this data under conditions reminiscent of the fair, reasonable and nondiscriminatory (FRAND) terms applied in EU competition law. In particular, researchers would have to align their own study designs to the agreed-upon questionnaire. Access to the data might be granted if they contribute their own data to an overall data set. Granting access to the data on a quid pro quo basis would reduce issues of moral hazard and free-riding of research efforts. At the same time, the researchers would still be free to add a proprietary set of questions when conducting their studies.

To sum up, large-scale empirical studies should be encouraged via standardization of study designs and methods, which would complement research conducted in the various disciplines. Particular efforts should be devoted to the question of efficiency of compliance programs, bearing in mind the variety of industry-, firm-, and employee-specific factors. Building on their enforcement experience, competition authorities should play a central role in the coordination of empirical studies.

59.4 DISCUSSION

This chapter challenges the idea that compliance cannot be rationalized. It shows that the complexity of compliance does not preclude the assessment of its effectiveness. A cost–benefit approach to compliance, as one element of firms' risk mitigation strategies, is necessary and can be done while acknowledging some essential challenges. In other words, the benefits of compliance (i.e., avoidance of penalties, nonmonetary costs of a violation, etc.) should outweigh the cost of compliance programs for the firm and its stakeholders. The compliance programs should be tailored to the risks internal and external to a firm, including the probability of detection.

This chapter advocates that efforts by firms and authorities should be structured so that *ex ante* and *ex post* assessment can be done consistently. Research along the lines of the model presented may help some inherent challenges to be apprehended:

Firstly, aspects such as legal uncertainty or imperfect information about the value of the sanctions or the different types of risk create challenges for the *ex ante* design of competition law compliance programs in terms of selecting the right intensity and composition of compliance efforts. This calls for more research on the types of parameters specifically associated with antitrust risk and how to measure these parameters better than today. Researchers should develop methods allowing practitioners to assess specific risks more accurately. While prior research has often been devoted to understanding the market forces contributing to cartel formation and sustainability, future research should concentrate more on measuring the effectiveness and the interaction effects of compliance mechanisms in the context of organizations differing in their corporate culture. Still, one must be prepared to deal with the persistence of at least some information imperfections in the foreseeable future, which creates another challenge.

Secondly, information imperfections may complicate the assessment of compliance *ex post* by competition authorities or external auditors. In some jurisdictions, firms may receive a reduction of the fine if they can demonstrate having an effective compliance program, or if they demonstrate that they made efforts to further raise its effectiveness. In other jurisdictions, such fine reductions have been called for or are being discussed.[11] Asymmetric information may then create divergent opinions about who should receive such a reduction. More research is thus needed on how to evaluate the effectiveness of a compliance program objectively taking into account both its tangible and its less-tangible components. Ideally, the assessment of external auditors or competition authorities and the assessment of the firms' compliance officers or consultants should converge. Similarly, the evaluation, ideally, should be sufficiently robust and standardized that the outcome depends as little as possible on the (actual or perceived) experience of the auditor. Although the evaluation should always be done on a case-by-case basis, a principled approach taking into account the complexity of compliance would considerably support the work of professionals involved in compliance. While this requires more research on the evaluation of compliance programs, competition authorities and firms should also work jointly on the methods used as part of their risk mitigation strategies and how these efforts can be appreciated best.

REFERENCES

Aguzzoni, Luca, Gregor Langus, and Massimo Motta. 2013. "The Effect of EU Antitrust Investigations and Fines on a Firm's Valuation." *The Journal of Industrial Economics* 61, No. 2: 290–338.

Beckenstein, Alan R., and H. Landis Gabel. 1986. "The Economics of Antitrust Compliance" *Southern Economic Journal* 53, No. 3: 673–92.

Bennett, Rebecca J., and Sandra L. Robinson. 2000. "Development of a Measure of Workplace Deviance." *Journal of Applied Psychology*, 85: 349–60.

Bénabou, Roland, and Jean Tirole. 2003. "Instrinsic and Extrinsic Motivation." *Review of Economic Studies* 70: 489–520.

Bryant, Peter G., and Woodrow Eckard. 1991. "Price Fixing: The Probability of Getting Caught." *Review of Economics and Statistics* 73: 531–6.

Bussmann, Kai-D. , Claudia Nestler, and Steffen Salvenmoser. 2018. "Wirtschaftskriminalität 2018." https://pwc.to/2FzlHEC.

Campello, Murillo, Daniel Ferrés, and Gaizka Ormazabal. 2017. "Whistle-Blowers on the Board? The Role of Independent Directors in Cartel Prosecutions." *Journal of Law and Economics* 60: 241–68.

[11] For example, the European Commission has for long refused to consider the existence of compliance programs as a mitigating factor in the context of a conviction, and as such no reduction in the level of fine is granted in the EU. In the US, until recently the DoJ was expressly excluding the reward of compliance programs in antitrust cases; although in recent cases, compliance programs implemented during the investigation were considered as mitigating factor in the amount of fines imposed. Among EU Member States only the UK and Italy may give credit to effective compliance programs, as part of investigations. In the UK, the basic amount of the fine may be reduced of up to 10% where adequate steps have been taken to ensure compliance. In Italy, effective compliance programs may constitute a mitigating factor, with a possible reduction of up to 15% of the amount of the fine. Until 2017, in France, companies also could be granted up to 10% fine reduction for compliance programs, as part of settlement procedures. For a more detailed overview of the discussion, see Thépot (2019: ch. 8).

Combe, Emmanuel, Constance Monnier, and Renaud Legal. 2008. "Cartels: The Probability of Getting Caught in the European Union." https://ssrn.com/abstract=1015061.

Deci, Edward L., Richard Koestner, and Richard M. Ryan. 1999. "A Meta-analytic Review of Experiments Examining the Effects of Extrinsic Rewards on Intrinsic Motivation." *Psychological Bulletin* 125: 627–68.

EY. 2018. "Integrity in the Spotlight. The Future of Compliance. 15th Global Fraud Survey." https://fraudsurveys.ey.com.

Fershtman, Chaim, and Kenneth Judd. 1987. "Equilibrium Incentives in Oligopoly." *American Economic Review* 77: 927–40.

Fisse, Brent, and John Braithwaite. 2010. *Corporations, Crime and Accountability*. Cambridge University Press.

Geradin, Damien. 2013. "Antitrust Compliance Programmes and Optimal Antitrust Enforcement: A Reply to Wouter Wils." *Journal of Antitrust Enforcement* 1: 325–46.

González, Tanja A., and Markus Schmid. 2012. "Corporate Governance and Antitrust Behavior." Swiss Institute of Banking and Finance, University of St. Gallen, Working Paper.

González, Tanja A., Markus Schmid, and David Yermack. 2017. "Does Price Fixing Benefit Corporate Managers?" NYU Working Paper No. FIN–13–002.

Götz, Georg, Daniel Herold, and Johannes Paha. 2016. "Results of a Survey in Germany, Austria, and Switzerland on How to Prevent Violations of Competition Laws." In *Competition Law Compliance Programmes – An Interdisciplinary Approach*, edited by Johannes Paha, 37–58. Springer.

Harrington, Joseph E., and Yanhao Wei. 2017. "What Can the Duration of Discovered Cartels Tell Us about the Duration of All Cartels?" *Economic Journal* 127: 1977–2005.

Herold, Daniel. 2016. "Compliance and Incentive Contracts." In *Competition Law Compliance Programmes – An Interdisciplinary Approach*, edited by Johannes Paha, 87–102. Springer.

Herold, Daniel, and Johannes Paha. 2018. "Cartels as Defensive Devices: Evidence from Decisions of the European Commission 2001–2010." *Review of Law and Economics* 14, No. 1: 1–31.

Ivaldi, Marc, Frédéric Jenny, and Aleksandra Khimich. 2016. "Cartel Damages to the Economy: An Assessment for Developing Countries." In *Competition Law Enforcement in the BRICS and in Developing Countries*, edited by Frédéric Jenny and Yannis Katsoulacos, 103–34. Springer.

Jensen, Michael C., and William H. Meckling. 1976. "Theory of the Firm: Managerial Behavior, Agency Costs and Ownership Structure." *Journal of Financial Economics* 3: 305–60.

KPMG. 2016. "Global Compliance Survey." https://bit.ly/2ZqxoFu.

Levenstein, Margaret C., and Valerie Y. Suslow. 2006. "What Determines Cartel Success?" *Journal of Economic Literature* 44, No. 1 (March): 43–95.

2015. "Cartels and Collusion, Empirical Evidence." In *The Oxford Handbook of International Antitrust Economics*, edited by Roger D. Blair and D. Daniel Sokol, 442–63. Oxford University Press.

Marcus, Bernd, Heinz Schuler, Patricia Quell, and Gerhardt Hümpfner. 2000. "Measuring Counterproductivity: Development and Initial Validation of a German Self-Report Questionnaire." *International Journal of Selection and Assessment* 1018–35.

McAdams, Richard H., and Rasmusen, Eric B. 2007. "Norms and the Law." In *Handbook of Law and Economics Vol. 2*, edited by A. Mitchell Polinsky and Steven Shavell, 1573–1618. Elsevier.

Murphy, Joseph E. 2010. "A Compliance & Ethics Program on a Dollar a Day: How Small Companies Can Have Effective Programs." Society of Corporate Compliance & Ethics. https://assets.corporatecompliance.org/Portals/1/PDF/Resources/CEProgramDollarADay-Murphy.pdf. (Available in different languages at www.corporatecompliance.org/compliance-ethics-program-dollar-day-how-small-companies-can-have-effective.)

2014. "Tone at the Top: How the CEO Can Do More Than Just Talk." *Compliance & Ethics Professional* (online magazine) (October): 80.

2017. "Policies in Conflict: Undermining Corporate Self-Policing." *Rutgers University Law Review* 69: 421–96.

van der Noll, Rob, and Barbara Baarsma. 2017. "Compliance with Cartel Laws and the Determinants of Deterrence – An Empirical Investigation." *European Competition Journal* 13, no. 2–3: 336–55.

Paha, Johannes, and Georg Götz. 2015. "Screening und das Compliance-Risikomodell: Konzepte zur unternehmensinternen Aufdeckung von Verstößen gegen das Kartellverbot." *Wirtschaft und Wettbewerb* 12: 1198–210.

Parker, Christine. 2002. *The Open Corporation: Effective Self-Regulation and Democracy*. Cambridge University Press.
Parker, Christine, and Vibeke Lehmann Nielsen. 2009. "Corporate Compliance Systems: Could They Make Any Difference?" *Administration & Society* 41, no. 1: 3–37.
Paruzel, Agnieszka, Barbara Steinmann, Annika Nübold, Sonja K. Ötting, and Günter W. Maier. 2016. "Psychological Contributions to Competition Law Compliance." In *Competition Law Compliance Programmes – An Interdisciplinary Approach*, edited by Johannes Paha, 215–41. Springer.
Riley, Anne, and Daniel Sokol. 2015 "Rethinking Compliance." *Journal of Antitrust Enforcement* 3: 3–57.
Rodger, Barry. 2015. "Competition Law Compliance: The CMA 2015 Study, Compliance Rationales and the Need for Increased Compliance Professionalism and Education." *European Competition Law Review* 36, No. 10: 423–9.
Rummel, Per. 2016. "Legal Incentives for Compliance Programmes: Stick or Carrot?" In *Competition Law Compliance Programmes – An Interdisciplinary Approach*, edited by Johannes Paha, 203–11. Springer.
Scheld, Denise, Johannes Paha, and Nicolas Fandrey. 2016. "Managing Antitrust Risks in the Banking Industry." *European Competition Journal* 12: 113–36.
Schwalbe, Ulrich. 2016. "Antitrust Compliance and Abusive Behaviour." In *Competition Law Compliance Programmes – An Interdisciplinary Approach*, edited by Johannes Paha, 103–20. Springer.
Simpson, Sally. 1986. "The Decomposition of Antitrust: Testing a Multi-level, Longitudinal Model of Profit-Squeeze." *American Sociological Review* 51, No. 6: 859–75.
2002. *Corporate Crime, Law, and Social Control*. Cambridge University Press.
Sokol, Daniel. 2012. "Cartels, Corporate Compliance, and What Practitioners Really Think about Enforcement." *Antitrust Law Journal* 78: 201–38.
Sonnenfeld, Jeffrey. 2002. "What Makes Great Boards Great." *Harvard Business Review* 2002 (September): 106–13.
Stephan, Andreas. 2010. "See No Evil: Cartels and the Limits of Antitrust Compliance Programs." *Company Lawyer* 31, no. 8: 231–9.
Stigler, Gregory J. 1964. "Theory of Oligopoly." *Journal of Political Economy* 72: 44–61.
Tayler, William B., and Robert J. Bloomfield. 2011. "Norms, Conformity, and Controls." *Journal of Accounting Research*, 49: 753–90.
Thépot, Florence. 2015."Antitrust v. Anti-corruption Policy Approaches to Compliance: Why Such a Gap?" *CPI Antitrust Chronicle* 6, no. 2.
2016. "Can Compliance Programmes Contribute to Effective Antitrust Enforcement?" In *Competition Law Compliance Programmes – An Interdisciplinary Approach*, edited by Johannes Paha, 191–202. Springer.
2019. *The Interaction between Competition Law and Corporate Governance: Opening the "Black Box."* Cambridge University Press.
Umphress, Elizabeth E., John B. Bingham, and Marie S. Mitchell. 2010. "Unethical Behavior in the Name of the Company: The Moderating Effect of Organizational Identification and Positive Reciprocity Beliefs on Unethical Pro-organizational Behavior. *Journal of Applied Psychology* 95: 769–80.
US Department of Justice, Criminal Division. 2019. "Evaluation of Corporate Compliance Programs. Guidance Document." https://bit.ly/2lEphmk.
Wagner-von Papp, Florian. 2016. "Compliance and Individual Sanctions in the Enforcement of Competition Law." In *Competition Law Compliance Programmes – An Interdisciplinary Approach*, edited by Johannes Paha, 135–88. Springer
Wils, Wouters. 2013. "Antitrust Compliance Programmes and Optimal Antitrust Enforcement." *Journal of Antitrust Enforcement* 1: 5–81.

60

Understanding AI Collusion and Compliance

Justin Johnson and D. Daniel Sokol

Abstract: Antitrust compliance scholarship, particularly with a focus on collusion, has been an area of study for some time (Beckenstein and Gabel 1986; Hylton 2015; Riley and Sokol 2015; Sokol 2017). Changes in technology and the rise of artificial intelligence (AI) and machine-learning have created new possibilities both for anticompetitive behavior and for detection of algorithmic collusion. To some extent, AI collusion takes traditional ideas of collusion and simply provides a technological overlay to them. However, in some instances, the mechanisms of both collusion and detection can be transformed using AI. This chapter discusses existing theoretical and empirical work, and identifies research gaps as well as avenues for new scholarship on how firms or competition authorities might invest in AI compliance to improve detection of wrongdoing. We suggest where AI collusion is possible and offer new twists to where prior work has not identified possible collusion. Specifically, we identify the importance of AI in addressing the "trust" issue in collusion. We also identify that AI collusion is possible across nonprice dimensions, such as manipulated product reviews and ratings, and discuss potential screens involving co-movements of prices and ratings. We further emphasize that AI may encourage entry, which may limit collusive prospects. Finally, we discuss how AI can be used to help with compliance both at the firm level and by competition authorities.

60.1 INTRODUCTION: FUNDAMENTALS OF AI COLLUSION

60.1.1 *What Do We Mean by AI Collusion?*

AI collusion is an emerging field of study. Although there is an increasing number of theory papers, most papers in the field focus on policy. To date, there has not been empirical work done on the topic of AI collusion. Rather, there are two examples of collusion cases that have occurred in online markets: *Topkins*, in which algorithms coordinated pricing using pricing software with settings that humans chose in advance to accomplish that purpose; and *Eturas*, in which rival travel agencies voluntarily participated in a booking system that, by design, limited discounts to 3 percent.

To better frame AI collusion, we must define it and its parameters. To do so, we begin by discussing existing theoretical and experimental work related to AI collusion. A preliminary question is "what is meant by 'AI collusion' as opposed to simply 'collusion'?" The answer is that AI collusion can mean different things. Consider the following (nonexhaustive) categorization.

First, AI collusion could be taken to mean collusion in the presence of certain market features that are commonly associated with computers in general or algorithms. For instance, we might ask how collusion is influenced when prices can be rapidly changed, or where prices are easily seen by all players in the market. We note that although computers and algorithms might make it more likely that prices could be easily observed and changed, from an abstract viewpoint these factors exist to some degree even without advanced technology (Kaplow 2013). Indeed, it has long been thought that easy price monitoring coupled with the ability to rapidly change prices may foster collusion, even without the involvement of computers. However, AI may reasonably represent an extreme case in which prices are observed and adjusted in real time, faster than humans might be able to operate. Because of the amount of data, it might be possible for collusion to be "hidden in plain sight" (such as coordinated as part of massive amounts of public information so that it is difficult to observe the collusive signals), which makes detection of collusion more difficult. As such, this represents one cause for concern regarding AI and collusion.

To understand why the ability to monitor and rapidly set prices may foster collusion, it is enough to know that the standard economic theory of cartels posits that a primary impediment to a collusive outcome is the ability and incentive of cartel members to cheat on a collusive agreement by either lowering price or expanding output. According to this theory (Green and Porter 1984), a potential cheater considers the short-term gain of so cheating and weighs it against the potential longer-term consequences of being caught cheating and in turn punished by the cartel (for example, other cartel members detecting a cheater may in turn lower their prices a substantial amount to punish the cheating firm).

If prices are quickly and easily observable, and also readily changed, then this theory suggests that the gains from cheating are small. The reason is that cheating is quickly detected and responded to, so the short-term gains are small and the punishment arrives soon. As noted already, this idea is independent of whether computers or humans are setting prices, so long as the prices are easily seen and are being set quickly.

Second, AI collusion could refer specifically to how algorithms may learn to collude as distinct from humans, putting aside issues related to price monitoring or the ability to rapidly change prices. The idea is that algorithms may use different processes than humans (or humans as idealized in the economics literature as perfectly rational and far-sighted) in setting prices or learning about the market environment. Indeed, there are different types of learning built into different types of algorithm, which may not necessarily be close to how humans would learn to play a game. Similarly, humans may not always operate entirely rationally. For example, consider a potential human colluder who might worry in an emotional sense about whether other firms can be trusted to not cheat on a collusive arrangement.

From this perspective, the issue becomes whether these particular processes used by algorithms can realistically lead to collusion, or what the likelihood of collusion would be compared to what might happen if only humans were involved. Other questions are what exactly it means for machines to collude and what intent or a collusive "agreement" means for machines (Ittoo and Petit 2017). For now, at least, we will sidestep these nuances and simply take collusive pricing to mean prices that are higher than they would be if the players interacted only on a short-run rather than a long-run basis.

Third, AI collusion could refer to the intersection of collusion by humans and machines. Most particularly, we can imagine circumstances in which humans influence the design of algorithms or online markets a way that intentionally encourages collusion. A simple example would be a situation in which multiple merchants use an algorithm and it is designed to limit competition, perhaps serving a role in a hub-and-spoke conspiracy. Both the *Topkins* and *Eturas* cases fit into this category.

Another example might be an algorithm that is programmed to elicit or teach cooperative behavior in competing players, be they humans or algorithms. For instance, an algorithm might be intentionally programmed to lead the market to higher prices in some manner, or to target punishments toward firms that lower their prices. In these cases, the algorithm is the agent of a human designer, who has a particular collusive desire in mind.

60.1.2 *What Does the Literature Suggest about AI Collusion?*

Mehra (2016) and Ezrachi and Stucke (2017) have recently sounded the alarm that the growing prevalence of pricing algorithms could lead to collusive outcomes. One emphasis of their work is that the interaction between human and computer may lead to harmful outcomes. We suggest the example of humans designing algorithms with collusive intent, as we note in Section 60.1.1. Similarly, humans might agree to use common algorithms as a part of a hub-and-spoke conspiracy. However, they also raise the concern that algorithms, even if not explicitly programmed to collude as such, may learn over time to do so.[1]

How realistic is it that algorithms not explicitly programmed to collude might nonetheless collude? For example, imagine algorithms that are simply programmed to maximize their profits over time, but not given explicit instructions about how to behave in order to reach the goal of maximizing these profits. Further imagine that these agents are capable of learning in some way about the strategic environment in which they operate.

Some observers have suggested that collusive outcomes are unlikely to be learned. Indeed, in some learning environments it is known that agents using simple rules will certainly not converge to collusive outcomes (see, for example, Milgrom and Roberts (1990) for an assessment of games in which agents use a particular learning technique called "fictitious play"). However, there are many different ways in which algorithms could behave and learn. Ittoo and Petit (2017) identify potential challenges to learning collusion, including computational difficulties with many pricing agents. Schwalbe (2018) also suggests some challenges to the emergence of cooperative behavior, for example, suggesting that a lack of communication may make it harder for collusive outcomes to emerge. Schwalbe (2018) also argues that communication between agents may be required for collusive outcomes to emerge. Related, Kühn and Tadelis (2018) argue that challenges in coordinating on a collusive equilibrium are such that collusion is unlikely. Coordination in a number of experimental games breaks down in the iterated games when there are more than two participants. Recent advances in computer science suggest that smart contracts may help limit collusion in certain areas such as in certain cloud computing applications (Dong et al. 2017).

Nonetheless, there exists a literature that suggests that simple algorithms may indeed learn to charge higher prices than those that economic theory predicts would be set by noncolluding (or short-term) players. Both Tesauro and Kephart (2002) and Waltman and Kaymak

[1] It has long been known that agents playing simple rules, such as might be implemented by either a human or a machine, can lead to collusion. An example is the *tit-for-tat* algorithm (Axelrod 1984), which would "cooperate" (say, by charging a high price) as long as rivals have also cooperated recently but otherwise would "punish" (say, by charging a low price) in response to a rival not cooperating. Axelrod's punch card programming shows that the possibility of computer-based collusion has been understood for a long time. Our focus here will instead be on algorithms that are not programmed as such to collude.

(2008) consider a type of reinforcement learning called Q-learning, which is commonly used in computer science. They both find that these algorithms may learn how to set high prices, without being programmed explicitly to do so.

Calvano et al. (2020) also consider pricing algorithms imbued with simple learning capabilities, in particular, Q-learning. These authors specifically model actions and payoffs in a manner that is consistent with a simple and standard demand system for differentiated products (in particular, logit demand) in which agents choose prices over time. They find that collusion in the form of supracompetitive prices readily emerges. An important additional contribution is that these authors study in great detail the actual strategies that algorithms converge to, for example, showing that price cuts by one player would be punished by the other algorithm in a manner consistent with what economic theory predicts.

Klein (2019) also finds evidence that learning algorithms in simple economic environments may end up charging average prices well above what would occur in the absence of repeated interactions. He considers a situation in which agents take turns changing their prices. In some simulations, the algorithms end up charging a single price that is greater than zero. In other simulations he finds that prices vary cyclically over time, reminiscent of the "Edgeworth price cycles" analyzed by Maskin and Tirole (1988), and that this is associated with supranormal profits.

The basic intuition behind the price cycles and resulting positive profits is simple: each algorithm learns that if prices are very low, then there is little loss today in raising its price (doing so further lowers its demand today, but, since profits were low, it doesn't matter too much). But, so raising its price leads its rival to raise its price. This gives the algorithms the opportunity to slowly lower the price over time until prices reach cost and the cycle repeats. Because prices are never below cost but sometimes above cost, profits are positive (even though in Klein's model there is zero product differentiation which would otherwise be associated with zero profits).

Works by Klein (2019) and Calvano et al. (2020) are important because they seek to move beyond the theoretical critiques of "pure" AI collusion, where AI that is not explicitly programmed to collude nonetheless ultimately sets supranormal prices. Although there are different types of learning that algorithms could employ, all of these authors use learning techniques that are commonly considered in the computer science literature and that may also be used in practice. Hence, their works represent important experimental evidence about what might happen when algorithms set prices.

Salcedo (2015) shows that collusive behavior may occur when algorithms can "decode" rival algorithms and when changing an algorithm takes time. Here the basic idea is that such conditions allow for a form of price commitment and communication of that intent, which can lead to collusion. Observe that this collusion might occur even if it is possible to change prices very rapidly, because the design of the algorithms can limit the types of pricing decisions that are made.

Brown and MacKay (2019) also examine how algorithms can serve as commitment devices. More precisely, they consider firms that compete not directly in prices but in algorithms which are in turn potentially functions of observables such as market prices. One possibility is that firms use this commitment power to soften competition, leading to higher prices. Related to this idea is that if one firm is more sophisticated than the other, in that it can more rapidly change prices, then the firm that is less sophisticated may gain by acting as a price leader. This means that the less sophisticated firm sets a higher price than it might otherwise, trusting that the more sophisticated firm will respond with its own high price. These authors also provide some empirical evidence supportive of their theories.

In the computer science literature, the possibility of AI collusion has not been uncovered with real-world cases. Crandall et al. (2018) suggest a number of reasons for this limitation in the real world:

> A successful algorithm should possess several properties. First, it must not be domain-specific – it must have superior performance in a wide variety of scenarios (generality). Second, the algorithm must learn to establish effective relationships with people and machines without prior knowledge of associates' behaviors (flexibility). To do this, it must be able to deter potentially exploitative behavior from its partner and, when beneficial, determine how to elicit cooperation from a (potentially distrustful) partner who might be disinclined to cooperate. Third, when associating with people, the algorithm must learn effective behavior within very short timescales – i.e., within only a few rounds of interaction (learning speed). These requirements create many technical challenges . . . including the need to deal with adaptive partners who may also be learning and the need to reason over multiple, potentially infinite, equilibria solutions within the large strategy spaces inherent of repeated games. The sum of these challenges often causes AI algorithms to fail to cooperate, even when doing so would be beneficial to the algorithm's long-term payoffs.

These real-world limitations suggest that if AI collusion exists, it needs to have overcome these various factors. With a new focus on data science degrees in various universities around the world and improved machine-learning tools, such a day may come (or may have happened covertly), implying that we need to take the possibility of AI collusion seriously.

Other work has focused on how AI may improve prediction capabilities, say about the current or future demand levels in a market, and how these changes in the information structure influence collusion among classical rational economic agents (as opposed to considering algorithms as such). See Miklos-Thal and Tucker (2019) and Wilson and O'Connor (2019). These works can be thought of as extensions to the classical work on collusion by Green and Porter (1984) and Rotemberg and Saloner (1986).

60.1.3 *The Effect of AI and Accompanying Technology on Entry and Investment*

Although our main contributions involve the connections between AI and trust and AI and screens for nonprice variables, here we note in passing that AI (along with other technological changes) may also influence decisions concerning entry and investment, with potentially nuanced results. To do this, let us return to one of the core theories of why AI may facilitate collusion: by speeding up pricing decisions and easing the monitoring of prices, the temptation to cheat on a collusive arrangement may be very low because such cheating can be readily detected and punished.

But these same technological advances may influence market structural features and other aspects of competition in ways that counter or even reverse any prospective collusion-enhancing effects. Consider the entry decision. It may be easier for prospective entrants to recognize the potential for high profits in a given market if prices are readily observed. Hence, AI may help potential entrants find profitable investment opportunities. A standard feature of models of collusion is that as the number of active firms increases, it becomes harder to maintain collusion.

AI may also make it easier to quickly and inexpensively enter markets, and then leave again if prices fall too much. That is, it may be easier to practice "hit-and-run entry."

Consider, for example, an online vendor that functions as one of many intermediaries to a variety of manufacturers, and suppose that the collusive concern involves pricing by such intermediaries (say, on an e-commerce platform). Any one vendor may be able to rapidly adjust its product line over time to take advantage of collusive attempts to raise prices in particular markets. Because such a vendor can exit quickly, it is not concerned about any punishment that might be meted out by the colluding parties. Another way of thinking about this is that a given disruptive player may be able to spread its disruptive behavior more effectively across more markets as a result of new technologies.

In addition to directly encouraging entry, AI and accompanying technological changes may alter investment and product-positioning incentives by allowing firms (incumbents or potential entrants) to better understand consumer demand. Most prominently, abundant online reviews and ratings of different products provide a rich source of data for firms, and this data (used alone or parsed with AI) may reasonably allow incumbents to more easily improve their products, or suggest to an entrant what a successful new product variant might be. In other words, for any given price level, the returns to innovation may be higher when firms have more abundant sources of data about what consumers prefer.

Such improved innovation and product design may, of course, benefit consumers. However, collusion remains a concern and indeed collusion may limit the benefits from innovation that flow to consumers. The exception is if such innovation itself encourages entry by new players, and thereby contributes to the disruption of collusive behavior.

60.1.4 *What Does This Mean for Compliance?*

Our discussion of the literature so far suggests that currently there is no clear answer as to whether AI collusion is (or will become) a significant concern. Nonetheless, some simple lessons emerge related to compliance.

First and most simply, it seems clear that there is the potential for mischief when humans work to use machines to facilitate collusion, for example, in hub-and-spoke style conspiracies. Ostensibly, competing managers might choose to use a common algorithm to facilitate collusion or join marketplaces with rules that are likely to lead to collusive outcomes.

Second, even in the absence of a clear hub-and-spoke-style conspiracy, humans may be tempted to design algorithms to facilitate collusion. Humans might, for example, directly program in features that would tend to encourage collusive play. The simplest example is programming in tit-for-tat behavior, or other behavior that seeks to lead a market to higher prices or punish rivals that charge low prices.

60.2 TRUST AND AI COLLUSION

Just as humans can collude, humans can directly program machines with the intent of encouraging collusion. With algorithms, however, it may be easier to move more markets toward collusion, simply by applying the same algorithm to different products. As more pricing is automated, fewer humans are involved within a given organization, suggesting, from a compliance perspective, that an organization may be able to expand collusive activity with less likelihood of internal detection (which may also limit external detection). But we note that this collusive risk is greater the more such behavior exists across organizations.

Because collusion involves multiple firms, it requires agents across those different firms to make the collusion work and compliance failures across multiple organizations. But should this occur, more products might be affected than would be true in the absence of AI.

Yet, AI may also make the cost of colluding higher or lower depending on a series of factors. From a traditional standpoint, firms are complex hierarchies, plagued with information and incentive problems. Coordination is therefore costly, possibly decreasing the profitability of wrongdoing. As an instance of costly coordination, we can think of a top manager instructing, and incentivizing through the promise of a reward, a middle manager to adopt a collusive pricing strategy and remain quiet about it (i.e., not blow the whistle). Coordination problems are typically solved by a combination of rewards and punishments (formal and informal) and are often viewed as agency costs. Some papers examine mechanisms across firms to show how this coordination works (Genesove and Mullin 2001; Levenstein 1997), but work remains to be done as to the particular mechanisms employed to address dynamics within firms to create this trust. The idea of building trust as part of AI has not explicitly been the focus of the AI collusion literature outside of noting the experimental economic literature on more general coordination.

AI collusion may be easier in that it may be more straightforward to solve than the internal agency cost problem. Firms often organize themselves by separating ownership from control, paving the way to informational frictions such as moral hazard. Owners cannot be certain that managers will act in their best interest without effective monitoring. In addition, as the firm grows in size and the hierarchy becomes more complex, informational asymmetries arise among different layers of management. Typically, a cartel must succeed in solving internal agency problems (avoiding detection by others within the firm). However, to achieve effective collusion for an industry, the cartel must also solve coordination across firms. AI collusion potentially creates mechanisms to get around the verification problem within the firm because it reduces the number of employees in any given firm who need to be involved in collusion and who might otherwise leave a trail for others within the firm to blow the whistle on the cartel.

Another possible solution to the trust problem is AI collusion across firms that does not require human intervention in the same industry. If AI can overcome the trust problem, it can make commitments to collude across firms more credible. Sociologists and economists (Greif 2006; Macaulay 1963; Tirole 1996) emphasize that a large share of incentives are informal (i.e., relational). These relational norms may be employed to either solve typical agency cost problems (including loyalty, trust, and hard work) and also to induce price fixing. Examples include promises of promotion, salary raises, or even side payments. Informal incentives are powerful in that they are difficult to establish in court. To be effective, however, these incentives must be credible. That is, employees must trust that it is in their best interest to honor their promises across firms. If machines can learn to trust, this reduces the possibility of defection from a cartel.

However, relational contracting might also make AI collusion less likely. Economics has highlighted the importance of relationships containing repeated and long-term promises that are honored (Williamson 1983). Since, even absent agency cost problems, cartels must be long-term sustainable, it is likely that they involve "patient" enough decision-makers. If firms are patient enough to sustain a cartel, it is also plausible to think that they are patient enough to enforce relational contracts to solve agency cost problems across firms. However, how do algorithms build trust across firms? Algorithms have difficulty in understanding humor, jealousy, kinship, envy, and other human emotions that create or reduce trust, as of yet.

The above discussion suggests that human involvement with automated pricing systems should be examined closely. Because such involvement may provide direct opportunities for managers to collude, effective compliance requires that overseers inquire as to the process that guided both the selection and the development of the algorithm. If evidence is uncovered that this selection or development process was motivated by the desire to reduce competition, there may be a serious and evident compliance risk. In other settings, machines may learn to collude on their own. This would create another set of compliance risks for which the current processes of compliance are not well equipped.

60.3 NEW IDEAS: SCREENS FOR DETECTION AND AI COLLUSION FOR NONPRICE COMPETITION

60.3.1 *What Are Screens?*

Screens are a mechanism for identifying anticompetitive behavior. A screen is a diagnostic tool that uses statistical testing based on an econometric model of anticompetitive behavior to identify patterns of collusion. Traditional screens require data such as prices, bids, market shares, volumes, etc. to be able to identify patterns of behavior that exhibit irregularities that suggest potential collusion.

Screening in competition cases employs two general strategies. The first strategy searches for improbable events. This type of screen is akin to a cheating poker player who wins every hand. The collusive equivalent examines improbable price movements within an industry that are likely explained through coordination. The second screening strategy uses a control group. That is, the prices in the control group seem anomalous as compared to other similar markets.

60.3.2 *How Can Screens Be Used for AI-Related Compliance?*

Screens are only as good as the assumptions made regarding the market and the screen for the model. Effective screens also require sufficient data to properly detect wrongdoing. Thus, screens will work better when there are large amounts of data. This suggests that AI can be used to have machines better determine situations where collusion may be likely. Certain types of characteristics make the use of AI to implement screening a worthwhile investment. The first is large amounts of data. The second goes to issues that are structural in nature. Structural features that are typically associated with a higher likelihood of collusion include homogenous products, lack of industry volatility, and at least moderate concentration (similarly, the presence of some leading players in terms of size in the industry). When such features are present then it may be that collusion is more likely and hence investing in detection is more sensible. Beyond structural factors, work on screens has examined behavioral factors (Harrington 2007) that suggest collusion based on behavioral deviations on price or nonprice factors.

Bajari and Ye (2003) and Porter and Zona (1999) both studied structural screens. Behavioral screens were looked into by Abrantes-Metz et al. (2012) and Jiménez and Periguero (2012).

Rather than AI serving as a collusive mechanism, it can be used to develop better models and gather data to improve prediction of where collusive behavior will occur. There is a series of areas in which screens can be used. In these areas, there is rich empirical literature on the applications of screens. One such area is bid rigging of otherwise competitive tenders. Screens have been used to identify bid rigging in milk (Porter and Zona 1999), frozen fish (Abrantes-Metz et al. 2006), consulting work contracts (Ishii 2009), and financial markets (Abrantes-Metz et al. 2012). Hendricks et al. (2015) review the literature on auctions and bid rigging generally.

Another area in which AI can be used to detect collusion is price fixing. Theory posits that successful collusion allows for higher prices and less volatility than prices that would prevail absent collusion (Harrington and Chen 2006). Sometimes unusual patterns in pricing suggest collusion, and pricing irregularities may indicate temporary breakdowns in collusion and consequent punishment phases. Thus, AI can more effectively identify situations in which there may be collusive explanations for unusual patterns based on structure or behavior.

Harrington (2018) suggests further study of AI collusion to better understand detecting and prosecuting it. The increasing prevalence of AI may also lead to effects not previously seen or well studied. For example, if it becomes possible to tell which vendors are using AI, it might be possible for authorities or private actors to look for interaction or hub-and-spoke effects. While established screens look for some sort of variance in price/quantities, there may be other areas in which AI could test for collusion. One way would be to test for "splitting the market over time" in terms of prices or potentially territorial restrictions. Another such test might be for "shill reviews as a tool for collusion" (see Section 60.3.3 for more details). The basic idea is that shill reviews can be used to support a cartel. If, for example, price cuts by a firm lead to "review attacks" against that firm, then this may be evidence of collusive behavior. The empirical marketing literature suggests that fraudulent reviews (often with low ratings) are common online (Anderson and Simester 2014; Lappas et al. 2016; Luca and Zervas 2016; Mayzlin et al. 2014). Most importantly, one such paper by Luca and Zervas (2016: 3413) notes that in the case of Yelp ratings, restaurants are more likely to receive negative reviews "when there is an increase in competition from independent restaurants serving similar types of food."

The great bulk of the existing discussion of AI collusion focuses solely on price effects of collusion and specifically whether and how AI will lead an existing set of competitors to raise their prices. Although this focus is reasonable as a starting point, it neglects not only that nonprice variables may be important for collusion but also that there is much data available regarding certain nonprice variables. We emphasize that we are not claiming to be the first to consider such variables (see, e.g., Schinkel and Spiegel 2017). However, we will focus in on the particular dimension of consumer reviews and ratings and discuss their role in collusion. We will also suggest potential new empirical screens along this dimension.

60.3.3 *Consumer Reviews as a Nonprice Variable, and Screening on Reviews and Prices*

Models of collusion typically consider only price-setting behavior. However, especially in online markets, an important additional variable is consumer reviews and ratings. Many online marketplaces allow consumers to provide such feedback, which is then prominently displayed for all to see. Such reviews are prone to deception and in a collusive environment might be used for purposes of punishment against cartel members. Because of the common presumption that collusion and punishment involve only price effects, many existing screening approaches to collusion would leave collusion along other dimensions undetected.

A feature of these reviews is that they are not necessarily authentic – firms can manipulate their own ratings and reviews or those of their rivals, most obviously by submitting fake reviews. Additionally, even if a review (say, a negative one aimed at a rival) is known by rivals to be fake, those rivals may be unsure which firm is behind the review. That is, a firm that generates a fake review may effectively be anonymous.

To better understand collusion in online markets, these ratings and reviews must be considered within a broader collusive framework that also involves prices. As we will explain, this suggests that new potential screens are needed to detect collusion, focusing not just on prices but also on ratings and co-movements in prices and ratings.

We suppose that firms are able and willing to use AI to automate the process of manipulating their own ratings, and those of their rivals, in the same way that price setting can be automated.[2] To understand the role of such manipulation, we first ask how these ratings would be chosen in the absence of collusion. In the absence of any dynamic considerations, how would firms manipulate reviews?

A leading possibility is that firms would choose their positive self-reviews and negative rival-reviews in whatever manner maximizes their own demand at the prevailing (or equilibrium) prices. If negative reviews are used, then it may be that the overall effect is to lower average ratings in this product category, compared to the situation in which no firms manipulate ratings. This would lead to an inward shift in the industry demand facing these firms. In turn, this would lower industry profits and possibly lower average prices.

We can therefore see that a collusive regime might seek both to increase aggregate product ratings (and hence shift demand outwards) and to raise prices. It seems natural that this regime would, from the cartel's perspective, preferably involve only positive fake product reviews, not attacks on rivals' ratings. It may also be that the overall quantity of fake reviews ideally would decline, although this is less certain because it might be optimal to do more total fake reviews but ones that are positive in nature. But, ideally, there would be fewer fake reviews in total or at least fewer fake negative reviews.

Although this may be the ideal outcome for a cartel, the fact that it is difficult to know the ultimate source of any fake review raises challenges for a cartel. In other words, even though prices may be readily observed and quickly changed, the anonymity of reviews gives cartel members another, possibly safer way to cheat on the cartel.[3] This temptation may increase when prices are higher, if fake negative reviews by one firm shift demand away from the target and toward other firms.

Nonetheless, even when monitoring of some feature of competition is imperfect, cartels may still be able to function, as Green and Porter (1984) show in the context of unobservable prices.[4] In the present context, to limit fake negative reviews, a cartel may enter a punishment phase if there is sufficient reason to believe that many fake negative reviews are being used. For example, an otherwise unexplained decline in the ratings for one or more firms might trigger a punishment phase, even though it is not known for certain whether fake reviews were used or what the source of any fake reviews is. To explain further, average ratings are likely to

[2] Of course, many firms would not engage in these tactics, but there may be some that would.

[3] To be entirely clear, when we say that reviews are anonymous, we don't mean that there is no name associated with a given review but instead that the reviewer may be a shill and that tying the reviewer to the firm behind the review might be difficult.

[4] Cartels may not be able to keep prices as high as they would prefer in all circumstances, due to either misunderstandings or other reasons. The ability of a cartel to recover from bouts of lower prices is important for maintaining long-term cartel profits. Green and Porter (1984) identify "equilibrium price wars" in cartels, in which demand uncertainty makes it difficult for a cartel to always know whether profits have fallen due to a deviation by a cartel member or instead due to a random demand shift, and the cartel must sometimes sharply lower prices in response. Similarly, Rotemberg and Saloner (1986) identify that forecast changes in the level of demand may lead to periods in which prices are much lower than in other periods, even with a cartel.

be somewhat random over time and, even if no fake reviews are used, it is possible that average reviews will decline. But because the cartel cannot be sure that fake reviews are not driving this decline, it may be necessary to enter a temporary punishment phase. The purpose of such a punishment phase is to deter cheating on the cartel in the first place. Such a punishment may involve price cuts by all firms or an increase in the number of negative reviews leveled by firms against one another.

However, the more successful the cartel is, the fewer fake negative reviews will be used. Such reviews could be part of any punishment phase that the cartel enters, even if this punishment phase occurs in the absence of definitive proof that cheating occurred. Because of a lack of focus on nonprice punishment from victims or competition authorities, such punishment may go undetected.

In other cases, it may be clear which firm has deviated from a collusive regime, in which case both price cuts and negative fake reviews targeted against the deviator may result. For instance, if a firm chooses to cut prices to a level lower than stipulated by the cartel then this will be clear to other members of the cartel. As the cartel recovers, we would expect both prices to rise and negative fake reviews to taper off.

We will now discuss potential empirical screens suggested by our informal analysis above. We can imagine that such screens might be used in ways similar to (price) variance screens. In particular, screens that look at reviews and ratings in addition to price might be used to detect formation of cartels within given markets over time. Importantly, it may be that such screens could be broadly implemented using AI itself.

There are two related types of empirical screen suggested by our informal discussion so far. The essence of the first screen is to detect such co-movements in prices and reviews. In markets that have become cartelized, not only should prices increase but also the number of fake negative reviews should decrease where this decrease is more significant the more successful the cartel is. Also, the total number of fake reviews, either positive or negative, may decrease. Overall, we might expect category rating averages to increase. Hence, otherwise unexplained increases in prices that are also accompanied by declines in negative fake reviews and increases in overall ratings may be evidence of cartelization (subject to considering other explanations as discussed later). Note that, in the absence of other factors, normally higher prices would likely be associated with lower overall ratings. Hence, the idea of this screen is to look for anomalous positive correlation between price and ratings.

This first screen also applies if the industry periodically enters punishment phases driven by unexplained declines in average reviews, where it is difficult to lay blame on any particular firm due to the anonymity of reviews. In fact, following up our discussion earlier, even if firms don't usually use fake reviews, overall randomness in the review process by regular consumers may sometimes lead to declines in average ratings. In these cases, because the cartel cannot definitely know whether a firm has sponsored fake reviews and so is behind these declines, the industry may need to enter a temporary punishment phase. Thus, prices may fall and fake negative reviews increase with a consequent decline in overall ratings, but only temporarily. Again, this suggests a positive correlation between prices and ratings, which is not what should be expected in the absence of other factors.

Of course, recognizing a fake negative review from a real negative review is not easy. However, we emphasize that a decline in fake negative reviews should mean a decline in overall negative reviews – and possibly a decrease in the raw number of ratings over time – and an increase in the level of ratings. So, it may be easier to look first at overall ratings and ratings activity (that is, the number of ratings). Moreover, it may be possible to probabilistically detect fake reviews using machine-learning capabilities. For example, fake reviews may on average be of lower quality or more generic than real reviews. Ideally, it would be possible to construct a measure of review quality and the frequency of fake reviews, positive or negative, being used at any point in time. And, indeed, this might be an important step somewhere in the process of screening, even if not the first step.

As for any screen, other possible explanations must be considered before reaching any conclusions. Thus, it is important to control for other factors that may explain simultaneous price increases and ratings increases. For instance, industry-wide improvements in products or customer service, or even increased review solicitations from legitimate purchasers, could explain simultaneous price increases and ratings increases. But these questions do not need to be considered to run the initial screen, and instead can be considered for cases that appear problematic. Most papers that focus on reviews focus on end-consumer reviews. They do not focus on reviews in business-to-business (B2B) platforms. Thus, the study of ratings as a retaliatory tool with which to harden a cartel is an area of potential future investigation.

The second type of empirical screen suggested by our discussion here involves detecting punishments directed at a specific firm. In particular, if a firm that cuts prices in turn suffers a sudden spike in the number of negative reviews, then this may be evidence of other firms in the cartel punishing the price cutter.[5] Similarly, if a specific firm cuts its price and is attacked in reviews, but then raises its price and experiences a decline in review attacks, then this may be further evidence of cartel behavior.

To conclude this section, we reiterate that compliance in online settings may benefit by considering not only prices but also reviews and ratings, at least if such ratings and reviews can be manipulated or falsified by firms in the market. In particular, we emphasized co-movements in prices and ratings. Both screens apply to cartels that may experience periods of instability, potentially followed by recovery of the cartel. The first screen also applies to the transition from a noncartelized regime to a cartelized one. Finally, screens might be used to detect ratings manipulation as identified by Mukherjee et al. (2011).

60.4 CONCLUSION

AI collusion research remains in its nascent stages. Assuming that it is possible to infer agreement for purposes of antitrust liability, AI collusion raises new possible mechanisms to create collusion. However, when used as a mechanism to detect collusion via screens, AI can help to solve collusion problems. This is particularly true for certain industries that are more prone to collusion for structural reasons or where certain patterns of behavior may be more likely to yield results with an investment in AI-screening technology.

Overall, the literature on AI collusion has focused on theory and policy arguments rather than on empirics. Nevertheless, the study of AI collusion is significant. If AI collusion does exist, the methods to detect such collusion must be tailored to the compliance risks specific to AI. Traditional organizational mechanisms that must be modified include internal controls, surveillance, and reporting systems.[6] Spending on AI compliance and the mechanisms used

[5] As already noted, a price cut on its own should probably not otherwise lead to a ratings decline for a firm (that is, in the absence of strategic behavior by rivals or other effects).

[6] Internal controls focus on monitoring of antitrust conduct, evaluating the potential risk of employees' conduct, and implementing various internal training programs that promote compliance. The surveillance system identifies whether employees' activities violate antitrust law and, if so, to cease the activity. In addition, once an illegal activity is observed, what the compliance literature and practice call a "surveillance system" is implemented within the firm. The reporting allows employees to report potential illegal antitrust activities.

to detect such collusion via AI-enabled screens would be different from that on traditional mechanisms of antitrust compliance. The cost of such AI compliance would also be significant.

One of the conclusions of this chapter is that AI should be utilized through screens only when the payoff of the effort is high based on the amount and the quality of data. This returns antitrust compliance to an earlier era in which structural concerns of collusion being more probable were far more central to antitrust enforcement. It also renews emphasis on behavioral markers such as irregular pricing or nonpricing patterns. From a policy perspective, one natural place to focus an AI compliance inquiry is procurement auctions by governments or large commercial buyers, or other environments with significant amounts of data.

REFERENCES

Abrantes-Metz, R., L. Froeb, J. Geweke, and C. Taylor. 2006. "A Variance Screen for Collusion." *International Journal of Industrial Organization* 24, no. 3 (May): 467–86.

Abrantes-Metz, Rosa, Michael Kraten, Albert Metz, and Gim Seow. 2012. "Libor Manipulation?" *Journal of Banking and Finance* 36, No. 1 (January): 136–50.

Anderson, E. T., and D. I. Simester. 2014. "Reviews without a Purchase: Low Ratings, Loyal Customers, and Deception." *Journal of Marketing Research* 51, No. 3 (June): 249–69.

Axelrod, R. 1984. *The Evolution of Cooperation*. New York: Basic Books.

Bajari, P., and L. Ye. 2003. "Deciding between Competition and Collusion." *Review of Economics and Statistics* 85, no. 4 (November): 971–89.

Beckenstein, A. R., and H. L. Gabel. 1986. "The Economics of Antitrust Compliance." *Southern Economics Journal* 52, no. 3 (January): 673–92.

Brown, Z. Y., and A. MacKay. 2019. "Competition in Pricing Algorithms." Working Paper.

Calvano, E., G. Calzolari, V. Denicolò, and S. Pastorello. 2020. "Artificial Intelligence, Algorithmic Pricing and Collusion." *American Economic Review* 110, no. 10: 3267–97.

Crandall, J. W., M. Oudah, Tennom, F. Ishowo-Oloko, S. Abdallah, J. F. Bonnefon, M. Cebrian, A. Shariff, M. A. Goodrich, and I. Rahwan. 2018. "Cooperating with Machines." *Nature Communications* 9: 233.

Dong, C., Y. Wang, A. Aldweesh, P. McCorry, and A. van Moorsel. 2017. "Betrayal, Distrust, and Rationality: Smart Counter-Collusion Contracts for Verifiable Cloud Computing." Proceedings of the 2017 ACM SIGSAC Conference on Computer and Communications Security, Dallas, TX, 30 October–3 November.

Ezrachi, A., and M. E. Stucke. 2017. "Artificial Intelligence and Collusion: When Computers Inhibit Competition." *Illinois Law Review* 2017: 1785–1810.

Genesove, D., and W. P. Mullin. 2001. "Rules, Communication, and Collusion: Narrative Evidence from the Sugar Institute Case." *American Economic Review* 91, No. 3: 379–98.

Green, E., and R. Porter. 1984. "Noncooperative Collusion under Imperfect Price Information." *Econometrica* 52, No. 1: 87–100.

Greif, A. 2006. *Institutions and the Path to the Modern Economy: Lessons from Medieval Trade*. New York: Cambridge University Press.

Harrington, J. 2007. "Behavioral Screening and the Detection of Cartels." In *European Competition Law Annual 2006: Enforcement of Prohibition of Cartels*, eds. Claus-Dieter Ehlermann and Isabela Atanasiu, 51–68. Oxford: Hart Publishing.

2018. "Antitrust in High Speed: Colluding through Algorithms and Other Technologies." New York, 8 January. https://joeharrington5201922.github.io/pdf/Antitrust%20in%20High%20Speed_Remarks_Harrington.pdf.

Harrington J., and J. Chen. 2006. "Cartel Pricing Dynamics with Cost Variability and Endogenous Buyer Detection." *International Journal of Industrial Organization* 24, No. 6: 347.

Hendricks, K., R. P. McAfee, and M. Williams. 2015. "Auctions and Bid Rigging." In *Oxford Handbook on International Antitrust Economics*, Vol. 2, eds. Roger D. Blair and D. Daniel Sokol, 498–522. New York: Oxford University Press.

Hylton, K. N. 2015. "Deterrence and Antitrust Punishment: Firms versus Agents." *Iowa Law Review* 100: 2069–83.
Ishii, R. 2009. "Favor Exchange in Collusion: Empirical Study of Repeated Procurement Auctions in Japan." *International Journal of Industrial Organization* 27: 137–44.
Ittoo, A., and N. Petit. 2017. "Algorithmic Pricing Agents and Tacit Collusion: A Technological Perspective." Working Paper.
Jiménez, J. L., and J. Perdiguero. 2012. "Does Rigidity Hide Collusion?" *Review of Industrial Organization* 41, no. 3: 223–48.
Lappas, T., G. Sabnis, and G. Valkanas. 2016. "The Impact of Fake Reviews on Online Visibility: A Vulnerability Assessment of the Hotel Industry." *Information Systems Research* 27, No. 4: 940–61.
Levenstein, M. 1997. "Price Wars and the Stability of Collusion: A Study of the Pre-World War I Bromine Industry." *Journal of Industrial Economics* 45, No. 2: 117–38.
Kaplow, L. 2013. *Competition Policy and Price Fixing*. Princeton, NJ: Princeton University Press.
Klein, T. 2019. "Autonomous Algorithmic Collusion: Q-Learning under Sequential Pricing." Working Paper.
Kühn, K. U., and S. Tadelis. 2018. "The Economics of Algorithmic Pricing: Is Collusion Really Inevitable?" Working Paper.
Luca, M., and G. Zervas. 2016. "Fake It Till You Make It: Reputation, Competition, and Yelp Review Fraud." *Management Science* 62, No. 12: 3412–27.
Macaulay, S. 1963. "Non-contractual Relations in Business: A Preliminary Study." *American Sociological Review* 28, No. 1: 55–67.
Maskin, E., and J. Tirole. 1988. "A Theory of Dynamic Oligopoly, II: Price Competition, Kinked Demand Curves, and Edgeworth Cycles." *Econometrica* 56, No. 3: 571–99.
Mayzlin, D., Y. Dover, and J. Chevalier. 2014. "Promotional Reviews: An Empirical Investigation of Online Review Manipulation." *American Economic Review* 104, No. 8: 2421–55.
Mehra, S. K. 2016. "Antitrust and the Robo-Seller: Competition in the Time of Algorithms." *Minnesota Law Review* 100: 1323–75.
Miklos-Thal, J., and C. Tucker. 2019. "Collusion by Algorithm: Does Better Demand Prediction Facilitate Coordination between Sellers?" *Management Science* 65, no. 4: 1552–61.
Milgrom, P., and J. Roberts. 1990. "Rationalizability, Learning, and Equilibrium in Games with Stochastic Complementarities." *Econometrica* 58, No. 6: 1255–77.
Mukherjee, A. B., Liu J. Wang, N. Glance, and N. Jindal. 2011. "Detecting Group Review Spam." *ACM Proceedings of the 20th International Conference Companion on World Wide Web*: 93–4.
Porter, R., and J. Zona. 1999. "Ohio School Milk Markets: An Analysis of Bidding." *RAND Journal of Economics* 30: 263–88.
Riley, A., and D. D. Sokol. 2015. "Rethinking Compliance." *Journal of Antitrust Enforcement* 3: 31–57.
Rotemberg, J., and G. Saloner. 1986. "A Supergame-Theoretic Model of Price Wars during Booms." *American Economic Review* 76, No. 3: 390–407.
Salcedo, B. 2015. "Pricing Algorithms and Tacit Collusion." Working paper.
Schinkel, M. P., and Y. Spiegel. 2017. "Can Collusion Promote Sustainable Consumption and Production?" *International Journal of Industrial Organization* 53: 371–98.
Schwalbe, U. 2018. "Algorithms, Machine Learning, and Collusion." Working Paper.
Sokol, D. D. 2017. "Antitrust Compliance." In *The Oxford Handbook of Strategy Implementation*, eds. Michael A. Hitt, Susan E. Jackson, Salvador Carmona, Leonard Bierman, Christina E. Shalley, and Mike Wright, 155–76. New York: Oxford University Press.
Tesauro, G., and J. O. Kephart. 2002. "Pricing in Economies Using Multi-agent Q-learning." *Autonomous Agents and Multi-agent Systems* 5: 289–304.
Tirole, J. 1996. "A Theory of Collective Reputations (with Applications to the Persistence of Corruption and to Firm Quality)." *Review of Economic Studies* 63, No. 1: 1–22.
Waltman, L., and U. Kaymak. 2008. "Q-learning Agents in a Cournot Oligopoly Model." *Journal of Economic Dynamics and Control* 32: 3275–93.
Wilson, N., and J. O'Connor. 2019. "Reduced Demand Uncertainty and the Sustainability of Collusion: How AI Could Affect Competition." Working Paper.
Williamson, Oliver. 1983. "Credible Commitments: Using Hostages to Support Exchange." *American Economic Review* 73, No. 4: 519–40.

61

HIPAA Compliance

Stacey A. Tovino

Abstract: Despite the federal Department of Health and Human Services' provision of considerable guidance and technical assistance to covered entities and business associates regarding their responsibilities under the HIPAA Privacy, Security, and Breach Notification Rules (HIPAA), little is known about the extent of compliance across the healthcare industry as well as reasons for noncompliance. This chapter reviews academic, industry, and government studies assessing HIPAA compliance and presents relevant insights. These insights relate to the extent to which small numbers of covered entities comply with the HIPAA Privacy Rule's plain language requirement, the HIPAA Privacy Rule's access to protected health information requirement, the HIPAA Security Rule's addressable encryption standard, and the HIPAA Security Rule's audit logs and access reports requirement. Additional insights relate to the extent to which covered hospitals and health systems believe that they are complying with the HIPAA Privacy and Security Rules, the impact of HITECH on data breaches involving business associates, the organizational strategies and institutional environments that influence compliance, and the extent to which institutional pressures and internal security needs assessments influence investment in security compliance.

61.1 INTRODUCTION

The available studies have significant limitations that affect their generalizability and, in some cases, their reliability. Most of the available studies focus on small subsets of regulated actors, leaving entire classes of covered entities and business associates unstudied. Many studies focus on compliance with discrete regulatory provisions, ignoring dozens of other HIPAA requirements. Many studies focus on compliance in narrow contexts, such as personal health records or text messaging, overlooking daily interactions between and among workforce members and the large-scale operations of covered entities and business associates. Several studies that rely on self-reported compliance data reveal substantial misunderstandings regarding HIPAA by regulated actors. Finally, some studies demonstrate misunderstandings regarding HIPAA by nonlawyer study authors, impacting both study design and data analysis. This chapter concludes by suggesting ways in which the HIPAA compliance literature could be further developed.

61.2 BACKGROUND

On August 21, 1996, President William J. Clinton signed the Health Insurance Portability and Accountability Act (HIPAA) into law. HIPAA directed the federal Department of Health and

Human Services (HHS) to promulgate regulations requiring covered entities, defined to include health plans, healthcare clearinghouses, and certain healthcare providers, to protect the privacy and security of protected health information (PHI) and electronic protected health information (ePHI), respectively. These regulations are known as the HIPAA Privacy Rule and the HIPAA Security Rule. (45 C.F.R. §§ 164.500–.534; 45 C.F.R. §§ 164.302–.318). Compliance by most, but not all, covered entities with the HIPAA Privacy Rule was required by April 14, 2003. Compliance by most, but not all, covered entities with the HIPAA Security Rule was required by April 20, 2005.

On February 17, 2009, President Barack Obama signed into law the American Recovery and Reinvestment Act (ARRA), which included the Health Information Technology for Economic and Clinical Health (HITECH) Act. HITECH directed HHS to promulgate regulations extending the application of the use and disclosure requirements within the HIPAA Privacy Rule and the administrative, physical, and technical safeguards within the HIPAA Security Rule to business associates. HITECH also directed HHS to promulgate regulations mandating covered entities and business associates to adhere to certain notification procedures in the event of a breach of unsecured protected health information (uPHI). These regulations are known as the HIPAA Breach Notification Rule (45 C.F.R. §§ 164.400–.414). Compliance with the HIPAA Breach Notification Rule was technically required by September 23, 2009; however, HHS used its technical discretion not to impose sanctions for a failure to make proper notification regarding breaches discovered before February 22, 2010.

As discussed in more detail in this chapter, the HIPAA compliance literature is not robust. A small number of academic, industry, and government studies have attempted to assess compliance by covered entities and business associates with all or portions of the HIPAA Privacy, Security, and Breach Notification Rules. These studies are summarized and analyzed in this chapter.

61.3 PLAIN LANGUAGE REQUIREMENT

The HIPAA Privacy Rule requires authorizations for the use and disclosure of PHI to be written in plain language (45 C.F.R. § 164.508(c)(3)). One study, published by Paasche-Orlow et al. in 2013, attempts to assesses compliance with this plain language requirement. In particular, Paasche-Orlow et al. (2013) searched the websites of the 126 US medical schools listed on the Association of American Medical Colleges (AAMC) web page and, between June 2009 and June 2010, obtained HIPAA authorization forms and consent-to-research templates from 100 (79 percent) and 106 (84 percent) medical schools' websites, respectively. The authors studied the text in these forms and templates that would be presented to adults eligible to participate in research, although the authors excluded forms designed for special populations (e.g., children) and special circumstances (e.g., pregnancy), which is one limitation of this study. The study authors assessed the readability of these forms and templates using the Flesch-Kincaid readability scale, which is automated and available through Microsoft Word.

Paasche-Orlow et al. (2013) found, with respect to the HIPAA authorization forms, that the average reading level was at the 11.6 grade level compared to the average reading level for the consent-to-research forms required by the Federal Policy for the Protection of Human Subjects (the Common Rule), which was at the 9.8 grade level. The study authors also found that "[i]n a given medical school, the HIPAA template text is 1.8 grade levels higher than [the] informed consent template text," and that the HIPAA template text of medical schools did not meet the schools' own (internal) readability standards in the vast majority of cases (Paasche-Orlow et al. 2013:15).

The study authors concluded: "The average reading level of research-related HIPAA template text is much higher than the average reading capacity of U.S. adults and fails to meet these institutions' own stated standards by a large margin" (Paasche-Orlow et al. 2013:17). The authors recommended "[m]ore explicit guidance for how to make consent and HIPAA text for research studies easier to read and understand" and "more intense federal supervision" (Paasche-Orlow et al. 2013:18).

61.4 ACCESS TO PHI REQUIREMENT

With a few exceptions, the HIPAA Privacy Rule gives an individual the right to inspect and obtain a copy of PHI about the individual (45 C.F.R. § 164.524(a)(1)). Covered entities must provide the individual with access to the individual's PHI in the form (e.g., paper or electric) and format (e.g., email, flash drive, compact disc, online patient portal) requested by the individual if the PHI is readily producible in that form and format (45 C.F.R. § 164.524(c)(2)(i)). The HIPAA Privacy Rule permits covered entities to charge a reasonable, cost-based access fee; however, the access fee may include only the costs of labor, supplies, and postage (45 C.F.R. § 164.524(c)(4)). In guidance posted to its website, HHS has stated that covered entities have the option of charging a flat fee not to exceed $6.50 if they do not want to go through the process of calculating the actual or average costs for requests for electronic copies of ePHI (HHS 2016). Some states more specifically regulate medical record access charges, including through maximum charges codified in statutes and/or regulations.

One study attempts to assess compliance with the HIPAA Privacy Rule's access to PHI requirement. In a cross-sectional study published in 2018, Lye et al.: (1) collected medical records release forms from eighty-three top-ranked US hospitals representing twenty-nine states; and (2) subsequently telephoned each hospital's medical records department to collect data on requestable information, formats of release, costs, and processing times using a predetermined script to minimize variation and biases across telephone calls. Telephone call respondents were either employees of the hospitals' medical records departments or representatives from an outsourced call center.

Lye et al. (2018) found discordance between the information provided by the covered entities on their medical records release forms and the information obtained during the simulated patient telephone calls in terms of requestable information, formats of release, and costs. On the medical records release forms, as few as nine hospitals (11 percent) provided the option of selecting particular categories of PHI to be released and only forty-four hospitals (53 percent) provided patients the option to acquire their entire medical records. During the telephone calls, all eighty-three hospitals stated that they were able to release entire medical records to patients.

Lye et al. (2018) also found discrepancies in terms of information given during telephone calls compared to information provided on the medical records release forms between the formats hospitals stated that they could use to release information: sixty-nine (83 percent) versus forty (48 percent) for pick-up in person; twenty (24 percent) versus fourteen (17 percent) for facsimile; thirty-nine (47 percent) versus twenty-seven (33 percent) for email; fifty-five (66 percent) versus thirty-five (42 percent) for compact disc; and twenty-one (25 percent) versus thirty-three (40 percent) for online patient portals. Lye et al. (2018) stated that their findings demonstrated noncompliance with the HIPAA Privacy Rule provision prohibiting a covered entity from refusing to provide an individual with access to PHI in the form and format requested by the individual (45 C.F.R. § 164.524(c)(2)(i)).

Lye et al. (2018) also found that forty-eight respondent hospitals had costs of release (as much as $541.50 for a 200-page record) above HHS's guidance recommendation of $6.50 for electronically maintained records (HHS 2016). In addition, at least six of the hospitals (7 percent) were noncompliant with state requirements for processing times. Lye et al. (2018) concluded that there are "discrepancies in the information provided to patients regarding the medical records release processes and noncompliance with federal and state regulations and recommendations. Policies focused on improving patient access may require stricter enforcement to ensure more transparent and less burdensome medical records request processes for patients" (Lye et al. 2018:2).

61.5 AUDIT LOG AND ACCESS REPORT REQUIREMENTS

The HIPAA Security Rule requires covered entities and business associates to implement procedures to regularly review records of information system activity, such as audit logs, access reports, and security incident tracking reports (45 C.F.R. § 164.308(a)(1)(ii)(D)). The HIPAA Security Rule also requires covered entities and business associates to implement hardware, software, and/or procedural mechanisms that record and examine activity in information systems that contain or use ePHI (45 C.F.R. § 164.312(b)). With several exceptions, the HIPAA Privacy Rule gives individuals the right to receive an accounting of disclosures (but not uses) of PHI made by a covered entity in the six years prior to the date on which the accounting is requested (45 C.F.R. § 164.528(a)(1)).

One study attempts to investigate compliance with these requirements, although it is not clear that the study authors correctly understand these requirements. In a study published in 2011, Carrion, Aleman, and Toval reviewed the privacy policies of twenty free, web-based personal health records (PHRs) with available privacy policies and purported to extract and assess privacy and security characteristics according to certain unreferenced standards within the HIPAA Privacy and Security Rules. The study authors reported that fourteen out of the twenty (70 percent) PHRs studied allowed individuals access to their PHI as required by the HIPAA Privacy Rule, as discussed in Section 61.4. The study authors also found, however, that only two out of the twenty (10 percent) PHRs "provide the individual with the ability to view a log of who has accessed his/her PHR" (Carrion, Aleman, and Toval 2011:2383). The study concluded that many of the PHRs do not meet HIPAA standards and that "[s]ome improvements can be made to current PHR privacy policies to enhance the audit and management of access to users' PHRs" (Carrion, Aleman, and Toval 2011:2380).

The Carrion, Aleman, and Toval (2011) study has several limitations. First, the study authors appear to misunderstand the requirements set forth in the HIPAA Privacy and Security Rules. Although *covered entities* have an obligation to review information system activity through audit logs and access reports under the HIPAA Security Rule (45 C.F.R. § 164.308(a)(1)(ii)(D)), *individuals* have a right only to request and receive an accounting of disclosures (but not uses) under the HIPAA Privacy Rule (45 C.F.R. 164.528(a)(1)). The study authors appear to think that the HIPAA Security Rule gives individuals the right to access any audit logs and access reports involving their PHI:

> Does the PHR provide the individual with the ability to view a log of who has accessed his/her PHR?: Only two of the PHRs reviewed (10%) meet this requirement. The majority of the PHRs analyzed (65%) do not allow the individual to see who has accessed his/her data. . . . Our requirements are not being met by the PHRs analyzed (Carrion, Aleman, and Toval 2011:2383).

In addition, Carrion, Aleman, and Toval (2011) only assessed the PHRs with respect to a few HIPAA standards, ignoring dozens of other important standards. For example, the study authors did not assess the PHRs with respect to the HIPAA Privacy Rule's notice of privacy practices requirement (45 C.F.R. § 164.520), additional privacy protections requirement (45 C.F.R. § 164.522), or amendment of incorrect or incomplete PHI requirement (45 C.F.R. § 164.526). The study authors also did not assess the PHRs with respect to the majority of the administrative, physical, and technical safeguards set forth within the HIPAA Security Rule. (45 C.F.R. §§ 164.308–.312).

61.6 SHARING PHI BY TEXT

The HIPAA Privacy Rule permits the use and disclosure of PHI for treatment purposes without the patient's prior written authorization (45 C.F.R. § 164.506(c)(1) and (2)). For example, the HIPAA Privacy Rule permits a resident physician to share PHI with a teaching physician if the purpose of the communication is to obtain guidance regarding the treatment of a patient or to otherwise share information regarding the treatment of a patient. Likewise, the HIPAA Privacy Rule permits a teaching physician to share PHI with a resident if the purpose of the data sharing is to train the resident or to assist with the treatment of the patient. With respect to the *method* of PHI sharing, the HIPAA Security Rule contains an addressable encryption standard (45 C.F.R. § 164.312(a)(2)(iv)). In particular, the HIPAA Security Rule requires a covered entity to implement encryption only if, after a risk assessment, the covered entity has determined that encryption is a reasonable and appropriate safeguard in its risk management of the confidentiality, integrity, and availability of e-PHI. If the covered entity decides that encryption is not reasonable and appropriate, the covered entity must document that determination and implement an equivalent alternative measure, presuming that the alternative is reasonable and appropriate.

Three studies have attempted to assess HIPAA compliance in the context of text messaging, although it is not clear that the authors of (and/or the respondents to) these studies understand the HIPAA Privacy and Security Rule treatment and encryption provisions discussed above. The first text messaging study, published by Drolet et al. in 2017), involved a cross-sectional survey of the American Society for Surgery of the Hand membership in March and April 2016. Drolet et al. (2017) found that 63 percent of the 409 respondent hand surgeons reported that they believe that text messaging does not comply with the HIPAA Security Rule and that 37 percent of hand surgeons reported that they do not use text messaging to communicate PHI. According to the study authors, younger surgeons and respondents who believed that their texting complied with the HIPAA Security Rule were significantly more like to report text messaging of PHI.

The second text messaging study, published by Freundlich, Freundlich, and Drolet in 2018, involved three rounds of a direct email survey of US designated institutional officials (DIOs). DIOs are individuals who lead sponsoring institutions in the oversight and administration of residency and fellowship training programs accredited by the Accreditation

Council for Graduate Medical Education (ACGME). The survey was designed to assess institutional practices for electronic communication among trainees and faculty, not DIOs. Respondents represented ACGME-accredited programs located in all fifty states, the District of Columbia, and Puerto Rico.

Freundlich, Freundlich, and Drolet (2018) found that more than half of respondent institutions (202/339, 59.6 percent) still provide trainees with one-way text pagers as a means of clinical communication, including communication of PHI and ePHI regulated by the HIPAA Privacy and Security Rules, respectively, while 121/339 (35.7 percent) provide a cellular/mobile device for this purpose. Meanwhile, more than two-thirds of respondents (231/339, 68.1 percent) reported that their institutions prohibit the use of personal cellular/mobile devices for text messaging of PHI. The authors stated: "There is ongoing debate about the appropriate use of SMS under the Health Insurance Portability and Accountability Act (HIPAA) at academic institutions and this is reflected in the survey results" (Freundlich, Freundlich, and Drolet 2018:9).

Respondents to the Freundlich, Freundlich, and Drolet (2018) study were evenly split in their belief that HIPAA prohibited (167/339, 49.3 percent) or did not prohibit (172/339, 50.7 percent) text messaging of PHI on personal mobile devices. "This disparity amongst institutional and academic leaders highlights a concerning lack of clarity on legislation guiding electronic transmission of PHI" (Freundlich, Freundlich, and Drolet 2018:9). Of respondents who believed that SMS violates HIPAA standards, 94/167 (56.3 percent) reported that their institution still uses one-way text paging. The study authors concluded: "This great paradox may represent an inertial phenomenon or miseducation regarding new technology. Regardless, clarification is needed regarding appropriate use parameters for electronic communication" (Freundlich, Freundlich, and Drolet 2018:9).

The third text messaging study, published by McKnight and Franko in 2016, also purported to study self-reported HIPAA compliance in the context of texting by medical residents, medical fellows, and attending physicians at Accreditation Council for Graduate Medical Education (ACGME) training programs. The McKnight and Franko (2016) study involved a digital survey sent to 678 academic institutions over a one-month period. The study authors reported that 58 percent of all resident respondents self-reported "violating HIPAA" by sharing protected health information (PHI) via text messaging with 27 percent reporting they do it "often" or "routinely" compared to 15–19 percent of attending physicians. According to the study authors: (1) 5 percent of respondents "often" or "routinely" used HIPAA compliant apps (HCApps) with no significant differences related to training level; (2) 20 percent of residents admitted to using nonencrypted email at some point; and (3) 53 percent of attending physicians and 41 percent of medical residents utilized encrypted email routinely. Physicians from surgical specialties compared to nonsurgical specialties demonstrated higher rates of "HIPAA violations" with SMS use (35 percent versus 17.7 percent), standard photo/video messages (16.3 percent versus 4.7 percent), HCApps (10.9 percent versus 4.9 percent), and non-HCApps (5.6 percent versus 1.5 percent).

McKnight and Franko (2016) also assessed barriers to HIPAA compliance, reporting that the most significant, self-reported barriers were inconvenience (58 percent), lack of knowledge (37 percent), unfamiliarity (34 percent), inaccessibility (29 percent), and habit (24 percent). The authors concluded that "[m]edical professionals must acknowledge that despite laws to protect patient confidentiality in the era of mobile technology, over 50% of current medical trainees knowingly violate these rules regularly despite the threat of severe consequences. The medical community must further examine the reason for these inconsistencies and work towards possible solutions" (McKnight and Franko 2016:129).

One limitation of the McKnight and Franko (2016) study is the lack of perfect information by the studied medical residents, medical fellows, and teaching physicians regarding HIPAA. As discussed above, encryption is not a required implementation specification under the HIPAA Security Rule; instead, encryption is just addressable (45 C.F.R. § 164.312(a)(2)(iv), 164.312(e)(2)(ii)). Neither the study authors nor the respondents appear to understand the difference between a required and an addressable implementation specification. To this end, the residents, fellows, and teaching physicians' self-reports of their beliefs regarding their behaviors (e.g., that they believe they are texting using HCApps or non-HCA apps) may be accurate; however, their beliefs regarding whether their behaviors are HIPAA compliant, or whether particular technologies are HIPAA compliant, may be incorrect.

61.7 GENERAL COMPLIANCE DATA

One professional association, the American Health Information Management Association (AHIMA), has attempted to study HIPAA compliance more generally. In February 2004, less than one year after most covered entities were required to comply with the HIPAA Privacy Rule, AHIMA sent an email to AHIMA members who were considered most likely to have participated significantly in the HIPAA implementation process and to non-members who had participated in various HIPAA-related educational opportunities provided by AHIMA (AHIMA 2004: 12–13). AHIMA received 1,192 qualified responses, 56 percent of which came from individuals working in the hospital setting. The remainder of responses came from individuals working in integrated delivery systems, ambulatory care, physician offices, behavioral health care, home health care, long-term care, and other healthcare settings. In terms of geographic diversity, qualified responses were received from all fifty states, the District of Columbia, and Puerto Rico. Of the 1,192 qualified respondents: (1) 58 percent were designated privacy or security officials; (2) 11 percent were functioning as privacy or security officials without formal titles; and (3) the remaining 31 percent served on HIPAA privacy and security teams or committees but were neither designated officials nor functioning as such officials.

After analyzing the data it received, AHIMA stated in an April 2004 report: (1) 23 percent of respondents felt that their organizations were "fully compliant" with the HIPAA Privacy Rule; (2) 68 percent of respondents felt that their organizations were "currently between 85 to 99 percent compliant"; and (3) 8 percent of respondents reported being "50 percent or less compliant at this time" (AHIMA 2004:5). Seventy percent of survey respondents agreed that attempts to comply with the HIPAA Privacy Rule had uncovered privacy problem areas within their organizations. Two of the most common problem areas identified by AHIMA related to the lack of standardized practices for the release of PHI in accordance with 45 C.F.R. § 164.524 and public access to PHI in accordance with 45 C.F.R. § 164.510 (AHIMA 2004:5).

When asked by AHIMA about current problems complying with the HIPAA Privacy Rule, no single area was identified by more than 39 percent of respondents. However, four areas emerged as more problematic than all of the other areas: (1) the accounting of disclosures requirement under 45 C.F.R. § 164.528 (39 percent); (2) obtaining PHI from other providers as permitted by 45 C.F.R. § 164.506(c) (33 percent); (3) access and release of information to relatives or significant others pursuant to 45 C.F.R. § 164.510 (32 percent); and (4) the business associate requirements set forth in 45 C.F.R. §§ 164.502–.504 (25 percent) (AHIMA 2004:5).

Three years after most covered entities were required to comply with the HIPAA Privacy Rule, AHIMA conducted a second study (AHIMA 2006) that essentially repeated the study conducted two years earlier (AHIMA 2004). In the 2006 study, AHIMA found that nearly 39 percent of hospitals and health systems self-reported "full privacy compliance," a considerable increase over the 23 percent finding from the 2004 study. Fifty-five percent of respondents indicated that resources are their most significant barrier to full privacy compliance. "Privacy officers particularly need support for education and training of new staff, while a lack of resources and competing priorities have led some hospital and health system staff to slack off regarding all aspects of the privacy rule" (AHIMA 2006:3). AHIMA reported that budgets appear to impact the level of privacy training and monitoring that a privacy officer or staff are capable of providing. Finally, privacy officers reported sensing a loss of support from senior management, both in ensuring that the facility staff is aware of the need for privacy and in ensuring sufficient budgeting for education. Most providers reported growing accustomed to the various provisions of the HIPAA Privacy Rule. However, the accounting of disclosures requirement codified at 45 C.F.R. § 164.528 was still proving difficult for many respondents (AHIMA 2006:3).

The pair of AHIMA studies have several limitations, two of which are worth highlighting. First, the compliance data collected and analyzed by AHIMA were self-reported by the respondent hospitals and health systems. Given the dozens of standards set forth in the HIPAA Privacy and Security Rules and the lack of perfect legal knowledge and compliance knowledge on the part of covered entities, self-reported data (in this context) should be viewed with skepticism. HIPAA compliance is an ongoing concern and noncompliance is not readily detectable by one individual at any point in time. In addition, a majority of the AHIMA study respondents were affiliated with hospitals, leaving many other types of covered entities (e.g., physician clinics, nursing homes, home health agencies, hospices, rehabilitation facilities, health plans, and healthcare clearinghouses) unstudied.

In addition to data provided by AHIMA, HHS has released to the public reports assessing HIPAA compliance as well as data that could be used to assess HIPAA compliance (HHS 2018, 2019). In a compliance report covering years 2015, 2016, and 2017, for example, HHS (2018) summarily discusses: (1) the number of HIPAA-related complaints received by HHS from the public; (2) the number of complaints resolved informally, a summary of the types of complaint so resolved, and the number of covered entities that received technical assistance from HHS during each of the three years covered by the report; (3) the number of complaints that resulted in the imposition of civil money penalties or that were resolved through monetary settlements, including the nature of the complaints involved and the amount paid in each penalty or settlement; (4) the number of compliance reviews that HHS conducted and the outcome of each such review; (5) the number of subpoenas or inquiries issued by HHS relating to HIPAA; (6) the number of HIPAA audits performed as required by HITECH; and (7) HHS's plan for improving HIPAA compliance and enforcement going forward. In addition to the information set forth in its 2018 report, HHS also makes available on its website a significant amount of complaint and enforcement data that are current through July 31, 2019 (HHS 2019).

These reports and data reveal that the compliance issues that are investigated most by HHS are, in order of frequency: (1) the impermissible use and disclosure of PHI as prohibited by 45 C.F.R. §§ 164.502–.514; (2) a lack of safeguards of PHI as required by 45 C.F.R. § 164.530(c);

(3) a lack of patient access to PHI as required by 45 C.F.R. § 164.524; (4) a lack of administrative safeguards for ePHI as required by 45 C.F.R. § 164.308; and (5) the use or disclosure of more than the minimum necessary amount of PHI as prohibited by 45 C.F.R. §164.502(b) (HHS 2018, 2019). These reports and data also reveal that the types of covered entity that have been required to take corrective action to achieve voluntary compliance are, in order of frequency: general hospitals, private practices and physicians, outpatient facilities, pharmacies, and health plans (HHS 2018, 2019).

61.8 EFFECT OF HITECH ON BUSINESS ASSOCIATES

As discussed in Section 61.2, the HITECH legislation signed into law by President Barack Obama on February 17, 2009, directed HHS to promulgate regulations extending the application of the use and disclosure requirements within the HIPAA Privacy Rule and the administrative, physical, and technical safeguards within the HIPAA Security Rule to business associates. HITECH also directed HHS to promulgate regulations mandating covered entities and business associates to adhere to certain notification procedures in the event of a breach of uPHI.

One study attempts to empirically examine the effects of HITECH's direct regulation of business associates on the frequency of privacy breaches by business associates. The particular goal of this study, published by Yaraghi and Gopal in 2018, was to shed light on whether and how shifts in regulatory application protect patient privacy. To this end, the study authors used data made publicly available by HHS's Office for Civil Rights (OCR) on breaches of uPHI that occurred between October 2009 and August 2017. During the time period studied, 2,010 uPHI breach incidents occurred, 291 of which occurred among business associates. The remaining incidents occurred among covered entities, including covered healthcare providers (1,410 incidents), health plans (253 incidents), and healthcare clearinghouses (4 incidents). Fifty-two incidents were not categorized as involving a covered entity or business associate.

Yaraghi and Gopal (2018:153) found that HITECH "had a strong and immediate effect on reducing the number of breaches among business associates by 14.41 units." Further: "Our results indicate that implementation of the [HITECH] rules could have led to a significant decrease in the number of incidents and thus has protected millions of Americans from unwanted privacy exposures. Therefore, we conclude that the federal policy appears to have achieved its intended goal of enhancing privacy protection efforts and reducing the number of breach incidents among business associates" (Yaraghi and Gopal 2018:161).

61.9 FACTORS INFLUENCING COMPLIANCE

One study attempts to investigate the factors that influence HIPAA compliance. Using data from the 2003 Health Information and Management Systems Society (HIMSS) Analytics Database, Anthony, Appari, and Johnson (2014) studied compliance with the HIPAA Privacy and Security Rules by 3,221 nonfederal, medium and large, acute-care hospitals in 2003, which was the initial year of mandatory compliance for the HIPAA Privacy Rule and the initial year of voluntary, but not mandatory, compliance for the HIPAA Security Rule.

Anthony, Appari, and Johnson (2014) found that approximately two-thirds of hospitals self-reported that they had achieved mandatory compliance with the HIPAA Privacy Rule in 2003, with for-profit hospitals being significantly more likely than nonprofit hospitals to be compliant. In contrast, only 16 percent of hospitals studied self-reported that they had achieved voluntary compliance with the HIPAA Security Rule in 2003, with for-profit hospitals being significantly less likely to be compliant than nonprofit hospitals. Consistent with a market logic, the authors suggested that for-profit hospitals were probably: (1) less likely than not-for-profit hospitals to invest in costly compliance activities with unclear benefits in 2003 with respect to the HIPAA Security Rule because compliance was not yet required; but (2) more likely to devote resources to mandatory compliance with respect to the HIPAA Privacy Rule that same year.

Anthony, Appari, and Johnson (2014) also found that hospitals that were located in competitive markets were more likely to engage in voluntary compliance with the HIPAA Security Rule. With respect to this finding, the authors suggested that perhaps these hospitals saw a competitive advantage in achieving early security compliance or were interested in gaining recognition as a technology leader in a competitive market. The study authors formally concluded that organizational strategies and institutional environments do influence hospital compliance, contributing to compliance variation across the US health care system.

The study conducted by Anthony, Appari, and Johnson (2014) has several limitations. As with other studies, the compliance data studied by the authors was self-reported by the respondent covered entities. Given the dozens of standards set forth in the HIPAA Privacy and Security Rules and the lack of legal knowledge and compliance knowledge on the part of the covered entities, self-reported data (in this context) should be viewed with skepticism. Second, the nonlawyer study authors made a legal error that impacted their study design. Recall that all covered healthcare providers (regardless of size) were required to comply with the HIPAA Privacy Rule by April 14, 2003. Small health plans (i.e., those insurers with less than $5 million in annual receipts) had one additional year to comply. Anthony, Appari, and Johnson (2014) misunderstood these rules, thinking that the later (2004) deadline applied to small healthcare providers, not small health plans: "[B]ecause the HIPAA regulations gave small hospitals extended time to achieve compliance, we restrict our analysis to hospitals with 50 or more beds (n = 3,321)" (Anthony, Appari, and Johnson 2014:114). Therefore, the study authors incorrectly excluded small hospitals from their study.

Third, Anthony, Appari, and Johnson (2014) only included acute-care hospitals in their study. The HIPAA Privacy and Security Rules apply to dozens of other types of provider entity, including most specialty hospitals, nursing homes, home health agencies, hospices, durable medical equipment providers, physician clinics, healthcare clearinghouses, and health plans, just to name a few. The study authors' findings are thus limited to non-small, acute-care hospitals and are not generalizable to all covered entities and, post-HITECH, business associates.

61.10 INVESTMENT IN SECURITY COMPLIANCE

One study attempts to investigate the factors that influence investment in security compliance. Drawing upon the resource-based view (RBV) of the firm, Cavusoglu et al. (2015) examined the nature of organizational resources deployed for better security; that is, information security control resources (ISCR). The study authors defined ISCR to include three distinct but interrelated sets of resources, including information security technologies (i.e., tangible resources), qualified information security personnel (i.e., human resources), and security awareness of organizational users (i.e., intangible resources). Second, based on institutional theory and its recent development, the study authors explicated antecedents of an organization's investment in ISCR. The study authors posited that organizations heterogeneously respond to institutional pressures related to information security by making different levels of investment in ISCR.

Based on data collected through a survey of one individual at each of 241 small and large for-profit organizations set in a variety of industries including, but not limited to, the healthcare industry, Cavusoglu et al. (2015) found that institutional pressures and internal security needs assessments (ISNA) significantly explain the variation in organizational investment in ISCR. According to the study authors, coercive pressures such as the HIPAA Rules and the European Union General Data Protection Regulation as well as normative pressures (i.e., beliefs regarding what is appropriate among members of social networks) were found to have not only a direct impact but also an indirect impact through ISNA on organizational investment in ISCR (Cavusoglu et al. 2015:395–6).

With respect to coercive pressures, the study authors specifically stated that they "influenced an organization's decision to invest in ISCR. This result is consistent with the emerging view that government regulations significantly affect organizations' information security practices" (Cavusoglu et al. 2015:395). According to the study authors, "coercive pressure has a strong effect on ISNA. Coercive pressure from government regulatory agencies and business partners seems to be successful in making a business case for organizational investment in ISCR and in determining how to address information security risks" (Cavusoglu et al. 2015:395).

Cavusoglu et al. (2015) also found that coercive pressure has a significant impact on information security technologies (i.e., tangible resources) and qualified security personnel (i.e., human resources), but not on security awareness of organizational users (i.e., intangible resources).

> This is presumably because government regulations and requests from business partners generally focus on security technologies and standards. To comply with such government regulations and business partner requests, we would expect that organizations also need to invest in qualified information security personnel with expertise and skills. However, such regulations and requests did not have a direct impact on the extent of security awareness of knowledge workers in our sample organizations (Cavusoglu et al. 2015:396).

The Cavusoglu et al. (2015) study has a number of limitations in terms of its contributions to the HIPAA compliance literature. For example, it is not clear from the published study how many of the respondent organizations were required to comply with HIPAA and which provisions within HIPAA (e.g., the administrative safeguards, the technical safeguards, the physical safeguards, the use and disclosure requirements, the individual rights, or the administrative requirements) were found to have applied coercive pressure to the HIPAA-regulated respondents. In addition, the study contains little discussion of the laws, or the content of such laws, that allegedly provided coercive pressure to the studied organizations.

61.11 PROFESSIONAL DISCOURSE

Finally, one study investigates healthcare professionals' discourse about privacy, including the definition and importance of privacy in health care as well as the role of privacy in day-to-day work. This study has interesting insights in terms of the impact of HIPAA (compared to long-standing privacy norms) on the behavior of different types of health care and health information professionals. In particular, Anthony and Stablein (2016) conducted in-depth, semi-structured interviews with a total of eighty-three individual respondents, among them thirty physicians, thirty-two nurses, and twenty-one health information professionals. The respondents were affiliated with two academic medical centers and one Veterans Administration hospital/clinic in the US Northeast. Interview responses were qualitatively coded for themes, and patterns across groups were identified.

Anthony and Stablein (2016) reported privacy discourse differences across the health professional groups. In particular, the study authors noted that the health information professional respondents actively adopted legal standards whereas the physician and nurse respondents were more likely to resist or be neutral regarding legal changes. For example, one health information professional respondent stated that health information professionals "very strictly live and die by HIPAA. It is a big deal, and it's very well respected, and everybody is very conscious of it" (Anthony and Stablein 2016:214). In comparison, one nurse stated: "A patient has a right to receive medical care and have his privacy maintained. There is a federal law [HIPAA] that addresses it. There are other laws that address it" (Anthony and Stablein 2016:214).

When specifically asked by the study authors about how new laws governing health information, including the HIPAA Privacy Rule, affect privacy, some respondents stated that such laws did not change anything. For example, one physician respondent stated: "I just continue what I have always done [regarding patient privacy]" (Anthony and Stablein 2016:218). Similarly, one nurse respondent stated: "I think you use your best judgment as a professional [regarding patient privacy]" (Anthony and Stablein 2016:218).

Other respondents stated that HIPAA and other laws highlighted the importance of patient privacy but did not necessarily or dramatically change their practices: "I think HIPAA introduced that we have to get serious about [patient privacy]" (Anthony and Stablein 2016:218). Still other respondents felt that new legal regulations actually undermined existing professional ethics and practices of privacy in health care by inserting federal law over and above professional standards that already existed: "The law [HIPAA] suggests to the patient that before this, physicians weren't respecting [privacy], and now they have to because it's the law. I think that is absolutely not accurate" (Anthony and Stablein 2016:218).

61.12 CONCLUSION

This chapter has presented insights from academic, industry, and government studies and reports that assess compliance with the HIPAA Privacy, Security, and Breach Notification Rules. These insights relate to the extent to which small numbers of covered entities comply with the HIPAA Privacy Rule's plain language requirement, the HIPAA Privacy Rule's access to protected health information requirement, the HIPAA Security Rule's addressable encryption standard, and the HIPAA Security Rule's audit logs and access reports requirement. Additional insights relate to the extent to which covered entities and business associates believe that they are complying with the HIPAA Privacy and Security Rules, the impact of HITECH on data breaches involving business associates, the organizational strategies and institutional environments that influence compliance, and the extent to which institutional pressures and internal security needs assessments influence investment in security compliance.

Most of the available studies focus on compliance by a limited group of regulated actors or institutions, such as medium and large acute-care hospitals (Anthony, Appari, and Johnson 2014), top-ranked hospitals (Lye et al. 2018), medical schools (Paasche-Orlow et al. 2013), academic medical centers (McKnight and Franko 2016; Freundlich, Freundlich, and Drolet 2018), small and large for-profit organizations (Cavusoglu et al. 2015), hand surgeons (Drolet et al. 2017), companies offering personal health records (Carrion, Aleman, and Toval 2011), and business associates (Yaraghi and Gopal 2018). However, other studies (or data sets) focus on (or could be used to assess) compliance by a wider range of regulated actors and institutions (AHIMA 2004, 2006; HHS 2018, 2019).

Many of these studies focused on particular uses and disclosures of PHI, such as uses and disclosures of PHI through personal health records (Carrion, Aleman, and Toval 2011) and text messaging (Drolet et al. 2017; Freundlich, Freundlich, and Drolet 2018; McKnight and Franko 2016). Within the HIPAA Privacy and Security Rules, some studies focus on particular provisions, such as the plain language requirement codified at 45 C.F.R. § 164.508 (c)(3) (Paasche-Orlow et al. 2013) and the access to PHI requirement codified at 45 C.F.R. § 164.524 (Lye et al. 2018; Carrion, Aleman, and Toval 2011).

The HIPAA compliance literature is not as robust as one might expect, especially given the length of time since the compliance date for the HIPAA Privacy Rule (i.e., seventeen years), the HIPAA Security Rule (i.e., fifteen years), and the HIPAA Breach Notification Rule (i.e., eleven years). In addition to limitations inherent in studies of this type (e.g., limitations regarding the number of respondents, the type of respondents, the survey questions and/or the availability of data, and the self-reported nature of much of the data), the nonlawyer authors' study designs and data analyses were significantly impacted by the authors' and/or the respondents' lack of perfect information regarding the HIPAA Privacy and Security Rules and/or their institutions' actual compliance with such rules.

Going forward, academic, industry, and government researchers investigating HIPAA compliance should attempt to study the compliance of health plans, healthcare clearinghouses, and nonhospital/nonacademic medical center covered entities, which have been largely ignored by the literature to date. Researchers who are intimately familiar with the proper application of the HIPAA Rules should develop and lead these studies so as to avoid errors in study design. Perhaps most importantly, researchers should attempt to obtain and evaluate nonself-reported compliance data. Other than the compliance data obtained and analyzed by HHS through its audit and enforcement efforts, most of the academic and industry compliance data were self-reported by the respondent covered entities.

REFERENCES

American Health Information Management Association (AHIMA). 2004. *The State of HIPAA Privacy and Security Compliance*. http://bok.ahima.org/PdfView?oid=23016.

American Health Information Management Association (AHIMA). 2006. *The State of HIPAA Privacy and Security Compliance*. http://bok.ahima.org/doc?oid=100517#.XW05lpNKiT8.

Anthony, Denise L., Ajit Appari, and M. Eric Johnson. 2014. "Institutionalizing HIPAA Compliance: Organizations and Competing Logics in U.S. Health Care." *Journal of Health and Social Behavior* 55: 108–24.

Anthony, Denise L., and Timothy Stablein. 2016. "Privacy in Practice: Professional Discourse about Information Control in Health Care." *Journal of Health Organization and Management* 30:207–26.

Carrion, Inmaculada, Jose Luis Fernandez Aleman, and Ambrosio Toval. 2011. "Assessing the HIPAA Standard in Practice: PHR Privacy Policies." *Annual Conference of the IEEE EMBS* 33 (August–September): 2380–3.

Cavusoglu, Huseyin, Hasan Cavusoglu, Jai-Yeol Son, and Izak Benbasat. 2015. "Institutional Pressures in Security Management: Direct and Indirect Influences on Organizational Investment in Information Security Control Resources." *Information and Management* 52: 385–400.

Drolet, Brian C., Jayson S. Marwaha, Brad Hyatt, Phillip E. Blazar, and Scott D. Lifchez. 2017. "Electronic Communication of Protected Health Information: Privacy, Security, and HIPAA Compliance." *Journal of Hand Surgery* 42, No. 6 (June): 411–16.

Freundlich, Robert E., Katherine L. Freundlich, and Brian C. Drolet. 2018. "Pagers, Smartphones, and HIPAA: Finding the Best Solution for Electronic Communication of Protected Health Information." *Journal of Medical Systems* 42:9.

Lye, Carolyn T., Howard P. Forman, Ruiyi Gao, Jodi G. Daniel, Allen L. Hsiao, Marilyn K. Mann, Dave deBronkart, Hugo O. Campos, and Harlan M. Krumholz. 2018. "Assessment of US Hospital Compliance with Regulations for Patients' Requests for Medical Records." *JAMA Open Network* (October 5): 1–12.

McKnight, Randall, and Orrin Franko. 2016. "HIPAA Compliance with Mobile Devices Among ACGME Programs." *Journal of Medical Systems* 40, No. 5 (May): 129.

Paasche-Orlow, Michael, Frederick L. Brancati, Holly A. Taylor, Sumati Jain, Anjali Pandit, and Michael S. Wolf. 2013. "Readability of Consent Form Templates: A Second Look." *IRB: Ethics and Human Research* 35, No. 4 (July–August): 12–19.

United States Department of Health and Human Services (HHS). 2016. *Individuals' Right Under HIPAA to Access Their Health Information 45 CFR § 164.524*. www.hhs.gov/hipaa/for-professionals/privacy/guidance/access/index.html.

United States Department of Health and Human Services (HHS). 2018. *Report to Congress on HIPAA Privacy, Security, and Breach Notification Rule Compliance for Calendar Years 2015, 2016, and 2017*. www.hhs.gov/sites/default/files/compliance-report-to-congress-2015–2016–2017.pdf.

United States Department of Health and Human Services (HHS). 2019. *HIPAA Compliance and Enforcement*. www.hhs.gov/hipaa/for-professionals/compliance-enforcement/index.html.

Yaraghi, Niam, and Ram D. Gopal. 2018. "The Role of HIPAA Omnibus Rules in Reducing the Frequency of Medical Data Breaches: Insights from an Empirical Study." *Milbank Quarterly* 96, No. 1: 144–66.

62

Biopharmaceutical Compliance

Jordan Paradise

Abstract: The global pharmaceutical market is projected to approach \$1170 billion by the year 2021;[1] the US market alone currently accounts for 45 percent of the market, at nearly \$500 billion.[2] International legal frameworks share fundamental characteristics governing the development, evaluation, and approval of drugs and biological products, including clinical trials demonstrating safety and efficacy; good laboratory, clinical, and manufacturing practices; appropriate labeling; and robust reporting and post-market surveillance. This chapter explores regulatory compliance in the pharmaceutical industry drawing from recent scholarship, federal agency reports and materials, and publicly available corporate resources. Coverage will focus specifically on the US market, with general discussion of international trends as well.

62.1 INTRODUCTION

The global pharmaceutical market is projected to approach \$1170 billion by the year 2021.[3] The US market alone currently accounts for 45 percent of this, at nearly \$500 billion.[4] The biopharmaceutical industry is highly regulated across the spectrum of research, product development, and eventual market entry. International legal frameworks share fundamental characteristics governing the development, evaluation, and approval of drugs and biological products, including clinical trials demonstrating safety and efficacy; good laboratory, clinical, and manufacturing practices; appropriate and truthful labeling; and robust reporting and post-market surveillance. Compliance with these legal frameworks is often tedious and expensive for industry yet has a significant impact on public health and safety. This chapter explores trends in legal and regulatory compliance in the biopharmaceutical industry drawing from recent scholarship, federal agency reports and materials, and publicly available corporate resources. Coverage will focus specifically on the US market.

The topic of compliance in the realm of pharmaceuticals and biologics is necessarily complex and wide-ranging. There is a spectrum of federal regulatory agencies involved, the statutory authority is broad, and agency actions vary depending on ever-changing factors, including appropriations and agency budget, agency priorities, public health emergencies, and presidential administrations. Compliance has been defined as the action not only of

1 The Business Research Company, "The Growing Pharmaceuticals Market: Expert Forecasts and Analysis, May 16, 2018, https://blog.marketresearch.com/the-growing-pharmaceuticals-market-expert-forecasts-and-analysis.

2 Matej Mikulic, "U.S. Pharmaceutical Industry – Statistics and Facts," *Statistica*, November 5, 2020, www.statista.com/topics/1719/pharmaceutical-industry/.

3 See note 1.

4 See note 2.

conforming to rules but also of identifying and comprehending the scope of obligations imposed by those rules (Hindin and Silberman 2016). The term compliance in this chapter refers to the adherence to law or policy set out by federal statute, agency regulations, and even "nonbinding" materials such as guidance documents and agency manuals.

Exploration of biopharmaceutical industry compliance is challenging. There are several significant barriers to access of comprehensive information regarding industry compliance in this realm. First, the propriety nature of the industry stifles public access to product information and industry practices. Market exclusivities, patent protection, and trade secrets provide incentives to develop products, but also foster secrecy. Second, the biopharmaceutical industry is ever-conscience of the potential for tort liability, which also hinders information-sharing. Third, compliance trends vary across time given myriad factors and thus there is no way to generalize. Compliance must be explored in specific contexts rather than wholescale. Fourth, there are limited resources from the federal government reporting on compliance trends and activities, likely given the proprietary and intensely competitive nature of the industry. Fifth, and relatedly, the terms and scope of consent decrees between the government and industry are not publicly available. These consent decrees are increasingly the means by which noncompliance is resolved.

62.2 THE FOOD AND DRUG ADMINISTRATION (FDA)

The biopharmaceutical industry is subject to a barrage of federal statutes, regulations, and policy. Industry activities are scrutinized by numerous federal administrative agencies, including the Department of Health and Human Services (HHS), the Office of the Inspector General (OIG), the Department of Justice (DOJ), the Federal Trade Commission (FTC), and the Securities and Exchange Commission (SEC), to name but a few. In addition to codified law and regulations, many of these agencies have published compliance-specific materials to guide and inform industry behavior. For example, the DOJ Criminal Division published a guidance document entitled *Evaluation of Corporate Compliance Programs* in April 2019; it was last updated in June 2020.[5] The guidance assists "prosecutors in making informed decisions as to whether, and to what extent, the corporation's compliance program was effective at the time of the offense, and is effective at the time of a charging decision or resolution" in order to inform prosecution, monetary penalty, and compliance obligations, and existing obligations contained within a corporate criminal resolution.

Likewise, the DOJ's Holder memorandum issued in 1999 contemplates the sufficiency of compliance programs when considering whether to federally prosecute an entity.[6] Examples of federal legislation of direct relevance to the industry in this context are provisions in the False Claims Act and the Anti-kickback statute regarding payments and reporting. And, in 2003, the OIG published a *Compliance Guidance for Pharmaceutical Manufacturers* setting forth seven fundamental elements that should be included in any effective compliance program for pharmaceutical manufacturers.[7] These seven elements are: (1) implementation

[5] www.justice.gov/criminal-fraud/page/file/937501/download.

[6] United States Department of Justice. 1999. Memorandum of Deputy Attorney General Eric. G. Holder. *Bringing Criminal Charges Against Corporations*. www.justice.gov/sites/default/files/criminal-fraud/legacy/2010/04/11/charging-corps.PDF.

[7] United States Office of the Inspector General. 2003. *Compliance Guidance for Pharmaceutical Manufacturers*. https://oig.hhs.gov/fraud/docs/complianceguidance/042803pharmacymfgnonfr.pdf.

of written policies and procedures; (2) designation of a compliance committee and officers; (3) provision of training and education; (4) establishment of effective communication mechanisms; (5) use of internal monitoring and auditing procedures; (6) creation and publication of disciplinary guidelines to enforce standards; and (7) prompt detection of and response to problems, including taking of corrective actions. In addition to mentioning fraud and kickbacks, the OIG guidance provides that manufacturers should prohibit sales agents from encouraging providers to bill for free drug samples and ensure appropriate labeling, packaging, and documentation of any free sample. These draft guidelines are all voluntary, but they send a strong signal of what is expected from a compliance program (Goldstein and Snyder 2003).

However, as a regulatory matter, the pharmaceutical and biologic industry is primarily governed by the US Food and Drug Administration (FDA). Congress established the FDA as a public health and safety agency, tasked with the dual mission of both promoting innovation and protecting the public health. Drugs and biologics are two of the most highly regulated product areas, subject to intense pre- and post-market requirements. The FDA is a classic command-and-control agency, directing requirements that apply across research and development, clinical trials, product review and approval, and post market. The basic legal structure involves Congressional authority set forth in both the Food, Drug and Cosmetic Act (FDCA)(21 U.S.C. §101 et seq.) and the Public Health Services Act (PHSA)(42 U.S.C. §262). The FDA has promulgated extensive regulations subject to the Administrative Procedure Act and its enabling statutes. Other statements of policy and procedure, while not legal binding, hold great importance for industry. These include guidance documents, compliance manuals, and general statements of policy.

62.3 THE FDA'S APPROACH TO REGULATION AND COMPLIANCE

The traditional command-and-control regulatory approach to compliance is grounded in applying punitive and deterrent regimes to achieve desired regulatory outcomes. There is a rich literature discussing approaches to regulation supporting industry compliance. Ian Ayres and John Braithwaite, for example, have framed a basic approach as "responsive regulation," depicted as an enforcement pyramid with a "range of interventions of ever-increasing intrusiveness (matched by ever-decreasing frequency of use)" (Ayers and Braithwaite 1992). Some commentators have characterized the FDA as specifically employing a "coercive approach" to enforcement (Glicksman and Earnhart 2015). In order to achieve outcomes, the agency has a range of administrative and enforcement tools at its disposal to monitor and respond to industry behaviors.

The statutes (both the FDCA and the PHSA) grant the FDA a variety of mechanisms with which to address and respond to industry activities. At a general administrative level, the FDA can communicate with consumers, industry, and medical professionals through publicity and outreach. The agency routinely utilizes the website to issue public alerts and share information about products or regulated entities. Letters and electronic communications are also directed to medical specialists and pharmacists. The agency has broad powers to enable product recalls, withdraw a product from the market, remove an approved product indication, and issue a hold on clinical trials. Once a violation is detected, the agency may issue a warning letter or cyber letter, triggering a specific follow-up and close-out process on the part of industry. Inspections of facilities and products are also commonplace, coupled to an official Form 483 identifying observations made by inspectors; these may result in warning letters or legal action. Enforcement may then be effectuated with the assistance of the courts through a seizure action or injunction.

Overall, the FDA operates at many levels to address compliance issues. Three historic key areas of FDA activity to explore compliance trends are warning letters, seizures, and injunctions. Inspections are the primary means of collecting information to support these three areas. Notably, there has been a sharp decline in the number of seizure and injunction actions pursued by the FDA since 1975 (Tyler 2013). The FDA has increasingly turned to consent decrees to address noncompliance in the event of repeated dereliction of agency communications, often provided in the form of warning letters or inspection observation reports. Consent decrees are entered by a judge, the US attorney representing the agency, and the company's top official; they are binding on the parties and subject to judicial enforcement. Most consent decrees involve violations of good manufacturing practices or distribution processes set forth by FDA regulations. The agency must demonstrate evidence that there has been an effort to work with the company to address the problems at issue prior to issuance of the consent decree.

There is considerable variability in the scope and content of consent decrees. A consent decree may require a company to cease production, limit production to essential products, assign quality assurance functions to third parties, and adhere to identified timeframes. Consent decrees have a significant effect on profitability by negatively impacting merger potential, production and sales, pending product applications, and company reputation. They typically include fines and the equitable remedies of disgorgement or restitution. The FDA must use its resources to enforce consent decrees, impacting other important processes that the agency engages in, like overseeing premarket compliance, inspections, product approval, post-market activity (Chrai and Burd 2004). There is no readily available data provided by the FDA on the number and content of consent decrees and there are no legal requirements regarding their publication or availability to the general public.

The richest statistics and supporting information regarding compliance are available directly from the government on the FDA's website. The FDA has developed an "FDA Data Dashboard" database that culls information about inspections, compliance actions, and recalls across all regulated product areas.[8]

62.4 FDA REPORTED STATISTICS: DRUGS

As mentioned at the end of the previous section, the FDA maintains a public electronic database, the FDA Data Dashboard, containing records of agency activity in several core areas. It is updated monthly, with the information "based upon transparency datasets and other data already available to the public through the FDA.gov website." Three areas relevant to compliance are reported on it: inspections; compliance actions, that is, warning letters, injunctions, and seizures; and product recalls.

Inspections are the primary focus of activity over the ten-year period reflected on the database. Between 2009 and May 2019, the FDA reports conducting a total of 26,334 inspections of drug facilities: 17,983 in the USA and 8,351 in foreign establishments.[9] Of these total inspections, no required action was indicated in 12,225 of those inspections; voluntary action was indicated in 1,714 inspections; and official action was indicated in 12,395 inspections. The FDA reports on five

[8] Inspections: https://datadashboard.fda.gov/ora/cd/inspections.htm; compliance actions: https://datadashboard.fda.gov/ora/cd/complianceactions.htm; recalls: https://datadashboard.fda.gov/ora/cd/recalls.htm.

[9] https://datadashboard.fda.gov/ora/cd/inspections.htm.

TABLE 62.1 *Inspections*

Inspections	Total	US domestic	Foreign
	26,334	17,983	8,351
NAI (no action)	12,225	8,773	3,452
VAI (voluntary action)	1,714	7,975	4,420
OAI (official action)	12,395	1,235	479

TABLE 62.2 *Official actions categories*

Official actions categories	Total
Bioresearch monitoring	220
Drug quality assurance	1,304
Over-the-counter drug evaluation	1
Post-market survey and epidemiology	24
Unapproved or misbranded	165

specific categories of observations in the official actions: bioresearch monitoring, drug quality assurance, over-the-counter drug evaluation, post-market survey and epidemiology, and unapproved or misbranded products. An official action may involve issues pertaining to more than one of the five categories. Tables 62.1 and 62.2 depict this information. As the database notes, not all inspections are included in the database. Those conducted by states, those conducted prior to approval of a product, and nonclinical lab inspections are not included.

During this same time frame, the FDA reports a total of 1,349 compliance actions divided into the following three areas: warning letters (1,305); injunctions (29); and seizures (15). A total of 942 compliance actions occurred in the USA while compliance actions occurred in 416 foreign establishments.[10] The FDA notes that compliance actions are primarily utilized in the USA, whereas actions pertaining to foreign firms are often dealt with through import alerts and other measures. The numbers reflect finalized and completed actions only. The 1,349 total was based on distinct compliance actions, while 1,358 was a total from all actions (those with the same case ID were counted separately for separate citations). The website notes: "Some actions are counted as both domestic and foreign when there are both domestic and foreign firms associated with the action." Tables 62.3 and 62.4 depict the number of compliance actions in years 2009–2019.

The FDA reports a total of 10,070 drug recalls between 2012 and 2019.[11] Table 62.5 depicts the number of recalls in each of the three recall classifications. Class I is the most urgent type of recall where there is a risk of death or serious injury from a dangerous or defective product; Class II is intermediate recall where there is no immediate risk of death although there are still health and safety risks involved; and Class III is the least urgent where a product is unlikely to cause an adverse reaction or pose a safety risk but nonetheless violates a labeling or manufacturing requirement. Recalls may be instituted at industry discretion or at the urging of the FDA.

10 https://datadashboard.fda.gov/ora/cd/complianceactions.htm.
11 https://datadashboard.fda.gov/ora/cd/recalls.htm.

TABLE 62.3 *Warning letters*

Year	Total
2009	112
2010	173
2011	109
2012	95
2013	86
2014	96
2015	77
2016	152
2017	160
2018	158
2019 (through May)	87
	1,305

TABLE 62.4 *Injunctions and seizures*

Year	Injunctions	Seizures
2009	4	3
2010	1	3
2011	5	3
2012	2	1
2013	3	1
2014	1	2
2015	3	1
2016	3	1
2017	5	N/A
2018	2	N/A
2019 (through May)	N/A	N/A
	29	**15**

TABLE 62.5 *Recalls*

Year	Class I	Class II	Class III	Total
2012	10	289	39	338
2013	62	848	156	1,065
2014	153	1,345	149	1,647
2015	118	1,584	120	1,822
2016	108	1,272	168	1,548
2017	75	908	193	1,176
2018	108	951	147	1,206
2019 (through May)	497	680	91	1,268
				10,070

62.5 FDA REPORTED STATISTICS: BIOLOGICS

The FDA reports separately on biologics information. Between 2009 and May 2019, it reports conducting a total of 20,636 inspections of biologics facilities: 20,118 in the USA and 518 in foreign establishments.[12] Of these total inspections, no required action was indicated in 16,344 inspections; voluntary action was indicated in 4,125 inspections; and official action was indicated in 167 inspections. The FDA reports on three categories of observations in the official actions: blood and blood products; human cellular, tissue, and gene therapies; and vaccines and allergenics. Vaccines and allergenics are those products familiar to most consumers as prescription medicines. On the other hand, blood and blood components and human cellular, tissue, and gene therapies are regulated differently based on highly specific and robust guidance documents and regulations. Tables 62.6 and 62.7 depict this information.

The FDA reports a total of 113 biologic compliance actions during this same time frame divided into the following three areas: 111 warning letters; 2 injunctions; and 0 seizures. A total of ninety-nine compliance actions occurred in the USA; compliance actions occurred in ten foreign establishments.[13] The numbers reflect finalized and completed actions only. Tables 62.8 and 62.9 depict the number of compliance actions in years 2009–2019.

The FDA reports a total of 8,548 biologics recalls between 2012 and 2019.[14] Table 62.10 depicts the number of recalls in each of the three classifications.

Taken together, the FDA statistics illustrate several important points. First is the striking comparison in the number of inspections resulting in official actions. Table 62.11 notes that while the total number of inspections in both realms exceeded 20,000 in the same time frame, there was significant difference in those resulting in official action: drugs (12,395) and biologics (167).

TABLE 62.6 *Inspections*

Inspections	Total	US domestic	Foreign
	20,636	20,118	518
NAI *(no action)*	16,344	16,136	208
VAI *(voluntary action)*	4,125	3,831	294
OAI *(official action)*	167	151	16

TABLE 62.7 *Official actions categories*

Official actions categories	Total
Blood and blood products	13,512
Human cellular, tissue, and gene therapies	6,470
Vaccines and allergenics	654

12 https://datadashboard.fda.gov/ora/cd/inspections.htm.
13 https://datadashboard.fda.gov/ora/cd/complianceactions.htm.
14 https://datadashboard.fda.gov/ora/cd/recalls.htm.

TABLE 62.8 *Warning letters*

Year	Total
2009	19
2010	15
2011	8
2012	21
2013	17
2014	8
2015	4
2016	4
2017	6
2018	4
2019 (through May)	5
	111

TABLE 62.9 *Injunctions and seizures*

Year	Injunctions	Seizures
2009	0	0
2010	2	0
2011	0	0
2012	0	0
2013	0	0
2014	0	0
2015	0	0
2016	0	0
2017	0	N/A
2018	0	N/A
2019 (through May)	N/A	N/A
	2	0

TABLE 62.10 *Recalls*

Year	Class I	Class II	Class III	Total
2012	N/A	574	399	973
2013	16	1880	682	2,578
2014	2	726	264	992
2015	2	667	301	970
2016	1	513	267	781
2017	N/A	607	293	900
2018	5	529	291	825
2019 (through May)	2	278	249	529
				8,548

TABLE 62.11 *Comparing total inspections for biologics and drugs*

Inspections	Total drugs	Total biologics
Total	26,334	20,636
NAI (no action)	12,225	16,344
VAI (voluntary action)	1,714	4,125
OAI (official action)	12,395	167

One explanation for the discrepancy may be enhancements to drug inspections introduced through agency programs, such as the pharmaceutical good manufacturing practices initiative. The FDA has installed a pharmaceutical inspectorate which consists of a team of individuals who are experts in drug product manufacturing technology. This team conduct inspections of pharmaceutical firms; the focus is almost exclusively on inspection of facilities that use complex manufacturing technologies (Niedelman 2005). It may also be that there are significantly more drug manufacturing facilities, given the complex nature of biologics manufacturing and storage.

A second point illustrated by the statistics is that injunctions and seizures are no longer important enforcement tools. Twenty-nine injunctions for drug violations and two for biologics over a ten-year period, and a mere fifteen seizures over that same period, all for drugs. The literature supports this shift away from injunctions and seizures and toward consent decrees (Tyler 2013). However, unlike an injunction granted by a judge, consent decrees are not documents typically made available to the public. They also allow industry to deny any wrongdoing as part of the terms.

Third, the FDA issued far more warning letters regarding drugs (1,305) than biologics (111) over the ten-year period. This is likely tied to the number of inspections, with the larger inspection numbers resulting in a corresponding increase in warning letters in the drug realm. Again, it may be due to the numbers of pharmaceutical facilities versus biologics facilities. Finally, recall numbers were comparable: 10,070 for drugs and 8,548 for biologics. There is no indication on how many of these were at the urging of the FDA or initiated by industry, or what type of defect was involved.

62.6 THEORETICAL LITERATURE REVIEW

There is a vast literature of agency behaviors in regulating, industry responses to regulation, the impact of regulation on industry and on innovation, and theories of compliance generally. This literature describes many factors that drive industry compliance, or noncompliance, such as the number and efficiency of inspections (Olson 1999); the financial costs of complying (Hale et al 2011); company risk-aversiveness (Hale et al 2011); fear of tort liability (Green 1997); and political climate, including the presidential administration and congressional oversight activities such as hearings and accountability investigations (Olson 1999). Experts have observed that "[s]ome corporate actors will only comply with the law if it is economically rational for them to do so; most corporate actors will comply with the law most of the time simply because it is the law" (Ayers and Braithwaite 1992). Scholars have also attributed problems with industry compliance to regulations that are vague, unclear, or inconsistent (Hale et al. 2011).

As a general matter, there is ample support in the literature for the view that compliance imposes direct burdens on industry. These burdens include time and money spent figuring out new regulations and how to implement mechanisms to adhere, training employees, and additional record-keeping and reporting. Utilizing a behavioral analysis approach, Hale et al. (2011) report that federal regulations impose a substantial burden on businesses, particularly smaller firms, in several ways. Companies must often spend time discovering whether a new regulation will apply to them and whether there is a gap between their current practices and the new practices. There are then costs associated with adopting methods, retraining employees, and buying materials and equipment. In addition to the financial costs, Hale et al. (2011) argue that regulations have the tendency to increase the effect of stifling innovation. Risk averseness coupled with companies not wanting to experiment with the rules leads to reduced innovations, and companies will replace higher-paid experts capable of innovation with lower-paid rule-followers (Hale et al. 2011).

Scholars examining regulation of the biopharmaceutical industry by the FDA have examined compliance across many domains. These studies, however, are typically limited to a narrow scope of inquiry and are relevant to a specific time frame. Examples of this domain-specific exploration of compliance include articles probing clinical trial reporting adherence and clinical trial transparency (Miller et al. 2017; Prayle et al. 2012), agency behaviors directly and indirectly impacting compliance (Olson 1995), the impact of recently enacted mandatory physician reporting provisions (Sclar and Keilty 2012), relationships between tort liability through state product liability litigation and compliance (Green 1997; Noah 2000; Rabin 2000), and responses to FDA observational reports (i.e., Form 483) as one means to mitigate subsequent FDA compliance actions (Poska and Graham 2009).

For example, Sclar and Keilty (2012) have explored the impact of the Patient Protection and Affordable Care Act (ACA) sunshine provisions on industry behaviors. The sunshine provisions in ACA shift the burden to the manufacturers to expose their own relationship with providers instead of relying on investigators and whistleblowers. The primary effect of the sunshine provisions is to require many life sciences companies to track and make known to (Centers for Medicare and Medicaid Services) CMS their financial arrangements with physicians. The federal sunshine provisions require the following: applicable manufacturers of drugs, devices, biologicals, or medical supplies covered by Medicare, Medicaid or Children's Health Insurance Program to report annually to CMS certain payments or transfers of value provided to covered recipients; and applicable manufacturers and applicable group purchasing organizations to report annually certain ownership and investment interests held by physicians (and their immediate family members) in these entities. State sunshine laws are broader and govern manufacturer conduct and/or require spending disclosures. Several operational challenges are set forth regarding these sunshine provisions, including development of enterprise-wide databases; identification and monitoring of HCP touch points and third-party vendor payments; and implementation of standard operating procedures, education, and auditing.

Sclar and Keilty (2012) also note an increase in warning letters and untitled letters for (Current Good Manufacturing Practice) cGMP noncompliance, yet a decrease in the number of letters issued for noncompliant drug advertising and marketing. An increase in letters issued to the industry seems focused on two areas of scandal: misleading off-label drug promotions and foreign drug manufacturing quality. Warning letters are looked at in the industry very harshly because companies or people typically only receive them when there has been particularly egregious noncompliance. However, these do not represent a comprehensive picture of compliance enforcement. The data being gathered are not comprehensive and some of the most important issues are not even being systematically tracked, but it demonstrates that there has been an increase in enforcement action. Companies with more visibility, larger advertising budgets, and more marketing personnel are more likely to be targeted for promotional noncompliance. Finally, the authors offer that fraudulent activities occurring against government and state health programs have resulted in 56 percent of fines and forfeitures collected by state federal governments due to pharmaceutical compliance investigations. Most of these have been civil fines (Sclar and Keilty 2012).

In a 2015 article, Page et al. explore instances of noncompliance in the pharmaceutical industry, identify prevalent areas of concern, and present a targeted enforcement model to maximize effective resource allocation for the FDA. In order to quantify noncompliance within the pharmaceutical industry, the authors examined inspectional observations, warning letters, untitled letters, criminal and civil litigation and settlements, and corporate integrity agreements (CIA). The following four areas were identified as areas of concern: failure to file, or falsifying, reports on safety data; noncompliance with cGMPs; off-label drug promotion; and violation of the False Claims Act. A particular emphasis was placed on CIAs because they are issued in the most egregious noncompliance settlements so using them for research data gives insight into major industry issues. The CIAs revealed that the act of falsely reporting or failing to report safety data to regulatory agencies and healthcare professionals has increased in recent years. The CIAs also demonstrate that career-ending penalties on individual executives have been used as deterrents for noncompliance (Page 2015).

M. K. Olson (1999) has done extensive empirical research regarding the FDA as a federal regulator. While dated, her findings warrant attention. Olson's work offers that Congressional oversight hearings and FDA inspection activity produce a deterrence effect among regulated industries. Political influences impact agency enforcement and influence firms' compliance. When there is a reduction in oversight and FDA inspection, there is in turn increased noncompliance. She has also demonstrated that the ebb and flow of agency rulemaking affects industry compliance trends (Olson 1999).

Often, measures and discussions of compliance costs are necessarily framed through the lens of documented noncompliance as an indicator of compliance trends. Olson (1999) notes:

> Firms chose their compliance investments to balance the incremental cost of additional compliance investments with the incremental benefits of increased compliance. Unfortunately, firms' compliance investments are unobservable. The true number of firms in violations of regulatory law is also unobservable. However, it is possible to observe regulatory outcomes such as the number of detected noncompliant firms.

Olson has also explored the "external signals theory," which explains that "regulatory agencies alter their actions to receive positive feedback from outside groups" (Olson 1996). Olson sets forth a framework explaining how agencies respond to changes in regulated industries, the political environment, and among consumers. These factors are highlighted as compelling drivers of adaptation in regulatory policy and enforcement actions during the timeframe 1972–92. Olson notes a movement from frequent inspections with legalistic enforcements to reduced inspections and flexible enforcement. Olson posits that this change most likely came from either a change in budget or a change in political costs and benefits. Olson proposes three hypotheses for these changes. First, increased applications for approval combined with reductions in budget led to reduced inspections and flexible enforcement. Second, increased fire alarms from consumers allowed the FDA to target inspections to reduce inspections and maintain deterrence. Third, the FDA has a tendency to target firms that have a history of noncompliance (Olson 1996).

Olson concludes that political and regulatory environment changes lead regulators to substitute some regulatory actions for others, altering strategies of regulation and producing changes in policy. Regulators are further responsive to diverse external interests which play a different role in influencing different FDA actions. So long as regulators may choose among different actions and these actions create trade-offs, there are opportunities for substitution inside the agency (Olson 1996).

In yet another article, Olson (1995) applies her external signals model to the context of drug approval by the FDA. She concludes that the FDA responds to multiple interests, including Congress, regulated industries, and consumers, although its response varies among industries. Further, bureaucratic discretion is highest for products with the greatest regulatory stringency. The FDA is more responsive to industry signals for medical device approvals, and more responsive to consumer signals for generic and new drugs due to adverse feedback (Olson 1995).

Comparative research has explored the features of the US regulatory system that impact agency activity. Hans and Gupta (2018) compare pharmacovigilance regulation of the USA and several other developed countries, finding dramatic differences across the multiple parameters measured. These include process for reporting, inspection and audit procedures, risk management systems, adverse event reporting requirements and procedures, and method and manner of safety communications (Hans and Gupta 2018). Another article notes that, unlike equivalent bodies in many other countries, the FDA can use adjudication to ensure product safety while at the same time limiting the ability of industry to participate in the policy-making process (Wiktorowicz 2003).

62.7 MARKET COMMENTARY

Market forecasting publications abound with insights on compliance trends and FDA enforcement activity, though again the foci vary depending on the publication date and the general administrative and political environment. Coverage by those representing or assessing industry is largely dependent on changes in federal legislation, market trends, and litigation landscape. A brief look at a few perspectives in this realm is informative. Recently, a 2018 business analysis by Deloitte summarizes findings regarding the impact of changing regulations in the pharmaceutical and medical device industries, offering recommendations to make company processes more transparent, including the establishment of procedures for constant reevaluation of practices in response to the shift toward self-reporting (Deloitte 2018). The report highlights drug pricing reporting at both the federal and the state level and regulation of combination products as two areas of potential significant change for biopharmaceutical companies.

The Deloitte report suggests that considering the federal ceiling price and the manufacturers' civil monetary penalties regulation that went into effect in 2019, manufacturers should consider revamping practices for Medicaid Drug Rebates Program restatements; true-up of estimated ceiling prices for new drugs; and offsetting the de minimis threshold. At the state level, legislation limiting drug costs by requiring reporting on pricing and pricing increases instructs that manufacturers should focus on additional reporting capability, including tracking and assessment of new requirements, reporting and documentation of compliance with requirements, and reevaluation of pricing strategies (Deloitte 2018).

For combination products, which are therapeutic, and diagnostic products that combine active ingredients and mechanisms of action of drugs, devices, and biological products, the regulatory landscape is complex, with agency regulations and expectations evolving globally at different speeds. To address the changing regulatory landscape and avoid compliance violations, Deloitte suggests that companies review the latest updated quality management regulatory requirements for combination products in order to ensure compliance going forward. As a means to accomplish this, the report identifies a holistic approach involving thorough review of current products for appropriate classification and identification; review of current and upcoming regulatory requirements coupled with a readiness assessment; establishment of effective controls for management, purchasing, and design; enhancement of corporate corrective action and preventative plans and post-market surveillance to identify, define, implement, and monitor processes and capabilities to meet combination product requirements; and a rigorous safety review followed by update of the processes to satisfy the requirements for combination products (Deloitte 2018).

The Deloitte report also offers several general recommendations for life science companies in the compliance realm on topics of data analytics, market access, and interactions with healthcare providers. First, companies should consider leveraging technology solutions to automate activities and controls and to assist with ongoing compliance monitoring, including workflow automation, use of cluster analysis in large data sets, and harnessing the power of cognitive technologies. Second, life sciences companies should view the Open Payments system as a valuable tool in their ongoing compliance efforts. At a minimum, life sciences manufacturers should be able to correlate supporting data and/or supporting documents to help: detect compliance patterns and take corrective actions before they become issues; explain any identified anomalies; use these findings to enhance compliance. They suggest focus on data cleansing; infrastructure, including processes, policies, and procedures; and cross-functional teams as compliance becomes more complex at the federal and state level (Deloitte 2018).

Another example of industry projection on compliance trends is KPMG International's *Pharma Outlook 2030: From Evolution to Revolution.*[15] Published in 2017 by the KPMG Global Strategy Group, the report depicts the pharmaceutical industry "at a crossroads" in a "heavily disrupted marketplace" and highlights several areas of long-term impact. Those relating to regulation include movements toward greater transparency in a variety of contexts and the resulting movement toward value-based models of care. The report also notes areas of research and development becoming more prevalent in the industry and thus potential targets for regulators in early stages of development. The first area is integration of medical devices and software. The FDA has recently published a "software as medical device" guidance document[16] and outlined a precertification process for device software[17] in the wake of escalating concerns about hacking of such devices. The second area is gene editing, a technology that is driving potential applications for detection, prevention, and treatment of

[15] KPMG, February 6, 2017, https://home.kpmg/uk/en/home/insights/2017/02/pharma-outlook-2030-from-evolution-to-revolution.html.

[16] United States Food & Drug Administration (FDA). 2017b. *Guidance for Industry: Software as a Medical Device (SaMD).*

[17] United States Food & Drug Administration (FDA). 2017a. *Digital Health Innovation Plan.*

genetic diseases and conditions. The third is immunotherapy innovations, where collaborative advances are being made in cancer and chronic disease treatments. Finally, the report characterizes models of oversight emerging to address developments. These include integration of lifecycle management, virtual offerings, and convergence of product focus.[18]

62.8 CONCLUSION

The biopharmaceutical industry is governed by complex layers of federal regulation. The primary regulatory agency is the FDA, which operates chiefly through a command-and-control mechanism. Compliance is sought using administrative and legal tools such as inspections, warning letters, and enforcement actions. Recent trends demonstrate consistent levels of inspections and warning letters and increasing use of consent decrees between the agency and industry to remedy alleged violations of the statute and regulations. Scholars have explored theoretical and empirical aspects of biopharmaceutical compliance, though the scholarship is narrow and out of date. The most useful up-to-date information on recent trends is offered by the FDA in an online database and through market analysis publications and projections.

REFERENCES

Ayres, Ian, and John Braithwaite. 1992. *Responsive Regulation: Transcending the Deregulation Debate.* Oxford University Press.

Chrai, Suffly S., and Michelle Burd. 2004. "Consent Decrees: Effects on Consumers, Companies, and Investors." *Pharmaceutical Technology* 28: 168–82.

Deloitte Center for Regulatory Strategy, Americas. 2019. *Leading in Times of Change: Life Sciences Regulatory Outlook 2019*, www2.deloitte.com/content/dam/Deloitte/us/Documents/regulatory/us-insurance-regulatory-outlook-2019.pdf.

Glicksman, Robert L., and Dietrich Earnhart. 2015. "Coercive vs. Cooperative Enforcement: Effect of Enforcement Approach on Environmental Management." *International Review of Law & Economy* 42: 135–46.

Goldstein, Wendy C., and Lynn Shapiro Snyder. 2003. "The OIG's Draft Compliance Guidance for Pharmaceutical Manufacturers: One More Compliance 'Script' for the Healthcare Industry." *Food and Drug Law Institute Update* 26–30.

Green, Michael D. 1997. "Statutory Compliance and Tort Liability: Examining the Strongest Case." *University of Michigan Journal of Legal Reform* 30: 461–510.

Hale, Andrew, David Borys, and Mark Adams. 2011. "Regulatory Overload: A Behavioral Analysis of Regulatory Compliance." Working Paper No. 11–47, Mercatus Center: George Mason University, 1–31.

Hans, Mohit, and Suresh Kumar Gupta. 2018. "Comparative Evaluation of Pharmacovigilence Regulation of the United States, United Kingdom, Canada, India, and the Need for Global Harmonized Practices." *Perspectives in Clinical Research* 9(4): 170–4.

Hindin, David A., and D. Silberman. 2016. "Designing More Effective Rules and Permits." *George Washington Journal of Energy and Environmental Law* 7: 103–23.

Miller, Jennifer E., Marc Wilenzick, Nolan Ritcey, Joseph S. Ross, and Michelle M. Mello. 2017. "Measuring Clinical Trial Transparency: An Empirical Analysis of Newly Approved Drugs and Large Pharmaceutical Companies." *British Medical Journal Open* 7: e017917. https://bmjopen.bmj.com/content/7/12/e017917.

Niedelman, Steven M. 2005. "Remarks at the Food and Drug Law Institute's 48th Annual Conference." *Food and Drug Law Journal* 60: 117.

[18] See note 19.

Noah, Lars. 2000. "Rewarding Regulatory Compliance: The Pursuit of Symmetry in Products Liability." *Georgetown Law Journal* 88: 2147–65.

Olson, Mary K. 1995. "Regulatory Discretion Among Competing Industries: Inside the FDA." *Journal of Law, Economics and Organization* 11: 379–405.

Olson, Mary K. 1996. "Substitution in Regulatory Agencies: FDA Enforcement Alternatives." *Journal of Law, Economics and Organization* 12: 376–407.

Olson, Mary K. 1999. "Agency Rulemaking, Political Influences, Regulation, and Industry Compliance." *Journal of Law, Economics and Organization* 15: 573–601.

Page, Jr., Robert A. et al. 2015. "Sustainability and Stratified Noncompliance in the Pharmaceutical Industry." *Journal of International Business Disciplines* 1: 18–40.

Poska, Richard, and Graham, Ballard. 2009. "FDA 483 Responses-Suggestions for Industry." *Journal of Validation Technology* 57–62.

Prayle, Andrew P., Matthew N. Hurly, and Alan R. Smyth. 2012. "Compliance with Mandatory Reporting of Clinical Trials Results on ClinicalTrials.gov: Cross Sectional Study." *British Medical Journal Open* 344: d7373. www.bmj.com/content/bmj/344/bmj.d7373.full.pdf.

Rabin, Robert L. 2000. "Reassessing Regulatory Compliance." *Georgetown Law Journal* 88: 2147–65.

Sclar, David, and Gary Keilty. 2012. "Sunshine and Strategy: Managing and Monitoring Compliance with PPACA's Sunshine Provisions – Evolving Legal Requirements and Operational Considerations." *Health Lawyer* 24: 14–24.

Tyler, Ralph S. 2013. "The Goals of FDA Regulation and the Challenges of Meeting Them." *Health Matrix* 22: 423–6.

Wiktorowicz, Mary E. 2003. "Emergent Patterns in the Regulation of Pharmaceuticals: Institutions and Interests in the United States, Canada, Britain and France." *Journal of Health Politics, Policy, and Law* 28(4): 615–58.

63

Transnational Anti-Bribery Law

Kevin E. Davis and Veronica Root Martinez *

Abstract: This chapter focuses on private firms' compliance with norms concerning transnational bribery. It begins with an overview of the regulatory context and obstacles to effective enforcement of norms against transnational bribery. It then reviews how compliance is defined, how it ought to be defined, and obstacles to the achievement of optimal compliance. Finally, it ends by focusing on the next steps forward in this space: (1) greater information sharing from private firms to outsiders in order to better analyze and evaluate the current efficacy of compliance programs targeting anti-bribery, and (2) increased coordination between enforcement agencies at the national and international levels to better tackle transnational bribery.

63.1 INTRODUCTION

Compliance with anti-bribery regulation is a pressing concern for organizations of all sizes and types, for good reason (Consero 2017). Since the beginning of the twenty-first century, dozens of states have adopted expansive anti-bribery laws and there has been a particularly dramatic increase in the level of enforcement of laws aimed at transnational bribery. There is also tremendous public interest in and concern about bribery, often prompted and sustained by reports and investigations conducted by the media and nongovernmental organizations (NGOs). As a result, firms that engage in corrupt activity risk severe and debilitating legal sanctions, as well as reputational harm and political disfavor. In the face of these pressures, companies have strong incentives to create and maintain anti-bribery compliance programs.

Four distinctive features of bribery and its regulation complicate both the definition and the implementation of compliance. First, corrupt conduct typically implicates multiple organizations, including firms whose employees or agents pay bribes, governments whose officials accept bribes, financial institutions which help corrupt officials to hold their assets, and various sorts of advisors and intermediaries who help to facilitate all these interactions. Second, since bribery typically has no obvious individual victims, it is difficult to detect. Third, bribery and its effects often cross national borders, in part because of the globalization of economic activity and in part because operating in multiple jurisdictions helps potentially culpable actors to avoid detection. Fourth, when bribery is transnational, compliance with anti-bribery laws requires organizations, including both states and firms, to take into account a diverse set of laws enforced and interpreted by multiple actors.

This chapter begins, in Section 63.2, with an overview of the regulatory context that governs transnational bribery across the globe. In Section 63.3, it discusses how compliance is defined

* Many thanks to Carol Li and Caitlin-Jean Juricic for invaluable research and editing assistance.

within the anti-bribery space. The chapter then questions how compliance ought to be defined, in Section 63.4. The chapter concludes by highlighting some obstacles to effective compliance with laws against transnational bribery, in Section 63.5, and then, in Section 63.6, suggesting some next steps.

63.2 REGULATORY CONTEXT

Corruption of public officials is the focus of an extensive body of regulation. Much of that regulation is driven by concerns about one of the most paradigmatic forms of corruption, namely, bribery.

Virtually every country in the world criminalizes bribery involving its own public officials. Countries also almost universally sanction people or firms who facilitate or promote corrupt activities such as bribery by laundering their proceeds. It is becoming increasingly common for states to sanction bribery and money laundering that involves foreign public officials. This trend is most often attributed to the enactment of the U.S. Foreign Corrupt Practices Act (FCPA), which became law in 1977 and sanctions the offering or payment of bribes to foreign public officials. Other countries agreed to adopt similar legislation by signing on to the Organisation for Economic Co-operation and Development Convention on Combating Bribery of Foreign Public Officials in International Business Transactions (OECD Convention),[1] which went into effect in 1997. Since then, most countries in the world have signed the United Nations Convention Against Corruption (UNCAC),[2] which contains commitments to regulate both domestic and transnational forms of bribery, embezzlement, and money laundering. The product of this combined set of initiatives is a multi-country ensemble of regulations with both territorial and extraterritorial scope. As a result, individuals and organizations that operate across borders can face liability from multiple sources for the same conduct.

Although virtually every country in the world has anti-bribery laws on the books, levels of enforcement vary considerably. Laws targeting private firms are new in many countries and enforcement is still uncommon. Nonetheless, there have been some prominent examples of anti-bribery enforcement actions aimed at corporations. A leading example of enforcement targeting firms for engaging in predominantly domestic bribery is Brazil's Operation Car Wash, which led to sanctions against sixteen of the country's largest construction firms.[3] However, in recent years there has been an especially marked growth in the intensity of enforcement of laws regulating transnational bribery. This was prompted by a significant increase in the level of enforcement of the FCPA that began in the mid-2000s, measured in terms of both the number of sanctions imposed and the level of sanctions (Martinez 2019:1205; Choi and Davis 2014:419; Warin et al. 2011:321). Recent settlements have topped $1.5 billion in combined monetary penalties.[4] A handful of other developed countries have

1 December 17, 1997, 37 I.L.M. 1.

2 U.N. Doc. A/58/422, Dec. 14, 2005.

3 Ministério Público Federal, "Caso Lava Jatos: Resultados," www.mpf.mp.br/grandes-casos/lava-jato/resultados.

4 See, e.g., U.S. Department of Justice (DOJ), "Petrobras Agrees to Pay More than $850 Million for FCPA Violations," press release September 27, 2018, www.justice.gov/opa/pr/petr-leo-brasileiro-sa-petrobras-agrees-pay-more-850-million-fcpa-violations; US Securities and Exchange Commission (SEC), "Petrobras Reaches Settlement with SEC for Misleading Investors," press release September 27, 2018, www.sec.gov/news/press-release/2018-215#:~:text=Petrobras%20Reaches%20Settlement%20With%20SEC%20for%20Misleading%20Investors,-FOR%20IMMEDIATE%20RELEASE&text=The%20Securities%20and%20Exchange%20Commission,rigging%20scheme%20at%20the%20company.

followed the lead of the United States and now actively enforce laws against bribery of foreign public officials. In 2018, Transparency International classified seven countries – Germany, Israel, Italy, Norway, Switzerland, the UK, and the USA – as active enforcers (Dell and McDevitt 2018; Heimann et al. 2015; Gilbert and Sharman 2014:75–89).

Corporate liability, both criminal and civil, is a prominent feature of anti-bribery law in the United States, and the OECD Convention demands that its signatories impose some form of corporate liability for transnational bribery. As a result, even countries such as Brazil that have traditionally been resistant to the concept have adopted some form of corporate liability for at least transnational bribery. For example, the UK Bribery Act and the Brazilian Clean Company Act explicitly adopt versions of strict liability enforcement regimes against companies for the acts of their employees.

Corporate liability regimes are designed to induce firms to adopt their own compliance programs. For example, the portion of the US Sentencing Guidelines that deals with organizations ("Organizational Guidelines") creates strong incentives for companies to adopt effective ethics and compliance programs, as having such a program can mitigate the potential fine range in the event of a violation by up to 95 percent (Desio n.d.). Similarly, the UK Bribery Act includes a defense for commercial organizations when an employee pays a bribe for the purpose of obtaining or retaining business or a business advantage if the firm has adequate procedures in place to prevent bribery.

As in other areas, firms' compliance efforts are influenced not only by official legal prohibitions but also by the ways in which those prohibitions are enforced. There are several important obstacles to the enforcement of anti-bribery norms.

Arguably, the most significant obstacle to enforcement of anti-bribery law is detection of the misconduct. It has long been accepted within legal scholarship that firms are in the best position to detect misconduct within their ranks, which requires reliance on the firm to police the actions of its employees and members (Root 2017:1011; Arlen and Kraakman 1997). This reality means that enforcement agencies are inherently limited in their ability to enforce anti-bribery laws, because they often cannot detect the misconduct without the participation of the firm itself. A primary tool, therefore, utilized by states is to encourage voluntary self-disclosure on the part of firms regarding misconduct they have detected (Root 2017:1011).

The incentive to self-disclose is, however, greatest for firms whose misconduct is most likely to be detected and sanctioned through other means. At present these seem to be firms that are publicly – as opposed to privately – held, and especially large financial institutions. For example, under US law, public firms are legally required to keep accurate books and records, retain auditors, adopt internal controls, and promptly disclose material information.[5] This body of laws is enforced by independent regulators, in multiple jurisdictions, who offer bounties to whistleblowers who report misconduct. Publicly held financial institutions are subject to additional scrutiny by specialized regulatory agencies. By comparison, private firms are subject to much less regulatory scrutiny – typically only from agencies charged with enforcing criminal prohibitions – and so the shortcomings of their efforts to combat bribery are much less likely to be detected and sanctioned. This disadvantage is made all the starker when one considers the diversity of industries and organizational types that are subject to worldwide anti-bribery laws.[6] For governmental authorities charged with enforcing anti-

[5] US DOJ Criminal Division and US SEC Enforcement Division, "A Resource Guide to the U.S. Foreign Corrupt Practices Act," July 2020, www.justice.gov/criminal-fraud/file/1292051/download.

[6] Gibson Dunn, "2017 Year-End FCPA Update," January 2, 2018, www.gibsondunn.com/wp-content/uploads/2018/01/2017-year-end-fcpa-update-1.pdf.

bribery norms, the underlying unlawful conduct may look quite different when committed by an oil company than when it is found within a financial institution. As a result, enforcement agencies may be at a disadvantage in identifying improper transactions simply because they are unfamiliar with a particular business structure and form.

Another obstacle to effective enforcement of anti-bribery laws is related to the global nature and diversity of the field. As explained earlier, the enforcement of anti-bribery laws is undertaken by a variety of enforcement agencies across the globe.[7] Similarly, the organizations that have engaged in bribery are found in countries worldwide, and many of these organizations have a presence in multiple countries. As a result, it may be difficult for an enforcement agency in Country X to get all the information it needs from Country Y to ensure a full investigation and sanction for a multinational organization's misconduct. The OECD has helped by encouraging coordination amongst states (Brewster and Dryden 2018:200–1), but different states have their own constituencies that they must satisfy, which may deter them from certain cooperative activities. And some states may be unwilling to assist an international enforcement agency, which may limit the reach and effectiveness of enforcement norms. Additionally, a variety of states with anti-bribery laws choose not to enforce those laws, whether that is because they lack the resources or for strategic reasons (Davis 2019:226–7; Stephan 2012:53). When the law is on paper only, the jurisdiction can become a haven for bribery (Spahn 2012:20). Moreover, a state may be concerned that another enforcement agency is overreaching in its attempts to sanction a particular organization, which can result in wrangling between two or more enforcement agencies over who should be vested with the responsibility of pursuing the enforcement action (Holtmeier 2015:493). Finally, an enforcement agency genuinely committed to enforcing anti-bribery laws may itself be corrupted or become captured by the company or industry, which could lead to a lower than optimal amount of enforcement activity (Spahn 2012:12–13). These concerns are exacerbated when one considers that judicial involvement, a common check on potential capture of regulatory or enforcement agencies, is often nonexistent in the anti-bribery space, leaving enforcement agencies with a tremendous amount of power.

63.3 HOW IS COMPLIANCE DEFINED?

For many areas of the law, one looks to the pronouncements of legislators and judges to determine what firms should and should not do. Within the field of anti-bribery law, however, conventional modes of legal analysis do not hold. One often cannot engage in a review of case law to determine what is and is not prohibited under anti-bribery law, because many of these matters are resolved without any significant judicial involvement (Brewster and Dryden 2018:243–6). Most violations of anti-bribery laws by private firms are settled prior to formal or active court involvement, and scholars have expressed skepticism about the practicality and efficacy of creating an international tribunal to deal with this type of misconduct (Brewster and Dryden 2018:250–3). As a result, the staff of enforcement agencies, together with firms' compliance personnel and advisors, play a significant role in defining compliance. Their views are in turn influenced by their conversations with members of a broader interpretive community that includes not only other enforcement and compliance professionals, but also

7 Jones Day, "Anti-Bribery Regulation Survey of 41 Countries 2017–2018," www.jonesday.com/en/insights/2018/04/anticorruption-regulation-survey-of-41-countries-2.

representatives of international organizations such as the OECD Working Group on Bribery and members of civil society.

The leading members of this interpretive community are law enforcement agencies in the United States – specifically, the Department of Justice (DOJ) and the Securities and Exchange Commission (SEC) – charged with enforcing the FCPA, mainly because they continue to be the most active enforcement agencies in the anti-bribery space (Brewster and Dryden 2018:248–50). Those agencies provide a range of both official and unofficial guidance regarding the FCPA, including: the DOJ's Justice Manual (JM) (previously known as the United States Attorneys' Manual);[8] the FCPA Resource Guide jointly authored by the DOJ and the SEC;[9] and various FCPA opinion releases that allow firms to get an opinion from the DOJ about whether prospective conduct conforms with the FCPA. US officials also provide unofficial guidance through various speeches, where they often explain the importance of the FCPA and detail coordination among the DOJ, the SEC, and other global actors in anti-bribery efforts.[10] Additionally, for a time the DOJ employed an internal compliance counsel to assist it in evaluating the effectiveness of compliance programs, which resulted in the publication of information by which the DOJ would evaluate corporate compliance programs.[11] While it appears that the DOJ will not continue to retain an internal compliance counsel, it continues to signal that it will carefully evaluate and assess the effectiveness of a firm's compliance program when determining the appropriate sanction for a violation of the FCPA.[12] Finally, information about what does not qualify as satisfactory compliance is provided, at least implicitly, when the DOJ and the SEC announce completed enforcement actions and publish documents that describe the misconduct that gave rise to those enforcement actions.

Although the United States has historically been dominant in the enforcement of transnational anti-bribery law, a number of other countries have re-tooled or adopted new anti-bribery laws within the last decade and are playing an increasing role in setting standards for organizational behavior.[13] For example, the UK Bribery Act of 2010 dramatically changed the UK's approach to anti-bribery enforcement (Cole and Roberts 2011). Additionally, the 2014 Brazil Clean Companies Act has proven quite important as it is a broadly drafted statute that expands the scope of liability beyond individuals to companies themselves. Most recently, France's Sapin II law, enacted in 2018, created a new anti-corruption authority and has created new compliance obligations for organizations to prevent and detect conduct outlawed by the act (Brunelle 2018). Each of these countries' enforcement agencies has issued guidance on how to comply with their legislation.

8 US DOJ, Justice Manual § 9–47.000 Foreign Corrupt Practices Act of 1977, www.justice.gov/jm/jm-9-47000-foreign-corrupt-practices-act-1977.

9 See note 5.

10 See, e.g., US DOJ, "Deputy Attorney General Rod J. Rosenstein Delivers Remarks at the American Conference Institute's 20th Anniversary New York Conference on the Foreign Corrupt Practice Act," May 9, 2018, www.justice.gov/opa/speech/deputy-attorney-general-rod-j-rosenstein-delivers-remarks-american-conference-institutes.

11 US DOJ, "Evaluation of Corporate Compliance Program," June 2020, www.justice.gov/criminal-fraud/page/file/937501/download.

12 US DOJ, "Assistant Attorney General Brian A. Benczkowski Delivers Remarks at NYU School of Law Program on Corporate Compliance and Enforcement Conference on Achieving Effective Compliance," October 12, 2018, www.justice.gov/opa/speech/assistant-attorney-general-brian-benczkowski-delivers-remarks-nyu-school-law-program.

13 Ernst & Young, "15th Global Fraud Survey," June 10, 2019, https://assets.ey.com/content/dam/ey-sites/ey-com/en_gl/topics/assurance/assurance-pdfs/ey-integrity-in-spotlight.pdf.

Under the auspices of the OECD Convention, the OECD Working Group on Bribery has issued formal recommendations related to anti-bribery efforts meant to assist member-states and others in creating robust enforcement norms. The OECD Working Group also coordinates rigorous peer review exercises that involve "an examination of one state's performance or practices in a particular area by other states" for the purpose of helping "the state under review improve its policymaking, adopt best practices and comply with established standards and principles."[14]

While the attention of enforcement agencies worldwide has greatly incentivized firms to adopt anti-bribery compliance programs, there are also private and extralegal sources of pressure on firms to engage in these compliance efforts. For instance, firms have incentives to conform to other firms' compliance practices if those practices are likely to be regarded as industry standards that may in turn be relied upon by state actors to evaluate compliance.

Private firms' trading partners can also be sources of pressure. Surveys within industry suggest that the biggest concerns of those charged with anti-bribery efforts are risks from third parties with whom they are engaged in business relationships. In one case, 35 percent of those surveyed indicated that "third-party violations top the list of perceived risks to an organization's anti-bribery and corruption program" (Kroll 2018:7). Importantly, "almost a quarter of respondents report[ed] that they do not feel confident in their organization's ability to catch third-party violations of anti-bribery and corruption laws" (Kroll 2018:7). This is a dramatic finding, because "45 percent of respondents work with at least 1,000 third parties per year" (Kroll 2018:7). As a result of these risks, firms often put affirmative requirements within their contracts with third parties to adhere to certain anti-bribery norms.[15]

Firms also consider information from various nongovernmental actors that monitor anti-bribery issues. For example, Transparency International's Corruption Perceptions Index (CPI) sends a strong signal within industry about what countries a company should be more or less concerned about when assessing the risk of public sector corruption. Additionally, the International Organization for Standardization (ISO) has established a mechanism for certifying a firm's anti-bribery management system, which requires adherence to certain requirements.[16] Activities undertaken by organizations like these serve as a form of private guidance for firms striving to create, implement, and maintain effective anti-bribery compliance programs.

The above efforts aimed at incentivizing firms to engage in robust anti-bribery efforts have largely been perceived as effective. There is particularly striking evidence that firms have reduced their investments in high-risk jurisdictions. Several studies suggest that relatively corrupt countries have experienced lower levels of foreign direct investment in and exports from countries that have signed the OECD Convention (Blundell-Wignell and Roulet 2017; D'Souza 2012:73; Cuervo-Cazurra 2006:807). Consistent with these findings, a recent study found that enactment of the UK Bribery Act reduced the value of UK-headquartered firms with exposure to countries perceived to be corrupt, increased the value of direct competitors of UK firms headquartered outside the OECD and without connections to the UK, and caused UK firms to reduce their engagement with corrupt countries (Zeume 2017:1457).

14 Organisation for Economic Co-operation and Development. "Peer Review at a Glance," www.oecd.org/site/peerreview/peerreviewataglance.htm.

15 See, e.g., Oracle, "Partner Code of Conduct and Business Ethics," www.oracle.com/partners/en/how-to-do-business/opn-agreements-and-policies/019520.pdf.

16 ISO, "ISO 37001:2016: Anti-Bribery Management Systems – Requirements with Guidance for Use," www.iso.org/standard/65034.html.

Another recent study suggests that the increase in enforcement of the FCPA that occurred shortly after the OECD Convention came into force discouraged firms from OECD countries – not just US firms – from investing in relatively corrupt countries and led to a net decline in aggregate foreign direct investment in those countries (relative to aggregate noncorrupt countries) (Christensen et al. 2019; cf. Trzcinski 2013).[17] There is less evidence of the impact of the law on misconduct. However, one study using data from Ghana found that firms whose home countries were parties to the OECD Convention were generally less likely to pay or be solicited for bribes (Spencer and Gomez 2011:280). Another study, using data from Vietnam, found that foreign investors in Vietnam whose home countries were parties to the OECD Convention demonstrated lower propensity to pay bribes after the increase in enforcement that accompanied Phase 3 of the Working Group's review process, which was initiated in 2010 (Jensen and Malesky 2018:33).

These studies are consistent with more general findings that firms spend a great deal of time and resources to ensure that their agents comply with various laws. While the exact figures are unknown, the costs do appear to be significant and rising. For example, a 2018 survey of financial institutions revealed that 24 percent of firms expected to spend more than 5 percent of revenue on compliance by 2023 and 11 percent expect to spend more than 10 percent by then.[18] Additionally, a 2017 survey of 900 compliance professionals worldwide indicated that firms expected their compliance team budgets to remain constant or increase over the next twelve months (English and Hammond 2017). Despite these expected increases to compliance budgets, a 2017 survey of ethics and compliance executives indicated that the greatest perceived impediment to their compliance departments, at a response rate of 38 percent, was access to budgetary resources (Consero 2017). These surveys' responses regarding the financial costs of compliance for firms encompass concerns beyond the anti-bribery context, but they are still instructive in that they demonstrate that firms are spending a significant amount of resources on their compliance efforts, and for many firms a significant portion of those efforts are aimed at the risk of bribery.

63.4 HOW SHOULD COMPLIANCE BE DEFINED?

We turn now from the legal question of what sort of conduct is required to comply with anti-bribery laws to the normative question of what sort of conduct ought to be required. In other words, what sorts of effort should organizations undertake to combat bribery?

The answer to this question clearly depends on the criteria for evaluation (Davis 2019). One obvious criterion is legality. It is important for organizations to comply with applicable laws in the course of trying to combat bribery. So, for example, a compliance strategy that violates laws against monitoring employees' email seems less appealing than one which complies with the law, all other things being equal.

[17] Trzcinski's (2013) study of firms subjected to FCPA enforcement actions between 2000 and 2010 found that 70 per cent continued to maintain facilities or offices in countries where misconduct had been identified. She interprets this as evidence that "companies who have been through FCPA enforcement actions are not necessarily pulling out of high-risk countries." However, it is difficult to know whether this is a valid interpretation in the absence of information on the rate of divestment among firms that were not the subjects of FCPA enforcement actions.

[18] Duff & Phelps, "Sixth Annual Global Regulatory Outlook Report," 2018, www.duffandphelps.com/-/media/assets/pdfs/publications/compliance-and-regulatory-consulting/global-regulatory-outlook-2018.pdf?la=en&hash=7754B63FF7CFFE22E46C57BDF9B9681949DCEA31.

Another intuitively appealing criterion is efficiency, meaning the extent to which an organization's anti-bribery efforts enhance overall social welfare, which in turn implies maximizing the differential between their associated benefits and costs. The tangible benefits include minimizing the harm caused by bribery, but there are also intangible benefits from punishing corrupt acts purely for the sake of making a moral statement. It is worth noting that in cases of transnational bribery the costs and benefits of compliance activities will accrue to people in different societies. For instance, the costs of a multinational enterprise's anti-bribery initiative might be borne by investors in the firm while the benefits accrue to the inhabitants of countries governed by corruptible officials. The efficiency of any given compliance activity depends on the resources invested in it and its cost-effectiveness. The effectiveness of a compliance activity is measured by the magnitude of the associated benefits, and its cost-effectiveness refers to the resources required to achieve any given level of effectiveness.

Compliance activity can also be evaluated in terms of legitimacy, meaning the extent to which the organization is justified in exercising power over people. Legitimacy is most commonly used to evaluate the actions of officials who wield the power of the state. However, private actors also wield great power over people's lives, particularly when they can invoke state power, mainly in the form of contract law, in their dealings with employees, suppliers, or customers. Consequently, some scholars argue that private compliance efforts also ought to be evaluated in terms of legitimacy. The sources of legitimacy are contested. Typically, it is considered to be a function of factors such as participation or consent of affected groups, transparency, legality reason-giving, and entitlements to recourse or review, as well as effectiveness.

The distinctive features of anti-bribery compliance make it difficult to arrive at any sort of consensus about the merits of any given compliance activity. First, it may be difficult to assess the legality of the compliance efforts of organizations that are subject to multiple laws. There are significant differences across jurisdictions in terms of laws that protect employees and trading partners against various forms of monitoring, investigation, and discipline (Arlen and Buell 2020). Consequently, practices that are legal in one jurisdiction may be illegal in another.

Second, and relatedly, organizations that operate in a transnational context will find their compliance efforts being evaluated by a broad and heterogeneous set of people, including not only anti-corruption regulators but also important stakeholders such as customers, trading partners, and governments. These people may have differential access to information about compliance activities, especially if costs and benefits accrue in different places. People in different places may also have different conceptions of legitimacy.

Third, the benefits and costs of compliance efforts are likely to be difficult to determine. One reason is that the harm associated with bribery can be difficult to assess. Another reason stems from the fact that bribery is difficult to detect. This in turn means that it is difficult to measure the preventive effect of any given compliance activity on either the volume or the magnitude of bribery. In addition, the expressive benefits of compliance activities are contested. Meanwhile, on the cost side of the equation, there is the familiar problem of isolating the costs of anti-bribery compliance from the costs of compliance with other norms. For instance, the same internal controls that limit employees' ability to steal from a company serve to limit their ability to pay bribes to public officials. Consequently, even assuming the costs of internal controls can be measured, it may not be obvious what portion of those costs ought to be attributed to anti-bribery compliance.

Fourth, when multiple organizations are involved in compliance and there are several equally effective combinations of compliance strategies, it will be impossible to identify the optimal compliance strategy for any single organization in isolation, and coordination may be difficult. For example, it might be efficient for either firms or governments to invest in auditing a particular set of transactions, but not both. In the absence of coordination there might be either excessive or suboptimal levels of auditing.

63.5 OBSTACLES TO EFFECTIVE COMPLIANCE

Within firms themselves, a number of challenges are associated with effective self-regulation. For example, the sheer scope and size of many firms has increased exponentially over the past several decades, which makes the task of monitoring a particularly complex endeavor (Martinez 2020:268–9). Today's firms are often made up of a dizzying array of complex corporate families with a variety of parent and subsidiary corporations across the globe (Martinez 2020:268). Many firms have adopted global compliance programs, but the steps necessary for creating effective compliance norms in Canada might look quite different from what is necessary for achieving that same goal in China or Nigeria. As firms move increasingly toward global compliance programs, they must find ways to both standardize and customize their compliance efforts to ensure that effective policies and procedures are adopted throughout the global firm (Martinez 2020:276–7).

Relatedly, firms are made up of heterogeneous individuals and groups that may have different beliefs about the prevalence of bribery, its appropriateness, and the costs and benefits of engaging in or tolerating it. Explaining why unlawful payments are improper in a country where unlawful payments are perceived to be a regular and necessary component of effectuating business transactions can be an especially challenging task. Indeed, ad hoc discussions with people in industry suggest that even after undergoing robust training on what is required by the FCPA and other anti-bribery regimes, employees will still often believe that certain payments that they perceive to be necessary for carrying out essential business tasks must qualify for an exemption. This is true even when the payments at issue are clearly in violation of the principles outlined in the training provided.

Additionally, those charged with compliance within firms may be subject to conflicts of interest and become corrupted if noncompliance with anti-bribery laws is perceived by the employee as beneficial in some way to himself or the firm (Arlen and Kraakman 1997). This is the most classic concern for those charged with creating compliance programs. If the employee puts his own short-term interests above the long-term interest of the organization, he may engage in behavior that is ultimately harmful for the firm. For example, if a sales manager receives a bonus for achieving a certain sales target, he may be incentivized to make an unlawful payment to a foreign official to ensure that the target is met. In the short term, the employee may believe that his interest in meeting the sales target is aligned with that of the organization, which also prefers robust sales numbers. In actuality, however, making an unlawful payment puts the organization at risk for later sanction from an enforcement agency and, perhaps, reputational harm.

Finally, yet another obstacle to achieving effective anti-bribery compliance programs is related to the relationships between a company and its third-party contracting partners (Kroll 2018:7–11). Many firms contract with third parties to perform certain tasks on behalf of the organization and these contractual relationships are lawful. If, however, a third-party contracting partner violates the FCPA or related laws, it puts the organization itself, not just the third-party contracting partner, at risk for investigation and sanction from enforcement agencies. As a result, firms are charged with monitoring not only themselves but also the conduct of their contracting partners. Firms have expressed concern about their ability to effectively monitor the actions of their third-party contracting partners, which reveals the challenge this particular point of risk creates for firms (Kroll 2018:7–11). These concerns may be particularly salient for small firms which are less able to bear the fixed costs of establishing a compliance program and are more likely to rely on third parties (Sykes and Pearlman 2017:171–4).

These are just a few of the many potential challenges associated with creating and maintaining an effective compliance program that will prevent corrupt behavior within firms. As globalization increases, the challenge for firms continues to expand as the scope of individuals and entities that must be monitored constantly increases.

63.6 NEXT STEPS IN TRANSNATIONAL ANTI-BRIBERY COMPLIANCE

As explained in this chapter, organizations, whether private firms or state actors, charged with responding to bribery have a daunting task before them. It requires coordination amongst state actors, private firms, their contracting partners, and the public (Yeung 2004).[19] As such, those charged with developing anti-bribery compliance programs have to make important decisions within a space that lacks clear-cut answers and guidance.

One approach that merits further consideration is to encourage private firms to work together to develop standards for compliance programs, including sharing information about the performance of their compliance practices (Baer 2009).[20] The benefit of relying upon firms to create a set of standards is that it allows those with access to the most precise information to evaluate the costs, risks, and benefits of different compliance activities.[21] The drawback, of course, is that those creating the standards that industries and governments will rely upon to evaluate the effectiveness of firms' compliance programs may have an incentive to adopt policies that are easy to implement but unlikely to deter bribery at optimal rates.

The challenge going forward is how to transfer information from private firms to those outside of those firms, so that proper evaluations can be made about what an effective anti-bribery program might look like. Attempts to harness this information have occurred both within the United States, through the DOJ's experiment with an internal compliance counsel as well as its policies addressing leniency and the imposition of monitorships,[22] and

[19] Yeung (2004:171) discusses the "centrality of dialogue and deliberation between stakeholders in the law enforcement process, primarily between the regulator and regulated, but in which other participants affected by the regulatory enterprise may (in certain circumstances) contribute."

[20] This approach is an extension of that advocated by new governance literature, which encourages private actors to find solutions to regulatory problems. Baer (2009) discusses how "New Governance regimes therefore grant regulated entities a fair amount of discretion to devise processes necessary to achieve the broad goals that private and public actors collaboratively debate."

[21] There are a variety of examples where members of industry work together to identify solutions to common compliance concerns. For example, IBM identified regulatory compliance challenges in the data protection and data privacy area and "launched a groundbreaking initiative in May 2017 to build an industry-standard cloud control framework for financial services." As of October 2017, 30 financial services organizations agreed to "join together to create a standard regulatory framework and controls for the financial services industry" (Meshell 2017). Another example is Anheuser-Busch InBev SA's efforts to develop artificial intelligence and data analytics tools that could detect risky or illegal payments. Notably, it hopes to "develop a consortium that enables companies to share insights from their data to boost the accuracy of their analytics models" (Tokar 2020).

[22] It is worth noting that even sources of information that could in theory create pools of information that could be shared across industry sometimes do not appear for a variety of reasons. For example, literature suggests that

internationally, through the OECD Working Group on Bribery and various NGOs. The reality, however, is that as anti-bribery efforts grow worldwide in response to more active enforcement activities by non-US states, the need to gather, interpret, and transmit information about anti-bribery compliance will continue to increase in importance (Davis 2019). Additionally, the need for interstate coordination in enforcement activities and international cooperation amongst practitioners and academics will be pivotal to ensuring that global anti-bribery and anti-bribery activities complement, as opposed to contradict or unnecessarily overlap with, one another.

REFERENCES

Arlen, Jennifer, and Reinier Kraakman. 1997. "Controlling Corporate Misconduct: An Analysis of Corporate Liability Regimes." *New York University Law Review* 72:687–779.

Arlen, Jennifer, and Samuel W. Buell. 2020. "The Law of Corporate Investigations and the Global Expansion of Corporate Criminal Liability." *University of Southern California Law Review* 93:697–761.

Baer, Miriam H. 2009. "Governing Corporate Compliance." *Boston College Law Review* 50:949–1019.

Blundell-Wignall, Adrian, and Caroline Roulet. 2017. "Foreign Direct Investment, Corruption and the OECD Anti-Bribery Convention." www.oecd-ilibrary.org/finance-and-investment/foreign-direct-investment-corruption-and-the-oecd-anti-bribery-convention_9cb3690c-en.

Brewster, Rachel, and Christine Dryden. 2018. "Building Multilateral Anticorruption Enforcement: Analogies between International Trade and Anti-Bribery Law." *Virginia Journal of International Law* 57:221–62.

Brunelle, Emmanuelle. 2018. "French Anti-Corruption Agency Provides Guidance on Sapin II Compliance." Freshfields Bruckhaus Deringer LLP. https://www.lexology.com/library/detail.aspx?g=d9d485e0-48e8-45ca-9e3b-1b1b443f2415.

Choi, Stephen J., and Kevin E. Davis. 2014. "Foreign Affairs and Enforcement of the Foreign Corrupt Practice Act." *Journal of Empirical Legal Studies* 11:409–45.

Christensen, Hans B., Mark G. Maffett, and Thomas Rauter. 2019. "Policeman for the World: US Enforcement of Foreign Corruption Regulation and Corporate Investment Policies." https://papers.ssrn.com/sol3/papers.cfm?abstract_id=3349272.

Cole, Jeremy, and Michael Roberts. 2011. "Changes in UK Corruption Enforcement – The Bribery Act of 2010." Hogan Lovells LLP. https://www.lexology.com/library/detail.aspx?g=2688ffe3-2aa3-4076-9701-768ea64d78f8.

Consero Group. 2017. "Corporate Compliance & Ethics Report." www.consero.com/august-2017-corporate-compliance-ethics-report/.

Cuervo-Cazurra, Alvaro. 2006. "Who Cares About Corruption?" *Journal of International Business Studies* 37:807–22.

Davis, Kevin E. 2019. *Between Impunity and Imperialism: The Regulation of Transnational Bribery*. New York: Oxford University Press.

Dell, Gillian, and Andrew McDevitt. 2018. "Exporting Corruption, Progress Report 2018: Assessing Enforcement of the OECD Anti-Bribery Convention." www.transparency.lt/wp-content/uploads/2018/09/TI_Exporting-Corruption-Report_2018.pdf.

Desio, Paula (Deputy General Counsel, US Sentencing Commission). "An Overview of the Organizational Guidelines." www.ussc.gov/sites/default/files/pdf/training/organizational-guidelines/ORGOVERVIEW.pdf (accessed December 11, 2020).

information gleaned by the government during monitorships that report to the DOJ does not result in broader information being disseminated to the public. For example, Ford and Hess discuss how "monitors learn by trial and error (at the company's expense) and without the benefit of other monitors' experience." Consulting with other monitors occurs only "rarely and on an ad hoc or informal basis," even though "[s]everal monitors expressed a strong desire for a forum in which to share their insights and learn from the experience of other monitors." (Ford and Hess 2009:679, 719).

D'Souza, Anna. 2012. "The OECD Anti-Bribery Convention: Changing the Currents of Trade." *Journal of Development Economics* 97:73–87.

English, Stacey, and Susannah Hammond. 2017. "Cost of Compliance." Thomson Reuters. https://legal.thomsonreuters.com/content/dam/ewp-m/documents/legal/en/pdf/reports/cost-of-compliance-2017.pdf.

Ford, Christie, and David Hess. 2009. "Can Corporate Monitorships Improve Corporate Compliance?" *Journal of Corporation Law* 34:679–737.

Gilbert, Jo-Anne, and J. C. Sharman. 2014. "Turning a Blind Eye to Bribery: Explaining Failures to Comply with the International Anti-corruption Regime." *Political Studies* 64:74–89.

Heimann, Fritz, Ádám Földes, and Sophia Coles. 2015. "Exporting Corruption, Progress Report 2015: Assessing Enforcement of the OECD Convention on Combatting Foreign Bribery." https://issuu.com/transparencyinternational/docs/2015_exportingcorruption_oecdprogre.

Holtmeier, Jay. 2015. "A Case for Measured Coordination among Multiple Enforcement Authorities." *Fordham Law Review* 84:493–523.

Jensen, Nathan M., and Edmund J. Malesky. 2018. "Nonstate Actors and Compliance with International Agreements: An Empirical Analysis of the OECD Anti-Bribery Convention." *International Organization* 72:33–69.

Kroll. 2018. "Anti-Bribery and Corruption Benchmarking Report" (April 1). www.kroll.com/en-us/abc-report.

Martinez, Veronica Root. 2019. "The Outsized Influence of the FCPA?" *Illinois Law Review* 2019:1205–25.

2020. "Complex Compliance Investigations." *Columbia Law Review* 120:249–307.

Meshell, Gary B. 2017. "Turning the Regulatory Challenges of Cloud Computing into Competitive Advantage" (October) IBM Security. https://hosteddocs.ittoolbox.com/cloud-regulatory-advantage.pdf.

Root, Veronica. 2017. "Coordinating Compliance Incentives." *Cornell Law Review* 102:1003–85.

Spahn, Elizabeth K. 2012. "Multijurisdiction Bribery Law Enforcement: The OECD Anti-Bribery Convention." *Virginia Journal of International Law* 53:1–52.

Spencer, Jennifer, and Carolina Gomez. 2011. "MNEs and Host Country Corruption." *Strategic Management Journal* 32:280–300.

Stephan, Paul B. 2012. "Regulatory Competition and Anticorruption Law." *Virginia Journal of International Law* 53:53–70.

Sykes, Alan, and Rebecca L. Pearlman. 2017. "The Political Economy of the Foreign Corrupt Practices Act: An Explanatory Analysis." *Journal of Legal Analysis* 9:153–82.

Tokar, Dylan. 2020. "AB InBev Taps Machine Learning to Root Out Corruption" (January 17), *Wall Street Journal*. https://www.wsj.com/articles/ab-inbev-taps-machine-learning-to-root-out-corruption-11579257001.

Trzcinski, Leah M. 2013. "The Impact of the Foreign Corrupt Practices Act on Emerging Markets: Company Decision-Making in a Regulated World." *New York University Journal of International Law & Politics* 45:1201–85.

Warin, Joseph, Michael Diamant, and Veronica Root. 2011. "Somebody's Watching Me: FCPA Monitorships and How They Can Work Better." *University of Pennsylvania Journal of Business Law* 13:321–81.

Yeung, Karen. 2004. *Securing Compliance: A Principled Approach*. Portland: Oxford.

Zeume, Stefan. 2017. "Bribes and Firm Value." *Review of Financial Studies* 30:1457–89.

64

Data Security, Data Breaches, and Compliance

Chirantan Chatterjee and D. Daniel Sokol

Abstract: This chapter explores the attributes of compliance in the context of data breaches. First, it identifies the sort of corporate governance problem that data breaches create. Then, it approaches the empirical work related to data breaches and to the organization of compliance-based responses in terms of risk assessment, training, and compliance, both preemptively and after a breach. Next, the chapter discusses the extant theoretical and empirical evidence about the short- and long-term impacts of IT security events on breached firms as well as corporate governance issues relating to data breaches. It also examines studies that evaluate the impact of different types of event on various types of firm and stakeholder. The chapter also explores how data breaches impact broader issues of corporate governance and compliance. In the end, it identifies potential research questions and avenues for future researchers on how firms or governments might have to think about their IT security investments and the necessary measures that have to be in place to respond effectively if such events occur.

64.1 INTRODUCTION

Computers and information technology impact daily life. Their growing role has led to greater investments in the infrastructure and safety of these systems. While investments in networking capabilities and the security of IT systems have increased over the years, threats to their security and the information that is stored in them also have increased and evolved. Governments and firms are now increasingly focusing on ensuring the security of the data that they collect from their citizens and customers respectively as part of a growing compliance infrastructure. According to a recent Gartner forecast report, global IT security spending is expected to grow by 8.7 percent to $124 billion in 2019, which will be greater than the general IT spending growth which is expected to be around 3.2 percent (Gartner, 2019).

Despite all these efforts related to information security, data breaches are increasingly more common. The risk of a data breach is now part of regular risk assessment by firms. However, the nature of how to conceptualize compliance with regard to data breaches is understudied in terms of both theory and empirics relative to other sorts of more traditional compliance function, such as the risk of audit or anti-bribery related wrongdoing. This chapter explores the attributes of compliance in the context of data breaches. First, it identifies the sort of corporate governance problem that data breaches create. Then, it approaches the empirical work related to data breaches and to the organization of compliance-based responses in terms of risk assessment, training, and compliance, both preemptively and after a breach.

Next, the chapter discusses the extant theoretical and empirical evidence about the short- and long-term impacts of IT security events on breached firms as well as corporate governance issues relating to data breaches. It also examines studies that evaluate the impact of different types of event on various types of firm and stakeholder. The chapter also explores how data breaches impact broader issues of corporate governance and compliance. In the end, it identifies potential research questions and avenues for future researchers on how firms or governments might have to think about their IT security investments and the necessary measures that have to be in place to respond effectively if such events occur.

Data breaches are one of the most prominent modes of attacking a company's or a government agency's website or server. The term "data breach" now encompasses a wide range of security-compromising activities and attacks.

64.2 WHAT IS A DATA BREACH?

The term "data breach" represents a whole gamut of internet or IT security violations that can be committed against individuals, companies, and governments. The nonprofit ITRC (Identity Theft Resource Center) defines a data breach as "an incident in which an individual's name plus a Social Security Number, driver's license number, medical record or financial record (including debit/credit cards) is potentially put at risk because of exposure." A broader definition comes from Cannon and Kessler (2007: 42), who define a data breach as "the unauthorized access to and acquisition of data in any form or format containing sensitive information that compromises the security or confidentiality of such information and creates a reasonable risk of its misuse."

Other authors have used the term "internet security breach" (Campbell et al., 2003; Cavusoglu et al., 2004; Kannan et al., 2007) or "privacy breach" (Acquisti et al., 2006). Spanos and Angelis (2016: 217)summarize information security breaches as "successful attempts by hackers to harm the confidentiality, integrity or the availability of a system" and also classify them further into sub-categories such as privacy breaches, denial-of-service (DOS) attacks, and website defacements. While privacy breaches are intended to affect the confidentiality of a system by allowing unauthorized access, DOS attacks target the availability of an information system and make it inoperable, and website defacements harm the visual appearance of a website and harm its integrity.

64.2.1 *Types of Data Breach*

Data breaches come in various forms and types. Over the years several authors have tried to classify and study the impact of different types of data breach. Spanos and Angelis (2016) classify the types of security event that have been studied in this area under four major categories: security breaches; phishing; IT security investments; and software vulnerabilities and IT security legislation. They further point out that "security breaches" (often used interchangeably with the terms "IT security breaches" and "data breaches") are the most widely studied category, with 81.1 percent of the thirty-seven papers that they reviewed while analyzing their impact.

Various studies in the area of information study breaches have been focused on a particular type of data breach. For instance, Campbell et al. (2003) classified breach events based on the involvement of confidential data, while Garg et al. (2003) classified them as website defacements, DoS attacks, theft of customer information, and theft of credit card information. Hovav and D'Arcy (2003) and Casuvoglu et al. (2004) focused mainly on the impact of DOS attacks. Quite recently, Romanosky (2016) classified all cyber-attack incidents as data breaches, security incidents, privacy violations, and phishing/skimming. Jacobs et al. (2019) offer an approach called an Exploit Prediction Scoring System (EPSS).

Various authors who have studied this area have used different ways to classify the type of security breach. This could be a potential reason why different authors seem to have varying results while explaining the impact of different types of security event on the stock market.

Data/security breaches have been further classified into several subcategories based on the type of damage inflicted on the victim's IT systems. The damages depend on the property or aspect of IT security that is compromised by the attacker(s). One of the most widely used frameworks for defining information security has been the CIA (Confidentiality, Integrity, Availability) Triad (Solomon and Chapple, 2005). Hackers attack any of these three important aspects of an IT system and it can lead to Disclosure, Alteration, and Denial of data or access to the IT system, known as the DAD Triad (Solomon and Chapple, 2005). Table 64.1 summarizes the different types of data breach based on the CIA and DAD frameworks with examples.

TABLE 64.1 *Data breach types and examples*

Compromised property – attack consequence	Description	Examples
Confidentiality – Disclosure	Attackers get unauthorized access to confidential data which can be used later for malicious purposes	Unauthorized access to: 1. *customer data* (social security number, contact information, credit card details, etc.) 2. *employee data* (names, contact information, salaries) 3. *company data* (designs, source code, documents)
Integrity – Alteration	Attackers manipulate, alter, corrupt, and delete the data and make it unavailable/inaccessible for subsequent use	1. *Website alteration* – hackers gain access to company's web servers and delete content or corrupt the sites with inappropriate information 2. *Website defacement* – hackers modify the visual appearance of a webpage and make it inaccessible
Availability – Denial	Attackers make a website inaccessible or unusable for legitimate users by flooding servers and networks with requests and traffic that overwhelms the breached firm's IT resources	1. *DoS* – an attacker creates a flood of information requests to a web server and makes it unavailable for regular use 2. *DDoS* – when multiple systems take part in a DoS attack, it is known as a distributed denial of service attack

64.2.2 *Cost and Impact of Breaches*

Information security events can cause multiple damages to a firm. Firms have always had to choose between investing in IT security before breaches occur and having to pay exorbitant costs after the event. However, they also have to decide how much to invest in IT security because too much investment might be considered unwanted if such events do not impact the firm seriously. For these reasons, scholars have been interested in quantifying the impact of such breaches to help firms better understand the cost and impact of IT breaches. Yayla and Hu (2011) highlight that firms have both tangible and intangible costs due to security breaches. While tangible costs include revenue and productivity loss and the cost of repair and replacement of hardware and software, intangible costs include loss of customer loyalty and trust, investor confidence, and competitive advantage in their industry.

One of the most prominent ways of studying the impact of security events is to study the short-term effects of breach announcements by analyzing the impact of a firm's stock price after a breach announcement. This has by far been the most widely studied mode of IT breach consequence. Using event study methodologies, multiple authors have highlighted the costs such as the loss in market capitalization (Cavusoglu et al., 2004) incident-specific losses (Garg et al., 2003), and loss in annual revenues (Romanosky, 2016). Some authors have also looked at the long-term impact of such breaches, which involves analyzing the impact three or four quarters after the actual breach incident (Ko and Dorantes, 2006; Kannan et al., 2007). Apart from calculating the losses in terms of stock price changes, another phenomenon that has been studied frequently is the impact of breach announcements by industry type and size – for instance, Cummins et al. (2006) examine this for banks and insurance companies, while Pirounias et al. (2014) examine this for technology firms. Related work by Romanosky et al. (2011) studies whether or not state-level disclosure laws impact identity theft. In the upcoming sections we will summarize these studies based on their key impact as analyzed.

64.2.3 *Short-Term Impact (Stock Market Returns)*

Since these attacks have adverse strategic and operational (and thereby profitability and potentially shareholder) consequences for the breached firm, several authors have attempted to study the impact of such breaches (Campbell et al., 2003; Casuvoglu et al., 2004; Hovav and D'Arcy, 2003) on these firms and also to validate whether the efficient market hypothesis works well to account for the impact on these affected companies' share prices.

The study of information security events' impact on the stock price of firms first began in the early 2000s (Spanos and Angelis, 2016) and the number of publications in this field of study have been increasing since then. While these early studies were focused on hacker attacks on internet firms, recent studies have broadened to include various types of information security event that compromise the confidentiality, integrity, and availability of data held by different types of firm, industry, and stakeholder.

A majority of the studies in the area of information security breach analysis have focused on studying the stock price impact before and after the announcement of a data breach. Pirounias et al. (2014) postulate that this is due to lack of objective quantitative data; as a consequence, stock price is used as a proxy for the costs of a cyberattack by academia. In a significant number of studies, the impact is calculated as abnormal stock returns, which is further defined as "the difference between the actual and the expected return of a security."

Garg et al. (2003) did some pioneering work in this area by studying twenty-two breach events between 1996 and 2002, and finding that the average loss was in the range of $17 million to $28 million. Another key finding from the study was that the most adverse market reactions (negative abnormal return) were in response to credit card information theft, which ranged between 9 percent and 15 percent of the twenty-two events.

In similar early work, Campbell et al. (2003) studied the impact of different types of breach between 1995 and 2000 and asserted that there was a significant negative market response when confidentiality was compromised but there wasn't any significant market reaction when there was no involvement of confidential information.

Cavusoglu et al. (2004) were the first to quantify the impact of internet security breaches on the market value of a firm. By analyzing over sixty-six events from 1996 to 2001, they pointed out that breached firms lose around 2.1 percent of their market value within two days of the breach announcement. While their study was not focused very much on the type of security breach, they showed that the market value of security developers increases when breaches are announced. They further showed a more adverse market impact on internet firms than conventional firms and a similar trend for smaller firms when compared with larger ones.

Other work examines stock market returns. Acquisti et al. (2006) demonstrated that even though there is a statistically negative market reaction which impacts the market value of firms within the first two days of the announcement of a breach, the cumulative effect reduces and loses statistical significance with time. They have also pointed out that a set of outlying firms were responsible for driving the significant impact of the results, which could have been due to larger and more visible firms possibly experiencing greater damage than others. Further, Telang and Wattal (2007) analyzed 147 security-related vulnerability incidents announced by software vendors between 1999 and 2004 and found that they lose an average 0.63 percent of their market value on the day of announcement of the vulnerability and that they specifically lose more value in competitive markets. They also described that larger vendors are more immune to vulnerability disclosures than smaller ones and that the severity of the breach is directly proportional to its negative impact.

In additional work, Goel and Shawky (2009) studied security breaches between 2004 and 2008 and observed a significant negative impact of 1 percent of the market value of the firm during the days surrounding the announcement of the security breach, while Pirounias et al. (2014) conducted one of the first studies on firm-specific breach events that happened between 2008 and 2011 and revealed the average total cost of a breach in their entire sample to be between $168 million and $200 million. Similar to the findings of Acquisti et al. (2006), they also highlighted that specific major events tend to have a larger and greater impact on the market value of a firm.

More recently, Romanosky et al. (2016) claimed that in spite of an increase in the number of breach events and legal actions that they analyzed in a ten-year period from 2005 to 2014, the actual costs of these events for firms were less than $200,000, which they estimated to be around 0.4 percent of firm revenues. Further, consumers regularly express concern with regard to their privacy; yet, Ablon et al. (2016) found that only 11 percent of consumers cease dealing with companies that have experienced privacy breaches.

64.2.4 *Long-Term Impact*

While a vast majority of authors have focused on studying the impact of breach events over a short time frame, some have focused on evaluating their long-term impact. Ko and Dorantes

(2006) performed a matched-sample comparison (unlike earlier studies that were based on an event study methodology) to study the impact of financial metrics like sales, operating income, return on assets, return on sales, and a few others for two groups of firms – breached and control (firms that were not breached but were very similar to those that were breached in terms of sales, number of employees, and industry), in the subsequent four quarters after a breach. They concluded that breaches have a minimal long-term impact on affected firms.

Ko et al. (2009) have also observed that while breaches affecting confidentiality and availability have a long-term negative impact, those affecting integrity do not have a long-term impact. Similarly, Hilary et al. (2016) also noted that despite increasing attention from both the public and regulators like the US Securities and Exchange Commission (SEC) on the topic of cyber risks, the market reactions to data breach announcements were limited – around -0.5 percent over a three-day window. Another interesting finding from their qualitative analysis of major data breaches at Sony, Target, Home Depot, and Anthem (all of which happened between 2011 and 2016) is that none of these high-profile breaches had any significant and long-term abnormal returns on their stock price, over a six-month and a twelve-month horizon.

64.2.5 *Reducing Costs of Information Security Breaches*

Gordon et al. (2011), apart from noting that breaches compromising availability have the most negative impact on stock returns, highlighted that there has been a significant downward shift in the costs of security breaches after the 9/11 attacks when compared to the period before it. Interestingly, other studies by Yayla and Hu (2011) and Priounias et al. (2014) found that breach events in more recent years have had less negative impact than those in the earlier years and that markets have started to react more maturely to such breach announcements by firms, respectively. In another stream of work, Buckman et al. (2019) found that firms that created stricter policies with regard to information breaches after they were the victims of a breach reduced a second breach by up to 50 percent, depending on the policy.

64.2.6 *Impact Based on Firm/Industry Type*

Another interesting topic for academic researchers within the area of information security breaches has been the study of the impact of these events for different firm types (large vs. small etc.) and industry types (internet-specific vs. others, e-commerce vs. bricks and mortar, etc.). Several studies have tried to analyze these distinctions.

One of the first studies in this regard was by Hovav and D'Arcy (2003), who showed that "internet-specific companies" were impacted more than other companies by DoS attack announcements and also indicated that larger non-internet-specific firms might be overreacting by investing resources into IT security the violation of which might have only a marginal shareholder impact. Further, Cummins et al. (2006) studied the impact of operational risk events that have been reported by public US-based banking and insurance firms between 1978 and 2003 and pointed out a significantly negative stock price reaction to announcements of operational loss events. They also found that the impact was larger for insurers than for banks and that the market value losses were higher in firms which had stronger growth prospects.

The roles of contingency factors like business and industry type, breach type, event year, and length of window were studied by Yayla and Hu (2011). Their analysis concluded that though e-commerce firms faced a greater negative impact when compared to those of bricks-and-mortar firms during the three- and seven-day event windows, it was not the case during a twelve-day window and hence the differences reduced quickly. Other work by Collins et al. (2011) studied the impact of the passage of data breach reporting legislation and observed that after the enforcement of the HITECH Act The Health Information Technology for Economic and Clinical Health Act in 2009, the frequency of security incidents reported by the medical industry improved; such incidents primarily included inside abuse, physical loss of records, compromised portable devices, and compromised stationary devices.

Additionally, Arcuri et al. (2014) analysed the impact of around 128 breaches of 81 firms classified into financial and other economic sectors and found no negative impact for financial institutions but found a negative impact for firms from the other sectors. As strange as it might sound, they also demonstrated that while firms in other sectors had a negative mean CAR (cumulative abnormal return) in seven- and three-day event windows, financial sector firms showed positive mean CARs in the same time period.

A more specific incident-level cost disparity between technological and non-technological firms (based on their SIC (Standard Industrial Classification) codes) was brought out in the study by Pirounias et al. (2014). They noted that the subset of technological firms within their sample had incurred an average total cost of $356 million to $381 million per security breach, which is $201 million to $243 million more than the average cost for a nontechnological firm.

Finally, Hinz et al. (2015) studied the stock price and systemic risk impact associated with security events targeting six consumer electronics companies between 2011 and 2012. They concluded that the average risk assessment of investors remained unchanged after these events, which might be an indication that the impact of such breaches is already priced under the operational risks associated with these stocks by investors. They further observed significant negative returns not only for the affected firms but also for other companies in the same industry, which implies that there is information transfer across consumer electronics companies.

64.3 OTHER STUDIES IN THE AREA OF INFORMATION SECURITY BREACH ANALYSIS

Apart from the abovementioned studies, others highlight the impact of breach announcements on other stakeholders within the ecosystem and also those of IT security investments by firms.

Cavusoglu et al. (2004) performed some of the first studies on the impact of data breaches on other stakeholders like security developers and posited that security developers on average gained 1.36 percent more than their normal gains within just days of announcement of security breaches by affected firms. Since that study, others have found interesting results. Chai et al. (2011) found a strong positive correlation between the announcement of IT security investments and positive abnormal returns for firms based on evidence from 101 investment announcements between 1997 and 2006 from firms whose stocks were publicly traded in the US market. They also pointed out that the results of such announcements had been more pronounced since the passage of the Sarbanes-Oxley Act of 2002 (SOX).

More recent work by Chen et al. (2012) studied the impact of IT breaches on the stock price of IT consulting firms and found that they experienced positive cumulative abnormal returns within two days of announcement of events by affected firms. However, breach events which involved a higher number of records negatively impacted the stock price of IT consulting firms, which might be attributable to the adverse reputational impact of such breaches. They also found the impact on the stock prices of IT consulting firms to be more pronounced when they involved firms from technology and retail industries.

Finally, Modi et al. (2015) analyzed the impact of customer data breaches that emerge from service provider failures in the case of triadic structures which involve buyer firms, front-end service providers, and customers. Their results revealed that stock market losses due to failures at the service provider's end are greater than those due to failures at the buyer's end.

In a different strand of research, work by Mitra and Ransbotham (2015) empirically details security vulnerabilities through both full-disclosure and limited-disclosure mechanisms. They find that full disclosure of information security attacks not only serves to accelerate the diffusion of attacks but also has two additional effects: increasing the penetration of attacks within the target population, and increasing the risk level of the first attack after the vulnerability is reported.

64.4 CORPORATE GOVERNANCE AND INCENTIVES

Data breach studies implicate broader issues of compliance and corporate governance. Whereas there has been a vast literature across fields on compliance and corporate governance, work specific to data breaches and its intersection with these issues remains in early stages. On the one hand, increasingly, corporate boards are paying attention to cybersecurity risks with 89 percent of directors in public companies saying that board meetings regularly include a discussion of cybersecurity (NACD, 2017). On the other hand, the compliance protocols and procedures are not as fleshed out for data breaches as they are for traditional compliance issues such as anti-bribery and audit fraud. Further, data breach-related compliance spending by firms remains much smaller than other traditional areas of compliance. This part of the chapter explores why data breach-related compliance languishes relative to other types of compliance.

64.4.1 *Incentives*

A core concept in the economics and corporate governance literature in finance is that of agency costs (Jensen and Meckling, 1976). Agency costs refer to incentive misalignment. Within a firm, an agent may have different incentives than that of management, which the agent will pursue. Thus, even if at the level of board directors, there is a desire to be pro-compliant, this may not translate to agents of the firm.

If we assume that current efforts at compliance in areas like audit and anti-bribery work to better align the incentives of agents to the board, they do so via efforts like the use of incentive contracts and the creation of robust compliance programs to better monitor agents of the firm. Such programs overall have certain common structures: internal controls, tone of top management, risk assessment, lines of communication, controls regarding oversight and responsibility, and implementation of policies and procedures, monitoring, response and prevention, auditing, training, and enforcement and discipline.

Data breaches often work differently. Even though the majority of cyberattacks are aided by insiders, their assistance is typically unintentional (Mangelsdorf, 2017). The traditional principal–agent problems and mechanisms that might therefore work more effectively for detection of audit-related fraud may not work as well for data breaches. As such, the nature of the mechanisms and procedures used as part of compliance and corporate governance may need to be modified.

There are well-established methods for board- and firm-level compliance for more traditional areas of compliance. It may not be as easy to define metrics to create effective assessments of cybersecurity compliance. Part of this may be due to there being less training on cybersecurity than on other types of risk management. In other cases, cybersecurity has been defined too narrowly, with focus solely on keeping hackers out rather than on how to address compliance after a breach (Rothrock et al., 2018). Translating issues of data security is also difficult if the chief information security officer (CISO) cannot adequately explain issues to the board for purposes of risk management. Semi-structured interviews by Moore et al. (2016) suggest that CISOs believe that firms underinvest in cybersecurity and do not use quantitative metrics to guide investment decisions, even though they use such metrics to improve operational security. Their survey is larger than the work by Libicki et al. (2015), which finds little buy-in from management and the board on the subject of cybersecurity.

Theoretical and empirical models of investment in security are relevant to a discussion of investments. Acemoglu et al. (2016) model security investments in a network of interconnected agents, while Kovenock and Roberson (2018) model the attack and defense of multiple networks of targets where there are intra-network strategic complementarities among targets. On the empirical side, Gordon et al. (2018) identify that more spending on IT is positively related to publicly traded company internal controls reporting.

From a compliance standpoint, externalities may be mentioned as well (the idea that if one user does not patch a security vulnerability, the entire network, potentially the whole Internet, becomes less secure). Related to this argument are the empirical work by Sombatruang et al. (2019), which finds that humans are the weakest link in terms of Wi-Fi access, as they do not seem to care about Wi-Fi security, and the survey work by Beautement et al. (2016), which shows that security policies are often written without effectively taking into account the goals and capabilities of the employees that must follow them.

64.4.2 *Identifying Cyber Risk and Data Breaches as Part of the Compliance Function*

A number of papers analyze cybersecurity risk and the investment intended to minimize it. Benaroch (2017) and Chronopoulos et al. (2018) offer a real options model approach to cybersecurity investment. Respectively, their policy-oriented and empirical papers show that firms do not treat cybersecurity risks in the same way that they treat other sorts of risk such as anti-corruption or audit fraud. A survey of IT professionals found that most US financial services firms deploy new technologies prior to creating the compliance apparatus necessary to ensure data security (Thales, 2017).

Cybersecurity issues are a problem of information asymmetries (Anderson and Moore, 2006). Not all cybercrime is reported and the lack of disclosure makes it difficult to manage risk properly. Buyers of security-related services may have a lemons problem (Akerlof, 1970) because they may not want to pay a premium for quality that they cannot easily measure. This leads to lower-level products with regard to cybersecurity (Anderson, 2001).

64.4.3 *The Problem of Data Lemons in Mergers and Acquisitions*

Increasingly, firms need to be concerned about data breaches that they acquire as a result of mergers and acquisitions (M&A) activity. (Chatterjee and Sokol (2019) identify a "data lemons" problem in the M&A context, where the buyer does not know the quality of the seller's data compliance due to asymmetric information being available. Increasingly, a seller's quality may be linked to the strength of its cybersecurity program and its compliance with data privacy regulations. Empirical work that identifies the consequences of data lemons, such as Marriott's acquisition of Starwood Hotels and Resorts' data breach, remains a research gap.

64.4.4 *Penalties*

Unlike the fines for more traditional areas of compliance, those for data breaches in Europe or the United States have not been particularly high. One of the reasons for the low levels of fines (which may be leading to underinvestment and lack of board-level focus) has to do with the nature of data collection and storage. There are a number of strong reasons why consumers share consumer data, including passing on improvements to products and services. However, data breaches impact consumers rather than the collectors of data, which creates a negative externality from seller to buyer, so that sellers may over-collect data and may not properly represent the quality of data protection (Jin, 2019).

Government enforcement of data breach charges against a collector of data may be difficult because of the causal link that the government would need to make to an actual harmful outcome (Jin, 2019) in which there must be economic effects directly linked to the data breach. Solove and Citron (2018) explore how courts have struggled with conceptualizing a coherent doctrine regarding data breach harms and suggest that courts are too dismissive of data breach claims. Nevertheless, government enforcement, though more active, often lacks the financial and non-financial penalties of other areas of compliance failure such as anti-bribery, antitrust, and audit fraud. Yet, the recent Facebook settlement suggests that penalties can be significant, as can the types of behavioral remedy available (a combination of GDPR[1]-like restrictions and SOX structures). More time will offer clarity on whether Facebook-style penalties are the new norm.

Empirical work on private rights of action in data breach cases is also at an early stage. Empirical work by Romanosky et al. (2014) on the frequency of data breach lawsuits found that there were 231 such federal suits between 2000 and 2011 and that the probability of a suit being brought is 3.5 times greater when an individual suffers financial harm, and 6 times lower when the firm that has been breached offers free credit monitoring. There has been no analogous empirical work done on state law data breach claims, to our knowledge.

64.5 FUTURE RESEARCH

Our assessment of the literature suggests the following areas for extended research. Information security research so far has been largely focused on the short-term impact of breach events on the stock price of affected firms and also their impact within a specific industry. Upcoming studies should focus more on the long-term impact (more than thirty days) of these events and on the costs incurred by firms in repairing damage to hardware and software, on the litigation costs associated with these breaches, on customer and reputation losses due to these events, and on other financial metrics including stock price. Further, empirical work is needed to better understand the changing nature of corporate governance and compliance programs specific to data security in terms of reporting structure, resources

[1] General Data Protection Regulations, under EU law, implemented May 25, 2018.

spent, and the various processes and procedures that firms use to create compliance programs. It would also be useful to estimate whether data breaches translate into the loss of firms' market share, thereby creating adverse implications for producer and consumer welfare in the long run. One useful database is the Privacy Right Clearinghouse.

Future research should also focus on the impact of data breach events on government agencies, universities, and other nonprofit institutions. Along with ransomware attacks, which have been on the rise since 2017 and have crippled national healthcare systems, railroads, airports, and vaccine manufacturing facilities, data breaches nowadays seem to have direr consequences than they did during the first decade of the twenty-first century. Organized studies that focus on the impact of such ransomware attacks might influence policymakers in proactively investing in IT security.

Along with the ever-growing use of social media, a growing amount of private information is now at the risk of getting breached. The exposure of 540 million Facebook user records on public storage servers in April 2018 and the Quora (the Q&A website) data breach in November 2018, which exposed the details of over 100 million users, have led to growing scrutiny into the ways and mechanisms through which these companies save and secure the private information that is at their disposal. Research in the coming years should also focus on the societal impact of these types of data breach and their impact on the trust that individuals place in their online and offline behaviour, to demonstrate the underlying heterogeneities.

Finally, empirical work on data security, privacy, and security breaches associated with the Internet of Things will be increasingly important. Already, there is policy and theoretical work on connected cars (Mulligan and Bamberger, 2016; Cao et al., 2019), medical devices (Slotwiner et al., 2018), and robotics (Calo, 2015).

REFERENCES

Ablon, L., Heaton, P., Lavery D., and Romanosky, S. 2016. *Consumer Attitudes Toward Data Breach Notifications and Loss of Personal Information*. Santa Monica, CA: RAND Corporation.

Acemoglu, D., Malekian, A., and Ozdaglar, A. 2016. "Network Security and Contagion." *Journal of Economic Theory* 166: 536–85.

Acquisti, A., Friedman, A., and Telang, R. 2006. "Is There a Cost to Privacy Breaches? An Event Study." Proceedings of the 3rd International Conference on Intelligent Systems (ICIS).

Akerlof, G. 1970. "The Market for Lemons: Quality Uncertainty and the Market Mechanism." *Quarterly Journal of Economics* 84: 488–500.

Anderson, R. 2001. "Why Information Security Is Hard – An Economic Perspective." Proceedings of the 17th Annual Computer Security.

Anderson, R. J., and Moore, T. 2006. "The Economics of Information Security." *Science* 314: 610–13.

Arcuri, M. C., Brogi, M., and Gandolfi, G. 2014. "The Effect of Information Security Breaches on Stock Returns: Is the Cyber Crime a Threat to Firms?" European Financial Management Association Meeting, Rome.

Beautement, A., Becker, I., Parkin, S., Krol, K., and Sasse, M. A. (2016). "Productive Security: A Scalable Methodology for Analysing Employee Security Behaviours." Proceedings of the Symposium on Usable Privacy and Security (SOUPS) (253–70).

Benaroch, M. 2017. "Real Options Models for Proactive Uncertainty: Reducing Mitigations and Applications in Cybersecurity Investment Decisionmaking." *Information Systems Research*, forthcoming. 10.1287/isre.2017.0714.

Buckman, J., Hashim, M. J., Woutersen, T., and Bockstedt, J. (2019). "Fool Me Twice? Data Breach Reductions Through Stricter Sanctions." Working paper, https://ssrn.com/abstract=3258599.

Campbell, K., Gordon, L. A., Loeb, M. P., and Zhou, L. 2003. "The Economic Cost of Publicly Announced Information Security Breaches: Empirical Evidence from the Stock Market." *Journal of Computer Security* 11(3): 431–48.

Cannon, D. M., and Kessler, L. 2007. "Danger–Corporate Data Breach!" *Journal of Corporate Accounting & Finance* 18(5): 41–9.

Calo, R. 2015. "Robotics and the Lessons of Cyberlaw." *California Law Review* 103(3): 513–63.

Cao, Y., Xiao, C., Cyr, B., Zhou, Y., Park, W., Rampazzi, S., Chen, Q. A., Fu, K., and Mao, Z. M. 2019. "Adversarial Sensor Attack on LiDAR-based Perception in Autonomous Driving." Proceedings of the 26th ACM Conference on Computer and Communications Security (ACM CCS), November.

Cavusoglu, H., Mishra, B., and Raghunathan, S. 2004. "The Effect of Internet Security Breach Announcements on Market Value: Capital Market Reactions for Breached Firms and Internet Security Developers." *International Journal of Electronic Commerce* 9(1): 70–104.

Chai, S., Kim, M., and Rao, H. R. 2011. "Firms' Information Security Investment Decisions: Stock Market Evidence of Investors' Behavior." *Decision Support Systems* 50(4): 651–61.

Chatterjee, C., and Sokol, D. D. 2019. "Don't Acquire a Company Until You Evaluate Its Data Security." Harvard Business Review. https://hbr.org/2019/04/dont-acquire-a-company-until-you-evaluate-its-data-security.

Chen, J. V., Li, H. C., Yen, D. C., Bata, K. V. 2012. "Did IT Consulting Firms Gain When Their Clients Were Breached?" *Computers in Human Behavior* 28(2): 456–64.

Chronopoulos, M., Panaousis, E., and Grossklags, J. 2018. "An Options Approach to Cybersecurity Investment." *IEEE Access* 6: 12175–86.

Collins, J. D., Sainato, V. A., and Khey, D. N. 2011. "Organizational Data Breaches 2005–2010: Applying SCP to the Healthcare and Education Sectors." *International Journal of Cyber Criminology* 5(1): 794–810.

Cummins, J. D., Lewis, C. M., and Wei, R.. 2006. "The Market Value Impact of Operational Loss Events for US Banks and Insurers." *Journal of Banking & Finance* 30(10): 2605–34.

Garg, A., Curtis, J., and Halper, H. 2003. "Quantifying the Financial Impact of IT Security Breaches." *Information Management and Computer Security* 11(2): 74–83.

Gartner. 2019. "Gartner Says IT Security Spending to Hit $124B in 2019." www.darkreading.com/2019-security-spending-outlook/d/did/1333826?image_number=2.

Goel, S., and Shawky, H. A. 2009. "Estimating the Market Impact of Security Breach Announcements on Firm Values." *Information & Management* 46(7): 404–10.

Gordon, L. A., Loeb, M. P., and Zhou, L. 2011. "The Impact of Information Security Breaches: Has There Been a Downward Shift in Costs?" *Journal of Computer Security* 19(1): 33–56.

Gordon, L. A., Loeb, M. P., Lucyshyn, W., and Zhou, L. 2018. "Empirical Evidence on the Determinants of Cybersecurity Investments in Private Sector Firms." *Journal of Information Security* 9(2): 133–53.

Hilary, G., Segal, B., and Zhang, May H. 2016. "Cyber-Risk Disclosure: Who Cares?" Georgetown McDonough School of Business Research Paper No. 2852519.

Hinz, O., Nofer, M., Schiereck, D., and Trillig, J. 2015. "The Influence of Data Theft on the Share Prices and Systematic Risk of Consumer Electronics Companies." *Information & Management* 52 (3): 337–47.

Hovav, A., and D'Arcy, J. 2003. "The Impact of Denial-of-Service Attack Announcements on the Market Value of Firms." *Risk Management and Insurance Review* 6(2): 97–121.

Jacobs, J., Romanosky, S., Edwards, B., Roytman, M., and Adjerid, I. 2019. "Exploit Prediction Scoring System (EPSS)." https://i.blackhat.com/USA-19/Thursday/us-19-Roytman-Predictive-Vulnerability-Scoring-System-wp.pdf.

Jensen, M. C., and Meckling, W. H. (1976). "Theory of the Firm: Managerial Behaviour, Agency Costs and Ownership Structure." *Journal of Financial Economics* 3(4): 305–60.

Jin, G. Z. 2019. "Artificial Intelligence and Consumer Privacy." in *The Economics of Artificial Intelligence: An Agenda*, edited by Ajay Agrawal, Avi Goldfarb, and Joshua Gans. Chicago: University of Chicago Press.

Kannan, K., Rees, J., and Sridhar, S. 2007. "Market Reactions to Information Security Breach Announcements: An Empirical Analysis." *International Journal of Electronic Commerce* 12(1): 69–91.

Ko, M., and Dorantes, C. 2006. “The Impact of Information Security Breaches on Financial Performance of the Breached Firms: An Empirical Investigation.” *Journal of Information Technology Management* 17(2): 13–22.

Ko, M., Osei-Bryson, K. M., and Dorantes, C. 2009. “Investigating the Impact of Publicly Announced Information Security Breaches on Three Performance Indicators of the Breached Firms.” *Information Resources Management Journal (IRMJ)* 22(2): 1–21.

Kovenock, D., and Roberson, B. 2018. “The Optimal Defense of Networks of Targets.” *Economic Inquiry* 56(4): 2195–2211.

Libicki, M. C., Ablon, L., and Webb, T. 2015. “The Defender’s Dilemma: Charting a Course Toward Cybersecurity.” Technical Report Research Report 1024, RAND Corporation.

Mangelsdorf, M. E. 2017. What Executives Get Wrong About Cybersecurity. *MIT Sloan Management Review* 58(2): 22.

Mitra, S., and Ransbotham, S. 2015. “Information Disclosure and the Diffusion of Information Security Attacks.” *Information Systems Research* 26(3): 565–84.

Modi, S. B., Wiles, M. A., and Mishra, S. 2015. “Shareholder Value Implications of Service Failures in Triads: The Case of Customer Information Security Breaches.” *Journal of Operations Management* 35: 21–39.

Moore, T., Moore, D., and Chang, F. 2016. “Identifying How Firms Manage Cybersecurity Investment.” In 15th Workshop on the Economics of Information Security (WEIS).

Mulligan, D. K., and Bamberger, K. A. 2016. “Public Values, Private Infrastructure and the Internet of Things: The Case of Automobiles.” *Journal of Law & Economic Regulation* 9(1): 7–44.

NACD (2017). Director’s Handbook on Cyber-Risk Oversight. www.nacdonline.org/insights/publications.cfm?ItemNumber=10687.

Pirounias, S., Mermigas, D., and Patsakis, C. 2014. “The Relation Between Information Security Events and Firm Market Value, Empirical Evidence on Recent Disclosures: An Extension of the GLZ Study.” *Journal of Information Security and Applications* 19(4): 257–71.

Romanosky, Sasha. 2016. “Examining the Costs and Causes of Cyber Incidents.” *Journal of Cybersecurity* 2(2): 121–35.

Romanosky, S., Telang, R., and Acquisti, A. 2011. “Do Data Breach Disclosure Laws Reduce Identity Theft?” *Journal of Policy Analysis and Management* 30(2): 256–86.

Romanosky, S., Hoffman, D., and Acquisti, A. 2014. “Empirical Analysis of Data Breach Litigation.” *Journal of Empirical Legal Studies* 11(1): 74–104.

Rothrock, R. A., Kaplan, J., and Van der Oord, F., 2018. “The Board’s Role in Managing Cybersecurity Risks.” *MIT Sloan Management Review* 59(2) (Winter): 12–15.

Slotwiner, D. J., Deering, F., Fu, K., Russo, A. M., Walsh, M. N., and Van Hare, G. F. 2018. “Cybersecurity Vulnerabilities of Cardiac Implantable Electronic Devices.” *Heart Rhythm* 15(7) (May): e61–e67.

Solomon, Michael G., and Chapple, M. 2005. *Information Security Illuminated*. Burlington, MA: Jones & Bartlett Learning.

Solove, Daniel J., and Citron, Danielle K. 2018. “Risk and Anxiety: A Theory of Data Breach Harms.” *Texas Law Review* 96: 737–86.

Sombatruang, N., Onwuzurike, L., Sasse, M. A., and Baddeley, M. 2019. “Factors Influencing Users to Use Unsecured Wi-Fi Networks: Evidence in the Wild.” WiSec 2019 – Proceedings of the 2019 Conference on Security and Privacy in Wireless and Mobile Networks, 203–14. http://dx.doi.org/10.1145/3317549.3323412.

Spanos, G., and Angelis, L. 2016. “The Impact of Information Security Events to the Stock Market: A Systematic Literature Review.” *Computers & Security* 58: 216–29.

Telang, R., and Wattal, S. 2007. “An Empirical Analysis of the Impact of Software Vulnerability Announcements on Firm Stock Price.” *IEEE Transactions on Software Engineering* 33(8): 544–57.

Thales. 2017. “2017 Thales Data Threat Report: Trends in Encryption and Data Security (Financial Services Edition).” https://dtr-fin.thalesesecurity.com/.

Yayla, A. A., and Hu, Q. 2011. “The Impact of Information Security Events on the Stock Value of Firms: The Effect of Contingency Factors.” *Journal of Information Technology* 26(1): 60–77.

65

Doping in Sports: A Compliance Conundrum

Jeffrey Cisyk and Pascal Courty

Abstract: This chapter reviews the history of doping regulations, contemporary anti-doping policies and the effectiveness thereof, as well as the public's perception of the current state of doping in sports. We discuss how detection, testing and punishment influence compliance and, ultimately, the prevalence of doping. We offer a general framework to understand why anti-doping objectives are difficult to achieve. Finally, we assess some of the proposed solutions to improve current anti-doping policies.

65.1 INTRODUCTION

What could be more disturbing than the revelation that one's beloved sports hero has used performance-enhancing drugs (PED) to cheat their way to victory? The illicit use of PEDs, the practice colloquially known as doping, compromises the credibility of fair competition and our faith in the spirit of sports. Our animosity towards doping co-exists with the silent truth that most of us know that doping is rampant in many sports. Although doping is the object of intense controversies within sporting bodies, the media and academia, it seems that the end of doping in sports is not within sight.

This chapter reviews the literature on doping and explains why compliance with doping regulations is controversial. Scholars from medicine, sports management, ethics, law and economics have different – and sometimes opposing – views on how to approach doping and how to improve anti-doping policies. While the consensus is still in favour of a zero-tolerance approach, this chapter will discuss why an outright elimination of doping is likely impossible.

Anti-doping raises a myriad of issues that cannot be adequately covered in a short chapter. While this chapter reviews the literature, we had to be selective, and we refer the reader to specialized sources for topics that cannot be given fair treatment. The main contribution of this chapter is to propose a simple framework to explain why compliance with doping regulations raises unique issues. At the heart of the problem is the very high aspiration of the anti-doping agenda (zero-tolerance) paired with great limitations in detection technologies (testing). We then summarize our analysis with a statement of the sports compliance conundrum.

We dedicate the end of this chapter to reviewing current proposals to improve doping regulations. While some of these proposals (e.g., collective responsibility, deferred compensation) have great potential, we conclude that what is most needed now are reliable, comparable measures of prevalence and systematic evaluations of anti-doping interventions.

65.2 CURRENT STATE OF ANTI-DOPING REGULATIONS

Although doping is not new to sports, formal anti-doping regulations are. The past thirty years have seen wide adoption of policies across countries, sport federations and sporting events that have evolved towards a detection-based deterrence approach established upon a list of banned substances. These deterrence regulations, known at secondary measures, complement primary interventions that attempt to educate athletes and the sports community about the consequences of doping and to establish drug-free norms. The current system is mostly repressive and punitive, where punishment takes, in many instances, the form of a participation ban.

However, there is still much variation across counties, federations and sporting events in the definition of doping and in the implementation of doping countermeasures. In 1999, the World Anti-Doping Agency (WADA) was created in part to standardize these rules and regulations for international sport. WADA's vision is "a world where all athletes can compete in a doping-free sporting environment," and the main justifications for anti-doping are to: (1a) protect the athlete to participate in doping-free sport and thus promote (1b) health and (1c) fairness (level playing field); (2) coordinate international anti-doping programs with regard to (2a) detection, deterrence, and punishment, and (2b) prevention (Møller 2016).

Despite its best intentions, there is considerable controversy and disagreement about fundamental questions regarding these aforementioned goals of WADA's code. While few would challenge the objectives stated in (1a–1c), many debate whether (2a) is the appropriate approach to achieve these objectives and whether these objectives are attainable at all. The literature has questioned the type of institutions needed to enforce anti-doping measures, what compliance means, whether to emphasize a preventative or a punitive approach, and so on. Another debate questions the current zero-tolerance and repressive approach to doping (Kayser, Mauron and Miah 2007; Mazanov and Connor 2010) due to high consumer demand for the opportunity to witness the exceptional events that PEDs are purported to produce.

65.3 THE BUILDING BLOCKS OF ANTI-DOPING REGULATIONS

There are fundamental challenges in answering basic empirical questions about the prevalence of drug use in most sports, let alone questions about compliance or about the effectiveness of anti-doping regulations. We review what we know about doping in sports starting from what we know best (detection and deterrence) and moving to issues for which we have less precise knowledge (prevalence and compliance).

65.3.1 *Detection*

The current standard in detecting PED use involves the testing of urine and/or blood samples against a list of banned substances. To be prohibited and featured on WADA's list of banned substances, known as a 'negative list', a substance must satisfy two of three requirements: (1) enhance performance; (2) have potential health risk; (3) violate the spirit of the sport (WADA 2019). A key criticism of the current enforcement approach is that it is hard to determine what should be on a negative list. Caffeine, for example, has been on some negative lists while other performance-enhancement techniques such as altitude training or hypobaric chambers are difficult to evaluate on the grounds of criteria (2) because they do not have well-understood

TABLE 65.1 *PED testing in the four major North American sports leagues*

	Baseball	Hockey	Football	Basketball
	MLB	NHL	NFL	NBA
Number of tests league-wide, per season	7,400	2,199	7,036	2,135
Size of testing pool approximate	750	713	1,696	450
Number of tests per athlete per season	≥3	≥3	≥1	≤6

Sources: MLB and MLBPA Joint Drug Prevention and Treatment Program, expiring 1 December 2021; NHLPA and NHL Collective Bargaining Agreement, 16 September 2012–15 September 2022; NFL Policy on Performance-Enhancing Substances, 2018; NBA and NBPA Collective Bargaining Agreement, 19 January 2017.

long-term effects (Vlad et al. 2018). A recent study supported by WADA even recommends that spinach be added to the negative list (Isenmann et al. 2019).

Anti-doping testing is not cheap: Maenning (2014) reports that WADA ran 270,000 tests in 2012. The laboratory cost of these tests was $228 million and adding the costs of administering each test brings the overall cost to about $500 million. Mountjoy et al. (2017) calculate that in 2015, 28 summer Olympic International Federations ran 33,000 tests at a cost of $27.7 million. These costs do not include costs associated with challenges to test outcomes and litigation around enforcement. Table 65.1 reports testing policies in the four major North American leagues. A large number of athletes are tested a couple of times each year.

Current regulations have given birth to a doping industry that tries to stay one step ahead of an anti-doping industry. New drugs and delivery methods are constantly arising. In an attempt to keep up, agencies update negative lists and design new testing protocols (Mazanov and Connor 2010). Therefore, a 'window of opportunity' emerges wherein a new drug may be used until it has been proven performance enhancing and/or risky and a testing protocol has been adopted. Firms have an incentive to innovate with ways to avoid existing tests and to develop 'designer drugs' that are not yet on negative lists. While many have questioned the accreditation of testing labs and the secrecy of testing protocols, there is a trade-off between test transparency and revealing weaknesses that could then pave the way for masking strategies and selective use of PEDs. A more fundamental problem is that athletes are not punished for the substances that are not on negative lists. Due to the cat-and-mouse nature of anti-doping, there is much debate over whether a negative list can ever be exhaustive (Müller 2010).

Adverse test rates are surprisingly low. In 2012, WADA reported a rate of adverse analytical finding of 1.76 per cent for a worldwide total of 267,000 samples analysed. Low adverse test rates hold for most sports and sporting events. Section 65.3.3 on prevalence will contrast the testing evidence with the widespread belief that a significant fraction of athletes use PEDs.

An important advancement in detecting technology is the biological passport wherein athletes are tested against their own baseline levels of various drug-markers. The athlete's passport records longitudinal results of, for example, blood or urine samples. Having a complete history of an athlete's test profile greatly increases the power of tests by using temporal deviation from the athlete's own normality: instead of using direct detection from a population norm, the passport allows intra-individual temporal variations in variables that are sensitive to drug use. Although building statistical models using a wide range of variables (longitudinal test results, behavioural variables, performance outcomes, etc.) is relatively new, it is a promising agenda for broader and more accurate detection technologies.

65.3.2 *Deterrence*

Deterrence incentives can take many forms. To start, athletes take into account health risk, and the perception and understanding of these risks increase with exposure to information and education campaigns (Mazanov, Huybers and Connor 2011). In addition, sports have adopted or have considered adopting a number of punishment mechanisms based on test outcomes:

1. competition ban
2. stripping medals and honours, and repayment of prize money
3. disclosure of test outcomes (negative impact on sponsorship)
4. fines and financial penalties.

Deterrence incentives vary greatly across sports and levels of competition. To illustrate, Table 65.2 reports the punishment in several of the major sports leagues. The first offence can have significant impact on most athletes' incomes. The third offence completely eliminates the value of the athlete's human capital in five out of seven leagues.

65.3.3 *Prevalence*

Low adverse test rates do not necessarily mean that most athletes comply with anti-doping rules. Because one would expect that athletes who dope do so strategically to minimize the chance of persecution, the incidence of positive tests should be lower than prevalence.

TABLE 65.2 *Competition bans for positive PED test as a percentage of a sport's season*

Sport	League	1st Offence	2nd Offence	3rd Offence
Football	CFL	11%	50%	100%
	NFL	25%	63%	200%
Hockey	NHL	24%	73%	Lifetime
Basketball	NBA	30%	67%	Lifetime
Baseball	MLB	49%	100%	Lifetime
College sports	NCAA	100%	Lifetime	
Soccer	FIFA	400%	800%	Lifetime

Sources: CFL Drug Policy at a Glance – www.cfl.ca/2015/05/05/cfl-drug-policy-glance/; NFL Policy on Performance-Enhancing Substances, 2018; NHLPA and NHL Collective Bargaining Agreement, 16 September 2012–15 September 2022; NBA and NBPA Collective Bargaining Agreement, 19 January 2017; MLB and MLBPA Joint Drug Prevention and Treatment Program, expires 1 December 2021; NCAA Frequently Asked Questions about Drug Testing – www.ncaa.org/sport-science-institute/topics/frequently-asked-questions-about-drug-testing; FIFA Anti-Doping Regulations, 2018 Edition.

In fact, there is little doubt that the prevalence of doping is much higher than positive test results would indicate. Even WADA acknowledges that "testing has not proven to be particularly effective in detecting doping." However, estimating the prevalence of an illegal practice is challenging. The simplest approach uses anonymous questionnaires of self-reported drug use. This relies, however, on a profound assumption that respondents are comfortable revealing compromising information. Some recent studies use the randomized response technique, which is a slightly more complicated survey approach that guarantees respondents' confidentiality (Pitsch and Emrich 2011; de Hon, Kuipers and van Bottenburg 2015; Ulrich et al. 2018). Other methods include inference from changes in athletic performance, models of biological parameters, response to remission incentives, and testimonies by retired athletes who fall outside statutes of limitations.

Pitsch and Emrich (2011), de Hon, Kuipers and van Bottenburg (2015) and Pielke (2018) review these various methods. Although there is much variation in estimates of doping prevalence, most studies agree that prevalence is high and most likely in the two-digit range. For example, de Hon, Kuipers and van Bottenburg (2015) conclude that 'the prevalence of doping in elite sports is likely to be between 14 and 39%'. Maennig (2014) offers a minimum bound, stating that 'at least 10% of all elite athletes are doping'.

65.3.4 *Test Validity: Sensitivity and Specificity*

The validity of a test is measured by its sensitivity and specificity. Sensitivity is the probability of a positive test conditional on actually doping: the probability of a 'true positive'. Sensitivity is therefore the probability of catching a non-complier. Conversely, specificity is a measure of true negative: the probability of a negative test conditional on not doping. We denote sensitivity by s and specificity by f. Together, sensitivity and specificity make up the adverse test rate, or the probability of a positive test.[1]

Although sensitivity and specificity are essential to understanding the deterrence effect of testing, WADA and test laboratories do not disclose this information (Mazanov and Connor 2010). Sensitivity has been estimated for specific drugs and testing protocols. Hermann and Henneberg (2014) review the literature and argue that 'the highest rates of success of doping detection have been reported as being 60% and 80% success rate', with rates being as low as 10 per cent for select drugs and testing protocols.

When sensitivity or specificity is not perfect ($s < 1$ and/or $f < 1$), making inference about doping from laboratory tests requires making a Bayesian inference, updating one's prior probability of prevalence. This inference may be based on a single or multiple test result(s). Berry (2008) argues that, 'due to inherent flaws in the testing practices of doping laboratories', it is not possible to conclude that an athlete is guilty of doping when they test positive. Pitsch (2009) comes to the similar conclusion that imperfect testing methods based on 'Bayesian logic lead to important ethical questioning of anti-doping policies'.

65.3.5 *Compliance*

The same way that low adverse test rates do not mean that most athletes comply with anti-doping rules, a high prevalence rate does not necessarily mean that compliance is low. For

[1] Let $d = 1$ if an athlete dopes and $d = 0$ otherwise, and let $t = 1$ if the athlete tests positive and $t = 0$ otherwise. We have: $s = \Pr(t = 1|d = 1)$, $f = \Pr(t = 0|d = 0)$, and $Pr(t = 1) = sPr(d = 1) + (1 - f)Pr(d = 0)$.

example, it may be that 70 per cent of athletes comply with anti-doping rules when prevalence is 30 per cent. Compliance should be measured as the reduction in doping associated with a specific regulation or enforcement mechanism. If all athletes dope in the absence of testing, the compliance rate is equal to one minus the rate of prevalence under anti-doping, as computed in the example in Section 65.3.4.

One may argue that compliance is high on the grounds that prevalence, without any doping regulations, would be much higher than current levels. In fact, historical evidence that predates the rigorous modern anti-doping detection (i.e., pre-1990s) suggests a high demand for doping. The Goldman dilemma points to the same conclusion wherein about half of surveyed elite athletes reported that they would take a drug that guarantees success even if it would cause death within five years (Goldman, Bush and Klatz 1984). Although Connor, Woolf and Mazanov (2013) have questioned the validity of the dilemma, other studies suggest that the demand for safe and undetectable doping is high (Overbye, Knudsen and Pfister 2013) and survey questionnaire responses point to the same conclusion.

Another approach to understanding compliance is to compute the probability that an athlete – who strategically dopes to avoid detection – is actually caught given existing testing rules. This probability accounts for a test's sensitivity, the window of detection (the time span when a drug can be detected) and the frequency of tests. Hermann and Henneberg (2014) conclude that this probability is low for most sporting events and for most drugs used. This is because, too often, test sensitivity is low, the window of detection is short, and tests are infrequent. They conclude that it is easy to avoid testing positive for 'narrow-window drugs'. This explains the low rates of adverse findings and points towards the fundamental problem that athletes can avoid detection.

65.4 SPORT'S COMPLIANCE CONUNDRUM

This section explains why compliance with anti-doping regulations in sports raises issues that are absent in standard applications of deterrence theory. The core of the discussion is technical and the reader not interested in the mechanics of compliance may move directly to the main results stated in our Proposition below.

Denote policy $p \ni\in \{a, \emptyset\}$, where $p = a$ if there is an anti-doping policy and $p = \emptyset$ otherwise. Let $d_i^p = 1$ if athlete $i \ni\in I$ dopes under policy p and $d_i^p = 0$ otherwise. There are three types of athlete:

1. unconditional non-compliers : $d_i^{\emptyset} = d_i^a = 1$
2. unconditional compliers : $d_i^{\emptyset} = d_i^a = 0$
3. conditional compliers: $d_i^{\emptyset} = 1$ and $d_i^a = 0$.

Doping prevalence under proposed anti-doping regulations is composed of the unconditional non-compliers, $Pr(d_i^a)$. The deterrence effect of anti-doping regulations is measured by the fraction of conditional compliers, $Pr(d_i^{\emptyset}) - \ Pr(d_i^a)$. If all athletes dope in the absence of anti-doping regulations ($Pr(d_i^{\emptyset}) = 1$), we obtain that the deterrence effect of anti-doping regulations is equal to one minus the prevalence rate under anti-doping, $1 - \ Pr(d_i^a)$.

If the benefit of doping is b and the cost of non-compliance is c, an athlete complies if $b \leq \ cs$ where s is the test's specificity as defined in Section 65.3.4. Deterrence theory says that athletes comply with doping regulations so long as the punishment when being caught is large enough, $c \ \ b/s$. To illustrate, take the evidence discussed in Table 65.2 and set the value of $s = 0.5$ and c to six months' salary loss. We obtain that athletes who can gain at least one year of additional salary from doping do not comply. This is plausible as compensation schemes in elite sports are characterized by high pay-offs from small, incremental performance improvements (Rosen 1981).

The punishment must increase as sensitivity decreases or as the benefit from doping increases. In the case of individual sport with a winner-takes-all prize scheme, for example, the benefit from doping is equal to the incremental probability of winning multiplied by the prize. Thus, until otherwise corrected, doping should prevail for effective drugs and within sports with high financial rewards. Circumstantial evidence supports this prediction. For example, Maennig (2014) argues that the commercialization of sports and the increase in benefit b should decrease compliance, consistent with the observation that doping is common in media sports with large financial rewards and in sports where doping has a significant impact on winning (e.g., weightlifting).

We now turn to our main result. Recall WADA's key objectives from Section 65.2:

Definition: Anti-doping aims for: (1) drug-free sport, defined as $Pr(d_i^a) = 0$; and (2) fair competition ('level playing field'), defined as drug-free sport without false negative test results, that is, $Pr(d_i^a) = 0$ and $f = 1$.

The drug-free sport condition embodies the zero-tolerance approach to doping. The level playing field condition adds the requirement that no athlete can be wrongly accused of doping. We can state the sport's compliance conundrum as follows:

Proposition: Anti-doping interventions based on testing and punishment fail to achieve WADA's key objectives for two reasons: (1) unlike standard deterrence applications, a drug-free sport objective does not value incremental increases in compliance, only absolute compliance (which is difficult to achieve with low test sensitivity and/or high benefits to doping); and (2) a level playing field cannot hold with imperfect specificity (f<1).

Three outcomes that we label the 'paradox of doping' can happen simultaneously: high deterrence ($Pr(d_i^{\varnothing} - d_i^a)$ is high); high prevalence ($Pr(d_i^a)$ is high); and low adverse test rate ($Pr(t = 1)$ is low). According to the literature, prevalence is around 30 per cent, an upper bound for the deterrence effect of anti-doping is 70 per cent, and the adverse test rate is 2 per cent. A low adverse test rate occurs because doping tests have low sensitivity. To achieve high deterrence, low sensitivity is balanced with powerful punishments (high costs to doping; see Table 65.2) that debase the value of a non-complier's human capital. The challenge is that the benefits to doping are large in commercialized sports. When combined with a low test sensitivity, full compliance is not achievable under realistic punishment schemes.

Although these three outcomes are expected in any use of deterrence elsewhere, they generate a paradox in sports because the objective of anti-doping is absolute, rather than incremental, compliance in order to eliminate the highly unpopular suspicion that a competition was won by a non-complier. To contrast compliance in doping with other domains, take crime deterrence as an illustration. An increase in the punishment may reduce crime's prevalence, and any incremental reduction in crime is valuable to society. Although important, incremental reduction in doping, however, is not the main concern in sports. The issue at stake is that doping gives some athletes an unfair advantage. While crimes can be seen as independent events that can be treated separately, the fact that athletes compete against one another makes doping a collective problem. The goal is not to reduce doping down to a given pre-set target level of non-compliance but to eliminate it outright so that no athlete can get an unfair advantage. Therefore, any non-zero level of prevalence compromises the spirit of competition. The high prevalence rate speculated to exist in many sports suggests that current penalties for doping are not sufficiently high. Worse, penalties would arguably have to be set at unrealistically high levels to achieve full compliance.

The other concern originates when imperfect specificity compromises the second objective of anti-doping regulations. When specificity is imperfect, athletes may be wrongly punished. This challenges a deterrence approach because it compromises fairness (Berry 2008; Delanghe et al. 2014). An anti-doping programme that deters doping and achieves low prevalence may fail the level playing field objective if some athletes who do not dope are wrongly punished due to imperfect testing.

As emphasized in the model, imperfect specificity goes against 'fairness and equality' because it introduces uncertainty to the competition. Considerations should be given to a substance's ability to enhance performance when specificity is low. The negative list should therefore trade-off specificity and performance enhancement.

65.5 CURRENT PROPOSALS

Many proposals have been made to improve current anti-doping programmes: Section 65.3.1 has already discussed progress in detection technologies with the recent introduction of the biological passport. We focus here on proposals that, to the best of our knowledge, have not yet been implemented.

65.5.1 *Collective Responsibility*

Teams, leagues and federations do not bear many of the costs of doping. Cisyk and Courty (2017) find small declines in attendance at Major League Baseball games following the announcement of a PED suspension and there is evidence of similar negative responses for television audiences or endorsements in other sports (Cisyk 2020; van Reeth 2013). Although such demand responses demonstrate that the public cares about PED use, the financial consequences are limited. Taking into account the positive impact of doping on performance and overall demand, it is not implausible that event organizers sometimes benefit from poorly detected non-compliance, or, stated differently, lose from taking an aggressive stance on doping (Mazanov and Connor 2010).[2] For example, random testing in the Ultimate Fighting Championship may negatively affect revenue when last-minute competition bans force cancellations to matches.

Maennig (2014) proposes holding all parties involved in a competition collectively responsible for doping outcomes. For example, one could ban the broadcast of high-doping-prevalence sports the same way that countries with state-sponsored doping programmes have been banned from participating in the Olympic Games. Broadcast bans would add financial consequences through loss of sponsorship and advertisement. One would expect sports to develop norms that would internally discipline or exclude non-compliers. Such norms are not unusual; for example, golfers have the obligation to report rule violations by competitors. Even informal sports, such as pick-up basketball, require each player to police others' actions under the 'call your own fouls' rule.[3]

[2] An exception is the cancellation of the 2009 Tour of Germany (cycling) which was attributed to the pull-out of public broadcasters after doping revelations.

[3] 'Call your own fouls' requires players to explicitly announce when their opponent has committed an infraction.

Along the same lines, Maennig (2014) suggests that funding for inter-sport anti-doping agencies should be proportional to the sport's prevalence rather than to its share of the testing pool. This would shift the burden on doping-prone sports to take a more active role against doping.

65.5.2 *Leniency and Self-Reporting*

An effective way to understand prevalence is to offer leniency for self-reporting and whistle-blowing. Such exemptions from punishment incentivize athletes to reveal shortcomings in existing testing protocols. The National Basketball Association (NBA), for example, allows for a one-time voluntary self-admission of any prohibited substance without penalty or public announcement. Following the NBA model, sports' governing bodies may handle self-reporting discreetly to reduce the risk of public backlash and boycott.

Another form of exemption from doping punishments includes statutes of limitation. Athletes tend to withhold information about doping until the end of their career. For example, Figure 65.1 shows that baseball players are more likely to admit to doping at or near the end of their career. However, remission incentives and statutes of limitation for self-reporting are double-edged because one would like to hold athletes accountable in order to preserve the credibility of deterrence.

65.5.3 *Life-Cycle Considerations*

When repression takes the form of a lifetime competition ban, athletes at the end of their career face a lower cost to exposure because their human capital fully depreciates at retirement. Moreover, athletes near the end of their career may benefit more from doping because they have to keep pace with younger athletes. For these reasons, the deterrence approach is less effective for athletes who are approaching retirement.

A solution to this problem would be to require athletes to contribute a portion of their annual earnings to a fund that would be used as a bond in the event of doping violations. In such a deferred compensation scheme, an athlete's earnings would be held in escrow until the culmination of a doping-free career in order to solve the end-of-career problem (Maennig 2014). As an aside, note that deferred compensation also solves the problem of fine enforcement. Many sports punish doping violations with fines or by requiring the athletes to repay prize awards. Collecting these fines, however, has proven difficult when, for example, an athlete is near bankruptcy. Enforcement would be easier if each athlete had a personal escrow fund.

65.5.4 *Governance*

While anti-doping agencies were originally created to protect athletes, some have since argued that these agencies perpetuate anti-doping rhetoric in hopes to gain legitimacy, public support and, ultimately, additional funding (Mazanov and Conner 2010). For example, with its strict laboratory accreditation process, WADA has created a monopoly over drug testing and has been accused of focusing on the quantity over quality of tests while keeping a veil of opacity over the science of testing (Maennig 2014).

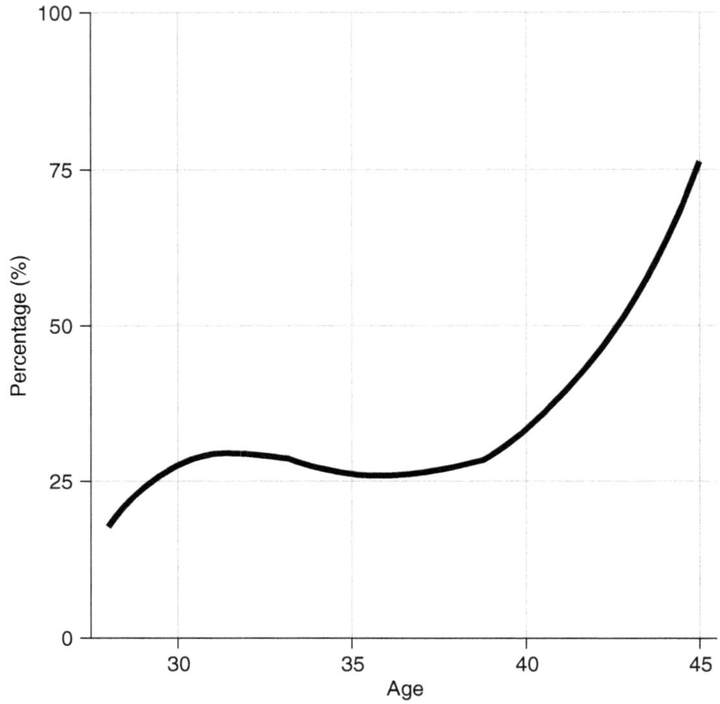

FIGURE 65.1 Age of MLB players who admitted to doping
Note: The figure displays the probability that one of the eighty-nine Major League Baseball (MLB) players admitted to doping after being accused by an independent investigation led by the US Congress in 2007. Of the implicated players, twenty-eight (31 per cent) admitted to PED use, noticeably those in the latter stages of their career or already retired.
Source: Report to the Commissioner of Baseball of an Independent Investigation into the Illegal Use of Steroids and Other Performance Enhancing Substances by Players in Major League Baseball, or 'Mitchell Report' (Mitchell 2007).

The WADA centralized model for anti-doping was established upon the urge to standardize doping regulations that were essential to allow athletes from different countries and sports to compete on a fair playing field. At the same time, a centralized approach to doping risks stifling innovation and experimentation to new anti-doping ideas. A mixed approach towards harmonization encourages federations, leagues and countries to adopt innovative and un-tested anti-doping policies. This is happening to some extent with the for-profit leagues that largely self-regulate (e.g., the leagues presented in Tables 65.1 and 65.2), although even in these instances there are pressures from politicians and sponsors to follow international anti-doping norms.

65.5.5 *Policy Evaluation*

We are not aware of standardized *ex post* evaluations that assess currently used anti-doping policies. Such policy evaluations are standard in other domains (e.g., education, welfare intervention, etc.) and established on well-accepted scientific methods (Athey and Imbens 2017). Estimation of the causal impact of an anti-doping intervention on compliance may now be possible given the current progress towards constructing reliable longitudinal measures of prevalence.

Surprisingly, much of the anti-doping resources is dedicated towards managing and implementing detection; anti-doping agencies have so far not bothered estimating prevalence using the methods described in Section 65.3.3, or, for that matter, the impact of their own interventions using modern methods of policy evaluation. Specifically, debates around the effectiveness of the current detection-based deterrence agenda rely on speculative theories rather than rigorous causal evidence (Kayser, Mauron and Miah 2007; Mazanov and Connor 2010).

A different and indirect way to evaluate the effectiveness of anti-doping programmes would be to use the simple framework presented in Section 65.4. We are not aware of any study that investigates whether fines and punishments respond as predicted by deterrence theory. The point would be to compare anti-doping programmes (using, for example, the information in Tables 65.1 and 65.2 in the case of North-American leagues) across sports, countries, federations and events and to investigate whether testing and punishment policies are designed to optimally deter doping. For example, punishment should increase with higher stakes and lower test sensitivity. The point would be to investigate whether anti-doping programmes are designed in a way that is consistent with the goal of minimizing doping.

65.6 SUMMARY AND CONCLUSIONS

We have reviewed current anti-doping policies and their effectiveness, the discontent about the state of doping in sports, and offered a general framework to understand why anti-doping objectives are difficult to achieve. Anti-doping in sports does not aim for an incremental reduction in doping but for a complete elimination as predicated under the 'doping-free sport' objective of most anti-doping policies falling under the umbrella of WADA. The current state of discontent with WADA's anti-doping approach is that a detection-based deterrence approach cannot eliminate doping given current detection technologies and high stakes.

However, significant improvement in testing technologies, such as the biological passport, could shift the balance in favour of the WADA agenda. Additional proposed methods including collective punishment, deferred compensation and laboratory competition could further WADA's goals. That being said, the public's knowledge regarding compliance with doping regulations will be incomplete until (i) modern methods to accurately measure prevalence are adopted and (ii) systematic evaluations of anti-doping interventions are undertaken.

REFERENCES

Athey, Susan, and Guido W. Imbens. 2017. 'The State of Applied Econometrics: Causality and Policy Evaluation'. *Journal of Economic Perspectives* 31, no. 2: 3–32. DOI: 10.1257/jep.31.2.3.

Berry, Donald A. 2008. 'The Science of Doping'. *Nature* 454, no. 7205: 692. DOI: 10.1038/454692a.

Cisyk, Jeffrey. 2020. 'Impacts of Performance-Enhancing Drug Suspensions on the Demand for Major League Baseball'. *Journal of Sports Economics* 21, no. 4: 391–419. DOI: 10.1177/1527002520906529.

Cisyk, Jeffrey, and Pascal Courty. 2017. 'Do Fans Care about Compliance to Doping Regulations in Sports? The Impact of PED Suspension in Baseball'. *Journal of Sports Economics* 18, No. 4: 323–50. DOI: 10.1177/1527002515587441.

Connor, James, Jules Woolf, and Jason Mazanov. 2013. 'Would They Dope? Revisiting the Goldman Dilemma'. *British Journal of Sports Medicine* 47, No. 11: 697–700. DOI: 10.1136/bjsports-2012-091826.

de Hon, Olivier, Harm Kuipers, and Maarten van Bottenburg. 2015. 'Prevalence of Doping Use in Elite Sports: A Review of Numbers and Methods'. *Sports Medicine* 45, No. 1: 57–69. DOI: 10.1007/s40279-014-0247-x.

Delanghe, Joris R., Thomas M. Maenhout, M. M. Speeckaert, and Marijn L. De Buyzere. 2014. 'Detecting Doping Use: More Than an Analytical Problem'. *Acta Clinica Belgica* 69, No. 1: 25–9. DOI: 10.1179/0001551213Z.0000000009.

Goldman, Bob, Patricia J. Bush, and Ronald Klatz. 1984. *Death in the Locker Room: Steroids and Sports*. London: Century.

Hermann, Aaron, and Maciej Henneberg. 2014. 'Anti-doping Systems in Sports Are Doomed to Fail: A Probability and Cost Analysis'. *Journal of Sports Medicine & Doping* 4, No. 5: 148. DOI: 10.4172/2161-0673.1000148.

Isenmann, Eduard, Gabriella Ambrosio, Jan Felix Joseph, Monica Mazzarino, Xavier de la Torre, Philipp Zimmer, Rymantas Kazlauskas et al. 2019. 'Ecdysteroids as Non-conventional Anabolic Agent: Performance Enhancement by Ecdysterone Supplementation in Humans'. *Archives of Toxicology* 93, No. 7: 1–10. DOI: 10.1007/s00204-019-02490-x.g.

Kayser, Bengt, Alexandre Mauron, and Andy Miah. 2007. 'Current Anti-doping Policy: A Critical Appraisal'. *BMC Medical Ethics* 8, No. 1: 2. DOI: 10.1186/1472-6939-8-2.

Maennig, Wolfgang. 2014. 'Inefficiency of the Anti-doping System: Cost Reduction Proposals'. *Substance Use & Misuse* 49, No. 9: 1201–5. DOI: 10.3109/10826084.2014.912065.

Mazanov, Jason, and James Connor. 2010. 'Rethinking the Management of Drugs in Sport'. *International Journal of Sport Policy* 2, No. 1: 49–63. DOI: 10.1080/19406941003634032.

Mazanov, Jason, Twan Huybers, and James Connor. 2011. 'Qualitative Evidence of a Primary Intervention Point for Elite Athlete Doping'. *Journal of Science and Medicine in Sport* 14, No. 2: 106–10. DOI: 10.1016/j.jsams.2010.06.003.

Mitchell, George John. 2007. 'Report to the Commissioner of Baseball of an Independent Investigation into the Illegal Use of Steroids and Other Performance Enhancing Substances by Players in Major League Baseball'.

Møller, Verner. 2016. 'The Road to Hell Is Paved with Good Intentions – A Critical Evaluation of WADA's Anti-doping Campaign'. *Performance Enhancement & Health* 4, no. 3–4: 111–15. DOI: 10.1016/j.peh.2016.05.001.

Mountjoy, Margo, Stuart Miller, Matteo Vallini, Jeremy Foster, and James Carr. 2017. 'International Sports Federation's Fight to Protect the Clean Athlete: Are We Doing Enough in the Fight against Doping?' *British Journal of Sports Medicine* 51: 1241–1242. DOI: 10.1136/bjsports-2017-097870.

Müller, Rudhard Klaus. 2010. 'History of Doping and Doping Control'. *Doping in Sports: Biochemical Principles, Effects and Analysis* 195: 1–23. DOI: 10.1007/978-3-540-79088-4_1.

Overbye, Marie, Mette Lykke Knudsen, and Gertrud Pfister. 2013. 'To Dope or Not to Dope: Elite Athletes' Perceptions of Doping Deterrents and Incentives.' *Performance Enhancement & Health* 2, no. 3: 119–34. DOI: 10.1016/j.peh.2013.07.001.

Pielke, Roger. 2018. 'Assessing Doping Prevalence Is Possible: So What Are We Waiting For?' *Sports Medicine* 48, No. 1: 207–9. DOI: 10.1007/s40279-017-0792-1.

Pitsch, Werner. 2009. '"The Science of Doping" Revisited: Fallacies of the Current Anti-doping Regime'. *European Journal of Sport Science* 9, No. 2: 87–95. DOI: 10.1080/17461390802702309.

Pitsch, Werner, and Eike Emrich. 2011. 'The Frequency of Doping in Elite Sport: Results of a Replication Study'. *International Review for the Sociology of Sport* 47, No. 5: 559–580. DOI: 10.1177/1012690211413969.

Rosen, Sherwin. 1981. 'The Economics of Superstars'. *American Economic Review* 71, No. 5: 845–58. www.jstor.org/stable/1803469.

Ulrich, Rolf, Harrison G. Pope, Léa Cléret, Andrea Petróczi, Tamás Nepusz, Jay Schaffer, Gen Kanayama, R. Dawn Comstock, and Perikles Simon. 2018. 'Doping in Two Elite Athletics Competitions Assessed by Randomized-Response Surveys'. *Sports Medicine* 48, No. 1: 211–19. DOI: 10.1007/s40279-017-0765-4.

Van Reeth, Daam. 2013. 'TV Demand for the Tour de France: The Importance of Stage Characteristics versus Outcome Uncertainty, Patriotism, and Doping'. *International Journal of Sport Finance* 8, No. 1: 39–60.

Vlad, Robert Alexandru, Gabriel Hancu, Gabriel Cosmin Popescu, and Ioana Andreea Lungu. 2018. 'Doping in Sports, a Never-Ending Story?' *Advanced Pharmaceutical Bulletin* 8, No. 4: 529. DOI: 10.15171/apb.2018.062.

World Anti-Doping Agency. 2019. 'Athlete Biological Passport Operating Guidelines'. www.wada-ama.org/en/resources/athlete-biological-passport/athlete-biological-passport-abp-operating-guidelines.

66

Food Safety Compliance

Donald Macrae and Florentin Blanc *

Abstract: The primary objective of food safety regulation is to reduce the risk of unsafe food making consumers ill. It is not always clear that rules produce the outcomes they aim at, and even when outcomes are achieved overall, it is far from certain that it is necessarily compliance with rules that makes the food safe, or that enforcement was the driving force behind it. Meaningful food safety compliance requires good alignment between regulatory design and desired outcomes. A key question for a policymaker intent on establishing a regulatory regime is "How much compliance will it need?". This issue of how much compliance is needed to deliver the regulatory objectives is a challenge. While there is a solid body of literature on modern food law, there is less research done specifically on food regulation compliance. Recent research has shown the complexity of enforcement and "regulatory delivery" systems in food, but the link between such enforcement systems and actual compliance is far from simple. Effective food safety compliance requires a complex set of factors – good regulation, well-designed enforcement and, possibly most importantly, competence, knowledge, and understanding of food safety's importance on the side of food business operators. The food safety regulatory regime presents a vast set of compliance issues, which makes it a useful domain in which to test models of compliance. This chapter discusses some of the existing literature on the topic, sets out this range of compliance issues as they have arisen in practice, and discusses some of the salient points arising.

66.1 INTRODUCTION: CONTEXTUAL OVERVIEW OF THE HISTORY AND GOALS OF FOOD SAFETY REGULATION

Norms and procedures regulating the supply and sale of food have existed for around a millennium at least (Ferrières 2005), reflecting some deeply held and widespread concerns about the safety of the food we eat, when produced by others (thus, these regulations were created for cities, which brought in their food from outside). Regulations largely predated advances in science, and thus (from a scientific perspective) often regulated the wrong thing in the wrong way (Young 1989; Coppin and High 1999). Even today, not all food regulations can be said to be "science-based," and there is significant disagreement on some issues such as genetically modified organisms (GMOs) (Blanc et al. 2015).

* The authors wish to gratefully thank their colleague Margarita Escobar for her help with finalizing and editing this chapter.

In spite of its imperfect relationship with science, food regulation's aim is to ensure that the food we buy is what it states to be, and is safe to eat. Expectations from regulations have tended to increase as consumers have become more remote from their food supply (Blanc 2018a). While the development of food regulations and institutions was clearly not always disinterested and may have reflected at different points in time regulatory capture, regulatory entrepreneurship, or other self-interest (Young 1989; Coppin and High 1999; Blanc 2018a), the public perception and stated intent of food regulation is indeed to ensure the safety (and "truthfulness") of the supply.

The link between regulation and outcomes is complex, and has often been assumed more than really studied. It is not always clear that rules produce the outcomes they aim at, and even when outcomes are achieved overall (i.e. food is generally safe), it is far from certain that it is necessarily compliance with rules that makes the food safe, or that enforcement was the driving force behind it. *Meaningful* food safety compliance requires good alignment between regulatory design and desired outcomes – that is, that rules are "fit for purpose" and science-based. While this is overall increasingly the case in many countries (Manion 2012), rules are never perfect, particularly when they aim at specific outcomes in complex systems (Ogus 1994; Baldwin 1995).

66.2 WHAT DISTINGUISHES FOOD SAFETY REGULATION COMPLIANCE?

The food safety regulatory regime presents a vast range of compliance issues, which makes it a useful domain in which to test models of compliance. Section 66.2 discusses some of the existing literature on the topic, while Section 66.3 sets out this range of compliance issues as they have arisen in practice, and Section 66.4 discusses some of the salient points arising.

Food safety raises acute compliance issues that mostly come down to the fundamental human need for food. From that flows:

- ***Ubiquity*** – practically every country and society that has any food surplus and trade has some form of food safety regulatory system, even without formal rules. That ubiquity extends inexorably to the highest level of global commerce.
- ***Segmentation*** – development of food safety regulatory systems has followed socioeconomic development as the markets have grown and matured, and as the national diets have evolved. That has, however, left many countries still facing food safety compliance issues that developed countries have dealt with, sometimes decades ago if not more, in some cases as long as 100 years ago. At the same time, some lower-income countries face the problem of regulating food producers and retailers integrated in global supply chains, as well as subsistence farmers and traditional food markets.
- ***Evolution*** – segmentation illustrates the diversity of issues arising from differential rates of evolution, according to socioeconomic development. But more advanced jurisdictions are also facing continuing evolution, which may even lead to regression. Having thought that the problem was solved, some developed countries are withdrawing resources and, at the same time, market complexity and volumes are rising, and new problems are emerging, such as plant-based "meat" or GMOs, or new outbreaks of hepatitis. What may seem to be clear lessons from the past now need to be applied in a different context from that in which the lessons were learned.
- ***Symbiosis*** – there is a strong relationship between the evolution of markets and the evolution of food safety regulatory systems – with regulation not having necessarily been

the cause of safety improvements but an important trust factor enabling market growth. There is a strong (and often uneasy) relationship between food markets and their regulatory supervisors. For many developing economies, agricultural and food products are the main exports, and agriculture (with or without processing) is the main source of employment. Avoiding poisoning customers is a shared objective between economic operators and regulators, in a way that does not occur in some other regulatory systems, such as environmental protection, even though this driver does not always exclude reckless behavior, or contamination through ignorance or incompetence, even in larger companies.

66.2.1 *Alignment of Regulatory and Commercial Objectives*

The primary objective of food safety regulation is to reduce the risk of unsafe food making consumers ill. A rational food business operator (FBO) should generally share that objective, even if its primary objective is to run a successful business. While not being the primary objective, it is almost a *sine qua non* in running a successful food business over the long term (conversely, it may be ignored by "rogue" actors aiming to make a quick profit and disappear). An FBO *can* therefore view compliance costs as valid expenses in running the business, as opposed to an externally imposed overhead – depending on the actual content of regulations, the level of competence of the FBO, and its confidence in regulators, as well as whether it has a long-term business perspective. This will be a question of degree but food safety compliance can in fact improve business performance, rather than be a net cost:

- Many FBOs are small or micro businesses, with limited management capacity. Applying food safety management systems (based on Hazard Analysis Critical Control Point (HACCP)) as part of compliance introduces them to applying a systematic approach, which can potentially extend to other aspects of their business – but it can be a very challenging undertaking. When the UK's Food Standards Agency introduced its "Safer Food, Better Business" compliance support package, a subsequent survey showed that 68 percent of the small FBOs that applied it also considered that their business had improved.[1]
- A successful regulatory inspection report can be a selling point for the FBO, if reports/ratings are made public. There will be other regulatory regimes where regulatory certificates, such as an elevator safety check or a license to operate, may be displayed, but these are not usually regarded as giving a market advantage. There is little research on how influential the food safety ratings actually are with consumers, but the catering industry seems to assume that to be the case, given the support for these schemes and their gradual spread across the world (Fuller et al. 2019: 12–13; Watts et al. 2019).[2]

[1] Short case study by the Chartered Institute of Environmental Health: https://web.archive.org/web/20071020072540/http://www.cieh.org/library/Knowledge/Food_safety_and_hygiene/Case_studies/Westminster%20CHIP.pdf.

[2] There are conflicting reports of consumers' awareness of the rating system and of its influence on their buying decisions. A 2017 report by the insurance company NFU Mutual found levels of awareness as low as 8 percent in some parts of the UK – www.dorsetfoodanddrink.org/wp-content/uploads/2018/05/nfu-mutual-food-hygiene-ratings-report-2018-double-page.pdf.

The existence of some degree of alignment between regulatory objectives and business interests regarding food safety does not, however, mean that all businesses will seek to ensure safe food, or succeed at it. Short-term profits may trump long-term perspectives, resulting in conscious disregard for rules. Probably more frequent is "incompetence" in the broadest sense, that is, the incapacity to properly perceive and address food safety hazards. This is not only a feature of micro, small and medium enterprises (MSMEs), as such problems can also be found in major companies. The difficulty in controlling *Listeria* in ice-cream production in the USA in the past few years is a good example of this, as was the 2018 US *E.coli* outbreak linked to romaine lettuce, or the *Salmonella* contamination of infant formula in France (Blanc 2018a: 70–3). Managing food contamination is difficult, and large facilities mean that a "small" problem can lead to a large outbreak. Inadequate prevention of irrigation water contamination was certainly not "in the business interest" of romaine lettuce producers, but it happened nonetheless. This shows the importance of continuously looking for more meaningful ways to "comply" (i.e. to better manage risks in the food chain), and of more effective ways to regulate and enforce (i.e. to better steer food operators in areas where problems remain).

Assessing the actual health impact of unsafe food is difficult because, in the absence of large-scale epidemiological surveys, it is very hard to assess prevalence of given diseases – and even harder to compare it across countries – given that most people do not report low-level food illnesses, and that not all acute cases lead to laboratory analysis. There is clear evidence, overall, that food is now much safer than 100 or (even more so) 150 years ago in developed countries (Wagstaff 1986: 624–31). Likewise, it is also clear that most low-income countries experience serious food safety problems. In both situations, however, the causality between compliance and food safety levels is unclear – improvements often preceded regulation, just as today's major contaminations often arise from nonregulatory issues (e.g. lack of access to safe water – Blanc 2018a: 268–71). The difficulty in assessing the exact level of influence of compliance issues on safety outcomes does not mean, of course, that there are none. It makes it, however, difficult to ascertain whether perceptions of relative safety or risk are accurate (Blanc and Cola 2017: 73–4).

Official healthcare data may, as indicated, be insufficient to detect low-level food illness and use this for risk-based targeting of inspections. These cases will often be mentioned on social media, and experiments have shown that automated analysis of such posts can yield good predictive results for detecting noncompliance (Schomberg et al. 2016; Sadilek et al. 2017). Such approaches are gaining interest as a source of improved risk-based targeting data for inspections and enforcement, but are also open to criticism for potential lack of rigor – and for their impact on privacy (Altenburger and Ho 2019). Whatever the impact on the behavior of regulatory authorities, social media reports of food-borne illness are in any case an increasing commercial hazard for FBOs.

66.2.2 *Prevalence and Diversity: Village to Global*

Eating and breathing are both basic human functions, yet food safety and air quality regulatory regimes operate differently. The latter is far more recent, partly because the link between business behaviors and harm has been less apparent in the case of air pollution, as well as less understood, and is strongly (but not entirely) linked to modern economic activities. Food safety regulation has grown to cover not only the most salient, industrial-scale risks but also those emerging from more "mundane" activities, in an effort to achieve better outcomes.

Food is a tradable product or commodity and this holds true from a rural village to global distribution systems. The regulatory regime also needs to stretch from street vendors to multinational chains. Compliance requirements can be very technical, whether full HACCP or ISO 22000, especially when applied to a complex production process, and may carry significant capital costs. But the same principles have to be applied to basic food handling operations at the simplest level, including in lower-income countries.

- At the technical high end, compliance is technically complex and requires expertise and investment, much like in other regulatory domains such as air pollution. What can be learned about compliance in major corporations will have some direct implication for food safety regulation at that level.
- At the lower end, the challenge of supporting compliance of micro businesses with regulatory requirements has required a new approach. In place of guidance notes that are barely distinguishable from the original regulations, there are now a number of illustrated materials of varying lengths and formats, YouTube videos, in different languages, etc.[3]

Indeed, another challenge of food safety compliance is the multilingualism needed even in the same city in a developed economy. The US Food and Drug Administration (USFDA) invested significant resource in developing practice guidance to accompany the Food Safety Modernization Act (FSMA) in a way that would not be seen by the regulatory authorities in sectors such as financial services.

At the very high end of food safety compliance is the "meta-market" in food safety that operates at a global level (e.g. the UK has established a new regulator to focus on this "meta-market," albeit as a subset of competition law rather than food safety law, called the Groceries Code Adjudicator). Global supply chains operate across many different national food safety regulatory systems and so have to comply with a set of higher standards that can also "satisfy" the national ones. Food safety is already distinct from many other regulatory regimes in having international standards set by various international organizations (*Codex Alimentarius* in particular), on which most national standards are based, but the "meta-market" goes beyond these in order to have consistency across the national markets that the meta-market transcends.[4]

Even at the national level, food safety compliance is needed for international trade, usually by matching the regulatory requirements of the more developed market in any bilateral transaction. These regulatory requirements can operate as nontariff barriers to trade and this is covered by the Sanitary and Phytosanitary agreement (SPS) under the World Trade Organization (WTO), which runs parallel to the Technical Barriers to Trade agreement (TBT) that applies to virtually all other products.

66.2.3 *Need for Positive Results, Delivered at Scale*

Food safety regimes may frame the goal negatively (preventing supply of unsafe food), but the intended outcome remains that of supplying safe food to large numbers of people. A number

[3] As an example, see the guidance infographics issued by the Association of Convenience Stores to its 33,500 members – www.acs.org.uk/advice. They cover eleven different regulatory regimes that these small corner shops have to comply with, including food safety.

[4] There are proprietary standards applied at this level that supersede national and even *Codex* standards, in order to give global traders confidence of being compliant across many markets. The Global Food Safety Initiative (GFSI) tried to supersede even these, so that meeting its standards will cover everything – https://mygfsi.com/.

of (though by no means all) other regulatory regimes still tend to define their outcomes "negatively" (avoiding cartels, pollution, or hazardous products) rather than in terms of ensuring efficient and effective markets. When scale is added, the regulatory objective is clearly that of ensuring supply of safe food. The beneficiaries of the regulatory system are the entire population of that state at any given time, or an even larger group if exports are included. The regulatory challenge is not so much to stop rogue operators who deliberately or recklessly endanger consumers as it is to improve the standards of vast numbers of FBOs who may unintentionally contaminate food. At scale, market forces will weed out the intentionally dangerous businesses (though they can still do short-term harm) but of themselves will not improve the practices of millions of small and micro FBOs.[5]

Comparison of the "policing" model of enforcement with the "advisory" model can be oversimplified, but there remains a real distinction between the two. To ensure safe food daily for 25 million people in Shanghai, it would be statistically insignificant to close down 100 unsafe street traders and small restaurants. Effective regulatory delivery in that case involves raising the standards and operating practices of tens of thousands of small FBOs. One-on-one inspection is inefficient and ineffective in these circumstances, except insofar as it may provide high-profile messaging. The key risk to manage is not that of deliberate endangering but that of unintended endangering. Deterrence does not remedy ignorance or lack of capacity, whereas advice and guidance often will.

66.2.4 *Regulations at One Remove from the Hazard*

Modern food safety legislation is moving away from simply banning unsafe food to a position of regulating the prevention of risks to food. In 2018, the most common violations found by USFDA were in relation to failures in preventative systems, regardless of whether any food was actually safe or not (Flynn 2019). The approach taken by modern food safety regulation is proactive prevention, based on risk management of food hazards. An FBO may supply totally safe food but may still face serious sanctions for failures in its food risk management systems.

66.2.5 *Continuing Evolution of New Hazards*

The scope of a food safety regulatory regime is potentially very broad because of the centrality of food in human life, but it also means that it almost "vanishes" in the overlapping regimes that it connects with. In developing economies, food contaminated by contaminated water is usually seen as a public health issue and not a food safety issue, primarily because the public health laws and institutions predate food safety as a discrete regulatory regime. It is often the junior partner in an "FDA"-style institution, loosely copied on the US model, in which the medicine part dominates, to the extent that practices used for enforcing medical regulations are applied – inappropriately – to food safety issues.

A recent study by the World Bank has tracked the development of food safety issues in parallel with the economic progress from low-income, through lower-middle to middle-income economies (Jaffee et al. 2019). Urbanization and change of dietary practices lead to new hazards, with extended supply chains, and more processed food. A rise in income usually

[5] India is trying to tackle this issue with campaigns seeking to mobilize hundreds of millions of people (from a population of 1.2 billion), run by its national regulator, Food Safety and Standards Authority for India (FSSAI). The "Eat Right India" campaign is perhaps the most central one, but FSSAI is promoting a range of interventions – https://eatrightindia.gov.in/index.

leads to replacing low-risk starchy staples with higher-risk meat and leafy greens, while the market systems remain mainly informal and difficult to steer toward orderly development.

Even in highly developed economies, new hazards are still appearing. One is novel foods, such as lab-grown "meat," as well as fashions for high-risk foods such as almost raw burgers.[6] Better surveillance and measurement systems, such as Whole Genome Sequencing (WGS), are also identifying hazard patterns and connections previously not understood. Even the highly developed food safety system in the European Union has faced failures in some outbreaks of food-borne illness that crossed many country boundaries. All this means that the nature and contents of "food safety compliance" change over time.

66.2.6 *Importance for Other Development Objectives*

In developing economies, reforms aimed at promoting food safety have to take account of the connections they will have with other development objectives. The World Bank has identified and mapped seven Sustainable Development Goals (SDGs) that are closely connected with food safety issues or changes in behaviors (compliance) that can have a positive or negative impact on these other objectives (Jaffee et al. 2019). For example, women tend to have a stronger role in food markets than in most other markets and so reforms to market systems for food will have a (positive or negative) impact on gender equality (SDG 5). Because of the global market in food products, poor countries can experience food safety changes driven by external businesses and benefiting elites in the country well before the government begins to regulate food safety in a way that may (if done properly) bring benefits to the majority.

Such interventions by multinationals are small (private) "regulatory systems" in themselves, especially where the business acts as a vertical integrator for a supply chain, supporting and monitoring the local producers, outside of government regulation. It will have its own version of compliance insofar as its suppliers have to adopt new behaviors and practices in order to participate in its supply chain. It is an element in the "meta-market" referred to earlier, beyond any specific government's regulatory regime but acting on suppliers to ensure that food products of sufficient safety and quality reach international markets (and possibly domestic markets as well).

66.2.7 *Broad Compliance*

A key question for a policymaker intent on establishing a regulatory regime is "How much compliance will it need?". Many actors and stakeholders of regulatory systems tend to assume or explicitly state that only full compliance is acceptable, and that it is achievable (and thus that any new norm adopted will lead to all its expected impact). In reality, compliance is never complete or universal, and the pathway from rules to effect is (at best) complex. The simplistic view of regulatory systems is that government (using "experts") defines rules that businesses should follow, in order that the cumulative effect of their compliance will deliver the policy objectives. Inspectors will then be sent in to check that the rules are being obeyed and to impose sanctions insofar as they are not.

[6] For one example, Scottish cheesemakers from raw milk have been litigating to prevent traditional inspection preventing their operation – www.foodstandards.gov.scot/downloads/SFELC_Document.pdf.

It is usually the case that not all requirements are of the same importance in managing the food risk and, even within that, the level of prescription may be excessive. As demonstrated by Diver (1983) and developed by Baldwin (1990, 1995), "optimal" rules are not possible, and any given rule will be either over- or underinclusive. In the first case, it constrains too much (costs are excessive); in the second, it does too little (hazards are left unchecked). The salience of each requirement may also vary with circumstances, which means that some enforcement discretion is indispensable to achieve optimal results (Baldwin 1995). Achieving even small increases in the total percentage of compliance with all applicable rules can have major effects on food safety – hence the importance of targeting improvements in terms of outcomes (decrease in prevalence of diseases, in number of outbreaks, etc.) rather than strictly of compliance levels (Blanc 2018b).

In 2007, the UK government set a target of businesses being "broadly compliant," rather than 100 percent compliant. This was based on the Food Hygiene Rating Scheme, which rated food businesses between 0 and 5, where 3 was a pass. Businesses scoring between 3 and 5 were good enough – "broadly compliant." It was also assumed that the market would push many of the 3s up toward 5. And just as it was not expected that any business needed to be better than 3, the national target was originally (2007) only 75 percent of food businesses nationally being "broadly compliant." Annual statistics from local government inspections have demonstrated a peak of 93 percent of food businesses being broadly compliant (although it has been dropping recently to nearer 90 percent) (Food Standards Agency 2019).

This issue of how much compliance is needed to deliver the regulatory objectives is a challenge not only to the policymakers but also to the compliance industry that has proliferated in developed and developing economies alike, and is predicated on 100 percent compliance as the assumed target. Compliance can come to replace outcomes as the purpose of the regulatory system. A genuine risk-based approach, by contrast, will consider the risks in the business and assess its level of compliance from this perspective, as in the UK system described above.

66.3 LITERATURE OVERVIEW

A range of research literature is relevant to understanding food safety compliance – but most of it approaches compliance only as an effect that is assumed to result from enforcement activities, implicitly assuming the full validity of the deterrence model. Some papers look at the development of modern food safety legislation, including in terms of scientific foundations, which matters in assessing the extent to which compliance with norms can result in effective safety. A significant amount of recent publications specifically discuss the interplay of public and private norms as well as private certification mechanisms – with some attention paid to "positive" compliance drivers (securing/strengthening market position), as well as civil and penal liability issues (if contaminated food is sold and results in an outbreak) (Fagotto 2015; Marks 2016). Some look at the challenges linked to urbanization and growth, and the difficulty in establishing trust – but not always considering the question of compliance promotion and enforcement approaches, and their relative effectiveness (Cheng 2017). Finally, a few publications do consider the questions of enforcement institutions and approaches, of different compliance motives and profiles, and of how a combination of "regulatory delivery" tools may contribute to improved outcomes (Yapp and Fairman 2006; Hutter and Amodu 2008; Blanc and Cola 2017).

A crucial limitation is thus that much of this literature assumes that "more enforcement" automatically leads to "higher compliance," which in turn is assumed to mean "increased safety." By contrast, there is evidence both that rules cannot (by definition) be always optimal (and thus that compliance cannot always be equated with safety) (Gunningham 2015) and that the links between enforcement activities and compliance are complex (Blanc 2018a).

Yapp and Fairman (2006) give an overview of different compliance models (Tyler 2003; Blanc 2018a: 45) and how they can be applied to food safety, and a list of SMEs' compliance challenges in food safety – in particular lack of money, time, experience, information, support, interest, and knowledge (Yapp and Fairman 2006: 44). The main reason for non-compliance appeared to be that "the majority of SMEs were therefore seen to be 'organizationally incompetent'. Non-compliance was due to failures of management, systems, trust and knowledge" (Yapp and Fairman 2006: 49). Primary motives for complying stated by SMEs were in "order to protect their reputation and their business from potential legal action, from adverse publicity or because of consumer demand" (2/3 of respondents) and "legal duty to comply" (3/4 of respondents) (Yapp and Fairman 2006: 48). The competence and credibility of inspectors appeared to play an important role in compliance decisions (Yapp and Fairman 2006). The authors also pointed to the challenge posed by the modern meaning of food safety compliance as a continued effort to self-control and improve, based on HACCP principles: "[W]hereas food SMEs see [compliance] in terms of completing whatever work has been specified ... during the formal food hygiene inspection, enforcing agencies and academics view it as a continual, evaluative process of the business operation" (Yapp and Fairman 2006: 48).

Hutter and Amodu (2008) confirmed Yapp and Fairman's findings on essential points regarding the importance of competence and knowledge:

> Several studies have found that SMEs generally have lower levels of knowledge of regulatory laws and state regulatory systems (BRTF 1999; Fairman and Yapp 2004; Food Standards Agency 2001; Gunningham 2002; Henson and Heasman 1998; Hutter and Jones 2007; Vickers et al. 2005). They also appeared to rely on state regulatory systems for education and advice [as they] have less contact with non-state sources which provide information and advice (Fairman and Yapp 2004; Genn 1993; Hutter and Jones 2007). (Hutter and Amodu 2008: 15)

They likewise emphasize the complexity of a HACCP-based approach – though it should be noted that, precisely in response to such findings, the Food Standards Agency (2007) had already introduced its "Safer Food, Better Business," which embeds HACCP principles into a simple, practical, well-explained tool that SMEs can (and do) easily use.

The question of compliance cannot be abstracted from that of regulation (what is being complied with) or of enforcement (what is being done to control and ensure compliance). The gradual emergence and development of food safety legislation and institutions for inspections and enforcement is summarized in Blanc and Cola (2017). The strong degree of path dependency, in particular, goes some way to explaining the persistence of structures and approaches that are suboptimal in terms of compliance promotion. Purnhagen (2014) has shown how major jurisprudential decisions drove the development of European legal approaches that, in turn, became essential foundations of modern food safety law (see also Blanc 2018a). Balancing these perspectives, Manion (2012) emphasizes the increasing importance of scientific foundations and references in food safety legislation.

The increasing (and sometimes uneasy) complementarity between public enforcement and private certification in food safety is an important trend, which Fagotto (2015) investigates in detail. Her analysis supports the idea of an alignment of public and private motives, and of their complementarity ("When we consider private food safety initiatives, it is beyond doubt that there is an *alignment of public and private interests* to provide food safety. Private actors have powerful incentives to achieve food safety because the economic repercussions of foodborne outbreaks can be devastating" Fagotto 2015: 206. Fagotto also points to the inherent limits of public enforcement (fragmentation and difficulty of working across borders). Her critical findings on the limitations of private sector audits are important, though not insuperable (announced audits mostly, cases of low competence of auditors, and possible conflicts of interest between keeping a client and enforcing strict standards). Overall, Fagotto (2015) sees third-party audits and private certification as useful complements to public regulation (provided they are designed and enforced adequately), and not substitutes or competitors. We would concur with this perspective, and add that some of the limitations she finds (of both public and private instruments) are inherent to any type of regulatory control and enforcement: inspectors/auditors (public or private) may be of very varying levels of competence and integrity, control visits cannot necessarily find all problems (whether they be announced or not), and, ultimately, continued compliance depends on the internal workings of the business operators (structures, culture, etc.) (Hodges 2015; Hodges and Steinholtz 2017).

The question of private standards and compliance schemes is also covered in Brunet Marks (2016). She sees private standards again as complementary to public regulation, but also sees them as (in a WTO perspective) the only way that countries can effectively go "beyond" the core requirements based on the FAO-WHO[7] *Codex Alimentarius*, in the context of the WTO SPS agreement. Without entering into the merits of this discussion (many matters are outside/beyond *Codex* standards, many others are subject to interpretation, and enforcement mechanisms for WTO agreements are not easy to use), it assumes that rule-setting is the main way to improve food safety. There are considerable reasons to doubt this: modern food safety legislation is mostly about internal controls (based on HACCP) because the challenge is to ensure adequate and constant compliance, whereas underlying requirements are mostly clear (what is needed to achieve is not so much the issue as "how to achieve it effectively and consistently") (Blanc 2018a).

In her monograph on food safety in China, Cheng (2017) shows the challenges posed to an authoritarian approach to food safety: it appears to have particular difficulties in improving trust, and more generally the authorities seems to fail at improving the situation in spite of both pressure from the top leadership *and* demand from the population. What her account, however, fails to question is the "how" behind "more enforcement." Deciding to enforce food safety "more strictly" or "more strongly" is insufficient – improving food safety requires a system-wide approach where, as indicated earlier, the "repressive" part can be only a (possibly minor) element, alongside enabling conditions (e.g. water quality), knowledge and capacity, strengthening the legitimacy of the regulatory system, etc.

Finally, many papers and monographs on food safety regulation start from a statement of the importance of the topic, emphasizing "increasing" food safety problems. While the importance given to food safety problems in public discussions and private considerations is high, it is not in any way "new" (as thoroughly demonstrated by Ferrières 2005). Public scares about food safety are at least centuries old – and the speed at which they spread, as well as their strength, was quite amazing already in premodern times. As for *actual* safety, while Cheng (2017) focuses on chemical safety, where there is certainly evidence of a worsening (at

7 Food and Agriculture Organization (FAO)-World Health Organization (WHO).

least in some countries) over the past few decades, microbiological safety has been dramatically improving over the past 150 years. Pre-industrial food production and distribution systems were not in any meaning of the word "safe" (Ferrières 2005; Blanc 2018a). What can be said is that food safety concerns are important, and impact both private and public behavior. Some reflect trust issues (founded or not in facts, but with real effects in any case); others reflect real risks to health (higher or not than before, most likely simply *different*); and still others correspond simply to the fact that food safety can never be 100 percent ensured at all points and at all times; it is a continuous, ever-renewed effort.

66.4 DISCUSSION: MANY FACTORS, COMPLEX INTERACTIONS

Compliance is inherently a complex phenomenon, and modifying behavior in a certain way requires a variety of drivers (Blanc 2018b: 142). While there is a solid body of literature on modern food law (Van der Meulen 2013; Purnhagen 2014), there is less research done specifically on food regulation compliance. Recent research has shown the complexity of enforcement and "regulatory delivery" systems in food (Corini et al. 2017), but the link between such enforcement systems and actual compliance is far from simple.

Regarding the interplay between private and public sectors discussed in this chapter, Fagotto (2015) exposes how they indeed can reinforce each other, and cautions that "one should not hastily conclude that PFSS [Private Food Safety Standards] should replace government regulation, or that public food safety functions should be entrusted to the industry, for example by delegating inspection responsibilities to private auditors," for reasons of conflict of interest, competence, and methods. We would add that, as indicated in Section 66.3, private auditors can also aim "100 percent compliance" (for liability issues in particular), which may be an aggregate result in a negative social impact, if marginal compliance costs exceed benefits (OECD 2000: 11: "full compliance may be so costly that it causes more damage than it remedies"). State regulators, by contrast, can adopt a risk-based approach and, when they do so, are better positioned to try to achieve optimal outcomes for a given level of public and private costs.

Much of the conversation on food safety is driven by assumptions that are not necessarily true. For instance, while globally food-borne diseases are an important burden, how true is it in developed economies? And is the food safety situation overall really worsening in terms of outcomes (deaths, disability, etc.)? Much food safety regulation literature also assumes that compliance is driven primarily by control and deterrence, even though many studies have shown the limitations of this vision (Tyler 2003; Blanc 2018a). Even the assumed rationality of economic actors is far from being perfect – as small and large economic operators regularly put themselves in situations where their business is irremediably harmed or destroyed by food safety lapses, by ignorance, or because they underestimated the risks (Kahneman et al. 1982).

Food safety results sometimes fit uneasily with compliance models. From a pure rational calculations perspective, stronger compliance could be expected in some than in other regulatory fields where the interests of business operators are far less aligned with regulatory goals – not necessarily because of enforcement by regulators but because of the probability of detection (through illness) and sanctions (through drop in sales) by consumers. While indeed many (most) FBOs tend to comply, at least with essential safe practices – and the majority of unsafe food globally results more from fundamental problems in equipment, supply, resources, and competence, rather than from willful malpractice – some egregious cases of noncompliance do happen, and not always by "fly by night" operators intending to make a quick profit before disappearing to avoid liability.

Some famous examples put the claim of rational alignment of goals into question – from the Chicago "meatpackers" scandal in 1906, brought to light by Upton Sinclair's *The Jungle* (a clear example of perfectly conscious and voluntary malpractice) (Young 1985), through Italy's 1986 methanol wine scandal (Barbera and Audifredi 2012; Giuliani et. al 2015) to the USA's romaine lettuce *E.Coli* outbreak in 2018 – and many more. Several issues seem to be involved in these situations:

- Difficulty in detecting the link between food and harm: consumers may not be able to know what sickened them, or may not see effects before a long time has elapsed. This could be applicable at least for *The Jungle*, where most meat would have been thoroughly cooked, and harmful bacteria killed, meaning that the harm would be through long-term chemical contamination. Similarly, in the famous "Horsegate" fraud case (which had mostly no food safety relevance), since no one would get sick, there was a very low probability of detection (Brooks et al. 2017).
- Bounded rationality: economic operators do not necessarily think "far ahead" or consider "black swans" – and, just as in financial markets, they tend to underestimate the probability of adverse events, as well as "how bad" they could get (Kahneman et al. 1982). They may also not necessarily "believe in science" – and this is true not only of managers without a technical education but of engineers, biologists, etc. As can be seen in many "pseudoscience" or "science-denialist" movements, always some of the people involved in such beliefs have a technical background but believe that they "know better" than the prevailing science. A somewhat similar case would be the "antivax" movement – from a rational perspective, parents should be vaccinating their children, but, in fact, many do not because they believe that "nothing bad will happen" from not doing so (on the contrary, even). Thus, some managers or technical operators may consciously decline to apply food safety rules because they do not believe that they matter (Hansson 2017).
- Lack of knowledge or competence: operators may be willing to do the right thing if given the necessary advice, but they lack the knowledge to apply safe practices if not given specific guidance. To some extent, the Italian methanol wine scandal seemed to result from this, based on the statements of the main culprit, who apparently thought that adulterating wine would not cause serious harm.

The romaine lettuce case would appear to combine insufficient competence (major company but spread-out operations with possibly limited competence "on the ground"), bounded rationality ("nothing will happen") and maybe the expectations that at most a few people would get mildly sick and that nothing would ensue. Given that regulatory follow-up on some previous outbreaks in the USA was often weak (Blanc 2018b), this may not have been a fully unrealistic expectation – but it also meant underestimating the potential market backlash. In any event, a combination of such factors can always happen again, and lead to similar consequences.

Given this, absolute confidence in food safety is impossible, even assuming a technically proficient, adequately funded, well-managed company. The complexity, number of potential risk factors, ever-changing physical environment, etc. mean that contamination *can happen* even if compliance appears adequate. This is why all modern food safety systems have been built to incorporate the possibility of failure, and thus feature two essential elements: the traceability requirement (to be able to identify the source of contamination, and other products that may have been contaminated) and the organization of recalls (voluntary and mandatory). This is why traceability is such a vital requirement (on which much emphasis is laid when checking compliance in food safety, at least in countries which have reached sufficient development to apply it), and why the EU's RASFF (Rapid Alert System for Food and Feed) was, when it was created, an innovation as important as institutional and regulatory changes that may have more "visibility" McKean 2001; Van der Meulen et al. 2015; 2–13; Blanc 2018b: 93–4. In a surprising way, given how it was received in public opinion and the media, one could argue that the "Horsegate" scandal proved that the system was (roughly, mostly) working: no serious health effect occurred, and once the fraud was detected it was possible to trace it back up the supply chain and identify other affected products and lots, and recall them.

The romaine lettuce outbreak also underlined the importance of the rules themselves – as the emphasis on compliance assumes that rules are "fit for purpose." Much discussion ensued about whether the delay in adopting new FDA rules on irrigation water was to blame for the outbreak, but it is worth underlining that the said rules only mandate bi-yearly testing of water, which probably would have done little to prevent the contamination. The EU, in this area, mandates only very broadly that the operator must have internal control to prevent contaminations, thus pointing again to the importance of *competence*, beyond formal requirements. Quality of rules is important, but improving the knowledge and understanding of operators is probably even more so.

As we have seen, rational calculations can play an important role in food safety because of the direct connection to market effects – but neither are these effects always linear, nor are rational calculations always sufficient. Human decision-making is far from being necessarily rational (Kahneman et al. 1982), and personal and business ethics (Hodges and Steinholtz 2017) often play a more important role in outcomes than formal rules and enforcement.

In conclusion, effective food safety compliance requires a complex set of factors – good regulation, well-designed enforcement, and, possibly most importantly, competence, knowledge, and understanding of food safety's importance on the side of FBOs. Because of the importance of consumer demand on operators, schemes such as food hygiene ratings can also be used (Simon 2005); integrating these better with widely used internet search tools (and emphasizing consumer education) could also make them more effective.

REFERENCES

Altenburger, K., and Ho, D. E. (2019) "Can Silicon Valley Save Food Safety? Maybe, but Not with Online Reviews Alone," Food Safety News, www.foodsafetynews.com/2019/01/can-silicon-valley-save-food-safety-maybe-but-not-with-online-reviews-alone/.

Baldwin, R. (1990) "Why Rules Don't Work." *Modern Law Review* 53: 321–37. https://doi.org/10.1111/j.1468–2230.1990.tb01815.x.

(1995) *Rules and Government*. Oxford: Clarendon Press.

Barbera, F., and Audifredi, S. (2012). "In Pursuit of Quality: The Institutional Change of Wine Production Market in Piedmont." *Sociologia Ruralis* 52: 311–31, https://doi.org/10.1111/j.1467–9523.2012.00567.x.

Blanc, F. (2018a) *From Chasing Violations to Managing Risks: Origins, challenges and evolutions in regulatory inspections*. Cheltenham, UK: Edward Elgar Publishing.

(2018b) "Tools for Effective Regulation: Is 'More' Always 'Better'?" *European Journal of Risk Regulation*, 9, no. 3: 465–82, https://doi.org/10.1017/err.2018.19.

Blanc, F., and Cola, G. (2017) "Inspections, Risks and Circumstances: Historical Development, Diversity of Structures and Practices in Food Safety." *Studi Parlamentari e di Politica Costituzionale* 3–4: 73–4.

Blanc, F., Macrae, D., and Ottimofiore, G. (2015) Understanding and Addressing the Risk Regulation Reflex: Lessons from International Experience in Dealing with Risk, Responsibility and

Regulation. Netherlands Ministry of Interior and Kingdom Relations. www.government.nl/documents/reports/2015/01/21/understanding-and-addressing-the-risk-regulation-reflex.

Brooks, S., Elliott, C. T., Spence, M. et al. (2017) "Four Years Post-Horsegate: An Update of Measures and Actions Put in Place Following the Horsemeat Incident of 2013." *Sci Food* 1, no. 5, https://doi.org/10.1038/s41538-017–0007-z.

Better Regulation Task Force (BRTF). (1999) *Regulation and Small Firms: a Progress Report.* London: Better Regulation Task Force. Cabinet Office Publications & Publicity Team. http://www.brc.gov.uk/.

Cheng, C. (2017) *The Politics of Food Safety: Detection and Perceptions of Food Safety Problems in China*, PhD dissertation, Duke University, https://dukespace.lib.duke.edu/dspace/bitstream/handle/10161/14527/Cheng_duke_0066D_14036.pdf?sequence=1&isAllowed=y.

Coppin, C. A., and High, J. C. (1999) *The Politics of Purity: Harvey Washington Wiley and the Origins of Federal Food Policy*. Ann Arbor: University of Michigan Press.

Corini, A., van der Meulen, B., Kets, F., Ottimofiore, G., and Blanc, F. (2017) "Enforcement of EU Food Law." In *Law Enforcement by EU Authorities – Implications for Political and Judicial Accountability*, edited by M. Scholten and M. Luchtman, 195–220. Cheltenham, UK: Edward Elgar Publishing. https://doi.org/10.4337/9781786434630.00014.

Diver, C. S. (1983) "The Optimal Precision of Administrative Rules." *Yale Law Journal* 93, no. 1: 65–109. https://doi.org/10.2307/796245.

Fagotto, E. (2015). "Are We Being Served? The Relationship between Public and Private Food Safety Regulation." In *The Changing Landscape of Food Governance*, edited by Tetty Havinga, Frans van Waarden, and Donal Casey, 201–22. Cheltenham, UK: Edward Elgar. https://doi.org/10.4337/9781784715410.00022.

Fairman, R. and Yapp, C. (2004) *The Evaluation of Effective Enforcement Approaches for Food Safety in SMEs*. University of London: King's College.

Ferrières, M. (2005) *Sacred Cow, Mad Cow: A History of Food Fears*. Translated by Jody Gladding. New York: Columbia University Press.

Flynn, D. (2019) "Report Details Most Common Violations at FDA-Regulated Food Facilities." Food Safety News, www.foodsafetynews.com/2019/01/can-silicon-valley-save-food-safety-maybe-but-not-with-online-reviews-alone/.

Food Standards Agency. (2001) *Task Force on the Burdens of Food Regulations on Small Food Businesses*. Food Standards Agency, London.

Food Standards Agency. (2019) Annual Report on Local Authority Food Law Enforcement, www.food.gov.uk/news-alerts/news/fsa-publishes-latest-annual-report-on-local-authority-food-law-enforcement.

Fuller, E., Bankiewicz, U., Davies, B., Mandalia, D., and Stocker, B. (2019) "The Food and You Survey," *Wave 5, Combined Report for England, Wales and Northern Ireland*, Food Standard Agency and NatCean Social Research, UK.

Genn, H. (1993) "Business Responses to the Regulation of Health and Safety in England." *Law and Policy* 15, no. 3: 219–233.

Giuliani, A., Lorenzoni, G., and Visentin, M. (2015) "New Wines in New Bottles: The 'Renaissance' of the Italian Wine Industry." *Industry and Innovation* 22, no. 8: 729–52, https://doi.org/10.1080/13662716.2015.1114914.

Gunningham, N. (2002) "Regulating Small and Medium Sized Enterprises." *Journal of Environmental Law* 14, no. 1: 3–32.

Gunningham, N. (2015) "Compliance, Deterrence and Beyond." In *Compliance and Enforcement in Environmental Law*, edited by Lee Paddock. Cheltenham, UK: Edward Elgar Publishers – SSRN RegNet Research Paper No. 2015/87, https://ssrn.com/abstract=2646427 or https://doi.org/10.2139/ssrn.264642.

Hansson, S. O. (2017) "Science Denial as a Form of Pseudoscience." *Studies in History and Philosophy of Science* Part A, 63: 39–47, https://doi.org/10.1016/j.shpsa.2017.05.002.

Henson, S. and Heasman, M. (1998) "Food Safety Regulation and the Firm: Understanding the Compliance Process." *Food Policy* 23, no. 1: 9–23.

Hutter, B. H., and Amodu, T. (2008) *Risk Regulation and Compliance: Food Safety in the UK*. London: London School of Economics and Political Science.

Hutter, B.M., and Jones, C. (2007) "From Government to Governance: External Influences on Business Risk Management." *International Journal of Regulation and Governance* 1, no. 1: 27–45.
Hodges, C. (2015) *Law and Corporate Behaviour*. London: Hart/Beck Bloomsbury Publishing.
Hodges, C., and Steinholtz, R. (2017) *Ethical Business Practice and Regulation*. London: Hart/Beck Bloomsbury Publishing.
Jaffee, S., Henson, S., Unnevehr, L., Grace, D., and Cassou, E. (2019) "The Safe Food Imperative: Accelerating Progress in Low- and Middle-Income Countries." Agriculture and Food Series. Washington, DC: World Bank.
Kahneman, D., Slovic, D., and Tversky, A. (1982) *Judgment under Uncertainty: Heuristics and Biases*. Cambridge: Cambridge University Press.
McKean, J. D. (2001) "The Importance of Traceability for Public Health and Consumer Protection." *Revue Scientifique et Technique (International Office of Epizootics)* 20, no. 2: 363–71, https://doi.org/10.20506/rst.20.2.1280.
Manion S. (2012) "A Science-Based Endeavor: Interpreting Contamination Prevention in the Food Safety Modernization Act." *Penn State Law Review* 117: 537–62. www.pennstatelawreview.org/117/2/117-2-Comment_Manion.pdf.
Marks, A. B. (2016) "A New Governance Recipe for Food Safety Regulation." *Loyola University Chicago Law Journal* 47, no. 3, https://ssrn.com/abstract=2802860.
OECD (Organisation for Co-operation and Economic Development). (2000) *Reducing the Risk of Policy Failure: Challenges for Regulatory Compliance*, www.oecd.org/regreform/regulatory-policy/1910833.pdf.
Ogus, A. (1994) *Regulation: Legal Form and Economic Theory*. Oxford: Clarendon Press.
Purnhagen, K. (2014) "The Virtue of Cassis De Dijon 25 Years Later – It Is Not Dead, It Just Smells Funny." In *Varieties of European Economic Law and Regulation*, edited by Kai Purnhagen and Peter Rott. Dordrecht: Springer.
Sadilek, A., Kautz, H., DiPrete, L., Labus, B., Portman, E., Teitel, J., and Silenzio, V. (2017) "Deploying nEmesis: Preventing Foodborne Illness by Data Mining Social Media." *AI Magazine* 38, no. 1: 37–48, https://doi.org/10.1609/aimag.v38i1.2711.
Schomberg, J. P., Haimson, O. L., Hayes, G. R., and Anton-Culver, H. (2016) "Supplementing Public Health Inspection via Social Media." *PloS one* 11, no. 3, https://doi.org/10.1371/journal.pone.0152117.
Simon, P. A., Leslie, P., Run, G., Jin, G. Z., Reporter, R., Aguirre, A., and Fielding, J. E. (2005) "Impact of Restaurant Hygiene Grade Cards on Foodborne-Disease Hospitalizations in Los Angeles County." *Journal of Environmental Health* 67, no. 7: 32–6, www.ncbi.nlm.nih.gov/pubmed/15794461.
Tyler, T. R. (2003) "Procedural Justice, Legitimacy, and the Effective Rule of Law." *Crime and Justice* 30: 283–357.
Van der Meulen, B. M. (2013) "The Structure of European Food Law." *Laws* 2, no. 2: 69–98, https://doi.org/10.3390/laws2020069.
Van der Meulen, S., Boin, G., Bousoula, I., Conte-Salinas, N., Paganizza, V., Montanari, F., Rodriguez Fuentes, V., and van der Meulen, B. (2015) "Fighting Food Fraud." *European Food and Feed Law Review* 10, no. 1: 2–13.
Vickers, I., James, P., Smallbone, D. and Baldock, R. (2005) "Understanding Small Firm Responses to Regulation." *Policy Studies* 26, no. 2: 149–169.
Wagstaff, D. J. (1986) "Public Health and Food Safety: A Historical Association." *Public Health Reports*, 101, no. 6, www.ncbi.nlm.nih.gov/pmc/articles/PMC1477676/pdf/pubhealthrep00180-0062.pdf.
Watts, R., Burgess, K., and Joiner, S. (2019) "Food Hygiene Ratings: Councils Struggle to Keep Up with Restaurant Inspections," *The Times*, October 15, www.thetimes.co.uk/article/food-hygiene-ratings-councils-struggle-to-keep-up-with-restaurant-inspections-spg9w8735.
Yapp, C., and Fairman, R. (2006) "Factors Affecting Food Safety Compliance within Small and Medium-Sized Enterprises: Implications for Regulatory and Enforcement Strategies." *Food Control* 17: 42–51, https://doi.org/10.1016/j.foodcont.2004.08.007.
Young, J. H. (1985) "The Pig That Fell into the Privy: Upton Sinclair's The Jungle and the Meat Inspection Amendments of 1906." *Bulletin of the History of Medicine* 59, no. 4: 467–80.
Young, J. H. (1989) *Pure Food: Securing the Federal Food and Drugs Act of 1906*. Princeton: Princeton University Press.

67

Global Supply Chain Auditing

Galit A. Sarfaty

Abstract: The governance of global supply chains is a ripe area of study for legal scholars. As part of an analysis of the governance of multi-tiered global supply chains and the implementation of recent supply chain transparency laws, this chapter analyzes the central role of supply chain auditors. These actors conduct human rights due diligence and implement supply chain policies on behalf of companies, which are in effect outsourcing their compliance obligations. In this chapter, I first discuss the emergence of a supply chain-audit regime in response to recent legislation, industry standards, and reputational pressure on companies to enhance their social and environmental performance. Next, I analyze concerns over the efficacy of supply chain auditors in incentivizing improvements in corporate compliance and behavior. Among the critiques are that audits advance the interests of downstream buyers; auditors are reluctant to report fraud; audits do not move beyond first-tier suppliers; audits are of limited duration; auditors fail to engage with workers; audit results are not released to the public; and suppliers have an incentive to cheat. Finally, I briefly offer remedies that have been proposed to address some of the major critiques and thereby enhance the effectiveness of the supply chain-auditing regime.

67.1 INTRODUCTION

Global outsourcing – the practice of subcontracting business to third parties in other countries – has become a trillion-dollar industry, with an annual growth rate of between 12 percent and 26 percent across functions (Deloitte 2014: 14). According to Peter Drucker (1998), whom many consider the father of modern management theory, outsourcing is one of the greatest industry structure shifts of the century. The governance of global supply chains is therefore a ripe area of study for legal scholars.

The globalization of business has led companies to increasingly outsource production to third-party suppliers in countries plagued by weak governance. Although the reliance on these often complex and multi-tiered global supply chains has provided economic benefits to workers in developing countries, recent tragedies – such as the 2013 Rana Plaza garment factory collapse in Bangladesh that killed over 1,100 workers and a string of suicides at Foxconn manufacturing plant, Apple's main supplier in China – highlight the human rights risks at stake when companies outsource. These abuses range from corporate complicity in labor rights violations to indirect support of corrupt or oppressive regimes (Holliday 2005; Schrempf 2011; Wettstein 2012). Abuses can occur at any level of a supply chain, from the first tier of direct suppliers to layers of subcontractors to the firms providing raw material inputs.

International and domestic legal instruments have emerged to regulate corporate management of third-party suppliers, particularly with respect to their human rights practices. While voluntary codes of conduct, third-party certification systems, and international soft law operate in this field, they have had a limited effect on corporate behavior (Simons and Macklin 2014; Short, Toffel, and Hugill 2016). Domestic legislation is emerging as an alternative method for regulating the extraterritorial human rights abuses of corporations and for achieving corporate accountability. State governments are demanding more information on the origins of a company's products and all its components. An ever-growing body of regulations reflects the growing trend toward supply chain transparency (Mares 2018; Sarfaty 2015). Recently passed and proposed regulations in a variety of jurisdictions require companies to publicly disclose information on their global supply chains, including due diligence measures that they have undertaken to prevent human rights violations by third-party suppliers.

As part of an analysis of the governance of multi-tiered global supply chains and the implementation of recent supply chain transparency laws, this chapter analyzes the central role of supply chain auditors. These actors conduct human rights due diligence and implement supply chain policies on behalf of companies, which are in effect outsourcing their compliance obligations. In this chapter, I will first discuss the emergence of a supply chain-audit regime in response to recent legislation, industry standards, and reputational pressure on companies to enhance their social and environmental performance. Next, I will analyze concerns over the efficacy of supply chain auditors in incentivizing improvements in corporate compliance and behavior. Among the critiques are that audits advance the interests of downstream buyers; auditors are reluctant to report fraud; audits do not move beyond first-tier suppliers; audits are of limited duration; auditors fail to engage with workers; audit results are not released to the public; and suppliers have an incentive to cheat. Finally, I will briefly offer remedies that have been proposed to address some of the major critiques and thereby enhance the effectiveness of the supply chain-auditing regime.

67.2 THE EMERGENCE OF A SUPPLY CHAIN-AUDIT REGIME

The modern trend in supply chain regulation and governance auditing has been the creation of a "benchmarking regime" in which auditors apply various sets of benchmarking standards (either internal or external to the buyer) to suppliers (LeBaron and Lister 2015). These standards can take many forms and range from corporate codes of conduct to third-party standards and certifications. I will describe the role of auditors in monitoring internal and third-party codes of conduct, and the development of a third-party assurance industry.

The rise of public condemnation for labor conditions in the 1990s led many large multinational corporations (MNCs), such as Nike and Hewlett Packard (HP), to adopt internal corporate codes of conduct (Esbenshade 2001; Bartley 2007; O'Rourke 2003). While most large companies have their own supplier codes of conduct and primarily utilize internal monitoring standards (Tsai and Wu 2018: 244), they have begun to rely on third-party auditors to conduct audit validation (Distelhorst et al. 2015; McAllister 2012). For example, HP "periodically employs professional third-party auditors in response to allegations of major problems at suppliers and also to validate their own internal auditing procedures" (Distelhorst et al. 2015: 227). However, according to Distelhorst et al.'s (2015) study, third-party audits comprised only 9 percent of all of HP's audits, and there was relatively no difference in audit quality.

The use of external auditors to monitor internal codes of conduct has gradually increased because it is viewed as more rigorous and objective than relying on internal auditors (McAllister 2014; Casey 2006). According to Islam, Deegan, and Gray (2018: 204–5), "the significance of employing external auditors is that they are believed to be relatively independent bodies and receiving assurance from these bodies creates a sense of legitimacy." Their study found that third-party auditors were regularly called in when firms came under threat of media exposure or sustained NGO campaigns. As one internal auditor is reported as saying, "[w]hen something goes wrong, you can imagine third party auditing is imminent" (Islam et al. 2018: 206). The authors conclude that "[t]he greater the media attention or perceptions about the severity of the potential crisis, the greater the perceived likelihood that third parties would be involved in the audit practice" (Islam et al. 2018: 206).

This proposition is also supported by the experience of Apple with regard to Foxconn, one of the company's largest suppliers in China. Apple only started utilizing third-party auditors to monitor working conditions after a spate of worker suicides at Foxconn led to a public relations crisis (Zenker 2018: 309). At that time, Apple brought in the reputable labor rights consulting firm Verité to investigate its production facilities in China. Prior to this incident, however, the company was internally monitoring its suppliers (Clarke and Boersma 2017: 120). This sort of responsive behavior suggests that third-party monitors are often used to legitimize CSR programs and to abate public criticism in the wake of a crisis.

When firms are not auditing to their own internal standards, the alternative is to have a third-party monitor audit to an external benchmark standard or certification. Using external certification standards allows downstream companies to ensure that they outsource only from suppliers with determined labor standards (Zenker 2018: 301). There is a plethora of standards that firms can seek to utilize, depending on the industry, raw commodity, or region of sourcing. As of 2017, the International Trade Center (ITC) listed a total 238 different "standards, codes, protocols" in a standards map intended to help companies align with frameworks that could apply for them (Meidinger 2019: 10).

The proliferation of private performance codes combined with a growing army of private inspectors, certifiers, and auditors has developed into a "third party assurance industry" (Blair, Williams, and Lin 2008: 329). The growing demand for third-party assurance services is due to a number of factors, including: 1) a growth in international trade and outsourcing; 2) increased complexity and division of labor within supply chains; 3) the need for assurance that suppliers can meet the various quality and delivery requirements of corporate buyers; and 4) a need to ensure that suppliers are meeting labor, human rights, and environmental standards (Blair et al. 2008: 329). Blair et al. (2008: 359) conclude that this alternative form of regulation is a means to impose norms and "rule of law values such as transparency and accountability" in the Global South.

Thus, third-party assurance provides "an enforcement mechanism that would otherwise be lacking in many countries" (Blair et al. 2008: 358). Private regulation via codes of conduct and monitoring may be the only way that workers' rights and labor conditions are addressed in many developing countries (Parella 2014: 792). Though many of these countries ostensibly have strong regulations on paper, they often lack the means to enforce their own laws in practice (Distelhorst et al. 2015). However, other scholars argue that labor standards imposed by Western companies and external auditors on suppliers in developing countries may be a form of "cultural imperialism" (Khan and Lund-Thomsen 2011). For instance, a grower from Zambia expressed apprehension about the fact that his farm was audited by Verité Asia, which utilized only Asian auditors who had no knowledge of the local language and imposed foreign working standards (for factories in Asia) with little regard to the local customs and traditions of African farming (Blowfield and Dolan 2008: 10–11).

67.3 CRITIQUES OF THE SUPPLY CHAIN-AUDITING REGIME

There are a number of important concerns over the efficacy of supply chain auditors in incentivizing improvements in corporate compliance and behavior. Critiques include auditors' limited scope and on-the-ground expertise, their reluctance to report fraud, the difficulty of auditing beyond first-tier suppliers, and the promotion of superficial compliance. In this section I will review these critiques and their implications for the use of auditors to monitor supply chains for human rights and labor violations.

67.3.1 *Audits Advance the Interests of Downstream Buyers*

One of the most devastating critiques of the supply chain auditing regime is that it does not advance the various social objectives (e.g., improving labor conditions, environmental compliance, etc.) that it was originally intended to promote. For example, LeBaron, Lister, and Dauvergne (2017) argue that the audit regime disproportionately benefits the MNCs that utilize auditing to protect their business interests. MNCs, they argue, are merely shaping the various auditing standards in ways that legitimate and protect their business. In other words, the problem is not with the methodology or application of auditing but rather with the interests of the auditing regime itself and the disproportionate power that MNCs have in dictating its application (LeBaron et al. 2017). At the core of the auditing regime is the interest of MNCs to answer to customer pressure and legal regimes and, as such, MNCs exert considerable control over the process, including: who to audit, when to audit, how far down the supply chain they will audit, which auditing standard to use, which corrective action plan (CAP) to implement in case of violation, and which auditors to deploy. This often results in a façade of social and environmental compliance that seeks to placate buyers, suppliers, and consumers without promoting real changes in behavior (Clarke and Boersma 2017: 126).

According to this critique, brand-conscious firms may be using ethical auditing programs to position themselves as socially responsible companies in order to gain the market advantage that comes from sourcing from responsible suppliers (LeBaron et al. 2017). The same firms may concurrently be placing large orders from noncompliant suppliers (LeBaron et al. 2017). As Koenig-Archibugi (2017: 345) elucidates, MNCs will place small orders with CSR-compliant Sri Lankan suppliers to claim that they source from "ethically safe countries" such as Sri Lanka, and yet place large orders from non-CSR-compliant suppliers in Bangladesh, China, etc.

Some of the more extreme critics have argued that the entire auditing framework is corrupt. As one of LeBaron and Lister's (2015: 915) informants explains: "[T]here is a whole industry of ethical auditors out there now who will find nothing if you pay them to go and find nothing." These critics argue that the auditors are trying to prove that violations are not occurring rather than that they are indeed occurring (LeBaron and Lister 2015: 915). The irony of the situation, as Esbenshade (2001: 106) notes, is that "those who profit from abuses within the system are in control of regulating it." Moreover, Islam et al. (2018: 205) view auditing as principally a mechanism for CSR legitimation in which the "human condition is reduced to 'the code' and then the code is reduced to a checklist which can be represented in rating, for example, three traffic light colors." Thus, they conclude that audits are effectively a strategy for buyers and their suppliers to advance their interests and are not actually advancing workers' rights (Islam et al. 2018: 205).

However, this extreme critique of ethical auditing and private compliance regimes is debated among scholars. According to Konefal and Hatanaka (2011: 125), supports of third-party certification cite its technical and objective character while critics argue that it is a political and power-laden process. Distelhorst and Locke (2018: 708) adopt a middle-ground position and found the existence of "economic incentives for compliance in industries characterized by strong activist campaigns and private regulatory responses from industry." Vogel (2010) also recognizes the achievements of private regulatory mechanisms in pressuring firms to adopt higher social and environmental standards, particularly those firms that have been the target of public criticism. Yet he argues that business compliance with codes has been uneven and that the overall impact on addressing social, environmental, and human rights problems is limited (Vogel 2010: 79–80).

67.3.2 *Auditors Fail to Engage with Workers*

Ever since O'Rourke's damning critique of the labor monitoring practices of PricewaterhouseCoopers (PwC) in 2000, there has been a constant and consistent line of criticism that auditors do not properly engage with workers and their findings are, therefore, tainted by the role of management. In this report, O'Rourke (2000: 3–4) highlights that PwC's auditors failed to speak with workers that had not been selected and coached by a factory's management. Most workers were interviewed in the workplace rather than in a safe environment (O'Rourke 2000: 3–4). This practice is deeply problematic as it allows management to identify which workers are being questioned and leads to potential threats of retaliation against workers. Both factors are clear deterrents to candor during the interview process (O'Rourke 2000: 3–4). Another study found that even though many workers often prefer to be interviewed off-site, auditors often do not remove them from their working environment because this requires more time and organization (Courville 2003: 276). Barrientos and Smith (2007: 725) identify a similar trend in their work on corporate codes falling under the UK Ethical Trading Initiative, as they find suppliers training their workforce in answering auditors.

Esbenshade's (2001: 98) fundamental critique of supply chain auditing in Los Angeles' garment industry was that it did not actively engage the workers in "any participatory defense of their rights." The trend of excluding workers from the table has resulted in what Esbenshade calls "the social accountability contract" which forms strictly between employers, their contractors, governments, and NGOs but excludes the workers themselves. While the social accountability contract aims to protect workers, it fails to empower them as participants in the monitoring system (Esbenshade 2001: 99).

67.3.3 *Audits Do Not Move Beyond First-Tier Suppliers*

Another crucial problem in the supply chain auditing framework is the fact that auditors rarely go beyond first-tier suppliers (LeBaron et al. 2017; LeBaron and Lister 2015; Nadvi and Raj-Reichert 2015). Auditors frequently "pass-the-buck" for auditing lower tier suppliers to the first-tier supplier, which creates the illusion of a rigorous auditing scheme but is deeply lacking in practice. When an upstream supplier is found to be violating labor conditions, the end purchaser and the first-tier supplier can often plead ignorance and hide behind their own CSR standards.

This gives little incentive to midstream suppliers or final purchasers to ensure that the factories below them have adequate human rights and labor protections (Zenker 2018: 302).

Furthermore, tier-one suppliers often turn to unauthorized subcontracting to avoid detection for violations during the auditing process (Mueller, Gomes dos Santos, and Seuring 2009). As evidenced by the Rana Plaza incident, unauthorized subcontracting can have dire consequences and is one of the principal reasons why buyers' audits have not been effective in detecting unsafe working conditions (Parella 2014: 790). Barrientos (2008) sees the use of third-party subcontracting as the "Achilles' heel" of corporate codes of conduct because if companies are exposed as having poor working conditions, then the buyer suffers the potential blowback from the media. Even when firms do audit and monitor the lower tiers of supply chains, industry codes of conduct and internal codes of conduct are largely absent beyond the first, or at best second, tier of suppliers (Nadvi and Raj-Reichert 2015; Casey 2006).

67.3.4 *Audits Are of Limited Duration*

One of the most prominent critiques of auditing is that it is, by its very nature, merely a window into factory conditions at any given point in time. Many scholars have recognized this inherent dilemma:

> Audits take a partial snapshot of a supplier on a given day; by their very nature audits cannot reveal the full picture of the operations of suppliers and sub-contractors. Because most audits are announced, or at least semi-announced, as one informant said, the factory usually "has the opportunity to drill their people on what they need to say" (LeBaron et al.: 969).
>
> [E]ven if a facility is audited several times annually, who is watching all of the other days of the year? (Parella 2014: 789).
>
> Private monitoring can, at best, offer very sporadic snapshots of conditions in factories and, at worst, convey only the appearance provided by the factory owner on the day of the visit (Esbenshade 2001: 116).

After conducting several interviews with professional auditors in Bangladesh, Islam et al. (2018: 204) concluded that the auditors had a clear intention of completing their on-site investigations within a single day. The time constraints for the audit, in other words, are often predetermined and are set irrespective of the on-the-ground circumstances. Similarly, Locke, Amengual, and Mangla (2009: 332) found that auditors only spent one working day per factory audit, with most of this time spent reviewing documents rather than inspecting the actual factory. Each factory was only audited once or twice per year with an average of 1.84 times globally. Moreover, because audits are often pre-announced, suppliers can prepare to comply for the duration of the audit only and then resume regular noncompliant operations when the auditors leave (Lund-Thomsen 2008; Blowfield and Dolan 2008).

67.3.5 *Auditors Are Reluctant to Report Fraud*

There are several dangers that come with third-party auditing and the principal-agent relationship that is created between them. Corona and Randhawa (2010) have utilized game theory to examine iterative interactions (repeat audits) between the auditor and the firm ordering the auditing. They argue that reputational concerns for the auditor will lead to "slippery-slope interactions" where the auditor is more reluctant to report fraud under certain circumstances.

If auditors fail to find violations during their first audit, they will be more reluctant to report violations during their second (or later) audit because it would bring a potential reputational impact that they had failed to detect the infraction on their prior visit. This problem is also influenced by the manager's reputation of the firm that is being audited. Where the manager's reputation is high, they find that auditors will become "handcuffed" in the second interaction and this allows for managers to commit fraud in the second interaction with great impunity.

The auditor has to worry not only about losing future contracts with that manager's firm but also about their reputation as an efficacious auditor in the marketplace. The auditor has an incentive to not report the potential infraction because the manager has a good reputation and the auditor's silence will be likely to go unnoticed. The manager can also get away with acting with greater impunity in later interactions because of the increased reputational costs to the auditor the longer the infraction goes unreported.

When the manager's reputation is low, however, the auditor, Corona and Randhawa (2010) argue, will be more willing to report fraudulent activity that they detect because the market would expect fraudulent activity to be reported. Yet, there is still increased reputational pressures on the auditor to avoid reporting later infractions the longer that the relationship goes on. This is because of the inherent suspicion that others will believe that the auditor failed to detect the infraction at an earlier point.

67.3.6 *Suppliers Have an Incentive to Cheat*

The current auditing system results in strong incentives for suppliers to cheat. Compliance does not pay for suppliers if they must cover the costs of auditing and suffer the financial losses associated with compliance (e.g., higher wages, reduced work hours, labor unions) with no guarantee of long-term business relationships with downstream purchasers (Gould 2005; Lund-Thomsen 2008). Because of the ever-present fear that a buyer will terminate a contract with a supplier that is not compliant with codes of conduct, suppliers are incentivized to cheat (Parella 2014: 789).

The supplier's principal objective is often merely to pass the audit rather than addressing the underlying issues that the audits are designed, in theory, to address (Jiang 2009: 88). Indeed, suppliers have found various ways of avoiding detection: for instance, preparing double sets of books and coaching workers before audits (Parella 2014: 804–5; O'Rourke 2000: 3–4). O'Rourke (2000: 3) notes that factory managers regularly prepped workers for interviews with PwC auditors and often provided them with falsified documents which could not be verified. Audit evasions regularly include hiding child laborers and other workers before the auditors arrive (Parella 2014; Moore, de Silva, and Hartmann 2012; Blowfield and Dolan 2008). The result of more rigorous auditing standards has only led to what LeBaron et al. (2017: 108) call an "arms race" between auditors and suppliers – the suppliers find new ways to deceive or bribe the auditors and the buyers try to find ways to keep auditing effective for their purposes. In fact, suppliers are now even hiring former auditors to help them avoid detection (LeBaron et al. 2017: 102).

67.3.7 *Audit Results Are Not Released to the Public*

As a form of private regulation, audits are most often conducted at the bequest of a buyer, and are not released to the public. Unless the parties are required to disclose the information of their audit findings by contract, or in very rare circumstances by governmental regulation, the information disclosed in audits remain private (Lin 2009). Auditors are regularly bound by rigid confidentiality clauses that are imposed by their principals and their wealth of information is left to the discretion of the firm to disclose (LeBaron and Lister 2015: 915). Confidentially allows firms to avoid "unfavorable and uncontrollable exposure to the public" and enables them to potentially correct noncompliance issues without "paying a reputational price" (Lin 2009: 727). Yet, as a result of this confidentiality, the information obtained during most audits cannot be verified by other researchers or NGOs, and is therefore of no use to public efforts to improve human rights and working conditions in factories (O'Rourke 2000: 7).

Moreover, third-party benchmarking organizations such as the Fair Labor Association (FLA) and Social Accountability International (SAI) have historically not published any substantive information on their regulatory practices (O'Rourke 2003: 21). They also do not disclose or provide lists of suppliers that have failed to pass their standards to the public (Lin 2009: 727). Similarly, commodities-specific multi-industry organizations such as the Responsible Minerals Initiative (RMI) do not provide audit reports to their corporate members, which can only access the level of conformance of a supplier. In a study of Bangladeshi suppliers, Islam et al. (2018: 204) found that audits were rarely disclosed to any form of third party outside of the factory owners and the MNC purchaser. They interviewed one internal auditor who pointed out that their audit teams were not required, or even permitted, to talk to NGOs or the local community unless they were formally instructed by their head office (Islam et al. 2018: 207).

67.4 THE FUTURE OF SUPPLY CHAIN AUDITING

The effectiveness of supply chain auditing moving forward depends on whether the regime can truly improve labor conditions and the human rights of local workers. There have been various remedies proposed to address some of the above critiques, which I briefly summarize now.

With regard to ensuring that audits do not advance the interests of buyers and do not engage with workers, Locke et al. (2009: 345) recommend that auditors should be "trained and empowered to engage in commitment rather than just traditional compliance." If the role of auditors were shifted from "box-ticking" to a deeper form of engagement with the supplier's factory, then, according to their reasoning, this would obviate the problems associated with the interests that are being advanced through auditing. Yet, even Locke et al. (2009: 346) admit that a commitment-oriented approach alone is no panacea.

Other scholars similarly call for firms to give workers a more central focus in monitoring practices and suggest that workers be given clear assurances and protections for reporting problems (O'Rourke 2000; Egels-Zandén 2007). Moreover, local NGOs and worker-support organizations should be involved in the process to verify that workers are being adequately protected (O'Rourke 2000: 8). Some auditing frameworks, such as the Fair Food Program (FFP), already require that third-party auditors speak with at least 50 percent of the workers on an audited farm. This style of engagement with the workers has been heralded as a potential solution by Parella (2014: 812), as it would represent a shift from "audit-based monitoring" to a more participatory and compliant form of monitoring that would engage with workers. Offering workers a grievance mechanism to express their concerns would further improve supplier compliance (Parella 2014: 812).

The nascent worker-driven social responsibility (WSR) programs, for example developed through the Florida-based Coalition for Immokalee Workers (CIW)'s FFP, puts the workers at the center of the auditing system, from design to implementation. As Asbed and Hitov (2017: 531) argue, if "backed by the purchasing decisions and power of multinational mega-corporations," the WSR system proves to be highly efficient to address human rights abuses in global supply chains.

The methodology of auditors also needs to be addressed. In order to move beyond first-tier suppliers, Zenker (2018: 329–30) suggests that private regulators should utilize governmental licensing resources to compile databases of the various suppliers and subcontractors. She posits that disclosure of subcontractors should be a requirement for achieving any form of CSR certification, and that downstream buyers should be required to audit each and every supplier and subcontractor in the chain. Yet it remains to be determined who pays for the expansive auditing costs of developing a database and moving all the way down the supply chain. One possibility is for MNCs to share the costs of auditing through joint or shared audits of the same supplier (Caro et al. 2018). The costs of auditing, in other words, could be split among many purchasers rather than pushed to the supplier. Passing the costs of auditing downstream to buyers would give suppliers less incentive to cheat (Parella 2014).

Auditors' reluctance to report fraud and suppliers' incentive to cheat are particularly difficult problems to address. McAllister (2012: 40) proposes that auditors could be barred from re-auditing for the same client for at least five years. This could reduce the incentive to fraudulently pass factories as compliant in order to obtain future work. The auditors would have to worry more about their reputation than the prospect of securing repeat work. In order to improve supplier performance and provide a disincentive to cheating, Jiang (2009: 78) suggests establishing long-term contractual relationships between suppliers and buyers. If suppliers did not have to fear losing their production orders as a result of audits, then they might be more willing to comply.

Another way to remove the incentive to cheat among suppliers would be for companies to apply less stringent timelines and reduce their production quotas and guidelines. For instance, Lin-Hi and Blumberg's (2017: 794) study of the Chinese toy industry highlights the fact that buyers often wait until the last minute before placing their toy orders before the holidays to maximize their market analysis. As a result, suppliers are often forced to turn to such mechanisms as ramping up overtime hours and unauthorized outsourcing in order to fill their short-notice and highly flexible orders (Jiang 2009: 79). Reducing the production demands on suppliers (e.g., quality control, turnaround time), combined with removing the fear of contract termination based on noncompliance, would give factory managers less of an incentive to evade auditing measures. However, MNCs may be unwilling to lower their commercial expectations for supplier performance as this would have the potential of minimizing profits. The general mindset that "buyers are only concerned with getting the right quality product at the right price and suppliers are concerned with supplying the right quality product at a profitable price" will likely continue to impede improvement in this area (Jiang 2009: 79).

While these proposed remedies are promising, there remain gaps in the literature with respect to how third-party monitoring could be used to protect human rights within global supply chains. For instance, what is the difference between the behavior of commercial versus not-for-profit auditors, as well as small or medium-sized buyers versus multinational firms? How does recent supply chain disclosure legislation improve or hinder the existing third-party auditing regime, which has primarily been studied in the context of voluntary schemes? Future scholars and advocates have significant room to expand both empirically and theoretically in this area.

REFERENCES

Asbed, Greg, and Steve Hitov. 2017. "Preventing Forced Labor in Corporate Supply Chains. The Fair Food Program and Worker-Driven Social Responsibility." *Wake Forest Law Review* 52:497–531.
Barrientos, Stephanie. 2008. "Contract Labor: The Achilles Heel of Corporate Codes in Commercial Value Chains." *Development & Change* 39(6):977–90.
Barrientos, Stephanie, and Sally Smith. 2007. "Do Workers Benefit from Ethical Trade? Assessing Codes of Labour Practice in Global Production Systems." *Third World Quarterly* 28(4):713–29.
Bartley, Tim. 2007. "Institutional Emergence in an Era of Globalization: The Rise of Transnational Private Regulation of Labor and Environmental Conditions," *American Journal of Sociology* 113 (2):297–351.
Blair, Margaret M., Cynthia A. Williams, and Li-Wen Lin. 2008. "The New Role for Assurance Services in Global Commerce." *Journal of Corporations Law* 33(2): 325–60.
Blowfield, Michael E., and Catherine S. Dolan. 2008. "Stewards of Virtue? The Ethical Dilemma of CSR in African Agriculture." *Development & Change* 39(1):1–23.
Caro, Felipe, Prashant Chintapalli, Kuman Rajaram, and Chris S. Tang. 2018. "Improving Supplier Compliance through Joint and Shared Audits with Collective Penalty." *Manufacturing and Service Operations Management* 20(2):363–80.
Casey, Roseann. 2006. "Meaningful Change – Raising the Bar in Supply Chain Workplace Standards." Corporate Social Responsibility Initiative, Working paper No. 29. Cambridge, MA: John F. Kennedy School of Government, Harvard University.
Clarke, Thomas, and Martjin Boersma. 2017. "The Governance of Global Value Chains: Unresolved Human Rights, Environmental and Ethical Dilemmas in the Apple Supply Chain." *Journal of Business Ethics* 143(1):111–31.
Corona, Carlos, and Ramandeep S. Randhawa. 2010. "The Auditor's Slippery Slope: An Analysis of Reputational Incentives." *Management Science* 56(6):924–37.
Courville, Sasha. 2003. "Social Accountability Audits: Challenging or Defending Democratic Governance?" *Law & Policy* 25(3):269–97.
Deloitte. 2014. "Deloitte's 2014 Global Outsourcing and Insourcing Survey." Accessed May 23, 2019. www2.deloitte.com/content/dam/Deloitte/us/Documents/strategy/us-2014-global-outsourcing-insourcing-survey-report-123114.pdf.
Distelhorst, Greg, and Richard M. Locke. 2018. "Does Compliance Pay? Social Standards and Firm-Level Trade." *American Journal of Political Science* 62(3):695–711.
Distelhorst, Greg, Richard M. Locke, Timea Pal, and Hiram Samel. 2015. "Production Goes Global, Compliance Stays Local: Private Regulation in the Global Electronics Industry." *Regulation & Governance* 9:224–42.
Drucker, Peter. 1998. *Peter Drucker on the Profession of Management*. Boston: Harvard Business School Press.
Egels-Zandén, Niklas. 2007. "Suppliers' Compliance with MNCs' Codes of Conduct: Behind the Scenes at Chinese Toy Suppliers." *Journal of Business Ethics* 75(1):45–62.
Esbenshade, Jill. 2001. "The Social Accountability Contract: Private Monitoring from Los Angeles to the Global Apparel Industry." *Labour Studies Journal* 26(1):98–120.
Gould, Daniella. 2005. "The Problem with Supplier Audits." *Corporate Responsibility Management* 2 (1):24–9.
Holliday, Ian. 2005. "Doing Business with Rights Violating Regimes Corporate Social Responsibility and Myanmar's Military Junta." *Journal of Business Ethics* 61:329–42.
Islam, Muhammad Azizul, Craig Deegan, and Rob Gray. 2018. "Social Compliance Audits and Multinational Corporation Supply Chain: Evidence from a Study of the Rituals of Social Audits." *Accounting and Business Research* 48(2):190–224.
Jiang, Bin. 2009. "Implementing Supplier Codes of Conduct in Global Supply Chains: Process Explanations from Theoretical and Empirical Perspectives." *Journal of Business Ethics* 85 (1):77–92.
Khan, Farzad Rafi, and Peter Lund-Thomsen. 2011. "CSR as Imperialism: Towards a Phenomenological Approach to CSR in the Developing World." *Journal of Change Management* 11(1): 73–90.

Koenig-Archibugi, Mathias. 2017. "Does Transnational Private Governance Reduce or Displace Labor Abuses? Addressing Sorting Dynamics Across Global Supply Chains." *Regulation and Governance* 11:343–52.

Konefal, Jason, and Maki Hatanaka. 2011. "Enacting Third-Party Certification: A Case Study of Science and Politics in Organic Shrimp Certification." *Journal of Rural Studies* 27:125–33.

LeBaron, Genevieve, and Jane Lister. 2015. "Benchmarking Global Supply Chain: The Power of the 'Ethical' Audit Regime." *Review of International Studies* 41:905–24.

LeBaron, Genevieve, Jane Lister, and Peter Dauvergne. 2017. "The New Gatekeeper: Ethical Audits as a Mechanism of Global Value Chain Governance." *In The Politics of Private Transnational Governance. by Contract*, eds. A. Claire Cutler and Thomas Dietz, 97–114. London: Routledge.

Lin, Li-Wen. 2009. "Legal Transplants through Private Contracting: Codes of Vendor Conduct in Global Supply Chains as an Example." *American Journal of Comparative Law* 57:711–44.

Lin-Hi, Nick, and Igor Blumberg. 2017. "The Power(lessness) of Industry Self-Regulation to Promote Responsible Labor Standards: Insights from the Chinese Toy Industry." *Journal of Business Ethics* 143:789–805.

Locke, Richard, Matthew Amengual, and Akshay Mangla. 2009. "Virtue Out of Necessity? Compliance, Commitment, and the Improvement of Labor Conditions in Global Supply Chains." *Politics and Society* 37(3):319–51.

Lund-Thomsen, Peter. 2008. "The Global Sourcing and Codes of Conduct Debate: Five Myths and Five Recommendations." *Development and Change* 39(6):1005–18.

Mares, Radu. 2018. "Corporate Transparency Laws: A Hollow Victory?" *Netherlands Quarterly of Human Rights* 36(2):189–213.

McAllister, Lesley K. 2012. "Regulation by Third-Party Verification." *Boston College Law Review* 53 (1):1–64.

2014. "Harnessing Private Regulation." *Michigan Journal of Environmental & Administrative Law* 3 (2):291–419.

Meidinger, Errol. 2019. "Governance Interactions in Sustainable Supply Chain Management." In *Transnational Business Governance Interactions: Enhancing Regulatory Capacity, Ratcheting Up Standards, and Empowering Marginalized Actors*, eds. Stepan Wood, Rebecca Schmidt, Errol Meidinger, Burkard Eberlein, and Kenneth Abbott. Cheltenham and Northampton, UK: Edward Elgar.

Moore, Lynda, Indrani de Silva, and Sara Hartmann. 2012. "An Investigation into the Financial Return on Corporate Social Responsibility in the Apparel Industry." *Journal of Corporate Citizenship* 45:105–22.

Mueller, Martin, Virginia Gomes dos Santos, and Stegan Seuring. 2009. "The Contribution of Environmental and Social Standards towards Ensuring Legitimacy in Supply Chain Governance." *Journal of Business Ethics* 89(4):509–23.

Nadvi, Khalid, and Gale Raj-Reichert. 2015. "Governing Health and Safety at Lower Tiers of the Computer Industry Global Value Chain." *Regulation & Governance* 9:243–58.

O'Rourke, Dara. 2000. "Monitoring the Monitors: A Critique of PricewaterhouseCoopers (PwC) Labor Monitoring." https://nature.berkeley.edu/orourke/PDF/pwc.pdf.

2003. "Outsourcing Regulation: Analyzing Nongovernmental Systems of Labor Standards and Monitoring." *Policy Studies Journal* 31:1–29.

Parella, Kishanthi. 2014. "Outsourcing Corporate Accountability." *Washington Law Review* 89 (3):747–818.

Sarfaty, Galit A. 2015. "Shining Light on Global Supply Chains." *Harvard International Law Journal* 56 (2):419–63.

Schrempf, Judith. 2011. "Nokia Siemens Networks: Just Doing Business – or Supporting an Oppressive Regime?" *Journal of Business Ethics* 103:95–110.

Short, Jodi, Michael Toffel, and Andrea Hugill. 2016. "Monitoring Global Supply Chains." *Strategic Management Journal* 37:1878–97.

Simons, Penelope, and Audrey Macklin. 2014. *The Governance Gap: Extractive Industries, Human Rights, and the Home State Advantage*. London: Routledge.

Tsai, Chang-hsien, and Yen-nung Wu. 2018. "What Conflict Mineral Rules Tell Us about the Legal Transplantation of Corporate Social Responsibility Standards without the State: From the United Nations to the United States to Taiwan." *Northwestern Journal of Law & Business* 38:233–84.

Vogel, David. 2010. "The Private Regulation of Global Corporate Conduct: Achievements and Limitations." *Business Society* 49(1):68–87.

Wettstein, Florian. 2012. "Silence as Complicity: Elements of a Corporate Duty to Speak Out against the Violation of Human Rights." *Business Ethics Quarterly* 22(1):37–61.

Zenker, Julia. 2018. "Made in Misery: Mandating Supply Chain Labor Compliance." *Vanderbilt Journal of Transnational Law* 51:297–331.

68

Corporations, Human Rights and Compliance

Wim Huisman

Abstract: In the last decades, human rights have entered the wide field of corporate social responsibilities and the subsequent standards that corporations have to comply with. While not yet in the form of hard law, international organizations such as the United Nations (UN) and the Organisation for Economic Co-operation and Development (OECD) have introduced principles and guidelines for business and human rights. The Special Rapporteur on Business and Human Rights for the UN Human Rights Council has designed the so-called 'Ruggie framework' in which corporations have the duty to respect human rights, while states have the duty to protect them. Many industries and corporations have adopted these principles and guidelines in their codes of conduct. While being non-enforceable, these principles and guidelines are often seen as embryonic law. Currently, a binding treaty on business and human rights is being debated by the UN. Also, on the national level, lawsuits against corporations for being involved in human rights abuses, both civil and criminal, have been brought to courts in various countries. Cases even amount to corporate involvement in breaches of international criminal law such as genocide, war crimes and crimes against humanity. As a response to the increasing awareness of the role of business in human rights violations, a plethora of judicial and non-judicial instruments has been introduced to hold corporations and their executives accountable and to ensure compliance with human rights standards. This chapter will first explore the human rights obligations of corporations and the ways in which corporations are responsible for the breach of these obligations. Second, we will explore what is known about actual corporate compliance with human rights standards and corporate involvement in human rights violations. Third, the chapter will discuss available instruments for enforcing corporate compliance with human rights standards and their use, before, fourth, assessing the various regulatory and non-regulatory interventions for potential effectiveness. Integrating contemporary models of business regulation and compliance management, the chapter will end by exploring possibilities to combine and order existing instruments into a coherent scheme of action.

68.1 INTRODUCTION

In the last decades, human rights have entered the wide field of corporate social responsibilities and the subsequent standards that corporations have to comply with. Business and human rights 'became an increasingly prominent feature on the international agenda in the 1990s' (Ruggie 2013: xxv). Owing to globalization, corporations became increasingly involved in human rights abuses in the low-wage countries they moved their production to, the developing nations they harvested their resources from and the fragile countries to which they supplied their goods or services, such goods and services possibly having been used for such abuses. Multinational corporations (MNCs) lacked awareness and the necessary instruments 'to manage the risks of their causing or contributing to human rights harm through their own activities and business relationships' (Ruggie 2013: xxvi). At the same time, business corporations were able to escape from the legal responsibilities of the companies involved with respect to the detrimental human rights or environmental impacts of business activities in their global value chains.

Yet, at the same time, a process of proliferation and consolidation of international human rights law and international criminal justice took hold, culminating in the Rome Statute and the establishment of the International Criminal Court (ICC) in 2002 and other international institutions such as the Tribunals for former Yugoslavia and Rwanda, as well as regional courts such as the Inter-American Court of Human Rights and national courts in Latin America. Corporate compliance with human rights standards became part of this international 'justice cascade' (Sikkink 2011). While not yet in the form of hard law, international organizations such as the United Nations (UN), the Organisation for Economic Co-operation and Development (OECD) and the International Labor Organization (ILO) have introduced principles and guidelines for business and human rights. The Special Rapporteur on Business and Human Rights for the UN Human Rights Council designed the so-called 'Ruggie framework' in which corporations have the duty to respect human rights, while states have the duty to protect them. Many industries and corporations have adopted these principles and guidelines in their codes of conduct. While they are non-enforceable, these principles and guidelines are often seen as embryonic law (Cerone 2016: 20). Currently, a binding treaty on business and human rights is being debated by the UN (Bilchitz 2016). Also, on the national level, lawsuits, both civil and criminal, against corporations for being involved in human rights abuses have been brought to courts in various countries (Kaleck and Saage-Maaß 2010). Cases even amount to corporate involvement in gross human rights violations and breaches of international criminal law, such as genocide, war crimes and crimes against humanity (Huisman and van Sliedregt 2010; Kelly 2016).

As a response to the increasing awareness of the role of business in these crimes, a plethora of judicial and non-judicial instruments has been introduced to hold corporations and their executives accountable and to ensure compliance with human rights standards. In this chapter, we explore the regulation, compliance and enforcement of the human rights obligations of business corporations.

This chapter first explores corporations' human rights obligations and the ways in which corporations are responsible for the breach of these obligations. For this, Section 68.2 discusses the leading benchmark for human rights standards for corporations, the UN Guiding Principles and the due diligence requirements they create for corporations to comply with. Second, we explore what is known about actual corporate (non-)compliance with human rights standards and corporate involvement in human rights violations. Section 68.3 presents the results of studies trying to measure the prevalence of corporate involvement in human rights abuses; it also compares such measurements and discusses the problems with them.

Third, the chapter looks at the available instruments for enforcing corporate compliance with human rights standards. After identifying a governance gap in enforcing corporate compliance with human rights standards, Section 68.4 explores the actual use of available instruments, including criminal and civil proceedings as well as non-judicial responses to abuses.

Fifth and finally, Section 68.5 aims towards building an integrative model for regulating business and human rights. Assessing the effects of current instruments and testing contemporary models of business regulation and compliance management, we propose a model to combine and order existing instruments into a coherent scheme of action. While effective regulation should be aimed at taking away the root causes of corporate involvement in human rights abuses, such as company-community conflicts over land and scarce resources (Macdonald, Marshall and Balaton-Chrimes 2017), this chapter does not address these underlying issues. Nor does it cover more fundamental issues of regulation of MNCs in the Global South (Dubash and Morgan 2013). The focus of this chapter is how international human rights standards translate to human rights obligations that corporations need to comply with and how to enforce these standards in cases where corporations are involved in human rights abuses.

68.2 HUMAN RIGHTS OBLIGATIONS OF CORPORATIONS

As public international law governs relations between states, states are subjects of international human rights law, as codified in treaties, conventions, covenants and statutes. Corporations do not owe direct human rights obligations. Yet, owing to globalization, large and multinational corporations can act as 'corporate sovereigns', enjoying rights in international law, exercising state functions in countries in which they operate and having turnovers that exceed the gross domestic product (GDP) of those countries (Garrett 2008). The UN Special Representative on Business and Human Rights, John Ruggie, stated that corporations increasingly function as actors on the international level, with the accessory capacity to carry rights and duties under international law.[1] And, also owing to globalization, MNCs have increasingly become involved in human rights violations in countries in which they operate, often fragile states and developing nations with poor human rights records owing to conflict and authoritarian rule. Especially the trade in 'blood diamonds' and other 'conflict commodities' in civil wars in Africa that emerged with the turn of the new millennium has framed the nexus of business and human rights (Le Billon 2012: 1). With Resolution 2005/69, the UN Office of the High Commissioner of Human Rights was required

> to identify and clarify standards of corporate responsibility and accountability for transnational corporations and other business enterprises with regard to human rights and to elaborate on the role of States in effectively regulating and adjudicating the role of transnational corporations and other business enterprises with regard to human rights, including through international cooperation.

68.2.1 *UN Guiding Principles on Business and Human Rights*

When asked to advise the UN Human Rights Council, the Special Representative on Business and Human Rights, Ruggie, recommended a three-pillar framework for improving the existing fragmentary and inconsistent approach: 'Protect, Respect and Remedy'. The three main pillars are: 1) the state duty to protect against human rights abuses by third parties, including business; 2) the corporate responsibility to respect human rights; and 3) greater

[1] UN Human Rights Council, A/HRC/035, 19 February 2007, para. 20.

access by victims to effective remedy, both judicial and non-judicial. The Human Rights Council unanimously approved the framework in 2008 and asked the Special Representative to 'operationalize' it, that is, provide concrete guidance and recommendations to states, businesses and other actors on the practical meaning and implications of the three pillars and their interrelationships.[2] For this purpose, Ruggie drafted the 'Guiding Principles on Business and Human Rights: Implementing the United Nations "Protect, Respect and Remedy" Framework', which were endorsed by the UN Human Rights Council in 2011. Ever since, this framework has been the leading reference for defining the human rights standards that corporations should adhere to as part of their 'social licence to operate' (Buhmann 2016). Buhmann shows that UN guidance has had a significant bearing on how public regulators seek to influence business conduct beyond human rights to broader corporate social responsibility concerns. This demonstrates a process of juridification entailing a legal framing of human rights expectations of companies, a proliferation of law into the field of business ethics, and an increased regulation by law of social actors and processes. And, as mentioned, the UN is currently exploring the next step of transforming the framework into a treaty that will directly bind and regulate business corporations (Bilchitz 2016). So when it comes to human rights, the Guiding Principles have become the benchmark for corporate compliance with human rights obligations.

Within the framework and Guiding Principles, the main focus for corporations is the responsibility to respect human rights. But what does being compliant with this principle mean? According to international law, the duty to respect requires that actors 'refrain from interfering directly or indirectly with the enjoyment' of human rights. This 'entails the prohibition of certain acts … that may undermine the enjoyment of rights' (Blitt 2012: 44). So far, the principle seems in line with the types of obligation generally found in criminal law, namely the obligation to refrain from harmful acts. And, indeed, the Guiding Principles first state that the responsibility to respect human rights requires that businesses should avoid infringing on the human rights of others. But they immediately add that corporations should '[s]eek to prevent or mitigate adverse human rights impacts that are directly linked to their operations, products or services by their business relationships' (Principle 13). Thus, according to the Guiding Principles, in order to be compliant, an organization has not only an obligation to refrain but also a duty to act.

68.2.2 *Compliance with Due Diligence Requirements*

This relates to the distinction between crimes of omission and those of commission traditionally made in criminal law (Hughes 1958). Crimes of commission involve doing something that the law says is wrong, while crimes of omission involve failing to fulfil a duty that the law has created. A common feature of corporate crime cases is an omission in meeting a regulatory obligation, that is, failing to take certain precautions to prevent harm to consumers, workers, the environment or competitors (Gobert and Punch 2003). Business regulation frequently imposes a duty on firms to take protective measures in their regular business processes. These measures involve extra time and money and therefore complicate business processes, thus creating opportunities to earn money by executing or offering services below the desired compliance level. Many law violations by legitimate organizations are therefore not crimes that require action; they are violations because a required action is

[2] UN Human Rights Council, A/HRC/14/27, 9 April 2010, para. 3.

not taken. Corporate offences, in other words, are more often crimes of omission rather than crimes of commission. Crimes of omission may be owing to organizational failure, but omissions may be more or less purposeful: sometimes, preventative action is purposefully left behind and rules are wilfully resisted; and, sometimes, a daily routine is continued without paying attention to rules that require extra investments (Huisman and van Erp 2013).

According to international law, the duty to respect obligates actors 'not to commit violations themselves' (Blitt 2012: 44). This is extra relevant, considering the finding in Section 68.3.2 that many known cases are of only indirect involvement in the human rights abuses committed by others. However, in the operationalization of this duty, the Guiding Principles draw a key distinction between obligation and responsibility. The responsibility to respect human rights means that business enterprises should act with due diligence to avoid infringing on the rights of others and to address adverse impacts with which they are involved. In order to meet this responsibility, business enterprises should have in place policies and processes, including due diligence processes to identify, prevent, mitigate and account for how they address their impacts on human rights; and processes to enable the remediation of any adverse human rights impacts they cause or to which they contribute (Principle 15). So the obligation to refrain in reality means the obligation to act and exercise due diligence, to prevent their own activities, or those of their local subsidiaries or suppliers, from having an adverse impact on the human rights of local employees, neighbours or communities. For this, the Guiding Principles stipulate that business enterprises should have policy measures and procedures in place and business models are to be made compatible with respect for human rights. In this light, not the legal entities but rather business strategy, organizational processes and managerial routines become constitutive elements of 'business enterprise' as meant in the Guiding Principles (Fasterling 2019). The operational programme for addressing human rights responsibilities is further spelled out in Principles 15 to 19 and may be viewed as a special form of risk management (Fasterling 2019: 21). For corporations, compliance with the principles on business and human rights boils down to implementing and maintaining a compliance management system, similar to the compliance management systems they use to comply with anti-bribery and anti-money laundering obligations and international standards such as the anti-money laundering guidelines of the Financial Action Task Force and the OECD anti-bribery convention (Chen and Soltes 2018; Bleker-van Eijk and Houben 2017).

68.2.3 *Embryonic Law*

The main point of criticism of the Guiding Principles as the leading instrument regulating business and human rights is that they are not legally binding and therefore are non-enforceable. Compliance with the obligations can be voluntary only and, as such, the Guiding Principles are discarded as non-effective in impacting and changing corporate human rights performances (Macleod and Lewis 2004). Yet, the validity of this mandatory–voluntary dichotomy is also criticized. First, the Guiding Principles have influenced other forms of public regulation of corporate social responsibilities, of which some are enforceable by law, especially on a national level (Buhmann 2016; Fasterling 2019). Second, the responsibilities and obligations laid out in the Guiding Principles may be enforceable in the near future and anticipating future liabilities may impact current corporate compliance policies. For this, Blitt (2012) refers to the 1948 Universal Declaration of Human Rights (UDHR), which is often credited as the first modern acknowledgement on the part of states that international law can in fact serve as a source of rights and responsibilities for individual as well as state actors. And while its content constituted an aspirational statement of human rights principles, rather than a binding treaty capable of establishing legally enforceable obligations on the part of states, it was slowly but gradually translated into law over the years (Blitt 2012: 38). According to Blitt (2012), the story of the UDHR is the story of how aspirational non-binding principles of 'soft law' can evolve continually over time into more durable and enforceable 'hard law', either in the form of a written treaty or in the consolidation of customary international practice. He predicts that the same will be true for the Guiding Principles. 'Put simply, although SRSG Ruggie's freshly minted Guiding Principles might strike one as plainly non-binding and aspirational today, these same principles can and will find surreptitious ways of growing up and becoming enforceable international norms that may carry serious repercussions for corporations, officers, and ill-prepared shareholders' (Blitt 2012: 41).

Finally, when the human rights violations that corporations can become involved in – not complying with the Guiding Principles – cross the threshold of international criminal law, being held legally liable for this involvement is already a reality. Gross human rights violations were criminalized as war crimes, crimes against humanity and genocide in the 1995 Rome Statute, which is the basis of the jurisdiction of the ICC (Stoitchkova 2010) and which has 139 states as signatories. And even those states that have not ratified the Rome Statute, such as the United States of America, still have implemented these core crimes of international criminal law into their domestic legal systems. As will be shown in Section 68.4, corporations and their executives can be and are being held liable for these gross human rights violations.

68.3 CORPORATE NON-COMPLIANCE

Research on the compliance of corporations with the human rights standards discussed in Section 68.2 is scarce. Specialized human rights groups such as the Business and Human Rights Resource Centre[3] and SOMO[4] monitor the compliance of individual corporations, but oversight of corporate compliance rates is missing. Available research surpassing the individual corporate level mostly focuses on non-compliance: corporations involved in human rights violations. Yet, available criminological studies aim not so much at the scale of violations but at identifying underlying causes of this form of corporate deviance (van Baar 2019), while legal studies usually limit themselves to mentioning a few contemporary cases before focusing on legal issues such as modes of liability (van der Wilt 2013).

68.3.1 *Corporate Human Rights Abuses*

A rare attempt to create some oversight of the prevalence of non-compliance was made by the Special Rapporteur on Business and Human Rights for the UN Human Rights Council. Ruggie collected and analysed 320 cases of alleged human rights abuses posted on the Business and Human Rights Resource Centre website from February 2005 to December 2007.[5] These entries connected alleged abuses to more than 250 companies. An initial coding of cases showed that all industry sectors were alleged to impact human rights, and impacts were alleged to occur in all regions. The final sample of allegations was sorted

3 www.business-humanrights.org/.
4 Centre for Research on Multinational Corporations, www.somo.nl.
5 UN Human Rights Council, A/HRC/8/5, Add. 2, 23 May 2008.

into eight industry sectors: extractive (28 per cent of cases), financial services (8 per cent), food and beverage (7 per cent), heavy manufacturing (4 per cent), infrastructure and utilities (9 per cent), electronics and ICT (5 per cent); pharmaceutical and chemical (12 per cent) and retail and consumer products (21 per cent).

Findings further include that corporations are alleged to impact the full range of human rights, including civil and political rights; economic, social and cultural rights; and labour rights. Other findings were that initial abuses seemed to lead to further related allegations of abuses and that environmental harms and corruption were connected to impacts on human rights: two 'classic' forms of corporate crime (Huisman and Sidoli 2019). Finally, Ruggie broadly categorized the manner in which the companies were involved – as directly or indirectly. For direct cases, the company's own actions or omissions were alleged to cause the abuse. In indirect cases, the company was perceived to contribute to or benefit from the violations of third parties, including suppliers, states or governmental agencies, and other companies. In Ruggie's sample, nearly 60 per cent of cases featured direct forms of company involvement in the alleged abuses.

Another assessment of prevalence was made in the context of the 'African World War' (1998–2003). A UN Panel of Experts, established by the UN Security Council, found that 157 corporations were directly or indirectly involved in illegal exploitation of natural resources.[6] The proceeds of these illegally exploited resources enabled the purchase of arms and, as such, the continuation of war crimes and crimes against humanity in the DRC (UN Doc S/2–3/1027, 2003).

68.3.2 *Corporate Involvement in International Crimes*

Another and more recent as well as longitudinal attempt to assess the prevalence of corporate involvement in human rights violations was made by Huisman, Karstedt and van Baar (in press). This study includes only cases in which corporations are allegedly involved in the most serious human rights violations that constitute breaches of international criminal law, including crimes against humanity, war crimes and genocide. While both moral and legal ambiguity have been defining characteristics of corporate and white-collar crime, in these cases at least the criminal nature of the human rights abuses is clear (Brants 2007). However, as in most cases, the corporations are only indirectly involved: since the crimes themselves are committed by others, the liability of the corporations remains ambiguous. Yet, as these are the most serious human rights violations, these cases require legal responses, holding the corporations accountable for their complicity in these crimes as well as for not complying with the business and human rights standards laid out in Section 68.2.

In this study, 103 cases in which corporations have been accused of involvement in international crimes are identified, coded and analysed (Huisman, Karstedt and van Baar in press). These have to be substantive accusations, and they are made either by non-governmental organizations (NGOs) and human rights advocacy groups in research reports or in the course of lawsuits and legal proceedings against corporations (often both). The study covers the period since World War II, as the phenomenon of corporations and their managers being involved in gross human rights violations was coined by the Nuremberg Trials, at which

[6] The Panel of Experts on the Illegal Exploitation of Natural Resources and Other Forms of Wealth of the Democratic Republic of the Congo (DRC).

executives of leading German corporations stood trial for their role in Nazi crimes (Bush 2009; Karstedt 2015).

Industry sectors differ widely in terms of involvement in international crimes. Corporations in the extractive industries sector are at high risk not only of violating human rights more generally, as Ruggie found, but also of leading involvement in international crimes with 40 per cent of all cases. About a fifth (21 per cent) of the corporations operate in manufacturing and industry, both heavy and light industries. Both the IT and telecommunications sector and the financial sector are represented with about 10 per cent of all cases, while the more obvious private military and security companies represent a mere 5 per cent.

Further, 15 per cent of cases allege direct involvement, which is less than the 61 per cent found by Ruggie. An obvious explanation is the selection criterion of international crimes, which includes only gross human rights violations that qualify as breaches of international criminal justice. In Ruggie's sample, many cases concern violations of labour rights, inflicted by the corporations themselves as employers. The violence that is associated with international crimes is typically committed by state agents who also serve as business partners of the companies involved.

68.3.3 *Problems of Measuring and Comparing Compliance*

Considering the limited number of studies and the differences between these studies, it is impossible to draw firm conclusions about the prevalence of business compliance with human rights standards. The scarce studies available looking at corporate involvement in human rights abuses, including those presented in Sections 68.3.1 and 68.3.2, do not take compliance as a measurement; they simply count numbers of accused corporations. With a company limiting union rights and a company facilitating a genocide, each counts as one case. Further, the broad range of abuses being studied and the different findings make comparisons that cut across types of human rights abuse, geographical locations and the nature of the corporate involvement very difficult; conclusions are no easier to draw. Ruggie (2013) used a random sample of all human rights abuses reported by the Business and Human Rights Resource Centre, while Huisman, Karstedt and van Baar (in press) used a targeted sample of the most serious abuses. Ruggie (2013) looked at cases from 2005 to 2007 while Huisman et al. (in press) collected cases from World War II onwards. Yet, considering these differences, it is striking that some similarities do seem to appear.

The first is that involvement in human rights abuses seems unevenly distributed over branches of industry. Some industries appear to be more risk prone. Risks of becoming involved in human rights abuses seem related to the nature of the business and the place where the business is found. Risks are high when products are directly linked to the commission of human rights abuses, such as supply of arms, chemicals (for the production of toxic weapons) and IT surveillance software (for tracking down dissidents). Less, but also risky are dual-use products for which the potential civil use can mask its actual military or security-related use. For instance, a Dutch businessman was convicted for selling chemical precursors he claimed were used for producing artificial fertilizers, while in reality they were used to produce chemical weapons which were used by Saddam Hoessein's regime in Iraq (Huisman and van Sliedregt 2010). Finally, apparently neutral products, such as money and finance, can also bring risks, illustrated by the cases involving banks in both samples.

Second, looking at geographical location, the bigger picture appears to be that corporations with home countries in the Global North get involved in the human rights abuses committed in host countries in the Global South. Risks are high when business is found in countries with poor human rights records, such as is often the case in countries rich in natural resources (Le Billon 2012). Over time, the recorded cases seem to follow a pattern of contexts of war or authoritarian rule in which gross human rights violations are committed and corporations get involved: from Nazi Germany in the 1950s, military juntas in Latin America in the 1970s, apartheid South Africa in the 1980s, African civil wars in the 1990s to conflicts sparked by the Arabic Spring in the new millennium (Huisman, Karstedt and van Baar in press). These findings underscore the challenges for states in the Global South when they regulate businesses in their midst (Dubash and Morgan 2013). As we will discuss in Section 68.5, compliance with due diligence requirements should be linked to the inherent risks associated with the nature of the industry and the country(ies) in which the company operates.

68.4 CURRENT ENFORCEMENT MECHANISMS

While the globalization of the twentieth century brought new challenges for MNCs in the socio-political contexts associated with human rights violations, the same era saw the emergence of an international human rights regime that gained momentum. With the beginning of the 1990s, a 'justice cascade' (Sikkink 2011) took hold, in which international criminal justice and regional and national courts interacted in a process of consolidation of norms and actions, to bring an end to impunity for gross human rights violations. The direction of this cascade was vertical from the international to the national level, with international standards implemented in domestic law, and horizontal across regions. The justice cascade was both decentralized and interactive, with multiple actors and a proliferation of diverse new institutions, ranging from international and hybrid tribunals, regional courts of human rights to national truth commissions (Huisman, Karstedt and van Baar in press). While this justice cascade made it more difficult for human rights abusers to escape justice, the enforcement of human rights has also been criticized as highly selective, with mostly military and political actors from the Global South standing trial in international courts and tribunals (De Hoon 2017). While the chief prosecutor of the ICC has repeatedly announced that the Court will start investigating businessmen involved in international crimes (Bernaz 2017) – this has still not occurred, at the time of writing – the Court itself does not have jurisdiction over corporations (Stoitchkova 2010). In general, a governance gap has been identified when enforcing corporate compliance with human rights standards, as there is no regulatory agency to monitor corporate compliance with human rights standards (Buhmann 2016).

Still, as the language of human rights has emerged as a powerful narrative in the wake of the justice cascade, advocacy groups have organized campaigns against MNCs and NGOs, often together with local communities starting to resist the detrimental impact of industrial production and international supply chains, besides human rights abuses including corruption and environmental degradation (Huisman and Sidoli 2019). Accountability occupies a central place within the complex of regulatory trends that are shaping the business and human rights nexus, with victims, advocacy groups, activist lawyers and local prosecutors trying to find ways of holding corporations accountable for the harms they are associated with, in order to seek redress, compensation and justice.

In theory, there are many ways to respond to corporate involvement in human rights abuses in general and in international crimes in particular and to hold corporations and their managers accountable for such involvement. Most countries have included the core crimes of international criminal justice into their domestic criminal code. Many countries acknowledge corporate criminal liability and if not, individual managers could be held liable (Ramasastry and Thompson 2006). Special sanctions legislation has been put in place to prevent corporations from doing business with 'bad actors' such as states and armed groups that commit gross human rights violations, creating the possibility of issuing administrative sanctions against corporations (Michalowski 2015). Several tort lawsuits have been initiated by victims claiming damages from companies involved in their abuses (Schrempf-Stirling and Wettstein 2017). And there are various non-judicial mechanisms for seeking redress against corporations (Ruggie 2013).

Although not always specified, lawsuits against corporations are motivated, on the one hand, by the principle of retribution, as the official goal of international criminal justice is 'to end all impunity' for international crimes (Stoitchkova 2010). On the other hand, the desire to sanction corporations is motivated by the expected deterrent effect not only on the corporation itself but also on other corporations potentially getting involved in human rights violations. Also, making corporations compensate the harms they were involved in contributes to the reconciliation towards victims. Legal scholars have extensively discussed the possibilities of holding corporations liable for international crimes and other human rights abuses (e.g. Kaleck and Saage-Maaß 2010; Van der Wilt 2013). The outcome is that there are certainly such possibilities – and possibilities for holding individual managers liable as well – but there are many legal and practical problems involved in doing so, creating a 'governance gap' (Simons and Macklin 2014). These boil down to two problems that are typical for corporate crime (Gobert and Punch 2003) and that are multiplied in cases of international crime (Brants 2007). The first is the problem of 'remoteness', which relates to the indirect ways of involvement and therefore the difficulty of establishing causality, that is, that the involvement caused the crime (in legal terms: the problem of establishing *actus reus*). Corporations are distanced in a number of ways from the harms produced by abuses. Geographically, timely and organizationally: the decision taken in a corporate boardroom in a Western capital to invest in a project in a developing country under authoritarian rule on the other side of the world might lead to harms years later. The second is the problem of 'neutral acts': corporations do not have the intent to do harm, they just want to make a profit (in legal terms: the problem of establishing *mens rea*; Burchard 2010). Inherent in international crimes is the intent to do harm, while the harms of corporate crime are generally the unwanted outcomes of corporate decisions or processes just intended to make profit.

68.4.1 *Criminal Proceedings*

Several criminal investigations into alleged corporate involvement in gross human rights violations have been initiated, mostly after complaints had been filed to local prosecutors by victims and/or human rights advocacy groups and activist law firms representing them. Most of these have been stopped for reasons that are not always clear, as it might not be compulsory for prosecutors to justify dropping a case.[7] If reasons are mentioned, these mostly relate to lack of evidence. In the case of Riwal, for alleged involvement in Israeli war crimes by contributing

7 Examples include the Australian investigation of mining company Anvil for alleged support to the Congolese army in killing at least seventy-three civilians in putting down protest; the Swiss investigation of Argor-Heraeus for alleged laundering of conflict gold from Congo; the German investigation into the role of Daimler-Chrysler for complicity in the kidnapping, torture and killing of union members by Argentinian security forces; and the Colombian investigation into the alleged complicity of Occidental Petroleum in the extrajudicial killings by the Colombian air force.

to the construction of the Annexation Wall and Israeli settlements, the Dutch prosecutor deemed the company's contribution too minor to prosecute.[8] Whether reasons for dropping cases are always true reasons is also not clear; political and economic interests might also hinder prosecutors investigating major corporations.[9]

A few cases are still pending. Amesys is under investigation by French prosecutors for facilitating extrajudicial arrests and torture by supplying surveillance software to Gadaffi's security forces in Libya.[10] A similar case of supplying surveillance software to Syrian security forces, this time involving the company Qosmos, is also pending in France.[11] And in 2018, cement producer LafargeHolcim was indicted for complicity with crimes against humanity committed by ISIS in Syria. Former executives were already under investigation.[12] In 2010, Sweden's public prosecutor opened a criminal investigation into allegations that the oil consortium led by Lundin Petroleum Swedes has been complicit in war crimes committed during the civil war in Sudan (Schoultz and Flyghed 2016). In 2017, criminal complaints were filed by human rights advocacy groups in the Netherlands and France against two banks, alleging that their financial transactions facilitated the commission of international crimes: respectively, Rabobank for complicity in crimes against humanity committed by Mexican drug cartels (Ryngaert 2018: 16) and BNP Paribas for complicity in the Rwandan genocide.[13]

While no corporation has yet been convicted for gross human rights violations, some individual managers or entrepreneurs have been, starting with German business executives at the Nuremberg Trials. In the Netherlands, two businessmen were convicted of complicity in war crimes, but these were not managers of large and multinational corporations (Huisman and van Sliedregt 2010). In 2018, two former managers of the Argentinean subsidiary of Ford motor company were convicted of complicity in crimes against humanity based on their having identified workers as union members to military security forces, after which these workers were tortured and disappeared.[14] Some managers have (also) been convicted of associated crimes: executives of Elf were convicted of bribing warring parties in Angola and some Daewoo executives were sentenced for supplying arms to the Burmese junta (Huisman 2010). In several other cases, indicted managers, such as Anvil Mining expats in Congo, were acquitted (Kyriakakis 2007).

68.4.2 *Civil Proceedings*

Many more civil suits have been brought against corporations. According to Schrempf-Stirling and Wettstein (2017: 548), since the 1980s, more than 120 foreign direct liability

8 www.om.nl/vaste-onderdelen/zoeken/@31796/no-further/.

9 In some cases, companies have been fined in the United States for breaching sanctions regulations, while their behaviour was also qualified as complicity in international crimes in other lawsuits. Chiquita settled a criminal complaint by the US government and agreed to pay a $25 million fine for paying paramilitaries in Colombia. BNP Paribas paid an $8.9 billion penalty for conducting business with Sudan, Iran and Cuba subject to sanctions.

10 www.fidh.org/IMG/pdf/report_amesys_case_eng.pdf.

11 www.ecchr.eu/en/case/surveillance-in-syria-european-firms-may-be-aiding-and-abetting-crimes-against-humanity/.

12 www.asso-sherpa.org/landmark-decision-company-lafarge-indicted-complicity-in-crimes-against-humanity-included.

13 www.economist.com/finance-and-economics/2017/07/08/bnp-paribas-faces-accusations-over-the-rwandan-genocide.

14 Cassandra Garrison and Nicolás Misculin (2018) 'Ex-Ford Argentina executives convicted in torture case; victims may sue in U.S.', *Reuters*, www.reuters.com/article/us-argentina-rights-ford-motor/ex-ford-argentina-executives-convicted-in-torture-case-victims-may-sue-in-u-s-idUSKBN1OA25H.

cases have been filed worldwide against MNCs for their alleged complicity in human rights abuses. Most cases have been filed in the United States under the Alien Tort Claims Act (ATCA). However, in 2013 the US Supreme Court ruled that ATCA presumptively does not apply extraterritorially.[15] Since then, most cases have been dismissed, with the exception of some cases against US-based corporations. Civil cases for damages are also pending in other countries, such as in France against Dalhoff Larsen and Horneman for buying timber from Liberian companies that provided support to Charles Taylor's government during the Liberian civil war. Some civil cases ended in settlements in which the victims received compensation from the corporations, under the condition that they give up any further litigation.

68.4.3 *Soft Law and Market Sanctions*

All in all, the results of legal action have been very modest, given the probable prevalence and seriousness of corporate involvement in international crimes, as discussed in Section 68.3. Attempts to hold corporations accountable for their involvement in human rights abuses have so far not been successful in the sense that they have not led to convictions or rulings establishing accountability. Other tools have also been used, such as non-judicial grievance mechanisms and arbitration procedures (Simon and Macklin 2013). These are often the extension of the soft law standards and norms on business and human rights presented in Section 68.2, such as the UN Guiding Principles on Business and Human Rights, the OECD Guidelines for Multinational Enterprises (OECD 2011) and the ILO Tripartite Declaration of Principles Concerning Multinational Enterprises and Social Policy. These instruments can contribute to creating generally accepted social norms regarding the protection of human rights by corporations. However, as discussed, compliance with these soft law norms is voluntary and non-enforceable (Macleod and Lewis 2004). Especially those corporations that are likely to be the worst offenders may not be compelled to take part (Hayman 2009).

Non-judicial grievance mechanisms and arbitration procedures include National Contact Points (NCPs). NCPs are complaints-handling institutions that states commit to setting up. NCPs have extraterritorial competence in that they may handle complaints of violation of the OECD Guidelines outside the company's home country (OECD 2011). The UN highlighted NCPs as an important modality for providing accountability in its three-pillar framework (United Nations 2008). Buhmann (2020) observes that there is broad variety in NCPs' composition, organization and degree of independence from the government. Studies have indicated that NCPs having such diverse institutional set-ups may affect their legitimacy with stakeholders, affecting trust in NCPs as remedy institutions able to deliver accountability (Buhmann 2020). Nevertheless, Buhmann (2016) suggests that their potential impact on the social licence to operate of transnational companies can be considerable. While NCPs are non-judicial institutions, they offer a formal, state-based remedy where national judicial remedies often do not reach owing to jurisdictional and territorial limitations. 'Being non-judicial institutions, NCPs should be assessed in regards to what they can do, not what they cannot' (Buhmann 2020: 53).

NCPs can make recommendations in their final statements and facilitate agreements between parties, which may include future compliance with the UN Guiding Principles. Specific soft law schemes, which may include forms of enforcement, may also be introduced

[15] *Kiobel* v. *Royal Dutch Petroleum Co.*, 133 S.Ct. 1659 (2013).

for particular branches of industry. Examples are the Kimberley certification process for diamonds and the Forest Stewardship Council (FSC) certificate for timber. To look at these further, the Kimberley process involves a global certification scheme implemented through domestic law. States ensure that the diamonds they trade are from Kimberley-compliant countries by requiring detailed packaging protocols and certification, coupled with chain-of-custody warranties by companies. Kimberley has established detailed public reporting requirements for participants, as well as multi-stakeholder monitoring. It carries out peer reviews of member states, often spurred by civil society reports of government-related performance shortfalls. Kimberley actually removed one government, effectively shutting it out of the international diamond trade – a measure permitted under World Trade Organization rules.

On the forestry side, the FSC certifies forestry products regarding their origin, guaranteeing that they are legal and sustainable. The FSC showed its teeth in a case in which Danish timber company Dalhoff Larsen and Horneman (DLH) was accused of buying timber during Liberia's civil war. According to allegations, DLH purchased timber harvested by companies that directly benefited the regime of president Charles Taylor. These companies were widely known for human rights abuses and several other crimes, and one of the directors DLH bought from was convicted for war crimes in the Netherlands.[16] NGO Global Witness submitted a complaint with a large amount of evidence to the FSC. In 2015, DLH was stripped of its certificate. The FSC also issued a statement to the effect that if DLH wants its certificate back, it first has to compensate the Liberian communities for their losses.[17] In a press statement released by DLH, the company signalled that it intended to get its certificate back by complying with the required steps. Once it had done that, DLH was re-certified by the FSC.[18]

NGOs have also attempted to generate market sanctions by exposing corporate involvement in human rights abuses. While large consumer boycotts were set up against the presence of Shell in apartheid South Africa and against blood diamonds originating from war-torn Sierra Leone, other attempts to create consumer boycotts were not successful. Also, activist shareholders as well as institutional investors such as pension funds have attempted to force divestment decisions upon corporations. The Norwegian Sovereign Fund, the world's largest sovereign wealth fund, sold off assets from companies that were accused of human rights violations, environmental pollution and corruption.[19] While some of these calls for divestment have been successful, the effect on stock value and therefore the deterrent power is still unclear, as will be discussed further in Section 68.5 (Long, Wann and Brockman 2016).

68.5 TOWARDS AN INTEGRATED MODEL

Section 68.4 shows that while many instruments exist and have been attempted, almost none of these attempts have led to holding corporations to account for their involvement in human rights violations. There are no internationally binding corporate human rights duties, existing soft laws are non-enforceable, the ICC has no jurisdiction over corporations, violations of UN-imposed trade embargoes have stimulated almost no legal scrutiny, there have been no

16 Court of Appeal of 's-Hertogenbosch, 21 April 2017, ECLI:NL:GHSHE:2017:1760.

17 www.globalwitness.org/en/archive/wartime-timber-company-dlh-penalized-trading-illegal-liberian-private-use-permit-logs-0/.

18 https://fsc.org/en/node/18805.

19 www.abc.net.au/news/2017–03-09/norway-sovereign-wealth-fund-threatens-unethical-firms/8341372.

criminal convictions of corporations or their executives, and of the many civil suits, so far none has successfully found the relevant corporation guilty of human rights violations. As a result, from a legal point of view, there appears to be de facto impunity for corporate involvement in human rights abuses. If compliance is conditional on there being effective law enforcement, such impunity will prevent corporations from complying with human rights standards. In this section, we first look at the relevance of deterrence for achieving corporate compliance, before wrapping up this chapter with discussion of how a smart mix of existing judicial and non-judicial instruments could compensate for the lack of formal regulation and enforcement.

68.5.1 *Corporate Deterrence*

'To end all impunity' is a main purpose of international criminal justice and, according to this principle, retribution is an important goal of punishment (Stoitchkova 2010). However, how this relates to future compliance with human rights standards is not clear. Increasingly, criminal justice is being portrayed as an instrument with which to force companies to work on and improve regulatory compliance. Setting up compliance management systems and appointing compliance officers and corporate monitors have been used in deferred prosecution agreements (DPAs) and conditional sentences in a wide range of corporate crime cases (Garrett 2014; Chen and Soltes 2018). In this view, prosecution and punishment serve as deterrents for corporations becoming involved in abuses. From a criminological perspective, we might question the deterrent effect of sanctioning corporations. In an early systemic review of corporate deterrence, Simpson et al. (2014) found hardly any significant effects of criminalization and sanctioning; these had minimal to no deterrent impact at the individual and company levels. Based on this outcome, the researchers stated: '[W]e cannot conclude that law has a deterrent effect on corporate offending.'

Having realized that sanctions lack a direct deterrent effect, law enforcement agencies have attempted to use legal sanctioning as a catalyst to generate reputational damage for the offending company, which is assumed to have a deterrent effect on businesses (van Erp 2008). However, in line with the lack of reputational cost in offences that externalize harm, such as foreign bribery and environmental pollution (Karpoff, Lott and Wehrly 2005, and in contrast with offences that internalize harm for shareholders, such as accounting fraud (Karpoff, Lee and Martin 2008), a study conducted by Van Baar, Enneking, van Erp and Engelen (unpublished) found no reputational costs brought about by publicized business involvement in human rights abuses.[20] It appears that shareholders do not mind – or even appreciate – corporations passing the harmful effects of their operations on to external parties, especially when these are not in power to effectively respond to that externalization. Besides the absence of market sanctions of corporate human rights abuses, one might question whether stock value is a good indicator of deterrent value. This is illustrated by the boycott against Shell for its presence in apartheid South Africa. Although widespread protests and consumer boycotts damaged the company's reputation and profits, Shell decided to ride out the boycott and pay the 'Apartheid Premium' (Katzin 1995: 333). The mechanisms of efforts to improve the human rights practices of businesses, including divestment, can be complex with

[20] Information derived from www.uu.nl/agenda/expert-meeting-corporate-human-rightsviolations-and-reputational-damage.

a number of possible pathways. This does not lead easily to simple measures (e.g. stock price) and hence clear-cut conclusions.

Besides the absence of a deterrent effect with any single sanctioning strategy, Simpson et al. (2014) found that studies examining multiple interventions produce a significant deterrent effect on individual- and corporate-level offending. Therefore, they determined that a mixture of agency interventions is apt to have the biggest impact. This is in line with 'smart regulation' of business, as was advocated by Gunningham, Grabosky and Sinclair (1998), who proposed a pluralistic approach to regulation that embraced innovative and flexible forms of social control. Smart regulation encompasses elements of both self- and co-regulation and promotes the combined efforts of government agencies, regulated entities, commercial third parties and non-commercial third parties in regulating corporate crime (Gunningham, Grabosky and Sinclair 1998). Applying herself to business and human rights, Buhmann (2016: 709) proposes a 'smart mix approach' to regulating them: 'States may employ a "smart mix" of regulatory modalities to promote business respect for human rights through both legal requirements and voluntary action.'

A word of warning here is that the studies about corporate deterrence mostly relate to research undertaken at the nation-state level and do not necessarily translate to the international level. The question is how these studies relate to the international level where, as law enforcement is often lacking, local laws are involved and the distance between the harm done and acknowledgement of that harm may be considerable. While this certainly needs further study, we would like to draw upon Buhmann's (2016: 710) observations 1) that public regulators increasingly promote corporate social responsibility, for example, leading to mandatory reporting; 2) that their efforts are based on the fact that conventional public law constrains them from implementing public policy objectives that affect businesses; and 3) that these efforts are evolving into a juridification that will function through diverse regulatory modalities with different regulatory organizations, ranging from soft law guidance to hard law requirements, and remedial institutions with extraterritorial reach. In other words, as international human rights standards become codified in national law, the findings on the deterrent effects of responses to breaches of national laws may be valid for non-compliance with human rights obligations as well.

68.5.2 *Civil Society Interventions*

Non-regulatory instruments have been suggested to prevent white-collar and corporate crime, based on analysis of the crime scripts and opportunities for corporate crime (Benson and Madensen 2007). Such instruments might also be available to prevent corporations from getting involved in situations in which they might become complicit in human rights abuses, by 'influencing the flow of events' and steering the flow of action in another direction (Parker and Braithwaite 2003: 119). Furthermore, these instruments might be operated by other, non-state actors: so-called third-party actors such as the human rights advocacy groups or corporate stakeholders presented earlier in the chapter. As a result of the difficulty that international organizations such as the UN have in filling governance gaps resulting from states' lack of will or capacity to regulate corporate adverse impacts, Scherer and Palazzo (2011) argue that a new form of transnational regulation is arising with private actors and multi-stakeholder initiatives filling governance gaps. Studies have highlighted how fast the NGO-represented regulation sector is growing at local, national and international levels, as well as the significant role that NGOs can play in influencing corporate behaviour through use of multiple adversarial strategies (Durbin and Welch 2002). NGOs and other third-party actors have been found to play an important role in executing regulatory mechanisms of social control, including behaviour-modification, information-gathering and standard-setting (Hutter and Jones 2006). The use of civil society actors in corporate regulation has been particularly advocated for transnational corporate offences and state-corporate crime (Green and Ward 2004). The concept of state-corporate crime is especially helpful in conceptualizing corporate involvement in human rights abuses, as state actors are often the principal perpetrators (van Baar 2019). Connor and Haines's (2013) case study of the Indonesian sports shoe industry analysed the capacity of global networks of civil society actors to supplement effectively weak state regulation, to reduce human rights abuses by MNCs. They found networked regulation to have a positive short-to-medium-term impact on respect for trade union rights among some manufacturers producing for MNCs.

68.5.3 *Responsive Regulation of Human Rights*

The lack of hard law and international enforcement bodies, combined with the inherent problems of regulating business and deterring corporate crime, and the potential impact of civil society actors, provides a strong business case for designing a 'smart mix' of interventions. The design of such a mix should include a certain sequencing of interventions (instead of randomly firing away interventions) in such a way that they are mutually reinforcing. Since no single regulatory theory, strategy or sanction is flawless, we need to invoke more than one strategy or sanction in an integrated fashion (Deva 2012: 200). Integrated theories for regulating business have been developed and could be applied to human rights. The integrated theory of responsive regulation by Ayres and Braithwaite (1992) is probably the most widely used model for business regulation and corporate crime prevention and is therefore an obvious candidate for regulating corporate human rights performance as well. Central to responsive regulation is the well-known enforcement pyramid that prescribes a hierarchy of regulatory interventions, as well as representing circumstances of interaction between regulators and corporations. Regulatory instruments situated at the bottom of the pyramid reflect the least severe regulatory responses, whereas instruments situated at the top of the pyramid represent the most severe regulatory responses. So the steps of the pyramid escalate from negotiation and persuasion, warning letters, and civil and administrative penalties, to criminal prosecution and licence suspension and revocation (Ayres and Braithwaite 1992).

As a case in point, the model has been suggested to overcome the failures of international human rights law in preventing human rights abuses. 'Responsive regulation translates productively in the field of human rights, highlighting the value of persuasion, education and capacity building as the first steps to achieving compliance with human rights norms' (Charlesworth 2017: 369). Applying the model to dealing with tyranny in the case of Timor-Leste, Braithwaite, Charlesworth and Soares (2012) show that it is possible for networks of states, aid donors, businesses, the media and NGOs to create webs of informal sanctions in a regulatory pyramid of human rights. Referring to Braithwaite (2011), Charlesworth observes that main principles of responsive regulation include flexibility, giving voice to stakeholders, engaging resisters with fairness, nurturing motivation, signalling but not threatening the possibility of escalation and enrolling powerful regulatory partners in networks. 'Thus, laggards may be willing to acknowledge problems complying with international human rights standards if they can see that this will protect them from more punitive forms of sanctions (Braithwaite 2011: 496)' (Charlesworth 2017: 369).

Considering the diversity in corporate involvement in human rights abuses found in Section 68.3, the responsiveness that the model prescribes in regulating companies in particular cases would be a great benefit. It would allow regulatory interventions to be tailored to the nature of the corporations' involvement in human rights abuse, by virtue of the supply chain relationships, the financing arrangements and a physical presence in the country in which the abuse takes place.

However, from the characteristics of regulation, compliance and enforcement in the field of business and human rights, as discussed in this chapter, flows that the application of the enforcement pyramid will have its limits, as a number of the preconditions for its efficacy are missing. First, and different from the well-regulated fields to which the model has so far been applied, the pyramid has no hard law foundation in the field of human rights. It will stand on the weak soil of soft law. Second, the pyramid has no top of severe sanctions: there is no international regulator to revoke a licence, the ICC has no jurisdiction and pending lawsuits have not yet led to any convictions. Braithwaite (2011: 475) notes the paradox that 'by having a capability to escalate to tough enforcement, most regulation can be about collaborative capacity building'. As the 'trick of successful regulation is to establish a synergy between punishment and persuasion', allowing regulators 'to speak softly while carrying a big stick' (Ayres and Braithwaite 1992: 25, 40), there is no deterrent 'big stick' in the case of non-compliance at lower levels. This problem is rooted in the foundation of the pyramid, as no hard law means no liability and therefore no enforcement. Third, the general criticism that the pyramid is one-dimensional and only looks at public regulators is extra valid in the field of business and human rights, as there is no international regulating body and home states not willing to regulate the human rights performances of corporate nationals abroad and host states are also not willing or not capable to do so.

The suitability of this theory to underpin a regulatory regime that could effectively make companies accountable for human rights violations was also critically assessed by Deva (2012). He concluded that although this theory provides a starting point, the usefulness of the progressive enforcement pyramid is limited. 'Although the progressively punitive regulatory pyramid looks impressive on paper, putting this into practice will not be that easy, especially when dealing with instances of human rights violations by MNCs' (Deva 2012: 188). Instead of a rigid hierarchical order of regulatory interventions, Devae proposed a 'simultaneous' and 'coordinated' integration. This integrated theory encompasses a mixture of both 'carrots' and 'sticks', brought together in a framework of potential incentives and sanctions to be administered on international, national and corporate levels. In practice, such a comprehensive model of interventions could run the risk of becoming a 'shot hail' strategy in trying to improve corporate human rights performance. More empirical research is needed on the effects of the various regulatory instruments and interventions on corporate behaviour and how these reinforce or oppose each other. A promising example is found in the review of more than forty corporate foreign direct liability cases and their effects on corporate human rights policies and conduct by Schrempf-Stirling and Wettstein (2017). The review shows that most corporations adjusted their human rights policies and adopted additional measures to cope with human rights issues during or shortly after the legal proceedings, even when these proceedings were unsuccessful from a legal point of view. Targeted companies improved their human rights reporting, their human rights policies, training and assessments and their collaboration with NGOs. Further research is needed to find the causal mechanism behind this correlation of unsuccessful civil litigation and corporate self-regulation and whether this could be an educational effect or a reputational one.

Besides co-ordinated multiplicity, Deva presents informality as a second underpinning of an integrated regulatory framework of business and human rights (Deva 2012: 15). While 'third parties' were already added in contemporary models of business regulation, the reliance on informal, non-legal tools and non-state institutions to ensure that companies comply with their human rights responsibilities is even more important. This underscores the point that 'regulation' should not be seen as linked exclusively to formal law, state and legal institutions. Third-party actors need to fill the regulatory gap in business and human rights.

68.5.4 *Weaving the Webs of Compliance*

Weaving the webs of compliance, 'smart' regulatory mixes should combine the sequenced principles for reinforcing interventions and, in doing so, combine public, civil society and market actors. Keeping the metaphor of the pyramid – but without the rigid hierarchical order – it can be noted that a 'real' pyramid consists of four sides.[21] Using the three-pillar framework of business and human rights, this translates into (i) a regulatory side with a duty to protect, (ii) a corporate side with a duty to respect, (iii) a civil side with access to remedies and (iv) a market side with economic incentives. On each side, the first step of the pyramid is norm awareness, communicating human rights standards and the corporate duty to respect. The second step is compliance management and compliance assistance, ensuring corporate ability to comply with the duty to respect human rights and due diligence obligations. The third step is monitoring compliance with the duty to avoid adverse human rights impacts and the obligation to implement policies and processes that will enable the exercising of due diligence. The fourth step is public reporting of corporations' efforts and outcomes concerning compliance with norms and the use of self-regulatory tools. The fifth step consists of sanctioning corporations' involvement in human rights abuses and failure to comply with the compliance management and reporting obligations.

The question remains whether such a pyramid needs a hard law basis, for example, in the form of a binding business and human rights treaty. Norm setting defines compliance, increases the risk of detection and helps to remove excuses. Is soft law sufficient in a well-designed – 'smart' – integrated framework of available instruments? And for enforcement, do we need corporate criminal liability in international criminal law? Not so much for single deterrence, as Simpson et al. (2014) established, but perhaps for reinforcing civil society and market-based interventions. However, home and host states do not seem fit for the task and could play a limited role, meaning that NGOs and international organizations will do the heavy lifting.

REFERENCES

Ayres, Ian, and John Braithwaite. 1992. *Responsive Regulation: Transcending the Deregulation Debate*. New York: Oxford University Press.

Benson, Michael, and Tamara Madensen. 2007. 'Situational Crime Prevention and White-Collar Crime'. In *International Handbook of Corporate and White Collar Crime*, edited by H. Pontell and G. Geis, 609–26. New York: Springer.

[21] This idea of a four-dimensional pyramid for preventing corporate involvement in human rights abuses was presented at the 2017 annual conference of the European Society of Criminology in the presentation 'Weaving the Webs of Compliance in Preventing Corporate Involvement in Atrocity Crimes' by Janet Ransley, Susanne Karstedt and Wim Huisman at Cardiff University.

Bernaz, Nadia. 2017. 'An Analysis of the ICC Office of the Prosecutor's Policy Paper on Case Selection and Prioritization from the Perspective of Business and Human Rights'. *Journal of International Criminal Justice* 15(3): 527–42.

Bilchitz, David. 2016. 'The Necessity for a Business and Human Rights Treaty'. *Business and Human Rights Journal* 1: 203–27.

Bleker-van Eijk, Sylvie, and Raf A. M. Houben. 2017. *Compliance and Integrity Management: Theory and Practice*. Alphen aan den Rijn: Wolters Kluwer.

Blitt, R. C. 2012. 'Beyond Ruggie's Guiding Principles on Business and Human Rights: Charting an Embracive Approach to Corporate Human Rights Compliance'. *Texas International Law Journal* 48: 33.

Braithwaite, John. 2011. 'The Essence of Responsive Regulation'. *University of British Columbia Law Review* 44(3): 475–520.

Braithwaite, John, Hilary Charlesworth and Adérito Soares. 2012. *Networked Governance of Freedom and Tyranny: Peace in Timor-Leste*. Canberra: ANU E Press.

Brants, Chrisje. 2007. 'Gold Collar Crime'. In *International Handbook of White-Collar Crime*, edited by Gilbert Geis and Henry Pontell, 309–26. New York: Springer.

Buhmann, Karin. 2016. 'Public Regulators and CSR: The 'Social Licence to Operate' in Recent United Nations Instruments on Business and Human Rights and the Juridification of CSR'. *Journal of Business Ethics* 136: 699–714.

Buhmann, Karin. 2020. 'National Contact Points under OECD's Guidelines for Multinational Enterprises: Institutional Diversity Affecting Assessments of the Delivery of Access to Remedy'. In *Accountability, International Business Operations, and the Law: Providing Justice for Corporate Human Rights Violations in Global Value Chains*, edited by Liesbeth Enneking, Ivo Giesen, Anne-Jetske Schaap, Cedric Ryngaert, François Kristen and Lucas Roorda, 39–59. New York: Routledge.

Burchard, Christoph. 2010. Ancillary and Neutral Business Contributions to 'Corporate–Political Core Crime': Initial Enquiries Concerning the Rome Statute. *Journal of International Criminal Justice* 8 (3): 919–46.

Bush, Jonathan A. 2009. 'The Prehistory of Corporations and Conspiracy in International Criminal Law: What Nuremberg Really Said'. *Columbia Law Review* 109(5): 1094–1262.

Cerone, John. 2016. 'A Taxonomy of Soft Law: Stipulating a Definition'. In *Tracing the Roles of Soft Law in Human Rights*, edited by Stéphanie Lagoutte, Thomas Gammeltoft-Hansen and John Cerone, 15–26. Oxford: Oxford University Press.

Charlesworth, Hilary. 2017. 'A Regulatory Perspective on the International Human Rights System'. In *Regulatory Theory: Foundations and Applications*, edited by Peter Drahos, 357–74. Acton ACT, Australia: ANU Press.

Chen, Hui, and Eugene Soltes. 2018. 'Why Compliance Programs Fail: And How to Fix Them'. *Harvard Business Review* 96(2): 116–25.

Connor, Tim, and Haines, Fiona. 2013. 'Networked Regulation as a Solution to Human Rights Abuse in Global Supply Chains? The Case of Trade Union Rights Violations by Indonesian Sports Shoe Manufacturers'. *Theoretical Criminology* 17: 197–214.

De Hoon, Marieke. 2017. 'The Future of the International Criminal Court: On Critique, Legalism and Strengthening the ICC's Legitimacy'. *International Criminal Law Review* 17: 591–614.

Deva, Surya. 2012. *Regulating Corporate Human Rights Violations: Humanizing Business*. New York: Routledge.

Dubash, Navroz K., and Bronwen Morgan. 2013. *The Rise of the Regulatory State of the South: Infrastructure and Development in Emerging Economies*. Oxford: Oxford University Press.

Durbin, Andrea, and Carol Welch. 2002. 'The Environmental Movement and Global Finance'. In *Civil Society and Global Finance*, edited by Jan Aart Scholte and Albrecht Schnabel, 213–27. New York: Routledge.

Easterling, Björn. 2019. 'Whose Responsibilities? The Responsibility of the 'Business Enterprise' to Respect Human Rights'. In *Accountability, International Business Operations, and the Law: Providing Justice for Corporate Human Rights Violations in Global Value Chains*, edited by Liesbeth Enneking, Ivo Giesen, Anne-Jetske Schaap, Cedric Ryngaert, François Kristen and Lucas Roorda, 18–37. New York: Routledge.

Garrett, Allison D. 2008. 'The Corporation as Sovereign'. *Maine Law Review* 60(1): 130–64.
Garrett, Brandon L. 2014. *Too Big to Jail: How Prosecutors Compromise with Corporations*. Cambridge, MA: Harvard University Press.
Gobert, James, and Maurice Punch. 2003. *Rethinking Corporate Crime*. London: Butterworths.
Green, Penny, and Tony Ward. 2004. *State Crime: Governments Violence and Corruption*. London: Pluto Press.
Gunningham, Neil, Peter Grabosky and David Sinclair. 1998. *Smart Regulation: Designing Environmental Policy*. Oxford: Clarendon Press.
Hayman, G. 2009. 'Corruption and Bribery in the Extractive Industries'. In *Transparency International Global Corruption Report 2009: Corruption and the Private Sector*, edited by Zinnbauer D., Dobson, R. and Despota, K., 54–56. Cambridge: Cambridge University Press.
Hughes, Graham. 1958. 'Criminal Omissions'. *Yale Law Journal* 67(4): 590–638.
Huisman, Wim. 2010. *Business as Usual? Corporate Involvement in International Crimes*. The Hague: Eleven International Publishing.
Huisman, Wim, Susanne Karstedt and Annika van Baar. In press. 'The Involvement of Corporations in Atrocity Crimes'. In Oxford Handbook on Atrocity Crimes, edited by Barbara Hola, Hollie N. Brehm and Maartje van Weerdesteijn. Oxford: Oxford University Press.
Huisman, Wim, and Daniel Sidoli. 2019. 'Corporations, Human Rights and the Environmental Degradation-Corruption Nexus'. *Asia Pacific Journal of Environmental Law* 22(1): 66–92.
Huisman, Wim, and Elies van Sliedregt. 2010. 'Rogue Traders – Dutch Businessmen and International Crimes'. *Journal of International Criminal Justice* 8: 803–28.
Huisman, Wim, and Judith van Erp. 2013. 'Opportunities for Environmental Crime: A Test of Situational Crime Prevention Theory'. *British Journal of Criminology* 53(6): 1178–1200.
Hutter, Bridget M., and Clive J. Jones. 2006. Business Risk Management Practices: The Influence of State Regulatory Agencies and Non-State Sources. London School of Economics and Political Science.
Kaleck, Wolfgang, and Miriam Saage-Maaß. 2010. 'Corporate Accountability for Human Rights Violations Amounting to International Crimes: The Status Quo and Its Challenges'. *Journal of International Criminal Justice* 8: 699–724.
Karpoff, Jonathan M., John R. Lott and Eric W. Wehrly. 2005. 'The Reputational Penalties for Environmental Violations: Empirical Evidence'. *Journal of Law and Economics* 68: 653–75.
Karpoff, J. M., J. Scott Lee and G. S. Martin. 2008. 'The Consequences to Managers for Financial Misrepresentation'. *Journal of Financial Economics* 88: 193–215.
Karstedt, Susanne. 2015. 'Managing Criminal Reputations: West German Elites after the Nuremberg Trials, 1946–1960'. *Journal of International Criminal Justice* 13(4): 723–43.
Katzin, Donna. 1995. 'Anatomy of a Boycott: The Royal Dutch/Shell Campaign in the US'. In Embargo: Apartheid's Oil Secrets Revealed, edited by Richard Hengeveld and Jaap Rodenburg, 327–37. Amsterdam: Amsterdam University Press.
Kelly, M. J. 2016. *Prosecuting Corporations for Genocide*. New York: Oxford University Press.
Kyriakakis, Joanna. 2007. 'Australian Prosecution of Corporations for International Crimes'. *Journal of International Criminal Justice* 5(4): 809–26.
Le Billon, Philippe. 2012. *Wars of Plunder: Conflicts, Profits and the Politics of Resources*. London: C. Hurst & Co.
Long, D. M., C. Wann and C. Brockman. 2016. 'Unethical Business Behaviour and Stock Performance'. *Academy of Accounting and Financial Studies Journal* 20(3): 115–22.
Macdonald, Kate, Shelley Marshall and Samantha Balaton-Chrimes. 2017. 'Demanding Rights in Company-Community Resource Extraction Conflicts: Examining the Cases of Vedanta and POSCO in Odisha, India'. In *Demanding Justice in the Global South: Claiming Rights*, edited by Jean Grugel, Jewellord Nem Singh, Lorenza Fontana and Anders Uhlin, 43–67. Cham: Springer International.
Macleod, Sorcha, and Douglas Lewis. 2004. 'Transnational Corporations: Power, Influence and Responsibility'. *Global Social Policy* 4: 77–98.
Michalowski, Sabine. 2015. 'Doing Business with a Bad Actor: How to Draw the Line between Legitimate Commercial Activities and Those that Trigger Corporate Complicity Liability'. *Texas International Law Journal* 50(3): 403–64.

OECD. 2011. *OECD Guidelines for Multinational Enterprises*. OECD Publishing. http://dx.doi.org/10.1787/9789264115415-en.

Parker, Christine, and John Braithwaite. 2003. 'Regulation'. In *The Oxford Handbook of Legal Studies*, edited by Peter Cane and Mark Tushnet, 119–45. Oxford: Oxford University Press.

Ramasastry, Anita, and Richard C. Thompson. 2006. *Commerce Crime and Conflict*. Oslo: Fafo.

Ruggie, John G. 2013. *Just Business: Multinational Corporations and Human Rights*. New York/London: W.W. Norton.

Ryngaert, Cedric. 2018. 'Accountability for Corporate Human Rights Abuses: Lessons from the Possible Exercise of Dutch National Criminal Jurisdiction over Multinational Corporations'. *Criminal Law Forum* 29(1): 1–24.

Scherer, Andreas G., and Guido Palazzo. 2011. 'The New Political Role of Business in a Globalized World: A Review of a New Perspective on CSR and Its Implications for the Firm, Governance and Democracy'. *Journal of Management Studies* 48(4): 899–931.

Schoultz, Isabel, and Janne Flyghed. 2016. 'Doing Business for a "Higher Loyalty"? How Swedish Transnational Corporations Neutralise Allegations of Crime'. *Crime, Law and Social Change* 66 (2): 183–98.

Schrempf-Stirling, Judith, and Florian Wettstein. 2017. 'Beyond Guilty Verdicts: Human Rights Litigation and Its Impact on Corporations' Human Rights Policies'. *Journal of Business Ethics* 145(3): 545–62.

Sikkink, Kathryn. 2011. *The Justice Cascade: How Human Rights Prosecutions Are Changing World Politics*. New York: W.W. Norton.

Simons, Penelope, and Audrey Macklin. 2014. *The Governance Gap: Extractive Industries, Human Rights, and the Home State Advantage*. Abingdon, UK and New York: Routledge.

Simpson, Sally, Melissa Rorie, Mariel Elise Alper, Natalie Schell-Busey, William Laufer and N. Craig Smith. 2014. Corporate Crime Deterrence: A Systematic Review, Campbell Collaboration.

Stoitchkova, Desi. 2010. *Towards Corporate Liability in International Criminal Law*. Utrecht: Intersentia.

UN Human Rights Council, 2010. UN Human Rights Council, A/HRC/14/27, 9 April 2010, para. 3.

van Baar, Annika. 2019. 'Corporate Involvement in International Crimes'. In Nazi Germany, Apartheid South Africa and the Democratic Republic of Congo, PhD Dissertation. VU University Amsterdam.

van Erp, Judith. 2008. 'Reputational Sanctions in Private and Public Regulation'. *Erasmus Law Review* 5: 145–63.

van der Wilt, H. 2013. 'Corporate Criminal Responsibility for International Crimes: Exploring the Possibilities'. *Chinese Journal of International Law* 21(1): 43–77.

69

Aiming for Integrity with Integrity

Jonathan E. Soeharno

Abstract: This chapter puts compliance into the perspective of its aim: achieving a culture of integrity. Integrity, however, is characterized by elusiveness and is difficult to operationalize. This chapter deals with two questions: What does one aim for when one aims for integrity? And how does one aim for integrity? First, the chapter explains how integrity is to be understood along the line of trustworthiness. It has an objective dimension – the particular values, norms or interests that form the object of trust in a particular organization, institution or profession – and a subjective dimension – the purposive ensuring that these remain beyond all doubt. Second, it explains how integrity requires continual articulation, interpretation and safeguarding of the object of integrity. In this context, this chapter emphasizes the reflexive nature of integrity.

Reputation, reputation, reputation! O! I have lost my reputation. I have lost the immortal part of myself, and what remains is bestial.

Shakespeare, *Othello* (Act II, Scene III)

69.1 GOING LONG ON INTEGRITY

In a famous speech to MBA students in 2006, investor Warren Buffett recalled: 'There was a guy, Pete Kiewit in Omaha, who used to say he looked for three things in hiring people: integrity, intelligence, and energy. And he said if the person did not have the first one, the latter two would kill him, because if they don't have integrity, you want them dumb and lazy' (Connors 2010: 171). To underline this statement, he challenged his audience members to choose a fellow student on whom to go long (for example buying 10 per cent of their earnings for the rest of their lifetime) or short. Buffett playfully analyzed that, above all other qualities – for example IQ, energy or grades – integrity is a reason to go long on someone (on 'the person who is generous, honest and who gave credit to other people for their own ideas') as much as non-integrity seems to be a reason to go short on someone (on 'the person who turned you off, the person who is egotistical, who is greedy, who cuts corners, who is slightly dishonest'). The essence of his speech is that if you want people to trust you enough to invest in you for a longer period of time, you don't need to have otherworldly intellect or energy, just a quality that is attainable to all: integrity.

This speech was held before the worldwide financial crises of the beginning of the twenty-first century. These crises were certainly not caused by a lack of intellect or energy. In fact, the mortgage-backed securities that played a central role in these crises were ingenious products fashioned by highly intelligent bankers (sometimes even with PhDs in theoretical physics) and implemented with great energy. Clearly, neither their *ingenuity* nor their *energy* was the issue here. The same seems to hold for later affairs in the financial sector, from manipulation of LIBOR (London Inter-Bank Offered Rate; Keenan 2012) to national affairs such as the recent findings of the Australian Royal Commission into Misconduct in the Banking, Superannuation and Financial Services Industry. In 2019 this Royal Commission revealed, among other things, that almost a billion dollars had been charged to clients as fees for services that were never rendered – including fees to people whom banks knew to have been dead for more than ten years (see Royal Commission into Misconduct in the Banking, Superannuation and Financial Services Industry 2019 and coverage in ABC News Australia 2018). In these examples, the affected clients would have probably preferred their bankers to have been dumb and lazy.

Over the years the financial sector has offered definitive proof of the importance of integrity over intellect or energy – and of how a lack of integrity can corrode trust in an entire sector. Even banks that had a myriad of state-of-the-art compliance instruments – from mission statements, codes of conduct and training programmes to ethical paragraphs in annual accounts, whistleblowing policies and more (I will come back to the instruments later) – could not prevent their credibility from being heavily tarnished. It is no surprise then that the focus of compliance within this sector has shifted – as it has for a long time in many other sectors – from (instruments of) strict compliance to a *culture of integrity*.

This aim sounds as simple as it is elusive. For what does one aim for exactly, when one aims for (a culture of) integrity? The concept of integrity is characterized by vagueness that makes it difficult to operationalize. For one, it is telling that even though integrity violations are easily alleged, it often appears difficult to normatively explain exactly *what* has allegedly been violated.

This short chapter focuses on integrity as the aim of compliance. It deals with two questions in particular: What does one aim for when aiming for integrity? And how does one aim for integrity?

69.2 THE NATURE OF INTEGRITY

69.2.1 *In Broad Strokes*

What does one aim for when one aims for integrity? Even though integrity has old connotations, the widespread manner in which it is used in society today is of the last decades: ranging from holding a prominent place in (corporate) codes of conduct, laws and regulations and enjoying fond usage in management discourse to serving as a low-threshold label for unwanted behaviour. In parallel, the *philosophical* use of integrity has developed from a rather dullish standard – think of incorruptibility, wholeness or unimpeachability – to include a colourful range of meanings including moral purpose and virtuousness itself (Blackburn 1994: 195; Calhoun 1995; Carr 1976; Carter 1996; Cox, la Caze and Levine 2003, 2017; Dobel 1999; Halfon 1989; Harcourt 1998; Harris 1974; Hepburn 1995: 410–11; Mautner 1996: 210; McFall 1987; Musschenga 2002; Ramsay 1997; Soeharno 2009: 27–46).

Integrity is understood to have both 'objective' and 'subjective' features. Looking at its objective features, integrity derives literally from the Latin *non-tangere* (no touching). At first glance, it would appear that integrity is apparently achieved when *nothing* happens – take, for example, the traditional meanings of *unimpeachability* or *incorruptibility*. Yet, apparently there is 'something' that should remain untouched. As the philosopher McFall once said: '[I]n order to sell one's soul, one must have something to sell' (McFall 1987: 10). In this metaphor, this 'soul that is not to be sold' forms the *object* of integrity.

Next to this 'objective' dimension of integrity, there is a 'subjective' dimension. Namely *ensuring* that this 'something' indeed remains untouched. This forms the *practice* of integrity. Chesire Calhoun argues, for example, that integrity should be described as 'standing for something' (Calhoun 1995; Carr 1976). This is not a 'static' exercise. The key ethical concept here is *prudence* and borrows from virtue ethical theory: the continuous, diligent assessment of what the object entails in concrete contexts and how it is not compromised (see Aristotle 1954; Aubenque 1963; Ebert 1995; Höffe 1995; MacIntyre 1981; Nussbaum 1994; Oksenberg Rorty 1980).

And how it is not *seen* to be compromised. In essence, integrity is about trustworthiness, namely 'ensuring' that the 'object' remains 'untouched'. In this context, appearances may matter as trustworthiness can be affected by a large number of factors. I will come back to that.

69.2.2 *The Object of Integrity*

So, how should one understand the 'object' of integrity – the 'something' that should remain untouched? Speaking about professions and institutions, sociologist Max Weber referred to an *honorary aspect* – a higher interest served by specific institutions or professions (Weber 1994: 42–6). Weber warned that if the honorary aspect is neglected, lost or compromised by other interests, trust may erode.

For example, if one consults a *doctor*, it must be beyond doubt that this doctor adheres to the core values of the medical profession – *respect for human life, respect for the patient, confidentiality* and *expertise* (World Medical Association 2017). None of these values are to be compromised by other interests, such as the making of profit, without the cost of trustworthiness. Similarly, if one appears before a judge, it must be beyond doubt that this judge is *impartial* and *independent* (UNODC 2002). No other interests – such as a judge's personal ambitions, moral convictions or financial interests – are to prevail over these core values. This may prove especially tricky in asymmetrical relationships. Take, for example, a lawyer who suggests that a client start not one but two sets of proceedings; how is it possible to know whether the lawyer is acting in the client's interest or primarily in the interest of adding to their billable hours (ABA 2020; CCBE 2013)?

Whereas the *object* can be expressed in values, it can be delineated with norms (Kekes 1983: 514; Taekema 2004). Simply put, values – or principles, standards – indicate what is *aspired* to by the institution, organization or profession. Norms or rules, on the other hand, mark the limits of what is no longer accepted behaviour or culture. For example, while academic researchers must always be committed to *honesty* and *reliability* (values), they should never be caught on *plagiarism*, *falsification* or *fabrication* (norms) (ALLEA 2017). As noted, judges must always be committed to *independence* and *impartiality*, yet must never break their duty of *confidentiality* (UNODC 2002). And for businesses: where contributing to the *stability* of the broader financial system is perceived as a societal responsibility of the banking sector (G30 2018: 7; Theissen 2013: 27, 80), the *manipulation of interest rate benchmarks* amounts to the selling of one's soul.

The 'soul' is not fixed. Rather, it depends on time and place. For example, to address present-day concerns about overconsumption of alcohol, Heineken, a beer brewer, introduced in 2018 along its core values the value of 'responsible drinking'. This is something that would not necessarily have been expected, say, half a century ago. And in response to shareholder activism that focuses on short-term gains, in 2019 major American companies via the Business Roundtable no longer held that *creating shareholder value* is the primary focus of the corporation: each company is to define its long-term purpose even if this comes at the cost of (short-term) shareholder interests (Mayer 2018).

Next to the specific purpose of each company, organization or institution, there are more generic standards, too. Take, for example, industry or sectoral standards. Or international efforts to codify or promulgate standards for (multisector) businesses or governments, such as the *United Nations Guiding Principles on Business and Human Rights* or the *Guidelines for Multinational Enterprises* of the Organisation for Economic Co-operation and Development (OECD). Also, there are values and norms that can be found broadly in (national, international, sectoral and multisectoral) codes and policies. These are values such as *truthfulness, transparency, candour, respect for the individual, diligence, loyalty, fair dealing* and *addressing concerns*, and norms in the sphere of *obedience to applicable laws and regulations, privacy and confidentiality, non-bribery and non-corruption, fair competition* and *health and safety rules* (Jackson 2013; Sharp Paine et al. 2005). Sometimes 'new standards' are promulgated as general standards, such as the currently trending values of *inclusiveness, social safety, diversity* or *sustainability*.

On a deeper level, there are standards that are so evident that they are often assumed rather than explicitly mentioned in codes of conduct or mission statements. These reflect basic achievements of civilization, such as the hearing of both sides, human dignity, objectivity (e.g. valuing fact over opinion), the presumption of innocence, the foreseeability of punishment and equal treatment. These have a long history, going back to, among others, Roman law and natural law traditions (cf. Friedmann 1953; Tamanaha 2004: 102–13). I note these because – as I will explain later – it unfortunately happens that (even) these standards risk being overlooked when responding to alleged violations of integrity.

There is much more to say about the object of integrity, but for now it suffices to note that integrity is – in essence – not a specific value or norm in itself but rather an undetermined value or norm that signals that *other* values and *other* norms – the *honorary aspect* or the *soul* of the profession or organization – must remain *untouched* (Calhoun 1995; Carr 1976: 260; McFall 1987: 14).

69.2.3 *The Subject of Integrity – Ensuring that the Soul Is Not Sold*

The object of integrity forms the normative basis of a culture of integrity, and therewith of compliance. From a subjective point of view, aiming for integrity starts with the articulation of its object.

Articulating the object of integrity is not a static exercise, as the abovementioned examples – Heineken (*more attention for responsible drinking*) and companies (*less focus on creating shareholder value*) – have shown. Rather, it is a matter of *prudence* – the continuous assessment of what the honorary aspect, the core values and basic norms of the organization, entails in concrete situations.

And how it is to be *interpreted*. Take, for example, the judicial value of *independence*. Depending on the legal culture in which the judge works, this may have different meanings. To what extent can a judge be active within – or donate to – a political party, or be a board member, a donator or a 'liker' on social media of organizations such as Greenpeace, the

American National Rifle Association or Sea Shepherd? The normative interpretation of this judicial value of independence depends on the specific (legal) culture in which the judge operates – it is a matter of contextual prudence.

Even when the object of integrity is successfully articulated and interpreted, this does not, of course, in itself ensure integrity. In fact, it may be perceived as window dressing or storytelling, rather than an ethical commitment to doing what an organization deems as right. By analogy, the Greek tragedy writer Aeschylus once wrote about the taking of oaths that the oath does not make people credible, but people make the oath credible (Fletcher 2012: 57; Soeharno 2020: 38–42). In a similar vein, just as the oath does not make credible but has to be *made* credible, so the object of integrity – whether articulated in core values, a mission statement, a code of conduct or soft law commitments – does not make credible but has to be *made* credible. For example, in order to ensure its new value *responsible drinking*, Heineken introduced a number of measures including media restrictions on marketing beer to minors. Without similar measures and the execution thereof, the value of *responsible drinking* would be nothing more than empty words.

In organizations, for leadership – eager to demonstrate results – it may be tempting to fall into the trap of making an integrity officer, compliance officer or general responsible for integrity. Or to translate the responsibility for culture into boxes that can be checked. Both strategies ultimately miss the mark. The responsibility for integrity lies with leadership (cf. Monitoring Committee Corporate Governance Code 2016: paras. 2.5.1–2) for the simple reason that it concerns the *object* of the trustworthiness of the organization. This cannot be delegated. Also, focusing on integrity instruments – about which much has been written (cf. Daimler 2018; Huberman Arnold, Arnold and Arnold 2010; Kaptein 2008, 2011; Kiel 2015; Lasthuizen, Huberts and Heres 2011; Vyakarnam et al. 1997; Weaver, Treviño and Cochran 1999) – can easily detract from the ultimate aim of a culture of integrity. For example, it is not the not-having of a conflict of interest policy that is the issue but the not-having of conflicts of interests. And a 'speak up' policy is not the real aim; the real aim is that people speak up.

This has an impact on governance models: any governance model that delegates the responsibility for integrity away from leadership or encourages leadership to focus on instruments rather than the aim of these instruments ultimately misses the mark, as it fails to acknowledge the necessity of ongoing prudential effort by leadership to ensure a culture of integrity.

Prudence does not merely concern the prudence of leadership. It also extends to the prudence of individuals, teams, groups, sectors, organizations, governments or institutions. Take the financial sector. When analyzing root causes for the 2008–9 financial crises, the top-heavy Group of Thirty (that includes the presidents of the European Central Bank and the Federal Reserve Bank, hereafter 'G30') concluded in 2015 that 'poor cultural foundations were a significant driver of the 2008–2009 financial crisis (in common with many past crises)' (G30 2015: 17, 18–21). Therefore the focus on culture became a top priority. Ensuring a culture of integrity within the banking sector, however, requires prudence at many levels. Traditionally, the focus was on prudence at management, shareholder and regulatory levels. In the last decades, however, more attention is being paid to prudence at the levels of the individual bank employee (some countries such as Australia and The Netherlands have even introduced oaths for individuals working in the banking sector to focus on proper individual conduct (Soeharno 2020: 7–9)), teams (Scholten 2017), clients, the sector, politics and societal stakeholders. On all these levels – and between these levels – prudence is required. This multilevel prudence shows how difficult it can be to realize a culture of integrity.

The Greek philosopher Aristotle once mused that the answer to the question who is virtuous cannot be given on the basis of one single right action: 'one swallow does not make a spring' (Aristotle 1954: I.7:1098a20). It takes time and effort to build a reputation of integrity. This requires that prudent assessments are made continuously and over a longer period of time. Unfortunately, the opposite is true as well. One failure to uphold the honorary aspect may cause the direct loss of a carefully built-up reputation of integrity.

69.3 DEALING WITH (NON-)INTEGRITY, WITH INTEGRITY

69.3.1 *Reflexive Integrity*

The ultimate test of integrity is whether it is handled with integrity. Integrity issues can cause great anxiety, as the quote from Shakespeare's *Othello*, at the start of this chapter, shows. After all, trustworthiness is at risk of being tarnished. In practice, however, this anxiety can cause the own core values to be overlooked.

Of course and above all, there may be a felt and justified need to act strongly when integrity is at stake. In Weber's words, one does not only swear loyalty to the 'honorary aspect' of the institution or the profession, one also *renounces its cardinal sins* (Weber 1994: 74–6). When adhering to core values, one undertakes not to *deviate* from them. But if one nevertheless does so, one can – in the heavy words of Sartre – be labelled a traitor, dissonant, fugitive, disgrace or outcast (Sartre 1982: 417–44; also Khurana and Nohria 2008: 4). For example, police officers who violate their codes of conduct by forging official police reports, only to be later rebuked by video footage, put not only their own integrity on the line but also that of the justice system. Logically then, according to Foucault (1975), the heaviest form of discipline is *removal* from the community: the sector, the organization or the profession. For if one violates its honorary aspect, one puts not just one's own honour at stake but also the honorary aspect of the sector, the organization or the profession.

Still, however, dealing with integrity issues must meet the demands of integrity. Not seldom does one see overresponses: immediate dismissals, a sacrifice of board members, the reversal of well-thought-through decisions or the closure of local branches. Actions that may later turn out to have been disproportionate. But under the felt pressure, and within the unfiltered panopticon of (social) media or stakeholders, the core values and norms of the organization may be compromised. Even deeper values may be compromised too, such as human dignity, the hearing of both sides, the foreseeability of punishment, objectivity (the placing of facts over opinions) or the presumption of innocence (Wexler 2019).

This harms the culture of integrity that one wishes to achieve, as I will explain with two examples of overlooked elements.

69.3.2 *The Vagueness of Values*

In 1817 the British lawyer and philosopher Jeremy Bentham pointed to the treacherous simplicity of the oath that he had taken when entering the University of Oxford. Apparently, the university chancellor was all too willing to impose various sanctions for all kinds of alleged violations of this broadly formulated oath. The broad formulation of the oath thus led to arbitrariness and uncertainty (Bentham 1817).

This is equally true for integrity. There is an old adage in law that there should be no unforeseen punishment (*nulla poene sine lege*). This foreseeability principle – that is to bring about certainty and reduce arbitrary punishments – may, however, conflict with the aspirational and broad nature of the values, principles or standards used to articulate the object of integrity.

For example, one may strive for sustainability, integrity, diversity, social safety, independence, honesty or trustworthiness, yet one can never 'fully meet' these values or standards. For it is always possible to be *more* sustainable, diverse, independent, honest or trustworthy. Moreover, these values are susceptible to hindsight bias. For example, the very complaint about a lack of social safety could in itself be used to justify the assessment that the atmosphere was apparently not socially safe enough. In other words: with these kinds of values, integrity is at risk of being always violated and anyone accused of an integrity violation is always at risk of 'punishment'.

This should lead to prudence and reticence on the side of those who write and enforce codes of conduct. Making a clear distinction between values – what is *aspired to* – and norms – what is the *limit* of acceptable behaviour – is an important first step.

69.3.3 *Integrity Violation, No Ethical Fault*

Second, there is the important notion that violations of integrity do not necessarily imply ethical fault on an individual level. Integrity does not translate directly to individual ethics as much as it does to the *trustworthiness* of a profession, role, sector, institution, organization or corporation. This nuance is highly important when dealing with alleged integrity violations.

Let me explain by using a judicial example. A basic tenet of the adjudication of law is fair trial by impartial judges. If a judge turns out not to have been impartial, this can have grave consequences: the judge may be held to recuse himself or the entire trial may be deemed to be void. But when is a judge partial? It is established case law of the European Court of Human Rights that an *appearance* of partiality may suffice, even if it has not been assessed that there was *in fact* partiality on the part of the individual judge. This is in a long-standing tradition of English natural justice, that justice must not only be done, it should also *be seen to be done* (Soeharno 2009: 77–100; Wade and Forsyth 2004: 439–558).

The landmark Danish case that was brought before the European Court of Human Rights concerned a judge who was involved in several stages of the same proceedings. First, this judge had taken a pre-trial decision ordering the detention of the suspect. Thereafter, the same judge formed part of the tribunal who convicted the suspect. This was at the time possible under Danish law. The question was whether the earlier pre-trial decision rendered the judge partial. The European Court of Human Rights judged that there was a violation of the standards of fair trial: decisive was the appearance created by objective factors – namely that the judge was involved in the pre-trial decision – irrespective of the question of whether the judge concerned was *in fact* partial (ECHR, 24 May 1989, *Hauschildt/Denmark* (Series A-154), § 48). In other words, the integrity of the judge was compromised owing to the objective appearance of partiality, while at the same time this did not imply ethical fault: the judge *himself* was not deemed partial.

This example shows that a violation of integrity does not necessarily imply ethical fault. And there are many other examples of structural faults – for example IT systems that are incompatible, changing management, conflicting policies – without ethical mistake on an individual level. Especially in the age of increasing digitalization it is better to be mindful of potential unintended consequences of technology (think of algorithms that cause inappropriate segmentation of customers, mis-selling of products through chatbots) where no mistake has been made by individuals in an ethical sense.

This dynamic has important consequences for dealing with (non-)integrity. For in these cases, 'punishing' individuals could amount to nothing more than finding scapegoats. And even though there may be nothing more than the *appearance* of an ethics violation, any punishment is not appearance but harsh reality.

It goes against basic values of civilization to blame people for mistakes that (objectively) *seem* to be their fault but in fact *are not*. It may, however, be very difficult for a leader or manager to admit and even more difficult for the public to understand that where things went wrong, there may be no one to blame. Yet this may be exactly what integrity requires.

69.4 WHEN IS IT RIGHT?

From times immemorial, the question is asked: when does one act *right*? It is not clear, however, who decides on the answer. Who decides on the content of the context-dependent 'object' of integrity that is to remain untouched? And who decides whether this object has indeed remained 'untouched'? Customers? Clients? Litigants? Shareholders? Non-governmental organizations (NGOs)? Politicians? Media? Perturbed citizens? Regulators? Integrity then, requires proactive articulation, interpretation and safeguarding.

When the philosopher Hegel describes the role of philosophy, he refers to the wife of Ulysses, Penelope. She was beset by suitors eager to marry her as Ulysses had not returned from Troy. Penelope told them that she would make her choice once the fabric that she was weaving was finished. Every night, however, she took the fabric apart and every day she started weaving anew. Philosophy, says Hegel, is like this fabric and the philosopher is like Penelope. Building on yesterday's experience, they start anew each day. Likewise, integrity is a continuous activity. To adequately demonstrate trustworthiness, each day, sectors, organizations, professions and individuals must prudently reweave their fabric of convictions.

REFERENCES

ABA. 2020. *American Bar Association Model Rules of Professional Conduct*.

ABC News Australia. 2018. 'Banking Royal Commission: Fees for the Dead and Cash Bribes – The Greatest Shocks (So Far)'. *ABC News Australia*, 7 September 2018. (See also 'Commonwealth Bank Charged Fees to Customer Who Had Been Dead for a Decade, Royal Commission Told'. *ABC News Australia*, 19 April 2018.)

ALLEA. All European Academies. 2017. *European Code of Conduct for Research Integrity* (revised edition).

Aristotle. 1954. *Aristotelis Ethica Nicomachea*, edited by I. Bywater. Oxford: Oxford University Press.

Aubenque, P. 1963. *La Prudence chez Aristote*. Paris: Presses Universitaires de France.

Bentham, J. 1817. *Swear Not at All: Containing an Exposure of the Needlessness and Mischievousness as Well as Antichristianity of the Ceremony of an Oath*. London: Hunter.

Blackburn, S. 1994. 'Integrity'. In *The Oxford Dictionary of Philosophy*. Oxford: Oxford University Press.

Calhoun, C. 1995. 'Standing for Something'. *Journal of Philosophy* 92(5): 235–60.

Carr, S. 1976. 'The Integrity of a Utilitarian'. *Ethics* 86(3): 241–6.

Carter, S. L. 1996. *Integrity*. New York: Basic Books.

CCBE. 2013. *Charter of Core Principles of the European Legal Profession and Code of Conduct for European Lawyers*.

Connors, R. J. 2010. *Warren Buffett on Business: Principles from the Sage of Omaha*. Hoboken: Wiley & Sons.

Cox, D., M. la Caze and M. Levine. 2003. *Integrity and the Fragile Self*. Aldershot: Ashgate.

2017. 'Integrity'. In Edward N. Zalta (ed.), *The Stanford Encyclopedia of Philosophy*. plato.stanford.edu/archives/spr2017/entries/integrity/ (first published 2001 and substantively revised in 2017).

Daimler, M. 2018. 'Why Great Employees Leave "Great Cultures"'. *Harvard Business Review*, 11 May 2018.

Dobel, J. 1999. *Public Integrity*. Baltimore: John Hopkins University Press.

Ebert, Th. 1995. 'Phronêsis. Anmerkungen zu einem Begriff der Aristotelischen Ethik (VI 5,8–13)'. In O. Höffe (ed.), *Aristoteles. Die Nikomachische Ethik*. Berlin: Akademie Verlag, 165–85.

Fletcher, J. 2012. *Performing Oaths in Classical Greek Drama*. Cambridge: Cambridge University Press.

Foucault, M. 1975. *Surveiller et punir, naissance de la prison*. Paris: Gallimard.

Friedmann, W. 1953. *Legal Theory*. London: Stevens & Sons.

G30 (Group of Thirty). 2015. *Banking Conduct and Culture: A Call for Sustained and Comprehensive Reform*. Washington: G30 Offices.

2018. *Banking Conduct and Culture. A Permanent Mindset Change*. Washington: G30 Offices.

Halfon, M. 1989. *Integrity: A Philosophical Inquiry*. Philadelphia: Temple University Press.

Harcourt, E. 1998. 'Integrity, Practical Deliberation and Utilitarianism'. *Philosophical Quarterly* 48(191): 189–98.

Harris, J. 1974. 'Williams on Negative Responsibility and Integrity'. *Philosophical Quarterly* 24(96): 265–73.

Hepburn, R. 1995. 'Integrity'. In T. Honderich (ed.), *The Oxford Companion to Philosophy*. Oxford: Oxford University Press, 410–11.

Höffe, O. (ed.). 1995. *Aristoteles, Die Nikomachische Ethik*. Berlin: Akademie Verlag.

Huberman Arnold, D., K. Arnold and V. J. Arnold. 2010. 'Managing Ethical Risks and Crises: Beyond Legal Compliance'. *Beijing Law Review* 1(1): 1–6.

Jackson, J. K. 2013. *Codes of Conduct for Multinational Organisations: An Overview*. CRS Report for US Congress, 16 April 2013.

Kaptein, M. 2008. 'Developing and Testing a Measure for the Ethical Culture of Organizations: The Corporate Ethical Virtues Model'. *Journal of Organizational Behavior* 29: 923–47.

2011. 'Understanding Unethical Behaviour by Unraveling Ethical Culture'. *Human Relations* 46(6): 843–69.

Keenan, Douglas. 2012. 'My Thwarted Attempt to Tell of Libor Shenanigans'. *Financial Times*, 27 July 2012. (See also 'U.S. Conducting Criminal Libor Probe'. *Reuters*, 28 February 2012; 'Libor Collusion Was Rife, Culture Went Right to the Top'. *Reuters*, 7 August 2012.)

Kekes, J. 1983. 'Constancy and Purity'. *Mind* XCII: 499–518.

Khurana R. and N. Nohria. 2008. 'It's Time to Make Management a True Profession'. *Harvard Business Review*, October 2008.

Kiel, F. 2015. *Return on Character: The Real Reason Leaders and Their Companies Win*. Boston: Harvard Business Review Press.

Lasthuizen, K., L. Huberts and L. Heres 2011. 'How to Measure Integrity Violations: Towards a Validated Typology of Unethical Behavior'. *Public Management Review* 13(3): 383–8.

MacIntyre, A. 1981. *After Virtue: A Study in Moral Theory*. London: Duckworth.

Mautner, T. 1996. 'Integrity'. In T. Mautner (ed.), *A Dictionary of Philosophy*. Oxford: Blackwell Publishers, 210.

Mayer, C. 2018. *Prosperity: Better Business Makes the Greater Good*. Oxford: Oxford University Press.

McFall, L. 1987. 'Integrity'. *Ethics* 98: 5–20.

Monitoring Committee Corporate Governance Code. 2016. *Dutch Corporate Governance Code*.

Musschenga, A. W. 2002. 'Integrity. Personal, Moral and Professional'. In A. W. Musschenga, W. van Haaften, B. Spiecker and M. Slors (eds.), *Personal and Moral Identity*. Dordrecht: Kluwer, 169–201.

Nussbaum, M. C. 1994. *Therapy of Desire: Theory and Practice in Hellenistic Ethics*. Princeton: Princeton University Press.

Oksenberg Rorty, A. (ed.). 1980. *Essays on Aristotle's Ethics*. Berkeley: University of California Press.

Ramsay, H. 1997. *Beyond Virtue: Integrity and Morality*. London: Macmillan.

Royal Commission into Misconduct in the Banking, Superannuation and Financial Services Industry. 2019. *Final Report*. Vol. 2.

Sartre, Jean-Paul. 1982. *Critique of Dialectical Reason*. Norfolk: Thetford.

Scholten, Wieke. 2017. *Banking on Team Ethics: A Team Climate Perspective on Root Causes of Misconduct in Financial Services*.

Sharp Paine, L., R. Deshpande, J. D. Margolis and K. Bettcher. 2005. "Up to code: Does your company's conduct meet world-Class standards?" *Harvard Business Review*: 122–35. Kurt Lewin Institute.

Soeharno, J. E. 2009. *The Integrity of the Judge. A Philosophical Inquiry*. Aldershot: Ashgate.

2020. *The Value of the Oath*. The Hague: Eleven.

Taekema, S. 2004. 'What Ideals Are: Ontological and Epistemological Issues'. In W. van der Burg and S. Taekema (eds.), *The Importance of Ideals: Debating Their Relevance in Law, Morality and Politics*. Brussels: Peter Lang, 39–58.

Tamanaha, B. Z. 2004. *On the Rule of Law: History, Politics, Theory*. Cambridge: Cambridge University Press.

Theissen. R. 2013. *Are EU Banks Safe?* The Hague: Eleven.

UNODC. 2002. *Bangalore Principles of Judicial Conduct*.

Vyakarnam, S., A. Bailey, A. Myers and D. Burnett. 1997. 'Towards an Understanding of Ethical Behavior in Small Firms'. *Journal of Business Ethics* 16(15): 1625–36.

Wade, H. and C. Forsyth. 2004. *Administrative Law* (9th ed.). Oxford: Oxford University Press.

Weaver, G. R., L. K. Treviño and P. Cochran. 1999. 'Corporate Ethics Programs as Control Systems: Influences of Executive Commitment and Environmental Factors'. *Academy of Management Journal* 42(1): 41–57.

Weber, M. 1994. *Wissenschaft als Beruf. Politiek als Beruf (Studienausgabe)*. Tübingen: Mohr Siebeck.

Wexler, L. 2019. '#MeToo and Procedural Justice'. *Richmond Public Interest Law Review* 22(2): 180–92.

World Medical Association. 2017. *Declaration of Geneva*.

THE CAMBRIDGE HANDBOOK OF COMPLIANCE

Compliance has become key to our contemporary markets, societies, and modes of governance across a variety of public and private domains. While this has stimulated a rich body of empirical and practical expertise on compliance, thus far, there has been no comprehensive understanding of what compliance is or how it influences various fields and sectors. The academic knowledge of compliance has remained siloed along different disciplinary domains, regulatory and legal spheres, and mechanisms and interventions. This handbook bridges these divides to provide the first one-stop overview of what compliance is, how we can best study it, and the core mechanisms that shape it. Written by leading experts, chapters offer perspectives from across law, regulatory studies, management science, criminology, economics, sociology, and psychology. This volume is the definitive and comprehensive account of compliance.

Benjamin van Rooij is Professor of Law and Society at the University of Amsterdam, and Global Professor of Law at the University of Cailfornia, Irvine, where he studies compliance and the way law shapes human and organizational conduct. He publishes in leading academic journals as well as in the *New York Times*, *Huffington Post*, *The Hill*, and NPR news radio.

D. Daniel Sokol is a professor of law at the University of Florida, an affiliate professor at the University of Florida Warrington College of Business, and the senior advisor to White & Case, LLP. Sokol is also among the top ten most cited antitrust law professors in the past five years and has lectured on compliance to governments, practitioners, and academics across five continents.